Neuropsychological
Foundations of
Learning Disabilities

Neuropsychological Foundations of Learning Disabilities

A Handbook of Issues, Methods, and Practice

Edited by

John E. Obrzut
College of Education
Division of Educational Foundations
and Administration
University of Arizona
Tucson, Arizona

George W. Hynd
College of Education
Division for the Education
of Exceptional Children
University of Georgia
Athens, Georgia

Academic Press
San Diego New York Boston
London Sydney Tokyo Toronto

Find Us on the Web!   http: //www.apnet.com

Academic Press
A Division of Harcourt Brace & Company
525 B Street, Suite 1900, San Diego, California 92101-4495

United Kingdom Edition published by
Academic Press Limited
24–28 Oval Road, London NW1 7DX

Library of Congress Cataloging-in-Publication Data

Obrzut, John E.
    Neuropsychological foundations of learning disabilities : a
handbook of issues, methods, and practice / John E. Obrzut, George
W. Hynd.
        p. cm.
    ISBN 0-12-524040-6 (case)   ISBN 0-12-524039-2 (paper)
    1. Learning disabilities--Physiological aspects. 2. Clinical
neuropsychology. 3. Neuropsychological tests. I. Hynd, George W.
II. Title.
    [DNLM: 1. Learning Disorders. 2. Neuropsychology--in infancy &
childhood. 3. Psychological Tests--in infancy & childhood. WM 145
013n]
RC394.L37O27 1991
616.85'889--dc20
DNLM/DLC
for Library of Congress   90-1250
                                                                      CIP

PRINTED IN THE UNITED STATES OF AMERICA
97 98 IBT 9 8 7 6 5 4 3

Dedication

To all the special students who may experience learning disabilities and to the teachers who help these children. Also, special thanks to Krystopher who continues to provide the motivation for these professional endeavors.

J.E.O.

To Jack, Ben, and the memory of Walt, my most valued colleagues. To Peg, Kelly, Naomi, and Ed who have all greatly facilitated our research efforts aimed at trying to understand the neurobiological basis of learning disabilities.

G.W.H.

Contents

CHAPTER TWENTY-ONE Specific Speech and Language
Disorders
Rachel E. Stark, James W. Montgomery, and
Jennifer Windsor

CHAPTER TWENTY-TWO Specific Nonverbal and
Social-Skills Deficits in Children with Learning Disabilities
Margaret Semrud-Clikeman and George W. Hynd

CHAPTER TWENTY-THREE Remediating Reading
Disabilities
Barbara W. Wise and Richard K. Olson

CHAPTER TWENTY-FOUR Academic Interventions with
Learning-Disabled Students: A Cognitive/Metacognitive
Approach
Candace S. Bos and Anthony K. Van Reusen

CHAPTER TWENTY-FIVE Neuropsychological
Assessment: Case Studies
Lawrence Lewandowski

CHAPTER TWENTY-SIX Neuropsychological Perspectives
in Special Education
John Kershner

CHAPTER TWENTY-SEVEN On the Relevance of
Neuropsychological Data to Learning Disabilities
Merrill Hiscock and Cheryl K. Hiscock

Contributors

Numbers in parentheses indicate the pages on which the author's contributions begin.

P.G. AARON (519), Educational and School Psychology, Indiana State University, Terre Haute, Indiana 47809

ERVIN S. BATCHELOR, JR. (309), Behavioral Neurology Unit, Beth Israel Hospital, Boston, Massachusetts 02215

CANDACE S. BOS (659), Division of Special Education and Rehabilitation, University of Arizona, Tucson, Arizona 85718

CHARLES J. BRAINERD (147), Educational Psychology Program, College of Education, University of Arizona, Tucson, Arizona 85721

IDALYN S. BROWN (387), Department of Neurology, Neuropsychology Section, The Bowman Gray School of Medicine, Winston-Salem, North Carolina 27103

M.P. BRYDEN (411), Department of Psychology, University of Waterloo, Waterloo, Ontario N2L 3G1, Canada

K. CARLAND-SAUCIER (49), RMT Inc., Greenville, South Carolina 29606

CHRISTOPHER H. CHASE (199), College of Communications and Cognitive Science, Hampshire College, Amherst, Massachusetts 01002

RAYMOND S. DEAN (309), Neuropsychology Laboratory, Ball State University, Muncie, Indiana 47306

JOHN C. DEFRIES (29), Institute for Behavioral Genetics, University of Colorado–Boulder, Boulder, Colorado 80309-0447

DRAKE D. DUANE (7), Institute for Human Development and Behavioral Neurology, Scottsdale, Arizona 85258

R. DUARA (49), Mailman Center for Child Development, Department of Pediatrics, Miami, Florida 33101

REBECCA H. FELTON (387), Department of Neurology, Neuropsychology Section, The Bowman Gray School of Medicine, Winston-Salem, North Carolina 27103

JACQELYN J. GILLIS (29), Institute for Behavioral Genetics, University of Colorado–Boulder, Boulder, Colorado 80309

KAREN GROSS-GLENN (49), Deceased

M. RUSSELL HARTER (437), Deceased

CHARLES P. HEATH (287), Deer Valley Unified School District, Phoenix, Arizona 85027

CHERYL K. HISCOCK (743), Department of Psychology and Philosophy, Sam Houston State University, Huntsville, Texas 77062

MERRILL HISCOCK (743), Department of Psychology, University of Houston, Houston, Texas 77004

GEORGE W. HYND (475, 603), Division of Exceptional Children, University of Georgia, Athens, Georgia 30602

CLAYTON E. KELLER (549), Department of Child and Family Development, College of Education and Human Service Professions, University of Minnesota, Duluth, Minnesota 55812

JOHN KERSHNER (711), Department of Special Education, The Ontario Institute for Studies in Education, Toronto, Ontario M5S 1V6, Canada

JOE C. KUSH (287), Deer Valley Unified School District, Phoenix, Arizona 85027

B. LEVIN (49), Mailman Center for Child Development, Department of Pediatrics, Miami, Florida 33101

LAWRENCE LEWANDOWSKI (685), Department of Psychology, College of Arts and Sciences, Syracuse University, Syracuse, New York 13244

HERBERT A. LUBS (49), Mailman Center for Child Development, Department of Pediatrics, Miami, Florida 33101

M.L. LUBS (49), Mailman Center for Child Development (D-820), Department of Pediatrics, Miami, Florida 33101

G. REID LYON (355), Department of Psychology, University of Vermont, Burlington, Vermont 05401

HEIKKI LYYTINEN (475), Department of Psychology, University of Jyvaskyla, SF 40100 Jyvaskyla 10, Finland

JAMES W. MONTGOMERY (573), Clinical Center for Study of Development & Learning, CB# 7255, BSRC, University of North Carolina, Chapel Hill, North Carolina 27599-7255

SYLVIA R. MORRISON (79), Department of Education, The Ontario Institute for Studies in Education, Toronto, Ontario M5S 1V6, Canada

ROBERT F. NEWBY (355), Curative Rehabilitation Center, Medical College of Wisconsin, Milwaukee, Wisconsin 53226

NAOMI NIEVES (113), Deceased

JAMES P. O'DONNELL (331), Department of Psychology, Southern Illinois University at Carbondale, Carbondale, Illinois 62901

JOHN E. OBRZUT (179), Division of Educational Psychology, College of Education, University of Arizona, Tucson, Arizona 85721

RICHARD K. OLSON (631), Department of Psychology, University of Colorado–Boulder, Boulder, Colorado, 80309

MARK RABIN (49), Mailman Center for Child Development, Department of Pediatrics, Miami, Florida 33101

VALERIE REYNA (147), Educational Psychology Program, College of Education, University of Arizona, Tucson, Arizona 85721

PAUL SATZ (99), Neuropsychiatric Institute and Hospital, Center for the Health Sciences, Unviersity of California Los Angeles, Los Angeles, California 90024

MARGARET SEMRUD-CLIKEMAN (471, 603), Department of Psychiatry, Massachusetts General Hospital, Boston, Massachusetts 02114

LINDA S. SIEGEL (79), Department of Education, The Ontario Institute for Studies in Education, Toronto, Ontario M5S 1V6, Canada

JOHN E. SIMURDAK (519), Porter School Psychology Clinic, Indiana State University, Terre Haute, Indiana 47809

RACHEL E. STARK (573), Department of Audiology and Speech Services, Steer Audiology and Speech-Language Center, Purdue University, West Lafayette, Indiana 47907

RUNA STEENHUIS (411), Department of Psychology, University Hospital, London, Ontario N6A 5A5, Canada

JOE P. SUTTON (549), Department of Special Education, Bob Jones University, Greenville, South Carolina 29614

H. LEE SWANSON (241), Department of Educational Psychology, Faculty of Education, University of British Columbia, Vancouver, British Columbia V6T 1Z5, Canada

PAULA TALLAL (199), Center for Molecular and Behavioral Neurosciences, The State University of New Jersey-Rutgers, Newark, New Jersey 07102

ANTHONY K. VAN REUSEN (659), Division of Special Education and Rehabilitation, University of Arizona, Tucson, Arizona 85718

X.L. WEN (49), Mailman Center for Child Development, Department of Pediatrics, Miami, Florida 33101

JENNIFER WINDSOR (573), Department of Audiology and Speech Services, Steer Audiology and Speech-Language Center, Purdue University, West Lafayette, Indiana 47907

BARBARA W. WISE (631), Department of Psychology, University of Colorado–Boulder, Boulder, Colorado, 80309

Preface

This volume is a comprehensive summary of the recent advances made in the neuropsychology of learning disabilities with regard to theory, diagnosis, and remediation. Its primary focus is on understanding the neurobiological and cognitive bases of the learning disability syndrome. The book presents current scientific perspectives derived from behavioral, genetic, eletrophysiological, and brain imaging studies in addition to providing new data regarding cognitive and memory functions, laterality mechanisms, neurodiagnostic assessment subtype analysis, and common specific disorders in such areas as reading, math, speech/language, and social skills. Many of the authors are nationally and internationally known scholars with a vested interest in the study of learning disabilities from theoretical and empirical perspectives.

The book is intended for researchers, practitioners, and students in psychology, neuroscience, and special education who are interested in working with children and adults who experience learning problems due primarily to central nervous system dysfunction. The volume is geared for graduate level courses in departments of Clinical Psychology, School Psychology, and Special Education. Because the book is large in scope and breadth, the material is technical in parts but less complex in others in an effort to encourage interest from a large readership.

The rationale for the volume derives from the fact that it is becoming more evident that learning disabilities are either the direct or indirect result of central nervous system dysfunction. This point is particularly underscored in the 1987 National Institutes of Health (NIH) Interagency Report to Congress. Yet few psychologists and educators have access to the recent advances that have been made in the articulating the neuropsychological nature of the learning disability syndrome. However, federal legislation (Public Law 94-

142 and, more recently, PL 99-457) have made it imperative that children and adolescents with specific learning disorders be evaluated, identified, and placed into special educational programs for appropriate educational services. This law, and associated shifts in federal funding expanding both research and educational services to these individuals, have made it necessary for a wider potential audience of researchers and practitioners to have a comprehensive and up-to-date volume relevant to their professional needs. Furthermore, a greater appreciation and recognition on the part of many professionals of brain–behavior relationships involved in the learning process has led to the need for such a text. The current interest in brain–behavior relationships is best exemplified by the numerous conferences, organizations, books, and journals that have evolved during the last decade.

While some of the earlier volumes in the field provided little or no knowledge about the neuro*biological* basis of learning disabilities, this volume attempts to fill the void by including critical discussions of state-of-the-art genetic, electrophysiological, and brain-imaging studies. The book offers a variety of theoretical positions, experimental methods, and ideas for practice that will stimulate ongoing research in the field of learning disabilities. Many individuals are responsible for the success of such a comprehensive volume. In addition to the authors of this volume, the editors wish to acknowledge all those individuals working with and/or conducting basic research with children and adolescents who experience learning disabilities and thereby have made significant contributions.

PART ONE

Foundations and Theoretical Issues in the Neuropsychology of Learning Disabilities

Historically it has long been recognized that there existed a group of children who suffered deficits in visual–spatial and semantic–linguistic processes which were remarkably similar to those of adult patients with known brain lesions. The published reports late in the 1800s documented the existence of a syndrome referred to as congenital word blindness, a term suggested by Kussmaul in 1877. Kussmaul's patient could not read but had adequate intellectual and perceptual abilities. A series of reports by Hinshelwood (1895, 1900), Bastian (1898), Clairborne (1906), and others (Jackson, 1906; Morgan, 1896; Stephenson, 1905) supported the existence of a syndrome characterized by a developmental inability to read in the presence of adequate opportunity, intellectual ability, and motivation.

A review of these cases suggests that by the end of the first decade of this century collective evidence supported the observations that (1) these children had some form of congenital learning problems; (2) more males than females were affected; (3) the disorder manifested variably in terms of severity and pattern of deficits; (4) normal classroom instruction was not adequate in meeting their educational needs; and (5) the disorder may be related to a developmental process affecting primarily left hemispheric central language processes (Hynd & Willis, 1988). Our current research efforts build on these early observations.

Orton (1928), Strauss and Lehtinen (1947), and more recent researchers have contributed to an evolving conceptualization of brain–behavior relations in these children such that the most recent federal definition of

1

learning disabilities recognizes the presumed neurobiological etiology (Wyngaarden, 1987). While the definition of learning disabilities continues to draw controversy and diagnosis still depends primarily on a psychometrically significant discrepancy between measured achievement and cognitive potential, significant progress has been made in articulating more clearly the etiological and neuropsychological nature of the many syndromes now recognized under the generic term "learning disabilities."

The chapters in the first part of this volume provide a current perspective as to recent advances in this regard. Duane, in Chapter One, provides a personal perspective as to the evolutionary process regarding our conceptualizations of the neurobiological nature of learning disabilities. Based on a broad but integrative perspective, Duane attempts to project into the near future as to what issues may arise as vital in increasing our understanding not only of the narrowly defined population of learning-disabled children, but also of how these various syndromes interact with the manifestations of psychiatric disturbance. Advances made in charting development and its variation in learning-disabled children's brains may shed light not only on the interaction between the genetic program and the environment, but may also provide us insight and models for how other neurologically based disorders evolve (e.g., attention-deficit disorders, Tourette's syndrome).

Clinicians have long been impressed with the fact that children with specific learning disabilities often have parents or a sibling who experience similiar difficulties in learning. In fact, early studies of twin concordance rates suggested a strong genetic link. Chapter Two by DeFries and Gillis describes the results of the ongoing Colorado Reading Project. By employing reading achievement data collected on reading-disabled MZ and DZ twin pairs, DeFries and Gillis provide strong evidence in support of the notion that individual differences in reading attainment are highly heritable. While additional data are required to test the specificity of reading deficits in these twin pairs with regard to the genetic etiology, these studies are vitally important in support of molecular genetic studies.

Based on the initial study reported by Smith, Kimberling, Pennington, and Lubs (1983), molecular genetic studies have been undertaken in several centers in the United States. Chapter Three by Lubs, Rabin, Carland-Saucier, Wen, Gross-Glenn, Duara, Levin, and Lubs addresses the current state of knowledge related to genetic linkage. As pointed out in this chapter, more than 15 years of work was required before heterogeneity and specific linkage to chromosome 15 were demonstrated. As further work has progressed, it has become evident that perhaps as many as five suggestive localizations may exist, perhaps each independently or interactively resulting in a relatively uniquely different phenotype. The collection not only of genetic information but of neuropsychological data as well is recognized as critical if the phenotype for the various manifestations of learning disabilities is to be accurately identified. Thus, more sophisticated and discriminative neuropsychological diagnostic procedures will aid both behavioral and molecular genetic studies in charting the nature of genetic transmission of learning disabilities. Ultimately, one might hope that genetic screening for learning disabilities might be a reality, but, as these authors point out, only after each gene has been localized, cloned, and sequenced.

As has been pointed out, defining learning disabilities has provoked much controversy over the years. Not only is an adequate definition essential in identifying the various syndromes for the genetic studies, but the definitions also reflect uniquely different perspectives as to which models one may evoke in conceptualizing learning disabilities. Needless to say, different definitions and diagnostic criteria may result in more or less restrictive populations being identified and served. Morrison and Siegel, in Chapter Four, discuss the assumptions related to most definitions of learning disabilities and offer an alternative definition which, they believe, provides some solutions to the problems raised by current definitions. While the specific criteria suggested by Morrison and Siegel may provoke yet more controversy, they have made a significant contribution in clearly recommending criteria that are supported by a growing body of research pertaining to the underlying deficits manifested by reading- and arithmetic-disabled children. The use of such specific diagnostic criteria by researchers would at least provide a common diagnostic reference point from which to more accurately define populations of learning-disabled children employed for research purposes.

Consistent with the perspective taken by Morrison and Seigel regarding the central disruption of phonological coding in reading-disabled children, Satz, in Chapter Five, discusses the Dejerine hypothesis and advances an etiological reformulation of the neurolinguistic–neurobiological interactions that may exist in these children. Satz addresses the important literature on language lateralization and how dyslexic children may suffer disruptions in the normal developmental processes associated with the maturation of dedicated unilateral cortical zones subserving linguistic processes. The literature on childhood aphasia is integrated into the neurobiological model advanced by Geschwind and colleagues. As Satz points out, the heuristic model which implicates the interaction between fetal testosterone and the microscopic abnormalities found in the autopsied dyslexic cases deserves further investigation, especially with regard to the manifestation of possible subtypes of dyslexia.

Nieves, in Chapter Six, extends the neuropsychological perspective by examining the relationships between childhood psychopathology and learning disabilities. While it has long been observed that many learning-disabled children suffer increasing emotional difficulties presumably associated with school failure, the co-occurrence of psychiatric disturbance in these children has been poorly studied from an empirical perspective. In this chapter, Nieves reviews the literature regarding the co-occurrence of learning disabilities and conduct disorders, attention-deficit disorders, anxiety disorders, and depression. As she points out, it may be that learning disabilities do not "cause" emotional problems, but it may be that learning disabilities and psychiatric disturbance may coexist, one interacting with the other. In fact, the nature of these possible associations may help researchers identify more clearly the various phenotypes associated with genetic transmission. However, it remains a fact that there is no consensus as to the nature of the interactions between learning disabilities and various forms of childhood psychopathology at this point in time. This conclusion should not inhibit the development of more sophisticated research designs aimed at addressing these interactions, however.

While learning disabilities are most frequently diagnosed on the basis of a significant difference between measured psychometric intelligence and achievement, many believe that learning-disabled children suffer from a dysfunction in basic psychological processes. Memory processes are most often implicated, as these children seem impaired in the ability to learn material and, when learning occurs, they seem to have difficulty in retrieval of previously learned concepts. In Chapter Seven, Brainerd and Reyna review the evidence regarding the acquisition process and the forgetting processes in learning-disabled children. From their research they conclude that learning-disabled children seem to have deficits in the rate at which information is stored into long-term memory. Further, deficits in storage of information into memory seem to increase with age when comparisons are made with normal children, and learning-disabled children seem to have difficulty in acquiring material in memory. These conclusions fit well with the notion that learning-disabled children suffer deficits in attention and automatized processes and some relationship may exist at a neurobiological level, as discussed by Satz in an earlier chapter, particularly with regard to the executive processes possibly disrupted through abberations in fetal brain ontogeny.

Consistent with the notion that learning-disabled children may have delayed or deficient language lateralization, Obrzut, in Chapter Eight, discusses the evidence regarding hemispheric activation and arousal. In this chapter he presents evidence from directed dichotic listening tasks that assess language activation processes associated with hemispheric asymmetries. The evidence supports the conclusion that, when compared to normal children, learning-disabled children are deficient in processing receptive language in the left hemisphere. By employing a directed-attention paradigm, Obrzut has demonstrated that right hemispheric attentional activation during language processing interferes with more appropriate processing in the left central language zones. This model is consistent with the modification of Dejerine's hypothesis as advanced by Satz in his chapter and is further supported by data discussed by Harter and Hynd, Semrud-Clikeman, and Lyytinen in their chapters in Part Two of this volume.

While perceptual-processing models of linguistic material may add to our understanding of the interactions between the allocation of hemispheric attentional resources in learning-disabled children, learning, and specifically reading, clearly involves a multitude of associated cognitive processes. Chase and Tallal, in Chapter Nine, discuss cognitive models that help us understand the interactions of these processes as they may be impaired in learning-disabled children. These authors review a complex literature and conclude that, while executive processes may well be impaired in reading-disabled children, the source of reading impairment lies in the lexical component of the language-input system. However, since language processing is such a complex and interactive network, a parallel distributed reading model best fits the available neurolinguistic data. This model is vitally important since it serves to integrate neurobiological and cognitive processing perspectives and provides a firm foundation for further study.

Swanson, in Chapter Ten, discusses an information-processing model that relates distinctive encoding deficits in learning-disabled children to deficient hemispheric processing. Consistent with the data provided by Obrzut, Swanson advances evidence that poor accessibility of information during recall in learning-disabled children is related to diffuse processing by the cerebral hemispheres. This diffuse processing of information may result from impaired allocation of hemispheric resources. Such a model may not be inconsistent with that proposed by Chase and Tallal in the previous chapter. It may well be that the allocation of interhemispheric attentional resources, as discussed by Obrzut, interferes with memory storage, recall, lexical processing, and information processing in general.

The chapters in the first part of this volume provide a multidisciplinary view of the neurobiological basis of learning disabilities. The perspectives brought to bear are intentionally from a diverse group of scholars. The perspectives represented in this section of the volume are derived from pediatric neurology, behavioral and molecular genetics, special education, neuropsychology, cognitive psychology, neurolinguistics, and educational psychology. It should be evident that, as long as learning disabilities are behaviorally diagnosed and are presumed to be due to central nervous system dysfunction, progress in understanding these children can only occur through a multidisciplinary effort. The contents of these chapters represent well our current state of knowledge and provide many possible directions for further, equally as productive, efforts aimed at better understanding learning-disabled children.

References

Bastian, H. C. (1898). *Aphasia and other speech defects*. London: H. K. Lewis.

Clairborne, J. H. (1906). Types of congenital symbol amblyopia. *JAMA, Journal of the American Medical Association, 47*, 1813–1816.

Hynd, G. W., & Willis, W. G. (1988). *Pediatric neuropsychology*. Orlando, FL: Grune & Stratton.

Hinshelwood, J. (1895). Word-blindness and visual memory. *Lancet, 2*, 1564–1570.

Hinshelwood, J. (1900). Congenital word-blindness. *Lancet, 1*, 1506–1508.

Jackson, E. (1906). Developmental alexia (congenital word blindness). *American Journal of Medical Science, 131*, 843–849.

Kussmaul, A. (1877). Disturbance of speech. *Cyclopedia of Practical Medicine, 14*, 581–875.

Morgan, W. P. (1896). A case of congenital word blindness. *British Medical Journal, 2*, 1378.

Orton, S. (1928). Specific reading disability–strephosymbolia. *JAMA, Journal of the American Medical Association, 90*, 1095–1099.

Smith, S. D., Kimberling, W. J., Pennington, B. F., & Lubs, H. A. (1983). Specific reading disability: Identification of an inherited form through linkage analysis. *Science, 219*, 1345–1347.

Stephenson, S. (1905). Six cases of congenital word blindness affecting three generations of one family. *Ophthalmoscope, 5*, 482–484.

Strauss, A. A., & Lehtinen, L. E. (1947). *Psychopathology and education of the brain-injured child* (Vol. 1). Orlando, FL: Grune & Stratton.

Wyngaarden, J. B. (Ed.). (1987). *Learning disabilities: A report to the U.S. Congress*. Washington, DC: National Institute of Health, Interagency Committee on Learning Disabilities.

CHAPTER ONE

Biological Foundations of Learning Disabilities

Drake D. Duane

To ignore the biological substrate of the learner in the study of learning and its vicissitudes is counterintuitive. The necessity of this co-investigation is powerfully exemplified in considering that group of conditions currently referred to as "learning disabilities" (LD). Indeed, the concept of LD is bred from the loins of clinical biology, that is, medicine, and specifically neurology. Defensiveness about medical models put aside, the notion of selectively handicapped learners is a direct product of nineteenth and twentieth century awareness of brain–behavior relationships as revealed by medical research. In order to anticipate as well as to participate in the next evolutionary phase of conceptualizing learning disorders, this chapter will survey the historical roots, current status, and probable near future of the biological basis of learning behavior.

I. History

A. Spoken Language

Hippocrates in the fifth century B.C. speculated that thought, language, and personality were products of the brain. Using the postulates of the time, he assumed physical properties such as moisture and temperature influenced characteristics such as reason. The speculation of Hippocrates was not confirmed until the nineteenth century, when direct evidence was provided that at least language was generated by the brain.

Pierre Paul Broca (1863, 1865) provided three enduring observations. The first was that aphasia, inability to speak, resulted from insults to the left hemisphere. The second was that verbal expression was not only lateralized to the left hemisphere but was localized to the second frontal convolution. The third observation was that this phenomenon was absolute in right-handed subjects. These three points still warrant clarification. That is, what are the precise relationships between localization of lateralized function and the handedness of a subject?

On the developmental side, Wilde (1853), just a few years before Broca's publication, described children who were mute but not deaf. Whether the observations from acquired disease in the adult as those of Broca on aphasia clarify mechanisms in developmental disorders as those of Wilde is still opaque. In the first half of the twentieth century debate raged between strict localizationists, that is, those who postulated specific functions in specific loci, and those who conceived of brain function as nonobligated or so-called cortical pluripotential. The latter perceives functional anatomy as mutable by experience. Currently, it is evident that central nervous system (CNS) function is asymmetric and, although lateralized, function is not diffusely lateralized. Further, it is evident that lateralization and localization are not identical in individuals who are biologically right versus left handed. It should not escape the awareness of investigators in learning disorders that their ontologic approach may prove more rewarding in explaining adult phenomena than adult lesions are in clarifying childhood brain function. Indeed the reverse may occur, namely the elucidation of developmental disorders may illuminate mechanisms of adult cerebral function, and more so than does analysis of function predicated on acquired disorders.

B. Written Language

The loss of the ability to read, or alexia, was described in adults in the late nineteenth century. Referred to initially as "word blindness," this condition, like the aphasias, was lateralized to disorders in the left hemisphere and localized to the posterior hemisphere. Invariably the disorder isolated the left hemisphere from the right and isolated the left hemisphere from its own angular gyrus.

The work of Dejerine on alexia (1892) was known to Morgan (1896) and Hinshelwood (1900) when they described what they thought was a "congenital" form of word blindness in school-aged children. These early as well as subsequent works noted an apparent discrepant occurrence of childhood reading disability in males, in those with anomalous hand preference, and in those with uncertainty in concepts of right and left space. Aside from gender and hand preferences, additional predictive correlates were family history of reading difficulty and virtually uniform coexistent underachievement in spelling (dysgraphia). Although spelling problems might be considered products of an inopportune symbol system, the occurrence of dyslexia/dysgraphia in diverse language cultures and in their familial nature argue for biological determinants, nonculturally dependent.

C. Mathematics

Acquired disorders of calculation were not recorded in the medical literature until 1920 (Henschen). This recognition latency between speech/writing and calculation disorders would be repeated in the literature regarding developmental disorders. The nonregularity of location in right or left hemisphere as well as the nonregularity of intrahemispheric localization from case to case led to the explanation either that arithmetic ability was widely interconnected between and within hemispheres or that a hierarchical classification of calculation difficulties would explain inconsistent patterns of lateralization and localization. Luria's (1966) classification of primary acalculia (left parietooccipital), acoustic aphasic acalculia (left temporal), motor aphasic acalculia (left frontal), and frontal acalculia was simplified by Hécaen (1962) to aphasic, visuospatial, and anarithmetica. The second form was said to account for those occurrences in the nonlanguage-dominant hemisphere.

But of all the disorders of calculation, it was that described by Gertsmann which captured attention in the medical jargon of acquired syndromes and influenced the perception of developmental disorders of calculation. The tetrad of dyscalculia, difficulty with finger recognition ("finger agnosia"), confusion of concept of right and left, and associated spelling difficulty (dysgraphia) Gerstmann (1940) suggested were necessarily interdependent and evolved from adult acquired disorders with solitary involvement of the left parietal lobe. Benton (1961) has shown that there is no special link between these four symptoms. Nonetheless, the impact of the concept influenced Kinsbourne and Warrington (1963) to postulate a developmental form of the Gerstmann syndrome. In their report, females outnumbered males, left handedness or "crossed dominance" was common, and family history of educational difficulty as well as early brain injury with signs of organic brain dysfunction were prevalent. Constructional difficulties were universal in these brain-injured children. Among the descriptors of children demonstrating the Gerstmann syndrome was a reversal of the verbal and performance IQ pattern from that which had been associated with developmental reading problems, in this instance, lower performance IQ than verbal IQ. Over the next two decades psychologists paid increasing sensitivity to IQ subscale score patterns, so-called factor analysis, in addition to verbal and performance IQ levels (Lezak, 1983). The heightened awareness of variability in patterns of function was in part also influenced by split-brain research which documented asymmetries of cerebral function in animals and man (Sperry, 1982).

D. Attention

Brain injury in children, whether traumatic or postinfectious, produces variable effects on cerebral function. Among the more common consequences are disturbances in motor control, for example, awkwardness and restlessness. The notion of hyperkinesis is as diffuse as the lesions which seem to produce it. Postnatal insults with widespread effects are prone to limit thinking and reasoning while exciting impulsivity and frenetic behavior.

The association between "injury" and "hyperactivity" seemed so regular that subsequent descriptions of hyperactivity in the context of developmental disorders assumed an acquired traumatic mechanism for both (Strauss & Lehtinen, 1947). It was for this reason that in the 1950s organizations devoted to handicapped learners were often labeled for the "brain injured."

The observation that hyperkinetic behavior "paradoxically" might be reduced by chemical stimulants added an important dimension to the approach to developmental disorders (Bradley, 1957). Successful pharmacologic intervention represents molecular therapy and suggests that molecular mechanisms underlie the behavior. If so, then whenever these molecular derangements may occur, from conception onward, molecularly dependent hyperactivity and attention-control disturbance may ensue. What is yet to be determined is what are the specific developmental stages in pre- and postnatal cerebral evolution at which chemically mediated attention-control disorders inevitably occur.

The stage was set in 1962 for the use of the term "learning disabilities" as an attempt to encompass the aforementioned conditions, states, and presumed mechanisms of production (Kirk, 1962). Classroom educators were enjoined to serve these differing handicapping conditions in which familial and acquired factors might be causal and in which the manifestation was selective academic underachievement with or without nonpsychiatrically induced incorrigible behavior. Within this context, still another large and somewhat heterogeneous group of disabled learners was described in whom language skills were intact, visual motor skills were impaired, visuospatial abilities were lacking, and, most disabling of all, there was an impairment below cognitive estimates in comprehending the social emotional milieu. Johnson and Myklebust (1967) referred to these as "nonverbal learning disabilities." This condition shared some properties of the acquired hemiattention syndromes following right cerebral acquired diseases in adolescence and adulthood (Denckla, 1978; Weinstein & Friedland, 1977). Curiously, they shared the low performance IQ, common occurrence in females, mixed handedness, and constructional apraxia, which had been observed in the developmental cases of the Gerstmann syndrome. These observations further shifted the suspected lateralization for attention and calculation from the left to the right hemisphere.

The factor or factors which underlie each of these conditions disabling to learning may influence their natural history, successful intervention, or even prevention. What follows is a discussion of the tools available for investigating the biology of these conditions with samples of data which have been generated.

II. Tools and Levels of Investigation

The biologic substrate of behavior is open to several direct and indirect means of investigation which define anatomic, physiologic, and chemical parameters. *In vivo* analyses include two-dimensional imaging of CNS shapes, areas, textures, and densities, from which volumes and surfaces may be estimated. Computed tomography (CT) employs X-ray, while magnetic resonance imaging (MRI) is based on magnetic field oscillation of hydrogen atoms. The magnetic field pulse can be adjusted so that chemical structures more complex than hydrogen may be assessed. This gives MRI the potential for neurochemical assessments including visualizing neurotransmitters. Overall sharper resolution as well as excellent imaging of subcortical structures, especially the brain stem, give MRI an advantage for *in vivo* gross anatomic study. Recent advances in MRI technology permit volumetric estimates which are remarkably similar to values obtained at post-mortem. Density differences as small as 3 mm may be visible by MRI.

Neurophysiologic assessment of brain function is less palpable than imaging but yields estimates more obviously correlated with function. In the extreme, electroencephalographic (EEG) studies may be used to define life, whereas MRI images do not decline for several hours post-mortem. Resting EEG affords gross estimates of generalized or localized physiologic function. The EEG is the sine qua non for defining risk for clinical seizure. However, not every clinical seizure disorder is associated with recorded epileptogenic activity, nor is every epileptiform discharge equivalent to a seizure disorder. Sharply contoured wave forms, however, are physiologic signs of increased cortical neuronal irritability whether due to developmental anomaly or acquired injury such as trauma or stroke. The presence of such sharp waves requires explanation as they are rare in the asymptomatic population.

The last two decades have witnessed increased attempts to enhance the descriptive power of the EEG. With computer techniques the multitude of wave-form frequencies present in the EEG may be precisely quantified by so-called power spectral analysis. Additionally, such analysis may be graphically displayed in color upon brain diagrams. They may then be contrasted with control populations in what is called significance probability mapping, that is, how different is this topography from that of the general population? Such "maps" are useful but should not be considered equivalent to anatomic depictions. For example, changes in the EEG may be observed at some distance from the site of physical injury because of conduction along axonal networks. Although influenced by the anatomy, these EEG-generated maps depict a topography of the electrical landscape rather than a geography of the physical form.

Another computer-assisted physiologic technique is the analysis of event-related potentials (ERP). These wave forms represent averaged responses to controlled environmental variations such as light flashes, clicks, or tones. One such clinically available format is the auditory oddball paradigm which generates an N100 (downward deflecting at 100 msec) and P300 (upward deflecting at 300 msec) response. The characteristics of response latency, wave-form configuration, and topographic distribution have proven to be useful correlates in clinical seizure disorders and in some developmental disorders of language or attention (D. D. Duane, personal observations).

Both power spectral analysis and ERP are influenced by underlying anatomy, whether the anatomic variation is developmental or acquired. Unlike CT or MRI, they also are sensitive to the metabolic state of the subject, including the effects of medication. For example, increased amounts of beta (14–24 Hz frequency on power spectral analysis) frontal EEG activity occurs with the use of benzodiazepine drugs. Contrariwise, shortened latencies, elevated amplitudes, and more widespread distribution of P300 responses may follow acute use of methylphenidate (Ritalin).

Precision of anatomic correlation may be enhanced with a new technique referred to as magnetoencephalography (MEG), by which magnetic field analysis records the ionic activity of the brain rather than its electrical potentials by EEG. More precise localization of seizure foci may be achieved by MEG (Lopes da Silva & Van Rotterdam, 1987). The magnetic recording can be superimposed upon MRI anatomic images. Torello, Phillips, Hunter, and Csuri (1987) have recently suggested a similar imaging technique for computer-assisted EEG by which the EEG activity is superimposed upon two- or three-dimensional magnetic resonance images of the patient's brain. The effects of CNS shape and volume upon physiology thereby can be assessed.

In vivo techniques of measuring cerebral metabolic activity may include cerebral blood flow studies (CBF) following gas inhalation, single photon emission computed tomography (SPECT), and positron emission tomography (PET). Among the advantages of regional cerebral blood flow studies is the ability to separate cortical from subcortical vascular perfusion and non-dependence on X-ray. SPECT is also a blood flow measurement but records subcortical as well as cortical perfusion. A slight detraction for the study is the necessity of X-ray exposure. Both gas inhalation CBF and SPECT record events over 4–10 minutes. This poses constraints on task selection for investigation but is not an unreasonable window of investigation. Anatomic resolution is somewhat superior by SPECT than by cerebral blood flow. PET requires the introduction of a labile radioactive iosotope, thus carrying a health risk to the subject. Rather precise information, however, is gathered with respect to either glucose or oxygen utilization at the tissue level. The poorly defined metabolic images may be sharpened by using an MRI template for anatomic detail. Several minutes to almost an hour may be required to collect data by some PET techniques, which is a disadvantage in attempting to capture brain events which are evanescent. The immediacy to task response is an advantage of EEG physiological studies.

Readers, therefore, should be mindful of the relative advantages and limitations of each of the above investigative tools. Further, one should recognize that the processes assessed by each are not identical. Consequently, nonidentical results between types of investigations should be expected and may not be incongruent. It is the knowledgeable integration of the results from various investigative probes creatively employed which will unveil the mystery linking brain structure and function with behavior.

A. In Vitro *Studies*

There is no more direct assessment of the brain than its physical appearance to the naked eye or as explored by the microscope or when revealed by its assayed chemical remnants. The validity of brain-surface symmetry–asymmetry at autopsy was rediscovered by Norman Geschwind and Walter Levitsky (1968). The significance of this observation still needs elucidation, but in light of the finding of left greater than right temporal plane surface area and left more than right lateralization for language in man, Geschwind and Levitsky speculated that the two phenomena may be related.

Five decades earlier, Brodmann (1909) defined variations in the microscopic anatomy of the cortical surface of the brain in which the thickness and density of the six nerve-cell layers expanded and contracted from region to region. Later these fluctuations in thickness of the cortex were correlated with specific functions. This was part of the investigation of cerebral localization of function, from which it was accepted that cortical architecture would influence function and, indeed, that architecture might be influenced by function.

A variety of dyes and pigments were applied to the microscopic sections which variously illuminated nerve cells, axons, dendrites, or the supporting tissues of the brain. These early twentieth century investigators believed that they were exploring the cellular tapestry which represented the cloth of human experience. Disease states distort this fabric, but how nonmetabolic developmental disorders might be reflected in gross or microscopic anatomy awaited the research of the past decade in dyslexia. Ultramicroscopy utilizing the electron microscope identifies cell organelles such as the nucleus, mitochondria, and synaptic vesicles. Some of these are distorted in adult disease and in some rare metabolic disorders of childhood. The ultramicroscopic appearance of these organelles in various developmental learning disorders is still unknown.

That nerve cells excite or inhibit one another chemically is a discovery of the 1930s. Chemical analyses of these neurotransmitters became possible by the 1960s. This resulted in new brain maps of chemical territories for compounds such as catecholamines. This knowledge proved essential in uncovering the chemical basis of Parkinson's disease. The distribution of some chemical substances is normally asymmetric (Amaducci, Sorbi, Albanese, & Gianotti, 1981; Oke, Keller, Mefford, & Adams, 1978). The lateralized distribution of these substances as factors in various disease states remains unknown, although asymmetric dopamine depletion is observed in asymmetric Parkinson's disease. But where and how the asymmetry of neurotransmitters influences functions such as attention and memory is, at best, speculative (Weinstein & Friedland, 1977). Developmental conditions such as learning problems with specific deficits in memory may provide additional insight into the general principles of memory function, supplementing what is learned from their devastating loss in Alzheimer's disease.

III. Developmental Syndrome Investigations

A. Dyslexia

It is perhaps fortuitous that reading disability should be the most fully studied of the learning disorders. This investigation makes the case that brain mechanisms and learning behavior are intimately related, and, further, that explicating such childhood-onset conditions provides insights into biological mechanisms which have broad implications.

In 1978 a group of clinicians and brain researchers met at the request of the Orton Dyslexia Society to discuss the worthiness and feasibility of an autopsy study of the brains of individuals who in life had been diagnosed dyslexic. Attended by Macdonald Critchley, Robert Joynt, Richard Masland, Lauretta Bender, Sandra Witelson, Margaret Rawson, Roger Saunders, Drake Duane, and others, Norman Geschwind presented work of two of his junior colleagues, Albert Galaburda and Thomas Kemper. Their work was published the following year (Galaburda & Kemper, 1979). They reported a detailed gross and microscopic analysis of the CNS of a young man believed to have been dyslexic. These findings were so compelling that private philanthropy was sought and funding provided within 2 years for the Orton Dyslexia Brain Research Laboratory at the Beth Israel Hospital in Boston. As of this writing, the brains of ten individuals, seven males and three females, who in life were dyslexic have been examined. The results have been remarkably consistent and powerfully suggest that there is a relationship between the structure of the brain and difficulty in the acquisition of reading skill.

Galaburda and his co-workers (Galaburda, Rosen, & Sherman, 1989; Galaburda, Sherman, Rosen, Aboitiz, & Geschwind, 1985) have defined the following characteristics in the dyslexic central nervous system. First, the temporal plane, a wedge-shaped region of the superior surface of the temporal lobe, is symmetric on the two sides in all ten cases. Second, all of the males demonstrate specific multiple microscopic alterations referred to as focal cortical dysgenesis. Third, two of the three females and one of the seven males demonstrate multiple cortical lesions referred to as fibromyelin plaques.

The issue of symmetry and its regularity in this population is of considerable interest. In the late 1960s Geschwind with Levitsky had demonstrated that in 65% of an adult autopsy population the left temporal plane was significantly larger than the right (Geschwind & Levitsky, 1968). An association with the leftward lateralization for language was an obvious possibility which did not escape the attention of later investigators (Galaburda, LeMay, Kemper, & Geschwind, 1978). That the findings were nonartifactual was supported by repeated studies over the next decade consistently showing similar percentages of symmetry and asymmetry (Chi, Dooling, & Gilles, 1977; Wada, Clarke, & Hamm, 1975; Witelson & Pallie, 1973): approximately 65% left larger than right temporal plane, approximately 10% right larger than left temporal plane, and the remaining 25% demonstrating symmetry. Recent work by Galaburda, Corsiglia, Rosen, and Sherman (1987) suggests that the figure for symmetry of the temporal plane may be closer to 15%. Consequently, that 10 consecutive nervous systems would show symmetry is an extremely unlikely probability. It is therefore probable that some characteristic of the symmetric nervous system is related to dyslexic performance. Interestingly, symmetry does not result from a volume reduction of the left hemisphere or from an increase in the size of individual nerve cells, but rather from an overabundance of nerve cells in the right hemisphere in contrast to those with an asymmetric left-greater-than-right nervous system. A right cerebral increment in neurons may well have implications for information processing. It has been speculated that this overdevelopment of the right hemisphere accounts for the frequent occurrence of relative competence in quantitative thinking and visuospatial skill among those with reading disability.

Multifocal cortical dysgenesis also warrants consideration. There are three components to these regions of cellular anomaly: first, ectopias, that is, superficial clumps of nerve cells left behind in regions from which they should have migrated during fetal development; second, dysplasias, in which the organization of neurons is in minor disarray; and third, polymicrogyria, many microscopic in-foldings of the brain trapped beneath the cortical surface. These three components tend to cluster together. The clusters are observed bilaterally but asymmetrically and are far more prevalent in the left hemisphere than in the right. Although commonly frontal, they are predominantly located along the Sylvian fissure, that region of the brain about which language function has a proclivity.

These regions of focal cortical dysgenesis are in all likelihood the result of neuronal migration anomalies which occur in the second half of fetal brain development. What provokes them is not obvious but a number of speculations have been raised, two of which have significant importance in reshaping concepts of brain structure, function, and behavior. The postulate which Geschwind and Galaburda (1985) originally proposed related to the role of testosterone. There is some evidence that the male sex steroid may have an adverse effect on neuronal cell migration. The male fetus generates testosterone during embryogenesis. More recently, testosterone has been reimplicated by Galaburda (1990) as having a reverse effect, that is, sparing the most severe effects of presumptive immunologic mechanisms which lead to fetal wastage. Either of these were thought to explain the increased male-to-female ratio observed in populations with reading disability.

An alternative hypothesis is even more intriguing. Immunologic mechanisms are proposed by which antigens in the maternal circulation cross the placental barrier, attach to neurons through fetal intracranial circulation, and influence the organization, migration, and subsequent connectivity of neurons. Animal studies using the New Zealand black mouse, an immune incompetent creature, demonstrate similar regions of focal cortical dysgenesis in that animal's CNS. The effects in that animal are widespread, with altered patterns of cortical lamination and interneuronal connections (Sherman, Rosen, & Galaburda, 1989). Perhaps analogously, in apes experimental fetal brain lesions induce a remarkable reorganization of intra- and interhemispheric connections and consequent overgrowth of the contralateral hemisphere (Goldman-Rakic & Rakic, 1984). Such a mechanism could account for the symmetry of the temporal plane consequent to asymmetric cortical developmental alteration.

The theory of an immunologic basis for dyslexia and perhaps other learning disabilities is reinforced by the observation by Pennington, Smith, Kimberling, Green, and Haith (1987) of elevated titers of antinuclear antibodies in 65% of mothers with dyslexic offspring. Furthermore, mothers with systemic lupus erythematosus have higher than anticipated rates of children with learning disorders (Lahita, 1988). Although these may be construed as pathological in a negative sense, one should recognize that immunologic mechanisms are apt to have been present in our species from earliest times. Rather, it may be more productive to consider these as epigenetic mechanisms by which nature may vary CNS structure and consequent physiology, chemistry, and function, for example, the determinants of aptitudes. This is not to say genetic factors are nonoperative. Gene mechanisms may influence the probability of or responsiveness to the aforementioned mechanisms. However, Nowakowski (1988) has noted that several strains of mice may generate neuronal ectopias in the hippocampus. He speculates that these ectopias are solely under genetic influence.

The finding of fibromyelin plaques in two of the three dyslexic females and in one of the seven dyslexic males assessed by Galaburda and co-workers (1989) may be the result of microcirculation alterations that occur either in the last trimester of fetal development or during the period prior to postnatal year two (P. Humphreys, W. E. Kaufman & A. M. Galaburda, 1990). The distribution of these lesions in what is called the watershed region, a curvilinear cortical zone affected by circulation failure, is reminiscent of the effects of the perinatal stressor of maternal hypotension. That is, a reduction in maternal blood pressure is associated with a reduction in perfusion of the fetus. In regions such as the "watershed," relative deprivation of circulation may occur leading to these ischemic-induced alterations. Alternately, the ischemia is induced by autoimmune mechanisms, whether they be maternal or fetal in origin.

It is not unreasonable to speculate that these three mechanisms—symmetry pattern, cortical dysgenesis, and fibromyelin plaque formation—operating independently or in concert and to varying degrees and in varying locations may result in a number of variations in brain morphology and physiology with consequent variation in aptitude pattern. The extent to which such mechanisms in actuality contribute to reading disability, much less other disorders now referred to as learning disabilities, remains unknown. But these observations in dyslexia are of heuristic value in constructing hypotheses regarding learning disorders in general.

The interpretation of the microscopic pathology in the dyslexic nervous system is strongly influenced by recent work regarding neocortical development, including the role of radial-based glial cells (Rakic, 1988) in the construction of the normal cortical laminar pattern and cell-adhesion molecules (CAMs) and substrate-adhesion molecules (SAMs) which guide the migrating cellular array (Edelman, 1987). Operating at differential periods of brain development, these processes include postnatal adjustments in cortical architecture by which neuronal loss naturally occurs, perhaps involving up to 20% of the normal child's cortical neuronal population. So wide a window in brain development creates innumerable opportunities for variations in cortical structure and, in all likelihood, function. Intuitively, such processes must have implications for cognition.

While on the topic of dyslexia, which historically has been associated with concerns regarding hand preference and is now complicated by issues of temporal plane symmetry and asymmetry of cortical lesions, is the question of handedness. Samuel T. Orton (1937), in his description of children with reading and other language problems, was impressed with the frequency of ambidexterity and crossed eye–hand preference. This was taken as evidence for insecurity of lateralization not only of limbs but in visuospatial lateralization of individual letters and letter strings. Such a notion has improbable validity (Vellutino, 1979). However, although the majority of impaired readers are right handed, the extent of handedness as measured quantitatively by laterality indices suggests weak right handedness is unusually common among those with reading disability (D. D. Duane, personal observations; Galaburda, 1990). Whether this is the result of left-more-than-right cortical dysgenesis, temporal plane symmetry, or other as yet undetermined factors is not clear. What is suggested by my own clinical observations is that other learning disabilities are similarly overrepresented with weak right handedness, weak left handedness, and pathologic right handedness. The last represents dysfunction in the right hemisphere which in some way limits lateralization of motor function to the left hand. It may be that non-right handedness is associated with a higher risk of immunologic dysfunction (Geschwind & Behan, 1982).

Morbid anatomy represents the archeology of the brain. Cellular arrays and hemispheric volumes are the remnant artifacts of the evolution of the civilization of cells whose growth was stopped at a given point in that evolutionary cycle. The sociology of that civilization of cells during its lifetime constitutes the work of *in vivo* physiology and metabolic investigation.

For a number of years it has been suggested that subtle EEG alterations were observable in the population of those with reading disability. Event-related potentials were also described as somehow peculiar between the two hemispheres in those with reading disability as opposed to age-matched controls without reading problems (for a review, see Duane, 1983). The most revealing physiologic investigation of dyslexia employed computer-assisted EEG at rest and while engaged in a number of mental activities. This work by Duffy, Denckla, Bartels, and Sandini (1980) suggests physiologic alterations in the dyslexic population in two regions, left parietal and bilateral paracentral. These results are not necessarily at odds with the post-mortem findings by Galaburda, Rosen and Sherman (1989) since they sample different informational strata. Further, there likely is some heterogeneity within the population of those called dyslexic. In my own clinical EEG laboratory, among the physiologic concomitants of the symmetric nervous system is an asymmetry of resting alpha energies, greater in the right posterior hemisphere than the left. The same phenomenon may be observed in those with weak or non-right handedness. Although Duffy's study is not without criticism (Nuwer, 1988) and falls short of making a diagnosis, it is well conceived and supports further investigation using computer-assisted EEG techniques utilizing multiple paradigms in carefully selected populations with learning disorders.

The National Institute of Child Health and Human Development has funded a small group of dyslexia institutes. The group at Bowman Gray is headed by Frank Wood. In addition to an investigation of early school-age children, the investigators are utilizing a unique opportunity to evaluate a group of adults who in childhood were diagnosed dyslexic by the late Mrs. June Orton (wife of Samuel T. Orton). Based on CBF studies, the adult dyslexics demonstrate enhanced left temporal–parietal cortical activity versus controls (F. Wood, personal communication, 1990). Event-related potential studies in the same patient population show selective lexical attention difficulty. Utilizing PET this group, in addition to reconfirming bilateral temporal lobe enhanced activity in lexical tasks, previously observed by the University of Miami group headed by Herbert Lubs, has defined a link between left temporal lobe and left caudate nucleus function (F. Wood, personal communication, 1990).

It is noteworthy that four different lines of investigation—post-mortem anatomy, *in vivo* anatomy, electrophysiology, and metabolism through cerebral blood flow and PET studies—suggest bilaterality of function in controls and dyslexics with asymmetric changes in that bilaterality among dyslexics. Although preliminary, these early observations reintegrate the two hemispheres in normal and dyslexic function. Observations like these force a reconsideration of theories of brain function and may adjust the recent perhaps overemphasis on hemispheric specialization which focuses on solitary unilateral dysfunction.

The morbid anatomy of dyslexia also has restimulated thinking with respect to general and local configuration of the CNS and its volume. As a result, MRI techniques now are directed toward quantitative measurement of cortical areas, lobar volumes, and ventricular volumes. Work in dyslexic subjects supports relative symmetry of the parietooccipital width, which bears a strong although imperfect correlation with the surface volume of the temporal plane (Rumsey *et al.,* 1986). A rigorous attempt at documenting quantitative brain measurements or "morphometry" has been led by Caviness and Filipek and their associates at the Massachusetts General Hospital. This technique has already been successfully applied to developmental disorders of receptive spoken language (Filipek, Kennedy, Caviness, Klein, & Rapin, 1987). Auditory verbal agnosia was associated with a bilateral reduction in volume of the superior temporal lobes. It is reasonable to expect that in the decade ahead, as technology improves and if subject selection is precise, the quantitative approach to MRI assessment of brain volume and configuration should add accuracy to clinical diagnoses as well as stimulate new theories of brain function. An example is the description of midcerebellar hypoplasia in autism (Courchesne, Yeung-Courchesne, Press, Hesselink, & Jernigan, 1988). Although this observation may simply serve as a temporal marker for the developmental derangement in autism, it necessitates a reevaluation of the role of the cerebellum in cognition as well as in motor behavior (Berntson & Torello, 1982).

B. Attention-Deficit Hyperactivity Disorder

A problem in establishing the essential mechanism to attention-deficit hyperactivity disorder (ADHD) (which is equivalent to attention deficit disorder (ADD) with and without hyperactivity or attention-control disorder) is the multiplicity of disorders with which it may co-occur. Early descriptions described hyperkinetic behavior as a sequela to head trauma, CNS infection, cerebrovascular accident (Strauss & Lehtinen, 1947), and, more recently, toxic mechanisms including lead (Needleman et al., 1979). That the behavior may occur in association with reading disability, calculation disability, selective memory disturbance, or without apparent academic impact also confounds defining an essential pathogenesis (Clements & Peters, 1962; D. D. Duane, personal observations). Presence of the behavior in early childhood strongly suggests developmental mechanisms. The apparent gender preference for males and not infrequent familial occurrence reinforce the probability of biologic mechanisms (Cantwell, 1975).

It is unclear whether or not there are morphometric correlates with any of the forms of attention-control disorder. Hypoperfusion effects related to maternal stress or immunologic factors, as have been suggested in dyslexia, may be a factor in ADHD. Emission CT studies utilizing xenon gas inhalation demonstrate bilateral frontal cortical and subcortical defects ascribed to hypoperfusion (Lou, Hendrickson, & Bruhn, 1984). However, the study population included children with language disabilities in addition to those with attention-deficit disorder. The fact that the hypoperfusion changes were partially corrected in some instances following administration of methylphenidate (Ritalin) supports the probable role of molecular neurochemical mechanisms in attention-deficit disorder. Clinically it is clear that in many instances the alerting agents, amphetamine (Dexedrine), methylphenidate (Ritalin), and pemoline (Cylert), have a salutary effect on the symptoms of ADHD. However, the nonuniversal effectiveness of medicinal management as well as the differential effectiveness of more than one class of pharmacologic agent reinforces a sense of heterogeneity within this group of conditions. Despite the work with Piracetam, there is no comparable pharmacologic mechanism which has been postulated in isolated reading disorders. The present dearth of information should not lead to an assumption that there are no coexistent morphologic and neurochemical factors in some or many of the specific developmental disorders. Rather, the question remains unanswered.

The effectiveness of pharmacologic agents which putatively activate neurotransmitters within the arousal system has led to the hypothesis that arousal mechanisms are among those disturbed in attention-deficit disorders

(Wender, 1971). A possible clinical correlate is an observed unusual frequency of daytime nonalertness among those with a variety of learning disorders but especially attention-deficit disorder. My co-workers and I at Mayo Clinic, Rochester, were able to assess alertness using the pupillometer, a device used to clinically assess alertness in adults with narcolepsy (D. D. Duane, N. Rasmussen, R. C. Colligan, & F. Yan-Go, personal observations). This device records pupil size, and pupil size is inverse to the level of alertness, that is, pupils which progressively become smaller signify loss of alertness (Yoss, Moyer, & Ogle, 1969). Narcolepsy is a disorder in which daytime non-alertness occurs despite adequate nocturnal rest and may coexist with cataplexy, hypnagogic hallucinations, and sleep paralysis. In narcolepsy it is possible to titrate to pupillary stability following dosages of alerting medications. An example is assessing pupil stability, that is, alertness, following a specific dose of methylphenidate. Presently my colleagues and I are titrating dosages of alerting compounds in ADHD patients with pupillometry-determined nonalertness and assessing concomitant cognitive function. If at a specific dose of an alerting substance alertness is achieved, and at the same time there is improvement in previously deficient cognitive function, then there is double reinforcement that a specific dose of a specific medication has acute positive effects. Similarly, acute negative side effects, cognitive, behavioral, and tic movements, can be quantified. What factor or factors underlie the observed nonalertness which is not explained by impaired nocturnal rest remains unknown. A prospective study is underway to clarify the frequency of non-wakefulness in various learning disorders and controls (D. D. Duane & L. Epcar, in preparation). The presence of quantifiable motor system anomalies within the hyperactive population is further evidence for organic CNS mechanisms, in this instance reflected in the reduced speed of fine alternate distal limb movements and balance (Denckla & Rudel, 1978).

In the last 20 years physiologic alterations ranging from nonspecific EEG changes to subtle changes in evoked and event-related potentials have been described in the ADHD population. Clinically, my co-workers and I have observed a high percentage of anomalies of the latency and topography of the P300 response in the auditory oddball paradigm among those with clinically defined ADHD. These commonly normalize following effective doses of alerting medication. The P300, however, may also be altered in some forms of depression, alcoholism, schizophrenia, and dementia. Thus, what component of ADHD may account for the P300 latency prolongation is unclear. That this ERP is altered in psychiatric states and that depression may be prevalent among those with ADHD, and further that some ADHD syndromes respond to antidepressant drugs such as imipramine (Tofranil) and fluoxetine (Prozac), raise the possibility of an association between this disorder and psychiatric states, especially depression. If confirmed, the association may be at a biological level (Duane, 1989). The next decade portends for further explication of these associations between biologically determined learning disorders and emotional states.

C. Nonverbal Learning Disorders

In all probability this is also a heterogeneous group of disorders. Cognitive features include lowered performance IQ versus verbal IQ and specifically a reduction in perceptual organization factor from the subscale IQ score factor analysis. Behaviorally, these patients are motorically awkward, dysrhythmic, flat in affect, speak and read reasonably well, demonstrate marked constructional difficulties, calculate poorly, and, most devastating, inappropriately interact socially (Johnson, 1987; Voeller, 1986; Weintraub & Mesulam, 1983). Although the effects of gender are unclear, a number of studies have suggested that affected females outnumber affected males. Although non-right handedness and weak right handedness occur within this population, it is not clear whether it is with any greater or lesser prevalence than with other learning disorders. There are instances in this population of "pathologic" right handedness, that is, right cerebral dysfunction presumably limiting the option of left-hand preference. Hyperactivity and difficulty with attention are not uncommon in this group. But whether this is distinct from other forms of such behavior needs to be determined. ADHD symptoms may respond to medication but the academic difficulties and social–emotional impairments in this group generally are not benefited by alerting drugs.

Components of this syndrome in which there is an apparent limitation in perception or expression of vocal and gestural emotional cues have been described in acquired diseases of the right hemisphere referred to as the aprosodias (Ross, 1981). Although the mechanisms thought to underlie nonverbal learning disabilities have been lateralized to the right hemisphere, it is apparent that these phenomena may occur within a broad spectrum of circumstances. Among these are closed-head injury, intracranial surgery, and whole-head X-irradiation (Rourke, 1987). This and other so-called "right hemisyndromes" have been associated with EEG abnormalities including periodic sharp wave discharges. These discharges may represent effects of cortical dysgenesis, perinatal stress, or postdelivery head trauma. In all three groups of learning problems discussed above (dyslexia, ADHD, and nonverbal LD) occasional, febrile, or nocturnal seizures may co-occur. The occurrence of clinical seizure and/or potentially epileptiform discharges during electroencephalography in these patients reinforces organic cerebral mechanisms at least concurrent with learning disabilities. In my own clinical laboratory there appears to be an increased frequency of epileptiform discharges (not equivalent to clinical seizure) both among those with a history of learning disorders and among those with psychiatric diagnoses with coexistent learning problems. Both groups are weakly right handed by the Edinburgh laterality quotient (D. D. Duane, personal observation). At what stage or stages of cortical development, beginning with early neuronal migration during the first trimester of gestation through the final trimming of neurons in or beyond the fourth year of life, these epileptiform discharges emanate remains to be determined.

The nonverbal learning disorders have been said to be associated with elevated rates of depression (Brumback & Staton, 1982; Rourke, Young & Leenaars, 1989; Rutter, 1974). However, it is difficult in many of these nonverbal learning disabilities to assess clearly the affective level as it commonly seems shallow. But that may not be equivalent to depression. A potential biological link exists not only between nonverbal learning disorders and depression but between other states such as Tourette's syndrome (TS) and forms of learning disabilities and other psychiatric states, in this instance attention-deficit hyperactivity disorder and obsessive compulsive disorder (OCD) (Kurlan, 1989). It has been speculated that the gene expression may in the same family produce some members with TS, others with ADHD, still others with OCD, and combinations of these within affected members. Anxiety symptoms and panic attack are not rare among those with learning disorders. The extent to which these are also biologically produced as opposed to situational reaction or consequence of life experience remains to be determined (Altshuler, Devinsky, Post, & Theodore, 1990). One of the three females in the dyslexia autopsy study experienced nonpsychotic visual hallucinosis. My colleagues and I have seen three similar cases of visual hallucinosis among those with a history of learning disability (D. D. Duane, C. Crawford, & M. J. Brennan, personal observation). Thus, psychiatric disorder may not only be in the differential diagnosis of learning disabilities but may be among the differential manifestations.

IV. Conclusion

The above brief survey should establish that there is every reason to accept the notion that many problems in learning are the product of neurodevelopmental aberrations within the central nervous system. Indeed, learning disorders offer model syndromes for investigation which may reveal much about the usual course of brain development that results in less extreme variations in aptitude, that is, idiosyncrasy. Further, developmental disorders of learning may afford a means of gaining insight into biologic mechanisms underlying psychiatric disorders. It is reasonable to assert that these biologically induced variations in brain morphology, physiology, and chemistry influence aptitude patterns, attention-control mechanisms, and internally generated levels of mood and anxiety. Comprehending these biologically engendered qualities within learners and anticipating the response that various environmental settings provoke provides the power to adjust the environment to set and achieve realistic educational goals. Such power may not only facilitate school success but may help ensure mental health. The unraveling of these mechanisms should reveal the brain as a unified organ integrated with the behavior it produces.

References

Altshuler, L. L., Devinsky, O., Post, R. M., & Theodore, W. (1990). Depression, anxiety, and temporal lobe epilepsy: Laterality of focus and symptoms. *Archives of Neurology (Chicago)*, *47*, 284–288.

Amaducci, L., Sorbi, S., Albanese, A., & Gianotti, G. (1981). Choline acetyltransferase (ChAT) activity differs in right and left human temporal lobes. *Neurology, 31*, 799–805.

Benton, A. L. (1961). The fiction of the Gerstmann syndrome. *Journal of Neurology, Neurosurgery and Psychiatry, 24*, 176–181.

Berntson, G. G., & Torello, M. W. (1982). The paleocerebellum and the integration of behavioral function. *Physiological Psychology, 10*(1), 2–12.

Bradley, C. (1957). Characteristics and management of children with behavioral problems associated with brain damage. *Pediatric Clinics of North America, 4*, 1049–1060.

Broca, P. P. (1863). Localisation des fonctions cérébrales: Siège du langage articule. *Bulletin de la Societe d'Anthropologie de Paris, 4*, 200–203.

Broca, P. P. (1865). Sur la siège du faculté de langage articule. *Bulletin de la Societe d'Anthropologie de Paris, 6*, 377–393.

Brodmann, K. (1909). *Vergleichende Localisationslehre de Grosshirnrinde in ihren Prinzipien dargestellt auf Grund des Zellenbaues.* Leipzig: Barth.

Brumback, R. A., & Staton, R. D. (1982). An hypothesis regarding the commonality of right hemisphere involvement in learning disability, attentional disorder, and childhood major depressive disorder. *Perceptual Motor Skills, 55*, 1091–1097.

Cantwell, D. P. (1975). *The hyperactive child: diagnosis, management, current research.* New York: Spectrum Publications.

Chi, J. G., Dooling, E. C., & Gilles, F. H. (1977). Left-right asymmetries of the temporal speech areas of the human fetus. *Archives of Neurology (Chicago), 34*, 346–348.

Clements, S. D., & Peters, J. E. (1962). Minimal brain dysfunctions in the school-age child: diagnosis and treatment. *Archives of General Psychiatry, 6*, 185–197.

Courchesne, E., Yeung-Courchesne, R., Press, G. A., Hesselink, J. R., & Jernigan, T. L. (1988). Hypoplasia of cerebellar vermal lobules VI and VII in autism. *New England Journal of Medicine, 318*, 349–354.

Dejerine, J. J. (1892). Contribution à l'étude de l'anatomie-pathologique et clinique des différentes variétés de cécite verbale. *Comptes Rendus des Seances et Memoires de la Societe de Biologie et de Ses Filiales, 44*, 61–90.

Denckla, M. B. (1978). Minimal brain dysfunction. In J. S. Chall & A. F. Mirsky (Eds.), *Education and the brain* (National Society for the Study of Education Yearbook, 77, Part II, pp. 223–268), Chicago, IL: University of Chicago Press.

Denckla, M. B., & Rudel, R. G. (1978). Anomalies of motor development in hyperactive boys. *Annals of Neurology, 3,* 231–233.

Duane, D. D. (1983). Neurobiological correlates of reading disorders. *Journal of Educational Research, 77,* 1–15.

Duane, D. D. (1989). Neurobiological correlates of learning disorders. *Journal of the American Academy of Child and Adolescent Psychiatry, 28,* 314–318.

Duffy, F. H., Denckla, M. B., Bartels, P. H., & Sandini, G. (1980). Dyslexia: Regional differences in brain electrical activity by topographic mapping. *Annals of Neurology, 7,* 412–420.

Edelman, G. M. (1987). *Neural Darwinism: The theory of neuronal group selection.* New York: Basic Books.

Filipek, P. A., Kennedy, D. N., Caviness, V. S., Klein, S., & Rapin, I. (1987). *In vivo* magnetic resonance imaging-based volumetric brain analysis in subjects with verbal auditory agnosia. *Annals of Neurology, 22,* 410–411.

Galaburda, A. M. (1990). The testosterone hypothesis: Assessment since Geschwind and Behan, 1982. *Annals of Dyslexia, 40,* 18–38.

Galaburda, A. M., & Kemper, T. L. (1979). Cytoarchitectonic abnormalities in developmental dyslexia: A case study. *Annals of Neurology, 6,* 94–100.

Galaburda, A. M., Corsiglia, J., Rosen, G. D., & Sherman, G. F. (1987). Planum temporale asymmetry: Re-appraisal since Geschwind and Levitsky. *Neuropsychologia, 25,* 853–868.

Galaburda, A. M., LeMay, M., Kemper, T. L., & Geschwind, N. (1978). Right-left asymmetries in the brain: Structural differences between the hemispheres may underlie cerebral dominance. *Science, 199,* 852–856.

Galaburda, A. M., Rosen, G. F., & Sherman, G. D. (1989). The neural origin of developmental dyslexia: Implications for medicine, neurology and cognition. In A. M. Galaburda (Ed.), *From reading to neurons* (pp. 376–388). Cambridge, MA: MIT Press.

Galaburda, A. M., Sherman, G. F., Rosen, G. D., Aboitiz, F., & Geschwind, N. (1985). Developmental dyslexia: Four consecutive patients with cortical anomalies. *Annals of Neurology, 18,* 222–233.

Gerstmann, J. (1940). Syndrome of finger agnosia, disorientation for right and left, agraphia and acalculia: Local diagnostic value. *Archives of Neurology and Psychiatry, 44,* 398–408.

Geschwind, H., & Behan, P. (1982). Left-handedness: Association with immune disease, migraine and Developmental learning disorders. *Proceedings of the National Academy of Sciences of the U.S.A., 79,* 5097–5100.

Geschwind, N., & Galaburda, A. M. (1985). Cerebral lateralization: Biological mechanisms, association and pathology. *Archives of Neurology (Chicago), 42,* 428–462, 521–556, 634–654.

Geschwind, N., & Levitsky, W. (1968). Human brain: Left-right asymmetries in temporal speech region. *Science, 161,* 186–187.

Goldman-Rakic, P. S., & Rakic, P. (1984). Experimental modification of gyral patterns. In N. Geschwind & A. M. Galaburda (Eds.), *Cerebral dominance: The biological foundations* (pp. 179–192). Cambridge, MA: Harvard University Press.

Hécaen, J. (1962). Clinical symptomatology in right and left hemisphere lesions. In V. B. Mountcastle (Ed.), *Interhemispheric relations and cerebral dominance* (pp. 215–243). Baltimore, MD: Johns Hopkins University Press.

Henschen, S. (1920). *Klinische und Pathologische Beitrage zur Pathologie des Gehirns.* Stockholm: Nordiska Bokhandeln.

Hinshelwood, J. (1900). Congenital word-blindness. *Lancet, 1,* 1506–1508.

Humphreys, P., Kaufman, W. E., & Galaburda, A. M. (1990). Developmental dyslexia in women: Neuropathological findings in three cases. *Annals of Neurology, 28,* (in press).

Johnson, D. J. (1987). Nonverbal learning disabilities. *Pediatric Annals, 16,* 133–141.

Johnson, D. J., & Myklebust, H. (1967). *Learning disabilities: Educational principles and practices.* New York: Grune & Stratton.

Kinsbourne, M., & Warrington, E. T. (1963). The developmental Gerstmann syndrome. *Archives of Neurology (Chicago), 8,* 490–501.

Kirk, S. A. (1962). pp. 242–275. *Educating Exceptional Children.* Houghton Mifflin, Boston.

Kurlan, R. (1989). Tourette's syndrome: Current concepts. *Neurology, 39,* 1625–1630.

Lahita, R. G. (1988). Systemic lupus erythematosus: Learning disability in the male offspring of female patients and relationship to laterality. *Psychoneuroendocrinology, 13,* 385–396.

Lezak, M. D. (1983). *Neuropsychological assessment* (2nd ed.). New York: Oxford University Press.

Lopes da Silva, F., & Van Rotterdam, A. (1987). The biophysical aspects of EEG and magnetoencephalogam generation. In E. Niedermeyer & F. Lopes da Silva (Eds.), *Electroencephalography: Basic principles, clinical applications, and related fields* (2nd ed., pp. 29–41). Baltimore, MD: Urban & Schwarzenberg.

Lou, H. C., Hendrickson, L., & Bruhn, P. (1984). Focal cerebral hypoperfusion in children with dysphasia and/or attention deficit disorder. *Archives of Neurology (Chicago), 41,* 825–829.

Luria, A. R. (1966). *Higher cortical functions in man* (B. Haigh, Trans.). New York: Basic Books.

Morgan, W. P. (1896). A case of congenital word blindness. *British Medical Journal, 2,* 1378.

Needleman, H. D., Gunnoe, C., Leviton, A., Reed, R., Peresie, H., Maher, C., & Barrett, P. (1979). Deficits in psychologic and classroom performance of children with elevated dentine lead levels. *New England Journal of Medicine, 300,* 689–695.

Nowakowski, R. S. (1988). Development of the hippocampal formation in mutant mice. *Drug Development Research, 15,* 315–336.

Nuwer, M. R. (1988). Quantitative EEG: II. Frequency analysis and topographic mapping in clinical settings. *Journal of Clinical Neurophysiology, 5,* 45–85.

Oke, A., Keller, R., Mefford, I., & Adams, R. N. (1978). Lateralization of norepinephrine in human thalamus. *Science, 200,* 1411–1413.

Orton, S. T. (1937). *Reading, writing and speech problems in children: a presentation of certain types of disorders in the development of the language faculty.* New York: Norton.

Pennington, B. F., Smith, S. D., Kimberling, W. J., Green, P. A., & Haith, M. M. (1987). Left-handedness and immune disorders in familial dyslexics. *Archives of Neurology (Chicago), 44,* 634–639.

Rakic, P. (1988). Specification of cerebral cortical areas. *Science, 241,* 170–176.

Ross, E. D. (1981). The aprosodias: Functional-anatomic organization of the affective components of language in the right hemisphere. *Archives of Neurology (Chicago), 38,* 561–569.

Rourke, B. P. (1987). Syndrome of nonverbal learning disabilities: The final common pathway of white-matter disease/dysfunction? *Clinical Neuropsychologist, 1,* 209–234.

Rourke, B. P., Young, G. C., & Leenaars, A. A. (1989). A childhood learning disability that predisposes those afflicted to adolescent and adult depression and suicide risk. *Journal of Learning Disabilities, 22,* 169–175.

Rumsey, J. M., Dorwart, R., Vermess, M., Denckla, M. B., Kruesi, M. J. P., & Rapoport, J. (1986). Magnetic resonance imaging of brain anatomy in severe developmental dyslexia. *Archives of Neurology (Chicago), 43,* 1045–1046.

Rutter, M. (1974). Emotional disorder and educational underachievement. *Archives of Diseases in Childhood, 49,* 249–256.

Sherman, G. D., Rosen, G. F., & Galaburda, A. M. (1989). Animal models of developmental dyslexia: Brain lateralization and cortical pathology. In A. M. Galaburda (Ed.), *From reading to neurons* (pp. 389–404). Cambridge, MA: MIT Press.

Sperry, R. (1982). Some effects of disconnecting the cerebral hemispheres. *Science, 217,* 1223–1226.

Strauss, A. A., & Lehtinen, L. E. (1947). *Psychopathology and education of the brain-injured child.* New York: Grune & Stratton.

Torello, M. P., Phillips, T., Hunter, W. W., & Csuri, C. (1987). Combinational imaging: Magnetic resonance imaging and EEG displayed simultaneously. *Journal of Clinical Neurophysiology, 4,* 274–275.

Vellutino, F. R. (1979). *Dyslexia: Theory and research.* Cambridge, MA: MIT Press.

Voeller, K. K. S. (1986). Right-hemisphere deficit syndrome in children. *American Journal of Psychiatry, 143,* 1004–1009.

Wada, J. A., Clarke, R., & Hamm, A. (1975). Cerebral hemispheric asymmetry in humans: Cortical speech zones in 100 adults and 100 infant brains. *Archives of Neurology (Chicago), 32,* 239–246.

Weinstein, E. A., & Friedland, R. P. (Eds.). (1977). *Hemi-inattention and hemispheric specialization,* Advances in Neurology, Vol. 18. New York: Raven Press.

Weintraub, S., & Mesulam, M. M. (1983). Developmental learning disabilities of the right hemisphere: Emotional, interpersonal and cognitive components. *Archives of Neurology (Chicago), 40,* 463–468.

CHAPTER TWO

Etiology of Reading Deficits in Learning Disabilities: Quantitative Genetic Analysis

J. C. DeFries
Jacquelyn J. Gillis

I. Introduction

Quantitative genetics is concerned primarily with the inheritance of individual differences that are of degree, rather than of kind (Falconer, 1981). Such differences among individuals are usually caused by many genes, each with a relatively small effect, and by environmental influences. The effects of individual "polygenes" on quantitative characters are not readily discernible using the methodology of classical quantitative genetics; however, the aggregate importance of such genes can be assessed by their contribution to observed (phenotypic) variability in a population. Moreover, the increasing availability of DNA chromosomal markers may eventually make possible the systematic genetic dissection of quantitative characters (Lander & Botstein, 1989).

Quantitative genetic theory was developed about half a century ago by applied geneticists faced with the practical problem of improving polygenic characteristics in domestic animals and plants (Falconer, 1960; Lush, 1937; Mather, 1949). Although the mathematical model of quantitative genetics has not been substantially altered in recent decades (cf. Falconer, 1981), it provides the basis for a general theory of the etiology of individual differences (Plomin, DeFries, & Fulker, 1988) and its utilitarian value remains (Weir, Eisen, Goodman, & Namkoong, 1988).

Individual differences in most behavioral characters are due to multifactorial influences (Plomin, DeFries, & McClearn, 1990). Reading performance, for example, is continuously distributed and its expression is likely to be influenced by many genes; thus, although the etiology of extreme scores may differ from that of variation within the normal range, the methodology of quantitative genetics is particularly applicable to the analysis of the continuum of variation of reading performance (Stanovich, 1989).

Since the publication of Galton's (1875) article, "The History of Twins, as a Criterion of the Relative Powers of Nature and Nurture," behavioral scientists have been employing twin studies to learn how heredity and environment influence behavioral development (Loehlin & Nichols, 1976). To date, twin studies of behavioral characters have been of two major types: (1) comparisons of identical and fraternal twin correlations to assess the etiology of individual differences within the normal range of variation; and (2) comparisons of identical and fraternal twin concordance rates to test for the genetic etiology of various pathological conditions. More recently, DeFries and Fulker (1985, 1988) proposed a multiple regression analysis of twin data that facilitates an alternative test of genetic etiology as well as a quantitative genetic analysis of individual differences.

DeFries and Fulker (1985) first formulated a "basic model" in which a cotwin's score is predicted from that of a proband (the member of a pair of twins selected because of a deviant score on a continuous variable) and the coefficient of relationship. It was shown that application of this very simple analysis provides a statistically powerful test of genetic etiology and a measure of the extent to which the deficit exhibited by probands is heritable. By fitting an "augmented model" containing an interaction term to these same data, within-group heritability (a measure of the extent to which individual differences within the selected group are due to heritable influences) and the proportion of variance due to environmental influences shared by members of twin pairs can also be estimated. Moreover, a simple transformation of twin data prior to regression analysis affords a test of the hypothesis that the etiology of extreme scores may differ from that of variation within the normal range. In this chapter we outline this methodology and employ it to analyze reading performance data from twin pairs tested as part of the ongoing Colorado Reading Project (DeFries, 1985; DeFries, Fulker, & LaBuda, 1987). Before discussing this new methodology, however, we briefly review previous twin studies of reading disability.

II. Twin Concordance Rates

Previous twin studies of reading disability employed comparisons of concordance rates as a test for genetic etiology. In such studies, samples of twins are ascertained because at least one member of each pair is reading disabled. A pair is concordant if both members of the pair are affected but discordant if only one member of the pair is affected. Although the computation of a concordance rate is conceptually very simple (the percentage of probands with affected cotwins), the method by which the sample was ascertained must be considered.

As shown in Table I, both members of a twin pair may be affected (i.e., Twin 1 and Twin 2 are both +), only one may be affected (+ − or − +), or neither may be affected (− −). If Twin 1 is an arbitrarily specified member of the pair (e.g., the member of the pair born first), it may be seen that there are two ways in which a twin pair may be discordant (+ − and − +) and we expect that such pairs should occur with equal frequency in the population. If an entire population of twins is tested (e.g., all school-age twin pairs in Colorado), ascertainment is "complete" and the resulting sample size is A + 2B + C. However, if a partial sample of twins has been ascertained in which at least one member of each pair is affected, two alternative types of "incomplete ascertainment" may have been employed: (1) "single selection," in which only one member of a pair could be selected as a proband (i.e., there is no possibility that any twin pair could be ascertained more than once for inclusion in the sample); and (2) "truncate selection," in which both affected members of the pair can be ascertained as probands (Thompson & Thompson, 1986).

In order to illustrate the difference between single and truncate selection, assume that only first-born twins have been tested for reading deficits and that twin pairs with an affected proband have been included in our sample.

TABLE I Twin Pair Concordance or Discordance[a]

Number of pairs	Twin 1	Twin 2
A	+	+
B	+	−
B	−	+
C	−	−

[a] A + or − indicates that a member of a twin pair is affected or not affected for a condition such as reading disability.

Therefore, only twin pairs in the first two rows of Table I would have been ascertained and the resulting sample size would be A + B. Consequently, the corresponding estimate of the *pairwise* concordance rate (Plomin *et al.*, 1990) for reading disability would be A/(A + B). However, if both members of the pair were tested and could potentially be identified as probands, the twin pairs in the third row of Table I would also be ascertained, with a resulting sample size of A + 2B. When this method of ascertainment is employed, *probandwise* concordance should be computed. To estimate probandwise concordance, each member of a concordant pair is counted twice, once as a proband and once as a cotwin, which effectively increases the sample size to 2A + 2B pairs. This "double entry" of concordant pairs adjusts for the increase in the number of discordant pairs ascertained by truncate selection and results in a proband-wise concordance rate comparable to that of pairwise concordance with single selection, that is, $2A/(2A + 2B) = A/(A + B)$.

Previous twin studies of reading disability have recently been reviewed by Stevenson, Graham, Fredman, and McLoughlin (1984), Harris (1986), and LaBuda and DeFries (1990). Although it is likely that truncate selection was employed in previous twin studies of reading disability, pairwise concordance rates were reported in each of these reviews. If truncate selection is employed to ascertain a sample but pairwise concordance is computed [i.e., A/(A + 2B)], both identical and fraternal twin concordances will be underestimated. However, for conditions such as reading disability in which identical twin concordance is relatively high and fraternal twin concordance is intermediate, the underestimate will be greater for the fraternal twin pairs. The resulting bias will thus tend to exaggerate somewhat the importance of genetic factors in the etiology of reading disability. For example, in Bakwin's (1973) twin study of reading disability reviewed in more detail below, the identical and fraternal twin pairwise concordance rates were 84 and 29%, respectively, whereas the probandwise concordance rates are 91 and 45%. Of course, when 100% of the twin pairs are concordant, pairwise and probandwise concordance rates will be equal.

A. Previous Twin Studies

Probandwise concordance rates are presented in Table II for each of three previous twin studies of reading disability and for the ongoing Colorado Reading Project. The report by Zerbin-Rüdin (1967) is actually based upon a review of earlier case studies. Because these cases had been referred to clinics, ascertainment bias is possible in this sample (Belmont & Birch, 1965). Referrals to clinics may be more affected than subjects ascertained from school populations and severely affected twins are more likely to be concordant. Moreover, case studies of concordant twin pairs are more likely to be reported

TABLE II Probandwise Concordance Rates for Reading Disability

Study	Number of pairs		Concordance (%)	
	Identical	Fraternal	Identical	Fraternal
Zerbin-Rüdin (1967)	17	34	100	52
Bakwin (1973)	31	31	91	45
Stevenson et al. (1987)	14–19	27–42	33–59	29–54
Colorado Reading Project	96	96	71	49

than those of discordant pairs (Harris, 1986). Thus, the concordance rates estimated from the Zerbin-Rüdin (1967) report are probably inflated at least to some extent.

In contrast to Zerbin-Rüdin's (1967) summary of previous case studies, Bakwin (1973) ascertained pairs of same-sex twins through mothers-of-twins clubs. Reading history was obtained via interviews with parents, telephone calls, and mail questionnaires. The prevalence rate for reading disability in this sample of 676 children was 14.3% and was highly similar for both identical and fraternal twin pairs. However, as shown in Table II, the probandwise concordance rates are considerably different (91 and 45%, respectively). Thus, results obtained in Bakwin's twin study also suggest substantial genetic influence; however, his definition of reading disability "as a reading level below the expectation derived from the child's performance in other school subjects" (p. 184) is rather vague and evidence for the validity of the parental reports used in his study was not presented.

More recently, Stevenson et al. (1984) and Stevenson, Graham, Fredman, and McLoughlin (1987) reported results of a twin study of reading ability and disability in a sample of 285 pairs of 13-year-old twins ascertained by screening hospital records in five London boroughs or through primary schools in the London area. Physical similarity and, when necessary, dermatoglyphics and blood-group testing were employed to assess zygosity. The Schonell Graded Word Reading and Spelling Tests and the Neale Analysis of Reading Ability were used to diagnose twins who were reading or spelling "backward," or reading or spelling "retarded." Reading or spelling "backwardness" was identified by the presence of reading or spelling age below chronological age, whereas reading or spelling "retardation" was defined by marked under achievement in reading or spelling relative to that predicted from IQ and chronological age. Unexpectedly, the prevalence of reading and spelling problems in fraternal twins was nearly twice that in identical twins. Although pairwise concordance rates were presented in the earlier report (Stevenson et al., 1984), probandwise concordances were presented in the later publication (Stevenson et al., 1987). As shown in Table II, these probandwise concordance rates for various diagnostic criteria ranged from 33 to 59% for identical twins and from 29 to 54% for fraternal twins. The authors speculated that the lower concordance rates for reading disability obtained in this study may have been due to differences in ascertainment, definition, or zygosity determination. Moreover, they suggested the interesting hypothesis that the genetic etiology for reading disability in children 13 years of age may be less important than in younger children.

The probandwise concordance rate for identical twin pairs exceeds that for fraternal twin pairs in each of the three previous twin studies summarized in Table II. Although this result is consistent with the hypothesis of a genetic etiology for reading disability, substantial variation in concordance rates occurred among studies. Results obtained from the Zerbin-Rüdin (1967) and Bakwin (1973) studies suggest that reading deficits may be highly heritable, whereas those of Stevenson et al. (1987) indicate less genetic influence. Such variation among studies substantiates the need for additional research. As Harris (1986) recently noted, ". . . in reading disability, a large and well ascertained sample of affected twins and their co-twins, whose affection status is documented and zygosity is determined by highly reliable methods, has not to my knowledge been described and would be a welcomed addition to research in this area. Ascertainment schemes that assure that the probability of being identified as a reading-disabled twin individual is not related to the affection status of the co-twin are essential" (Harris, 1986, p. 16).

B. The Colorado Reading Project

Because of the paucity of well-designed twin studies of reading problems, a twin study of reading disability was initiated in 1982 as part of the ongoing Colorado Reading Project (Decker & Vandenberg, 1985; DeFries, 1985). An extensive psychometric test battery is currently being administered to identical and fraternal twin pairs in which at least one member of each pair is reading disabled and to a comparison group of twins who are normal readers. In order to minimize the possibility of ascertainment bias, this sample of twins is being systematically obtained through cooperating school districts in Colorado.

Twin pairs are identified by school district administrators and permission is then sought from parents to review the school records of each twin for evidence of reading problems. Such evidence includes low reading achievement test scores, referral to a reading therapist because of poor reading performance, reports by classroom teachers or school psychologists, and parental interviews (Gillis & DeFries, 1989). Pairs of twins in which at least one member has a reading problem are then asked to complete an extensive battery of psychometric tests in our laboratory at the University of Colorado. Included in this psychometric test battery are the Wechsler Intelligence Scale for

Children-Revised (WISC-R) (Wechsler, 1974) or the Wechsler Adult Intelligence Scale-Revised (WAIS-R) (Wechsler, 1981) and the Peabody Individual Achievement Test (PIAT) (Dunn & Markwardt, 1970). Using data from the PIAT Reading Recognition, Reading Comprehension, and Spelling subtests, a discriminant function score is computed for each member of the pair. The discriminant weights employed in this computation were estimated from an analysis of data obtained from an independent sample of 140 reading-disabled and 140 control nontwin children. In order for a twin pair to be included in the proband sample, at least one member with a positive school history for reading problems must also be classified as affected by the discriminant score. In addition, probands must have an IQ score of at least 90 on either the Verbal or the Performance Scale of the WISC-R or WAIS-R; have no diagnosed neurological, emotional, or behavioral problems; and have no uncorrected visual or auditory acuity deficits. Control twins are matched to probands on the basis of age, gender, and school district; must have a negative school history for reading problems; and must be classified by the discriminant analysis as unaffected.

Zygosity of the twin pairs is determined by selected items from the Nichols and Bilbro (1966) questionnaire, which has a reported accuracy of 95%. In doubtful cases, zygosity is confirmed by analysis of blood samples. The twin pairs are all reared in English-speaking, middle-class homes, and they range in age from 8 to 20 years at the time of testing. To date, a total of 96 pairs of identical (monozygotic, or MZ) twins, 72 pairs of same-sex fraternal (dizygotic, or DZ) twins, and 24 pairs of opposite-sex DZ twins meet our criteria for inclusion in the proband sample. As a comparison group, we have also tested a total of 96 pairs of MZ twins and 67 pairs of same-sex DZ twins that meet our criteria for inclusion in the control sample.

In contrast to our nontwin sample in which the gender ratio is 3.8 males to each female, the numbers of male and female probands in the twin sample are 137 and 139, respectively. This lower gender ratio for members of twin pairs may be due to a differential volunteer rate of male and female twin pairs; female MZ pairs tend to be overrepresented in twin studies (Lykken, Tellegen, & DeRubeis, 1978). On the other hand, it is also possible that the excess of male subjects invariably found in referred samples of reading-disabled children may be due at least in part to a referral bias (Finucci & Childs, 1981).

From Table II it may be seen that the number of affected twin pairs tested to date in the Colorado Reading Project exceeds the total number of reading-disabled twin pairs tested in all previous studies. Thus, considerable confidence can be placed in the results of this single study. The probandwise concordance rate of 71% for MZ twin pairs is substantially greater than that for DZ twins (49%), thereby confirming the evidence for a genetic etiology of reading disability obtained in previous twin studies.

III. Multiple Regression Analyses of Twin Data

A comparison of concordance rates as a test for genetic etiology is especially appropriate for categorical variables, for example, presence or absence of a psychiatric illness. However, reading disability is operationally defined (Wong, 1986) and the diagnosis is made on the basis of a continuous measure (e.g., reading performance) with arbitrary cutoff points (Stevenson *et al.*, 1987). Transformation of a quantitative scale such as reading performance into a categorical variable (e.g., reading disabled versus normal) obviously results in a loss of important information pertaining to differences both between and within the two categories.

A methodology that facilitates the analysis of both between-group and within-group variation should be preferable to one that ignores the continuum of variation in reading performance. Recently, DeFries and Fulker (1985) proposed such a methodology as indicated above. A multiple regression analysis of twin data was advocated in which a cotwin's score is predicted from that of a proband (the member of the pair selected because of a deviant score on a continuous measure such as reading performance) and the coefficient of relationship ($R = 1.0$ for MZ twin pairs and 0.5 for DZ twin pairs). Two models were formulated: (1) a basic model in which the partial regression of cotwin's score on the coefficient of relationship provides a test for genetic etiology, and (2) an augmented model containing an interaction term between proband's score and relationship that yields direct estimates of heritability (h^2) and the proportion of variance due to environmental influences shared by members of twin pairs (c^2) potentially relevant to the unselected population.

DeFries and Fulker (1985) also illustrated how the results of fitting the basic model to selected twin data could be used to obtain an estimate of h_g^2, a measure of the extent to which the deficit of probands is due to heritable influences. Moreover, it was suggested that a comparison of h_g^2 and h^2 could be used to test the hypothesis that the etiology of extreme scores differs from that of variation within the normal range. Unexpectedly low reading performance, for example, could be due to a major gene effect, to a chromosomal anomaly, or to some environmental insult, whereas individual differences within the selected group may be due to polygenic or multifactorial influences. In such a case, h_g^2 and h^2 would be expected to differ in magnitude. On the other hand, if the probands merely represent the lower tail of a normal distribution of individual differences, h_g^2 and h^2 should be similar in magnitude. Subsequently, DeFries and Fulker (1988) noted that a simple transformation of twin data prior to multiple regression analysis facilitates direct estimates of both h_g^2 and h^2, as well as a test of their difference.

A. Models

In contrast to the comparison of concordance rates in identical (MZ) and fraternal (DZ) twin pairs that had been used as a test for genetic etiology in previous studies, DeFries and Fulker (1985) proposed that a comparison of MZ and DZ cotwin means is more appropriate. As shown in Fig. 1, when probands have been ascertained because of extreme scores on a continuous measure such as reading performance, the scores of both the MZ and the DZ cotwins are expected to regress toward the mean of the unselected population. However, to the extent that the condition has a genetic etiology, this regression toward the mean should differ for MZ and DZ cotwins. Because the coefficient of relationship is 1 for MZ twins, but only .5 for DZ twins, scores of DZ cotwins should regress more toward the mean of the unselected population. Therefore, if the means for the MZ and DZ probands are equal, a simple t test of the difference between the means of the MZ and DZ cotwins would suffice as a test for genetic etiology. However, the partial regression of cotwin's score on the coefficient of relationship, independent of proband's score, provides a more general, statistically powerful, and flexible test (DeFries & Fulker, 1988). In addition, by adding the product of the proband's score and the coefficient of relationship to the model during a second step in the analysis, direct estimates of h^2 and c^2 can also be obtained. Because regression coefficients are less influenced by restriction of range of the independent variables (e.g., reading performance scores of reading-disabled children), regression analyses of such attenuated data are more appropriate than correlation analyses (Cohen & Cohen, 1975; Morton, 1982).

The basic model in which a cotwin's score (C) is predicted from the proband's score (P) and the coefficient of relationship (R) is as follows:

$$C = B_1P + B_2R + A \tag{1}$$

where B_1 is the partial regression of cotwin's score on proband's score, B_2 is the partial regression of cotwin's score on relationship, and A is the regression constant.

As shown in Eq. 2, the augmented model is the basic model plus an interaction term:

$$C = B_3P + B_4R + B_5PR + A \tag{2}$$

where PR is the product of proband's score and the coefficient of relationship. Because inclusion of the interaction term in the augmented model changes the expectations for the partial regression coefficients estimated from the basic model, the coefficients of P and R are symbolized B_3 and B_4 in Eq. 2.

DeFries and Fulker (1985) asserted that B_1 is a measure of average twin resemblance and that B_2 equals twice the difference between the means for

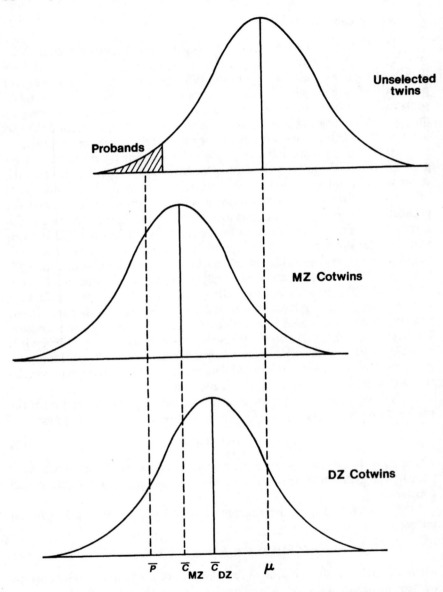

FIGURE 1 Hypothetical distributions for reading performance of an unselected sample of twins and of the identical (MZ) and fraternal (DZ) cotwins of probands with a reading disability. The differential regression of the MZ and DZ cotwin means toward the mean of the unselected population (μ) provides a test of genetic etiology. [From DeFries, Fulker, and LaBuda, (1987). Reprinted by permission from *Nature*, Vol. 329, p. 537. Copyright (c) 1987, Macmillan Magazines Ltd.]

MZ and DZ cotwins after covariance adjustment for any difference between MZ and DZ probands. Therefore, B_2 was advocated as a test of significance for genetic etiology. In addition, it was suggested that the ratio of B_2 to the difference between the mean for probands and that for the unselected population could be used to estimate h_g^2. Moreover, they demonstrated that B_3 and B_5 provide direct estimates of c^2 and h^2.

LaBuda, DeFries, and Fulker (1986) subsequently derived the expected partial regression coefficients for the basic and augmented models as functions of additive genetic variance (V_A), variance due to environmental influences shared by members of twin pairs (V_C), phenotypic variance (V_P), and the cotwin and proband means. Given the standard assumptions of quantitative genetic analyses of twin data (e.g., a linear polygenic model, little or no assortative mating, and equal shared environmental influences for MZ and DZ twin pairs), they showed that B_1 is a weighted average of twin resemblance in the combined sample of MZ and DZ twin pairs and that B_2 equals twice the difference between the means for MZ and DZ cotwins after covariance adjustment for the difference between the means for MZ and DZ probands.

The expected partial regression coefficients estimated from the fit of the augmented model were shown to be as follows:

$$B_3 = V_C/V_P = c^2 \tag{3}$$

$$B_4 = 2\{(\overline{C}_{MZ} - \overline{C}_{DZ}) - [\overline{P}_{MZ}(h^2 + c^2) - \overline{P}_{DZ}(h^2/2 + c^2)]\} \tag{4}$$

$$B_5 = V_A/V_P = h^2 \tag{5}$$

Thus, B_3 and B_5 provide unbiased estimates of c^2 and h^2, respectively. B_4 is a function of twice the difference between the means for MZ and DZ cotwins; however, unlike B_2, it does not provide a test for genetic etiology. In fact, when the twin data are transformed by expressing each score as a deviation from the mean of the unselected population and dividing by the proband mean, B_2 directly estimates h_g^2 and B_4 estimates $h_g^2 - h^2$ (DeFries & Fulker, 1988). Thus, by fitting the basic and augmented models to selected MZ and DZ twin data transformed in this very simple manner, direct estimates of h_g^2 (an index of the extent to which the difference between the mean for probands and that for the unselected population is heritable), c^2, h^2, and $h_g^2 - h^2$ (a test of the hypothesis that the etiology of extreme scores differs from that of variation within the normal range) are obtained.

B. Application

To illustrate the application of this methodology, the basic and augmented models were fitted to discriminant function data from twin pairs tested in the Colorado Reading Project. Because the probands were selected

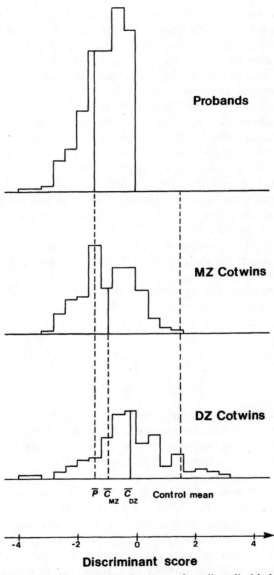

FIGURE 2 Discriminant score distributions of reading-disabled probands, MZ cotwins, and DZ cotwins tested in the Colorado Reading Project.

TABLE III Mean Discriminant Scores of
96 Pairs of Identical Twins and 96 Pairs of
Fraternal Twins in Which at Least One
Member of Each Pair is Reading Disabled[a]

	Probands	Cotwins
Identical	−3.28	−3.04
Fraternal	−3.07	−2.12

[a] Expressed as standardized deviations from control
mean.

on the basis of their discriminant scores (a composite measure of performance
on the Reading Recognition, Reading Comprehension, and Spelling subtests
of the PIAT), the fit of the basic model to data for that measure is most
appropriate as a test of genetic etiology.

Discriminant score distributions for the probands, the MZ cotwins, and
the DZ cotwins are depicted in Fig. 2. From this figure it may be seen that the
scores of the MZ and DZ cotwins have regressed differentially toward the
mean of the control sample. The average discriminant scores of the MZ and
DZ probands and cotwins, expressed as standardized deviations from the
control mean, are presented in Table III. (Because truncate selection was
employed to ascertain this sample of affected twins, concordant pairs have
been double entered for all analyses in a manner analogous to that used for
computation of the probandwise concordance rates.) From Table III it may be
seen that the average discriminant scores of the MZ and DZ probands are
highly similar and over three standard deviations below the mean of the
matched comparison sample of unaffected twins. It may also be seen that the
scores of the DZ cotwins have regressed 0.95 standard deviation units on the
average toward the control mean, whereas those of the MZ cotwins have
regressed only 0.24 standard deviation units. When the basic model was fitted
to these data, the resulting highly significant B_2 estimate of -1.60 ± 0.35
($p < .001$, one tailed) was a function of this differential regression of the MZ
and DZ cotwin scores and it provides the best evidence to date for the
heritable nature of reading disability. Moreover, when the basic model was
fitted to transformed data in which each score is expressed as a deviation from
the control mean and divided by the proband mean, $B_2 = h_g^2 = 0.50 \pm 0.11$.
This result suggests that about half of the reading performance deficit of
probands, on average, is due to heritable factors.

The regressions of cotwin's score on proband's score for the MZ and DZ
twin pairs are presented in Table IV, as are the results of fitting the augmented
model to the transformed discriminant function score data. As expected,

TABLE IV MZ and DZ Regressions for Discriminant Score and Results of the Augmented Regression Analysis

Regression of cotwin's score on proband's score	MZ twins: .83 ± .10	DZ twins: .42 ± .16
Results of augmented regression analysis	$B_3 = c^2 = .00 ± .29$	
	$B_4 = h^2_g - h^2 = -.32 ± .39 \ (p > .40)$	
	$B_5 = h^2 = .82 ± .37 \ (p < .05)$	

$B_5 = h^2$ is twice the difference between the MZ and DZ regression coefficients. The resulting estimate of $h^2 = 0.82$ suggests that individual differences within the selected group are highly heritable. In contrast, environmental influences that are shared by members of twin pairs ($c^2 = 0.00$) are not an important source of variation within the selected group. It is interesting to note that highly similar estimates ($h^2 = 0.69 ± 0.30$ and $c^2 = -0.01 ± 0.25$) were obtained when the augmented model was fitted to reading performance data from the 96 pairs of MZ twins and 67 pairs of same-sex DZ twins included in the control sample.

Finally, and perhaps most importantly, estimates of h^2_g and h^2 can be compared to test the hypothesis that the etiology of extreme scores differs from that of variation within the normal range. Although the obtained estimates of 0.50 and 0.82 are rather discrepant, suggesting that probands may not merely represent the lower tail of a normal distribution of individual differences, the B_4 term in Table IV is nonsignificant. Because the statistical power to detect a significant difference between h^2_g and h^2 is relatively low (DeFries & Fulker, 1988), a larger sample of twins will be needed to test this hypothesis more rigorously.

IV. Discussion

Previous twin studies of reading disability employed a comparison of MZ and DZ concordance rates as a test for genetic etiology. A pair is concordant if both members of the pair are affected but discordant if only one member of the pair has a disability. Previous reviews of these twin studies reported pairwise concordance rates. If "single selection" is employed to ascertain a twin sample (i.e., if only one member of a twin pair could be ascertained as a proband), pairwise concordance would be appropriate. However, if "truncate selection" is employed in which both affected members of each pair could have been ascertained as probands, probandwise concordance should be reported. In order to compute probandwise concordance, each member of a concordant pair is counted twice, once as a proband and once as a cotwin. Because it is likely that truncate selection was employed in previous twin studies of reading disability, probandwise concordance rates are reported in this chapter.

Probandwise concordance rates are higher for pairs of MZ twins than for DZ twin pairs in each of the three previous studies reviewed in this chapter. However, considerable variation exists among studies and the most recent study (Stevenson et al., 1987) suggests little genetic influence. The sample of reading-disabled twin pairs tested in the ongoing Colorado Reading Project (96 pairs of MZ twins and 96 pairs of DZ twins) is larger than the total number of twin pairs with reading disability reported in the previous world's literature. Thus, the results obtained from this single study should be especially informative. The estimated probandwise concordance rates for these MZ and DZ twin pairs are 71 and 49%, respectively, suggesting a substantial genetic etiology for reading disability.

As outlined in this chapter, the multiple regression analysis of selected twin data provides a more powerful and flexible test of genetic etiology than does a comparison of concordance rates. When probands are identified because of deviant scores on a continuous variable such as reading performance, the differential regression of scores of MZ and DZ cotwins toward the mean of the unselected population provides a test for genetic etiology. When the basic model in which a cotwin's score is predicted from the proband's score and the coefficient of relationship is fitted to such data, the partial regression of cotwin's score on relationship estimates twice the difference between the means of the MZ and DZ cotwins after covariance adjustment for any difference between the MZ and DZ probands. If each score is transformed by expressing it as a deviation from the mean of the unselected population and dividing by the proband mean, this regression coefficient directly estimates h_g^2, a measure of the extent to which the deficit of probands is due to heritable influences. When the basic model was fitted to transformed reading performance data from reading-disabled MZ and DZ twin pairs tested in the Colorado Reading Project, an estimate of $h_g^2 = 0.50 \pm 0.11$ was obtained. This result suggests that about half of the deficit in the reading performance of probands is due to heritable influences.

In order to estimate h_g^2 for a particular variable, probands are diagnosed because of deviant scores for that measure. Then, the basic model is fitted to the probands' and cotwins' scores for that variable. In contrast to this univariate analysis, it would also be possible to select probands on the basis of their performance on some character (X) and then fit the basic model to data for a correlated character (Y). For example, Olson, Wise, Conners, Rack, and Fulker (1989) recently used such an approach to analyze phonological and orthographic coding deficits in our sample of reading-disabled twins. For these analyses they selected probands on the basis of their deficits in PIAT Reading Recognition and then fitted the basic model twice, once to the phonological data and once to the orthographic data. A very interesting pattern of differential results was obtained for the two correlated characters: The "heritability" estimate obtained for the phonological coding measure was large (0.93) and highly significant, whereas that for orthographic coding was small (-0.16) and nonsignificant. These bivariate "heritability estimates" are functions of the genetic covariance between the selected variable and the correlated variable. Therefore, the pattern of results obtained by Olson et al. (1989) suggests that the phonological coding and word recognition deficits of probands are largely due to the same genetic factors, whereas the deficit of probands with regard to orthographic coding is primarily due to environmental influences.

The basic model for the multiple regression analysis of twin data can be easily extended to include other main effects and interactions (Cohen & Cohen, 1975) in order to test for differential genetic etiology as a function of group membership. For example, Harris (1986) suggested that twin analyses of reading disability should be conducted separately for males and females because of the possibility of differential genetic etiology as a function of gender. However, this hypothesis can be tested more explicitly by fitting a basic regression model that includes an interaction between gender (a dummy variable) and relationship to data from male and female twin pairs simultaneously.

Age adjustment could be easily accomplished by including age of proband as another independent variable in the regression model. Moreover, by including the product of age and the coefficient of relationship in the basic model, it would be possible to test Stevenson et al.'s (1987) hypothesis of differential genetic etiology as a function of age. In a similar manner, data from probands of ostensibly different subtypes could be analyzed to test for differential genetic etiology. Such analyses could be employed to validate alternative typologies and to test the "assumption of specificity" (Stanovich, 1986).

By fitting an augmented model containing an interaction term between proband's score and the coefficient of relationship to twin data, direct estimates of h^2 and c^2 can also be obtained. When the augmented model was fitted to reading performance data from reading-disabled MZ and DZ twin pairs tested in the Colorado Reading Project, estimates of $h^2 = 0.82 \pm 0.37$ and $c^2 = 0.00 \pm 0.29$ were obtained. These results suggest that individual differences in reading performance within the affected sample are highly heritable.

A simple transformation of selected twin data prior to multiple regression analysis facilitates a test of the hypothesis that the etiology of extreme scores differs from that of variation within the normal range. When the augmented model is fitted to twin data transformed by expressing each score as a deviation from the proband mean and dividing by the proband mean, the partial regression of cotwin's score on the coefficient of relationship tests the significance of the difference between h_g^2 and h^2. Because the power to detect a significant difference between these two genetic parameters is relatively low (DeFries & Fulker, 1988), data from a large sample of probands and cotwins would be required to test this hypothesis rigorously. Nevertheless, because such a test is of considerable theoretical interest, especially with regard to the issue of specificity of the deficit in reading disability (Foorman, 1989), additional testing of twins in which at least one member is reading disabled is clearly warranted.

Acknowledgment

This work was supported in part by a program project grant from NICHD (HD-11681), and the report was prepared while J. Gillis was supported by NICHD training grant HD-07289. The invaluable contributions of staff members of the many Colorado school districts and of the families who participated in this study are gratefully acknowledged. We also thank Drs. Robin P. Corley and Michele C. LaBuda for aid with the statistical analyses and Rebecca G. Miles for expert editorial assistance.

References

Bakwin, H. (1973). Reading disability in twins. *Developmental Medicine and Child Neurology, 15,* 184–187.

Belmont, L., & Birch, H. G. (1965). Lateral dominance, lateral awareness and reading disability. *Child Development, 36,* 57–72.

Cohen, J., & Cohen, P. (1975). *Applied multiple regression/correlation analysis for the behavioral sciences.* Hillsdale, NJ: Lawrence Erlbaum Associates.

Decker, S. N., & Vandenberg, S. G. (1985). Colorado twin study of reading disability. In D. B. Gray & J. F. Kavanagh (Eds.), *Biobehavioral measures of dyslexia* (pp. 123–135). Parkton, MD: York Press.

DeFries, J. C. (1985). Colorado reading project. In D. B. Gray & J. F. Kavanagh (Eds.), *Biobehavioral measures of dyslexia* (pp. 107–122). Parkton, MD: York Press.

DeFries, J. C., & Fulker, D. W. (1985). Multiple regression analysis of twin data. *Behavior Genetics, 15,* 467–473.

DeFries, J. C., & Fulker, D. W. (1988). Multiple regression analysis of twin data: Etiology of deviant scores versus individual differences. *Acta Geneticae Medicae et Gemellologiae: Twin Research, 37,* 205–216.

DeFries, J. C., Fulker, D. W., & LaBuda, M. C. (1987). Evidence for a genetic aetiology in reading disability of twins. *Nature (London), 329,* 537–539.

Dunn, L. M., & Markwardt, F. C. (1970). *Examiner's manual: Peabody Individual Achievement Test.* Circle Pines, MN: American Guidance Service.

Falconer, D. S. (1960). *Introduction to quantitative genetics.* New York: Ronald Press.

Falconer, D. S. (1981). *Introduction to quantitative genetics* (2nd ed.). London: Longman.

Finucci, J. M., & Childs, B. (1981). Are there really more dyslexic boys than girls? In A. Ansara, N. Geschwind, A. Galaburda, M. Albert, & N. Gartrell (Eds.), *Sex differences in dyslexia* (pp. 11–19). Towson, MD: Orton Dyslexia Society.

Foorman, B. R. (1989). What's specific about specific reading disability: An introduction to the special series. *Journal of Learning Disabilities, 22,* 332–333.

Galton, F. (1875). The history of twins, as a criterion of the relative powers of nature and nurture. *Fraser's Magazine, 92,* 566–576.

Gillis, J. J., & DeFries, J. C. (1989). Validity of school history as a diagnostic criterion for reading disability. *Reading and Writing: An Interdisciplinary Journal, 1,* 93–101.

Harris, E. L. (1986). The contribution of twin research to the study of the etiology of reading disability. In S. D. Smith (Ed.), *Genetics and learning disabilities* (pp. 3–19). San Diego, CA: College-Hill Press.

LaBuda, M. C., & DeFries, J. C. (1990). Genetic etiology of reading disability: Evidence from a twin study. In G. Th. Pavlidis (ed.), *Perspectives on dyslexia: Vol. 1. Neurology, neuropsychology and genetics* (pp. 47–76). Chichester, England: Wiley.

LaBuda, M. C., DeFries, J. C., & Fulker, D. W. (1986). Multiple regression analysis of twin data obtained from selected samples. *Genetic Epidemiology, 3,* 425–433.

Lander, E. S., & Botstein, D. (1989). Mapping Mendelian factors underlying quantitative traits using RFLP linkage maps. *Genetics, 121,* 185–199.

Loehlin, J. C., & Nichols, R. C. (1976). *Heredity, environment, and personality.* Austin: University of Texas Press.

Lush, J. L. (1937). *Animal breeding plans.* Ames, IA: Collegiate Press.

Lykken, D. T., Tellegen, A., & DeRubeis, R. (1978). Volunteer bias in twin research: The rule of two-thirds. *Social Biology, 25,* 1–9.

Mather, K. (1949). *Biometrical genetics: The study of continuous variation.* London: Methuen.

Morton, N. E. (1982). *Outline of genetic epidemiology.* New York: Karger.

Nichols, R. C., & Bilbro, W. C. (1966). The diagnosis of twin zygosity. *Acta Genetica et Statistica Medica, 16,* 265–275.

Olson, R., Wise, B., Conners, F., Rack, J., & Fulker, D. (1989). Specific deficits in component reading and language skills: Genetic and environmental influences. *Journal of Learning Disabilities, 22,* 339–348.

Plomin, R., DeFries, J. C., & Fulker, D. W. (1988). *Nature and nurture during infancy and early childhood.* Cambridge: Cambridge University Press.

Plomin, R., DeFries, J. C., & McClearn, G. E. (1990). *Behavioral genetics: A primer* (2nd ed.). New York: Freeman.

Stanovich, K. E. (1986). Cognitive processes and the reading problems of learning-disabled children: Evaluating the assumption of specificity. In J. K. Torgesen & B. Y. L. Wong (Eds.), *Psychological and educational perspectives on learning disabilities* (pp. 87–131). Orlando, FL: Academic Press.

Stanovich, K. E. (1989). Various varying views on variation. *Journal of Learning Disabilities, 22,* 366–369.

Stevenson, J., Graham, P., Fredman, G., & McLoughlin, V. (1984). The genetics of reading disability. In C. J. Turner & H. B. Miles (Eds.), *The biology of human intelligence* (pp. 85–97). Nafferton, England: Nafferton Books Limited.

Stevenson, J., Graham, P., Fredman, G., & McLoughlin, V. (1987). A twin study of genetic influences on reading and spelling ability and disability. *Journal of Child Psychology and Psychiatry, 28,* 229–247.

Thompson, J. S., & Thompson, M. W. (1986). *Genetics in medicine.* Philadelphia, PA: Saunders.

Wechsler, D. (1974). *Examiner's manual: Wechsler Intelligence Scale for Children-Revised.* New York: Psychological Corporation.

Wechsler, D. (1981). *Examiner's manual: Wechsler Adult Intelligence Scale-Revised.* New York: Psychological Corporation.

Weir, B. S., Eisen, E. J., Goodman, M. M., & Namkoong, G. (1988). *Proceedings of the Second International Conference on Quantitative Genetics.* Sunderland, MA: Sinauer Associates.

Wong, B. Y. L. (1986). Problems and issues in the definition of learning disabilities. In J. K. Torgesen & B. Y. L. Wong (Eds.), *Psychological and educational perspectives on learning disabilities* (pp. 3–26). Orlando, FL: Academic Press.

Zerbin-Rüdin, E. (1967). Kongenitale Wortblindheit oder spezifische dyslixie (congenital word-blindness). *Bulletin of the Orton Society, 17,* 47–56.

CHAPTER THREE

Genetic Bases of Developmental Dyslexia: Molecular Studies

H. A. Lubs
M. Rabin,
K. Carland-Saucier
X. L. Wen
K. Gross-Glenn[1]
R. Duara
B. Levin
M. L. Lubs

I. Introduction

A. *Historical Background*

1. GENETIC STUDIES

Since the study of Hallgren in 1950, data have been available which are consistent with, and strongly suggestive of, an autosomal dominant mode of inheritance for many cases of specific developmental dyslexia. Other studies such as those of Zahalkova, Vrzal, and Klobovkova (1972) and Omenn and Weber (1978) presented smaller but similar family studies. These studies, however, were not regarded by many as proof of this mode of inheritance for several reasons: The definitions of affected versus unaffected were often not well defined and this mode of inheritance did not clearly explain the male preponderance found in many nonfamilial studies of dyslexia. Moreover, no

---

1 The editors and publishers regret the untimely death of Karen Gross-Glenn during the publication of this book.

Neuropsychological Foundations of Learning Disabilities, copyright © 1991 by Academic Press Inc. All rights of reproduction in any form reserved.

laboratory or psychological test was available to provide a definitive means of diagnosis.

The study by Smith Kimberling, Pennington, and Lubs (1983), however, demonstrated autosomal dominant inheritance. Although more males were affected than females, the sex ratio was not significantly different from 1.0 when the (largely male) probands were omitted. Thus, this study provided direct evidence of autosomal dominant inheritance and indirect confirmation of at least one possible specific gene causing one general type of dyslexia by the linkage studies.

Several studies have approached the genetic transmission of dyslexia by accepting all patients with normal intelligence, evidence of a relatively pure reading disability, and absence of other etiologic factors into a genetic study of dyslexia. This predictably resulted in a combination of families which includes generation-to-generation transmission (autosomal dominant inheritance), affected siblings with normal parents (autosomal recessive inheritance), and sporadic cases (often multifactorial) (DeFries & Decker, 1982; Finucci, Guthrie, Childs, Abbey, & Childs, 1976; Finucci & Childs, 1981). The statistical techniques necessary to justify different genetic mechanisms in the presence of phenotypic similarities are inadequate for the task, although they may show a "significant" genetic component and may be consistent with a major gene effect (DeFries & Decker, 1982). Conclusions will vary widely depending on the proportion of families with each type of inheritance that were included in a particular study.

It is well known, however, that autosomal dominant disorders are highly variable within a family and that this variability encompasses both absence of any effect of a gene (decreased penetrance) and highly variable manifestations (expressivity). In the autosomal dominant form of osteogenesis imperfecta, for example, some individuals have few or no broken bones but do have blue sclera; others may have no clinical manifestations but show decreased bone density by X-ray and still transmit the disorder. The genetic analysis in one type of osteogenesis is consistent with this mode of inheritance. Thus, it is to be anticipated that there would be variability rather than complete uniformity in the behavioral manifestations of the portion of cases of dyslexia that are inherited as an autosomal dominant disorder and that some would show minimal to no effects of the gene. For reasons that are still a matter of speculation, this occurs more frequently in females carrying a gene for dyslexia.

It is unclear what proportion of developmental dyslexia may be due to an autosomal dominant or major gene effect. This question can only be answered when a reliable test is available to define specific subtypes. The great majority of cases ascertained by Hallgren (1950), however, appeared to be dominantly inherited and most experienced teachers of learning-disabled children with dyslexia will ask not whether other members of the family have dyslexia, but who has it. The Colorado family study (Volger, DeFries, & Decker, 1984) recently has shown that slightly less than half of unselected dyslexics had a parent with a similar history of reading disability. Using a multiple regression analysis, a regression score of 0.83 was found in identical twins, one of whom had dyslexia (DeFries & Fulker, 1985). If obvious cases of birth injury and environmental damage are excluded, it is very likely that many, if not the majority of cases remaining, will have an autosomal dominant genetic etiology. With a thorough review of more distant relations, this proportion will likely increase.

2. SUBTYPING EFFORTS

Efforts were also made using data from three-generation families to determine the validity of the Mattis (1978) and Boder (1973) subtyping systems. These results have been reported elsewhere (Smith & Pennington, 1983; Pennington Smith, McCabe, Kimberling, & Lubs, 1984), and were recently summarized by Smith (1986). Inspection of the pedigrees did not show a consistent subtyping within a specific family.

A second analysis was also carried out using a more liberal classification of individual profiles as suggestive of a given subtype and was reported by Smith (1986). Similarly, in this study, inspection did not show an intrafamily consistency and the analysis of variance on the overall group was not greatly different from the initial analysis. Thus, no evidence to support these subtypes in these large families was obtained.

B. Interaction with Maternal Environment and Other Factors

Recently we have been able to begin analyzing the mechanisms by which interactions of a gene with the remaining genome and environment influence phenotypes. For example, the suggestion by Geschwind and Galaburda (1985a, 1985b, 1985c) that the reported male predominance of dyslexia might be influenced by increased testosterone levels at critical periods during development provides a reasonable hypothesis for the further study of such an interaction.

Data are also emerging which associate brain lateralization, dyslexia, and immune dysfunction. Geschwind and Behan (1982) observed an increased frequency of immune dysfunction in strongly left-handed individuals (27/253) compared to strongly right-handed individuals (10/253). Learning disabilities were also found significantly more often in the left handers. A subsequent follow-up of immune disorders, verified by medical records, showed a $2\frac{1}{2}$ times increased frequency of immune disorders in left-handed individuals. Results from a later study by the same group (Geschwind & Behan, 1984) revealed an increased frequency of immune disorders of the digestive tract (ulcerative colitis, regional ileitis, and celiac disease) and thyroid autoimmu-

nity in individuals and families with marked sinistrality, absence of lateralization, or ambidexterity. No difference was found in rheumatoid arthritis.
Pennington, Smith, and Haith (1985) showed an increase of autoimmune
disorders in 10 families with dyslexia. Two of 42 dyslexics had rheumatoid
arthritis, 1 had ulcerative colitis, and 1 had Hashimoto's thyroiditis. Only 1
nondyslexic of 43 had an autoimmune disorder (rheumatoid arthritis). Although the frequency of left-handedness was increased in dyslexics, there
appeared to be no difference in autoimmune disease in dyslexic left handers
compared to right handers. From these studies it appears that autoimmune
disorders may be increased in families with dyslexia and may possibly affect up
to 10% of adult dyslexics.

In the study by Pennington et al. (1985) there was also a suggestion of
an increase of atopic disorders (asthma and hay fever) in dyslexics. This has
occurred particularly in those families in which the gene for dyslexia was on
chromosome 15. No increase was found in the frequency of migraine. The
possible clinical significance of these findings cannot yet be assessed since the
numbers were small and the information was gathered by personal interview
rather than documented by medical records.

Further progress in understanding this information depends on our
ability to identify specific environmental factors on the one hand and specific
genetic factors on the other hand. A specific diagnostic laboratory test for an
autosomal dominant disorder depends on the identification of a factor closely
associated with the basic defect. Although it is possible that certain psychophysical or brain-imaging studies might approach such a diagnostic usefulness, it is most likely that only a direct molecular genetic analysis will permit
unequivocal diagnosis.

II. Use of Linkage Studies in Dyslexia

A. Principles

Present data suggest that multiple genetic entities etiologically associated with dyslexia may be defined through linkage studies. This approach
depends initially on identification of the chromosome loci of the defective
genes and subsequently on incremental refinement of their map positions to
identify the primary genetic defect responsible for subtypes of this disorder
(Fig. 1). Genetic linkage, therefore, appears to be one of the most promising
routes to the resolution of the problem of diagnosis and subtyping of developmental dyslexia. By establishing one or more specific genetic subtypes, the
phenotype of these subgroups may be described in detail by behavioral,
psychophysical, and other techniques.

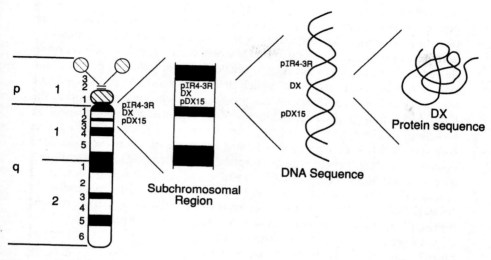

Chromosome 15

FIGURE 1 Genetic linkage. Illustration of the tentative linkage of a gene on chromosome 15 linked to the dyslexic phenotype (DX). Initial linkage studies, using heteromorphisms of the short arm (labeled p) of chromosome 15, localized a DX gene to this chromosome (Smith, Kimberling, Pennington, & Lubs, 1983). Molecular genetic studies in progress have permitted this gene to be further localized to a small region (i.e., 15q11-q13) just below the centromere. Additional studies will be required to determine the order of DNA probes at this locus, to identify the primary gene defect responsible for dyslexia at the level of DNA sequence, and ultimately to identify the corresponding protein which the gene encodes.

To understand the strategies employed in ascertaining the identity of the putative "dyslexia gene(s)", it is essential to define basic genetic terminology and principles. Deoxyribonucleic acid (DNA) is the macromolecule which encodes the genetic information in all cells. DNA is comprised of units called nucleotide bases and is organized as two complementary polynucleotide chains in a double helical structure. A gene is a segment of DNA representing a hereditary unit, that is, encoding a protein product which defines a genetic trait (such as a blood group). The DNA, containing the genes in linear sequence, is organized into chromosomes. Human cells contain two (homologous) copies of each of 22 autosomal chromosomes and 2 sex chromosomes (i.e., 2 X chromosomes for females and 1 X chromosome plus 1 Y chromosome for males). An individual inherits one complete set of chromosomes from his or her mother and one set from his or her father.

Genes can mutate to yield different alleles. The alleles encoding specific gene products can be determined directly by DNA analysis or indirectly by biochemical characterization of the corresponding protein. Chromosomes inherited from maternal and paternal sex cells carry alleles corresponding to those of the respective parent. A trait (phenotype) is specified by the combination of the two parental alleles, which define the genotype for that genetic locus. When both chromosomes carry the same allele for a given locus, the individual is homozygous for the locus. When different alleles are present on homologous chromosomes, the individual is heterozygous. If one allele is sufficient to define a particular phenotype, the mode of inheritance is defined as dominant. If the phenotype is expressed only when one allele is homozygous, the mode of inheritance is defined as recessive. If a gene sustains a mutation such that it no longer encodes a functional protein product, a "disease phenotype" may result. If alleles at one genetic locus define a specific disease phenotype, the disorder is termed a single-gene defect.

Genetic linkage implies that genes (DNA sequences) at two or more loci on the same chromosome tend to be co-inherited and therefore segregate together in families. The farther apart two gene loci are located on the same chromosome, the less likely that DNA sequences (gene markers) at these loci will be inherited together because of their separation by genetic recombination (i.e., the exchange of genetic material between homologous chromosomes at meiosis). The frequency of recombination is determined by family studies and is a measure of genetic distance between two loci. This is demonstrated in Fig. 2. Distance on the genetic map is expressed in units called Morgans (or centiMorgans). A Morgan is defined as the average distance over which one genetic exchange or crossing-over occurs in a large number of meioses. One centiMorgan corresponds to a 1% recombination rate (a recombination frequency of 0.01), which is approximately equivalent to 10^6 nucleotide base pairs of DNA. A recombination frequency of 0.5 indicates the two loci are sufficiently far apart that there is no linkage and that the gene markers are inherited independently, that is, no different from chance. Two or more genes are said to be linked when they are sufficiently close together on a chromosome that independent segregation between them does not occur, that is, they are transmitted together more frequently than expected by chance. A recombination frequency of 0.05 indicates co-inheritance of gene markers 95% of the time.

The likelihood of two distant gene markers being transmitted together through 10 matings (where one parent has both markers) is comparable to tossing 2 heads 10 times in a row ($1/2^{10} = 1/1000$). These are the odds expected by chance. If two traits are extremely close on the same chromosome, however, then the probability that both will be inherited together is 1, that is, by definition there will be 10 pairs of heads in a row. Thus, the odds of linkage

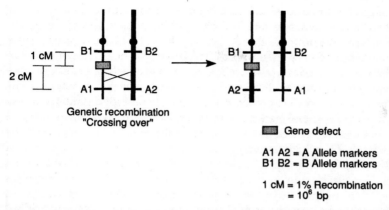

FIGURE 2 Genetic recombination. Given two DNA markers A and B, each having two allelic forms 1 and 2, the likelihood that either marker will be separated from a linked gene defect by genetic recombination is dependent on the distance between them. The closer the marker is to the defective gene of interest (i.e., the more tightly it is linked to the defective gene), the more likely that the marker will be inherited with the gene defect in an affected family. Markers at greater distances from the gene defect are more frequently separated from the gene during meiotic recombination.

versus random inheritance in the latter case would be 1.0/.001, or 10^3. This is expressed as a lod score, which is the logarithm of the odds for linkage over a random outcome in this example. The odds for linkage (10^3 to 1) would be expressed as a lod score of 3. In contrast, two unlinked gene loci show 50% recombination or random assortment. Linkage is detected by evaluating the distribution of gene markers in offspring from a series of matings where at least one parent has both markers (is heterozygous). The likelihood that the resultant offspring could be produced by chance is compared with the likelihood that the distribution could be produced by linkage at different recombination frequencies. Since these odds are expressed as logarithmic values, the lod scores from a series of families can be summed to yield a total value for all families studied. A lod score of at least 3.0 (odds 1000 : 1 favoring linkage) is usually considered as initial proof of linkage, while a lod score of -2.0 (100 : 1 against linkage) is considered strong evidence against linkage. Lod score calculations are routinely performed using computer programs such as LIPED (Ott, 1974) or LINKAGE (Lathrop, Lalovel, Julier & Ott, 1984) which allow family data to be evaluated at defined recombination frequencies. Because of the required odds of 1000 : 1 in favor of linkage, a false positive result will occur infrequently. Confirmation, nevertheless, by a second study or a different method remains a critical procedure.

Linkage studies of dyslexia have been performed using three classes of genetic markers: (1) chromosomal heteromorphisms (i.e., morphologic differences of chromosomes 1, 9, 13, 14, 15, 16, 21, 22), (2) polymorphic protein markers, and (3) polymorphic DNA markers. The criteria these different markers share is that they all are inherited as Mendelian traits. Chromosomal heteromorphisms are detected by direct cytogenetic analysis of metaphase chromosome spreads prepared from peripheral blood lymphocytes of family members. Protein markers may be divided into two general classes: (1) cell-surface proteins, such as ABO blood-group determinants, and (2) polymorphic forms of cellular enzymes (isosymes). The former group may be detected using immunologic reagents specific for particular cell-surface proteins. The latter group is defined using electrophoretic separation techniques which distinguish isozymes based on molecular charge characteristics. DNA marker studies are performed using a technique called blot hybridization (Fig. 3). Human genomic DNA is digested with a restriction endonuclease. Restriction enzymes recognize specific nucleotide sequences in DNA. Therefore, nucleotide changes in DNA at a genetic locus can result in the appearance or disappearance of recognition sites in the DNA, altering the sizes of DNA fragments, restriction-fragment-length polymorphisms (RFLPs), derived from the locus. The restriction fragments are separated based on molecular size by agarose gel electrophoresis, and the size-fractionated fragments are transferred to a hybridization membrane by capillary blotting. DNA fragments on the membrane are hybridized to a radio-labeled probe, which specifically reanneals to complementary genomic DNA sequences. Hybridized fragments are visualized by autoradiography. The distribution of alleles detected in families by a DNA probe using this approach is analyzed using the LINKAGE computer program to test for genetic linkage (Lathrop et al., 1984).

In addition to defining the chromosomal locus of a single-gene defect, linkage studies can also be used to detect genetic heterogeneity in disorders which may arise from defects in any one of a number of genes. If data in a number of large families with the same apparent inherited disorder show linkage to genes on different chromosomes in different families, or only a portion of families show linkage to the same locus, genetic heterogeneity is present and can be confirmed by statistical analysis (Morton, 1956; Ott, 1983; 1985). The computer program most frequently used for testing lod score heterogeneity is the HOMOG program (Ott, 1985). The pooling of lod scores from several clinically similar but genetically different entities will often obscure the detection of a linkage, as occurred with the study of Smith, Kimberling et al. (1983). More than 15 years of work was required before heterogeneity and a specific linkage to chromosome 15 were demonstrated; however, this linkage must still be confirmed.

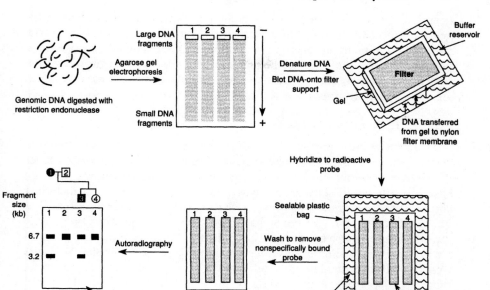

FIGURE 3 Detection of restriction fragment length polymorphisms (RFLPs) by blot hybridization. The pattern of alleles of the DNA marker inherited from the affected mother (1) and normal father (2) by the affected son (3) and normal daughter (4) in this family can be determined by visual inspection of the hybridization data after autoradiography. Hence the normal individuals are homozygous for a 6.7-kb allele (i.e., they have one copy on this allele on each of their two homologous chromosomes). The affected mother and her affected son are heterozygous and share a 3.2-kb allele which is diagnostic for the disease phenotype in this family.

The likelihood of detecting a linkage increases directly with the number of available markers. The entire human genome spans about 3300 centiMorgans. If the genome were to be covered with highly polymorphic (variable) marker loci at 20-cM intervals, a minimum of 165 marker loci would be needed to detect synteny (two genes on the same chromosome). The probability that a random locus is within a specific map distance of at least one marker can be roughly estimated (Conneally & Rivas, 1980). Given 165 markers, this probability is about 0.84. Determining the prior probability of finding linkage between a genetic disease, however, and a series of genetic markers is not as straightforward as it may appear because (1) the autosomes are of different genetic lengths, (2) available markers are not distributed at random in the genome, and (3) the actual frequency of polymorphism at each locus varies widely, and in many instances markers are only minimally informative if the polymorphism is rare. A close linkage can be the basis of diagnostic testing until a gene is isolated and a direct, definitive test developed. These approaches are discussed in detail below.

B. Prior Linkage Studies

Smith, Kimberling et al. (1983) initiated genetic linkage studies to provide an indirect test of the hypothesis of autosomal dominant inheritance of dyslexia. For this study, the linkage analyses were performed between specific reading disability and a battery of known genetic traits including chromosomal heteromorphism and polymorphic protein markers (Table I, Fig. 4). For the corresponding phenotype analysis, the participating family members were given a battery of achievement and neuropsychological tests to see if there was consistency of subtype within and between families. Subtypes were tentatively defined in three different ways: on the basis of spelling errors, using an adaptation of the criteria of Boder (1973) and newly developed criteria (Pennington, Smith, McCabe, Kimberling, & Lubs, 1984); using neuropsychological tests to replicate the work of Mattis, French, and Rapin (1975) and Mattis (1978); and using cluster analysis. This study design permitted the testing and analysis of these prior subtyping systems on family data to determine whether consistent types were found within a family.

The ascertainment and diagnosis of subjects in these studies has been reported elsewhere (Smith, Kimberling et al., 1983; Smith & Pennington, 1983; Smith, Pennington, Kimberling, & Lubs, 1983) but will be reviewed here. Families were solicited from parents' groups, from special schools for the learning disabled, and through referral from educators and other professionals. The following criteria were established for inclusion in the study: a history of specific reading disability in three generations of one side of a family in an autosomal dominant pattern; verbal and performance IQ of at least 90 on Wechsler or equivalent test for all members; native English speaking; both biological parents and at least two children over age 7 had to be available for study; no evident cause of dyslexia by history or examination other than family history was detected. Known neurological, psychiatric, or environmental deprivation which might influence reading ability prohibited their inclusion in the study. All families included were middle or upper class. Diagnosis of reading disability was based upon two criteria: psychoeducational test results and historical information. For children, diagnosis as affected required a history of reading disability from the time reading was introduced and performance on the Gray Oral Reading Test at least 2 years below the mean grade level of the PIAT mathematics and general information scores. Similar criteria

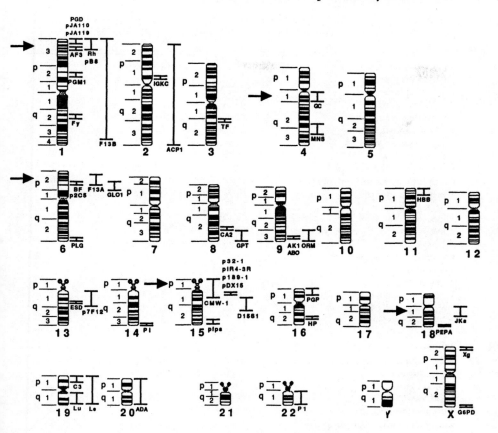

FIGURE 4 Map of genetic markers. Chromosomal distribution of polymorphic protein markers (solid text) and DNA markers (outline text) used in the study of Smith, Kimberling, Pennington, and Lubs (1983) and the University of Miami linkage studies. Subchromosomal localization of respective probes is indicated. Heteromorphic regions on chromosomes 1, 9, 13, 14, 15, 16, 21, and 22 (hatched areas) were used as markers in the previous study (Smith, Kimberling *et al.*, 1983). Abbreviations are indicated in Table I.

were used for adults; however, if an adult gave a history of early and persistent difficulty learning to read but passed the tests, the possibility of compensation for an earlier disability was considered. In that case, the adult had to have an affected child and sibling or parent who could be documented to be affected. The compensated adult would then be an "obligate carrier" of the putative gene if he had an affected child. Genotyping markers (blood and enzyme types) and Q- and C-band chromosomal heteromorphisms were analyzed

TABLE I Polymorphic Protein Markers

System	Symbol	Chromosome Locus	No. Alleles
α_1-Antitrypsin	PI	14q32.1	5
ABO blood group[b]	ABO	9q34.1-q34.2	4
Acid phosphatase[b]	ACP1	2	2
Adenosine deaminase[b]	ADA	20	2
Adenylate kinase	AK1	9q34.1-q34.2	2
Carbonic anhydrase[a]	CA2	9q22	2
Coagulation Factor 13A	F13A	6p24-p21.3	3
Coagulation Factor 13B	F13B	1	3
Complement (third component)	C3	1p13.3-p13.2	2
Complement (fourth component)	C4	6p21.3	28
Duffy blood group[b]	FY1	q22-q23	3
Esterase D[b]	ESD	13q14.1-q14.2	2
Glucose-6-phosphate dehydrogenase[a,b]	G6PD	Xq28	3
Glutamic pyruvic transaminase	GPT	8q23-qter	2
Glyoxylase	GLO1	6p21.3-p21.1	3
Group-specific component[b]	GC	4q12-q13	2
Haptoglobin +	HP	16q22	2
Hemoglobin[a]	HBB	11p15.5	2
Immunoglobulin Gm[b]	IGHG	14q32,3	3
Immunoglobulin Km	IGKC	2p12	2
Kidd blood group[b]	Jk	18q11-q12	2
Lewis blood group	Le	19	2
Lutheran blood group	Lu	19q12-q13	2
MNS blood group[b]	MNS	4q28-q31	4
Orosomucoid	ORM	9q31-qter	2
P blood group	P1	22q11.2-qter	2
Peptidase A[a]	PEPA	18q23	3
Phosphoglucomutase[b]	PGM1	1p22.1	4
Phosphogluconate dehydrogenase	PGD	1p36.2-p36.13	2
Phosphoglycolate phosphatase	PGP	16p13	3
Plasminogen	PLG	6q26-q27	3
Properdin Factor B	BF	6p21.3	2
Rhesus blood group[b]	Rh	1p36.2-p34	5
Transferrin[b]	TF	3q21	3
Xg blood group	Xg	Xp22.3	2

[a] Blacks only.
[b] Smith, Kimberling, Pennington, and Lubs (1983).

(Table I, Fig. 4). The inheritance of these markers was compared with the transmission of reading disability using the linkage program LIPED (Ott, 1974).

Researchers Smith, Kimberling, and Pennington are continuing their efforts to extend and further study the original families from Denver, Colorado to provide more informative matings. Pennington has also iden-

TABLE II Linkage between Dyslexia and Chromosome 15 Heteromorphisms

Family	Recombination Fraction				
	.00	.10	.20	.30	.40
1000	.292	.208	.129	.062	.016
1001	$-\infty$	-.229	-.060	-.011	-.001
1002	.292	.208	.129	-.062	.016
6371	.602	.465	.318	.170	.049
6372	$-\infty$	-1.718	-.571	-.097	.059
6375	-.194	-.081	-.038	-.016	-.005
6432	3.215	2.661	2.083	1.470	.792
6484	$-\infty$	-2.085	-.540	.055	.193
6491	$-\infty$	-1.322	-.582	-.228	-.054
6596	.523	.334	.180	.071	.015
8001	$-\infty$	-1.351	-.641	-.307	-.115
8002	$-\infty$	-.123	.105	.086	.030
8005	$-\infty$	-.335	-.122	-.038	-.006
8006	$-\infty$	.159	.232	.182	.093
8007	.301	.255	.204	.146	.079
8008	.903	.725	.541	.356	.175
8010	$-\infty$	-.252	-.092	-.036	-.010
9007	$-\infty$	-.384	-.047	.032	.020
9008	$-\infty$	-.264	-.109	-.049	-.015
9102	$-\infty$	-.957	-.426	-.168	-.040
Total	$-\infty$	-4.096	.693	1.742	1.291

tified additional Denver families for study. Current results of their linkage analysis using centromeric heteromorphisms of the short arm of chromosome 15 as a marker are shown in Table II. Of the 20 informative families, 12 show crossovers ($-\infty$ at a recombination frequency of 0.00) and 5 of these are clearly not linked. Of the 12 positive families, 4 are large enough to have suggestively positive lod scores and 1 (Family 6432) is clearly linked. The program HOMOG (Ott, 1985), however, operating on this data has now demonstrated significant heterogeneity of the lod scores. Two parameters were considered: α, the proportion of linked families, and θ, the recombination fraction. Three hypotheses were formulated and tested (Table III). The null hypothesis was that there was no linkage. α was set at 0 and θ at 50% (i.e., no linkage). The second hypothesis was that there was linkage, with homogeneous families. α was set at 1 (all families) and the program estimates the maximum value of θ over all families. Smith, Pennington, Kimberling, and Ing (in press) obtained a maximum recombination frequency of 0.30 (which was the same as was obtained with the traditional linkage analysis (Tables II, and III). The third hypothesis was that there was heterogeneity, with a proportion of families showing linkage. Both α and θ were estimated from the

TABLE III Test of Heterogeneity [a,b]:
Reading Disability Versus Chromosome 15
Heteromorphisms

	df	X^2	p value
H_2 vs H_1	1	2.588	.0538
H_1 vs H_0	1	8.022	.0023
H_2 vs H_0	2	10.610	.0006

[a] Using the program HOMOG (Ott, 1985).
[b] H_0: No linkage ($\alpha = .00$, $\theta = .50$)
   H_1: Linkage with homogeneity ($\alpha = 1.00$, $\theta = .30$)
   H_2: Linkage with heterogeneity ($\alpha = .20$, $\theta = .00$)

data. These maximized at an α of 30% and at a θ of 0. The null hypothesis was rejected when compared with either of the alternate hypotheses. In addition, the hypothesis of homogeneity was rejected when it was compared with the hypothesis of heterogeneity. Thus the hypothesis that there is heterogeneity, with 30% of the population showing linkage, provided the best fit to the lod score data. The HOMOG program also estimated the probability that each family was linked to chromosome 15 by converting the lod scores to a direct probability statement (Table IV). One family (6432) had a probability of 0.998 and another family (8008) had a probability of linkage of 0.667. Sixteen were considered unlinked and two were equivocal, with probabilities between 0.40 and 0.60. Recent data presented by S. D. Smith et al., (1986 personal communication) indicate a weak linkage between reading disability and the RFLP probe D15S1. Although the lod scores derived using D15S1 are lower than those obtained calculated with the chromosome 15 heteromorphism as marker, it is likely that the DNA marker D15S1 is at a greater distance from the gene defect associated with the dyslexic phenotype, and hence such a result would be expected. Additional studies with DNA markers nearer to the centromere will be required to confirm the chromosome 15 linkage data using DNA markers closer to the putative dyslexia gene.

Comparable disorders in clinical genetics have already been resolved by molecular genetic techniques. Hyperextensible joints, for example, occur in a continuum of clinical severity and complexity. Isolated hyperextensibility is very common and causes no medical problems. More severe cases are generally classified as Ehlers–Danlos syndrome. On the basis of clinical grouping, there was considerable overlap between clinical types and difficulty classifying specific families even though more than 10 clinical subtypes were proposed. Recently, molecular genetics studies have related the spectrum of severity

TABLE IV Posterior Probability of
Linkage of SRD to Chromosome 15
Heteromorphisms[a]

Family number	Probability
9007	.000
9008	.000
9102	.000
6371	.500
6372	.000
6375	.138
6432	.998
6484	.000
6491	.000
6576	.455
8001	.000
8002	.000
8005	.000
8006	.000
8007	.333
8008	.667
8010	.000
1000	.329
1001	.000
1002	.329

[a] $\alpha = .20$; $\theta = .00$.

to a sequence of different mutations in the procollagen genes (Prokop &
Kivirikko, 1984). A mutation at the 5' end of the gene causes severe problems
(since nearly all of the collagen chain is then coded incorrectly). A mutation
toward the 3' end of the gene (at the end of the sequence) may cause only
minor problems, such as benign hyperextension of the joints, since only a
small portion of the molecule is abnormal. More than 20 mutations of varying
sizes, locations, and effects have now been identified. The problem is in many
ways analogous to dyslexia, and both disorders can ultimately be understood
in terms of molecular genetics.

III. The Present Study

A. Purpose

The purpose of the study is first to confirm or reject the available linkage
data regarding dyslexia and chromosome 15 and, if the linkage is confirmed,
to further define and extend linkage relationships between types of dyslexia

and chromosome 15 markers (i.e., develop more useful and closely linked markers).

The second goal is to identify other linkages in the remaining 2/3 of families not linked to chromosome 15 markers which present a three-generation history of dyslexia. The study is also designed to define the clinical phenotypes of any subtypes detected using a combination of clinical, behavioral, visual–auditory, and brain-imaging studies and to determine whether there is a correlation between autoimmune or atopic disorders and dyslexia. The long-term goals involve isolation and characterization of the gene(s) causing inherited dyslexia and development of both a specific genetic and a specific functional test for each type of dyslexia that would make possible early, definitive diagnosis.

This is a significantly more ambitious study than the first study by Smith, Kimberling et al. (1983) in that both detection of linkages and description of the phenotype of each gene by neuropsychological, brain-imaging, and other studies is being undertaken.

B. Selection of Families and Initial Evaluation

1. SCREENING OF FAMILIES

A genetic counselor is the first member of the research team to formally contact a member of a prospective participant family. She describes the study and gains enough preliminary information to draw up a tentative pedigree. After review of the pedigree by the geneticists and psychologists, families are further contacted if it appears that there are likely to be enough family members who will both meet our criteria for dyslexia and be sufficiently interested and available to participate in the study. Each family member is contacted in order to gain more detailed information directly from that individual. An extensive questionnaire is administered that forms the basis for a semistructured screening interview. Two parallel forms of the questionnaire have been developed, one suitable for an adult, speaking about him or herself, and one suitable for a parent, providing information about a son or daughter who is less than 18 years of age. Table V shows the categories of information that are addressed by the questionnaire.

The diagnostic questionnaire serves a dual purpose. First, information is sought regarding nonhereditary factors that may have contributed to a person's reading difficulties, for example, brain trauma or lack of educational opportunity. This allows us to rule out the possibility of reading disorders that may be caused by confounding variables. Second, the questionnaire addresses related problems that may be common to several members within one family, for example, attention-deficit hyperactivity disorder (ADHD) or thyroid problems. Because screening for all associated physical and psychological

TABLE V Categories of Information on Questionnaires

History of problems in the following areas:
  Congenital
    Prenatal: Indicates presence of serious illness (rubella, toxemia, seizure disorder); use of
      medication; smoking, alcohol, or other drug use by mother during pregnancy
    Perinatal: Indicates unusual or notable problems occurring during or shortly after
      delivery
  Sensory/motor
    Speech, language, or hearing: Speech, language, or hearing problems; infantile ear
      infections; difficulty in conveying spoken ideas or meanings; problems requiring
      speech therapy
    Oculomotor/visual: History of visual or oculomotor problems, e.g., crossed eyes, vision
      not normal or correctable to normal
    Handedness: Indicates presence of non-right handedness
  Neurological
    History of head injury, symptoms of Tourette syndrome, migraines, seizure disorders; or
      consultation with a neurologist for another problem
  Psychiatric
    Attention/hyperactivity: History of attention-deficit disorder, with or without
      hyperactivity
  Educational history
    Indicates remedial/tutorial classes for academic problems; special teachers; held back in a
      grade; diagnosed by specialist as dyslexic, learning disabled, minimal dysfunction,
      attention disorder
    Reading/spelling and writing/history: Indicates self-reported history of difficulty with
      reading, spelling, and/or writing
  Other psychiatric
    Includes positive diagnosis for psychiatric disorder, mental retardation, panic or anxiety
      attacks, recurring disturbing thoughts, inability to get along with others or with
      authorities
  Other medical
    Indicates report of medical problems such as allergies, autoimmune, or other inherited
      diseases

disorders would be an inordinately lengthy endeavor, we have selected disorders that have been noted by other workers to coexist with dyslexia (e.g., autoimmune disorders, non-right handedness). This information will allow us to explore the inheritance of these conditions across generations and relate them to the presence or absence of dyslexia. Ultimately, inheritance of these coexisting factors may provide markers for distinguishing different genetic subtypes of dyslexia.

2. DIAGNOSTIC CRITERIA

Following completion of the questionnaire, family members are scheduled for individual diagnostic testing on a battery that includes a standardized (Wechsler) IQ test and reading and spelling tests. Participation in the study

TABLE VI Diagnostic Reading Battery and Criteria for Diagnosis of Dyslexia

Oral reading	Gray Oral Reading Test, Revised Letter–Word Identification subtest (Woodcock–Johnson Psychoeducational Battery)
Comprehension	Passage Comprehension subtest (Woodcock–Johnson Psychoeducational Battery)
Decoding	Word Attack subtest (Woodcock–Johnson Psychoeducational Battery) Nonsense Passages (adult only)
Spelling	Spelling subtest (Wide-Range Achievement Test-Revised)

requires at least average intellectual ability (full-scale IQ >90). The reading and spelling tests have been selected to tap four major subskill areas believed to be essential for adequate reading and spelling: decoding, oral reading, comprehension, and spelling.

A diagnosis of dyslexia requires observation of a discrepancy between an individual's full-scale IQ score and his or her performance on tests measuring at least two of the four subskill areas. Table VI summarizes the diagnostic test battery. The degree to which reading/spelling abilities must be lower than overall cognitive ability is age dependent (Table VII), increasing from .5 standard deviation (SD) up to age 9, to 1.0 SD between ages 9 and 14, to 1.5 SD for age 15 and above. With the exception of Nonsense Passages, a test which is administered only to adults, all of the tests are standardized across a wide range of ages. All yield standard scores that are used for comparison with the individual's full-scale IQ score.[1] Adults must also report a childhood history of reading and/or spelling problems. Young children are not diagnosed until they have had adequate opportunity to attempt to learn to read, usually between ages 6 and 6.5 or at the end of the first grade. Because of

---

1 We are indebted to George Hynd for his help in devising these criteria.

TABLE VII Age-Graded Cutoffs

Age (years)	IQ discrepancy[a]
≤8	.5 standard deviation less than expected score based on IQ in at least one category in Table VI
9–14	1.0 standard deviation less than expected score based on IQ in two of four categories in Table VI
>15	1.5 standard deviation less than expected score based on IQ in two of four categories in Table VI (plus history of childhood reading and spelling problems)

[a] Relative to full-scale IQ score on WAIS-R or WISC-R test.

"floor effects" that often characterize standardized tests, these diagnoses are generally considered as tentative, with plans made for future testing when the child is a year older.

3. DIAGNOSIS OF DYSLEXIA IN ADULTS

Genetic studies of dyslexia involve making a diagnostic decision regarding the presence or absence of dyslexia in as many members of each family as possible. Using linkage analysis requires studying families across several generations, therefore, most of the individuals in these studies will be adults. Although a diagnosis of dyslexia in a child who is currently experiencing difficulty in learning to read and spell can often be made with some degree of certainty, diagnosis of dyslexia in an adult presents some special problems. First, if the individual was born more than about twenty years ago, an earlier diagnosis will probably not have been made, as prior to the mid-1960s there was little awareness of reading disability as a specific cognitive disorder. For these individuals, information regarding their childhood educational experiences must be gained through retrospective questionnaires that probe their relative success or difficulty with reading, spelling, and writing. As self reports can be notoriously inaccurate, one also needs more objective indices of school difficulty, for example, having had tutors, special classes, repeating a grade, or premature withdrawal from school.

A second problem associated with diagnosing dyslexia in adults is that many dyslexic children eventually do learn to read and spell adequately. This is, in fact, only a problem for the researchers. This is especially true for individuals who have pursued careers that require considerable amounts of reading and writing. For such people, we find that very few standardized tests are suited to tap what remains of a reading disability that was quite pronounced in childhood. Indeed, it appears that such persons have "compensated" for their earlier disability, either through effective remediation and/or by sheer perseverance. In our earlier family studies, we used the "stress tests" (so named by analogy to EKG stress tests used in cardiology) as a means of circumventing this diagnostic problem (Finucci et al., 1976). The idea behind these tests is that of the need to stress a system in order to observe an abnormality of functioning that might have otherwise gone unnoticed. The test is made up of two short paragraphs, adapted from part of an early version of the Gray Oral Reading Test. It has been modified to incorporate about 30 pronounceable nonsense words, interspersed throughout the meaningful text. These "nonsense passages" elicit dysfluent oral reading in compensated adult dyslexics, who otherwise read quite fluently. Over several years, we and others have tested many nondyslexic adults on the nonsense passages in order to amass normative data for adults without a childhood history of reading problems. Relative to normal readers, dyslexic adults' reading usually shows a "speed/accuracy trade-off," with a normal reading rate but many errors or conversely with a slow reading rate but few errors (Gross-Glenn, Jallad, Novoa, Helgren-Lempesis, & Lubs, 1990). Because of their good discriminability between adults with and without a childhood history of reading problems, the nonsense passages have been added to our test battery.

C. Phenotype Definitions: Behavior, Brain-Imaging, Neuropsychologic, and Immunologic Studies

1. BEHAVIORAL STUDIES

A wide variety of studies is being carried out to determine the phenotype associated with each (presumed) different genetic type. Details of these studies will not be fully discussed and are presented only as examples of studies in progress that will eventually be used to define each genetic subtype, as discussed below.

To better define the differences between families, a variety of functional studies is being carried out. In addition to the diagnostic measures described above, we have used psychophysical measures of visual and speech system functioning that are sensitive enough to distinguish subtle differences from normal that characterize dyslexic individuals.

Results from the visual studies (Gross-Glenn et al., 1989) have shown that dyslexics require more time than normal readers to perceive high-spatial-frequency (fine detail) information. This very specific spatiotemporal visual deficit may be part of a dyslexia phenotype associated with only certain genetic markers. Studies are underway in our laboratory to make this (and other) correlations between phenotypic and genotypic data.

2. BRAIN IMAGING

Because the genetic differences for dyslexia are likely to lead to neural differences, we have used two neuroimaging techniques to study differences in both brain structure and function. Magnetic resonance imaging (MRI) provides a series of clear images of the brain in many planes, permitting a noninvasive means for quantifying differences in brain anatomy between dyslexia and normals. Thus far our studies have indicated variations in both cerebral asymmetry and corpus callosum area for dyslexic individuals (Gross-Glenn et al., 1989).

Differences in brain function were evaluated by positron emission tomography (PET) (Duara et al., 1989; Gross-Glenn et al., 1989). PET scans yielded metabolic data for different brain regions during a serial-word-reading task. Consistent with results from MRI and visual psychophysical studies, PET scans for dyslexic individuals revealed differences in metabolic activity from those observed in normal readers that were very specific. These differences were localized to extrastriate visual regions and to prefrontal cortext. Work is underway to determine how results of these neuroimaging studies relate to genetic as well as other behavioral data.

3. NEUROPSYCHOLOGICAL STUDIES

An example of the neuropsychological test data in five families will be presented here. The test battery, grouped according to skills, is shown in Table VIII. Initially adult dyslexics were compared to adult nondyslexics within these families using a *t* test. Those tests which, on this preliminary analysis, have yielded a significant difference in adult dylexics are indicated in Fig. 5 by an asterisk. These results were somewhat surprising since better verbal fluency has not been described in dyslexics. The poor results by dyslexics with the Menyuk tests on the other hand were not unexpected since this involved comprehension of simple sentences. As shown in Fig. 5, all of the "FAS"

TABLE VIII Neuropsychological Test
Battery

Language-based skills
   Peabody Picture Vocabulary
   Boston Naming
   "FAS" Verbal Fluency[a]
   Rapid Automatized Naming
   Menyuk Syntactic Comprehension[a]
Visual–spatial/constructive skills
   Berry Visual–Motor Integration
   Rey-Osterreith Complex Figure
   Judgment of Line Orientation
Executive Function/set Shifting
   Rapid Alternating Stimuli
   Stroop
   Mazes
Verbal Memory
   Sentence Memory
   Object Memory
   Wechsler Memory Scale
   California Verbal Learning
Nonverbal Memory
   Benton Visual Retention
   Bead Memory[a]
   Wechsler Memory Scale
Attention
   Auditory Consonant Trigrams[a]

[a] Differences betweeen normal and dyslexic adult family members.

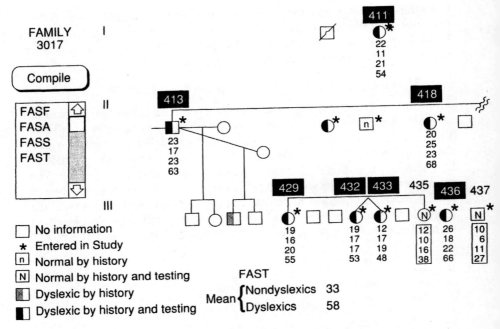

FAST

Mean { Nondyslexics 33
       Dyslexics   58 }

FIGURE 5 Computer printout of Family 3017 pedigree. The results of "FAS" tests are printed out below each appropriate circle (females) or square (males). (Half-black circles or squares indicate individuals with dyslexia and their study numbers are indicated with a black background.) For individual 413, the results indicated 23 "F" words, 17 "A" words, 23 "S" words, for a total of 63 words. Any of the 300 variables can be selected for such a printout using the "compile" index shown to the left. The means for all adult nondyslexics (33) and dyslexics(58) are shown at the bottom. This family contributed nearly all of the high total values in the study.

differences in verbal fluency were due to the superior performance by Family 3017. The results for the normals are shown in the boxes and these can be compared to results for spouses or siblings by inspection. The mean value in the two nondyslexics in this family was 33 F, A, or S words produced; this was comparable to the other normal and dyslexic subjects in the other four families. In contrast, the seven dyslexics in this family all have superior performance, with an average of 58 words produced. The current interpretation of these data is not that the FAS verbal fluency test results are better in dyslexics. Rather, in a subset of families, or at least in one family, superior abilities appear to be present in those with a gene for dyslexia. Similarly, results on the Menyuk test (Table IX) and the Auditory Consonant Trigrams were different only in two of the five families, each of which produced poor performance in

TABLE IX Summary of Neuropsychological Test Results by Family (Dyslexics versus Nondyslexics)

Test	Variant Families	Performance
FAS	1 family (3017)	Better verbal memory
Menyuk	2 families (3001, 3015)	Poorer syntactic comprehension
Auditory consonant trigrams (18 seconds, total)	2 families (3014, 3015)	Poorer nonmeaningful verbal memory

dyslexics. The remaining families were unremarkable both with respect to their overall results and with respect to the absence of differences between normals and affected individuals. Thus, a combination of genetic and statistical techniques is critical to the initial evaluation and to the final assessment of such information in this stage of the study.

4. IMMUNOLOGIC STUDIES

An increased prevalence of allergic symptoms and other immunologic dysfunction has been noted in dyslexic subjects (Geschwind & Behan, 1982; Pennington et al., 1985). It is possible that this association is present only in some genetic types of dyslexia and not others. For this reason we are evaluating the following variables in all subjects: ANA if positive further testing for autoimmune dysfunction is done, and T-cell subsets and allergic disorders by questionnaire. If associations exist in some families and not in others, it would help to further delineate difficult phenotype subtypes of dyslexia.

5. MOLECULAR AND GENETIC STUDIES

The general use of linkage studies has been discussed above. Such studies, however, are expensive and time consuming. One approach used to focus on a limited genomic region involves utilization of genetic clues (i.e., observation of a chromosome marker in affected individuals) and suggestive data (i.e., possible involvement of previously identified gene/gene product in the etiology of the disorder) prior to initiation of linkage studies. This strategy of "making an educated guess" is critical to permit the most efficient and rapid detection of linkages, in contrast with a systematic global screening approach which would require the analysis of about 165 probes on each family and all families.

Our studies have combined aspects of both strategies. A combination of blood group and protein polymorphic markers comparable to those utilized in the study of Smith, Kimberling *et al.* 1983) (Fig. 4) has been employed because such studies are a relatively inexpensive and efficient way to screen globally. Other studies have utilized molecular genetics to identify DNA markers on chromosome 15, which may be linked to the dyslexic phenotype. Additional molecular analyses have been directed at defining genetic linkages on other chromosomes.

DNA polymorphism studies have focused on chromosome 15 and the development of new probes for the region of the long arm of this chromosome (15q11) where the putative dyslexia gene is thought to reside. Polymorphic markers utilized for these studies are indicated (with their chromosomal map locations) on the ideogram shown in Fig. 4. To date, we have screened five new families identified in Miami using three previously characterized DNA probes (p32-1, pIR4-3R, and p189-1) as well as a polymorphic DNA probe isolated in our own lab (pDX15). In none of these families do we detect linkage to these chromosome 15q11-specific DNA markers. Restudy of Family 6432 (Tables I and II) with these probes is planned.

Protein polymorphism studies have been carried out in parallel with the molecular analyses. The chromosomal distribution of these markers is shown in Fig. 4 and the marker designations are listed in Table I. Linkage analyses (Table X) of the family data obtained using these markers revealed a possible explanation for the absence of detectable linkage of the dyslexia phenotype to chromosome 15-specific DNA markers in these new families. In three of the families (3001, 3006 and 3014) the lod scores suggest linkage with chromosomes other than chromosome 15; that is, chromosome 6 in family 3001, chromosome 4 in Family 3006, and chromosome 1 in Family 3014. It is of interest to note that preliminary data of Smith *et al.* (in press) suggest linkage to the same region of chromosome 6 in other families. No other chromosomes are implicated as potential loci for a dyslexia gene in these families. In Family

TABLE X Maximal Lod Scores for Polymorphic Markers in Miami Families[a]

		Family				
Chromosome	Marker	3001	3006	3014	3015	3017
1q22-q23	Fy	.00	.29	.18	.10	$-\infty$
1p22.1	PGM1	$-\infty$	.00	.27	$-\infty$	.00
1p36.2-p34	Rh	$-\infty$	$-\infty$	.98	$-\infty$	.54
4q12-q13	GC	$-\infty$	.90	.06	$-\infty$	.45
6p21.3	BF	.00	.00	-2.07	$-.27$	.046
6p24-p21.3	F13A	.00	.00	.06	.08	.00
6p-21.3-p21.1	GLO1	.60	$-\infty$	$-\infty$	.70	$-\infty$
18q11-q12	Jk	$-.62$	.02	$-.43$	.70	-2.20

[a] $\theta = .00$

3014, there is reasonable evidence (i.e., a lod score of −2.07) to exclude chromosome 6p with respect to linkage to a dyslexia gene in this family. In family 3015 suggestive lod scores were obtained for two markers (GL01 and Jk). A lod score of −2.2 in Family 3017 with the Jk marker excludes chromosome 18 in this family. These data support the hypothesis of genetic heterogeneity in the etiology of the dyslexic phenotype.

Linkage analysis is being carried out by the standard LIPED technique as will be heterogeneity testing (Ott, 1985) after linkage is found. This test is required before it can be demonstrated on a statistical basis that more than one linkage group is involved. An alternative approach, however, is planned which will permit free pooling of family and linkage data based on the first one-third to one-half of the study. Thus, if three families appear to have a suggestive or significant lod score with a classical marker, such as Rh, a preliminary evaluation of their phenotypic data will be made. If correlations are found, these can be tested in families ascertained in the future. In addition, more precise linkage studies will be done to determine the validity of this pooling process. If the linkage is a true one, this will be demonstrable by significant lod scores at smaller recombination fractions. If spurious, that is, based on chance variation of lod scores, the linkage will not be confirmed and the preliminary analyses will be discarded. This compromise permits interim generation of hypotheses from findings during the study.

6. DATA SYNTHESIS: PHENOTYPE/GENOTYPE

A variety of approaches is being used to analyze the more than 300 variables that are recorded in the data base. The overall goal, once several linkages are established, is to develop a sophisticated description of similarities and differences between each genetic type. Until such time as the larger amount of data are available, however, several approaches can be utilized. All families can be tentatively lumped in general questions concerning the differences between affected and unaffected, males and females, varying ages, etc. When significant differences are shown, the results can then be inspected on a family-by-family basis using the available programs to print out pertinent data on a pedigree basis. This approach was illustrated in the previous section and illustrates clearly the need to do both types of preliminary analyses.

Simple inspection of data on a pedigree basis, even without prior statistical analysis, however, may identify unique differences between families that would be obscured on analysis of the overall data. The "automated" pedigree approach, which permits inspection of all 300 variables on this basis, is extremely powerful. It is likely to lead to a number of tentative observations that can subsequently be evaluated more thoroughly as the gene localization studies proceed and several families are known with the same genotype. This approach also permits inspection of data on a "rational" or organized basis.

For example, appropriate neuropsychological and brain-imaging data can be similarly inspected on a pedigree basis to see if certain psychological, psycho-physical, or brain-imaging variations here appear in the same individuals persistently or recur within affected members of a particular, or all, families. Finally, the degree to which the planned discriminant function analyses will prove helpful will depend on the number and type of gene localizations that evolve and the closeness of the linkage relationships and the size of the families that are included in the study.

IV. Significance of the Genetic Study of Dyslexia

Developmental dyslexia is a heterogeneous group of disorders, some of which are inherited. Past efforts to subtype this group of disorders using behavioral parameters have not resulted in consistent findings within specific families. Further progress in studying this group of disorders depends upon the development of specific descriptive or diagnostic tests which will provide a clear basis for subtyping specific individuals or families. By analogy to other inherited disorders, two phases of studies and levels of understanding will occur. First, linkage studies will delineate the location by chromosome and chromosome band of several different genes, each of which leads to a disorder which currently falls within the definition of specific developmental dyslexia. Currently, there are five suggestive localizations. As each of these specific genetic subtypes is identified, the phenotype of each genotype can be de-scribed in detail by the behavioral, psychophysiologic, and brain-imaging techniques described above. If specific functional or anatomical differences can be established between these types, it is possible that specific therapies can be designed for each type. Moreover, it should ultimately be possible to develop early, preschool diagnostic techniques and to prevent early loss of basic academic subskills and potential emotional problems associated with reading difficulties because of an unrecognized dyslexia. It is possible, based on the reports of neuronal loss over the first years of life, such as those by Huttenlocher (1979), that early detection (based on genetic studies) could lead to remediation procedures that might alter the persistence of critical pathways.

Identification of specific mutational changes in these genes will permit the development of relatively inexpensive screening tests for dyslexia and related dysfunctions. These will permit determining the frequency of this group of disorders and serve as early diagnostic tests. These techniques, however, will only become available after each gene has not only been local-ized, but also has been cloned and sequenced.

References

Boder, E. (1973). Developmental dyslexia: A diagnostic approach based on three atypical reading-spelling patterns. *Developmental Medicine and Child Neurology, 15,* 663–687.

Conneally, P. M., & Rivas, M. L. (1980). Linkage analysis in man. *Advances in Human Genetics, 10,* 209.

DeFries, J. C., & Decker, S. N. (1982). Genetic aspects of reading disability: A family study. In R. N. Malatesha & P. G. Aaron (Eds.), *Reading disorders: Varieties and Treatments* (p. 255). New York: Academic Press.

DeFries, J. C., & Fulker, D. W. (1985). Multiple regression analysis of twin data. *Behavior Genetics, 15*(5), 467.

Duara, R., Gross-Glenn, K., Barker, W., Loewenstein, D., Chang, Y., Apicella, A., Yoshii, F., Pascal, S., & Lubs, H. (1989). PET studies during reading in dyslexics and controls [Abstract] *Journal of Nuclear Medicine, 30*(5), 802.

Finucci, J. M., Guthrie, J. T., Childs, A. L., Abbey, H., & Childs, B. (1976). The genetics of specific reading disability. *Annals of Human Genetics, 40,* 123.

Finucci, J. M., & Childs, B. (1981). Are there really more dyslexic boys than girls? In A. Ansara, N. Geschwind, A. Galaburda, M. Albert, N. Gartrell (Eds.), *Sex Differences in Dyslexia, 1.*

Forest, M. G., Sizonenko, P. C., Cathiard, A. M., & Bertrand, J. (1974). Hypophyso-gonadal function in humans during the first year of life: I. Evidence for testicular activity in early infancy. *Journal of Clinical Investigations, 53,* 819–828.

Geschwind, N., & Behan, P. O. (1982). Left-handedness: Association with immune disease, migraine, and developmental learning disorder. *Proceedings of the National Academy of Sciences of the U.S.A., 79,* 5097.

Geschwind, N., & Behan, P. O. (1984). Laterality, hormones and immunity In N. Geschwind & A. M. Galaburda (Eds.) *Cerebral dominance: The Biological Foundations.* Cambridge, MA: Harvard University Press.

Geschwind, N., & Galaburda, A. M. (1985a). Cerebral lateralization—Biological mechanisms, associations, and pathology: I. A hypothesis and a program for research. *Archives of Neurology (Chicago), 42,* 428.

Geschwind, N., & Galaburda, A. M. (1985b). Cerebral lateralization—Biological mechanisms, associations, and pathology: II. A hypothesis and a program for research. *Archives of Neurology (Chicago), 42,* 521.

Geschwind, N., & Galaburda, A. M. (1985c). Cerebral lateralization—Biological mechanisms, associations, and pathology: III. A hypothesis and a program for research. *Archives of Neurology (Chicago), 42,* 634.

Gross-Glenn, K., Duara, R., Kushch, A., Pascal, S., Barker, W., Jallad, B., & Lubs, H. A. (1989). MRI and visual psychophysical studies of inherited dyslexia. *Society for Neuroscience Abstracts,* XV(196.10), 482.

Gross-Glenn, K., Duara, R., Yoshii, F., Barker, W., Chang, J., Apicella, A., Boothe, T., & Lubs, H. (1990). PET-Scan Reading Studies: Familial Dyslexics. In G. T. Pavlidis Ed.), *Dyslexia: A neuropsychological and learning perspective.* New York: Wiley. Vol. 1, 109–118.

Gross-Glenn, K., Jallad, B., Novoa, L., Helgren-Lempesis, V., & Lubs, H. (1990). Nonsense passage reading as an aid to the diagnosis of familial dyslexia in adults. *Reading and Writing: An Interdisciplinary Journal, 2,* 161–173.

Grossman, C. J. (1985). Interactions between the gonadal steroids and the immune system. *Science, 227,* 257.

Gusella, J. F. (1981). *Dyslexia: Theory and research.* Cambridge, MA: MIT Press.

Hallgren, B. (1950). Specific dyslexia (congenital word-blindness): A clinical and genetic study. *Acta Psychiatrica et Neurologica Scandinavica, Supplementum,* 65(1).

Huttenlocher, P. R. (1979). Synaptic density in human frontal cortex—Developmental changes and effects of aging. *Brain Research, 163,* 195–205.

Lathrop, G. M., Lalovel, J. M., Julier, C., & Ott, J. (1984). Strategies for multilocus linkage analysis in humans. *Proceedings of the National Academy of Sciences of the U.S.A., 81,* 3443–3446.

Mattis, S. (1978). Dyslexia syndromes: A working hypothesis that works. In A. L. Benton & D. Pearl (Eds.), *Dyslexia: An appraisal of current knowledge.* New York: Oxford University Press.

Mattis, S., French, J. H., & Rapin, I. (1975). Dyslexia in children and young adults: Three independent neuropsychological syndromes. *Developmental Medicine and Child Neurology, 17,* 150.

Morton, N. E. (1956). Genetic tests under incomplete ascertainment. *American Journal of Human Genetics, 11,* 1.

Omenn, G. S., & Weber, B. A. (1978). Dyslexia: Search for phenotypic and genetic heterogeneity. *American Journal of Medical Genetics, 1,* 333.

Ott, J. (1974). Estimation of the recombination fraction in human pedigrees: Efficient computation of the likelihood for human studies. *American Journal of Human Genetics, 26,* 588.

Ott, J. (1983). Linkage analysis and family classification under heterogeneity. *Anatomy of Human Genetics, 47,* 311.

Ott, J. (1985). *Analysis of human genetic linkage.* Baltimore, MD: Johns Hopkins University Press.

Pennington, B. F., & Smith, S. D. (1983). Genetic influences on learning disabilities and speech and language disorders. *Child Development, 54,* 369.

Pennington, B. F., Smith, S. D., McCabe, L. L., Kimberling, W. J., & Lubs, H. A. (1984). Developmental continuities in a form of familial dyslexia. In R. Emde & R. Harmons, (Eds.), *Continuities and discontinuities in development* (p. 123). New York: Plenum.

Pennington, B. F., Smith, S. D., & Haith, M. M. (1985, October). *Frequency of left-handedness, immune disease, and migraine in a sample of dyslexic families.* Personal communication presented at the Charter and Scientific Meeting of Rodin Remediation, St. Andrews, Scotland.

Prockop, D. J., & Kivirikko, K. I. (1984). Heritable diseases of collagen. *New England Journal of Medicine, 311*(6), 376–386.

Smith, S. D. (1978). *Genetic studies and linkage analysis of specific dyslexia: Evaluation of inheritance in kindreds selected for apparent autosomal dominant transmission.*

Doctoral thesis, Indiana University, Department of Medical Genetics, Bloomington.

Smith, S. D. (1986). Analysis of subtypes. In G. T. Pavlidis & D. F. Fisher (Eds.), *Dyslexia: Its neuropsychology and treatment*. London: Wiley.

Smith, S. D., Kimberling, W. J., Pennington, B. F., & Lubs, H. A. (1983). Specific reading disability: Identification of an inherited form through linkage analysis. *Science, 219,* 1345.

Smith, S. D., & Pennington, B. F. (1983). Genetic influences on learning disabilities: I. Clinical genetics. *Learning Disabilities, 2,* 31.

Smith, S. D., Pennington, B. F., Kimberling, W. J., & Ing, P. S. (in press). Familial dyslexia: Use of genetic linkage data to define subtypes. *Journal of the American Academy of Child and Adolscent Psychiatry.*

Smith, S. D., Pennington, B. F., Kimberling, W. J., & Lubs, H. A. (1983). A genetic analysis of specific reading disability. In J. A. Cooper & C. L. Ludlow (Eds.), *Genetic aspects of speech and language disorders*. New York: Academic Press.

Southern, E. M. (1979). Gel electrophoresis of restriction fragments. In R. Wu (Ed.), *Methods in enzymology* (Vol. 68, p. 152). New York: Academic Press.

Volger, G. P., DeFries, J. C., & Decker, S. N. (1984). Family history as an indicator of risk for reading disability. *Journal of Learning Disabilities, 10,* 616.

Zahalkova, M., Vrzal, V., & Klobovkova, E. (1972). Genetic investigations in dyslexia. *Journal of Medical Genetics, 9,* 48.

CHAPTER FOUR

Learning Disabilities: A Critical Review of Definitional and Assessment Issues

Sylvia R. Morrison
Linda S. Siegel

I. Introduction

The field of special education has faced and continues to face what have appeared to be overwhelming difficulties in the definition and classification of learning disabilities (e.g., Algozzine & Ysseldyke, 1988; Cruickshank, 1981; Epps, Ysseldyke, & Algozzine, 1985; Fletcher & Morris, 1986; Kavale, 1980, 1987; Keogh, 1983, 1986, 1987; Wong, 1979, 1986, 1988). In part this must be due to its broad constituency consisting of teachers, psychologists, physicians, and educational administrators. Each of these groups has differing needs and expectations. Thus the purpose of this chapter will be to (1) briefly review the history of these difficulties, (2) discuss the assumptions of most current definitions of learning disabilities, and (3) offer an alternative definition which we feel provides a solution to many of the problems.

II. History of the Definitional Issue

Historically, Cruickshank (1981) has suggested that the term "learning disabilities" is "one of the most interesting accidents of our professional times" (p. 81). It was never used before 1963 and developed from "prepared but informal remarks" (Cruickshank, 1981, p.81) made by Samuel A. Kirk at a dinner for concerned parents of children with learning problems in Chicago, Illinois. Shortly after the dinner, the parents organized themselves on a national level under the banner of Association for Children with Learning Disabilities. Therefore, the term "learning disabilities" (LD) was adopted as a "functional term without precedents to guide those who attempted to define it and without research or common usage which would assist in its appropriate formulation as a functional term" (Cruickshank, 1981, p.81).

In light of this historical background Cruickshank (1981) has argued that there are a variety of possible definitions: (1) diagnostic and etiological; (2) educational, pedagogical, pediatric, or biochemical; and (3) legislative. Keogh (1983) has suggested that LD classification must serve at least three purposes: (1) to focus attention on the problem and ensure advocacy, (2) as a category or mechanism for providing services to a population, and (3) as a condition or set of conditions that requires further research. Therefore definitions may be operationalized in different manners depending on their purposes. Keogh (1987) has argued that problems develop when "we assume that the definitions are comparable, that exemplars of one are automatically exemplars of another" (p. 5). For example, school districts need to be able to categorize children in order to provide service. They are not concerned with ensuring the homogeneity within these classifications needed for research.

This problem is complicated by the confusion in terms used to describe some or all of the LD population. Cruickshank (1972) observed that more than 40 English terms have been used in the literature to refer to some or all of the children subsumed under the LD label. Hammill, Leigh, McNutt, and Larsen (1981) also noted that a variety of terms such as minimal brain dysfunction/injury, psychoneurological learning disorders, dyslexia, or perceptual handicap, to name a few, all have been used to refer to LD populations.

In response to the confusion within the definitional issue, in 1981 the National Joint Committee for Learning Disabilities (NJCLD) adopted the following definition:

> Learning disabilities is a generic term that refers to a heterogeneous group of disorders manifested by significant difficulties in the acquisition and use of listening, speaking, reading, writing, reasoning, or mathematical abilities. These disorders are intrinsic to the individual and are presumed to be due to central nervous system dysfunction. Even though a learning disability may occur concomitantly with other handicapping conditions (e.g., sensory impairment, mental retardation, social or emotional disturbance) or environmental influences (e.g., cultural

differences, insufficient/inappropriate instruction, psychogenic factors), it is not the direct result of these conditions or influences. (Hammill *et al.*, 1981, p. 336)

However, as a number of investigators have suggested (e.g., Fletcher & Morris, 1986; Siegel & Heaven, 1986; Wong, 1986), this definition also is difficult to operationalize because it is vague and unspecific. Wong (1986) and Keogh (1986, 1987) note that in spite of this definition and *The rules and regulations for implementing Public Law 94-142* (Federal Register, 1977), special-education categories still differ from state to state and even within states from district to district. To complicate matters further, Epps *et al.* (1985) found that states using different category names to classify learning-disabled children may actually be using the same criteria to identify these children and some states using the same category names may be using different identification criteria.

Mann, Davis, Boyer, Metz, and Wolford (1983), in a survey of Child Service Demonstration Centers (CSDC), found that although most of the CSDCs used the federal criterion of academic underachievement, only two-thirds of the centers used even two of the three other criteria and only three of the 61 centers used all of the diagnostic criteria. Furthermore, 36 CSDCs did not distinctly state discernible diagnostic criteria.

In 1985, the U.S. Congress passed an act (PL 99-158) forming the Interagency Committee on Learning Disabilities (ICLD) "to review and assess Federal research priorities, activities, and findings regarding learning disabilities" (Silver, 1988, p. 73). According to Silver (1988) three specific mandates were identified by Congress: (1) the determination of the number of people with learning disabilities and a demographic description of them; (2) a review of the current research findings on the cause, diagnosis, treatment, and prevention of learning disabilities; and (3) suggestions for legislation and administration actions that would (a) increase the effectiveness of research on learning disabilities and improve the dissemination of the findings of such research, and (b) prioritize research on the cause, diagnosis, treatment, and prevention of learning disabilities.

In 1987, the committee presented its report to Congress. In this report, the ICLD recommended a legislated definition of LD based on a revision of the 1981 NJCLD's definition. The new definition was to include (changes are in italics) "significant difficulties in . . . *social skills*." As well the final sentence was changed to read as follows: ". . . with *socio*environmental influences (e.g., cultural differences, insufficient, or inappropriate instruction, psychogenic factors), and *especially with attention deficit disorder, all of which may cause learning problems, a learning disability* is not the direct result of those conditions or influences" (Silver, 1988, p. 79).

In addition the committee argued that prevalence studies on learning disabilities should not and could not accurately be undertaken until there was national consensus on a definition of learning disabilities. However, since the publication of the report only one member of the NJCLD has supported the revised definition, while the others have voted for nonsupport. At issue appears to be the phase "significant difficulties in . . . social skills." In spite of all the work and research, Silver (1988) concludes that a lack of a uniform definition and set of diagnostic criteria is one of the most crucial factors inhibiting current and future research efforts. This problem must be addressed before further epidemiological, clinical, basic, and educational research can result in meaningful, generalizable findings.

III. Assumptions in LD Definitions

In spite of these definitional problems, inherent in most definitions of learning problems, including that by NJCLD and its revision by the ICLD, U.S. Public Law 94-142, and Ontario's Bill 82, are three main assumptions:

1. *Specificity.* The learning problem is specific, generally confined to one or two cognitive areas.
2. *IQ–achievement discrepancy.* The child's achievement (usually as measured by one or more standardized achievement tests) is not commensurate with his/her ability (usually as measured by a standardized IQ test) or chronological age.
3. *Exclusionary Criteria.* The learning difficulty is *not* a result of some other, frequently inconsistent, condition.

Each of these assumptions is controversial and will be discussed separately.

A. Specificity

Siegel (1988a) has argued that there are two types of specificity. The first involves the degree to which the individual's problem is specific to one or more cognitive areas. A number of authors (Hall & Humphreys, 1982; Stanovich, 1986a, 1988; Swanson, 1988b, 1989) have maintained that one of the essential concepts of a learning disability is its specificity. That is, a learning disability is presumed to be caused by a neurological inefficiency which affects a narrow group of subskills of cognitive processes. This affects a specific domain of academic skills but leaves intellectual ability intact. In other words, a learning disability reflects a cognitive deficit possibly due to a neurological dysfunction that is comparatively specific to a particular domain (e.g., reading or arithmetic). Swanson (1988a) has suggested that these specific deficits must not stray too far into other cognitive domains or the concept of a specific learning disability will blend with other more generalized conditions (e.g, mental retardation). As well, Stanovich (1986a, 1986b) maintains that definitions of "dyslexia" must rest on an assumption of specificity. He contends that "dyslexia" results from a brain/cognitive deficit that is reasonably specific to reading. Further clear differences exist between the "dyslexic" reader (one with a relatively high IQ for that level of reading) and the "garden-variety" poor reader (one with a lower and more typical IQ score as compared to his/her reading level). In addition the concept of "dyslexia" requires that deficits found in such readers must not extend too far into other domains of cognitive functioning. However, Siegel (1989) has demonstrated that there are no differences in reading, language, spelling, and memory processes between dyslexic and garden-variety poor readers.

Siegel (1988a) and L. Brown and Bryant (1985) argue that this type of specificity is unrealistic. Siegel (1988a) maintains that if children have problems in working memory this could affect a variety of academic tasks especially in areas such as reading, spelling, and arithmetic. L. Brown and Bryant (1985) suggest that if a child has a severe language problem this could influence a large number of cognitive areas: reading, writing, speaking, and/or listening. As well, Siegel (1988a) contends that implicit in the specificity assumption is a second assumption that domains such as reading and arithmetic are entirely independent cognitive processes. She argues this is invalid as working memory as well as recognizing and labeling abstract symbols are involved in both reading and arithmetic skills, and a child who has difficulty with these cognitive processes is likely to have problems with tasks involving such skills (Siegel, 1988a).

Although Rourke (1982) has cautioned that not enough is known about the relevant parameters of children's learning and its disabilities to develop a comprehensive theory or model, he and a colleague (Rourke & Fisk, 1988) maintain that the concept of learning disabilities should be considered in the broadest possible context and "any model that purports to deal adequately with the manner in which central processing deficiencies hamper learning in the developing child must take into consideration, encompass, and explain all aspects of the child's developmental (learning) demands" (Rourke & Fisk, 1988, p. 547).

Siegel (1988a) suggests that a second type of specificity involves questions about the degree to which all LD children have the same problems or whether there are subtypes. She argues that the concept of a generalized homogeneous group labeled LD children should be abandoned and that the LD child should be considered as part of a smaller more clearly defined subtype (Siegel, 1988a). As well, other theorists (e.g., Bateman, 1969; Benton, 1978; Boder, 1973; Kinsbourne & Warrington, 1963; Rourke,

1983, 1985) have contended that differences within the population of children with learning disabilities may reflect the existence of distinguishable subtypes. In other words, not all learning-disabled children have the same types of disabilities and independent subtypes include distinctive characteristics and antecedent conditions that consistently predict specific patterns of learning difficulties. Therefore, failure to differentiate among types of learning disabilities can lead to inaccurate conclusions. For example, Siegel and Ryan (1984, 1988) found that certain reading-disabled children [as defined by having scores equal to or below the 25th percentile on the Reading Subtest of the Wide Range Achievement Test (WRAT)] have difficulty processing certain aspects of syntax, while specific arithmetic-disabled children (as defined by having scores equal to or below the 25th percentile on the Arithmetic Subtest of the WRAT while having normal reading scores, equal to or above the 30th percentile on the Reading Subtest of the WRAT) do not. Differences between the same two groups have been found in working memory (Fletcher, 1985a; Siegel & Linder, 1984; Siegel & Ryan, 1989). Swanson (1988b) found that LD readers may be characterized by different patterns of memory dysfunction. These differences are reflected on measures of achievement in reading and arithmetic. If all these children had been considered together as a homogeneous group, these differences might have been obscured.

In light of the above controversy and research findings the use of a specificity assumption in the definition of learning disabilities is questionable. This is true regardless of whether one refers to domain specificity (the limitation of the disability to one or two cognitive areas) or population specificity (failure to use subtypes).

B. IQ–Achievement Discrepancy

Another assumption of many LD definitions, including U.S. Public Law 94-142, Ontario's Bill 82, and the NJCLD's definition, is that there must be an IQ–achievement discrepancy. In other words the child's achievement is not commensurate with his/her ability or intelligence (IQ). Many investigators (e.g., Fletcher & Morris, 1986; Reynolds, 1984–1985, 1985; Siegel, 1985, 1988a, 1988b, 1990) argue that not only is this assumption controversial but it also may be invalid. Resnick (1979) argues that scientific evidence for sorting mildly handicapped children on the basis of IQ test results is weak.

Siegel (1989) contends that the following four basic assumptions are inherent in many IQ–achievement discrepancy definitions: (1) IQ tests are measures of intelligence; (2) intelligence and achievements are independent and the scores on IQ tests will not be affected by the presence of a learning disability; (3) reading is predicted by IQ test scores, that is, normal children with low IQ scores should be poor readers while those children with high IQ scores should be good readers; and (4) reading-disabled children with discrepant IQ scores will have different cognitive processes and information-processing skills than reading-disabled children with nondiscrepant IQ scores. Specifically there are clear, measurable differences between children who have poor reading scores and low IQ scores and those who have poor reading scores and higher IQ scores.

The first of Siegel's assumptions involves the ability of IQ tests to measure intelligence or ability. Neisser (1979) suggests that according to Rosch's theory of concepts, one's intelligence is just the degree to which one resembles a prototypically intelligent person. Further, because no single characteristic defines the prototype, there can be no adequate process-based definition of intelligence. Neisser (1979) states that it is impossible to explicitly define the concept of intelligence because of the nature of intelligence and the nature of concepts. Lezak (1988) argues that IQ is a construct and does not measure any real function or structure. However, that has not prevented psychometricians from measuring "it." But what is being measured?

Historically, the purpose of IQ tests has been to predict school success. According to some investigators (e.g., A. L. Brown & French, 1979) they fulfill that function well for normal children. However, they were never designed as measures of general intelligence and are composed mainly of items that are representative of the kinds of problems that traditionally dominate school curricula (A. L. Brown & French, 1979). Further while they may correlate well with school success in normal children, they are hardly good predictors of achievement in disabled learners (Sattler, 1982).

Fletcher and Morris (1986) also question the ability of IQ tests to measure potential or intelligence. They and others (e.g., Fletcher et al., 1989) suggest that performance on IQ tests is influenced by past learning, genetic endowment, and a host of situation factors. As well, some investigators (Fletcher et al., 1989; Fletcher & Morris, 1986, Neisser, 1979; Siegel, in press; Siegel & Heaven, 1986) argue that IQ tests such as the Wechsler Intelligence Scale for Children-Revised (WISC-R) do not measure all aspects of a child's adaptive functioning such as social behavior, problem solving, and information-processing skills. Specifically Hunt (1980) claims that IQ tests were not designed as measures of information-processing skills. Siegel (1989) argues that IQ tests include virtually no skills that are identifiable as problem-solving and/or logical-reasoning skills. In fact she claims they are measures of expressive language skills, memory, fine-motor abilities, and specific factual knowledge.

In their review of intelligence tests, Siegel and Heaven (1986) suggest that a wide variety of abilities is measured and that the same abilities are not measured by all IQ tests. Specifically a number of tests which have been designated as intelligence tests measure a variety of different functions and it is conceivably possible for a child to have one IQ score on one test and a different score on a second test. As well, others (Fletcher *et al.*, 1989; Fletcher & Morris, 1986) argue that IQ tests often represent measurements of several covarying abilities—hardly a measure of a single construct called "potential."

Finally, if intelligence is a measure of some stable construct of ability or potential and IQ tests measure it, then these test results should be stable over time. Elliott and Boeve (1987) found that, at least for mildly handicapped students, the variable time has a statistically significant effect on both children's WISC-R verbal and performance scores. Therefore for these students, at least, it is questionable if the WISC-R is measuring a stable construct.

The second assumption of the discrepancy definition is that measures of intelligence and measures of achievement are independent. Although this assumption has been questioned by some investigators (see Lyon, 1987, for a complete discussion), we maintain that it is necessary if a discrepancy definition is to be meaningful. If you accept the argument that intelligence is not orthogonal to achievement, then there would be no reason to expect a discrepancy. Therefore a discrepancy definition is logical if and only if the presence of a learning disability will not affect IQ test scores but will affect achievement test scores. Then LD children will have a discrepancy between the scores on their IQ tests and the scores on their achievement tests while normally achieving children and those with other disabilities will have scores on these tests which are similar (not discrepant).

A number of investigators (Green, 1974; Hopkins & Stanley, 1981; Siegel, 1988a, 1988b) have suggested that this assumption of independence is questionable. Green (1974) argues, for example, that comparisons of scores for ability and achievement are meaningful only to the extent to which unique elements are measured. Fletcher *et al.* (1989) maintains that it has not been clearly demonstrated that children with discrepancies in IQ and achievement have more specific disabilities than do poor achievers whose IQ scores were not discrepant. In fact, they contend that there is relatively little empirical evidence to show that similarly defined children differ on measures other than IQ. In an epidemiological study on the influence of various definitions of learning disabilities on the selection of children, Shaywitz, Shaywitz, Barnes, and Fletcher (1986) found that, although variations in the use of IQ indices lead to the identification of different children as learning disabled, there were few differences in cognitive abilities. As well, there were few differences among identified LD children with discrepant and not-discrepant IQ scores.

Hopkins and Stanley (1981) examined the overlapping variance in a well-constructed intelligence test (the Lorge–Thorndike) and in two subtests (the reading and the arithmetic) of a well-constructed achievement test (the Iowa Test of Basic Skills). On average, 47% of the variance was found to overlap. This suggests that when one ability test and one achievement test are used, about 50% of the time the same concept is being measured. This clearly violates the assumption of independence among concepts measured by the ability and achievement tests. It can only be hoped that the other 50% of the variance is tapping something different which can provide insight to the "true" differences revealed by the comparison.

In addition, Siegel (1989) argues that expressive language skills, short-term memory abilities, speed of information processing, speed of responding, and knowledge of specific facts are among the abilities measured by IQ tests. These tend to be the same abilities which appear to be measured by many standardized achievement tests. In a review of achievement tests said to measure a variety of aspects of reading, many tests (e.g., Gates–MacGintrie, Monroe–Sherman, Stanford Achievement Test) were timed, which classifies them as measures of speed of information processing and/or speed of re-sponding. Others, such as the Peabody Individual Achievement Test (PIAT), measure short-term memory and working memory, as the student is not permitted to look back over the text once the question is asked. In addition, these abilities tend to be the ones which investigators (e.g., Fletcher, 1985b; Siegel, 1985; Siegel & Linder, 1984; Siegel & Ryan, 1984, 1988; Swanson, 1988b) have found to be deficient in many LD individuals.

These criticisms of the discrepancy criteria have not gone unchallenged. Stanovich (1989) suggests that, historically, many theorists have considered verbal comprehension, fluency, and knowledge to be components of their global construct of intelligence. Therefore it is only logical that these concepts be measured, as they are an integral part of the defined construct. Specifically he contends if our definition of the construct intelligence includes components of verbal comprehension, fluency, and knowledge, then we must construct intelligence tests accordingly. If this means that some children for what-ever reason (i.e., poor expressive language skills) receive a low score on the test, then they are less intelligent according to that definition. According to Stanovich (1989) what is crucial to the discrepancy criteria is the hypothesis that LD individuals with low IQ scores have cognitive processes that are different from LD individuals with high IQ scores. However, as we will demonstrate in the next section, evidence for this hypothesis is questionable at best.

Discrepancy definitions also have been questioned on statistical grounds. Reynolds (1984–1985, 1985) notes that many discrepancy models are based on grade equivalents. He points out that these models have prob-lems in two areas. First, neither age nor grade-equivalent scores provide adequate mathematical properties (cannot be added, subtracted, multiplied, or divided) for use in discrepancy analysis. Second, the amount of retardation reflected by "2 years below grade level" changes with increasing grade level. A much greater level of retardation is reflected by a 2-year deficit at grade two than at grade seven and even less retardation would be reflected at grade eleven. Therefore a much greater deficit would be needed for a grade-three child to be identified as LD than for one in grade ten.

Finally, Lyon (1987) suggests that the maintenance of the use of a discrepancy definition has been largely for administrative and social reasons rather than because of its usefulness in diagnosis, educational planning, and instruction. Clearly, based on the above evidence IQ–achievement discrepancy assumptions must be questioned as a means of defining learning-disabled children. (See also this volume, Chapter 11).

C. Exclusionary Criteria

The final assumption of most definitions of LD is frequently an exclusionary statement that the learning disability is not primarily a result of some vague, specific condition. A number of investigators (Fletcher et al., 1989; Kavale, 1980; Siegel & Heaven, 1986) have argued that this is invalid for a number of reasons. Kavale (1980) suggests that learning disabilities should most properly be viewed as a complex interrelationship between brain dysfunction and cultural–economic disadvantage. He contends that there is a strong association between learning disabilities and cultural–economic disadvantage. This is rarely recognized because the use of an exclusionary criterion prevents culturally–economically disadvantaged children from being identified as LD. Kavale (1980) argues that comparisons between LD and cultural–economically disadvantaged groups in terms of symptomatology show that the two groups are more alike than different.

Others (Fletcher et al., 1989; Fletcher & Morris, 1986; Siegel, 1988b, 1990; Siegel & Heaven, 1986) contend that IQ cutoffs are inappropriate for a variety of reasons. Siegel (1988b, in press) suggests that arbitrary cutoffs are inappropriate because IQ tests measure the same abilities in which LD children are known to be deficient (see previous section for detailed discussion). In a study which compared two groups of children, one group whose reading scores were discrepant when compared to their IQ scores and the other whose scores were consistent, Fletcher et al. (1989) found that differences in neuropsychological performance were small and nonspecific. As well, Siegel (1988b) found that cognitive processes involving reading, spelling, language, and memory tasks do not appear to be predicted well by IQ test scores. It is more useful to use detailed analyses of specific skills and information-processing abilities. Specifically Siegel (1988b) has found in a reading learning-disabled population aged 7–16 years that IQ scores did not appear to be good predictors of the cognitive processing needed for reading, spelling, language, or memory tasks. In addition, there were few significant differences in a variety of reading, spelling, language, and short-term and working memory tasks among disabled readers of different IQ levels, suggesting that there are no differences in cognitive abilities in basic information-processing skills of disabled readers with differing IQ levels. Siegel (1988b) and Share, McGee, and Silva (1989) have both found in their work children with low IQs but age-appropriate reading levels, indicating that low IQ does not preclude normal reading levels.

In light of the failure of the exclusionary criteria to allow for the differentiation of a specific group, the use of it as a criteria to define LD must remain at best an open question and at worst an invalid one.

IV. An Alternative to Current Definitions

Clearly the field of special education continues to have problems defining and classifying children with learning disabilities. Current discrepancy definitions are problematic and should be reconsidered, as they cannot be justified in light of their illogical nature. But where does that leave us and where can we go from here?

One way in which meaning is given to a concept is by defining it operationally. Specifically an operational definition explains a concept solely in terms of the operations used to produce and measure it. Recognizing that there are problems inherent in operational definitions (e.g., the meaning of the concept is restricted to the narrowly described operations used for measuring it), we suggest that learning disabilities should be defined operationally. Further these definitions of learning disabilities (1) need to have an IQ threshold because we recognize that the field is not ready to accept Siegel's (1989) challenge to the use of IQ tests; (2) should refer to a significant difficulty in a school-related area; and (3) exclude only severe emotional disorders, second-language background, sensory disabilities, and/or neurological deficits.

Evidence (Siegel, Levey, & Ferris, 1985; Siegel & Ryan, 1989b) suggests that the type of operational definition used for the concept may influence the outcome and conclusions of the study. Siegel and Ryan (1989b) have argued that the actual definition used for a reading disability can make a difference in the conclusions that are drawn about information-processing characteristics of the children and whether there are reading-disability subtypes. In one study, poor readers (all with IQ scores equal to or above 80) were divided into four groups as follows: (1) those with phonics deficits—inadequate phonics skills based on the reading of pseudowords, (2) those with word-recognition deficits—inadequate word-recognition skills based on performance on the reading subtest of the WRAT, (3) those with comprehension-only deficits—inadequate reading comprehension skills but adequate word-recognition skills, and (4) those with rate-only deficits—slow reading speed but adequate word-recognition skills. When each disabled group was compared to an age-matched normally achieving group distinct cognitive differences appeared. For example, children with a phonics deficit or a word-recognition deficit had significantly below-normal scores on all cognitive tasks except for visual–spatial tasks, while those in the comprehension-only group were significantly lower than normal readers on short-term memory tasks but not on language tasks. The readers with rate-only deficits had cognitive profiles similar to normally achieving children. Therefore the ones with word-recognition problems are probably the ones with language deficits and those with only a reading comprehension problem probably do not have language problems.

In addition there was approximately a 25% overlap between poor comprehenders and poor readers. Therefore had a reading comprehension test been used to define the learning-disabled group and word recognition not been used as a control, the reading-disabled group would have consisted of some children with word-recognition problems and some without.

This leads to the question, how should a reading disability be defined? Like Stanovich (1986a, 1989) we suggest that the core deficits in a reading disability are problems in phonological processing. While we recognize that reading is more than simply decoding and recognizing words (one has to remember what was read, put it into context, and so on), unfortunately currently there no accurate tests to measure these variables (see Siegel & Heaven, 1986, for a complete discussion of this issue). Further empirical evidence suggests that when a difficulty with phonics and/or word recognition is used as the basis of the definition of a reading problem, then disabled readers appear to have reasonably homogeneous cognitive profiles and, in particular, deficits in the language areas (e.g., Fletcher, 1985a, 1985b; Rourke & Finlayson, 1978; Rourke & Strang, 1978; Siegel & Ryan, 1984, 1988, 1989; Strang & Rourke, 1983). Therefore we and others (e.g., Siegel & Heaven, 1986; Siegel & Ryan, 1989a; Velluntino, 1978, 1979) argue that single-word or nonword reading constitute the purest measures of reading and that an operational definition of a reading disability should be based on nonword tests to measure phonics skills and/or single-word tests to measure word-recognition skills.

The classification of children with arithmetic problems is equally problematic. As Siegel and Ryan (1989a) point out, it is almost impossible to find a group of reading-disabled children who also do not have severe deficits in arithmetic. At the same time, a number of investigators (Fletcher, 1985b; Rourke & Finlayson, 1978; Rourke & Strang, 1978; Siegel & Feldman, 1983; Siegel & Linder, 1984; Siegel & Ryan, 1984, 1988, 1989a) have found a group of learning-disabled children with difficulties in arithmetic but with average or above-average reading scores (as measured on the reading subtest of the WRAT, a word-recognition test). Some evidence (e.g., Fletcher, 1985a; Rourke & Finlayson, 1978; Rourke & Strang, 1978; Siegel & Feldman, 1983; Siegel & Linder, 1984; Siegel & Ryan, 1984, 1988, 1989a) suggests that these children with arithmetic deficits but normal reading (word recognition) have different cognitive profiles than those with reading difficulties. Therefore, it is important that children designated as arithmetic learning disabled not have problems that are confounded by difficulties in reading. Obviously if an arithmetic problem-solving test is used to define the group, some so-called "arithmetic-disabled" children will have problems with the arithmetic and others will have problems with arithmetic that result from their reading problems. Again the type of arithmetic test used to define the problem will have a significant impact on the conclusions that are reached about the arithmetic-disabled child.

In light of these findings we suggest that an operational definition of learning disabilities incorporate a reading disability and an arithmetic disability. In addition, a third category—attention-deficit disorders—should be added, as many investigators, physicians, and educators have evidence to suggest that these children constitute a distinct subtype of the LD population (e.g., Gillberg & Gillberg, 1989; Meints, 1989; Szatmari, Offord, & Boyle, 1989a, 1989b). With these criteria in mind, we suggest that learning disabilities be operationally defined as follows: a term which refers to a group of children who have severe academic difficulties as demonstrated by systematic measurements of achievement (reading and arithmetic) that are reasonable and do not confound reading with attention or memory skills or context clues (percentile or standard score cutoffs, not grade-levels discrepancy, should be used). Specifically they should (1) have IQ scores equal to or above 80, and (2) have one or more of the following: (a) WRAT reading subtest score equal to or below the 25th percentile, (b) WRAT arithmetic subtest score equal to or below the 25th percentile and WRAT reading subtest score equal to or above the 30th percentile, (Jastak & Wilkinson, 1984) and/or (c) a score greater than two standard deviations above the mean for age and sex on the Parent and/or Teacher Questionnaire (Goyette, Conners, & Ulrich, 1978). The use of this classification scheme provides the broad constituency of educators, school administrators, physicians, and investigators with three clearly defined types of disorders: (1) reading (word recognition), (2) arithmetic (computation, written work), and (3) attention deficit. Each of these disorders has been shown to have distinctive neurological and cognitive profiles (e.g., Fletcher, 1985b; Rourke & Finlayson, 1978; Rourke & Strang, 1978; Siegel & Feldman, 1983; Siegel & Linder, 1984; Siegel & Ryan, 1984, 1988, 1989a; Spellacy & Peters, 1978).

While we recognize the limitations of categorizing reading as phonological processing and arithmetic as simple computation, we suggest that given the current state of testing they provide the purest measures from which to work. In addition, although the WRAT-R (Jastak & Wilkinson, 1984) has been criticized in the literature (e.g., Reid, 1986; Reynolds, 1986), others

(Geist, 1986; Spruill & Beck, 1986; Witt, 1986) maintain that it is a useful screening device. As well, there is evidence that for whatever reason, the WRAT-R consistently divides the LD population into subtypes with distinctive cognitive and neuropsychological profiles (e.g., Fletcher, 1985a; Rourke & Finlayson, 1978; Rourke & Strang, 1978; Share, Moffitt, & Silva, 1988; Siegel & Linder, 1984; Siegel & Ryan, 1984, 1988, 1989a).

V. Conclusions

In this chapter we have demonstrated that there is little consensus among teachers, psychologists, and educational administrators regarding the definition of learning disabilities and its interpretation. Further the common practice of computing a discrepancy between achievement and ability (usually as measured by an IQ test score) seems illogical because (1) discrepancy formulas are subject to methodological flaws, (2) there appear to be few if any cognitive differences between children with discrepancy scores and those without discrepancy scores, and (3) discrepancy scores exist within other exceptionalities as well as in normal children. As have other investigators (e.g., Stanovich, 1986a), we have suggested that definitions of reading disability need to be based on measures of phonological processing. Further we have argued that those with arithmetic disabilities must be considered separately from those with reading disabilities and that a definition of arithmetic disability be based on computation measures which are not confounded by a reading component. We maintain that the use of these operational definitions of learning disabilities avoids the problems inherent in discrepancy definitions as well as those problems related to reading comprehension and problem-solving measures. Further these definitions are easily identifiable and practical for the broad constituency of legislators, educators, physicians, and investigators working with learning-disabled children.

Acknowledgment

The preparation of this chapter and the research on which it was based were supported by a grant from the Natural Sciences and Engineering Research Council of Canada to Linda S. Siegel.

References

Algozzine, B., & Ysseldyke, J. E. (1988). Questioning discrepancies; Retaking the first step 20 years later. *Learning Disability Quarterly, 11,* 307–318.

Bateman, B. (1969). Reading: A controversial view: Research and rationale. In L. Tarnopol (Ed.), *Learning disabilities: Introduction to education and medical management* (pp. 289–304). Springfield, IL: Thomas

Benton, A. (1978). Some conclusions about dyslexia. In A. L. Benton & D. Pearl (Eds.), *Dyslexia: An appraisal of current knowledge* (pp. 453–476). New York: Oxford University Press.

Boder, E. (1973). Developmental dyslexia: A diagnostic approach based on three atypical reading-spelling patterns. *Developmental Medicine and Child Neurology, 15,* 663–687.

Brown, A. L., & French, L. A. (1979). The zone of potential development: Implications of intelligence testing in the year 2000. *Intelligence, 3,* 255–273.

Brown, L., & Bryant, B. (1985). Focus on appraisal: Measuring the aptitude-achievement discrepancy in learning disability diagnosis. *Remedial and Special Education, 6,* 37.

Cruickshank, W. M. (1972). Some issues facing the field of learning disability. *Journal of Learning Disabilities, 5,* 380–388.

Cruickshank, W. M. (1981). Learning disabilities: A definitional statement. In W. M. Cruickshank (Ed.), *Concepts in learning disabilities.* Syracuse, NY: Syracuse University Press.

Elliott, S. N., & Boeve, K. (1987). Stability of WISC-R IQ's: An investigation of ethnic differences over time. *Educational and Psychological Measurement, 47,* 461–466.

Epps, S., Ysseldyke, J., & Algozzine, B. (1985). An analysis of the conceptual Framework underlying definitions of learning disabilities. *Journal of School Psychology, 23,* 133–144.

Federal Register. (1977). *The rules and regulations for implementing Public Law 94-142.* Washington, DC: U.S. Government Printing Office.

Fletcher, J. M. (1985a). External validity of learning disability subtypes. In B. P. Rourke (Ed.), *Neuropsychology of learning disabilities: Essentials of subtype analysis.* (pp. 187–211). New York: Guilford Press.

Fletcher, J. M. (1985b). Memory for verbal and nonverbal stimuli in learning disability subgroups: Analysis of selective reminding. *Journal of Experimental Child Psychology, 40,* 244–259.

Fletcher, J. M., Espy, K. A., Francis, D. J., Davidson, K. C., Rourke, B. P., & Shaywitz, S. A. (1989). Comparisons of cutoff and regression-based definitions of reading disabilities. *Journal of Learning Disabilities, 22,* 334–338.

Fletcher, J. M., & Morris, R. (1986). Classification of disabled learners: Beyond exclusionary definitions. In S. J. Ceci (Ed.), *Handbook of cognitive, social, and neuropsychological aspects of learning disabilities.* Hillsdale, NJ: Erlbaum.

Geist, H. (1986). Reaction to Reid and Reynolds. *Journal of Counseling and Development, 65,* 118.

Gillberg, C. I., & Gillberg, C. (1989). Children with preschool minor neuro-developmental disorders: IV. Behavior and school achievement at age 13. *Developmental Medicine and Child Neurology, 31,* 3–13.

Goyette, G. H., Conners, C. K., & Ulrich, R. F. (1978). Normative data on the revised Conners Parent and Teacher Rating Scales. *Journal of Abnormal Child Psychology, 6,* 221–236.

Green, D. R. (1974). *The aptitude-achievement distinction.* Moneterey, CA: CTB/McGraw-Hill.

94 / SYLVIA R. MORRISON AND LINDA S. SIEGEL

Hall, J., & Humphreys, M. (1982). Research on specific learning disabilities: Deficits and remediation. *Topics in Learning and Learning Disabilities, 2,* 68–78.

Hamill, D. D., Leigh, J. E., McNutt, G., & Larsen, S. C. (1981). A new definition of learning disabilities. *Learning Disability Quarterly, 4,* 336–342.

Hopkins, K. D., & Stanley, J. C. (1981). *Educational and psychological measurement* (6th ed.). Englewood Cliffs, NJ: Prentice-Hall.

Hunt, E. B. (1980). Intelligence as an information-processing concept. *British Journal of Psychology, 71,* 449–474.

Jastak, S. R., & Wilkinson, N. L. (1984). *Wide Range Achievement Test—Revised.* Wilmington, DE: Jastak Associates.

Kavale, K. A. (1980). Learning disability and cultural-economic disadvantage: The case for a relationship. *Learning Disability Quarterly, 3,* 97–112.

Kavale, K. A. (1987). Theoretical issues surrounding severe discrepancy. *Learning Disability Research, 3,* 12–20.

Keogh, B. K. (1983). Classification, compliance, and confusion. *Journal of Learning Disabilities, 16,* 25.

Keogh, B. K. (1986). Future of the LD field: Research and practice. *Journal of Learning Disabilities, 19,* 455–460.

Keogh, B. K. (1987). Learning disabilities: In defense of a construct. *Learning Disabilities Research, 3,* 4–9.

Kinsbourne, M., & Warrington, E. J. K. (1963). The developmental Gerstmann syndrome. *Archives of Neurology (Chicago) 8,* 490–501.

Lezak, M. D. (1988). IQ: R.I.P. *Journal of Clinical and Experimental Neuropsychology, 10,* 351–361.

Lyon, G. R. (1987). Severe discrepancy: Theoretical psychometric, developmental, and educational issues. *Learning Disability Research, 3,* 10–11.

Mann, L., Davis, C. H., Boyer, C. W., Jr., Metz, C. M., & Wolford, B. (1983). LD or not LD, that was the question: A retrospective analysis of child service demonstration centers' compliance with the federal definition of learning disabilities. *Journal of Learning Disabilities, 16,* 14–17.

Meints, C. K. (1989). Attention Deficit Disorder: A review of the literature. *Psychology in the Schools, 26,* 168–178.

Neisser, U. (1979). The concept of intelligence. *Intelligence, 3,* 217–227.

Reid, N. (1986). Wide Range Achievement Test: 1984 revised edition. *Journal of Counseling and Development, 64,* 538–539.

Resnick, L. B. (1979). The future of IQ testing in education. *Intelligence, 3,* 241–253.

Reynolds, C. R. (1984–1985). Critical measurement issues in learning disabilities. *Journal of Special Education, 18,* 453–476.

Reynolds, C. R. (1985). Measuring the aptitude-achievement discrepancy in learning disability diagnosis. *Remedial and Special Education, 6,* 38–55.

Reynolds, C. R. (1986). Wide Range Achievement Test (WRAT-R): 1984 edition. *Journal of Counseling and Development, 64,* 540–541.

Rourke, B. P. (1982). Central processing deficiencies in children: Toward a developmental neuropsychological model. *Journal of Clinical Neuropsychology, 4,* 1–18.

Rourke, B. P. (1983). Outstanding issues in learning disabilities research. In M. Rutter (Ed.), *Developmental neuropsychiatry* (pp. 1–25). New York: Guilford Press.

Rourke, B. P. (1985). *Neuropsychology of learning disabilities: Essentials of subtype analysis.* New York: Guilford Press.

Rourke, B. P., & Finlayson, M. A. J. (1978). Neuropsychological significance of variations in patterns of academic performance: Verbal and visual-spatial abilities. *Journal of Abnormal Child Psychology, 6,* 121–133.

Rourke, B. P., & Fisk, J. L. (1988). Subtypes of learning-disabled children: Implications for a neurodevelopmental model of differential hemispheric processing. In D. L. Molfese & S. J. Segalowitz (Eds.), *Brain lateralization in children: Developmental implications.* New York: Guilford Press.

Rourke, B. P., & Strang, J. D. (1978). Neuropsychological significance of variations in patterns of academic performance: Motor, psychomotor, and tactile-perceptual abilities. *Journal of Pediatric Psychology, 2,* 62–66.

Sattler, J. M. (1982). *Assessment of children's intelligence and special abilities* (2nd ed.). Boston, MA: Allyn & Bacon.

Share, D. L., McGee, R., & Silva, P. A. (1989). IQ and reading progress: A test of the capacity notion of IQ. *Journal of the American Academy of Child and Adolescent Psychiatry, 28,* 97–100.

Share, D. L., Moffitt, T. E., & Silva, P. A. (1988). Factors associated with arithmetic-and-reading disability and specific arithmetic disability. *Journal of Learning Disabilities, 21,* 313–321.

Shaywitz, S. E., Shaywitz, B. A., Barnes, M., & Fletcher, J. M. (1986, October). *Prevalence of dyslexia in a epidemiological sample.* Child Neurological Society.

Siegel, L. S. (1985). Psycholinguistic aspects of reading disabilities. In L. S. Siegel & F. J. Morrison (Eds.), *Cognitive development in atypical children* (pp. 45–66). New York: Springer-Verlag.

Siegel, L. S. (1988a). Definitional and theoretical issues and research on learning disabilities. *Journal of Learning Disabilities, 21,* 264–266.

Siegel, L. S. (1988b). Evidence that IQ tests are irrelevant to the definition and analysis of reading disabilities. *Canadian Journal of Psychology, 42,* 201–215.

Siegel, L. S. (1989). IQ is irrelevant of the definition of learning disabilities. *Journal of Learning Disabilities, 22,* 469–478.

Siegel, L. S. (1990). IQ and learning disabilities: R.I.P. In H. L. Swanson & B. Keogh (Eds.), *Learning disabilities: Theoretical and research issues.* (pp. 112–128) Hillsdale, NJ: Erlbaum.

Siegel, L. S., & Feldman, W. (1983). Nondyslexic children with combined and arithmetic learning disabilities. *Clinical Pediatrics, 22,* 200–207.

Siegel, L. S., & Heaven, R. K. (1986). Categorization of learning disabilities. In S. J. Ceci (Ed.), *Handbook of cognitive, social, and neuropsychological aspects of learning disabilities.* Hillsdale, NJ: Erlbaum.

Siegel, L. S., Levey, P., & Ferris, H. (1985). Subtypes of developmental dyslexia: Do they exist? In F. J. Morrison (Ed.), *Applied Developmental Psychology* Vol. 2 (pp. 169–190) Orlando: Academic Press.

Siegel, L. S., & Linder, B. A. (1984). Short term memory processes in children with reading and arithmetic learning disabilities. *Developmental Psychology, 20,* 200–207.

Siegel, L. S., & Ryan, E. B. (1984). Reading disability as a language disorder. *Remedial and Special Education, 5,* 25–33.

Siegel, L. S., & Ryan, E. B. (1988). Development of grammatical sensitivity, phonological, and short-term memory skills in normally achieving and learning disabled children. *Developmental Psychology, 24,* 28–37.

Siegel, L. S., & Ryan, E. B. (1989a). The development of working memory in normally achieving and subtypes of learning disabled children. *Child Development, 60,* 973–980.

Siegel, L. S., & Ryan, E. S. (1989b). Subtypes of developmental dyslexia: The influence of definitional variables. *Reading and Writing: An Interdisciplinary Journal, 2,* 257–287.

Silver, L. (1988). A review of the Federal Government's Inter Agency Committee on learning Disabilities: Report to the U.S. Congress. *Learning Disabilities Focus, 3,* 73–81.

Spellacy, F., & Peter, B. (1978). Dyscalculia and elements of developmental Gerstmann Syndrome in school children. *Cortex, 14,* 197–206.

Spruill, J., & Beck, B. (1986). Relationship between WRAT and WRAT-R. *Psychology in the Schools, 23,* 357–360.

Stanovich, K. E. (1986a). Cognitive processes and the reading problems of learning disabled children: Evaluation the assumption of specificity. In J. Torgesen & B. Wong (Eds.), *Psychological and educational perspectives on learning disabilities* (pp. 87–113). Orlando, FL: Academic Press.

Stanovich, K. E. (1986b). Matthew effects in reading: Some consequences of individual differences in the acquisition of literacy. *Reading Research Quarterly, 21,* 360–407.

Stanovich, K. E. (1988). Explaining the differences between the dyslexic and the garden-variety poor reader: The phonological-core variable-difference model. *Journal of Learning Disabilities, 21,* 590–604.

Stanovich, K. E. (1989). Has the learning disabilities field lost its intelligence? *Journal of Learning Disabilities, 22,* 487–492.

Strang, J. D., & Rourke, B. P. (1983). Concept-formation/non-verbal reasoning abilities of children who exhibit specific academic problems with arithmetic. *Journal of Clinical Child Psychology, 12,* 33–39.

Swanson, H. L. (1988a). Memory subtypes in learning disabled readers. *Learning Disability Quarterly, 11,* 342–357.

Swanson, H. L. (1988b). Toward a metatheory of learning disabilities. *Journal of Learning Disabilities, 21,* 196–209.

Swanson, H. L. (1989). Phonological processes and other routes. *Journal of Learning Disabilities, 22,* 495–497.

Szatmari, P., Offord, D. R., & Boyle, M. H. (1989a). Correlates, associated impairments and patterns of service utilization of children with attention deficit disorder: Findings from the Ontario Child Health Study. *Journal of Child Psychology and Psychiatry and Allied Disciplines, 30,* 205–217.

Szatmari, P., Offord, D. R., & Boyle, M. H., (1989b). Ontario Health Study: Prevalence of attention deficit disorder with hyperactivity. *Journal of Child Psychology and Psychiatry and Allied Disciplines, 30,* 219–230.

Vellutino, F. (1978). Toward an understanding of dyslexia: Psychological factors in specific reading disability. In A. L. Benton & D. Pearl (Eds.), *Dyslexia: An appraisal of current knowledge.* (pp. 61–112). New York: Oxford University Press.

Vellutino, F. R. (1979). *Dyslexia: Theory and research.* Cambridge, MA: MIT Press.

Witt, J. C. (1986). Review of the Wide Range Achievement Test—Revised. *Journal of Psychoeducational Assessment, 4,* 87–90.

Wong, B. Y. (1979). Research and educational implications of some recent conceptualizations in learning disabilities. *Learning Disabilities Quarterly, 2,* 63–68.

Wong, B. Y. (1985). Problems and issues in the definition of learning disabilities. In J. Torgesen & B. Y. Wong (Eds.), *Psychological and educational perspectives on learning disabilities.* Orlando, FL: Academic Press.

Wong, B. Y. (1988). Basic research in learning disabilities: An introduction to the special series. *Journal of Learning Disabilities, 21,* 195.

CHAPTER FIVE

The Dejerine Hypothesis: Implications for an Etiological Reformulation of Developmental Dyslexia

Paul Satz

I. Introduction

Since the seminal report of Dejerine (1892), which observed the onset of alexia with agraphia following an adult lesion of the left angular gyrus, investigators have long suspected that this neural substrate, in the posterior left cerebral hemisphere, may play a key role in the understanding of childhood developmental dyslexia. Later reports by Morgan (1896) and Hinshelwood (1900) postulated a similar locus for the first cases of congenital word blindness. Throughout the twentieth century this view was shared by those who conceptualized reading as a language or left-hemisphere process. The strongest advocates of this view were those who observed the selected losses in reading, spelling, and writing following acquired focal lesions in adults (Benson & Geschwind, 1969). In fact, some of the more formal theories of reading sprang from these reports (Coltheart, Patterson, & Marshall, 1980; Liberman, 1982; Marshall & Newcombe, 1981; Vellutino, 1987).

With the advent of the neurolinguistic movement in the early 1970s, further attention focused on the role of the left hemisphere as a putative substrate for childhood dyslexia. Despite general agreement as to a possible locus, the mechanism presumed to underlie this "congenital" form of the disorder remained unknown.

It was not until 1968 that Drake reported a post-mortem analysis of the brain of a dyslexic which revealed abnormal subcortical neurons in *both* temporal lobes. These anomalous cellular migrations were later confirmed by Galaburda and Kemper (1979), who showed the first relatively convincing evidence of a *unilateral* congenital abnormality of the left posterior temporal lobe. According to Geschwind (1985, p. 22) ". . . this patient was a 20 year old man still severely dyslexic at the time of death in an accident. The patient was left-handed, a highly-skilled metalsmith and had two dyslexic brothers, as well as a mother with rheumatoid arthritis."

It was not long after this initial report that Geschwind and his colleagues (Geschwind, 1985; Geschwind & Behan, 1982; Geschwind & Galaburda, 1985a, 1985b) advanced the first formal neurobiological theory of childhood dyslexia. Briefly, the theory states that the disorder is due to an excess of testosterone during prenatal development which, in some males, slows the maturation of the left hemisphere, leading to structural anomalies of cell migration (heterotopias) and organization (dysplasias). It is further hypothesized that because of this anomalous cellular migration in the left hemisphere, certain compensatory functions in the right hemisphere are activated, leading to a shift in hand preference (left) and the development of superior visuospatial abilities. However, the substrate for speech and language remains in the left hemisphere, leading to later reading and writing disturbances. The theory also postulates that testosterone has an impact on the thymus gland, leading to an increased risk for autoimmune disorder in later life. In sum, the theory predicts a triadic association involving handedness (left), cognition (reading/language disability), and immunological status (autoimmune disorder) in males who are exposed prenatally to excessive amounts of testosterone.

The differential effect of testosterone on the left hemisphere is explained, in part, as a function of the right hemisphere's advantage in maturational rate, especially in males, which leaves the left hemisphere at greater risk during this early critical developmental period (Taylor & Ounsted, 1972). Additionally, the left hemisphere is invoked, probably because of its dominant role in language and reading processes.

The latter position represents an important theoretical advance that reaffirms traditional claims for a unilateral neural substrate in developmental dyslexia. Despite the obvious appeal and heuristic importance of this position, it does assume, implicitly or otherwise, that brain structures outside of the critical speech/language zones (both intra- and interhemispheric) lack the capacity to compensate for the putative left temporal–parietal insult in dyslexia (presumably congenital). This assumption, however, deserves closer scrutiny.

Why, for example, should the *reading* process be more vulnerable to a focal brain lesion (pre- or early postnatal) than other *related* cognitive functions? With respect to *speech* and *language*, it has long been reported that early left focal brain insult (pre- or postnatal) produces no long-term deficits in these functions. Rapid recovery from aphasia is the rule, although the status of other cognitive functions, especially reading and writing, is less clear (see review by Satz & Bullard-Bates, 1981). A more recent review of this literature as it relates to the proposed etiological reformulation of the Dejerine (1892) dyslexia hypothesis was reported by Satz (1987, in press).

According to Satz (in press), spontaneous recovery was reported in the vast majority of children who acquired aphasia after early left-hemisphere insult. Recovery from aphasia ranged from a low of 50% (Van Dongen & Loonen, 1979) to a high of 100% (Basser, 1962; Byers & McLean, 1962). Most of the studies reported spontaneous recovery in approximately 75% of the cases. Spontaneous recovery was also shown to be unrelated to the presence of severity of hemiparesis. A majority of the cases improved despite the residual presence of hemiparesis (Alajouanine & Lhermitte, 1965; Basser, 1962; Byers & McLean, 1962; Woods & Carey, 1979; Woods & Teuber, 1978). No studies disconfirmed this finding. It was also shown that when the left lesion occurred before the first birthday, the child was usually *spared* of any aphasia onset or subsequent linguistic impairment (Woods & Carey, 1979). Unfortunately, many of the studies failed to document the age of lesion onset which, if after age 8 years, may have accounted for some of the infrequent cases of residual aphasia. In fact, when age of lesion onset was documented, no reports of residual aphasia were observed before ages 6–8. Although the recovery from childhood aphasia seems both dramatic and consistent in these reports, the effects on subsequent cognitive and academic skills, especially reading, remain unknown. While some of the studies reported instances of cognitive and/or academic difficulties in these children (Alajouanine & Lhermitte, 1965; Byers & McLean, 1962; Hécean, 1976; Woods & Carey, 1979), the reports were largely qualitative or anecdotal in nature. No study provided any objective data on achievement variables, including word recognition, reading comprehension, spelling, or math. However, when academic difficulties were reported, they may have been associated with cases of later lesion onset (i.e., after 6–8 years).

What brain mechanism(s) might account for the preceding instances of sparing or recovery of speech after early injury to the left cerebral hemisphere? The strongest evidence comes from studies that have investigated the status and/or hemispheric representation of speech and language functions after focal injury to the *left* hemisphere during infancy or childhood. Some of these studies, including the seminal reports by Rasmussen and Milner (1977) and

Penfield and Roberts (1959), were reviewed in a recent paper by Satz, Strauss, Wada, and Orsini (1988).

The most striking finding from this review is that the earlier the left hemisphere perturbation (i.e., before 12 months), the greater the likelihood of an interhemispheric shift or reorganization in both speech and handedness. Lesions occurring between the ages of 12 and 72 months (6 years) are more likely to result in a unimodal interhemispheric shift in speech, a bilateral or less complete form of hemispheric speech reorganization, or an intrahemispheric reorganization, primarily speech. In each of the latter three cases, the likelihood of a corresponding shift in handedness is lower than with lesions occurring before the first birthday, which are more likely to result in a bimodal hemispheric reorganization. It is hypothesized that this latter type of hemispheric reorganization probably accounts for instances of *sparing* following left-hemisphere injury, while the former modes of reorganization account for instances of *recovery* in speech. Unfortunately, it is unclear whether the rate and/or degree of recovery is related to the type of inter- or intrahemispheric reorganization. This question has yet to be tested empirically.

Although the sodium amytal studies provide the clearest evidence for an interhemispheric mode of speech reorganization, they provide only indirect evidence with respect to an intrahemispheric mode. It is primarily the data from Penfield and Roberts (1959) that address the latter issue. In fact, the seminal chapter by Penfield and Roberts, which is seldom cited, provides the most direct evidence for an intrahemispheric mode of speech reorganization. The data (Table I) have been retabulated here to illustrate the hypothesized effect. The table reports the presence or absence of an aphasia after left temporal lobectomy in an adult sample of nonaphasic patients with early- (< age 2) or later- (> age 2) occurring epileptogenic lesions of the left hemisphere. Inspection of this table shows that with later-onset lesions (> age 2) most of the patients (right and left handed) became aphasic after operation on the side of the lesion (approximately 75%). However, with early-onset lesions only 22% (16/71) of the adult patients became aphasic after surgical removal of brain tissue on the side of the old epileptogenic lesion (i.e., the left side). The onset of aphasia in these cases strongly suggests that speech reorganization had been mediated by adjacent structures in the same hemisphere that were activated after the initial brain perturbation. We have recently hypothesized (Satz, Whitaker, & Strauss, in press) that these structures, that is, posterior association cortex, represent equipotential substrates that were not functionally committed at the time of the initial perturbation. Similar viewpoints have also been expressed by Hécaen, Perenin, and Jeannerod (1984).

Table I also presents data indirectly on the presence of an interhemispheric mode of reorganization. In contrast to the later-occurring lesions,

TABLE I Aphasia Onset after Left Lobectomy by Age of Lesion and Handedness[a]

	Early (< age 2)				Late > age 2		
Hand	N	No. Aphasic	%	Hand	N	No. Aphasic	%
Right	22	10	46	Right	157	115	73
Left	49	6	12	Left	18	13	72

[a] From Penfield and Roberts (1959).

most of the early left-sided lesion cases (12 right handers, 43 left handed = 55/71 = 78%) had no aphasia whatsoever after resection of brain tissue on the side of the original lesion. This *sparing* was most probably mediated by an interhemispheric shift in both speech (right) and handedness (left). Consistent with the amobarbital data, this more dramatic type of interhemispheric reorganization is associated with a much earlier focal perturbation.

II. Reading and Writing Status

What continues to remain unclear, however, is the status of other cognitive functions—namely, reading and writing. As noted earlier, few studies have addressed this topic systematically or empirically. Also the few reports available are largely anecdotal in nature, leaving ambiguous the status or side of lesion onset (i.e., left or bilateral). The only study available which meets most of the criteria necessary for addressing this issue was reported recently by Aram and Ekelman (1988). The authors report scholastic aptitude and academic achievement data for 32 children with carefully documented focal vascular lesions (20 left, 12 right) ranging from prenatal to childhood onset. In addition, the authors employed an individually matched control child for each of the lesion cases. The majority of lesions consisted of cerebral vascular accidents usually sustained after cardiac catheterization or surgery (11 left, 10 right), but there were also six children with prenatal insults (4 left, 2 right), four children with arteriovenous malformations (all left), and one child with a subcortical lesion. Table II presents the adjusted percentiles (by full-scale IQ) on the *scholastic aptitude* measures (reading, math, written language, and knowledge) and *academic achievement* measures (reading, math, and written language) for the two lesion and control groups. The aptitude and achievement clusters were assessed by subtest from the Woodcock–Johnson Psychoeducational Battery (Woodcock & Johnson, 1977). For brevity, the table excludes data on the cognitive cluster (verbal, reasoning, perceptual speed, and memory).

TABLE II Mean Percentile Aptitude and Achievement Scores[a] by Lesion Side and Controls

Test	Scores	Left	Control	Right	Control
	Reading	61.9	66.9	59.7	59.3
	Math	68.1[b]	82.5	60.5[b]	76.7
Aptitude	Written language	70.9	79.0	60.7	73.2
	Knowledge	70.6	7.55	62.6	73.2
	Reading	55.3	58.7	52.9	57.1
Achievement	Math	65.8	68.9	45.7	60.2
	Written language	62.6	72.5	53.3[b]	70.3

[a] Adjusted by full-scale IQ.
[b] Score lower than control, $p = \leq .01$.

Inspection of this table reveals only three instances (3/14) in which the lesioned group was lower than the matched control. Two of the instances involved math aptitude (one with left lesions and the other with right lesions) and the other involved written language on achievement (right-lesion group). All other comparisons were nonsignificant. In fact, inspection of the percentile scores reveals relatively high scores for both lesion and control groups on the scholastic aptitude and academic achievement measures. These percentile levels clearly contradict any overall evidence of a major reading or learning disability in either lesioned group. However, Aram and Ekelman (1988) correctly noted that the relatively high performance scores tended to mask instances of academic difficulty in some of the unilateral cases. With respect to grade repetition, four of the left- (20%) and four of the right-lesion group (33%) had been held back. Also, with respect to special class placement, six of the left- (30%) and four of the right-lesion group (33%) were receiving remedial help. However, these difficulties, while infrequent, were not related to lesion side.

Although these findings are based on a single report, no matter how meritorious, they should be replicated. At the same time, it should be recognized that the lesions sustained by these children, while unilateral, were quite severe, and predominately of vascular etiology. Yet, they failed to produce any striking evidence of reading or learning failure. Furthermore, as a group, neither the left- nor the right-lesioned children showed formal signs of a developmental dyslexia. Why? The most reasonable explanation, and one consistent with the previous section on speech and language, is that the onset of the damage in most of Aram and Ekelman's cases (27/32 = 85%) was before age 8. In fact, the frequency of late onset of damage was slightly higher in their left-lesioned group (25% versus 0%) which, if anything, would tend to bias the effect in favor of traditional views of developmental dyslexia—namely, a putative left-hemisphere substrate.

Is there any clinical evidence that an acquired *early* left-hemisphere lesion can produce a major reading or learning disability? A recent study by Levine, Hier, and Calvanio (1981) provides one of the few reports on this question. The authors described the case of a 33-year-old right-handed man who had no family history of reading, speech, or spelling disorder and whose development was normal until age 5 years 8 months, when he had an abrupt onset of symptoms including nocturnal spells of screaming, pallor, and stiffening of the arms. At age 6 years 1 month he had his first seizure followed by bilateral retinal hemorrhages and increasing confusion. Ventriculography revealed a mass in the left temporal lobe which, after frontotemporal craniotomy, disclosed a large hemorrhage which was then resected. He returned to school but was unable to learn to read or write and was referred to special classes. At age 7 years 8 months, EEG revealed an epileptogenic focus in the left temporal lobe anterior to the original cortical scar. Following left anterior lobectomy, the patient became *aphasic* but *recovered* within 3 months. However, he was never able to make any academic progress, primarily in reading, despite several years of remedial intervention. Interestingly, at age 17, while asymptomatic, an amobarbitol test of the right carotid artery was conducted. While producing a dense left hemiplegia, the test revealed no arrest of speech, suggesting that his recovery from aphasia was mediated by an intrahemispheric mode of reorganization, probably adjacent to the original lesions. As noted earlier in this chapter, this mode of reorganization, primarily unimodal, is more often associated with a later-childhood-onset lesion (i.e., ages 4–6). In fact, the patient remained right handed despite two lesions in the critical speech/hand zones of the left hemisphere. This finding further strengthens the importance of time of lesion onset (i.e., before age 1) in inducing a more complete and bimodal form of hemispheric reorganization.

A. Theoretical Clue

Although the later onset of the lesions (ages 6 years 1 month and 7 years 8 months) probably accounts for the occurrence of a less complete form of hemispheric reorganization, as well as speech recovery, one must ask why the patient never managed to learn to read or write. The report indicates that the patient's right hemisphere was intact and therefore capable of taking over speech and language functions. However, an intrahemispheric mode of reorganization occurred. The answer probably lies in the later onset of the initial lesion (approximately 6 years) followed relatively soon by the second lesion (age 7 years, 8 months) which may have further compromised the degree of intrahemispheric reorganization, especially the acquisition of a new and later-developing skill—namely, reading. Furthermore, the child's seizure disorder and multiple symptoms after the initial lesion probably interfered with or delayed the acquisition of reading prior to the onset of the second lesion, which occurred perilously close to the *critical period* for recovery. As noted earlier, this period generally marks the onset of more permanent sequelae in speech and language functions following injury to the left cerebral hemisphere. It is also the period (approximately 8 years) during which the adult pattern of acquired aphasia—and alexia—are more likely to be observed (Benson & Geschwind, 1969).

If early focal insult to the left hemisphere (before ages 6–8) leads to relative sparing and/or recovery of speech, language, and reading processes, and similar lesions after this critical period do not, then what neural substrate, if any, might account for the relatively severe and permanent form of developmental or congenital dyslexia? The answer most probably involves some insult to *both* cerebral hemispheres, either prenatally or during early postnatal life when the nervous system is still immature and undergoing major morphogenesis. Despite the plasticity of the nervous system during this period, the presence of a bilateral lesion or neurodevelopmental anomaly prevents the establishment of a hemispheric reorganization that would permit some form of sparing or recovery of speech, language, or reading processes. It is now commonly accepted that developmental or congenital *aphasia* is caused by a bilateral lesion, primarily affecting the temporal lobes, either prenatally or during early postnatal life (Dennis & Whitaker, 1976; Kinsbourne & Hiscock, 1977, 1981; Sarno, 1981; Witelson, 1977). Unfortunately, the traditional claim, as well as appeal, for a left-hemisphere substrate in developmental dyslexia has remained so dominant that it has probably dampened inquiry into alternative etiologic explanations.

Is there any evidence to support the presence of a bilateral hemispheric substrate in developmental dyslexia? Interestingly, the strongest support comes from the pioneering post-mortem cytoarchtectonic studies in Boston by Galaburda, Geschwind, and associates (Galaburda, 1986; Galaburda & Edelberg, 1982; Galaburda & Kemper, 1979; Galaburda, Sherman, Rosen, Aboitiz, & Geschwind, 1985; Geschwind, Signoret, & Ronthal, 1985). The particular data of relevance concern the presence of structural anomalies of cell migration (heterotopias) and organization (dysplasias) in the cerebral hemispheres of the first four autopsied cases of adult dyslexics reported by Galaburda, Sherman *et al.,* (1985). Although the frequency of anomalies clearly favored the left hemisphere approximately 3 : 1, there were striking anomalies in the right hemisphere in each of the cases. In fact, the areas of maximum involvement included the *bilateral* frontal cortex and the left temporal cortex. Note also that Drake (1968) reported the presence of bilateral temporal lobe anomalies in the first autopsied case of an adult dyslexic. It should also be mentioned that additional cases of bilateral asymmetric anomalies have been reported by Galaburda (1987). Although Galaburda's recent efforts

(Galaburda, 1987; Galaburda, Sherman *et al.*, 1985; Galaburda, Signoret, & Ronthal, 1985) have focused on the atypical presence of symmetry in the planum temporale of his autopsied dyslexic brains, the fact remains that heterotopias and dysplasias have been observed in both cerebral hemispheres. It is also worth noting that a recent positron emission tomography (PET) study examining rCMRGLu in dyslexics during reading revealed an active participation of the insular cortex bilaterally (Gross-Glenn *et al.*, 1986). Also, two recent regional cerebral blood flow (rCBF) studies by Hynd and colleagues (Hynd, Hynd, Sullivan, & Kingsburg, 1987; Huettner, Rosenthal, & Hynd, 1989) have revealed an active participation of the right central and posterior cortex (as well as the left) during the reading of narrative text. Some evidence of bilateral temporal indices in spontaneous EEG has also been suggested in learning-disabled children (Morris, Obrzut, Coulthard-Morris, 1989).

A critical review of the literature on dyslexia and brain morphology can be found in a recent and incisive paper by Hynd and Semrud-Clickeman (1989). With respect to the bilateral ectopias and dysphasias, the authors state:

> The bilateral nature of these neurodevelopmental anomalies is not the focus of discussion in Galaburda, Sherman *et al.*'s (1985) report. Rather the symmetrical plana found in their patients receive the most attention, in large part one presumes because every case reportedly had large symmetrical plana which is at odds with normative findings. . . . thus, the potential importance of these findings seems observed by the focus on symmetry of the central-posterior cortex.
>
> From a behavioral perspective, the bilateral involvement of the anterior cortex is not without relevance. The frontal lobes have long been recognized as important on tasks requiring sustained attention, regulating emotional tone, maze learning, conceptual set shifting, and strategic planning . . . the distribution of ectopias in the frontal cortex seems to cluster in the orbitofrontal and dorsolateral cortex both of which have extensive afferent input from the medical dorsal thalamic nucleus. The orbitofrontal cortex is part of the limbic association system while the dorsolateral cortex is considered part of the prefrontal association cortex. . . . There is accumulating evidence that the right anterior cortex, in addition to the left, is involved to a significant degree in a functional-linguistic system. In particular, it appears that the affective components of language are a characteristic feature of the right hemisphere encompassing the frontal and central perisylvian cortex. . . . The components of language that seem related to right hemispheric structures include prosody and emotional gesturing . . . thus, it might

tentatively be hypothesized that the language disturbance in develop-mental dyslexia may not just reflect left anterior-central structures but may also involve right hemisphere systems as well. Galaburda, Sherman et al.'s (1985) studies show significant involvement of both frontal regions." [p. 57]

These studies, in sum, provide increasing evidence for a bilateral hemi-spheric substrate in at least a subset, if not a majority, of congenital dyslexics. Although the initial autopsied cases have revealed more extensive left-hemisphere anomalies—which have been cited as evidence for the traditional unilateral brain substrate (Geschwind, 1984; Geschwind & Behan, 1982)—the fact remains that both cerebral hemispheres have been involved. The present reformulation provides a more heuristic framework for explaining much of the heterogeneity, if not diagnostic subtypes, that has been observed in reading-disabled children (Bakker, 1979; Lyon, 1985; Rourke, 1985; Satz & Morris, 1981). In cases of predominant left-hemisphere anomaly one might expect to find the characteristic language-disorder subtype that has been observed in at least 50–60% of dyslexic children (Doehring, 1978; Lyon & Watson, 1981; Rourke, 1985; Satz & Morris, 1981). This subtype is also compatible with Bakker's (1979, 1984) P type, which is characterized by overreliance on perceptual strategies because of the delay or impairment in linguistic processing. In cases of predominant right-hemisphere anomaly, one might expect to find the characteristic visuospatial-disorder subtype that has been observed in approximately 10–30% of dyslexic children (Lyon, 1985; Rourke, 1985; Satz & Morris, 1981). This subtype is also compatible with Bakker's (1979, 1984) L type, which is characterized by overreliance on left-hemisphere strategies because of the delay or impairment in abstracting perceptual features from script. In cases of predominant bifrontal lobe anom-aly, as reported in some of the Galaburda cases (Galaburda, Sherman et al., 1985; Galaburda, Signoret, & Ronthal, 1985), one might expect to find some of the attentional and disinhibition difficulties observed in some dyslexic children with attention-deficit disorders (ADD) (Connors, 1987; Harter, 1987).

With respect to developmental dyslexia, it is likely that the disorder can spring from a structural lesion or brain anomaly that occurs either pre- or postnatally, as long as the neural substrate is bilateral. If bilateral asymmetric, the subtype of dyslexia may vary as noted above. Lesions occurring after the critical period for speech and language recovery—probably between ages 6 and 8—need not be bilateral. At such time, a unilateral lesion to the left hemisphere can produce the developmental equivalent—namely, an acquired alexia.

It is of course possible that the majority of cases of developmental dyslexia spring from prenatal microscopic cellular anomalies. This is the position advanced by Geschwind and associates (Galaburda, Sherman *et al.*, 1985; Galaburda, Signoret, & Ronthal, 1985; Geschwind & Behan, 1982; Geschwind & Galaburda, 1985a,b) and it is yet to be disconfirmed. The role of testosterone, which these authors cite as the trigger mechanism, is also an interesting and heuristic hypothesis that deserves further investigation. What remains unclear is the role of other putative trigger mechanisms (e.g., genetic) in the etiology of this baffling childhood disorder. It is hoped that this reformulation helps to stimulate alternative hypotheses that can be integrated within the context of other theoretical positions.

Acknowledgment

Some of the original ideas for this chapter spring from an earlier invited presentation at the Third World Congress of Dyslexia in Crete, Greece, in 1987 which my dear friend, Professor George Th. Pavlidis, urged me to write in more expanded format for his forthcoming book, *Perspectives in Dyslexia*, John Wiley & Sons. This chapter represents a critical abbreviation, with some modifications, of the Pavlidis chapter.

References

Alajouanine, T., & Lhermitte, F. (1965). Acquired aphasia in children. *Brain, 88,* 653–662.

Aram, D. M., & Ekelman, B. L. (1988). Scholastic aptitude and achievement among children with unilateral brain lesions. *Neuropsychologia, 26,* 903–916.

Bakker, D. (1979). Hemispheric differences & reading strategies: Two dyslexias? *Bulletin of the Orton Society, 29,* 84–100.

Bakker, D. (1984). The brain as a dependent variable. *Journal of Clinical Neuropsychology, 6,* 1–16.

Basser, L. S. (1962). Hemiplegia of early onset and the faculty of speech with special reference to the effects of hemispherectomy. *Brain, 85,* 427–460.

Benson, D. F., and Geschwind, N. (1969). The alexias. In P. J. Vinken & G. W. Bruyn (Eds.), *Handbook of clinical neurology* (Vol. 4). Amsterdam: North-Holland Publ.

Byers, R. K., & McLean, W. (1962). Etiology and course of certain hemiplegias with aphasia in childhood. *Pediatrics, 29,* 376–383.

Coltheart, M., Patterson, K., & Marshall, J. C. (Eds.). (1980). *Deep dyslexia.* London: Routledge & Kegan Paul.

Connors, K. (1987). Dyslexia and the neurophysiology of attention. *Third World Congress on Dyslexia, Crete, Greece.*

Dejerine, J. (1892). Contribution à l-étude anatamie-pathologique et clinique des différentes variétés de cécite verbale. *Comptes Rendus des Seances et Memoires de la Societe de Biologie, 44*, 61.

Dennis, M., & Whitaker, H. (1976). Language acquisition following hemidecortication: Linguistic superiority of the left over the right hemisphere. *Brain & Language, 3*, 404–433.

Doehring, D. G. (1978). The tangled web of behavioral research on developmental dyslexia. In A. L. Benton & D. Pearl (Eds.), *Dyslexia: An appraisal of current knowledge*. New York: Oxford University press.

Drake, W. E. (1968). Clinical and pathological findings in a child with a developmental learning disability. *Journal of Learning Disabilities, 1*, 486–502.

Galaburda, A. M. (1986, November). *Human studies on the anatomy of dyslexia*. Paper presented at the annual conference of the Orton Dyslexia Society, Philadelphia, PA.

Galaburda, A. M. (1987). Morphological advances in dyslexia. *International Conference on Child's Learning Disabilities and Brain Function, Stavanger, Norway*.

Galaburda, A. M., & Eidelberg, P. (1982). Symmetry and asymmetry in the human posterior thalamus. II. Thalamic lesions in a case of developmental dyslexia. *Archives of Neurology (Chicago), 39*, 333–336.

Galaburda, A. M., & Kemper, T. L. (1979). Cytoarchitectonic abnormalities in developmental dyslexia: A case study. *Annals of Neurology, 6*, 94–100.

Galaburda, A. M., Sherman, G. F., Rosen, G. D., Aboitiz, F., & Geschwind, N. (1985). Developmental dyslexia: Four consecutive patients with cortical anomalies. *Annals of Neurology, 18*, 222–233.

Galaburda, A. M., Signoret, J. C., & Ronthal, M. (1985). Left posterior angiomatous anomaly and developmental dyslexia: Report of five cases. *Neurology (Cleveland), 35*(Suppl.), 198.

Geschwind, N. (1984). Cerebral dominance in biological perspective. *Neuropsychologia, 22*, 675–683.

Geschwind, N. (1985). The biology of dyslexia: The unfinished manuscript. In D. G. Gray & J. F. Kavanagh (Eds.), *Biobehavioral measures of dyslexia*. Parkton, MD: York Press.

Geschwind, N., & Behan, P. O. (1982). Left handedness: Association with immune disease, migraine, and developmental learning disorders. *Proceedings of the National Academy of Sciences of the U.S.A., 79*, 5097–5100.

Geschwind, N., & Galaburda, A. M. (1985a). Cerebral lateralization: Biological mechanisms, associations, and pathology. I. A hypothesis and a program for research *Archives of Neurology (Chicago), 42*, 428–459.

Geschwind, N., & Galaburda, A. M. (1985b). Cerebral lateralization: Biological mechanisms, associations and pathology. II. A hypothesis and a program for research. *Archives of Neurology (Chicago) 42*, 521–552.

Gross-Glenn, K., Duara, R., Yoshii, F., Barker, W. W., Chang, J. Y., Apicella, A., Boothe, T., & Lubs, H. A. (1986). PET-Scan studies during reading in dyslexic and non-dyslexic adults [Abstract]. *Neuroscience*.

Harter, R. M. (1987). Distinct even-related potential indicants of reading disability and attention deficit disorder. *Third World Congress on Dyslexia, Crete, Greece*.

Hécaen, H. (1976). Acquired aphasia in children and the autogenesis of hemispheric functional specialization. *Brain & Language, 3,* 114–134.

Hécaen, H., Perenin, M. T., & Jeannerod, M. (1984). The effects of cortical lesions in children: Language and visual functions. In C. R. Almli & S. Finger (Eds.), *Early brain damage* (pp. 277–298). Orlando, FL: Academic Press.

Hinshelwood, J. (1900). Congenital word-blindness. *Lancet, 1,* 1506–1508.

Huettner, M. I. S., Rosenthal, B. L., & Hynd, G. W. (1989). Regional cerebral blood flow (rCBF) in normal readers: Bilateral activation with narrative speech. *Archives of Clinical Neuropsychology, 4,* 71–78.

Hynd, G. W., Hynd, C. R., Sullivan, H. G., & Kingsbury, T., Jr. (1987). Regional cerebral blood flow (rCBF) in developmental dyslexia: Activation during reading in a surface and deep dyslexic. *Journal of Learning Disabilities, 20,* 294–300.

Hynd, G. W., & Semrud-Clickeman, M. (1989). Dyslexia and brain morphology. *Psychological Bulletin, 106,* 447–482.

Kinsbourne, M., & Hiscock, M. (1977). Does cerebral dominance develop? In S. J. Segalowitz & F. A. Gruber (Eds.), *Language development and neurological theory.* New York: Academic Press.

Levine, D. W., Hier, D. B., & Calvanio, R. (1981). Acquired learning disability for reading after left temporal lobe damage in childhood. *Neurology, 31,* 257–264.

Liberman, I. (1982). A language-oriented view of reading and its disabilities. In H. Myklebust (Ed.), *Progress in learning disabilities* (Vol. 5, pp. 81–101). New York: Grune & Stratton.

Lyon, R. (1985). Educational validation studies of learning disability subtypes. In B. P. Rourke (Ed.), *Neuropsychology of learning disabilities.* New York: Guilford Press.

Lyon, R., & Watson, B. (1981). Empirically derived subgroups of learning disabled readers: Diagnostic considerations. *Journal of Learning Disabilities, 14,* 256–261.

Marshall, J. C., & Newcombe, F. (1981). Lexical access: A perspective from pathology. *Cognition, 10,* 209–214.

Morgan, W. P. (1896). A case of congenital word-blindness. *British Medical Journal, 2,* 1378.

Morris, G. L., Obrzut, J. E., & Coulthand-Morris, L. (1989). Electroencephalographic and brain stem evoked responses from learning-disabled and control children. *Developmental Neuropsychology, 5,* 187–206.

Penfield, W., & Roberts, L. (1959). *Speech and brain mechanisms.* Princeton, NJ: Princeton University Press.

Rasmussen, T., & Milner, B. (1977). The role of early left brain injury in determining lateralization of cerebral speech functions. *Annals of the New York Academy of Sciences, 299,* 355–379.

Rourke, B. (1985). *Neuropsychology of learning disabilities.* New York: Guilford Press.

Sarno, M. T. (1981). *Acquired aphasia.* New York: Academic Press.

Satz, P. (1987). Developmental dyslexia: An etiological reformulation. Invited address, *Third World Congress of Dyslexia, Crete, Greece.*

Satz, P. (1989). Developmental Dyslexia: An etiological reformulation. In G. Pavlidis (Ed.), *Dyslexia: A Neuropsychological & Learning Perspective.* New York: John Wiley, 1–26.

Satz, P., & Bullard-Bates, C. (1981). Acquired aphasia in children. In M. T. Sarno (Ed.), *Acquired aphasia* (pp. 399–426). New York: Academic Press.

Satz, P., & Morris, R. (1981). Learning disability subtypes: A review. In F. J. Pirozzolo & M. C. Wittrock (Eds.), *Neuropsychological and cognitive processes in reading* (pp. 109–141). New York: Academic Press.

Satz, P., Strauss, E., Wada, J., & Orsini, D. (1988). Some correlates of intra- and interhemispheric speech organization after left focal brain injury. *Neuropsychologia, 26,* 345–350.

Satz, P., Whitaker, H., & Strauss, E. (in press). The ontogeny of hemispheric specialization: Some old hypotheses revisited. *Brain & Language, 38,* 596–614.

Taylor, D., & Ounsted, 1972). *The nature of gender differences explored through ontogenetic analyses of sex ratios in disease.* Unpublished manuscript.

Van Dongen, H. R., & Loonen, M. C. (1979). Neurological factors related to prognosis of acquired aphasia in childhood. In Y. Lebrun & R. Hoops (Eds.), *Recovery in aphasics.* Amsterdam: Swetz & Zeitlinger.

Vellutino, F. R. (1987). Dyslexia. *Scientific American, 256,* 34–41.

Witelson, S. (1977). Early hemisphere specialization and interhemispheric plasticity: An empirical and theoretical review. In S. J. Segalowitz & F. A. Gruber (Eds.), *Language development and neurological theory.* New York: Academic Press.

Woodcock, R. W., & Johnson, M. D. (1977). *Woodcock-Johnson Psycho-Educational Battery:* Hingham, MA: Teaching Resources.

Woods, B. T., & Carey, S. (1979). Language deficits after apparent recovery from childhood aphasia. *Annals of Neurology, 5,* 405–409.

Woods, B. T., & Teuber, H. L. (1978). Changing patterns of childhood aphasia. *Annals of Neurology, 3,* 273–280.

CHAPTER SIX

Childhood Psychopathology and Learning Disabilities: Neuropsychological Relationships

Naomi Nieves[1]

I. Introduction

While there is much controversy regarding what constitutes a learning disability (LD), it is generally agreed that children who manifest the symptoms of this disorder are significantly below their peers in academic achievement despite average intelligence. Further, it is thought that the etiology of the disorder is a neurological one.

In addition, there is a general belief that these children often experience emotional problems and, in particular, low self-esteem. Difficulties with self-concept are often thought to arise because of the child's persistent experiences with failure in school, as well as his or her perceptions of expectancies by significant others (Chapman & Boersma, 1980).

Children with learning disabilities also have been found to exhibit social-skills deficits as well as the behavioral deficits associated with emotional difficulties. It is often thought that these children experience such problems secondary to their poor self-concept and constant academic failure.

Although psychopathology has been linked with LD, research on this issue has been inconclusive and, according to Schonhaut and Satz (1983), uncertain, as most researchers have not appropriately measured behavioral and emotional variables. A major problem that arises when reviewing the LD literature with regard to the socioemotional development of this group is the

---

1 The editors and publishers regret the untimely death of Naomi Nieves during the publication of this book.

varied terminology used. Such terms as *minimal brain dysfunction, hyperactivity,* and especially *underachievement* have often been used synonymously with LD and can still be found. Thus, there has been a tendency to believe that they are the same disorder or at least concurrent disorders.

The purpose of this chapter, then, is to review some of the research dealing with childhood psychopathology and LD. Keeping in mind that the terms *LD* and *underachievement* are not necessarily synonymous, the literature with respect to underachievement and psychopathology will also be reviewed, since the terms have often been used interchangeably.

II. Relationship between Academic Underachievement/LD and Psychopathology

Some researchers argue that there is a causal relationship between some types of psychopathology and underachievement. Rutter, Tizard, and Whitmore (1970) posit that underachievement in general leads to a poor self-concept, often resulting in aggression. The relationship between LD and emotional/behavioral disorders, however, is unclear and needs further exploration. For example, many studies that have investigated such a relationship have not clearly defined diagnostic criteria for inclusion in the LD classification. The National Joint Committee for Learning Disabilities (NJCLD) has defined LD as "a generic term that refers to a heterogeneous group of disorders manifested by significant difficulties in the acquisition and use of listening, speaking, reading, writing, reasoning, or mathematical abilities. These disorders are intrinsic to the individual and presumed to be due to central nervous system dysfunction" (Hammill, Leigh, McNutt, & Larsen, 1981). This definition expands on the federal definition of LD, which does not include a statement regarding its neurological etiology. Therefore, such labels as *learning* or *reading disorder* used in the literature may or may not reflect a learning disability, according to this definition. Another nosological system (DSM-III-R) [American Psychiatric Association (APA), 1987], for instance, uses the term *developmental disorders* to include reading, math, writing, and communication difficulties but no other criterion is offered than "markedly below the expected level, given the person's schooling and intellectual capacity." It is assumed that many LD children are included in these categories, but one is uncertain of prevalence rates. Therefore, it is difficult to compare across studies and derive a clear understanding of the findings if diagnostic criteria are inconsistent. Further, because of the heterogeneity of the disorder and the variability in which it is expressed, it is evident that establishing such relationships can be a difficult task.

In this context, a question one may ask is: Are children with severe LD more at risk of developing psychopathology than children with mild to moderate LD? Additionally, are different types of LD associated with different types of psychopathology? For instance, Johnson and Myklebust (1967, p. 272) identified yet another type of learning disability that is a deficit in "social perception." They describe this deficiency as "the inability which precludes acquiring the significance of basic nonverbal aspects of daily living, though his verbal level of intelligence falls within or above the average." This child is unable to learn meaning from cues in his environment (e.g., facial expressions, gestures). Although the child is able to use language, the words are described as "empty," as the child is unable to experience the objects that they symbolize. This type of disability is problematic with respect to the socialization process, as the child is unable to "read" cues from his environment and may often be oblivious to the impact of his behavior on others. In an early study conducted by Boshes and Myklebust (1964), one of the variables that correlated most significantly with neurological dysfunction in children with LD was social maturity. Johnson and Myklebust (1967) suggest that social maturity was seen as significantly below chronological age because experiences are often distorted in these children, even when spoken and written language are intact. More specifically, they regard this type of noverbal disability as falling at the levels of perception and imagery, rather than at the symbolization and conceptualization levels, which are more typically deficient in the verbal-learning disorders. Based on their model regarding the development of experiences, these researchers propose that the lowest level developed is sensation, followed by perception, imagery, symbolization, and conceptualization. Thus, disabilities involving faulty perception and imagery produce a more fundamental distortion of the experience.

Juvenile delinquency is often thought to co-occur with LD and also deserves mention. In addition, although it is a legal term and not a psychiatric one, juvenile delinquency is often the result of some types of child and adolescent psychopathology. It has been estimated that 75% of juvenile delinquents are significantly deficient in reading (Kline, as cited in Satz, 1977). While reading difficulties are not always attributable to LD, there is considerable evidence that links emotional and behavioral disturbances to learning-disabled populations (Eisenberg, 1967; Giffin, 1968; Rappaport, 1966; Satz, 1977).

Different perspectives have been advanced by researchers regarding the psychological development of children with LD. In particular, the psychodynamic (Giffin, 1968; Rappaport, 1966) and behavioral views (Ferster, as cited in McLean, 1981; Lewinsohn, 1974; Rachlin, 1976; Seligman, 1975) have been prominent in attempting to explain socioemotional and behavioral aspects of LD. Briefly, from the psychodynamic perspective, it appears that children with LD do not escape unscathed from the emotional disturbances that can be attributed to learning handicaps. Children with LD are not only unable to satisfy themselves with regard to normal achievement, but they often experience the rejection and anxiety that they stimulate in significant others.

Behaviorism, which is based on the principles of reinforcement, espouses the theory of insufficient reinforcement among LD children. More specifically, since LD children so often experience academic failure, they do not come in contact with the positive contingencies that are generally produced by good academic performance and appropriate social interactions. Since organisms seek reinforcement in diverse ways, maladaptive or deviant behaviors can often serve this function if rewards are not attained through more appropriate means.

Thus, regardless of theoretical orientation, it has generally been the notion that children with LD tend to also exhibit signs of emotional or behavioral disturbances. Furthermore, the psychopathology related to LD has often been viewed as a consequence of their repeated failures.

Other researchers believe, however, that psychopathology precedes school failure (Patterson, DeBaryshe, & Ramsey, 1989) and, in particular, reading disorders (McGee, Williams, Share, Andersen, & Silva 1986; Richman, Stevenson, & Graham, 1982). Unfortunately, in reviewing studies that examine socioemotional and academic issues in school-aged children, terms associated with LD (e.g., underachievement) have often not been differentiated from LD. Further, when diagnostic criteria are reported in LD populations they vary across studies, making results difficult to compare. For example, in the United States discrepancy formulas vary across states. While some utilize a regression formula, others depend on IQ–achievement standard-score discrepancies to classify LD children. Still others, as stated earlier, do not attempt to categorize LD children, but rather use general terms such as underachievement or more specific terms such as reading disability/disorder, reading retardation, and developmental (reading, arithmetic, writing) disorder. For this reason, studies that examine academic underachievement in these domains will be presented, since it is believed that LD children are overrepresented in these samples.

While the cause-and-effect controversy regarding LD and psychopathology continues to be of some concern to researchers (Rutter et al., 1970; Wilson & Herrnstein, 1985), another theory with regard to LD and psychopathology has been offered by Spreen (1989). His theory of cerebral dysfunction proposes a third variable, a biological one. Emotional disorders and learning disabilities both can be the result of changes in the brain, and one disorder need not precede the other. This theory will be discussed in more detail later in this chapter, but first an overview of studies linking different types of psychopathology and LD and/or learning disorders will be offered. These studies are summarized in Table I.

TABLE I Studies Linking Different Types of Psychopathology and Learning Disabilities

Reference	N	Population	Sex	Age range (years)	Assessment instruments/ diagnostic criteria	Major findings
Reiss and Rhodes (1961)	9238	Junior and senior high school students	M	12 and older	IQ, official records, socioeconomic status (SES) index	Significant relationship between IQ and delinquency regardless of social class (subjects with lower IQs had higher rates of delinquent offenses, except for traffic-only violations).
Boshes and Myklebust (1964)	85	LD (3 subgroups) 1. Negative neurological signs 2. Suspect neurological signs 3. Positive neurological signs	Not reported	7–18	WISC IQ neurological exam, social maturity test, Gates Reading Test, Gates Diagnostic Test	1. Social maturity, spelling, auditory blending more frequently showed a relationship with neurological status. 2. The more positive neurological signs exhibited, the more social maturity correlated with IQ and achievement variables.
Rutter et al. (1970)	3519	School-age children	M = 1766 F = 1753	9–11	Developmental history, medical exam, WISC IQ, achievement, health questionnaire, behavior questionnaires (parent and teacher forms)	1. Prevalence of educational problems was 7.9%. 2. Prevalence of handicapped children (educational, intellectual, physical, psychiatric) was 17%. 3. 25% of handicapped children had at least two handicaps. 4. 45% of antisocial boys had specific reading retardation (28 months below expected for age and IQ). 5. 25% of children with specific reading retardation also exhibited antisocial behaviors.
West and Farrington (1973)	411	Delinquent (84) and nondelinquent (327) boys	M	8–10 through adolescence	Delinquency scale, police records, teacher ratings, peer ratings, developmental and health history, Raven's Progressive matrices, achievement measures.	1. Five background factors associated with delinquency were low family income, large family size, parent criminality, low IQ, and poor parental behavior. The last four factors were associated with delinquency independent of the other factors. 2. Delinquent boys scored 6 points lower than nondelinquent boys on the Raven and Porter Maze and were mainly recidivist delinquents.

(continued)

TABLE I *Continued*

Reference	N	Population	Sex	Age range (years)	Assessment instruments/ diagnostic criteria	Major findings

Keogh and Margolis (1976)	151	1. Educationally handicapped (EH) subjects (73)
		  a. EH hyperactives
		  b. EH nonhyperactives
		2. Normal achieving (NA) subjects (78)
			M	Not reported— Grades 3–8	Behavior checklist, IQ tests (Lorge—Thorndike or Standford–Binet or WISC), achievement [Cooperative Primary Tests or Comprehensive Test of Basic Skills (CTBS), Peabody Individual Achievement Test (PIAT), Children's Embedded Figures Test (CEFT), Matching Familiar Figures Test (MFFT), Children's Checking Test (CCT)]	1. EH subjects significantly differed from NA subjects in attentional tasks, but EH hyperactives and EH nonhyperactives did not.
						2. Errors rather than response speed differentiated the NA and EH groups. Hyperactive boys obtained lower achievement scores than did nonhyperactives and NAs.

Cantwell and Satterfield (1978)	148	1. Hyperactive subjects (94) 2. Normal controls (54)	M	6–11	WISC-R, Wide-Range Achievement Test (WRAT), semistructured parent and child interviews, parent and teacher rating scales. No psychosis or gross neurological disease	1. Hyperactive subjects obtained lower mean full-scale IQs than did controls (107 vs. 114). 2. Three-fourths of the hyperactive subjects were underachieving in math, reading, and spelling
Loney *et al.* (1981)	135	Minimal brain dysfunction	M	4–12 ($\bar{X}$ = 8.2) through adolescence	Intake form completed by child, parents, and teacher; behavior ratings and questionnaires; structured interview; cognitive, personality, and achievement (WRAT) tests	1. Ecological and family variables (i.e., SES, family intactness, number of children in family) and child aggression were the best predictors of adolescent aggressive symptoms, hyperactive symptoms, and delinquent behaviors. 2. Two-thirds of their sample scored 2 or more years below grade placement on the WRAT.

Study	Sample (N)	Groups	Age	Sex	Measures	Results
Moffitt et al. (1981)	Study I = 129	Danish population of children at high risk for antisocial behavior (72) and matched controls (57)	11–13	M	WISC, SES	Low IQ correlated with delinquent acts independent of SES effects.
	Study II = 4552	Danish males with height greater than 184 cm.	19–25	M	Borge Priens Prover (BBP) IQ, SES, police register, karyotyping	Low IQ correlated with delinquency independent of SES effects.
Ackerman et al. (1983)	102	1. Hyperactive H 2. Reading disabled (RD) 3. Hyperactive and reading disabled (H & RD) 4. Attention-deficit disorder (ADD)	7–10	M = 24 F = 9 M = 19 F = 10 M = 10 F = 6 M = 12 F = 12	WISC-R, WRAT, Gray Oral Reading Test, Conners parent and teacher forms, Children's Personality Questionnaire (CPQ), MFFT, CEFT, Color Naming Test, House Test of Leveling—Sharpening, Augmentation—Reduction Test, Reaction Time Measures	1. Girls obtained lower WISC-R IQs than did boys referred for same problems. 2. Groups of normal readers (H and ADD) scored higher on WISC-R verbal and sequential factors than did groups of disabled readers. 3. Reading and spelling were more strongly correlated with Verbal Factor for girls but with Sequential Factor for boys. 4. Groups could be reliably separated within the girls' sample by their CPQ profiles. 5. Solely hyperactive subjects were the most sensitive to omission of details. Aggressivity Factor reliability separated the hyperactives from the nonhyperactives.
Forness et al. (1983)	92	Emotional and behavior-disordered subjects	7–12	M = 69 F = 23	WISC-R, PIAT	One-third of the sample had deficits in achievement when expected achievement was adjusted for mental age.
C. Gillberg et al. (1983)	108	1. Attention and motor-perception disorder (MBD) = 41 2. Motor-perception disorder (MPD) = 6 3. Attention-deficit disorder (ADD) = 12 4. Comparison group = 49	9½–10½	M and F	Teacher reports, grades, WISC	1. Approximately 80% of MBD subjects (vs. 16% of controls) had school achievement deficits. 2. 93% of MBD subjects had either behavior or achievement problems. 3. 79% of the severe MBD group and 33% of the moderate MBD group were also deficient in reading and writing
Quay and Peterson (1983)	143	School-age children grades 4, 5, and 6 (subsample of the standardization sample of the Revised Behavior Problem Checklist)	Not reported	Not reported	Revised Behavior Problem Checklist (RBPC), short form of the Test of Academic Aptitude (IQ), and CTBS (achievement)	Attention (AP) factor showed a negative correlation with achievement independent of aptitude measure.

(continued)

119

TABLE I Continued

Reference	N	Population	Sex	Age range (years)	Assessment instruments/ diagnostic criteria	Major findings
Shepard et al. (1983)	790	Learning-disabled, school-age subjects across Colorado	Not reported	Not reported	Various IQ and achievement tests, perceptual and psychological processing tests, medical data	More than one-half of the sample had characteristics (e.g., other categories) that did not conform with federal guidelines for LD. Other categories included brain injured, hyperactive, mild mental retardation, emotionally disturbed, and language impaired.
August and Holmes (1984)	70	1. Hyperactive (H) = 14 2. Hyperactive and unsocialized aggression (H-USA) = 24 3. Specific reading disabilities (SRD) = 17 4. Normal controls (NC) = 15	M	10–16	Behavior rating scales, parent structured interview, MFFT, Stanford Diagnostic Reading Test, WRAT (word recognition and spelling), medical reports.	1. Hyperactive groups scored higher in overactivity, inattention, and reactivity. 2. SRD group scored high on inattention factor and similar to H group 3. H-USA group was significantly more deviant than SRD group in all categories 4. SRDs scored lower on academic measures than did all other groups 5. Hyperactive groups achieved commensurate with IQ and were not viewed as LD.
Edelbrock et al. (1984)	87	1. ADD with (18) and without (7) hyperactivity 2. Other clinic-referred children (CC) = 62	M	7–11	Teacher report form of the Child Behavior Checklist (CBCL) (Achenbach), DSM-III	1. ADD subjects obtained significantly higher scores on inattentive scale than did CC subjects. 2. ADD/H and ADD/WO both obtained high inattentive scores but ADD/H also scored high on nervous–overactive scale. 3. ADD/Hs were found to be more aggressive than were ADD/WOs. 4. ADD/WOs were more socially withdrawn, less happy, had poorer school performance, and were at greater risk for failure in school.
Harris et al. (1984)	60	1. Learning disabled (LD) = 30 2. Emotionally disturbed (ED) = 30	M	6–12	Teacher report form of CBCL (Achenbach)	1. Behavior profiles were similar in both groups, but LDs were less deviant. 2. EDs had significantly higher (deviant) total scores, externalizing and internalizing scales, and social-withdrawl, self-destructive inattentive, and nervous–overactive scales. 3. Aggressive scale was the most frequently elevated scale for LDs and more elevated than for EDs.

Study	N	Sample	Sex	Age/Grade	Measures	Findings
Ledingham and Schwartzman (1984)	753	1. Aggressive = 122 2. Withdrawn = 150 3. Aggressive–withdrawn =182 4. Control group = 299	M = 367 F = 386	Not reported (grades 1, 4, 7)	Pupil evaluation inventory	1. Aggressive and aggressive–withdrawn were more likely to fail a grade or be in a special placement. 2. Fewer males than females were in a regular class at the expected grade level. 3. Older aggressive–withdrawn and control subjects had higher rates of failure and special placement
McGee et al. (1984)	489	1. Aggressive = 21 2. Hyperactive = 18 3. Aggressive–hyperactive = 24 4. Normal control = 426	M	Longitudinal study (ages 3, 5, 7)	WISC-R, Burt Reading Test, Illinois Test of Psycholinguistic Abilities (ITPA), spelling test, Rutter Scales, Basic Motor Test, self-reports	1. Only the aggressive–hyperactive group differed significantly from normals in reading. 2. The order of groups with regard to behavior problems from least to most severe were: normals, hyperactives, aggressives, and aggressive–hyperactives. 3. Both hyperactive groups showed poorer cognitive abilities at ages 3 and 5 than did normals but did not differ from each other.
McGee et al. (1985)	926	Nonclinic-referred sample	M and F	9	Parent and teacher ratings (Rutter Scales A and B), WISC-R, Burt Reading, Spelling, Dunedin Articulation Check, Basic Motor Abilities	1. Separate factors of inattention, hyperactivity, and antisocial behaviors were identified. 2. Cognitive (PIQ), academic, and speech–motor variables predicted inattention but not hyperactivity or antisocial behaviors.
Goldstein et al. (1985)	82	Learning disabled (LD): 1. LD only = 44 2. LD with low IQ = 11 3. LD with sociocmotional disturbance = 17 4. LD with hyperactivity = 10	Not reported	$\bar{X} = 9$	WISC-R, Keymath Diagnostic Test, Woodcock Reading Test, Child Depression Inventory (CDI)	1. No relationship found between depression and achievement and IQ for subtype 1. 2. Subtype 2: Relationship between CDI and verbal/performance. 3. Subtype 3: Relationship between CDI and IQ and achievement. 4. Subtype 4: Relationship between CDI and IQ and math achievement.

Porter and Rourke (1985)	100	Learning disabled	M = 87
			F = 13
				6–15	WISC, WRAT, Personality Inventory for Children (PIC)	1. Four subtypes of personality patterns, accounting for 77% of the sample.
						  Subtype 1: Good social/emotional adjustment (44%).
						  Subtype 2: Serious internalized psychopathology (26%).
						  Subtype 3: Somatic complaints (13%).
						  Subtype 4: Externalized psychopathology (17%).
						2. No cognitive or academic differences among subtypes.

(continued)

TABLE I *Continued*

Reference	N	Population	Sex	Age range (years)	Assessment instruments/ diagnostic criteria	Major findings
Mattison *et al.* (1986)	177	1. Referred and placed in class for socioemotional disturbance (SED) 2. Referred and *not* placed in class for social emotional disturbance (NSED)	M = 152 F = 25	6–18	WISC-R, WRAT, Bender Gestalt Test, projectives, Family History Research Diagnostic Criteria, Schedule for Affective Disorders and Schizophrenia for School-Age Children (K-SADS) DSM-III	1. Both SED and NSED groups had a high prevalence of serious psychopathology, but SED group was more deviant. 2. In children ages 6–12, the most frequently occurring diagnosis was ADD. 3. In children ages 13–18, the most frequently occurring diagnoses were affective disorders. 4. There were significantly lower reading scores in the 12–18 age group.
Weiss and Hechtman (1986)	119	1. Attention-deficit-disordered children (ADD) = 75 2. Normal controls (NC) = 44.	M = 90% F = 10%	6–12 with a 10-year follow-up longitudinal study.	Psychiatric interview, brief psychiatric rating scale, California Psychological Inventory, SCL-90	1. 66% of ADD subjects (vs. 7% of NC subjects) still had at least one disabling symptom of the hyperactive diagnosis at follow-up. 2. Hyperactivity in childhood did not predispose psychosis in adulthood. 3. 23% of ADDs had antisocial personality disorder as adults. No other diagnosis distinguished ADD from normals. 4. ADDs had significantly more adjustment problems and less formal education as adults, average marks were lower than controls, discontinued high school, and were expelled from school more often than were controls.

Study	N	Sample	Age	Measures	Findings
Hynd *et al.* (in press)	20	1. Attention-deficit disorder hyperactivity (ADD-H) = 10 2. Attention-/deficit disorder without hyperactivity (ADD/WO) = 10	M = 17 F = 3	$\bar{X}$ = 11.5 $\bar{X}$ = 12.9	WISC-R, Basic Achievement Skills Individual Screener (BASIS), Rapid Alternating Naming (RAN), Rapid Alternating Stimulus (RAS), K-SADs revision, SNAP checklist, PIC DSM-III criteria	1. Academic underachievement was found in 60% of ADD-WOs. 2. ADD-WOs obtained lower math scores than ADD-Hs. 3. ADD-WOs obtained lower scores in RAN and RAS tasks. 4. Parents' ratings of motor activity and impulsivity were significantly different (ADD-H > ADD-WO). 5. 40% of ADD-Hs also had a codiagnosis of conduct disorder (vs. zero in ADD-WO subjects). 6. ADD-Hs' parents expressed more concerns regarding age-appropriate social-skills development than did parents of ADD-WOs.
Nieves *et al.* (submitted for publication)	74	1. Attention-deficit disorder hyperactivity (ADD-H) = 21 2. Conduct disorder (CD) = 7 3. Attention-deficit disorder with hyperactivity and conduct disorder (ADD-H + CD) = 27 4. Clinic control (CC) = 18	M and F M = 76% M = 71% M = 89% M = 72%	6–13	WISC-R, BASIS, K-SADs revision, Conners (parent & teacher forms), Revised Behavior Problem Checklist, SNAP checklist, Child & Behavior Rating Scale, DSM-III criteria	1. SES significantly correlated with low IQ and achievement. 2. CD was associated with lower verbal IQ. 3. ADD-H + CD subjects had lower IQ and achievement scores. 4. ADD-H subjects underachieved in reading and spelling relative to IQ.

Spreen (1989)	255	1. Learning disabled (LD) = 203, 3 subtypes:
		  a. LD with hard neurological signs
		  b. LD with soft neurological signs
		  c. LD with no neurological signs
		2. Normal controls (NC) = 52
			M and F	10–25 longitudinal study	Bell Adjustment Inventory, MMPI, structured interview (parent & subject)	1. No clear relationships were found among neurological dysfunction, type of LD, and presence or absence of emotional disorder.
						2. Age trends were found with
						  (a) fewer behavior problems in early school years;
						  (b) behavior problems increasing with age; and
						  (c) decreasing again after leaving school.
						3. In childhood, LD and NC subjects differed in prevalence of behavior problems (LD > NC), but LD subtypes did not differ from each other.

III. Overview of Studies Linking Psychopathology and LD

As previously stated, studies that have examined children with socio-emotional and behavioral problems as well as LD have often not been adequate in providing clear criteria for group inclusion. Since academic underachievement is part of the LD definition, and since it has often been the case that the terms have been used interchangeably, studies that have examined the relationship between underachievement and types of psychopathology will also be reviewed in the following sections.

A. *Association between Academic Underachievement and Conduct Disorder*

In espousing a developmental perspective of antisocial behavior, Patterson *et al.* (1989) proposed that coercive child behaviors are likely to produce two types of reactions from the environment: (1) rejection by their normal peer group, and (2) academic failure. They believe that antisocial behaviors directly cause learning problems and that efforts to reduce antisocial behaviors through the enhancement of academic skills have been futile. Wilson and Herrnstein (1985), however, support the opposite view, stating that academic failure causes conduct problems. Regardless of which perspective is taken, several studies have shown a strong association between academic underachievement and conduct disorder in childhood and adolescence. The following studies summarize general findings regarding this relationship.

In a large epidemiological study conducted by Rutter *et al.* (1970), one-fourth of the children manifesting specific reading retardation (at least a 28-month deficit in reading relative to chronological age and IQ) were also rated by their teachers as exhibiting antisocial behaviors. In addition, when male subjects showing antisocial behaviors were examined, 45% were found to be deficient in reading. This incidence of reading disorders is extremely high, especially in light of the fact that only 4% of the general population in this study was disabled in reading.

Using a hospitalized population of emotionally and behaviorally disordered children age 7 through 12, Forness, Bennett, and Tose (1983) found that one-third of their sample had significant deficits in academic achievement. More specifically, these subjects were underachieving in all academic areas, as measured by the Peabody Individual Achievement Test (PIAT) (Dunn & Markwardt, 1970). Although psychiatric diagnoses were not reported for these subjects, the researchers report that most of them exhibited conduct problems. Unfortunately, this study does not differentiate among disorders, making it difficult to compare the incidence of academic underachievement across diagnostic categories.

Among other measures, peer ratings have been successfully used in predicting academic performance in children with conduct problems. In a 3-year follow-up study, Ledingham and Schwartzman (1984) reviewed school records of subjects ($N = 753$) who were rated by their peers as aggressive, withdrawn, and aggressive–withdrawn. A normal control group was also included. These researchers found that aggressive and aggressive–withdrawn groups were more likely to have failed a grade or to have been referred to special classes by the time of the follow-up 3 years later. However, special class placement was not elaborated upon, and IQ scores were not reported. It is therefore difficult to draw conclusions regarding the nature of their exceptionality (i.e., cognitive, behavioral, socioemotional, or mixed).

Studies that have reported IQ measures in their samples have found similar results, however. For example, Mattison and colleagues (1986) examined clinic-referred schoolchildren who were being assessed for placement in classes for the socially and emotionally disturbed (SED). This group was then subdivided into those who were placed and those who were not placed (NSED) in a special class. Their general findings indicated that more children in the SED group showed more school-related problems and more grade repetitions than did those in the NSED group. Further, using DSM-III diagnostic criteria they found that younger children (ages 6–12) were mostly referred for attentional deficits (44%), affective disorders (23%), and conduct disorders (19%). Older children (13 years and higher) were most often referred for affective disorders (49%), attention deficits (16%), and conduct disorders (14%). Thus, there appears to be a significant age difference with respect to the presence of different behavioral manifestations of psychiatric disturbance. It may be that since overt behaviors such as conduct problems and hyperactivity are so salient, they are less likely to be ignored by educators. Children with affective disorders, however, do not attract attention upon themselves and may often be identified incidentally or later when symptoms become more severe. This finding may have important implications for the early diagnosis and treatment of affective disorders in children. It may also help explain the highly variable differences in reported behavioral and emotional disturbances in many of the studies addressing the co-occurrence of LD and psychopathology.

While there is a high co-occurrence of conduct problems and academic failure among the LD population, there is also the belief that children with conduct disorder (CD) typically obtain lower verbal scores on measures of intelligence than do their peers. This association deserves further mention. The following section will address Verbal IQ in CD populations. Because children with CD tend to be overrepresented in delinquent populations, especially as adolescents, an overview of studies on delinquency and IQ will also be provided.

B. *Association between Lower Verbal IQ and Conduct Disorder*

Academic underachievement in learning disabilities cannot be discussed in the absence of intelligence data, as it is presumed that learning-disabled children possess normal intelligence. A significant number of studies dealing with the relationship between CD and underachievement have found that intelligence is often lower in this population. Specifically, lower verbal IQs have been reported for children with CD (Nieves, Connor, Hynd, Lahey, & Town, submitted for publication) and especially for juvenile-delinquent populations (Hirschi & Hindelang, 1977; Moffitt, Mednick, Gabrielli, & Schulsinger, 1981; Reiss & Rhodes, 1961; West & Farrington, 1973; Wilson & Herrnstein, 1985). Even when the variance from socioeconomic status (SES) is taken into account, lower verbal IQ continues to correlate strongly with conduct problems.

In view of these findings with CD populations, can we then say that they are also learning-disabled if they indeed have lower verbal IQs? The issue is not that simple, however, when one considers that many children with learning disabilities have language-based difficulties and will display these deficits on verbally laden tasks. Further, verbal subscales tend to tap acquired knowledge, and this is often poor in deficient readers. Additionally, children with conduct problems have been found to score in the average range in performance IQ (Nieves *et al.*, submitted for publication; Sattler, 1982). Thus, we can conclude that there are many LD children who perform poorly on measures of verbal intelligence and also display conduct problems, and that these groups are not mutually exclusive. Taking these factors into consideration, the studies that follow describe IQ findings in CD and juvenile-delinquent populations as they relate to poor achievement and learning deficits.

As previously stated, Wilson and Herrnstein (1985, p. 171) have taken the position that lower achievement and lower IQ precipitate conduct problems and delinquency in youth. They posit that defiance, violence, and reported illegalities are a result of feelings of unfairness due to constant school failure. The individual may then "feel justified in settling the score outside," since there is little to be gained from noncriminal acts (i.e., academic efforts are not reinforced). Therefore, school failure predicts criminal activity in juvenile delinquents. They report that, on the average, delinquents score 10 points lower on IQ tests than do nonoffenders.

Hirschi and Hindelang (1977) also argue that lower IQ and poor school achievement in juveniles affect the likelihood that delinquent acts will be committed. These factors are stronger predictors, in their view, than are social class and race variables. Related to this issue, in a Danish sample of a homogeneous group of males, Moffitt *et al.* (1981) found significant negative correlations between verbal IQ, full-scale IQ, and number of delinquent offenses. These correlations were also independent of SES. Reiss and Rhodes (1961) have reported similar findings in a large sample of junior and senior high school boys. Consequently, regardless of social class and race variables, delinquency rates are highest among children with lower verbal intelligence.

Nonverbal intelligence has also been found to be lower among delinquent boys. In their longitudinal survey, West and Farrington (1973) reported that, on the average, delinquent boys scored 6 points lower than nondelinquent boys on the Raven's Progressive Matrices and the Porteus Maze tests. In addition, the main contributors to this contrast were the recidivist delinquents who obtained the lowest IQ scores. Lower IQs were more typical of those children who had been convicted of crimes at an early age and continued to repeat their offenses. Lower IQs were not noted at age 14 and higher. This latter group may be more representative of the group type of conduct disorder (DSM-III-R) (APA, 1987) or the socialized aggressive type (DSM-III) (APA, 1980) who, according to Quay and Werry (1986), have unimpaired cognitive or learning abilities. Thus, one can see, as other researchers have noted, that the earlier the onset of criminal activities, the worse the prognosis in terms of delinquency (Loeber, 1985; Offord, Sullivan, Allen, & Abrams, 1979; Walker, Lahey, Hynd, & Frame, 1987).

There is a substantial amount of evidence that suggests a strong link between CD and underachievement. However, many of these studies have focused on children with conduct problems and their related underachievement. The picture is not as clear when one examines studies that primarily look at identified LD subjects and their related behavior disorders. For example, in a review of longitudinal studies on the prognosis for children with LD, Schonhaut and Satz (1983) concluded that the relationship between LD and antisocial behaviors was uncertain. This conclusion was based on mixed findings that emerged from the 18 studies reviewed.

Schonhaut and Satz (1983) evaluated the studies in three ways. First, studies were rated in terms of outcome results: favorable, unfavorable, or mixed. The studies were further rated in terms of methodological criteria. Finally, the third evaluation rated the studies based on a composite scale— examining outcome results in light of the methodological criteria. Of the five best-rated studies, four were found to have unfavorable results. These results included school failure, school suspensions, high drop-out rate, less-skilled jobs, and more psychopathology. It should be noted, however, that only 3 of the 18 reported studies included emotional or behavioral assessment instruments in their follow-up measures. In addition, SES was the best predictor with respect to academic prognosis, with lower-SES subjects having a worse prognosis. Therefore, it seems clear that if the prognosis of LD children is to be examined, a wide variety of outcome measures should be employed throughout their development. These should include academic, socioemotional, behavioral, and occupational measures in order to get the best overview regarding the long-term outcome in LD populations.

In summary, since so much of the literature reports that a strong association between antisocial behaviors and LD exists, it is imperative that, at the least, behavioral and socioemotional assessment routinely be conducted in future studies that examine characteristics of LD subjects. In this context, the following section provides an overview of studies that have utilized behavioral and socioemotional measures as well as achievement measures in examining the prevalence of LD and underachievement in children with attention-deficit disorders (ADD).

C. Association between Attention-Deficit Disorder and Learning Disabilities

The prevalence of attention-deficit hyperactivity disorder (ADHD) has been estimated to be approximately 3% (DSM-III-R) (APA, 1987), although estimates vary. Academic underachievement is so prevalent in children with ADHD that some researchers have conceptualized LD and ADHD as the same disorder since often the distinction has not been made between academic underachievement and LD. For this reason, results of these studies should be viewed with caution. Keeping in mind that problems with diagnosing LD do exist because of inconsistencies with diagnostic criteria across studies, studies that deal with ADHD and LD populations will be reviewed.

While there is a significant overlap between the two disorders, ADHD and LD, it is noteworthy that some ADHD children do not demonstrate cognitive and academic deficits. Conversely, many LD children do not display ADHD symptoms. However, the vast majority of studies thus far have demonstrated that ADHD children exhibit academic deficits (Ackerman, Dykman, & Oglesby, 1983; Cantwell & Satterfield, 1978; I. C. Gillberg, Gillberg, & Rasmussen, 1983; Hynd *et al.*, submitted for publication; Keogh & Margolis, 1976; Loney, Kramer, & Milich, 1981; Nieves *et al.*, submitted for publication).

For example, C. Gillberg *et al.* (1983) examined school achievement in four groups of children. These groups were classified as minimal brain dysfunction (MBD), motor-perception dysfunction (MPD), attention-deficit disorder (ADD), and a comparison group of undiagnosed school-age children. The MBD group was further subdivided into a severe subgroup and a mild/moderate subgroup. The MBD diagnosis required the presence of both attentional deficits and motor-perception dysfunction, which refers to behaviors associated with hyperactivity. In this sample the researchers found that the group that demonstrated the most deficits in academic achievement was the group of children who had both attentional deficits and hyperactivity (MBD). Seventy-nine percent of the severe group and 33% of the mild/moderate group displayed severe deficits in reading and writing, while 6% of the comparison group displayed such deficits. Furthermore, 80% of the total MBD group was also found to have co-occurring behavior problems. Severe behavior problems among children with ADHD have been reported quite frequently in the hyperactivity literature and will be addressed in a later section.

Similar to C. Gillberg *et al.* (1983), Cantwell and Satterfield (1978) investigated the prevalence of academic underachievement in a group of hyperactive boys. Results of this study indicated that, compared to normal controls, three-fourths of the hyperactive group was significantly underachieving in reading, spelling, and arithmetic, as measured by the Wide Range Achievement Test (WRAT). Underachievement in this study was defined using a prediction equation as 1 year below the grade level predicted for an average child of the same chronological age and full-scale IQ. Thus, this study provides further evidence that children with ADHD are significantly underachieving relative to their normal peers.

These general findings have been supported by Keogh and Margolis (1976), who also found significant reading deficits in hyperactive versus nonhyperactive boys. These researchers compared a group of normally achieving regular classroom children with a group of educationally handicapped (EH) boys in grades three through eight. The EH group was also subdivided according to teacher ratings into a hyperactive or a not-hyperactive group. Overall, the hyperactive EH boys obtained lower achievement scores than did the nonhyperactive EH boys. While IQ scores were not significantly different among groups, reading achievement was found to be significantly lower in the hyperactive group.

In addition to these investigations, longitudinal studies following hyperactive children have provided evidence that these subjects continue to experience academic deficits and school failure. In a follow-up study of hyperactive boys, Loney *et al.* (1981) found that two-thirds of their sample scored 2 or more years below grade placement on the WRAT. At the initial sample selection, 62% of these subjects were rated by their teachers as functioning at borderline or poor in academic areas on a 5-point scale ranging from poor to excellent.

Similarly, results of a 10-year prospective study conducted by Weiss and Hechtman (1986) lend support to Loney and colleagues' (1981) findings regarding poor academic achievement in hyperactive children. Their findings revealed that hyperactives had less education than did controls at follow-up, average marks were lower than those of controls, and they tended to discontinue high school for this reason and were expelled from school more often.

This indicates that children with ADHD do not outgrow their academic deficiencies and that a large percentage of these children may have coexisting learning disabilities.

In summarizing the previous studies, we can conclude that underachievement is frequently associated with the diagnosis of ADHD. However, while LD may be a frequently co-occurring disorder in the ADHD population, prevalence rates are unclear due to different criteria used to arrive at an LD diagnosis.

In addition to the frequent associations between LD and ADHD, CD has frequently been found to co-occur with ADHD. It is important to note this latter association, as it has further confounded studies that examine LD and underachievement in general in several ways. First, studies have often been lenient when categorizing ADHD subjects by depending either on only one informant or on one measurement instrument. Ackerman *et al.* (1983), for instance, employed the Conners Rating Scale to categorize their subgroups of boys and girls who were pure hyperactive, reading disabled, hyperactive/reading disabled, and attention disordered. The main findings to emerge were sex differences. Except for the reading-disabled group, boys obtained higher arithmetic standard scores than did girls. Furthermore, whereas reading/spelling achievement correlated highest with verbal IQ on the WISC-R in girls, achievement in boys correlated highest with sequential memory (arithmetic, digit span, and coding).

A further and most important finding by Ackerman *et al.* (1983), however, and one germane to this discussion, was that when using the Conners Rating Scale, the Aggressivity Factor was found to reliably separate the hyperactives from the nonhyperactives. This is an important finding as it points out that perhaps the parents' and teachers' ratings were reflecting aggression, not hyperactivity. High intercorrelations of these two factors have been reported in the Conners Scale (Lahey, Green, & Forehand, 1980); for this reason, a multiassessment approach is preferred to increase the validity of the diagnosis. Further, the notion that hyperactivity and aggression or CD are synonymous has been the topic of much debate in the past. This issue is reflected in the second point, which is that while low academic achievement has been strongly linked with ADHD, many studies have not differentiated children with ADHD from children with ADHD and the co-occurring diagnosis of CD. However, it has been well substantiated that these two disorders are separate, albeit their overwhelming co-occurrence (Hynd *et al.*, submitted for publication; Lahey, Schaughency, Hynd, Carlson, & Nieves, 1987; Stewart, Cummings, Singer, & de Blois, 1981). Because CD and ADHD have not been reliably differentiated as two distinct disorders in many studies, it has not been clear to what extent either disorder is associated with LD. Since children with ADHD and those with ADHD and CD manifest different social, emotional, and behavioral symptoms, as well as different prognosis, this topic will now be addressed as it pertains to the incidence of LD in these two populations.

D. Comorbidity of Conduct Disorder and Attention-Deficit Hyperactivity Disorder

Studies that have examined school achievement and have differentiated CD and ADHD have been few. One such study conducted by McGee, Williams, and Silva (1984) assessed behavioral and cognitive characteristics of 7-year-old boys who were identified as (1) hyperactive, (2) aggressive, and (3) hyperactive–aggressive. Although there were no significant IQ differences between the hyperactive and hyperactive–aggressive groups, specific reading retardation (defined as a reading score more than 1.5 standard deviations below that predicted by IQ) was more prevalent in the hyperactive–aggressive group. These results, however, have not been consistent in the literature, as other researchers have found that these groups do not differ significantly in achievement measures.

For instance, in another study that differentiated hyperactive subjects from hyperactives with conduct problems, August and Holmes (1984) examined underachievement using measures of achievement and behavioral ratings. In addition, a clinic control group consisting of reading-disabled boys and a normal control group including normal siblings from the three selected groups was included. There were no significant differences in IQ among groups. The researchers were specifically interested in the incidence of learning disabilities in hyperactive boys. They found no differences in measures of achievement (reading and spelling) between the hyperactives and the hyperactives with conduct problems. Further, they found that both groups were achieving commensurate with their measured potential. Finally, August and Holmes found the incidence of learning disabilities to be as low as 7 and 8% for both groups, respectively.

Thus, we can summarize the results of these two well-designed studies and conclude that they have yielded different results with regard to underachievement in general and specific reading disability in particular in populations of ADHD and ADHD with CD. While McGee and colleagues (1984) found a high prevalence of reading disabilities in their hyperactive–aggressive group, August and Holmes found no differences in groups in reading and spelling or in LD in general. It is likely that the different diagnostic criteria employed by these two studies may have contributed to the difference in results. August and Holmes report that the diagnosis of hyperactivity did not reflect the current (DSM-III) criteria for Attention-Deficit Disorder with Hyperactivity (ADD-H), which maintain that the core features of the disorder are problems with inattention. McGee *et al.* (1985) used the Rutter Scales A (parent) and B (teacher) to arrive at the diagnoses of hyperactivity and hyperactivity with aggression. Since these results differed, a further attempt was made to assess whether CD, ADD/H, or both disorders are associated with academic underachievement in the following study.

Nieves and colleagues (submitted for publication) examined groups of clinic-referred children who were reliably diagnosed according to the DSM-III (APA, 1980) nosology. Using multimodal, multiinformant diagnostic procedures, children with a diagnosis of (1) CD, (2) ADD/H, (3) CD and ADD/H, and (4) a clinic control group were examined on IQ and achievement measures. Results indicated that while children with ADD/H and CD obtained lower achievement scores in reading and spelling, standard scores in these measures were commensurate with full-scale IQ. However, SES was significantly lower in this group and, while a different perspective was proposed to explain low SES and psychopathology (Dohrenwend & Dohrenwend, 1969) rather than the environmental perspective, these results should be viewed with caution. Further results revealed that CD was associated with verbal–performance discrepancies, with verbal IQ being lower. However, ADD/H was found to be significantly associated with underachievement in reading and spelling relative to performance and full-scale IQ, even after the effects of SES were partialled out. It appears, then, that while CD is associated with lower verbal IQ, ADD/H is associated with underachievement in reading and spelling. In addition, children with the codiagnoses of ADD/H and CD not only achieve less than their peers but also have lower IQs. Therefore, it is likely that the incidence of LD in this latter group is low, since IQ–achievement discrepancies are not generally seen in this group. Future studies that control SES factors and employ the same reliable and current procedures to carefully identify these groups in the natural environment (e.g., schools) will perhaps provide more consistent information regarding these disorders and their relationship to underachievement and LD.

The previous studies have yielded different results when examining learning disorders in ADHD populations. One obvious confound discussed was the high comorbidity of CD in the ADHD groups and the failure of some researchers to differentiate among these groups.

While the issue of underachievement remains to be resolved in this population, still other studies have recently provided evidence that learning difficulties are associated with the attentional rather than the hyperactivity component of the disorder (Edelbrock, Costello, & Kessler, 1984; Hynd *et al.*, submitted for publication; McGee *et al.*, 1985; Quay & Peterson, 1983). This finding is an important one and is relevant to this discussion because it may help to further clarify why there is conflicting evidence in the literature regarding ADHD and learning disorders. Additionally, it refutes the notion that attention-deficit disorder without hyperactivity (ADD/WO) is not a valid subtype, as is reflected in the more recent unidimensional view of ADHD (DSM-III-R) (APA, 1987) since there is evidence to suggest that children with the diagnosis of ADD/WO can be reliably diagnosed. This latter issue will now be discussed as it relates to difficulties in assessing and classifying groups of ADD subjects. A brief review of studies that have assessed children with ADD/H and ADD/WO on measures of achievement will then follow.

E. Association between Attention-Deficit Disorder without Hyperactivity and Learning Disabilities

The distinction between ADD/H and ADD/WO has been the topic of controversy in the recent child psychopathology literature and deserves further elaboration before studies including ADD/WO subjects are reviewed. Specifically, some researchers have concluded that there is no empirical evidence to suggest that the two subtypes differ (Routh, 1983; Spitzer & Cantwell, 1980) or that they only differ in the presence or absence of hyperactivity (Mauer & Stewart, 1980). Others, however, maintain that the two disorders are quite dissimilar and can be reliably differentiated (Edelbrock *et al.*, 1984; Hynd *et al.*, submitted for publication; King & Young, 1982; Lahey, Schaughency, Frame, & Strauss, 1985; Lahey *et al.*, 1987). As a result of the former perspective, current diagnostic classification of the attention-deficit disorders by DSM-III-R (APA, 1987) reflects the view that these two disorders are not dissimilar. For instance, the category of ADHD has replaced ADD/H, and this has resulted in some changes in diagnostic procedures. While the diagnosis of ADD/H required the presence of some symptoms from each of the three dimensions (inattention, impulsivity, and motor hyperactivity) (DSM-III) (APA, 1980), the category of ADHD includes eight symptoms from all three dimensions, regardless of the cluster of dimensions. The ADD/WO category has been replaced by the term *undifferentiated ADD* but does not have diagnostic criteria. Therefore, it is possible that diagnosticians may include children with ADD/WO in the ADHD category since those eight symptoms may also describe the ADD/WO subtype. Since more recent evidence has emerged to suggest that the category of ADD/WO is a valid one, it seems reasonable that it should be differentiated from ADD/H. Studies that make this distinction will now be discussed.

Research by Edelbrock *et al.* (1984) suggests that boys with the diagnosis of ADD/WO score lower on teacher ratings of school performance and are more likely to repeat grades than are boys with ADD/H. In addition, while those who received a diagnosis of ADD/H were less popular, self-destructive, and aggressive, they found the ADD/WO subgroup was described as less happy, more socially withdrawn, and at greater risk for academic failure. Thus, children with ADD/WO tend to exhibit more internalizing disorders and can be distinguished from groups of ADD/H peers who, as a group, display behaviors more typical of the externalizing dimension.

Further evidence of underachievement in groups of ADD/WO has been reported by Quay and Peterson (1983) in a subsample of their standardization population of the Revised Behavior Problem Checklist (RBPC). They found that the dimension of attention problems/immaturity (AP) was the only factor that negatively correlated with achievement, even when ability was partialled out. These researchers obtained intelligence and achievement measures in a group of children grades four through six. All children were rated by their teachers with the RBPC, which has resulted in four major scales after factor analysis: (1) conduct disorder (CD), (2) socialized aggression (SA), (3) attention problems/immaturity (AP), and (4) anxiety–withdrawal. Two minor scales include psychotic behavior (PB) and motor-tension excess (ME). The AP scale represents ADD, according to DSM-III, with the ME scale representing hyperactivity. Therefore, the AP factor alone can be conceptualized as ADD/WO. While all of the scales were negatively correlated with the ability measure initially, AP was the only scale that consistently showed a negative relationship with the achievement measure after ability was partialled out. This finding further indicates that the relationship that exists between underachievement and ADD can be explained by problems with inattention without the hyperactivity (ME) component.

These findings were also replicated by McGee *et al.* (1985) in their longitudinal study examining 7- and 9-year-old children. They found that reading, spelling, and performance IQ were only related to the inattention ratings of both parents and teachers, independent of hyperactivity or impulsivity.

A recent study conducted by Hynd *et al.* (submitted for publication not only examined academic, intellectual, and behavioral characteristics, but also assessed neuropsychological functioning in children reliably diagnosed as having ADD/H and ADD/WO. While there were no significant differences in ability on the WISC-R, the ADD/WO group was found to be significantly deficient in mathematics as well as in rapid naming tasks. The groups also differed in the co-occurrence of developmental reading and arithmetic disorders in accordance with DSM-III criteria (APA, 1980), with 60% of the ADD/WO children obtaining a developmental learning disorder diagnosis versus none of the ADD/H children. On the other hand, 40% of the ADD/H children had a codiagnosis of CD. The fact that the ADD/WO children did poorly in comparison to the ADD/H children on rapid naming tasks is of considerable interest because evidence suggests that LD children perform more slowly and with more errors than other children (Wolf, Bally, & Morris, 1986). Thus, the association between ADD/WO and LD may be significant, and the failure of many studies to assess for neurocognitive deficits in subtypes of ADD may have contributed to the low incidence rates of LD in some studies. Neurocognitive assessment may assist in providing a more careful delineation of how these disorders co-occur. To summarize, this study also supports Edelbrock *et al*'s. (1984) findings that learning difficulties are more typical of children diagnosed as ADD/WO, while ADD/H children tend to exhibit more conduct problems.

It appears, then, that the dimension of attention plays a significant role in the development of learning disorders, while the hyperactivity component is less important, if not tangential. This makes sense when one conceptualizes LD as a deficit in the basic neuropsychological processes, which involve higher cortical functions such as attention and memory. While deficits in these areas may have a negative impact on new learning, excessive motor activity may only interfere with learning if the individual is not in the proper environment (e.g., out of his or her seat) in which learning is to occur. It remains to be seen whether future studies confirm the relationship between ADD/WO and learning disabilities, as there are very few studies to date that address this issue.

In summary, the attention-deficit disorders are significantly associated with underachievement and learning disabilities. It is less clear, however, which subtype of the disorder is associated with LD, although evidence is leaning toward the notion that LD children are overrepresented in the ADD/WO category. Reliable diagnostic procedures are needed across studies in order to assess the effects of subtypes of psychopathology on academic achievement. In particular, the main effects of CD, ADD/H, and ADD/WO should be examined separately in order to decrease confounding variables.

The preceding sections have focused on literature that examined the relationship of learning disabilities and/or academic underachievement and overt or the broader externalizing dimension. Less is known about the internalizing dimension, especially with affective disorders in children. A brief summary will be presented as these disorders relate to LD.

IV. Internalizing Disorders and Learning Disabilities

Although research in the area of LD and socioemotional functioning has often been contradictory, in general the literature has demonstrated that LD children experience interpersonal difficulties and are not as well adjusted as are their normal peers. Specifically, problems with self-esteem in LD populations are often attributed to their constant failure and the resulting negative treatment they receive in their environment. Porter and Rourke (1985) concluded on the basis of studies reviewed that LD children (1) are perceived as less pleasant and less desirable by parents, teachers, and peers, (2) receive more negative communications, (3) are ignored and rejected more often by their teachers, (4) are treated more punitively by parents, and (5) live in families similar to those of emotionally disturbed children. Of particular relevance here is the notion that while LD children often do not exhibit overt maladaptive behaviors, at some point they begin to exhibit signs of internalizing disorders such as anxiety and depression. However, the fact is that to date very little is known about the incidence of these disorders in the LD population, perhaps because the disorders within the internalizing dimension are more difficult to measure. For instance, while research clearly supports that there is a broad internalizing dimension with regard to psychopathology, the subtypes of this dimension have been found to have questionable diagnostic reliability (Quay & Werry, 1986). One obvious reason is that the behaviors associated with anxiety and depression are more difficult to observe since they are not overt as is the case with conduct problems. Another reason may be that multiple sources of information are not obtained or that the appropriate informant is not interviewed. However, there is accumulating evidence that subtypes of anxiety and depression can be found among children. Although the literature is scant with respect to these disorders in LD subjects, a brief review will be offered here.

A. Anxiety Disorders

Although one may suppose that anxiety disorders are associated with academic underachievement, this association has typically not been found in the literature. Highly anxious students, however, have been found to do poorly on tests, whereas their performance is more adequate in less stressful situations (Hill, 1972). Some anxious children have been found to under-achieve, but it may be the case, as with school refusal in children with separation anxiety disorder, that academic performance is hindered by lack of instruction rather than by a learning disorder. More research is needed in this area to examine achievement in different subtypes of anxiety disorders (e.g., avoidant disorder, overanxious disorder, separation anxiety disorder). Since anxiety disorders often co-occur with other disorders such as depression, they may be superimposed or not diagnosed as readily as the more serious disorder (Quay & Werry, 1986). To summarize, little is known about anxiety in children with LD. Although anxiety disorders have been found to be associ-ated with test taking in some children, these children seem to perform better when placed in less stressful conditions.

B. Depression

Depression has been conceptualized in various ways, depending on the individual's theoretical framework. For example, from the operant perspec-tive, depression has been viewed as a set of maladaptive behaviors. An illustration of this concept can be seen in the theory of "learned helplessness" proposed by Seligman (1975), according to which depression is a result of the belief by the individual that responding is useless. Depression is then a natural consequence of a reduction in the amount of positive reinforcement that an individual receives. (Ferster, as cited in McLean, 1981) identified several reasons why there is a decrease in reinforcement, including (1) sudden environmental changes, (2) becoming involved in negative interpersonal exchanges that decrease the opportunity for positive reinforcement, and (3) inability to attend to environmental cues in order to interact in socially appropriate ways (Ferster, as cited in McLean, 1981). This theory of insufficient reinforcement has been investigated by Lewinsohn (1974), who found that depressed individuals are less skilled in social situations, receive less response-contingent reinforcement, and in general become involved in fewer reinforcing activities. It may be the case that many LD students who experience failure are not coming in contact with positive reinforcement that is generally produced by good academic performance and appropriate social interactions. Depression and anxiety may often be the result.

Whatever causes depression to occur, its symptoms are fairly reliable among individuals. Until recently, however, depression was viewed as primarily an adult disorder. Improved methods of assessing children have facilitated researchers in investigating affective disorders of children and adolescents so that there is now convincing evidence that it occurs in this young population. According to Kovacs (1989), depression in children directly affects their abilities by disrupting the development of age-appropriate competencies. For example, cognitive development and subsequent achievement appear to be slowed down in children who display symptoms of major depressive disorders.

Mattison *et al.*'s (1986) study reviewed earlier with respect to overt antisocial behaviors provides us with some evidence that there is a large percentage of depressed children, particularly in adolescence, who exhibit academic problems significant enough to warrant special placement. Forty-nine percent of the children who were referred at 13 years and older in their study were diagnosed as having affective disorders. A lesser yet considerable percentage of children 6 through 12 years of age (23%) were also classified as having affective disorders. These researchers argue that the chronicity of their learning problems, especially poor reading, contributes to the high incidence of dysthymic disorders found in the older group. These and other findings further point out the need for early identification of learning-disabled children with coexisting affective disorders, as they do not seem to attenuate through development. For example, although children may recover from the episode for which the referral was made, it has been shown that these children continue to exhibit residual effects that interfere with social and academic functioning (Puig-Antich *et al.*, 1985).

More recently, researchers in the area of LD have focused on examining psychopathology in the different subtypes of learning-disabled children. Goldstein, Paul, and Sanfilippo-Cohn (1985) reported that, while depression and achievement were not correlated in their LD-only group, there was a strong inverse correlation between depression and achievement in their subgroup of children who exhibited learning disabilities and social–emotional disturbance (LD/SED). In addition, depression in the LD group was seen as transient, while it was more stable in the LD/SED group.

Porter and Rourke (1985) also examined socioemotional factors among subtypes of LD. They assessed 100 LD children, using the Personality Inventory for Children. Using a Q-type factor analysis, they identified 77 subjects that could be categorized into four subtypes of LD. These subjects did not differ on academic or cognitive measures. While 44% were classified as normal, 26% were classified as having a serious internalizing disorder including depression, anxiety, psychosis, and deficits in social skills. Research linking subtypes of LD with emotional disorders is relatively recent, and what is available to date indicates that there is little agreement in the literature about these subtypes and differential emotional disorders (Spreen, 1989). These studies are reviewed elsewhere (Hooper & Willis, 1989) and should provide a basis for future investigation of the nature of emotional disorders in different subtypes of learning-disabled populations.

Although the current definition of learning disabilities includes the notion that the disorder is due to a central nervous system dysfunction, some researchers and practitioners continue to disregard the importance of this etiological factor when diagnosing school-aged children. In a study designed to describe characteristics of children identified as learning disabled in the state of Colorado, Shepard and colleagues (Shepard, Smith, & Vojir, 1983) found that 31% of this population had behavioral problems and that close to 6% had strong evidence of emotional disturbance that was not considered to be secondary to the learning disability. On the basis of these and other data obtained, these researchers concluded that LD is not a valid label when applied for the purposes of providing services. Although there are significant problems with the definition and the impreciseness of measures for diagnosing LD, it seems inappropriate to think of the diagnosis of LD as useless. It is to be expected that ambiguities should persist given the nature and the heterogeneity of the disorder. Because of exclusionary criteria, the authors conclude that other related disorders should not be part of the LD definition. However, as is true with many disorders, recent research points to the hypothesis that an LD can often coexist with a behavioral or emotional disorder, and neither of the two needs to be a causative agent of the other (Spreen, 1989). In addition, other researchers have found that carefully diagnosed LD children have behavioral profiles quite similar to emotionally handicapped children, although not as severe.

Harris, King, Reifler, and Rosenberg (1984), for instance, compared behavioral profiles of children diagnosed as LD and children diagnosed as emotionally disturbed (ED). These subjects were in special day schools for their respective disabilities. The Teacher Form of the Child Behavior Checklist (CBCL) (Achenbach & Edelbrock, 1981) was employed to answer the following: (1) are behavioral profiles different in these two populations, and (2) do externalizing factors reach significant clinical ranges (T score >70) in either group? Results indicated that 50% of LD children had one or more scales falling in the clinical range and that overall the LD group scored at the 85th percentile (T score >60), which is approximately 1 standard deviation from the mean. Seventy-three percent of the ED population had scores in the clinical range (T score >70). However, the profiles were quite similar when the individual scales were inspected. Of interest, the aggressive scale was found to be more deviant in the LD group. Harris et al. (1984) question whether these LD children are more aggressive or more depressed. Although depression is not assessed with the Teacher Form of the CBCL, the authors discuss Puig-Antich's (1982) theory regarding the relationship between depression and conduct disorder. According to this theory, conduct problems may be symptoms of depression, which is the main disorder. When depression is alleviated, conduct problems disappear. This question, however, cannot be addressed on the basis of the findings from this study, although it is an interesting hypothesis. Regardless, this study provides more evidence that both emotional disorders and LD frequently co-occur, while there is no convincing evidence to imply causality in either direction in these two groups. This latter point will now be expanded upon, with a brief discussion of the cerebral dysfunction hypothesis.

V. Cerebral Dysfunction Hypothesis

Since LD has been found to frequently co-occur with emotional and behavioral disorders in children, different models to explain this relationship have been advanced. The two main traditional models have been described as the (1) primary disorder theory, and (2) secondary reaction theory. The former theory explains psychopathology as an "emotional block which impedes learning," while the latter hypothesizes that secondary emotional reactions are the result of school failure (Spreen, 1989, pp. 117–118). Most of the studies reviewed thus far have reflected these two theoretical perspectives.

Spreen (1989), however, proposes a third alternative—the cerebral dysfunction theory—which states that there may be constitutional as well as pre-, peri-, and postnatal factors contributing to brain dysfunction in both LD and emotionally disturbed populations. This conclusion is partially based on Geschwind and Galaburda's (1985) hypothesis of defective neuronal migration during embryonic development. Anomalies in the process of cell migration result in dysplasias, ectopias, and arteriovenous malformations. Thus, the underlying pathology is responsible for LD, emotional disturbances, and a host of other disorders that can occur concurrently. In his longitudinal study, Spreen followed 203 LD subjects and 52 normal controls from age 10 into adulthood (age 25). The LD group was further subdivided into three groups—those with neurological hard signs, those with soft signs, and those with no neurological signs. At age 18, all LD groups differed significantly from the normal control group on socioemotional measures. In addition, all LD subjects obtained elevated scores on the Bell Adjustment Inventory, specifically for home, social, and emotional adjustment. Within the LD groups, differences were reported between subjects with neurological signs and subjects without neurological signs on parent ratings of emotional dependency, disorganizations, and social interactions. At age 25, life dissatisfaction was high in all LD groups. While life stresses were lessened between ages 18 and 25 (after school termination), Minnesota Multiphasic Personality Inventory (MMPI) scales indicated similar elevations for all LD groups that significantly differed from the control group. Overall, their findings suggest that while there is a high degree of psychopathology coexisting with the learning disability, there is no overwhelming evidence that different subtypes of LD and/or lateralized lesions are associated with particular types of psychopathology. It appears that more longitudinal studies need to be undertaken to gain more knowledge about LD subtypes and their relationship to other disorders including emotional and behavioral disturbances.

VI. Conclusion

A number of studies have been reviewed concerning the relationship between psychopathology and learning disorders. Psychopathology in LD populations has been traditionally viewed based on two theoretical models: (1) a primary disorder theory, whereby the primary emotional disturbance interferes with learning, and (2) a secondary reaction theory, whereby secondary emotional problems develop as a result of school failure (Spreen, 1989). A third theory proposed by Spreen entertains the notion that both LD and emotional disorders can coexist without one being the primary cause of the other. Based on constitutional or biological factors, a variety of syndromes, including LD and emotional disorders, can develop concurrently. All three theories could be at least equally viable, according to Spreen, and need not account for all types of emotional disturbances in LD populations. Both the primary disorder theory and the secondary reaction theory propose that one disorder causes the other to occur as a result of the child's psychological development. These theories, however, do not take into account that structural differences in the brain could be detected in early development and infancy (Molfese & Molfese, 1986). In light of the evidence that LD (Geschwind & Galaburda, 1985) as well as some subtypes of psychopathology are biologically based—such as ADD/H (Ferguson & Rapoport, 1983; C. Gillberg, Carlstrom, & Rassmussen, 1983)—the cerebral dysfunction hypothesis seems to best explain the frequent co-occurrence of psychopathology among LD populations.

While much of the past research has examined externalizing disorders in LD subjects, more recently some of the literature with LD subtypes has suggested a high incidence of internalizing disorders among different subtypes of LD. To date there is no convincing evidence that consistently and reliably associates certain subtypes of LD with different types of psychopathology. Research in this area is relatively recent but will surely continue to grow in the next decade. It is hoped that our understanding will be enhanced as more longitudinal data on LD populations that include emotional and behavioral measures become available.

References

Achenbach, T. M., & Edelbrock, C. S. (1981). Behavioral problems and competencies reported by parents of normal and disturbed children aged four through sixteen. *Monographs of the Society for Research in Child Development, 46*(1, No. 188).

Ackerman, P. T., Dykman, R. A., & Oglesby, D. M. (1983). Sex and group differences in reading and attention disordered children with and without hyperkinesis. *Journal of Learning Disabilities, 16*(7), 407–415.

American Psychiatric Association (APA) (1980). *Diagnostic and statistical manual of mental disorders* (3rd ed.). Washington, DC: American Psychiatric Association.

American Psychiatric Association (APA) (1987). *Diagnostic and statistical manual of mental disorders revised* (4th ed.). Washington, DC: American Psychiatric Association.

August, G. J., & Holmes, C. S. (1984). Behavior and academic achievement in hyperactive subgroups and learning disabled boys. *American Journal of Diseases in Children, 138*, 1025–1029.

Boshes, B., & Myklebust, H. R. (1964). A neurological and behavioral study of children with learning disorders. *Neurology, 14*(1), 7–12.

Cantwell, D. P., & Satterfield, J. H. (1978). The prevalence of academic underachievement in hyperactive children. *Journal of Pediatric Psychology, 3*(4), 168–171.

Chapman, J. W., & Boersma, F. J. (1980). *Affective correlates of learning disabilities*. Amsterdam: Swets & Zeitlinger.

Dohrenwend, B. P., & Dohrenwend, B. S. (1969). *Social status and psychological disorder: A cause inquiry*. New York: Wiley.

Dunn, L. M., & Markwardt, F. C. (1970). *Peabody Individual Achievement Test.* Circle Pines, MN: American Guidance Service.

Edelbrock, C., Costello, A. J., & Kessler, M. D. (1984). Empirical corroboration of attention deficit disorder. *Journal of the American Academy of Child Psychiatry, 23*(3), 285–290.

Eisenberg, L. (1967). Psychiatric implications of brain damage in children. In E. Frierson & W. Barbe (Eds.), *Educating children with learning disabilities* (pp. 171–187). New York: Appleton-Century-Crofts.

Ferguson, H. B., & Rapoport, J. L. (1983). Nosological issues and biological validation. In M. Rutter (Ed.), *Developmental neuropsychiatry* (p. 369–384). New York: Guilford Press.

Forness, S. R., Bennett, L., & Tose, J. (1983). Academic deficits in emotionally disturbed children revisited. *Journal of the American Academy of Child Psychiatry, 22*(2), 140–144.

Geschwind, N., & Galaburda, A. M. (1985). Cerebral lateralization, biological mechanisms, associations, and pathology. *Archives of Neurology (Chicago), 42,* 428–459.

Giffin, M. (1968). The role of child psychiatry in learning disabilities. In H. R. Myklebust (Ed.), *Progress in learning disabilities* (Vol. 1, pp. 75–97). Boston, MA: Houghton-Mifflin.

Gillberg, C., Carlstrom, G. E., & Rasmussen, P. (1983). Hyperkinetic disorders in seven-year-old children with perceptual, motor, and attentional disorders. *Journal of Child Psychology and Psychiatry, 24,* 233–246.

Gillberg, I. C., Gillberg, C., & Rasmussen, P. (1983). Three-year follow-up at age 10 of children with minor neurodevelopmental disorders: II. School achievement problems. *Developmental Medicine and Child Neurology, 25,* 566–573.

Goldstein, D., Paul, G. G., & Sanfilippo-Cohn, S. (1985). Depression and achievement in subgroups of children with learning disabilities. *Journal of Applied Developmental Psychology, 6,* 263–275.

Hammill, D. D., Leigh, J. E., McNutt, G., & Larsen, S. C. (1981). A new definition of learning disabilities. *Learning Disability Quarterly, 4,* 336–342.

Harris, J. C., King, S. L., Reifler, J. P., & Rosenberg, L. A. (1984). Emotional and learning disorders in 6–12 year old boys attending special schools. *Journal of the American Academy of Child Psychiatry, 23*(4), 431–437.

Hill, K. T. (1972). Anxiety in the evaluative context. In W. W. Hartup (Ed.), *The young child: Reviews of research* (Vol. 2, pp. 255–263). Washington, DC: National Association for the Education of Young Children.

Hirschi, T., & Hindelang, M. J. (1977). Intelligence and delinquency: A revisionist review. *American Sociological Review, 42,* 571–587.

Hooper, S. R., & Willis, W. G. (1989). *Learning disability subtyping: Neuropsychological foundations, conceptual models, and issues in clinical differentiation.* New York: Springer-Verlag.

Hynd, G. W., Lorys-Vernon, A. R., Semrud-Clikeman, M., Nieves, N., Huettner, M. I. S., & Lahey, B. B. (1990). Attention deficit disorder without hyperactivity (ADD/WO: A distinct neuro-cognitive syndrome). *Journal of Child Neurology.*

Johnson, D. J., & Myklebust, H. R. (1967). *Learning disabilities: Educational principles and practices*. New York: Grune & Stratton.

Keogh, B. K., & Margolis, J. S. (1976). A component analysis of attentional problems of educationally handicapped boys. *Journal of Abnormal Child Psychology, 4*(4), 349–359.

King, C. S., & Young, R. D. (1982). Attentional deficits with and without hyperactivity: Teacher and peer perceptions. *Journal of Abnormal Child Psychology, 10*, 483–495.

Kovacs, M. (1989). Affective disorders in children and adolescents. *American Psychologist, 44*(2), 209–215.

Lahey, B. B., Green, K. D., & Forehand, R. (1980). On the independence of ratings of hyperactivity, conduct problems, and attention deficits in children: A multiple regression analysis. *Journal of Consulting and Clinical Psychology, 48*, 566–574.

Lahey, B. B., Schaughency, E. A., Frame, C. L., & Strauss, C. C. (1985). Teacher ratings of attention problems in children experimentally classified as exhibiting attention deficit disorder with and without hyperactivity. *Journal of the American Academy of Child Psychiatry, 24*(5), 613–616.

Lahey, B. B., Schaughency, E. A., Hynd, G. W., Carlson, C. L., & Nieves, N. (1987). Attention deficit disorder with and without hyperactivity: Comparison of behavioral characteristics of clinic referred children. *Journal of the American Academy of Child and Adolescent Psychiatry, 26*(5), 718–723.

Ledingham, J. E., & Schwartzman, A. E. (1984). A three-year follow-up of aggressive and withdrawn behavior in childhood: Preliminary findings. *Journal of Abnormal Child Psychology, 12*(1), 157–168.

Lewinsohn, P. M. (1974). Clinical and theoretical aspects of depression. In K. S. Calhoun, H. E. Adams, & K. M. Mitchell (Eds.), *Innovative treatment methods in psychopathology*. New York: Wiley.

Loeber, R. (1985). Patterns and development of antisocial child behavior. In G. J. Whitehurst (Ed.), *Annals of child development* (Vol. 2). Greenwich, CT: JAI Press.

Loney, J., Kramer, J., & Milich, R. S. (1981). The hyperactive child grows up: Predictors of symptoms, delinquency and achievement at follow-up. In K. D. Gadow & J. Loney (Eds.), *Psychosocial aspects of drug treatment for hyperactivity* (pp. 381–415). Boulder, CO: Westview Press.

Mattison, R. E., Humphrey, F. J., Kales, S. N., Handford, H. A., Finkenbinder, R. L., & Hernit, R. C. (1986). Psychiatric background and diagnoses of children evaluated for special class placement. *Journal of the American Academy of Child Psychiatry, 25*(4), 514–520.

Mauer, R. G., & Stewart, M. A. (1980). Attention deficit without hyperactivity in a child psychiatry clinic. *Journal of Clinical Psychiatry, 417*, 232–233.

McGee, R., Williams, S. & Silva, P. A. (1984). Behavioral and developmental characteristics of aggressive, hyperactive, and aggressive-hyperactive boys. *Journal of the American Academy of Child Psychiatry, 23*(3), 270–279.

McGee, R., Williams, S., Share, D. L., Anderson, J., & Silva, P. A. (1986). The relationship between specific reading retardation, general reading backwardness and behavioural problems in a large sample of Dunedin boys: A longitudinal study from five to eleven years. *Journal of Child Psychology and Psychiatry, 27,* 597–610.

McGee, R., Williams, S., & Silva, P. A. (1985). Factor structure and correlates of ratings of inattention, hyperactivity, and antisocial behavior in a large sample of 9-year-old children from the general population. *Journal of Consulting and Clinical Psychology, 53*(4), 480–490.

McLean, P. D. (1981). Behavioral treatment of depression. In W. E. Craighead, A. E. Kazdin, & M. J. Mahoney (Eds.), *Behavior modification: Principles, issues, and applications* (2nd ed., pp. 223–242). Boston, MA: Houghton-Mifflin.

Moffitt, T. E., Gabrielli, W. F., Mednick, S. A., & Schulsinger, F. (1981). Socio-economic status, IQ, and delinquency. *Journal of Abnormal Psychology, 90*(2), 152–156.

Molfese, D. L., & Molfese, V. J. (1986). Psychophysiological indices of early cognitive processes and their relationship to language. In J. E. Obrzut & G. W. Hynd (Eds.), *Child neuropsychology: Theory and research* (Vol. 1, pp. 95–115). Orlando, FL: Academic Press.

Nieves, N., Connor, R. T., Hynd, G. W., Lahey, B. B., & Town, P. (1990). *Academic underachievement and intellectual ability in children with conduct disorder (CD) and attention deficit disorder with hyperactivity (ADD/H).* In press.

Offord, D. R., Sullivan, K., Allen, N., & Abrams, N. (1979). Delinquency and hyperactivity. *Journal of Nervous and Mental Disease, 167*(12), 734–741.

Patterson, G. R., DeBaryshe, B. D., & Ramsey, E. (1989). A developmental perspective on antisocial behavior. *American Psychologist, 44*(2), 329–335.

Porter, J. E., & Rourke, B. P. (1985). Socioemotional functioning of learning disabled children: A subtypal analysis of personality patterns. In B. P. Rourke (Ed.), *Neuropsychology of learning disabilities: Essentials of subtype analysis* (pp. 257–280). New York: Guilford Press.

Puig-Antich, J. (1982). Major depression and conduct disorder in prepuberty. *Journal of the American Academy of Child Psychiatry, 21,* 118–128.

Puig-Antich, J., Lukens, E., Davies, M., Goetz, D., Brennan-Quattrock, J., & Todak, G. (1985). Psychosocial functioning in prepubertal major depressive disorders: II. Inter-personal relationships after sustained recovery from the affective episode. *Archives of General Psychiatry, 42,* 511–517.

Quay, H. C., & Peterson, D. R. (1983). *Interim manual of the Revised Behavior Problem Checklist.* Miami, FL: University of Miami.

Quay, H. C., & Werry, J. S. (1986). *Psychopathological disorders of childhood* (3rd ed.). New York: Wiley.

Rachlin, H. (1976). *Introduction to modern behaviorism* (2nd ed.). San Francisco, CA: Freeman.

Rappaport, S. R. (1966). Personality factors teachers need for relationship structure. In W. Cruickshank (Ed.), *The teacher of brain-injured children: A discussion of the bases of competency* (pp. 45–55). Syracuse, NY: Syracuse University Press.

Reiss, A. J., & Rhodes, A. L. (1961). The distribution of juvenile delinquency in the social class structure. *American Sociological Review, 26,* 720–732.

Richman, N., Stevenson, J., & Graham, J. P. (1982). *Pre-school to school: A behavioural study*. New York: Academic Press.

Routh, D. K. (1983). Attention deficit disorder: Its relationships with activity, aggression, and achievement. *Advances in Developmental Behavioral Pediatrics, 4,* 125–163.

Rutter, M., Tizard, J., & Whitmore, K. (1970). *Education, health and behaviour*. New York: Wiley.

Sattler, J. M. (1982). *Assessment of children's intelligence and special abilities* (2nd ed.). Boston, MA: Allyn & Bacon.

Satz, P. (1977). Reading problems in perspective. In W. Otto, C. W. Peters, & N. Peters (Eds.), *Reading problems: A multidisciplinary perspective* (pp. 42–73). Reading, MA: Addison-Wesley.

Schonhaut, S., & Satz, P. (1983). Prognosis for children with learning disabilities: A review of follow-up studies. In M. Rutter (Ed.), *Developmental neuropsychiatry* (pp. 542–563). New York: Guilford Press.

Seligman, M. E. P. (1975). *Helplessness: On depression, development, and death*. San Francisco, CA: Freeman.

Shepard, L. A., Smith, M. L., & Vojir, C. P. (1983). Characteristics of pupils identified as learning disabled. *American Educational Research Journal, 20*(3), 309–331.

Spitzer, R. L., & Cantwell, D. P. (1980). The DSM-III classification of the psychiatric disorders of infancy, childhood, and adolescence. *Journal of the American Academy of Child Psychiatry, 19,* 356–370.

Spreen, O. (1989). The relationship between learning disability, emotional disorders, and neuropsychology: Some results and observations. *Journal of Clinical and Experimental Neuropsychology, 11*(1), 117–140.

Stewart, M. A., Cummings, C., Singer, S., & de Blois, C. S. (1981). The overlap between hyperactive and unsocialized aggressive children. *Journal of Child Psychology and Psychiatry, 22,* 35–45.

Walker, J. L., Lahey, B. B., Hynd, G. W., & Frame, C. L. (1987). Comparison of specific patterns of antisocial behaviors in children with conduct disorder with and without co-existing hyperactivity. *Journal of Consulting and Clinical Psychology, 55*(6), 910–913.

Weiss, G., & Hechtman, L. T. (1986). *Hyperactive children growing up*. New York: Guilford Press.

West, D. J., & Farrington, D. P. (1973). *Who becomes delinquent?* London: Heinemann.

Wilson, J. Q., & Herrnstein, R. J. (1985). *Crime and human nature*. New York: Simon & Schuster.

Wolf, M., Bally, H., & Morris, R. (1986). Automaticity, retrieval process, and reading: A longitudinal study in average and impaired readers. *Child Development, 56,* 988–1000.

CHAPTER SEVEN

Acquisition and Forgetting Processes in Normal and Learning-Disabled Children: A Disintegration/ Redintegration Theory

C. J. Brainerd
V. F. Reyna

I. Introduction

Historically, the study of childhood learning disabilities focused on deficits that were presumed to be specific to circumscribed domains, such as reading, mathematics, or language. Although some controversy has always surrounded the classification of learning disabilities (e.g., Fletcher & Morris, 1986; Siegel & Heaven, 1986), the notion that a learning-disabled child is one who possesses normal psychometric intelligence but is subject to localized cognitive deficits has remained fundamental to the field (e.g., Doris, 1986). It is theoretically possible, however, that learning-disabled children may possess normal intelligence, localized cognitive deficits, *and generalized cognitive deficits*. Here, the only logical restriction would be that generalized cognitive deficits, whatever they may be, must be uncorrelated with psychometric intelligence.

To many investigators, it has seemed that basic short- and long-term memory abilities—for example, span of immediate recall, rehearsal in short-term memory, storage in long-term memory, and retrievability of information from long-term memory—are prudent places to begin the search for such generalized cognitive deficits. Research of this ilk has flourished in recent years (e.g., Bauer, 1977; Brainerd, Kingma, & Howe, 1986; Dallago & Moely, 1980; Howe, Brainerd, & Kingma, 1985; Kail & Leonard, 1986; Swanson, 1984; Wong, Wong, & Foth, 1977). To be sure, such studies have not always been successful in identifying generalized memory deficits in learning-disabled children. For instance, measures of short-term memory span often fail to differentiate disabled from nondisabled populations, particularly when the to-be-remembered items are semantically impoverished (e.g., nonsense trigrams). On the other hand, disabled and nondisabled children have been routinely found to differ on other memory abilities, and long-term memory abilities have produced especially robust differences. Our own research program on children's learning disabilities falls within this latter area.

To date, our research has gone through three stages. First, we developed a family of mathematical models that would allow us to secure precise quantitative measurements of certain long-term memory abilities across a broad range of laboratory memory tasks (Brainerd, 1983, 1985; Brainerd & Howe, 1980, 1982; Brainerd, Howe, & Desrochers, 1982; Brainerd, Howe, & Kingma, 1982). The pool of tasks included such familiar procedures as associative recall, cued recall, free recall, serial anticipation, and relearning. Next, we exploited these models in an attempt to isolate long-term memory abilities on which learning-disabled and nondisabled children seemed to differ *at acquisition*. That is, we conducted experiments in which children learned materials in circumstances that were already known to produce disabled/nondisabled differences, and we used our models to disentangle the various memorial sources of these differences (Brainerd *et al.*, 1986; Howe *et al.*, 1985; Howe, O'Sullivan, Brainerd, & Kingma, 1989). Finally, we have recently begun studying the complementary issue of long-term memory abilities that control everyday *forgetting*, abilities that may also differentiate disabled and nondisabled children. It is this particular research that serves as the impetus for this chapter. But since this research was directly motivated by our prior experiments on acquisition, we summarize the acquisition work before taking up forgetting.

II. Acquisition

In this section, we first examine the theoretical concepts and models that have guided our acquisition studies. We then sketch the principal findings that have been obtained in studies where these techniques were applied to disabled/nondisabled comparisons.

A. Concepts and Models

Since the appearance of a paper by Melton (1963), the distinction between the processes whereby stable traces are formed (storage) and the processes whereby humans gain access to those traces on memory tests (retrieval) has been a central issue to students of long-term memory: "What, then, are the principal issues in a theory of memory? These are about either the storage or the retrieval of traces" (p. 4). Nowadays, the separation of storage in and retrieval from memory is the most primitive of all theoretical distinctions. Our own experiments have focused on elucidating the role that this distinction plays in children's memories. In keeping with the aims of this volume, we assume that the storage–retrieval distinction is best viewed as fundamental to the neuropsychology of memory rather than as a by-product of cognitive aspects of memory (e.g., strategic intervention).

As an antecedent to our research, it was necessary to develop modeling techniques that were capable of factoring storage processes from retrieval processes within standard long-term memory paradigms (associative recall, free recall, etc.). The particular model that we selected originally appeared in the literature nearly three decades ago (Theios, 1961). Since then it has been applied to a large group of animal and human learning situations, some of them long-term memory paradigms (see Greeno, James, DaPolito, & Polson, 1978), a fact that reinforces the supposition that basic neuropsychological distinctions are being captured. What all of these situations have in common is that it is not typically possible for subjects to make a correct response by guessing at the start of the experiment (before any learning trials have been administered). The guessing probability is zero because these paradigms are *production tasks* that require subjects to generate their own responses, not *selection tasks* in which subjects can respond by choosing among the members of a small set of alternatives. Examples of animal production tasks include Pavlovian conditioning, escape conditioning, and avoidance conditioning. Examples of memory paradigms that are production tasks include virtually all list-learning procedures where the response measure is some sort of recall.

Suppose that subjects are administered a memory task of this type and that they must achieve a perfect-recall criterion—that is, alternating cycles of study and test trials are administered until subjects are able to recall every list item perfectly. The error–success data that are obtained across trials for individual items conform to three general patterns. Some items will exhibit a string of successes without any errors, other items will exhibit an initial run of errors followed by a criterion run of successes, and still other items will exhibit an initial run of errors followed by a sequence of alternating errors and successes followed by a criterion run of successes. For example, imagine a hypothetical free-recall experiment in which children memorize a list of 16 words to a criterion of two consecutive errorless free-recall tests. Table I contains the data of an actual subject from such an experiment (a 7-year-old) who required 14 trials to meet the perfect-recall criterion. Note that each of the three types of error–success patterns was exhibited by some of the 16

TABLE I Error–Success Data for a Child
Memorizing a 16-Item Free-Recall List to a
Criterion of Two Consecutive Errorless Test
Cycles

List Item	Trial-by-Trial Responses[a]
1	11110000000000
2	11000010110000
3	00001001000000
4	11111111111100
5	11101010110000
6	00000000000000
7	11111000000100
8	11000110000000
9	01110010101100
10	00000000000000
11	11000000000000
12	00000000000000
13	11111100001100
14	11000000100000
15	11111100000000
16	01100010100100

[a] 1, recall error; 0, recall success.

items. Note further, however, that the third pattern predominated, as it often does in production tasks with children (Brainerd, 1985).

Our initial studies of normal children's performance on such tasks showed that the structure of error–success sequences could be accounted for by a remarkably simple memory model. The model assumes that memorization consists of only three, discrete states and that learning involves all-or-none transitions between these states. The three states are:

1. U, an initial "unmemorized" state in which only recall errors occur,
2. P, an intermediate "partially memorized" state in which both recall errors (substate P_E) and recall successes (substate P_S) occur, and
3. L, a terminal "memorized" state in which only recall successes occur.

A number of studies with children showed that this simple model delivered surprisingly exact accounts of the fine-grain structure of recall data (e.g., Brainerd, Howe, & Desrochers, 1982; Brainerd, Howe, Kingma, & Brainerd, 1984).

To us and to other investigators (e.g., Greeno *et al.*, 1978) it has seemed natural to identify the states of this model with the constructs of storage and retrieval. In any recall memorization experiment, as we have said, the guessing probability is zero at the outset. In order for the probability of recalling an item to be greater than zero, the minimum precondition would appear to be that *a permanent trace of that item should be deposited in long-term memory*. So, we identify escape from the "unmemorized" state *U* with the event of storing a durable trace. When storage has been achieved, the target trace will presumably be retrievable at least some of the time, but there is no reason to suppose that subjects will be able to gain access to the trace infallibly on memory tests. Further learning may be required before subjects secure a retrieval algorithm for the trace. This leads us to identify escape from the "partially memorized" state *P* with acquiring a retrieval algorithm for a stored trace. Between the time that an item enters state *P* and escapes to state *L*, recall is successful with some average probability $0 < p < 1$. Hence, we identify the value of *p* with the accuracy of retrieval between the time that a trace is stored and the time that a retrieval algorithm is acquired. Finally, when an item enters the terminal "memorized" state *L*, it is assumed that a trace is in storage and that a retrieval algorithm is available for that trace.

Now that these basic definitions are in hand, we may proceed to the full-blown model and the specific memory processes that it measures. These processes, along with the parameters of the model that measure each, are displayed in Table II. The processes can be grouped into three categories: storage/storage failure, retrieval learning, and retrieval performance.

1. STORAGE/STORAGE FAILURE

These are three parameters in Table II that measure storage-related processes. The parameter *a'* is the probability of depositing a stable trace of an item on the very *first* study trial. The parameter *a* is the probability of depositing a trace on any study trial *after* the first one. The parameter *f* is the storage-failure parameter. Since a trace might be inclined to disintegrate when it is first stored and may require further study trials to stabilize, *f* is the probability that a trace is lost between the trial on which it is first stored and the very next trial.

2. RETRIEVAL LEARNING

Assuming that the acquisition of retrieval algorithms must await trace storage, there are two points at which such learning can take place, and our model provides separate measures of each. First, a retrieval algorithm may be learned *on the same study trial on which the trace is stored*. The parameter *b'* is the probability of learning a retrieval algorithm on the same trial on which a trace is stored if that trial is Trial 1. The parameter *b* is the probability of learning a retrieval algorithm on the same trial on which a trace is stored if storage occurs on any trial *after* Trial 1. Second, a retrieval algorithm may also be learned *on*

TABLE II Memory Processes Measured by the Acquisition Model

Parameter	Definition
Storage	
a'	The probability that a stable trace is stored in the first study trial.
a	The probability that a stable trace is stored on any study trial after the first.
f	The probability that a trace is lost after it is stored on the first study trial.
Retrieval learning	
b'	The probability that a retrieval algorithm is learned on Trial 1 for a trace stored on that trial.
b	The probability that a retrieval algorithm is learned on any subsequent trial for a trace stored on that trial.
c	For traces stored on some earlier trial, the probability that a retrieval algorithm is learned following a successful recall.
d	For traces stored on some earlier trial, the probability that a retrieval algorithm is learned following a recall error.
Retrieval performance	
$1 - e$	For traces stored on some trial after Trial 1, the probability of successful retrieval if a retrieval algorithm was not learned on that trial.
$1 - r$	For traces stored on Trial 1, the probability of successful retrieval if a retrieval algorithm was not learned on Trial 1.
g	On any pair of trials between the trial on which storage occurs and the trial on which a retrieval algorithm is learned, the probability that a success follows an error.
h	On any pair of consecutive trials between the trial on which storage occurs and the trial on which a retrieval algorithm is learned, the probability that a success follows a success.

some trial after the trial on which the trace is stored. The parameter c is the probability of learning a retrieval algorithm for a previously stored trace if that trace was successfully retrieved on the immediately preceding trial. The parameter d is the probability of learning a retrieval algorithm for a previously stored trace if that trace was not successfully retrieved on the immediately preceding trial.

3. RETRIEVAL PERFORMANCE

Finally, the model provides four different ways of measuring the accuracy with which a trace is retrieved between the time of its storage and the time that a retrieval algorithm is finally acquired. The parameter $1 - r$ is the probability of successful retrieval on Trial 1 of traces that were stored on Trial 1. The parameter $1 - e$ is the probability of successful retrieval on any trial *after* Trial 1 of traces that were stored on that trial. For traces that were stored on some previous trial, g is the probability of a retrieval success if a retrieval error occurred on the immediately preceding trial. For traces that were stored on some previous trial, h is the probability of a retrieval success if retrieval was also successful on the immediately preceding trial.

B. Comparisons of Disabled and Nondisabled Children

Extensive applications of the model in Table II to normal children, college students, and aging populations have produced a number of developmental findings that generalize across several tasks (for reviews, see Brainerd, 1983, 1985). Our concern here, however, is with those particular applications in which children who were classified as learning disabled were compared to their nondisabled peers. We summarize the results of these experiments in the order in which they were published.

Howe et al. (1985) In this study, disabled/nondisabled comparisons were carried out with second-grade children (7- and 8-year-olds) and sixth-grade children (11- and 12-year-olds). The second-grade sample consisted of 60 normally achieving children and 61 children who had been classified by their schools as being at least 1 year behind their classmates in either reading or arithmetic, but not in both. The sixth-grade sample consisted of 60 normally achieving children and 82 children who had been classified by their schools as being at least 1 year behind their classmates in reading or arithmetic, but not in both. All of the children at both age levels had measured IQs in the 97–106 range, and there were no differences between the disabled and nondisabled samples in this variable.

All of the children at both age levels memorized lists of 16 items under standard free-recall conditions. On each study trial, the experimenter presented the items one at a time at a 5-sec rate. To control for age and ability differences in reading, the experimenter read each item aloud as it appeared. After each item had been presented, 30 sec of distractor activity (letter shadowing) was interpolated to empty short-term memory. Following the distractor activity, the child was instructed to recall as many items as could be remembered in any order. The free-recall test continued until all 16 items had been recalled or until 30 sec had elapsed without the production of a new word. This procedure of study–distractor–test continued in successive cycles until the child reached a criterion of two consecutive free-recall tests on which all 16 items were recalled.

The types of items memorized by individual children varied. Half the children (both disabled and nondisabled) at each age level memorized lists of highly familiar (A or AA on the Thorndike–Lorge count) concrete nouns. Examples include words such as *baby, chair, snake, trumpet*. The other half of the children (both disabled and nondisabled) at each age level memorized lists of pictures (line drawings). For the sake of comparability, the pictures depicted the same objects that were named in the words being memorized by the children in the word condition. The picture–word manipulation was included as a test of the familiar hypothesis that the memory deficits of learning-disabled children are largely semantic in origin. Under this hypothesis, disabled/nondisabled differences should be far more pronounced with words than with pictures.

The results of this experiment are reported at the top of Table III in the form of values of the storage and retrieval parameters of our model. We consider the general results that bear upon ability differences first and then discuss qualifications that arise from the picture–word manipulation.

The most interesting pattern was one of developmental change in the memorial locus of disabled/nondisabled differences. As expected, free recall was more difficult for disabled children than for nondisabled children. However, this difference appeared to be storage based in younger children and retrieval based in older children. Concerning storage, the average values of the two storage parameters in younger children were $a' = .47$ (nondisabled) and .41 (disabled), and $a = .60$ (nondisabled) and .48 (disabled). The latter difference was reliable, and the former difference approached significance. Hence, disabled second graders had difficulty, relative to nondisabled second graders, depositing stable traces. However, they did not encounter similar difficulty in either retrieval performance or acquiring retrieval algorithms. Concerning the former, the average values of the retrieval performance parameters were .64 (nondisabled) and .69 (disabled). Concerning the latter, the average values of the retrieval learning parameters were .23 (nondisabled) and .18 (disabled).

Turning to the sixth-grade data, the average values of the two storage parameters were $a' = .48$ (nondisabled) and .45 (disabled), and $a = .63$ (nondisabled) and .58 (disabled). As neither difference was reliable, older disabled children were storing information at the same rate as nondisabled children. With respect to retrieval learning, however, the average values of the relevant parameters were .33 (nondisabled) and .23 (disabled), a highly reliable difference. The individual parameters that produced reliable differences were b', c, and d. Thus, although older disabled and nondisabled children deposited traces in long-term memory at the same rate, it was more difficult for disabled children to learn how to access those traces reliably on memory tests. Finally, disabled and nondisabled sixth graders did not differ in the values of the retrieval performance parameters.

These general trends varied somewhat as a function of whether picture lists or word lists were being memorized. With word lists, second-grade nondisabled children were better at storage than disabled children by both storage measures (a' and a). With pictures, however, nondisabled second graders were only superior on the *a* measure of storage. Although there were no *overall* differences in storage between disabled and nondisabled sixth graders, there were differences on the word lists. Specifically, parameter *a* was reliably larger for the nondisabled sixth graders.

In sum, the developmental pattern of disabled/nondisabled differences in long-term memory processes was somewhat different for pictures and words. For words, the developmental trend was deficit *addition* in the sense that storage was better in nondisabled children at both age levels but retrieval was also better in older nondisabled children. With pictures, however, the developmental pattern was deficit *replacement* in the sense that retrieval learning supplanted storage as the locus of disabled/nondisabled differences.

Brainerd et al. (1986) Five additional experiments were reported in which disabled/nondisabled comparisons were made with second- and sixth-grade children. Experiments 1–4 were analogous to Howe *et al.* (1985) in that lists were memorized under standard free-recall conditions. In Experiment 5, however, lists were memorized under cued-recall conditions. In Experiment 1, the children (30 disabled subjects and 30 nondisabled subjects at each age level) memorized lists of unrelated nouns drawn from the Battig–Montague pool. In Experiments 2 and 3, the children memorized concrete noun lists (Experiment 2) and picture lists (Experiment 3) like those administered by Howe *et al.* (1985). There were again 30 nondisabled and 30 disabled children at each age level in each experiment. In Experiments 4 and 5, the children memorized lists of categorized nouns under either free-recall conditions (Experiment 4) or cued-recall conditions (Experiment 5). As in the other three experiments, there were 30 nondisabled and 30 disabled children at each age level. The disabled and nondisabled children in all of these experiments had measured IQs in the normal range, and none of the groups differed reliably on this variable.

Although disabled/nondisabled differences varied somewhat from experiment to experiment, we only consider global trends that bear on the pattern that emerged in the study by Howe *et al.* (1985). First, as with the word lists of Howe *et al.*, nondisabled children stored items more easily than disabled children did at both age levels, though this difference was confined to the later storage parameter, *a*. Moreover, the superior storage ability of nondisabled children tended to increase with age: The average values of *a* for second graders were .56 (nondisabled) and .46 (disabled), whereas these values for sixth graders were .70 (nondisabled) and .47 (disabled). Thus, the increasing storage superiority of nondisabled children was due to the fact that their storage ability improved with age, but the storage ability of disabled children remained frozen.

Second, although the retrieval learning abilities of younger nondisabled and disabled children were equivalent in Howe *et al.* (1985), there was some

TABLE III Disabled/Nondisabled Comparisons for Acquisition

Experiment					Parameter						
	a	a'	f	b'	b	c	d	$1-e$	$1-r$	g	b
Howe et al. (1985)											
Younger words											
Disabled	.33	.46	0	.17	.01	.16	.36	.68	.88	.50	.67
Nondisabled	.44	.5	0	.23	0	.19	.45	.60	.73	.45	.62
Older words											
Disabled	.40	.49	0	.15	0	.23	.32	.93	.92	.54	.72
Nondisabled	.39	.59	0	.31	.19	.26	.61	.70	.94	.56	.65
Younger pictures											
Disabled	.48	.49	.03	.22	0	.22	.31	.77	.82	.48	.73
Nondisabled	.49	.63	.0	.29	0	.25	.41	.54	.88	.56	.71
Older pictures											
Disabled	.40	.67	0	.30	.27	.20	.36	.57	.86	.59	.69
Nondisabled	.57	.67	0	.37	0	.35	.48	.79	.88	.68	.72
Brainerd et al. (1986) Experiment 1											
Younger											
Disabled	.39	.44	0	.29	.15	.06	.42	.56	.78	.25	.55
Nondisabled	.39	.46	0	.34	.17	.18	.58	.73	.79	.28	.57
Older											
Disabled	.34	.47	0	.07	0	.28	.52	.93	.90	.31	.70
Nondisabled	.41	.78	0	.20	.05	.36	.49	.58	.88	.48	.66
Brainerd et al. (1986), Experiment 2											
Younger											
Disabled	.35	.50	0	.14	.04	.17	.41	.69	.81	.27	.66
Nondisabled	.49	.53	0	.07	0	.27	.47	.79	.68	.26	.67
Older											
Disabled	.42	.47	0	0	0	.29	.41	1.00	.90	.28	.73
Nondisabled	.39	.58	0	.24	.18	.68	.68	.69	.93	.33	.62
Brainerd et al. (1986), Experiment 3											
Younger											
Disabled	.54	.43	0	0	0	.31	.38	1.00	.75	.21	.85
Nondisabled	.51	.73	0	.10	0	.32	.50	.63	.86	.31	.73
Older											
Disabled	.52	.66	0	.24	.17	.21	.47	.60	.82	.33	.66
Nondisabled	.59	.74	0	.32	.06	.38	.62	.72	.87	.45	.66

Brainerd et al. (1986), Experiment 4

Younger										
Disabled	.38	.40	0	.17	.12	.14	.33	.89	.69	.47	.59
Nondisabled	.43	.48	0	.15	.09	.25	.50	.81	.87	.42	.63
Older										
Disabled	.41	.49	0	.16	.29	.22	.21	.93	.90	.47	.66
Nondisabled	.51	.67	0	.29	.26	.16	.53	.57	.83	.51	.62

Brainerd et al. (1986), Experiment 5

Younger										
Disabled	.52	.73	0	.25	.41	.28	.59	.67	.77	.50	.71
Nondisabled	.53	.72	0	.38	.47	.47	.69	.81	.77	.69	.81
Older										
Disabled	.52	.73	0	.25	.41	.28	.59	.67	.77	.50	.71
Nondisabled	.53	.72	0	.38	.47	.47	.69	.81	.77	.69	.81

Howe et al. (1989)

Younger disabled										
Unrelated	.37	.48	0	.31	.14	.06	.62	.48	.84	.40	.56
2-car FR*	.27	.40	0	.20	.21	.14	.33	.69	.79	.47	.60
2-car CR	.38	.52	0	.26	.20	.30	.37	.69	.86	.47	.65
4-car FR	.44	.47	0	.19	.12	.23	.27	.85	.90	.58	.74
Younger nondisabled										
Unrelated	.37	.52	0	.38	.11	.17	.55	.61	.82	.47	.59
2-car FR	.43	.48	0	.25	.20	.25	.50	.71	.87	.42	.67
2-car CR	.45	.61	0	.43	.44	.25	.59	.53	.73	.45	.64
4-car FR	.48	.67	0	.45	.07	.33	.63	.68	.88	.47	.63
4-car CR	.52	.89	0	.62	.77	.77	.98	.50	.65	.76	.72
Older disabled										
Unrelated	.32	.47	0	.21	.20	.25	.34	.85	.92	.57	.69
2-car FR	.41	.49	0	.16	.29	.21	.37	.93	.90	.47	.66
2-car CR	.52	.73	0	.25	.41	.28	.60	.67	.77	.50	.71
4-car FR	.40	.46	0	.12	.16	.26	.25	1.00	.88	.59	.75
4-car CR	.72	.98	0	.38	.55	.56	.19	.47	.62	.47	.85
Older nondisabled										
Unrelated	.40	.66	0	.39	.12	.29	.47	.52	.86	.66	.67
2-car FR	.57	.67	0	.29	.26	.16	.53	.57	.83	.51	.62
2-car CR	.53	.72	0	.38	.47	.47	.69	.81	.77	.69	.81
4-car FR	.46	.60	0	.36	.12	.59	.59	.85	.92	.65	.85
4-car CR	.79	.98	0	.53	.76	.83	.90	.08	.22	.10	.67

* 2-car FR, 2-category free recall; 2-car CR, 2-category cued recall; 4-car FR, 4-category free recall; 4-car CR, 4-category cued recall.

evidence of superior retrieval learning among the younger nondisabled children in this experiment. Three of the four retrieval learning measures (b', b, and c) did not differentiate the groups, though their grand means favored nondisabled second graders. The fourth parameter, d, however, was reliably larger overall in nondisabled children.

Third, as in Howe *et al.* (1985), there was overwhelming evidence of superior retrieval learning in older nondisabled children than in older disabled children. The average values of the four retrieval learning parameters for the older children across the five experiments were b' = .29 (nondisabled) and .14 (disabled), b = .20 (nondisabled) and .17 (disabled), c = .41 (nondisabled) and .26 (disabled), and d = .60 (nondisabled) and .44 (disabled). Except for parameter b, each of these differences was reliable.

Fourth, retrieval performance parameters did not differentiate nondisabled and disabled children at either age level. Although there were a few scattered differences within particular experiments, there were no global differences favoring one ability group over the other.

So far, then, the following picture has emerged in connection with the long-term memory deficits of disabled children. Developmentally, it is storage ability that first differentiates disabled from nondisabled children. The storage differences that show up in younger children are preserved in older children and, indeed, they may increase with age. An even more important developmental change involves the ability to learn how to retrieve traces. Younger disabled children do not exhibit major deficits on this variable. They lose ground with age, however, and these children display pervasive deficits in retrieval learning by age 11 or 12. So, the sheer number of long-term memory processes that differentiate disabled from nondisabled children grows with age. But there is an important category of long-term memory abilities that disabled and nondisabled children *never* seem to differ on. Between the time that a trace is stored and the time that an algorithm for accessing the trace has been acquired, children are able to retrieve the trace with some level of accuracy. The data consistently indicated that this level is the same for disabled and nondisabled children, regardless of age. Thus, although disabled children exhibit limitations in general long-term memory abilities, these limitations are confined to abilities that would be broadly termed "learning" rather than to steady-state memory performance (*Howe et al*, 1989).

Except for the last two experiments of Brainerd *et al.* (1986), the bulk of the preceding studies dealt with disabled/nondisabled differences in memory for unrelated items. There are theorists, however, who contend that learning-disabled children are at a particular disadvantage with semantically related material (e.g., categorized lists), and some of Brainerd *et al.*'s (1986) data were consistent with this claim. An experiment by Howe *et al.* (1989) was designed to focus squarely on this issue.

Howe *et al.* (1989) studied 150 normally achieving second-grade children, 150 second-grade children who had been classified as learning disabled, 150 normally achieving sixth-grade children, and 150 sixth-grade children who had been classified as learning disabled. At each age level, 60 of the 300 children (30 nondisabled, 30 disabled) memorized one of the following five types of lists: (1) unrelated nouns under free-recall conditions, (2) nouns belonging to two familiar categories under free-recall conditions, (3) nouns belonging to two familiar categories under cued-recall conditions, (4) nouns belonging to four familiar categories under free-recall conditions, and (5) nouns belonging to four familiar categories under cued-recall conditions. The results are displayed at the bottom of Table III.

In reporting their results, Howe *et al.* (1989) placed particular emphasis on developmental and disabled/nondisabled differences in the effects of implicit and explicit category structure. The normal finding is that, relative to unrelated lists, recall of categorized lists is better, whether category structure is implicit (free recall) or explicit (cued recall). Howe *et al.* (1989) found that both of these effects were present in nondisabled children and tended to increase with age. However, both second-grade and sixth-grade disabled children were deficient in their ability to benefit from either implicit or explicit category structure. In fact, neither the older nor the younger disabled children derived *any* benefit from categorized lists when category structure was implicit. Although both groups displayed superior recall of categorized lists when the categories were cued, this superiority was not nearly as great as in the corresponding nondisabled samples. A final, developmental result was especially interesting. Whereas the nondisabled children showed the usual age improvement in implicit and explicit category structure, disabled children did not. This outcome lends considerable support to the view that learning-disabled children are especially deficient in organizational aspects of long-term memory.

C. Summary

Our model-based analyses argue for certain general conclusions about long-term memory limitations of learning-disabled children. First, from a fairly early age, disabled children show deficits in the rates at which they store information in long-term memory. However, this effort is confined to traces that are deposited after the first trial. In other words, the effect does not materialize until prior attempts have been made to store the target items. Second, memory differences between nondisabled and disabled children tend to increase with age. The differences in storage rate seem to increase somewhat, and differences in retrieval learning appear at older age levels that are not observed earlier. In fact, retrieval learning (parameters b', b, c, and d) is a far more powerful source of disabled/nondisabled differences than storage is in older children. Third, disabled/nondisabled differences, particularly differences in retrieval learning ability, are acute when lists are taxonomically organized. Disabled children display arrested development in connection with such materials. Whereas nondisabled children derive progressively more benefit from taxonomic organization with age, disabled children do not.

III. Forgetting

When it comes to children's learning, especially in the classroom, acquisition is only half the story. Once children have been induced to acquire certain information or skills, we want them to retain what they have acquired as long as possible. This is the question of forgetting or, alternatively, the question of long-term retention.

In this section, we summarize our research on basic forgetting processes in disabled and nondisabled children. We set the stage for this work in the first two subsections, initially by considering the curious asymmetry between acquisition and forgetting, and then by considering certain theoretical issues that figure in the developmental analysis of forgetting. In the third subsection, we describe the specific model that we have used to measure different types of forgetting processes in children. Finally, we report some new experiments in which this model was used to pinpoint disabled/nondisabled differences in forgetting.

A. Acquisition/Forgetting Asymmetries

The standard laboratory tool for studying everyday forgetting, whether in children or in adults, is the Ebbinghaus long-term retention paradigm. This procedure consists of an initial acquisition session followed by one or more retention sessions. During the acquisition session, the subjects memorize some material—usually meaningful material such as concrete nouns, pictures, or sentences—to some criterion of accuracy (e.g., 75% correct). Next, a retention interval of several hours, days, weeks, or months ensues. At the end of this interval, the subjects are administered a series of tests for the previously memorized material. Importantly, no further opportunities to study the material are provided during the retention session. The slope of the line that connects performance at the end of the acquisition session with average performance during the retention session is the standard measure of forgetting—for example, if the acquisition criterion was 100% correct and average performance during the retention session was 75%, we say that the forgetting rate was 25% (see Brainerd & Reyna, 1990).

To lay persons and memory researchers alike, it seems natural to regard acquisition processes and forgetting processes as symmetrical. In general, the symmetry position assumes that variables that affect acquisition rate have the same effect on forgetting rate (e.g., materials that are easier to learn are easier to retain) and that individual differences in acquisition rate control individual differences in forgetting rate (e.g., subjects who acquire material faster in the first place also retain it better). If the symmetry assumption were true, then, of course, there would be far less motivation for studying disabled/nondisabled differences in forgetting: Acquisition data such as those that we have reviewed would be sufficient to convince us both that there are disabled/nondisabled differences in long-term memory processes and that we know the locus of those differences at specific age levels. Despite the intuitive appeal of the symmetry assumption, it has been repeatedly disconfirmed in experimentation and, consequently, data on disabled/nondisabled differences in acquisition do not tell us anything definitive about corresponding differences in forgetting.

The relevant findings come from a recent series of experiments on the development of forgetting in normal children (Brainerd *et al.*, 1985; Brainerd & Reyna, 1989, 1990). As mentioned, the symmetry hypothesis makes two claims, one about symmetrical effects of experimental manipulations and the other about symmetrical effects of individual differences. Both claims were disconfirmed in these experiments. Concerning manipulations, Brainerd *et al.* (1985) and Brainerd and Reyna (1989) reported that certain treatments that enhanced children's acquisition rates either had no effect on their retention rates or, more dramatically, *interfered* with retention. For instance, Brainerd *et al.* (1985) found that 7-year-olds acquired lists of unrelated word pairs more rapidly than lists of categorized word pairs, but they forgot the two types of lists at the same rate. Brainerd *et al.* (1985) also found that 7- and 12-year-olds acquired categorized word pairs more rapidly when words were typical exemplars of categories than when they were atypical examplars, but that categorized word pairs were retained better when they were atypical exemplars than when they were typical exemplars. Concerning individual differences, Brainerd and Reyna (1990) used path analysis to study the possibility that age differences in forgetting rates were due to correlated individual differences in acquisition rates (i.e., were due to the fact that older children acquire items more rapidly than younger children, together with the symmetry principle that faster learning means better retention). They found no evidence for this possibility. In their experiments, they pitted three causal models against each other: (1) a model that assumed that age produces improvements in learning rate which in turn produces improvements in retention, (2) a model that assumed that age produces improvements in learning rate and retention rate and improvements in learning rate also affect retention rate, and (3) a model that assumes that age produces improvements in learning and retention rates that are completely independent of each other. The data favored the third model. For present purposes, the importance of these data lies in the fact that the rate at which Brainerd and Reyna's (1990) children (7- and 12-year-olds) acquired the target material (concrete and abstract nouns) bore no relationship at all to the rate at which they forgot the same material.

These are but a few examples of many asymmetries that are known to exist between acquisition and forgetting (for reviews, see Brainerd *et al.*, 1985; Howe & Brainerd, 1989). The existence of these asymmetries makes forgetting a very interesting topic of study in its own right and suggests that disabled/nondisabled differences in forgetting, if any, are apt to be different than the aforementioned differences in acquisition.

B. *Concepts and Controversies*

Throughout this century, the study of forgetting, both in adults and in children, has been accompanied by certain fundamental controversies. Two of these are instructive in the present context, and we briefly examine them before taking up our approach to forgetting.

1. PROCESS LOCI OF FORGETTING

Theorists have long disagreed as to whether forgetting is chiefly due to alterations in the traces themselves (usually called *storage failure*) or to alterations in the ability to gain access to intact traces (usually called *retrieval failure*). Traditionally, storage-based explanations of forgetting have focused on what might be called the unlearning of previous material via either spontaneous decay processes or destructive overwriting by subsequent learning (Howe & Brainerd, 1989). Retrieval-based explanations, on the other hand, center on "confusions" that arise between previously stored traces and subsequently stored traces, both of which coexist in memory and must be differentially accessed on memory tests (Brainerd, Reyna, Kingma, & Howe, 1989). The hallmark of such explanations is the notion that subsequently stored traces do not affect previously stored traces and that, once they are stored, all traces survive intact.

Although both types of explanations can be found in the contemporary forgetting literature, retrieval failure has traditionally been the preeminent position (Loftus & Loftus, 1980). Freud's theory of childhood amnesia is a classic illustration of a developmental version of this position: Adults were said to be able to access intact childhood memories in specialized retrieval environments (e.g., in hypnotic states, during psychoanalysis). Freudian claims notwithstanding, the simple fact of reminiscence provides the most compelling support for this approach. A familiar experience, one that we have every day, is remembering something at Time 2 that could not be remembered at Time 1, despite having no intervening opportunity to relearn the target information. The retrieval-failure interpretation of this prosaic experience is that the information was in storage all along, but access was only gained on the second occasion. Developmentally, retrieval-based accounts of ontogenetic changes in forgetting rely on the hypothesis that forgetting diminishes because retrieval strategies improve with age (Howe & Brainerd, 1989).

Despite the fact that the retrieval-failure hypothesis is preeminent, there are also influential examples of storage-failure approaches, particularly in research on eyewitness testimony (e.g., Ceci, Ross, & Toglia, 1987; Loftus & Hoffman, 1989). A strong version of storage failure says that all forgetting is due to trace absence, either because traces decay spontaneously or because they are destroyed by subsequently stored traces (Howe & Brainerd, 1989). Gestalt theory, which assumed that spontaneous "reorganization" of traces takes place, provides an early illustration. A less extreme view is that trace mutation (storage failure) and growing inaccessibility (retrieval failure) both contribute to forgetting, with the issue of their relative contributions being regarded as a question to be answered by experimentation (Brainerd *et al.*, 1985; 1989).

Unlike the study of acquisition, therefore, where everyone concurs that storage and retrieval processes both contribute to performance, there is no such agreement when it comes to forgetting. Obviously, this dispute beclouds both the study of forgetting development in normal children and the study of disabled/nondisabled differences in forgetting rates. For progress to be made on either topic, it is critical that studies be designed in such a way that they supply data on the relative contributions of storage versus retrieval failures to forgetting.

2. DOES FORGETTING DEVELOP?

Virtually every major theory of memory development implies that forgetting rates change with age, with rates decreasing during birth-to-adult development and accelerating thereafter (Brainerd & Reyna, 1990; Howe & Brainerd, 1989; Howe & Hunter, 1986). Surprisingly, however, when we began our studies of children's forgetting, it was widely imagined that forgetting from long-term memory is age invariant (for reviews, see Brainerd, *et al.*, 1985; Howe & Brainerd, 1989). As late as 1985, for example, Lehman, Mikesell, and Doherty had summarized the conventional wisdom of the extant literature with the statement that "information is not lost more rapidly by children than by adults. Forgetting rates . . . were invariant from middle childhood to young adulthood" (p. 27). This supposed lack of developmental trends in forgetting has serious implications for disabled/nondisabled comparisons because if nondisabled subjects of very different ages do not differ in forgetting rates, it is unlikely that disabled and nondisabled children of the same age will differ either.

Fortunately, recent research has established that this view was unduly pessimistic. Although the number of published studies in which null age effects were reported is quite sizeable, reviewers have identified certain methodological anomalies that stacked the deck in favor of developmental invariance (see Brainerd, *et al.*, 1985; Howe & Brainerd, 1989). The three most common problems were (1) recognition insensitivity, (2) low forgetting rates, and (3) stages-of-learning artifacts. With respect to the first problem, the memory tests that were administered during the retention sessions of these studies were recognition tests. One of the first rules of developmental research is that if one seeks to diagnose age changes, one must use dependent variables that are highly sensitive to such changes. There is a large developmental literature on recognition, and null age effects have been the standard finding with such tests (e.g., Ornstein & Corsale, 1979). So, regardless of what sort of memory ability one is studying, recognition tests are not apt to provide evidence of age change. Concerning the second problem, it turns out that the acquisition-to-retention declines in most studies were small *and in some cases were not statistically reliable* (e.g., Morrison, Haith, & Kagan, 1980). It goes without saying that age changes in forgetting cannot be observed when the amounts of forgetting are not reliable, and they are very difficult to observe when the amounts of forgetting are reliable but minuscule. Last, concerning the third problem, stages-of-learning confounds arose from the fact that small, fixed numbers of learning trials were administered during the acquisition sessions of all studies, with one-trial designs being the rule. This means that the older children in such studies reached more advanced stages of learning than the younger children by the end of the acquisition session for the simple reason that older children learn at faster rates than younger children. Suppose that forgetting rates are always lower for the initial, "primary" things that children learn about an item than they are for the subsequent, "secondary" things that children learn about it. Under this scenario, it would be extremely difficult to detect age differences in forgetting rates with fixed-trials designs because stages-of-learning confounds (older children reach more advanced stages of learning and forgetting rates are higher for more advanced stages) and the underlying developmental trend in forgetting (older children forget more slowly than younger children for given stages of learning) have opposite effects on retention performance (Brainerd & Reyna, in press).

These design anomalies have been eliminated in a series of studies conducted since 1985, and we have obtained robust age differences in forgetting rates between early childhood and young adulthood. The problem of recognition insensitivity has been dealt with by switching to recall tests. Low forgetting rates were eliminated by adjusting list difficulty and the length of the retention interval so as to ensure substantial amounts of forgetting. Stages-of-learning artifacts were controlled by using criterion-learning designs during the acquisition session. Here, the rationale is that since learning curves are negatively accelerated, age disparities in completeness of acquisition-phase learning will become vanishingly small as learning approaches asymptote. Six experiments have now been published with nondisabled children, four using associative recall and two using free recall, in which developmental trends in forgetting rates were secured.

The four associative-recall experiments were reported by Brainerd *et al.* (1985). In these studies, children of different ages memorized paired-associate lists of various types to a perfect-recall criterion during the acquisition session, and they were then administered a series of paced recall tests (no further study trials) 1 week later during the retention session. In three studies with elementary schoolers, forgetting rates dropped 45% between the ages of 7 and 12. In one study with adolescents, forgetting rates dropped an additional 18% between the ages of 11 and 17. The two free-recall experiments were reported by Brainerd and Reyna (1990). The children in both experiments memorized free-recall lists to a perfect-recall criterion during the acquisition session and then received a series of free-recall tests (no study trials) 2 weeks later. When the items were concrete nouns, forgetting rates declined by 69% between the ages of 7 and 12. When the items were abstract nouns, forgetting rates declined by 22% across the same age range.

To sum up, it has been believed for some years that forgetting rates do not develop, and this hypothesis is still widely accepted. We now know, however, that the null age effects of early studies were probably procedural artifacts and that there are robust age trends in forgetting when these confounds are eliminated. This, in turn, suggests that the study of disabled/nondisabled differences in forgetting will prove to be a productive topic.

C. *Theory and Models*

Our studies of age differences in forgetting and of disabled/nondisabled differences in forgetting are both guided by an explicit theoretical interpretation of forgetting that is implemented in a mathematical model. We summarize the theory first and then exhibit the model that captures the theory's main constructs.

1. THE DISINTEGRATION/ REDINTEGRATION HYPOTHESIS

The disintegration/redintegration hypothesis is a quasiperceptual view of children's forgetting that assumes that the storage and retrieval processes of acquisition lead to the construction of traces whose constituent features are so tightly integrated that they "stand out" well against the background of competing memory noise. The storage-failure and retrieval-failure mechanisms that produce forgetting are assumed to involve a systematic disintegration of the bonds that hold features together to form traces, which causes traces to "stretch" and "fade out" against the background of memory noise. The test-induced recoveries in memory performance that normally occur across a sequence of retention tests (e.g., Brainerd, Desrochers, & Howe, 1981) are assumed to reflect subjects' ability to redintegrate traces that have undergone featural disintegration during the retention interval.

The disintegration/redintegration hypothesis unites the notions of storage failure and retrieval failure under a single process metaphor for forgetting, namely, featural disintegration (Brainerd et al., 1989). The level of featural integration in traces (the strength of the "glue" that holds the features together) is the chief determinant of performance on retention tests. Storage failures and retrieval failures are simply different stages in the disintegration process. In all of our experiments, children are required to meet a perfect-recall criterion during acquisition, which means that it can safely be assumed that stable traces have been stored and retrieval algorithms have been learned for those traces. During the retention interval, featural bonds may weaken to the point that a trace can no longer be perfectly retrieved, but it can be retrieved some of the time. We say that such traces have undergone *retrieval failure*. However, featural bonds may become so weakened that a trace falls below the zero-recall threshold. We say that *storage failure* has occurred for such traces. Even traces that have fallen below the zero-recall threshold, however, are assumed to retain some integrity as distinct memorial structures.

During the retention session, the disintegration/redintegration hypothesis postulates that certain types of test-induced recovery are possible as a consequence of redintegration (Brainerd & Reyna, 1989; Brainerd et al., 1989; Howe & Brainerd, 1989). Redintegration is a mechanism whereby the activation of some of a trace's features on a retention test spreads to other features, which produces net increases in the general level of featural integration. The improvements in retention-test performance that accrue from redintegration are grouped into two categories, *restorage* and *retrieval relearning*. For traces that fall below the zero-recall threshold during the retention interval (storage failures), redintegration may induce sufficient refurbishment to cause these traces to migrate back across the threshold, in which event restorage is said to have occurred. For traces that fall below the perfect-recall threshold but remain above the zero-recall threshold (retrieval failures), redintegration may force those traces back across the perfect-recall threshold, in which event retrieval relearning is said to have occurred.

Relative to other interpretations of forgetting, the disintegration/redintegration hypothesis has two unique attributes. First, it does not conceptualize storage failure as trace eradication, viewing it instead as process of gradual stretching and fading. This eliminates most of the criticisms that have traditionally been leveled at the notion of storage failure by proponents of the retrieval-failure position (Howe & Brainerd, 1989). Second, thanks to the fading metaphor, the possibility of restorage can be allowed on long-term retention tests, and the question of the relative contributions of restorage and retrieval relearning to performance on such tests can be studied (Brainerd & Ornstein, in press). In contrast, because subjects do not restudy the target material on retention tests, the notion of restorage is an oxymoron if a trace-destruction metaphor is used for storage failure (Brainerd *et al.*, 1989).

2. TRACE-INTEGRITY MODEL

We have seen that the disintegration/redintegration hypothesis interprets performance on retention tests in terms of four basic memory processes. Two of them, storage failure and retrieval failure, are what could reasonably be termed *true forgetting processes* because they refer to events that occur during the retention interval. The other two, restorage and retrieval relearning, are test-induced recovery processes because they refer to events that occur on the retention tests. Disabled/nondisabled differences in retention performance might be due to any or all of these factors and, hence, it is desirable to measure each independently of the others. In our studies, we do this with a mathematical model called the trace-integrity model. The model's parameters are exhibited and defined in Table IV.

To explicate this model, consider a hypothetical Ebbinghaus-type design in which children memorize a list to a stringent acquisition criterion and then receive a series of retention tests (without further learning opportunities) some days/weeks/months later. True forgetting processes are measured by the parameters S and R in Table IV. S is the storage-failure rate. Specifically, it is the probability that a trace has fallen below the zero-recall threshold during the retention interval and, consequently, that the probability of recalling the relevant item on the first retention test is zero. R is the retrieval-failure parameter. For traces that have *not* fallen below the zero-recall threshold during the retention interval (i.e., traces for which storage has not failed), R is the probability that the relevant items cannot be recalled on the first retention test. Conceptually, S is the *unconditional* probability that an item is completely unavailable for recall on the first retention test, and R is the *conditional* probability that an item that is available for recall on the first retention test cannot be accessed.

The remaining parameters in Table IV measure the two forms of redintegration. Restorage is measured by the parameter a. For traces for which storage failed (with probability S) during the retention interval, a is the probability that redintegration causes the trace to migrate back across the

TABLE IV   Memory Processes Measured by the Forgetting Model

Parameter	Definition
Forgetting	
S	Probability of storage failure during the retention interval.
R	Probability of retrieval failure during the retention interval for items for which storage did not fail.
Test-induced processes	
a	Probability that a trace for which storage failed during the retention interval is restored on any retention test.
r_1	Probability that a stored trace is retrieved on a retention test that is preceded by a success on the prior retention test.
r_2	Probability that a stored trace is retrieved on a retention test after two consecutive previous successes.
r_3	Probability that a stored trace is retrieved on a retention test after three consecutive previous successes.
f_1	Probability that a stored trace is retrieved on a retention test if there was an error on the immediately preceding retention test.
f_2	Probability that a stored trace is retrieved on a retention test after two consecutive previous errors.
f_3	Probability that a stored trace is retrieved on a retention test after three consecutive previous errors.

zero-recall barrier on any retention test. Retrieval learning, on the other hand, is measured by the parameter sets r_1, r_2, r_3 and f_1, f_2, f_3. Each of these latter parameters captures information that is pertinent to a trace's retrieval history *after the first retention test*. The parameters in the first set are called *recall-success parameters*, and they measure the probability of two consecutive successes (r_1) three consecutive successes (r_2), or four consecutive successes (r_3). The parameters in the second set are called *recall-error parameters*, and they measure the probability of a success following an immediately preceding error (f_1), a success following two immediately preceding errors (f_2), and a success following three immediately preceding errors (f_3). Retrieval relearning is assessed by simply comparing the values of the r_i and the f_i to the value of $1 - R$. Since $1 - R$ is the probability of successful retrieval on the first retention test and the r_i and the f_i are concerned with retrieval on later retention tests, retrieval learning has occurred if either the r_i or the f_i is larger than $1 - R$.

The parameters of the model in Table IV can be estimated and the model's degree of fit to long-term retention data can be assessed using maximum likelihood procedures that we have developed elsewhere (Brainerd *et al.*, 1989; Howe & Brainerd, 1989). A discussion of these procedures is not necessary to understanding our findings on forgetting in disabled and nondisabled children, however.

3. COMPARISONS OF FORGETTING RATES IN DISABLED AND NONDISABLED CHILDREN

Forgetting research that involves disabled/nondisabled comparisons is even thinner in the literature than forgetting research involving between-age comparisons of nondisabled children. We were able to locate only one previously published study in this area (Hall, Humphreys, & Wilson, 1983), a study that was subject to the same methodological problems that we described earlier. In this subsection, therefore, we report two large-scale experiments concerned with the respective forgetting rates of disabled and nondisabled children of different ages (7- to 12-year-olds). The two experiments were very similar procedurally, with the key differences being that the children in Experiment 1 were Dutch elementary schoolers who memorized picture lists, and the children in Experiment 2 were American elementary schoolers who memorized word lists. The data of the nondisabled children in Experiment 1 have been reported by Brainerd *et al.* (in press), and the data of Experiment 2 have been reported by Brown (1988).

The subjects in Experiment 1 were 80 nondisabled Dutch second graders (mean age 7 years, 7 months), 80 disabled Dutch second graders (mean age 7 years, 9 months), 80 nondisabled Dutch sixth graders (mean age 11 years, 8 months), and 80 disabled Dutch sixth graders (mean age 11 years, 9 months). All children were pupils of elementary schools in Enschede, a city in northern Holland. All the children at both age levels had measured IQs in the 97–106 range. The children in the disabled samples had been classified by their schools as being at least one year behind their normally achieving peers in reading or arithmetic, but not in both. The experiment consisted of two sessions, an initial acquisition session followed by a long-term retention session 2 weeks later. During the acquisition phase, half the children at each age level (40 nondisabled, 40 disabled) memorized lists of 16 unrelated pictures of familiar objects under standard free-recall conditions. The acquisition procedure was identical to the free-recall experiments that we reported earlier, and memorization continued until each child was able to meet a criterion of two consecutive errorless free-recall tests. The other half of the children at each age level memorized lists of 16 pictures of familiar objects, where each picture belonged to one of four everyday categories (e.g., things to wear, furniture, vehicles, animals). The children in the categorized conditions were also required to meet a criterion of two consecutive errorless free-recall tests. After the criterion had been met, the acquisition session was terminated and a 2-week retention interval ensued. At the end of 2 weeks, each child returned to the laboratory for a series of five long-term retention tests. The procedure consisted of individual free-recall tests interspersed with irrelevant buffer activity (30 sec of letter shadowing) to empty short-term memory. At the start of the session, some simple retention instructions were read by the experimenter. The first free-recall test was then administered, followed by the first buffer activity. This alternating cycle of test/buffer was continued until five free-recall tests had been administered. So, the complete sequence of events was $T_1B_1T_2B_2T_3B_3T_4B_4T_5$, where T denotes a free-recall test and B denotes buffer activity.

In Experiment 2, the subject sample consisted of 50 disabled children and 56 nondisabled children in the 7–12 age range. For purposes of analysis, they were divided into a younger sample (mean age 8 years, 3 months) and an older sample (mean age 10 years, 8 months). The disabled children were initially selected through their schools' special-education files. Disabled children who were included in the study were required to possess at least average intelligence as measured by the WISC-R or the Stanford–Binet. All of these children had been identified as reading disabled, and none had been identified as arithmetic disabled. The procedure for Experiment 2 was the same as for Experiment 1, except for the following changes: All children memorized 16-item word lists rather than picture lists; the buffer activity consisted of counting backward from 10 to 1; and cued recall rather than free recall was used with the categorized lists during both the acquisition and the retention sessions.

To pinpoint disabled/nondisabled differences in forgetting rates, we estimated the parameters of the forgetting model (Table IV). These estimates are reported by experiment, age level, disability grouping, and list condition in Table V. Before considering these model-based results, however, we note three qualitative findings of general interest.

First, although there were disabled/nondisabled differences in forgetting rates in both experiments, such that nondisabled children displayed less forgetting than disabled children, these differences were much smaller than those that are typically observed in initial acquisition rates (see above). In Experiment 2, for instance, younger disabled and nondisabled children who memorized categorized lists did not differ reliably in their forgetting rates. All other disabled/nondisabled comparisons at both age levels showed reliable differences in forgetting, but the sizes of these differences were in the 10–20% range. It is as though disabled children, who take much longer to learn material in the first place, have to retain the material at levels that much more closely approach the retention levels of nondisabled children. [It might be thought that disabled/nondisabled differences in forgetting would necessarily be smaller than acquisition differences because disabled children require more learning trials to meet the acquisition criterion. Here, recall that Brainerd and Reyna (1990) showed that children's forgetting rates did not vary as a function of number of trials to criterion.] Second, we remarked earlier that disabled children are at a particular disadvantage when it comes to acquiring

TABLE V Disabled/Nondisabled Comparisons for Retention Data

Experiment	S	R	a	r_1	r_2	r_3	f_1	f_2	f_3
Experiment 1									
Younger unrelated									
Disabled	.59	.16	0	.92	.96	.98	.61	.22	.51
Nondisabled	.47	.15	.06	.91	.88	.95	.66	.15	.70
Older unrelated									
Disabled	.45	.09	0	.97	.97	.99	.74	.50	.42
Nondisabled	.36	.12	.07	.96	.96	.96	.68	.35	.37
Younger categorized									
Disabled	.42	.05	.29	.96	.98	1.00	.66	.72	.21
Nondisabled	.26	.02	.35	.97	.99	.99	.81	.50	.02
Older categorized									
Disabled	.19	.11	.65	1.00	1.00	1.00	.73	.48	.37
Nondisabled	.05	.07	.68	.99	1.00	1.00	.63	.72	.05
Experiment 2									
Younger unrelated									
Disabled	.61	.24	0	.86	.93	.92	.55	.74	.43
Nondisabled	.49	.17	.02	.93	.96	.95	.35	.70	.63
Older unrelated									
Disabled	.63	.18	.03	.95	.88	.94	.36	.63	.72
Nondisabled	.44	.24	.01	.94	.95	.91	.40	.31	.96
Younger categorized									
Disabled	.16	.09	.12	.97	.99	.98	.56	.79	1.00
Nondisabled	.08	.18	.06	.97	1.00	1.00	.80	.95	.90
Older categorized									
Disabled	.17	.04	.06	.97	1.00	1.00	.48	.26	.27
Nondisabled	.06	.06	.09	.99	1.00	1.00	.30	.96	.64

categorized items as opposed to unrelated items. The reverse is true, however, when it comes to forgetting. In Experiment 1, disabled/nondisabled differences in forgetting rates were much smaller for categorized than for unrelated materials at both age levels. In Experiment 2, there was no disabled/nondisabled difference for categorized lists among younger children and only a small difference among older children (9%). Thus there is a noteworthy asymmetry between the effects of semantic relatedness on disabled/nondisabled comparisons of acquisition versus forgetting. This asymmetry is of considerable theoretical significance: While the greater difficulty that disabled children encounter *acquiring* categorized lists may be said to support the familiar conjecture of deficient semantic organization in long-term memory, the fact that the disabled/nondisabled difference in forgetting rates shrinks with categorized lists argues against this conjecture.

Third, the spread between the respective forgetting rates of disabled and nondisabled children did not tend to vary with age. As we mentioned earlier, it is fairly common to find that disabled/nondisabled differences in acquisition rates diverge with age. The fact that this did not happen in the present forgetting data constitutes another major asymmetry in ability differences at acquisition versus retention.

Turning to the model-based analysis, since disabled/nondisabled differences in forgetting rates were smaller than differences in acquisition rates, one would expect that these differences would be confined to fewer memory processes. This was the case and, indeed, only one process appeared to be involved. In Experiment 1, the disabled children at both age levels exhibited higher rates of storage failure (parameter S in Tables IV and V) across the retention interval than did their nondisabled peers. This was true for both unrelated and categorized lists. In addition, the disabled children at both age levels were less able to restore a failed trace (parameter a in Tables IV and V) when lists were unrelated, but not when they were categorized. None of the other parameters varied reliably between the two ability groupings at either age level. Thus, there was no evidence of higher rates of retrieval failure among disabled children, and there was no evidence that disabled children were less able to relearn how to retrieve traces on retention tests. In Experiment 2 the results were similar, except for the fact that disabled/nondisabled differences were smaller. With unrelated lists, younger disabled children displayed higher rates of storage failure than younger nondisabled children, and older nondisabled children displayed higher rates of storage failure than older disabled children. No other differences were reliable. With categorized lists, older disabled children displayed higher rates of storage failure than older nondisabled children, but there were no disabled/nondisabled differences among younger children. Thus, the experiments concurred in showing that storage failure was more apt to occur in disabled children, and there was some related evidence that nondisabled children might be better at test-induced restorage. However, there was a consistent lack of evidence for disabled/nondisabled differences in retrieval-based processes.

These results for disabled/nondisabled differences in forgetting comprise yet another asymmetry between acquisition and retention data. As we have seen, disabled/nondisabled differences in acquisition tend to be broadly distributed across all of our measures of retrieval learning, and ability differences in these parameters tend to increase with age. Ability differences in storage are inclined to be much smaller and are confined to later phases of the storage process (parameter a in Tables IV and V). In contrast, retrieval processes, in the sense of either retrieval failure during the retention interval or retrieval relearning on the retention tests, seem to have nothing to do with disabled/nondisabled differences in forgetting, such differences being exclusively due to storage processes.

IV. Final Remarks

During the past decade, it has become widely understood that children with specialized learning disabilities also exhibit generalized memory deficits, especially long-term memory deficits. This datum has profound implications for theoretical conceptions of learning disabilities. For instance, Stanovich (1986) remarked in connection with the memory deficits that have been observed in reading-disabled children that

> The plethora of deficits that have been uncovered are indirectly threatening to the assumption of specialty because they suggest widespread cognitive difficulties rather than highly localized dysfunction that selectively impairs reading and virtually nothing else. . . . Indeed, some of the "specific" deficit areas that are now routinely discussed in the learning-disabilities literature are so broad that they actually serve to undermine the assumption of specificity and thus might simply add fuel to the definitional disputes that have marked the field from the beginning. [p. 233]

Although disabled children's poorer performance on such familiar tasks as free and cued recall has led researchers to acknowledge the existence of generalized memory deficits, the exact nature of those deficits has remained in doubt. In our research program, we have sought to shed some light on this problem by the simple device of factoring it into more manageable proportions. We have factored it in two ways. First, we have segregated the memory processes that might be associated with learning disability into two broad categories—namely, processes that are responsible for the acquisition of information and processes that are responsible for its retention over extended time intervals. Second, within each domain, candidate processes have been further divided into those that are involved in fixing representations in long-term memory (storage mechanisms) and those that are involved in reading out those representations on memory tests (retrieval processes). So far, our experiments have identified disabled/nondisabled differences in both acquisition and forgetting that were consistently localized within particular memory processes.

Concerning acquisition, we believe that there is converging support for three conclusions that are of some theoretical significance. First, it is retrieval learning, the ability to acquire algorithms for gaining access to previously stored traces, that is the most persistent source of disabled/nondisabled differences. Across various types of material, our disabled samples have encountered repeated difficulty in getting information out of storage once they have gotten it in. This deficit is broadly based, with all four of the retrieval learning parameters of our model exhibiting disabled/nondisabled differences in one experiment or another, and the breadth of the deficit increases with age. Second, deficits have also been observed in storage abilities. On the one hand, these deficits have shown up with sufficient regularity that they cannot be dismissed as chimerical. On the other hand, storage deficits have been much more circumscribed than retrieval deficits. They are not observed when children first begin studying target material, emerging instead after one or more study opportunities. When it comes to depositing information, then, it is as though disabled and nondisabled children begin on equal footing, but disabled children fall behind as learning unfolds. Third, the retrieval differences between disabled and nondisabled children do not extend to retrieval performance. We have argued that once a durable trace of an item has been stored, the concept of retrieval can be factored into two separate ideas—retrieval *learning* and steady-state retrieval *performance*. The former refers to the rate at which subjects learn algorithmic retrieval operations for traces, and the latter refers to the average accuracy levels of the fallible retrieval operations that are employed between the time of storage and the time that a retrieval algorithm is acquired.

Turning to forgetting, the extant data are very thin and extrapolation from them is correspondingly hazardous. Nevertheless, there are three further conclusions that we would like to mention that, though the data are modest, enjoy some credibility because they fit with the established pattern of asymmetries in acquisition versus forgetting (e.g., Brainerd, *et al.*, 1985, Brainerd *et al.*, 1989; Howe & Brainerd, 1989). To begin with, disabled/nondisabled differences in forgetting performance tend to be smaller in magnitude than the corresponding differences in acquisition. Of the eight disabled/nondisabled comparisons that we reported (2 experiments × 2 list types × 2 ability groups), one of them was not reliable (Experiment 2, younger children, categorized lists) and the other seven were smaller than the acquisition differences were. The important implication, of course, is that although learning-disabled children may have difficulty acquiring information in the first place, especially in learning how to retrieve it, they have far less difficulty retaining information once it is learned. Second, the retention deficits of disabled children were confined to storage-related processes: Storage was more likely to fail during the retention interval for disabled children, and disabled children were less able to restore failed traces across a series of retention tests. Third, although it has been consistently found that disabled children's acquisition deficits are more pronounced for taxonomically related materials than for unrelated materials, we found no evidence of this in our retention data. In fact, the reverse was true, with disabled/nondisabled differences being less marked for categorized materials. This outcome, assuming that it stands the test of replication, is of considerable interest because it would challenge, or at least sharply delimit, one of the most popular explanations of disabled/nondisabled differences in long-term memory. According to this explanation, disabled children are deficient in basic semantic organization, and this deficiency translates into performance difficulties on many memory tasks. If this hypothesis were true, then, naturally, one would expect that learning-disabled children would be at a particular disadvantage in retaining as well as in acquiring taxonomically related materials. They are not and, actually, the opposite is true.

Finally, the chief value of the disintegration/redintegration hypothesis for the study of memory deficits in learning-disabled children is that it allows the study of acquisition and retention deficits to proceed under a unified set of theoretical constructs. Acquisition is viewed as a process whereby features are tightly integrated so as to form traces that stand out against the background of competing memory information, with storage being the initial phase of featural integration and retrieval learning being the terminal phase of featural integration. Retention is said to consist of an initial reversal of the featural integration process, disintegration, across the retention interval, followed by subsequent featural redintegration across a series of retention tests. Our general objective in promulgating the disintegration/redintegration metaphor is to increase the chances that studies of learning-disabled deficits at acquisition will aid in the interpretation of retention deficits and that studies of deficits at retention will aid in the interpretation of acquisition deficits.

References

Bauer, R. H. (1977). Memory processes in children with learning disabilities: Evidence for deficient rehearsal. *Journal of Experimental Child Psychology, 24,* 415–430.

Brainerd, C. J. (1983). Structural invariance in the developmental analysis of learning. In J. Bisanz, G. L. Bisanz, & R. V. Kail, Jr. (Eds.), *Learning in children* (pp. 1–36). New York: Springer-Verlag.

Brainerd, C. J. (1985). Model-based approaches to storage and retrieval development. In C. J. Brainerd & M. Pressley (Eds.), *Basic processes in memory development* (pp. 143–208). New York: Springer-Verlag.

Brainerd, C. J., Desrochers, A., & Howe, M. L. (1981). Stages-of-learning analysis of picture-word effects in associative memory. *Journal of Experimental Psychology: Human Learning and Memory, 7*, 1–14.

Brainerd, C. J., & Howe, M. L. (1980). Developmental invariance in a mathematical model of associative learning. *Child Development, 51*, 349–363.

Brainerd, C. J., & Howe, M. L. (1982). Stages-of-learning analysis of developmental interactions in memory, with illustrations from developmental interactions in picture-word effects. *Developmental Review, 2*, 251–273.

Brainerd, C. J., Howe, M. L., & Desrochers, A. (1982). The general theory of two-stage learning: A mathematical review with illustrations from memory development. *Psychological Bulletin, 91*, 634–665.

Brainerd, C. J., Howe, M. L., & Kingma, J. (1982). An identifiable model of two-stage learning. *Journal of Mathematical Psychology, 26*, 263–293.

Brainerd, C. J., Howe, M. L., Kingma, J., & Brainerd, S. H. (1984). On the measurement of storage and retrieval factors in memory development. *Journal of Experimental Child Psychology, 37*, 478–499.

Brainerd, C. J., Kingma, J., & Howe, M. L. (1985). On the development of forgetting. *Child Development, 56*, 1103–1119.

Brainerd, C. J., Kingma, J., & Howe, M. L. (1986). Long-term memory development and learning disability: Storage and retrieval loci of disabled/nondisabled differences. In S. J. Ceci (Ed.), *Handbook of cognitive, social, and neuropsychological aspects of learning disabilities* (Vol. 1, pp. 161–184). Hillsdale, NJ: Erlbaum.

Brainerd, C. J., & Ornstein, P. A. (in press). Children's memory for witnessed events: The developmental backdrop. In J. L. Doris (Ed.), *The suggestibility of children's recollections with a view toward children's testimony*. Washington, DC: American Psychological Association.

Brainerd, C. J., & Reyna, V. F. (1989). *Development of forgetting, reminiscence, and hypermnesia: A disintegration/redintegration theory.* Manuscript submitted for publication.

Brainerd, C. J., & Reyna, V. F. (1990). Can age x learnability interactions explain the development of forgetting? *Developmental Psychology. 26*, 194–203.

Brainerd, C. J., Reyna, V. F., Kingma, J., & Howe, M. L. (1989). *Development of forgetting and reminiscence: Evaluating the disintegration/redintegration hypothesis.* Manuscript submitted for publication.

Brown, K. F. (1988). *Development of long-term memory retention processes among learning disabled and non-disabled children.* Unpublished doctoral dissertation, University of Arizona, Tucson.

Ceci, S. J., Ross, D. F., & Toglia, M. P. (1987). Suggestibility in children's memory: Psycholegal implications. *Journal of Experimental Psychology: General, 116*, 38–49.

Dallago, M. L. L., & Moely, B. E. (1980). Free recall in boys of normal and poor reading levels as a function of task manipulations. *Journal of Experimental Child Psychology, 30,* 62–78.

Doris, J. (1986). Learning disabilities. In S. J. Ceci (Ed.), *Handbook of cognitive, social, and neuropsychological aspects of learning disabilities* (Vol. 1, pp. 3–54). Hillsdale, NJ: Erlbaum.

Fletcher, J. M., & Morris, R. (1986). Classification of disabled learners: Beyond exclusionary definitions. In S. J. Ceci (Ed.), *Handbook of cognitive, social, and neuropsychological aspects of learning disabilities* (Vol. 1, pp. 55–80). Hillsdale, NJ: Erlbaum.

Greeno, J. G., James, C. T., DaPolito, F. J., & Polson, P. G. (1978). *Associative learning: A cognitive analysis.* Englewood Cliffs, NJ: Prentice-Hall.

Hall, J. W., Humphreys, M. S., & Wilson, K. P. (1983). Differences in long-term retention in relation to early school achievement. *American Journal of Psychology, 96,* 267–287.

Howe, M. L., & Brainerd, C. J. (1989). Development of children's long-term retention. *Developmental Review, 9,* 301–340.

Howe, M. L., Brainerd, C. J., & Kingma, J. (1985). Storage-retrieval processes of normal and learning-disabled children: A stages-of-learning analysis. *Child Development, 56,* 1120–1133.

Howe, M. L., & Hunter, M. A. (1986). Long-term memory in adulthood: An examination of storage/retrieval processes at acquisition and retention. *Developmental Review, 6,* 334–364.

Howe, M. L., O'Sullivan, J. T., Brainerd, C. J., & Kingma, J. (1989). Localizing the development of ability differences in organized memory. *Contemporary Educational Psychology, 14,* 336–356.

Kail, R., & Leonard, L. B. (1986). Sources of word-finding problems in language-impaired children. In S. J. Ceci (Ed.), *Handbook of cognitive, social, and neuropsychological aspects of learning disabilities* (Vol. 1, pp. 185–202). Hillsdale, NJ: Erlbaum.

Lehman, E. B., Mikesell, J. W., & Doherty, S. C. (1985). Long-term retention of information about presentation modality by children and adults. *Memory & Cognition, 13,* 21–28.

Loftus, E. F., & Hoffman, H. G. (1989). Misinformation in memory: The creation of new memories. *Journal of Experimental Psychology: General, 118,* 100–104.

Loftus, E. F., & Loftus, G. R. (1980). On the permanence of stored information in the human brain. *American Psychologist, 35,* 409–420.

Melton, A. (1963). On the permanence of stored information in the human brain. *American Psychologist, 35,* 409–420.

Morrison, F. J., Haith, M., & Kagan, J. (1980). Age trends in recognition memory for pictures: The effects of delay and testing procedure. *Bulletin of the Psychonomic Society, 16,* 480–483.

Ornstein, P. A., & Corsale, K. (1979). Organizational factors in children's memory. In C. R. Puff (Ed.), *Memory organization and structure.* New York: Academic Press.

Siegel, L. S., & Heaven, R. K. (1986). Categorization of learning disabilities. In S. J. Ceci (Ed.), *Handbook of cognitive, social, and neuropsychological aspects of learning disabilities* (Vol. 1, pp. 95–122). Hillsdale, NJ: Erlbaum.

Stanovich, K. E. (1986). Commentary: New beginnings, old problems. *In* S. J. Ceci (Ed.), *Handbook of cognitive, social, and neuropsychological aspects of learning disabilities* (pp. 229–238). Hillsdale, NJ: Erlbaum.

Swanson, L. J. (1984). Semantic and visual memory codes in learning disabled readers. *Journal of Experimental Child Psychology, 37,* 124–140.

Theios, J. (1961). *A three-state Markov model for learning* (Tech. Rep. No. 40). Stanford, CA: Stanford University, Institute for Mathematical Studies in the Social Sciences.

Wong, B., Wong, R., & Foth, D. (1977). Recall and clustering of verbal materials among normal and poor readers. *Bulletin of the Psychonomic Society, 10,* 375–378.

CHAPTER EIGHT

Hemispheric Activation and Arousal Asymmetry in Learning-Disabled Children

John E. Obrzut

I. Introduction

The notion that children with learning disabilities have presumed neuro-developmental anomalies has recently been the focus of much concern. Since we know that acquired deficits in language or cognition occur when there is damage to certain areas of the intact brain, it is likely that developmental dysfunction of these same brain areas may be at the basis of the syndrome known as learning disability. The main assumption is that deficiencies in cognitive tasks such as those requiring reading and language skills are the result of deficient lateralization in this group of children. Despite several critical reviews regarding this assumption (Hiscock & Kinsbourne, 1982; Naylor, 1980; Young & Ellis, 1981), more recent reviews confirm the belief that learning-disabled children have an abnormal or weak pattern of hemispheric lateralization (Corballis, 1983; Obrzut, 1988), as originally suggested by Orton (1937).

The basic data for this conclusion are derived from those studies which compare normal and learning-disabled children on some laterality task as assessed by noninvasive techniques such as dichotic listening, visual half-field, verbal–manual timesharing, or tactile dichhaptic tasks. Generally speaking, the evidence has led to the hypothesis that learning-disabled children are less

Neuropsychological Foundations of Learning Disabilities, copyright © 1991 by Academic Press Inc. All rights of reproduction in any form reserved.

lateralized than normal children (see Bryden, 1988, and Obrzut, 1988, for reviews), although much ambiguity exists among the findings. For example, in the review conducted by Bryden (1988), of 51 studies, which employed some relatively common behavioral measure of cerebral lateralization, 30 were found to show, to a greater or lesser extent, that poor readers were less lateralized than good readers. However, 14 showed no difference between the groups, and 7 reported that poor readers were more lateralized. Thus, it appears the majority of the assessed samples indicate poor readers are less lateralized than normal readers.

From this conclusion at least two issues remain to be answered. The first issue is a theoretical one, while the second issue is a practical one. On a theoretical level, we need to discover why learning-disabled children display a deficient pattern of lateralization, while on a practical level, we need to know how these abnormal patterns of lateralization are related to deficiencies in certain academic tasks such as reading.

The most common and valid technique for assessing auditory laterality is dichotic listening, which is essentially a technique used to measure how the brain processes linguistic and nonlinguistic auditory information. By use of data derived from dichotic listening studies it is becoming possible to infer how the brain processes information and whether deficiencies experienced by learning-disabled children in academic tasks are primarily due to abnormal cerebral organization.

The intent of this chapter is to further our theoretical and practical understanding of brain lateralization in learning-disabled children. Specifically, this chapter will discuss the hemispheric activation or arousal hypothesis of information processing as it relates to this clinical population. Discussion of methodological considerations will precede a summary of the available data derived from the dichotic listening technique used with learning-disabled children, and inferences about the data in relation to overall brain organization will be provided.

A. Basis for Deficient Hemispheric Lateralization

It has been suggested before that learning-disabled children display a deficient pattern of lateralization, which results in their inability to acquire adequate academic skills. Two competing hypotheses have been advanced to account for this weakness in lateralization: a developmental lag hypothesis and an abnormal cerebral organization hypothesis. To summarize, the developmental lag hypothesis suggests that the learning disabled lag behind their normal counterparts in the development of verbal–linguistic skills necessary for the reading task. Thus, language has not fully lateralized to the left hemisphere, leading to weak asymmetries on tests of perceptual laterality. The competing hypothesis suggests that dysfunction in the structure of cerebral organization, either prenatally or during early postnatal development, has led to abnormal cerebral organization. Since learning-disabled children demonstrate deficit performance, that is, weak lateralization, on tasks involving all modalities (auditory, visual, concurrent verbal–manual), I have concluded that the developmental lag hypothesis is quite untenable and am in agreement with Corballis (1983) that abnormal cerebral organization may underlie the learning-disability syndrome (Obrzut, 1988).

Previous summaries of the literature by Bryden (1988), Obrzut, Hynd, and Boliek (1986), and Obrzut (1988) indicate various reasons why one might expect to find abnormal patterns of cerebral lateralization in learning-disabled children relative to normal learners. Generally, it has been thought that learning-disabled children may have expected patterns of brain organization, but due to interhemispheric communication deficits, and/or intra- and interhemispheric resource allocation (Kershner, 1988), or inadequate hemispheric patterns of activation and/or arousal (Obrzut, 1988), appropriate hemispheric specialization is compromised. Thus, learning disability may be a function of unusual laterality patterns or speed of information processing. In recent years, we have presented many empirical summaries on the relationship between reading and other related language skills and hemispheric lateralization and have concluded that a large subset of learning-disabled children experience inadequate hemispheric patterns of cerebral activation and/or arousal which negatively affects their auditory information-processing ability. Nevertheless, despite the many hypotheses generated on this topic, this particular hypothesis merits further empirical examination. The following section will discuss methodological considerations in undertaking such studies.

II. Methodological Considerations

A. Preferred Laterality Measure

While the most popular measures of cerebral lateralization include handedness, dichotic listening, visual half-field, and dichhaptic techniques, according to Bryden (1988) and Obrzut (1988) directed-attention dichotic listening is the most preferred method for measuring receptive speech and nonspeech lateralization in learning-disabled children. The right-ear advantage (REA) in dichotic performance is implicitly assumed to represent the linguistic specialization of the left cerebral hemisphere. This inference is based on the fact that (1) the contralateral pathways are prepotent over ipsilateral auditory pathways, and (2) the left hemisphere is preprogrammed when activated differentially for attending selectively to the right side of space (i.e., right ear). Thus, auditory–verbal information perceived dichotically at the right ear is more readily perceived than the same information perceived at the left ear.

In contrast to free-recall procedures in dichotic listening, which permit strategy and memory effects to exert an influence over performance, dichotic directed attention controls task parameters used by children in their report strategies. Specifically, directed attention requires the subject to report the information received in each ear in a predetermined sequence. In this regard, ear order becomes a counterbalanced grouping factor as one-half of the subjects attend first to the right ear and one-half attend first to the left ear. Thus, the procedure controls for ambient and strategic fluctuations in deployment of attention.

According to Hiscock and Decter (1988) signal-detection procedures also eliminate some of the problems inherent in the free-report paradigm. A signal-detection task in dichotic listening requires the subject to listen for a single target that occurs randomly at either ear. Analysis of the data from this type of experimental design allows the researcher to differentiate between asymmetric sensitivity and asymmetric response bias. Research also has been conducted to demonstrate the simultaneous use of signal-detection and directed-attention methods. Geffen and Sexton (1978) and Sexton and Geffen (1979), for example, instructed children to monitor one ear and to indicate the presence of a target at that ear.

B. Preferred Stimulus Material

Most of the data generated from learning-disabled populations involves the presentation of speech sounds consisting of CV syllables formed with the six stop consonants \b\, \d\, \g\, \p\, \t\, and \k\ and the vowel \a\, or lists of two, three, or four pairs of digits or words. However, according to Bryden (1978), group differences in the REA obtained with list procedures may not reflect group differences in cerebral lateralization. More recent support for this contention has been garnered by Obrzut, Boliek, and Obrzut (1986), who administered four types of dichotic stimuli (words, digits, CV syllables, melodies) in three experimental conditions (free recall, directed left, directed right) to a sample of high academically performing children. Whereas the expected REA for words and CV syllables was found under free recall, the directed conditions produced varied results depending on the nature of the stimuli. Directed condition had no effect on recall of CV syllables but had a dramatic effect on recall of digits. Word stimuli and directed condition interacted to produce an inconsistent pattern of perceptual asymmetries. These findings appear to support the hypothesis that perceptual asymmetries can be strongly influenced by the type of stimulus material used and the effect of the attentional strategy employed.

C. Index of Selective Attention and Laterality

One of the most common conclusions that can be inferred from a review of dichotic listening studies with learning-disabled children is that these children demonstrate a degraded performance when compared to age-matched, normal controls in their overall performance level. According to Bryden (1988) this difference leads to confusion in the interpretation of the data. Most analyses are conducted on the difference between right- and left-ear scores and yield a significant effect if this difference is greater for one group than for the other. However, if the dichotic task is too easy or too hard, differences between the ear scores will be small. On the other hand, if performance is at an intermediate level, both large and small ear differences are likely to exist.

Since we are concerned with the relative distribution of errors and how report bias (shifting) may interact with group laterality differences, a laterality measure that is independent of overall level of accuracy should be used. The selective attention and laterality index (lambda) developed by Bryden and Sprott (1981) is one such signal-detection measure which adjusts for group differences in performance and yields selective attention scores for each ear in addition to an overall laterality score. This logs-odds ratio, or lambda (λ) = (Log)(right correct/left correct) ln (RC/LC), can be used in tests of significance on individual subjects as well as on a group (see for example, Obrzut, Obrzut, Bryden, & Bartels, 1985). In the directed-attention conditions (DL, DR), the lambda ratio of correct responses to intrusion errors reflects the strength of attending to a precued side and thus is considered a measure of selective attention. The lambda laterality index, (Log)(right correct)(left intrusion)/(left correct)(right correct) ln (RC)(LI)/(LC)(RC), provides a single measure of lateralization. This index reflects the relative odds with which left- and right-side items are identified when attending to a particular channel. Thus, attention is controlled and the effect of systematically shifting channels can be estimated in a concise analysis by testing for order effects (see for example, Kershner & Morton, 1990).

D. Criteria for Subject Selection

In order to produce a valid study with regard to cerebral asymmetry and lateralization of function in learning-disabled students, studies need to be carried out with well-defined samples of the target group. Past reviews of this literature have indicated that the heterogeneous nature of these samples selected in most research does not allow for valid generalization across studies (Bryden, 1988; Obrzut, 1988; Obrzut & Boliek, 1988). On a smaller scale, sample selection for laterality studies has proceeded without the consistent use of objective criteria for inclusion. On a more global level, sample selection has included individuals from school as well as clinic/hospital settings. As was indicated elsewhere (Obrzut, 1988), children chosen from the latter institutions are often very different (i.e., more severe) in their presenting symptomatology. Thus, the results from these populations are inconsistent with the results of studies that use school populations. The recommended identifying criteria that these samples must meet in order to be valid are the following:

1. Full-scale IQ (FSIQ) should be within or above normal limits (>85) for both normal and learning-disabled subjects;
2. A learning-disabled subject should evidence a processing deficit in reception, discrimination, association, organization/integration, retention, or application of information, resulting in an achievement deficit on one or more standardized individual tests of reading or mathematics (defined as a criteria of >20 standard score units below FSIQ);
3. Learning-disabled and normal children should be able to read at least at the third-grade level (see Moscovitch, 1987);
4. Normal control subjects should be matched on the basis of chronological age and IQ and also should include younger children matched for reading age as recommended by Backman, Mamen, and Ferguson (1984); and
5. Data should be analyzed separately for boys and girls as well as by handedness groups (see, for example, Obrzut, Conrad & Boliek, 1989; Obrzut, Conrad, Bryden, & Boliek, 1988).

The rationale behind each of these criteria are fairly obvious and do not require further explanation. However, one may consult the papers by Moscovitch (1987) and Bryden (1988) for clarification of these criteria. As noted earlier, with adherence to these recommended criteria for subject selection, the data gathered from learning-disabled children should prove to be less equivocal in nature and prove useful in making stronger assertions about language lateralization.

III. Hemispheric Activation and Arousal Theory

With the advent of the dichotic listening paradigm, it has become possible to generate viable hypotheses concerning the relationship between cerebral laterality and learning disabilities. The early studies using the dichotic technique, without sufficient control over task parameters and response strategies, hypothesized that learning-disabled children were less lateralized than their normal counterparts due to incomplete cerebral dominance or to a lag in development. However, studies using school-age normal and learning-disabled children did not support the notion that differences between the groups in lateralized language processes were due to delayed cerebral dominance or to basic developmental delays (Hynd, Obrzut, Hynd, & Weed, 1979; Obrzut, Hynd, Obrzut, & Leitgeb, 1980; Obrzut, Hynd, Obrzut, & Pirozzolo, 1981). Rather, these studies concluded, albeit post hoc, that deficiencies in lateralization experienced by learning-disabled children were likely due to attentional deficits or dysfunction.

In the decade of the 1980s research reporting overall differences in performance on dichotic tasks led to a new body of literature aimed at examining the effect of selective attention and/or arousal in hemispheric laterality. Based primarily on Kinsbourne's (1970) attentional model of functional asymmetry, researchers have revised the traditional dichotic paradigm by introducing prestimulus cuing (directed attention) in addition to the free-report condition (e.g., Hiscock & Kinsbourne, 1980; Obrzut et al., 1981) in an attempt to control for the effects of variability in selective attention. The major hypothesis generated by this research is that the nondominant hemisphere is suppressed when there is an expectancy for verbal or nonverbal stimuli. Since learning-disabled children are viewed as having potential attentional deficits, they are more likely to be unable to suppress the nondominant hemisphere during information processing.

So what has been the outcome of such studies with learning-disabled children? At least in the early studies conducted by Obrzut and his colleagues (e.g., Obrzut, Hynd, & Obrzut, 1983; Obrzut et al., 1981) normal children demonstrated an REA in all conditions: free recall, directed left, directed right. Learning-disabled children, however, showed variable performance. When attention was directed to the right ear, they dramatically increased their REA; when it was directed to the left ear, a left-ear advantage (LEA) was found. Thus, normal children were not influenced by directed attention, as they were better able to report verbal information from the right ear while simultaneously attending to the left ear. This finding reflects the inherent REA and is consistent with the structural hypothesis predicting that the left hemisphere is prewired for language. When attention was directed, the learning-disabled children performed as if there were minimal interaction between the two cerebral hemispheres in processing the dichotic stimuli.

The results of these studies have indicated that, perhaps, in normal children, the mechanism of suppression of information from the nondominant hemisphere is established. Thus, the normal children cannot willingly attend to verbal stimuli with facility in an incompatible perceptual field. In contrast, the learning-disabled children, because of a failure of the linguistic information to be shared efficiently across the corpus callosum, have not established a mechanism for reciprocal inhibition and divide or direct attention to stimuli presented in either perceptual field. Further, these studies as well as others (e.g., Kershner, Henninger, & Cooke, 1984) have shown that when learning-disabled children are compared to normal children, they can be either more or less lateralized and that the same child can shift lateralization in dichotic performance, as a means of coping with task demands, from a left-hemisphere advantage to a right-hemisphere advantage. Thus, it appears that learning-disabled children show greater changes in brain processing with altered demands of a learning task. Although these studies do not identify a specific anatomical etiology of the learning-disability syndrome, they suggest a task-related attentional dysfunction which may interfere with language processing. That is, recent studies have begun to identify different levels of activation or arousal in learning-disabled children which may interfere with their systems controlling auditory–linguistic attention and lateral orienting. This may help explain two viable competing hypotheses that (1) learning-disabled children have language lateralized to the left hemisphere, as do normal children, but the language mechanisms within the left hemisphere are deficient, and (2) learning-disabled children have normal hemispheric lateral-ization of cognitive functions but have impaired interhemispheric commu-nication.

A. Group Differences in Hemispheric Activation

Some evidence exists that the two cerebral hemispheres can be differen-tially activated or aroused and that this pattern of activation and/or arousal may account for differences in asymmetrical performance (Levine, Banich, & Kim, 1987; Levy & Heller, 1987). The idiosyncratic patterns of arousal asymmetries are thought to influence performance on perceptual laterality tasks such as dichotic listening and are independent of one's underlying direction and/or degree of hemispheric dominance.

To the extent that individual differences in hemispheric arousal exist, they may have implications for the mode of processing that is employed by a subject when stimulus conditions allow performance to be controlled by either cerebral hemisphere (O'Boyle & Hellige, 1989). Thus, two individuals or two groups (normal and learning disabled) with the same underlying pattern of cerebral dominance may vary in the extent to which one or both hemispheres are aroused and/or suppressed with the introduction of relevant stimulus information. From this perspective, learning-disabled children would not be thought to suffer from a fixed laterality deficit, but rather would experience an arousal bias or attentional deficit which interferes with left-hemisphere lan-guage processes by over- or underengaging either hemisphere.

Several studies have attempted to control various task parameters and strategies used by children in performing dichotic listening tasks so that the neuropsychological mechanisms underlying these performances can be better identified. Such studies have introduced more neurological variance by using homogeneous clinical groups such as left handers and bilinguals. The dichotic tasks have controlled for type of stimuli, attentional and memory factors, spatial localization, and spatial orientation of the subject. In this manner the issue of whether all verbal and nonverbal tasks measure the same underlying REA or LEA has begun to be addressed. More importantly, these studies have begun to investigate the dynamics of activation asymmetries (i.e., the role of attention) and its relation to cerebral processing in learning-disabled children.

IV. Data Analysis and Conceptualization

A review of past dichotic studies that have used the directed-attention paradigm with learning-disabled children has indicated that these children exhibit a degraded performance when compared to age-matched, normal controls in their strength of processing auditory receptive language unilaterally in the left hemisphere (Obrzut, 1988). However, by further controlling subject and task parameters, the recent results are consistent with the view that an attentional dysfunction which interferes with left-hemisphere language processing is primarily responsible for the impaired performance of learning-disabled children. This conclusion is derived from a series of studies which examined the interactions of attentional strategy effects with lateralized processing by learning-disabled children. Specifically, these studies have compared the verbal processing ability of learning-disabled children (1) in relation to performance by other presumed anomalous groups of bilingual and left-handed children (Obrzut et al., 1988), (2) in relation to various task parameters such as visual–spatial lateral orientation (Boliek, Obrzut, & Shaw, 1988), and (3) in relation to stimuli differing in physical attributes (Boliek, Obrzut, & Bryden, 1989) and nonverbal stimuli (Obrzut, Boliek, & Bryden, 1990; Obrzut et al., 1989).

A. Theoretical Models of Maladaptive Laterality

Presumably these studies as well as others have led Kershner and Morton (1990) to formulate more specific learning-disability models of maladaptive lateralization. Table I summarizes these models and indicates the associative predictions with dichotic listening data. The authors refer to the first model as the poor structural lateralization model (PSL). This model implies that the dichotic test measures a hard-wired neural substrate for linguistic processing and that language is represented more bilaterally at the level of cerebral structure in learning-disabled children. Some support for this model was derived from a study by Obrzut et al. (1985), who compared a group of auditory–linguistic disabled readers to a control group of above-average readers matched on the basis of chronological age, gender, and right handed-

TABLE I Learning-Disability Models of Maladaptive Lateralization and Predicted Directed-Attention Dichotic Listening Outcomes

Model	Predicted outcome
Poor structural lateralization (PSL)	Reduced overall REA due to combined increased recall in left-attend condition and decreased recall in right-attend condition
Right-hemisphere excessive activation (RHA)	Reduced overall REA due to increased recall in left-attend condition with no reduction in recall in right-attend condition
Left-hemisphere excessive activation (LHA)	Enhanced overall REA due to decreased recall in left-attend condition with no increase in recall in right-attend condition
Bidirectional excessive hemisphere activation (BHA)	Reduced or enhanced overall REA due to combined dysfunctional effects of RHA and LHA models, that is, either increased recall in left-attend condition with no reduction in right-attend condition or decreased recall in left-attend condition with no increase in recall in right-attend condition

ness. The learning-disabled children were found to be poorer in reporting CV syllables when precued to attend to the right dichotic channel and were better in attending selectively to the left channel. Consequently, both selective attention conditions contributed to their overall diminished REA. In the context of the PSL model, the degraded bilateral performance by the learning-disabled group could indicate a less established structural organization.

Kershner and Morton (1990) refer to the second model as the right-hemisphere excessive-activation model (RHA). This model has its basis in the hypothesis that learning-disabled children may fail to suppress the right hemisphere during verbal tasks. This model implies that the dichotic test measures hemispheric activation coexisting with the underlying structural system and that, unlike the PSL model, the cortical structure for language in learning-disabled children is normal in its geographical distribution but weaker in its ability to inherit attentional bias and subsequent right-hemisphere engagement in verbal processing. The RHA model is similar to the PSL model in that both assume that right-hemisphere activation interferes with the efficiency of left-hemisphere language processing. However, unlike the PSL model, which entails a structurally fixed reduction in the degree of left-hemisphere specialization, the RHA model assumes a dynamic difference in the balance of activation between hemispheres during linguistic processing. In terms of dichotic listening, while both models predict a smaller REA in learning-disabled children, the RHA model predicts that the diminished REA will result from an increase in correct recall from the directed left condition coupled with fewer intrusions from the right ear, without interference with selective report from the directed right condition.

Support for this model is derived from two studies in which learning-disabled children demonstrated a lower REA than control children (Boliek *et al.*, 1988; Obrzut *et al.*, 1988). However, in these experiments there were no group differences in recall from the directed right condition. The diminished REA was produced solely by the superior ability of the learning-disabled children to recall CV and CVC stimuli in the directed left condition (see also Hugdahl & Andersson, 1987). Additional support for the RHA model was obtained in the Obrzut *et al.* (1988) study which demonstrated that left-handed children were susceptible to attentional shifts in unilateral processing similar to learning-disabled children. Furthermore, Boliek *et al.* (1988) showed that lateralized performance by learning-disabled children was influenced more by the verbal nature of the attentional strategy than by the hemispatial nature of the strategy.

The third model as described by Kershner and Morton (1990) is referred to as the left-hemisphere excessive-activation model (LHA). This model implies that the dichotic test measures hemispheric activation coexisting with an underlying structural system and that the cortical structure for language in learning-disabled children is normal in its geographical distribution but that an unusually high level of left-hemisphere activation is necessary to carry out language tasks. In comparison to control children learning-disabled children are hypothesized to generate heightened levels of left-hemisphere involvement with a concomitant suppression of right-hemisphere involvement. In this view, learning-disabled children may be too lateralized. Unlike the previous models, the LHA model hypothesizes exactly opposite predictions for dichotic performance between learning-disabled and normal control children.

Support for this model is derived from Aylward (1984), who found a larger REA in two subtypes of dyslexic subjects (dysphonetic and dyseidetic) which was produced by their poorer ability to recall post-cued, digit names from the left channel. Studies employing CV syllables as stimuli also have demonstrated a stronger REA by learning-disabled than control children (Obrzut *et al.*, 1981, 1983). The learning-disabled children recalled more CV stimuli than control children from both the left and the right channels in the directed-attention conditions. Aside from dichotic listening studies the LHA model has additional support from an electrophysiological experiment (Shucard, Cummings, & McGee, 1984) and from a regional cerebral blood flow study with adult dyslexic subjects (Hynd, Hynd, Sulliven, & Kingsbury, 1987).

A fourth model described by Kershner and Morton (1990) is referred to as the bidirectional excessive hemisphere activation model (BHA). This model presumes that an instability in left-hemisphere language processing in learning-disabled children may cause them to be vulnerable to bidirectional attentional demands which may promote excessive activation in either the left or the right hemisphere. The assumption is that the overabundance of arousal and/or activation would produce less efficient processing and make it more difficult to "reallocate" the focus of processing between separate neural areas. The BHA model implies that the dichotic test measures hemispheric activation coexisting with an underlying structural system, and that the cortical structure for language in learning-disabled children is normal in its geographical distribution but that hemispatial attentional and response requirements of verbal tasks can induce both weaker- or stronger-than-normal lateralized processing. The BHA model combines the left- and right-hemisphere dysfunctions in attentional control of the LHA and RHA models in a more integrative fashion. Thus, according to the BHA model, the difference in lateralized performance between learning-disabled and normal children will depend on the asymmetrical attentional, processing, and response demands of the dichotic task.

Some support for this model was obtained by Boliek *et al.* (1988), who found that while right hemispatial orientation increased the magnitude of the REA for both control and learning-disabled subjects, left hemispatial orientation increased the magnitude of the left-ear report only in learning-disabled subjects. Conversely, whereas focused attention to the right ear also increased left-hemisphere efficiency for both groups of children, focused attention to the left ear produced *symmetrical* functioning by learning-disabled subjects. Thus, hemispatial and asymmetrically focused attention strategies interact with structural mechanisms in producing the observed REA in dichotic listening and do so differentially for learning-disabled children. A more direct test of hypotheses associated with the BHA model was provided by Kershner and Morton (1990). In two experiments, these authors assessed the effects of priming bias on dichotic listening performance and found, independent of attentional bias, that learning-disabled children were more strongly lateralized than control children. More importantly, although the net effect was much stronger when shifting from left to right, the learning-disabled children were poorer shifting attention bidirectionally between ears, which produced both weaker and stronger REAs compared to normal children. That is, in left-ear recall the learning-disabled children were poorer generally compared to normal children, but they were equivalent in right-ear recall when the right ear was monitored first. Thus, Kershner and Morton (1990) concluded that these results support the BHA model over the other models.

Regardless of the particular model one subscribes to, the results support the view that, in contrast to a fixed laterality deficit, learning-disabled children experience an attentional dysfunction which interferes with left-hemisphere language processing by overengaging either hemisphere. In addition, the pronounced asymmetry in the relative magnitude of the ear effects at each channel also suggests greater interference in learning-disabled children between the systems controlling auditory–linguistic attention and lateral orienting. As a further test of these hypotheses, several recent studies have begun to identify trends in listening asymmetries in relation to handedness, gender, reading ability, and attentional mechanisms on verbal and nonverbal processing tasks.

B. Recent Laterality Studies

In one such study, Obrzut et al. (1989) assessed the cerebral lateralization of left- and right-handed good readers in contrast to left- and right-handed reading-disabled children using verbal (CV) and nonverbal (tonal) stimuli. The results indicated that males outperformed females across stimuli and dichotic selective-attention conditions (free recall, directed left, directed right) regardless of handedness, and all subjects recalled more tonal stimuli than CV stimuli. More importantly, the expected REA (left-hemisphere processing) was found for CV stimuli only by right-handed good readers across all three dichotic conditions. The left-handed good readers and left-handed reading-disabled children were left-ear dominant in free recall and in the directed-left condition but were right-ear dominant in the directed-right condition. Conversely, right-handed reading-disabled children produced an REA during free-recall and directed-right conditions but were left-ear dominant in the directed-left condition. In contrast, a significant LEA (right-hemisphere processing) was found for tonal stimuli across all dichotic conditions for all four groups. Thus, these findings lend support to the hypothesis that attentional factors have a greater influence on auditory processing of verbal than nonverbal stimuli for various groups of children and also suggest reversed or bilateralized processing abilities for language in familial left-handed children. In essence, right-hemisphere processing is generally unaffected by left-hemisphere dysfunction and neither handedness nor attentional manipulation affects such processing for any of the groups. This strongly suggests that the source of the reading-disabled child's difficulties may be primarily in the inability of either the left or the right hemisphere to assume a dominant role in the processing of only verbal information.

In a further attempt to specify the nature of the interaction between left- or right-hemisphere processing and attention with learning-disabled children, Obrzut et al. (1990) studied verbal and nonverbal dichotic performance in children under different attentional and stimulus conditions concurrently.

The verbal material consisted of CV stimuli presented with an additional spectral separation (i.e., male-voiced CV versus female-voiced CV simultaneously presented). This separation of competing messages differing only in physical attributes (voice) allowed for the examination of spatial separation of stimuli and was speculated to provide a more direct test of an attentional-deficit hypothesis. The nonverbal stimuli consisted of simple square wave tones (STs). Simple STs had frequencies corresponding to the six notes in the octave between C4 and C5 on the major scale D (297 Hz), E (330 Hz), F (352 Hz), G (396 Hz), A (440 Hz), B (495 Hz).

The results from this experiment seem to suggest that for learning-disabled children spatial separation of stimuli in conjunction with divided attention can affect the degree and/or direction of cerebral specialization as hypothesized. Figures 1 and 2 show, for the free-recall condition only, that

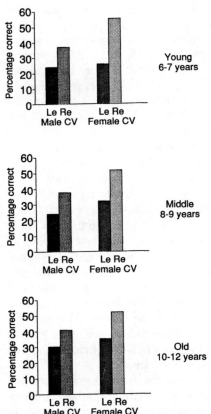

FIGURE 1   Percentage left- and right-ear free-recall reports of CV stimuli across age for control subjects.

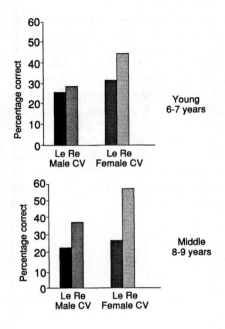

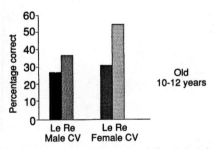

FIGURE 2 Percentage left- and right-ear free-recall reports of CV stimuli across age for learning-disabled subjects.

while the REA was found across both control and learning-disabled groups and for male-voiced and female-voiced stimuli, left-ear and right-ear reports were greater for the female-voiced stimuli. Also, the REA was greater for older learning-disabled children but smaller for younger learning-disabled children. This in turn arises because control children accurately produced more left-ear but not right-ear reports with advancing age, while learning-disabled children increased their right-ear but not their left-ear reports with age. Furthermore, ear reports of the younger children were less influenced by attentional and voice manipulation, whereas older children were more sensitive to such manipulation, but differently depending on sex.

For nonverbal processing, as shown in Fig. 3, much larger LEAs were found for control children than for learning-disabled children and this effect was independent of development. However, young learning-disabled children appeared to be bilateral for processing tonal stimuli whereas older learning-disabled children demonstrated lateralized performance with such stimuli.

Figure 4 shows the number of control and learning-disabled children that changed ear advantages when reporting CV versus tonal stimuli compared with subjects who maintained the same ear advantage for both stimuli. From these results it was concluded that control children are "oppositely lateralized" for the two types of stimuli, whereas learning-disabled children show a general processing bias to the "same hemisphere" regardless of type of stimuli and attentional instruction. These findings provide further evidence of

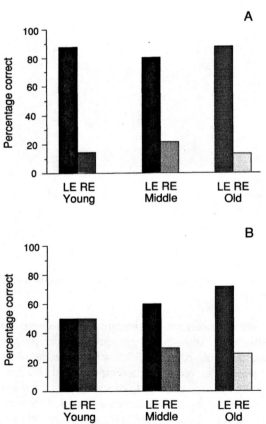

FIGURE 3 Percentage left- and right-ear reports of tonal stimuli across age for (A) control and (B) learning-disabled subjects.

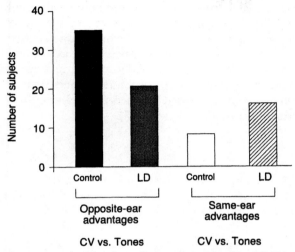

FIGURE 4 Number of control and learning-disabled subjects that changed ear advantage when reporting CV and tonal stimuli versus those who maintained the same ear advantage for both stimuli.

the complex relationship among hemisphere asymmetry, reading ability, and attentional biases than is generally acknowledged in the literature.

V. Concluding Remarks

Through systematic study with listening asymmetries, the relationship between cognitive deficits in learning-disabled children and cerebral organization is becoming clearer. Based on a review of studies that have used the dichotic selective-attention paradigm, it can be inferred that learning-disabled children, in comparison to age-matched, normal control children, are deficient in their ability to process auditory receptive language unilaterally in the left hemisphere. Clearly, the systematic control of subject and task parameters has allowed for more direct tests of specific learning-disability models of abnormal lateralization. These particular studies have indicated it is likely that right-hemisphere attentional activation interferes with left-hemisphere verbal processing in learning-disabled children. In addition, learning-disabled children experience a greater imbalance in activation between hemispheres suggestive of an attentional-control dysfunction. Thus, hemispheric processes involved in selective-attention strategies as employed in the dichotic task may share common neuronal mechanisms with cognitive processes that are important for successful completion of academic tasks. The fact that control children were found to be "oppositively lateralized" for verbal and nonverbal stimuli whereas learning-disabled children exhibited a general processing bias to the "same hemisphere" regardless of stimuli necessitates further study of activation and attention mechanisms in this population. Future research should investigate whether learning-disabled children experience an imbalance in activation between hemispheres or have dysfunctional interconnected attention systems. This issue is in part being addressed by others using electrophysiological measures (see Harter, this volume, Chapter 17).

Acknowledgment

I wish to thank Carol Boliek for her editorial comments and suggestions on an earlier draft of this chapter. Her insight into this research area was invaluable to this writing and greatly appreciated.

References

Aylward, E. (1984). Lateral asymmetry in subgroups of dyslexic children. *Brain & Language, 22,* 221–231.

Backman, J. E., Mamen, M., & Ferguson, H. B. (1984). Reading level design: Conceptual and methodological issues in reading research. *Psychological Bulletin, 96,* 560–568.

Boliek, C. A., Obrzut, J. E., & Bryden, M. P. (1989, February). *Effects of spatial location and focused attention on dichotic listening with learning- and non-disabled children.* Paper presented at the Seventeenth annual meeting of the International Neuropsychological Society, Vancouver, British Columbia, Canada.

Boliek, C. A., Obrzut, J. E., & Shaw, D. (1988). The effects of hemispatial and asymmetrically focused attention on dichotic listening with normal and learning-disabled children. *Neuropsychologia, 26,* 417–423.

Bryden, M. P. (1978). Strategy effects in the assessment of hemispheric asymmetry. In G. Underwood (Ed.), *Strategies of information processing.* London: Academic Press.

Bryden, M. P. (1988). Does laterality make any difference? Thoughts on the relation between cerebral asymmetry and reading. In D. L. Molfese & S. J. Segalowitz (Eds.), *Brain lateralization in children: Developmental implications* (pp. 509–525). New York: Guilford Press.

Bryden, M. P., & Sprott, D. A. (1981). Statistical determination of degree of laterality. *Neuropsychologia, 19,* 571–681.

Corballis, M. C. (1983). *Human laterality.* New York: Academic Press.

Geffen, G., & Sexton, M. A. (1978). The development of auditory strategies of attention. *Developmental Psychology, 14,* 11–17.

Hiscock, M., & Decter, M. H. (1988). Dichotic listening in children. In K. Hugdahl (Ed.), *Handbook of dichotic listening: Theory, methods and research* (pp. 431–473). Chichester, London: Wiley.

Hiscock, M., & Kinsbourne, M. (1980). Asymmetries of selective listening and attention switching in children. *Developmental Psychology, 16,* 70–82.

Hiscock, M., & Kinsbourne, M. (1982). Laterality and dyslexia: A critical review. *Annals of Dyslexia, 32,* 177–226.

Hugdahl, K., & Andersson, L. (1987). Dichotic listening and reading acquisition in children: A one-year follow-up. *Journal of Clinical and Experimental Neuropsychology, 9,* 631–649.

Hynd, G. W., Obrzut, J. E., Weed, W., & Hynd, C. R. (1979). Development of cerebral dominance: Dichotic listening asymmetry in normal and learning disabled children. *Journal of Experimental Child Psychology, 28,* 445–454.

Hynd, G. W., Hynd, C. R., Sullivan, H. G., & Kingsbury, T., Jr. (1987). Regional cerebral blood flow ($_r$CBF) in developmental dyslexic: Activation during reading in a surface and deep dyslexic. *Journal of Learning Disabilities, 20,* 294–300.

Kershner, J. R. (1988). Dual processing models of learning disability. In D. L. Molfese & S. J. Segalowitz (Eds.), *Brain lateralization in children: Developmental implications* (pp. 527–546). New York: Guilford Press.

Kershner, J. R., Henninger, P., & Cooke, W. (1984). Written recall induces a right hemisphere linguistic advantage for digits in dyslexic children. *Brain & Language, 21,* 105–122.

Kershner, J. R., & Morton, L. L. (1990). Directed attention dichotic listening in reading disabled children: A test of four models of maladaptive lateralization. *Neuropsychologia, 28,* 181–198.

Kinsbourne, M. (1970). The cerebral basis of lateral asymmetries in attention. *Acta Psychologica, 33,* 193–201.

Levine, S. C., Banich, M. T., & Kim, H. (1987). Variations in arousal asymmetry: Implications for face processing. In D. Ottoson (Ed.), *Duality and unity of the brain: Unified functioning and specialization of the hemispheres* (pp. 207–222). London: Macmillan.

Levy, J., & Heller, W. (1987). Diversities in right-handers in left-hemisphere processing. In D. Ottoson (Ed.), *Duality and unity of the brain: Unified functioning and specialization of the hemispheres* (pp. 71–82). London: Macmillan.

Moscovitch, M. (1987). Lateralization of language in children with developmental dyslexia: A critical review of visual half-field studies. In D. Ottoson (Ed.), *Duality and unity of the brain: Unified functioning and specialization of the hemispheres* (pp. 324–346). London: Macmillan.

Naylor, H. (1980). Reading disability and lateral asymmetry: An information processing analysis. *Psychological Bulletin, 87,* 531–545.

O'Boyle, M., & Hellige, J. (1989). Cerebral hemisphere asymmetry and individual differences in cognition. *Learning and Individual Differences, 1,* 7–35.

Obrzut, J. E. (1988). Deficient lateralization in learning-disabled children: Developmental lag or abnormal cerebral organization? In D. L. Molfese & S. J. Segalowitz (Eds.), *Brain lateralization in children: Developmental implications* (pp. 567–589). New York: Guilford Press.

Obrzut, J. E., & Boliek, C. A. (1988). Dichotic listening: Evidence from learning and reading disabled children. In K. Hugdahl (Ed.), *Handbook of dichotic listening: Theory, methods and research* (pp. 475–511). Chichester, London: Wiley.

198 / JOHN E. OBRZUT

Obrzut, J. E., Boliek, C. A., & Bryden, M. P. (1990, February). *Focused attention and voice frequency change in dichotic listening: A developmental analysis of verbal and nonverbal processing*. Paper presented at the Eighteenth annual meeting of the International Neuropsychological Society, Kissimmee, FL.

Obrzut, J. E., Boliek, C. A., & Obrzut, A. (1986). The effect of stimulus type and directed attention on dichotic listening with children. *Journal of Experimental Child Psychology, 41,* 198–209.

Obrzut, J. E., Conrad, P. F., & Boliek, C. A. (1989). Verbal and nonverbal auditory processing among left- and right-handed good readers and reading-disabled children. *Neuropsychologia, 27,* 1357–1371.

Obrzut, J. E., Conrad, P. F., Bryden, M. P., & Boliek, C. A. (1988). Cued dichotic listening with right-handed, left-handed, bilingual and learning-disabled children. *Neuropsychologia, 26,* 119–131.

Obrzut, J. E., Hynd, G. W., & Boliek, C. A. (1986). Lateralized asymmetries in learning-disabled children's processing. In S. J. Ceci (Ed.), *Handbook of cognitive, social, and neuropsychological aspects of learning disability* (pp. 441–474). Hillsdale, NJ: Erlbaum.

Obrzut, J. E., Hynd, G. W., & Obrzut, A. (1983). Neuropsychological assessment of learning disabilities: A discriminant analysis. *Journal of Experimental Child Psychology, 35,* 46–55.

Obrzut, J. E., Hynd, G. W., Obrzut, A., & Leitgeb, J. L. (1980). Time-sharing and dichotic listening asymmetry in normal and learning-disabled children. *Brain & Language, 11,* 181–194.

Obrzut, J. E., Hynd, G. W., Obrzut, A., & Pirozzolo, F. J. (1981). Effect of directed attention on cerebral asymmetries in normal and learning disabled children. *Developmental Psychology, 17,* 118–125.

Obrzut, J. E., & Obrzut, A., Bryden, M. P., & Bartels, S. G. (1985). Information processing and speech lateralization in learning disabled children. *Brain & Language, 25,* 87–101.

Orton, S. T. (1937). *Reading, writing and speech problems in children*. New York: Norton.

Sexton, M. A., & Geffen, G. (1979). Development of three strategies of attention in dichotic monitoring. *Developmental Psychology, 15,* 299–310.

Shucard, D., Cummings, K., & McGee, M. (1984). Event-related brain potentials differentiate normal and disabled readers. *Brain & Language, 21,* 318–334.

Young, A. W., & Ellis, A. W. (1981). Asymmetry of cerebral hemisphere function in normal and poor readers. *Psychological Bulletin, 89,* 183–190.

CHAPTER NINE

Cognitive Models of Developmental Reading Disorders

Christopher H. Chase
Paula Tallal

I. Introduction

Cognitive psychology is experiencing a paradigm shift with the advent of connectionist or distributed models of cognitive processes (Mandler, 1985). In place of serial box models, made up of modular symbol-oriented subsystems connected by arrows, several researchers (Hinton & Anderson, 1981; McClelland, Rumelhart, & Hinton, 1986) have begun to model information-processing and memory functions through the use of a very large number of simple processing elements that are highly interconnected and simultaneously interactive. Traditional serial box reading models have been challenged by evidence from many adult studies which question the sequential framework of their processing systems and modular designs (e.g., Rumelhart, 1977). In response to these problems, new reading models with parallel distributed processing (PDP) features have been designed (McClelland & Rumelhart, 1981; Seidenberg & McClelland, 1989).

Little of this new modeling work has been extended to the study of reading development. Most investigations of young normal and impaired readers have focused either on the study of reading error patterns (Boder, 1973; Doehring & Hoshko, 1977; Temple, 1984) or on the analysis of neuropsychological correlations (Mattis, French, & Rapin, 1975; Petrauskas & Rourke, 1979) without making reference to models of reading behavior (Lovett, 1984). Without a theoretical framework to guide the interpretation

Neuropsychological Foundations of Learning Disabilities, copyright © 1991 by Academic Press Inc. All rights of reproduction in any form reserved.

of the data, it is difficult to build a bridge between our understanding of the structural abnormalities found in the dyslexic brain (Galaburda, Sherman, Rosen, Aboitiz, & Geschwind, 1985) and the functional impairments associated with specific reading disabilities (see Coltheart, 1982).

This chapter will familiarize the reader with some of the thoretical issues surrounding the modeling of reading development. A well-known, dual-route model of word recognition will be reviewed and its application to normal and impaired reading development discussed. Evidence and arguments against its serial box approach will be presented. Then a brief introduction to some of the PDP models of word recognition will be presented and results of their application to normal and dyslexic reading development discussed.

II. Dual-Route Reading Model

A. Serial Box Design

Traditional reading models (Newcombe & Marshall, 1984) have employed a sequential, modular design in which processing subsystems provide highly specialized functions that break down the reading task into different components (see Fig. 1). These models have sometimes been referred to as dual-route systems, drawing attention to the fact that parallel but independent processing routes are present to handle familiar and unfamiliar verbal material. The lexical system (labeled A) visually decodes the word and accesses pronunciation and meaning by way of a look-up lexical table. The phonologic system (labeled B) segments pseudowords or ones not in the lexicon into orthographic segments that are then phonologically translated using grapheme–phoneme conversion (GPC) rules based on functionally spelling units acquired through experience. Phonemic units are then blended together for pronunciation.

Reading in the dual-route model is strictly a bottom-up process where information moves through a series of stages of analysis in which processing at any level can only affect the immediate level above. Information is always analyzed by a sequentially ordered set of operations that proceed in computer-like fashion. Activation in the two routes remains discrete and is not distributed outside of the proper channel. Cross-talk between lexical and phonologic systems does not exist in current models. Each system handles the letter string differently. Presumably, the lexical system analyzes the letter string and searches its memory register until the proper orthographic address is found and meaning is attached. Unfamiliar words or nonwords produce no activation. Simultaneously, the phonologic system decodes the string using GPC rules. In addition, activation is not distributed within a system, so consequently orthographic neighbors that may look or sound like the word input

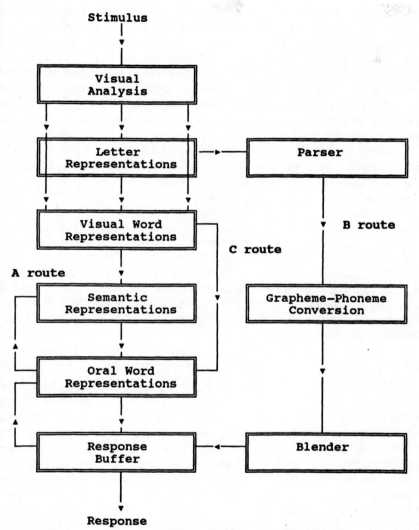

FIGURE 1　The dual-route model of reading.

may be scanned as part of the lexical or phonologic addressing procedures but are not activated by the system.

The justification for using modular subsystems for reading (lexical versus phonologic) comes from several sources. First, pseudowords take longer to read than words (Frederiksen & Kroll, 1976). Since pseudoword pronunciation cannot be retrieved directly from memory, it must be strategically constructed in another way that requires more time.

Second, irregular or exception words, those whose pronunciation is difficult to predict from the spelling-to-sound rules of the language, for example, words such as *pint* where the long "i" vowel sound is unique among words that end in *int*, take longer to read than regular words (Baron, 1979; Stanovich & Bauer, 1978). Because lexical information for a regular word is consistent with the phonologic analysis, processing is thought to take less time. However, conflicting results between the two mechanisms, which occur with exception words, must be resolved by the output system, resulting in more processing time.

Third, studies of acquired dyslexia in adults suggest a dissociation in performance between words and nonwords. On the one hand, *surface dyslexia* patients retain the ability to orally read familiar, regular words and pseudo-words with greater accuracy than matched irregular words. Since the lexical system contains the pronunciation specific to an irregular word, as the GPC rules would regularize the way the word sounds, this performance patterns suggests damage which is specific to the lexical system (Coltheart, Masterson, Byng, Prior, & Riddoch, 1984; J. M. Holmes, 1978; Marshall & Newcombe, 1973). On the other hand, the ability to read pseudowords is more impaired than the ability to read familiar words for a *phonologic* dyslexic, suggesting that they predominately read by lexical routes because of damage to their phono-logic system (Beauvois & Derouesne, 1979; Shallice & Warrington, 1980; Temple & Marshall, 1983).

B. Sequential Model of Reading Development

Most theories about the acquisition of reading skills adopt the same structural design and processing procedures used in the dual-route reading model. The learning process is described as a series of sequential, hierarchical stages. Frith (1985) identifies three phases in reading development: logo-graphic, alphabetic, and orthographic. A logographic strategy involves reading by the visual or graphic features of the letters and words, relying on visual memory to develop a "sight vocabulary." Alphabetic reading involves phonologic decoding of GPC through systematic analysis. Orthographic reading uses morpheme units organized into a syllabus and available for systematic recombination as needed. The difference between alphabetic and orthographic reading involves the size and type of unit used for decoding.

In terms of the sequential, modular reading model (Fig. 1), logographic reading involves the lexical route. The alphabetic and orthographic strategies can be related to the phonologic mechanisms as described above, although Frith defined orthographic reading as being nonphonologic and therefore part of a separate system associated with the analysis of word components (Shallice & McCarthy, 1985).

According to Frith, reading skills are acquired in a strict sequential order which progresses from logographic to orthographic procedures, each stage building on the previous one. At first a child develops a sight vocabulary. Then phonemic awareness (I. Y. Liberman, Shankweiler, Liberman, Fowler, & Fischer, 1977) and formal training produce a transition into alphabetic reading, a stage of great importance for developing fluent reading skills (Gough & Hillinger, 1980; I. Liberman, 1982). Finally, orthographic reading strategies are adopted as children increase their syllabus, allowing them to speed up the decoding process by using larger morphemic units.

C. Dual-Route Model of Developmental Dyslexia

Studies of feature-detection mechanisms of dyslexic children have produced inconclusive and controversial results. Although some attention was given to sequencing and reversal errors (was/saw, b/d) as evidence of possible feature-detection dysfunction (see Stanovich, 1982), systematic studies of the distribution of error types have indicated that dyslexic patterns of mistakes are no different from those of normal developing readers of the same skill level (Cohn & Stricker, 1979; Harman, 1982; Schlieper, 1980; Vellutino, 1979). Other studies involving backward masking and temporal-integration tasks have suggested that dyslexic children process both visual (DiLollo, Hanson, & McIntyre, 1983; Lovegrove, Martin & Slaghuis, 1986) and auditory (Tallal, 1980) information more slowly, resulting in a bottleneck of incomplete processing and impaired perception. However, conflicting results (Arnett & DiLollo, 1979; D. Fisher & Frankfurter, 1977) and alternative explanations have been given that suggest that differences in maturation, criterion shifts, attention and motivation, and changing mechanisms of masking may account for these findings (Ericksen, 1980; Lawrence, Kee, & Hellige, 1980; Vellutino, 1979). Despite these conflicting interpretations, the fact remains that dyslexic children are consistently slower than normal readers on perceptual-input and motor-output tasks (Tallal, 1988).

The lexical system of most dyslexic children appears to develop normally. Many studies using simple memory tasks with words, have found dyslexic children have no difficulty storing semantic information. Several paired-associate learning experiments found dyslexics to learn at a normal rate with word–word pairs (Budoff & Quinlan, 1964), spoken words and letter-like symbols (Firth, 1972; Jorm, 1977), and spoken words and visual digit strings (Jorm, 1981). D. Holmes and McKeever (1979) also reported adolescent dyslexics had no difficulty recognizing written words previously presented to them.

However, several psycholinguistic studies have suggested that lexical impairments do exist within the developmentally dyslexic population. J. M. Holmes (1973) described four developmental cases of surface dyslexia, evidenced by relatively good performance with regular words and pseudowords but greater difficulty with reading irregular matched words.

Temple (1984, 1985) recently described four new cases of developmental surface dyslexia that showed consistent regularity effects. In addition, she reported two types of error patterns, characteristic of the syndrome. First, the majority of errors (64% in one case) were neologistic (nonwords) rather than paralexic (resembling a word). This pattern was thought to occur because a phonologic reading strategy was primarily being used without lexical access to check the validity of the pronunciations. Second, homophone confusions (mistaking two words that are pronounced alike, e.g., thrown/throne) were common because phonologic mechanisms have no way to tell them apart. In three of the cases, Temple (1985) also reported a variety of phonologic impairments.

In a larger study of 32 dyslexic boys, Baddeley, Logie, and Ellis (1988) reported the children's performance to resemble surface dyslexia because of poorly developed sight vocabularies. However, the dyslexic pattern of reading performance was remarkably similar to a control group matched on reading age, suggesting that the process of reading development in normal children may provide a better model than the performance of acquired dyslexic adults.

Substantial evidence indicates the phonologic mechanism of most dyslexic readers functions poorly. Better readers are more adversely affected by the phonologic ambiguity of items, suggesting that poorer readers may have more difficulty accessing phonologic codes (Mann, Liberman, & Shankweiler, 1980; Shankweiler, Liberman, Mark, Fowler, & Fischer, 1979). Several studies have found dyslexic readers have difficulty reading nonsense words (Done & Miles, 1978; Gascon & Goodglass, 1970; Otto, 1961; Vellutino, Harding, Phillips, & Steger, 1975). Studies of error patterns on such tasks revealed that normal novice readers attempt to phonologically encode the stimuli, making more neologistic mistakes, whereas dyslexics relied more on their lexical system, as evidenced by their tendency to make paralexic errors and give real words as responses (Vellutino, Steger, Harding, & Phillips, 1975). Dyslexic readers also have been shown to be very poor at utilizing their phonologic systems to make GPC as evidenced by their inability to orally read pseudowords (Firth, 1972; Jorm, 1981; Snowling, 1980). Tallal (1980) has reported a strong relationship between pseudoword reading and the rate of nonverbal auditory processing, suggesting that deficits in the temporal analysis of auditory information may interfere with the development of the phonologic system for some children. Three developmental phonologic dyslexic cases, with psycholinguistic profiles which are similar to the acquired syndrome, also have been reported (Temple, 1984; Temple & Marshall, 1983).

At least two other reading-impaired subtypes have been reported (see Malatesha & Dougan, 1982, for a comprehensive review), however, these subtypes have difficulty finding a place in the dual-route system. The first has been described as a perceptual–motor deficit as demonstrated by relatively poor performance on visual-pattern recognition or figure-drawing tasks but normal performance on language measures (see Mattis, 1978; Satz, Morris, & Fletcher, 1985). The second has been described as an "unexpected" subtype (Satz & Morris, 1981), with normal performance on both language and visuospatial tasks. As the dual-route system emphasizes the linguistic aspects of reading, neither of these two subtypes can be easily accounted for within its processing framework.

In summary, although recent studies have drawn attention to a developmental dyslexic subtype with lexical impairments, most of the evidence points to a breakdown in the phonologic mechanisms of dyslexic children. Practice in "phonics" may improve their ability to use spelling-to-sound correspondence rules for reading; however, such a strategy will always require more effort and be slow and variable. Dyslexic children predominantly read by using what Frith described as logographic skills. Individual phonemes and graphemes are ignored, as the child attends to the graphic features of the word. Reading is accomplished by relying on visual memory, using a large "sight" vocabulary.

D. Challenges to the Serial Box Design

Over the last 15 years, two kinds of empirical evidence have accumulated which seriously challenge the sequential, modular model framework. One type contends that sequential, bottom-up processing models of reading cannot account for experimental results which suggest that knowledge structures at higher levels of analysis affect how letters and words are processed at lower levels (Rumelhart, 1977). Another set of data questions the modular reading structure for processing lexical and nonlexical information (e.g., Glushko, 1979; Seidenberg, Bruck, Fornarolo, & Backman, 1985; Seidenberg, Waters, Barnes, & Tanenhaus, 1984). In addition, theorists have been critical that the dual-route processing mechanisms and representation architecture are too loosely defined and unconstrained, making it difficult to determine how the system will actually function.

1. INTERACTIVE VERSUS SEQUENTIAL PROCESSING

In 1977, Rumelhart summarized several types of evidence that suggest letter and word perception and reading comprehension are affected by the visual, semantic, syntactic, and pragmatic environments in which the reading occurs. Results from many adult and developmental reading studies demonstrate a common finding. Higher levels of analysis involving lexical and semantic levels of meaning affect perceptual processing at lower levels (Gibson &

Levin, 1975; Reicher, 1969; Rumelhart & McClelland, 1982; Schank, 1973; Schvaneveldt & Meyer, 1973; Tanenhaus, Leiman, & Seidenberg, 1979). Reading is seen as a complex, interactive process in which information is not only processed from the bottom up, but also from the top down. It may be best described as a process of simultaneous interactions between multiple levels of analysis resulting in constraints that produce a probabilistic interpretation of the letter string.

One of the most extensively studied "top-down" phenomena is known as the word-superiority effect (WSE). Substantial evidence has accumulated to suggest that letter perception can be enhanced by presentation in the context of a word (Allegretti & Puglisi, 1982; Baron & Thurston, 1973; Chastain, 1981; Johnston, 1981; Johnston & McClelland, 1973; Juola, Schadler, Chabot, & McCaughey, 1978; Paap, Newsome, McDonald, & Schvaneveldt, 1982; Purcell & Stanovich, 1982; Reicher, 1969; Rumelhart & McClelland, 1982; Williams, Gaffney, & Solman, 1985); that is, adults have been shown to identify a letter significantly faster and more accurately when it is presented in a word than in isolation.

a. Interactive Reading Processes in Children. Many studies have shown that the word-recognition skills of young readers are affected by the types of contextual cues outlined by Rumelhart (1977). In a review of the developmental word-recognition literature, Barron (1981) concluded that between the second and fourth grades children begin to use contextual cues to facilitate word recognition. Using lexical priming and lexical-decision tasks, many studies have shown children as young as second grade can use orthographic structure and benefit from semantically related primes for word recognition (Allington, 1978; Horn & Manis, 1985; Leslie & Shannon, 1981; Rosinski & Wheeler, 1972; Schvaneveldt, Ackerman, & Semlear, 1977; Schwantes, 1981; Simpson & Lorsbach, 1983; Simpson, Lorsbach, & Whitehouse, 1983; Zecker & Zinner, 1987). Tachistoscopic studies involving whole-word or letter recognition report similar conclusions (Allegretti & Puglisi, 1982; Chase & Tallal, in press; Gibson, Osser, & Pick, 1963; Gibson, & Hammond, 1962; Johnston, 1981; Juola *et al.*, 1978; Lefton & Spragins, 1974). Like adults, children's pronunciation latencies of target words have been consistently reported to improve when preceded by a congruous sentence context (Merrill, Sperber, & McCauley, 1981; Perfetti, Goldman, & Hogaboam, 1979; Raduege & Schwantes, 1987; Schwantes, 1982; Simons & Leu, 1987; Stanovich, Nathan, West, & Vala-Rossi, 1985; Stanovich, West, & Feeman, 1981; West & Stanovich, 1978). However, unlike adults, children also appear to be significantly impaired by an incongruous context (Schwantes, 1981; Stanovich *et al.*, 1985; West & Stanovich, 1978), which has been interpreted as the interference of postlexical processes.

Stanovich (1980) has suggested that compared to older, better readers, younger and less skilled readers may place a greater reliance on postlexical processing using contextual semantic and syntactic cues provided from their comprehension of the sentences or passages to aid them in word recognition. His interactive–compensatory hypothesis proposed that inexperienced readers compensate for their poorer perceptual decoding skills and weaker intralexical spreading activation by using orthographic redundancy and context to facilitate word recognition. As the perceptual encoding of orthographical and phonological information improves with age and reading skill, children place less reliance on postlexical context (Simpson et al., 1983; Stanovich et al., 1981).

b. Reading Development Is Interactive. Barron (1986) has argued that the dual-route model fails to provide an adequate account of how beginning readers develop word-recognition skills. The traditional model provides only two independent methods for word recognition: either a direct lexical route in which whole-word correspondences are used or a phonological route involving the application of GPC rules. Such a sharp distinction does not adequately describe the variety of perceptual units utilized by beginning readers. Several studies (Ehri & Wilce, 1985; Masonheimer, Drum, & Ehri, 1984) have suggested that letter–sound associations and the names of the letters play an important role in the early acquisition of word-recognition skills (particularly as consonants in the initial or final positions in a word). Presumably as rudimentary sound-blending skills are acquired, children then move from individual letters to graphemes, grapheme clusters, and then syllables. However, as the perceptual unit changes size in English, the sounds associated with its proper pronunciation vary as well. If children make use of so many different heterogeneous structures while learning, it becomes difficult to conceive how mastery of sight–sound correspondences at one level can be built upon at the next level to produce a coherent formulation of spelling–sound rules (Venezky, 1970) that are supposed to form the basis for phonologic decoding.

A recent longitudinal study by Stuart and Coltheart (1988) questions the notion that children learn reading in discrete stages that proceed from orthography to phonology as described by Frith (1985). Stuart and Coltheart (1988) assessed phonological skills in children before and during the first year they were learning to read. Their results demonstrated the children do not always begin reading "logographically" because prereading phonological skills were a significant predictor of reading development. Rather they proposed an interactive relationship between phonological and orthographic analyses. Children with advanced phonemic awareness make use of their skill to develop their grapheme-parsing abilities, utilizing reading strategies that decode from sound to print as well as from print to sound. Such developmental data suggest that reading models for the young must also incorporate processing systems which are interactive rather than sequentially discrete.

2. DISTRIBUTED VERSUS MODULAR STRUCTURE

Several adult studies support the notion of a more distributed lexical network. Recent data suggest considerable interaction between effects attributable to the separate lexical and phonologic processing structures. Pseudo-word pronounciation has been shown to be affected by syntactic constraints (Campbell & Besner, 1981) as well as by orthographically similar lexical items (Glushko, 1979; Kay & Marcel, 1981; Rosson, 1983). In addition word familiarity, which is considered a lexical effect because it is associated with whole-word representations, appears to interact with the effects of pronunciation regularity, which are due to GPC rules (Seidenberg *et al.*, 1984, 1985).

a. Distributed Reading Processes in Children. There are many sources of evidence which suggest children's phonologic decoding skills interact with their lexical knowledge. Marcel (1980) claims that many oral reading errors of children (less than 10 years old) cannot be adequately described as misapplication of GPC rules but rather appear to be an attempt to make "(aural–oral) lexical sense," that is, to produce an utterance which captures as many of the letter sounds as possible and still produce a word known to their lexicon. So for example, *gaol* is pronounced *goal,* or *campaign* as *camping.* These kinds of errors are difficult for the dual-route model to explain because GPC rules do not include a method for incorporating and using lexical information.

Two studies have directly examined for interactive effects between lexical and phonologic systems in developing readers. First, Reitsma (1983) provided evidence that beginning readers form a memory for word-specific spelling patterns when learning to pronounce unfamiliar words. With a moderate amount of practice, first-grade Dutch children (7–8 years old) read nonwords more rapidly than unpracticed homophonic control words. Since the control words had the same pronunciation, the difference could only be due to orthographic alterations. However, unfamiliar or nonwords are supposed to be decoded only by GPC rules in the phonologic system; consequently, both visual and phonologic decoding appear to be interactively involved. Second, Waters, Seidenberg, and Bruck (1984) reported that third graders read regular high-frequency words more accurately than low-frequency words. Regular words are decoded by GPC rules, yet word frequency is associated with whole-word correspondences in the lexicon, thus providing further evidence of interactions between phonologic and lexical codes in young readers.

Several studies have suggested that word recognition undergoes a developmental shift from phonologic to lexical analysis between second and fourth grade. Doctor and Coltheart (1980) showed children less than 9 years old were more prone to homophonic confusions in a sentence-comprehension task, suggesting phonological mediation plays a greater role in word recognition for younger readers. Backman, Bruck, Hebert, and Seidenberg (1984) studied children's abilities to read words and nonwords of different pronunciation regularity. A regular spelling pattern has a single pronunciation (e.g., *-ust, -ane*). Homographic patterns are associated with irregular or multiple pronunciations. They can be exception words with irregular spelling patterns (e.g., *yacht*), words with regular spelling patterns but pronunciations which are inconsistent with orthographic neighbors (e.g., *have*), or words with multiple ambiguous pronunciations (e.g., *-ove, -own*). Results showed younger readers made more errors with words containing homographic spelling patterns than with regular words; however, by fourth grade there were no differences between word types for normally developing readers. As the homographic words violate GPC rules, improved performance on this word class suggests a developmental shift to lexical analysis. Together, these studies suggest younger readers rely more upon phonology for decoding, whereas older readers primarily recognize words on a visual basis.

In the dual-route model, such age- and skill-dependent transitions give the appearance that the lexical route eventually replaces the phonologic route during development. This notion mistakenly places the emphasis for successful reading acquisition upon the lexical route, despite evidence which shows the importance of phonics in learning to read (see Barron, 1986, for a review).

Word recognition then depends upon the interaction and time course of the two processing systems. For the most part, fluent adult readers base their recognition on orthographic features because their visual decoding skills are rapid. Children, however, utilize both visual and auditory codes because of their slower rates of processing.

E. Computationally Inexplicit

While the dual-route model can be adapted to accommodate some of these empirical findings by adding new modules and processing pathways (see Norris & Brown, 1985, or Jorm & Share, 1983), proponents have been accused of too frequently making ad hoc changes to account for new bits of data without really understanding what are the model's processing capabilities and limitations. Some theorists have been critical of the lack of specificity concerning the nature of the dual-route processing mechanisms and representation architecture (Seidenberg, 1985a, 1985b, 1985c, 1988). Expressing a cognitive model in the form of a computer program provides a means for dealing with the complexity of interaction among processing subsystems and for focusing attention on the causally relevant features which may not be apparent from a symbolic description alone (Pylyshyn, 1984). For example, word-recognition models which are more distributed have demonstrated the feasibility of allowing many lexical effects to emerge from the complex interactions of simple processing units without using specialized processing components to code for orthographic differences in the input (McClelland & Rumelhart, 1981). Unless the computational assumptions about the processing components in dual-route systems are made explicit, it becomes very difficult to accept the attributes assigned to a particular structure as being good representations of how the reading system functions. As such, the dual-route model offers little evidence that the system will work as designed. Further, the dual-route model adopts procedures for controlling processing that are poorly suited for the task. Processing is rigidly prescribed through a hierarchical structure using a sequence of instructions that are carried out following a predetermined course with control being passed from one module to the next. However, the research reviewed above suggests word recognition involves a different kind of processing, one in which representational components are less specialized and communicate more flexibly.

F. Biologically Implausible

The dual-route model has been applied to the study of brain function to describe the neural basis of reading (Benson, 1984; Geschwind, 1962). In doing so, modelers have followed a localist approach that postulates specific regions of the brain as specialized for particular language functions. Figure 2 presents a diagram of such a cortical processing system. Visual input is serially processed from occipital to temporal and then frontal regions, undergoing auditory recoding that utilizes the semantic and articulatory language areas of Wernicke and Broca. Reading is conceived as a language-based activity in which visual features are transformed to auditory code by the use of the GPC mechanism in the angular gyrus region of the temporal lobe. Evidence for this position comes from studies of acquired adult dyslexia wherein patients have suffered cortical focal lesions that damaged their language-dominant hemisphere (Coltheart, Patterson, & Marshall, 1987; Patterson, Marshall, & Coltheart, 1985).

Recent studies (Aram Ekelman, & Gillespie, in press; Dennis, Lovett, & Wiegel-Grump, 1981) have challenged the localist position of assigning particular reading functions to specific anatomical locations. New neurologic studies demonstrate the cerebral cortex has far more plasticity than was previsously thought (Merzenich et al., 1983).

Studies of reading skills in children with acquired focal cortical lesions present a very different clinical picture from the one portrayed by adults. The few studies that have been conducted (Alajouanine & Lhermitte, 1965; Aram

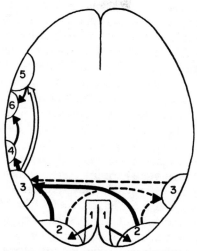

FIGURE 2 Cross-section diagram of cerebral hemispheres illustrating the major pathways for reading processes. Heavy lines indicate left-hemisphere connections; lighter lines are right hemisphere connections. (1) Visual cortex, (2) visual associative cortex, (3) angular gyrus, (4) left temporal lobe language area, (5) left frontal lobe language area, (6) Left frontal lobe motor language area. [From D. F. Benson (1982). *The Alexias.* In H. S. Kirshner & F. R. Fremon (Eds.), *The neurology of aphasia.* Copyright 1982 by Swets and Zeitlinger. Reprinted by permission.]

et al., in press; Hécaen, 1976; Kershner & King, 1974; Vargha-Khadem, O'Gorman, & Watters, 1985) present conflicting results, but most are methodologically flawed. Some studies (e.g., Hécaen, 1976) are based on clinical judgment and lack standardized measures of reading. Others have included children with probable diffuse brain damage (Alajouanine & Lhermitte, 1965; Hécaen, 1976; Vargha-Khadem *et al.*, 1985). In some cases (e.g., Kershner & King, 1974; Vargha-Khadem *et al.*, 1985) diagnosis has been made only on the basis of neurologic examination without the support of radiologic findings. In other studies (Alajouanine & Lhermitte, 1965; Hécaen, 1976; Vargha-Khadem *et al.*, 1985) many of the children's lesions were secondary to other neurologic disorders, such as seizures, or were the result of closed-head trauma, tumors, or meningioencephalitis.

Aram and colleagues (in press), however, have used very stringent selection criteria aimed at excluding children with bilateral or more diffuse brain damage. They report that focal cortical lesions acquired before puberty failed to produce significant reading impairments, even when the damage involved the temporal lobe of the language-dominant hemisphere, but that left-hemisphere subcortical damage involving the head of caudate, putamen, external, and internal capsule did result in reading, language, and memory dysfunction. In previous accounts (Lenneberg, 1967), recovery of normal language development has been found in children whose lesions were acquired before puberty. Aram's data extend these findings to reading development, presenting a similar clinical picture that marks puberty as a turning point for functional recovery. Indeed, even when the left hemisphere is surgically removed in infancy, one study (Dennis *et al.*, 1981) showed that reading skills can continue to develop normally (patient, S.M.). Together these results question the assumption that reading functions are localized to (or limited to) specific cortical regions during development and encourage the consideration of models that involve a more flexible representational network.

In addition, recent animal studies have revealed that representational maps in cerebral cortex may dynamically reorganize with new experience. Studies with monkeys (Jenkins, Merzenich, & Ochs, 1984; Merzenich *et al.*, 1983) have demonstrated the surface of the hand has a corresponding spatial map on the surface of the primary somatosensory cortex. Experimentally induced changes in somatic stimulation or hand activity will topographically reorganize the corticospatial map over a period of several weeks without producing confused perception of the hand surface (Merzenich & Kaas, 1982). These results imply that, within a cortical sensory region, representational systems cannot be localized to particular neural pathways. Rather representational maps are more dynamically interactive with the environment and involve a broader distributed network that can change with experience. Reading representation can be expected to be no less dynamic in its plasticity of functioning.

Neurologic evidence also exists to challenge the sequential design of the serial box reading model. A positron emission tomography (PET) study (Peterson, Fox, Posner, Mintun, & Raichle, 1988) for measuring activity-related changes in regional cerebral blood flow has suggested that single-word reading activates widely separated areas of cerebral cortex as well as subcortical structures. Results showed that visual and auditory input activated separate cortical regions during a passive word-recognition task. Visual tasks produced no activation near Wernicke's area or the region of the angular gyrus. These findings are inconsistent with aspects of the serial model that involve cross-modal translation and support a parallel design with separate sensory perceptual systems.

Further, to model reading as a series of discrete cortical subsystems that complete their analysis before passing the information on to another region of cortex is implausible given what is known about neurophysiology and neuroanatomy. Almost all information transmitted by neurons over a distance of 1 mm or more is carried by an action potential, which provides an excitatory or inhibitory signal lasting about 1 msec. Most connections are short and broadly distributed, activating other neurons in surrounding columns or laminae, although myelinated fiber tracks exist for longer transmissions. Neuronal transmissions spread in cascade fashion with central regions activated by the output of peripheral systems even while perceptual analysis is still ongoing (see Crick & Asanuma, 1986; Shepherd, 1979).

The dual-route model includes computer-styled subsystems that use a variety of computational paradigms. For example, some modules are storage buffers that must integrate information from several different sources. Other modules act as central processing units to modify the letter string input by either breaking it down into smaller components (such as phonologic units) or attaching new meaning through the use of a content-addressable memory system. However, it is difficult to conceive how such designs could be implemented by the central nervous system. While separate cortical areas are specialized for processing different sensory information, they have a similar anatomical structure which makes them more similar to one another than to other subcortical structures. This relative uniformity in cortical architecture suggests the capacity for utilizing a general-purpose processing design that can handle perceptual as well as analytical functions. In addition, the cortex uses the same neural circuits for memory and computational processing. Learning occurs through modification in the connections of the circuits (Cotman & Lynch, 1988). Therefore, computer-styled models with physically separated memory buffers and central processing units are a poor paradigm for describing brain function.

The time available for processing while reading also places constraints on the type of designs that can be used. Reading processes are rapid in adults. Tachistoscopic experiments indicate that recognition of familiar words can occur in less than 50 msec (Rayner & Duffy, 1988). A visual signal traveling from retina to visual cortex undergoes only four or five synaptic relays but takes about 25–50 msec due to slow photoreceptors (Sejnowski, 1986). Consequently, serial processing in word recognition must be shallow, probably less than 10 steps deep. With communication channels limited to a simple binary signal, it is difficult to conceive how complex visual patterns of words and the auditory codes associated with them can be analyzed in so few steps without massive parallel processing occurring simultaneously.

III. Parallel Distributed Reading Model

To address some of the criticisms of serial box models, researchers recently have begun to construct reading models out of simple processing units that are more distributed in their representational architecture and interactive in their processing. A parallel distributed processing (PDP) model

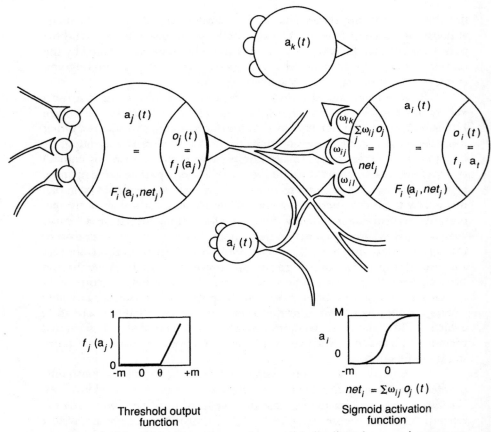

FIGURE 3 The basic components of a parallel distributed processing system. [From D. E. Rumelhart, J. L. McClelland, & the PDP Research Group (1986). *Parallel distributed processing: Explorations in the microstructures of cognition,* Vol. 1, p. 47. Copyright 1986 by MIT Press. Reprinted by permission.]

is comprised of a neural-like network of simple processing units that mutually excite and inhibit one another to produce a pattern of activation as a means of representation. Figure 3 illustrates the basic components of a PDP system. A set of processing units (seen as circles in the diagram) exists with each unit u_i containing a level of activation at a moment in time $d_i(t)$. All of the processing in a PDP model is handled by the units. Each unit's function is to distribute output and receive input to and from neighboring units. Processing goes on simultaneously, so the system has parallel functioning. There is no executive unit coordinating the functioning of a neighborhood of units. Rather the system processes information dynamically by shifting and settling into different patterns of activation over time in an effort to maintain a state of equilibrium. The pattern of activity distributed throughout all the units of the system as a whole is the way to meaningfully represent what occurs in a PDP system.

The level of activation for a unit can vary, for example, taking in any real-number value between some minimum and maximum interval. Activation also can be modified by an internal threshold function F_i. To produce output from the unit $o_i(t)$, the level of activation must exceed a certain value. For example, output can be the difference between threshold and current level of activation when it is above threshold, but equal to zero when below threshold. Output can take the form of excitation or inhibition and passes through unidirectional connections (seen as lines in Fig. 3) as input to another system unit u_j.

The pattern of connections determines what the system knows and how it will respond to stimulation from outside the system. In some systems, units are organized into levels with patterns of connections occurring between neighboring units within a level and connections spreading out to units at neighboring levels. Such an organization is described as interactive because connections are both top down and bottom up with information usually only passing between adjacent levels. Connections are most often arranged so that units which are consistent with one another have excitatory relationships, whereas inconsistent units inhibit one another.

The connection from unit u_i to unit u_j can change. Such changes are reflected in the weight or strength, w_{ij}, associated with the connection. Weights can undergo change as a function of experience, resulting in a rearrangement in the patterns of connections between units to produce a different processing structure.

Networks are arranged among units in the system so that each unit receives multiple inputs and sends multiple outputs to its neighbors. Input can be combined by adding them together to produce the net input total. For unit u_i, the net input equals the sum of all outputs from unit u_j at time t or $o_j(t)$ multiplied by the weight associated in the connection between the two units (w_{ij}), or:

$$\text{net}_i = \Sigma \ w_{ij} * o_j(t)$$

This net input value must then be combined with the previous level of activation of u_i by function F_i to produce the new activation value. The degree of the effect the net input has on u_i can be adjusted to keep the unit from exceeding its minimum and maximum values. In addition, the new activation value $a_i(t+1)$ can be adjusted to reflect the fact that $a_i(t)$ is decaying to a resting level.

A. *Interactive Activation Model of Reading*

The interactive activation model of McClelland and Rumelhart (1981) and Rumelhart and McClelland (1982) approaches the phenomenon of word perception from a PDP framework. The central feature of this model assumes that the processing of information during reading consists of series of levels corresponding to visual features, letters, and words. Figure 4 presents the general concept of the system. The arrows in the figure represent excitatory connections, whereas the circular ends of the connections represent inhibitory pathways. The complete model consists of parallel orthographic and phono-logic systems that segment each letter string for perceptual analyses and pass their information on to a common lexical system.

At the first level of processing, units detect the visual and acoustical features that distinguish letters and sounds from one another. Units also act as letters, phonemes, and words at subsequent levels of analyses. In the ortho-graphic system, each of the letters in a 4-letter string is assumed to be

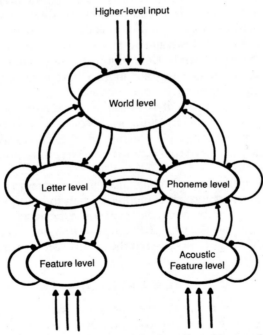

FIGURE 4 Interactive activation model of reading. Lines ending with arrows represent excitation and dots indicate inhibition. [From McClelland & Rumelhart (1981). Copyright 1981 by the American Psychological Association. Reprinted by permission.]

processed simultaneously by four sets of detectors at the feature and letter level, one for each letter position in the string. Analogous segmentation takes place acoustically in the phonologic system. Processing is assumed to be parallel and to proceed through the different levels at the same time in cascade fashion (McClelland, 1979), so that feature analyses occur concurrently with processing at the word level. In addition, processing is interactive, with information flowing in both directions at once—from lower (feature) to higher (word) levels and from higher to lower levels.

To the extent that two units are mutually consistent, they support one another by excitatory activation. For example, in the orthographic system the letter "w" in the first position of a 4-letter string is consistent with the word *work,* and their corresponding units would have mutually excitatory connections. However, to the extent that two units are mutually inconsistent, they weaken one another by inhibitory activation, as in the case of the letter "w" and the word test. Mutual inhibitory relationships also occur between units within the same level of processing; for example, different orthographic letter units that correspond to the first position of a 4-letter string must necessarily weaken one another because a word can only begin with one letter. As letter units from the same string position inhibit each other, word units also compete through lateral inhibitory connections.

Figure 5 illustrates these principles of excitatory and inhibitory interactions for the unit of the letter "t" in the first position of a 4-letter string and

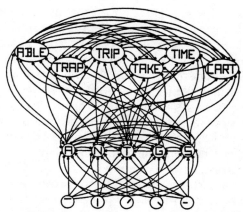

FIGURE 5 The unit for the letter "T" in the first serial position and some of its neighbors. Note that only words with "T" in the first position receive activation. A complete display would include four full sets of feature detectors. [From McClelland & Rumelhart (1981). Copyright 1981 by the American Psychological Association. Reprinted by permission.]

some of its orthographic neighbors. In the interactive activation model, the processing necessary to identify the letter "t" is distributed across the activations of a large network of units. The pattern of activation, partially represented in Fig. 5, is the way the letter "t" is represented in this model.

B. IA Model of the Word-Superiority Effect

The IA model was specifically constructed to simulate the WSE, one of the interactive reading phenomena described above. Rumelhart and McClelland (1982) chose to concentrate on the orthographic route of processing, studying the interactive relationships between the letter and word subsystems. Consideration of the effects of higher-level input and a phonologic system was omitted from their initial set of experiments. They conducted many WSE experiments using a variation on a backward masking paradigm as a means for testing the capabilities of the IA model. During its initial operation, model parameters were selected to simulate the experimental data. Simulations were performed by computer program.

The IA model accounted for the WSE in the following way. Letter strings activated a neighborhood of word units that shared letter patterns (e.g., *word* and *work*). Recognition for both words and pseudowords occurred through the synthesis of the partial activation of all the word units in the neighborhood. In the case where the letter string was a word, its word unit rapidly reached a higher level of activation than other word units in the neighborhood and, through lateral inhibition, activation among similar-looking neighbors decreased. However, in the case of a pseudoword letter string, no single word unit became stronger than the others, and so a neighborhood of word units that shared two or three letter patterns with the letter string remained activated. The combined activation of the pseudoword neighborhood produced about the same degree of activation at the word level as was produced when the letter string was a word (hence the WSE with pseudowords is equal to that with words). Through top-down feedback, the neighborhood of word units strengthened the activation of its corresponding letter units. Thus in the IA model, information from a higher-level unit, such as a word, can affect the processing at a lower-level unit, such as a letter. Through this feedback, letter recognition is facilitated by word or pseudoword context. The model predicted that wordlike consonant strings (like *spct*) which are orthographically irregular and unpronounceable also should produce a WSE because they would activate an orthographic neighborhood of word units as occurred with pseudowords. A subsequent experiment with such letter strings confirmed the predicted WSE (Rumelhart & McClelland, 1982).

C. Studying Lexical Development with the IA Model

As previously discussed, many studies have suggested that less skilled readers may place a greater reliance on top-down processing using contextual semantic cues provided from their comprehension of the sentences or passages to aid them in word recognition (Allington & Fleming, 1978; Schvaneveldt *et al.*, 1977; Stanovich *et al.*, 1981; West & Stanovich, 1978). However, these studies are not directly applicable to the lexical processes being modeled by IA because they were concerned with the top-down effects produced by conscious expectations rather than with the automatic spreading-activation process operating within lexical memory.

Other studies have attempted to measure lexical processes more directly by examining children's use of orthographic structure. Some have compared good readers to poor readers who were at most 6 months or a year retarded in their reading (Allington, 1978; Backman *et al.*, 1984; Reitsma, 1983; Simpson *et al.*, 1983; Waters *et al.*, 1984). Most of these studies report poorer readers' performance was similar to that of younger, good readers who had the same level of reading skill. However, Reitsma (1983) found they also were much slower to learn about graphemic composition of words.

A few studies have specifically examined developmentally dyslexic children (Horn & Manis, 1985; Seidenberg *et al.*, 1985; Seymour & Porpodas, 1980; Zecker & Zinner, 1987), but their results have been more equivocal. In a study of four dyslexic children (ages 8–9), Seymour and Porpodas (1980) employed a physical matching task ("same" or "different") with letter strings that varied in orthographic regularity (e.g., *slart* versus *lrtsa*). They reported chronological- and reading-age-matched children showed consistently better response times with orthographically regular letter strings, whereas the dyslexic children showed no regularity effects. Zecker and Zinner (1987) showed a similar result using a lexical-decision task with orally presented words that varied for semantic relatedness. Chronological-age-matched controls benefited more from the semantic relation between word pairs than the dyslexic children, with only 9 of the 20 poor readers showing facilitation. However, other studies employing lexical-decision and naming tasks suggested dyslexic performance was similar to that of younger non-disabled children (Horn & Manis, 1985; Seidenberg *et al.*, 1985).

Studying the development of the WSE can provide important data about how the lexical system organizes itself during reading acquisition. The WSE specifically appears to be a lexical effect. By using a tachistoscopic, backward masking paradigm the time course of processing can be limited to lexical analysis, providing information about lexical organization without the interference of postlexical judgments (Doyle & Leach, 1988). Although lexical-decision and naming tasks more closely resemble normal reading, they carry the additional burden of involving postlexical processes (Seidenberg, 1985c). As reviewed above, most theories suggest novice readers have weaker or undeveloped interactions among the lexical units, although ideas about how these units and the connections between them are formed during the course of reading development are never specified.

The IA model provides a sophisticated way to analyze the interactive relationship among the orthorgraphic units within the lexical memory system of developing readers. This model gives a detailed account of processing during a simple letter-identification task. In addition, the experiments of Rumelhart and McClelland (1982) provide us with parameters for use in the simulation of a normal adult reader. Conducting similar experiments with developing normal and impaired readers provides an opportunity to more closely examine these processes in children and model them. Conversely, experimental data from children can provide information pertaining to how the IA model learns and may suggest which parts of the model are more affected by developmental changes in reading skill.

We conducted an experiment to examine the WSE in an older and younger group of normal readers, comparing their performance with high-frequency words, pseudowords, and nonwords (Chase & Tallal, 1990). The same experimental data also were collected on a group of dyslexics who are the same age as the older group of normal readers but have reading skills comparable to the younger group. In addition, the robustness of the IA model also was tested through computer simulation to see if it could model the developmental data.

In studying the WSE in children, we compared the interactive and sequential processing functions to determine which provides a better model for the way beginning readers process letter strings. We also were testing the relative merits of a distributed or modular structure for modeling beginning reading by comparing performance with words and pseudowords to a nonword condition.

If normal young readers utilize interactive processing within the lexical system during letter analysis, then word context should facilitate letter recognition, and performance should be better with words than with matched nonwords. Since words and matched pseudowords share the same neighborhood, their patterns of distributed activation could be similar and result in comparable pseudoword performance. However, developmental differences in threshold activation or connection strengths between letter and word units may reduce the WSE for pseudowords.

Dyslexic readers may perform quite differently from both the chronological- and the reading-age-matched groups, depending upon the degree of abnormality in system parameters. If the lexical systems of dyslexic children are merely functionally immature, then their results should be similar to those of the younger, reading-age-matched control group. However, if the dyslexics are unable to attend to orthographic regularity, then they may not show a WSE. For example, weak word-to-letter feedback could result in no WSE.

IV. IA Model of Developing Readers

A. Experimental Data

In the WSE, the word type determines how much the perception of the target letter is facilitated. The general method used had two main features: (1) tachistoscopically present 4-letter strings, following the offset by a patterned mask, and (2) test the perceptibility of a single letter in the display on each trial using a forced-choice test. A series of experiments was conducted using word, pseudoword (pronounceable nonword), and unpronounceable nonword 4-letter displays. Dyslexic children's performance was compared to adults, and chronological- (CA) and reading-age (RA) matched groups. To facilitate group comparisons and control for practice and fatigue effects, subject performance was calculated after each block of trials and exposure duration was adjusted to maintain each subject's accuracy at 75% throughout the experiment.

Results showed that the two groups of normally developing readers (average ages of 8 and 10 years old) demonstrated a strong WSE for both words and pseudowords over nonwords. However, their pseudoword advantage was about half the word advantage. In contrast, the adult word and pseudoword scores were equal, a finding supported by other studies (Carr, Davidson, & Hawkins, 1978; Rumelhart & McClelland, 1982). Dyslexic readers failed to demonstrate any WSE. They appeared to process nonwords in the same way as real ones, even though they had sufficient skills to read accurately about 90% of the words with almost 100% comprehension of their meaning. Their absence of a WSE could not be attributed to factors of age, IQ, SES, sex, reading ability, or stimulus-exposure duration, as all these variables were matched in the two control groups.

Figure 6 presents graphs of all four groups comparing their performance for the three word types at the four different positions in the letter strings. The degree of top-down feedback from the lexical memory system is reflected not only in the word-type differences, but also in the shape of the serial-position curves. Performance in the first three serial positions for adults and for the CA group is more uniform because, according to the IA model, top-down feedback from word units has accelerated the processing strength of these letter units. Due to the pattern mask, insufficient time was available to provide the same enhancement to the fourth serial position. In contrast, the RA and dyslexic groups show serial-position curves similar to the nonword decay

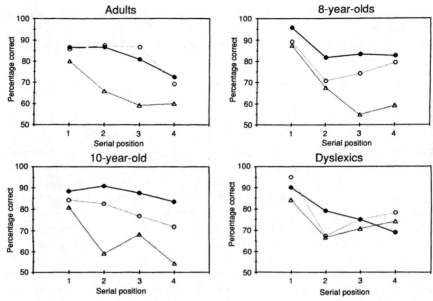

FIGURE 6   Letter-identification performance for adults, dyslexic children, chronological-age-matched controls (10 yr-olds), and reading-aged-matched Controls (8 yr-olds). Performance with words (●), pseudowords (○), and nonword (△) stimuli are displayed at the four different serial positions.

function. Word-type differences in the RA group clearly indicate that lexical feedback has been at work to enhance word and pseudoword performance, but the serial-position curves graphically illustrate that the top-down feedback is weaker for these younger readers. The dyslexic group shows no lexical feedback at all, as evidenced by the fact that serial-position curves all decay and there are no word-type differences.

B. IA Model Results

Modeling results suggested the following predictions about the way lexical systems are organized in developing readers. First, the amount of top-down feedback from word units to letter units varies with reading skill, appearing to be more than twice as strong with the older children as with the younger group. The dyslexic children show hardly any benefit from word context, and their top-down feedback is only 10% as strong as normal readers their own age. Second, bottom-up input to word units also appears to be affected by age or reading skill. Adults produce a more distributed pattern of excitation, resulting in partial activation of many word units, whereas younger

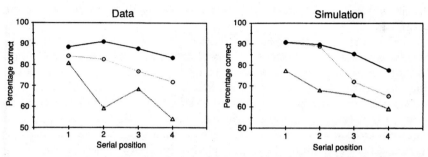

FIGURE 7 Letter-identification performance for the chronological-age-matched controls (data) and the computer simulation of their performance.

readers tend to be more selective and activate only those word units that closely resembled the stimulus input. The dyslexic children, like the adults, produce a distributed pattern of activation over many word units; however, the amount of activation among word units is almost half of the adult level.

Overall, the IA model did a reasonably good job simulating the differences in word-type performance. Figure 7 illustrates the model's success by presenting the experimental and simulation results for the CA-matched group of 10-year-olds. Results for the other three groups were reasonably close as well (see Chase & Tallal, 1990, for further details).

C. Sequential versus Distributed Model Predictions

The results of this study strongly support a parallel distributed processing approach to modeling reading development. The dual-route model with its independent and stimulus-specific lexical and phonologic systems has a very difficult time accounting for the normal readers' data. The dual-route model proposes that real words are processed by a lexical system which is faster and more efficient than a phonologic system. Performance with unfamiliar word types such as pseudowords or nonwords is expected to be poorer because they are supposed to be processed by the slower phonologic system. If the modular principle is to be maintained, the present data would suggest three different processing systems that operate at three varying degrees of efficiency and change during development. Such proliferation of new processing modules for every new set of data lacks the constraint necessary to be a viable, working model. Another possibility within the dual-system framework is for word types to activate the two processing systems to differing degrees; that is, the lexical system is highly stimulated by real words, partially active for pseudowords, and not at all active for nonwords, whereas the opposite is true for the phonologic system. However, using all systems for processing each input is distributed and parallel in design, thus abandoning the modular framework entirely.

The dual-route model fared no better with the dyslexic data, unless one treats their reading impairment as a global deficit that affected both the lexical and the phonologic systems. Nevertheless, the lack of a WSE for the dyslexics does suggest that selective study of reading-impaired populations can provide a distorted view of reading processing systems. Marshall and Newcombe's modular framework was almost exclusively developed through the study of an acquired dyslexic adult population. Perhaps their success with the modular and sequential approach was in part a reflection of the types of processing impairments found within the population they studied.

D. IA Model Criticisms

1. SERIAL-POSITION EFFECTS

Although word-type averages generated by the IA model were good simulations, capturing the serial-position effects proved to be much more problematic. In general, model simulations consistently underestimated performance in the first serial position while overestimating scores in the third and fourth position (see Fig. 5). The model assumes that information from all four serial positions is processed simultaneously with each position having equal input. However, strong linear trends for serial position suggest a left-to-right processing strategy in which information on the left side of the display was processed before that on the right side. The differences in serial-position curves between groups may reflect changes which are important in the development of reading skills, as several studies have shown the size of perceptual spans improves with reading ability (Bouma & Legein, 1977; D. F. Fisher & Lefton, 1976; Gibson & Levin, 1975; Haber, 1978; Patberg & Yonas, 1978).

These serial-position effects probably are not the result of eye movements during reading. When normal adults read, their eyes come to rest for periods that last from 150 to 500 msec (Rayner & Pollatsek, 1989). Between these periods of visual fixation, the eyes make rapid (20–35 msec) forward jumps of about seven to nine character spaces in a movement called a saccade. The display durations used in our experiments are very brief and, for all but the youngest reading group, are significantly less than the shortest fixation period.

Since letter recognition was occurring with very brief exposure durations in our experiments and took place under backward masking conditions, which presumably would limit postlexical effects, it is more plausible that the serial-position effect is happening in the early stages of processing during the perceptual analysis of the visual features. This interpretation involves treating each letter position as activating at different rates which are contolled by attentional factors. Posner and colleagues (Posner, Inhoff, Friedrich, & Cohen, 1987; Posner, Rafal, Choate, & Vaughan, 1985; Posner, Walker, Friedrich, & Rafal, 1987; Sieroff, Pollatsek, & Posner, 1988; Sieroff & Posner, 1988) have demonstrated that covert shifts of spatial attention that do not involve oculomotor movements can improve visual processing performance and recently proposed a modulatory role for attention in the sensory registration of letters (Sieroff & Posner, 1988). Processing input could accumulate gradually for each serial position in proportion to the amount of attention it receives, slowly activating on a sigmoid function curve. The serial-position effects would reflect the rate of activation or the rise of the function curve; that is, serial positions 1 and 2 would rise very rapidly, approximating a step function, whereas serial positions 3 and 4 would be more slowly activating and not reach their maximum until a later period of time.

Attentional differences remain an important variable for modeling and further study. If developing readers do not fixate on the target location as consistently as mature readers or have narrower perceptual spans, then the quality and amount of their stimulus reception will be degraded. Younger readers may have required much more stimulation before feature detectors could resolve the ambiguity. Further work is needed to more fully explore the role that feature detection plays in processing systems of developing readers.

2. LEARNING CONNECTION STRENGTHS

Another criticism of the IA model, first expressed by it creators, concerns its excessive flexibility by allowing too many parameters or connection strengths between units to be modifiable by the experimenter to fit a particular data set (Massaro, 1988; Seidenberg, 1985b, 1985c). Some have expressed concerns that such latitude provides too much power so that the model cannot be falsified as it has the capability of simulating results from mutually exclusive and inconsistent psychological models.

The recent introduction of models that can learn to adjust their own connection strengths through supervised learning provides a more parsimonious solution to this problem. Since 1986, several algorithms have been proposed for training networks. Supervised learning schemes are ones in which the network is given repeated examples of the desired input–output mapping, and the network adjusts the weights between units to produce the desired function. The network thus programs itself to solve the task. Back propagation (Rumelhart, Hinton, & Williams, 1986), a supervised learning scheme for PDP networks, is the most widely used technique. The basic idea is to change the weights between the units in such a way as to reduce the error in the output. An input pattern is presented to the network, and activation is propagated forward through the network to the output units. The correct output pattern is provided to the output units in the form of a teaching signal. Back propagation provides a rule for propagating an error signal back through the network from the output units, which tells units layered between input and output levels which way to change their weights.

With the development of back-propagation procedures, we are now in a position to examine ways in which the IA model can learn to recognize words. Building such a model would be very important in gaining a broader understanding of the normal course of reading development and may potentially provide us a method for dynamically modeling changes associated with the cognitive development of better reading skills.

3. LOCALIST REPRESENTATION

The IA model adopted a local representational scheme in which each processing unit took on the identity of a particular feature, letter, or word. This type of coding scheme is relatively efficient for tasks that involve English orthography because many of the network's units may be simultaneously activated by a single display input, and the knowledge base requires each unit to respond to a set of information which is not representationally shared by other units (Hinton, 1988). However, some researchers (Rumelhart & McClelland, 1986; Seidenberg & McClelland, 1989; Sejnowski & Rosenberg, 1986) have adopted a scheme of coarse-coded, distributed representations (Hinton, McClelland, & Rumelhart, 1986) in which code identity is patterned across many computing units. For lexical tasks, many studies have used a Wickelgren's triplet scheme (Wickelgren, 1969), in which words are broken down into combinations of letter triplets. For example, *make* is represented by the orthographic units _ma, mak, ake, and ke_, where _ is a symbol for the beginning or ending of a word. These Wickelfeatures are sensitive to the local contexts, encouraging the network to pay attention to the sequential pattern of letters. As a result, such systems can produce unique responses for words that share the same letter input (e.g., *god* versus *dog*). In addition, distributed representations are much more biologically plausible, as it is very unlikely that a single neuron or cell assembly would specifically code for a letter or word.

4. MULTIPLE WORD RECOGNITION

The IA model also is limited because it was designed only to recognize a single 4-letter word without any consideration of retinal position. A more complete model that can simulate normal reading must be able to process multiple words appearing at various places in a visual image. Such a model faces a problem known as *translation-invariant recognition* (Neisser, 1967); that is, a word must be identified regardless of spatial location, print size, or other kinds of spatial transformations.

V. Other Connectionist Word-Recognition Models

Several other connectionist or PDP word-recognition models have been developed which address some of the shortcomings found in the IA model. Only four of these models will be briefly discussed, although several others deserve consideration as well (e.g., Cottrell, 1988; Kawamoto, 1988). Two of the models discussed were developed to provide learning capabilities, and two were constructed for multiple word recognition.

A. Models That Learn

Sejnowski and Rosenberg (1986) constructed a simple feed-forward, 3-layer PDP network that could learn to read out loud by using back-propagation learning procedures. Rather than applying phonologic rules, they trained the model to map from letter input to the correct phoneme output using continuous informal speech. The model achieved a good performance and generalized well on new words. During the early stages of learning, the model produced sounds that were reported to be similar to early speech patterns in children.

Seidenberg and McClelland (1989) developed a more elaborate word-recognition model that offers both an orthographic and a phonologic coding system which can learn the correct pronunciation of letter strings through back-propagation procedures. The basic architecture is made up of ortho-graphic and phonologic units as well as an intervening level of "hidden" units, so called because they are layered between input and output levels within the system. The hidden units map correspondences between the letters and pho-nemes through training. The representational system is fairly insensitive to spatial position. It encodes letters using a variant of Wickelfeature triplets in both the orthographic and the phonologic systems. While this coding scheme has made the model more sensitive to local contextual letters, it is also rela-tively insensitive to the serial position in which letters appear. Consequently, serial-position effects have a difficult time finding their way into this modeling system. In addition, by using a single encoding scheme of triplets the model assumes a fixed perceptual span of three letters; however, the developmental data presented here suggest that such encoding skills may change with age and reading ability. The strength of the model is found in its capability to decode words by sight and by sound, providing a representational architecture that can simulate data from visual word recognition as well as from pronunciation experiments.

Since the Seidenberg and McClelland model must be trained to pro-nounce words, it can simulate the performance of developing readers. Pro-nunciation latencies of the model were estimated for a given word, and experiments were conducted to examine the effects of word frequency and regularity of pronunciation on the model's performance.

Several of Seidenberg's studies provided the experimental data from normal and impaired developing readers (Backman *et al.*, 1984; Seidenberg *et al.*, 1985; Waters *et al.*, 1984). They report that unskilled readers make more errors pronouncing exception words (i.e., words with irregular spelling–sound correspondences) than regular words. However, normally developing readers' performance with high-frequency words improves more rapidly than that with low-frequency words, so that by the age of 10, performance on high-frequency exception words is as good as on regular words. Dyslexic children fail to show this improvement.

When the model's performance was sampled early in training, to simulate the behavior of unskilled readers, results showed the model to behave in a similar fashion by producing longer latencies even on high-frequency exception words. After training, however, the model was able to encode enough information about specific exception words to perform as well as the better readers. Developmental dyslexia was simulated by reducing the number of hidden units in half, making it more difficult for the network to acquire a map between orthography and phonology. Eliminating these units produced the expected general decrement in performance but also made it more difficult to encode specific information about exception words. Consequently the model had the same problem with high-frequency exception words as the dyslexics, even with prolonged training.

These modeling results suggest that some developmental changes in reading behavior can be simulated by simple processing units that adopt a distributed and interactive processing architecture. In this context, dyslexic performance was simulated by providing fewer hidden units, suggesting that reading impairments could be caused by limited lexical capacity for encoding GPC. While this hypothesis has received considerable research support from behavior studies (see review above), this model provides computational evidence that such an impairment can produce a very specific pattern of reading that simulates dyslexic performance on high-frequency exception words. Such computational sophistication has the potential to provide a unified explanation for a wide range of behavior phenomena.

B. Multiple Word-Recognition Models

McClelland (1985, 1986) was one of the first to attempt to build a model which could recognize more than one word at a time. He modified the IA model so that connections between units were not static, but dynamically programmed by weighted feedback provided from a central knowledge store of letter and word units. These central units were not specialized to respond to one word register or one serial position, but rather would reflect a systemic degree of activation in response to any word or letter currently being processed by the system. Such a scheme allowed multiple word inputs. He called this model PABLO, for programmable blackboard.

Through feedback PABLO was quickly able to tune itself to inputs, even if seriously degraded, and bottom-up inhibition, which is used in the IA model to sharpen word-unit activation, was not necessary. Nevertheless, the pattern of activation at the word level was quite similar. Word units in PABLO received the same degree of partial activation that was produced by the IA model.

Although PABLO's central knowledge store provides the means for processing several words simultaneously, considerable hardware is required to provide letter-recognition capabilities to all areas of the visual field. Such hardware also requires specific recurrent connections between the local-letter units and the central word units. For a visual field that can simultaneously hold 24 letters, Mozer (1988) has estimated PABLO would require a total of 776,600 different letter and word units and a total of 120,482,496 connections between them. Consequently, implementing a complete system on computer becomes economically unfeasible at this time.

Mozer (1988) has designed a model he called MORSEL to perform multiple word recognition with greater economy. Using the Wickelfeature representational scheme, triplet letter units respond to local letter patterns but are not sensitive to word contexts or spatial location. The complete model has many processing modules, one of which is an attentional mechanism capable of controlling the temporal order by gating early stages of processing from particular spatial locations. The attentional system can be sequentially directed to particular serial positions, providing a means for producing the left-to-right serial-position effects previously reported. However, when displays are brief, the attentional system may have insufficient time to process for spatial location. As a result, the MORSEL model has difficulty determining what appeared where because the letter clusters do not encode for spatial location.

VI. Summary and Conclusions

Many of the criticisms directed at adult reading models apply equally well to the field of reading development. Children's reading models are often simplified adaptations of adult systems, providing little understanding of how such a complex structure evolved. Without an explicit description of normal reading development, impairments cannot be described in the context of normal function. Many of the difficulties in defining reliable subtypes of developmental dyslexia may be the result of using models that fail to account for many empirical data and lack computational sophistication. By combining psychological experimentation with computationally implemented models, researchers are provided the means to simulate reading behavior in greater detail, allowing a more fine-grained analysis of cognitive processing than was previously possible.

Swanson (1988) also has stressed the importance placing the study of learning disabilities on a firmer theoretical foundation, however, his ideas about modeling are quite different from the PDP approach described above. Although Swanson acknowledges the importance of perceptual abilities and other knowledge-based factors, he appears to emphasize deficits in strategic planning, self-perception, and self-monitoring behaviors as the source for academic problems. We agree with Stanovich (1988) that these types of executive control functions are much too global to provide the basis for a learning disability in such a specific area as reading. Disruption of central cognitive functions should be associated with more global intellectual dysfunction, whereas dyslexia's diagnostic criteria specifically exclude children with intellectual impairments.

We believe the data suggest dyslexic reading impairments to be more peripherally located and encapsulated from other cognitive systems (Stanovich, 1985). However, this conclusion does not imply that dyslexic impairments are simple. Fodor (1983) has argued that for perceptual input systems to perform rapid and automatic identification considerable complexity and computational elaboration are required. By placing the source of reading impairment in the lexical component of the language-input system, as many of the studies reviewed have suggested, we are studying an enormously complex and interactive network. The PDP approach provides sufficient computational sophistication to implement working models of such a system.

In addition, PDP models adopt design features which Rumelhart & McClelland (1986) have described as "brain-style processing." Processing units are neuronlike with simple excitatory and inhibitory connections; output from the system is continuous; activation is distributed and massively parallel; the system operates by constraint satisfaction to settle into a solution. Although these models adopt strategies which grossly simplify the neurobiology of reading, this approach can provide a conceptual framework that may be able to isolate the basic computational problems facing developing readers and offer insights as to the functional significance of dyslexic neurologic abnormalities.

Acknowledgments

The experimental results reported were part of the first author's dissertation, completed at the University of California, San Diego, Department of Neurosciences. Discussion of the experimental data is adapted from "A developmental, interactive activation model of the word superiority effect" by Chris Chase and Paula Tallal, which appears in *Journal of Experimental Child Psychology, 49,* 448–487 (1990).

References

Alajouanine, T. H., & Lhermitte, F. (1965). Acquired aphasia in children. *Brain, 88,* 653–662.

Allegretti, C. L., & Puglisi, J. T. (1982). Recognition of letters in words and non-words. *Journal of General Psychology, 107,* 139–148.

Allington, R. L. (1978). Sensitivity to orthographic structure as a function of grade and reading ability. *Journal of Reading Behavior, 10,* 437–439.

Allington, R. L., & Fleming, J. (1978). The misreading of high-frequency words. *Journal of Special Education, 12,* 417–421.

Aram, D. M., Ekelman, B. L., & Gillespie, L. L. (1989). Reading and lateralized brain lesions in children. In K. von Euler, I. Lumberg & G. Leunerstrand (Eds.), *Brain & reading.* Hampshire, England: Macmillan.

Arnett, J. L., & DiLollo, V. (1979). Visual information processing in relation to age and to reading ability. *Journal of Experimental Child Psychology, 27,* 143–152.

Backman, J., Bruck, M., Hebert, M., & Seidenberg, M. (1984). Acquisition and use of spelling-sound information in reading. *Journal of Experimental Child Psychology, 38,* 114–133.

Baddeley, A. D., Logie, R. H., & Ellis, N. C. (1988). Characteristics of developmental dyslexia. *Cognition, 29,* 197–228.

Baron, J. (1979). Orthographic and word-specific mechanisms in children's reading of words. *Child Development, 50,* 60–72.

Baron, J., & Thurston, I. (1973). An analysis of the word- superiority effect. *Cognitive Psychology, 4,* 207–228.

Barron, R. W. (1981). Development of visual word recognition: A review. In G. E. MacKinnon & T. G. Waller (Eds.), *Reading research: Advances in theory and practice* (Vol. 3, pp. 119–158). New York: Academic Press.

Barron, R. W. (1986). Word recognition in early reading: A review of the direct and indirect access hypotheses. *Cognition, 24,* 93–119.

Beauvois, M. F., & Derouesne, J. (1979). Phonological alexia: Three dissociations. *Journal of Neurology, Neurosurgery and Psychiatry, 42,* 1115–1124.

Benson, D. F. (1984). Alexia and the neural basis of reading. *Annals of Dyslexia, 34,* 3–13.

Boder, E. (1973). Developmental dyslexia: A diagnostic approach based on three atypical reading-spelling patterns. *Developmental Medicine and Child Neurology, 15,* 663–687.

Bouma, H., & Legein, C. P. (1977). Foveal and parafoveal recognition of letters and words by dyslexics and by average readers. *Neuropsychologia, 15,* 69–80.

Budoff, M., & Quinlan, D. (1964). Reading progress as related to efficiency of visual and aural learning in the primary grades. *Journal of Educational Psychology, 55,* 247–252.

Campbell, R., & Besner, D. (1981). This and Thap—Constraints on the pronunciation of new, written words. *Quarterly Journal of Experimental Psychology, 33A,* 375–396.

Carr, T. H., Davidson, B. J., & Hawkins, H. L. (1978). Perceptual flexibility in word recognition: Strategies affect orthographic computation but no lexical access. *Journal of Experimental Psychology: Human Perception and Performance, 4,* 674–690.

Chase, C. H., & Tallal, P. (1990). A developmental, interactive activation model of the word superiority effect. *Journal of Experimental Child Psychology, 49,* 448–487.

Chastain, G. (1981). Phonological and orthographic factors in the word superiority effect. *Memory & Cognition, 9,* 389–397.

Cohn, M., & Stricker, G. (1979). Reversal errors in strong, average, and weak letter namers. *Journal of Learning Disabilities, 12,* 533–537.

Coltheart, M. (1981). Disorders or reading and their implications for models of normal reading. *Visible Language, 15,* 245–286.

Coltheart, M. (1982). The psycholinguistic analysis of acquired dyslexias: Some illustrations. *Philosophical Transactions of the Royal Society of London, Series B, 298,* 151–164.

Coltheart, M., Masterson, J., Byng, S., Prior, M., & Riddoch, J. (1984). Surface dyslexia. *Quarterly Journal of Experimental Psychology, 35,* 489–508.

Coltheart, M., Patterson, K., & Marshall, J. C. (1987). *Deep dyslexia.* London: Routledge & Kegan Paul.

Cotman, C. W., & Lynch, G. F. (1988). The neurobiology of learning and memory. In J. F. Kavanagh & T. J. Truss (Eds.), *Learning disabilities: Proceeding of the National Conference* (pp. 1–69). Parkton, MD: York Press.

Cottrell, G. W. (1988). A model of lexical access of ambiguous words. In S. I. Small, G. W. Cottrell, & M. K. Tanenhaus (Eds.), *Lexical ambiguity resolution* (pp. 179–194). San Mateo, CA: Morgan Kaufmann Publishers.

Crick, F. H., & Asanuma, C. (1986). Certain aspects of the anatomy and physiology of the cerebral cortex. In J. L. McClelland & D. E. Rumelhart (Eds.), *Parallel distributed processing: Exploration in the microstructure of cognition* (Vol. 2, pp. 333–371). Cambridge, MA: MIT Press.

Dennis, M., Lovett, M., & Wiegel-Crump, C. A. (1981). Written language acquisition after left or right hemidecortication in infancy. *Brain & Language, 12,* 54–91.

DiLollo, V., Hanson, D., & McIntyre, J. S. (1983). Initial stages of visual information processing in dyslexia. *Journal of Experimental Psychology: Human Perception and Performance, 9,* 923–935.

Doctor, E. A., & Coltheart, M. (1980). Children's use of phonological encoding when reading for meaning. *Memory & Cognition, 8,* 195–209.

Doehring, D. G., & Hoshko, I. M. (1977). Classification of reading problems by the Q technique of factor analysis. *Cortex, 13,* 281–294.

Done, D. J., & Miles, T. R. (1978). Learning, memory and dyslexia. In M. M. Gruneberg, P. E. Morris, & R. N. Sykes (Eds.), *Practical aspects of memory.* London: Academic Press.

Doyle, J. R., & Leach, C. (1988). Word superiority in signal detection: Barely a glimpse, yet reading nonetheless. *Cognitive Psychology, 20,* 283–318.

Ehri, L. C., & Wilce, L. S. (1985). Movement into reading: Is the first stage of printed word learning visual or phonetic? *Reading Research Quarterly, 20,* 327–350.

Ericksen, C. (1980). The use of a visual mask may seriously confound your experiment. *Perception and Psychophysics, 28,* 89–92.

Firth, I. (1972). *Components of reading disability*. Unpublished doctoral dissertation, University of New South Wales.

Fischler, I., & Bloom, P. A. (1980). Rapid processing of the meaning of sentences. *Memory & Cognition, 8,* 216–225.

Fisher, D. F., & Frankfurter, A. (1977). Normal and disabled readers can locate and identify letters: Where's the perceptual deficit? *Journal of Reading Behavior, 9,* 31–43.

Fisher, D. F., & Lefton, L. A. (1976). Peripheral information extraction: A developmental examination of reading processes. *Journal of Experimental Child Psychology, 21,* 77–93.

Fodor, J. A. (1983). *The Modularity of Mind*. Cambridge, MA: MIT Press.

Frederiksen, J. R., & Kroll, J. F. (1976). Spelling and sound: Approaches to the internal lexicon. *Journal of Experimental Psychology: Human Perception and Performance, 2,* 361–379.

Frith, U. (1985). Beneath the surface of developmental dyslexia. In K. E. Patterson, J. C. Marshall, & M. Coltheart (Eds.), *Surface dyslexia*. London: Erlbaum.

Galaburda, A. M., Sherman, G. F., Rosen, G. D., Aboitiz, F., & Geschwind, N. (1985). Developmental dyslexia: Four consecutive patients with cortical anomalies. *Annals of Neurology, 18,* 222–233.

Gascon, G., & Goodglass, H. (1970). Reading retardation and the information content of stimuli in paired associate learning. *Cortex, 6,* 417–429.

Geschwind, N. (1962). The anatomy of acquired disorders of reading. In J. Money (Ed.), *Reading disability*. Baltimore, MD: Johns Hopkins University Press.

Gibson, E. J., & Levin, H. (1975). *The psychology of reading*. Cambridge, MA: MIT Press.

Gibson, E. J., Osser, H., & Pick, A. D. (1963). A study of the development of grapheme-phoneme correspondences. *Journal of Verbal Learning and Verbal Behavior, 2,* 142–146.

Gibson, E. J., Pick, A., Osser, H., & Hammond, M. (1962). The role of grapheme-phoneme correspondence in the perception of words. *American Journal of Psychology, 75,* 554–570.

Glushko, R. J. (1979). The organization and activation of orthographic knowledge in reading aloud. *Journal of Experimental Psychology: Human Perception and Performance, 5,* 674–691.

Gough, P., & Hillinger, M. (1980). Learning to read: An unnatural act. *Bulletin of the Orton Society, 30,* 171–196.

Haber, R. N. (1978). Visual perception. *Annual Review of Psychology, 29,* 31–59.

Harman, S. (1982). Are reversals a symptom of dyslexia? *Reading Teacher, 35,* 424–428.

Hécaen, H. (1976). Acquired aphasia in children and the ontogenesis of hemispheric functional specialization. *Brain & Language, 3,* 114–134.

Hinton, G. E. (1988). *Representing part-whole hierarchies in connectionist networks* (Tech. Rep. No. CRG-TR-88-2). Toronto: University of Toronto, Computer Science Department.

Hinton, G. E., & Anderson, J. A. (Eds.). (1981). *Parallel models of associative memory*. Hillsdale, NJ: Erlbaum.

Hinton, G. E., McClelland, J. L., & Rumelhart, D. E. (1986). Distributed representations. In D. E. Rumelhart & J. L. McClelland (Eds.), *Parallel distributed processing: Exploration in the microstructure of cognition* (Vol. 1, pp. 77–109). Cambridge, MA: MIT Press.

Holmes, D., & McKeever, W. (1979). Material specific serial memory deficit in adolescent dyslexics. *Cortex, 15,* 51–62.

Holmes, J. M. (1973). *Dyslexia: A neurolinguistic study of traumatic and developmental disorders of reading.* Unpublished doctoral dissertation, University of Edinburgh.

Holmes, J. M. (1978). "Regression" and reading breakdown. In A. Caramazza & E. B. Zurif (Eds.), *Language acquisition and language breakdown: Parallels and divergences.* Baltimore, MD: Johns Hopkins Press.

Horn, C. C., & Manis, F. R. (1985). Normal and disabled readers' use of orthographic structure in processing print. *Journal of Reading Behavior, 17,* 143–161.

Jenkins, W. M., Merzenich, M. M., & Ochs, M. T. (1984). Behaviorally controlled differential use of restricted hand surfaces induces changes in the cortical representation of the hand area 3b of adult owl monkeys. *Society for Neuroscience Abstracts, 10,* 665.

Johnston, J. C. (1981). Effects of advance precuing of alternatives on the perception of letters alone and in words. *Journal of Experimental Psychology: Human Perception and Performance, 7,* 560–572.

Johnston, J. C., & McClelland, J. L. (1973). Visual factors in word perception. *Perception and Psychophysics, 14,* 123–154.

Jorm, A. F. (1977). The effect of word imagery on reading performance as a function of reader ability. *Journal of Educational Psychology, 69,* 46–54.

Jorm, A. F. (1981). Children with reading and spelling retardation: Functioning of whole-word and correspondence-rule mechanisms. *Journal of Child Psychology and Psychiatry, 22,* 171–178.

Jorm, A. F., & Share, D. L. (1983). Phonological recoding and reading acquisition. *Applied Psycholinguistics, 4,* 103–147.

Juola, J. F., Schadler, M., Chabot, R. J., & McCaughey, M. W. (1978). The development of visual information processing skills related to reading. *Journal of Experimental Child Psychology, 25,* 459–476.

Kawamoto, A. H. (1988). Distributed representations of ambiguous words and their resolution in a connectionist network. In S. I. Small, G. W. Cottrell, & M. K. Tanenhaus (Eds.), *Lexical ambiguity resolution* (pp. 195–228). San Mateo, CA: Morgan Kaufmann Publishers.

Kay, J., & Marcel, A. (1981). One process, not two, in reading aloud: Lexical analogies do the work of non-lexical rules. *Quarterly Journal of Experimental Psychology, 33A,* 397–413.

Kershner, J. R., & King, A. J. (1974). Laterality of cognitive functions in achieving hemiplegic children. *Perceptual and Motor Skills, 39,* 1283–1289.

Lawrence, Y., Kee, D., & Hellige, J. (1980). Developmental differences in visual backward masking. *Child Development, 51,* 1081–1089.

Lefton, L. A., & Spragins, A. B. (1974). Orthographic structure and reading experience affect the transfer from iconic to short-term memory. *Journal of Experimental Psychology, 103,* 775–781.

Lenneberg, E. H. (1967). *Biological foundations of language*. New York: Wiley.

Leslie, L., & Shannon, A. J. (1981). Recognition of orthographic structure during beginning reading. *Journal of Reading Behavior, 13,* 313–324.

Liberman, I. (1982). A language-oriented view of reading and its disabilities. In H. Myklebust (Ed.), *Progress in learning disabilities* (Vol. 5). New York: Grune & Stratton.

Liberman, I. Y., Shankweiler, D., Liberman, A. M., Fowler, C., & Fischer, F. W. (1977). Phonetic segmentation and recoding in the beginning reader. In A. S. Reber & D. L. Scarborough (Eds.), *Toward a psychology of reading: The proceedings of the CUNY conference*. Hillsdale, NJ: Erlbaum.

Lovegrove, W., Martin, F., & Slaghuis, W. (1986). A theoretical and experimental case for a visual deficit in specific reading disability. *Cognitive Neuropsychology, 3,* 225–267.

Lovett, M. W. (1984). The search for subtypes of specific reading disability: Reflections from a cognitive perspective. *Annals of Dyslexia, 34,* 155–178.

Malatesha, R. N., & Dougan, D. R. (1982). Clinical Subtypes of developmental dyslexia: Resolution of an irresolute problem. In R. N. Malatesha & P. G. Aaron (Eds.), *Reading disorders: Varieties and treatments*. San Diego, CA: Academic Press.

Mandler, G. (1985). *Cognitive psychology*. Hillsdale, NJ: Erlbaum.

Mann, V., Liberman, I., & Shankweiler, D. (1980). Children's memory for sentences and word strings in relation to reading ability. *Memory & Cognition, 8,* 329–335.

Marcel, A. J. (1980). Surface dyslexia and beginning reading: A revised hypothesis of the pronunciation of print and its impairments. In M. Coltheart, K. E. Patterson, & J. C. Marshall (Eds.), *Deep dyslexia* (pp. 227–258). London: Routledge & Kegan Paul.

Marshall, J. C., & Newcombe, F. (1973). Patterns of paralexia: A psycholinguistic approach. *Journal of Psycholinguistic Research, 2,* 175–199.

Masonheimer, P. E., Drum, P. A., & Ehri, L. C. (1984). Does environmental print identification lead children into word reading? *Journal of Reading Behavior, 16,* 257–271.

Massaro, D. W. (1988). Some criticisms of connectionist models of human performance. *Journal of Memory and Language, 27,* 213–234.

Mattis, S. (1978). Dyslexia syndromes: A working hypothesis that works. In A. L. Benton & D. Pearls (Eds.), *Dyslexia: An appraisal of current knowledge*. New York: Oxford University Press.

Mattis, S., French, J. H., & Rapin, I. (1975). Dyslexia in children and young adults: Three independent neuropsychological syndromes. *Developmental Medicine and Child Neurology, 17,* 150–163.

McClelland, J. L. (1979). On the time relations of mental processes: An examination of systems of processes in cascade. *Psychological Review, 86,* 287–330.

McClelland, J. L. (1985). Putting knowledge in its place: A scheme for programming parallel processing structures on the fly. *Cognitive Science, 9,* 113–146.

McClelland, J. L. (1986). The programmable blackboard model of reading. In J. L. McClelland & D. E. Rumelhart (Eds.), *Parallel distributed processing: Exploration in the microstructure of cognition* (Vol. 2, pp. 122–169). Cambridge, MA: MIT Press.

McClelland, J. L., & Rumelhart, D. E. (1981). An interactive activation model of context effects in letter perception: Part 1. An account of basic findings. *Psychological Review, 88,* 375–407.

McClelland, J. L., Rumelhart, D. E., & Hinton, G. E. (1986). The appeal of parallel distributed processing. In D. E. Rumelhart & J. L. McClelland (Eds.), *Parallel distributed processing: Exploration in the microstructure of cognition* (Vol. 1, pp. 3–44). Cambridge, MA: MIT Press.

Merrill, E. C., Sperber, R. D., & McCauley, C. (1981). Differences in semantic encoding as a function of reading comprehension skill. *Memory & Cognition, 9,* 618–624.

Merzenich, M. M., & Kaas, J. H. (1982). Reorganization of mammalian somatosensory cortex following peripheral nerve injury. *Trends in Neuroscience, 5,* 434–436.

Merzenich, M. M., Kaas, J. H., Wall, J. T., Sur, M., Nelson, R. J., & Felleman, D. J. (1983). Progression of change following median nerve section in the cortical representation of the hand in areas 3b and 1 in adult owl and squirrel monkeys. *Neuroscience, 10,* 639–665.

Mozer, M. C. (1988). *The perception of multiple objects: A parallel distributed processing approach* (ICS Tech. Rep. No. 8803). University of California, San Diego, Institute for Cognitive Science.

Neisser, U. (1967). *Cognitive psychology.* New York: Appleton-Century-Crofts.

Newcombe, F., & Marshall, J. C. (1984). Varieties of acquired dyslexia: A linguistic approach. *Seminars in Neurology, 4,* 181–195.

Norris, D., & Brown, G. (1985). Race models and analogy theories: A dead heat? Reply to Seidenberg. *Cognition, 20,* 155–168.

Otto, W. (1961). The acquisition and retention of paired associates by good, average and poor readers. *Journal of Education Psychology, 52,* 241–248.

Paap, K. R., Newsome, S. L., McDonald, J. E., & Schvaneveldt, R. W. (1982). An activation-verification model for letter and word recognition: The word superiority effect. *Psychology Review, 89,* 573–594.

Patberg, J. P., & Yonas, A. (1978). The effects of the reader's skill and the difficulty of the text on the perceptual span in reading. *Journal of Experimental Psychology: Human Perception and Performance, 4,* 545–552.

Patterson, K. E., Marshall, J. C., & Coltheart, M. (Eds.). (1985). *Surface dyslexia.* London: Erlbaum.

Perfetti, C. A., Goldman, S. R., & Hogaboam, T. W. (1979). Reading skill and the identification words in discourse context. *Memory & Cognition, 7,* 273–282.

Peterson, S. E., Fox, P. T., Posner, M. I., Mintun, M., & Raichle, M. E. (1988). Positron emission tomographic studies of the cortical anatomy of single-word processing. *Nature (London), 331,* 585–589.

Petrauskas, R., & Rourke, B. (1979). Identification of subtypes of retarded readers: A neuropsychological, multivariate approach. *Journal of Clinical Neuropsychology, 1,* 17–37.

Posner, M. I., Inhoff, A. W., Friedrich, F. J., & Cohen, A. (1987). Isolating attentional systems: A cognitive anatomical analysis. *Psychobiology, 15,* 107–121.

Posner, M. I., Rafal, R. D., Choate, L. S., & Vaughan, J. (1985). Inhibition of return: Neural basis and function. *Cognitive Neuropsychology, 2,* 211–228.

Posner, M. I., Walker, J. A., Friedrich, F. A., & Rafal, R. D. (1987). How do the parietal lobes direct covert attention? *Neuropsychologia, 25,* 135–145.

Purcell, D. G., & Stanovich, K. E. (1982). Some boundary conditions for a word superiority effect. *Quarterly Journal of Experimental Psychology: Human Experimental Psychology, 34A,* 117–134.

Pylyshyn, Z. (1984). *Computation and cognition.* Cambridge, MA: MIT Press.

Raduege, T. A., & Schwantes, F. M. (1987). Effects of rapid word recognition training on sentence context effects in children. *Journal of Reading Behavior, 19,* 395–414.

Rayner, K., & Duffy, S. A. (1988). On-line comprehension processes and eye movements during reading. In M. Daneman, G. E. MacKinnon, & T. G. Waller (Eds.), *Reading research: Advances in theory and practice* (Vol. 6, pp. 13–66). San Diego, CA: Academic Press.

Rayner, K., & Pollatsek, A. (1989). *The psychology of reading.* Englewood Cliffs, NJ: Prentice-Hall.

Reicher, G. M. (1969). Perceptual recognition as a function of meaningfulness of stimulus material. *Journal of Experimental Psychology, 81,* 274–280.

Reitsma, P. (1983). Printed word learning in beginning readers. *Journal of Experimental Child Psychology, 36,* 321–339.

Rosinski, R. R., & Wheeler, K. E. (1972). Children's use of orthographic structure in word discrimination. *Psychonomic Science, 26,* 97–98.

Rosson, M. B. (1983). From SOFA to LOURCH: Lexical contributions to pseudo-word pronunciation. *Memory & Cognition, 11,* 152–160.

Rumelhart, D. E. (1977). Toward an interactive model of reading. In S. Dornic (Ed.), *Attention and performance VI* (pp. 573–603). Hillsdale, NJ: Erlbaum.

Rumelhart, D. E., Hinton, G. E., & Williams, R. J. (1986). Learning representations by back-propagating errors. *Nature (London) 323,* 533–536.

Rumelhart, D. E., & McClelland, J. L. (1982). An interactive activation model of context effects in letter perception: Part 2. The contextual enhancement effect and some tests and extensions of the model. *Psychological Review, 89,* 60–94.

Rumelhart, D. E., & McClelland, J. L. (1986). On learning the past tenses of English verbs. In J. L. McClelland & D. E. Rumelhart (Eds.) *Parallel distributed processing: Explorations in the microstructure of cognition* (Vol. 2, pp. 216–271). Cambridge, MA: MIT Press.

Rumelhart, D. E., & McClelland, J. L. (1986). PDP models and general issues in cognitive science. In D. E. Rumelhart & J. L. McClelland (Eds.). Parallel distributed processing: Explorations in the microstructure of cognition (Vol. 1, pp. 110–146). Cambridge, MA: MIT Press.

Satz, P., & Morris, R. (1981). Learning disability subtypes: A review. In F. J. Pirozzolo & M. C. Wittrock (Eds.), *Neuropsychological and cognitive processes in reading.* New York: Academic Press.

Satz, P., Morris, R., & Fletcher, J. (1985). Hypotheses, subtypes, and individual differences in dyslexia: Some reflections. In D. B. Gray & J. F. Kavanagh (Eds.), *Biobehavioral measures of dyslexia*. Parkton, MD: York Press.

Schank, R. C. (1973). Identification of conceptualizations underlying natural language. In R. C. Schank & K. M. Colby (Eds.), *Computer models of thought and language*. San Francisco, CA: Freeman.

Schlieper, A. (1980). Reversal and sequence errors in meaningful text. *Reading Improvement, 17*, 74–79.

Schvaneveldt, R. W., Ackerman, B. P., & Semlear, T. (1977). The effect of semantic context on children's word recognition. *Child Development, 48*, 612–616.

Schvaneveldt, R. W., & Meyer, D. E. (1973). Retrieval and comparison processes in semantic memory. In S. Kornblum (Ed.), *Attention and performance IV*. New York: Academic Press.

Schwantes, F. M. (1981). Locus of the context effect in children's word recognition. *Child Development, 52*, 895–903.

Schwantes, F. M. (1982). Text readability level and developmental differences in context effects. *Journal of Reading Behavior, 14*, 5–12.

Seidenberg, M. S. (1985a). The time course of phonological code activation in two writing systems. *Cognition, 19*, 1–30.

Seidenberg, M. S. (1985b). Constraining models of word recognition. *Cognition, 20*, 169–190.

Seidenberg, M. S. (1985c). The time course of information activation and utilization in visual word recognition. In D. Besner, T. G. Waller, & G. E. MacKinnon (Eds.), *Reading research: Advances in theory and practice* (Vol. 5, pp. 200–252). Orlando, FL: Academic Press.

Seidenberg, M. S. (1988). Cognitive neuropsychology and language: The state of the art. *Cognitive Neuropsychology, 5*, 403–426.

Seidenberg, M. S., Bruck, M., Fornarolo, G., & Backman, J. (1985). Word recognition processes of poor and disabled readers: Do they necessarily differ? *Applied Psycholinguistics, 6*, 161–180.

Seidenberg, M. S., & McClelland, J. L. (1989). A distributed, developmental model of word recognition and naming. *Psychological Review, 96*, 523–568.

Seidenberg, M. S., Waters, G. S., Barnes, M. A., & Tanenhaus, M. K. (1984). When does irregular spelling or pronunciation influence word recognition? *Journal of Verbal Learning and Verbal Behavior, 23*, 383–404.

Sejnowski, T. J. (1986). Open questions about computation in cerebral cortex. In J. L. McClelland & D. E. Rumelhart (Eds.) *Parallel distributed processing: Explorations in the microstructure of cognition* (Vol. 2, pp. 372–389). Cambridge, MA: MIT Press.

Sejnowski, T. J., & Rosenberg, C. R. (1986). *NETtalk: A parallel network that learns to read aloud* (Tech. Rep. No. 13). Baltimore, MD: Johns Hopkins University, Cognitive Neuropsychology Laboratory.

Seymour, P. H. K., & Porpodas, C. D. (1980). Lexical and non-lexical processing of spelling in dyslexia. In U. Frith (Ed.), *Cognitive processes in spelling*. New York: Academic Press.

Shallice, T., & McCarthy, R. (1985). Phonological reading: From patterns of impairment to possible procedures. In K. E. Patterson, J. C., Marshall, & M. Coltheart (Eds.), *Surface dyslexia.* London: Erlbaum.

Shallice, T., & Warrington, E. K. (1980). Single and multiple component central dyslexic syndromes. In M. Coltheart, K. E. Patterson, & J. C. Marshall (Eds.), *Deep dyslexia.* London: Routledge & Kegan Paul.

Shankweiler, D., Liberman, I. Y., Mark, L. S., Fowler, C. A., & Fischer, F. W. (1979). The speech code and learning to read. *Journal of Experimental Psychology: Human Learning and Memory, 5,* 531–545.

Shepherd, G. M. (1979). *The synaptic organization of the brain.* New York: Oxford University Press.

Sieroff, E., Pollatsek, A., & Posner, M. I. (1988). Recognition of visual letter strings following injury to the posterior visual spatial attention system. *Cognitive Neuropsychology, 5,* 427–449.

Sieroff, E., & Posner, M. I. (1988). Cueing spatial attention during processing of words and letter strings in normals. *Cognitive Neuropsychology, 5,* 451–472.

Simons, H. D., & Leu, D. J. (1987). The use of contextual and graphic information in word recognition by second-, fourth-, and sixth-grade readers. *Journal of Reading Behavior, 19,* 33–47.

Simpson, G. B., & Lorsbach, T. C. (1983). The development of automatic and conscious components of contextual facilitation. *Child Development, 54,* 760–772.

Simpson, G. B., Lorsbach, T. C., & Whitehouse, D. (1983). Encoding and contextual components word recognition in good and poor readers. *Journal of Experimental and Child Psychology, 35,* 161–171.

Snowling, M. J. (1980). The development of grapheme-phoneme correspondence in normal and dyslexic readers. *Journal of Experimental Child Psychology, 29,* 294–305.

Stanovich, K. E. (1980). Toward an interactive-compensatory model of individual differences the development of reading fluency. *Reading Research Quarterly, 16,* 32–71.

Stanovich, K. E. (1982). Individual differences in the cognitive processes of reading: I. Word decoding. *Journal of Learning Disabilities, 15,* 485–493.

Stanovich, K. E. (1985). Cognitive processes and the reading problems of learning disabled children: Evaluating the assumption of specificity. In J. Torgesen & B. Wong (Eds.), *Psychological and educational perspectives on learning disabilities* (pp. 87–113). Orlando, FL: Academic Press.

Stanovich, K. E. (1988). Science and learning disabilities. *Journal of Learning Disabilities, 21,* 210–214.

Stanovich, K. E., & Bauer, D. W. (1978). Experiments on the spelling- to sound regularity effect in word recognition. *Memory & Cognition, 6,* 410–415.

Stanovich, K. E., Nathan, R. G., West, R. F., & Vala-Rossi, M. (1985). Children's word recognition in context: Spreading activation, expectancy, and modularity. *Child Development, 56,* 1418–1428.

Stanovich, K. E., West, R. F., & Feeman, D. J. (1981). A longitudinal study of sentence context effects in second-grad children: Tests of an interactive-compensatory model. *Journal of Experimental Child Psychology, 13,* 185–199.

Stuart, M., & Coltheart, M. (1988). Does reading develop in a sequence of stages? *Cognition, 30,* 139–181.

Swanson, H. L. (1988). Toward a metatheory of learning disabilities. *Journal of Learning Disabilities, 21,* 196–209.

Tallal, P. (1980). Language and reading: Some perceptual prerequisites. *Bulletin of the Orton Society, 30,* 170–178.

Tallal, P. (1988). Developmental language disorders. In J. F. Kavanagh & T. J. Truss (Eds.) *Learning disabilities: Proceedings of the National Conference* (pp. 181–272). Parkton, MD: York Press.

Tanenhaus, M., Leiman, J., & Seidenberg, M. (1979). Evidence for multiple stages in the processing of ambiguous words in syntactic contexts. *Journal of Verbal Learning and Verbal Behavior, 18,* 427–441.

Temple, C. M. (1984). New approaches to the developmental dyslexias. *Advances in Neurology, 42,* 223–232.

Temple, C. M. (1985). Surface dyslexia: Variations within a syndrome. In K. E. Patterson, J. C. Marshall, & M. Coltheart (Eds.), *Surface dyslexia.* London: Erlbaum.

Temple, C. M., & Marshall, J. C. (1983). A case study of developmental phonological dyslexia. *British Journal of Psychology, 74,* 517–533.

Vargha-Khadem, F., O'Gorman, A. M., & Watters, G. V. (1985). Aphasia and handedness in relation to hemispheric side, age at injury and severity of cerebral lesion during childhood. *Brain, 108,* 677–696.

Vellutino, F. R. (1979). *Dyslexia: Theory and research.* Cambridge, MA: MIT Press.

Vellutino, F. R., Harding, C. J., Phillips, F., & Steger, J. A. (1975). Differential transfer in poor and normal readers. *Journal of Genetic Psychology, 126,* 3–18.

Vellutino, F. R., Steger, J. A., Harding, C. J., & Phillips, F. (1975). Verbal vs. non-verbal paired-associates learning in poor and normal readers. *Neuropsychologia, 13,* 75–82.

Venezky, R. L. (1970). *The structure of English orthography.* The Hague: Mouton.

Waters, G. S., Seidenberg, M. S., & Bruck, M. (1984). Children's and adults' use of spelling-sound information in three reading tasks. *Memory & Cognition, 12,* 293–305.

West, R. F., & Stanovich, K. E. (1978). Automatic contextual facilitation in readers of three ages. *Child Development, 49,* 717–727.

Wickelgren, W. A. (1969). Context-sensitive coding, associative memory, and serial order in (speech) behavior. *Psychological Review, 76,* 1–15.

Williams, M. C., Gaffney, J. B., & Solman, R. T. (1985). The word- superiority effect under conditions that approximate reading. *Brain & Language, 25,* 160–166.

Zecker, S. G., & Zinner, T. E. (1987). Semantic code deficit for reading disabled children on an auditory lexical decision task. *Journal of Reading Behavior, 19,* 177–189.

CHAPTER TEN

Learning Disabilities, Distinctive Encoding, and Hemispheric Resources: An Information-Processing Perspective

H. Lee Swanson

I. Introduction

Traditionally, theories of children's memory have relied almost exclusively on data from normal subjects. However, recent years have seen a growing realization that performance of subjects with information-processing deficits, such as the learning disabled, represent an important source of information about memory performance (e.g., Ceci, Lea, & Ringstrom, 1980). The impaired memory performance of such subjects may be brought to bear on theories that emanate from both cognitive and neuropsychological frameworks. For example, learning-disabled (LD) children's memory deficiencies have been documented in the cognitive and neuropsychological literature (e.g., see Ceci, 1986, for a review). The research to date suggests that such children have an impairment in memory encoding (e.g., Swanson, 1987c), possibly due to semantic memory deficiencies (e.g., Baker, Ceci, & Herrmann, 1987; Bub, Black, Hampson, & Kertesz, 1988; Chabot, Petros, & McCord, 1983; Swanson, 1986, in press), as well as problems in interhemispheric processing (transmitting information across the corpus callosum) (e.g., Boliek, Obrzut, & Shaw, 1988; Hynd, Obrzut, & Bowen, 1987; Obrzut, Hynd, & Zellner, 1983; Obrzut, Obrzut, Bryden, & Bartels, 1985).

Findings on unique populations such as these provide an opportunity to relate cognitive theories of memory encoding to neuropsychological data. One methodology by which this can occur is to vary distinctive encoding demands on dichotic listening tasks. Such a methodology permits the uncovering of particular processes that are responsible for variations in distinctive encoding as well as the extent to which encoding activities draw limited sources from one or the other cerebral hemisphere. In this chapter, the memory encoding hypothesis will be reviewed under conditions that manipulate the demands made on hemispheric resources. Of particular interest was how LD readers distinctively encode information.

The chapter is organized around three themes. First, the question of how hemispheric resources coordinate information-processing will be addressed. Three information-processing models are considered as a means to understand how hemispheric resources are activated during the recall of words. Second, the interaction between structure, as defined in terms of hemispheric resources, and process, as defined by the level of word processing and retrieval organization, is considered. The findings consider the inadequacy of an isolated focus on structure and process as an account for learning disabilities. Third, the role of semantic memory in hemispheric processing is outlined. It is suggested that semantic memory may account for the hemispheric processing and inefficiencies noted in LD readers. A distinctive coding hypothesis is presented as one of the manifestations of poor semantic memory in LD readers.

A. Information-Processing Models

Hemispheric asymmetries from an information-processing perspective have been studied with LD children (Kershner, Henninger, & Cooke, 1984; Swanson & Mullen, 1983). Within the information-processing perspective, however, at least three models may be invoked to explain the role of encoding an LD readers' hemispheric processing. One model suggests that these children are less able (capable) than nondisabled children in dividing their attention between the two hemispheres (e.g., Obrzut, Hynd, Obrzut, & Pirozzolo, 1981). Evidence to support this selective-attention model comes from dichotic listening tasks employing both undirected- and directed-attention conditions. These studies suggest that both LD and nondisabled children show a right-ear advantage (REA), but LD children have more difficulty demonstrating an REA when attention is directed to the left ear (see Hynd et al., 1987, for a review). In contrast, nondisabled children produce the REA regardless of attention conditions. Results such as these suggest that the LD children's selective attention difficulties are related to their inability to process simultaneous information from both hemispheres across the corpus callosum (e.g., see Obrzut et al., 1981).

Another model that may account for LD readers' hemispheric process-ing deficits may be related to resource allocation (Kershner et al., 1984). That is, nondisabled children allocate a smaller proportion of their limited atten-tional resources to an encoding task than do LD children. Support for the attentional-capacity model is applied to learning disabilities is indirect. Studies with nondisabled subjects have shown that attentional capacity is important to efficient hemispheric performance and that the conservation of attentional resources is dependent on a division of "labor" between hemispheres (e.g., Friedman, Polson, Defoe, & Gaskill, 1988). This resource-allocation model captures some of the aspects of the selective-attention model discussed earlier but is more inclusive because the processing dynamics of a limited-capacity system are proposed (see Friedman & Polson, 1981, for a review).

Finally, the amount of word knowledge activated from long-term mem-ory may influence disabled readers' hemispheric processing (Swanson & Mullen, 1983; Swanson & Obrzut, 1985). For example, Swanson (1986) proposed a distinctive-encoding hypothesis that viewed LD children as failing to activate word features in semantic memory that presumably regulated their level of word encoding and locus of hemispheric processing. As an extension of this hypothesis, it may be assumed that an impoverished activation of word knowledge (i.e., semantic memory) influences what items can be selectively attended to and what attentional resources can be effectively allocated during hemispheric processing. There is sufficient evidence supporting the notion that an impoverished knowledge base influences memory encoding (e.g., Baker et al., 1987; Riddoch & Humphreys, 1987; Swanson, 1986). There is also indirect information suggesting that LD children have long-term mem-ory deficiencies in the amount of information contained (e.g., Swanson & Mullen, 1983), the internal coherence of that information (e.g., Dallago & Moely, 1980), and the number of available routes by which that information can be retrieved (e.g., Cermak, 1983; Shankweiler, Liberman, Fowler, & Fisher, 1979). These "knowledge" deficiencies in long-term memory may impose several limitations on LD children's information-processing abilities and therefore it may be reasoned that such limitations influence hemispheric processing.

Based on these three information-processing models, two hypotheses involving attentional resources are thought to be illuminating regarding ability-group differences in memory encoding. First, LD readers' poor encod-ing is characterized by an attentional-resource deficit. Such a global resource deficit has been recently established in the literature (Swanson, 1986; 1989; Swanson, Cochran, & Ewars, 1989). Later in the chapter, studies to deter-mine if this attentional deficit is characterized in terms of reciprocity, inte-grality, and/or resource-allocation strategies will be reviewed.

The second hypothesis is that the distinctive-encoding and attentional-capacity deficits of LD readers may be linked to the availability of stored information. The basis for this hypothesis is somewhat more tentative than the first, since a common assumption is that LD readers' encoding deficiencies reflect problems with accessing adequately stored information (i.e., the use of control processes) (Bauer & Emhert, 1984; Dallago & Moely, 1980). Recent research has indicated, however, that LD readers' encoding of information, which relies on the accessing of word information from semantic memory or other resource pools, is more diffuse and thus the memory trace more fragmented than that of skilled readers (Swanson, 1986; Swanson & Obrzut, 1985). Some earlier studies initially supporting these hypotheses will now be discussed.

II. Interaction of Structure and Process

Numerous studies have addressed possible memory differences between LD and nondisabled readers (e.g., Dallago & Moeley, 1980; Swanson, in press; Torgesen, 1977). Within these studies of LD readers' memory development, two broad theories may be distinguished. The structural-deficiency hypothesis suggests that faulty memory of LD children is caused by inherent limitations, such as atypical hemispheric processing (e.g., Beaumont & Rugg, 1978; Witelson, 1977), and the strategic-deficiency hypothesis suggests that LD children perform poorly on word-recall tasks because of their inability or lack of inclination to effectively cluster or organize information (e.g., Dallago & Moely, 1980). The difficulty of both explanations, of course, is that these theories are not particularly useful in accounting for LD readers' recall because they provide limited information on the *interaction* of both structural and strategic deficiencies. A hypothesis is needed that integrates both the structural and the organizational deficiency notions to explain LD readers' faulty recall. The first study reviewed will address this issue.

A. Study 1

The assumption of the first study is that neither the structural- nor the strategic- deficit hypothesis adequately explains LD children's faulty memory performance. Thus, a hypothesis that incorporates the mechanisms of both cognitive and physiological theory must be invoked to explain LD children's information processing. One possible mechanism that may bridge the two theories is that LD children suffer from a limited word-knowledge structure (semantic memory). In support of this notion, several authors (e.g., Riddoch, Humphreys, Coltheart, & Funnel, 1988; Tulving & Thomson, 1973) suggest that a word has a representation in semantic memory representing various sets of features (i.e., orthographic, phonemic, semantic). These features form an integrated referent or word-knowledge structure. During word encoding, there is an activation of some subset of features from that referent (e.g., Hunt & Mitchell, 1978; Kintsch, 1974; Ratcliff & McKoon, 1989). Certain word features are activated within hemispheres or interchanges between the hemispheres across the callosum (cf. Sidtis, Volpe, Holtzman, Wilson, & Gazzaniga, 1981). Adequacy of word recall, then, is a product of the structures of the child's word knowledge in interaction with processes directing attention to some feature of that word. One possible mechanism affecting both hemispheric and strategic processing of word features may be related to the word-knowledge resources (referred to in this chapter as semantic memory) that can be effectively *activated* to meet task demands.

Swanson and Mullen (1983) provide a preliminary test of this hypothesis, and of the inadequacy of the structural- and strategic-deficiency hypotheses in isolation in accounting for LD readers' recall. To this end, learning-disabled and nondisabled readers were compared on diotic and dichotic listening recall tasks for semantically organized, phonemically organized, and categorically unrelated word lists presented in the left, the right, or both ears. Two age levels were included in the present study because recall deficiencies of learning-disabled readers have been attributed to developmental factors such as lateralization (e.g., Satz, 1976; Satz & Sparrow, 1970) and organizational strategy (e.g., Dallago & Moely, 1980; Tarver, Hallahan, Kauffman, & Ball, 1976; see Swanson & Rathgeber, 1986, for a review).

Word-processing strategies were operationally defined in the present study by the clustering availability of word lists (see Dallago & Moely, 1980, for rationale). Clustering is assumed to function as a retrieval plan for generation at output (e.g., Anderson, 1976). Tentative support would be found for a structural-deficit hypothesis if similar lateral asymmetries and clusterings occurred between reading groups, whereas LD readers are inferior in recall to nondisabled readers. That is, when the same lateral asymmetries occur between LD and nondisabled readers we can reasonably assume that the organization of cerebral functions is the same and differences in recall can be attributed to capacity. Tentative support for strategic-deficit hypothesis would be found when different lateral asymmetries and organization abilities exist between the reading groups.

An attempt was also made to understand the mechanisms that may contribute to both the structural and the strategic recall deficiencies of LD readers. A testable construct of word knowledge is the child's ability to form and retrieve an interrelated network of nodes and links (see Anderson, 1976). One such network is the retrieval of superordinate relationships. For example, the word *chair* is a distinct word but related to a superordinate rhyme node of *air*. Because the superordinate classification has been linked to a child's word knowledge (Chi, 1983), this may represent one (of many) mechanisms related to LD readers' faulty retrieval.

TABLE I Mean Percentage Correct Recall as a Function of Age, Group, Mode or Presentation, and Level of Word Processing[a]

	Both ears			Right ear			Left ear		
	Semantic	Phonemic	Unrelated	Semantic	Phonemic	Unrelated	Semantic	Phonemic	Unrelated
Older									
Disabled	.44	.28	.29	.36	.36	.26	.44	.33	.26
	(.11)[b]	(.09)	(.11)	(.16)	(.14)	(.11)	(.16)	(.11)	(.06)
Nondisabled	.45	.38	.35	.44	.42	.35	.43	.33	.30
	(.18)	(.12)	(.08)	(.13)	(.13)	(.13)	(.13)	(.11)	(.07)
Younger									
Disabled	.37	.28	23	.29	.24	.26	.38	.28	.26
	(.12)	(.11)	(.12)	(.11)	(.13)	(.09)	(.12)	(.08)	(.06)
Nondisabled	.33	.30	.20	.42	.29	.22	.37	.31	.29
	(.12)	(.10)	(.04)	(.16)	(.09)	(.05)	(.11)	(.11)	(.09)

[a] From Swanson and Mullen (1983).
[b] Standard deviation in parentheses.

246

B. *Subjects, Method, and Results*

Subjects in this study consisted of nondisabled and LD boys separated into two age groups (8 and 10 years), with each subject age-group-matched on the basis of IQ and chronological age. Percentage correct recall as a function of age, reader group (nondisabled versus disabled), mode of presentation (diotic, both ears; dichotic, left ear, then right ear), and level of word processing (semantic, phonemic, unrelated) is presented in Table I. Increases in recall were a function of age and level of word processing (semantically organized words were recalled more effectively than phonemically organized or categorically unrelated words). The results indicate that higher recall occurred for nondisabled than LD readers on the both-ear phonemically organized, the right-ear semantically organized, and the right-ear phonemically organized word-lists conditions. No significant difference between group recall occurred on other levels of word processing. Learning-disabled readers recalled more words on the both-ear and left-ear than right-ear presentation. Another analysis was done to more closely analyze organizational patterns of LD and nondisabled readers' retrieval of words. The percentage of superordinate categories recalled was computed and only one significant main effect occurred: Nondisabled readers recalled more categories than LD readers.

C. *Summary*

This preliminary study indicated that LD and nondisabled readers' recall differences are due to *both* asymmetric organization of cerebral functions and organization processes used to encode words. Thus, the structural- and strategic-deficiency hypotheses in isolation do not appear to explain recall differences. One possible explanation for the results, to be developed later in the chapter, is that individual differences between ability groups are directly related to existing word structures in semantic memory. The extent to which LD and nondisabled children employ word-knowledge structures depends on the fit between their preferred hemispheric specialization and their strategies to organize words for retrieval. The next study reviewed, however, extends this earlier work by suggesting that LD readers compensate for their inadequate knowledge base (semantic memory) by the way they coordinate information across the cerebral hemispheres.

III. Coordination of Resources

Next, research on *how* the combination of multiple hemispheric resources characterize LD and skilled readers' memory performance is reviewed. Hemispheric resources may be conceptualized as those processes, strategies, or mechanisms from two independent cerebral spheres that influence memory performance (e.g., Friedman & Polson, 1981; Hellige & Wong, 1983). A focus on how multiple hemispheric resources aggregate (combine) to influence individual differences in memory performance has been of theoretical interest (e.g., Friedman & Polson, 1981; Hynd, Obrzut, Weed, & Hynd, 1979; Kerschner et al., 1984). For example, the wide range of individual differences in the degree of lateralization on dichotic listening tasks has led some theorists (e.g., Friedman & Polson, 1981; Somberg & Salthouse, 1982) to suggest that memory performance is characterized by different hemispheric resource combinations, which may or may not require supplies primarily from one or both cerebral hemispheres. Therefore, because the human system develops a number of alternative means of combining hemispheric resources, it appears necessary to compare a number of information-processing models in hopes of capturing ability-group differences in performance.

In considering the possible models that may capture the diversity of performance between ability groups, the following question must be asked: Can retrieval performance which draws resources from a particular cerebral hemisphere predict performance on a memory task that simultaneously activates the resources from both hemispheres? That is, can dichotic or unilateral encoding conditions predict recall performance on simultaneous (i.e., diotic) encoding conditions? The question is important for two reasons. First, the range of individual differences in lateralization on dichotic tasks suggests that few tasks require hemisphere-specific resources to attain an acceptable level of performance (e.g., Carswell & Wickens, 1985; Friedman & Polson, 1981; Herdman & Friedman, 1985). Thus, it may be argued that unilateral tasks do not demand qualitatively different resources than those that are activated during simultaneous encoding conditions. The major implication is that unilateral presentations may accurately predict ability-group performance during simultaneous processing.

Second, a comparison between unilateral and simultaneous processing is useful in assessing theories about the LD readers' memory performance. For example, several earlier studies (Beaumont & Rugg, 1978; Orton, 1937; see Satz, 1976; Witelson, 1977, for a review) suggest that LD readers' memory difficulties are related to incomplete lateralization. It is assumed that ability-group differences result from the fact that language representations become more unilateral (i.e., left hemisphere) in specialization for skilled readers than for LD readers. However, recent studies suggest that LD readers' recall difficulties are related to interhemispheric processing difficulties which result from the shifting of attention from one ear to the other (Hynd et al., 1979; Obrzut, Hynd, Obrzut, & Leitgeb, 1980). One means of testing these competing assumptions is to compare ability-group recall on tasks which present stimuli unilaterally or monaurally (thus to minimize the attentional shift from one ear to the other) to their recall on tasks that require simultaneous processing of the same stimuli (thus to maximize conditions which encourage shifting of attention).

A. Resource Competition

No doubt, predictions about ability-group performance relative to the research question are difficult to answer since it may be argued that successful unilateral encoding creates a *competition* for independent hemispheric resources while successful simultaneous encoding is related to a *coordination* of hemispheric resources (e.g., Friedman *et al.,* 1982). Specifically, when unilateral encoding conditions are used (i.e., in this case when subjects are asked to respond to stimulus presented to one ear) it is necessary to consider each ear presentation (right versus left) as a different task, for which the resources demanded from each hemisphere may differ. This occurs because the two independent hemispheres compete (thus, resources for each hemisphere potentially differ) for the type of resources the task requires. Therefore, any ear advantage noted between ability groups reflects the relative efficiency of applying different resources to the same memory task. On the other hand, simultaneous encoding depends less on the efficiency of resources than on the *coordination* of independent resources (Friedman *et al.,* 1982). This has implications for the kinds of hemispheric sharing of trade-off effects that would be observed in LD and non-LD ability groups. Specifically, when information is simultaneously presented to both ears (i.e., both hemispheres), ability-group differences in performance reflect the fact that (1) performance depends less on the degree of lateralization than on the concurrent demands for resources from both hemispheres, and (2) the hemispheric resources demanded by a particular task may overlap with those from another either partially, completely, or not at all. Thus, an important task when predicting ability-group performance from unilateral to simultaneous encoding conditions is to characterize *how* the two cerebral hemispheres in both ability groups combine (or do not combine) to perform memory operations. In this regard, three information-processing models must be considered.

One possible model for conceptualizing the flexibility of processing among ability groups is to determine the manner in which multiple resources contribute to recall in an "additive" fashion (Swanson, 1984b, 1987b, 1987c). The premises of this model are borrowed largely from Paivio (1971) and Tulving and Watkins (1975). An additive hypothesis, applied to hemispheric functioning, assumes that some aspect of a task (word recall in this case) requires resources from one hemisphere and other aspects of the task require resources from the opposite or both hemispheres. Consider a memory trace that draws complementary resources from both the left and right hemispheres (LR), L but not R resources (L*R* component), R but not L resources, (R*L*), or neither L nor R resources (*LR,* or null component). If a word is encoded in either the right or the left hemisphere, retrieval of that word will occur if any of the non-null components are present. If the same word is presented simultaneously to both ears, retrieval of that word is greatly enhanced over unilateral encoding conditions, because the resources of both hemispheres are combined to form an integrated or complementary set of memorial information. Viewing the combination of resources as probabilities, the probability of recall for simultaneous encoding, $p(R = L)$, is greater than $[p(R), p(L)]$ for encoding in isolation. Thus, recall of simultaneous presentations provides an additive component in recall when compared to unilateral encoding presentations (i.e., directed listening to the right or left ear). As a consequence, simultaneous encoding conditions should increase recall over unilateral encoding conditions.

A second additive model may again view information from the hemispheres as independent but not as complementary fragments that form an aggregate of memorial information. That is, the two hemispheres may be considered to combine resources that are distinct and nonoverlapping. A prediction of this model is that simultaneous encoding improves recall when compared to unilateral encoding conditions. Hence, during simultaneous encoding the right and left hemispheres may be seen to combine independent information in an additive fashion (see Friedman & Polson, 1981, for a rationale). A formula for determining the additive function of two independent resources is provided in the literature on adult subjects using cued recall (e.g., Bruce, 1980). Adapting a formula from Bruce (1980), the prediction of simultaneous encoding from unilateral encoding conditions is $p(R = L) = [p(R) = p(L)] - [p(R) \times p(L)]$.

The third model, unlike the previous two where the hemispheres function in an additive fashion during simultaneous encoding, suggests that the two hemispheres are correlated in terms of processing efficiency. Assumptions for this model, the maximum-rule model, may be derived from the literature on adult memory (e.g., Bruce, 1980) and Gibson's (1971) model of perceptual coding. Two assumptions are related to the maximum-rule model when applied to hemispheric processing. First, the correlated relationship between the two hemispheres represents two resources of differing potency. For example, if a particular linguistic feature is retrieved by a hemisphere that does not specialize in linguistic processing, then it will also be retrieved when encoded in the specialized hemisphere. Second, as a consequence of this correlation, regardless of hemispheric specialization, simultaneous encoding would not increase recall when compared to unilateral encoding. This is because the less potent hemisphere adds nothing to the effectiveness of simultaneous encoding. Thus $p(R = L)$ is equal to $p(L), p(R)$.

B. Study 2

The additive, independence, and maximum-rule hypotheses were tested as possible information-processing models that would predict ability-group differences on a simultaneous processing task from unilateral encoding conditions (Swanson, 1987a). Learning-disabled and nondisabled readers were compared on simultaneous (diotic) and unilateral (dichotic) listening tasks for categorically unrelated stimuli. Unrelated word lists were used in the present study because these materials require more active and deliberate attempts at activating memory resources than taxonomically related items. Thus, it was assumed that intense processing demands would be placed on hemispheric resources and therefore the relative contribution of each hemisphere would be more adequately assessed. Serial-position performance was analyzed, since such functions have a large data base in the literature.

C. Summary of Results

Figure 1 presents the amount recalled by LD and nondisabled children as a function of ear presentation (left ear versus right ear versus both ears) and serial position. As shown in Fig. 1, nondisabled readers recalled more words than the LD readers, and the recency positions (last four positions) were recalled better than middle and primacy positions. The above results on ability-group differences in hemispheric processing must be viewed tentatively, however, since no index of laterality has been provided. Consequently, RE and LE total correct recall scores (collapsed across serial positions) on the dichotic listening task converted to a laterality index. The index was calculated as RE performance minus LE performance divided by their sum. A positive

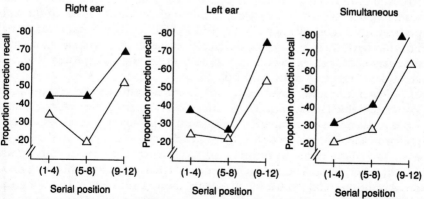

FIGURE 1   Mean serial-recall performance as a function of ability group and ear presentation. From Swanson (1987a).

TABLE II   Mean Observed and Predicted Scores by Serial Position and Ability Group[a]

	Learning-disabled readers				Nondisabled readers			
	Mean	Correlations			Mean	Correlations		
Observed performance	LE[b,c]	RE	LE		LE	RE	LE/RE	
Simultaneous encoding								
Primacy	− .24	−.40	−.25	.01	.30	−.14	.08	−.51
Middle	.28	.16	.02	.26	.41	.20	−.42	−.12
Recency	.65	.25	.20	.55	.78	.17	−.19	−.02
Predictive performance								
Additive		*t* Test				*t* Test		
Primacy	.62	5.47 $p < .01$			.78	5.42 $p < .01$		
Middle	.50	3.68 $p < .01$			.67	3.16 $p < .01$		
Recency	1.00[d]	3.60 $p < .01$			1.00[d]	5.58 $p < .01$		
Independence								
Primacy	.53	5.20 $p < .01$			.65	4.51 $p < .01$		
Middle	.43	3.10 $p < .01$			.57	2.28$p < .01$		
Recency	.79	1.61 N.S.			.91	2.08 N.S.		
Maximum								
Primacy	.31	N.S.			.38	1.26 N.S.		
Middle	.25	N.S.			.34	1.19 N.S.		
Recency	.54	N.S.			.78	.96 N.S.		

[a] From Swanson (1987a)
[b] Additive rule = LE + RE; independence rule = (RE + LE) − (RE × LE); maximum rule = RE, LE.
[c] rs between simultaneous and left-ear (LE) and right-ear (RE) presentations and between LE and RE (LE/RE).
[d] Scores corrected to yield an additive effect no greater than 1.00.

score indicates an REA; a negative score indicates an LEA. Mean laterality scores did not differ significantly between LD ($M = .015$) and nondisabled readers ($M = .046$). As expected, both ability groups showed an REA for processing categorically unrelated word lists. Thus, in conjunction with serial-position performance, residual differences in recall do not appear related to qualitative differences in the organization of hemispheric process (i.e., laterality) and memory strategy in isolation.

When the serial-recall values scores are substituted into the equations shown in Table II, the predictions differ somewhat from the observed scores. Each prediction was compared to observed serial-position recall within each ability group. The results suggest that (1) the maximum-rule hypothesis did not differ significantly from observed recall scores for either ability group, (2) the additive model clearly overpredicted ability-group performance for all serial positions, and (3) the independence model overpredicted ability-group performance except for the recall of recency positions. An examination of the Pearson product–moment correlation coefficients revealed some unique ability-group differences (see Table II). It was assumed that if ability groups differed in their coordination of weak/dominant hemispheric resources, these differences would be reflected in the direction of the correlation coefficients. Since each correlation is based on only 12 pairs of data, r must be large to achieve a significant outcome; in particular, for a one-tailed test, $r \geq .497$ is required for the .05 level of significance. By this criterion, only two correlations were significant (i.e., one positive for LE/RE for LD readers on the recency positions, one negative for LE/RE for primacy positions). Beyond this, 66% of the correlations were negative for nondisabled readers, while 22% were for LD readers. Thus, clear support is found for the notion that ability groups differ in how resources are coordinated.

In sum, the maximum-rule model predicted both reading-ability groups' simultaneous encoding performances better than the additive or independent models. In addition, simultaneous encoding produced no higher recall than unilateral encoding conditions. This finding implies that, for both ability groups, the combination of hemispheric processes is done in a weak/dominant manner. That is, simultaneous encoding demands bear a *nonadditive* relationship to unilateral encoding. The present findings are in contrast with general studies which suggest that LD readers differ from the nondisabled in the general processes (i.e., weak/dominant processing) they use to combine hemispheric information. However, an analysis of correlation patterns within this general processing does suggest that both ability groups differ in how they *coordinate* such hemispheric resources during word retrieval. The next study considers whether LD readers' difficulties in coordinating resources may be related to problems in semantic memory.

IV. Do Semantic Deficiencies Underlie Memory Deficiencies?

Although semantic memory may be an important mechanism mediating encoding processes (as suggested in Swanson & Mullen, 1983) and the coordination of hemispheric resources (Swanson, 1987a), it has not been established in the literature that LD readers' semantic memory is deficient. The following study tested three assumptions related to LD readers' semantic memory. First, it was assumed that learning-disabled readers are deficient in the amount of information (i.e., word knowledge) contained in semantic memory. Some indirect evidence supports this assumption (e.g., McFarland & Rhodes, 1978; Morrison, 1984; Swanson & Mullen, 1983; Torgesen & Houck, 1980). Second, LD readers are deficient in the organization or internal coherence of information stored in semantic memory. Related to this assumption, several studies (e.g., Dallago & Moely, 1980) view LD readers as having inefficient organization strategies (see Pressley & Levin, 1987, for a review). Finally, this next study explored the assumption that LD readers have an inefficient "means" by which to activate resources in semantic memory (Swanson, 1988a, 1988b). Consistent with others (Friedman & Polson, 1981), it is assumed that the cerebral cortex is highly adaptive and that individuals have at their disposal a number of means for achieving recall (e.g., Friedman & Polson, 1981). Two mechanisms that may reflect this "alternative means" of information processing are selective attention (e.g., Ceci & Tishman, 1984) and the efficiency with which attentional resources from each hemisphere are allocated (i.e., correlated) to process particular word features (e.g., Friedman & Polson, 1981; Friedman *et al.*, 1982; Hellige & Wong, 1983; Kershner *et al.*, 1984).

A. Study 3

In order to make inferences about the amount of information contained in LD readers' semantic memory (i.e., word knowledge), the effects of orienting activities on word recall were examined. Several studies suggest that an orienting task influences performance by controlling the *distinctive* encoding (e.g., Ackerman, 1984; Craik & Simon, 1980; Kintsch, 1974; Swanson, 1984a). Distinctiveness refers to the extent to which the word features in semantic memory are specific to the to-be-remembered items. To stage distinctive encoding in the present study, 4 words from a list of 12 words were isolated, via orienting activities, on semantic, phonemic, or structural word features. Support for the hypothesis that ability-group differences in the recall of word features are related to the quality of memory trace would be found if both ability groups significantly benefit from orienting instructions, but in a different fashion. That is, when both ability groups benefit from encoding processes that direct attention toward isolated word features, any residual differences in recall between ability groups reflect the quantity (as well as quality) of information embedded in the memory trace. The clustering of target words was examined to determine if LD readers were inferior in their organization of word knowledge in semantic memory compared to nondisabled readers. To determine if LD readers vary from nondisabled readers in their means of accessing resources from semantic memory, selective attention to particular word features within (intrahemispheric) and across (interhemispheric) dichotic ear presentations were examined. To determine ability-group efficiency in the accessing of semantic memory resources, central and incidental recall scores were correlated within ear (intrahemispheric) and across ear (interhemispheric) presentations.

B. Method and Results

Learning-disabled and nondisabled readers in two age groups were compared on dichotic listening recall tasks that included orienting and non-orienting instructions. Orienting instructions directed children's attention

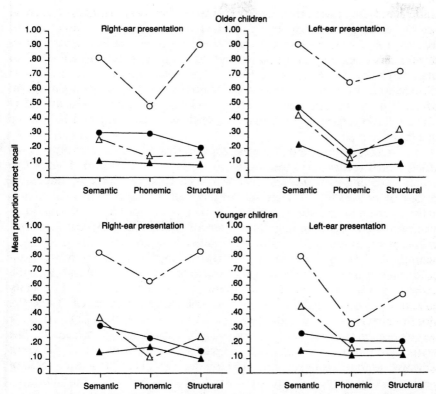

FIGURE 2 Proportion of correct recall of the target words as a function of age, ability group, hemispheric presentation, word organization, and orienting instructions (learning disabled: △, orienting; ▲, nonorienting; nondisabled: ○, orienting; ●, nonorienting). From Swanson (1986).

toward semantic, phonemic, or structural word features. As shown in Fig. 2, nondisabled readers outperformed LD readers regardless of ear presentation. Nondisabled readers had higher recall scores for RE than for all LE presentations, whereas LD readers had no ear effect ($M = .19$, left ear versus $M = .16$ right ear presentation). An important finding was that nondisabled readers significantly benefited from orienting instructions compared to nonorienting instructions for LE ($M = .63$ versus $M = .26$) and RE ($M = .73$ versus $M = .29$) presentations. Learning-disabled readers benefited from orienting compared to nonorienting instructions for both ear presentations, but significant results were found only for LE ($M = .27$ versus $M = .12$) but not RE presentation ($M = .19$ versus $M = .13$).

A test was made of the notion that the organizational coherence of information recalled may account for ability-group differences. To better understand the organization of retrieval word features independent of recall scores, adjusted ratio of clustering (ARC) scores (see Roenker, Thompson, & Brown, 1971) were computed. Perfect clustering is set at an ARC score of 1.0, chance clustering is set at 0, and negative values represent clustering less than expected by chance. As shown in Table III, all mean cluster scores were above chance. Regardless of condition, nondisabled readers had higher organization scores than the learning disabled. These results support the prediction that LD semantic memory is organizationally deficient when compared to that of nondisabled readers.

Another analysis tested the assumption that LD readers are inferior to nondisabled readers in activating word features from semantic memory to match encoding demands and therefore such children utilize an alternative means of processing information. An index of such processing activities is reflected in children's selective attention to targeted word features. This index was calculated by determining the proportion of correctly recalled target items minus the proportion of correctly recalled background items $[P_c$ (target words) $- P_c$ (background words)]. It was assumed that if the activated word features in semantic memory were consistent with the orienting task, then the index scores would be positive. In contrast, negative scores reflect a difficulty in activating the targeted distinctive word features. As shown in Table IV, nondisabled readers had higher selective-attention scores than LD readers for words organized by semantic, phonemic, and structural word features. The results support the prediction that LD readers manifest qualitatively different selective-attention patterns compared to nondisabled readers in their recall of semantic, phonemic, and structural word features. An important finding related to the processing of semantic, phonemic, and structural word features was that LD readers are inferior in their ability to attend to word features congruent with the orienting task. Disabled readers are less selective to relevant word features when background information can be processed interhemispherically, while skilled readers effectively access targeted word features under both intra- and interhemispheric conditions.

The previous findings support studies (e.g., Hynd *et al.*, 1979; Obrzut *et al.*, 1981) suggesting that interhemispheric processing difficulties in the processing of verbal information occur in LD readers. However, it has not been established that there is a trade-off between the acquisition of central and incidental information, and thus the notion that orienting instructions place demands on verbal resources is in question. The efficient allocation of resources to remember target word features reflects a negative correlation between the target and nontarget words. Positive correlations represent less efficient processing of the targeted words and thus resources are reallocated to process incidental word features. Zero correlations reflect the fact that no recall scores occurred for nontargeted words. As shown in Table V, a high

TABLE III Mean Adjusted Ratio of Clustering Score as a Function of Age, Group, Ear Presentation, Orienting Instruction, and Type of Word Feathre[a]

| | Orienting instructions | | Nonorienting instructions | | |
	Left ear	Right ear	Left ear	Right ear	M
Younger children					
Learning disabled					
Semantic	.21	.25	.16	.16	.20
Phonemic	.04	.04	.03	.14	.06
Structural	.12	.10	.05	.12	.08
M	.12	.13	.08	.14	
Nondisabled					
Semantic	.25	.23	.18	.27	.23
Phonemic	.24	.27	.19	.19	.22
Structural	.24	.25	.10	.14	.18
M	.24	.25	.16	.20	
Older children					
Learning disabled					
Semantic	.24	.12	.11	.17	.16
Phonemic	.12	.11	.11	.17	.13
Structural	.24	.11	.11	.15	.15
M	.20	.11	.11	.16	
Nondisabled					
Semantic	.26	.22	.21	.15	.21
Phonemic	.21	.23	.19	.19	.21
Structual	.26	.21	.20	.36	.26
M	.24	.22	.20	.23	

[a] From Swanson (1986).

number of negative and zero correlations occurred. Thus, there appears to be a trade-off between the acquisition of targeted and background words (e.g., when targeted word recall is high and recall of background words is low). The frequency (quantity) of negative and zero correlations did not differ between the ability groups, $x^2 < 1.0$. However, a visual analysis of the coefficients revealed some qualitative differences in ability-group patterns. When items were attended to in the targeted ear, a number of highly significant negative correlations occurred for nontarget words that shared similar features. When the targeted and nontargeted items differed in word features (with the exception of the nondisabled readers' structural–semantic comparison, left ear) correlations were weak or unrelated. These patterns (e.g., negative correlation of similar word features) held for both ear presentations (assuming $-.32$

TABLE IV Mean Selective-Attention Index as a Function of Ear Presentation for the Target Words, Hemispheric Attention (Intrahemispheric versus Interhemispheric), Type of Encoding for Target Items (Semantic, Phonemic, Structural), Age and Ability Group[a]

| | Learning disabled | | | | | | | Nondisabled | | | | | | |
| | Semantic | | Phonemic | | Structural | | | Semantic | | Phonemic | | Structural | | |
Ear presentation	R	L	R	L	R	L	M	R	L	R	L	R	L	M
Younger children														
Intrahemispheric	.32	.42	.00	-.02	.20	.09	.17	.78	.75	.62	.26	.77	.48	.61
Interhemispheric	.21	.34	-.10	-.08	.13	.02	.09	.75	.74	.64	.25	.78	.44	.60
M	.27	.38	-.05	-.05	.17	.06		.77	.75	.63	.26	.78	.46	
Older children														
Intrahemispheric	.16	.43	.06	.05	.10	.29	.26	.72	.87	.34	.53	.94	.67	.68
Interhemispheric	.04	.30	-.03	.01	-.05	.19	.08	.81	.85	.40	.61	.95	.73	.73
M	.10	.37	.02	.03	.03	.24		.77	.86	.37	.57	.95	.70	

[a] From Swanson (1986).

TABLE V Resource Allocation of Attentional Resources to Target Items as Correlated to Recall of Background Items as a Function of Type of Encoding Ear Presentation, and Ability Group[a]

| | Learning Disabled | | | | | | Nondisabled | | | | | |
| | Semantic | | Phonemic | | Structural | | Semantic | | Phonemic | | Structural | |
Ear presentation	R	L	R	L	R	L	R	L	R	L	R	L
Intrahemispheric organization of background items												
Semantic			−.11	−.11	−.26	.00			−.12	−.24	−.63*	.48
Phonemic	.00	−.47*			−.18	−.30	.17	−.25			−.21	−.37*
Structural	.18	.03	−.08	−.15			−.28	−.25	−.18	−.28		
Interhemispheric organization of background items												
Semantic	−.40**	.01	.38**	−.18	−.18	−.23	−.70**	−.76**	.00	.00	.00	−.37*
Phonemic	.00	.05	−.47**	.08	−.18	−.23	.08	−.24	−.77***	−.32	−.24	.00
Structural	−.11	−.32	.68***	−.17	−.50***	.12	.00	.00	−.12	−.19	−.52***	−.59***

[a] From Swanson (1986).
* $p < .10$.
** $p < .05$.
*** $p < .01$.

259

approaches significance) for nondisabled readers, but only for the right-ear presentation in LD. Another finding was that when target words were isolated by phonemic features in the right ear, LD readers increased their recall of nontarget words in the left ear. No such pattern occurred for target words presented in the left ear, and this paradoxical pattern was not found for nondisabled readers. Thus, support is found for the notion that resource-allocation differences (i.e., trade-off effects) do exist between ability groups.

C. Summary

The previous study supports the notion that semantic memory deficiencies underlie LD readers' encoding processes. On the assumption that orienting activities direct the encoding of information against a featural representation of that information in semantic memory (e.g., Kintsch, 1974), and that such activities define the quality of the memory trace (e.g., Craik & Simon, 1980; Eysenck & Eysenck, 1979; Hunt & Mitchell, 1978), the results suggest that deficiencies in semantic memory influence LD readers' word recall. Specifically, the results indicate that (1) LD readers' lateralization patterns vary from those of disabled readers during orienting activities; (2) LD readers recall fewer words than nondisabled readers even though both ability groups benefited from orienting compared to nonorienting activities (i.e., LD readers' recall improved for the LE presentation; nondisabled readers' recall improved for both ear presentations); (3) LE readers' clustering scores were lower than those of nondisabled readers although both ability groups benefited from orienting activities for the LE but not the RE presentation; (4) LD readers were inferior to nondisabled readers in their selective attention to target word features, especially when incidental word features were processed interhemispherically; and (5) the efficiency of processing targeted and nontargeted information for the two ear presentations produced different patterns (i.e., trade-off effects) between reading-ability groups. Based on the previous results of the three studies, how can they be summarized within information-processing framework that accounts for problems in word encoding?

V. Distinctive Encoding

The previous studies reviewed suggest that LD readers fail to efficiently activate word features in semantic memory, which in turn regulates their encoding and hemispheric processing of particular word features. The hypothesis assumes that the to-be-recalled word has a representation in semantic memory, perhaps in the form of a set of qualitatively different features— orthographic, phonemic, and semantic. Learning-disabled readers' encoding of words fails to effectively activate a subset of those features. No doubt, when these word features are inadequately activated, the memory trace is weakened. This weakened memory trace is most apparent during interhemispheric processing. Thus, LD readers' hemispheric processing is viewed as a product of semantic memory representation in interaction with encoding processes. On the other hand, nondisabled readers' performance reflects a greater degree of general knowledge or accumulation of facts about words which become increasingly accessible by means of well-trodden information-processing routes. This framework replaces past studies which have focused exclusively on lateralization or encoding processes by directing attention to how LD children's existing word knowledge contributes to their difficulties in information processing.

A major problem with the previous research from this laboratory is that it is strongly assumed that semantic deficits underlie the encoding difficulties of LD readers. Unfortunately, it has not been established that LD readers suffer from encoding deficits. Specifically, it has not been established that LD readers have difficulty processing specific, or if you will, distinctive word information. To address this issue, two recently completed studies will be summarized. First, a review of what is meant by distinctive encoding must be considered.

A. What is Meant by Distinctive Encoding?

Several descriptions of encoding processes have converged on the concept of distinctiveness (e.g., Hunt & Mitchell, 1982; Ratcliff & McCoon, 1989; Schmidt, 1985). The distinctiveness of an encoded item refers to its discriminability from other items in the semantic memory system (Hunt & Mitchell, 1978). That is, the item shares few memory traces with other items (Nelson, 1979), is less susceptible to interference (Eysenk & Eysenk, 1979), and is more likely to facilitate retrieval (Hunt & Mitchell, 1982) when compared to nondistinctive traces in the memory system. One possible underlying mechanism for why distinctive events are remembered is related to the limited memory system (e.g., Ellis, Roger, & Rodriguez, 1984; Eysenk & Eysenk, 1979). More resources are allocated to distinctive items than to nondistinctive items, which in turn places demands on memory capacity.

In a detailed account of the effects of distinctiveness on attentional capacity, Hunt and Mitchell (1982) have made a distinction between relational (conceptual) information and item-specific information. Relational information is shared among items, while item-specific information discriminates between items. Both memory traces combine to make an item distinct, however, only relational information appears to make demands on the memory system. In contrast, item-specific information, if automatically processed, demands little memory capacity. For example, when a word such as *car* or *bike* is encoded, both relational and item-specific information are encoded. When the word *car* is conceptually related with the other item (e.g., car and bike are forms of transportation), there is an increase in relational processing of the word *car* which in turn leads to enhanced recall of targeted words from the conceptual category. Background words (those not associated with the categories) are less likely to be recalled since few attentional resources are available for processing those items (Hunt & Einstein, 1981).

From previous work (e.g., Swanson, 1986), it is uncertain whether skilled and disabled readers' recall-relational information reflects an excessive depletion of semantic resources, as shown by the negative correlations between the recall of targeted and background items, or whether it merely reflects resource-allocation strategies (e.g., Schmidt, 1985). The finding that distinctively encoded items are better accessed and recalled by some individuals than others may be evidence that some individuals are less able to *divide* their attention among various items. One means of determining an individual's ability to divide attention is related to the degree of trade-offs (negative correlations) that occur between the quantities of resources allocated to each to-be-remembered item (Kahneman, 1973). An alternative possibility is that individual differences reflect the strategic allocation of monitoring of resources and that some individuals allocate a smaller proportion of their limited resources to the task than others. One means of monitoring resources is to selectively attend to isolated features (Lane, 1980).

The next two studies further analyze recall for targeted information as a function of performance on background (nontargeted) information. If individual differences reflect the depletion of semantic resources, one would hypothesize that as more resources are demanded, negative correlations would be more frequent between the target and nontarget information and that the frequency and magnitude of such correlations would vary across clinical subgroups of learners. However, if ability-group differences in distinctive encoding are a function of changes in the cognitive monitoring of resources, it should be possible to show ability-group differences in selective-attention strategies.

B. Study 4

The following study (Swanson & Cochran, in press) introduced item distinctiveness by manipulating the orientation to various features of words. Item distinctiveness was manipulated along structural (orthographic), phonemic, and semantic (categorical) feature dimensions. In Study 4, item-specific word information was defined in terms of semantic, phonemic, and structural (orthographic) dimensions. Item-specific processing was introduced in the orienting task by requiring the subject to attend to specific word features. Relational processing was determined from the recall of targeted and background items, where both types of items shared the same word features (e.g., semantic, structural). To this end, LD and skilled readers were given orienting and nonorienting instructions related to specific features of words presented in lists in a dichotic listening task. The reciprocal relations between RE and LE presentations as a function of word features were analogous to the resource trade-offs presumed to underlie target–background word decrements. Dependent measures were based on target and background word recall. Reading-ability groups, within a split-plot design, received all presentations (right ear versus left ear), orienting instructions (orienting versus nonorienting), and types of encoding (semantic versus phonemic versus structural).

C. Summary of Results

The mean proportion of correct recall for target words as a function of ability group, orienting instructions, and type of word feature is shown in Fig. 3. The important results were that skilled readers were superior to disabled readers during orienting instructions, while the reverse effect occurred for nonorienting instructions. Skilled readers had higher recall for orienting when compared to nonorienting instructions, as did disabled readers. The results suggest that phonemic word features were better recalled for RE than LE presentations, and semantic word features were better recalled in LE than RE presentations. Within orienting conditions, different levels of recall were related to word features of left-ear (semantic > structural > phonemic) and right-ear (semantic = phonemic > structural) presentations.

The above findings suggest that skilled readers perform better than disabled readers with orienting instructions, but disabled readers were better than skilled readers with nonorienting instructions. Why disabled children actually outperform skilled readers on the nonorienting task is uncertain. As shown in Fig. 3, disabled readers recall more semantically related words than skilled readers without orienting instructions. It is possible that skilled readers may have attended to the semantic as well as other word features, which in turn compounded the difficulty of the task.

A selective-attention index, as in the previous study, was used to assess ability-group variations in intra- and interhemispheric processing demands. The results indicated that skilled readers had higher selective-attention scores than disabled readers during both intrahemispheric and interhemispheric processing. Disabled readers had higher selective-attention scores during intrahemispheric than interhemispheric attention. No significant differences in hemispheric attention were found for skilled readers.

These results support the prediction that LD readers manifest qualitatively different selective-attention patterns compared to nondisabled readers in their recall of semantic, phonemic, and structural word features (Table VI). Learning-disabled readers are diffuse in their selective attention to relevant word features when background information can be processed interhemi-

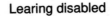

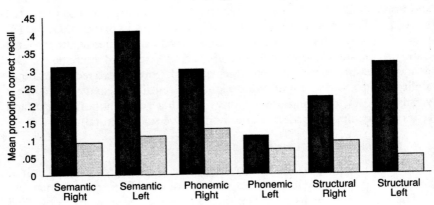

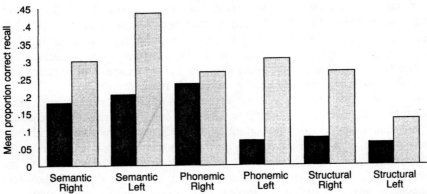

FIGURE 3 Proportion of correct recall of the target words as a function of ability group, hemispheric presentation, word organization, and orienting instructions. ■, nonorienting; □, orienting.

spherically. In contrast, skilled readers effectively access (selectively attend to) targeted word features under both intra- and interhemispheric conditions.

The present study has not established, however, what types of memory demands are made on the acquisition of targeted and nontargeted information. In this study, the reciprocity of resources is reflected by a negative correlation between the target and nontarget words, and it was expected that these correlations would occur between words that share similar conceptual features. Positive correlations represent the integrality of resources and it was expected that these correlations would occur between words that do not share

TABLE VI Mean Selective-Attention Scores and Correlation Coefficients as a Function of Ear Presentation for the Target Words, Hemispheric Attention (Intra- versus Interhemispheric), Type of Word Feature (Semantic, Phonemic, Structural), and Ability Group

	Learning disabled						Skilled					
	Semantic		Phonemic		Structural		Semantic		Phonemic		Structural	
Ear presentation	R	L	R	L	R	L	R	L	R	L	R	L
Selective attention												
Intrahemispheric	.03	.07	-.01	.03	-.05	.05	.17	.07	-.03	-.02	.05	.03
Interhemispheric	.07	.14	.01	.04	.01	.19	.30	.14	.19	.11	.22	.20
Correlations												
Intrahemispheric												
Semantic	—	—	.00	-.22	.05	-.17	—	—	.00	-.50	.16	-.19
Phonemic	.11	-.19	—	—	.23	.00	-.42	-.15	—	—	.14	.00
Structural	-.17	-.55*	-.10	.36	—	—	-.20	-.26	.44	-.52	—	—
Interhemispheric												
Semantic	-.11	.00	-.36	-.06	-.34	-.28	.30	.21	-.50	.66*	.26	-.41
Phonemic	.13	-.11	-.20	-.37	-.34	-.24	.53	.00	.16	.37	.29	-.53
Structural	-.56	-.42	-.37	-.28	.00	.14	-.50	-.64*	.75*	.27	-.12	.60

** p < .05.

TABLE VII Correlations between Target Words and Background Words as a Function of Type of Encoding, Ear Presentation, and Ability Group for the Orienting Conditions

	Learning disabled						Skilled					
	Semantic		Phonemic		Structural		Semantic		Phonemic		Structural	
Ear presentation	R	L	R	L	R	L	R	L	R	L	R	L
Intrahemispheric organization of background items												
Semantic	—	—	.07	.08	.23	-.19	—	—	-.56**	-.06	.14	-.49**
Phonemic	-.21	.35	—	—	.00	-.35	-.10	.23	—	—	.02	-.45**
Structural	.02	.48**	.11	-.12	—	—	.09	.09	.17	-.06	—	—
Interhemispheric organization of background items												
Semantic	-.25	-.36	.00	.05	-.38	-.43**	-.69**	-.31	-.45*	.00	-.10	-.14
Phonemic	.02	.53**	.10	-.15	-.12	-.18	-.48**	-.19	-.46*	-.34**	.14	-.41**
Structural	.10	.00	-.03	.40	-.24	-.19	.14	.23	.00	-.07	.00	.00

* $p < .05$.
** $p < .01$.

266

similar features. Approximately half the corrections reflect a trade-off between acquisition of targeted and background words, that is, when target-word recall is high and recall of background words is low or nonexistent (Table VII). Most critically, when items were attended to in the targeted ear (intra-hemispheric), a frequent number of zero and negative correlations (11 of 12 correlations) occurred for words that shared similar features (with the exception of the disabled readers' phonetic right ear) in the nontargeted ear (inter-hemispheric). The frequency of negative and zero correlations did not differ between ability groups. This finding is important since it suggests that ability groups were using similar processing resources to perform the task. Thus, other sources of processing must account for ability-group differences in distinctive encoding.

VI. Problems of Access or Item Availability in Semantic Memory

The findings of the previous study are consistent with the notion that both skilled and disabled readers' memory traces contain information not necessarily congruent with the orienting task. Disabled readers' memory traces, as reflected in the selective-attention scores, appear to be more diffuse than those of skilled readers. The results suggest that resource reciprocity and integrality between target and background items is somewhat comparable between groups, suggesting that resource-allocation strategies rather than resource-capacity demands may underlie ability-group differences.

A logical alternative to the suggestion that individual differences in distinctive encoding reflect resource-allocation strategies, which in turn weakens the memory trace, is that encoding is related to context biases (e.g., Tulving & Thomson, 1973). Thus, an alternative explanation for the effects of distinctive encoding is that the encoding context has not been reinstated in the retrieval phase. Some authors argue that input and storage systems in disabled readers are intact (see Bauer & Emhert, 1984; Dallago & Moely, 1980), and consequently any major difficulties in recall might involve the matching of retrieval cues to the encoded memory trace. Cued-recall may be seen as benefiting disabled readers' retrieval by narrowing the range of competing responses between the retrieval and encoding phase and thereby improving the match between the two memory processes (see Tulving & Thomson, 1973).

In addition to using cued recall to test this alternative explanation, the next study directed subjects to process all word features prior to recall. Al-though it was assumed that the ability groups are biased toward encoding of particular word features (skilled readers prefer semantic word features and disabled readers prefer structural) (Ceci *et al.,* 1980), it is possible that an automatic activation occurs on certain features. This automatic activation reflects the fact that the memory trace includes features not directly related to the orienting task. To capitalize on this phenomenon, children's attention was directed toward all word features in the word lists. It was assumed that by inducing the activation of multiple word features, rather than relying on incidental processing, a more direct assessment of the salient word features that form a memory trace would be possible, and the formation of a memory trace could be examined thoroughly via the orthogonal use of various types of word-feature cues. It was also assumed that presenting multiple word features would increase the difficulty of remembering some word features, thus reducing capacity that would have been used to process others. Thus, a negative correlation would be expected between the recall of salient and nonsalient word features.

A. Study 5

Subjects consisted of skilled and LD readers matched on CA and IQ. Selection criteria (chronological age, IQ, reading scores, laterality quotients) for this group were comparable to those for subjects in Study 4 and no group differences were present.

As part of the encoding instructions, children were told that some words could be grouped by (1) words that are (e.g., *animals* or *furniture*), (2) words that rhyme with (e.g., *hat* or *big*), and (3) words that start with the letter (e.g., "s" or "b"). In short, for each particular ear presentation, children were told the number of words, the type and number of categories, and the number of words per category in the list they were going to learn.

For this recall task, two phases of assessment were used. In the first phase, the noncued recall phase, children were directed to recall as many words as possible. After subjects had recalled as many words as possible and had performed a brief 1-minute distractor task that included the calculation of simple addition problems (according to teacher records, all arithmetic problems were considered easy calculations for LD readers), they were told that they had forgotten some of the words from a particular category. They were asked (cued) to remember words not produced during the noncued phase that went with, for example, *animals* or *furniture or* rhymed with, for example, *hat* or *big or* started with, for example, "s" or "b". The amount of time between the noncued recall phase and the cued recall phase was approximately 1 minute.

B. Summary of Results

Figure 4 presents the proportion of correct free recall and cued recall (cued recall following the free-recall phase) and adjusted (to be discussed) cued recall scores. In order to simplify the analysis, the results of free recall and cued recall were examined separately.

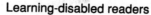

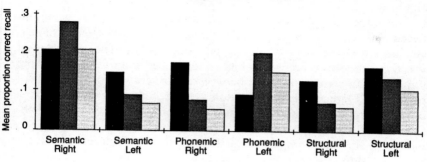

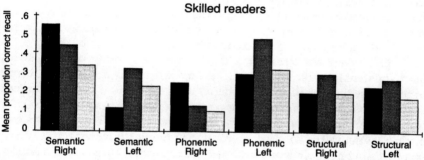

FIGURE 4 Proportion of correct recall of the target words as a function of ability group, hemispheric presentation, word organization, and orienting instructions. Free recall, ■; cued recall, ■; adjusted recall, □.

1. FREE RECALL

The proportion of correct recall for skilled readers was higher than that for LD readers overall. The ability group × type of word feature interaction indicated that skilled readers recalled more words for semantic features than LD readers, suggesting that ability-group differences in item availability may be restricted to words that are semantically organized. The above analysis is limited, however, in that minimal information is provided on the *retrieval* strategies used to recall word features. To better understand the retrieval strategies (i.e., clustering), independent of the number of words recalled, the ARC scores were computed. The results produced no reliable effects and therefore the scores are not reported. Taken together, these findings suggest that recall differences between ability groups for the semantically organized words are not due to retrieval strategies (as suggested by the ARC scores) but rather reflect the availability of semantic word features for recall (see Tulving & Pearlstone, 1966, for the distinction between accessibility and availability). The results also indicate that semantic word features are more likely to be remembered when presented in the left than in the right ear.

Another analysis was conducted to determine whether variations between ability groups occurred in selective attention. The index of selective attention was the same as in my previous studies. The interhemispheric selective-attention scores were higher for skilled than for LD readers. No significant differences occurred between ability groups for intrahemispheric processing. Higher selective-attention scores occurred for skilled readers during interhemispheric than intrahemispheric processing, while no reliable effects related to hemispheric processing occurred for LD readers. These results indicate that, when compared to LD readers, skilled readers' selective attention is less diffuse for processing target items in the target ear when compared to comparable item features in the opposite ear (Table VIII).

In terms of correlations between target and nontargeted words, negative and zero correlations were approximately 50% of the total number of correlations, and ability groups were comparable in the frequency of those correlations. Of interest was the finding that integrality (positive correlation) was more apparent for skilled than for LD readers when background word features of the competing ear (interhemispheric) were similar to the word features of the targeted ear. This finding seems reasonable because orienting instructions (as in Study 4) isolate particular word features and make those items more distinct, as compared to instructions in the present study that direct subjects on processing multiple word features. The reciprocity (negative correlations) between hemispheres in the processing of similar word features that emerged for LD readers reflects the fact that they have difficulty coordinating the use of multiple resource pools and/or suffer for depletion of certain resource pools. In comparison with Study 4, the present findings suggest that when multiple word features are encoded, an integrality (positive correlation) between word features sharing the same features is found.

2. CUED RECALL

Figure 4 shows the mean proportion of correct cued recall as a function of ability groups and type of word feature that was cued. A significant main effect was found for ability group and for type of word feature. As shown in Fig. 4, skilled readers were able to recall more items previously forgotten than disabled readers. This preliminary analysis of cued recall suggests that disabled readers' access to a memory trace may be inferior to that of skilled readers. To more directly test this assumption, a trace analysis, via the reduction method, was performed by comparing the cued-recall phase to the noncued (free-recall) phase (see Tulving & Watkins, 1975; Watkins, 1979; Watkins & Gardner, 1982, for a detailed discussion of the reduction method). The procedure, which can be applied to various cued-recall paradigms, allows data

TABLE VIII Mean Selective-Attention Scores as a Function of Ear Presentation for the Target Words, Hemispheric Attention (Intrahemispheric versus Interhemispheric), Type of Encoding for Target Items (Semantic, Phonemic, Structural), and Ability Group

Ear presentation	Learning-disabled readers						Skilled readers					
	Semantic		Phonemic		Structural		Semantic		Phonemic		Structural	
	R	L	R	L	R	L	R	L	R	L	R	L
Intrahemispheric	.25	.47	.05	.00	.13	.10	.68	.75	.45	.50	.63	.84
Interhemispheric	.14	.35	−.02	−.07	.05	−.04	.73	.75	.49	.51	.64	.85

on the noncued and cued recall phases to be arranged directly into a cuegram or contingency table. This contingency table allows for the calculation of an unbiased estimate of the relation between noncued and cued recall. Three known proportions for the contingency table include the total proportion of correct recall for both noncued and cued recall combined, for noncued recall but not cued recall (i.e., the noncued response is assumed to be unaltered by cued responding), and for the proportion of noncued and cued items forgotten. The remaining proportion is derived by simple subtraction, thus completing the contingency table. This final proportion represents the effectiveness of cued recall (item accessibility) adjusted by the influence of noncued recall (item availability). The adjusted recall scores indicated that LD readers were lower in cued-recall performance than skilled readers. These results, in conjunction with the analysis of the free-recall phase, suggest that retrieval cues provided access to memory traces for LD readers but that such memory traces may be inferior to those of skilled readers. For both ability groups, higher accessibility to cued information was related to the type of cue. Semantic cues were more effective than phonemic or structural cues, although phonemic and structural cues produced comparable levels of recall.

In sum, the previous analysis indicates that LD readers can access information previously forgotten and that this access to information is independent of the direction of ear presentation (i.e., no significant ear-presentation effects occurred). In addition, structural, phonemic, and semantic cues can be seen to have the same relative effect on recall for LD readers as they do for skilled readers (i.e., no interactions). Therefore, when the results of cued-recall and adjusted cued-recall scores are taken together, it appears that LD readers' poor accessibility to information when compared to skilled readers is related to the quality or structure of their memory trace.

The previous results of the free-recall (noncued) phase suggest that LD readers are inferior in their ability to selectively attend to information presented interhemispherically. Consequently, the impaired ability of LD readers to retrieve forgotten words may be related to the diffusion of attentional resources between the cerebral hemispheres that occurs during free recall prior to cued recall.

VII. Summary and Discussion

The important findings of the five studies need to be briefly summarized. The results indicate the following: (1) Skilled readers' recall is superior to that of LD readers during orienting instructions. This finding suggests that skilled readers are more likely to processes multiple features of words, but when directed to isolated word features they are more able than LD readers to access those features. (2) In some cases, lateralization patterns are comparable between ability groups, suggesting that both groups are relying on the same hemisphere processing resources for accessing word features, but LD readers have less resources to access overall. (3) Disabled readers are more diffuse than skilled readers in their selective attention to targeted word features, especially when background word features were processed interhemispherically. This finding suggests that ability groups may vary in strategies for allocating resources across the cerebral hemispheres. (4) Resource reciprocity was comparable between ability groups only during semantic and structural processing, while skilled readers had more negative correlations than disabled readers during phonemic processing.

The results of these studies will now be placed in theoretical perspective. The distinctive encoding framework, as inferred from the dichotic listening task, provides a theoretical account of the effects of distinctive encoding on individual differences in recall. It is assumed that the ear presentations and target and background item recall provide a measure of demands placed on semantic memory. In general, the amount of recall of background items decreases in the opposite ear with increases in recall in the targeted ear and with increases in recall of target word features; recall of background items in the primary ear decreases with increases in recall in the target item. The resources allocated to the target information were inferred from changes in the direction of the correlation coefficients. The results obtained in the present study suggest that some correlations depend on the ability group and the type of distinctive encoding. For example, LD readers had more positive correlations between target and background items within and between ear presentations of phonemic word features than skilled readers.

Overall, however, the results suggest that the reciprocity and/or integrality between tasks may not adequately capture ability-group differences in distinctive encoding. A more appropriate explanation is that ability-group differences reflect resource-allocation strategies. One such strategy is to selectively attend to word features. Several investigators have shown that it is difficult to selectively attend to one feature of an object while ignoring other dimensions (e.g., Hunt & Mitchell, 1978; Kahneman & Chajczyk, 1983). In the present study, processing of irrelevant dimensions was carried out regardless of their effect on the target task. High levels of target-word recall by skilled readers also had a facilitating effect on nontargeted background items. In contrast, LD readers were affected negatively from resource-allocation strategies that debilitated target and nontarget item recall. This finding suggests that individual differences in distinctive encoding are not so much a matter of resource demands as they are of resource-allocation strategies. Further, these allocation strategies emerge because LD readers have a meager representation of word features in semantic memory.

There are a number of alternative interpretations to our account of the locus of individual differences in distinctive encoding. First, one possibility may be related to a lack of congruence (or mismatch) between the encoding and retrieval phases. Based on the encoding specificity model (Tulving & Thomson, 1973), it may be argued that encoding operations determine what is stored and "retrieval cues provide access to what is stored" (p. 369). No doubt, it may be argued that the LD readers in Study 5 used retrieval cues that were incompatible with the experimenter-provided cues. However, if certain word features (e.g., semantic) were not adequately processed at input, cuing these word features (e.g., semantic) might prove debilitating, as in a case where a subject is cued at retrieval by a semantic cue when he/she originally encoded or preferred to encode words that were phonemically or structurally organized. This argument lacks support, however, in that experimental cues did not produce qualitatively different patterns across ability groups during the cued-recall phase (i.e., no interactions). Thus, an explanation of ability-group differences in terms of a mismatch between encoding and retrieval processes seems unlikely.

A second interpretation is that the effectiveness of retrieval cues on the recall of forgotten words cannot be specified independently of the *type* of cue used. That is, retrieval cues may augment the effects of any type of initial encoding (e.g., Craik & Lockhart, 1972; Moscovitch & Craik, 1976; Tulving & Watkins, 1975) so that certain retrieval cues may be superior to others even when the initial encoding of word features is incongruent with the retrieval cue (e.g., Moscovitch & Craik, 1976). There is evidence that LD readers may prefer superficial cues (e.g., structural) over more elaborative cues (e.g., semantic). For example, several studies (e.g., McFarland & Rhodes, 1978) have suggested that LD readers rely less heavily on semantic and phonemic information and therefore may prefer to process words in terms of their nonsemantic (e.g., structural) features. This hypothesis suggests that LD readers can learn normally, provided they are induced to retrieve in an appropriate manner. In general, the results summarized in this chapter suggest that the semantic organization of words facilitated recall for both ability groups when compared to other types of word organizations. Further, there was no evidence (i.e., no interaction) to suggest that semantic cues differently reduced LD readers' cued recall, as would be predicted from the assumption that their memory deficiency stemmed from a failure to effectively use semantic information. This conclusion was reinforced by an analysis of recall errors, which again showed no difference between the groups in the proportion of errors related to the semantic, phonemic, or structural word features.

A final theoretical model, the one favored by these results, is that poor accessibility of information during cued recall has something to do with the storage of a memory trace in semantic memory and the resource-allocation dynamics of interhemispheric information processing. That is, LD readers paradoxically supplement inferior memory traces prior to retrieval, by processing information in a diffuse manner. This diffuse processing is reflected in the transmission of information between the two cerebral hemispheres. In contrast to LD readers, skilled readers are more likely to ignore irrelevant information in the competing hemisphere. Such processing not only provides an immediate advantage in the availability of information (as indicated by noncued recall performance), but retrieval cues continue to access additional information from the previously stored memory traces. Thus, skilled readers allocate less diffuse attention to word features during interhemispheric processing prior to cuing than LD readers and such processing is reflected in the fact that memory traces are sufficiently intact to support cued recall.

Conclusions related to this model are supported since an ability group × hemispheric-attention interaction occurred for selective-attention scores across a number of experiments. The reader is reminded, however, that the allocation of attentional resources is task dependent and varies under a particular set of encoding and retrieval demands (e.g., Friedman & Polson, 1981; Kahneman, 1973). Regardless, there is some evidence to suggest that memory resources (e.g., see Wickens, 1980), such as word knowledge or semantic memory, play an active part in the formation of the memory trace which in turn influences how hemispheric resources are combined and/or attended to. Thus, perhaps all that can be safely stated is that inferences about individual differences in memory ability cannot be made without reference to how interhemispheric processing is influenced by previously stored information, the quality of information stored in semantic memory, and the mechanisms by which resources are allocated.

References

Ackerman, B. P. (1984). Encoding effects on recall and recognition. *Journal of Experimental Child Psychology, 37,* 426–450.

Anderson, J. (1976). *Language, memory and thought.* Hillsdale, NJ: Erlbaum.

Baker, J. G., Ceci, S. J., & Hermann, N. D. (1987). Semantic structure and processing: Implications for the learning disabled child. In H. L. Swanson (Ed.), *Memory and learning disabilities.* (Greenwich, CT: JAI Press.

Bauer, R. H., & Emhert, J. (1984). Information processing in reading-disabled and nondisabled children. *Journal of Experimental Child Psychology, 37,* 271–281.

Beaumont, J., & Rugg, M. (1978). Neuropsychological laterality of function and dyslexia: A new hypothesis. *Dyslexia Review, 1,* 18–21.

Boliek, C. A., Obrzut, J. E., & Shaw, D. (1988). The effects of hemispatial and asymmetrically focused attention on dichotic listening with normal and learning-disabled children *Neuropsychologia, 26,* 417–433.

Bruce, D. (1980). Single probes, double probes, and the structure of memory traces. *Journal of Experimental Psychology: Human Learning and Memory, 6,* 276–292.

Bub, D., Black, S., Hampson, E., & Kertesz, A. (1988). Semantic encoding of pictures and words: Some neuropsychological observations. *Cognitive Neuropsychology, 5,* 27–66.

Carswell, C. M., & Wickens, C. D. (1985). Lateral task segregation and the task-hemispheric integrity effect. *Human Factors, 27,* 695–700.

Ceci, S. J., & Tishman, J. (1984). hyperactivity and incidental memory: Evidence for attentional diffusion. *Child Development, 55,* 2192–2203.

Ceci, S. J., Lea, S., & Ringstrom, M. (1980). Coding processes in normal and learning disabled children: Evidence for modality-specific pathway to the cognitive system. *Journal of Experimental Psychology: Human Learning and Memory, 6,* 785–795.

Cermak, L. (1983). Information processing deficits in children with learning disabilities. *Journal of Learning Disabilities, 16,* 599–605.

Chabot, R. M., Petros, T. V., & McCord, G. (1983). Developmental and reading ability differences in accessing information from semantic memory. *Journal of Experimental Child Psychology, 35,* 128–142.

Chi, M. T. H. (1983). A learning framework for development. In M. T. H. Chi (Ed.), *Trends in memory development* pp. 71–107. New York: Karger.

Craik, F. I., & Lockhart, R. S. (1972). Levels of processing: A framework for memory research. *Journal of Verbal Learning and Verbal Behavior, 11,* 671–684.

Craik, F. I., & Simon, E. (1980). Age difference in memory: The roles of attention and depth processing. In L. Poon *et al.,* (Eds.), *New directions in memory and aging* (pp. 95–112). Hillsdale, NJ: Erlbaum.

Dallago, M., & Moely, B. (1980). Free recall in boys of normal and poor reading levels as a function of task manipulation. *Journal of Experimental Child Psychology, 30,* 62–78.

Ellis, J. C., Roger, L. T., & Rodriguez, I. A. (1984). Emotional mood states and memory: Elaborative encoding, semantic processing, and cognitive effect. *Journal of Experimental Psychology: Learning Memory and Cognition, 10,* 470–482.

Eysenk, M. W., & Eysenk, M. C. (1979). Processing depth, elaboration of encoding, memory stores, and expanded processing capacity. *Journal of Experimental Psychology: Human Learning and Memory, 5,* 472–484.

Friedman, A., & Polson, M. C. (1981). Hemispheres as independent resource systems: Limited-capacity processing and cerebral specialization. *Journal of Experimental Psychology: Human Perception and Performance, 7,* 1031–1058.

Friedman, A., Polson, M. C., & Dafoe, C. G. (1988). Dividing attention between the hands and the head: Performance trade-offs between rapid finger tapping and verbal memory. *Journal of Experimental Psychology: Human Perception and Performance, 14,* 60–68.

Friedman, A., Polson, M. C., Dafoe, C. G. & Gaskill, S. (1982). Dividing attention within and between hemispheres: Testing a multiple resources approach to limited-capacity information processing. *Journal of Experimental Psychology: Human Perception and Performance, 8,* 625–650.

Gibson, E. J. (1971). Perceptual learning and the theory of word perception. *Cognitive Psychology, 2,* 351–368.

Hellige, J. B., & Wong, T. M. (1983). Hemisphere-specific interference in dichotic listening: Task variables and individual differences. *Journal of Experimental Psychology: General, 112,* 218–239.

Herdman, C. D., & Friedman, A. (1985). Multiple resources in divided attention: A cross-modal test of the independence of hemispheric resources. *Journal of Experimental Psychology: Human Perception and Performance, 11,* 40–49.

Hunt, R. R., & Einstein, G. O. (1981). Relational and item-specific information in memory. *Journal of Verbal Learning and Verbal Behavior, 20,* 497–514.

Hunt, R. R., & Mitchell, D. B. (1978). Specificity in nonsemantic orienting tasks and distinctive memory traces. *Journal of Experimental Psychology: Human Learning and Memory, 4,* 121–135.

Hunt, R. R., & Mitchell, D. B. (1982). Independent effects of semantic and nonsemantic distinctiveness. *Journal of Experimental Psychology: Human Learning and Memory, 8,* 81–87.

Hynd, G. W., Obrzut, J. E., & Bowen, S. M. (1987). Neurological basis of attention and memory in learning disabilities. In H. L. Swanson Ed.), *Memory and learning disabilities.* Greenwich, CT: JAI Press.

Hynd, G. W., Obrzut, J. E., Weed, W. & Hynd, C. (1979). Development of cerebral dominance: Dichotic listening asymmetry in normal and learning disabled children. *Journal of Experimental Child Psychology, 16,* 445–454.

Johnston, R. S., Rugg, M., & Scott, T. (1987). The influence of phonology on good and poor readers when reading for meaning. *Journal of Memory and Language, 26,* 57–68.

Jones, B. (1983). Measuring degree of cerebral lateralization in children as a function of age. *Developmental Psychology, 19,* 237–242.

Kahneman, D. (1973). *Attention and effort.* Englewood Cliffs, NJ: Prentice-Hall.

Kahneman, D., & Chajczyk, D. (1983). Tests of the automaticity of reading: Dilution of Stroop effects by color-irrelevant stimuli, *Journal of Experimental Psychology: Human Perception and Performance, 9,* 497–509.

Kershner, J. R., Henninger, P., & Cooke, W. (1984). Writing induces a right hemisphere linguistic advantage in dysphonetic dyslexic children: Implications for attention and capacity models of laterality. *Brain & Language, 21,* 105–122.

Kimura, D. (1973). Functional asymmetry of the brain. *Scientific American, 228,* 70–78.

Kinsbourne, M., & Hicks, R. E. (1978). Functional cerebral: A model for overflow, transfer and interference effects in human performance: A tutorial review. In J. Requin (Ed.), *Attention and performance VII.* Hillsdale, NJ: Erlbaum.

Kintsch, W. (1974). *The representation of meaning in memory.* Potomac, MD: Erlbaum.

Lane, D. M. (1980). Incidental learning and the development of selective attention. *Psychological Review, 87,* 316–319.

McFarland, C., & Rhodes, D. (1978). Memory for meaning in skilled and unskilled readers. *Journal of Experimental Child Psychology, 24,* 199–207.

Morrison, F. J. (1984). Reading disability: A problem in rule learning and word decoding. *Developmental Review, 4,* 36–47.

Moscovitch, M., & Craik, F. I. (1976). Depth of processing, retrieval cues and uniqueness of encoding. *Journal of Verbal Learning and Verbal Behavior, 15*, 447–458.

Nelson, D. L. (1979). Remembering pictures and words: Appearance, significance and name. In L. S. Cermak & F. I. M. Craik (Eds.), *Levels of processing in human memory* (pp. 45–76). Hillsdale, NJ: Erlbaum.

Obrzut, J. E., Conrad, P. F., Bryden, M. P., & Boliek, C. A. (1988). Cued dichotic listening with right-handed, left-handed, bilingual and learning-disabled children. *Neuropsychologia, 26*, 119–131.

Obrzut, J. E., Hynd, G. W., Obrzut, A., & Leitgeb, J. L. (1980). Time sharing and dichotic listening in normal and learning disabled children. *Brain & Language, 11*, 181–194.

Obrzut, J. E., Hynd, G. W., Obrzut, A., & Pirozzolo, F. J. (1981). Effect of directed attention on cerebral asymmetries in normal and learning disabled children. *Developmental Psychology, 17*, 118–125.

Obrzut, J. E., Hynd, G. W., & Zellner, R. D. (1983). Attentional deficit in learning-disabled children: Evidence from visual half-field assymmetries. *Brain & Cognition, 2*, 89–101.

Obrzut, J. E., Obrzut, A., Bryden, M. P., & Bartels, S. G. (1985). Information processing and speech lateralization in learning disabled children. *Brain & Language, 25*, 87–101.

Orton, S. T. (1937). *Reading, writing, and speech problems in children*. New York: Norton.

Paivio, A. (1971). *Imagery and verbal processes*. New York: Holt, Rinehart, & Winston.

Pressley, M., & Levin, J. R. (1987). Elaborative learning strategies for the inefficient learner. In S. J. Ceci (Ed.), *Handbook of cognitive, social, and neuropsychological aspects of learning disabilities*. Hillsdale, NJ: Erlbaum.

Ratcliff, R., & McKoon, G. (1989). Similarity information versus relational information: Differences in the time course of retrieval. *Cognitive Psychology, 21*, 139–155.

Riddoch, M. J., Humphreys, G., Coltheart, M., & Funnell, E. (1988). Semantic systems or system? Neuropsychological evidence re-examined. *Cognitive Neuropsychology, 5*, 3–25.

Roenker, D. L., Thomson, L., & Brown, S. C. (1971). Comparison of measures for the estimation of clustering in free recall. *Psychological Bulletin, 76*, 45–48.

Rourke, B. P. (1985). *Neuropsychology of learning disabilities: Essentials of subtype analysis*. New York: Guilford Press.

Satz, P. (1976). Cerebral dominance and reading disability. An old problem revisited. In R. Knights & D. Baker (Eds.), *The neuropsychology of learning disorders*. Baltimore, MD: William & Wilkins.

Satz, P., & Sparrow, S. (1970). Specific developmental dyslexia: A theoretical formulation. In D. Bakker & P. Satz (Eds.), *Specific reading disability: Advances in theory and method*. Rotterdam: Rotterdam University Press.

Schmidt, S. R. (1985). Encoding and retrieval processes in the memory for conceptually distinct events. *Journal of Experimental Psychology: Learning, Memory and Cognition, 11*, 565–578.

Shankweiler, D., Liberman, I. M., Fowler, L. C., & Fisher, F. (1979). The speech code and learning to read. *Journal of Experimental Psychology: Human Learning and Memory, 5*, 531–545.

Sidtis, J., Volpe, B., Holtzman, J., Wilson, D., & Gazzaniga, M. (1981). Cognitive interaction after stages of collosal section: Evidence for transfer of semantic activation. *Science, 212*, 344–346.

Somberg, B., & Salthouse, T. (1982). Divided attention abilities in young and older subjects. *Journal of Experimental Psychology: Human Perception and Performance, 8*, 90–100.

Swanson, H. L. (1984a). Effects of cognitive effort and word distinctiveness on learning disabled and nondisabled readers' recall. *Journal of Educational Psychology, 76*, 894–908.

Swanson, H. L. (1984b). Semantic and visual codes in learning disabled readers. *Journal of Experimental Child Psychology, 37*, 124–140.

Swanson, H. L. (1986). Do semantic memory deficiencies underlie learning disabled readers' encoding processes? *Journal of Experimental Child Psychology, 76*, 461–488.

Swanson, H. L. (1987a). The combining of multiple hemispheric resources in learning disabled and skilled readers' recall of words: A test of three information processing models. *Brain & Cognition, 6*, 41–54.

Swanson, H. L. (1987b). Verbal coding deficits in the recall of pictorial information for learning disabled readers: The influence of a lexical system. *American Educational Research Journal, 24*, 143–170.

Swanson, H. L. (1988a). The development of word recall and hemispheric specialization: Capacity, strategy, or high order cognitive process? *Bulletin of the Psychonomic Society, 26*, 97–99.

Swanson, H. L. (1988b). Learning disabled children's problem solving: An information processing analysis of intellectual performance. *Intelligence, 12*, 261–278.

Swanson, H. L. (1989). Central processing strategy differences in gifted, average, learning disabled and mentally retarded children. *Journal of Experimental Child Psychology, 47*, 370–397.

Swanson, H. L. (in press). Semantic coding deficits and learning disabilities. *Educational Psychology Review*.

Swanson, H. L., & Cochran, K. (in press). Learning disabilities, distinctive encoding and hemispheric resource. *Brain & Language*.

Swanson, H. L., Cochran, K., & Ewers, C. (1989). Working memory and reading disabilities. *Journal of Abnormal Child Psychology, 17*, 145–156.

Swanson, H. L., & Mullen, R. C. (1983). Hemispheric specialization in learning disabled readers' recall as a function of age and level of processing. *Journal of Experimental Child Psychology, 35*, 457–477.

Swanson, H. L., & Obrzut, J. E. (1985). Learning disabled readers' recall as a function of distinctive encoding, hemispheric processing and selective attention. *Journal of Learning Disabilities, 18*, 409–418.

Swanson, H. L., & Rathgeber, A. (1986). The effects of organizational dimensions on learning disabled readers' recall. *Journal of Educational Research, 79*, 155–162.

Tarver, S., Hallahan, D., Kauffman, J., & Ball, D. (1976). Verbal rehearsal and selective attention in children with learning disabilities: A developmental lag. *Journal of Experimental Child Psychology, 22*, 375–385.

Torgesen, J. (1977). Memorization processes in reading disabled children. *Journal of Educational Psychology, 690*, 471–478.

Torgesen, J., & Houck, G. (1980). Processing deficiencies in learning disabled children who perform poorly on the digit span test. *Journal of Educational Psychology, 72*, 141–160.

Tulving, E., & Pearlstone, Z. (1966). Availability versus accessibility of information in memory for words. *Journal of Verbal Learning and Verbal Behavior, 5*, 381–391.

Tulving, E., & Thomson, D. (1973). Encoding specificity and retrieval process in episodic memory. *Psychological Review, 82*, 261–275.

Tulving, E., & Watkins, M. J. (1975). Structure of memory traces. *Psychological Review, 82*, 261–275.

Watkins, M. J. (1979). Engrams as cuegrams and forgetting as cue overload: A cuing approach to the structure of memory. In C. R. Puff (Ed.), *Memory organization and structure* (pp. 347–370). New York: Academic Press.

Watkins, M. J., & Gardner, J. M. (1982). Cued recall. In C. R. Puff (Ed.), *Handbook of research methods in human memory and cognition* (pp. 173–195). New York: Academic Press.

Wickens, C. D. (1980). The structure of attentional resources. In R. Nickerson (Ed.), *Attention and Performance VII* (pp. 239–257). Hillsdale, NJ: Erlbaum.

Wickens, C. D. (1984). Processing resources in attention. In R. Parasuraman & D. R. Davies (Eds.), *Varieites of attention*. Orlando, FL: Academic Press.

Wickens, C. D., Mountford, S. J., & Schreiner, W. S. (1981). Time-sharing efficiency: Evidence for multiple resources, task-hemispheric integrity, and against a general ability. *Human Factors, 22*, 211–229.

Wickens, C. D., & Sandry, D. (1982). Task-hemispheric integrity in dual task performance. *Acta Psychologica, 52*, 227–248.

Witelson, S. (1977). Developmental dyslexia: Two right hemispheres and move left. *Science, 195*, 309–311.

Young, A., & Ellis, A. (1981). Asymmetry of cerebral hemispheric function in normal and poor readers. *Psychological Bulletin, 89*, 183–190.

Zecker, S., & Zinner, T. E. (1987). Semantic code deficit for reading disabled children on an auditory lexical decision task. *Journal of Reading Behavior, 19*, 177–188.

PART TWO

Methodologies and Assessment Techniques in the Diagnosis of Learning Disabilities

Despite the phenomenal growth of learning disabilities as a special educational category, the field continues to generate much controversy with regard to the appropriateness of current assessment and classification practices. At the center of this controversy is the lack of consensus among professionals and researchers as to what constitutes the most critical variables in the identification of children who experience learning disabilities. Thus, whereas the initial section of this volume addressed important etiological and theoretical issues related to the neuropsychological bases of learning disabilities, this section focuses on methodologies and techniques currently being employed in both assessment and research practice. The particular methodologies and techniques used, however, are derived from one's conceptual definition of the syndrome known as specific learning disability.

For most special educators, the trend in the learning disabilities field is toward more concise and constrained assessment and identification procedures. Academic achievement level and ability–achievement discrepancy variables become most significant in the diagnostic process, while neurological, social-skills, and psychological-processing deficits play a less significant role (see Merrell & Shinn, 1990). In contrast, neuroeducators conceptualize learning disabilities as neurologically based perceptual-processing difficulties which result in a significant ability–achievement discrepancy with concomitant low academic achievement.

Contrary to popular opinion, considerable agreement exists today among those involved in defining the field of learning disabilities as recently suggested by Hammill (1990). Hammill argues that of approximately 11 definitions, the one written by the National Joint Committee on Learning Disabilities (NJCLD, 1981) is the most precise and acceptable in becoming the consensus definition in the years ahead. Among its attributes is the fact that learning disabilities are defined as disorders intrinsic to the individual, presumed to be due to central nervous system (CNS) dysfunction. Even though data accumulated over a long period of time have failed to demonstrate a consistent relationship between CNS dysfunction and learning disabilities, there seems to be enough indirect neurological evidence to further pursue such analysis.

Whether or not learning disability constitutes a unique behavioral syndrome is an issue of validity. However, many of the problems concerning the validity of learning-disability diagnosis stem from assessment procedures which identify children in an inconsistent and unreliable manner. Although there is little argument that some form of discrepancy criteria is needed, it is not needed to determine the presence of a learning disability, but rather to validate the severity level and effects upon learning. Various methods of determining significant discrepancy between learning-disabled students' expected and actual academic performance have been promoted. Included are such methods as statistically based regression formulas, the Woodcock–Johnson Achievement/Aptitude dichotomy, and curriculum-based measurement. In Chapter Eleven, Heath and Kush strongly suggest the regression approach to the quantification of ability–achievement discrepancies as a necessary but not sufficient condition for the diagnosis of a learning disability over more familiar but less reliable methods. Regardless of the discrepancy method used, perhaps the larger issue may be the lack of reliable and valid formal and informal psychoeducational tests to identify learning disabilities.

But beyond the problems concerned with ambiguous definitions of learning disabilities and determining severity of the disorder, new directions are needed in the assessment of childhood learning disabilities to resolve the conflicting results. An empirical approach to assessment is provided in Chapter Twelve by Batchelor and Dean, who show how a standardized fixed-battery strategy to diagnosis is useful in subtyping achievement deficits and predicting diffuse or specific neuropsychological dysfunction in children. However, few data are available to indicate whether neuropsychological deficits associated with childhood learning disabilities are also associated with learning disabilities in young adulthood. Although it is suspected that academic deficits and their associated neuropsychological deficits persist into young adulthood, the precise nature of the change in these deficits for individuals at the secondary and postsecondary levels is not widely known. In Chapter Thirteen O'Donnell has presented empirical evidence to demonstrate that learning-disabled young adults do experience mild cerebral dysfunction and can be grouped into homogeneous subtypes.

Research devoted to the establishment of empirically derived subtypes has intensified over the past several decades with the recognition that learning disabilities reflect a highly heterogeneous array of developmental disorders. These efforts have helped enrich neurocognitive explanations for why children who experience learning disabilities are similar to or differ from one another. Newby and Lyon, in Chapter Fourteen, suggest that both the clinical–inferential and empirical approaches to subtyping of learning disabilities have made important contributions in the identification process. But rather than searching for discrete subtypes, the field is currently moving toward a more dimensional view of individual differences in learning disabilities and in early identification.

Research in early identification of learning disabilities showed little progress in the 1980s although federal legislation was passed and signed into law. This legislation encourages states to provide services to at-risk and handicapped infants, toddlers, and their families (Education of the Handicapped Act Amendments of the 1986, PL99-457). Thus, appropriate methods of early identification are still a vital need in the field of learning disability. The existing literature suggests that neuropsychological measures are not only useful in isolating the precise deficits present in a wide range of learning disabilities, but they are also useful in identifying young children at risk for learning problems and are helpful in predicting prognosis and treatment. In Chapter Fifteen, Felton and Brown have provided converging evidence for the role of phonological processing in the prediction of early reading skills and in defining subtypes, respectively. These researchers contend that neuropsychological assessment has excellent potential for contributing to the diagnostic and treatment components of learning disabilities as well.

Interest in the assessment of handedness has long interested researchers and clinicians in neuropsychology and has increased even more with the recent work advanced by Geschwind and Galaburda (1987). These theorists have argued that left handedness is a result of increased levels of testosterone during fetal development and have suggested that immune-system dysfunction, left handedness, and certain learning-disability subtypes were highly associated. In addition, handedness has been thought to be related to lateralization of language functions in the brain and thus might help one predict the likely pattern of language lateralization in an individual. In their work, Bryden and Steenhuis (Chapter Sixteen) argue that if these hypotheses are to be evaluated properly, there must be some consistency in the way manual preference is measured.

While learning disabilities have historically been linked to neurological dysfunction, most of the data have been correlative in nature. That is, children who experience severe learning disabilities frequently exhibit behaviors similar to those individuals with known brain damage. But the causative factor for some individuals may be at the level of basic structural anatomy, whereas for other individuals the causative factor may reside at the physiological or behavioral levels. Questions about cognitive performance are dissimilar from questions about brain physiology and are addressed at different levels of analysis (i.e., behavioral, physiological, structural), with different techniques required to answer the various questions posed. Thus, for example, if children with learning disabilities have deficiencies in phonological processing, as Newby and Lyon and Felton and Brown have suggested, it might be hypothesized that dysfunction in the superior, posterior dominant temporal lobe and in the region of the angular gyrus produced the deficits. More direct evidence of structural variation is needed in order to show a neurological basis for this type of learning disability.

In this regard, the last decade has literally been unprecedented in terms of the technological advances that have been achieved in the study of the underlying physiology of the brain. Not only has there been refinement of computerized tomographic (CT) scanning, but separate imaging techniques of the CNS structure such as magnetic resonance imaging (MRI) and positron emission tomography (PET) scanning techniques offer yet a better understanding of the mechanics of brain anatomy. For example, CT scans suggest another dimension of variation in anatomic structure relating to symmetry and asymmetry which is not comparable to the data documented at postmortem examination. However, this technology, used to assess brain morphology, cannot readily be used with learning-disabled children in the public school sector. Likewise, invasive procedures, such as the sodium amytal or regional cerebral blood flow (rCBF) techniques, entail the use of barbiturates or radioactive substances, respectively, and cannot be readily used with children. As a result, researchers may have to be content with less direct evidence of actual brain involvement in searching for the causes of learning disabilities.

Although neurophysiological measurement of brain electrical activity taken from dyslexic subjects through electroencephalogram (EEG), event-related potential (ERP), and the more recent brain electrical activity mapping (BEAM) has yielded inconsistent results, current work is being conducted in an effort to provide more reliable data. While in Chapter Seventeen, Harter demonstrates that a relationship exists between ERP indicants of information processing, dyslexia, attention-deficit disorder (ADD), sex, and intelligence, Hynd, Semrud-Clikeman, and Lyytinen, in Chapter Eighteen, discuss what is known about brain imaging (using CT/MRI) and electrophysiological properties (BEAM) of the brains of learning-disabled persons. Taken together this work indicates that morphological differences frequently associated with dyslexia may be due to factors that tend to coexist with dyslexia, for example, hyperactivity and ADD. Perhaps the data obtained with these techniques, which are at the cutting edge of scientific awareness regarding the neurologic principals underlying human behavior, might lend to a more consistent data base with regard to the development of better definitions of learning disabilities.

References

Geschwind, N., & Galaburda, A. M. (1987). *Cerebral lateralization*. Cambridge, MA: MIT Press.

Hammill, D. D. (1990). On defining learning disabilities: An emerging consensus. *Journal of Learning Disabilities, 23,* 74–84.

Merrell, K. W., & Shinn, M. R. (1990). Critical variables in the learning disabilities identification process. *School Psychology Review, 19,* 74–82.

National Joint Committee on Learning Disabilities (NJCLD). (1981). *Learning disabilities: Issues on definition.* Unpublished manuscript. [Reprinted in *Journal of Learning Disabilities,* (1987) *20,* 107–108.]

CHAPTER ELEVEN

Use of Discrepancy Formulas in the Assessment of Learning Disabilities

Charles P. Heath
Joseph C. Kush

I. Introduction

There currently exists no consensus among professionals as to an established definition of a learning disability. In fact, there continues to be some disagreement as to whether or not learning disabilities (LD) even exist! While some researchers argue that learning-disabled children do not constitute a homogeneous population and should be characterized instead by a collection of subtypes (Rourke, 1975, 1978, 1983), other researchers (Algozzine and Ysseldyke, 1986) have argued that LD may not constitute a unique behavioral syndrome and should not be considered a handicapping condition. Arguments of this type, as well as other attempts to more precisely conceptualize LD, are concerned primarily with the validity of the diagnosis. However, before questions of validity can be adequately examined, researchers and clinicians must first focus on improving the reliability of making an LD diagnosis.

Many of the problems concerning the validity of LD diagnoses can be traced to procedures which identify children in an inconsistent or unreliable manner. Both neuropsychological and psychoeducational models of LD often utilize assessment procedures that are psychometrically flawed with regard to reliability and validity (Coles, 1978).

This chapter describes the procedure which we suggest will identify IQ–achievement discrepancies in children in the most statistically reliable manner. Questions concerning the validity of the LD definition will remain to be answered. Only after the same population of students is defined by clinicians and researchers, and after a homogeneous group of students is identified by clinicians, can the question of validity be addressed.

A. Learning Disabilities from an Educational Perspective

Learning disabilities are the most frequently diagnosed handicapping condition of school-aged children in the United States. The number of school-aged children diagnosed learning disabled in the United States has tripled from 1976 to 1982 (Reynolds, 1984). Currently, more than 40% of the school-aged, special-education population is classified LD. This represents 4% of all school-aged children nationally (Chalfant, 1989). Individual state prevalence rates range from 26 to 40% of the special-education population. As a result, many states have attempted to respond to the ever-increasing LD population by adopting stricter qualification criteria. Vague and subjective LD definitions are being replaced with more stringent and statistically rigorous procedures. A review by Frankenberger and Harper (1987) indicated that in 1981–82 achievement-discrepancy criteria were specified by 16 (33%) of the states. By 1985–86 these numbers had increased to 28 (57%), with a large percentage using discrepancy analysis rather than utilizing an arbitrary cutoff score. However, there currently exist no data to determine whether or not more stringent discrepancy criteria will have an effect on decreasing the incidence of LD in the public school setting.

The variation among states speaks to the wide diversity of LD definitions and diagnostic criteria used by the individual state Departments of Education. While most states do agree that an LD definition must include a significant ability–achievement discrepancy, there is little consensus among the states as to how to diagnose or quantify this discrepancy. A study by Epps, Ysseldyke, and Algozzine (1983) examined 14 different operational definitions of LD and found that each definition tended to identify significantly different numbers of students.

The current federal definition of LD was first presented to Congress in 1969 and subsequently was incorporated into Public Law 94-142, the Education for All Handicapped Children Act. Although the federal definition of LD indicates that a learning-disabled child must demonstrate a "severe discrepancy between achievement and intellectual ability in one or more of [seven achievement] areas" (USOE, 1977, p. 65,083), there continue to exist no established procedural guidelines for measuring this discrepancy. In fact, when considering LD criteria, the current federal definition is one of exclusion, *describing what a learning disability is not rather than identifying what a learning disability is*. The responsibility for further defining and specifying diagnostic procedures has been left to the individual states.

B. Neuropsychological Definitions from an Educational Perspective

Over the past 25 years both clinicians and researchers have shown an inability to agree upon a precise and unambiguous definition of learning disabilities which can be clearly and consistently operationalized. Considerable research has been based upon the presumption of a neurologically based LD definition. Currently however, an evolution in the field of LD has led to a shift in orientation regarding the causal status of neurological factors. The National Joint Committee for Learning Disabilities (NJCLD) has recently redefined LD to include an emphasis on central nervous system dysfunction. This new definition has been adopted by Congress and defines LD as referring to "a heterogeneous group of disorders manifested by significant difficulties in the acquisition and use of listening, speaking, reading, writing, reasoning or mathematical abilities. These disorders are intrinsic to the individual and presumed to be due to central nervous system dysfunction" (NJCLD, 1987).

The discrepancy between these two federal definitions has resulted in much confusion for researchers and practitioners. The PL 94-142 definition eliminates the etiological role of neurological factors and emphasizes instead the role of academics. Learning disabilities by the PL 94-142 definition cannot be diagnosed except after adequate instruction has been attempted. In contrast, the NJCLD definition takes a broader view of LD, emphasizing causative factors (presumed to be neurologically based) whether or not they impact academic performance. Both definitions continue to present difficulties in that PL 94-142 fails to operationalize "significant discrepancy" and the NJCLD similarly fails to operationalize "significant difficulties."

There has been some criticism of neurologically based definitions of LD because there has yet to be demonstrated any consistent neurological pattern associated with LD children defined by psychometric properties (Arter & Jenkins, 1977; Satz & Morris, 1981). Recently, educational settings have begun to operationalize LD as a discrepancy between expected and actual achievement as a criterion for identifying a student as learning disabled (Mercer, Hughes, & Mercer, 1985). However, this emphasis does not preclude the origin from being neurological.

C. Need for Improved Research Methodology

Neuropsychological research within the field of LD has reached a point where the sophistication of studying the underlying physiology of the brain is unprecedented. Use of computerized (CT) scanning, magnetic resonance imaging (MRI), and positron emission tomography (PET) scanning is possible in numerous clinical and research settings. Even genetic influences on LD have been investigated through linkage analysis (Pennington & Smith, 1988). Attempts to psychometrically quantify physiological procedures into LD diagnoses, however, have led to inconsistent and inconclusive results. The confusion of results may stem from an inconsistency in identifying research populations.

In neuropsychology it is clear that a consistent operational definition must be agreed upon if knowledge is to be accumulated scientifically. The process of making an accurate diagnosis requires that there be some degree of consistency or reliability among diagnosticians or researchers in their decision-making processes. Researchers, however, have been relatively unable to distinguish learning-disabled students from nonhandicapped students (Ysseldyke, Algozzine, & Epps, 1983) and low achievers (Algozzine & Ysseldyke, 1982; Ysseldyke, Algozzine, Shinn, & McGue, 1982). Distinguishing learning-disabled students from other categories of handicapped students has also been shown to be difficult (O'Donnell, 1980). Much of this confusion concerning diagnostic and classification issues can be directly traced to definitions which are hard to operationalize and classification criteria which produce inconsistent and unreliably defined LD populations.

II. Operationally Defining a Significant Discrepancy

Cone and Wilson (1981) have compared state guidelines used to quantify the discrepancy between ability and achievement that is typically displayed by LD populations. They found that state guidelines could be grouped into four categories: (1) deviation from grade level, (2) expectancy formula, (3) standard-score comparisons, and (4) regression analyses. Each of these definitions will be reviewed and the diagnostic implications presented.

A. Deviation-from-Grade-Level Method

Although currently not used on a widespread basis, the simplest but least sophisticated definition is one which identified a child as learning disabled if his/her achievement fell below current grade placement by some predetermined number of years. While the magnitude of this "significant" difference has varied considerably (often 1 to 2 years below grade level), the deviation-from-grade-level definition has tended to utilize one of the following variations: (1) the use of a fixed or constant level of deviation or, (2) the use of a graduated deviation where older children are required to be further behind academically.

At first glance this approach appeared to be objective and easily quantifiable. Similarly this definition was extremely easy to calculate and required that only one test (academic achievement) be administered. From a research standpoint, too, this approach seemed to have merit since the replication of research could be done in a seemingly clear and consistent manner. In fact, until recently, research which adopted the below-grade-level definition was relatively common (Chapman & Boersma, 1979; Gottesman, 1979; Selz & Reitan, 1979; Smith & Rogers, 1978) and was presented as the basic LD definition in a popular text in neuropsychology (Kolb & Whishaw, 1980).

However, significant problems exist with this definition of LD, as the deviation-from-grade-level method only considers academic deviation and ignores variation in intelligence. By ignoring intellectual factors the deviation-from-grade-level identifies slow learners (including those with below-average intelligence) instead of students whose achievement is significantly discrepant from their potential. Even when graded deviations are considered (e.g., LD defined as academic achievement below one-half of the child's grade level), low-IQ children will remain more likely to be identified than will high-IQ children. Although children who are reading below grade level may require additional academic remediation, definitions which only focus on how far below grade level the student is achieving without also considering general ability are actually definitions of low achievement and should not be used in the diagnosis of LD.

B. Expectancy-Formula Method

A second attempt at quantifying significant academic discrepancies has included a variety of expectancy formulas. With this approach students' expected achievement levels are predicted from their mental age (MA) and/or chronological age (CA) and are subsequently compared to their actual levels of achievement. The evolution of this approach occurred over several years beginning with the Bond and Tinker (1957) method developed specifically for identifying a reading disability. Their formula was Standard Age × IQ/100 − 6.2 + 1.0 but was later (1973) modified to Reading Expectancy Level = Years in School × IQ/100 + 1.0. While the original formula was based on the notion that the average student entering first grade was 6.2 years old, the revised formula attempted to correct for inflated expectancy scores and a restricted IQ range (90–110).

Later, Harris (1970) offered an alternative formula, Expected Age = (2 MA + CA)/3, which again was later modified to Severe Discrepancy = CA × (IQ/300 + .17) − 2.5. This revision was proposed by the U.S. Office of Education and was subsequently widely adopted by many state Departments of Education. It is interesting to note that Harris failed to provide any information concerning how large a discrepancy could be considered clinically meaningful. In reviewing this approach several years later Danielson and Bauer (1978) found that below-average IQ (80–90) children were, again, much more likely to be identified by this formula than were average or above-average peers and that students younger than 8 years old were also overrepresented.

By directly comparing how a student was actually performing with how the student should be or was expected to be performing, the expectancy approach was an important improvement over the deviation-from-grade-level method. As recently as 1985, 42 of 50 state Departments of Education had adopted some type of discrepancy component in their definition of LD (Mercer *et al.*, 1985). The expectancy approach, however, retains a number of serious limitations. First of all, this approach fails to take into account the correlation between the IQ and achievement measures. This problem is compounded severely by the use of grade-equivalent scores which often distort academic performance. While grade-equivalent scores do reflect a student's relative academic standing, they are limited to ordinal levels of measurement and are not as precise as ratio-scale measurements such as standard scores.

Grade-equivalent scores (like age equivalents) can often result in misleading interpretations. While one may expect two children with the same mental-age score to think similarly, this is not true. There are important intellectual differences of a qualitative nature between a 3-year-old with a mental age of three and a 6-year-old with a mental age of three. Similarly, a first-grade student who is reading 1 year above grade level will receive a percentile rank near 85 while a tenth-grade student who is also reading 1 year above grade level may only be near the 65th percentile. By failing to recognize that achievement tests do not exhibit identical grade-equivalent scores it is quite possible that a student may qualify for special education services as LD with one achievement test but might not qualify for placement when another achievement test is administered. For example, Reynolds (1981, p. 352) has shown that a seventh-grade student who is 2 years below grade level in reading will receive very different percentile ranks (WRAT, 18; PIAT, 23; WRMT, 34; SDRT, 30), which may lead to significantly different interpretations.

C. Standard-Score Difference Method

The standard-score difference method of identifying a severe discrepancy consists of a direct comparison between a child's intellectual ability and his/her academic achievement. This approach requires converting both scores to a common metric (a significant improvement over the previous models) and the difference score is computed by subtracting the child's achievement score from his/her IQ score. This difference score is most often obtained by utilizing standard scores with both the IQ and the achievement measures having a mean of 100 and a standard deviation of 15. This permits a simple and uniform comparison of scores.

The standard-score difference definition is currently the approach most widely used to calculate a discrepancy between IQ and achievement (Chalfant, 1984). In order to qualify for LD services the student must demonstrate a difference of some predetermined amount between IQ and achievement; an IQ–achievement difference of 15 points (one WISC-R standard deviation) is a common criterion used by many states and/or individual school districts.

The difference-score definition is widely used in many states because it is easily computed. Although it is an improvement over expectancy formula and below-grade-level models, the standard-score method also suffers from serious limitations, including a lack of consideration of the correlation between the two measures. The standard-score approach assumes that a child's intelligence test score, on the average, will be identical to his or her achievement test score (a child with an IQ of 130 should have a reading and math achievement score of 130). While this would be true if IQ and achievement were perfectly correlated ($r = 1.00$), the actual correlation between most IQ and achievement measures is between .50 and .65. Because of the effect of regression to the mean, if we take into account the IQ–achievement correlation (.60 to .70), a student with an IQ of 130 would not have an expected achievement score of 130, it would instead by around 122. With low-IQ children the opposite effect happens. An 85 IQ student would actually have an expected achievement level of approximately 88.

By simply subtracting a student's achievement from his/her IQ score a fixed, standard-score discrepancy approach will always have a systematic bias (Thorndike, 1963) such that it will overidentify a disproportionate number of high-ability underachievers and will underidentify low-ability achievers who may in fact be learning disabled. Standard-score difference methods have been shown, in this regard, to produce disproportionate racial representation in LD classes (Braden, 1987).

Like previously mentioned LD definitions, the standard-score approach also fails to take into account measurement errors. Obviously, different instruments will yield different IQ and achievement scores. Even when clinicians and researchers use a constant discrepancy formula (15 points) but different tests, they are likely to come to different conclusions. For example, Bishop and Butterworth (1980) found that particular IQ tests identified more students as reading disabled than did others. Compounding the confusion is research that suggests the size of the discrepancy increases over time (Badlen, 1988; O'Shea & Valcante, 1986). These measurement errors result because IQ and achievement measures are not perfectly correlated. Even when the same test is administered on two separate occasions differences in motivation, attending, and guessing will occur such that identical scores cannot be expected. These errors are further compounded when two different tests are administered.

Without examining the reliability of this "newly" created score, the difference score, clinicians cannot be sure that the discrepancy did not in fact occur by chance. Difference-score reliabilities are *less* reliable than either of the two scores used to calculate the difference score. For example, IQ and achievement tests with individual reliabilities of .90 will produce a difference score with a reliability of approximately .78. Difference-score reliability is influenced by the reliability of the individual tests used to determine the reliability as well as the correlation between the two measures. Therefore it is desirable to use IQ and achievement tests which have high reliability (greater than .80) and which are highly correlated. Several examples include the Kaufman Test of Educational Achievement (K-TEA) (1985), the Basic Achievement Skills Individual Screener (BASIS) (1983), and the Woodcock–Johnson Psychoeducational Battery, Part Two, (Woodcock, 1977). Instruments which demonstrate low correlations with measures of intelligence should not be used; in particular, criticism concerning the reliability and validity of the Wide-Range Achievement Test (WRAT) has been well established (Salvia & Ysseldyke, 1985).

D. Scatter-Analysis Method

Many researchers and clinicians have attempted to establish a diagnosis of LD based on the pattern or profile formed by subtest scores from an individual or battery of assessment measures. The Weschler Intelligence Scale for Children-Revised (WISC-R) has been used frequently, in this regard, in an attempt to diagnose areas of specific strengths and weaknesses and to differentiate LD populations from normal and underachieving populations on the basis of the scatter or profile on a series of subtests. At the simplest level verbal–performance discrepancies have been hypothesized to reflect LD characteristics, while at a more complex level various groupings of WISC-R subtests (e.g., ACID: low Arithmetic, Coding, Information, and Digit Span) have also been thought to reflect common LD profiles.

The clinical use of this approach has been questioned (Gutkin, 1979; Kaufman, 1979; Kavale & Forness, 1984). The hypothesis of profile uniqueness assumes that the average profile for a group of learning-disabled children is characteristic of the LD population as a whole or that the LD subtest profile varies significantly from an overall normal population. Research findings have shown that this simply is not the case.

The major problem with examining the WISC-R, verbal IQ–performance IQ (VIQ–PIQ) split is usually one of overinterpretation. That is, a very large percentage of the normally functioning population has a rather large VIQ–PIQ split. Between the ages of 6 and 16, 25% of the normal population will show a WISC-R VIQ–PIQ difference of 14 points and 10% of the normal population will have a 20-point VIQ–PIQ difference (Sattler, 1989, p. 819). Surely not a full 25% of all children are learning disabled! In addition, the factor structure of the WISC-R has been shown to be similar for learning-disabled and normal children (Blaha & Vance, 1979; Naglieri, 1981; Sutter & Bishop, 1986).

Without establishing a normative subtest profile, which commonly exists in children, we cannot know whether clinically revealed subtest profiles are uncommon, distinctive, or clinically meaningful (McDermott, Glutting, Jones, Watkins, & Kush, 1989). Because studies have failed to find a unique

WISC-R pattern in learning-disabled children (Kavale & Forness, 1984; Mueller, Matheson, & Short, 1983; Sattler, 1989) and because this approach fails to consider academic achievement, WISC-R patterns or profiles, in isolation, should not be used to establish the diagnosis of a LD.

III. Regression Definition

Despite the wide variety of available definitions, procedures which apply a regression approach to quantify IQ–achievement discrepancies are regarded as the most psychometrically defensible (Reynolds, 1984; Shepard, 1980; Thorndike, 1963; Wilson & Cone, 1984) yet are rarely used by clinicians or researchers. The regression method utilizes a prediction equation based upon the correlation between IQ and achievement scores. For each specific IQ, an expected or predicted achievement score is estimated and then compared with the student's actual level of achievement. Regression, as related to correlation, indicates that when a dependent variable (academic achievement) is predicted from a correlated measure (IQ), the predicted value of the dependent variable will over time regress toward the mean. While most children will have academic scores which fail near this predicted score, only those who have scores which fall considerably below this level will be considered to be "significantly" below level. Not only does this approach take into account regression to the mean, but measurement error can be controlled as well.

A. Regression Formula

The regression model most appropriate for establishing an IQ–achievement discrepancy indicates that a significant discrepancy exists when the difference between the student's predicted achievement score and the student's actual achievement score exceeds a certain value. This value is computed by multiplying the standard deviation of the IQ and achievement measures by a prespecified z value and then multiplying by the square root of 1 minus the IQ–achievement correlation:

$$(\hat{y} - y) > 15z \sqrt{(1 - r_{x,y})}$$

While this formula may appear somewhat complicated, each component of the equation will be explained in the following sections and will be followed by a step-by-step example. This formula assumes that both IQ and achievement measures are expressed as standard scores ($\overline{X} = 100$; SD = 15).

This particular regression formula has been previously recommended by Cone and Wilson (1981) as well as by the United States Department of Education, Special Education Programs Work Group on Measurement Issues in the Assessment of Learning Disabilities (Reynolds, 1984).

B. Statistical Components of the Equation

1. STANDARD ERROR OF MEASUREMENT

Psychometric theory assumes that no measurement is precise. Because of various types of measurement error related to test unreliability, statisticians usually describe a person's obtained score, on any measurement, as consisting of two parts: true score and error score. A true score is never known exactly, so it is always inferred from the obtained score. The error component of a person's obtained score can be referred to as the standard error of measurement (SEM). Standard errors of measurement represent bands or ranges placed around single scores to increase the precision of measurement. The SEM is an estimate of the amount of error associated with the person's obtained score. Large SEM's are associated with less precise measurement. The formula for calculating the SEM multiplies the standard deviation (SD) of the test by the square root of 1 minus the reliability of the test:

$$\text{SEM} = \text{SD} \sqrt{(1 - r_{x,x})}$$

After the SEM is calculated, it is applied (added and subtracted) to the individual's obtained score to form a band or range around the score. This range of scores is called the confidence interval and reflects a range within which we would expect to find the individual's "true" score. The formula for constructing a confidence interval is:

$$\text{Confidence interval} = \text{obtained score} \pm z \, (\text{SEM})$$

The z score is obtained from a normal curve table. The most frequently used z values are $z = 1.00$ (68% level), $z = 1.65$ (90% level), $z = 1.96$ (95% level), and $z = 2.58$ (99% level).

Confidence intervals can be small or large depending on the degree of confidence desired. For example, if a student obtains an IQ score of 104 and it is known that the SEM for that IQ measure is 3 points, the confidence interval would be 104 ± 3 ($101 - 107$) at the 68% confidence level. Or, a larger confidence interval of 104 ± 8 ($96 - 112$) at the 99% confidence level could be calculated. The latter interval would be interpreted by saying that the chances are 99 out of 100 that the student's true score falls within the range of 96 to 112. The more confidence desired, the larger the confidence level must be.

2. STANDARD ERROR OF ESTIMATE

In the case of two scores where one score is used to predict the second, a different statistic, standard error of estimate (SEE), is used. The logic behind the SEE is exactly the same as for the standard error of measurement. The SEE increases the accuracy of prediction by placing a confidence interval around the predicted score. With a less-than-perfect correlation some prediction error will occur. As with the SEM, the larger the correlation between the two measures the smaller the SEE. The SEE is computed by multiplying the standard deviation of the achievement test by the square root of 1 minus the squared correlation between the IQ and achievement measures:

$$\text{SEE} = \text{SD} \sqrt{(1 - r_{x,y}^2)}$$

Again, if a z value of 1.00 is employed, it would be stated that the student's predicted score would fall within this range 68% of the time. That is, the obtained values of the achievement score (Y) will be scattered around the predicted value and the standard deviation of this scatter is the SEE. Two-thirds of the obtained Y values will fall within the range of 1 SEE.

3. REGRESSION TO THE MEAN

When two measures are correlated (such as IQ and achievement) certain predictions can be made. One prediction reflects what happens to the pair of scores as they occur farther and farther from the mean. When one score is exceptionally far from the mean, there is a very high probability that the score with which it is correlated will "regress to the mean," or be closer to the mean than the original score.

This phenomenon was first identified by Galton in the nineteenth century. Regression indicates that when two scores are positively correlated (as IQ and achievement tests typically are), individuals who obtain an extreme score on one test will on the average obtain a score closer to the population average on the second test.

McLeod (1979) has shown, for example, that for a group of students who each obtain a score of 130 on a test of intelligence, their average reading quotient is near 115, not 130. While some of the students will have reading scores higher than 130, one-half of the students are mathematically determined to be 15 or more points behind their IQ in reading. In contrast to a regression approach, LD definitions that adopt a fixed-score cutoff are discriminatory against such students, as they identify a disproportionate number of high-IQ students as being significantly deficient.

If both IQ and achievement measures are expressed as standard scores with means of 100 and standard deviations of 15, predicted achievement ($\hat{y}$) is computed by multiplying the IQ–achievement correlation by the obtained IQ minus the mean of the IQ test, which is then added to the mean of the achievement test:

$$\hat{y} = r_{x,y} (\text{IQ} - 100) + 100$$

C. Putting It All Together: An Example

In summary, the regression definition takes 5 steps:

$$(\hat{y} - y) > 15z \sqrt{(1 - r_{x,y})}$$

1. Measure the child's IQ.
2. Predict the child's achievement level ($\hat{y}$) by means of the correlation ($r_{x,y}$) between the IQ score and the achievement score.
3. Measure the child's achievement score (y).
4. Establish confidence intervals around the predicted achievement score using the SEE.
5. Compare the predicted and actual achievement scores ($\hat{y} - y$). The significance of this difference is evaluated by the SEE.

Two examples will be provided. The first will calculate a significant discrepancy using the five above steps as an outline. The second example will utilize a table of critical values which indicate the criteria needed for a significant discrepancy.

For the first example, assume the research literature indicates that the correlation between the IQ and achievement measures selected is .54. Next, the child obtains an IQ of 115, which yields a predicted achievement score of 108.1. This calculation is derived by the formula for predicted achievement, previously provided [Predicted Achievement = .54 (115 − 100) + 100]. Because the child was referred due to problems in only one area of achievement, we select a z value of 1.65. By multiplying 15 by 1.65 by the square root of 1 minus .54 we obtain a value of 18.9. Next, a confidence interval of 89.2 − 127 is established by adding and subtracting 18.9 to our predicted achievement score of 108.1. Because the student's actual achievement score of 85 is less than the lower end of the confidence interval (89.2), it is determined that a significant discrepancy does exist.

To eliminate the possibility of mathematical error, several computer programs are available that calculate significant IQ–achievement discrepancies using a regression approach for the IBM (McDermott & Watkins, 1987) and Apple (McDermott & Watkins, 1985; Reynolds & Snow, 1985; Watkins & Kush, 1988) microcomputers. In several of these programs, extensive literature reviews were conducted and correlations for many different IQ–achievement combinations are provided by the program.

Table I was developed using the Watkins and Kush (1988) program and presents critical values needed to establish a significant discrepancy for various IQ scores and various IQ–achievement correlations. A z value of 1.50 was specified for all computations (see Table I). While disagreement exists as to whether or not students with above-average intelligence who are academically at grade level (gifted LD) should receive LD services, the arbitrary exclusion of students from LD placements based entirely on IQ scores is inappropriate and discriminatory. As such, Table I provides scores across a broad range of mental abilities.

Table I is interpreted in the following manner. First, locate the student's IQ score in the first column. Follow that score across to the column with the correlational value closest to the correlation between the chosen measures of IQ and achievement. The resulting value represents the value needed to establish a significant discrepancy (based upon the SEE around the predicted achievement level). For example, if the student's IQ score is 105 and the IQ–achievement correlation is .68 (rounded to .70), an actual achievement score of 87 or below is required for a significant discrepancy to exist.

The concept of regression to the mean is displayed quite clearly in Table I. If a constant correlation of .50 is assumed, for example, a 135 IQ student must have an achievement score of less than 98 (a 37-point discrepancy) for a significant discrepancy to exist, while a 110 IQ student must only demonstrate a 24-point discrepancy (actual achievement less than 86) and a 100 IQ student only needs a 19-point discrepancy. Similarly, if IQ and achievement measures are selected with a higher correlation, .80 for example, the actual versus expected achievement difference needed to establish a significant discrepancy is greatly reduced (20, 15, and 13 points, respectively).

D. Related Issues

1. SELECTION OF IQ MEASURE

Often it may be unclear as to which IQ score to use in making the expected achievement estimation. In most cases the use of the full-scale IQ score is preferred since it reflects the highest predictive validity coefficient with achievement. In selecting a subscale IQ score to predict academic achievement, the clinician should be certain that the verbal-performance IQ score difference is statistically significant and diagnostically meaningful. Typically, subscale differences of 1.5 standard deviations or larger (WISC-R VIQ–PIQ difference of at least 23.8 points) will satisfy both criteria and occur in approximately 5% of the child population (Sattler, 1989). When such differences do exist, however, the verbal IQ will almost always be a better estimate of academic achievement. The decision to use a subscale IQ score should always be supported by additional assessment data (Kaufman, 1979).

2. SELECTION OF CORRELATION

Cone and Wilson (1981) advocate that when correlations between IQ and achievement measures have not been adequately investigated, a standard-score difference approach may be appropriate. However, when information concerning IQ–achievement correlations is not yet fully investigated a re-

TABLE I Observed Achievement Levels Necessary for IQ–Achievement Discrepancy Using Standard Scores[a]

	Correlations Between Intellectual and Achievement Measures										
	.80	.75·	.70	.65	.60	.55	.50	.45	.40	.35	.30
IQ	Achievement Test Score Necessary for Discrepancy										
135	115	111	108	106	103	100	98	96	93	91	89
134	114	111	108	105	102	100	98	95	93	91	89
133	113	110	107	104	102	99	97	95	93	90	88
132	112	109	106	104	101	99	97	94	92	90	88
131	111	108	106	103	101	98	96	94	92	90	88
130	111	108	105	102	100	98	96	93	91	89	88
129	110	107	104	102	99	97	95	93	91	89	87
128	109	106	104	101	99	97	95	93	91	89	87
127	108	105	103	100	98	96	94	92	90	88	87
126	107	105	102	100	98	96	94	92	90	88	86
125	107	104	101	99	97	95	93	91	89	88	86
124	106	103	101	99	96	94	93	91	89	87	86
123	105	102	100	98	96	94	92	90	89	87	85
122	104	102	99	97	95	93	92	90	88·	87	85
121	103	101	99	97	95	93	91	89	88	86	85
120	103	100	98	96	94	92	91	89	87	86	85
119	102	99	97	95	93	92	90	88	87	86	84
118	101	99	97	95	93	91	90	88	87	85	84
117	100	98	96	94	92	91	89	88	86	85	84
116	99	97	95	93	92	90	89	87	86	85	83
115	99	96	94	93	91	89	88	87	85	84	83
114	98	96	94	92	90	89	88	86	85	84	83
113	97	95	93	91	90	88	87	86	85	83	82
112	96	94	92	91	89	88	87	85	84	83	82
111	95	93	92	90	89	87	86	85	84	83	82
110	95	93	91	89	88	87	86	84	83	82	82
109	94	92	90	89	87	86	85	84	83	82	81
108	93	91	90	88	87	86	85	84	83	82	81
107	92	90	89	87	86	85	84	83	82	81	81
106	91	90	88	87	86	85	84	83	82	81	80
105	91	89	87	86	85	84	83	82	81	81	80
104	90	88	87	86	84	83	83	82	81	80	80
103	89	87	86	84	83	82	81	81	81	80	79
102	88	87	85	84	83	82	82	81	80	80	79
101	87	86	85	84	83	82	81	80	80	79	79
100	87	85	84	83	82	81	81	80	79	79	79
99	86	84	83	82	81	81	80	79	79	79	78
98	85	84	83	82	81	80	80	79	79	78	78
97	84	83	82	81	80	80	79	79	78	78	78
96	83	82	81	80	80	79	79	79	78	78	77
95	83	81	80	80	80	79	78	78	77	77	77
94	82	81	80	79	78	78	78	77	77	77	77

TABLE I *Continued*

	Correlations Between Intellectual and Achievement Measures										
	.80	.75	.70	.65	.60	.55	.50	.45	.40	.35	.30
IQ	Achievement Test Score Necessary for Discrepancy										
93	81	80	79	78	78	77	77	77	77	76	76
92	80	79	78	78	77	77	77.	76	76	76	76
91	79	78	78	77	77	76	76	76	76	76	76
90	79	78	77	76	76	76	76	75	75	75	76
89	78	77	76	76	75	75	75	75	75	75	75
88	77	76	76	75	75	75	75	75	75	75	75
87	76	75	75	74	74	74	74	74	74	74	75
86	75	75	74	74	74	74	74	74	74	74	74
85	75	74	73	73	73	73	73	73	73	74	74
84	74	73	73	73	72	72	73	73	73	73	74
83	73	72	72	72	72	72	72	72	73	73	73
82	72	72	71	71	71	72	72	72	72	73	73
81	71	71	71	71	71	71	71	71	72	72	73
80	71	70	70	70	70	70	71	71	71	72	73
79	70	69	69	69	69	70	70	70	71	72	72
78	69	69	69	69	69	69	70	70	71	71	72
77	68	68	68	68	68	69	69	70	70	71	72
76	67	67	67	67	68	68	69	69	70	71	71
75	67	66	66	67	67	67	68	69	69	70	71
74	66	66	66	66	66	67	68	68	69	70	71
73	65	65	65	65	66	66	67	68	69	69	70
72	64	64	64	65	65	66	67	67	68	69	70
71	63	63	64	64	65	65	66	67	68	69	70

a Standard scores with M = 100 and SD = 15.

gression approach is still the preferred method. Many factors influence the IQ–achievement correlation. Determination of this correlation should recognize the variation in IQ–achievement correlations across various ages, ethnic backgrounds, and special populations. In instances where the IQ–achievement correlation has yet to be established, the use of a correlation of .65 (approximate median correlation of existing IQ-correlation measures) is recommended.

Obviously, caution is needed when utilizing unsubstantiated measures in clinical or research practice. Consistent with established legal and ethical standards of clinical practice, the selection of the appropriate validity coefficient between IQ and achievement measures should be based on a large, stratified, random sample of normal children. Correlations derived from clinically referred or existing LD populations will be spuriously small due to the restricted range of the population and should only be used with caution. Every attempt should be made to identify correlations appropriate for the sample.

3. SELECTION OF AN APPROPRIATE Z VALUE

The number of a priori comparisons desired should lead directly to the level of confidence that surrounds these comparisons. In determining confidence intervals, the selection of the appropriate z-score should consider, among other things, the number of IQ–achievement comparisons that is going to be made. The failure to consider multiple comparisons will lead to an inflated alpha level. Unless this factor is considered, a significantly larger number of children will be identified as having a significant discrepancy. When making one IQ–achievement comparison the 90% confidence level (1.65 × SEE) is recommended; when making two or three comparisons the 95% confidence level (1.96 × SEE) should be used; when making more than three comparisons the 99% confidence level (2.58 × SEE) should be employed. This procedure is essentially the same as the Bonferroni technique typically used in research to control for errors introduced when making multiple comparisons within the same experimental data set. This recommendation also attempts to balance the risk of making a false-positive error (identifying a nonlearning-disabled child as learning disabled) with the risk of making a false-negative error (failing to identify a learning-disabled child). There is no consensus as to which is the more serious error (Reynolds, 1984). The recommendation presented here is based in part on the assumptions that (1) a "significant discrepancy" should occur relatively infrequently, and (2) not all children who exhibit a statistically significant discrepancy, based upon a regression approach, are necessarily learning disabled.

E. Advantages of a Regression Approach

The regression method offers several advantages over other less sophisticated diagnostic approaches. By taking into account the correlation between IQ and achievement measures, children across all IQ levels can be assessed and can be clearly distinguished from slow learners. Although student achievement is influenced by many different factors (e.g., motivation), IQ remains the best single predictor of academic achievement, and the prediction provided can be thought of as expected achievement (Thorndike & Hagen, 1977). Regression methods have also been shown to produce more proportionate racial representation in LD classes than do fixed standard-score definitions (Braden, 1987).

Too often a "fishing net" approach is used clinically in attempting to assess and diagnose a learning disability. Rather than determining a priori which specific measures will be used, based on the reason for referral, in many cases an entire achievement battery is administered and the highest IQ score is compared with the lowest achievement score. This "throw out the net and see what we pull in" approach significantly increases the likelihood that a discrepancy will be found even in an area in which the student is achieving successfully. These discrepancies may occur due to chance rather than due to a "true" discrepancy. A student referred for evaluation only because of suspected reading difficulties may actually have nine comparisons made if given the WISC-R (FSIQ, VIQ, PIQ) and the entire Woodcock–Johnson achievement battery (reading, math, written expression). Those who favor this method may argue that an undiscovered learning disability may be overlooked if an entire assessment battery is not undertaken. While psychoeducational evaluations should be comprehensive, the practice of assessing LD based only on the "test scores," while disregarding the specific reason for referral, classroom observations, and preassessment interventions, is clearly inappropriate and may be considered a form of statistical Russian roulette.

The regression approach suggests that prior to the administration of either the IQ or the achievement test a decision needs to be made as to exactly what type and how many suspected areas of disability are to be assessed so that the scope of the assessment is limited only to those comparisons. This decision should lead directly to the selection of the appropriate z value, as discussed earlier.

IV. Summary

One must agree with Reynolds (1984) that the determination of a significant discrepancy is a necessary but not sufficient condition for the diagnosis of a learning disability. Only after reliable IQ–achievement discrepancies are identified can researchers attempt to describe the common characteristics of the group so that issues related to etiology can be further investigated.

The diagnostic and classification process outlined in this chapter addresses the call of Rivers and Smith (1988) for consistency in eligibility criteria for placing students in LD programs. Consistent criteria are essential for reducing both the under- and the overclassification of students as learning disabled. Additionally, the consistency in eligibility criteria between school-based and clinical samples will lead toward more replicability of research in the area of neuropsychology. However, it is essential to keep in mind that the classification procedures presented in this chapter are only one variable that needs to be addressed in the determination of a learning disability. Both PL 94-142 and the NJCLD definition have exclusionary clauses which need to be considered.

Following a more consistent diagnostic procedure in determining a significant discrepancy should support efforts to more clearly define LD subtypes. Specific subtype identification and the documentation of equipment and procedures being used in the measurement of electrical activity may result in more consistency of research findings dealing with neurodevelopmental pathology.

Even after statistically reliable methods like the regression approach are adopted, additional research must be conducted to compare the extent of agreement between these approaches and other means of identification as well as to study the effects of measurement error, instrument selection, and the utility of varying cutoff scores used to define learning-disabled students. By comparing the regression approach, for example, with other identification techniques one may be better able to determine whether or not different populations of students are identified. Some of this research is now being done [Bennett & Clarizio, 1988; Macmann & Barnett, 1985; Shaywitz, Shaywitz, Barnes, & Fletcher 1986 (cited in Fletcher *et al.*, 1989); Sinclair & Alexson, 1986], in an attempt to explore various IQ and reading cutoff scores while varying the degree of discrepancy. This is an important step in the right direction and one which future research should pursue.

References

Algozzine, B., & Ysseldyke, J. (1982). Classification decisions in learning disabilities. *Educational and Psychological Research, 2*, 117–129.

Algozzine, B., & Ysseldyke, J. (1986). The future of the LD field: Screening and diagnosis. *Journal of Learning Disabilities, 19*, 394–398.

Arter, J. A., & Jenkins, J. R. (1977). Examining the benefits and prevalence of modality considerations in special education. *Journal of Special Education, 11*, 281–298.

Badien, N. A. (1988). The prediction of good and poor reading before kindergarten entry: A nine-year follow-up. *Journal of Learning Disabilities, 21*, 98–103.

Bennett, D. E., & Clarizio, H. F. (1988). A comparison of methods for calculating a severe discrepancy. *Journal of School Psychology, 26*, 359–369.

Bishop, D. V. & Butterworth, G. E. (1980). Verbal-performance discrepencies: Relationship to birth risk and specific reading retardation. *Cortex, 16*, 375–389.

Blaha, J., & Vance, H. (1979). The hierarchial factor structure of the WISC-R for learning disabled children. *Learning Disability Quarterly, 2*, 71–75.

Bond, G. L., & Tinker, M. A. (1957). *Reading difficulties, their diagnosis and corrections.* New York: Appleton-Century-Crofts.

Bond, G. L., & Tinker, M. A. (1973). *Reading difficulties, their diagnosis and corrections* (3rd ed.). New York: Appleton-Century-Crofts.

Braden, J. P. (1987). A comparison of regression and standard score discrepancy methods for learning disabilities identification: Effects on racial representation. *Journal of School Psychology, 25*, 23–29.

Chalfant, J. C. (1984). *Identifying Learning Disabled students: Guidelines for decision making.* Andover, MA: Network of Innovative Schools. (ERIC Document Reproduction Service No. ED 258390).

Chalfant, J. C. (1989). Learning disabilities: Policy issues and promising approaches. *American Psychologist, 44,* 392–398.

Chapman, J. S., & Boersma, F. J. (1979). Learning disabilities, locus of control, and mother attitudes. *Journal of Educational Psychology, 71,* 250–258.

Coles, G. S. (1978). The learning disabilities test battery: Empirical and social issues. *Harvard Educational Review, 48,* 313–340.

Cone, T. E., & Wilson, L. R. (1981). Quantifying a severe discrepancy: A critical analysis. *Learning Disability Quarterly, 4,* 359–371.

Danielson, L. C., & Bauer, J. N. (1978). A formula-based classification of learning disabled children: An examination of the issues. *Journal of Learning Disabilities, 11,* 163–176.

Epps, S., Ysseldyke, J., & Algozzine, B. (1983). Impact of different definitions of learning disabilities on the number of students identified. *Journal of Psychoeducational Assessment, 1,* 341–352.

Fletcher, J. M., Espy, K. A., Francis, D. J., Davidson, K. C., Rouke, B. P., & Shaywitz, S. E. (1989). Comparisons of cutoff and regression-based definitions of reading disabilities. *Journal of Learning Disabilities, 22,* 334–338, 355.

Frankenberger, W., & Harper, J. (1987). States' criteria and procedures for identifying learning disabled children: A comparison of 1981/82 and 1985/86 guidelines. *Journal of Learning Disabilities, 20,* 118–121.

Gottesman, R. C. (1979). Follow-up of learning disabled children. *Learning Disability Quarterly, 2,* 60–69.

Gutkin, T. B. (1979). WISC-R scatter indices: Useful information for differential diagnosis? *Journal of School Psychology, 17,* 368–371.

Harris, A. (1970). *How to increase reading abilities* (5th ed.). New York: David McKay.

Kaufman, A. S. (1979). *Intelligence testing with the WISC-R.* New York: Wiley (Interscience).

Kaufman, A. S., & Kaufman, N. L. (1985). *Kaufman Test of Educational Achievement.* Circle Pines, MN: American Guidance Service.

Kavale, K. A., & Forness, S. R. (1984). A meta-analysis of the validity of Wechsler Scale profiles and recategorizations: Patterns or parodies? *Learning Disability Quarterly, 7,* 136–156.

Kolb, B., & Whishaw, I. (1980). *Fundamentals of human neuropsychology.* San Francisco, CA: Freeman.

Macmann, G. M., & Barnett, D. W. (1985). Discrepancy score analysis: A computer simulation of classification stability. *Journal of Psychoeducational Assessment, 4,* 363–375.

McDermott, P. A., Glutting, J. J., Jones, J. N., Watkins, M. W., & Kush, J. C. (1989). Core profile types in the WISC-R national sample: Structure, membership, and applications. *Psychological Assessment: A Journal of Consulting and Clinical Psychology, 1,* 292–299.

McDermott, P. A., & Watkins, M. (1985). *McDermott Multidimensional Assessment of Children: 1985 Apple II version* [Computer programs]. New York: Psychological Corporation.

McDermott, P. A., & Watkins, M. (1987). *McDermott Multidimensional Assessment of Children: 1987 IBM version* [Computer programs]. New York: Psychological Corporation.

McLeod, J. (1979). Educational underachievement: Toward a defensible psychometric definition. *Journal of Learning Disabilities, 12,* 42–50.

Mercer, C. D., Hughes, C., & Mercer, A. R. (1985). Learning disability definitions used by state education departments. *Learning Disability Quarterly, 8,* 45–55.

Mueller, H. H., Matheson, D. W., & Short, R. H. (1983). Bannatyne-recatagorized WISC-R patterns of mentally retarded, learning disabled, normal, and intellectually superior children: A meta-analysis. *Mental Retardation and Learning Disability Bulletin, 11,* 60–78.

Naglieri, J. A. (1981). Factor structure of the WISC-R for children identified as learning disabled. *Psychological Reports, 49,* 891–895.

National Joint Committee on Learning Disabilities (NJCLD). (1987). Learning disabilities: Issues on definition. A position paper. *Journal of Learning Disabilities, 20,* 107–108.

O'Donnell, L. E. (1980). Intra-individual discrepancy in diagnosing specific learning disabilities. *Learning Disability Quarterly, 3,* 10–18.

O'Shea, L. J., & Valcante, G. (1986). A comparison over time of relative discrepancy scores of low achievers. *Exceptional Children, 53,* 253–259.

Pennington, B. F., & Smith, S. D. (1988). Genetic influences on learning disabilities: An update. *Journal of Consulting and Clinical psychology, 56,* 817–823.

Reynolds, C. (1981). The fallacy of "two years below grade level for age" as a diagnostic criterion for reading disorders. *Journal of School Psychology, 19,* 350–358.

Reynolds, C. (1984). Critical measurement issues in learning disabilities. *Journal of Special Education, 18,* 451–475.

Reynolds, C., & Snow, M. (1985). *Severe Discrepancy Analysis:* [Computer program]. College Station, TX: TRAIN.

Rivers, D., & Smith, T. (1988). Traditional eligibility criteria for identifying students as specific learning disabled. *Journal of Learning Disabilities, 21,* 642–644.

Rourke, B. P. (1975). Brain-behavior relationships in children with learning disabilities: A research program. *American Psychologist, 30,* 911–920.

Rourke, B. P. (1978). Reading, spelling and arithmetic disabilities: A neuropsychologic perspective. In H. R. Myklebust (Ed.), *Progress in learning disabilities* (Vol. 4). New York: Grune & Stratton.

Rourke, B. P. (1983). Reading and spelling disabilities: A developmental neuropsychological perspective. In U. Kirk (Ed.), *Neuropsychology of language, reading and spelling.* New York: Academic Press.

Salvia, J., & Ysseldyke, J. (1985). *Assessment in special and remedial education* (3rd ed.), Boston, MA: Houghton-Mifflin.

Sattler, J. M. (1989). *Assessment of Children* (3rd ed.). San Diego, CA: Jerome M. Sattler Publisher.

Satz, P., & Morris, R. (1981). Learning disability subtypes: A review. In F. J. Pirozzolo & M. C. Wittrock (Eds.), *Neuropsychological and cognitive processes in reading.* New York: Academic Press.

Seiz, M., & Reitan, R. (1979). Rules for neuropsychological diagnosis: Classification of brain function in older children. *Journal of Consulting and Clinical Psychology, 47,* 258–264.

Shepard, L. A. (1980). An evaluation of the regression discrepancy method for identifying children with learning disabilities. *Journal of Special Education, 14,* 79–91.

Sinclair, E., & Alexson, J. (1986). Learning disability discrepancy formulas: Similarities and differences among them. *Learning Disabilities Research, 1,* 112–118.

Smith, M. D., & Rogers, C. M. (1978). Reliability of standardized assessment instruments when used with learning disabled children. *Learning Disability Quarterly, 1,* 23–31.

Sonnenschein, J. L. (1983). *Basic Achievement Skills Individual Screener* (BASIS). (1983). San Antonio, TX: Psychological Corporation.

Sutter, E. G. & Bishop, P. C. (1986). Factor structure of the WISC-R and ITPA for learning disabled, emotionally disturbed, and control children. *Journal of Clinical Psychology, 42,* 975–978.

Thorndike, R. L. (1963). *The concepts of over- and under-achievement.* Bureau of Publications, Teachers College, Columbia University, New York.

Thorndike, R. L., & Hagen, E. P. (1977). *Measurement and evaluation in psychology and education (4th ed.).* New York: Wiley.

U.S.O.E. (1977). Assistance to states for education of handicapped children: Procedures for evaluating specific learning disabilities. *Federal Register, 42,* 65082–65085.

Watkins, M., & Kush, J. (1988). *The Research Assistant:* (Computer program]. Phoenix, AZ: SouthWest EdPsych Inc.

Wilson, L. R., & Cone, T. (1984). The regression equation method of determining academic discrepancy. *Journal of School Psychology, 22,* 95–110.

Woodcock, R. W. (1977). *Woodcock-Johnson Psycho-Educational Battery, Tech. Rep.* DLM Teaching Resources, Allen, TX.

Ysseldyke, J. E., Algozzine, B., & Epps, S. (1983). A logical and empirical analysis of current practice in classifying students as handicapped. *Exceptional Children, 50,* 160–170.

Ysseldyke, J. E., Algozzine, B., Shinn, M. R., & McGue, M. (1982). Similarities and differences between low achievers and students classified learning disabled. *Journal of Special Education, 16,* 73–85.

CHAPTER TWELVE

Neuropsychological Assessment of Learning Disorders in Children

Ervin S. Batchelor, Jr.
Raymond S. Dean

I. Introduction

Numerous reports have been published recently on the neuropsychologic assessment of childhood learning disabilities (e.g., Batchelor & Dean, 1989a; Fisk & Rourke, 1983; Fletcher, Satz, & Morris, 1984; Frith, 1983; Morris, Blashfield, & Satz, 1986; Obrzut, Hynd, & Boliek, 1986; Pirozollo, 1981; Reynolds, 1985; Rourke, 1983. Interestingly, studies in the area have yielded conflicting results (e.g., Batchelor & Dean, 1989a; Morris *et al.*, 1986). Several reasons for discrepancies among reports can be offered. One major problem has concerned ambiguous definitions of learning disabilities which are difficult to apply in subject selection (Batchelor & Dean, 1989a; Morris *et al.*, 1986; Rourke, 1983). Indeed, criteria which have been offered for diagnoses of learning disorders have lacked rigor (e.g., Batchelor & Dean, 1989a; Hynd & Hynd, 1984; Morris *et al.*, 1986; Rourke, 1983). As a result, the disorders represented by subjects have differed greatly across studies (e.g., Morris *et al.*, 1986; Rattan & Dean, 1987). Related to this problem is the fact that the severity of disorders varies with the setting from which subjects are studied (e.g., school versus clinic) (Batchelor & Dean, 1989a; Batchelor, Gray, & Dean, in press-a). It has also become clear that developmental level, general ability, and neuropsychological functioning, may play major roles in understanding learning disabilities. However, only recently have researchers begun to consider the implications of development of neuropsychological functioning and intelligence in the study of children with learning disorders (see Batchelor & Dean, 1989a; D'Amato, Gray, & Dean, 1988; Kelly, Batchelor, & Dean, 1989; Morris *et al.,* 1986; Spreen & Haaf, 1986). In addition to these subject-related problems, methodology and data analyses have varied widely across laboratories (e.g., Batchelor & Dean, 1989a, Batchelor, Dean, & Williams, 1989, Fletcher & Satz, 1985; Morris *et al.,* 1986). Considered together these factors limit the generalizability of many findings to a respective laboratory and then only with a specific sample. With this as a backdrop, this chapter examines issues in designing and implementing a program of study in children's learning disorders. The purpose here is to clarify the issues and obstacles in researching childhood learning disabilities and to discuss the implications of a program of research in neuropsychological assessment.

From a research viewpoint, assessment is one of the most essential aspects of the diagnostic process. Exacting definitions evolve from rigorous empirical testing of hypotheses formed from detailed clinical observation (Rourke, 1983). This process is essential if reliable nosological classification system of learning disorders is to be established (Rourke, 1983). In turn, scientific investigations and clinical acumen in the diagnosis of learning disorders are predicated upon a precise, unambiguous definition (Rourke, 1983). However, it would seem that lawmakers and administrators funneling program funds have been less than sympathetic to such a scientific method. Indeed, clinicians often have been limited to a most controversial set of criteria upon which to make diagnoses of learning disorders (e.g., PL 94-142). As a result, the terms "learning disability" and "learning disorder" have rendered different meanings in the research and applied settings (Hynd & Hynd, 1984).

Practically speaking, many have adopted use of an exclusionary definition for learning disabilities (e.g., PL 94-142 or World Federation of Neurology). Such definitions typically characterize a learning disability as any severe discrepancy between relatively normal intelligence and poor achievement which is not due to cultural deprivation, sensory impairment, behavioral–emotional disorders, or impoverished educational settings. From this view, diagnoses are obtained from arbitrary cutoff scores and a process of elimination. The psychometric validity of this approach is highly questionable (see Braden & Algina, 1989; Reynolds, 1985; Schultz & Borich, 1984; Wilson & Cone, 1984) (see also Heath & Kush, this volume, Chapter 11).

It would seem that with the use of an exclusionary definition of learning disabilities comes inherent measurement and clinical confusion (e.g., Morris *et al.,* 1986; Rourke, 1983; Rutter, 1978; Taylor, Satz, & Friel, 1979). Taylor *et al.* (1979) have shown that reading-disabled children meeting exclusionary criteria did not differ significantly on neuropsychological test performance from children with reading problems who did not meet these exclusionary criteria. Morris *et al.* (1986) have argued that use of exclusionary definitions in the research setting often results in the selection of a heterogeneous sample which may not be representative of the existing population of children with learning disorders.

The National Joint Committee for Learning Disabilities (NJCLD) argued that learning disorders "are intrinsic to the individual and presumed to be due to a central nervous system dysfunction" (Hammil, Leigh, McNutt, & Larsen, 1981). From this view, the diagnoses of learning disorders would require demonstration of achievement deficits concomitant with neurologic and neuropsychological dysfunction (see Hynd & Hynd, 1984). It is on this premise that we have conceptualized and implemented a research program for children with learning disorders. Recognizing that many clinicians are restricted to using exclusionary criteria for diagnosing children with learning disorders in the public schools, we felt it necessary to use large samples from this population to strengthen external validity. At the same time, we realized the methodological limitations of exclusionary definitions in the research setting (e.g., heterogeneity within and between samples associated with differences in achievement–intelligence discrepancy formulas and measurement tools applied in different settings). To avoid confusion between definitions, learning disorders are considered here to be related in various degrees to neuropsychological dysfunction. In addition, learning deficits are considered more realistically as continuous rather than dichotomous constructs (i.e., disordered versus normal). This approach has led us to consider questions regarding the nature of the relationship between severity of achievement deficits and neuropsychological dysfunction, the influence of intelligence and age on measures, and the neuropsychological underpinnings of achievement deficits.

In an attempt to formulate a replicable research program, we have selected a standardized fixed battery approach recommended by Reitan (1969). Specifically, all children in our studies were administered the Halstead–Reitan Neuropsychological Battery for Older Children (HRNB-C) (ages 9–14 years) (Reitan 1969), the Wechsler Intelligence Scale for Children-Revised (WISC-R) (Wechsler, 1974), the Wide-Range Achievement Test (WRAT) (Jastak & Jastak, 1978), and the Lateral Dominance Examination (LDE) (Reitan, 1969) by qualified examiners. The sample sizes ranged from some 435 to 1400 subjects. There was a ratio of 3.5 males to 1 female in studies where gender was combined (D'Amato, Dean, Rattan, & Nickell, in press). Subjects typically were from lower-middle to middle class backgrounds. No subject was diagnosed with frank neurologic or psychiatric disorders. All subjects were considered learning disabled (in accord with PL 94-142) by a multidisciplinary team of educational specialists.

II. Subtyping Efforts of Children with Learning Deficits

Perhaps the most controversial topic in the area of learning disabilities is the characterization of subgroups. Early attempts to identify a unitary constellation of symptoms or etiological factors underlying a single disorder in learning have met with little success (e.g., Fletcher & Satz, 1979). With few exceptions, researchers agree that children with learning disabilities encompass a heterogeneous group of learning problems (e.g., Doehring, 1978; Fisk & Rourke, 1983; Gaddes, 1985; Morris et al., 1986; Rattan & Dean, 1987; Rourke, 1983). Dissatisfied with exclusionary criteria (e.g., PL 94-142), many researchers have advocated subtyping learning disorders with the goal of identifying individual disorders (e.g., Fisk & Rourke, 1983; Morris et al., 1986; Rourke, 1983, Satz & Morris, 1984; Spreen & Haaf, 1986). Along this same line, several researchers have argued that the goal of subtyping should be the formation of homogeneous groups of learning-disabled children independent of exclusionary criteria (e.g., Fisk & Rourke, 1983; Fletcher & Satz, 1985; Morris et al., 1986; Rourke, 1983; Rourke & Strang, 1983). The value of this approach is in improved research methodology, design, data analysis, outcome, and eventually a clearer understanding of learning deficits (see Fletcher & Satz, 1985; Morris et al., 1986). However, the methods for deriving homogeneous subtypes are far less agreed upon (see Batchelor & Dean, 1989a, in press-a; Fletcher & Satz, 1985; Rourke & Adams, 1984).

One approach to subtyping learning problems has been the clinical derivation of groups (e.g., Batchelor, Dean & Williams, 1989; Boder, 1973; Frith, 1983; Rourke & Finlayson, 1978; Rourke & Strang, 1978; Strang & Rourke, 1983). While this approach allows the researcher to test hypotheses formed from clinical observations (Rourke, 1983), it compromises certain aspects of empirical rigor (e.g., Fletcher & Satz, 1985). Some have argued that a priori groups may reflect the researcher's bias regarding patterns of performance deficits (e.g., Fletcher & Satz, 1985). In some cases, the clinical approach has failed to account for midrange variability in learning deficits (e.g., Batchelor, Dean & Williams, 1989; Batchelor, Gray & Dean, in press-a). With these limitations in mind some interesting considerations have emerged from studies of clinically derived subgroups (e.g., Batchelor, Dean & Williams, 1989; Boder, 1973; Strang & Rourke, 1983) (see also Newby & Lyon, this volume, Chapter 14).

To illustrate, in one recent study a priori subgroups were based upon the child's discrepancy between expected grade-equivalent performance and an obtained grade-equivalent score on each of the three WRAT subtests (see Batchelor, Dean & Williams, 1989). Three levels of achievement were considered: grade level and higher, grade level to 1 year below expected grade-equivalent performance, and greater than 1 year below expected grade-equivalent performance. All possible combinations and permutations of performance levels for each subtest on the WRAT were considered in forming 14 groups (i.e., ranging from reading, spelling, and arithmetic greater than or equal to two grade-equivalent scores below grade placement being the most severe achievement-deficit group, to reading, spelling, and arithmetic grade-level performance being the least deficient group in achievement). Such an approach considered midrange variability while blocking on a dimension of severity of achievement deficits (see Batchelor, Dean & Williams, 1989). Neuropsychological variables were used in a discriminant analysis to predict group membership. Two significant ($p < .05$) discriminant functions obtained which were successful in predicting some 32% of the cases (Batchelor, Dean & Williams, 1989). The greatest number of false positives and false negatives occurred between groups differing in severity. Clearly, these data showed that patterns of achievement deficits were of little clinical use in characterizing a priori subgroups of children with learning problems. However, the pattern of misclassifications suggested that neuropsychological functioning may be linked more to a dimension of severity (Batchelor & Dean, 1989b).

To further consider severity as a salient factor relating neuropsychological and achievement deficits, groups were collapsed across areas of achievement (i.e., reading, spelling, and arithmetic) to form three groups separated by degree of severity (i.e., marginal to mild, moderate, and severe). The two significant discriminant functions were found to predict group membership on the basis of severity in achievement scores. The subjects considered severely and moderately deficient in achievement were classified with 64 and 63% accuracy, respectively. However, only 25% of the marginally to mildly deficient subjects were correctly identified (Batchelor, Dean & Williams, 1989). These results showed that neuropsychological data were more successful in predicting moderate and severe achievement deficits. Furthermore, it would seem that neuropsychological and achievement deficits may increase along a continuum of severity. Other support for this notion may be found in studies showing a much greater overlap in variability between the subtests of the HRNB-C and the WRAT (e.g., Davis, Dean, & Krug, 1989) as compared to the subtests of the WISC-R and the HRNB-C (e.g., D'Amato, Gray, & Dean, 1988). Thus, it may be argued that severity of achievement deficit (not type) suggests neuropsychological dysfunction (Davis, Dean, & Krug, 1989).

A second approach to subtyping children with learning deficits has involved empirical methods (see Morris et al., 1986; Satz & Morris, 1981). At first glance, this vantage appears to be psychometrically well founded. However, a number of issues should be considered in such research. First, statistical approaches (i.e., Q-factor and analysis cluster analysis) to subtyping offer a paradigm for classification that involves a rather complex set of assumptions which are rarely met outside of Monte Carlo studies. The number of measures obtained on each subject may influence the type of analysis (Q-factor or cluster) chosen (see Fletcher & Satz, 1985). The decision-making process for retaining factors or clusters may also affect the characterization of groups (Morris *et al.*, 1986). A comparison of Q-factor and cluster analyses has shown that each yields a different number of subtypes with different characteristics. There are more specific concerns unique to each approach (Q-factor or cluster) which the interested reader may find in Adams' (1985), Fletcher and Satz's (1985), and Rourke and Adams' (1984) work.

One final issue concerning statistical derivation of subgroups has to do with its clinical utility. From an empirical standpoint, Morris and his colleagues' (1986) work was an excellent example of a statistical approach to the derivation of subtypes of normal and learning-disabled readers. Indeed, this paper sets a precedent and offers direction for future attempts to redefine learning disorders. However, this venue may be of little practical value to clinicians limited to using exclusionary criteria in the diagnosis of childhood learning disability (McKinney, 1984). Thus, a more practical approach would entail empirical derivation and classification of children diagnosed with learning disorders using exclusionary criteria (e.g., PL 94-142). Two such projects have been undertaken in our laboratory.

The first study was designed to consider Morris *et al.*'s (1986) argument that reading-disabled children's neuropsychological deficits may change with age (Batchelor & Dean, 1989a). In this research, subjects were grouped by age level (i.e., 9–10, 11–12, 13–14 years of age). Cluster analyses and discriminant analyses were performed at each age level (Batchelor & Dean, 1989a). When like clusters were identified and collapsed across age level, predictive validity diminished (Batchelor & Dean, 1989a).

In support of previous studies, these data suggested that age differences in neuropsychological performance may be important in the clinical understanding and diagnosis of childhood learning disorders (e.g., Batchelor & Dean 1989a; Fletcher & Satz, 1980; Morris *et al.*, 1986; Satz, Taylor, Friel, & Fletcher, 1978). However, unlike most previous subtyping studies (e.g., Fisk & Rourke, 1979; Morris *et al.*, 1986; Petrauskas & Rourke, 1979) showing three subtypes of learning disorders, only two subgroups emerged from this study (Batchelor & Dean, 1989a). Similar to Fisk and Rourke's (1979) subtype B, one cluster showed diffuse deficits in auditory–verbal abilities, simple fine-motor skills, and spatial memory (Batchelor & Dean, 1989a). In contrast, subjects in cluster 2 showed specific neuropsychological weaknesses across age. For example, members of cluster 2 were deficient in the ability to perform spatial memory tasks at each age level. The 9 to 12-year-old subjects in cluster 2 also had relatively poor simple fine-motor skills. However, only the

11 to 12-year-old subjects in cluster 2 were impaired on visual tracking and mental flexibility tasks.

A second subtyping study attempted to consider the effects of intelligence on neuropsychological performance in learning-disabled children. This investigation seemed important in that full-scale intelligence scores (FSIQ) have been shown to significantly ($p < .05$) correlate with neuropsychological measures (Kelly et al., 1989). In addition, Adams (1985) has criticized clustering approaches to subtyping learning disorders for failing to control levels of performance between groups (Davis, Krug, & Dean, 1989). Cluster analyses were performed on HRNB scores for a group of learning-disabled children, ages 9–14, at the following FSIQ levels: less than 80, 80–89, 90–99, and 100–110. Two clusters obtained at each FSIQ level with the exception of 1 for the lowest group (Davis, Krug, & Dean, 1989). A Multivariate Analysis of Variance (MANOVA) showed that the two clusters differed at each FSIQ level when measures of the HRNB-C were dependent variables. A significant interaction between cluster membership and FSIQ level was found (Davis, Krug, & Dean, 1989). Clarification of this interaction suggested that clusters within each FSIQ group differed in that one was more impaired than the other. Discriminant analysis was performed in an effort to predict cluster membership. The resulting patterns of false positives and false negatives suggested similarities between clusters across FSIQ levels (Davis, Krug, & Dean 1989). Like clusters were collapsed across FSIQ level and predicted group membership using discriminant analysis. The results of this analysis allowed correct placement of subjects with some 93% accuracy (Davis, Krug, & Dean, 1989).

These data showed that when the effects of FSIQ were controlled, two clusters emerged for learning-disabled children with FSIQs of 80 and greater. One group showed distinct neuropsychological impairment and the other did not. Only one cluster was found for subjects with FSIQs less than 80 and the entire group was neuropsychologically impaired (Davis, Krug, & Dean, 1989).

In overview, the two subtyping studies generated from our laboratory lend support for Doehring, Hoshko, and Bryan's (1979) findings of two subtypes of children with learning deficits. Our findings are unique in that they generalize to the public school setting where exclusionary criteria are used to diagnose learning disorders. Subtyping efforts in our laboratory would suggest that once diagnosed as learning disabled in the public schools, an actuarial approach may be useful in predicting the child as experiencing diffuse or specific neuropsychological dysfunction. These data also suggested that subtyping must be sensitive to the effects of age (Batchelor & Dean, 1989a; Morris et al., 1986; Satz et al., 1978) and the level of FSIQ (Davis,

Krug, & Dean, 1989). However, the choice of statistical analyses for derivation of subtypes may also influence outcomes (Fletcher & Satz, 1985; Rourke & Adams, 1984). Thus, it would seem fair to conclude that results of subtyping studies must be carefully weighed given the potential for differences due to methodology and subject variables.

III. Comments on the Neuropsychological Implications of Intelligence

The neuropsychological implications of intelligence measures have been a topic of much debate (Kelly *et al.*, 1989). A number of studies have shown that the WISC-R and the HRNB-C offer mutually exclusive information concerning the functioning of the learning-disabled child (D'Amato, Gray, & Dean, 1988; Klonoff, 1971). In fact, D'Amato showed there to be but 10% overlap of the variance between WISC-R subtests and HRNB-C for children with learning deficits (D'Amato, Gray, & Dean, 1988). In contrast with these data, other studies have indicated the WISC-R summary scores (verbal, performance, full scale) to be the most salient indicators of child neuropsychological dysfunction (Klonoff & Law, 1974). Indeed, when the effects of FSIQ were controlled, differences in neuropsychological performance decreased between groups of normals and brain-damaged children (Klonoff & Law, 1974). A canonical analysis of WISC-R summary scores and HRNB-C variables for children with learning deficits showed some 29% common variability (Kelly *et al.*, 1989). Clearly, FSIQ was the most salient predictor of HRNB-C measures (Kelly *et al.*, 1989). Along these same lines, there seems to be little relationship between VSIQ–PSIQ discrepancies and neuropsychological measures for children with learning deficits (Batchelor & Dean, 1989b; Lueger, Albott, Hilgendorf, & Gill, 1985). In one recent study, neuropsychological measures accounted for a mere 13% of the variability in VSIQ–PSIQ differences (Batchelor & Dean, 1989b).

Taken together, these data would suggest that the HRNB-C and WISC-R subtests measure relatively independent functions for children with learning problems (Kelly *et al.*, 1989). However, FSIQ and the HRNB-C seem to share common variability and possibly a general intellectual functioning underpinning (Kelly *et al.*, 1989). Practically speaking, the clinician would do well to first consider the patient's overall level of intellectual performance (FSIQ) as an indication of neuropsychological dysfunction. In general, VSIQ–PSIQ differences would appear to offer little regarding the integrity of neuropsychological functioning for children with learning problems.

Neuropsychological Underpinnings of the HRNB-C

Clearly, assessment data must be both psychometrically sound (see Barker & Barker, 1984; Stevens, 1986) and clinically meaningful to be of value. Historically, actuarial apparatus have demonstrated the utility of the HRNB-C in separating children with learning disorders from brain-damaged children and normals (e.g., Reitan & Wolfson, 1988; Selz & Reitan, 1979). However, few studies have examined the neuropsychological constructs measured by the HRNB-C (Batchelor, Sowles, Dean, & Fischer, in press). Previous attempts at factor analyzing the HRNB-C have been problematic in that either additional subtests were included (Klonoff, 1971) or some of the measures recommended by Reitan (1969) were excluded (D'Amato, Gray, & Dean, 1988) from analyses (Batchelor et al., in press). Previous studies have failed to consider the effects of age on the factor structure of the HRNB-C (Batchelor et al., in press). Given longitudinal data on children with learning disorders (e.g., Morris et al., 1986; Spreen & Haaf, 1986) showing changes in neuropsychological functioning over time, one would expect that factor loadings for HRNB-C measures may change with age. Thus, we thought it appropriate to examine the neuropsychological constructs measured by the HRNB-C as recommended by Reitan (1969) (i.e., HRNB-C, WISC-R, and WRAT) for children with learning disorders at separate age levels (i.e., Batchelor et al., in press). Such a study was considered necessary in order to demonstrate that the HRNB-C (Reitan, 1969) offered meaningful information.

An exploratory factor analysis was performed using a principle-components approach for each of three age groups (i.e., 9–10, 11–12, and 13–14 years) and then for the entire sample (Batchelor et al., in press). Variables with loadings .40 and greater were used to characterize each factor (see Gorsuch, 1983). Eigen values 1.0 and greater were used as criteria for retaining factors (see Gorsuch, 1983). A relatively pure, orthogonal solution obtained for analysis of each age level and the entire sample. Rummel's (1970) criteria were used for determining like factors across age. Coefficients of congruence were calculated for similar factors at separate age levels and then with the solution for the entire sample. Six factors were retained for the 9 to 10-year-old group, and seven factors were interpreted for the 11 to 12-year-old and 13 to 14-year-old groups. (Batchelor et al., in press). Table I offers a summary of the like factors interpretable across age levels and factors specific to each age group.

A review of Table I suggested that many of the factors underlying the HRNB-C were unaffected by age (i.e., simple motor skills, verbal organization/concept formation, symbolic language integration, spatial organization, and complex visually guided motor activities). However, constructs such

TABLE I Common and Unique Factors and Salient Variable Loadings
Underlying the HRNB-C for Children 9 to 14 Years of Age

Factors	Salient Variables	Loading
Common factors for the entire sample[a]		
Simple motor skills	Tapping, right	.755
	Tapping, left	.774
	Grip strength, right	.824
	Grip strength, left	.812
Verbal organizational/concept formation	Information	.704
	Comprehension	.804
	Similarities	.771
	Vocabulary	.841
Symbolic language integration	Speech-sounds errors	−.651
	Arithmetic (WRAT)	.517
	Reading	.881
	Spelling	.895
Spatial organization/integration	Tactual perception test, total time	.934
	Tactual perception test, right time	.805
	Tactual perception test, left time	.794
Complex visually guided motor skills	Trails A time	−.653
	Trails B time	−.650
	Coding	.641
Age group and unique factors	Tactual perception test memory	.683
9–10; visual–spatial organization	Tactual perception test location	.682
	Picture completion	.551
	Picture arrangement	.475
	Block design	.668
	Object assembly	.684
9–10 and 13–14; complex attentional processing	Seashore rhythm test	.637
	Digit span	.752
	Arithmetic (WISC-R)	.487
11–14; visual organization	Category errors	−.447
	Picture completion	.553
	Picture arrangement	.460
	Block design	.787
	Object assembly	.756
11–14; spatial memory	Tactual perception memory	.852
	Tactual perception location	.837

[a] Factors are presented in a hierarchical fashion for percentage of variance accounted for in the overall variance/covariance matrix.

as complex attentional processing and visual–spatial organization/spatial memory seemed to be more sensitive to age effects (Batchelor *et al.*, in press). This study supported the notion that the HRNB-C offers meaningful information regarding measurement of constructs underlying neuropsychological functioning in children with learning deficits. Taken together with Reitan's (e.g., Reitan & Wolfson, 1988; Selz & Reitan, 1979) work, Batchelor *et al.*'s (in press) findings would argue for interpreting neuropsychological constructs of the HRNB-C in the assessment of childhood learning difficulties.

IV. Comments on the Neuropsychological Implications of Achievement Deficits

The following discussion of neuropsychological underpinnings of reading, spelling, and arithmetic deficits in children should be considered with several caveats. First, these studies were based on a heterogeneous sample of children with learning problems. Second, the relationship between reading, spelling, and arithmetic performance in these studies was at best minimally controlled. And finally, subgroups or subtypes of children seeming to have specific achievement deficits were not identified prior to these investigations. In response to these potential criticisms, we offer these points to consider. Subtyping efforts suggest that subgrouping children with learning problems based on achievement performance alone offers little clinical or empirical value (e.g., Batchelor & Dean, 1989a, Batchelor, Dean & Williams, 1989). Statistically derived, homogeneous subgroups may not generalize to the clinical setting, where the neuropsychologist must assess a heterogeneous population of children with achievement deficits ranging from marginal to quite severe (Batchelor & Dean, 1989a; McKinney, 1984). Furthermore, it is clear that severity and not type of achievement deficit seems to be the important link to neuropsychological functioning (Batchelor, Dean & Williams, 1989). From this view, we would argue that studies examining neuropsychological underpinnings of achievement functions based on a large heterogeneous sample of children with learning deficits would offer more practical value in applied settings and toward efforts to redefine learning disorders.

A. Neuropsychological Aspects of Reading and Spelling Deficits

Since Orton's (1937) early report, childhood reading and spelling problems have been the focus of a vast body of research on learning disorders. While many have conceptualized reading and spelling deficits as symptoms of a more pervasive language disorder (see Hooper & Boyd, 1986; Hynd & Hynd, 1984), there is evidence to suggest that reading and spelling problems can be differentiated on the basis of neuropsychological functioning (e.g., Naidoo, 1972; Nelson & Warrington, 1974). In order to better understand aberrations in reading and spelling performance, it would seem that the neuropsychological underpinnings of these academic areas must be considered. Efforts to investigate these functions have been limited due to methodological constraints (Stanovich, 1986). Indeed, a multivariate approach is necessary for adequate analysis of the relationship between reading and spelling deficits and neuropsychological functioning (Batchelor, Kixmiller, & Dean, 1990; Stanovich, Nathan, & Vala-Rossi, 1986). However, few researchers have had the resources required to examine the results of a comprehensive neuropsychological battery for a large sample of children with reading and spelling deficits (Stanovich, 1986).

In an attempt to consider the relationship between neuropsychological measures and reading and spelling performance, data from the HRNB-C, WISC-R, and WRAT were submitted to a multiple regression (Batchelor, Kixmiller & Dean, 1990) and a canonical analysis (Batchelor & Dean, 1989c). Results of these studies showed that the most salient neuropsychological predictors were common to both reading and spelling performance. It would seem that measures of complex verbal (i.e., verbal attention and short-term memory, remote verbal memory, symbolic language integration) and nonverbal functions (i.e., nonverbal concept formation) and simple motor skills (i.e., dominant gross motor strength and nondominant fine-motor speed and dexterity) contributed significantly ($p < .05$) to the prediction of both reading and spelling achievement scores (Batchelor et al., 1990; Batchelor & Dean, 1989c). Complex visually guided motor skills were uniquely related to reading performance (Batchelor et al., 1990), whereas, for spelling, visual sequencing was the only orthogonal predictor (Batchelor et al., 1990).

These data offered some support for a unitary functional system hypothesis (e.g., Hynd & Hynd, 1984). However, additional neuropsychological functions uniquely related to reading and spelling were identified. In light of a functional systems view, an additional analysis was performed considering reading and spelling on a continuum (see Batchelor et al., 1990). A simple index was formed from subjects' reading and spelling scores to create a single continuous variable. Neuropsychological measures were then regressed upon this index. Results of this analysis suggested that when reading and spelling performance were considered as a single construct, important information involving common and unique neuropsychological functions underpinning performance in both academic areas were lost (Batchelor et al., 1990). These data would imply that, for children with learning problems, reading and spelling should be viewed as separate functions sharing some common elements.

Practically speaking, these two studies (i.e., Batchelor et al., 1990; Batchelor & Dean, 1989c) would appear to have implications for children presenting with reading and spelling difficulty in the public schools. One may expect to find a combination of verbal, nonverbal, and simple motor-skills deficits in children with reading and spelling difficulty. (Batchelor & Dean, 1989c). Indeed, children with concomitant reading and spelling deficits may account for the largest percentage of the learning-disabled population in the public schools (Batchelor, Dean & Williams, 1989). Less frequently seen in the schools, children with only spelling problems may be likely to show visual sequencing deficits (Batchelor & Dean, 1989c). Rarely, it seems, do reading problems occur in isolation (Batchelor, Dean & Williams, 1989). However, in such cases, deficits in complex visually guided motor skills (i.e., visual tracking, short-term visual memory, psychomotor speed, spatial integration and organization) may be anticipated (Batchelor & Dean, 1989c).

B. Neuropsychological Aspects of Arithmetic Deficits

As compared to the volume of research on reading and spelling disabilities, learning problems in arithmetic have been largely overlooked (e.g., Batchelor, 1989; Batchelor, Gray, & Dean, in press-a; Rourke & Strang, 1983). This is an interesting fact, in that children referred for reading and spelling problems often show performance deficits in arithmetic as well (Batchelor, 1989; Batchelor, Dean & Williams, 1989; Fletcher & Loveland, 1986; Rourke & Strang, 1983; Satz & Morris, 1981). Indeed children with concomitant arithmetic, reading, and spelling deficits account for some 20% of the learning-disabled population in the public schools (Batchelor, Dean & Williams, 1989). Thus, assessment of arithmetic deficits would seem to be an important consideration to both the researcher and the practitioner.

Early investigations (e.g., Cohn; 1968; Guttmann, 1937) viewed arithmetic problems as characteristic of a generalized language disorder related to left-hemisphere dysfunction (Batchelor, 1989; Rourke & Strang, 1983). However, Batsche (1979), Rourke and Weintraub (Weintraub & Mesulam, 1983) have offered evidence that written arithmetic performance is bilaterally served by hemispheres of the brain. More recent studies (e.g., Batchelor, Gray, & Dean, in press-a, in press-b, 1990) have examined both written and verbal arithmetic performance in a multivariate fashion for children with learning problems. Such an approach was seen as heuristic in that neuropsychological performance patterns may be different depending on the deficit response mode exhibited by the child (Tuoko, 1982).

In an effort to examine the relationship between neuropsychological functions and written and verbal arithmetic performance, a multiple regression (Batchelor, Gray, & Dean, in press-a) and a canonical analysis (Batchelor, Gray, & Dean, in press-b) were performed using the HRNB-C, WISC-R, and WRAT scores. The results of these studies confirmed and extended previous findings (e.g., Batche, 1979; Rourke & Finlayson, 1978; Rourke & Strang, 1978; Strang & Rourke, 1983; Weintraub & Mesulam, 1983) suggesting that both verbal and nonverbal functions were required in solving arithmetic problems (Batchelor, 1989; Batchelor, Gray, & Dean, in press-a, 1990). Moreover, verbal and written arithmetic performance seemed to involve both right and left hemispheric processing (e.g., Batchelor, 1989; Batchelor, Gray, & Dean, in press-a). Neuropsychological functions of verbal attention and short-term memory, remote verbal memory, symbolic language integration, mental flexibility, and nonverbal abstract reasoning were linked to both oral and written arithmetic performance (Batchelor, Gray, & Dean, in press-b). The unique element of the written arithmetic performance depended most heavily on nonverbal attention and intermediate spatial memory (Batchelor, Gray, & Dean, 1990). In contrast, functions such as verbal facility, abstract verbal reasoning, nonverbal short-term memory, and nonverbal concept formation seemed important in solving verbal arithmetic tasks (Batchelor, Gray, & Dean, 1990).

In an attempt to investigate the importance of verbal and written arithmetic deficits, the neuropsychological implications of these performance patterns were considered oral (see Batchelor, Gray, & Dean, in press-c). Based on Tuoko's (1982) work, three groups of children with arithmetic performance deficits were identified based on a discrepancy between verbal (WISC-R) and written (WRAT) arithmetic scores. Groups 1 and 2 were considered severely deficient in written and verbal arithmetic, respectively. Group 3 was seen as severely deficient in both written and verbal arithmetic performance (see Batchelor, Gray, & Dean, in press-b). Using the HRNB-C and WISC-R variables (save WISC-R arithmetic), a discriminant analysis was used to predict group membership. Results of this study suggested that Groups 2 and 3 were more neuropsychologically impaired than Group 1 (Batchelor, Gray, & Dean, in press-b). Interestingly, Group 1 had the largest membership, whereas Group 2 yielded the smallest number of subjects. Groups differed significantly on neuropsychological measures of verbal attention, symbolic language integration, mental flexibility, verbal and nonverbal short-term memory and abstract reasoning, nonverbal concept formation, visual tracking, and sequencing. The overall percentage of correct group placement was 80% (see Batchelor, Gray, & Dean, in press-b).

These studies of the arithmetic process (Batchelor, Gray, & Dean, in press-a, in press-b) suggest that written and verbal arithmetic performance were highly related to verbal, nonverbal, and higher-order neuropsychological functioning. While some common neuropsychological elements are shared by written and oral arithmetic problem solving, task variations may require access of unique neuropsychological functions (Batchelor, Gray, & Dean, in press-a). Like reading and spelling performance, it would seem that arithmetic performance may be sensitive to a number of neuropsychological dysfunctions. Moreover, deficits in attention, verbal, nonverbal, and complex processing may influence arithmetic performance (Batchelor, 1989; Mesulam, 1985).

Public school children with deficient performance only in written arithmetic are probably seen more often than cohorts with only verbal or generalized arithmetic deficits. However, children with only written arithmetic deficits may show less severe neuropsychological impairment. From this view, it would appear that assessment of both written and verbal arithmetic should precede neuropsychological testing when arithmetic disorders are suspected (Batchelor, Gray, & Dean, in press-b).

V. Summary

The results of studies investigating the neuropsychological underpinnings of reading, spelling, and arithmetic performance converge to offer some conclusions. There would appear to be some common neuropsychological elements to reading, spelling, and arithmetic performance, including auditory attention and short-term memory, remote verbal memory, and symbolic language integration (Batchelor & Dean, 1989c; Batchelor, Gray, & Dean, in press-a; Batchelor, Kixmiller & Dean, 1990). Clearly, measures of symbolic language integration and auditory–verbal attention have been shown to be the salient predictors of achievement deficits across studies (Batchelor & Dean, 1989c; Batchelor, Gray, & Dean, in press-a; Batchelor, Kixmiller & Dean, 1990). These data are consistent with the early notion that reading, spelling, and arithmetic deficits may reflect a more pervasive language disorder (e.g., Cohn, 1968; Guttmann, 1937). However, there is a proponderence of clinical and empirical evidence suggesting that reading, spelling, and arithmetic are very complex functions that may be sensitive to deficits in specific nonverbal abilities, other higher-order processes (e.g., mental flexibility, psychomotor speed, and executive planning) (e.g., Batchelor, Gray, & Dean, in press-a; Batsche, 1979; Mesulam, 1985; Rourke & Strang, 1983; Weintraub & Mesulam, 1983). Such findings cast light upon confusion in subtyping efforts. Our data would suggest that achievement problems could be related to any number of combinations of neuropsychological dysfunctions. Thus, in any given approach to subtyping, one would expect overlap between characteristics of clusters (i.e., cluster analysis), subjects loading on more than one factor (i.e., Q-factor analysis), or problems with Type I and Type II error in predicting a priori formed groups (i.e., multivariate analysis of variance). In light of these findings and methodological problems associated with subtyping (i.e., definition, criteria for diagnosis, data analyses, etc.), researchers and clinicians would do well to take a more conservative approach to existing data in this area. From this standpoint, it would seem that future research efforts might be redirected toward corroboration of multivariate data (e.g., Batchelor, Gray, & Dean, in press-a, 1990; Morris *et al.*, 1986; Stanovich *et al.*, 1986; Strang & Rourke, 1983) with neuroradiological, electrophysiological, regional cerebral blood flow, and post-mortem findings (e.g., Denkla, LeMay, & Chapman, 1985; Drake, 1968; Galaburda, Sherman, Rosen, Aboitiz, & Geschwind, 1985; Hynd, Hynd, Sullivan, & Kingsbury, 1987). As Hynd has noted (e.g., Hynd & Hynd, 1984; Hynd & Willis, 1988), it would seem that we have adequate neurologic data to begin formulating neuroanatomical maps of reading functions. Along this same line, in conjunction with others, our data may contribute to the development of statistical paths of neuropsychological functions underlying reading, spelling, and arithmetic. Considering the current state of affairs, a synthesis of paradigms may be a viable option for future research attempts at evaluating and understanding children with learning problems.

References

Adams, K. M. (1985). Theoretical, methodological and statistical issues. In B. P. Rourke (Ed.). *Neuropsychology of learning disorders: Essentials of subtype analysis.* New York; Guilford.

Barker, H. R., & Barker, B. M. (1984). *Multivariate analysis of variance (MANOVA): A practical guide to its use in scientific decision making.* Tuscaloosa: University of Alabama Press.

Batche, G. M. (1979). Patterns of psychological and neuropsychological measures of performance in inter and intra group comparisons in children with variations in reading and arithmetic achievement (Doctoral dissertation, Ball State University, 1978). *Dissertation Abstracts International, 40A*(1–2), 746A.

Batchelor, E. S. (1989). Neuropsychology of childhood arithmetic disorders. *International Journal of Neuroscience, 44*, 27–41.

Batchelor, E. S., & Dean, R. S. (1989a). *Empirical derivation and classification of subgroups of children with learning deficits at separate age levels.* Manuscript submitted for publication.

Batchelor, E. S., & Dean, R. S. (1989b, November). *Neuropsychological performance differences for males and females with reading deficits.* Paper presented at the annual convention of the National Academy of Neuropsychologists, Washington, DC.

Batchelor, E. S., & Dean, R. S. (1989c). *Lexical integration in children with learning disorders.* Paper submitted for publication.

Batchelor, E. S., & Dean, R. S. (in press). A discrepancy between verbal and performance scores on the WISC-R for learning disabled children. *International Journal of Neuroscience.*

Batchelor, E. S. & Dean, R. S. & Williams, R. (1989). *Severity of neuropsychological functioning in clinically derived groups of learning disabled children.* Paper presented at the annual convention of the National Academy of Neuropsychology, Washington, DC.

Batchelor, E. S., Gray, J. W. & Dean, R. S. (in press a). Neuropsychological aspects of arithmetic performance in learning disability. *International Journal of Clinical Neuropsychology.*

Batchelor, E. S., Gray, J. W. & Dean, R. S. (in press b). Differential diagnosis of arithmetic disorders: A neuropsychological approach. *International Journal of Clinical Neuropsychology.*

Batchelor, E. S., Gray, J. W. & Dean, R. S. (1990). Empirical testing of a cognitive model to account for neuropsychological functioning underlying arithmetic problem solving. *Journal of Learning Disabilities, 23,* 38–42.

Batchelor, E. S., Kixmiller, J., & Dean, R. S. (1990). *Neuropsychological aspects of reading and spelling performance in children with learning disorders.* Paper submitted for publication.

Batchelor, E. S., Sowles, G., Dean, R. S. & Fischer, W. (in press). Construct validity of the Halstead-Reitan Neuropsychological Battery for Children with Learning Disorders. *Journal of Psychoeducational Assessment.*

Boder, E. (1973). Developmental dyslexia: A diagnostic approach based on three atypical reading-spelling patterns. *Developmental Medicine and Child Neurology, 15,* 663–687.

Braden, J. P., & Algina, J. (1989). A method for determining the probability. *Journal of School Psychology, 27,* 5–13.

Cohn, R. (1968). Developmental dyscalculia. *Pediatric Clinics of North America, 15,* 651–668.

D'Amato, R. C., Dean, R. S., Rattan, G., & Nikell, K. A. (in press). A study of psychological referrals for learning problem children. *Journal of Psychoeducational assessment.*

D'Amato, R. C., Gray, J. W., & Dean, R. S. (1988). A comparison between intelligence and neuropsychological functioning. *Journal of School Psychology, 26,* 283–292.

Davis, B., Dean, R. & Krug, D. (1989). *Subtests of the Wechsler Intelligence Scale for children-revised as predictors of neuropsychological impairment.* Unpublished manuscript.

Davis, B., Krug, D. & Dean, R. S. (1989). *Differential intelligence levels and corresponding neuropsychological clusters.* Unpublished manuscript.

Denkla, M. B., LeMay, M., & Chapman, C. A. (1985). Few CT scan abnormalities found in neurologically impaired learning disabled children. *Journal of Learning Disabilities, 18,* 132–135.

Doehring, D. G. (1978). The tangled web of behavioral research in developmental dyslexia. In A. L. Benton & D. Pearl (Eds.). *Dyslexia: An appraisal of current knowledge.* New York: Oxford University Press.

Doehring, D. G., Hoshko, T. M., & Bryans, B. N. (1979). Statistical classification of children with reading problems. *Journal of Clinical Neuropsychology, 1,* 5–16.

Drake, W. E. (1968). Clinical and pathological findings in a child with developmental learning disability. *Journal of Learning Disabilities, 1,* 486–475.

Fisk, J. L. & Rourke, B. P. (1979). Identification of subtypes of learning disabled children at three age levels: A neuropsychological, multivariate approach. *Journal of Clinical Neuropsychology, 1,* 289–310.

Fisk, J. L., & Rourke, B. P. (1983). Neuropsychological subtyping of learning-disabled children: History, methods, implications. *Journal of Learning Disabilities, 16,* 529–531.

Fletcher, J. & Satz, P. (1979). Unitary deficit hypothesis of reading disabilities: Has Vellutino leads us astray? *Journal of Learning Disabilities, 12,* 155–159.

Fletcher, J. & Satz, P. (1980). Developmental changes in neuropsychological correlates of reading achievements. A six year longitudinal follow-up. *Journal of Clinical Neuropsychology, 2,* 23–37.

Fletcher, J., Satz, P. & Morris, R. (1984). The Florida Longitudinal Project: A review. In S. A. Mednick & M. A. Harway (Eds.). *U.S. Longitudinal projects.* New York: Praeger.

Fletcher, J. & Satz, P. (1985). Cluster analysis and the search for learning disability subtypes. In B. P. Rourke (Ed.), *Essentials for subtype analysis.* New York: Guilford.

Fletcher, J. M. & Loveland, V. A. (1986). Neuropsychology of arithmetic disabilities in children. *Focus on Learning Problems, 8,* (2), 23–40.

Frith, U. (1983). The similarities and differences between reading and spelling problems. In M. Rutter (Ed.) *Developmental neuropsychiatry.* New York: Guilford Press.

Gaddes, W. H. (1985). *Learning disabilities and brain function: A neuropsychological approach,* pp. 23–35. New York: Springer-Verlag.

Galaburda, A. M., Sherman, G. F., Rosen, G. D., Aboitiz, F., & Geschwind, N. (1985). Developmental dyslexia: Four consecutive patients with cortical anomalies. *Annals of Neurology, 18,* 222–223.

Gorsuch, R. L. (1983). *Factor analysis.* New Jersey: Lawrence Erlbaum Associates.

Guttmann, E. (1937). Congenital arithmetic disability and acalculia (Henschen). *British Journal of Medical Psychology, 16,* 16–35.

Hamil, D. D., Leigh, J. McNutt, G. & Larson, S. C. (1981). A new definition of learning disabilities. *Learning Disabilities Quarterly, 4,* 336–342.

Hooper, S., & Boyd, T. (1986). Neurodevelopmental learning disorders. In J. Obrzut, & G. Hynd (Eds.), *Child Neuropsychology,* pp. 15–58. New York: Academic Press.

Hynd, G. W., & Hynd, L. R. (1984). Dyslexia: Neuroanatomical/neurolinguistic perspectives. *Reading Research Quarterly, 19,* 482–498.

Hynd, G. W., Hynd, C. R., Sullivan, H. G., & Kingsbury, T. (1987). Regional cerebral blood flow (rcBF) in developmental dyslexics: Activation during reading in surface and deep dyslexic. *Journal of Learning Disabilities, 20,* 294–300.

Hynd, G. W., & Willis, U. G. (1988). *Pediatric Neuropsychology.* Orlando, Grune & Stratton.

Jastak, J. & Jastak, S. (1978). *Wide range achievement test manual.* Wilmington, DE: Guidane Associates.

Kelly, M., Batchelor, E. S., & Dean, R. S. (1989). *Neuropsychological significance of intelligence summary scores.* Paper submitted for publication.

Klonoff, H. (1971). Factor analysis of a neuropsychological battery for children aged 9–15. *Perceptual Motor Skills, 32,* 603–616.

Klonoff, H., & Law, M. (1974). Disordered brain formation in young children and early adolescents. Neuropsychological and Hectroencephalographic correlates.

In R. M. Retain & L. A. Davidson (Eds.), *Clinical neuropsychology: Current status and applications* (pp. 121–165). New York: Wiley.

Lueger, R. J., Albott, W. C., Hilgendorf, W. A., & Gill, U. J. (1985). Neuropsychological and academic WISC-R Verbal-Performance discrepancies. *Journal of Clinical Psychology, 80,* 708–713.

McKinney, T. D. (1984). The search for subtypes of learning disability. *Journal of Learning Disabilities, 19,* 39–45.

Mesulam, M. M. (1985). Attention, confusional states, and neglect. In M. M. Mesulam (Ed.) *Principles of behavioral neurology,* (pp. 125–168). Philadelphia: F. A. Davis.

Morris, R., Blashfield, R. & Satz, P. (1986). Developmental classification of reading disabeled children. *Journal of Clinical and Experimental Neuropsychology, 8,* 271–292.

Naidoo, S. (1972). *Specific dyslexia.* New York: Wiley.

Nelson, H. E. & Warrington, E. K. (1974). Developmental spelling retardation and its relation to other cognitive abilities. *British Journal of Psychology, 65,* 265–274.

Obrzut, J., Hynd, G., & Boliek, C. A. (1986). Lateral asymmetrics in learning disabled children: A review. In S. J. Ceci (Ed.), *Handbook of cognitive, social, and neuropsychological aspects of learning disabilities.* Hillsdale, NJ: Erlbaum.

Orton, J. T. (1937). Specific reading disability-stephsymbalia. *JAMA, Journal of the American Medical Association, 90,* 1095–1099.

Petrauskas, R. & Rourke, B. P. (1979). Identification of subgroups of retarded readers: A neuropsychological multivariate approach. *Journal of Clinical Neuropsychology, 1,* 289–310.

Pirozzolo, F. J. (1981). Language and brain: Neuropsychological aspect of developmental reading disability. *School Psychology Review, 10,* 350–355.

Rattan, G. & Dean, R. S. (1987). The neuropsychology of children's learning disorders. In M. J. Williams & C. C. Long (Eds.), *The rehabilitation of cognitive disabilities.* New York: Plenum Press.

Reitan, R. M. (1969). *Manual for administration of neuropsychological test batteries for adults and children.* Indianapolis: Author.

Reitan, R., & Wolfson, D. (1988, August). *Neuropsychological functions of learning disabled, brain damaged and normal children.* Paper presented at the annual convention of the American Psychological Association, Atlanta, GA.

Reynolds, O. R. (1985). Critical measurement issues in learning disabilities. *Journal of Special Education, 18,* 451–487.

Rourke, B. P. (1978). *Essentials of subtype analysis.* pp. 5–21. New York: Guilford.

Rourke, B. P. (1983). Outstanding issues in research on learning disabilities. In M. J. Ratter (Ed.), *Developmental neuropsychiatry* (pp. 564–573). New York: Guilford Press.

Rourke, B. P., & Adams, K. M. (1984). Quantitative approaches to the neuropsychological assessment of children. In R. E. Tarter & G. Goldstein (Eds.), *Advances in clinical neuropsychology* (Vol. 2). New York: Plenum.

Rourke, B. P. & Finlayson, M. A. (1978). Neuropsychological significance of varitions in patterns of academic performance: Verbal and visual-spatial abilities. *Journal of Abnormal Child Psychology, 6, (1)*, 121–133.

Rourke, B. P. & Strang, J. (1987). Neuropsychological significance of variations in patterns of academic performance: Motor, psychomotor and tactile-perceptual abilities. *Journal of Pediatric Psychology, 3, (2)*, 62–66.

Rourke, B. P. & Strang, J. (1983). Subtypes of reading and arithmetic disabilities: A neuropsychological analysis. In M. Rutter (Ed.), *Developmental neuropsychiatry* (pp. 473–487). New York: Guilford Press.

Rummel, R. J. (1970). *Applied factor analysis*. Evanston, IL: Northwestern University Press.

Rutter, M. (1978). Prevalence and types of dyslexia. In A. C. Benton & D. Pearl (Eds.), *Dyslexia. An appraisal of current knowledge*, (pp. 5–28). New York: Oxford University Press.

Satz, P. & Morris, R. (1981). Learning desability subtypes: A review. In F. J. Piorzzolo & M. C. Wittrock (Eds.) *Neuropsychological and cognitive processes in reading*. New York: Academic Press.

Satz, P., Taylor, H. G., Friel, J., & Fletcher, J. (1978). Some developmental and precursors of reading disabilities: A six year follow-up. In A. C. Benton & D. Pearl (Eds.). *Dyslexia: An appraisal of current knowledge*, (pp. 313–347). New York: Oxford.

Schultz, A., & Borich, G. D. (1984). Considerations in the use of different scores to identify learning disabled children. *Journal of School Psychology, 22*, 381–390.

Selz, M., & Reitan, R. (1979). Rules for neuropsychological diagnosis: Classification of brain function in older children. *Journal of Consulting and Clinical Psychology, 47*, 258–264.

Spreen, O. & Haaf, R. G. (1986). Empirically derived learning disability subtypes: A replication attempt and longitudinal patterns over 15 years. *Journal of Learning Disabilities, 19*, 170–180.

Stanovich, K. E. (1986). Matthew effects in reading: Some consequences of individual differences in the acquisition of literacy. *Reading Research Quarterly, 21*, 360–406.

Stanovich, K. E., Nathan, R. G., & Vala-Rossi, M. (1986). Developmental changes in the cognitive correlates of reading ability and the developmental log hypothesis. *Reading Research Quarterly, 21*, 267–283.

Stevens, J. (1986). *Applied multivariate statistics for behavioral sciences*. Hillsdale, NJ: Erlbaum.

Strang, J. & Rourke, B. P. (1983). Concept formation/nonverbal reasoning abilities of children who exhibit specific academic problems with arithmetic. *Journal of Clinical Child Psychology, 12*, 33–39.

Taylor, H. G., Satz, P., & Friel, J. (1979). Developmental dyslexia in relation to other childhood reading disorders: Significance and clinical utility. *Reading Research Quarterly, 15*, 84–101.

Tuoko, H. (1982). Cognitive correlates of arithmetic performance in clinical referred children. Unpublished doctoral dissertation, University of Victoria.

Weintraub, S., & Mesulam, M. M. (1983). Developmental learning disabilities of the right hemisphere: Emotional, interpersonal and cognitive components. *Archives of Neurology (Chicago), 40*, 463–468.

Wechsler, D. (1974). *Wechsler Intelligence Scale for Children–Revised.* New York: Psychological Corporation.

Wilson, H. R., & Cone, T. (1984). The regression equation method of determining academic discrepancy. *Journal of School Psychology, 22*, 95–110.

CHAPTER THIRTEEN

Neuropsychological Assessment of Learning-Disabled Adolescents and Young Adults

James P. O'Donnell

I. Introduction

Early etiological hypotheses concerning impaired academic skill acquisition were modeled on the neurological findings in acquired aphasia. These hypotheses proposed that a lesion in the left cerebral hemisphere, usually in the region of the angular gyrus, could account for children's difficulties in acquiring reading, spelling, or computational skills (Benton, 1980; Hynd & Cohen, 1983, pp. 11–16). However, when neurological examinations failed to demonstrate focal lesions in most learning-disabled (LD) children (e.g., Money, 1966, pp. 32–34), this hypothesis was supplanted by the proposal that learning disabilities might be the result of a neuromaturational lag (e.g., Money, 1966, p. 34). Implicit in this "developmental lag" hypothesis was the idea that these deficits might be outgrown as children attained maturity (Rourke, 1976). Supporting data showed that underlying deficit patterns and subtype memberships seem to undergo developmental change (Fletcher, Satz, & Scholes, 1981; Morris, Blashfield, & Satz, 1986; Satz, Rardin, & Ross, 1971). Nevertheless, it became apparent from long-term follow-up studies that, for many LD persons, these disabilities persist into adulthood (e.g., Horn, O'Donnell, & Vitulano, 1983). Furthermore, many of the neuropsychological deficits associated with childhood LD (Selz & Reitan, 1979a, 1979b) are also associated with LD in young adulthood (O'Donnell, Kurtz,

& Ramanaiah, 1983). Therefore, since academic deficits and their associated neuropsychological deficits persist into young adulthood, and since the nature of the deficits changes for individual children, planning educational support services for secondary and postsecondary LD students will require reevaluation of their central processing deficits.

Coles (1978) thoroughly critiqued the use of neuropsychological test batteries for assessing LD persons on the grounds that such batteries lacked construct and discriminant validity and that the neurological substrate for LD might be an unproved assumption. Although substantial research published during the intervening decade challenges Coles' critique as it applies to childhood LD, rigorously controlled, systematic research is not available to show that neuropsychological measures can differentiate young-adult LD from their nondisabled peers, that such neuropsychological measures might be related to academic skills and abilities, or that such neuropsychological measures are related to neurological status. This chapter reports a series of related studies to address these important issues.

II. Purposes

The present research was undertaken in order to address four issues critical to the understanding of learning disabilities in young adults. The first purpose was to determine whether widely used neuropsychological measures might reflect underlying ability dimensions that are academically relevant for LD young adults. Addressing this issue would establish the construct validity of a neuropsychological test battery. The second purpose was to determine whether neuropsychological measures could differentiate normal young adults from young adults independently diagnosed as being learning disabled or head injured. Research on this issue would establish the discriminant validity of a neuropsychological test battery. The third purpose of this research was to use neuropsychological measures to identify academically related homogeneous subgroups among learning-disabled young adults. Information on this subject could be used to plan individually appropriate interventions. The final purpose of this research was to determine whether socioemotional factors might be associated with LD status during young adulthood. Data on this subject would be appropriate to both preventive and remedial efforts.

III. Assessment Methods and Procedures

The Halstead–Reitan Neuropsychological Test Battery and Allied Procedures (HRNTB) is a valid measure of brain–behavior relationships (Klove, 1974; Reitan, 1986) and has been successfully used in the assessment of LD children (Selz & Reitan, 1979a, 1979b). The tests comprising this battery [Category Test, Tactual Performance Test (time, memory, location scores), Seashore Rhythm Test, Speech–Sounds Perception Test, Finger-Tapping Test, Strength of Grip Trail-Making Test (Parts A & B), Finger Recognition Test, Fingertip Number Writing Test, Aphasia Screening Test] have been described (e.g., Reitan & Wolfson, 1985, pp. 15–89).

Our research has resulted in three modifications to the standard battery. First, the Aphasia Screening Test has been abbreviated to its naming, pronunciation, and sentence-interpretation items. This abbreviated instrument correlates with other measures of language ability, reliably discriminates normal from LD groups, and correlates with measures of reading and spelling (O'Donnell, 1985; O'Donnell, Romero, & Leicht, in press). Second, the Speech–Sounds Perception Test (SSPT) has been shortened to its first 30 items (O'Donnell, Randazzo, & Ramanaiah, in press). The abbreviated version (i.e., SSPT-30) is as reliable and valid as the full-length test (i.e., SSPT-60), and it correlates as strongly as SSPT-60 with other measures of language ability. Finally, each subject produced three drawings of the Greek cross and these drawings have been quantified. The quantitative score is reliable and it discriminates normal from clinical groups (O'Donnell, 1985).

Additional neuropsychological tests were incorporated into the battery. The Verbal Fluency Test (F–A–S) (Lezak, 1983, pp. 330–332) was included to measure verbal productivity. The Spatial Relations Test (Woodcock, 1978) was included as a measure of visual–spatial synthesis. The Grooved Pegboard (Lafayette Instruments, Model 32025) was included to make left–right comparisons and to measure dexterity.

The phonetic inaccuracy of a person's spelling (PI Errors) was measured. The PI score is reliable, discriminates normal from LD groups, and correlates with other measures of language (Horn, O'Donnell, & Leicht, 1988). Finally, the Wechsler Adult Intelligence Scale (WAIS) and the Wide-Range Achievement Test (WRAT) were included.

The Learning-Disability Sample

Applicants to an LD college support program (31 female; 202 male) (Cordoni, 1982) had been independently diagnosed by interdisciplinary staff conferences during the primary or secondary grades and these diagnoses had been continued through high school. Thus, they met federal government criteria for diagnosing LD. Among these LD, 79% had at least one score (reading, spelling, or arithmetic) from the WRAT which was 15 or more standard-score points less than their FSIQ; 83% had at least one WRAT score below the 20th percentile, and 93% met one of these criteria. Thus, most of these people also met research criteria for being classified as LD. These LD persons are probably typical of those attempting a postsecondary education.

However, they may not be typical of LD young adults generally. For example, only 35% had deficient scores on the WRAT reading subtest (i.e., less than the 20th percentile), while 83% had deficient spelling scores and 72% had deficient math scores. Parent and personal interviews showed that none of these persons had a history of brain injury, seizures, sensory deficits, drug abuse, or severe emotional problems. All had either graduated from high school or were within two semesters of high school graduation (mean education = 11.8; SD = 0.9). They averaged 18.6 (SD = 1.8) years in age (range = 16–28 years). Their WAIS full-scale IQs averaged 103.4 (SD = 9.6).

IV. Construct Validity of the Neuropsychological Test Battery

The construct validity of an LD battery is particularly important because test interpretation depends heavily upon the patterns and profiles of test performances. In the absence of empirically established construct validity, test interpretations are limited to psychometrically weak face validity (e.g., Heaton & Pendleton, 1981).

Factor analysis was used to investigate the dimensions underlying the present neuropsychological test battery. Previous factor analyses of the HRNTB have typically relied on data from groups of neurological and/or psychiatric inpatients averaging 35 or more years in age (e.g., Goldstein & Shelly, 1972; Swiercinsky, 1979; Swiercinsky & Hallenbeck, 1975) or on young children (Gamble, Mishra, & Obrzut, 1988). Since age affects many HRNTB test performances (e.g., Heaton, Grant, & Matthews, 1986) and since different diagnostic groups produce different neuropsychological test patterns (e.g., Reitan & Wolfson, 1985), prior factor analyses might not be generalizable to young-adult LD.

Carolyn Wiebe assisted in factor analyzing these data. Recommended procedures for conducting sound factor-analysis studies (Cattell, 1978) were adopted in analyzing the data. The intercorrelation matrix was submitted to iterative principal-axis factor analysis, using squared multiple correlations as diagonal elements. The scree test (Cattell, 1978) was used to assist in deciding the number of factors. Four-, five-, and six-factor solutions were rotated to orthogonal (varimax) and oblique (promax; direct quartimin) criteria. The varimax-rotated six-factor solution yielded the best simple structure. Scores with factor loadings of .40 or greater were selected for interpretation.

The right- and left-hand scores from motor and somatosensory tests were summed. Entering summed scores into the factor analysis minimized the liklihood that method-specific factors might appear, as has happened in previous factor-analysis studies (e.g., Goldstein & Shelly, 1972; Swiercinsky, 1979).

The six varimax-rotated factors accounted for 92.3% of the total variance and are shown in Table I. The first factor accounted for 24.8% of the variance and was defined by measures of psychomotor problem solving, logical reasoning, mental flexibility, and visual–spatial ability. This factor seemed to define a dimension of general adaptive abilities possibly characterized by nonverbal reasoning. The second factor accounted for 17.9% of the variance. Three of the four tests defining this factor (Digit Span, SSPT-30[2], and Rhythm) involved the perception of auditory material; two of the tests (SSPT-30, PI Errors) involved phonemic processing; and one test (Digit Span) involved auditory short-term memory. In an alternate analysis, SSPT-60 also saturated this factor. Factor 2 seemed to reflect deficits in auditory processing abilities. The saturation of the qualitative PI Error variable on this factor especially lends itself to this interpretation. Factor 3, accounting for 15.2% of the variance, was saturated by relatively pure measures of motor abilities (i.e., Finger Tapping and Grip Strength). It is clearly a "motor-abilities" factor. Factor 4 accounted for 15.1% of the variance and received loadings from somatosensory measures (Finger Recognition, Finger Number

TABLE I Varimax-Rotated Principal-Axis Factors for 18 Neuropsychological Test Scores[a]

	Factors						
	1	2	3	4	5	6	h²
TPT-Time	75	07	−09	37	−02	−07	72
TPT-Location	−59	−10	06	−15	−07	−14	42
Category	56	16	−09	29	02	−10	44
Trails-B	49	29	14	01	−33	−11	47
Spatial Relations	−48	−02	13	−21	19	20	36
Grooved Pegboard (Right and Left)	38	−08	−14	10	−21	05	23
Digit Span	01	−66	04	−06	−03	15	46
SSPT-30 (Errors)	10	57	−05	−00	−06	05	34
P.I. Errors	02	52	00	17	04	−10	32
Rhythm (Correct)	−10	−44	15	−31	06	15	35
Tapping (Right and Left)	−07	−05	93	−23	18	07	96
Grip (Right and Left)	−17	00	50	−10	−08	03	30
Finger Number Writing	28	16	−07	53	−14	−01	41
Finger Recognition	20	14	−11	51	−02	−02	34
Dyscopia	22	03	−13	46	−03	06	28
Digit Symbol	−10	−06	02	−10	76	00	60
Verbal Fluency	−04	−17	07	01	01	78	65
Dysphasic Errors	07	25	13	02	−08	02	09
% of Variance	43	16	13	9	7	4	

[a] Decimals have been omitted.

Writing) and from a measure of visual–motor abilities (Dyscopia). This seems to be a "sensory-motor" factor.

Factors 5 and 6 were singlets and cannot be interpreted apart from the validity of the individual tests. Factor 5 (saturated by Digit Symbol) accounted for 10.1% of the variance. Lezak (1983, pp. 272–274) has suggested that successful performance on Digit Symbol requires attention and response speed. Factor 6 (defined by F-A-S) accounted for 9.2% of the variance. Lezak (1983, pp. 329–333) suggested that F-A-S may reflect verbal production. In the present sample, F-A-S was independent of other language-related measures (e.g., Factor 2, Dysphasic Errors).

V. Criterion Validity of the Neuropsychological Test Battery

Clinical useful neuropsychological constructs must be anchored in a network of relationships with other relevant academic and cognitive variables. Therefore, we examined correlations between neuropsychological dimensions on the one hand and cognitive abilities and academic skills on the other.

T scores (M = 50; SD = 10) were computed for each LD subject using data from normals. The T scores were summed across salient items in a factor and divided by the number of salient items yielding 6-factor scores for each subject. Higher scores reflected better test performance.

Correlations were computed between the factor scores on the one hand and the WAIS and WRAT scores on the other. The WAIS variables examined were verbal comprehension (VC: information, comprehension, similarities, vocabulary) and perceptual organization (PO: picture completion, picture arrangement, block design, object assembly). The VC and PO cluster scores were used (rather than VIQ, PIQ, or FSIQ) because these clusters do not contain the Digit Span and Digit Symbol subtests used in the factor analysis. For the WRAT, standard scores (M = 100; SD = 15) from the reading, spelling, and arithmetic subtests were used.

The correlations between the factor scores for Factors 1 through 6, respectively, and VC were .17, .18, .12, .13, −.12, and .27. These correlations show that the factor scores overlap minimally with the WAIS VC cluster (i.e., 1.4 to 7.3% of the variance in common).

The correlations between the factor scores for Factors 1 through 6, respectively, and PO were .60, .16, .44, .29, .12, and .09 (i.e., 0.8 to 36% of the variance in common). The moderately high correlation between Factor 1 and PO suggests that Factor 1 shared some (but not all) of the same nonverbal reasoning processes subsumed by the WAIS PO subtests. In an alternate analysis, PO saturated Factor 1.

The correlations between WRAT reading and Factors 1 through 6, respectively, were .06, .46, −.04, .09, .08, and .22. The correlations between WRAT spelling and Factors 1 through 6 were −.04, .40, .06, .11, and .16. The correlations between WRAT arithmetic and Factors 1 through 6 were .28, .16, −.02, .20, .24, and .12. Both VC and PO were also correlated with the WRAT scores. (The correlations between WRAT reading, spelling, and arithmetic, respectively, and VC were .21, .05, and .19. The correlations between WRAT reading, spelling, and arithmetic, respectively, and PO were .00, −.08, and .24.) Therefore, partial correlations were computed to remove statistically the higher of the two WAIS cluster scores from the factor score–WRAT correlations. Partialling out VC left the Factor 2–reading (partial $r = .43$) and Factor 2–spelling (partial $r = .37$) correlations virtually unchanged. The Factor 5–arithmetic correlation was also almost the same (VC partial $r = .27$; PO partial $r = .22$). The partial r's of Factor 1 with arithmetic (partial $r = .18$) and Factor 6 with reading (partial $r = .17$) were low but significant. Thus, Factors 2 and 6 were related to reading and spelling and Factors 1 and 5 were related to arithmetic.

VI. Discriminant Validity of the Neuropsychological Test Battery

The ability of the HRNTB to discriminate normal adults from those suffering from various neurological conditions has been determined (e.g., Klove, 1974; Reitan, 1986). However, the sensitivity of this battery for discriminating LD children and adults from their normal or neurologically damaged counterparts has been examined in only two studies (O'Donnell *et al.*, 1983; Selz & Reitan, 1979a, 1979b). In both studies, the LD group differed from the contrast groups in terms of FSIQ. As a result, the discriminative efficiency of the HRNTB was confounded with the cognitive levels of the groups in these studies. The purpose of the next investigation was to determine whether the neuropsychological battery could discriminate LD from groups of normal and head-injured young adults. Josue Romero assisted in conducting this analysis.

Normal, LD, and head-injured groups were matched for FSIQ and balanced for gender (males : females = 2 : 1). Twenty female and 40 male LD young adults were selected for this study. Their average WAIS FSIQ was 103.4 (SD = 5.8). The head-injured (HI) group was composed of 20 males and 10 females who had sustained head trauma. They averaged 55.3 days (SD = 50.2 days) of unconsciousness, 90% for 1 week or longer. All had received neurological diagnoses of brain injury. They had suffered cerebral and brain-stem contusions, mass lesions, and anoxia so that it may be assumed that they had experienced bilateral and diffuse damage (e.g., Lezak, 1983, p. 170). In age and education, respectively, they averaged 24.6 (SD = 3.2 years) and 13.2 years (SD = 1.4 years) and in WAIS FSIQ they averaged 101.1 (SD = 6.6).

Finally, there was a group of 10 female and 20 male normal college students. According to their verbal reports, none had a history of learning problems or had experienced, following a blow to the head, either seizures or unconsciousness. They averaged 20.9 (SD = 4.1) years in age, had an average of 13.3 (SD = 1.2) years of education, and averaged 103.9 (SD = 5.0) in FSIQ. The groups did not differ in FSIQ [$F(2, 117) = 2.1; p > .10$]. On the WRAT, the LD had significantly lower reading, spelling, and arithmetic scores than the other groups.

In order to maintain an adequate variables-to-subjects ratio, 12 scores were retained from the factor analysis. Linear discriminant function analysis (LDFA) (full model, direct method) was performed on the 12 scores for the 120 subjects. In order to ensure that the results were not due to fluctuations in random error, the total sample was randomly divided and the results from the first half were cross-validated on the second half.

One discriminant function was significant and the Wilk's Lambda (λ) for this function was significant both for the total sample [$\lambda = .28$; $F(24, 212) = 8.0$, $p < .001$] and for each random half [first half: $\lambda = .13$; $F(24, 98) = 7.4$, $p < .001$; second half: $\lambda = 33$; $F(24, 86) = 2.6$, $p < .001$]. Thus, the profile of test scores significantly differentiated the groups.

The LDFA also performs a multivariate analysis of variance (MANOVA). Table II summarizes the results of the MANOVA. The univariate F values (Table II) show that all of the scores contributed significantly to group differentiation. Bonferroni's test was used to make post hoc comparisons among treatment means. The results from these post hoc tests (indicated by subscripts in Table II) indicated that 10 of the scores discriminated the normal and HI groups. The HI group was more deficient on each measure. These findings confirm the sensitivity of the neuropsychological battery for detecting differences between normal and brain-damaged persons (Klove, 1974; Reitan, 1986).

The post hoc tests also showed that five scores (Digit Span, PI Errors, Dyscopia, Digit Symbol, and Aphasic Errors) differentiated the normal group from the LD group, with the LD group being more deficient on each measure. These results confirm our previous studies (Horn et al., 1988; O'Donnell, 1985; O'Donnell et al., 1983) in showing that LD young adults tend to earn less adequate neuropsychological test scores than nondisabled persons.

Seven scores differentiated the LD group from the HI group. The HI group was deficient relative to the LD group on TPT-Time, Trails-B, SSPT-

TABLE II Results of Linear Discriminant Function Analysis of Neuropsychological Test Scores for Three Groups[a]

	Normal		Learning Disabled		Head Injured		
	M	(SD)	M	(SD)	M	(SD)	F
Category	34.0a	(17.0)	41.5a,b	(21.6)	50.4b	(24.9)	4.4**
TPT-T	11.8a	(13.2)	14.0a	(6.1)	22.6b	(7.8)	27.8***
Trails-B	57.1a	(14.2)	71.3a	(19.1)	129.5b	(68.9)	33.1***
SSPT-30	2.1a	(1.2)	3.4a	(1.9)	5.8b	(7.0)	5.8**
Digit Span	10.3a	(2.6)	8.9b	(2.3)	10.4a	(2.2)	5.7**
PI Errors (%)	42.1a	(17.2)	55.4b	(24.2)	49.4a,b	(24.6)	3.5*
Finger Recognition	1.1a	(2.1)	2.1a,b	(3.0)	3.4b	(4.7)	3.9*
Dyscopia	3.6a	(2.3)	4.7b	(1.6)	5.5b	(2.3)	8.8***
Tap Sum	99.2a	(10.2)	94.3a	(11.5)	63.1b	(23.5)	53.7***
Grip Sum	89.2a	(24.1)	83.3a	(24.9)	68.1b	(31.4)	5.2**
Digit Symbol	11.8a	(2.6)	9.6b	(5.8)	6.6c	(2.6)	31.7***
Aphasia	0.2a	(0.5)	1.0b	(1.0)	1.2b	(1.0)	10.5***

[a] Within a row, means with different subscripts differ significantly at $p < .05$.
$*p < .05$; $**p < .01$; $***p < .001$.

30, Finger Tapping, Grip Strength, and Digit Symbol; the LD group was more impaired than the HI group on Digit Span. Thus, this neuropsychological test battery is sensitive to differences between clinical groups.

The LD and HI groups did not differ on five measures (Category, PI Errors, Finger-Recognition Errors, Dyscopia, and Dysphasic Errors) even though all of these measures differentiated the HI and normal groups. It is not surprising that HI victims of severe craniocerebral trauma performed worse than the LD on several measures sensitive to the integrity of the cerebral hemispheres. What is important is that the LD were more impaired than the HI on one measure and did not differ from the HI on five measures *despite* the severity of injury of the HI persons. Thus, at least some LD persons are experiencing measurable neuropsychological dysfunction.

Ninety-two percent of all subjects were correctly classified by the LDFA. For the normal, LD, and HI groups, respectively, 100, 93, and 80% were correctly classified. Seven percent of the LD and HI groups were misclassified as normal, and 13% of the HI were misclassified as LD. In other words, this neuropsychological test battery was more likely to misdiagnose impaired persons as normal than it was to misdiagnose normal persons as impaired. Selz and Reitan (1979a) obtained similar results for children.

Halstead's Impairment Index (HII) is one of the most sensitive indicators of the presence of cerebral impairment derived from the HRNTB (Reitan, 1986, p. 19). Figure 1 shows the percentage of persons in each group

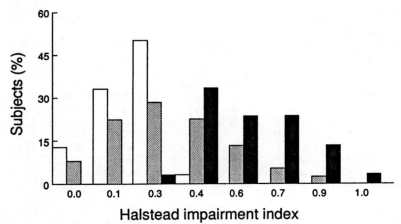

FIGURE 1 Halstead's Impairment Index by group (open bars, normals; hatched bars, learning disabled; filled bars, head injured).

with varying levels of HII. Ninety-seven percent of the normals were below and 97% of the HI were above an HII of 0.4. Adopting HII = 0.4 as a cutoff score, 42% of the LD group exhibited HII scores in the impaired range. A one-way analysis of variance $[F(2, 117) = 37.2, p < .001]$ showed that the HI (M = 0.6, SD = 0.2) had higher HII than the LD (M = 0.3, SD = 0.2), who had higher HII than the normals (M = 0.1, SD = 0.1). The analysis of HII and the LDFA showed that some LD young adults experience demonstrable neuropsychological dysfunction and tend to be similar to some HI in this respect.

VII. Subtypes of Learning-Disabled Young Adults

Early research assumed that LD persons had one underlying deficit. However, by the middle 1970s it had become apparent that the LD population was heterogeneous (e.g., Benton, 1975). This recognition prompted investigators to search for stable and replicable LD subtypes. Although early LD subtyping studies used clinical–inferential approaches (summarized by Hooper & Willis, 1989, pp. 42–44), these approaches were unable to analyze the multivariate relationships in large data sets and they were susceptible to subjective biases during the clustering process (Fletcher & Satz, 1985). Next, several investigators used Q-factor analysis in order to study subtypes of LD children (summarized by Hooper & Willis, 1989, pp. 64–68). Although Q-factor analysis was an improvement over the clinical–inferential approach, it is insensitive to elevations in the data, it cannot treat subjects who load highly on more than one factor, and it artificially restricts the number of subtypes that can be found in a data set (Fletcher & Satz, 1985).

Recent subtyping studies (Hooper & Willis, 1989, pp. 64–68) used cluster analysis, a family of multivariate statistical techniques that seeks to group people into clusters defined by the data rather than by a priori considerations. It is sensitive to elevations in the data, is appropriate when the assumption of linearity is not met, and is not limited to a fixed number of clusters. Discussions of cluster analysis methodology have been presented (Blashfield, 1976; Everitt, 1984).

Phillips (1986) cluster analyzed the test protocols of 143 male and 20 female LD applicants to Project Achieve. These were all of the subjects available at that time for whom complete data were available. They averaged 18.8 years in age (SD = 1.7) and 104.5 in WAIS FSIQ (SD = 9.4). She used variables from the HRNTB (Category; Tactual Performance, Total Time; Seashore Rhythm Test; Speech-Sounds Perception Test; Trail-Making Test, Part B) and from the WAIS (Information, Arithmetic, Digit Span, Block Design, and Digit Symbol). She also used the sum of naming and pronunciation errors from the Aphasia Screening Test (i.e., Aphasia), ratings of the Greek Cross (Dyscopia; O'Donnell, 1985), the Spatial Relations Test (Woodcock, 1978), and the proportion of phonetically accurate spelling errors from the WRAT (PA) (Horn et al., 1988). Raw scores were converted into T scores (M = 50; SD = 10) based on data derived from normal college-student volunteers. Higher scores represented better performance.

Phillips (1986) used Ward's Method and Average Linkage to determine the number of clusters in the data and to define the centers of the clusters. She then used these data as input into a K-means iterative partitioning method. The K-means analyses of the Ward's and Average Linkage methods both yielded five clusters. A contingency coefficient (C = .89, $p < .001$) showed that these clusters replicated. Twelve subjects were not consistently classified across the two algorithms and were dropped from the remaining analyses.

Phillips cross-validated the cluster results on random sample halves. With Ward's Method, 71 and 86% of the cases were placed into the same cluster in the half samples as in the full sample. With Average Linkage, 63 and 66% of the cases were placed into the same cluster in the half samples as in the full sample.

Table III shows the five subtypes emerging from the K-means iterated Ward's Method. Mean test scores for Subtype 1 (normal), were in the average range (i.e., $\geq 40T$). The other clusters had at least one mean test score ≤ 1.5 SD below the mean. Subtype 2 (auditory processing deficits) exhibited deficient performances on WAIS Digit Span, SSPT-60, Phonetically Accurate Spelling, and Trails-B. It parallels Factor 2 as described earlier. Subtype 3 (spatial processing deficits) subjects exhibited deficient performances on the

TABLE III Means and Standard Deviations (in T-Score Units) for Five Neuropsychological Subtypes

| | Subtypes | | | | | | | | |
| | Normal | | Auditory Processing | | Spatial Processing | | Global Deficit | | Language Processing | |
	M	(SD)	M	(SD)	M	(SD)	M	(SD)	M	(SD)
Digit Span	46.0	(10.0)	35.4	(7.1)	43.6	(9.1)	36.8	(10.9)	39.5	(8.1)
PA Errors	51.7	(12.7)	30.1	(10.8)	41.0	(14.5)	35.8	(12.8)	40.3	(12.2)
SSPT-60	49.4	(9.5)	18.6	(20.6)	44.6	(12.6)	30.7	(6.9)	48.7	(10.5)
Trails-B	40.3	(12.6)	28.6	(18.7)	26.6	(13.0)	2.2	(25.9)	35.8	(9.6)
TPT-T	57.0	(9.5)	48.5	(8.9)	17.4	(13.5)	-5.4	(15.2)	46.6	(9.6)
Spatial Rel.	48.3	(11.3)	41.1	(9.4)	34.3	(11.1)	26.1	(12.3)	38.6	(9.3)
Category	50.7	(8.4)	48.1	(10.0)	38.2	(12.5)	10.0	(12.1)	41.6	(14.4)
Digit Symbol	40.8	(9.4)	39.3	(7.2)	38.5	(8.1)	33.9	(8.1)	36.7	(8.1)
Dyscopia	47.4	(11.7)	39.5	(10.1)	40.6	(13.9)	29.8	(13.8)	37.4	(7.3)
Block Design	56.0	(9.2)	46.1	(8.8)	41.4	(7.4)	31.7	(7.2)	46.0	(9.5)
Aphasia	43.1	(12.3)	39.2	(12.6)	44.4	(12.0)	34.2	(19.3)	16.6	(12.4)
Rhythm Test	50.2	(11.1)	36.9	(13.5)	42.1	(13.4)	34.7	(12.8)	33.7	(11.6)
WAIS Infor.	46.2	(8.0)	43.0	(9.5)	43.7	(11.3)	37.9	(10.4)	41.4	(9.8)
WAIS Arit.	47.2	(9.6)	42.1	(11.9)	38.9	(8.9)	35.4	(6.9)	43.9	(10.8)

TPT-T, Spatial Relations Test, and Trails-B. All of these measures saturated Factor 1 from the previous analysis, implying that LD with spatial deficits might also experience general adaptive deficits. Subtype 4 (global deficits) had deficient performances on 10 of the 12 measures. The tests on which Subtype 4 subjects were most deficient (Tactual Performance Test, Trails-B, Category) were also the most salient scores defining Factor 1. Subjects in subtype 5 (language processing deficits) had deficits on the Aphasia Screening Test and had deficient scores on both the Rhythm Test and the Trails-B Test.

Two additional points are worth making. First, Subtype 2 had normal performances on the visual–spatial measures; Subtype 3 had normal performances on the auditory and language measures. This highlights the relative independence of these LD subtypes. Second, all subtypes except Subtype 1 exhibited relatively deficient performance on Trails-B. Therefore, it appears that all neuropsychological deficit LD subtypes experience a problem with flexibility and sequential processing.

To examine external subtype validity, Phillips (1986) applied cross-validated LDFA to a variable set including the WRAT reading, WRAT spelling, WRAT arithmetic, and Total Lateralized Sensorimotor Asymmetries score. The latter score was a summation of asymmetrical dominant- versus nondominant-hand performances on Finger Tapping, Grip Strength, Tactual Performance Test, Grooved Pegboard, Finger Recognition, and Finger Number Writing. O'Donnell (1983) showed that LD with an impairment index $\geq$ 0.4 and head-injured victims had a significantly greater number of asymmetries than normals, thus suggesting that higher numbers of asymmetries are associated with greater probabilities of cerebral impairment.

Table IV summarizes this LDFA. Two functions were significant ($p < .001$; $p < .002$). Function 1 was significant during cross-validation

TABLE IV Results of Discriminant Analysis of Achievement and Asymmetries Scores for Learning-Disability Subtypes[a]

Subtype	WRAT Reading		WRAT Spelling		WRAT Arithmetic		Lateralized Asymmetries	
	M	(SD)	M	(SD)	M	(SD)	M	SD
Normal	102.6a	(14.0)	86.9d	(13.4)	87.7a	(9.7)	1.9a	(0.9)
Auditory	86.8d	(11.0)	77.0c	(8.7)	87.7a	(10.5)	2.3a,b	(0.8)
Spatial	98.4a,b	(14.6)	87.6a	(14.4)	83.6a,b	(8.8)	2.6b	(1.2)
Global	94.4b,c	(8.8)	84.1a,b	(10.0)	81.0b	(5.1)	2.8b	(1.0)
Language	89.2c,d	(12.1)	79.8b,c	(10.7)	88.5a	(9.8)	2.3a,b	(1.0)
F values	8.6***		4.6**		2.9*		3.8**	

[a] Within a row, means with the same subscript do not differ.
*$p < .05$; **$p < .01$; ***$p < .001$.

($p < .002$). Function 2 was marginally significant ($p = .06$) during cross-validation. The univariate Fs show that all variables contributed to group differentiation. Subtypes 2 and 5 had the lowest reading and spelling scores. These results are consistent with the correlations between Factor 2 and WRAT reading/spelling. Subtype 4 had the lowest arithmetic score followed by Subtype 3. The correlational and subtype findings parallel Strang and Rourke (1985) in showing that nonverbal reasoning and visual–spatial deficits are related to impaired computational arithmetic.

The external validation also showed that Subtype 1 had the lowest mean Lateralized Asymmetries score and that Subtypes 3 and 4 had the highest Lateralized Asymmetries scores. This result suggests that the members of Subtypes 3 and 4 would be the most likely to be experiencing compromised brain functions. An ancillary ANOVA of the HII [$F(4, 158) = 38.3$, $p < .001$] score confirmed this suggestion. The normal subtype (mean HII = 0.1) differed from all others; the auditory and language subtypes (mean HII = .3 and .3, respectively) differed from the spatial and global subtypes (mean HII = .4 and .7, respectively). In turn the spatial subtype differed from the global subtype.

VIII. Personality and Social Problems among LD Young Adults

Learning-disabled children differ from their normally achieving peers in terms of a variety of affective, interpersonal, and behavior problems (e.g., Kronick, 1981) and these problems may persist into adolescence and young adulthood (Horn et al., 1983; Rourke, Young, Strang, & Russell, 1986; Spreen, 1989). Subtyping LD on the basis of their socioemotional problems has been done (Porter & Rourke, 1985; Speece, McKinney, & Appelbaum, 1985) for children but not for young adults. Leicht's (1987) study compared the personality and social functioning of normal and LD young adults, performed a subtype analysis of their personality/social problems, and examined whether such subtypes might be related to neuropsychological subtypes.

Consecutive applicants to Project Achieve (23 females, 129 males) completed the Personality Screening Inventory (PSI) (Lanyon, 1978) and the achievement and endurance scales from the Personality Research Form (PRF) (Jackson, 1974). The reliability and validity of these scales have been established (reviewed by Leicht, 1987, pp. 83–93 and 94–95). These scales were also completed by 21 female and 34 male college undergraduates, whose scores did not differ from published data (e.g., Jackson, 1974; Lanyon, 1978).

Leicht (1987) first compared the two groups on the PSI scales [alienation (AL), social nonconformity (SN), discomfort (DI), expression (EX), defensiveness (DE)] and on the severity index (a weighted sum of raw

PSI-scale scores derived by Overall (1974) for measuring severity of maladjustment). An LDFA performed on the PSI data showed that the test-score profiles were significantly different ($p < .001$). On AL, SN, EX, and DE, respectively, the learning disabled (M = 51.1, SD = 10.2; M = 51.1, SD = 9.9; M = 50.9, SD = 10.2; M = 51.0, SD = 9.8) had higher scores than the normals (M = 47.4, SD = 9.3; M = 47.0, SD = 9.5; M = 47.7, SD = 8.9; M = 47.2, SD = 10.0). However, the accuracy of classification was low, with 32.9% of the LD and 27.3% of the normals being misclassified. The LD also scored higher (M = 9.5, SD = 1.8) than the normals (M = 8.6, SD = 1.6) on the severity index. However, LDFA indicated that the severity index misclassified 48.0% of the LD and 23.6% of the normals. These results are consistent with other reports (e.g., Spreen, 1989) showing that LD young adults, as a group, have higher scores on a screening test for personal–social adjustment than their normal peers. However, the mean PSI-scale scores were in the average range and PSI scales and the severity index did not accurately discriminate individual LD from normal college students.

Leicht (1987) also cluster analyzed the PSI-scaled scores for the LD subjects, using the same clustering procedures as Phillips (1986). Ward's Method yielded six clusters, Average Linkage yielded seven clusters, and 85% of the subjects were consistently classified across the two algorithms (C = .89, $p < .001$). The clusters of both algorithms were stable during split-sample cross-validation. Leicht selected the six clusters from Ward's method for interpretation.

Table V summarizes the results from the cluster analysis. The high-score (i.e., $\geq 60T$) profile for Subtype 1 (extraverted social nonconformist) suggested impulsive, socially dominant persons with a disregard for social con-

TABLE V Means and Standard Deviations (in T-Score Units) for PSI Scales for Six Personal–Social Subtypes

PSI Scales		Subtype					
		1 (11%)	2 (13%)	3 (18%)	4 (30%)	5 (16%)	6 (12%)
AL	M	58.7	50.1	61.6	47.7	66.2	41.8
	(SD)	(6.6)	(3.2)	(8.5)	(6.2)	(7.7)	(5.8)
SN	M	61.2	43.6	64.0	51.0	47.4	62.0
	(SD)	(7.8)	(6.2)	(6.3)	(7.9)	(6.1)	(9.6)
DI	M	44.7	37.1	63.1	48.6	53.3	58.4
	(SD)	(5.3)	(6.1)	(8.4)	(7.1)	(11.1)	(9.9)
EX	M	72.1	55.7	52.9	49.1	41.0	64.0
	(SD)	(6.6)	(10.3)	(7.6)	(6.3)	(6.8)	(6.5)
DE	M	50.3	69.2	46.5	54.3	54.6	48.7
	(SD)	(8.9)	(6.1)	(7.1)	(6.3)	(6.9)	(10.3)

ventions. The Subtype 2 (defensive adjusted) scaled scores suggested persons who deny negative feelings (low DI) and who concomitantly view themselves as well adjusted (high DE). The Subtype 3 (alienated anxious nonconformist) high-score profile described individuals who were oversensitive, who had poor interpersonal skills, who were dissatisfied with the world, and who were anxious. Subtype 4 (normal) had no scales with clinically significant scores. The single high-scaled score for Subtype 5 (social isolation) suggested over-sensitivity and poor interpersonal skills. The high-score profile for Subtype 6 (extraverted anxious nonconformist) suggested an impulsive, unconventional, anxious style similar to Subtype 1 individuals.

An ANOVA [$F(5, 146) = 20.3, p < .001$) of the severity index showed that Subtype 3 (M 11.2, SD = 1.6) and Subtype 5 (M = 10.9, SD = 1.7) were above Overall's (1974) cutoff score (10.89) and were significantly higher than Subtype 1 (M = 9.5, SD = 1.0), Subtype 2 (M = 8.8, SD = 1.2), Subtype 4 (M = 8.5, SD = 1.7), or Subtype 6 (M = 8.8, SD = 1.6). Thus, most maladjusted LD were found in two subtypes and characterized by poor interpersonal skills and feelings of oversensitivity.

Leicht (1987) attempted external validation against the PRF achievement and endurance scales, against the WRAT subtests, and against Phillips' (1986) neuropsychological subtypes. For PRF achievement, the means and standard deviations of Subtypes 1 through 6, respectively, were as follows: (1) 54.3, 8.5; (2) 59.5, 6.6; (3) 47.6, 9.9; (4) 52.1, 7.8; (5) 49.3, 9.0; and (6) 49.0, 9.0. For PRF endurance, the means and standard deviations for Subtypes 1 through 6, respectively, were as follows: (1) 50.9, 7.8; (2) 57.0, 6.2; (3) 42.8, 8.5; (4) 46.9, 8.5; (5) 47.3, 8.9; and (6) 46.9, 7.4. A MANOVA with post hoc tests showed the same pattern for both PRF scales. Subtype 2 had the highest scores and Subtype 3 had the lowest scores. Thus, LD who were most defensive (or who had the most resilient ego defenses?) also had the highest achievement motivation and the highest level of perseverance. The LD who were most alienated, unhappy, anxious, and dissatisfied were also the least achievement oriented and the least persevering.

Leicht (1987) performed a personal–social subtype by WRAT achievement subtest MANOVA. The Wilk's Lambda [$\lambda = .92, F(15, 367)$] as well as the univariate F's were all nonsignificant. Thus, the data offered no support for the idea that personal–social subtypes might be related to academic skill deficits. Leicht attempted to examine relationships between his personal–social subtypes and neuropsychological subtypes based on Phillips' (1986) research. The resulting chi-square test was not significant [$\chi^2(20, N = 141) = 21.1$). Thus, these data offered no support for the idea that some neuropsychological LD subtypes might be more maladjusted than others. Finally, the correlation ($r = .04$) between the PSI severity index and the HRNTB impairment index indicated independence between likelihood of cerebral impairment and severity of socioemotional problems.

IX. General Discussion

This research attempted to address several research questions relevant to the neuropsychological assessment of LD young adults. The initial question asked whether a neuropsychological battery would define academically related neuropsychological constructs. Factor analysis showed that for LD young adults, neuropsychological test scores could be reduced to six orthogonal dimensions, three of which were related to academic achievement. Dimensions subsuming nonverbal reasoning/visual–spatial abilities (Factor 1) and attention–response speed (Factor 5) were associated with computational skill. Nonverbal reasoning may also be relevant to vocational success (Heaton & Pendleton, 1981). The auditory processing dimension (Factor 2) was associated with reading and spelling. Additional analyses of the abbreviated Aphasia Screening Test (O'Donnell *et al.*, 1990) showed that items measuring phoneme articulation (but not naming or sentence-interpretation items) were correlated with reading and spelling. These findings are consistent with previous research (e.g., Mann & Brady, 1988; Wagner & Torgesen, 1987) that showed that aspects of auditory processing are related (perhaps causally) to developmental reading/spelling disorders. Associations between the neuropsychological dimensions and academic skills were independent of general cognitive ability.

A second question asked whether the neuropsychological test battery could discriminate young-adult LD from normals. The linear discriminant function analysis correctly identified 93% of the LD and 100% of the normal groups. Since the groups were matched for FSIQ and for gender distribution and because split-sample cross-validation was performed, these results could not have been due to differences in cognitive ability, to gender-related ability, or to error perturbations in the data. Thus, the neuropsychological test battery can accurately discriminate LD from normal young adults. The strongest contributions to this discrimination came from measures of auditory processing, language, visual–motor ability, and attention–response speed. Deficiencies in these abilities have traditionally been associated with LD (e.g., Benton, 1975). The variety of deficient abilities suggests heterogeneity among these LD persons.

This research question also asked whether variables distinguishing LD from normals would also be related to neurological integrity. The LDFA showed that with FSIQ and gender controlled, the neuropsychological battery was extremely accurate in discriminating normals from severely injured victims of craniocerebral trauma, the distribution of Halstead Impairment Index (HII) scores showing incorrect identification of only 3% of each group. Thus, consistent with previous research (Klove, 1974; Reitan, 1986), this neuropsychological battery is sensitive to neurological impairment.

Figure 1 showed that 42% of LD earned HII scores in the impaired range. This indicates a nonchance probability of neurological impairment for some LD individuals. Phillips' (1986) study showed that these "high-impaired LD" clustered in the spatial (mean HII = 0.4) and global (mean HII = 0.7) subtypes (i.e., cerebral impairment is present for some, but not for all LD). The significant excess of sensorimotor asymmetries in the "high-impaired LD" (O'Donnell, 1983) and in the spatial and global subtypes (Phillips, 1986) also suggested that some LD experience neurological impairment. HII does not reveal the severity of impairment. However, the means in Table I showed that the LD were intermediate between the normal and head-injured groups on 10 of 12 variables, thus suggesting a severity of impairment greater than the normals but less than the HI group. In these respects, the data indicate that some, but not all, LD young adults experience "mild cerebral dysfunction."

The third question inquired as to whether there might be homogeneous subgroupings of LD young adults. Phillips' (1986) study showed that the neuropsychological test scores could be used to subdivide LD young adults into five subtypes. These subtypes were stable across clustering methods and across split-half cross-validation, and they were differentially associated with academic skills. The auditory and language subtypes were relatively more deficient in reading and spelling; the global and language subtypes were relatively more deficient in computational skill. Therefore, on the basis of correlations between factor scores and WRAT scores for a heterogeneous LD group, or on the basis of ANOVAs among homogeneous LD subtypes, reading and spelling deficits were associated with auditory and language deficits, and computational deficits were associated with visuospatial and generalized reasoning deficits. These results are generally consistent with results obtained for LD children (Hooper & Willis, 1989).

The final question, addressed by Leicht's (1987) study, asked whether socioemotional factors might be importantly associated with LD status. Using an instrument (PSI) with established reliability and validity (Lanyon, 1978; Leicht, 1987), Leicht found that LD had significantly higher scores than normals on four of five PSI scales. This finding was consistent with other research (e.g., Spreen, 1987, pp. 70–80; Spreen, 1989). However, Leicht's subtyping study showed that only two subtypes, both characterized by over-sensitivity and poor interpersonal skills, were actually "maladjusted" in the sense that their salient scales and severity index scores were in the clinically significant range. Thus, some LD young adults, but not all, experience socio-emotional problems.

Two of Phillips' subtypes (spatial, global) were characterized by deficits in visual–spatial and/or nonverbal reasoning abilities) and had more impaired arithmetic than reading/spelling. There was a correspondence between these subtypes and LD subtypes described by Rourke *et al.* (1986) as being susceptible to personal–social maladjustment. However, Leicht failed to find a relationship between his personal–social adjustment subtypes and Phillips' neuropsychological subtypes or between his personal–social subtypes and WRAT achievement. Therefore, in contrast with previous reports (Rourke *et al.*, 1986; Spreen, 1989), personal–social maladjustment in the present LD sample was independent of neuropsychological subtype membership and independent of achievement level. Finally, in contrast to Spreen (1989), Leicht failed to find a correlation between maladjustment among LD (PSI severity index) and neuropsychological impairment (HRNTB impairment index). Because of differences in cognitive functioning (mean FSIQ of present sample = 103; mean Victoria sample FSIQ = 87) and neurological status (42% of present sample impaired; 80% of Victoria group impaired), it is difficult to interpret differences between these two LD samples.

From his literature review, Coles (1978) concluded that the discriminative and construct validity of LD tests was unproven and that the neurological-dysfunction hypothesis was unsupported. He has reiterated these conclusions following a more recent and comprehensive review (Coles, 1987). The present research is relevant to these conclusions. The present results showed that the neuropsychological test battery defines academically relevant constructs, it accurately discriminates LD from normal young adults, it shows that a proportion (perhaps as many as 40%) of LD young adults exhibit mild neuropsychological dysfunction, and it shows that the dysfunctional LD fall into defined subgroups (Phillips Subtypes 3 and 4) with predictable educational deficits. Although some LD were maladjusted (Leicht's Subtypes 3 and 5), these maladjustments were unrelated to academic skills or to neuropsychological status. In other words, the present research seems to support the continued viability of the neurological hypothesis.

X. Summary

This chapter reported the results of a research program directed at understanding the neuropsychological and personality correlates of learning disabilities among young adults. Orthogonal dimensions from a factor analysis of the Halstead–Reitan Battery were correlated with skills in reading, spelling, and computational arithmetic. Neuropsychological test scores accurately discriminated 92% of the normal, LD, and head-injured subjects, and 42% of the LD had Halstead Impairment Index scores in the impaired range. These findings demonstrated that the construct and discriminant validities of this test battery applied to learning-disabled young adults and suggested that as many as 42% of LD young adults experience mild cerebral dysfunction.

Cluster analyses of neuropsychological and personality test scores showed that young-adult LD can be grouped into homogeneous subtypes. Both neuropsychological and personality subtypes were internally consistent. The extrinsic validity of the neuropsychological subtypes was demonstrated against academic test scores. The extrinsic validity of the personality subtypes was demonstrated against other personality test scores. However, the personality subtypes were independent of academic and neuropsychological test scores.

The present findings confirm the validity of the Halstead–Reitan Neuropsychological Test Battery in the assessment of young adults with learning disabilities. However, important issues not addressed in this research program need to be examined in future studies. One issue concerns the extent to which neuropsychological subtypes might be responsive to differential instructional methods. A second issue concerns whether and to what extent profiles of neuropsychological test scores can be used to predict educational and vocational outcomes for learning-disabled young adults. Answers to these questions could enhance the postsecondary adjustment of LD young adults.

Acknowledgments

This research was supported in part by Grant No. 2-10897 from the Graduate School at Southern Illinois University and in part by Grant No. G008001911 from the Bureau for the Education of the Handicapped, U.S. Office of Education. In addition, this research has received continuous support and encouragement from the Clinical Center at Southern Illinois University–Carbondale.

References

Benton, A. L. (1975). Developmental dyslexia: Neurological aspects. *Advances in Neurology, 7,* 1–47.

Benton, A. L. (1980). Dyslexia: Evolution of a concept. *Bulletin of the Orton Society, 30,* 10–26.

Blashfield, R. K. (1976). Mixture model tests of cluster analysis: Accuracy of four agglomerative hierarchical methods. *Psychological Bulletin, 83,* 377–388.

Cattell, R. B. (1978). *The scientific use of factor analysis in the behavioral and life sciences.* New York: Plenum.

Coles, G. (1978). The learning-disabilities test battery: Empirical and social issues. *Harvard Educational Review, 48,* 313–340.

Coles, G. (1987). *The learning mystique.* New York: Pantheon Books.

Cordoni, B. K. (1982). Services for college dyslexics. In R. N. Malatesha & P. G. Aaron (Eds.) (pp. 435–448). *Reading disorders: Varieties and treatments.* New York: Academic Press.

Everitt, B. (1984). *Cluster analysis* (2nd ed.). London: Heinemann Educational Books.

Fletcher, J. M., & Satz, P. (1985). Cluster analysis and the search for subtypes. In B. P. Rourke (Ed.), *Neuropsychology of learning disabilities: Essentials of subtype analysis.* New York: Guilford Press.

Fletcher, J. M., Satz, P., & Scholes, R. J. (1981). Developmental changes in the linguistic performance correlates of reading achievement. *Brain & Language, 13,* 78–90.

Gamble, C. M., Mishra, S. P., & Obrzut, J. E. (1988). Construct validity of neuropsychological instrumentation with a learning disabled population. *Archives of Clinical Neuropsychology, 3,* 359–368.

Goldstein, G., & Shelly, C. H. (1972). Statistical and normative studies of the Halstead Neuropsychological Test Battery relevant to a neuropsychiatric hospital setting. *Perceptual and Motor Skills, 34,* 603–620.

Heaton, R. K., Grant, I., & Matthews, C. G. (1986). Differences in neuropsychological test performance associated with age, education, and sex. In I. Grant & K. M. Adams (Eds.), *Neuropsychological assessment of neuropsychiatric disorders.* New York: Oxford University Press.

Heaton, R. K., & Pendleton, M. G. (1981). Use of neuropsychological tests to predict adult patients' everyday functioning. *Journal of Consulting and Clinical Psychology, 49,* 807–821.

Hooper, S. R., & Willis, W. G. (1989). *Learning disability subtyping: Neuropsychological foundations, conceptual models, and issues in clinical differentiation.* New York: Springer-Verlag.

Horn, J. L., O'Donnell, J. P., & Leicht, D. J. (1988). Phonetically inaccurate spelling among learning-disabled, head-injured, and nondisabled young adults. *Brain & Language, 33,* 55–64.

Horn, W. F., O'Donnell, J. P., & Vitulano, L. (1983). Long-term follow-up studies of learning-disabled persons. *Journal of Learning Disabilities, 16,* 542–555.

Hynd, G. W., & Cohen, M. (1983). *Dyslexia: Neuropsychological theory, research, and clinical differentiation.* New York: Grune & Straton.

Jackson, D. N. (1974). *Personality Research Form Manual.* Goshen, NY: Research Psychologists Press.

Klove, H. (1974). Validation studies in adult clinical neuropsychology. In R. M. Reitan & L. A. Davison (Eds.), *Clinical neuropsychology: Current status and applications.* New York: Wiley.

Kronick, D. (1981). *Social development in learning disabled persons.* San Francisco, CA: Jossey-Bass.

Lanyon, R. I. (1978). *Psychological Screening Inventory: Manual* (2nd ed.). Goshen, NY: Research Psychologists Press.

Leicht, D. J. (1987). *Personality/social/behavior subtypes of learning disabled young adults.* Unpublished doctoral dissertation, Southern Illinois University-Carbondale.

Lezak, M. D. (1983). *Neuropsychological assessment.* New York: Oxford University Press.

Mann, V. A., & Brady, S. (1988). Reading disability: The role of language deficiencies. *Journal of Consulting and Clinical Psychology, 56,* 811–816.

Money, J. (1966). On learning and not learning to read. In J. Money (Ed.), *The disabled reader: Education of the dyslexic child.* Baltimore, MD: Johns Hopkins University Press.

Morris, R., Blashfield, R., & Satz, P. (1986). Developmental classification of reading-disabled children. *Journal of Clinical and Experimental Clinical Neuropsychology, 8,* 371–392.

O'Donnell, J. P. (1983). Lateralized sensorimotor asymmetries in normal, learning-disabled, and brain-damaged young adults. *Perceptual and Motor Skills, 57,* 227–232.

O'Donnell, J. P. (1985). Language and visuospatial abilities in learning-disabled, brain-damaged, and nondisabled young adults. *Perceptual and Motor Skills, 60,* 807–814.

O'Donnell, J. P., Kurtz, J., & Ramanaiah, N. V. (1983). Neuropsychological test findings for normal, learning-disabled, and brain-damaged young adults. *Journal of Consulting and Clinical Psychology, 51,* 726–729.

O'Donnell, J. P., Randazzo, C. E., & Ramanaiah, N. V. (in press). *International Journal of Clinical Neuropsychology.*

O'Donnell, J. P., Romero, J., & Leicht, D. J. (1990). A comparison of language deficits in learning-disabled, head-injured, and nondisabled young adults: Results from an abbreviated Aphasia Screening Test. *Journal of Clinical Psychology, 46,* 310–315.

Overall, J. E. (1974). Validity of the Psychological Screening Inventory for psychiatric screening. *Journal of Consulting and Clinical Psychology, 42,* 717–179.

Phillips, F. L. (1986). *Subtypes among learning-disabled college students: A neuropsychological multivariate approach.* Unpublished doctoral dissertation, Southern Illinois University-Carbondale.

Porter, J. E., & Rourke, B. P. (1985). Socioemotional functioning of learning-disabled children: A subtypal analysis of personality patterns. In B. P. Rourke (Ed.), *Neuropsychology of learning disabilities: Essentials of subtype analysis.* New York: Guilford Press.

Reitan, R. M. (1986). Theoretical and methodological bases of the Halstead-Reitan Neuropsychological Test Battery. In I. Grant & K. M. Adams (Eds.), *Neuropsychological assessment of neuropsychiatric disorders* (pp. 3–30). New York: Oxford University Press.

Reitan, R. M., & Wolfson, D. (1985). *The Halstead-Reitan Neuropsychological Test Battery: Theory and clinical interpretation.* Tucson, AZ: Neuropsychology Press.

Rourke, B. P. (1976). Reading retardation in children: Developmental lag or deficit? In R. M. Knights & D. J. Bakker (Eds.), *Neuropsychology of learning disorders: Theoretical approaches.* Baltimore, MD: University Park Press.

Rourke, B. P., Young, G. C., Strang, J. D., & Russell, D. L. (1986). Adult outcomes of central processing deficiencies in childhood. In I. Grant & K. M. Adams (Eds.), *Neuropsychological assessment of neuropsychiatric disorders* (pp. 244–267). New York: Oxford University Press.

Satz, P., Rardin, D., & Ross, J. (1971). An evaluation of a theory of specific developmental dyslexia. *Child Development, 42,* 2009–2021.

Selz, M., & Reitan, R. M. (1979a). Rules for neuropsychological diagnosis: Classification of brain function in older children. *Journal of Consulting and Clinical Psychology, 47,* 258–264.

Selz, M., & Reitan, R. M. (1979b). Neuropsychological test performance of normal, learning-disabled, and brain-damaged children. *Journal of Nervous and Mental Disease, 167,* 298–302.

Speece, D. L., McKinney, J. D., & Appelbaum, M. I. (1985). Classification and validation of behavioral subtypes of learning disabled children. *Journal of Educational Psychology, 77,* 67–77.

Spreen, O. (1987). *Learning disabled children growing up: A follow-up into adulthood.* Berwyn, PA.: Swets North America.

Spreen, O. (1989). The relationship between learning disability, emotional disorders, and neuropsychology: Some results and observations. *Journal of Clinical and Experimental Neuropsychology, 11,* 117–140.

Strang, J. D., & Rourke, B. P. (1985). Arithmetic disability subtypes: the neuropsychological significance of specific arithmetical impairment in childhood. In B. P. Rourke (Ed.), *Neuropsychology of learning disabilities: Essentials of subtype analysis* (pp. 167–183). New York: Guilford Press.

Swiercinsky, D. P. (1979). Factorial pattern descriptions and comparison of factorial abilities in neuropsychological assessment. *Perceptual and Motor Skills, 48,* 231–241.

Swiercinsky, D. P., & Hallenbeck, C. E. (1975). A factorial approach to neuropsychological assessment. *Journal of Clinical Psychology, 31,* 610–618.

Wagner, R. K., & Torgesen, J. K. (1987). The nature of phonological processing and its causal role in the acquisition of reading skills. *Psychological Bulletin, 101,* 192–212.

Woodcock, R. W. (1978). *Development and standardization of the Woodcock-Johnson Psychoeducational Battery.* New York: Psychological Corporation.

CHAPTER FOURTEEN

Neuropsychological Subtypes of Learning Disabilities

Robert F. Newby
G. Reid Lyon

I. Introduction

It has been increasingly recognized over the last 25 years that the condition known as learning disabilities (LD) reflects a highly heterogeneous array of developmental disorders rather than a single entity. Several of the chapters in this volume illustrate this perspective by highlighting different types and dimensions of LD. Examination of subtypes is important in a volume on the neuropsychology of LD for two main reasons. First, one of the main contributions of neuropsychology to the LD field has been to identify and validate new taxonomies of LD subtypes (e.g., Rourke, 1985). Second, neuropsychological subtype systems have helped enrich neurocognitive explanations for why children with LD are similar to or different from each other (e.g., Bakker, 1984; Doehring, Trites, Patel, & Fiedorowicz, 1981).

This chapter will begin by presenting conceptual and methodological criteria for the identification of LD subtypes. The next two sections will outline major findings from relevant neuropsychological subtyping research with LD individuals. The reader should note that several recent reviews have covered this area in detail (e.g., Lyon, 1983; Lyon & Risucci, 1988; McKinney, 1984; Satz & Morris, 1981), with the most comprehensive review recently completed by Hooper and Willis (1989). Lyon and Flynn (1989b) also examined conceptual and validity requirements in conducting subtyping research. Given that these reviews are readily available and the literature in this area is quite extensive, this review is designed to be representative but not exhaustive. Within this context, 5 research programs are selected from over 100 available studies. These five were chosen because of their methodological characteristics, theoretical strengths, and/or representative standing in the subtyping literature. Although space does not permit a detailed methodological critique of each program, some evaluative comments will be provided.

The remainder of the chapter will focus on two selected topics. The first is a comparative analysis of several reading-disability subtype schemes. Reading is chosen because it represents a central problem for a significant number of LD children. Moreover, other content areas such as mathematics (Chapter 20) and nonverbal learning disabilities (Chapter 22) are addressed elsewhere in this volume. While no generally accepted consensus has been achieved on what are the most valid or useful reading-disability subtypes, we will suggest several lines of convergence in the field. Finally, a relatively new large collaborative program in Milwaukee, Wisconsin, on subtypes of dyslexia will be described, primarily to illustrate important steps that are needed to further validate LD subtypes in general.

II. General Considerations for Neuropsychological Subtyping

As LD subtype research has progressed over the years, increasingly rigorous conceptual and methodological demands have understandably been proposed by critical reviewers. Lyon and Flynn (1989b) outlined five criteria for an adequate subtype system:

A review of the development of classification systems in the behavioral and social sciences suggests that if a classification is to have predictive and communicative power, it should (1) be theory driven (Fletcher & Morris, 1986; Kavale & Forness, 1987b; Lyon, 1987; Skinner, 1981); (2) be based on variables that have theoretical relevance and adequate psychometric properties (Aldenderfer & Blashfield, 1986; Lyon & Risucci, 1989); (3) be developed on samples that are operationally defined (Fletcher & Morris, 1986; Speece, 1989); (4) be replicable and internally valid (Blashfield & Draguns, 1976; Skinner, 1981); and (5) be externally valid and thus useful for description, prediction, and clinical practice (Lyon, Moats, & Flynn, 1989; Lyon & Risucci, 1989).

At present, these criteria should be viewed as partially fulfilled goals rather than standard practice.

Most reviews of neuropsychological LD subtypes have divided them into clinical–inferential subtypes, those that are derived from clinical observation or theories relating to LD, and empirical subtypes, those that are derived through multivariate statistical methods. An alternative hypothesis to the notion that LD can be parceled into discrete subtypes is that LD children differ along one or more dimensions in continuous distributions (R. K. Olson, 1989; Stanovich, 1988). This notion is particularly relevant to certain kinds of reading disabilities and will be discussed further in the comparative analysis section.

III. Clinical–Inferential Subtypes

Early pioneers in LD subtype research used clinical observations to identify subtypes of disabled readers, often employing concepts from behavioral neurology. The clinical–inferential method begins with a concept or theory on what defines the different subtypes. Tests of the relevant mental processing variables that are hypothesized to differentiate the subtypes are then administered to a sample of LD children to study factors such as the prevalence of the different subtypes and the proportion of classifiable subjects. For instance, Kinsbourne and Warrington (1963, 1966) linked cerebral deficits with aphasia and the Gerstmann syndrome to reading disabilities with language retardation and sequential processing deficits, respectively. Mattis' group (Mattis, 1978; Mattis, French, & Rapin, 1975) distinguished dyslexics with language disorder, articulatory/graphomotor discoordination, and visual–spatial perceptual disorder. These early clinical–inferential schemes represented an alternative from previous views which implied or explicitly hypothesized that LD was a unitary homogeneous concept.

A mixture of support and criticism of these early ideas emerged over the years. Support has included frequent parallels between different systems, which are discussed further in the comparative analysis section below, and a number of educational validation studies. Educational validation (Lyon, 1985a; Lyon et al., 1989) refers to the clinically important process of testing whether different subtypes respond differently to alternative intervention methods. Criticisms of the clinical–inferential research have included small sample sizes, large age ranges, inadequate attention to gender, lack of normal comparisons or other carefully defined control groups, exclusion or absence of mixed syndrome groups from some studies, and questionable generalizability of the samples to more representative populations of learning-disabled children typically seen in schools (Lyon, 1983). In spite of being subject to many of these criticisms, the model provided by Boder is the first reviewed here because of its historical importance and extensive citation in the literature. More recent clinical–inferential subtype systems have addressed some of these problems, and several have illustrated strong grounding in theories of reading development, including the Bakker and Lovett programs, which are reviewed here in turn.

A. Boder's System

Boder (1970, 1971a, 1971b, 1973; Boder & Jarrico, 1982) classified children into a normal reading group, a group of nonspecific retarded readers, and three specific dyslexic subtypes on the basis of their word recognition and spelling performance. The reading problems of nonspecific retarded readers are not considered due to cognitive deficits. Dysphonetic dyslexics show deficient word analysis and word-attack skills resulting in an inability to sound out and blend the component letters and syllables of a word. Early problems with learning individual letter sounds often improve, but higher-order phonological processes such as holding sounds in working memory and integrating them into entire words continue. These problems with auditory analysis lead to frequent word substitutions based on minimal phonetic cues, such as *talk* for *toy*.

Dyseidetic dyslexics have problems with what Boder terms "whole-word gestalts," in the face of adequate phonetic decoding strategies. Their weak visual perception and visual memory for letters and for whole-word configurations impair the development of efficient sight-word vocabulary. Visuospatial letter and word reversals, the misconstrued "classic" sign of dyslexia in popular conceptions, are reported to be typical of this group. They have particular problems reading phonetically irregular words. For instance, dyseidetic dyslexics might produce the phonetic rendition *talc* for *talk*.

Mixed dysphonetic–dyseidetic dyslexics, or alexics, combine the cognitive deficits of the other two subtypes. Their typical misreadings are wild guesses from minimal morphological clues, such as *street* for *card*. Boder viewed this subtype as the most severely impaired, postulating that they seldom learned to read at all without aggressive intervention.

Through qualitative observations of children referred to neurology clinics for learning problems, Boder and Jarrico (1982) hypothesized that the mental processes in reading and spelling are interdependent and show characteristic patterns of deficits in dyslexia. Diagnosis is made primarily through comparing how many sight-read words can be spelled correctly versus how many nonsight-read words can be reproduced correctly or with good phonetic-equivalent misspellings. Qualitative analysis of reading miscues (oral reading errors) and of the balance of correctly read phonetically regular versus irregular words supplements the spelling test in diagnosis.

Boder's (1973) scheme has been one of the most heavily critiqued and widely researched of the LD subtype systems. Satz and Morris (1981) complimented her detailed clinical analyses and rational delineation of teaching methods. However, her classification procedures have been faulted because they are not theoretically grounded. Moreover, the Boder Test of Reading–Spelling Patterns (Boder & Jarrico, 1982), the primary tool for classification of readers, depends heavily on examiner judgment, has psychometric reliability weaknesses, and is not well normed (Alexander, 1984; Bing, 1985; Reynolds, 1984). It has also been reported that a dyseidetic pattern is sometimes indistinguishable from a mixed pattern until children receive training in phonics skills, and the differences in reading and spelling errors between groups could easily reflect differences in previous teaching and curricula rather than inherent mental processing deficits (Barr, 1974; Lyon, 1983). Some investigators (e.g., Roeltgen, 1985) have also questioned how closely reading and spelling symptoms parallel each other. Comprehensive reviews (e.g., Hooper & Willis, 1989, pp. 46–47) cited mixed validity support in approximately 20 research studies using the Boder diagnostic test, including comparisons among subtypes on electrophysiological measures, dichotic listening, and various neuropsychological tests; Boder's initial prevalence estimates that the dyslexic population is approximately 2/3 dysphonetic, 1/10 dyseidetic, and 1/4 mixed have received some support. While intuitively appealing, Boder's system needs further refinement to better reflect the complexity of the reading process (Hooper & Willis, 1989) and requires further educational validation along lines such as those in progress by Flynn (Lyon *et al.*, 1989).

B. Bakker's Balance Model

Bakker and colleagues (Bakker, 1980, 1983, 1984, 1988; Bakker & Licht, 1985; Bakker, Moerland, & Goekoop-Hoefkens, 1981; Bakker & Vinke, 1985) have extensively researched a two-subtype model for dyslexia based on a specific neuropsychological theory of reading development. In the early stages of normal reading acquisition, children are hypothesized to emphasize right-hemisphere-based perceptual strategies to learn letter shapes and interpret script. In order to become more efficient readers, however, they need to switch to presumably faster, left-hemisphere-based linguistic strategies to process text. As the reading process develops from single letters to words to sentences, there should be a normal shift from right- to left-hemisphere-mediated reading strategies (Hooper & Willis, 1989). Event-related potential studies of children at different grade-school levels have lent some support to this notion (Licht, Bakker, Kok, & Bouma, 1984), which is termed the *balance model,* based on the dynamic balance between the two underlying emphases at different points in reading development.

In the balance model, reading deficits are thought to develop when the child does not emphasize the correct process/hemisphere at the proper time. When the beginning reader relies on linguistic/left processing prematurely, linguistic or L-type dyslexia develops, characterized by fast but inaccurate reading with substantive errors such as omissions, additions, and substitutions. When the child has correctly emphasized perceptual/right processes early but fails to switch to more linguistic routes later, perceptual or P-type dyslexia ensues, with slow but generally accurate reading and time-consuming errors such as fragmentations and repetitions. Whereas virtually all other LD subtypes are labeled by their area of deficit (e.g., dysphonetic has deficit in phonics), Bakker's subtypes are labeled by the realm of cognitive overreliance or cerebral hemisphere of functional overdevelopment (e.g., L-type has left-hemisphere strength). Bakker and Licht (1985) have compared learning to read with learning to ride a horse, which works best when the rider begins with a slow, calm animal and then switches to a livelier, more quick steed as expertise is gained. In this metaphor, L types represent novice equestrians trying to learn to ride with too frisky a horse, whereas P types start with an appropriately slow, calm horse but fail to switch when they should.

The Bakker program presents a clear theoretical basis and provides multidimensional external validation evidence, although its internal validation is less strongly documented (Lyon & Risucci, 1989). Specifically, subtype diagnosis is made by measurement of ear advantage in dichotic listening tasks and miscue analysis of oral reading errors, each of which may have reliability problems. Mentally retarded children have been excluded, but mean IQs of research samples have been below average and no discrepancy between IQ and reading achievement is required. Thus, it is unclear how comparable these groups are to more conventionally defined LD samples.

Educational validation of the Bakker classification scheme has been strong. In a large study (Bakker & Vinke, 1985; Bakker et al., 1981) reading accuracy and efficiency of L types improved significantly after direct laboratory stimulation of the right hemisphere by flashing training words on computer monitors in their left visual fields only and by transmitting words to their left ears only with headphones. Analogous classroom methods to selectively stimulate the right hemisphere included mixing typefaces in text, but these had a less strong effect. P types tend to respond better to classroom methods that presumably stimulate the left hemisphere, such as rhyming exercises, than to direct laboratory left-hemisphere stimulation (Bakker, 1987). Significant correlations between changes in achievement and visual-event-related potential patterns in response to treatment are reported for both subtypes, in the direction predicted by the model (Bakker et al., 1981; Bakker & Vinke, 1985). Both types tend to become even more imbalanced in hemispheric reliance without intervention (Bakker & Vinke, 1985). More recent work by Bakker's group has considered hemisphere-specific tactile stimulation (Bouma, Bakker, & Gardien, 1988) and family factors (Van Strien, Bakker, Bouma, & Koops, 1988) in dyslexic subtypes.

Bakker et al.'s clear theoretical basis, elegant intertwining of electrophysiological and reading factors, and extensive branching into different aspects of dyslexia such as family histories represent strengths of this program. While creative, many of the instructional methods are too technical to apply pragmatically in school settings and involve elemental aspects of the reading process that may be too far removed from the ultimate goal of reading comprehension. Bakker *et al.*'s research on the balance model has been extensive, but there is a strong need for the model to be further validated in other research centers and cultural contexts.

C. Lovett and Colleagues' Investigations

Lovett (1984, 1987) proposed two subtypes of reading disability, building on the theory that word recognition develops in three successive phases. The three phases are related to response accuracy in identifying printed words, automatic recognition without the need to "sound out" words, followed by developmentally appropriate maximum speed as components of the reading process become consolidated in memory (Ehri & Wilce, 1983). Children who fail at the first phase are labeled accuracy disabled, and those who achieve age-appropriate word recognition but are markedly deficient in the second or third phase are called rate disabled. Accuracy disability does not result from an accuracy/speed trade-off, as children in this group are both inaccurate *and* slow readers. It is clear that Lovett's model satisfies the first of the general criteria for LD subtypes outlined above, that is, it is theory driven.

To avoid classification artifacts due to variations in the regularity, number, and complexity of stimuli among various standardized reading tests, children are classified as accuracy disabled only if they are substandard on four of five measures of untimed word recognition. Similar criteria are used to classify rate-disabled readers using tests of reading speed. Reading comprehension is not considered in diagnosis. Conventional criteria such as WISC-R verbal and performance IQ's within one standard deviation of the mean and a restricted age range of 8 to 13 years are specified.

Perhaps the greatest strength of the Lovett program is its extensive external validation. In a study of the two subtypes and a normal sample matched on word-recognition ability to the rate-disabled group ($N = 32$ per group), accuracy-disabled readers were deficient in a wide array of oral and written language areas. On the other hand, rate-disabled readers' deficiencies were more restricted to deficient connected text reading and spelling under some conditions (Lovett, 1987). Reading comprehension was impaired on all measures for the accuracy-disabled group and was highly correlated with word-recognition skill, but the rate-disabled group was impaired on only some comprehension measures.

In a well-designed large intervention study ($N = 110$) (Lovett, 1988; Lovett, Ransby, & Barron, 1988) the two subtypes responded differently to various treatment methods. The treatments consisted of (1) a decoding-skills

(DS) program which emphasized single-word recognition for both phonetically regular and exception words, (2) an oral and written language program (OWLS) which stressed contextual reading, listening and reading comprehension, vocabulary development, syntactical elaboration, and written composition, and (3) a classroom survival-skills program (CSS) which involved social skills, organizational strategies, and other instruction unrelated to reading development. The CSS program served as a control condition for nonspecific treatment effects. Word recognition improved significantly for both groups in the DS program, but only the rate-disabled group benefited substantially from the OWLS program. These findings suggested that children need better-developed overall language abilities to benefit from OWLS as compared to DS. Greater gains on exception words than on regular words in both groups suggested that the success of the DS program may relate to greater reliance on orthographic pattern recognition in dyslexics and/or the greater opportunity to develop automaticity that the exception instruction procedure afforded over the word-family regular-word instruction procedure. As neither group increased reading speed in response to any treatment, it was speculated that interventions longer than the 40 hours afforded would be necessary to improve rate/automaticity. In an expanded study with a larger sample ($N = 178$) (Lovett, Ransby, Hardwick, & Johns, 1989), the DS program yielded greater generalization of word-recognition skills than the OWLS program. However, this was not attributable to gains in knowledge of grapheme–phoneme correspondence rules, as the latter did not change. Vocabulary-knowledge improvements in the OWLS program were limited to words that were directly trained, but these gains could not be detected on standardized tests of the same skills. Interestingly, the two subtypes in the expanded sample were combined for all analyses because preliminary analyses suggested similar responses to all treatments across subtypes.

Lovett's program is founded on an explicit developmental reading theory, illustrates methodological robustness, and offers detailed, thoughtful alternative explanations for the voluminous, complex external validation findings. Important treatment-outcome findings are muted somewhat by clinically minimal reading gains on standardized measures, such as WRAT-R word recognition, in spite of statistically significant results (Lyon & Flynn, 1989a) and by the lack of subtype × treatment interactions in the final study. As with Bakker's work, Lovett's program needs to be validated by other researchers in other centers to increase confidence in the generalizability of her findings. Lovett and her colleagues are moving away from reliance on a scheme of discrete subtypes in favor of individual-difference models involving continuous distributions along various dimensions (Lovett, Benson, & Olds, in press).

IV. Empirical Subtypes

Two research programs illustrate the care, thoroughness, and interpretive caution that are necessary in deriving LD subtypes empirically with multivariate statistics. The basic approach here has been to use statistical clustering or sorting algorithms to group large numbers of subjects with similar profiles on a battery of tests into relatively homogeneous groups. These methods can address more complex performance patterns with greater reliability than the clinical–inferential approach. Statistical methods also can be used to identify underlying natural relationships in the data that may escape detection by human judges.

The most extensive discussion and illustration of these methods to date is an edited volume by Rourke (1985). Typically, a large number of scores on tests of mental functions or questionnaire ratings of behavioral problem areas is used to sort a large sample of subjects into homogeneous groups using Q-type factor analysis or cluster analysis. Rourke's own extensive subtyping programs have illustrated both methods. Q-type factor analysis, used in an early empirical study that replicated several LD subtypes across three age groups (Fisk & Rourke, 1979), has the advantage of calculating the similarity of profile patterns in a population. However, the Q-factor method has been criticized because it assumes that a linear model applies to all people, yields ambiguous classification when a subject loads on more than one factor, and artificially limits the number of factors to one less than the number of tests. Due to these criticisms, cluster analysis has predominated in more recent studies by Rourke and other research groups in the 1980s, such as a study of children who had the ACID pattern on the WISC (Del Dotto & Rourke, 1985). Cluster analysis has come into favor because multiple clustering methods can be compared for internal validation. However, cluster analysis is not based on a clearly articulated, generally accepted statistical foundation, as is factor analysis (Fletcher & Satz, 1985), and does not address construct validity completely (see Obrzut, 1987). Occasionally, Q-type factor analysis and cluster analysis have replicated subtypes in the same set of data (e.g., Del Dotto & Rourke, 1985), but such convergence is rare (Fletcher & Satz, 1985).

It is well recognized that these statistical procedures contain a critical potential pitfall. Specifically, they can yield apparently meaningful classifications even with random data. Therefore, considerable care must go into choosing the most appropriate subjects, variables, criteria for similarity, cluster methods, number of clusters interpreted, and validation procedures (Morris, Satz, & Blashfield, 1981). One particularly important theoretical issue is whether to base the subtypes on manifest academic variables or on more "underlying" neuropsychological variables. Doehring's group (Doehring & Hoshko, 1977; Doehring et al., 1981), for instance, defined its subtypes by Q-factor analysis of reading behaviors. In a second phase, Doehring et al. externally validated their groups by comparing them on an extensive set of language measures and a neuropsychological battery. More extensive discussion of both theoretical and technical issues regarding empirical classification methods is beyond the scope of this chapter and is available elsewhere (Aldenderfer & Blashfield, 1986; Fletcher & Satz, 1985; Speece, 1989).

Two series of studies are reviewed here to illustrate the empirical approach to classification. Satz et al.'s program uses a longitudinal design, and Lyon et al.'s program emphasizes educational-validation studies.

A. The Florida Longitudinal Program and Related Studies

Satz and colleagues (Fletcher & Satz, 1985; Morris, Blashfield, & Satz, 1986; Morris et al., 1981) used data from the Florida Longitudinal Project to define subtypes of both normal and LD students. The Florida study was designed to examine neuropsychological, achievement, developmental, and other aspects of the groups under study and to identify early predictors of reading disability. Thus reading development was longitudinally studied across the elementary school grades, beginning with extensive examination of virtually all of the white males entering kindergarten in one county. Classification research was initiated at a later point by applying cluster analyses to subsamples at grades two and five. A unique contribution of this program was its inclusion of both normal and LD children, which verified that cluster-analysis methods can identify valid LD subtypes which are distinct from variants of normal learning patterns.

In the first of a series of classification studies (Fletcher & Satz, 1985; Morris et al., 1981), average-linkage hierarchical agglomerative cluster analysis with iterative partitioning on the reading, spelling, and arithmetic subtests of the Wide-Range Achievement Test (WRAT) yielded nine subgroups at grade two ($N = 236$). Six of these had normal achievement, one was average in reading and spelling but deficient in math, and two showed global learning problems in all three academic areas. Only 4% of the sample was not classifiable and were considered "outliers." Data from the two global-learning-problem groups ($N = 89$) were submitted to a "second stage" cluster analysis, which analyzed performance scores from a number of verbal (receptive vocabulary, word similarities, verbal fluency) and visual–spatial (geometric copying, recognition–discrimination) neuropsychological variables. Five reliable LD subtypes were identified: globally verbally impaired (30%), specifically verbally impaired in verbal fluency only (16%), visuospatially impaired (26%), impaired both verbally and visually (11%), and an unexpected subtype with normal neuropsychological performance with the existence of poor achievement (14%). This latter group was achieving at normal levels by fifth grade (Satz & Morris, 1981).

Internal validity of both the nine- and five-group solutions was demonstrated in several ways. Alternative cluster-analysis methods and split-sample analyses yielded similar subgroups with minimal group-membership changes for individuals. Adding subjects from the subtype that was deficient in arithmetic only or from a superior-achieving subtype maintained the stability of the initial cluster structures and created new clusters for the added subjects. Adding measures to the analyses did not change cluster-profile shape and changed membership for only 12% of the sample. Monte Carlo simulation studies with randomly generated data suggested that the subtypes were not artifacts of the methods or sample, although the correspondence between some simulated and some actual profiles raised questions about this. The five LD clusters were externally validated by observing significant differences on various neuropsychological variables, neurological soft signs and stigmata, parental achievement-test performance, and socioeconomic status. Impressively, the cluster structures from this study were largely, though not completely, replicated in a separate U.S. research center that included females in the sample (Johnston, Fennell, & Satz, 1987) and in a Dutch sample (Van der Vlugt & Satz, 1985). The LD children in the latter sample in particular were lower than the original Florida children on both achievement and neuropsychological measures.

One of the most productive uses of the Florida data was the development of a longitudinal cluster-analysis method (Fletcher & Satz, 1985; Morris *et al.*, 1986). This represented a separate study using the same data set outlined above. Instead of clustering on a set of tests taken all at the same time, eight neuropsychological measures (four verbal, four visual–spatial) at three different ages (kindergarten, grade two, grade five) were combined in one analysis. This method defines clusters on the basis of patterns of neuropsychological performances *and* changes in these patterns across time. Similar clustering methods as used in the previous studies by this research group yielded three learning-problem clusters and two clusters of average to above-average students. Two of the LD clusters were characterized by important changes in selected neuropsychological functions across time. For example, one LD cluster, while initially manifesting both verbal and visual–spatial deficits at preschool and early school ages, markedly improved visual–spatial skills to average to above-average levels by the fifth grade. Conversely, a second LD cluster with average verbal and below-average visual–spatial skills at preschool age declined in verbal capabilities over time. Children in two normal clusters and the general-cognitive-deficiency cluster demonstrated stable neuropsychological characteristics over time.

Satz *et al.*'s (Fletcher & Satz, 1985; Morris *et al.*, 1981, 1986) subtype research demonstrates psychometric adequacy and internal validity. In addition, an elegant elaboration of cluster-analysis methodology and partial replication with diverse samples are features of these studies. The authors acknowledge that more recent developments in LD research would make measures of attention, memory, and psycholinguistic skills advisable in this type of subtype derivation (Fletcher & Satz, 1985). On the other hand, while some theoretical notions such as Bakker's (1979) developmental model for reading are drawn into the cluster interpretations post hoc, the Satz program's theoretical foundation is relatively weak. External validation is demonstrated in several ways, but not in the critical area of treatment response. The longitudinal nature of this set of studies is particularly commendable.

B. Lyon and Colleagues' Cluster and Educational-Validation Studies

Lyon and co-workers defined six reading-disability subtypes with cluster analyses of neuropsychological tests (Lyon & Watson, 1981). The theoretical viewpoint guiding this subtype research was based on Luria's (1966, 1973) notion that reading ability is a complex behavior effected by means of a complex functional system of cooperating zones of the cerebral cortex and subcortical structures. Within the context of this theoretical framework, a deficit in any one or several zones of the functional system may impede the acquisition of fluent reading behavior. As such, one could hypothesize the existence of several subtypes of disabled readers, each characterized by different patterns of neuropsychological deficits in subskills relevant to reading acquisition (i.e., linguistic abilities, perceptual skills, attentional mechanisms). The reader is referred to Lyon (1983) for a discussion of neuropsychological functional-systems theory and subtype research in LD.

The subtype solution obtained in the Lyon and Watson (1981) study was then externally validated with achievement measures (Lyon, Rietta, Watson, Borch, & Rhodes, 1981). A second subtype study was carried out with a younger sample of LD readers (Lyon, Stewart, & Freedman, 1982), and the subtype solutions obtained with older and younger subjects were educationally validated through a series of subtype-teaching-method intervention studies (Lyon, 1983, 1985b). Lyon's quantitative, qualitative, and theoretical analysis of derived subtypes and intervention programs is highlighted here. The overall research program has been summarized in detail elsewhere (Lyon, 1983, 1985a; Lyon & Flynn, 1989a; Lyon & Moats, 1988).

Over the course of this research program, the linguistic and perceptual-test performance of two separate samples of 11- to 12-year-old children ($N = 100$ each) (Lyon, 1983; Lyon & Watson, 1981) and one sample of 6- to 9-year-old children ($N = 75$) (Lyon *et al.*, 1982) was cluster analyzed to define LD reading subtypes. The measures selected for subtype-pattern identification were chosen for use because of (1) their previous use in empirical and clinical neuropsychological subtype research, (2) their availability for use in the public schools, and (3) their usefulness in assessing selected linguistic and perceptual components of the neuropsychological functions hypothesized to subserve the developmental reading process (see Luria, 1973; Lyon, 1983). A description of each of the measures and their relationship to specific reading impairments is provided in Lyon *et al.* (1982).

As in the Satz *et al.* studies, consistent results with different variable subsets and clustering algorithms supported the internal validity of the six older and five younger subtypes that were found. Cluster solutions from standardized scores based on local normal control samples were compared to solutions using raw test scores. Univariate and multivariate analyses of variance of the neuropsychological and academic test-score differences among groups provided validation, as did discriminant analyses defining dimensions that contributed to separation of the subtypes.

Lyon provided detailed qualitative descriptions of the subtypes and compared them to subtypes found by other researchers such as Satz (Satz & Morris, 1981) and Mattis (Mattis *et al.*, 1975) (see especially Lyon *et al.*, 1982). For instance, one subtype was depressed on all language measures but strong on visual–perceptual skills. Another subtype showed selective deficits in language comprehension and sound blending. These groups were similar to Satz's (Morris *et al.*, 1981) general and specific language-deficit types in that they understandably tended to show poor word-attack (phonetic) skills in reading and spelling errors. In contrast, a subtype that was deficient only on a visual–motor integration task made most of their oral reading errors when attempting to read phonetically irregular words, with less impaired reading in context and reading comprehension. Mixed verbal–perceptual deficit groups and an "unexpected" group with normal neuropsychological profiles were also found. The mixed groups had problems with both sight-vocabulary and word-attack skills. Groups with severe auditory comprehension and verbal memory-span deficits tended to have the lowest reading skills. Neuropsychological hypotheses for the differences among subtypes were offered tentatively and relied heavily on Luria's (1966, 1973) functional systems theory.

Following the identification of subtypes, the Lyon group attempted to externally validate the subtype solutions with a series of subtype-intervention studies. With the older LD group (Lyon, 1983), matched samples of five children from each of six subtypes received 1 hour per week of instruction in synthetic phonics (Traub & Bloom, 1975) for 26 weeks, in addition to their regular classroom instruction. Synthetic phonics teaches major phonics concepts in a sequence of reading and writing exercises beginning with individual letters and then progressing to increasingly complex consonant and vowel combinations in words. The subtypes with isolated visual–motor deficits and normal neuropsychological profiles were the only ones to show significant gains in individual word recognition after instruction. It was hypothesized that an absence of auditory–verbal deficits was associated with better response to a linguistically/phonetically oriented intervention.

The intervention study with the younger LD group (Lyon, 1985b) used only the subtype with selective linguistic and verbal expressive deficits, in the context of robust visual–perceptual–motor–memory strengths. This group had been likened to Boder's (Boder & Jarrico, 1982) dysphonetic dyslexics and other similar subtypes from several clinical–inferential and empirical subtype systems (Lyon *et al.*, 1982). Ten subjects were randomly assigned to one of two different 30-hour treatment programs over a 10-week period. The first program was synthetic phonics, described above. The second combined sight word, contextual analysis, structural analysis, and analytic phonics. This included rapid whole-word recognition, syntactic analysis of suffixes, and emphasis on metalinguistic awareness that reading is a meaningful language skill. Over the course of instruction, children in the combined method gained an average of 11 percentile points in word recognition versus 1 percentile point for the synthetic-phonics group; these differences were statistically significant. Apparently, the auditory receptive and auditory expressive language deficits that characterized these children impeded response to a reading instructional method that required learning letter–sound correspondences in isolation followed by blending and contextual reading components. Whole-word reading may have placed less linguistic demand on these readers.

Several limitations of these outcome studies must be acknowledged. First, pragmatics of subject availability necessitated small sample sizes and precluded full examination of possible aptitude × treatment interactions. Second, it is difficult to determine if the effects should be attributed to subtype characteristics, the instructional program, the interaction between the two, the teacher, the time spent in remediation, or previous or concomitant educational experience. Third, the subtype identification itself was limited by the range and kinds of tasks that provided data for the cluster analysis. For example, the test battery did not provide adequate fine-grained coverage of some linguistic factors (particularly phonology) implicated in the developmental reading process (Lyon & Flynn, 1989a). Nonetheless, these studies represent an important beginning in the important task of determining the pragmatic instructional implications of LD subtype research.

V. Comparative Analysis of Reading Subtype Programs

Hynd and Cohen (1983) summarized many lines of research suggesting that three broad subtypes of reading disabilities have predominated in the literature. These are a dichotomy of auditory–linguistic dyslexics with difficulties in verbal aspects of reading versus a visuospatial group with visual processing deficits (Pirozzolo, 1979), and a group with mixed deficits of both types. The preponderance of clinical–inferential schemes posit dichotomies along these lines. Several empirical subtype researchers who have compared their derived groups to subtypes proposed or derived in other studies (e.g., Fisk & Rourke, 1979; Fletcher & Satz, 1985; Lyon et al., 1982) have addressed this dichotomy. While this dichotomous characterization may ultimately represent an oversimplification of the most valuable reading-disabilities subtypes that can be educationally validated, the convergence deserves some examination. As Lyon (1983) cautioned, however, conceptual comparisons among subtypes in different research programs do not constitute stringent validation, because of differences in critical issues such as test variables, subject ages, and sample-selection criteria. No judgment about the relative overall superiority of one subtype scheme over others is intended here. The discussion is intended to focus only on the auditory–linguistic versus visuospatial distinction rather than to reflect a comprehensive analysis and comparison of all reported subtype possibilities.[1]

Boder's dysphonetic, Satz's and Lyon's general and specific language deficit, Bakker's P type, and Lovett's accuracy-disabled subgroups all manifest features characteristic of the auditory–linguistic category. Boder's definition is the most elemental, focusing specifically on the deficit in phonological processing in reading and spelling. Researchers have criticized Boder's weak psychometrics and her assumption that basic reading processes can be distinguished using spelling-error analysis. However, a significant set of researchers has paralleled her focus and supported the finding that the most prevalent reading-disability subtype is distinguished by deficits in phonological skills, to include deficiencies in sound segmentation, holding multiple phonemes in working memory, and blending or integrating sounds. The large amount of data supporting the importance of phonological deficits in specific reading disability is exemplified by the work of Stanovich (1988) and in a review by Wagner and Torgeson (1987).

Within a language-deficit model, phonological processing difficulties can be separated from concerns about broader language issues. Satz's and Lyon's empirically derived general language-deficit groups represent the other end of a continuum in their reference to a broad array of language problems including comprehension, vocabulary, fluency, and naming. This is probably because they were derived on the basis of more broad cognitive/

---

1 For purposes of brevity, references to the models discussed are omitted in this section. Readers should consult the sections above for references to original works by the researchers and models cited.

neuropsychological measures rather than on detailed aspects of the reading process itself. The specific language-deficit groups found by Satz and Lyon are based more directly on problems with verbal fluency and sequential comprehension, respectively, than on phonology; both researchers pointed out that fine-grained tests of phonology were not included in the neuropsychological batteries in their studies. Bakker's system defines P types in yet a different way, that is, lateralized preference in speech perception and qualitative analysis of reading miscues. Data from these measures identify a group that he interprets as overemphasizing the perceptual basis of reading but may also have a deficit in some aspect of language processing. Lovett's extensive external validation work clearly indicates broad oral and written language deficits in accuracy-disabled readers, including phonology.

Boder's dyseidetic, Satz's and Lyon's visual–perceptual, Bakker's L type, and (less obviously) Lovett's rate-disabled groups can be related to the general concept of visual–spatial dyslexia. Boder's concept relates most closely to the dimension of orthographic processing, that is, recognition and memory of exact word configurations, largely because her diagnostic procedures are the only ones that rely heavily on spelling. Full orthographic representation of words is necessary for accurate spelling and for irregular word reading, whereas phonological processing and/or partial orthographic representations of words are sufficient (albeit slow) for most word recognition (Frith, 1983).

Because Satz's and Lyon's visual–perceptual subtypes were based on tests with only indirect relationship to reading (e.g., drawing and visual form recognition), they are probably identifying an overlapping but largely different visual–spatial group from Boder. Convergence among the Boder versus empirically based findings is supported by the predominance of irregular-word (versus phonetically regular word) oral reading errors in the visual–perceptual group (Lyon & Flynn, 1989a). However Satz and Lyon found a much higher prevalence of their visual–spatial subtypes within reading-disabled samples than dyseidetics have typically shown, suggesting that there is overlap but not identity between the different schemes in this area. Olson *et al.* (R. K. Olson, 1989; R. Olson, Wise, Conners, & Rack, 1988) presented twin-study data indicating a much higher genetic heritability for phonological than orthographic reading skills, which were more closely related to environmental factors such as instructional history. J. M. Flynn (personal communication, April 21, 1988; Flynn & Deering, 1989) found increased theta activity in EEG measures of dyseidetics versus other normal and disabled readers during reading and reading-related tasks. She suggested that the dyseidetic group may be distinguished by a maladaptive overuse of phonics rather than a specific visual–spatial deficit per se. At least some children who fall into subtypes related to visual–spatial factors may have had an overemphasis on phonics in prior instruction. Lovett's rate-disabled group resembles dyseidetics in their slow word-recognition skills. However, external validation research suggested that this group's core deficit was in speed of naming of visually presented symbols and pictures (Lovett, 1987). Thus, rate disability is probably more validly interpreted as a language deficit than as a visual–spatial problem.

Several additional issues place important contexts and limitations on the interpretation of the broad auditory–linguistic versus visuospatial subtype conceptualizations. First, the dichotomy is not exhaustive of what has been proposed and found in the literature. For instance, Mattis's subtype with naming problems was important in their studies, though they have not been replicated by the empirical methods discussed above. Both Satz and Lyon found "unexpected" subtypes with learning deficits in otherwise normal neuropsychological profiles, which may represent developmental variants or students who were misidentified as LD because of environmental, instructional, and/or poor reading-strategy factors rather than central-processing deficits. Although it may be argued that the particular neuropsychological batteries used in Satz's and Lyon's studies were not sensitive enough or did not assess the appropriate areas of underlying deficit, the fact that Satz's unexpected group normalized their reading by fifth grade would argue that neuropsychological deficits may not in fact exist in this group.

In addition to "unexpected" subtypes, globally impaired mixed subtypes have been identified in both clinical–inferential and empirical programs. Mixed dyslexics may be interpreted as truly a combination of some linguistic deficits and perceptual or orthographic deficits or, more parsimoniously, as more severe manifestations of a single core deficit such as phonological processing. In fact, the only difference between the dysphonetic and mixed groups in Boder's test criteria is severity of reading level, not pattern of strengths and weaknesses. The clinical importance of the distinction between milder and more severe mixed groups in the empirical studies is unknown.

The recurrent verbal–visual subtype dichotomy outlined here may be more appropriately seen as two continuous dimensions of reading ability rather than as discrete subtypes. Stanovich (1988) argues for the dimensional view because individual performances on measures of phonological and orthographic processing appear to be more widely scattered than discretely clumped. Kavale and Forness (1987a) actually suggest that classification of LD children is premature at this stage and that more fundamental description of underlying dimensions of reading disability should be identified first.

Finally, some of the subtype schemes reviewed here embody explicit or implicit theories of reading development, which often differ in spite of superficial similarities in their descriptions of the manifest characteristics of the subtypes. One of the most striking instances of this is Boder's (implicit) model that slower, phonetic reading is supplemented with quicker, visual reading over the course of development. This is in contrast to Bakker's (explicit) theory that early perceptual emphasis gives way to more efficient linguistic processing as reading matures. Bakker's theory would predict that L-type problems should be more apparent at younger ages and P-type problems might not be likely to emerge until later in reading development. Satz's developmental subtype that improved visual–spatial functioning over time might, given Boder's implicit model, be expected to increase reading proficiency at later ages. Data relevant to these predictions have not been presented to date. Satz's second developmental subtype, with persistent yet stable visual–spatial deficits and declining verbal functioning over time, may represent a "Matthew effect" (Stanovich, 1986), whereby deficient specific reading subskills (e.g., visual–spatial) lead to declining cognitive functioning in other areas (e.g., verbal) in part because of reduced exposure to information and other sources of language development in print over time. Lovett's developmental theory, among the most explicitly elaborated of those reviewed here, bears more relationship with information-processing models of automatic and effortful processing than with the linguistic–perceptual dichotomy.

VI. The Milwaukee Dyslexia Research and Instruction Program

This large intervention program illustrates the clinical–inferential approach to defining reading-disability subtypes and a multifaceted procedure for validating the subtypes. The subtypes represent the two primary strains discussed in the previous section and are here labeled phonological and orthographic dyslexia. It is clearly acknowledged that we may be dealing with dimensions of the reading deficit rather than discrete groupings of children. In fact, the labels for the two groups considered in this program are derived from dimensional conceptualizations discussed by R. Olson *et al.* (1988) and R. K. Olson 1985; R. K. Olson, Kliegl, Davidson, & Foltz, 1985). The discrete-subtype approach is taken here for pragmatic instructional and heuristic reasons. Early results of this research program have been reported previously (Caldwell, Recht, & Newby, 1987; Newby, Caldwell, & Recht, 1989; Newby, Recht, & Caldwell, 1989; Recht, Caldwell, & Newby, 1988).

The theory underlying this program of investigation has two tiers. The first was based primarily on Boder's dysphonetic and dyseidetic subtypes, in connection with the broader themes relevant to these groups outlined in the previous section. The existence and importance of mixed and/or other subtypes was acknowledged but not included in the program for the purpose of focusing intensively on what were felt to be the essential deficits or dimensions for most dyslexic children. It was hypothesized that phonological dyslexic children might have relative weaknesses in sequential mental processing (Das, Kirby, & Jarman, 1975; Kaufman & Kaufman, 1983) and/or verbal processing, with relative strengths in simultaneous mental processing and/or visual–spatial functions. Orthographic dyslexics were presumed to have the opposite pattern, that is, simultaneous and/or visual–spatial weaknesses versus sequential and/or verbal strengths. Neuropsychologically based conceptions of rehabilitation (Ellis, 1985) and predominant trends in the LD field suggest that core deficit areas in LD children may not be trainable to a great extent, thus instruction should focus on compensating for weak mental processing areas by enhancing stronger areas. Besides the converse areas of relative strength for the two subtypes just outlined, dyslexic children of both subtypes were hypothesized to have relatively intact higher-order comprehension and metacognitive processes, in contrast with "garden-variety" poor readers who have many low general cognitive skills along with poor component reading skills (Stanovich, 1988). Both the general and subtype-specific areas of presumed strength guided the design of intervention strategies.

The second theoretical tier draws from Mason's (1984) and Frith's (1985) models of reading development and from Perfetti's (1988) theory of the nature of the reading process. This tier bears partial relationship to the discrete subtypes themselves, but it is central to conceptualization of instruction and remediation. Reading is presumed to develop through several stages. The first, logographic, involves learning the visual forms of the letters of the alphabet, memorizing visual gestalts of a few simple words and using pictures accompanying text as an aid to word recognition. Then the child moves into the alphabetic phase, where phonetic analysis predominates in increasing complexity. Word recognition then needs to become more efficient and automatic, which occurs in the orthographic phase, when whole-word perception or sight vocabulary is emphasized. The latter two phases represent the two main routes to word recognition, and both are important underpinnings for reading efficiency and for the development of higher-order reading skills, even though the phonological route is the most frequently observed prime obstacle in most recent studies of specific reading disability (Stanovich, 1988).

In addition to shifting from phonological to orthographic emphases in the decoding process, good readers need to become automatic in some aspects of their encoding of the semantic elements of text. This proceeds in four phases. The first is single-word meaning assignment. Next propositions are extracted; these are several-word actor–action or descriptor–object units in text (for instance, "The brown dog barked" has two propositions: "The dog barked" and "the dog is brown"). Third, the meaning of groups of propositions across sentences is integrated. This phase is evidenced by the habit of good readers remembering semantics, not syntax, when recalling what they have read. Fourth, readers must become aware of the construction and constraints of different text structures, such as narrative (story) versus expository (descriptive, explanatory) texts. Because higher-level meaning integration and construction of text models require dedicated attention, which has limitations in human mental processing, the steps of single-word and propositional encoding must become automatic. This hierarchical model of automatic and attended-to processes in reading is termed verbal efficiency theory (Perfetti, 1988).

The instruction program outlined below uses training in basic word recognition, comprehension, and strategies for reading in an attempt to dedicate more attention to the critical higher-order reading processes that strengthen meaning acquisition. Training in word recognition alone has been painfully slow or limited in successfully remediating dyslexia in previous research. The question of how much higher-order instruction dyslexics can productively use has yet to be answered, although some of Lovett *et al.*'s (1988) findings have suggested that some types of dyslexics fail to benefit from a complex whole-language type of approach.

In addition to the above theoretical foundations, the Milwaukee program embodies several pragmatic assumptions and educational values. First, reading is ultimately a meaning-acquisition process, so both word recognition and comprehension should be crucial aspects of instruction programs. Second, we wanted to use teaching methods that are relevant and available to the typical LD or reading specialist in schools. The myriad of methods in current reading practice afforded a wide choice on this criterion. Third, diagnostic criteria were designed using established, reliable clinical instruments. This was done to maximize applicability and to take advantage of presently available normative data rather than relying on experimental tests. Finally, we believe that educational validation is the most important test of LD subtype systems.

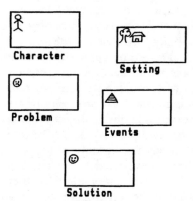

FIGURE 1   Story map for phonological dyslexia.

Following these theoretical notions and assumptions, two treatment methods were designed to match each subtype's presumed processing strengths. These methods have been applied in twice-weekly 60-minute individual tutoring sessions with reading specialists. Certain general procedures are the same for both methods. Each session focuses on one 200- to 800-word narrative story at the child's reading instructional level and on 3 to 5 vocabulary words which have been preselected to be among the most meaning-bearing units in the story and which the child cannot read in isolation. Reading comprehension is emphasized by teaching children story-grammar mapping. Story grammar (Baker & Stein, 1978) describes the parts of a well-formed story: setting, characters, problem, events, and resolution of the problem. These parts are intuitively understood by adults (Stein, 1979) but are not well understood or utilized by children (Spiegel & Fitzgerald, 1986). Explicit instruction and directed practice in selecting and recording the story-grammar elements has enhanced the reading comprehension of average readers (Whaley, 1981) and generally poor readers (Fitzgerald & Spiegel, 1983) but has not been studied with a specific dyslexic population. Tutors place an emphasis on teaching children to be strategic in their reading, to problem solve, to verbalize processes that have been efficient for them, and to use a meaning-vocabulary approach to new words. The students' conscious recall of these metacognitive elements of the instruction is assessed periodically. In instruction for phonological dyslexics, children are taught to first focus on the main idea or gestalt of the story and then to visually image the story and to draw or outline the story on key cards (see Fig. 1) in any order. Word instruction is a multisensory sight-word approach using visual–auditory and tracing elements. In instruction for orthographic dyslexics, children verbally rehearse the story and map the essential elements in sequential order (see Fig. 2). Word instruction is an analytic phonics approach emphasizing word

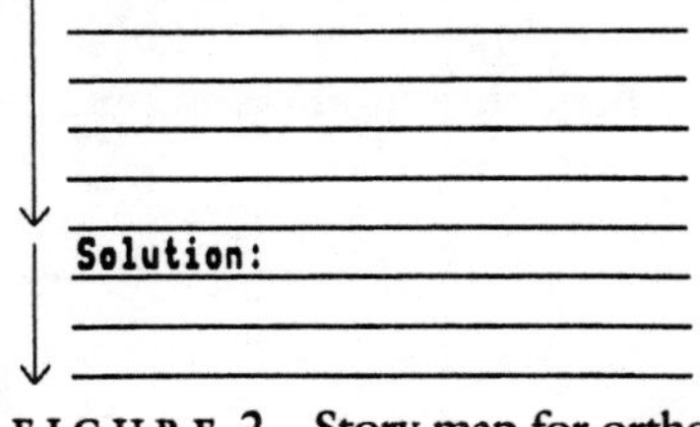

FIGURE 2   Story map for orthographic dyslexia.

sounds, roots, and blending. In both methods, teachers use the initial stories to illustrate each component and then gradually shift responsibility for identification to the students.

An initial study (Caldwell *et al.,* 1987; Newby, Caldwell, & Recht, 1989) demonstrated significant treatment gains in reading comprehension for four out of five subjects using a single-subject multiple baseline design. Subtype assignment at this stage of the project relied primarily on the Boder test (Boder & Jarrico, 1982) (and the original manuscript used Boder's labels for the subtypes), so diagnostic reliability questions may be raised. In this study, most subjects exhibited the hypothesized pattern of strengths in sequential and simultaneous mental processing (Kaufman & Kaufman, 1983). However, a study by Hooper and Hynd (1985) showed a lack of correspondence between Boder's (Boder & Jarrico, 1982) classifications and the KABC[2]. In addition, our own experience was that the correspondence between the subtypes' sequential–simultaneous processing often did not hold up in subsequent pilot work, thus we presumed that subtypes of basic word-identification deficits may not parallel types of higher-order cognitive processing. These considerations led to deemphasis of the sequential–simultaneous distinction in diagnostic criteria in later evolutions of the program outlined below.

Baseline treatment in the initial study consisted of 2 to 6 1-hour individual tutoring sessions with traditional remedial reading methods. Experimental treatment involved 8 to 12 sessions using only the treatment type matched to each subject's strength, thus it is unknown if treatment effects were attributable to specific strength-matched methods or to strategies instruction in general. It should also be noted that three of the four subjects who improved were in the orthographic subtype, suggesting that this group may be easier to help than those with core phonological problems.

A larger study currently in progress has the following parameters. Subjects are 92 children aged 8 to 11 years who meet historically conventional criteria for diagnosis of dyslexia. All have average intelligence (WISC-R verbal or performance IQ ≥ 90) and marked delay on a number of reading measures [standard scores < 90 on three out of four of the following: Woodcock Reading Mastery-Revised (WRMT-R), Word Identification and Passage Comprehension (Woodcock, 1987); Qualitative Reading Inventory (QRI) (Leslie & Caldwell, 1989), word recognition and reading comprehension in connected text]. Children with primary emotional/behavioral disturbance, uncorrected vision or hearing problems, or inadequate educational opportunity were excluded.

---

2 Kaufman Assessment Battery for Children.

Subtypes are assigned by two of the following three criteria:

Phonological	*Orthographic*
1. Dysphonetic spelling pattern on modified Boder test with a restricted range of eligible unknown spelling words.	1. Dyseidetic spelling pattern on modified Boder test with a restricted range of eligible unknown spelling words.
2. WRMT-R word-attack standard score < 85.	2. WRMT-R word-attack standard score > 85.
3. Discrepancy between regular and irregular words correct at frustrational level on Boder > 25%.	3. Discrepancy between regular and irregular words correct at frustrational level on Boder < 25%.

The psychometric weaknesses of the Boder test were addressed by modifying the selection of spelling words on the Boder (J. M. Flynn, personal communication, April 21, 1988) and by adding the psychometrically stronger Woodcock word-attack paradigm. These additions probably contributed to the present evidence for the validity of the subtypes.

Initial external validation was demonstrated on the first set of 31 phonological children and 18 orthographic children. The two groups were not significantly different on age (M = 9.5 years, range 7.4 to 11.3), sex (80% male), grade placement (M = 3.2, range 2 to 6), overall reading instructional level (M = second grade, range preprimer to third grade), socioeconomic status (M Hollingshead 4-factor = 44, range 23 to 66), or any IQ measures (full-scale IQ M = 103.4, range 85 to 124). Measures of rhyming, word segmentation, phonological integration, orthographic and phonological processing (R. K. Olson *et al.*, 1985), verbal and nonverbal memory storage and retrieval (selective reminding paradigm), and parent-rated and clinically tested attention were given to each group. Reliable differences between the groups in higher-level phonological skills, and trends toward developmental differences in lower-level phonological skills and toward an orthographic/phonological double dissociation, supported the validity of the subtypes. Memory and attention measures did not differ between the groups. Caution should be used in interpreting these results from a subsample of the entire study.

Treatment outcome will be investigated by randomly assigning subjects to one of three treatment conditions, that is, 12 weeks of twice-weekly 1-hour individual tutoring sessions using the two different methods outlined above or a 12 week period of no intervention. Control for concurrent classroom instruction in school programs is not practical, and effects of ongoing classroom instruction are assumed to be randomly distributed across groups and conditions. Multiple tests of reading skills will be taken, using matched alternate forms pre and post. The WRMT-R word identification, word attack, and passage comprehension will be used as standardized measures of achievement performance. Full-length stories at students' instructional and frustrational reading levels were constructed specifically for this study; miscue analysis of the total number of oral reading errors as well as a separate count of those errors that changed meaning, reading speed, and propositional analysis of free recall are derived from these stories. Timed and untimed readings of individually tailored lists of words taught in sessions evaluate treatment-specific word-recognition effects. The main analysis will incorporate a dyslexia subtype × treatment condition MANOVA on posttest scores, with pretest scores as covariates. The design will also include a no-treatment wait period or treatment with the alternate tutoring method for all subjects after the initial experimental period, allowing follow-up analysis of maintenance of skills and analysis of additive, interference, or carryover effects of the different treatments.

Continuous dimensions versus discrete subtypes As an alternative to the analyses of variance outlined above, the external and educational validation measures will also be examined with regression analysis, using composite indicators of phonological and orthographic processing that score subjects on continua of these dimensions.

Diagnostic stability over time will be assessed by readministering all diagnostic instruments at program exit. In general, it is hypothesized that subjects will maintain their initial subtype status in spite of treatment interventions, although changes in reading levels may move some subjects out of the initial diagnostic criteria range. This is an internal validation procedure. In addition, test–retest reliability and interscorer reliability on the Boder (Boder & Jarrico, 1982) spelling patterns will be examined.

Topographic brain mapping during rest, reading, and orthographic and phonological nonword identification tasks will compare the two subtypes and two normal control groups (age-matched and reading-level matched) on EEG and event-related potential measures.

VII. Conclusions

Neuropsychological research over the past two decades clearly supports the idea that subtypes of learning disabilities exist. Attempts to define these subtypes have been grouped into clinical–inferential and empirical methods. Criteria for the reliability and validity of subtype schemes have been proposed. At this point in time, it is unclear what balance between differences on manifest academic behaviors versus associated linguistic or other neuropsychological dimensions will be critical for defining the most useful or valid subtypes. Both the clinical–inferential and the empirical approach to this problem have made important contributions.

An integrated analysis of several prominent reading-disability subtype systems that have been intensively investigated in recent years suggests some areas of convergence in the literature. In particular, phonological and orthographic processing in reading appear to be central in defining subtypes. Although a dichotomy of auditory–linguistic versus visuospatial reading-disability subtypes has commonly been proposed, the field may be moving from a search for discrete subtypes toward a more dimensional view of individual differences in LD. Nonreading subtypes are also important and are addressed elsewhere in this volume.

Both neuropsychological concepts and intervention research are of central importance in the validation of LD subtypes. Several recent research programs have begun to test if different subtypes respond differently to various intervention methods. The Milwaukee program illustrates many of the procedures necessary to validate neuropsychological subtype systems, with an emphasis on intervention evaluation. Further research should integrate neuropsychological, academic, and biobehavioral measures related to LD, with clear theory-driven hypotheses about the relationships among these different spheres in LD children's mental processing.

Acknowledgments

We gratefully appreciate the comments on this manuscript by Donna Recht and JoAnne Caldwell. The Milwaukee Dyslexia Research and Instruction Program is supported by grants from the Faye McBeath Foundation, the R. J. and Linda Peters Foundation, the Herrick Foundation, and the Milwaukee Foundation.

References

Alenderfer, M. S., & Blashfield, R. K. (1986). *Cluster analysis*. Beverly Hills, CA: Sage Publications.

Alexander, P. A. (1984). Enlarging the gap between theory and practice: A review of the Boder Test of Reading-Spelling Patterns. *School Psychology Review, 13,* 529–533.

Baker, L., & Stein, N. (1978). The development of prose comprehension skills. In C. Santa & B. Hayes (Eds.), *Children's prose comprehension: Research and practice*. Newark, DE: International Reading Association.

Bakker, D. J. (1979). Hemispheric differences and reading strategies: Two dyslexias? *Bulletin of the Orton Society, 29,* 84–100.

Bakker, D. J. (1980). Hemisphere-specific dyslexia models. In R. N. Malatesha & L. C. Hastlage (Eds.), *Lateralization of language in the child* (pp. 310–351). Amsterdam: Swets & Zeitlinger.

Bakker, D. J. (1983). Hemispheric specialization and specific reading retardation. In M. Rutter (Ed.), *Developmental neuropsychiatry* (pp. 498–506). New York: Guilford Press.

Bakker, D. J. (1984). The brain as a dependent variable. *Journal of Clinical Neuropsychology, 6,* 1–16.

Bakker, D. J. (1987, June). *Electrophysiological variables in learning disability subtypes.* Paper presented at the Third World Congress on Dyslexia, Chania, Greece (unpublished manuscript).

Bakker, D. J. (1988, July). *Neuropsychological treatment of dyslexia subtypes.* Paper presented as part of the Symposium "Subtyping in Developmental Dyslexia" at the Eleventh European Conference of the International Neuropsychological Society, Lahti, Finland (unpublished manuscript).

Bakker, D. J., & Licht, R. (1985). Learning to read: Changing horses midstream. In G. T. Pavlidis & D. F. Fisher (Eds.), *Dyslexia: Neuropsychology and treatment* London: Wiley.

Bakker, D. J., Moerland, R., & Goekoop-Hoefkens, M. (1981). Effects of hemisphere-specific stimulation on the reading performance of dyslexic boys: A pilot study. *Journal of Clinical Neuropsychology, 3,* 155–159.

Bakker, D. J., & Vinke, J. (1985). Effects of hemisphere-specific stimulation on brain activity and reading in dyslexics. *Journal of Clinical and Experimental Neuropsychology, 7,* 505–525.

Barr, R. (1974). The effect of instruction on pupil reading strategies. *Reading Research Quarterly, 10,* 555–582.

Bing, S. B. (1985). A review of the Boder Test of Reading-Spelling Patterns: A diagnostic screening test for subtypes of reading disability. *Psychology in the Schools, 22,* 488–489.

Blashfield, R. K., & Draguns, J. (1976). Evaluative criteria for psychiatric classification. *Journal of Abnormal Psychology, 85,* 140–150.

Boder, E. (1970). Developmental dyslexia: A new diagnostic approach based on the identification of three subtypes. *Journal of School Health, 40,* 289–290.

Boder, E. (1971a). Developmental dyslexia: A diagnostic screening procedure based on three characteristic patterns of reading and spelling. In B. Bateman (Ed.), *Learning disorders* (Vol. 4). Seattle, WA: Special Child Publications.

Boder, E. (1971b). Developmental dyslexia: Prevailing diagnostic concepts and a new diagnostic approach. In H. R. Myklebust (Ed.), *Progress in learning disabilities* (Vol. 2). New York: Grune & Stratton.

Boder, E. (1973). Developmental dyslexia: A diagnostic approach based on three atypical reading-spelling patterns. *Developmental Medicine and Child Neurology, 15,* 663–687.

Boder, E., & Jarrico, S. (1982). *The Boder Test of Reading-Spelling Patterns: A diagnostic screening test for subtypes of reading disability.* New York: Grune & Stratton.

Bouma, A., Bakker, D. J., & Gardien, C. J. (1988, July). *Hemisphere-specific stimulation through tactile modality in dyslexics.* Paper presented at the Eleventh European Meeting of the International Neuropsychological Society, Lahti, Finland (unpublished manuscript).

Caldwell, J., Recht, D. R., & Newby, R. F. (1987, June). *Improving the reading comprehension of dysphonetic and dyseidetic dyslexics using story grammar.* Paper presented at the Third World Congress on Dyslexia, Chania, Greece (unpublished manuscript).

Das, J. P., Kirby, J. R., & Jarman, R. F. (1975). Simultaneous and successive syntheses: An alternative model for cognitive abilities. *Psychological Bulletin, 82,* 87–103.

Del Dotto, J. E., & Rourke, B. P. (1985). Subtypes of left-handed learning-disabled children. In B. P. Rourke (Ed.), *Neuropsychology of learning disabilities: Essentials of subtype analysis* (pp. 89–130). New York: Guilford Press.

Denckla, M. B. (1977). Minimal brain dysfunction and dyslexia: Beyond diagnosis by exclusion. In M. E. Blaw, I. Rapin, & M. Kinsbourne (Eds.), *Topics in child neurology.* Jamaica, NY: Spectrum Publ.

Doehring, D. G., & Hoshko, I. M. (1977). Classification of reading problems by the Q-technique of factor analysis. *Cortex, 13,* 281–294.

Doehring, D. G., Trites, R. L., Patel, P. G., & Fiedorowicz, C. A. M. (1981). *Reading disabilities: The interaction of reading, language and neuropsychological deficits.* New York: Academic Press.

Ehri, L. C., & Wilce, L. S. (1983). Development of word identification speed in skilled and less skilled beginning readers. *Journal of Educational Psychology, 75,* 3–18.

Ellis, A. W. (1985). The cognitive neuropsychology of developmental (and acquired) dyslexia: A critical survey. *Cognitive Neuropsychology, 2,* 169–205.

Fisk, J. L., & Rourke, B. P. (1979). Identification of subtypes of learning disabled children at three age levels: A neuropsychological multivariate approach. *Journal of Clinical Neuropsychology, 1,* 289–310.

Fitzgerald, J., & Spiegel, D. (1983). Enhancing children's reading comprehension through instruction in narrative structure. *Journal of Reading Behavior, 15,* 1–17.

Fletcher, J. M., & Morris, R. (1986). Classification of disabled learners: Beyond exclusionary definitions. In S. J. Cici (Ed.), *Handbook of cognitive, social and neuropsychological aspects of learning disabilities* (pp. 55–80). Hillsdale, NJ: Erlbaum.

Fletcher, J. M., & Satz, P. (1985). Cluster analysis and the search for learning disability subtypes. In B. P. Rourke (Ed.), *Neuropsychology of learning disabilities: Essentials of subtype analysis* (pp. 40–64). New York: Guilford Press.

Flynn, J. M., & Deering, W. M. (1989). Subtypes of dyslexia: Investigation of Boder's system using quantitative neurophysiology. *Developmental Medicine and Child Neurology, 31,* 215–223.

Frith, U. (1983). The similarities and differences between reading and spelling problems. In M. Rutter (Ed.), *Developmental neuropsychiatry* (pp. 453–472). New York: Guilford Press.

Frith, U. (1985). Beneath the surface of developmental dyslexia. In K. Patterson, J. Marshall, & M. Coltheart (Eds.), *Surface dyslexia.* London: Erlbaum.

Hooper, S. R., & Hynd, G. W. (1985). Differential diagnosis of subtypes of developmental dyslexia with the Kaufman Assessment Battery for Children (K-ABC). *Journal of Clinical Child Psychology, 14,* 145–152.

Hooper, S. R., & Willis, W. G. (1989). *Learning disability subtyping: Neuropsychological foundations, conceptual models, and issues in clinical differentiation*. New York: Springer-Verlag.

Hynd, G. W., & Cohen, M. J. (1983). *Dyslexia: Neuropsychological theory, research, and clinical differentiation*. New York: Grune & Stratton.

Johnston, C. S., Fennell, E. B., & Satz, P. (1987, February). *Learning disability subtypes: A cross-validation*. Paper presented at the 15th annual meeting of the International Neuropsychological Society, Washington, DC (unpublished manuscript).

Kaufman, A. S., & Kaufman, N. L. (1983). *Kaufman Assessment Battery for Children*. Circle Pines, MN: American Guidance Service.

Kavale, K. A., & Forness, S. R. (1987a). The far side of heterogeneity: A critical analysis of empirical subtyping research in learning disabilities. *Journal of Learning Disabilities, 20,* 374–382.

Kavale, K. A., & Forness, S. R. (1987b). Substance over style: Assessing the efficacy of modality testing and teaching. *Exceptional Children, 54,* 228–239.

Kinsbourne, M., & Warrington, E. K. (1963). Developmental factors in reading and writing backwardness. *British Journal of Psychology, 54,* 145–156.

Kinsbourne, M., & Warrington, E. (1966). Disorders of spelling. In J. Money (Ed.), *The disabled reader* (pp. 73–81). Baltimore, MD: Johns Hopkins Press.

Leslie, L., & Caldwell, J. (1989). *Qualitative Reading Inventory*. Glenview, IL: Scott Foresman.

Licht, R., Bakker, D. J., Kok, A., & Bouma, A. (1984, February). *Hemispheric asymmetry and learning to read: A longitudinal event related potential study*. Paper presented at the 12th annual meeting of the International Neuropsychological Society, Houston, TX (unpublished manuscript).

Lovett, M. W. (1984). A developmental perspective on reading dysfunction: Accuracy and rate criteria in the subtyping of dyslexic children. *Brain & Language, 22,* 67–91.

Lovett, M. W. (1987). A developmental approach to reading disability: Accuracy and speed criteria of normal and deficient reading skill. *Child Development, 58,* 234–260.

Lovett, M. W. (1988, May). Treatment effects and individual difference predictors of treatment outcome in the remediation of developmental dyslexia. Paper presented at the First annual conference on Research and Theory in Learning Disabilities, University Park, PA (unpublished manuscript).

Lovett, M. W., Benson, N. J., & Olds, J. (in press). Individual difference predictors of treatment outcome in the remediation of specific reading disability. *Unknown. Learning and Individual Differences*.

Lovett, M. W., Ransby, M. J., & Barron, R. W. (1988). Treatment, subtype, and word type effects in dyslexic children's response to remediation. *Brain & Language, 34,* 328–349.

Lovett, M. W., Ransby, M. J., Hardwick, N., & Johns, M. S. (1989). Can dyslexia be treated? Treatment-specific and generalized treatment effects in dyslexic children's response to remediation. *Brain & Language, 37,* 90–121.

Luria, A. R. (1966). *Higher cortical functions in man.* New York: Basic Books.

Luria, A. R. (1973). *The working brain.* New York: Basic Books.

Lyon, G. R. (1983). Learning-disabled readers: Identification of subgroups. In H. R. Myklebust (Ed.), *Progress in learning disabilities* (Vol. 5, pp. 103–134). New York: Grune & Stratton.

Lyon, G. R. (1985a). Educational validation of learning disability subtypes. In B. P. Rourke (Ed.), *Neuropsychology of learning disabilities: Essentials of subtype analysis* (pp. 228–256). New York: Guilford Press.

Lyon, G. R. (1985b). Identification and remediation of learning disability subtypes: Preliminary findings. *Learning Disabilities Focus, 1,* 21–35.

Lyon, G. R. (1987). Learning disabilities research: False starts and broken promises. In S. Vaughn & C. Bos (Eds.), *Research in learning disabilities: Issues and future directions* (pp. 69–85). San Diego, CA: College Hill Press.

Lyon, G. R., & Flynn, J. M. (1989a). Educational validation of studies with subtypes of learning disabled readers. In B. P. Rourke (Ed.), *Learning disabilities in children: Neuropsychological validity studies.* New York: Guilford Press.

Lyon, G. R., & Flynn, J. M. (1989b). Assessing subtypes of learning disabilities. In H. L. Swanson (Ed.), *Handbook on the assessment of learning disabilities: Theory, research, and practice.* San Diego, CA: College Hill Press.

Lyon, G. R., & Moats, L. C. (1988). Critical issues in the instruction of the learning disabled. *Journal of Clinical and Consulting Psychology, 56,* 830–835.

Lyon, G. R., Moats, L. C., & Flynn, J. M. (1989). From assessment to treatment: Linkage to interventions with children. In M. Tramontana & S. Hooper (Eds.), *Issues in child neuropsychology: From assessment to treatment.* New York: Plenum.

Lyon, G. R., Rietta, S., Watson, B., Borch, B., & Rhodes, J. (1981). Selected linguistic and perceptual abilities of empirically derived subgroups of learning disabled readers. *Journal of School Psychology, 19,* 152–166.

Lyon, G. R., & Risucci, D. (1989). Classification of learning disabilities. In K. A. Kavale (Ed.), *Learning disabilities: State of the art and practice* (pp. 44–70). San Diego, CA: College Hill Press.

Lyon, G. R., Stewart, N., & Freedman, D. (1982). Neuropsychological characteristics of empirically derived subgroups of learning disabled readers. *Journal of Clinical Neuropsychology, 4,* 343–365.

Lyon, G. R., & Watson, B. (1981). Empirically derived subgroups of learning disabled readers: Diagnostic characteristics. *Journal of Learning Disabilities, 14,* 256–261.

Mason, J. M. (1984). Early reading from a developmental perspective. In D. P. Pearson (Ed.), *Handbook of reading research* (pp. 505–544). New York: Longman.

Mattis, S. (1978). Dyslexia syndromes: A working hypothesis that works. In A. L. Benton & D. Pearl (Eds.), *Dyslexia: An appraisal of current knowledge.* New York: Oxford University Press.

Mattis, S., French, J. H., & Rapin, T. (1975). Dyslexia in children and adults: Three independent neuropsychological syndromes. *Developmental Medicine and Child Neurology, 17,* 150–163.

McKinney, J. D. (1984). The search for subtypes of specific learning disabilities. *Journal of Learning Disabilities, 17,* 43–50.

Morris, R., Blashfield, R. K., & Satz, P. (1986). Developmental classification of reading-disabled children. *Journal of Clinical and Experimental Neuropsychology, 8,* 371–392.

Morris, R., Satz, P., & Blashfield, R. K. (1981). Neuropsychology and cluster analysis: Potentials and problems. *Journal of Clinical Neuropsychology, 3,* 77–79.

Newby, R. F., Caldwell, J., & Recht, D. R. (1989). Improving the reading comprehension of children with dysphonetic and dyseidetic dyslexia using story grammar. *Journal of Learning Disabilities, 22,* 373–380.

Newby, R. F., Recht, D. R., & Caldwell, J. (1989, May/June). *Phonological processing, verbal and nonverbal memory, and attention in dysphonetic and dyseidetic dyslexics.* Paper presented at the biennial meeting of the Society for Research in Child Development, Kansas City, MO.

Obrzut, J. E. (1987). Neuropsychology of learning disabilities: Essentials of subtype analysis [Review of book]. *Journal of Clinical and Experimental Neuropsychology, 9,* 228–234.

Olson, R. K., Wise, B., Conners, F., & Rack, J. (1988, April). *Specific deficits in component reading and language skills: Genetic and environmental influences.* Paper presented in the Symposium on "What's Specific about Specific Reading Disability?" at the annual meeting of the American Educational Research Association, New Orleans, LA (unpublished manuscript).

Olson, R. K. (1985). Disabled reading processes and cognitive profiles. In D. B. Gray & J. F. Kavanagh (Eds.), *Biobehavioral measures of dyslexia* (pp. 215–244). Parkton, MD: York Press.

Olson, R. K. (1989, April). *Genetic and environmental influences on deficits in word recognition and component coding skills.* Paper presented as part of the Symposium "Normal and disabled readers: The role of phonological processing deficits" at the biennial meeting of the Society for Research in Child Development, Kansas City (unpublished manuscript).

Olson, R. K., Kliegl, R., Davidson, B. J., & Foltz, G. (1985). Individual and developmental differences in reading disability. In G. E. MacKinnon & T. G. Waller (Eds.), *Reading research: Advances in theory and practice* (Vol. 4, pp. 1–64). Orlando, FL: Academic Press.

Perfetti, C. A. (1988). Verbal efficiency in reading ability. In (Eds.), *Reading research: Advances in theory and practice* (Vol. 6, pp. 109–143). San Diego, CA: Academic Press.

Pirozzolo, F. J. (1979). *The neuropsychology of developmental reading disorders.* New York: Praeger.

Recht, D. R., Caldwell, J., & Newby, R. F. (1988, May). *Improving the reading comprehension of dysphonetic and dyseidetic dyslexics using story grammar.* Paper presented at the First annual conference on Research and Theory in Learning Disabilities, University Park, PA (unpublished manuscript).

Reynolds, C. R. (1984). Psychometric characteristics of the Boder Test of Reading-Spelling Patterns: Take one giant step backwards. *School Psychology Review, 13,* 526–529.

Roeltgen, D. (1985). Agraphia. In K. M. Heilman & E. Valenstein (Eds.), *Clinical neuropsychology* (pp. 75–96). New York: Oxford University Press.

Rourke, B. P. (1975). Brain-behavior relationships in children with learning disabilities: A research program. *American Psychologist, 30,* 911–920.

Rourke, B. P. (1985). *Neuropsychology of learning disabilities: Essentials of subtype analysis.* New York: Guilford Press.

Satz, P., & Morris, R. (1981). Learning disability subtypes: A review. In F. J. Pirozzolo & M. C. Wittrock (Eds.), *Neuropsychological and cognitive processes in reading* (pp. 109–141). New York: Academic Press.

Skinner, H. (1981). Toward the integration of classification theory and methods. *Journal of Abnormal Psychology, 90,* 68–87.

Speece, D. L. (1989). Methodological issues in cluster analysis: How clusters become real. In H. L. Swanson & K. Keogh (Eds.), *Learning disabilities: Theoretical and research issues.* Hillsdale, NJ: Erlbaum.

Spiegel, D., & Fitzgerald, J. (1986). Improving reading comprehension through instruction about story parts. *Reading Teacher, 39,* 676–682.

Stanovich, K. E. (1986). Matthew effects in reading: Some consequences of individual differences in the acquisition of literacy. *Reading Research Quarterly, 21,* 360–406.

Stanovich, K. E. (1988). Explaining the differences between the dyslexic and the garden-variety poor reader: The phonological-core variable-difference model. *Journal of Learning Disabilities, 21,* 590–612.

Stein, N. (1979). How children understand stories: A developmental analysis. In L. Katz (Ed.), *Current topics in early childhood education.* Hillsdale, NY: Ablex.

Traub, M., & Bloom, F. (1975). *Recipe for reading.* Cambridge, MA: Educators Publishing Service.

Van der Vlugt, H., & Satz, P. (1985). Subgroups and subtypes of learning disabled and normal children: A cross-cultural replication. In B. P. Rourke (Ed.), *Neuropsychology of learning disabilities: Essentials of subtype analysis* (pp. 212–227). New York: Guilford Press.

Van Strien, J. W., Bakker, D. J., Bouma, A., & Koops, W. (1988, July). *Familial antecedents of P- and L-type dyslexia.* Paper presented at the Eleventh European meeting of the International Neuropsychological Society, Lahti, Finland (unpublished manuscript).

Wagner, R. K., & Torgesen, J. K. (1987). The nature of phonological processing and its causal role in the acquisition of reading skills. *Psychological Bulletin, 101,* 192–212.

Whaley, J. (1981). Story grammar and reading instruction. *Reading Teacher, 34,* 762–771.

Woodcock, R. W. (1987). *Woodcock Reading Mastery Tests—Revised.* Circle Pines, MN: American Guidance Service.

CHAPTER FIFTEEN

Neuropsychological Prediction of Reading Disabilities

Rebecca H. Felton
Idalyn S. Brown

I. Introduction

The early 1970s saw the beginning of considerable research on early identification of children at risk for reading problems. The consensus of most studies was that early identification resulted in better outcome at follow-up, and the earlier the intervention, the more positive the outcome (Satz & Fletcher, 1988). However, in our experience, and as Satz and Fletcher observe, "the tragedy . . . is that most children with reading and learning problems are not referred for diagnostic evaluations until approximately 10 years of age, when they are maturationally less ready and have already been exposed to years of academic failure" (p. 824). A major factor in this current state of affairs is that IQ–achievement discrepancy guidelines for the identification of reading-disabled children make early identification difficult (but see Heath and Kush, this volume, Chapter 11). In addition, there is a lack of agreement in the educational community concerning appropriate methods of treatment for children who are evaluated early in their academic careers and declared to be either reading disabled or at risk for such a label in the future.

Despite considerable interest in early risk detection and subsequent intervention, research in early identification showed little progress in the 1980s (Satz & Fletcher, 1988). Thus, the determination of appropriate methods of early identification is still a major need in the field of reading disability.

Obviously, accurate prediction requires precise definition, and definitional issues continue to be controversial in the field of learning disabilities in general (Kavanaugh & Truss, 1988; Rourke & Gates, 1981). Fortunately, in the field of reading disability there is a growing consensus that language deficits are at the core of specific reading disability (Catts, 1989) and that research should focus on identifying the specific deficits associated with acquisition of lower-level word-identification skills (Stanovich, 1988).

II. The Role of Neuropsychology in Early Prediction of Risk

Over the past decade there has been increasing interest in the role of neuropsychological factors in reading disabilities. Researchers have used measures of neuropsychological functioning in classification and subtyping of reading disabilities and have looked at issues including developmental trends and hemispheric differentiation. H. G. Taylor (1988) makes a strong case for the use of neuropsychological testing in the field of learning disabilities, noting that such tests can provide useful information about a child which cannot be obtained from other sources. In addition, Taylor suggests that neuropsychological tests are useful in isolating correlates of learning problems that are of primary etiological significance; these correlates will be helpful not only in identifying subtypes of disability, but in predicting prognosis and treatment.

The existing literature suggests that neuropsychological measures do show promise as a means of identifying the precise deficits present in a wide range of learning disabilities (Hinshaw, Carte, & Morrison, 1986); moreover, research has shown that such tests are useful in identifying young children at risk for learning disability and in recommending treatment (Satz, Taylor, Friel, & Fletcher, 1978; H. G. Taylor, 1988). Clearly, this is true of specific reading disability as well.

III. Problems with Neuropsychological Tests

Despite the documented utility of neuropsychological testing in diagnosing the predicting learning disabilities, there are difficulties with such tests. For example, there are particular problems with neuropsychological data gathered from children, including effects of age and developmental changes on performance (Hinshaw *et al.*, 1986). Indeed, our knowledge of the "relevant neuropsychological dimensions of the ability structures of younger children" is relatively limited (Rourke & Gates, 1981, p. 10). Additional problems are lack of adequate reliability and normative data and lack of evidence that such tests can explain independent sources of variance in academic abilities. Thus, interpretability of test findings is a major concern (H. G. Taylor, 1988).

Shortcomings of individual tests and test batteries represent only a portion of the difficulties involved in prediction studies. In addition, such studies are beset by numerous problems in methodology. In an excellent critique of the current state of the art, Satz and Fletcher (1988) have outlined quite clearly and succinctly some of the major flaws in existing studies. These include the need for a theoretical basis for developing screening instruments and a need to distinguish between screening and diagnosis in the prediction of learning disability. Other major methodological flaws are problems in sample selection (e.g., size, representation of population) and test validity and utility, particularly as these may be affected by false positives and false negatives. Moreover, adequate standardization and validation of early screening measures have been jeopardized by failure to employ longitudinal designs, insufficient temporal interval from initial assessment to follow-up, and confounding of predictor and outcome variables such as might occur if results of early screening are allowed to affect determination of criterion outcome at follow-up.

IV. Review of Prediction Research

In general, prediction studies have employed both cross-sectional and longitudinal designs and have addressed the relative predictive utility of a variety of measurement techniques including multiple-instrument batteries, single instruments, teacher ratings, and parent involvement (Johnson, 1988). In a review of neuropsychological issues of interest to school psychologists, Rourke and Gates (1981) conclude that cross-sectional studies have failed to yield sufficient information to permit adequate generalization about the "neuropsychological dimensions that are relevant for intervention" (p. 10) and cite the need for longitudinal studies. The many advantages to be gained from longitudinal research include investigation of developmental precursors of reading difficulty, developmental changes and persistence of deficits over time, and immediate and long-term effects of intervention or failure to intervene.

While a number of studies have investigated the relationship between neuropsychological tests and reading difficulties, there have been few studies involving the use of a comprehensive battery of neuropsychological tests in a prospective, longitudinal study of reading disabilities. In addition, the results of existing prediction studies of reading failure have been informative but certainly not definitive. Rather than attempt an exhaustive review of the literature, we have selected for discussion studies which have incorporated methodological components critical to the prediction of reading disabilities. All of the studies described utilized a prospective, longitudinal design and predicted early reading skill with a broad-based neuropsychological assessment administered to children either prior to or early in their school career.

The theoretical basis of a large longitudinal study in Florida was the developmental-lag theory of reading difficulty (Satz & Sparrow, 1970). According to this theory, certain developmentally appropriate perceptual and sensorimotor abilities may be expected to emerge at about the time most children begin to learn to read. Due to a maturational lag, these abilities are less well developed in children who have difficulty in acquiring beginning reading skills. This maturational lag is postulated to delay acquisition of skills involving visual–perceptual and sensorimotor skills considered critical for beginning reading. By the time such children are exposed to the more complex aspects of reading they show deficits in verbal–conceptual abilities, although they may, by this time, have "caught up" with their peers in sensorimotor–perceptual functioning. The substrate of the observed difficulties in reading-disabled children was postulated to be delayed maturation of the left hemisphere.

In the Florida study (Satz et al., 1978) more than 400 white male kindergarten students in a county school system were tested over a 6-year period. Satz and his colleagues (1978) reported that the best kindergarten predictors of later reading achievement were alphabet recitation, a visual recognition–discrimination task, and a finger-localization task. In a subsequent analysis of this data, Fletcher and Satz (1980) demonstrated that perceptual, linguistic, and conceptual skills were all related to acquisition of reading but that the neuropsychological correlates of reading achievement changed with age. In predicting reading achievement from kindergarten tests, sensorimotor–perceptual skill accounted for a major portion of the variance. However, reading in fifth grade was most highly correlated with concurrent (fifth-grade) measures of verbal–conceptual ability. In a modification of their earlier theory, Fletcher and Satz (1980) state that these results do not support a developmental-lag hypothesis but "merely illustrate that the neuropsychological correlates of reading achievement change with age in a direction predicted by known variations in the acquisition of reading-related skills" (p. 35).

Wilson and Risucci (1988) studied 74 children with developmental language disorders (DLD) and average IQ to determine the predictive utility of neuropsychological assessment during the preschool years for reading (decoding and comprehension) during early elementary grades. Neuropsychological testing included specific language and visual constructs (i.e., auditory perception and cognition, short-term auditory memory, semantic word retrieval, visual match-to-sample discrimination, visual–spatial skills, visual discrimination and problem solving, and visual short-term memory). Results of these measures were used to validate five developmental language disorder subtypes. In correlating test results obtained in preschool with later performance on reading tests, they found that reading ability in the primary grades was best predicted by visual spatial skill, whereas in the higher grades (third and fourth) verbal measures were the best predictors, especially for reading comprehension. Based on these results, they concluded that early acquisition of reading skills is dependent upon the ability to use visual–spatial analysis and constructional and memory skills, whereas older children rely primarily on verbal (left-hemisphere) skills. Wilson and Risucci viewed these data as supportive of the developmental-lag theory of Satz (Satz *et al.*, 1978) and of Bakker's (1988) hypothesis of a shift in reading strategy from primarily visual–spatial (right hemisphere) to primarily verbal (left hemisphere), a shift purported to occur at about second or third grade.

In contrast to the preceding two studies, other researchers have shown that phonological processes are more important for early reading acquisition than sensorimotor–perceptual abilities. Phonological processes are linguistic operations that utilize information about the phonological (speech sound) structure of the language. Such operations are relatively independent of general intelligence and correlate well with reading, and thus are logical candidates as specific causes of reading disability (Stanovich, 1988). Measures of phonological processing have been found to be good predictors of reading by many researchers (e.g., Bradley & Bryant, 1985; Lundberg, Olofsson, & Wall, 1980; Mann & Liberman, 1984; Stanovich, Cunningham, & Cramer, 1984; Wolf, Bally, & Morris, 1986). Studies focusing specifically on the relationship of phonological processes to reading have been extensively reviewed by Wagner and Torgesen (1987) and Catts (1989).

In view of these recent findings, the longitudinal study of various sources of individual differences in reading achievement in a large group of Australian children (Share, Jorm, Maclean, & Matthews, 1984) is of great interest. At entry into kindergarten, more than 500 children were evaluated on a number of individual attributes, including home background, reading readiness skills, phonological processing, motor and language skills, and personality. Children were retested on reading at the end of kindergarten and the end of first grade. The best predictors of kindergarten and first-grade reading were ability to name letters, phoneme segmentation, letter copying, and finger localization. Collectively, individual differences accounted for 63% of the variance in end-of-kindergarten reading and 59% at the end of first grade. Overall, Share, and colleagues, conclude that "individual differences in reading achievement appear to arise from two principal sources: phonological processing skills and interdigital dexterity" (p. 1315). In the authors' opinion, these two sources of variance in reading represent very different types of abilities (i.e., language and motor) and, therefore, provide a framework for reconciling theories supporting the role of sensorimotor skills as determinants of reading with those supporting the importance of language processes. In addition, they noted that the Peabody Picture Vocabulary Test (PPVT), often used as a measure of verbal intelligence, accounted for only half as much variance as did phoneneme segmentation and letter naming, suggesting that undue importance has been attached to intelligence as a factor in early reading.

V. Bowman Gray Project

The studies to be described here were conducted as part of the Bowman Gray Project, one purpose of which is to study definition and subtyping of dyslexia. Based upon our clinical observations and supported by findings in the literature, a major hypothesis of this project is that chronic reading disability can be predicted by an appropriate combination of language tests, in particular those involving phonological processes. Since studies of early prediction of reading disability have been plagued by methodological problems, we have attempted to address some of these problems. First, the project is longitudinal, with children tested at various intervals over a 5-year period. In addition, we are studying several different populations (e.g., a randomly selected, normal sample of schoolchildren, a sample of children with documented reading problems, and a sample of children thought to be at risk for reading difficulty) and have included an intervention component. Finally, we have attempted to design our studies so that results may readily compared to those of prior studies.

A. Study 1

Study 1 (Felton & Brown, 1989) investigated the relationship of phonological processing ability to early reading skills in children designated as at risk for reading disabilities. Of particular interest was the differential prediction of two aspects of early reading skill, that is, sight-word identification and word-attack skills. Prior studies had suggested that estimates of the variance in reading explained by phonological tasks might be largely accounted for by the performance of good readers (Keogh, Sears, & Royal, 1988). Thus, we were particularly interested in the ability of tests of phonological processing to predict reading skill in a sample of children in which the expected reading outcome would be more restricted than in a typical school sample.

Subjects were 81 children (51 males and 30 females) who had been identified as at risk based on (1) teacher ratings, and (2) performance on tests shown in previous studies to be correlates of early reading skill. During first grade, approximately half of these children participated in a study of the effects of different methods of teaching reading to at-risk children and, therefore, received more intensive levels of instruction than typical for public school classrooms.

Subjects were evaluated in the spring of their kindergarten year with a battery of neuropsychological and readiness tests and were again evaluated at the end of first grade to determine reading skill. Assessment instruments administered in kindergarten were selected to reflect three major types of phonological processes which have been found to be good predictors of reading skill in young children:

1. Phonological awareness. Measured by tasks requiring rhyming, syllable counting, identification of words with different beginning or ending sounds, and manipulation of phonemes within syllables.
2. Phonological recoding in lexical access. Measured by tests of rapid automatized naming of colors, numbers, objects, and letters and confrontational naming.
3. Phonetic recoding in working memory. Measured by performance on a test of memory for strings of rhyming (WSM-rhyming) and nonrhyming (WSM-nonrhyming) words.

In addition, measures of early literacy (alphabet recitation and the Auditory Skills subtest of the Metropolitan Readiness Test), intelligence (Otis–Lennon Mental Ability Test), and somatosensory skill (finger localization) were obtained in kindergarten. At the end of first grade, the word-identification (sight words) and word-attack (decoding of nonwords) subtests of the Woodcock Reading Mastery Test were administered.

1. RESULTS AND DISCUSSION

One of the most notable aspects of this study is the lack of congruence with other studies which have investigated the relationship between phonological processing and reading in young children. Although all of the tests in the kindergarten battery were selected on the basis of their strong correlation with reading in previous prediction studies, when we controlled for general intelligence the only phonological processing measure that remained significantly correlated with reading was rapid automatized naming of numbers, letters, and objects, which predicted reading of sight words. Moreover, these correlations, although significant, accounted for no more than 15% of the variance. In addition, the correlations between reading outcome and the phonological processing measures were smaller than those reported in other studies, with no simple or partial correlations greater than .39. In contrast to the Florida and Australian studies, alphabet recitation and finger localization were unrelated to reading outcome. Simple bivariate and partial correlations

TABLE I Correlations Between Kindergarten Predictors and
End-of-First-Grade Reading

	Simple		Partial[a]	
Predictor	Word Identification	Word Attack	Word Identification	Word Attack
Initial consonant	.27*	.26*	.16	.15
Final consonant	.06	−.003	.03	−.03
Rhyme	−.02	−.13	−.05	−.16
Lindamood	.27*	.32**	.11	.18
Syllable count 1	−.23*	−.19	−.19	−.16
Syllable count 2	−.22	−.12	−.19	−.08
RAN color	−.30**	−.19	−.21	−.09
RAN number	−.39***	−.24*	−.38***	−.21
RAN object	−.27*	−.24*	−.24*	−.21
RAN letter	−.37***	−.19	−.39***	−.19
Boston naming	.17	.20	.07	.11
WSM/nonrhyming	−.04	.01	−.06	.01
WSM/rhyming	−.23*	−.22	−.18	−.17
Alphabet recitation	.12	−.08	.10	−.11
Finger localization	.01	.05	−.02	.02

[a] With IQ partialled out.
*$p < .05$.
**$p < .01$.
***$p < .001$.

for each of the kindergarten predictors with reading measures are shown in Table I.

An interesting and unanticipated finding was that both word identification and word attack were correlated with performance on the Auditory Skills subtest of the Metropolitan Readiness Test (MRT). This subtest, which measures knowledge of sound–symbol correspondences and discrimination of beginning sounds, may be considered an index of early literacy skills. This was the only kindergarten measure that was significantly correlated with both reading measures (for word identification partial $r = .40, p < .001$; for word attack partial $r = .32, p < .001$). Interestingly, the MRT measure and the rapid-naming tests explained approximately the same amount of the variance in word-identification scores (i.e., 15 to 16%).

The amount of variance in reading skill explained by various combinations of predictors was also investigated in this study. Stepwise regression analysis revealed that the best combination of kindergarten variables for predicting word identification was IQ, rapid naming of letters and numbers, and the Auditory Skills subtest of the MRT, which together accounted for 38% of the variance. The addition of three phonological awareness measures and the word-string memory for rhyming words increased the variance explained to 43%. For predicting word attack, the best model consisted of memory for rhyming words, manipulation of phonemes, and the MRT subtest. Together these variables accounted for 28% of the variance in reading, and the addition of IQ and the other phonological awareness tasks increased the total r^2 to only 30%.

These results reveal that a much smaller amount of the total variance in reading skill was explained by the predictors than has generally been reported in other prediction studies (e.g., Mann, 1984; Stanovich, Cunningham, & Cramer, 1984). Although there was a certain amount of heterogeneity in the at-risk group, this sample certainly presented a more restricted range of cognitive processing skills and reading outcomes than samples encompassing the entire range of reading ability. The inevitable statistical consequence, then, is smaller correlations than are found in samples with greater variance. A more substantive difference from earlier studies is the partialling of IQ, leaving a more accurate—although smaller—estimate of the variance attributable to specific processes.

Another important factor affecting the outcome of this study concerns the impact of an intervention program in which a subset of the sample received intensive reading instruction designed to make explicit the alphabetic code and the phonological underpinnings of our language system. Our initial selection process resulted in a group of children with poor prognosis for reading outcome for a variety of reasons, including poor home and preschool experiences, cognitive deficits, and inefficiencies in various phonological processing skills. Because phonological awareness requires metacognitive abilities, it is sensitive to the impact of environmental experience and training, particularly the process of being taught to read (Pennington, 1986). Thus it seems likely that the reading instruction used in the intervention program promoted reading skills in those children who initially demonstrated phonological awareness deficits. The result of such an interaction between instruction and deficit would be a decrease in the relationship between awareness and reading outcome. Although limiting the generalization of these results, this is an important finding in terms of the potential impact of treatment with at-risk children.

In summary, this study supports the importance of lexical access ability —specifically, rapid naming—for early reading acquisition and indicates that different aspects of reading may be predicted by different types of phonological processing. More importantly, these results suggest that the prediction of reading outcome for at-risk children is quite complex and may require the investigation of many factors in addition to the skills typically assessed by neuropsychological test batteries. Clearly, early literacy skills are one important source of variance in such a group. Our observations of the children in this study indicate several other factors which may interact with reading acquisition. These include the child's ability to meet the demands of the classroom in terms of the attentional skills required and the impact of instructional methods used to teach reading.

B. *Study 2*

Study 2 predicts third-grade reading ability from first-grade neuropsychological tests in a sample representative of the entire spectrum of children in regular educational programs in the public schools. Rather than focusing on the prediction of specific reading disability (i.e., reading discrepant from IQ), we chose to study the predictive power of neuropsychological tests across a wide range of cognitive abilities and reading skill. Thus, we did not restrict our sample in terms of intelligence but evaluated general ability and included this information in our analyses of the data. Although we classified subjects according to third-grade reading ability (severely disabled, poor, average, and superior readers), we recognize that such classifications are, to a degree, arbitrary and subject to change over time (Satz *et al.*, 1978).

1. METHOD

A sample of 800 children was randomly selected from the entire population ($N = 3011$) of first graders in a city/county school system. Permission to participate in the study was obtained for 485 children, who were then evaluated as first graders during the 1986–87 school year. During the 1988–89 school year, 348 subjects (72% of the original sample) were available for third-grade follow-up testing. Of these, 321 had complete data and comprised the sample for the present longitudinal study. Of these 321 subjects, 52% ($N = 167$) were males, 48% ($N = 154$) females, and the mean age at the third-grade evaluation was 8.9 years. Eighty-six (27%) of the study participants were minority students. T tests between means for males and females showed statistically significant differences only on the Meier Circles, Judgment of Line, Raven's Progressive Matrices, Boston Naming Test, and Rapid Naming (RAN) of objects. With the exception of RAN objects, boys performed better than girls, although the differences were functionally quite small in all cases. Notably, there were no sex differences in third-grade reading scores. Therefore, the data were analyzed without regard to gender.

T tests indicated small but statistically significant differences between the subjects lost to follow-up or deleted for missing data and the final sample on race, sex, age, and IQ. In general, deleted subjects were a bit older, included somewhat more males and nonwhites, and earned slightly lower scores on measures of general ability. The surviving sample had a mean Peabody Picture Vocabulary Test-Revised (PPVT-R) standard score of 102.6 (SD = 17.0), with scores ranging from 54 to 141. On the Raven's Coloured Progressive Matrices (RPM), the mean raw score was 20.9 (SD = 5.5) with scores ranging from 7 to 36. Scores on both measures were relatively normally distributed, with skewness values of −.34 for the PPVT-R and .08 for the Raven's Matrices. These two measures, the PPVT-R (Dunn & Dunn, 1981) and the RPM (Raven, 1965), provided converging indices of general intelligence. These tests in conjunction "should account for virtually all of the reading achievement variance that can reasonably be apportioned to general intelligence" (Stanovich, Cunningham, & Feeman, 1984).

Neuropsychological tests administered in first grade were selected as measures of the following categories of function.

1. Language processing and verbal memory and learning:
   Phonological awareness. Tasks included Final Consonant Different and Strip Initial Consonant tasks (Stanovich, Cunningham, & Cramer, 1984), Lindamood Auditory Conceptualization Test (Lindamood & Lindamood, 1971), and syllable-counting test (Mann & Liberman, 1984).
   Phonological recoding in lexical access. Measures included the rapid automatized naming of colors, digits, objects, and letters (Denckla & Rudel, 1976) and the Boston Naming Test (Kaplan, Goodglass, & Weintraub, 1982) a measure of confrontation naming of pictures of objects.
   Phonetic recoding in working memory. In our adaptation of the word-string memory test of Mann and Liberman (1984) subjects were required to listen to strings of four nonrhyming words and to repeat the entire string in the exact order heard. Scores on word-string memory reflect number of items correct.
   Verbal learning and memory. Rote verbal learning and memory were evaluated by the Rey Auditory Verbal Learning Test (Rey, 1964; E. M. Taylor, 1959). Scores reflect number correct on Trial 5 (free recall after five learning trials) and on Trial 7 (free recall on the postdistractor trial). Immediate and delayed memory for a prose passage were assessed by "The Lion Story" (Barbizet & Cany, 1968).
2. Visual–spatial processing and visual memory:
   Perceptual organization and visual memory. The Complex Figure Test (Rey, 1964) requires the ability to copy a complex figure and to recall the figure from memory (immediate and delayed).
   Visual–spatial skills. Spatial perception and visual analysis were measured by the Judgment of Line Orientation Test (Benton, Hamsher, Varney, & Spreen, 1883) and the Meier Visual Discrimination Test (M. J. Meier, personal communication, 1980). The Meier measures ability to detect subtle similarities and differences among four sets of concentric circles with randomly distributed gaps.

In third grade, subjects' reading skills were measured by the Woodcock–Johnson Psychoeducational Battery (WJPB)-Reading Cluster (Woodcock & Johnson, 1977). The reading cluster of the Woodcock is a composite of letter–word identification, word attack, and passage comprehension.

Subjects were tested individually in their schools by a psychologist. Testing of the first-grade sample began in late November and was completed in the summer following grade one. Third-grade testing was carried out over a 10-month period, between September and June.

2. RESULTS

a. Performance on Neuropsychological Predictor Variables and Reading-Criterion Variables. Descriptive statistics for all of the first-grade neuropsychological predictor variables are presented in Table II. Although the majority of scores were relatively normally distributed, several distributions were markedly skewed. On Strip Initial Consonant and syllable counting, the majority of children performed at or close to ceiling. On the Strip Initial Consonant test this resulted in a strong negative skew with more than half of the subjects performing at the ceiling of 10 items correct. On the syllable-

TABLE II First-Grade Predictor Variables

Predictor	Mean	Standard Deviation	Median	Skewness	Interquartile Range
Strip initial consonant	7.96	3.02	10	−1.48	7–10
Final consonant	6.69	2.43	7	−.46	5–9
Lindamood	53.43	21.99	49	.24	37–70
Syllable counting[a]	5.66	5.17	4	1.33	2–8
RAN color[b]	56.34	15.79	53	1.75	45–63
RAN number[b]	40.52	13.88	38	4.17	32–46
RAN object[b]	78.47	22.39	75	1.25	63–89
RAN letter[b]	40.04	13.18	37	2.01	31–45
Boston naming test	30.53	7.26	31	−.18	26–36
Word string memory	12.09	3.21	13	−.79	10–15
RAVLT Trial 5	9.97	2.48	10	−.34	8–11
RAVLT recall	8.45	2.53	8	.07	7–10
Prose immediate recall	10.31	4.67	10	.27	7–13.5
Prose delayed recall	10.08	4.43	10	.22	7–13
Rey figure copy	22.61	5.71	23	−.43	19–26.5
Rey immediate recall	15.03	6.18	15	.10	10.25–19.25
Rey delayed recall	13.94	5.97	13	.23	9.5–18.5
Meier circles	9.37	2.70	10	−.33	8–11
Judgment of lines	7.74	6.54	9	.02	0–14

[a] Error scores.
[b] Scores represent time in seconds. Thus, higher scores indicate slower naming.

counting test, on which the score is the number of errors, most of the subjects made very few errors, resulting in a strong positive skew.

All tests of rapid automatized naming (RAN) were positively skewed, as is typical for time measures. Using the criterion of 4 standard deviations from the mean (Morris & Fletcher, 1988) and visual inspection of the data, seven subjects could be classified as outliers on at least one of the RAN tests. However, because of the previously documented strong relationship between retrieval speed and later reading outcome (Mann, 1984), and the possibility that children with extreme scores might well be the most interesting in terms of the impact of naming on reading acquisition, we chose not to remove these subjects from the data set.

Scores on the Lindamood Test of Auditory Conceptualization showed a bimodal distribution, with the larger mode at the lower end of the distribution. Scores below 61 (the minimum grade-one score recommended by the test manual) were earned by 64% of the subjects. The distribution of scores on the Judgment of Line test was distinctive in that almost half (46%) of the subjects were unable to perform the task and received scores of zero. However, the remainder of the scores were fairly evenly spread across the entire range of possible scores.

Reading outcome in third grade is summarized in Table III. The reading cluster score, derived directly from the subtest raw scores, reflects a subject's combined performance on the three reading subtests (word identification, word attack, and passage comprehension) and, as recommended by Woodcock and Johnson (1977), was used for all statistical analyses in this study.

In order to facilitate comparisons between this sample and samples utilized in other studies, standard scores (corrected for age) and grade-equivalence scores are also reported in Table III. Although more than half of the sample (55%) earned grade equivalents of fourth grade or above, only 22% earned scores at the third-grade level, with 23% of the children scoring at the first- or second-grade level. These scores were positively skewed with a modal grade equivalent of 2.8 and with 11 subjects earning grade equivalents

TABLE III   End-of-Third-Grade Reading Outcome as Measured by the Woodcock–Johnson Psychoeducational Battery

	Reading Cluster Score	Standard Scores (Age)	Grade Equivalents
Mean (SD)	493.46 (17.7)	104.55 (14.3)	4.47 (1.90)
Mode	480	113	2.8
Skewness	−.42	.06	1.34
Range	428–533	65–135	1.3–12.8

of ninth grade or above. Obtained standard scores represented the entire range of possible scores (65 to 135).

b. Correlations between First-Grade Neuropsychological Tests and Third-Grade Reading. Simple (bivariate) correlations between neuropsychological tests administered in first grade and reading cluster scores obtained in third grade were all significant at the .0001 level (Table IV). The highest correlations were obtained between reading and phonological awareness measures (particularly the Lindamood, Strip Initial Consonant, and Final Consonant Different tests) and between reading and and confrontation naming (Boston Naming). Substantial correlations were also found between reading and PPVT-R ($r = .55, p < .0001$) and RPM ($r = .56, p < .0001$).

To control for effects of time of testing and general ability, correlations were calculated with the effects of PPVT-R, RPM, and age at first-grade

TABLE IV Correlations Between First-Grade Predictors and Third-Grade Reading

Predictor	Woodcock–Johnson Reading Cluster Score	
	Simple	Partial[a]
Strip initial consonant	.61†	.46†
Final consonant	.50†	.34†
Lindamood	.63†	.41†
Syllable counting	−.44†	−.24†
RAN color	−.29†	−.29†
RAN number	−.37†	−.39†
RAN object	−.45†	−.42†
RAN letter	−.44†	−.39†
Boston naming	.60†	.30†
Word-string memory	.34†	.20***
RAVLT Trial 5	.26†	.13*
RAVLT recall	.23†	.10
Prose immediate recall	.22†	.03
Prose delayed recall	.23†	.02
Rey figure copy	.40†	.14**
Rey immediate recall	.29†	.08
Rey delayed recall	.33†	.13*
Meier circles	.39†	.16**
Judgment of lines	.40†	.15**

[a] With PPVT-R, Raven's, and age partialled out.
*$p < .05$.
**$p < .01$.
***$p < .001$.
†$p \leq .0001$.

evaluation partialled out (see Table III). These controls rendered insignificant the relationships between reading and several measures of memory: immediate and delayed recall of a prose passage, immediate recall of a complex figure, and delayed recall on the Rey Auditory Verbal Learning Test (RAVLT). Correlations between reading and measures of verbal learning (RAVLT Trial 5) and visual–spatial ability (Judgment of Line and the Meier Circles) were substantially reduced by the IQ and age controls.

The highest partial correlations were between reading and measures of phonological awareness (particularly the Strip Initial Consonant and Lindamood tests). Tests of rapid naming of numbers and letters were relatively unaffected by IQ and age and remained moderately well correlated with general reading ability.

   c. Prediction of Third-Grade Reading Classification. Subjects were classified according to third-grade reading ability based on the Woodcock–Johnson reading standard score for age. The empirical distribution of reading standard scores for the entire sample was cut at the 5th, 16th, and 84th percentiles, thus establishing four levels: severely disabled readers (scores at or below the 5th percentile), mildly disabled readers (scores from the 6th to the 16th percentile), average readers (scores from the 17th to the 83rd percentile), and superior readers (scores at or above the 84th percentile). This procedure resulted in the following distribution of subjects within reading groups: severe ($N = 18$), mild ($N = 37$), average ($N = 212$), and Superior ($N = 54$). Combining the severe and mild categories ($N = 55$), this classification yielded a 17% overall incidence of reading difficulty. As expected, the groups differed greatly on a measure of vocabulary (PPVT-R) and reading. In addition, the superior readers were younger than the other subjects (see Table V).

   A four-group discriminant function analysis was computed on reading level (severe, mild, average, or superior) in order to compare the predictive ability of the first-grade tests against the actual third-grade reading-level criterion. All of the first-grade tests along with age at time of testing were entered into this analysis. The results of this analysis are presented in a prediction–performance matrix (Table VI). In this matrix, test predictions (rows) are compared to the actual reading groups (columns) utilizing the column (or vertical) method of calculation (Mercer, Algozzine, & Trifiletti, 1988). This method compares the observed values (i.e., within the cells) with the actual performance levels (based on third-grade outcome). As the matrix indicates, the first-grade tests were most accurate in predicting risk status for children who subsequently were classified as severely disabled or superior readers. For example, of the 18 children who were classified as severely disabled readers in the third grade, the first-grade tests predicted that 17 (94%) of them were at risk. Only one child who was actually a severely

TABLE V Descriptive Statistics for Reading-Level Groups

| | Reading-Level Groups (Grade 3) | | | | | | | | | | | |
| | Severe | | | Mild | | | Average | | | Superior | | |
Variable	M	(SD)	Range	M	(SD)	Range	M	(SD)	Range	M	(SD)	Range
First grade PPVT-R standard score	80.22	(18.00)	54.00–116.00	89.24	(16.72)	63.00–124.00	103.01	(14.23)	68.00–136.00	117.72	(10.78)	94.00–141.00
Third grade Age	9.45	(.46)	8.67–10.33	9.13	(.48)	8.08–10.25	8.84	(.41)	7.92–10.42	8.79	(.38)	8.17–10.25
Reading grade equivalent	2.04	(.36)	1.30–2.40	2.65	(.32)	1.90–3.30	4.20	(1.03)	2.30–7.60	7.59	(1.75)	5.40–12.80
Reading standard score (age)	77.72	(5.23)	65–82	87.30	(2.53)	83–91	104.36	(8.23)	92–118	126.01	(5.67)	119–135

TABLE VI   Predictive Classification of Children into Reading-Level Groups (Grade 3) Based on Discriminant-Function Composite Scores (Grade 1)

Prediction (Grade 1)	Reading-Level Groups (Grade 3)			
	Severe	Mild	Average	Superior
Risk				
N	17	31	29	0
Percentage[a]	94	84	14	0
No risk				
N	1	6	183	54
Percentage	6	16	86	100
Total	18	37	212	54

[a] Percentages based on vertical method of calculation.

disabled reader in third grade was missed by the first-grade tests (i.e., was predicted to be no risk). No superior readers were predicted to be at risk based on first-grade tests. For the mildly disabled readers ($N = 37$), the first-grade tests correctly predicted risk status for 84% ($N = 31$) and missed or incorrectly classified only 6 children. In the group of average readers ($N = 212$), the first-grade test prediction was accurate for 86% ($N = 183$) and inaccurate for only 29 children. In terms of overall hit rate (valid positives plus valid negatives), the first-grade tests accurately predicted 89% of the sample.

Although the vertical method of analysis has been utilized in reading-prediction research and strongly recommended (Mercer et al. 1988; Satz et al., 1978), the horizontal method has frequently been used in prediction studies (Mercer, 1975) and yields different but useful information. In this method of analysis, the observed values (i.e., within the cells) are compared to the prediction levels (i.e., risk or no risk). Risk status was predicted for 24% ($N = 77$) of the entire sample. Results of the horizontal method of analysis are presented in Table VII, in which the reading outcome data are collapsed into poor (severe and mild) and good (average and superior) reader groups. Of the 77 children predicted by the tests to be at risk, 62% ($N = 48$) were actually classified as poor readers based on third-grade criteria. Conversely, 38% ($N = 29$) of the children predicted to be at risk were classified as good readers in the third grade. A high percentage (97%) of the children who were good readers in third grade correctly predicted by the tests to be no risk. Only 3% of the children predicted to be no risk actually were classified as poor readers in the third grade.

While the above analyses provide information about the combined predictive accuracy of the entire battery of neuropsychological tests, an additional issue concerns the relative importance of individual tests as predictors. Therefore, a stepwise discriminant function analysis was computed on the

TABLE VII Predictive Classification of Good and Poor Readers (Grade 3) Based on Discriminant-Function Composite Scores (Grade 1)

| | Reading Outcome (Grade 3) | | |
Prediction (Grade 1)	Poor Readers (Severe and Mild)	Good Readers (Average and Superior)	Total
Risk			
N	48	29	77
Percentage[a]	62	38	
No risk			
N	7	237	244
Percentage	3	97	

[a] Percentages based on horizontal method of calculation.

total test battery to determine the ranking of the predictor variables in terms of their discrimination of reading outcome levels. Of the 22 possible first-grade predictors (including age), the stepwise procedure selected 8 variables for entry. In addition to the measures of general ability (PPVT-R and RPM), the procedure selected two phonological tests (Strip Initial Consonant and Linda-mood), two rapid naming tests (letters and numbers), age at testing, and the Boston Naming Test. When the Boston was entered, the PPVT-R was removed, indicating that these variables accounted for overlapping portions of variance in the prediction of reading level. With age removed from the model, the stepwise procedure selected the same variables except for the exclusion of the RPM and the inclusion of RAN-colors rather than RAN-numbers. The results of these two procedures are presented in Table VIII.

TABLE VIII Stepwise Discriminant Function Analysis Predicting Reading-Level Groups

| | Model with Age | | | | Model without Age | | |
| | Variable | | Partial | | Variable | | Partial |
Step	Entered	Removed	r^2	Step	Entered	Removed	r^2
1	PPVT-R		.30	1	PPVT-R		.30
2	Strip initial consonant		.15	2	Strip initial consonant		.15
3	Age		.12	3	Lindamood		.09
4	Lindamood		.10	4	RAN letter		.08
5	RAN letter		.09	5	Boston naming		.06
6	Boston naming		.08	6	RAN color		.05
7	PPVT-R		.01				
8	RAN numbers		.05				
9	Raven's matrices		.05				

3. DISCUSSION

These results demonstrate that, without controls for general ability and with a large, representative sample, a broad range of neuropsychological tests will be significantly correlated with reading outcome. This information, however, is relatively meaningless in terms of predicting reading difficulties in individual children. More promising is the finding that, with controls for age and IQ, a fairly small subset of measures taken in the first grade contributed substantially to the variance in third-grade reading. Measures of phonological processing, both phonological awareness and lexical access, were the best predictors of reading and accounted for between 15 and 21% of the variance in composite reading scores. Measures of phonetic recoding in working memory, verbal learning and memory, perceptual organization and visual memory, and visual–spatial skills each accounted for less than 3% of the variance in reading.

Clearly, these data fail to support studies (e.g., Satz *et al.,* 1978; Wilson & Risucci, 1988) which have found nonverbal (i.e., visual–spatial, sensorimotor–perceptual) skills to be the best predictors of early reading. It should be noted that neither the Satz *et al.* nor the Wilson and Risucci studies utilized statistical controls for the effects of IQ and neither of the test batteries included measures of phonological processing. In addition, the Wilson and Risucci study failed to take into account the impact of a language-impaired sample (with the resulting reduction in variance in language ability) on the study of relationships between predictors and reading. In our study, the phonological processing measures were the only variables that remained viable after the effects of IQ were removed. Thus, it is likely that the failure of other studies to include these tests and to control adequately for IQ is a major factor in differences in the obtained results.

In contrast, this study provides strong support for investigations which have demonstrated the importance of phonological awareness and phonological recoding in lexical access as contributors to individual differences in reading ability. For example, there were many similarities between the results of this study and those reported for the Australian study (Share *et al.,* 1984). In both studies, the best predictor of reading was a measure of phonological awareness (specifically phoneme segmentation) and the simple correlations were around .6 in both cases. In addition, the measures of rapid naming showed moderate (around .3 to .4) correlations with reading in both studies.

Both the current study and a subsequent analysis of the Australian study data (Jorm, Share, Maclean, & Matthews, 1986) address the issue of the impact of IQ on the prediction of reading. Although the methodologies employed to evaluate this question are quite different, the results of the two studies are similar. In the Australian study, backward readers (reading discrepant for age only), retarded readers (reading discrepant for age and IQ), and normal readers were compared in order to determine the predictors of reading difficulty independent of IQ. In comparison to normal readers, both the backward and the retarded readers were characterized by deficits in oral language (e.g., phoneme segmentation and naming) and early literacy (e.g., ability to name and write letters). The backward readers also demonstrated deficits in motor and memory skills (as would be expected given their lower level of general ability). The reading skills of the two types of poor readers were also similar in that both showed difficulty in reading of nonsense words and in spelling. Jorm and colleagues concluded that phonological processing problems were an important factor in the difficulties of both groups in acquiring lower-level reading skills.

These results, along with those of the current study, provide converging evidence for the role of phonological processing and early literacy in the prediction of poor reading in children regardless of intellectual level. Although the cognitive deficits of backward readers are more broadly based than those of IQ-discrepant readers, it would appear that the deficits that are specific to problems in the early stages of reading are the same for both groups. This is not, of course, to suggest that readers with lower levels of general ability are no different from readers with more selective cognitive deficits. Clearly, the more selectively impaired children should have a different prognosis in terms of their ability to compensate for their difficulties in learning to read. These studies do suggest, however, that failure to succeed in the early stages of reading (where phonological recoding is of great importance) is related to selective cognitive deficits in children relatively independent of general intellectual level (see Stanovich, 1988, for a discussion of this issue).

Although the relative contribution of intelligence and specific cognitive abilities to reading ability is an important issue, for the purposes of prediction it is much more important to evaluate the ability of various measures to predict reading outcome for individual children. This study along with the Florida longitudinal study (Fletcher & Satz, 1980; Satz et al., 1978) support a role for neuropsychological tests in such endeavors. Despite differences in methodology (e.g., subject pool, reading instruments, and methods of determining reading level), there were similarities in the predictive utility of the test batteries. Both the Florida study (kindergarten to second-grade prediction) and the current study (first- to third-grade prediction) resulted in respectable overall hit rates (76 and 89%, respectively) and were most successful in predicting reading outcome for children in the severe and superior groups.

However, in terms of the conclusions concerning the best neuropsychological indices of reading outcome and in ability to accurately predict outcome for the mildly impaired and average readers, the two studies differed greatly. In the Florida study the best predictors for classification were measures of sensorimotor–perceptual skills and alphabet recitation while, in the current study, measures of phonological processing and general ability were the best tests for predicting reading-group membership. These two very different sets of tests produced quite different results in terms of predicting reading level for the mildly impaired and average readers. The Florida study's prediction of second-grade reading produced a valid positive rate of only 66% for the mildly impaired readers and a valid negative rate of only 68% for the average readers. In comparison, the set of tests used in the current study resulted in much higher hit rates (i.e., a valid positive rate of 84% for the mild group and a valid negative rate of 86% for the average readers).

In terms of initial screening of children for possible reading problems, the current study suggests that neuropsychological tests in combination with simple measures of general ability are useful indicators of subsequent reading performance. Screening should aim for the identification of as many risk children as possible with a very low rate of false negatives (i.e., children classified as no risk who subsequently have difficulty in reading). This study meets these criteria in that only 3% ($N = 7$) of the children predicted to do well (no risk) by the tests were actually in the poor-reader group in third grade and only one of these was classified as a severely impaired reader. Another consideration in determining the utility of prediction instruments is the false-positive rate (i.e., prediction of risk with good outcome). Utilizing the more stringent horizontal method of analysis, the false-positive rate for this study was 38%. That is, 29 of the 77 children identified by the tests as at risk actually performed satisfactorily in the third grade. Such a rate is acceptable only if the advantages of screening outweigh the disadvantages of possible labeling of children. Ideally, the initial screening should lead to more in-depth evaluation of possible risk children and the determination of appropriate intervention programs. At this point, neuropsychological tests might play a different, but also vital, role in the assessment process.

VI. General Conclusion

Measures of phonological awareness and rapid automatized naming emerged as good predictors of reading after the effects of general ability were accounted for. Thus, the Bowman Gray studies provide converging evidence for the role of phonological processing in the prediction of early reading skills. In addition, our data illustrate the impact of restricted sample variance on results obtained from correlational studies and support the need for statistical control of general ability. A comparison of Studies 1 and 2 points to the importance of investigating differences in the predictive validity and utility of neuropsychological tests in different target groups. Clearly, the at-risk sample described in Study 1 presents quite a different challenge to neuropsychological prediction research than the normal sample of Study 2.

The high predictive accuracy of the phonological processing measures in combination with other measures (e.g., general ability and early literacy) is encouraging. Nonetheless, it must be remembered that these findings are useful only if paired with careful diagnostic studies of at-risk children which in turn result in effective interventions. In our opinion, neuropsychological assessment has excellent potential for contributing to the diagnostic and treatment components of this process. The finding in Study 1 of different predictors for word-attack and sight-word skills is certainly an indication that specific cognitive abilities may be sensitive to difficulties in different aspects of early reading. This potential will be reached, however, only through the application of sound methodological principles to studies that evaluate the role of neuropsychological assessment in the screening, diagnosis, and early treatment of at-risk children in actual school settings.

Acknowledgments

This research was supported by PHS Grant HD21887 to Bowman Gray School of Medicine and by PHS Grant NS19413 to UNC–Greensboro, Subcontract to Bowman Gray School of Medicine.

References

Bakker, D. J. (1988). Invoking precursors of deficient reading. In R. L. Masland & M. W. Masland (Eds.), *Preschool prevention of reading failure* (pp. 177–186). Parkton: MD: York Press.

Barbizet, J., & Cany, E. (1968). Psychometrical study of a patient with memory disturbances. *International Journal of Neurology, 7,* 44–54.

Benton, A. L., Hamsher, K. deS., Varney, N. R., & Spreen, O. (1983). *Contributions to neuropsychological assessment.* New York: Oxford University Press.

Bradley, L., & Bryant, P. (1985). *Rhyme and reason in reading and spelling.* Ann Arbor: University of Michigan Press.

Catts, H. W. (1989). Phonological processing deficits and reading disabilities. In S. Kamhi & H. Catts (Eds.), *Reading disabilities: A developmental perspective.* Boston, MA: College-Hill Press.

Denckla, M. B., & Rudel, R. G. (1976). Naming of object drawings by dyslexic and other learning disabled children. *Brain & Language, 3,* 1–16.

Dunn, L. M., & Dunn, L. M. (1981). *Peabody Picture Vocabulary Test-Revised.* Circle Pines, MN: American Guidance Service.

Felton, R. H., & Brown, I. B. (1989). Phonological processes as predictors of specific reading skills in children at risk for reading failure. *Reading and Writing: An Interdisciplinary Journal, 2,* 3–23.

Fletcher, J. M., & Satz, P. (1980). Developmental changes in the neuropsychological correlates of reading achievement: A six-year longitudinal followup. *Journal of Clinical Neuropsychology, 2*(1), 23–37.

Hinshaw, S. P., Carte, E. T., & Morrison, D. C. (1986). Concurrent prediction of academic achievement in reading disabled children: The role of neuropsychological and intellectual measures at different ages. *International Journal of Clinical Neuropsychology, 8*(1), 3–8.

Johnson, D. J. (1988). Review of research on specific reading, writing, and mathematics disorders. In J. F. Kavanaugh & T. J. Truss, Jr. (Eds.), *Learning disabilities: Proceedings of the National Conference.* Parkton, MD: York Press.

Jorm, A. F., Share, D. L., Maclean, R., & Matthews, R. (1986). Cognitive factors at school entry predictive of specific reading retardation and general reading backwardness: A research note. *Journal of Child Psychology and Psychiatry, 27* (1), 45–54.

Kaplan, E., Goodglass, H., & Weintraub, S. (1982). *Boston naming test.* Philadelphia, PA: Lea & Febiger.

Kavanaugh, J. F., & Truss, T. J., Jr. (Eds.). (1988). *Learning disabilities: Proceedings of the National Conference.* Parkton, MD: York Press.

Keogh, B. K., Sears, S., & Royal, N. (1988). Slingerland screening and instructional approaches for children at-risk for school. In R. L. Masland & M. W. Masland (Eds.), *Preschool prevention of reading failure* (pp. 107–120). Parkton, MD: York Press.

Lindamood, C. H., & Lindamood, P. C. (1971). *Lindamood auditory conceptualization test.* Boston, MA: Teaching Resources Corporation.

Lundberg, I., Olofsson, A., & Wall, S. (1980). Reading and spelling skills in the first school years predicted from phonemic awareness skills in kindergarten. *Scandinavian Journal of Psychology, 21,* 159–173.

Mann, V. A. (1984). Longitudinal prediction and prevention of early reading difficulty. *Annals of Dyslexia, 34,* 117–136.

Mann, V. A., & Liberman, I. Y. (1984). Phonological awareness and verbal short-term memory. *Journal of Learning Disabilities, 10,* 592–599.

Mercer, C. D. (1975, October). *Preliminary review of early identification indices for learning disabled children.* Paper presented at the meeting of the Conference of the State of Florida Association for Children with Learning Disabilities, Tampa.

Mercer, C. D., Algozzine, B., & Trifiletti, J. (1988). Early identification: An analysis of the research. *Learning Disability Quarterly, 11*(3), 176–188.

Morris, R., & Fletcher, J. (1988). Classification in neuropsychology: A theoretical framework and research paradigm. *Journal of Clinical and Experimental Neuropsychology, 10*(5), 640–658.

Pennington, B. F. (1986). Issues in the diagnosis and phenotype analysis of dyslexia: Implications for family studies. In S. D. Smith (Ed.), *Genetics and learning disabilities* (pp. 69–96). San Diego, CA: College-Hill Press.

Raven, J. C. (1965). *Guide to using the coloured progressive matrices.* London: H. K. Lewis.

Rey, A. (1964). *L'examen clinique en psychologie.* Paris: Presses Universitaires de France.

Rourke, B. P., & Gates, R. D. (1981). Neuropsychological research and school psychology. In G. W. Hynd & J. E. Obrzut (Eds.), *Neuropsychological assessment and the school-age child* (pp. 3–25). New York: Grune & Stratton.

Sarazin, F. A., & Spreen, O. (1986). Fifteen-year stability of some neuropsychological tests in learning disabled subjects with and without neurological impairment. *Journal of Clinical and Experimental Neuropsychology, 8*(3), 190–200.

Satz, P., & Fletcher, J. M. (1988). Early identification of learning disabled children: An old problem revisited. *Journal of Consulting and Clinical Psychology, 56*(6), 824–829.

Satz, P., & Sparrow, S. S. (1970). Specific developmental dyslexia: A theoretical formulation. In D. J. Bakker & P. Satz (Eds.), *Specific reading disability: Advances in theory and method*. Rotterdam: Rotterdam University Press.

Satz, P., Taylor, G. H., Friel, J., & Fletcher, J. M. (1978). Some developmental and predictive precursors of reading disabilities: A six year follow-up. In A. L. Benton & D. Pearl (Eds.), *Dyslexia: An appraisal of current knowledge*. New York: Oxford University Press.

Share, D. L., Jorm, A. F., Maclean, R., & Matthews, R. (1984). Sources of individual differences in reading acquisition. *Journal of Educational Psychology, 76*(6), 1309–1324.

Stanovich, K. E. (1988, March). *The right and wrong places to look for the cognitive locus of reading disability*. Paper presented at the 15th annual conference of the New York Branch of the Orton Dyslexia Society, New York.

Stanovich, K. E., Cunningham, A. E., & Cramer, B. B. (1984). Assessing phonological awareness in kindergarten children: Issues of task comparability. *Journal of Experimental Child Psychology, 38,* 175–190.

Stanovich, K. E., Cunningham, A. E., & Feeman, D. J. (1984). Intelligence, cognitive skills, and early reading progress. *Reading Research Quarterly, 193,* 278–303.

Taylor, E. M. (1959). *The appraisal of children with cerebral deficits*. Cambridge, MA: Harvard University Press.

Taylor, H. G. (1988). Neuropsychological testing: Relevance for assessing children's learning disabilities. *Journal of Consulting and Clinical Psychology, 56*(6), 795–800.

Wagner, R. K., & Torgesen, J. K. (1987). The nature of phonological processing and its causal role in the acquisition of reading skills. *Psychological Bulletin, 101,* 192–212.

Wilson, B. C., & Risucci, D. A. (1988). The early identification of developmental language disorders and the prediction of the acquisition of reading skills. In R. L. Masland & M. W. Masland (Eds.), *Preschool prevention of reading failure* (pp. 187–203). Parkton, MD: York Press.

Wolf, M., Bally, H., & Morris, R. (1986). Automaticity, retrieval processes, and reading: A longitudinal study in average and impaired readers. *Child Development, 57,* 988–1000.

Woodcock, R. W., & Johnson, M. B. (1977). *Woodcock-Johnson Psycho-educational Battery*. Hingham, MA: Teaching Resources.

The Assessment of Handedness in Children

M. P. Bryden
Runa Steenhuis

I. Introduction

There are many reasons why one might wish to have an adequate assessment of handedness in children and why one might wish to have a conceptual understanding of children's handedness. For example, handedness appears to be related to the lateralization of language functions in the brain (Rasmussen & Milner, 1977; Segalowitz & Bryden, 1983), and there are frequent suggestions that language lateralization may be related to certain developmental language disorders (e.g., Bryden, 1988; Geschwind & Galaburda, 1987; Gladstone & Best, 1985). Therefore, a knowledge of handedness might help one predict the likely pattern of language lateralization in an individual. Furthermore, one might well be interested in handedness in its own right, in that a well-developed sense of handedness may be related to the ability to make left–right discriminations (cf. Palmer, 1964). Thus, for instance, children who have a clearly developed handedness may also show better discrimination of left and right and a better directional sense. They, therefore, may also find it easier to learn the left-to-right reading convention and acquire the distinction between mirror-imaged letters such as "b" and "d" (cf. Corballis & Beale, 1976). Most recently, interest in handedness has increased because of the theorizing of Geschwind and Galaburda (1987). Based on data from Geschwind and Behan (1982), Geschwind and Galaburda have claimed a relationship between handedness, dyslexia, other forms of

Neuropsychological Foundations of Learning Disabilities, copyright © 1991 by Academic Press Inc. All rights of reproduction in any form reserved.

language disturbance, and immune disorders. These speculations have led to a recent surge of interest in the incidence of left-handedness in special populations of children, such as the autistic and dyslexic.

II. Is This Relevant to Developmental Neuropsychology?

Why should one be interested in accurately assessing handedness in children? Over the years, many clinicians and researchers have felt that there is an abnormally high incidence of left-handedness among those children manifesting various pathologies. It is often argued that left-handers are more likely to be poor readers, to suffer from developmental language disabilities, and to be stutterers or autistic. In general, it is often felt that left-handers are generally less intelligent and able than are right-handers. These arguments have recently come to the forefront with the publication of the Geschwind and Galaburda (1987) theory of cerebral lateralization, in which it is argued that left-handedness is a consequence of abnormally high levels of fetal testosterone and that therefore there are links between handedness, learning disabilities, and disorders of the immune system. However, Satz's (1972) concept of pathological left-handedness and his more recent arguments about ambiguous handedness (Soper *et al.,* 1986) also suggest important links between handedness, language development, and mental retardation.

If such arguments are to be evaluated properly, there must be some consistency in the way in which handedness is measured. Many children (and adults) prefer to use one hand for the majority of activities, but opt to employ the otherwise nondominant hand for certain actions. Thus, one may find people who perform the majority of activities left-handed, but have been taught to write with the right hand, or people who do most things right-handed, but elect to throw a ball left-handed. If one is to assess handedness properly, one needs to sample a variety of activities and to use the same measuring instrument with both pathological groups and normal controls.

The literature on reading disability is a particularly striking example of measurement problems. Geschwind and Behan (1982) surveyed a large number of adults and reported that only 1.1% of strong right-handers claimed to have had learning disabilities, while 11.8% of strong left-handers did so. In a survey of over 1000 professionals, Schacter, Ransil, and Geschwind (1987) indicate that dyslexia was reported in 3% of strong right-handers but in 9% of left-handers and weak right-handers. In children, Hallgren (1950) found that 18% of Swedish dyslexics were left-handed as opposed to 9% of his controls. Similar figures were reported by Naidoo (1972). Rutter, Tizard, and Whitmore (1970) found 9% left-handers in a specific reading retardation group and only 5% in their controls. While these differences were not statistically significant given the sample size, they follow the same general pattern as the preceding two studies. Annett and Turner (1974) also suggested that there were an excess of left-handers in schoolchildren severely deficient in reading.

In contrast, most large-scale studies of unselected samples of schoolchildren have not found much evidence for an association between reading ability and left-handedness. Satz and Fletcher (1987), for example, reported data on 571 children whose handedness and reading ability were assessed at the end of grade two. On the Harris Tests of Lateral Dominance (Harris, 1958), 85 (14.9%) preferred the left hand for the majority of 10 tasks, 481 (84.2%) preferred the right hand, and 5 (.9%) used the right hand for 5 activities and the left for 5. No differences were observed between the 425 strongly right-handed children and the 48 strongly left-handed children on either measures of reading achievement or on teachers' ratings of the likelihood of learning disability. When children performing 1 standard deviation or more below the population average in reading were examined, they were found to include 17% of the strongly right-handed group, but only 6% of the strongly left-handed group. Unfortunately, Satz and Fletcher (1987) do not report data for the 98 children (17%) who manifested varying degrees of "mixed" handedness, 59 of whom performed only a single activity with the otherwise nondominant hand.

Belmont and Birch (1965) also failed to find any difference between good readers and poor readers in a Scottish sample. Several other studies have compared left-handers and right-handers from school samples and have failed to find differences in reading level (e.g., Lyle & Johnson, 1976; Richardson & Firlej, 1979). Pennington, Smith, Kimberling, Green, and Haith (1987) found no differences in the incidence of left-handedness in their dyslexics and controls.

In addition, there are often claims that left-handers are cognitively deficient as compared to right-handers. Admittedly, there has been little support for this view (Hardyck, 1977; Hardyck, Petrinovich, & Goldman, 1976; Sheehan & Smith, 1986). Nevertheless, there are some data suggesting an elevated incidence of left-handedness in certain clinical groups. For example, there are claims that stutterers are more likely to be left-handed than nonstutterers (e.g., Christiansen & Sacco, 1989) and that autistic children are more likely to be left-handed (Soper *et al.*, 1986).

Notions about pathological left-handedness and evidence that there are sex differences in cerebral organization has also led researchers to examine the interaction of sex with handedness as related to cognitive ability in the general population. While sex does not interact with handedness in predicting cognitive ability in some studies (e.g., Calnan & Richardson, 1976), it does in others (e.g., Gillberg, Waldenström, & Rasmussen, 1984). In the latter study, males selected for poor motor performance in the nonpreferred hand had low scores on tests of school performance and more behavioral problems, especially the left-handers. Similarly, inconsistency of hand preference was found to be associated with lower scores on intelligence tests in females between the ages of 18 and 42 months, but not in males of the same age (Gottfried & Bathurst, 1983). A follow-up study on this sample at ages 5 and 6 years showed that consistency of hand preference related to purported left-hemisphere specialization only in females (Kee, Gottfried, Bathurst, & Brown, 1987).

III. Pathological Left-Handedness

An increased incidence of left-handedness and/or mixed handedness has been reported in a number of different groups, including premature infants (O'Callaghan et al., 1987; Ross, Lipper, & Auld, 1987) and the mentally handicapped (Batheja & McManus, 1985; Pipe, 1987; Rider, Imworld, Griffin, & Sander, 1985). This has led some researchers to suggest that members of these groups have suffered some form of early brain damage that has led to their becoming left-handed.

The most extreme version of this view is that all left-handedness is pathological (Bakan, Dibb, & Reed, 1973). By this argument, all left-handers were originally right-handers in whom early brain damage produced cerebral reorganization for motor function. A less extreme position has been put forth by Satz (1972), who argues that only a proportion of left-handers are what he terms pathological left-handers (see also Soper et al., 1986). To other researchers, excessively poor performance with the nondominant hand is thought to be an indication of unilateral brain damage (Bishop, 1980). Gillberg et al. (1984) tested this notion and concluded that there was increased pathological left-handedness in children with poor motor coordination in their nonpreferred hand because those children, especially if male and left-handed, had lower scores for spelling, reading, and writing. Since the authors report a significant correlation between the performance of the two hands, it is unclear that these children were not simply less coordinated. This might be considered a symptom of a more generalized pathology rather than of unilateral brain damage. A similar criticism has been raised by Batheja and McManus (1985), who have challenged Satz by pointing out that unilateral brain damage is the necessary condition for pathological left-handedness, but that while left-handedness is increased in Down syndrome children, the pathology is diffuse.

Batheja and McManus (1985) provide an alternative explanation. They believe that early in development the genetic predisposition towards a directional asymmetry (right-sidedness) can be disrupted. They state that "biological insults of any form at this critical point can result in increased biological *noise* and hence a reversion to a more atavistic state of 'fluctuating asymmetry', in the ultimate form of which 50 per cent of the population is left handed" (Batheja & McManus, 1985, p. 66). They concluded that these people are "left-handers de novo" and not "ex-right-handers."

Although Batheja and McManus (1985) are probably correct in their view that pathological left-handedness of the sort Satz (1972) proposes is likely to be uncommon, clarification is needed of the length of the proposed critical period, as is some indication of the nature of the process that is disrupted by biological insult. In addition, if genetic mechanisms determine the rightward bias, one still has the difficulty of discriminating between a genetic right-hander who becomes a left-hander "de novo" and phenotypic left-handers who have a genetic predisposition for left-handedness (if such a thing exists).

Furthermore, given some kind of an unbiased state, why do such children develop a preference for one particular hand at all? Does this mean that there is something about the environment that favors the use of a single hand for most activities in addition to an initial genetic nudge? Ideas of this sort would be consistent with McManus *et al.*'s (1988) view that "degree" of hand preference is an environmentally driven phenomenon and not genetically based. On the other hand, Bryden (1987) has provided some data to indicate that degree of hand preference is at least as heritable as direction and argued that degree and direction must be considered to be separate components of handedness.

From the developmental perspective there is some evidence of the conditions that might produce an unbiased state of the sort that McManus proposes. There is a suggestion that factors affecting the emergence of the tonic neck reflex might also influence the development of lateralized manual preference. Fox and Lewis (1982) found that infants with respiratory distress and poor muscle tone did not assume the head-right position even as late as 39 weeks. O'Callaghan *et al.* (1987) reported that among preterm infants whose weights were less than 1000 grams, 61% were left-handers at 4 years of age, while only 9.8% of their counterparts weighing more than 1500 grams at birth were left-handed. Illness alone did not seem to be the factor influencing handedness, since many of the heavier infants had been seriously ill. Rather, conditions associated with decreased muscle tone were thought to be important.

IV. Development of Lateral Preference

When differences that might be associated with different criteria for establishing preference are taken into account, it becomes clear that there is substantial agreement among many of the studies examining handedness and other lateral preferences. For children from about 3 years of age up to 11, there is a population bias toward right-sidedness (Coren, Porac, & Duncan, 1981; Groden, 1969; Hebben, Benjamins, & Milberg, 1981; Longoni & Orsini, 1988; Van Camp & Bixby, 1977; Whittington & Richards, 1987). When dichotomous classification of hand preference is used, estimates of the incidence of right-handedness are around 91%, with about 88% being right-footed, 60% right-eyed, and 60% right-eared. The data suggest little or no association between handedness and either ear or eye preference (Coren *et al.*, 1981), although footedness does seem to be related to handedness (Peters, 1988).

As in the study reported here, there are numerous reports of significantly increased incidence of left-handedness in males (see Hildreth, 1949, for a review of earlier work; Annett, 1970; Calnan & Richardson, 1976; Gillberg *et al.*, 1984; Neale, 1988; Peters, 1986; Whittington & Richards, 1987) even in cultures where the base rate of left-handedness is reduced (Rymar, Kameyama, Niwa, Hiramatsu, Saitoh (1984); Teng, Lee, Yang, & Chang, 1979). Some studies report nonsignificant differences between males and females, but even these indicate a greater incidence of left-handedness in boys (Longoni & Orsini, 1988). As Annett (1985) points out, the differences are small but significant in large samples.

Table I summarizes six studies in which sex differences in children's hand preference has been investigated. In all of these studies, the incidence of left-handedness is greater in boys than in girls, and in five the difference is statistically significant. Variations in procedure and in sample size make it very difficult to combine the data from the different studies, but, very roughly, these studies indicate that the incidence of left-handedness is about 25% higher in boys than in girls. The specific values, of course, will depend on the criteria for classifying children as showing "mixed" handedness. As Table I indicates, the procedures employed by Annett (1970) yield a very high incidence of mixed handedness, while Peters (1986) and Longoni and Orsini (1988) did not make use of a mixed category. Not only did the study to be reported later in this chapter also find a higher incidence of left-handedness in boys, but similar sex differences have been reported in children as young as 2 or 3 years of age (Annett, 1970; Hildreth, 1949). It thus appears that sex differences in handedness are robust and are unlikely to be a function of selective sampling.

There are few data available to examine sex differences in handedness in children under 2 years of age. In most studies, the samples are small and of limited power. A notable exception is that of Rice, Plomin, and Defries (1984), who examined several hundred 12- and 24-month-old infants and reported a tendency for more males to be left-handed. In other studies with similar-aged infants but much smaller samples, sex differences have not been

TABLE I Sex Differences in Children's Hand Preferences

Study	Age (yr)	Preference Measure	Sex (N)	Handedness (Percentage)			Statistical Test
				L	M	R	
Annett (1970)	3.5–15	5–7 Actions observed	M (99)	6.1	32.3	61.6	$X^2 = 6.28$
			F (120)	3.3	20.8	75.8	$p < .05$
Calnan and Richardson (1976)	11	Parental interview	M (5800)	11.7	6.6	81.7	$X^2 = 64.2$
			F (5576)	8.5	4.5	87.0	$p < .001$
Teng *et al.* (1979)	11	Questionnaire	M (1048)	2	17[a]	81	$X^2 = 24.35$
			F (1054)	1	19	80	$p < .001$
Peters (1986)	Grades 1–4	Teacher classified	M (1115)	9.5		90.5	$z = 2.93$
			F (1079)	6.9		93.1	$p < .01$
Whittington and Richards (1987)	7	Observation	M[b]	8.9	12.3	78.8	Not given
			F	6.0	14.1	79.9	
	11[c]	Observation, parent report	M[b]	9.4	5.2	85.4	Not given
			F	6.5	4.2	89.2	
Longoni and Orsini (1988)	4–6	6 Actions observed	M (145)	9.0		91.0	$X^2 = 1.29$
			F (126)	7.2		92.8	n.s.

[a] Combination of weak left and weak right groups.
[b] Only the total N (11,032) was given.
[c] The same subjects who had been tested at age 7.

found (Archer, Campbell, & Segalowitz, 1988a); Bates, 1986; Michel, Ovrut, & Harkins, 1986; Ramsay, 1979). While the evidence is limited, it seems that sex differences in infancy favor increased left-handedness in males just as they do in older children and adults.

Some investigators have attributed this sex difference to increased social pressure for right-handedness (conformity) in females (Hildreth, 1949; Neale, 1988) or the idea that males and females respond differently to that pressure (Porac, Coren, & Searleman, 1986). If we accept the report of Rice *et al.* (1984) of sex differences in very young children, such a claim seems less likely. An alternative view is that sex differences in left-handedness are related to differences in cerebral specialization attributable to elevated levels of prenatal testosterone (Geschwind & Galaburda, 1987).

Age trends in handedness are rather more difficult to determine. Most researchers have investigated "children" and have not presented their data by differing age groups. Figure 1 shows the data from one such study, that of Kilshaw and Annett (1983). While the sex difference is evident in this figure, there is no obvious trend for the incidence of left-handedness to either increase or decrease with age in the range from 4 to 15 that is represented in this study. Although the figure suggests an increase in left-handedness with age in boys, Kilshaw and Annett (1983) found no significant changes with age. Further, the data from the children's samples shown in Fig. 1 and in Table I are in general agreement with those from adult studies (e.g., Steenhuis & Bryden, 1989a).

Our understanding of the development of hand preference is further restricted by the fact that there are few longitudinal studies (see Young, 1977, for a similar point). Even in those that exist, sample sizes were small or the data

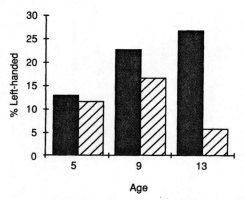

FIGURE 1 Changes in the incidence of left-handedness as a function of age and sex. Data from Kilshaw and Annett (1983).

were collected infrequently. For example, Gesell and Ames (1947) tested children 23 times between the ages of 23 weeks and 10 years but employed only 7 subjects. In contrast, Whittington and Richards (1987) sampled 11,000 children but tested them only twice. As a consequence of such practices, we have only a poor understanding of the course of development of hand preference. For instance, infants and young children are often characterized as exhibiting instability of hand preference (Gesell & Ames, 1947; Harris, 1983; Hildreth, 1949). However, other researchers claim that their preferences are relatively stable (Archer, Campbell, & Segalowitz, 1988b; Michel, 1983).

The relation between hand preference and the emergence of language function has received recent attention (see Harris, 1983, for a review of early studies) as an approach to help resolve the question of the relation between cerebral lateralization for language and the development of hand preference. Although an association between aspects of speech production and hand preference is supported, it is clear that the relation is not a simple or direct one (Archer *et al.*, 1988b; Bates, O'Connell, Vaid, Sledge, & Oakes, 1985; Ramsay, 1980a,b). Archer *et al.* (1988b) suggest that sex and the type of language function (expressive or receptive) were important variables in establishing the relation between hand preference and language development.

V. Lateral Preference in Infants

Aside from interest in the development of hand preference, the impetus for measuring lateralized preferences in infants is the possibility that in this group one can differentiate between those lateralized phenomena that are unlearned and innate and those that are influenced by learning and social pressure.

Harris (1983) has presented an interesting historical account of investigations of infant lateral preference; while it is clear from this review that our interest in the development of handedness has a long history, it is equally clear that we have much to learn. In very young infants, newborn to a few days old, inventive investigators (see Michel, 1983, for a review) have measured such variables as supine head position (Coryell, 1985; Coryell & Michel, 1978) and head turning to visual, auditory, and gustatory stimuli (e.g., Liederman & Kinsbourne, 1980) and to perioral stimulation (Turkiewicz, Moreau, & Birch, 1968; Viviani, Turkiewicz, & Karp, 1978). Consistent population preferences for the right side have been found on these measures.

Since the early work of Gesell and Ames (1947), there has been interest in the tonic neck reflex (TNR) as a rudimentary measure of lateralized motor preference. The position of the head and neck are thought to influence the position of the arms and body. The hand and arm ipsilateral to the direction that the head is turned are held in view, while the other hand is held out of view and close to the body. TNR is present *in utero* and lasts until about 20 weeks of age (Gesell & Ames, 1947). In a study of preterm infants, Fox and Lewis (1982) reported that a right postural asymmetry was present at 34 weeks after conception (Gesell & Ames, 1947, suggest 28 weeks) and that lateralized turning was present at 36 weeks.

Handedness at ages 1, 5, and 10 years was predicted by the direction of TNR in 14 of 19 cases in Gesell and Ames' (1947) longitudinal data. Another more recent study found that 74% of infants with a right-sided TNR at 2 days of age were right-handed at 7 years and that all of the neonates with a left-sided TNR were later left-handed (Viviani *et al.*, 1978). When head turning and hand visualization biases measured in infants under 12 weeks of age were followed up at 3.5 to 6 years of age, all six infants with a consistent right bias were right-handed, while both infants with mixed head-turning and visualization biases were left-handed (Coryell, 1985).

A number of investigators have cautioned that the tasks used to assess lateral preferences in infants and children must take into account performance limitations at each level of motor development (Palmer, 1964). While this may reflect the reality of testing across developmental stages, one makes the assumption that the same underlying construct is being measured with different tasks. This is especially problematic for longitudinal studies that begin in infancy. Nevertheless, the apparent strength of the relation between infancy measures, such as the TNR and laterlized turning, and child hand preferences (Gesell & Ames, 1947; Viviani *et al.*, 1978) provide good reason for optimism. However, there remains the question as to whether the relatively newly learned skills evaluated in infants and young children are equivalent to the overlearned tasks typically evaluated on adult hand-preference inventories.

VI. Measurement of Handedness

What procedures can we use to measure handedness in children, and does it make a difference which procedure we select? To answer such questions, one must be interested in the fine details of the measurement of handedness. While some researchers are satisfied to classify children as being either left-handed or right-handed (e.g., McManus, 1985), most people feel that it is necessary to be concerned with the distribution of scores along some continuum. To complicate matters further, a wide variety of different approaches has been used. These include assessment by parents or teachers (Calnan & Richardson, 1976; Peters, 1986), classification by writing hand (McManus, 1985), the use of performance tests such as peg moving (Annett, 1985), "demonstration" tests in which the child carries out or pantomines various unimanual activities (Tan, 1985), observation of all activities (Provins, Dalzeil, & Higginbottom, 1987), and preference inventories in which children indicate which hand they prefer for different activities (Dean, 1978; Roszkowski & Snelbeker, 1982).

Each of these approaches has its characteristic problems. We all have heard tales of individuals who have been encouraged or even forced to use their right hands for writing. While it would be nice to believe that such attitudes are a thing of the past (cf. Beukelaar & Kroonenberg, 1986), subtle pressures remain for writing with the right hand (Peters, 1986; Porac, Coren, & Searleman, 1986). Thus, classification by writing hand may not be the most appropriate means of grouping subjects, for it will miss the many right-handed writers who perform other activities left-handed. Similarly, classification by parents or teachers is likely to focus on the writing hand. Both of these approaches lead to a binary classification of children into left-handed and right-handed. Such binary classification schemes may be adequate for some purposes, especially if there is a very large sample in which meaningful effects will not be obscured by the misclassification of a few subjects. However, binary classification makes it impossible to distinguish between those children who are consistently unimanual and those who use the preferred hand for the majority of activities and the other hand for a few. Thus, any investigation of the effects of degree of handedness is suborned (Bryden & Steenhuis, 1988).

Observation of all activities (Provins et al., 1987) may provide a wealth of information, but it is a time-consuming and difficult chore, and perhaps unrealistic to use in most cases.

Annett (1985) has championed the use of a peg-moving task to obtain objective data about the relative proficiency of the two hands. However, Zung's (1985) work suggests that there is diminished motor asymmetry in subjects with slower overall performance. Furthermore, our work (Steenhuis & Bryden, 1989b) indicates that while performance measures are closely related to preference measures for comparable activities, they may not be so well related to preferences for other activities. Thus, for example, peg moving is related to other relatively unskilled reaching activities but less strongly to writing or to strength preferences, while a task like dot filling (Tapley & Bryden, 1985) is related more closely to writing than it is to strength or to unskilled reaching activities. In other words, performance measures relate to preference questions concerning similar activities, but not to those relating to quite different activities. This poses a problem for the use of performance measures such as those employed by Annett (1985) and Tapley and Bryden (1985), for it is customary to use only a single performance measure, and this measure will relate only to a limited set of manual preferences. Since several recent authors have emphasized the multidimensional nature of hand preference (e.g., Healey, Liederman, & Geschwind, 1986; Steenhuis & Bryden, 1989a), and Krombholz (1989) has shown a dissociation between the hand more skilled for dot filling and that with greater grip strength, a single performance measure may tap only a limited component of handedness.

Tests in which children demonstrate to the examiner a variety of manual preferences are also common (cf. Annett, 1970; Longoni & Orsini, 1988). Such procedures have the advantage that they tap a variety of different activities but suffer from the problem that, since each activity is generally tested only once, reliability is questionable. Furthermore, demonstration tests do not provide any means of distinguishing degree of preference within activities. With preschool and early primary school children and those with limited language skills, demonstration tests may provide the best measure of handedness.

One good example of a demonstration test is that employed by Satz and his colleagues (Satz, Nelson, & Green, 1989; Soper & Satz, 1984; Soper *et al.*, 1986). In this test, a subject is asked to show how he/she executes eight simple tasks: eating with a spoon, drinking from a cup, brushing the teeth with a toothbrush, drawing with a pencil, throwing a ball, hammering the table with a plastic hammer, picking up a piece of candy, and picking up a dime. Each of these activities is tested several times, in quasirandom order. This permits some measure of gradations of hand preference within each activity as well as between activities. For instance, if each activity were tested four times, the response distribution could be mapped onto the 5-point preference scale we have used. A consistent selection of left or right hand on all four trials would correspond to the "always" categories, a use of one hand on three of the four trials would correspond to the "usually" categories, and the use of each hand twice would correspond to the "equals" category. To overcome the drawbacks mentioned above and to link demonstration tests more closely to preference inventories, the procedures for administering demonstration tests need to be improved and standardized so that they will assess consistency within tasks as well as between tasks and so that the relation to questionnaire performance is well understood.

The problem with preference questionnaires is twofold. First, most questionnaires involve relatively complex decisions, such as to differentiate between when one "always" uses a particular hand for an activity and when one "usually" uses a particular hand. Young children may find such scales difficult or impossible to use in a consistent fashion. Second, most common handedness questionnaires involve reading and comprehending fairly difficult text, often referring to activities that children rarely perform, and may be unreliable for this reason. As we shall show, however, it is reasonable to give preference inventories to children at least as young as 10 years of age.

Unfortunately, as is the case with adults (Coren & Porac, 1978; Liederman & Healey, 1986; McMeekan & Lishman, 1975; Raczkowski, Kalat, & Nebes, 1974; Steenhuis, Bryden, Schwartz, & Lawson, 1990), there are few data on the reliability of lateral preference measures in children (Dean, 1978; Roszkowski & Snelbecker, 1982). For a small sample of grade-one and grade-two children, Roszkowski and Snelbecker (1982) administered a 5-item preference questionnaire (based on Bryden, 1977) with a 1-month interval. They reported that writing and drawing showed the greatest consistency (r = .82 and .76), while lower values were reported for throwing (.58), using scissors (.51), and brushing one's teeth (.40). Moreover, there is a fine line between studies that establish test–retest reliability of a particular measure and those that are investigating developmental changes. For example, Krombholz (1989) presents data for a dot-filling task and for grip force in a large sample of children tested three times in their first 2 years at school and reports that left-handers were most likely to change their hand preference, and then only within their first year at school. Krombholz attributes these changes to external pressures to be right-handed. It clearly is not necessary to conclude that dot-filling and grip strength are poor measures of hand preference because of developmental instability.

VII. Some Data on a Preference Inventory for Children

In order to determine whether or not it is reasonable to use a standardized preference inventory with children, we recently administered a slightly revised version of the questionnaire employed with adults by Steenhuis and Bryden (1989a) with a large sample of schoolchildren (see Table II). Our sample consisted of 522 children in grades four, six, and eight in the Ontario public school system. The children in these grades would be approximately 10, 12, and 14 years of age at the time of testing, $+/-$ 0.5 years at each grade. Questionnaires were completed by 51 boys and 58 girls in grade four, 93 boys and 98 girls in grade six, and 117 boys and 105 girls in grade eight. The handedness questionnaire employed was a 32-item questionnaire previously used with university undergraduates by Steenhuis and Bryden (1989a). Each question was followed by a 5-point scale ranging from "always use left hand" through "usually use left hand," "use both hands about equally," "usually use right hand," to "always use right hand." Scoring was from -2 to $+2$ for each item.

Steenhuis and Bryden (1989a) identified three major factors in their analysis of this questionnaire. A primary factor was identified as relating to skilled manual activities and included such items as writing, throwing a ball, and using a toothbrush. In general, this factor elicited relatively extreme responses, with most people claiming to use one hand for the action exclusively. A second factor was related to more unskilled and less practiced activities and primarily included questions relating to picking up small objects such as a pen or a piece of paper. The items loading on this factor were endorsed

TABLE II The Waterloo Handedness Questionnaire

Name				Age

Instructions: Answer each of the following questions as best you can. If you *always* use one hand to perform the described activity, circle **Ra** or **La** (for **right always** or **left always**). If you **usually** use one hand circle **Ru** or **Lu,** as appropriate. If you use **both hands equally often,** circle **Eq.**

Do not simply circle one answer for all questions, but imagine yourself performing each activity in turn, and then mark the appropriate answer. If necessary, stop and pantomime the activity.

1. Which hand do you use for writing?	La	Lu	Eq	Ru	Ra
2. In which hand would you hold a heavy object?	La	Lu	Eq	Ru	Ra
3. With which hand would you unscrew a tight jar lid?	La	Lu	Eq	Ru	Ra
4. In which hand do you hold your toothbrush?	La	Lu	Eq	Ru	Ra
5. With which hand would you pick up a penny off a desk?	La	Lu	Eq	Ru	Ra
6. In which hand would you hold a match to strike it?	La	Lu	Eq	Ru	Ra
7. With which hand do you throw a baseball?	La	Lu	Eq	Ru	Ra
8. With which hand would you pet a cat or dog?	La	Lu	Eq	Ru	Ra
9. Which hand would you use to pick up a nut or washer?	La	Lu	Eq	Ru	Ra
10. Which hand do you consider the strongest?	La	Lu	Eq	Ru	Ra
11. Over which shoulder would you swing an axe?	La	Lu	Eq	Ru	Ra
12. With which hand would you pick up a comb?	La	Lu	Eq	Ru	Ra
13. With which hand would you wind a stopwatch?	La	Lu	Eq	Ru	Ra
14. With which hand would you pick up a (baseball) bat?	La	Lu	Eq	Ru	Ra
15. With which hand would you pick up a piece of paper?	La	Lu	Eq	Ru	Ra
16. With which hand do you use a pair of tweezers?	La	Lu	Eq	Ru	Ra
17. With which hand would you throw a spear?	La	Lu	Eq	Ru	Ra
18. With which hand would you hold a cloth when dusting the furniture?	La	Lu	Eq	Ru	Ra
19. With which hand do you flip a coin?	La	Lu	Eq	Ru	Ra
20. In which hand would you hold a knife to cut bread?	La	Lu	Eq	Ru	Ra
21. With which hand do you use the eraser on the end of a pencil?	La	Lu	Eq	Ru	Ra
22. With which hand would you pick up a toothbrush?	La	Lu	Eq	Ru	Ra
23. With which hand would you hold a needle when sewing?	La	Lu	Eq	Ru	Ra
24. On which shoulder do you rest a baseball bat when batting?	La	Lu	Eq	Ru	Ra
25. In which hand would you carry a briefcase full of books?	La	Lu	Eq	Ru	Ra
26. With which hand would you pick up a jar?	La	Lu	Eq	Ru	Ra
27. With which hand do you hold a comb when combing your hair?	La	Lu	Eq	Ru	Ra
28. With which hand would you pick up a pen?	La	Lu	Eq	Ru	Ra
29. Which hand do you use to manipulate implements such as tools?	La	Lu	Eq	Ru	Ra

TABLE II *Continued*

30. Which hand would you use to put a nut or washer on a bolt?	La	Lu	Eq	Ru	Ra
31. With which hand would you pick up a baseball?	La	Lu	Eq	Ru	Ra
32. Which hand do you use to pick up objects?	La	Lu	Eq	Ru	Ra

33. Is there any reason (i.e., injury) why you do *not* use the hand you prefer to use for any of the above activities? YES / NO (circle one)

If yes, please explain why you do not use your preferred hand and which activities are affected.

Note: This questionnaire is a modified version of that appearing in Steenhuis and Bryden (1989a).

with less extreme responses, with people claiming to use one hand "usually" or to use both hands equally. The third factor was specifically related to the manner in which baseball bats and axes were swung. Like the first factor, these items tended to receive "extreme" endorsements, with an increased proportion of nonpreferred hand use in both right- and left-handers.

The data obtained from our children's sample was subjected to a factor analysis similar to the one we had done with adults (Steenhuis & Bryden, 1989a); this yielded four factors, as indicated in Table III.

It is clear that the three major factors identified in adults by Steenhuis and Bryden (1989a) are also present in school-age children. The one factor (Factor 3) seems to be largely specific to the question about winding a (stop)watch, an activity which is becoming increasingly less familiar. The other two items which load most heavily on this factor have weak loadings at best. Figures 2 through 5 show the distribution of responses given by left- and right-handers to the items on each factor. These figures generally substantiate the observations made by Steenhuis and Bryden (1989a). Factor 1 items (Fig. 2) lead to extreme responses (73.8% extreme responses in right-handers, 67.3% in left-handers), and the distributions for left-handers and right-handers are only moderately different. Factor 2 items (Fig. 3) lead to fewer extreme responses (34.0% in right-handers, 34.4% in left-handers). On Factor 3 (Fig. 4), right-handers generally endorse the extreme right-handed position, but left-handers use all categories. Factor 4 items (Fig. 5) again show mostly extreme responses (73.1% in right-handers and 67.1% in left-handers), but subjects are more likely to prefer the nondominant side than they are with Factor 1 items.

For each factor, using only the items loading .60 or greater on that factor, the distribution of factor sums was obtained. The distribution of scores as positive (right-handed), negative (left-handed), or zero (indeterminate) was then obtained for each of the four factors; the incidence of left-handedness on each factor is shown in Table IV. On Factor 1, the incidence of left-

TABLE III Factor Distribution and Grade and Sex Effects for Children's
Questionnaire

	Factor Loading	Grade Effect	Sex Effect	Overall Effect
Write	1			
Eraser	1		.05	
Cut bread	1		.10	
Hold toothbrush	1			
Needle	1		.05	
Throw spear	1		.001	.01
Throw baseball	1		.05	
Tools	1			
Pick up pen	1(2)[a]	.01		
Tweezer	1			
Comb	1(2)			
Hold a match	1			
Strong	1			
Dust	1(2)			
Flip	1(2)			
Pick up small object	2			
Pick up jar	2	.10	.10	.05
Pick up paper	2	.05		.05
Pick up nut	2		.01	.05
Pick up penny	2			
Pick up baseball	2		.001	.05
Pick up baseball bat	2	.001	.01	.001
Pet a cat/dog	2			
Pick up comb	2(1)	.05		.10
Carry briefcase	2			
Pick up toothbrush	2(1)		.10	.10
Carry heavy object	2			
Wind a watch	3	.10		
Hold jarlid to unscrew	3		.01	.05
Screw on a nut	3(1)			
Bat in baseball	4			
Swing an axe	4			

a Figures in parenthesis indicate a minor loading on a second factor.

handedness is slightly higher in grade four than in grades six or eight (but this difference is not significant), and there are substantially more left-handed boys than left-handed girls.

The same sex difference is evident for Factor 2. As grade increases, the number of right-handers decreases and the number of ambidextrous people increases. On Factor 3, there are again fewer right-handed boys than girls, and age trends are inconsistent, presumably because but a single question loads on

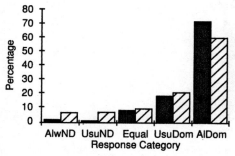

FIGURE 2 Distribution of responses for Factor 1 (skilled activities) items.

this factor. Finally, on Factor 4 (bats/axes), there are substantially more left-handed boys than girls and higher numbers of left-handers in grade four and ambidexters in grade eight.

As a further step in analyzing the data, the responses for each question were cast into a 6 × 5 table, with the grade/sex groupings as one factor and the categories endorsed as the second factor, and subjected to a chi-square test with 20*df*. This was then partitioned into separate tables to compare boys and girls and to make comparisons across grade levels (see Table III).

Four items (pick up comb, pick up paper, pick up baseball bat, and pick up pen) showed significant differences among the three grades. However, in none of these cases were the differences due to shifts in the proportion of left- or right-handers. Rather, these effects were all in the direction of the older children endorsing less extreme responses. Averaged across all the four questions, 51% of the grade-four responses were in one of the two extreme categories, while only 40% of the grade-six and 34% of the grade-eight responses were in the extreme categories. Thus, for these items at least, the older children were less extreme than the younger children in their responses.

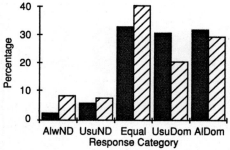

FIGURE 3 Distribution of responses for Factor 2 (unskilled activities) items.

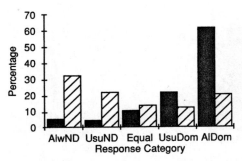

FIGURE 4   Distribution of responses for Factor 3 (strength) items.

As children get older, they may become more fully aware that they use the nonpreferred hand for many seemingly minor activities. This shift contrasts with the data of Whittington and Richards (1987), who found a decrease in the incidence of mixed-handers between the ages of 7 and 11, and those of McManus *et al.* (1988), who argued that children become more lateralized as they age rather than less so.

Eight of the items showed significant sex differences (throwing and picking up a baseball, using an eraser, holding a needle, unscrewing a jarlid, throwing a spear, picking up a nut, and picking up a baseball bat). In part, these sex differences were due to the common finding that there are fewer left-handed girls than there are left-handed boys. It is noteworthy, however, that only a few of the items show statistically reliable sex differences. Furthermore, some of the differences are degree effects rather than direction effects. Items such as throwing a baseball, throwing a spear, using an eraser, and picking up a baseball or baseball bat elicited less extreme responses from the girls than from the boys, while threading a needle elicited more extreme responses from the girls than from the boys.

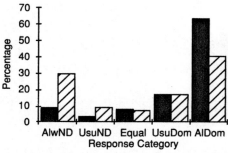

FIGURE 5   Distribution of responses for Factor 4 (bats/axes) items.

TABLE IV   Incidence of Left-Handedness and Mixed Handedness in Children

	Factor 1 Skilled (%)		Factor 2 Unskilled (%)		Factor 3 Strength (%)		Factor 4 Bats/Axes (%)	
	L	E	L	E	L	E	L	E
Grade 4 boys	17.6	0.0	13.7	5.9	17.6	11.8	19.6	7.9
Grade 4 girls	12.1	0.0	8.6	3.5	12.1	15.5	15.5	6.9
Grade 6 boys	15.1	0.0	14.0	4.3	7.5	10.8	17.2	6.5
Grade 6 girls	9.2	0.0	12.2	7.2	8.2	6.1	9.2	5.1
Grade 8 boys	15.4	0.0	15.4	8.5	13.7	10.3	18.8	9.4
Grade 8 girls	8.6	0.9	7.6	12.5	8.6	4.8	8.6	11.4
Grade 4	14.8	0.0	11.2	4.7	14.8	13.7	17.6	7.4
Grade 6	12.2	0.0	13.1	5.7	7.9	8.4	13.2	5.8
Grade 8	12.0	0.4	11.5	10.5	11.1	7.5	13.7	10.4
Boys	16.0	0.0	14.6	6.2	12.9	11.0	18.5	7.9
Girls	10.0	0.3	9.5	7.7	9.5	8.8	11.1	7.8

For none of the questions was there any significant residual interaction between grade level and sex. Further, the majority of the questions ($N = 19$) showed neither sex nor grade effects.

The data from this study suggest that it is reasonable to use a preference inventory with children as young as 10 years of age. The results indicate that the general pattern observed in adults (Steenhuis & Bryden, 1989a) is also found in children, that sex differences in the incidence of left-handedness are found, and that a few items show clear developmental trends in the pattern of responses.

VIII. Conclusions

Presumably those reading a handbook on the neuropsychology of learning disabilities are seeking guidance as to when they should be concerned about assessing handedness and how they should measure it. Our review of the literature has indicated a variety of areas in which there is at least suggestive evidence to indicate that handedness is a potentially important variable. However, any clear statements about the relation of handedness to specific cognitive variables or to specific neuropsychological disorders remain premature because of the lack of clear developmental data about hand preference and the wide variety of different measures that have been employed.

Although we foresee a great increase in studies relating handedness to neuropsychological dysfunction in the next few years, due in large part to the

Geschwind and Galaburda (1987) theory, our review of the literature has uncovered only equivocal evidence for any relation between handedness and cognitive abilities in normal children. Further, it seems one cannot assume that handedness serves as an index of a "pathological" state or atypical lateralization of other functions. Until we understand the variables that lead to the development of "normal" hand preference or divert the course of its development, we stand little chance of elucidating the relation between handedness and cognitive ability. This means that we will need careful, large-scale developmental studies of handedness using both observational and questionnaire techniques and, in particular, we need good longitudinal studies.

The evidence presented in this chapter indicates that a paper-and-pencil handedness questionnaire can be reliably administered to children as young as 10 years of age. With younger groups, demonstration tests are almost certainly the most appropriate means for assessing handedness. A good demonstration test should sample activities related to both of our first two factors (skilled and unskilled activities) (see Steenhuis & Bryden, 1989a). It should also permit a separation of degree and direction of handedness. At present, perhaps the best of these tests is that employed by Satz (Satz *et al.*, 1989; Soper & Satz, 1984). Because this test involves multiple presentations of a limited number of items, it permits one to distinguish between those who are inconsistent in their hand preferences in the sense of doing some activities with one hand and other activities with the other hand, and those who are ambiguous in their handedness, in the sense of being inconsistent within activities. Unfortunately, however, there are no large-sample studies showing just how hand preferences change through the primary school years, nor are there good studies linking performance on demonstration tests to performance on handedness inventories.

What advice can we give to people who are concerned with the measurement of handedness in children? We have provided some normative data for a handedness questionnaire and indicated directions in which we think research should proceed. If one's goal is to compare a group of children with a specific pathology against normal children, it is clear that one should use a standardized measuring instrument and choose one's control group wisely. However, clinicians are daily faced with the problem of assessing individual cases and reaching some decision. It is far too easy to note that a child does perform some activity in a relatively unique way and to leap to the conclusion that they are left-handed or anomalous in their dominance. While the need is for both better standardized tests and normative data based on large sample, we have at least made a beginning. How we interpret our measures is another question. In our present state of knowledge, we can say that if children are left-handed on some standard measure, such as our questionnaire or the Soper and Satz (1984) tests, they are in a minority. Whether being in this minority is of any diagnostic value remains an open issue.

Acknowledgments

Preparation of this chapter was aided in part by a grant from the Natural Sciences and Engineering Research Council of Canada, by a Killam Research Fellowship from the Canada Council, and by a Bilateral Exchange Award from the Royal Society of London to M. P. B. M. P. B. should like to thank I. Howarth and G. Underwood of the University of Nottingham for making facilities available to him.

References

Annett, M. (1970). The growth of manual preference and speed. *British Journal of Psychology, 61,* 545–558.

Annett, M. (1985). *Left, right, hand and brain: The right shift theory.* London: Erlbaum.

Annett, M., & Turner, A. (1974). Laterality and the growth of intellectual abilities. *British Journal of Educational Psychology, 44,* 37–46.

Archer, L. A., Campbell, D., & Segalowitz, S. J. (1988a). A prospective study of hand preference and language development in 18- to 30-month olds: I. Hand preference. *Developmental Neuropsychology, 4,* 85–92.

Archer, L. A., Campbell, D., & Segalowitz, S. J. (1988b). A prospective study of hand preference and language development in 18- to 30-month olds: II. Relations between hand preference and language development. *Developmental Neuropsychology, 4,* 93–102.

Bakan, P., Dibb, G., & Reed, P. (1973). Handedness and birth stress. *Neuropsychologia, 11,* 363–366.

Bates, E., O'Connell, B., Vaid, J., Sledge, P., & Oakes, L. (1986). Language and hand preference in early development. *Developmental Neuropsychology, 2,* 1–15.

Batheja, M., & McManus, I. C. (1985). Handedness in the mentally handicapped. *Developmental Medicine and Child Neurology, 27,* 63–68.

Belmont, L., & Birch, H. G. (1965). Lateral dominance, lateral awareness, and reading disability. *Child Development, 36,* 57–71.

Beukelaar, L. J., & Kroonenberg, P. M. (1986). Changes over time in the relationship between hand preference and writing hand among left-handers. *Neuropsychologia, 24,* 301–303.

Bishop, D. V. M. (1980). Measuring familial sinistrality. *Cortex, 16,* 311–313.

Bryden, M. P. (1977). Measuring handedness with questionnaires. *Neuropsychologia, 15,* 617–624.

Bryden, M. P. (1987). Handedness and cerebral organization: Data from clinical and normal populations. In D. Ottoson (Ed.), *Duality and unity of the brain* (pp. 55–70). Harmondsworth, UK: Macmillan.

Bryden, M. P. (1988). Does laterality make any difference? Thoughts on the relation between cerebral asymmetry and reading. In D. L. Molfese & S. J. Segalowitz (Eds.), *Brain lateralization in children: Developmental implications* (pp. 509–525). New York: Guilford Press.

Bryden, M. P., & Steenhuis, R. E. (1988). Handedness is a matter of degree. *Behavioral and Brain Sciences, 10:* 266–267.

Calnan, M., & Richardson, K. (1976). Developmental correlates of handedness in a national sample of 11-year-olds. *Annals of Human Biology, 3:* 329–342.

Christiansen, J. M., & Sacco, P. R. (1989). Association of hair and eye color with handedness and stuttering. *Journal of Fluency Disorders, 14,* 37–45.

Corballis, M. C., & Beale, I. L. (1976). *The psychology of left and right.* Hillsdale, NJ: Erlbaum.

Coren, S., & Porac, C. (1978). The validity and reliability of self-report items for the measurement of lateral preference. *British Journal of Psychology, 69,* 207–211.

Coren, S., Porac, C., & Duncan, P. (1981). Lateral preference behaviors in preschool children and young adults. *Child Development, 52,* 433–450.

Coryell, J. (1985). Infant rightward asymmetrics predict right-handedness in childhood. *Neuropsychologia, 23,* 269–271.

Coryell, J. F., & Michel, G. F. (1978). How supine postural preferences of infants can contribute toward the development of handedness. *Infant Behavioral Development, 1,* 245–257.

Dean, R. (1978). Reliability and predictive validity of the Dean Laterality Preference Schedule with preadolescents. *Perceptual and Motor Skills, 47,* 1345–1346.

Fox, N., & Lewis, M. (1982). Motor asymmetries in preterm infants: Effects of prematurity and illness. *Developmental Psychobiology, 15,* 19–23.

Geschwind, N., & Behan, P. (1982). Left-handedness: Association with immune disease, migraine and developmental learning disorder. *Proceedings of the National Academy of Sciences of the U.S.A., 79,* 5097–5100.

Geschwind, N., & Behan, P. (1984). Laterality, hormones, and immunity. In N. Geschwind & A. Galaburda (Eds.), *Cerebral dominance: The biological foundations* (pp. 211–224). Cambridge, MA: Harvard University Press.

Geschwind, N., & Galaburda, A. M. (1987). *Cerebral lateralization.* Cambridge, MA: MIT Press.

Gesell, A., & Ames, L. B. (1947). The development of handedness. *Journal of Genetic Psychology, 70,* 155–176.

Gillberg, C., Waldenström, E., & Rasmussen, P. (1984). Handedness in Swedish 10-year-olds. Some background and associated factors. *Journal of Child Psychology and Psychiatry, 25,* 421–432.

Gladstone, M., & Best, C. (1985). Developmental dyslexia: The potential role of interhemispheric collaboration in reading acquisition. In C. T. Best (Ed.), *Hemispheric function and collaboration in the child* (pp. 87–118). Orlando, FL: Academic Press.

Gottfried, A. W., & Bathurst, K. (1983). Hand preference across time is related to intelligence in young girls, not boys. *Science, 221,* 1074–1076.

Groden, G. (1969). Lateral preferences in normal children. *Perceptual and Motor Skills, 28,* 213–214.

Hallgren, B. (1950). Specific dyslexia: A clinical and genetic study. *Acta Psychiatrica et Neurologia Scandinavica Supplementum, 65,* 1–287.

Hardyck, C. (1977). Laterality and intellectual ability: A just not noticeable difference. *British Journal of Educational Psychology, 47:* 305–311.

Hardyck, C., Petrinovich, L. F., & Goldman, R. D. (1976). Left handedness and cognitive deficit. *Cortex, 12:* 266–279.

Harris, A. J. (1958). *Harris tests of lateral dominance: Manual of directions for administration and interpretation* (3rd ed.). New York: Psychological Corporation.

Harris, L. J. (1983). Laterality of function in the infant: Historical and contemporary trends in theory and research. In G. Young, S. J. Segalowitz, S. E. Trehub, & C. M. Corter (Eds.), *Manual specialization and the developing brain* (pp. 177–247). New York: Academic Press.

Healey, J. M., Liederman, J., & Geschwind, N. (1986). Handedness is not a unidimentional trait. *Cortex, 22,* 33–53.

Hebben, N., Benjamins, D., & Milberg, W. P. (1981). The relationship among handedness, sighting dominance, and acuity dominance in elementary school children. *Cortex, 17,* 441–446.

Hildreth, G. (1949). The development and training of hand dominance: II. Developmental tendencies in handedness. *Journal of Genetic Psychology, 75,* 221–254.

Kee, D. W., Gottfried, A. W., Bathurst, K., & Brown, K. (1987). Left-hemisphere language specialization: Consistency in hand preference and sex differences. *Child Development, 58,* 718–724.

Kilshaw, D., & Annett, M. (1983). Right- and left-hand skill: I. Effects of age, sex and hand preference showing superior skill in left-handers. *British Journal of Psychology, 74,* 253–268.

Krombholz, H. (1989). Laterality and force of handgrip during the first two years at school. *Perceptual and Motor Skills, 68,* 955–962.

Lewandowski, L., & Kohlbrenner, R. (1985). Lateralization in gifted children. *Developmental Neuropsychology, 1,* 277–282.

Liederman, J., & Healey, J. M. (1986). Independent dimensions of hand preference: Reliability of the factor structure and the handedness inventory. *Archives of Clinical Neuropsychology, 1,* 371–386.

Liederman, J., & Kinsbourne, M. (1980). Rightward motor bias in newborns depends upon parental right-handedness. *Neuropsychologia, 18,* 579–584.

Longoni, A. M., & Orsini, L. (1988). Lateral preferences in preschool children: A research note. *Journal of Child Psychology & Psychiatry and Allied Disciplines, 29,* 533–539.

Lyle, J. G., & Johnson, E. G. (1976). Development of lateral consistency and its relation to reading and reversals. *Perceptual and Motor Skills, 43,* 695–698.

McManus, I. C. (1985). Handedness, language dominance and aphasia: A genetic model. *Psychological Medicine: Monograph Supplement, 8.*

McManus, I. C., Sik, G., Cole, D. R., Mellon, A. F., Wong, J., & Kloss, J. (1988). The development of handedness in children. *British Journal of Developmental Psychology, 6,* 257–273.

McMeekan, E. R., & Lishman, W. A. (1975). Retest reliabilities and interrelationship of the Annett Hand Preference Questionnaire and the Edinburgh Handedness Inventory. *British Journal of Psychology, 66,* 53–59.

Michel, G. F. (1983). Development of hand-use preference during infancy. In G. Young, S. J. Segalowitz, C. M. Corter, & S. E. Trehub (Eds.), *Manual specialization and the developing brain* (pp. 33–70). New York: Academic Press.

Michel, G. F., Ovrut, M. R., & Harkins, D. A. (1986). Hand-use for reaching and object manipulation in 6- through 13-month-old infants. *Genetic, Social, and General Psychology Monographs, 111,* 407–427.

Naidoo, S. (1972). *Specific dyslexia.* London: Pitman.

Neale, M. C. (1988). Handedness in a sample of volunteer twins. *Behavior Genetics, 18,* 69–79.

O'Callaghan, M. J., Tudehope, D. I., Dugdale, A. E., Mohay, H., Burns, Y., & Cook, F. (1987). Handedness in children with birthweights below 1000 g. *Lancet, 1* (8542): 1155.

Palmer, R. D. (1964). Development of a differentiated handedness. *Psychological Bulletin, 62,* 257–272.

Pennington, B. F., Smith, S. D., Kimberling, W. F., Green, P. A., & Haith, M. M. (1987). Left-handedness and immune disorders in familial dyslexics. *Archives of Neurology (Chicago), 44,* 634–639.

Peters, M. (1986). Incidence of left-handed writers and the inverted writing position in a sample of 2194 German elementary school children. *Neuropsychologia, 24:* 429–433.

Peters, M. (1988). Footedness: Asymmetries in foot preference and skill and neuro-psychological assessment of foot movement. *Psychological Bulletin, 103,* 251–261.

Pipe, M. E. (1987). Pathological left-handedness: Is it familial? *Neuropsychologia, 25,* 571–577.

Porac, C., Coren, S., & Searleman, A. (1986). Environmental factors in hand preference formation: Evidence from attempts to switch the preferred hand. *Behavior Genetics, 16,* 251–261.

Provins, K. A., Dalziel, F. R., & Higginbottom, G. (1987). Asymmetrical hand useage in infancy: An ethological approach. *Infant Behavior and Development, 10,* 165–172.

Rackowski, D., Kalat, J. W., & Nebes, R. (1974). Reliability and validity of some handedness questionnaire items. *Neuropsychologia, 12,* 43–47.

Ramsay, D. S. (1979). Manual preference for tapping in infants. *Developmental Psychology, 15,* 437–442.

Ramsay, D. S. (1980a). Beginnings of bimanual handedness and speech in infants. *Infant Behavior and Development, 3,* 67–77.

Ramsay, D. S. (1980b). Onset of unimanual handedness in infants. *Infant Behavior and Development, 3,* 377–385.

Rasmussen, T., & Milner, B. (1977). The role of early left-brain injury in determining lateralization of cerebral speech functions. *Annals of the New York Academy of Sciences, 299,* 355–369.

Rice, T., Plomin, R., & DeFries, J. C. (1984). Development of hand preference in the Colorado Adoption Project. *Perceptual and Motor Skills, 58,* 683–689.

Richardson, J. T. E., & Firlej, M. D. E. (1979). Laterality and reading attainment. *Cortex, 15,* 581–595.

Rider, R. A., Imwold, C. H., Griffin, M., & Sander, A. (1985). Comparison of hand preference in trainable mentally handicapped and nonhandicapped children. *Perceptual and Motor Skills, 61,* 1280–1282.

Ross, G., Lipper, E. G., & Auld, P. A. (1987). Hand preference of four-year-old children: Its relationship to premature birth and neurodevelopmental outcome. *Developmental Medicine and Child Neurology, 29,* 615–622.

Roszkowski, M. J., & Snelbecker, G. E. (1982). Temporal stability and predictive validity of self-assessed hand preference with first and second graders. *Brain & Cognition, 1,* 405–409.

Rutter, M., Tizard, J., & Whitmore, K. (1970). *Education, health, and behaviour.* London: Longman.

Rymar, K., Kameyama, T., Niwa, S.-I., Hiramatsu, K.-I., & Saitoh, O. (1984). Hand and eye preference patterns in elementary and junior high school students. *Cortex, 20,* 441–446.

Satz, P. (1972). Pathological left-handedness: An explanatory model. *Cortex, 8,* 121–135.

Satz, P., & Fletcher, J. M. (1987). Left-handedness and dyslexia: An old myth revisited. *Journal of Pediatric Psychology, 12,* 291–298.

Satz, P., Nelson, L., & Green, M. (1989). Ambiguous-handedness: Incidence in a non-clinical sample. *Neuropsychologia, 27,* 1309–1310.

Schachter, S. C., Ransil, B. J., & Geschwind, N. (1987). Associations of handedness with hair color and learning disabilities. *Neuropsychologia, 25,* 269–276.

Segalowitz, S. J., & Bryden, M. P. (1983). Individual differences in hemispheric representation of language. In S. J. Segalowitz (Ed.), *Language functions and brain organization* (pp. 341–372). New York: Academic Press.

Sheehan, E. P., & Smith, H. V. (1986). Cerebral lateralization and handedness and their effects on verbal and spatial reasoning. *Neuropsychologia, 24,* 531–540.

Soper, H. V., & Satz, P. (1984). Pathological left-handedness and ambiguous handedness: A new explanatory model. *Neuropsychologia, 22,* 511–515.

Soper, H. V., Satz, P., Orsini, D. L., Henry, R. R., Zvi, J. C., & Schulman, M. (1986). Handedness patterns in autism suggest subtypes. *Journal of Autism and Developmental Disorders, 16,* 155–167.

Steenhuis, R. E., & Bryden, M. P. (1989a). Different dimensions of hand preference that relate to skilled and unskilled activities. *Cortex, 25,* 289–304.

Steenhuis, R. E., & Bryden, M. P. (1989b). Hand preference and performance: Right-handers, left-handers, and left-handers who are not consistently left-handed. *Journal of Clinical and Experimental Neuropsychology, 11,* 37.

Steenhuis, R. E., Bryden, M. P., Schwartz, M. & Lawson, S. (1990). Reliability of hand preference items and factors. *Journal of Clinical and Experimental Neuropsychology.*

Tan, L. E. (1985). Laterality and motor skills in four-year-olds. *Child Development, 56,* 119–124.

Tapley, S. M., & Bryden, M. P. (1985). A group test for the assessment of performance between the hands. *Neuropsychologia, 23,* 215–221.

Teng, E. L., Lee, P.-H., Yang, K.-S., & Chang, P. C. (1979). Lateral preferences for hand, foot, and eye and their lack of association with scholastic achievement in 4143 Chinese. *Neuropsychologia, 17,* 41–48.

Turkewitz, G., Moreau, T., & Birch, K. G. (1968). Relation between birth condition and neurobehavioral organization in the neonate. *Pediatric Research, 2,* 243–249.

Van Camp, S. S., & Bixby, M. B. (1977). Eye and hand dominance in kindergarten and first-grade children. *Merrill-Palmer Quarterly, 23,* 129–139.

Viviani, J., Turkewitz, G., & Karp, E. (1978). A relationship between laterality of functioning at 2 days and at 7 years of age. *Bulletin of the Psychonomic Society, 12,* 189–192.

Whittington, J. E., & Richards, P. N. (1987). The stability of children's laterality prevalences and their relationship to measures of performance. *British Journal of Educational Psychology, 57,* 45–55.

Young, G. (1977). Manual specialization in infancy: Implications for lateralization of brain functions. In S. J. Segalowitz & F. A. Gruber (Eds.), *Language development and neurological theory* (pp. 289–311). New York: Academic Press.

Zung, B. J. (1985). Left-right comparison and children's performance on sensorimotor tests. *Journal of Clinical Psychology, 41,* 788–795.

CHAPTER SEVENTEEN

Event-Related Potential Indices: Learning Disabilities and Visual Processing

M. Russell Harter[1]

I. Reading Disabilities and the Neural Specificity Theory of Event-Related Potential Indicants of Selective Attention

This chapter will focus on event-related potential (ERP) indicants of individual differences in various types of visual selective attention. Reading ability, including dyslexia and reading disability (RD), will be the individual difference of primary concern. Differences in ERPs associated with attention-deficit disorder (ADD), sex, and intelligence also will be considered. "Selective attention" is broadly defined as the predisposition of an organism to process selectively relevant, compared to irrelevant, information. In this context, the enhanced ERPs to relevant, compared to irrelevant, information are measures of neural selection and of active neural information processing.

There are many reviews, which represent other perspectives and sensory modalities, of ERP measures of reading ability and related topics (Duane, 1986; Duffy, Denckla, McAnulty, & Holmes, 1988; Harter, Anllo-Vento, Wood, & Schroeder, 1988; Harter, Diering, & Wood, 1988; Hughes, 1985; John, Prichep, Ahn, Easton, Fridman, & Kaye, 1983; Molfese & Betz, 1988;

---

[1] Deceased.

Ollo & Squires, 1986; Shucard, Cummins, Gay, Lairsmith, & Welanko, 1985). Many of these papers note that the data have been inconclusive because of the following types of problems: tasks did not involve the disability; hemispheric differences were not considered; more electrodes were needed; behavioral measures were not taken; ERP measures were poorly defined; individual differences that may contribute to reading disability (for example, gender and ADD) were not considered or controlled; different types of learning disabilities (for example, RD and ADD) were not dissociated; and the contribution of within-subject, trial-to-trial variability in ERP waveform to specific ERP measures was not considered. This chapter demonstrates biases toward experiments which have addressed many of these concerns and which reflect consistent trends.

The following discussion will reveal that the relationships between reading ability and ERP indicants of information processing are extremely complex. They depend on the characteristics of the subject, the ERP component considered, and the nature of information processed. Furthermore, ERP components traditionally associated with both sensory and cognitive processes relate to reading ability. These factors must be incorporated into any theoretical framework used to relate specific ERP components to reading ability and RD.

The theoretical importance of an ERP component or measure depends on how it is identified and defined. Investigators have used two general approaches to identify such measures in the context of reading ability (see Ollo & Squires, 1986, and Harter, Anllo-Vento et al., 1988, for a discussion of this topic). The most frequently used approach is to identify the subject groups of interest (for example, those with and without RD), measure ERPs from these groups, and establish which portion of the ERP waveform distinguishes the groups. The significance probability mapping procedure is one example of this approach (Duffy et al., 1988), although it revealed little between-group difference in visual ERPs.

Event-related potential components or measures defined in this manner are clinically important. For example, they can be used to classify subjects into reading groups. They have limitations, however. First, they reveal little about functional differences in neural processing in the groups of interest. Second, due to the complicated relationship between the scalp distribution of ERPs and their underlying sources, the distribution of such components may not reflect their neural sources. Finally, given the empirical nature of this approach and the almost infinite number of ways ERPs might reflect group differences, the risk of committing a Type I statistical error is high.

The theoretical approach emphasized here lessens the risks and problems mentioned above. It is central to the neural specificity theory of ERP indicants of attention. This theory provides a theoretical framework for interpreting specific ERP components and, thus, for interpreting differences in ERPs associated with reading ability.

A. Description of the Neural Specificity Theory

Harter and Aine (1984) proposed the neural specificity theory. Hillyard and Mangun (1986), Naatanen (1986), and Harter and Aine (1986) critically reviewed this theory. Its central assumption is that if a specific function is mediated by a known neural source, that neural source contributes to the functional ERP component associated with the activation of that specific function.

The following steps establish the functional validity of ERP components and measures. First, identify some function (letter identification) that involves the ability of interest (reading) and is localized in a particular cortical area (presumably the left posterior hemisphere). Second, determine the effects of this function on ERP waveform. For example, subjects could selectively attend to letters (relevant stimuli) mixed with nonletter patterns (irrelevant stimuli). The difference in ERP waveform to the relevant letters compared to irrelevant nonletter patterns then would define a functional component.

Such functional components presumably reflect the differential response, due to attention, of those neurons that normally represent the relevant and the irrelevant stimuli. Thus, they are a measure of active and selective neural information processing (neural selection). Given how they are defined, they relate to a specific cognitive function which has been localized in a particular cortical area. They not only may distinguish between subjects with and without RD, but they also may reveal the neurophysiological processes that underlie the distinction.

Executive centers outside of the sensory projection systems, possibly in prefrontal and parietal cortex, initiate and control the selection processes reflected by the functional ERP components. Long-term memories of the relevant and irrelevant information may activate these executive centers. Such activation, therefore, may take place in the absence of the actual relevant and irrelevant stimuli.

We proposed that there are two main classes of functional components associated with the function of two main cortical systems. Ungerleider and Mishkin (1982) reviewed the electrophysiological data from primates which serve as the bases for these two cortical systems. These systems have a number of characteristics pertinent to the present discussion.

The *"where"* system primarily consists of the dorsal or occipitoparietal pathways. It also includes projections from the tectofugal system, but these are of less importance in primates. It represents where an object is located across the entire visual field. Posterior parietal neurons tend to have receptive fields in the contralateral hemifield and generally do not receive input from the ipsilateral hemifield via the corpus callosum. The posterior parietal cortex equally represents both the central and the peripheral visual fields. The higher-association areas of the right parietal cortex (for example, Broadmann's areas 7, 39, and 4), which mediate spatial function, presumably receive their major visual input from this system.

The *"what" system* consists of the occipitotemporal pathways. It identifies complex objects regardless of their spatial location. Most inferior temporal neurons have bilateral receptive fields—due to connections through the corpus callosum—with very complex trigger features. They receive their major input from the central visual field. The bilateral transfer of information provides the opportunity for hemispheric specialization. The higher-association areas of the left temporal lobe (for example, Broadmann's areas 21, 22, 37, and 38), which mediate language function, presumably receive their major visual input from this system.

The "where" and "what" cortical systems have many characteristics in common with other closely related conceptualizations of dual visual processing systems—for example, transient versus sustained channels, Neisser's preattentive versus focal attentive processes, and the functions of the right parietal versus the left temporal cortical hemispheres. Transient versus sustained channels differ along the following dimensions: short versus long response latency, sensitive to moving versus stationary stimuli, large versus small receptive fields, input from the peripheral versus the central retina, sensitive to low versus high spatial frequencies, sensitive to flickering versus steady-state stimulation, and insensitive versus sensitive to image sharpness (Haber & Hershenson, 1980, pp. 115–117). Transient channels can inhibit sustained channels. Preattentive versus focal processes are distinguished along the dimensions of global versus specific segmentation of visual field, parallel versus serial processing, location detection versus object recognition, and ground versus figure (Haber & Hershenson, 1980, pp. 327–328). Preattentive processes direct focal attention. In the present context, the "where" and "what" systems will be expanded to include these additional characteristics.

Harter, Aine, and Schroeder (1982), Harter and Aine (1984), and Neville, and Lawson (1987) were some of the first investigators to note that the effects of selective attention on different ERP[2] components reflect activity in these two cortical systems. The enhanced positivity between about 100 and 200 msec (DP1) and enhanced negativity between about 180 and 200 msec

---

2 The effects of stimulus relevance on measures of neural activity are illustrated as differences in ERP amplitude, i.e., relevant minus irrelevant ERP waveforms are displayed as DP1, etc.

(DN1) in response to peripheral stimuli seemingly reflect activity in the occipitoparietal "where" system (see below). The effects of attending versus not attending the location of the evoking stimulus on ERP waveform defined these components. Thus, they are measures of *location selection*.

The enhanced negativity between about 200 and 240 msec (DN2 or DN230) and enhanced positivity between about 300 and 400 msec (DP3) in response to central stimuli seemingly reflect activity in the occipitotemporal "what" system (see below). The effects of attending versus not attending to the type of stimulus at a given location on ERP waveform defined these measures. They, thus, are measures of *type selection*.

B. Reading Ability and the Cortical Visual Systems: Hypotheses and Purposes

The discussion that follows provides the rationale for two main hypotheses:

H1: *Dyslexics or poor readers have either normal or superior processing in the occipitoparietal "where" system.*

H2: *Dyslexics or poor readers have deficient processing at one or more levels in the occipitotemporal "what" system.*

For the remainder of this section, findings supportive of either of these two hypotheses will be discussed.

Dyslexics have the most difficulty performing tasks that require verbal and language ability and that involve the posterior-temporal regions of the left hemisphere (H2); their performance is normal or less impaired on tasks that require visuospatial ability and that presumably involve the parietal regions of the right hemisphere (H1) (Kolb & Whishaw, 1985, pp. 713–717). Some investigators have hypothesized that dyslexics may have superior right-hemisphere and visuospatial abilities (H1) (see reviews by Bradshaw & Nettleton, 1983; Geschwind & Galaburda, 1985).

Morphological and anatomical data (see reviews by Duane, 1986; Hynd & Semrud-Clikeman, 1989), in part, support these findings and hypotheses. In about 80% of normal, right-handed individuals, the left posterior hemisphere is longer and wider than the right posterior hemisphere; in the brains of dyslexics, however, there is an increased incidence of symmetry in this region (H2). Hier, LeMay, Rosenberger, and Perlo (1978) reported that the usual morphological asymmetries of the brain even are reversed (right wider than left posterior hemisphere) more often in severe dyslexics (about 42%) than in normal (20–25%) subjects (H2). Geschwind and Galaburda (1985), however, did not find such increased incidence of reversed asymmetry in dyslexics, yet dyslexics still were atypical in that many displayed symmetry of the planum temporale (H2). These last two findings support the second hypothesis, H2, assuming that the atypical asymmetry is due to a reduction in the size of the left hemisphere. Geschwind and Galaburda did find bilateral neural anomalies and arteriovenous malformations in the temporal and parietal regions of dyslexics, these anomalies being more frequent in the left than the right hemispheres (H2).

Hynd and Semrud-Clikeman (1989) critically reviewed cytoarchitectonic computed tomography (CT) and magnetic resonance imaging (MRI) studies on dyslexia and brain morphology. Many studies contained methodological deficiencies, particularly for the diagnosis of dyslexia. They concluded that the morphological differences frequently associated with dyslexia may be due to factors that tend to coexist with dyslexia—for example, hyperactivity and attention-deficit disorder.

Behavioral measures of laterality also suggest reduced or reversed asymmetry in dyslexics. Normal reading subjects tend to reflect a right perceptual field (left-hemisphere) advantage. In contrast, dyslexics tend to show a reduction or reversal of this advantage (H2) (see below for a discussion of laterality and reading disability).

Some studies of basic, visual–perceptual abilities suggest that normal readers have greater sensitivity in sustained channels (H2), whereas disabled readers have greater sensitivity in transient channels (H1). The maximum contrast sensitivity was to relatively low spatial frequencies 2 cycles per degree (c/d) in disabled readers and to relatively high spatial frequencies (4 c/d) in normal readers (Lovegrove, Bowling, Badcock, & Blackwood, 1980). Visual persistence was longer for low than for high spatial frequencies for disabled readers and longer for high than for low spatial frequencies for normal readers (Lovegrove, Heddle, & Slaghuis, 1980). Poor readers had stronger perceptual grouping effects, effects interpreted as reflecting greater processing in the global, peripheral system (Williams & Bologna, 1985). Finally, in a letter-search task, poor and good readers performed equally well when the letters were blurred—that is, the letters had to be discriminated on the basis of lower spatial frequencies. Poor readers did less well than good readers when the letters were sharp—that is, the letters contained high spatial frequencies (Williams, Brannan, & Lartigue, 1987).

As stated earlier, the purposes of this chapter are to review recent findings on reading ability and ERPs and to consider these findings within the context of the above conceptual framework. First, reading ability is considered in relationship to ERP indicants of location selection in the "where" system. A new experiment is described and discussed in relation to our earlier one. Second, reading ability is considered in relationship to ERP indicants of type selection in the "what" system. This section primarily considers the many published studies on this topic. Finally, some of the individual differences in ERPs which may confound the effects of reading ability are noted.

II. Method for Spatial Orienting Experiment

Harter, Miller, Price, LaLonde, and Keyes (1989) described the procedures in detail. In brief, they were as follows.

A. Subjects

A random sample of 84 children served as subjects. Felton and Wood (1989, Study 3) and Felton and Brown (this volume, Chapter 15, Study 2) described the characteristics of the larger sample from which these subjects were selected. Subjects were a stratified random subsample of 84 children matched for age and intelligence: the 51 boys ranged in age from 6.4 to 8.5 years (mean = 7.3) and had a mean Peabody Picture Vocabulary Test-Revised (PPVT-R) score of 102; the 33 girls ranged in age from 6.5 to 7.8 years (mean = 7.1) and had a mean PPVT-R score of 101.

Two procedures were used to statistically assess the variability attributable to individual differences—that is, to reading ability, ADD score, and gender. The first was a classification procedure used in conjunction with an analysis of variance (BMDP 2V). The Woodcock–Johnson Total Cluster Score determined the reading-group classification. Low and high readers had scores below and above the mean (450), respectively. The Diagnostic Interview for Children and Adolescents-Parent Interview assessed the presence of ADD. The number of positive responses on this test served as an "ADD score." To have a sufficient number of subjects in subgroups, low- and high-ADD subjects had scores below and above the 56th percentile.

Correlation coefficients between the various dependent measures was a second statistical procedure. Since subjects are not classified in this type of procedure, it avoids the problems inherent in classification procedures.

B. Stimuli and Task

This experiment differed somewhat from the spatial-attention task used by Harter, Anllo-Vento, and Wood (1989). It did not require a discrimination between relevant and irrelevant targets presented at the same location (type or intralocation selection).

A trial consisted of presenting on a computer monitor first an arrow in the central visual field and then, 600 msec later, a target in the peripheral visual field. These stimuli were white (against a black background) and subtended about 42 minutes of visual angle.

The arrow occurred at the fixation point and randomly pointed to either the left or the right visual field ($p = .50$). The arrow direction defined the relevant visual field and was a cue for the subjects to direct their attention to the cued visual field (without moving their eyes). The targets were squares

flashed (50 msec in duration) 8° randomly to the left or the right of the arrow
(p = .50).

The task was to respond to a target only if it flashed in the relevant visual
field—that is, the field cued by the direction of the arrow. The reaction-time
response was to lift the right index finger off a microswitch key as quickly and
accurately as possible. Data from adults show that the hand of response and
the reference electrodes cannot account for the spatial-attention effects reported here (Harter, in press).

C. Event-Related Potentials and Electrooculograms

Subjects wore International Electro-caps. Event-related potentials were
recorded from the left and right occipital (O1 and O2), parietal (P3 and P4),
central (C3' and C4'), and frontal (F3 and F4) electrode locations. Eye
movements and blinks were monitored with an electrode placed 2 cm to the
left and 2 cm below the left corner of the left eye. All electrodes were refer-
enced to yoked ears. Movement artifacts or behavioral errors resulted in the
data being rejected.

The potentials were quantified following arrow onset by determining
the average ERP amplitude, in reference to zero-voltage baseline, for the
following epochs: 0–60 msec (A30), 120–160 msec (A140), 160–240 msec
(A190), 260–340 msec (A290), 360–440 msec (A290), 460–540 msec
(A490), and 560–640 msec (A590). Event-related potentials to targets were
quantified by measuring (1) the average amplitude from 120 to 140 msec after
the target (P1), (2) the average amplitude from 180 to 200 msec (N1) and
180 to 220 msec (DN1) after the target (these included the peaks of the raw
and difference waveforms, respectively), and (3) the average amplitude from
300 to 320 msec following the target (P3).

When reading ability or ADD significantly influenced a particular measure in the ANOVA, that effect was quantified and submitted to correlational
analyses. In the abbreviations below, "A" refers to an area under the waveform
measure, the numbers refer to the latency or average latency of the measure,
"N" and "P" refer to the polarity of component measures, "D" refers to the
difference or increase in ERP amplitude due to the relevance of the evoking
stimulus, and "O," "C," and "H" refer to occipital, arrow-cue direction, and
hemispheres, respectively.

The measures selected were as follows:
1. A30 averaged across all electrodes (CNV);
2. Occipital A140 (OA140);
3. A290 averaged across all electrodes (A290);
4,5,6. The interaction between arrow direction (left minus right) and
   hemispheres (left minus right) for A290 averaged across the occipital, central, and parietal electrodes (OPC290HC), for A390 aver-

aged across the central and parietal electrodes (PC390HC), and for occipital A590 (O590HC);

7. Occipital DN1 minus frontal DN1 (EDN1);
8. DP3 amplitude averaged across all electrodes (DP3);
9. Within-subject and condition variability in ERP waveform, as indicated by the standard deviation at the occipital electrode (OSD);
10. Behavioral reaction time to targets (rt);
11. Percentage of time the subject responded correctly to targets (hits); and
12. percentage of time the subjects responded to nontargets (fa).

These measures were correlated with

13. Age,
14. Woodcock Psychoeducational Battery Total Cluster Score (WTCL),
15. Woodcock Total Standard Score (Age) (WTSSA),
16. Woodcock Letter–Word Identification Raw Score (WLWID),
17. Woodcock Word-Attack Raw Score (WWAR),
18. Woodcock Passage-Comprehension Raw Score (WJPCR),
19. Peabody Picture Vocabulary Test-Revised Total Standard Score (PPVTTS), and
20. Diagnostic Interview for Children and Adolescents-Parents Interview (DICA).

Felton and Wood (1989) described the neuropsychological tests and procedures in detail.

It should be noted that many investigators have studied the effects of various types of attention on the CNV, P1, N1, and P3 ERP components (see reviews by Donchin, Ritter, & McCallum, 1978; Harter & Aine, 1984; Harter *et al.,* 1982; Hillyard & Munte, 1984; Hillyard & Picton, 1979; Naatanen, 1982; Neville & Lawson, 1987). The present study and review will focus on individual differences in these effects.

III. Reading Ability and Location Selection in the "Where" System: ERPs to Stimuli in the Peripheral Visual Field

In the context of ERP measures of visual–spatial attention, it was hypothesized that *dyslexics or poor readers should reflect normal or superior location selection* as indicated by the DP1 or DN1 ERP measures.

There has been only one previous study of ERP indicants of visual–spatial attention in children with and without RD (Harter, Anllo-Vento, & Wood, 1989). Boys, 12 with RD and 15 without RD, quickly shifted their attention to the left or right visual field. Boys with RD had greater DN1 compared to boys without RD. Reading ability negatively correlated with DN1 in this dichotomous sample of boys ($r = -.54$). These electrophysiological data provide some support for the hypothesis of greater visual–spatial attention and processing in the occipitoparietal system in RD children.

The study reported here assessed the relationship between ERP indicants of visual–spatial attention and potential reading ability in a younger, random sample. The sample consisted of first-grade boys and girls (see above). Relatively few children in this sample will become reading disabled or dyslexic at a higher grade (probably less that 10%), given it was a normal sample.

Three main types of location selection are discussed in relationship to reading ability: the selective preparation for the relevant stimulus before it occurs (the directing of attention and sensory readiness), the selective sensory processing of information presented at the location of the relevant stimulus (early selection and DN1), and the more cognitive processing of the relevant information per se (late selection and DP3). [The main effects of attention and sex differences have been published elsewhere (Harter, Miller et al., 1989).]

A. Behavioral Data from Present Experiment

The low compared to high readers revealed the following differences in behavioral measures: low readers had a lower percentage of hits [92 versus 96%, $F(1, 80) = 10.49$, $p = .0017$]; they required more practice trials to reach the criterion (75% correct) before starting the experiment [52 versus 38 trials, $F(1, 80) = 4.38$, $p = .0396$]; and more of their trials were rejected because of movement and other kinds of artifacts [88 versus 71 trials, $F(1, 80) = 5.52$, $p = .0213$]. Mean reaction time was faster for low than for high reading boys (432 versus 444 msec); in contrast, it was slower for low than for high reading girls (498 versus 438 msec) [Sex × Reading: $F(1, 80) = 7.46$, $p = .0077$].

Since this task had multiple parts and the behavioral results were complex, no simple conclusion can be drawn as to how reading ability related to task performance. Low readers may have had more difficulty discriminating arrow direction and its meaning, yet their reaction time to the peripheral targets at the relevant location was faster, at least for the boys.

B. Preparatory Activity: Contingent Negative Variation (CNV) and Contralateral Directing-Attention Negativity (DAN) and Positivity (DAP)

1. CNVs (MEASURE A30)

The negativity at arrow onset presumably reflects a CNV before the arrow cue. Contingent negative variations, which occur before and end shortly after an expected stimulus, are generally greatest over the vertex and presumably reflect an increase in general cortical arousal (Deecke et al., 1984; Naatanen & Michie, 1979; Ritter, Ford, Gaillard, Harter, Kutas, Naatanen,

Polich, & Renault, 1984; Tecce, 1972). Such general arousal would involve both the "where" and the "what" cortical systems.

The ERP waveforms associated with this task are shown for low and high readers in Figs. 1 and 2. The negative activity at the time of arrow onset (A30 measure) was greater for the low than for the high reading groups [Reading: $F(1, 80) = 4.75$, $p = .0322$]. This activity correlated negatively with several measures of reading ability (see Table I) and positively with EDN1 to the target ($r = .237$).

The greater negativity at the start of the trial for low readers suggests a greater state of preparation in these subjects. Possibly this task was more interesting for the low readers. Or, they were compensating for difficulty they had on portions of the task. Previous research generally shows decreased CNV

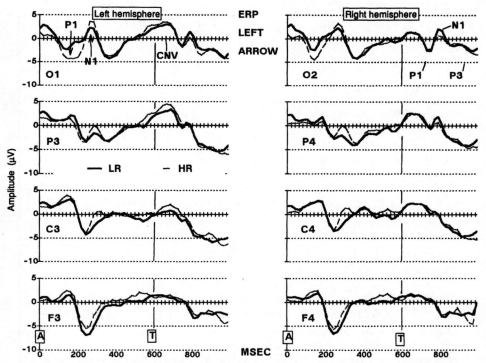

FIGURE 1 The superimposed tracings are from low readers (LR, solid line) and high readers (HR, dotted line) following the left arrow (A). ERPs are from the left (LT.) and right (RT.) hemisphere (HEMI.) over the occipital (O1 and O2), parietal (P3 and P4), central (C3 and C4), and frontal (F3 and F4) regions. Horizontal axis indicates when the arrow (A) and target (T) were presented in msec. Data have been averaged across 35 LR, 49 HR, and 2 target locations (left and right). Negativity up.

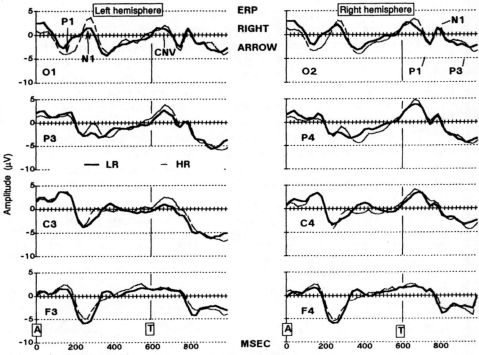

FIGURE 2 Same as Fig. 1 but ERPs following the right arrow.

in dyslexic and learning-disabled subjects (Hughes, 1985). The present results, thus, may be specific to the visual–spatial attention task employed.

2. EDAN AND LDAP

Harter, Miller *et al.* (1989) and Harter (in press) identified two slow potentials associated with a shift in the direction of attention. They were more negative and positive, respectively, over the hemisphere contralateral to the direction of attention. We labeled them directing-attention contralateral early negativity (EDAN) and late positivity (LDAP). EDAN and LDAP were greatest over the right central-parietal and occipital regions, respectively. Harter and colleagues interpreted right central-parietal EDAN as reflecting the greater involvement of these areas in controlling and directing spatial attention (Heilman, 1979; Knight, 1985; Kolb & Whishaw, 1985, pp. 389–390 and 573–591; Mesulam, 1981). Occipital LDAP appeared to reflect sensory-specific cortical priming of the relevant hemifield. Many other measures suggest such priming, for example, the activity of parietal neurons in the cortex of monkeys in a visual task (Bushnell, Goldberg, & Robinson, 1981; Lynch, Mountcastle, Talbot, & Yin, 1977) and the regional cerebral blood

TABLE I Correlation Matrix[a]

		CNV 1	OA140 2	A290 3	OPC290HC 4	PC390HC 5	O590HC 6	EDN1 7	DP3 8	OSD 9	rt 10	His 11	fa 12
ERP measures													
CNV	1	1.000											
OA140	2	-0.331	1.000										
A290	3	0.170	-0.193	1.000									
OPC290HC	4	-0.228	0.112	-0.114	1.000								
PC390HC	5	0.075	0.050	-0.033	-0.052	1.000							
O590HC	6	-0.009	0.086	-0.004	-0.040	-0.080	1.000						
EDN1	7	0.237	-0.191	0.190	-0.000	0.042	-0.025	1.000					
DP3	8	-0.106	-0.066	0.104	-0.078	0.092	0.128	-0.032	1.000				
OSD	9	0.170	-0.277	0.300	-0.161	0.020	-0.273	0.009	0.234	1.000			
Behavioral and neuropsychological measures													
rt	10	0.045	-0.055	-0.229	-0.025	0.092	-0.146	-0.140	-0.209	0.027	1.000		
His	11	-0.149	0.115	0.045	0.052	0.107	0.181	-0.030	0.225	0.044	-0.551	1.000	
fa	12	0.037	-0.111	0.195	-0.041	-0.037	0.011	0.051	-0.117	-0.078	0.070	-0.287	1.000
Age	13	-0.168	0.138	-0.092	0.149	-0.127	0.111	-0.060	0.075	-0.197	-0.120	0.038	-0.277
WTCL	14	-0.244	0.273	-0.209	0.158	0.059	-0.203	-0.266	0.094	-0.201	-0.028	0.230	-0.158
WTSSA	15	-0.091	0.150	-0.125	0.011	0.106	-0.279	-0.173	0.061	-0.042	0.057	0.113	0.028
WLWID	16	-0.197	0.293	-0.175	0.101	0.082	-0.155	-0.218	0.053	-0.229	-0.044	0.234	-0.125
WWAR	17	-0.176	0.250	-0.211	0.137	-0.037	-0.255	-0.241	0.088	-0.136	0.035	0.197	-0.228
WJPCR	18	-0.301	0.267	-0.200	0.200	0.096	-0.179	-0.268	0.067	-0.243	-0.035	0.245	-0.112
PPVTTS	19	-0.076	0.068	-0.078	-0.069	0.253	0.001	-0.215	-0.040	-0.121	0.064	0.109	-0.054
DICA	20	0.050	0.007	-0.055	-0.019	-0.085	0.029	0.277	-0.128	-0.139	-0.006	-0.118	0.137

[a] df = 82, $r = .18$, $p < .05$.

flow in the somesthetic cortical areas in man during a cutaneous task (Roland, 1981).

The difference in ERP waveforms, associated with directing attention to the left versus the right visual field, may best be seen in difference ERPs (DERPs) obtained by substracting these two waveforms. In Fig. 3, the ERPs following the right arrow were subtracted from the ERPs following the left arrow (LA − RA); such DERPs functionally reflect the effects of shifting attention to the left.

The effects of reading ability on the DERPs following the arrows depended on the electrode pair considered [activity 260–440 msec after arrow cue, Arrow Direction × Hemisphere × Electrode × Reading, $F(3, 240) = 4.21, p = .0082$]. Over the central regions, there was a slow, negative wave over the right hemisphere—the hemifield contralateral to the direction of the shift of attention (left) (EDAN, Fig. 3). EDAN was greater in size and longer in duration for high than for low readers.

Analysis of the occipital data revealed a second type of group difference. Low but not high readers reflected greater positivity over the right (contralateral) than left (ipsilateral) hemisphere (LDAP, Fig. 3) [occipital activity 260–440 msec after arrow cue, Arrow Direction × Hemisphere × Reading, $F(1, 80) = 6.71, p = .0114$]. Later in time, good readers also reflected LDAP.

One possible interpretation of the effects of reading ability on EDAN and LDAP is consistent with the main hypothesis stated above. Poor readers primed their attended occipital–parietal hemifields (the "where" system") more quickly than high readers. They had shorter-duration EDAN (which presumably reflects the directing of attention) and earlier-onset LDAP (which presumably reflects regional cortical priming).

Note than an analysis of covariance, using the PPVT total standard score as a covariate, suggests that PPVT-R accounts for the relationship between reading level and the size of central-parietal EDAN ($r = .253$ between PPVTTS and PC390HC, Table I). EDAN, therefore, relates to factors other than simply directing attention—for example, the ability to process arrow direction and meaning (involving the "what" system).

The effects of reading ability on the later portion of LDAP (A590 or activity between 560 and 640 msec) did not approach statistical significance ($p > .05$).

C. Effects of Target Relevance on N1 (DN1)

Investigators attribute the effects of attention on the negativity between 180 and 220 msec (DN1), in response to peripheral targets, to the modulation of sensory processing in the portion of the visual system that projects primarily from the peripheral retina to the posterior parietal areas—that is, processing in the "where" system (Harter, in press; Harter & Aine, 1984; Harter et al.,

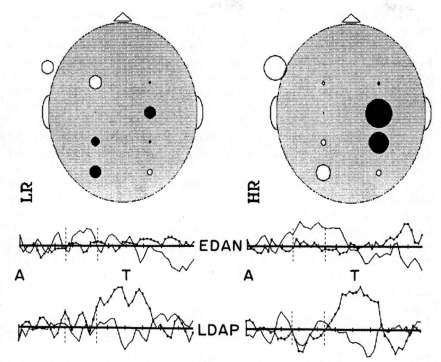

FIGURE 3 Difference ERPs derived by subtracting the ERPs following the right arrow from the ERPs following the left arrow and reflecting directing-attention contralateral negativity (EDAN, electrodes C3 and C4) and positivity (LDAP, electrodes O1 and O2). The dotted and solid tracings under the heads are from the left and right hemispheres, respectively. Negativity up. Left and right heads/tracings are for low (LR) and high (HR) readers. Each dot illustrates DERP amplitude at a given electrode location (see Fig. 1) averaged over the time specified by the two vertical dashed lines on the DERP waveform (260–420 msec after arrow onset). The dot in front of the left ear represents the eye electrode. Dot diameter represents DERP amplitude. The half-length of the vertical dashed lines through the ERP waveforms (baseline to minus or plus values) and the largest dot equal 1.1 μV. Open and solid dots represent positive and negative polarity, respectively. The target (T) was presented 600 msec after the arrow (A). Remainder same as Fig. 1.

1982; Harter, Anllo-Vento, & Wood, 1989; Harter, Miller *et al.*, 1989). Visual attention modulates the responsivity of neurons in the posterior parietal cortex (Bushnell *et al.*, 1981; Lynch *et al.*, 1977; Moran & Desimone, 1985). Cells in striate cortex, however, reportedly are unaffected by visual attention (Moran & Desimone, 1985).

As shown in Fig. 4, N1 amplitude following irrelevant targets was virtually identical for the low and high reading groups; N1 amplitude following relevant targets, however, was greater for the low than for the high reading group. The anterior-to-posterior gradient of this task-relevant effect, at 180–200 msec following targets (DN180), also was greater for the low than for the high reading subjects [Reading × Electrode × Relevance: $F(3,240) = 4.57$, $p = .0149$].

The Electrode × Relevance interaction, as measured by EDN1, correlated negatively with both reading ability ($r = -.266$) and PPVT scores ($r = -.215$) (see Table I). An analysis of covariance, using PPVT-R total standard scores as a covariate, showed that the negative relationship between DN1 amplitude and reading level remained even after removal of the contribution of PPVT scores ($p < .05$).

The greater location selection for low compared to high readers, as reflected by DN180, supports the hypothesis of greater processing in the occipitoparietal "where" system for low readers and dyslexics. It also replicates the negative relationship between DN1 and reading ability in older children with and without RD reported by Harter, Anllo-Vento, and Wood (1989). Note that this trend was unique to ERPs in response to the peripheral targets. P1N1 amplitude to the central arrow was greater for the high than for the low reading group, as discussed below.

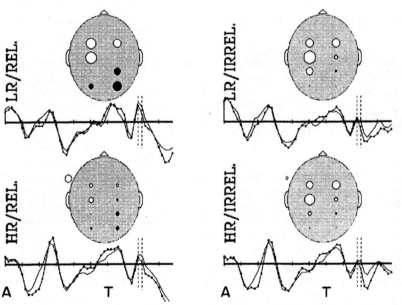

FIGURE 4 Dot maps of the scalp distribution of N1 amplitude following the targets (T) for the low (LR, top) and high (HR, bottom) readers, and relevant (REL., left) and irrelevant (IRREL., right) targets. The largest dot equals 3.9 μV. The ERP waveforms are from O1 and O2. Remainder same as Fig. 3.

The enhanced DN1 for poor readers could reflect several underlying neural changes. One possibility is that the modulation of the sensitivity of cortical areas receiving input from the relevant and irrelevant visual fields is more effective in RD subjects. This possibility is supported by the earlier onset of LDAP in low readers. The greater modulation could be due to either enhanced neural priming or greater regional cerebral blood flow.

If a focal lesion in the temporal areas is one cause of RD (as discussed below), such a lesion could result in functional cortical reorganization. The lesion could release previously masked functional plasticity of neurons (1) within the same hemisphere in areas adjacent to the lesion (e.g., occipital and parietal areas), or (2) in the opposite hemisphere in areas comparable to that lesioned. The enhanced DN1 over the right central areas, for example, could reflect a reduction of interhemispheric competition or inhibition due to a lesion in the left temporal region. Others have discussed interhemispheric inhibition in this context (Bradshaw & Nettleton, 1983, pp. 236–237; Bullock, Liederman, & Todorovic, 1987).

Superior location selection of peripheral stimuli in poor readers, as reflected by DN1, is consistent with and may explain several findings in the literature. Geiger and Lettvin (1987) reported that dyslexic compared to normal subjects were superior in their ability to correctly identify letters in the peripheral visual field. This was not the case with centrally presented letters. Given the nature of the Geiger and Lettvin design, it is not clear whether the superior ability of dyslexics was due to their superior spatial attention or letter-identification ability (in the peripheral visual field only). The effects of spatial attention (location selection) and letter-identification ability (type selection) should be unconfounded in future research on reading ability. This research should include central and peripheral visual-field viewing conditions.

J. E. Obrzut, Hynd, Obrzut, and Pirozzolo (1981) also reported that learning-disabled children were better able to direct their attention to either their left or their right perceptual space. In a dichotic listening task, normal children attended to the right ear (had a right-ear advantage) regardless of which ear they were instructed to attend; in contrast, the learning-disabled children shifted their attention with the instructional set. J. E. Obrzut, Hynd, and Zellner (1983) performed a similar study on visual half-field asymmetries in normal and learning-disabled children. Although the stimulus conditions (unilateral, cued unilateral versus bilateral presentation) did not interact significantly with groups (normal versus learning disabled), the results reflected a trend of greater attention effects—that is, greater differences between the cued versus noncued unilateral conditions—in the learning-disabled children.

J. E. Obrzut et al. (1981) noted that attention has not been controlled in most laterality experiments. Reading-disabled children, therefore, might attend to either the left or the right ear (or visual field). This could account for the reduced or deficient right-ear advantage or "laterality" in dyslexics or poor readers as a group. J. E. Obrzut (1988) discussed how these attentional-field differences might account for the reported "laterality" differences in reading-disabled compared to normal reading subjects.

Kinsbourne (1988) claimed that "left hemisphere activation difficulty is the best available explanation of the findings of J. E. Obrzut *et al.* (1981, p. 18)." The enhanced DN1 effects in RD subjects require modification of this conclusion; RD compared to no-RD subjects had greater left- (or right-) hemisphere activation, as reflected by DN1, when they attended to the right (or left) visual field. The above data, in fact, suggest right-hemisphere activation difficulty in subjects without RD when they attend to the left visual field (also see below).

Brannan and Williams (1987) investigated behavioral measures of the allocation of visual attention in good and poor readers using a Posner-type paradigm. Peripheral cues (2° from central fixation) signaled the direction of letter targets (also presented 2° from central fixation). They varied the probability of the correctness of the signal and the stimulus onset asynchrony (SOA) between the cue and the target. Six good and six poor readers were subjects. Poor readers reflected less accuracy at 0–50 msec SOA and nonsignificantly greater accuracy at 170 msec SOA as compared to good readers. Given that some time is required for a cue to be processed and attention directed, the effects at 0 msec SOA (and probably 50 msec SOA) reflected other than attentional processes. Had Brannan and Williams used a longer SOA and more peripheral stimuli, the poor readers may have shown significantly better performance than the good readers on their spatial-attention task. Thus, stimuli were presented at 8° and the SOA was 600 msec in the present study.

1. INTERACTION BETWEEN READING ABILITY AND GENDER

Harter, Anllo-Vento, and Wood (1989) reported greater differences in DN1 in their subjects with and without RD (about 6 μV) than in the low and high reading subjects in the present study (about 1.5 μV). The correlations between DN1 and reading level were $-.54$ and $-.27$ for these two studies, respectively. The smaller effects in the present study could be due to a number of factors. One such factor could be differences in the reading ability of subjects in the two experiments. The tasks also differed in that the previous task required type selection.

Sex differences in the subjects used in these two studies clearly are an important factor. Both boys and girls participated in the present study; only boys participated in our earlier one. In the present study, the effects of reading ability on occipital and parietal DN1 depended on gender [Relevance × Sex × Reading: $F(1, 80) = 10.53, p = .0017$]. DN1 was greater for low than high reading boys. In contrast, it was greater for high than low reading girls as shown in Fig. 5. The behavioral reaction-time data reflected a similar trend. Reaction time was faster for low than for high reading boys and for high than for low reading girls, as noted above. This interaction did not approach statistical significance for the percentage of hits or false alarms ($p > .05$).

The hypothesized enhanced processing in the "where" occipitoparietal system for low versus high readers, therefore, may apply mainly to boys. Unfortunately, the contribution of gender to the behavioral data reviewed in support of this hypothesis is inconclusive. Most of the studies simply did not report how many males and females were in the different reading groups (Geiger & Lettvin, 1987; Lovegrove, Heddle, & Slaghuis, 1980; Williams & Bologna, 1985; Williams et al., 1987). More males (8) than females (4) participated in one study (Brannan & Williams, 1987). An equal number of males and females were in both reading groups for only one study (J. E. Obrzut et al., 1981).

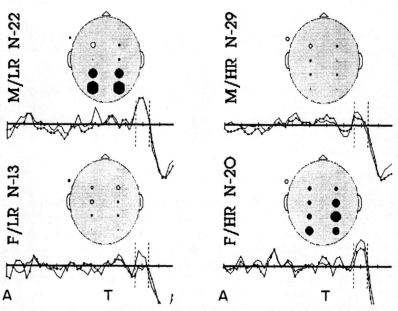

FIGURE 5 Dot maps of the scalp distribution of DN1 following the target (T). DN1 is the difference in N1 amplitude following relevant versus irrelevant targets. Males (M) top, females (F) bottom. Low readers (LR) left, high readers (HR) right. Tracings are DERPs from P3 and P4. The largest dot equals 3 μV. Remainder same as Fig. 3.

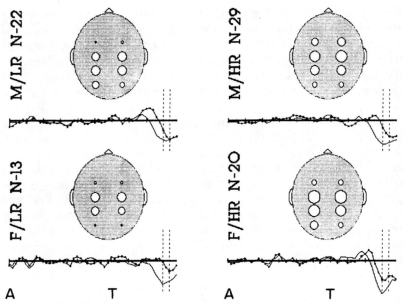

FIGURE 6 Dot maps of the scalp distribution of DP3. DERPs are from O1 (dotted) and C3 (solid). Largest dot equals 9.3 μV. Remainder same as Fig. 5.

The striking interaction between the effects of reading ability and gender on both DN1 and reaction time in the present study strongly implies a different functional cortical organization for the groups. Future work on reading ability clearly should consider gender differences in processes contributing to this ability.

D. Effects of Target Relevance on P3 (DP3)

The increase in P3 amplitude to the relevant compared to irrelevant targets (DP3) was slightly greater in the high than in the low reading subjects [Reading × Relevance: $F(1, 80) = 4.19, p = .0490$] as shown in Fig. 6. The correlations between DP3 and reading ability, however, did not approach statistical significance ($p > .05$).

Note that occipital DP3 revealed a Sex × Reading Ability interaction similar to that reflected by DN1 [Occipital Sex × Reading × Relevance: $F(1, 80) = 5.66, p = .0197$]. Occipital DP3 was greater for low than for high reading boys; in contrast, it was greater for high than for low reading girls (see Fig. 6). Again, such findings emphasize the need to consider gender differences in research on RD.

The positive relationship between DP3 amplitude and reading ability replicates previous findings. This relationship, however, was small compared to tasks requiring type selection, particularly when letter versus nonletter patterns must be attended (Harter, Anllo-Vento et al., 1988).

IV. Reading Ability and Type Selection in the "What" System: ERPs to Stimuli in the Central Visual Field

The discussion of the neural specificity theory above leads to the hypothesis that *dyslexics or poor readers should reflect deficient type selection, particularly over the left hemisphere,* as shown primarily by DP3. The results of many P3 studies support this hypothesis (see below). The results of the present study replicate and add to this previous literature.

A. Occipital P1 (120–140 msec) and N1 (260–290 msec)

In the present study, P1 (the A140 measure) and N1 (the A290 measure) amplitude to the arrows were smaller for the low than for the high readers, particularly over the occipital regions as shown by Figs. 1, 2, and 7 [A140, Reading × Electrode: $F(3, 240) = 5.13, p = .0092$; A290, Reading: $F(1, 80) = 6.64, p = .0118$]. Occipital P1 (OA140) and N1 (A290) both correlated positively with many of the Woodcock–Johnson measures of reading ability (see Table I).

Previous data also show smaller occipital P1 in poor readers, although this reduction was not always discussed or interpreted (Harter, Anllo-Vento et al., 1988; Holcomb, Ackerman, & Dykman, 1985; Hughes, 1985; Naylor, 1987). P1 is an early ERP component generally associated with sensory processes. P1 reduction occurred in response to the central arrows only; the response to the peripheral targets reflected the opposite trend (see Fig. 7). Such reduction, therefore, suggests some form of reduced sensory processing in poor readers in the occipital region of the occipitotemporal system.

Note that P1, N1, and the Woodcock–Johnson measures of reading ability all correlated negatively with the variability in ERP waveform (OSD) (see Table I). Such variability could reduce the amplitude of P1 and N1. In a previous study of intralocation or type selection, however, RD subjects had less variability in ERPs but still had smaller P1 amplitude (Harter, Anllo-Vento et al., 1988). The smaller P1 to central stimulation for RD subjects, therefore, probably is due to factors other than ERP variability.

B. Central P240

The ERP over central cortex, in response to stimulation of the central retina, contains a positive peak at or about 240 msec (central P240). In two previous studies, central P240 was smaller in amplitude for RD than for no-RD children (Harter, Diering, & Wood, 1988) and adults (Naylor,

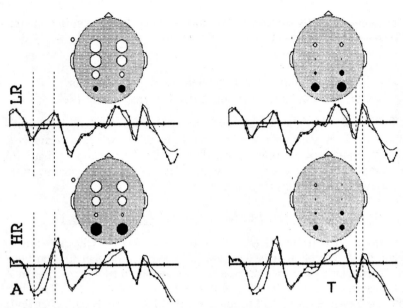

FIGURE 7 P1 to N1 amplitude following the central arrow (left) and peripheral targets (right). Relevant arrow–target conditions only. Low (LR, top) and high (HR, bottom) readers. ERPs are from O1 and O2. Largest dot equals 8 μV P1-to-N1 amplitude. The first and second vertical dashed lines indicate P1 and N1, respectively. Remainder same as Fig. 3.

1987). This effect in children was greater over the left than right central hemisphere.

The effect of RD on central P240, particularly over the left hemisphere, is consistent with the hypothesis that RD children have a deficit in the occipitotemporal "what" cortical system—that is, a temporal-lobe deficit, particularly in the left hemisphere. In the adult study, the reduced P240 associated with reading disability was symmetrical over the two hemispheres. This suggests that the early left-hemisphere deficit reflected by P240 becomes more bilateral with development.

C. Late Positivity and P3

An extensive literature focuses on the cognitive interpretations of P3 (see reviews by Donchin & Coles, 1988; Donchin et al., 1978). P3 amplitude is sensitive to whether or not the evoking stimulus shares any cue (spatial or nonspatial) in common with the relevant stimulus. In this sense, it is an indicant of the information content or meaningfulness associated with some aspect of the stimulus.

The neural sources of the various positive potentials, which include P3, are uncertain. Primarily on the basis of functional specificity of single-unit activity in monkeys, Harter and Aine (1984) proposed that the DP3 indicants of type-selection reflect activity in the portion of the visual system that projects primarily from the central retina to the inferior temporal cortical regions— that is, the higher levels of the "what" system. Data from intracranial recordings made from awake human subjects suggest that P3 recorded at the surface of the scalp in part may reflect sources in the medial temporal lobe (see Regan, 1989, pp. 244–245).

Many studies have reported that dyslexic and poor readers have reduced-amplitude positive waves between 200 and 500 msec after stimulation (Harter, Diering, & Wood, 1988; Holcomb et al., 1985; Johnston et al., 1984; Preston, Guthrie, Kirsch, Gertman, & Childs, 1977). The effects of attention on the amplitude of this positivity (DP3) also are smaller in poor readers and dyslexics (Danier et al., 1981; Harter, Anllo-Vento et al., 1988; Lovrich & Stamm, 1983; Naylor, 1987; Ollo & Squires, 1986). The reduced P3 and DP3 in poor readers, therefore, are consistent findings. Virtually all of these studies required subjects to attend to stimuli presented to the central visual field—that is, the tasks did not require location selection. These findings, therefore, support the main hypothesis of deficient neural processing in the "what" cortical system of dyslexic and poor readers.

The statistically significant effect of reading ability on DP3 amplitude following targets in the present study further replicates these results (see Figs. 1, 2, and 6). The correlation between DP3 and reading ability in this spatial-attention study, however, was small and nonsignificant as discussed above. P3 amplitude following the arrow also was similar for both reading groups (see Fig. 7).

In contrast, Harter, Anllo-Vento et al. (1988) reported larger and significant correlations between reading ability and DP3 indicants of type selection. Boys (25 without and 27 with RD) participated in three experiments. Each experiment required the selection of a different type of information presented to the central visual field. The magnitude of the correlation depended on the nature of the task—the selection of black versus white color ($r = .12$), the selection of 2 letters versus 2 patterns ($r = .44$), and the selection of 12 letters versus 12 patterns ($r = .49$). All tasks resulted in a positive relationship between DP3 and reading ability. This relationship, however, was greatest for the task most akin to reading.

Preston et al. (1977) and Harter, Anllo-Vento et al. (1988) reported that the enhanced DP3 for normal compared to disabled readers was greater over the left than the right occipital hemisphere. The hemispheric difference in DP3 correlated highly with reading ability in this study as well ($r = .43$). The reduced occipital DP3 (and central P240) in RD subjects, particularly over the left hemisphere, may reflect the structural anomalies discussed above. For example, it could reflect the neural anomalies and arteriovenous malformations in the temporal and parietal regions, particularly of the left hemisphere, of dyslexics (Geschwind & Galaburda, 1985).

D. Laterality

Orton proposed that dyslexia and deficiencies in reading and language skills are a result of incomplete or deficient language dominance in the left hemisphere. Reviews of the neuropsychological literature provide some support, although inconclusive, for this proposal (Bradshaw & Nettleton, 1983, pp. 348–351; Molfese & Segalowitz, 1988; J. E. Obrzut, 1988). Some ERP studies also support this hypothesis. Poor or disabled readers did not show the typical left- greater than right-hemisphere central P240 or DP3 found in normal reading subjects, as discussed above.

Kinsbourne (1988) suggested that "weakness in maintaining selective activation of the left hemisphere could explain the dyslexic child's problem not only in performing difficult verbal tasks, but also in consistently maintaining a verbal mental set" (p. 17). The reduced left-hemisphere P240 and DP3 in RD children performing letter-discrimination tasks supports this suggestion.

Other data indicate factors in addition to abnormal laterality of language function may account for RD. First, the smaller left hemisphere P240 and DP3 in RD children occurred in tasks not requiring language function (Harter, Anllo-Vento, & Wood, 1989; Harter, Anllo-Vento et al., 1988). According to Kinsbourne's hypothesis, these nonlanguage tasks should have activated the right hemisphere and should not have differentiated the subjects with and without RD. Unfortunately, virtually all of the behavioral studies of laterality in relationship to reading ability used only verbal-type stimuli—that is, digits and letters (as reviewed by J. E. Obrzut, 1988, Tables 21-1 and 21-4). The left-hemisphere deficit, therefore, may not be specific to language function.

And, second, many of the ERP components described here, that were sensitive to reading ability and RD (for example, P1, N1, and the early portions of P3), were symmetrical over the two hemispheres. Some factors contributing to RD, therefore, are bilateral and not specific to the left hemisphere.

V. Individual Differences in ERPs Which May Confound the Effects of Reading Ability and RD Gender or Sex Differences

Recent reviews of the ERP literature revealed few studies on sex differences (Picton, 1988; Regan, 1989). Behavioral data generally indicate, however, that males tend to have superior spatial abilities and inferior verbal abilities compared to females (see reviews by Bradshaw & Nettleton, 1983, pp. 214–226, and Kolb & Whishaw, 1985, pp. 363–372).

Harter, Miller *et al.* (1989) reported in detail the sex differences in the present study. The enhancement of N1, due to spatial attention, was earlier and greater for boys than for girls and the boys tended to have faster reaction times than the girls. (Note that reading ability was not considered in our earlier report; these trends apply primarily to low readers as discussed above and shown in Fig. 5).

Price (1988) investigated sex differences in ERPs associated with type selection. Her subjects attended either to a color or to letters flashed to the central visual field. Both P3 amplitude and the effects of stimulus relevance on P3 amplitude (DP3) were much larger for females than for males. These effects were reduced or absent, however, when the contribution of verbal ability (estimated by PPVT-R) was covaried out. The sex differences in P3, therefore, may simply reflect differences in verbal ability. Consistent with this interpretation, sex differences in P3 in the spatial-attention task were small and marginally significant (Harter, Miller *et al.*, 1989) (also see Fig. 6).

Harter, Miller *et al.* (1989) reported that following the onset of an arrow cue, males generally had a higher-amplitude, slow negativity over the posterior regions than did females. This negativity was interpreted as reflecting a contingent negative variation (CNV). Assuming CNV reflects a transient increase in general cortical arousal, the larger CNV for boys implies that, in general, they became more aroused and ready during the arrow-target interval. Some behavioral data also suggest that males are more vigilant than females (Davies, Jones, & Taylor, 1984).

If boys become more aroused in anticipating the targets, as suggested by measures of the CNV, their enhanced DN1 response to the targets also could be the consequence of this increased arousal. This interpretation is supported by the correlation ($r = .237$) between CNV and EDN1 (see Table I). This possibility, however, cannot explain the fact that the group differences in DN1 were specific to the relevant hemifield.

If more males than females are RD and this variable is not controlled, most samples of subjects with RD will contain more males than females. The above sex differences, some of which interacted with RD, reinforce the suggestion that such differences should be considered when interpreting previous results and designing future work on RD.

A. Attention-Deficit Disorder (ADD)

The interaction effects between ADD level and either arrow direction or target relevance were not statistically significant for any of the ERP measures in the experiment reported here. One apparent exception to this conclusion was the correlation between the DICA score and EDN1 ($r = .277$, shown in Table I). The relationship between DICA scores and reading ability

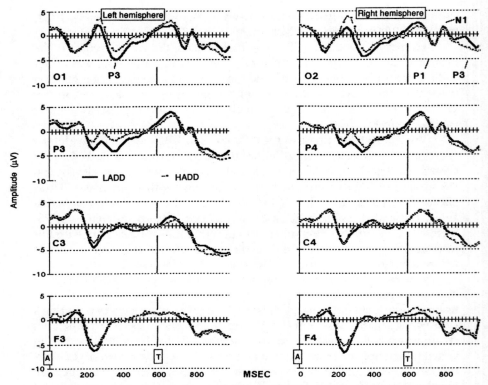

FIGURE 8 ERPs from subjects with low (LADD, solid line) and high (HADD, dotted line) ADD scores. Data have been averaged across the two arrow and two target conditions. Remainder same as Fig. 1.

($r = -.259$), however, accounts for this correlation. When the variability associated with reading ability was controlled statistically with an analysis of covariance, the effects of ADD level were not statistically significant ($p > .05$). The effects of RD on DN1, thus, cannot be attributed to differences in ADD.

As can be seen in Fig. 8 (P3), the most striking effect of ADD level in the present study was on a broad positive wave from about 250 to 400 msec following the arrow. The positivity was greatest over the occipital and parietal cortex. Initially it was larger for low- than for high-ADD subjects [A290: ADD Level, $F(1, 80) = 7.98, p = .0060$], this difference becoming greater over the left than the right hemisphere (A390: ADD Level × Hemisphere, $F(1, 80) = 6.46, p = .0130$). The low-ADD subjects also had a greater percentage of hits than the high-ADD subjects (95 versus 92%) in response to relevant targets.

The reduced positivity following the arrow cue in high-ADD subjects is consistent with previous results on P3 amplitude following relevant stimuli (Harter, Anllo-Vento et al., 1988; Holcomb et al., 1985; Klorman, Salzman, Pass, Borgstedt, & Dainer, 1979; Loiselle, Stamm, Maitinsky, & Whipple, 1980; Ollo & Squires, 1986). In most of these studies, the ADD subjects compared to normal subjects also performed the task at a lower level. Holcomb et al. (1985) proposed that the reduced P3 in ADD subjects may reflect an inappropriate allocation of attentional resources in these subjects, thus resulting in poorer performance.

The relationship between ADD and stimulus-relevance effects on P3 (DP3) is less clear. This interaction was not significant for DP3 following targets in the present study. Several studies report smaller DP3 and poorer performance in ADD, hyperactive, and hyperkinetic children (Holcomb et al., 1985; Klorman et al., 1979; Loiselle et al., 1980; Ollo & Squires, 1986). Two studies on the same population reported larger DP3 and no difference in performance in boys with as compared to without ADD (Harter, Anllo-Vento & Wood, 1989; Harter, Anllo-Vento et al., 1988). This ADD effect had a central-frontal distribution in these two studies and did not appear to involve the more traditional posterior P3 component. These differences in results may depend on the relationship between P3, task performance, and ADD.

Note that both RD and ADD have been considered in our studies and that the effects of these variables did not interact significantly. Also, RD influenced measures that were not influenced by ADD. The neural substrates of these two characteristics, therefore, appear to be distinct—even when ADD is concurrent with reading ability.

In the present study, higher ADD levels (DICA score) were associated with lower reading ability (WTCL score) ($r = -.259$). Unless these variables are controlled and unconfounded, therefore, samples of RD subjects will tend to have a disproportionately large number of ADD subjects. Given RD and ADD appear to be distinct disorders, they must be unconfounded to understand how each contributes to reading ability.

B. Intelligence

The interdependence of RD and verbal intelligence is a major issue. Our experiments were not designed to directly address this issue. Their results, however, clearly support the view that the contribution of verbal intelligence to reading ability must be considered in any study of RD.

In the present spatial-attention study, verbal intelligence (estimated by PPVT-R) was correlated negatively with the location selection of peripheral stimuli, as indicated by EDN1 ($r = -.215$), and positively with the percentage of hits ($r = .109$). Our earlier study of location selection similarly found correlations of $r = -.45$ and .36, respectively (Harter, Anllo-Vento, & Wood, 1989). When the contribution of intelligence to these relationships was removed with analyses of covariance, however, reading ability generally still influenced measures of location selection. The DN1 measure of location selection in the occipitoparietal "where" system, therefore, indicates that factors in addition to low verbal intelligence contribute to RD.

In our previous experiments requiring intralocation or type selection, PPVT-R correlated positively with many measures of processing in the occipitotemporal "where" system—DP3 ($r = .438$), hemispheric differences in occipital DP3 ($r = .339$) and central P240 ($r = .340$), and the accuracy of behavioral performance (Harter, Anllo-Vento *et al.*, 1988; Harter, Diering, & Wood, 1988). These correlations generally were greatest for those tasks requiring the selection of letters. Analyses of covariance, using verbal intelligence (estimated by PPVT-R) as a covariate, generally indicate that PPVT-R accounts for the relationships between reading ability and these measures of activity in the "what" system.

C. Within-Subject and Condition Variability in ERP Waveform (ERPV)

The within-subject and condition variability of the single-trial ERP waveforms (a minimum of 24 single trials) about the average ERP waveform (ERPV) has been computed in all of our studies of RD. This was done by computing the standard deviation of ERP amplitude across trials for each of the 50 digital samples of the ERP waveform.

Group differences in ERPV for the present spatial-attention experiment are shown in Fig. 9. ERPV decreased slightly after arrow presentation for all groups. ERPV was generally greater for the low than for the high readers [Reading: $F(1, 80) = 4.42, p = .0387$], particularly over the occipital regions [Reading × Electrode: $F(3, 240) = 4.49, p = .0118$]. ERPV was less for high- than for low-ADD subjects [ADD: $F(1, 80) = 4.00, p = .0489$], particularly over the occipital region [ADD × Electrode: $F(3, 240) = 5.98, p = .0028$] (see Fig. 9).

Event-related potential waveform, in part, could reflect variability due to the spontaneous changes in EEG frequency and amplitude. The alpha rhythm has an occipital–parietal maximum and blocks or desynchronizes (onset latency of about 160 msec) in response to novel or meaningful stimuli (Kolb & Whishaw, 1985, pp. 50–51). This desynchronization is one measure of cortical activation and would be associated with a decrease in ERPV. The absence of movement and other artifacts also could cause a decrease in ERPV.

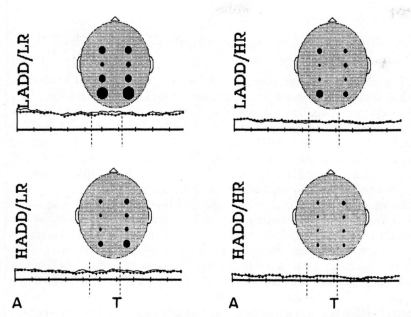

FIGURE 9 Within subject and condition, trial-to-trial variability in ERP waveform. Subjects with low ADD (LADD, top) and high ADD (HADD, bottom) scores, and low (LR, left) and high (HR, right) reading ability. Tracings are from O1 and O2. The largest dot equals a standard deviation of 22.8 μV. Data have been averaged across the two arrow and two target conditions. Remainder same as Fig. 3.

The greater ERPV for low as compared to high readers, therefore, could indicate they were either less aroused (had more alpha activity) or more "fidgety" during this spatial-attention task. The greater number of "noise rejections" for the low readers, discussed above, supports the latter possibility.

Note, however, that the effects of reading ability on ERPV appear to be task specific. During a type-selection attention task, ERPV was greater for normal than for RD subjects (Harter, Diering, & Wood, 1988).

The low ERPV for the high-ADD subjects is consistent with the view that these subjects are in a higher state of arousal, assuming low ERPV reflects a high state of cortical arousal (as discussed above). The alternative interpretation—that the low ERPV reflects fewer artifacts in the ERP data from the high-ADD subjects—is less plausible.

More information is needed before the sources of the group differences in ERPV can be identified. Clearly ERPV should be monitored to ensure that it cannot account for group differences in ERP amplitude.

VI. Conclusions

A. Reading Disability and Attention-Deficit Disorder Have Distinct Neural Substrates

The above results give neural validity to RD and ADD as distinct disorders with distinct underlying neural processes. Measures sensitive to RD mostly were not sensitive to ADD. When RD and ADD did influence the same measure, these two effects were statistically independent. These findings provide a direct electrophysiological parallel to the neuropsychological/behavioral data reported by Felton and Wood (1989) and Felton, Wood, Brown, Campbell, and Harter (1987). Investigators should distinguish between these disorders and their effects on reading ability.

Dykman, Ackerman, and Holcomb (1985) proposed (1) that ADD children have a deficit of sustained attention associated with frontal limbic dysfunction, and (2) that RD children have a deficit of selective attention associated with a left temporal-lobe deficit. Although the effects of ADD on ERPs have been inconsistent and inconclusive, little support for ADD being a frontal-lobe deficit could be found in the ERP. Poor and disabled readers did have reduced type selection, one measure of selective attention, over the left posterior cortical regions. Measures of selective visual–spatial attention (location selection), however, did not support the proposed deficit of selective attention in RD children. Poor and disabled readers, in fact, had enhanced location selection over the occipital and parietal areas. The differential effects of RD on location versus type selection, therefore, require qualification of their second proposal.

B. The "Where" and "What" Cortical Systems and Reading Ability

According to the neural specificity theory, the relationship between reading ability and ERPs depends on three main factors: (1) the nature of the task, particularly the extent to which it involves the occipitoparietal "where" or occipitotemporal "what" cortical systems, (2) the ERP component considered, and (3) the characteristics of the subject that determine his or her reading ability. We hypothesized that poor or disabled readers have normal or superior processing in the occipitoparietal "where" system but deficient processing in the occipitotemporal "what" system. Processes at multiple levels in both systems—for example, levels associated with sensory and cognitive processes—may contribute to different aspects of reading ability.

In tasks requiring the directing of spatial attention to peripheral targets, low or disabled readers reflected early regional cortical priming (earlier LDAP) and greater location selection (larger DN1 to targets). In tasks requiring the selection of a particular type of information in the central visual field, low or disabled readers reflected reduced processing—smaller P1, N1, P3, and DP3.

The results, therefore, supported our main hypotheses as to how reading ability influences processing at different levels of the "what" and "where" cortical systems. Note that the subjects were only in the first grade and they did not have to read to perform the tasks used in most of the experiments discussed. The various ERP measures appeared to reflect the sensory and cognitive processes that contribute to reading ability, not reading ability per se.

Low or disabled readers also had reduced hemispheric asymmetry in central P240 and occipital DP3 (reduced left-greater-than-right responses) in type-selection tasks. These findings support the hypothesis of abnormal or deficient lateralization of language function to the left hemisphere in dyslexics. Other ERP measures, however, suggested RD also results from bilateral deficits in lower levels of the "what" system.

Processing in the occipitoparietal and occipitotemporal cortical systems appeared to be independent. Although reading ability correlated with measures of both location and type selection, these two kinds of selection did not correlate with one another. For example, reading ability correlated with both DN1 ($r = -.45$) and hemispheric differences in DP3 ($r = .49$), but these ERP measures did not correlate with one another ($r = -.03$). The highest multiple correlation between reading ability and ERPs ($r = .78$) incorporated both location- and type-selection ERP measures (Harter, Anllo-Vento, & Wood, 1989). The independence of such ERP indicants of reading ability has implications for RD subtypes.

C. Subtypes and Reading Disability

Classification of subjects into dichotomous reading groups—for example, with versus without RD or low versus high readers—resulted in large and significant group differences in ERPs. This implies that all RD subjects have neurophysiological characteristics in common.

Some investigators have proposed ERP subtype systems (Duffy et al., 1988; Licht, Kok, Bakker, & Bouma, 1986; Shucard et al., 1985). These should be considered with caution, however, until they have been replicated on independent, large samples. The ERP measures differentiating the subtypes were identified by the empirical approach described above, an approach associated with a high risk of a Type I statistical error. The present results and discussion reveal several factors which should be considered as part of any subtyping system.

Individual differences in ERP components associated with both RD and ADD accounted for some variability in reading ability; yet, variations in ERP indicants of RD and ADD generally were not correlated with one another. In this context, ERP indicants of RD and ADD reflect distinct subtypes of learning-disabled children.

The ERP indicants of location and type selection suggest two possible groups of RD subtypes. One is associated with enhanced processing in the occipitoparietal "where" cortical system. The ERP indicants of enhanced location selection (for example, DN1 to peripheral targets) reflect this subtype. Verbal intelligence (estimated by PPVT-R) generally did not account for the relationship between DN1 and reading ability. Enhanced sensitivity of the "where" cortical system could inappropriately cause a shift in attention away from the central to the peripheral visual field (away from the material being read to distracting stimuli in the peripheral visual field). This subtype is distinct from ADD since ERP measures of location selection generally were not sensitive to ADD.

Deficient processing in the occipitotemporal "what" cortical system may reflect a second group of subtypes. Reduced ERPs associated with the discrimination of stimuli presented to the central visual field could reflect these subtypes, for example, reduced P1, N1, P240, P3, and hemispheric differences in P240 and DP3. Verbal intelligence (estimated by PPVT-R) accounted for the relationship between most of these ERP measures and reading ability. Additional research must be conducted to assess the independence of these ERP indicants of poor reading and how they might relate to behavioral measures of RD subtypes.

The sex differences in ERP measures of both location and type selection further complicate the subtyping problem. Such differences may either confound or interact with the effects of reading ability.

The above selective review of the literature implies that many individual differences—for example, verbal intelligence, ADD, and gender—account for variability in reading ability and ERP indicants of this ability. The multitude of such factors creates a serious, practical problem for researchers interested in RD subtypes. A large number of subjects must participate in subtype experiments in order to unconfound the contribution of such individual differences to reading ability. Even if only three dichotomous between-subject variables are considered—for example, RD versus no RD, ADD versus no ADD, and male versus female—a minimum of at least 80 subjects would be required. This problem may account for the sparsity of definitive ERP studies of RD subtypes.

Acknowledgments

This research was supported by NIH Grant RO1 NS19413 and NIH Grant PO1 HD21887. I thank Lourdes Anllo-Vento, Steven Miller, Margaret LaLonde,

Alvin Keyes, and Barbara Rudy for their contribution to various aspects of the research discussed here.

References

Bradshaw, J. L., & Nettleton, N. C. (1983). *Human cerebral asymmetry*. Englewood Cliffs, NJ: Prentice-Hall.

Brannan, J. R., & Williams, M. C. (1987). Allocation of visual attention in good and poor readers. *Perception and Psychophysics, 41,* 23–28.

Bullock, D., Liederman, J., & Todorovic, D. (1987). Reconciling stable asymmetry with recovery of function: An adaptive systems perspective on functional plasticity. *Child Development, 58,* 689–697.

Bushnell, M. C., Goldberg, M. E., & Robinson, D. L. (1981). Behavioral enhancement of visual responses in monkey cerebral cortex. I. Modulation in posterior parietal cortex related to selective visual attention. *Journal of Neurophysiology, 46,* 755–787.

Danier, K., Klorman, R., Salzman, F., Hess, D. W., Davidson, P. W., & Michael, R. L. (1981). Learning disordered children's evoked potentials during sustained attention. *Journal of Abnormal Child Psychology, 9,* 79–91.

Davies, D. R., Jones, D. M., & Taylor, A. (1984). Selective- and sustained-attention tasks: Individual and group differences. In R. Parasuraman & D. R. Davies (Eds.), *Varieties of attention* (pp. 395–448). Orlando, FL: Academic Press.

Deecke, L., Bashore, T., Brunia, C. H. M., Grunewald-Zuberbier, E., Grunewald, G., & Kristeva, R. (1984). Movement-associated potentials and motor control. *Annals of the New York Academy of Sciences, 306,* 398–428.

Donchin, E., & Coles, M. G. H. (1988). Precommentary: Is the P300 component a manifestation of context updating? *Behavioral and Brain Sciences, 11,* 355–425.

Donchin, E., Ritter, W., & McCallum, W. (1978). Cognitive psychophysiology: the endogenous components. In E. Callaway, P. Tueting, & S. H. Koslow (Eds.), *Event-related brain potentials in man* (pp. 349–441). New York: Academic Press.

Duane, D. D. (1986). Neurodiagnostic tools in dyslexic syndromes in children: Pitfalls and proposed comparative study of computed tomography, nuclear magnetic resonance, and brain electrical activity mapping. In G. T. Pavlidis & D. F. Fisher (Eds.), *Dyslexia: Its neuropsychology and treatment* (pp. 65–84). New York: Wiley.

Duffy, F. H., Denckla, M. B., McAnulty, G. B., & Holmes, J. A. (1988). Neurophysiological studies in dyslexia. In F. Plum (Ed.), *Language, communication, and the brain* (pp. 149–170). New York: Raven Press.

Dykman, R. A., Ackerman, P. T., & Holcomb, P. J. (1985). Reading disabled and ADD children: Similarities and differences. In D. B. Gray & J. F. Kavanagh (Eds.), *Biobehavioral measures of dyslexia* (pp. 47–62). Parkton, MD: York Press.

Felton, R. H., & Wood, F. B. (1989). Cognitive deficits in reading disability and attention deficit disorder. *Journal of Learning Disabilities, 22,* 3–22.

Felton, R. H., Wood, F. B., Brown, I., Campbell, S., & Harter, M. R. (1987). Separate verbal memory and naming deficits in attention deficit disorder and reading disability. *Brain & Language, 31,* 171–184.

Geiger, G., & Lettvin, J. (1987). Peripheral vision in persons with dyslexia. *New England Journal of Medicine, 316,* 1238–1243.

Geschwind, N., & Galaburda, A. M. (1985). Cerebral lateralization—biological mechanisms, associations, and pathology: I. A. hypothesis and a program for research. *Archives of Neurology (Chicago), 42,* 428–459.

Haber, R. N., & Hershenson, M. (1980). *The psychology of visual perception* (2nd ed.). New York: Holt, Rinehart, & Winston.

Harter, M. R. (in press). Visual-spatial attention: Preparation and selection in children and adults. In C. H. M. Brunia, A. W. K. Gaillard, A. Kok, & G. Mulder (Eds.), *Proceedings of the EPIC IX Conference.* New York: Elsevier.

Harter, M. R., & Aine, C. J. (1984). Brain mechanisms of visual selective attention. In R. Parasuraman & D. R. Davies (Eds.), *Varieties of attention* (pp. 293–321). Orlando, FL: Academic Press.

Harter, M. R., & Aine, C. J. (1986). Discussion of neural-specificity model of selective attention: A response to Hillyard and Mangun and to Naatanen. *Biological Psychology, 23,* 297–312.

Harter, M. R., Aine, C., & Schroeder, C. (1982). Hemispheric differences in the neural processing of stimulus location and type: Effects of selective attention on visual evoked potentials. *Neuropsychologia, 20,* 421–437.

Harter, M. R., Anllo-Vento, L., & Wood, F. B. (1989). Event-related potentials, spatial orienting, and reading disabilities. *Psychophysiology, 26,* 404–421.

Harter, M. R., Anllo-Vento, L., Wood, F. B., & Schroeder, M. M. (1988). II. Separate brain potential characteristics in children with reading disability and attention deficit disorder: Color and letter relevance effects. *Brain & Cognition, 7,* 115–140.

Harter, M. R., Diering, S., & Wood, F. B. (1988). I. Separate brain potential characteristics in children with reading disability and attention deficit disorder: relevance-independent effects. *Brain & Cognition, 7,* 54–86.

Harter, M. R., Miller, S. L., Price, N. J., LaLonde, M. E., & Keyes, A. L. (1989). Neural processes involved in directing attention. *Journal of Cognitive Neuroscience, 3,* 223–237.

Heilman, K. M. (1979). Neglect and related disorders. In K. M. Heilman & E. Valenstein (Eds.), *Clinical neuropsychology* (pp. 268–307). New York: Oxford University Press.

Hier, D. B., LeMay, M., Rosenberger, P. B., & Perlo, V. P. (1978). Developmental dyslexia. *Archives of Neurology (Chicago), 35,* 90–92.

Hillyard, S. A., & Mangun, G. R. (1986). The neural basis of visual selective attention: A commentary on Harter and Aine. *Biological Psychology, 23,* 265–279.

Hillyard, S. A., & Munte, T. (1984). Selective attention to color and location: An analysis with event-related brain potentials. *Perception and Psychophysics, 36,* 185–198.

Hillyard, S. A., & Picton, T. W. (1979). Event-related brain potentials and selective information processing in man. In J. E. Desmedt (Ed.), *Cognitive components in cerebral event-related potentials and seletive attention* (Progress in Clinical Neurophysiology, pp. 1–52). Basel: Karger.

Holcomb, P. J., Ackerman, P. T., & Dykman, R. A. (1985). Cognitive event-related brain potentials in children with attention and reading deficits. *Psychophysiology, 22,* 656–665.

Hughes, J. R. (1985). Evaluation of electrophysiological studies on dyslexia. In D. B. Gray & J. F. Kavanagh (Eds.), *Biobehavioral measures of dyslexia* (pp. 71–86). Parkton, MD: York Press.

Hynd, G. W., & Semrud-Clikeman, M. (1989). Dyslexia and brain morphology. *Psychological Bulletin, 106,* 447–482.

John, E. R., Prichep, L., Ahn, H., Easton, P., Fridman, J., & Kaye, H. (1983). Neurometric evaluation of cognitive dysfunction and neurological disorders in children. *Progress in Neurobiology, 21,* 239–290.

Johnstone, J., Galin, D., Fein, G., Yingling, C., Herron, J., & Marcus, M. (1984). Regional brain activity in dyslexic and control children during reading tasks: Visual probe event-related potentials. *Brain & Language, 21,* 233–254.

Kinsbourne, M. (1988). Developmental language and learning problems. *Journal of Neurolinguistics, 3,* 1–27.

Klorman, R., Salzman, L. F., Pass, H. L., Borgstedt, A. D., & Dainer, K. B. (1979). Effects of methylphenidate on hyperactive children's evoked responses during passive and active attention. *Psychophysiology, 16,* 23–29.

Knight, R. T. (1985). Electrophysiology in behavioral neurology. In M. M. Mesulm (Ed.), *Principles of behavioral neurology* (pp. 327–346). Philadelphia, PA: Davis.

Kolb, B., & Whishaw, I. Q. (1985). *Fundamentals of human neuropsychology* (2nd ed.). New York: Freeman.

Licht, R., Kok, A., Bakker, D. J., & Bouma, A. (1986). Hemispheric distribution of ERP components and word naming in preschool children. *Brain & Language, 27,* 101–116.

Loiselle, D. L., Stamm, J. S., Maitinsky, S., & Whipple, S. C. (1980). Evoked potential and behavioral signs of attentive dysfunction in hyperactive boys. *Psychophysiology, 17,* 193–201.

Lovegrove, W. J., Bowling, A., Badcock, D., & Blackwood, M. (1980). Specific reading disability: Differences in contrast sensitivity as a function of spatial frequency. *Science, 210,* 439–440.

Lovegrove, W. J., Heddle, M., & Slaghuis, W. (1980). Reading disability: Spatial frequency specific deficits in visual information store. *Neuropsychologia, 18,* 111–115.

Lovrich, D., & Stamm, J. S. (1983). Event-related potential and behavioral correlates of attention in reading retardation. *Journal of Clinical Neuropsychology, 5,* 13–37.

Lynch, J. C., Mountcastle, V. B., Talbot, W. H., & Yin, T. C. T. (1977). Parietal lobe mechanisms for directed visual attention. *Neurophysiology, 40,* 362–389.

Mesulam, M. M. (1981). A cortical network for directed attention and unilateral neglect. *Annals of Neurology, 10,* 309–325.

Molfese, D. L., & Betz, J. C. (1988). Electrophysiological indices of the early development of lateralization for language and cognition, and their implications for predicting later development. In D. L. Molfese & S. J. Segalowitz (Eds.), *Brain lateralization in children* (pp. 171–190). New York: Guilford Press.

Molfese, D. L., & Segalowitz, S. J. (Eds.). (1988). *Brain lateralization in children*. New York: Guilford Press.

Moran, J., & Desimone, R. (1985). Selective attention gates visual processing in the extrastriate cortex. *Science, 229*, 91–93.

Naatanen, R. (1982). Processing negativity: an evoked-potential reflection of selective attention. *Psychological Bulletin, 92*, 605–640.

Naatanen, R. (1986). The neural-specificity theory of visual selective attention evaluated. A commentary on Harter and Aine. *Biological Psychology, 23*, 281–295.

Naatanen, R., & Michie, P. T. (1979). Different variants of endogenous negative brain potentials in performance situations: A review and classification. In D. Lehmann & E. Callaway (Eds.), *Human evoked potentials* (pp. 251–267). New York: Plenum.

Naylor, C. E. (1987). *Event-related potentials and behavioral assessment: A 20 year follow-up of adults who were diagnosed as RD in childhood*. Unpublished doctoral dissertation, University of North Carolina at Greensboro.

Neville, H. J., & Lawson, D. (1987). Attention to central and peripheral visual space in a movement detection task. I. Normal hearing adults. *Brain Research, 405*, 253–267.

Obrzut, J. E., Hynd, G. W., Obrzut, A., & Pirozzolo, F. J. (1981). Effect of directed attention on cerebral asymmetries in normal and learning-disabled children. *Developmental Psychology, 17*, 118–125.

Obrzut, J. E. (1988). Deficient lateralization in learning-disabled children: developmental lag or abnormal cerebral organization. In D. L. Molfese & S. J. Segalowitz (Eds.), *Brain lateralization in children* (pp. 567–589). New York: Guilford Press.

Obrzut, J. E., Hynd, G. W., & Zellner, R. D. (1983). Attentional deficit in learning-disabled children: Evidence from visual half-field asymmetries. *Brain & Cognition, 2*, 89–101.

Ollo, C., & Squires, N. (1986). Event-related potentials in learning disabilities. In R. Cracco & I. Bodis-Wollner (Eds.), *Frontiers in clinical neurosciences: Evoked potentials*. New York: Liss.

Picton, T. W. (Ed.). (1988). *Handbook of electroencephalography and clinical neurophysiology: Human event-related potentials*. New York: Elsevier.

Preston, M. S., Guthrie, J. T., Kirsch, I., Gertman, D., & Childs, B. (1977). VERs in normal and disabled adult readers. *Psychophysiology, 14*, 8–14.

Price, N. J. (1988). *Event-related potentials: An investigation of sex differences in lateralization of information processing*. Unpublished master's thesis, University of North Carolina at Greensboro.

Regan, D. (1989). *Human brain electrophysiology: Evoked potentials and evoked magnetic fields in science and medicine*. New York Elsevier:.

Ritter, W., Ford, J., Gaillard, A. W. K., Harter, M. R., Kutas, M., Naatanen, R., Polich, J., & Renault, B. (1984). Cognition and event-related potentials: I. The relation of negative potentials and cognitive processes. In R. Karrer, J. Cohen, &

P. Tueting (Eds.), *Brain and information: Event-related potentials* (pp. 24–38). New York: New York Academy of Sciences.

Roland, P. E. (1981). Somatotopical tuning of postcentral gyrus during focal attention in man: A regional cerebral blood flow study. *Journal of Neurophysiology, 46,* 744–754.

Shucard, D. W., Cummins, K. R., Gay, E., Lairsmith, J., & Welanko, P. (1985). Electrophysiological studies of reading disabled children: In search of subtypes. In D. B. Gray & J. F. Kavanagh (Eds.), *Biobehavioral measures of dyslexia* (pp. 87–106). Parkton, MD: York Press.

Tecce, J. J. (1972). Contingent negative variation (CNV) and psychological processes in man. *Psychological Bulletin, 77,* 73–108.

Ungerleider, L. G., & Mishkin, M. (1982). Two cortical visual systems. In D. J. Ingle, M. A. Goodale, R. J. W. Mansfield (Eds.), *Analysis of visual behavior* (pp. 549–586). Cambridge, MA: MIT Press.

Williams, M. C., & Bologna, N. B. (1985). Perceptual grouping in good and poor readers. *Perception and Psychophysics, 38,* 367–374.

Williams, M. C., Brannan, J. R., & Lartigue, E. K. (1987). Visual search in good and poor readers. *Clinical Vision Science, 1,* 367–371.

CHAPTER EIGHTEEN

Brain Imaging in Learning Disabilities

George W. Hynd
Margaret Semrud-Clikeman
Heikki Lyytinen

I. Introduction

Although learning disabilities have historically been linked to neurological dysfunction (Bastian, 1898; Hinshelwood, 1900, 1902; Morgan, 1896), until recently, most of the evidence has been inferential. Children who experienced severe learning disabilities frequently demonstrated behaviors characteristic of patients with known brain lesions. Most often, the lesions that produced the perceptual and cognitive deficits similar to those found in learning-disabled children involved the left posterior and central language zones in the left cerebral hemisphere (Hynd & Semrud-Clikeman, 1989a).

As Taylor and Fletcher (1983) and others (e.g., Golden, 1982) have pointed out in their critical reviews, the evidence that learning disabilities are due to some defect in the brain has relied on correlative data. If, for example, a child had poor language comprehension, deficits in naming, and documented deficiencies in phonological coding, it might be hypothesized that dysfunction in the superior, posterior dominant temporal lobe and in the region of the angular gyrus produced the deficits. This hypothesis may be reasonable to some based on our knowledge of acquired aphasia, but it may have little relationship to disrupted neurological systems subserving these processes in

Neuropsychological Foundations of Learning Disabilities, copyright © 1991 by Academic Press Inc. All rights of reproduction in any form reserved.

children with developmental learning disabilities. At least until recently, the evidence that similar structures are involved in children's learning disabilities as are found in adults with acquired disorders has indeed been correlative.

The importance in documenting neurological systems implicated in childhood learning disabilities is important for two interrelated reasons. First, and most obvious, if learning disabilities are believed to be ". . . intrinsic to the individual and presumed to be due to central nervous system dysfunction . . . ," as the most recent federal definition suggests (Wyngaarden, 1987), then more direct evidence as to neurological involvement should be sought than is represented by the volumes of studies providing correlative data. Clearly, considering the technical advantages in the past two decades in imaging the brain through computed tomography (CT) and magnetic resonance imaging (MRI), more direct evidence of structural variation should be available if these disorders do have a neurological basis. Other brain-imaging procedures such as positron emission tomography (PET), regional cerebral blood flow (rCBF), or multichannel topographic brain electrical activity mapping (BEAM) may be useful, not necessarily in providing evidence of disordered structure, but rather evidence of disordered metabolic or electrophysiological systems.

A second reason why it is so important to document the precise neurological basis of learning disabilities in that some insight into etiology may be provided. If, in fact, as some of the post-mortem/cytoarchitectonic studies would suggest (Galaburda, Sherman, Rosen, Aboitiz, & Geschwind, 1985), developmental deviations in the evolving brain occur between the fifth and seventh gestational month in the brains of learning-disabled persons, then factors (e.g., environmental, genetic, etc.) associated with fetal development during this period need to be further articulated. If the "trigger" for disordered brain development can be found, then perhaps prevention may eventually be a reasonable goal.

In this context then, brain imaging in children with learning disabilities has a potentially important role. Additionally, such studies may shed light on the relationships between behavioral–psychometric data and deviations in brain morphology among learning-disabled children, should in fact such deviations indeed exist.

The purpose of this chapter is to provide a critical review of two methodologies that have been utilized to image the structure (using CT/MRI) and electrophysiological properties (BEAM) of the brains of learning-disabled persons. It needs to be emphasized that traditionally the research in this area has focused on developmental dyslexia. Thus, what is known about brain imaging in learning disabilities is derived primarily from studies focusing on developmental dyslexics. Consequently, potential deviations in the brains of other learning-disabled children (e.g., nonverbal learning disabled, children with arithmetic disabilities, etc.) have not been documented because research efforts have initially been directed at severe reading disabilities.

To place these studies in their proper theoretical context, we will first briefly address neurobiological theory upon which the neuroimaging studies are based. Then a critical review of the CT/MRI studies will be provided. Electrical brain mapping studies will also be reviewed, followed by a concluding comment.

II. Neurobiological Theory

To a very significant degree, the studies that directly examine deviations in brain morphology in learning disabilities, particularly developmental dyslexia, are an extension of a growing body of evidence that documents reliable patterns of asymmetry in the human brain. These asymmetries, particularly those favoring the left central language area, are believed to be vital to the development of language (Campbell & Whitaker, 1986).

On the basis of the observations of early investigators (Flechsig, 1908; von Economo & Horn, 1930), Geschwind and Levitsky (1968) provided documentation that in 100 normal adult brains the region of the planum temporale (posterior aspect of the superior temporal lobe) is larger on the left in 65% of brains; on the right it is larger in only 11% of brains. Also, they found that the left planum is about one-third longer on the average than is the right planum. Because the left temporal cortex is known to be associated with language, these findings were interpreted as reflecting a natural neurobiological substrata important to language. Similar studies by other investigators documented these findings in both adult and infant brains (Kopp, Michel, Carrier, Biron, & Duvillard, 1977; Wada, Clarke, & Hamm, 1975; Witelson & Pallie, 1973).

Other asymmetries in brain morphology exist. For example, Weinberger, Luchins, Morihisa, and Wyatt (1982) and LeMay (1976) provided evidence that in the majority of cases (approximately 75%) the volume of the right frontal cortex exceeds that of the left frontal cortex. Furthermore, this pattern of asymmetry, as well as that first documented by Geschwind and Levitsky (1968), appears in fetal development as early as 20 weeks (Weinberger et al., 1982).

However, it is clearly the asymmetry of the left central language cortex that has attracted the most attention of researchers. Geschwind (1974, 1984) and Geschwind and Galaburda (1985a, 1985b, 1985c), in particular, argued that natural asymmetries in brain morphology may be associated in a meaningful fashion with language and deficits in learning, particularly with regard to severe reading disorders or dyslexia. Specifically, it has been proposed that there are relations between male gender differentiation, the effects of testosterone on neuronal assemblies, and correlated asymmetries in brain morphology, immune function, and left-handedness. These possible relations are outlined in detail in Geschwind and Galaburda (1985a, 1985b, 1985c). Although a critical overview of these possible relations is beyond the scope of this chapter, it should be noted that the hypotheses advanced by Geschwind, and especially the limited data supporting these proposed interrelations (Behan & Geschwind, 1985; Geschwind & Behan, 1982), have been criticized for significant design and methodological deficiencies (Satz & Soper, 1986). However, the point that seems essential in the context of this chapter is the idea that deviations in normal patterns of brain asymmetry and function are meaningfully associated with developmental dyslexia.

The following discussion focuses on the evidence that has the potential to document these hypothesized relations in brain morphology and developmental dyslexia. Specifically, the CT/MRI studies will be addressed and discussed in the theoretical context noted above.

III. Neuroimaging Studies (CT/MRI)

The neuroimaging studies have the potential to reveal a number of important correlates of learning and behavioral disorders. Originally developed over two decades ago (Hounsfield, 1973), CT has proven to be of great clinical value with infants, children, and adults. Indexes of pathology include, but are not limited to, changes in tissue-density values, enlarged ventricular or cistern size, observable shifts in midline structures, alterations of normal vascular patterns (observed with contrast), and a prominent sulcal pattern.

It is important to note, however, that CT has not been found to be consistently useful in evaluating children with disorders of developmental such as nonspecific mental retardation (Moeschler, Bennett, & Cromwell, 1981). On the basis of this consideration and our prior observations regarding the neurobiological foundation of language and reading disorders, it seems that to contribute to this literature CT studies would need to (1) provide evidence of a deviation in brain architecture that is a reliable finding across studies using similar diagnostic criteria, (2) link the pathology in a meaningful fashion to current theory, and (3) provide evidence that the deviation in brain morphology is unique to the dyslexic syndrome. To facilitate a consideration of the CT/MRI studies such that their findings may be viewed from this perspective, the following discussion provides a critical overview of the findings of these neuroimaging studies.

IV. Clinical and Methodological Procedures

In the past decade, eight neuroradiological studies of the brains of dyslexics have been reported. Across these eight studies, over 200 children or adults with severe reading and learning problems have been evaluated.

It is important to note that many of these studies were preliminary investigations or employed samples of questionable inclusion. Hynd and Semrud-Clikeman (1989b) provide a critical review of the methodological procedures employed in these studies in which concerns over appropriate control groups, age range of subjects, appraisal of handedness, variation in cognitive ability, and diagnosis were raised. Recognizing that there are indeed serious methodological concerns regarding these studies, the results should nonetheless be informative.

V. CT/MRI Findings

In considering the results of these studies, it is important to keep in mind that, typically, the scans were evaluated for (1) obvious neurostructural abnormalities, and (2) deviations in normal patterns of parietooccipital asymmetry (L > R) that, according to neurobiological theory (Geschwind, 1974, 1984; Geschwind & Behan, 1982; Geschwind & Levitsky, 1968), correlate with unique neurolinguistic processes such as are evidenced in reading.

A. Brain Morphology

Tables I and II summarize these studies. In considering the presence of symmetry or asymmetry in these studies, two general approaches were used. Two of these eight studies represent poorly controlled attempts at judging brain morphology in any quantifiable manner (Leisman & Ashkenazi, 1980; Rumsey *et al.*, 1986). In the Leisman and Ashkenazi (1980) study, no report exists as to how asymmetries or symmetry were judged for the eight dyslexics and two controls. Rumsey *et al.* (1986) noted that in their uncontrolled study, MRI scans were clinically evaluated by two radiologists for ventricular organization, symmetry of the temporal lobe, symmetry of the signal intensity from the brain matter, presence of mass effects, and prominence of cortical sulci. Metric data regarding interrater agreement of the two radiologists were not provided.

In contrast are the more carefully evaluated studies in which quantitative procedures were used in order to reach quantifiable indexes of brain morphology. Furthermore, in some of these studies, two radiologists independently read the CT scans and reached judgments as to the presence or absence of pathology and brain asymmetry or symmetry (Denckla, LeMay, & Chapman,

TABLE I Summary of the Clinical and Methodological Characteristics of the Neuroimaging (CI and MRI) Studies of Developmental Dyslexia[a]

Reference	Type of Study	N	Notes on Population	Mean Chronological age (years)	Mean IQ	Handedness	Diagnostic Criteria	Neurological Abnormalities
Hier, LeMay, Rosenberger, and Perlo (1978)	CT	24 Dyslexics (22 male, 2 female)	Three Parietooccipital width groups formed: R > L = 10, R = L = 6, R < L = 8	25	Full-scale IQs not reported Verbal performance: R. parietooccipital > left: 87±13 96±10 L. parietooccipital > right: 99±11 103 ± 12	6 LH 18 RH	Less than 5th grade performance on Gray Oral Reading Test or 2-grade-level delay in reading while in school	All had normal neurological examinations.
LeMay (1981)[b]	CT	27 Dyslexics 317 Controls	24 dyslexics from Hier et al. (1978) plus 3 new subjects	N/R	N/R	RH dyslexics = 21 RH controls = 150 LH dyslexics = 6 LH controls = 167	N/R	Very few or no neurological findings except for developmental dyslexia. Three dyslexics (2 left-handed) had a history of seizure.
Leisman and Ashkenazi (1980)	CT	8 Dyslexics 2 Normals	Subjects for CT study selected from larger population (N = 20) of dyslexics in EEG study	8.2 Dyslexics 7.6 Normals	Not directly reported[c]	N/R	1. Each dyslexic demonstrated one of Boder's clinical subtypes and had better than 20/30 visual acuity. 2. Two or more years delay in reading in relation to mental age.	None
Rosenberger and Hier (1980)[d]	CT	53 Learning disabled (39 males, 14 females)	22 subjects had delayed speech. Immediate families of 38 had history of reading and/or speech disorders	Age range of 6–45	VIQ PIQ FSIQ RH: 97.2 93.1 102.6 LH: 99.4 102.6 97.1	45 RH 8 LH	1. Achievement deficits of at least 2 grade levels in reading at some point in school. 2. Large discrepancies between VIQ and PIQ (mean discrepancy 15.8 ± 8.7).	No gross neurological deficits; 11 showed some L–R confusion.

480

Study	Method	N	Subgroups	Age	IQ	Handedness	Diagnostic criteria	Comments
Haslam, Dalby, Johns, and Rademaker (1981)	CT	26 Dyslexics 8 Controls	Boder's subtypes: 8 dysphonetic 8 dyseidetic 10 nonspecific 8 controls	11.7 Dyslexics 9.8 Controls	VIQ PIQ FSIQ Dysphonetic 85.5 105.6 95.2 Dyseidetic 97.9 100.2 98.5 Nonspecific 96.4 99.0 97.3 Controls N/R	RH only	Reading performance at least 2 years behind expected level of performance based on WISC-R IQ.	46% of dyslexics had history of abnormal pregnancy or delivery. 50% showed soft neurological signs. Controls were referred for headaches.
Denckla, LeMay, and Chapman (1985)[e]	CT	32 Learning disabled	Right hemisyndrome: 12 males, 4 females Left hemisyndrome: 11 males, 5 females	11.1 (right) 11.1 (left)	98.5 (right) 106.6 (left)	N/R	Measured difference between expected (by IQ) and observed academic achievement in one or more subjects.	Hemisyndromes were assessed by a point system assigned for right- or left-sided subtle but definite neurological signs. Children with bilateral signs were excluded. A score of 4 points was minimum needed for assignment to hemisyndrome.
Rumsey (1986)	MRI	10 Dyslexics (males only)	Education level ranged from 10th grade to Master's Degree. Average was 13 yr of education.	22.60	105	All RH	1. Childhood history of reading disability. Median score on Gray Oral was 3.7 grade. 2. Meet DSM III criteria for developmental reading disability	Nine of 10 were clinically normal. One showed focal finding considered to be incidental to dyslexia. Three patients had neurodevelopmentally anomalous signs.
Parkins, Roberts, Reinarz, and Varney (1987)	CT	44 Dyslexics (males only) 254 Controls[f]		57	WAIS IQ for dyslexics mean = 97; when age corrected on Similarities & Block Design mean IQ = 103. (No IQ data on controls.)	RH Dyslexics = 35 RH Controls = 151 LH Dyslexics = 9 LH Controls = 103	1. History of poor reading and spelling dating from childhood through adulthood. 2. Psychometric evidence of dyslexia. 3. CT scans, availability of good quality.	None reported

[a] Abbreviations: N/R, not reported; RH, right-handed; LH, left-handed; VIQ, verbal IQ; PIQ, performance IQ.

[b] Includes subjects from Hier et al. (1978) plus additional subjects.

[c] IQs reported for larger group (N = 20) full-scale IQ = 104.23 for dyslexics, 103.9 for controls.

[d] Although Rosenberger and Hier (1980) refer to their sample as learning disabled, they report that all subjects demonstrated a deficit of at least two grade levels in reading skills. It is for this reason that their study is included in this table.

[e] Denckla et al.'s (1985) study is included since one of the "hemisyndromes" included in the learning-disabled population examined had a higher frequency of global achievement deficit, particularly in reading (right hemisyndrome group).

[f] Data from unselected males from previous studies (Chui & Damasio, 1980; Koff et al., 1986; LeMay, 1977).

TABLE II CT and MRI Findings in Developmental Dyslexia

Reference	Type of study	CT regions specified for study (scanner employed)	Classification Criteria	Presence of Brain Injury	Ventricular Asymmetries	Other CT Abnormalities	CT Results Left (% wider)	Right (% wider)	Equivalent (%)	Comments
Hier, LeMay, Rosenberger, and Perlo (1978)	CT	A 25° angle with respect to anthropological base of the skull was used for 4–6 transaxial sections through the cerebral hemispheres. Brain sections were reduced in size 3.3 times. (Type of scanner not reported.)	Brains were classified wider in left parietooccipital region if left was 1 mm ≥ right; wider in the right parietooccipital region if right was 1 mm ≥ left; symmetrical if the 2 widths were within 1 mm of each other. See Hier et al. (1978)	None reported	N/R[a]	None reported	33	42	25	Dyslexic subjects with reversed cerebral asymmetry had a lower mean verbal IQ. Conclusion was that this reversal may contribute to reading disability and also be a reflection of language disabilities experienced by 4 of the 10 subjects. Hier et al. (1978) suggested that patients with reversed cerebral asymmetry may have 5 times as great a risk factor for dyslexia.
LeMay (1980)	CT	See Hier et al. (1978). Type of scanner not reported.)	See Hier et al. (1978).	See Hier et al. (1978). LeMay suggested that findings of ventricular asymmetries raise possibility of developmental abnormalities or mild early brain damage. Three	Ventricle size was with normal ranges. Unusual asymmetries were seen in over 1/3 of patients (right ventricle > left; left ventricle >	See Hier et al. (1978).	RH dyslexics 33.3 RH controls 70 LH controls 40	33.3 20 29	33 10 31	LeMay concluded that there may be a higher incidence of early, slight morphological changes in brains of dyslexics but they are not necessarily

Study		Scanning procedure	Asymmetry measurement	patients had a history of seizures suggestive of possible impairment	right more than is normally seen			diagnostic of dyslexia
Leisman and Ashkenazi (1980)	CT	N/R	N/R	N/R	N/R	N/R	Normals 100 0 Dyslexics 0 25 0 75	Leisman and Ashkenazi concluded that dyslexics' parietooccipital regions show reversed symmetry or lack of symmetry.
Rosenberger and Hier (1980)[b]	CT	Each subject had 8 to 10 transaxial CT scan sections, each 8 mm thick from the canthometal line. (EMI CT 1005 scanner employing 160 × 160 grid.)	Cerebral asymmetry was judged by the LeMay (1977) criteria. A positive quotient from the formula $[(L - R)/(L + \times 100)]$ indicated left or unusual asymmetry; negative quotient, right or reversed asymmetry; and zero, assymmetrical brain. Blind assessment of CT scans not used.	None reported	N/R	None reported	42 L≥R:48	Asymmetry index correlated with the verbal–performance IQ discrepancy ($r = .38$, $p < .02$). Rosenberger and Hier (1980) concluded that reversal of cerebral asymmetry was associated with VIQ–PIQ asymmetries. Lower VIQ for those with reversed asymmetry.
Haslam, Dalby, Johns, and Rademaker (1981)	CT	Four scans were performed for each subject (8 transaxial sections) with a 15° angle with respect to the acanthomedial line. (Type of scanner not reported.)	Two methods were used, the modified LeMay technique and the technique of Hier et al. (1978). Both methods were consistent. Hemispheres were considered asymmetric if	None reported	None reported	There was an increased ratio of symmetric brians for all three reading-disabled types compared to the control	(see sub-table below)	No difference was found in verbal ability and relative posterior width of the hemispheres. Children with

Sub-table for Haslam, Dalby, Johns, and Rademaker (1981):

	Oc	Fro	Oc	Fro	Oc	Fro
Reading Disabled	46	8	12	69	42	23
Controls	87	12	0	75	12	12

(continued)

483

TABLE II (*Continued*)

Reference	Type of study	CT regions specified for study (scanner employed)	Classification Criteria	Presence of Brain Injury	Ventricular Asymmetries	Other CT Abnormalities	Left (% wider)	Right (% wider)	Equivalent (%)	Comments
										CT Results (spanning Left, Right, Equivalent, and preceding abnormalities columns)
			they differed by 1 mm or more in width. Borderline cases were consulted with an independent observer and complete agreement was obtained.			group and previously established norms.				reversed asymmetry were not found to be performing at lower reading levels as had been found in other studies. The suggestion was made that relative cerebral size may be influenced by genetics. Conclusion was that CT scans with the reading disabled without significant neurological signs are unwarranted. Language delay was found unrelated to brain measurements.
Denckla, LeMay, and Chapman (1985)	CT	A 0–15° angle inclined toward the feet with relation to the orbitomeatal line. A series consisted of 4 scanning runs. (EMI CT Mark I or 1005 scanner employed.)	Two independent radiologists blind to neurological or historical facts read 25 CT scans. Seven additional CT scans were read by one radiologist.	No reported brain injury but all subjects had neuropsychological deficits in areas of praxic-motor, perceptual, attentional, linguistic, or memory functioning.	One subject's ventricle measurements fell outside normal ranges. Twelve of 32 CTs had slight or minor asymmetries in widths of lateral	Five scans out of 25 (20%) were read as slightly abnormal. Two had basilar cisterns enlarged. One showed slight	Data not analyzed in this fashion.			Conclusion from the data was that most LD children with subtle, classical neurological signs which lateralize can have normal CT scans. However, advances in CT

(continued)

Study	Technique	Methods	Subjects		Results	Conclusions
		ventricles.[c] Four of these 12 had wider ventricles discordant with all findings. Left-handedness was equally divided between CT concordant and CT discordant subject groups.			dysgenesis. One showed midline shift 2 mm to right.	resolution may reveal more specific findings.
Rumsey et al. (1986)	MRI	MRI scans were 10 mm thick. Four patients scanned coronally and transversally; six patients scanned transversally only. (0.5 Tesla) Two radiologists clinically evaluated scans for ventricular size and configuration, temporal lobe symmetry, prominence of cortical sulci, mass effects, and symmetry of signal intensity of brain parenchyma.	All free of severe head injury, seizures, or other significant history.	90	Four patients showed mild reversals of lateral (R > L) ventricle asymmetry; two showed the usual asymmetry pattern (L > R). One subject showed a small white-matter lesion in right frontal lobe; another subject showed equivocal increase in T1 and T2 signal intensities in right hippocampal region. Rescanning was normal.	Concluded that coronal MRI scans may be better able to evaluate macroscopic brain asymmetry. They further suggest studies with MRI of dyslexic subjects with a history of significant speech delay and/or seizures may reveal meaningful results.
Parkins, Roberts, Reinarz, and Varney (1987)	CT	CT slices were obtained at a 15° angle from the canthomeatal line. Determination of asymmetry was from the CT level corresponding most closely to SM of Naesar. 48 CT scans were reviewed by neuroradiologists for symmetry of head position. Four CT scans eliminated due to gross distortions. Two raters independently judged the asymmetry	None reported		None reported Nondyslexics showed an increased frequency of R > L asymmetry on frontal length measures ($\chi^2 = 13.5$, $p < .05$); left-handed	Concluded that reversed occipital asymmetries are not characteristic of right-handed dyslexics. Suggest that posterior portions of the brains of some

	Fro	Oc	Fro	Oc	Fro	Oc
RH dyslexics	29	63	37	14	34	23
RH controls	18	61	48	13	34	26
LH dyslexics	33	22	22	33	45	45
LH controls	24	46	42	16	34	38

TABLE II (Continued)

Reference	Type of study	CT regions specified for study (scanner employed)	Classification Criteria	Presence of Brain Injury	Ventricular Asymmetries	Other CT Abnormalities	CT Results Left (% wider)	Right (% wider)	Equivalent (%)	Comments
		and Hayward (1978). An overhead projector was used for enlargement. Asymmetry was judged if corresponding measurement varied by > 1 mm from one hemisphere to the next. (Majority of scans from a Picker 1200 scanner. Others from an EMI 1005 scanner.)	ratings. Consensus was reached by assuming no asymmetry (91% agreement).			dyslexics differed significantly from RH dyslexics in that fewer LH dyslexics manifested typical L > R occipital width measure ($p = .03$).				LH dyslexics may be anatomically atypically organized.

[a] N/R, not reported.

[b] Rosenberger and Hier's (1980) study examined cerebral asymmetries and verbal intellectual performance in learning-disabled subjects. While these subjects were not diagnosed specifically as having developmental dyslexia, all had evidenced a 2-year delay in reading achievement in school. It is for this reason they are included in this review.

[c] Biventricular ratios were calculated employing the Fukuyama, Miyao, Ishizu, and Maruyama (1979) method, by the ratio of the length of a line drawn between the caudate nuclei heads and the width of the cerebral hemispheres at the same level. Evans's ratio (right and left anterior horn width/maximum internal skull width) was used for the frontal measurements.

1985; Parkins, Roberts, Reinarz, & Varney, 1987). Significant differences exist in these two studies with regard to interrater reliability.

In the Denckla *et al.* (1985) study, only 48% agreement was reached as to judgments made independently on 25 CT scans. In the Parkins *et al.* (1987) study, 91% agreement was reached by two independent raters with no disagreement as to the direction of asymmetry. Insofar as can be determined, these differences may reflect the task required of the two independent raters. In the Denckla *et al.* (1985) study, the raters were required to reach clinical interpretations as to whether the CT scans were normal or abnormal. In the Parkins *et al.* (1987) study, however, the raters were to make measurements regarding the presence of asymmetry. Not surprisingly, independent judgments based on metric procedures resulted in considerably higher interrater reliability than did those in the Denckla *et al.* (1985) study, in which the clinical agreement, though above chance levels, is not particularly impressive. In fact, it should be pointed out that the calculation of Cohen's kappa reveals an unacceptable degree of diagnostic agreement (Spitzer, Foreman, & Nee, 1979) in the Denckla *et al.* (1985) study.

The quantitative procedures used in these studies most frequently include LeMay's (1977) method or a modified version thereof (Haslam, Dalby, Johns, & Rademaker, 1981), Fukuyama, Miyao, Ishizu, and Maruyama's (1979) bicaudate measure for determination of the width of the lateral ventricles, and Pelicci, Bedrick, Cruse, and Vannucci's (1979) frontal biventricular index. Generally, it can be said that these indexes represent accepted procedures often used to determine intracranial dimensions.

Consequently, the quantitative procedures used for the determination of intracranial dimensions seem adequate, particularly in the Denckla *et al.* (1985), Hier, LeMay, Rosenberger, and Perlo (1978), Haslam *et al.* (1981), Parkins *et al.* (1987), and Rosenberger and Hier (1980) studies, but the data are very poorly reported with the exception of the number of cases showing right or left asymmetry or only symmetry. Furthermore, only in the Parkins *et al.* (1987) study was interrater reliability examined with regard to the determination of these measures. Notwithstanding the preceding considerations, these results are of clinical and theoretical interest.

It should be noted that in seven out of eight of these studies, no evidence of detectable brain injury is reported. Thus, insofar as the resolution and transaxial CT slices selected for study allow, it is notable that brain injury or obvious pathology does not characterize the patients in these neuroimaging studies. This, of course, is consistent with the notion that dyslexia is associated with some pathological process during neurological development and is not due to brain injury.

Enlarged or displaced ventricles may suggest the presence of pathology, and it is only in Denckla *et al.*'s (1985) study that several of their 32 subjects were judged to have ventricle measurements outside of normal limits. Also in this study, which focused on children whose learning deficits were found in association with either a right or a left hemisyndrome (diagnosed on the basis of lateralizing sensorimotor neurological signs), 5 out of 25 (20%) scans were read as abnormal by both radiologists. These abnormalities included two children who had enlarged basilar cisterns, one who showed a slight hemispheric dysgenesis, and another who showed a midline shift 2 mm to the right. While the radiologists in the Denckla et al. (1985) study judged the ventricles of 5 children to be enlarged, in applying the norms established by Pelicci et al. (1979), Fukuyama et al. (1979), and Pedersen, Gyldensted, and Gyldensted (1979), it was found that 4 out of these 5 fell within normal limits. Thus, consistent with Denckla et al.'s (1985) conclusion, it seems reasonable to conclude that few CT scan abnormalities exist in the brains of learning-disabled children with reading problems (presumably children likely to manifest a right hemisyndrome). The other CT/MRI scan studies support this conclusion, and this is one of few consistent findings to emerge from these studies. However, neurobiological theory would predict that the variables of importance are patterns of symmetry or asymmetry that are at variance with established norms.

Patterns of cerebral asymmetry as revealed by CT scans have been well documented. LeMay (1976), for example, examined 100 right-handed men and found that 78% evidenced L > R occipital length and only 5% showed the reversed R > L pattern. With regard to occipital width, 67% showed L > R, and 13.3% had the reverse (R > L) pattern.

Anterior asymmetries also exist. In LeMay's (1976) study, 70% had greater R > L frontal lengths, and 13% showed the reverse (L > R) pattern. Width measurements revealed that 53% had R > L frontal hemispheres, and 15% demonstrated a reverse (L > R) pattern. Of relevance, left-handed men showed different patterns of CT asymmetries in that more symmetry was found (e.g., occipital lengths; 37% L > R; 39% R > L; 24% L = R), suggesting that handedness may well be an important variable in these studies. The results of these neuroimaging studies of the brains of developmental dyslexics appear to be at odds with these normative figures.

A consistent finding in six out of eight of these studies is that in nonconsecutively diagnosed dyslexics varying in age from 8 to over 57 years, significantly less L > R asymmetry is present, and there is an increased degree of symmetry or, to a lesser extent, reversed R > L parietooccipital asymmetry. Figure 1 shows such symmetry in the brain of a dyslexic boy. In the two studies that fail to report this finding (Denckla et al., 1985; Parkins et al., 1987), it should be noted that in one case (Denckla et al., 1985) cerebral asymmetries were not appraised and in the other (Parkins et al., 1987) this finding was reportedly observed only in left-handed dyslexics.

Keeping in mind that most of these studies only examined parietooccipi-

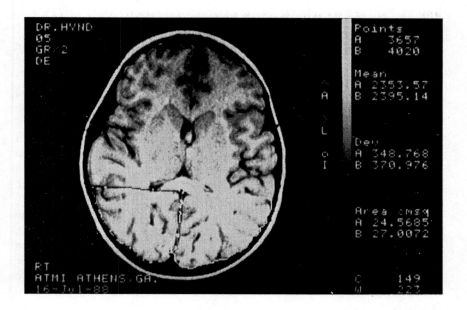

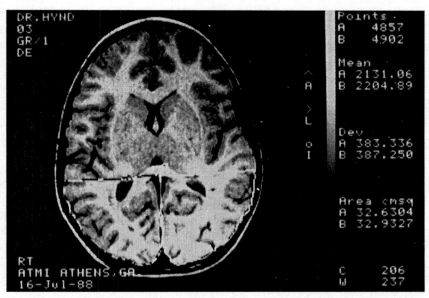

FIGURE 1 MRI scan of a child with normal (L > R) posterior asymmetry (top) (area of the left parietooccipital region = 27.0072 cm^2; right = 24.5685 cm^2) and a child with developmental dyslexia (bottom) showing symmetry (L = R) of the posterior area (left = 32.9327 cm^2; right = 32.6304 cm^2). Note that MRI scans are traditionally reversed in orientation such that right = left and left = right.

tal asymmetries and that LeMay (1976) found in her control population that 67% evidenced L > R width patterns, among the dyslexics examined in these studies the same pattern of asymmetry was noted to be present in only 33.3% of the Hier *et al.* (1978) dyslexics and in 46% of the Haslam *et al.* (1981) subjects. In the Leisman and Ashkenazi (1980) study, seven of the dyslexics had the reversed (R > L) pattern, and one had equivalent cerebral hemispheres. The degree of reversed cerebral asymmetry in three studies for which comparable data are reported (Haslam *et al.*, 1981; Hier *et al.*, 1978; Leisman & Ashkenazi, 1980) averages 19.67%, which is not greatly more than the 13.3% found in LeMay (1976). Comparable to this, and perhaps adding strength to the argument that symmetry (Haslam *et al.*, 1981) or asymmetry (Hier *et al.*, 1978; Rosenberger & Hier, 1980) is more often found in the brains of dyslexics, is the fact that across four studies (Haslam *et al.*, 1981; Hier *et al.*, 1978; Leisman & Ashkenazi, 1980; Rumsey *et al.*, 1986), an average of 58% of the CT scans were determined to be symmetrical in the parietooccipital region among the dyslexics. This high percentage of dyslexic brains showing equivalent or symmetrical parietooccipital CT regions is considerably greater than what LeMay (1976) reported or than what, somewhat more recently, she (LeMay, 1981) reported in her dyslexic control population which, across handedness (left-handed = 31%; right-handed = 10%), averaged 20.5%.

Only two studies reported frontal asymmetries in their developmental dyslexics (Haslam *et al.*, 1981; Parkins *et al.*, 1987), and it appears that Denckla *et al.* (1985) used Evans's index (Evans, 1942; Synek, Reuben, & DuBoulay, 1976) to examine frontal horn abnormalities. The data derived from Denckla *et al.*'s (1985) study were not reported, although Denckla *et al.* noted that Evans's ratio fell within the normal range for children with learning disabilities, including those with the right hemisyndrome.

In the Haslam *et al.* (1981) study, there do not appear to be very significant differences in frontal asymmetry between the developmental dyslexics and the control subjects. There were, however, proportionately more dyslexic children with equivalent frontal hemispheres than would be expected from LeMay's (1976) earlier normative findings, but because the original data are not provided, it is impossible to determine if this is a statistically significant finding. Parkins *et al.* (1987) did analyze their data regarding frontal measurements and reported that, for the developmental dyslexics, no significant differences existed with respect to previously collected (Chui & Damasio, 1980) normative data on any frontal measure.

Consequently, it does appear that developmental dyslexics may evidence an increased incidence of posterior symmetry (Haslam *et al.*, 1981; Rumsey *et al.*, 1986) or, in dyslexics with serious expressive language delay (as measured by history and verbal IQ), perhaps a higher incidence of reversed parietooccipital asymmetry (Hier *et al.*, 1978; Leisman & Ashkenazi, 1980; LeMay, 1981; Rosenberger & Hier, 1980). Although these conclusions are suggested by these studies, they clearly are at variance with the findings recently reported by Parkins *et al.* (1987), who examined 44 CT scans of developmental dyslexic adults.

As can be seen in Table II, Parkins *et al.* (1987) found it was only among left-handed dyslexics that there were proportionately fewer cases of L > R parietooccipital asymmetry; this finding was particularly significant regarding the length measurement. Thus, in the sample of adults examined by Parkins *et al.* (1987), the finding of less posterior asymmetry is only relevant in left-handed dyslexics.

Across these studies there seems to be some agreement that dyslexics may evidence increased degrees of symmetry of the posterior cortex, but the various studies differ with respect to the influence of handedness, with the Parkins *et al.* (1987) study standing alone in suggesting that this effect is only observed in left-handed developmental dyslexics.

It is quite possible that the adults in the Parkins *et al.* (1987) study are representative of a uniquely different population of developmental dyslexics. Several points argue in favor of this hypothesis. First, it is unusual that in all of these studies, but most notably in the Parkins *et al.* (1987) study, these dyslexic subjects have a normal IQ. Considerable evidence suggests that, on the average, the mean IQ for reading-disabled persons is usually attenuated and closer to 90 than to 100 (Camp & Dolcourt, 1977; Stanovich, 1985). This observation alone argues for the conclusion that across these studies— and especially with the Hier *et al.* (1978), Parkins *et al.* (1987), and Rumsey *et al.* (1986) studies, which all used adults—the subjects used in the neuro-imaging studies had higher levels of general ability than would be expected on the basis of prior studies of severely reading-disabled populations.

A second and related point is that evidence suggests a strong age effect with regard to the predictive validity of IQ measures. For example, Stanovich, Cunningham, and Feeman (1984) found that the correlation between IQ and reading achievement in the early elementary grades ranges from .3 to .5 but increases significantly in adulthood to .6 to .75. Other studies support this finding of age-related predictive relations (see Stanovich, 1985).

Consequently, normal intelligence (i.e., IQ = 103) in the presence of very severely deficient reading achievement (WRAT standard score = 79) in 57-year-old men suggests that these individuals are very unusual indeed because they score normally on a measure that correlates highly with reading achievement, particularly at their age. In other words, although all dyslexics could probably be considered statistical outliers in the present sense, these older dyslexics are potentially even more deviant than those at younger ages, as found in the Haslam *et al.* (1981) study, for example, in which the mean age was 11.7 years. Furthermore, the mere fact that the dyslexia persisted to such a degree into adulthood raises the question of whether these dyslexics might not represent a potentially more severe expression of this syndrome.

Although the possible long-term developmental interactions between severity of dyslexia, cognitive ability, handedness, and cerebral asymmetries are unknown, it may be postulated that among fairly young right-handed dyslexics (<8–25 years), symmetry or an increased incidence of reversed asymmetry may characterize some subjects. Furthermore, should interactions exist between handedness and cerebral asymmetries among dyslexics, age and severity may be important variables. To date, however, only the Parkins *et al.* (1987) study suggests that this may be a consideration.

B. *Neurolinguistic Relations*

Demonstration of morphologically different brains in developmental dyslexia is clearly an important contribution to theoretical perspectives regarding this disorder. However, morphological variation must be tied to some productive conceptualization if it is to assist in explaining why these individuals do not read at expected levels. It was on the basis of neurobiological theory that Hier *et al.* (1978) examined the possible relations between brain morphology and language ability. Although some of the studies that followed did not specifically examine the possible relations between measures of brain asymmetry and language proficiency (e.g., Denckla *et al.*, 1985; Leisman & Ashkenazi, 1980; LeMay, 1981; Parkins *et al.*, 1987; Rumsey *et al.*, 1986), others did. Of these studies, the majority were primarily concerned with examining whether the brains of developmental dyslexics were characterized by a unique pattern of brain asymmetry that presumably underlies linguistic specialization (Geschwind, 1974, 1984; Geschwind & Galaburda, 1985a, 1985b, 1985c; Geschwind & Levitsky, 1968).

The studies by Hier *et al.* (1978), Haslam *et al.* (1981), and Rosenberger and Hier (1980) provide conflicting data in this regard. The Hier *et al.* (1978) and Rosenberger and Hier (1980) studies provide provocative data that suggest a relation between these two groups of dyslexics when performance IQ was considered. On the basis of this evidence, Hier *et al.* (1978) concluded that reversed cerebral asymmetries in male dyslexics may serve as an added risk factor that potentially interacts with other variables to produce a more serious language deficit.

Rosenberger and Hier (1980) provided what at first glance appears to be supporting data. They found in examining the IQ scores of 53 learning-disabled subjects (all were reported to suffer a severe reading achievement deficit) not only depressed verbal IQ but also depressed performance IQ in the dyslexics with reversed asymmetry (R > L) in comparison to those dyslexics with normal patterns of asymmetry (L > R). No differences were found between these two groups on full-scale IQ.

Although this finding seems to be consistent with Hier *et al.*'s (1978) hypothesis that reversed cerebral asymmetry is associated with linguistic deficits as measured by verbal IQ, it may not be. Data in this regard are provided inadvertently by Rosenberger and Hier (1980). In an attempt to analyze the IQ data according to scores suggested by factor-analytic studies (Cohen, 1959), verbal comprehension and perceptual-organizational factors were examined. The resulting factor scores, using Cohen's (1959) factors, reveal that the dyslexics with reversed posterior asymmetry differed from those with typical asymmetry by only .7 of a scale-score point (L > R = 9.9; R > L = 8.6), which is well within the ±3 criterion suggested by Kaufman (1979) for interpreting statistically and potentially clinically meaningful differences. With regard to Cohen's (1959) factors, Sattler (1974) noted that the standard deviation of these factors is 2-1/2 scale-score points, thus suggesting the relative insignificance of the actual difference found in these factor scores in these populations.

On the perceptual-organizational factor, these two groups differ by only .5 of a scale-score point (L > R = 11.4; R > L = 11.9). In fact, according to both Sattler's (1974) and Kaufman's (1979) criteria, the only statistically meaningful difference is not between the hemispheric asymmetry groups but rather between the verbal comprehension factor score (8.6) and the perceptual-organizational factor score (11.9) in those dyslexics with reversed asymmetry.

The point to derive from this is that, although Rosenberger and Hier (1980) reported statistically significant differences between their hemispheric groups, the actual mean factor-score differences fall well within the standard error of the mean, and it is for this reason that Kaufman (1979) recommended ±3 scale-score points as a minimal difference in making clinical interpretations regarding these abilities. Sattler's (1974) recommendations are similar. Simply put, these reported factor-score differences may be meaningless in revealing differences in neuropsychological functioning.

However, Rosenberger and Hier's (1980) argument that verbal–performance IQ differences exist between dyslexics with different cerebral asymmetries was strengthened considerably only when Rosenberger and Hier (1980) compared those subjects with delayed language onset to those who acquired language (first 2-word phrases) before 36 months of age. When only those subjects with reversed asymmetry are considered, those with normal language development achieved a verbal IQ of 100.2, whereas those with seriously delayed language onset (>36 months) had a mean verbal IQ of 83.3. This is a statistically (Sattler, 1974) significant difference ($p < .01$) and may be clinically meaningful (Kaufman, 1979). Performance and full-scale discrepancies were equally as large and in the same direction. When the children with severely delayed speech were omitted from consideration, the differences in proportion of reversed asymmetry between the dyslexics and the controls disappeared.

Haslam *et al.* (1981) examined these same basic issues and found no support for the idea that normal or reversed hemispheric asymmetries are related to verbal or performance abilities. Their study, though generally well controlled, included fewer disabled subjects, and the criteria for severe language delay were not as strict as those used by Rosenberger and Hier (1980). Haslam *et al.* (1981) defined language delay as the failure to speak in 2-word phrases by 2 years of age or in simple sentences by 3 years of age. Also, a majority (71.7%) of Rosenberger and Hier's (1980) subjects (38 out of 53) had a positive family history (first-, second-, and third-degree relatives) of reading failure, speech disorders, or both reading and speech problems. Consequently, it may be that Rosenberger and Hier's (1980) subjects included a more seriously deficient subgroup of developmental dyslexics, whose significantly delayed onset of language was found in association with reversed cerebral asymmetries and lower levels of verbal, performance, and full-scale IQ. It is reasonable, therefore, to conclude that if a relation exists in dyslexics between reversed cerebral asymmetries of the parietooccipital cortex and verbal intelligence, it is primarily among those with rather severely delayed language onset.

A final point in this regard is made by Hier *et al.* (1978). They correctly noted that of the 10 subjects in the R > L group, 4 had evidence of language delay, whereas out of the remaining 14 subjects in the study, only 1 had a reported history of delay in speech acquisition.

C. Conclusions

Despite the fact that concerns exist over how the subjects in these studies were diagnosed (Hynd & Semrud-Clikeman, 1989b), the use of CT/MRI procedures has provided some limited evidence that alterations in normal patterns of brain asymmetry in the region of the left planum temporale and parietooccipital cortex may correlate with the behaviorally defined syndrome of developmental dyslexia. Future neuroimaging studies may provide validating evidence and examine the relative importance of variables that are poorly controlled in these studies.

VI. Brain Electrical Activity Mapping

Deviations in brain electrical activity may reflect dysfunctional neurological structures or systems, although the correlation is not necessarily robust. However, electroencephalographic mapping procedures are included in this chapter since there is a long history of using EEG in investigating neurologic dysfunction and since recent topographic mapping procedures allow us to visualize deviations that may implicate dysfunctional neurological processes. Traditionally, deviations in brain electrical activity have been reflected in abnormal amplitude, latency (as in event-related potentials), and frequency. More recently, topography of activity has become an area of focus in investigating electrophysiological differences in learning-disabled persons' brains. Similar to the CT/MRI studies, most investigators have focused on developmental dyslexics as the clinical group of interest. It should be noted, however, that there are relatively few studies in this area even in comparison to the CT/MRI literature.

A. Background

A technique capable of imaging the momentary fluctuation of brain activity participating in forming the functional basis of cognitive processes should have a high temporal resolution. Presently, only electrical activity of the brain can be recorded rapidly enough. Brain-activity mapping based on electroencephalographic (EEG) signals uses 10–124 electrodes spread on the head surface to collect a representative sample of measurable electrical brain activity. Its history is decades long (Lehman, 1971; Livanov, 1969; Petsche & Shaw, 1972; Remond, 1955), but only during the last 10 years have the data-reduction facilities and methods allowed the huge amount of data to be reduced to features that contain some practical value for study (Duffy, Burchfiel, & Lombroso, 1979; Duffy, Denckla, Bartels, Sandini, & Kiessling, 1980; John, 1977).

One of the first foci for clinical research was the brain functions of learning-disabled children (Ahn *et al.,* 1980; Duffy, Denckla, Bartels, & Sandini, 1980). Thus far, the frequency-domain EEG changes have been the main dependent variable, although it is the amplitude domain which may be more promising and which offers excellent temporal resolution. Direct comparisons of these two data domains have shown that the amplitude fluctuations studied in terms of event-related potentials (ERP) may contrast learning-disabled children better than do the frequency-domain features of EEG (Duffy, Denckla, Bartels, & Sandini, 1980; Duffy, Denckla, Bartels, Sandini, & Kessling, 1980). They may also have value in diagnosing subtypes of learning-disabled children (Duffy, Denckla, McAnulty, & Holmes, 1988).

This section concentrates on reviewing the multichannel frequency- and amplitude-domain EEG mapping studies completed with learning-disabled children.

B. Pros and Cons of Brain Electrical-Activity Mapping

There is plenty of empirical data showing that different clinical groups differ from each other in terms of the distribution of the frequency, the amplitude, or both aspects of brain electrical activity either at rest and/or under stimulus–task conditions (John, 1989). In these studies, EEG data have been used objectively using fixed data-selection algorithms and statistical analyses for conclusions instead of using traditional clinical EEG inspection based on subjective visual analysis. Not all of these mapping results, however, are based on a sufficiently credible empirical validation. The problems in these objective studies relate to the paucity of explicit theories and poor knowledge about the nature of generation of EEG activity in the brain. This means that the contrasts employed in the study must be selected empirically.

Consequently, empirical validation is difficult. First, any unexpectedly found contrast between groups will not be acceptable as such and, second, the EEG data easily produce unexpected differences. This is because conclusions are based on statistical testing of thousands of contrasts. These come from the product of (often many) measurement situations × (typically at least 20) electrodes × (many) response scores. The number of contrasts is unavoidably large, depending on the number of electrodes, and they often become unmanageable when ERPs based on hundreds of temporal samples are used as data. Large numbers of subjects, sophisticated analyses (see John, 1977; John, Prichep, & Easton, 1987), and a critical mind (Oken & Chiappa, 1986) are needed to avoid reliance on randomly occurring significant differences.

The ERP studies have had a different starting point. They share a common conceptual basis in that the phenomenon of interest in ERP research is relevant to learning-disabled problems. Basic knowledge about the behavior of ERPs in situations of attentional or arousal variation is quite large and relevant to theoretical developments regarding attention (see Näätänen, 1990, for a comprehensive summary).

In as many learning-disabled children as are believed to suffer attentional and accompanying problems in memory, ERP paradims are of potential use in documenting associated electrophysiological dysfunction. To date, many of the studies have employed single-channel ERP recordings (Harmony, 1989). There are, however, many problems in that the developmental course of children's ERPs is poorly documented and most of the data using these procedures have employed adults. Second, most of the ERP studies have used midline (F_z, C_z, P_z, O_z) electrodes that allow for poor measures of topography. Consequently, there is a need for topographic studies using ERPs with both normal and learning-disabled children who are matched for chronological age.

C. Brain Imaging Using ERP Paradigms

The first studies on mapping of ERPs in learning-disabled children have been published during the last few years. As a good example of these efforts, the Satterfield, Schell, Nicholas, and Backs (1988) study will be briefly described. They compared 6- to 7-year-old attention-deficit disorder with hyperactivity (ADD/H) boys, many of whom may have associated learning disabilities, with age-matched controls using a paradigm where ERP maps to attended and unattended stimuli were compared.

Subjects were instructed to actively attend to a designated stimulus source. Visual and auditory stimuli, namely checkerboard flashes and 1000-Hz tones, were used as stimuli. Stimuli lasted 10 msec and were presented with a constant interval of 2 sec. Twenty-five percent of the stimuli were of higher intensity—16.1 versus 16 lux for flashes and 85 versus 75 dB for tones—which, in turn, were targets in the attended modality. Subjects were taught to press a hand-held reaction-time button whenever a target occurred.

Electrodes were designated from the International 10–20 system and a suborbital electrode on the left cheek allowed for the monitoring of eye movements. Trials with artifacts and those following a button press or the target stimulus were excluded from averaging. Averages were presented for 1000 msec poststimulus corrected to the baseline of 75 msec mean of prestimulus time. A number of typical ERP component scores were separated.

Group (2) × attention (2) × auditory target/nontarget (2) × electrode site (19) ANOVAs were computed for each score separately with Greenhouse–Geisser correction for the repeated measures. The Bonferroni procedure was applied to the probability levels to correct for the large number of contrasts performed.

The N2 component (peak latency at 265 msec) was shown to be significantly lower in ADD/H children independent of electrode site. Follow-up analyses revealed that it was based on the ERP to the target stimulus in the auditory attend condition. Significant differences prevailed on the left-side and midline electrodes from frontal to parietal areas. The target–nontarget difference contrasted the groups, with the highly significant difference occurring at the left centroposterior regions.

Only control groups showed the expected processing negativity (PN) wave to the attended stimuli. The ERP results were consistent with the behavioral target-detection responses, some measures of which (commission errors) also contrasted the groups (ADD/H < controls). Thus, the well-known ERP responses, N2 to the target stimulus and PN to the attended stimuli, were consistently lower in the boys showing ADD/H.

These results make it possible to describe the functional significance of ERP components to the interpretation of the nature of ADD/H problems.

The results are consistent with other psychophysiological findings showing that unselective responsivity to critical (target) and less critical (nontarget) stimuli is a feature of the attentional problems in learning-disabled subjects (e.g., Lyytinen & Lorys-Vernon, 1988). Unfortunately, Satterfield *et al.* (1988) have not reported the ERP averages to unattended tones. These would make it possible to examine the more automatic aspect of N2 process, namely mismatch negativity (MMN), whose potential applicability to learning-disabled research has been proposed (Lyytinen & Lorys-Vernon, 1988) and which has direct relevance to attention theories (Näätänen, 1990). Satterfield *et al.* (1988) interpret the N2 and PN result to reflect poor discrimination and poor processing of the attended stimulus. The failure to find frontal PN in the ADD/H boys is interpreted as support for the contention that ADD/H is related to frontal dysfunction. It must be added that the amplitude topography of the ERP waves does not reveal the possible generator mechanisms. Developments in ERP methodology, like the current density mapping and dipole fitting allowing for better source localization, are still underway (see Fender, 1987, for a review). Topographic information may, however, be needed when no source localization is intended. Thus, in the preceding study, N2 and MMN components, which have different functional roles, can be separated by examining the MMN's polarity reversal between electrodes positioned above and below the approximate location of MMN generation (in the primary auditory cortex).

Mismatch negativity offers an interesting component for study in learning-disabled children because its potential generation is better known than that of many other components and it reflects the basic mechanism of automatic attention switching to stimulus changes (i.e., without conscious attention) (for details see Näätänen, 1990). Mismatch negativity has been shown to occur to any stimulus change within a sequence of auditory stimulation within the limits of sensory memory (up to 5–10 sec), including phonetic stimuli. Within sequences of phonetic stimuli, which the human brain is well prepared to process, a very small change elicits MMN, as shown by Aaltonen, Niemi, Nyrke, and Tuhkanen (1987). Mapping of the well-known MMN–ERP component to phonetic deviant stimuli offers an unexplored and theoretically interesting example from basic ERP research for application to the study of neurocognitive difficulties in phonetic discrimination often found in learning-disabled children (Hynd & Semrud-Clikeman, 1989a).

D. Using Multivariate Procedures to Contrast Learning-Disabled Groups

The most advanced examples of approaches emphasizing the purely empirical, statistical means for finding the critical differences between clinical and nonclinical groups are John's neurometrics (1977) and Duffy's Statistical Probability Mapping methods (Duffy *et al.*, 1979).

The "neurometrics" strategy refers to the quantitative methods John and his co-workers (1983) have developed to extract clinically valuable features from the EEG and ERP data. It is aimed at providing information about anatomical integrity, developmental maturation, and the mediation of sensory, perceptual, and cognitive processes (Harmony, 1984; John, 1977). It is seen as one of the most important applications of the imaging of brain electrical activity (John, Prichep, Fridman, & Easton, 1988). These procedures are based on collecting normative data from large samples of healthy, normally functioning individuals, thus allowing for comparison to clinical cases. The values of any feature of interest can then be expressed as a z score to contrast a clinical patient to normative data. The suggested testing and measuring procedures not only add to the objectivity of the EEG analysis but also assist in generating features independent from others that can be used as new dependent variables in the topographic maps. Additionally, the neurometrics strategy allows one to construct multivariate component features by combining several EEG/ERP-based data of potential relevance to construct multivariate composites for diagnostic contrasts.

One of the most important empirical contributions of the John's group thus far for learning-disabled research has been the collection of the basic EEG frequency-domain norms for ages 6–16 years from a resting condition. For EEG, this was accomplished earlier using a very carefully screened Swedish sample from ages 1–21 years (Matousek & Petersen, 1973).

The normative data provide regression equations to correct for age effects. The next step in these studies was to examine how a number of learning-disabled related groups deviated from normal EEG maturation lines (Ahn *et al.*, 1980). Two groups of control children ($N = 306 + 91$) were compared to (1) 474 consecutive visitors to a pediatric neurology outpatient service (percentage of neurological dysfunction not known), (2) 143 (>85 IQ) children who had multiple problems in learning and attended a school for learning-disabled children, and (3) 163 children whose learning problems were specific (in one area only, such as reading) and whose deficit in achievement scores showed a delay of not less than 2 years). The results revealed that the number of significantly deviating scores from the predicted normal scores was more than twice as many predicted by chance in about 58% of children in the first group and 54% and 52%, respectively, of children in the general and specific learning-disabled groups. A discriminant function computed for two independent replications of the learning-disabled samples demonstrated a total classification success rate of 65% (John *et al.*, 1983).

The methodological complexities of these neurometric approaches have indeed been considerable and lead to problems in replication (Galin, 1989;

Yingling, Fein, Galin, Peltzman, & Davenport, 1986). In general, it seems that the more neurologically involved a patient is (e.g., mildly retarded), the higher the probability that differences will be documented using these procedures (Gasser, Mochs, Lenard, Bacher, & Verleger, 1983).

Duffy and his co-workers' studies represent the other tradition of relevance that emphasizes the search of a comprehensive number of EEG/ERP indices and the use of advanced statistical techniques to find features contrasting clinical groups. A number of studies have been published describing brain electrical activity mapping (BEAM) hardware and significance probability mapping (SPM) software in addition to the results from a dyslexia study (Duffy, Denckla, Bartels, & Sandini, 1980; Duffy, Denckla, Bartels, Sandini, & Kessling, 1980; Duffy et al., 1988; Duffy & McAnulty, 1985) which are highly relevant here.

As in neurometrics, the basic contrasts in Duffy's approach are formed by computing z transforms on the basis of age-matched controls. Then, z scores and p values based on t- and/or F-based contrast values are used in the map plottings. The areas where the differences reach significant levels are visible from the brain map.

The first study (Duffy, Denckle, Bartels, & Sandini, 1980; Duffy, Denckla, Bartels, Sandini, & Kessling, 1980) of dyslexics using BEAM technology was made using eight 9– to 10.7-year-old "dyslexia-pure" boys (oral reading score > 1.5 years below expectations and no other learning-disabled features, such as hyperactivity; IQ between 94 and 114) and controls matched on age, IQ, socioeconomic status, and handedness. Twenty EEG electrodes placed in the standard 10–20 format and four electrodes for eye movement and muscle-artifact detection were used. Both frequency domain and ERP analyses were computed.

The frequency-domain recordings consisted of taking 3-minute samples from 10 different testing conditions or states. Brain electrical activity was recorded for six frequency bands from delta to beta (last divided into three parts) using equally wide windows from 0 to 23.5 Hz. The ERP recordings were made (1) to visual flash stimuli, (2) to 40-msec, 1000-Hz 92-dB tones, and (3) to words *tight* and *tyke*.

The only significant results of the frequency-domain recording (EEG) were found from areas which were not expected, namely from left medial frontal and left midtemporal regions, which showed more theta in dyslexics especially during reading. Consistent (less alpha suppression in dyslexic) differences were found also in other states, including naming and speech, and surprisingly also in the left frontotemporal areas during baseline conditions.

The ERP results contrasted the groups better, although an index based on a composite summary of variables was still better than the ERP variables alone (Duffy, Denckla, Bartels, Sandini, & Kessling, 1980). An examination of SPMs using 12-msec time windows revealed that the variables of greatest contribution in discriminating the groups were from ERPs to words and to flashes. The first showed the difference at a latency of 186 msec at postero-lateral locations (controls showing more positive and dyslexic negative volt-age) and the second at a latency of 282 msec, where the midline parietooccipi-tal values were more negative in controls than in dyslexics. These two variables were able to classify successfully 92% of cases. Additionally, in the ERP to tones, the late left temporo-parietal wave at 342 msec was significantly more negative in controls.

Although Duffy, Denckla, Bartels, and Sandini (1980) and Duffy, Denckla, Bartels, Sandini, and Kessling (1980) suggest that these results implicate the supplemental motor area, Broca's and Wernicke's areas, and the central language zones, insufficient evidence supports such a broad conclu-sion. It is tempting, however, to accept such a conclusion since these regions would be consistent with those traditionally implicated in developmental dyslexia (Hynd & Cohen, 1983). One of the problems in this study is that the dyslexic-pure subjects were inadequately described, thus one does not know what neuropsychological deficits characterized these subjects. More recently, however, this issue has been partially addressed.

In a recent report, Duffy *et al.* (1988) reported findings from an interest-ing dyslexia subgroup study using the same methodology. Forty-four dyslexic boys were divided into subgroups defined by Denckla (1979) as anomic-repetition disorder, dysphonemic sequencing, and global-mixed language so that 30 (13, 8, and 9, respectively) categorized cases were accepted into the BEAM study. When each subgroup was compared with a control group (not specified) and with the other subgroups a total of 149 contrasting features was detected. A further analysis was made to find statistically those features where each group was different from the combined group of the other two sub-groups. Of the 34 features separating the groups, 30 were based on ERP data and 18 on ERPs to word stimuli. Next, these neurophysiological contrasting features were correlated with the 6 neuropsychological variables (Boston Naming, Peabody, Token, Menyuk Syntactic Comprehension Test, Stanford –Binet's Sentence Memory, and WISC-R's Digit Span) characterizing the group separation on a psychological level. Thirty-six of the 272 correlations reached significance. All 11 (from 12) global subgroups' features correlated significantly with at least one neuropsychological variable and were in the "correct" direction (i.e., the lower the neuropsychological score the more deviant the neurophysiological score from the controls). Surprisingly, all the comparable scores (6 for anomic and 10 for dysphonemic) from the two other subgroups correlated in the opposite direction. The interpretation is that the aberrant electrical activity may represent compensatory overactivity rather than a simple pathological one. This shows how the interpretation of the electrical brain-imaging results may raise complex questions. This type of explanation may indeed be valid, as it is supported by a comparable compensatory activity reported by Rumsey, Coppola, Denckla, Hamburger, and Kruesi (1989).

An interesting feature from the subgroups study was that there was no evidence about asymmetric differences between groups or about left-sided aberration, although all of the groups showed language-related disorders. Also important is that the subgroups clearly differed from each other both neuropsychologically and neurophysiologically. The electrical activity of the bilateral medial frontal areas characterized the anomic group, that of the bilateral centroparietal the dysphonetics, and the spatial regions the global dyslexic from other dyslexic boys.

These studies have been reviewed in some detail because there are very few studies that have examined the topography of brain electrical activity in learning-disabled children's brains. Duffy and his colleagues represent a small group of investigators who are attempting to image electrophysiological differences in this context. However, it is clear that replications regarding the utility of BEAM or SPM both theoretically and clinically are urgently needed.

E. Conclusion

The approaches described above each have their strong and weak points. Research based on accumulated data of cognitive psychophysiology is theoretically the most promising. Problems remain, however. For example, is existing ERP knowledge sufficiently specific in offering fruitful hypotheses in relation to learning-disabled research? It seems that a subgroup analysis is the level at which to begin with learning-disabled samples.

Duffy's work offers a starting point if one only wants to find features from the brain's electrical activity that differentiate learning-disabled subgroups. The problem arises when one wants to interpret the results because the abstractions resulting from the multivariate composite variables may not allow generalization to known ERP components. These abstractions may, however, offer critically important cues as complementary data to neuropsychological methods. A combination of the different approaches will produce theoretically and methodologically efficient tools for electrical brain mapping in learning-disabled research. However, the temptation to view these maps of regional brain activity and accept uncritically that they reflect dysfunction in theoretically consistent neurological structures implicated in learning disabilities may be the most significant challenge of researchers and clinicians alike.

VII. Comment

Brain-imaging studies in learning disabilities are relatively few in number. While other methodologies exist (e.g., rCBF, PET), there are even fewer studies employing these procedures than in the CT/MRI or EEG/ERP literature. Thus, considering the relatively few studies available, any conclusions must be viewed as preliminary. Nonetheless, however, these studies do attempt to address the notion that learning disabilities are related to central nervous system dysfunction (Wyngaarden, 1987).

At the beginning of this chapter it was pointed out that, based on Geschwind's (1984) ideas, deviations in normal patterns of brain asymmetry should characterize dyslexia. Are deviations in normal patterns of brain asymmetry characteristic of developmental dyslexia? Posing the question in this fashion requires that the answer be no, the brains of developmental dyslexics are not characterized by deviations in normal brain asymmetry. Although there should be no doubt that the neuroimaging studies (Haslam et al., 1981; Hier et al., 1978; Parkins et al., 1987; Rosenberger & Hier, 1980; Rumsey et al., 1986) specifically suggest that symmetry in the region of the planum temporale and parietooccipital cortex is found with significantly greater frequency in the learning-disabled than in the normal population (Geschwind & Levitsky, 1968; Wada et al., 1975; Witelson & Pallie, 1973), there is not sufficient agreement among the neuroimaging studies findings to be more affirmative with regard to this question. It is relevant to recall that neither Denckla et al. (1985) nor Parkins et al. (1987) provided support for this general conclusion, thus underscoring the need for caution in interpreting this literature.

Although the findings of these studies suggest some consistencies with some aspects of evolving theory linking brain symmetry to behavioral manifestations of developmental dyslexia, it should be emphasized that in none of these studies have patients with other differentially diagnosed behavioral disorders (e.g., attention-deficit disorder/hyperactivity, infantile autism, mild mental retardation) been included as clinic controls. Examining brain morphology in such children would allow for the implication of different neurobehavioral systems, lending substantially more credibility to the findings of these studies. It would also be worthwhile in future studies to examine children who have large verbal—performance discrepancies but do not have dyslexia. Furthermore, neuropsychological examinations of children with documented posterior symmetry or reversed asymmetry would be helpful in determining whether relations exist between degree of deviation from normal patterns of asymmetry and the dyslexic syndrome.

Thus, to a certain degree, it is not yet known if this specific pattern of symmetry (Haslam *et al.*, 1981; Rumsey *et al.*, 1986) is indeed unique to children or adults with severe reading disability and is not similarly associated with other clinical developmental syndromes such as mild mental retardation, hyperactivity, or infantile autism. A recent MRI study by Hynd, Semrud-Clikeman, Lorys, Novey, and Eliopolos (1990) employing dyslexic, ADD/H, and normal control children does provide further evidence that symmetry-reversed asymmetry of the plana length is indeed unique to dyslexia. Ninety percent of the dyslexics showed such a pattern while only 30% of the ADD/H and normals showed such a pattern. Additionally, when subjects were grouped according to the pattern of anterior asymmetry (L ≥ R; L < R), those with reversed or symmetrical frontal regions had deficits in word attack but not passage comprehension (see Fig. 2). Thus, patterns of brain morphology may be related to neurolinguistic (reading) performance. It must be concluded that available evidence is highly suggestive and justifies further, more carefully controlled and reported studies.

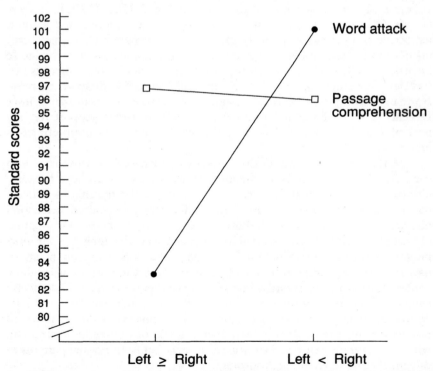

FIGURE 2 Word attack and passage-comprehension performance of children classified according to patterns of anterior width asymmetry.

What do the topographic brain electrical studies contribute to our knowledge about the presumed neurological basis of learning disabilities? While research in electrophysiology has been intense over the past 50 years, only recently have neurometric procedures been integrated in assessing the topographic distribution of brain electrical activity in children with learning disabilities. The work of Duffy *et al.* (Duffy, Denckla, Bartels, & Sandini, 1980; Duffy, Denckla, Bartels, Sandini, & Kessling, 1980; Duffy *et al.*, 1988) provides initial support for the ideas that not only are reading disabilities related to a disturbance in the central language zones, but perhaps differentially so among subgroups of disabled readers. Duffy *et al.* (1988) have examined neurolinguistic correlates to deviations in ERP components and found conceptually consistent results.

However, similar to the CT/MRI imaging studies, there are significant problems. There is, at present, no independent validation of Duffy *et al.*'s (1988) findings in carefully diagnosed subgroups of dyslexics. Second, Clinic contrast groups have not been employed in these neurometric studies of BEAM to confirm that the differences reported are indeed unique to the dyslexic syndrome and are not merely reflective of children referred to clinics for general learning or behavioral problems. Finally, can the results reported using BEAM be demonstrated to be differentially sensitive using conceptually relevant stimuli? For example, are only dyslexics identified as different electrophysiologically in the region of the left central language zones on auditory-linguistic ERP tasks while they perform similarly to control groups on tasks not reflective of their disability? Such differentiation on neuropsychologically meaningful tasks would add considerable confidence to the results of topographic mapping studies.

These research paradigms can and should be employed to investigate brain–behavior relations in other populations of learning-disabled children. To some extent, the imaging procedures employed in the studies noted in this chapter have revealed findings generally consistent with Geschwind's (1984) ideas about the neurobiological basis of developmental dyslexia.

There now exist sufficient theoretical formulations about the possible neurological foundations of other learning disabilities that similar neuro-imaging studies could be productively undertaken (Semrud-Clikeman & Hynd, 1990). Furthermore, brain-imaging procedures that allow for the superimposition of neurometabolic (PET) images on structural (MRI) images may be more revealing about how deviations in structure relate to disruptions in functional systems in these children (Duara *et al.*, 1988). Finally, more advanced morphometric procedures may be used on three-dimensional MRI scans, thus allowing for more accurate localization of structures possibly implicated in learning disabilities.

Brain-imaging procedures hold much promise in more clearly articulating brain–behavior relations in learning-disabled children. As differences emerge through brain-imaging procedures, they will only be relevant if they advance theory and assist us in more fully understanding possible etiological factors in children with learning disabilities.

Acknowledgment

Portions of this chapter are reprinted with permission from G. W. Hynd and M. Semrud-Clikeman (1989). Dyslexia and brain morphology. *Psychological Bulletin, 106,* 447–482.

References

Aaltonen, O., Niemi, P., Nyrke, T., & Tuhkanen, M. (1987). Event-related brain potentials and the perception of a phonetic continuum. *Biological Psychology, 24,* 197–207.

Ahn, H., Princhep, L., John, E. R., Baird, H., Trepetin, M., & Kaye, H. (1980). Developmental equations reflect brain dysfunctions. *Science, 210,* 1259–1262.

Bastian, H. C. (1898). *Aphasia and other speech defects.* London: H. K. Lewis.

Behan, P., & Geschwind, N. (1985). Dyslexia, congenital anomalies, and immune disorders: The role of the fetal environment. *Annals of the New York Academy of Sciences, 457,* 13–18.

Camp, B., & Dolcourt, J. (1977). Reading and spelling in good and poor readers. *Journal of Learning Disabilities, 10,* 300–307.

Campbell, S., & Whitaker, H. (1986). Cortical maturation and developmental neuro-linguistics. In J. E. Obrzut & G. W. Hynd (Eds.), *Child neuropsychology: Theory and research* (Vol. 1, pp. 55–72). Orlando, FL: Academic Press.

Chui, H. C., & Damasio, A. R. (1980). Human cerebral asymmetries evaluated by computerized tomography. *Journal of Neurology, Neurosurgery and Psychiatry, 43,* 873–878.

Cohen, J. (1959). The factorial structure of the WISC at ages 7-6, 10-6, and 13-6. *Journal of Consulting Psychology, 23,* 285–299.

Denckla, M. B. (1979). Childhood learning disabilities. In K. Heilman & E. Valenstein (Eds.), *Clinical neuropsychology* (pp. 535–573). New York: Oxford University Press.

Denckla, M. B., LeMay, M., & Chapman, C. A. (1985). Few CT scan abnormalities found even in neurologically impaired learning disabled children. *Journal of Learning Disabilities, 18,* 132–135.

Duara, R., Apicella, A., Smith, D. W., Chang, J. Y., Barker, W., & Yoshii, F. (1988). Anatomical definition in PET using superimposed MR images. *Journal of Mind and Behavior, 9,* 299–310.

Duffy, F. H., Burchfiel, J. L., & Lombroso, C. T. (1979). Brain electrical activity mapping (BEAM): A new method for extending the clinical utility of EEG and evoked potential data. *Annals of Neurology, 5,* 309–321.

Duffy, F. H., Denckla, M. B., Bartels, P. H., & Sandini, G. (1980). Dyslexia: Regional differences in brain electrical activity by topographic mapping. *Annals of Neurology, 7,* 412–420.

Duffy, F. H., Denckla, M. B., Bartels, P. H., Sandini, G., & Kessling, L. S. (1980). Dyslexia: Automated diagnosis by computerized classification of brain electrical activity. *Annals of Neurology, 7,* 421–428.

Duffy, F. H., Denckla, M. B., McAnulty, G. B., & Holmes, J. A. (1988). Neurophysiological studies in dyslexia. In F. Plum (Ed.), *Language, communication and the brain* (pp. 149–170). New York: Raven Press.

Duffy, F. H., & McAnulty, G. B. (1985). Brain electrical activity mapping (BEAM): The search for a physiological signature of dyslexia. In F. H. Duffy & N. Geschwind (Eds.), *Dyslexia: A neuroscientific approach to clinical evaluation* (pp. 105–122). Boston/Toronto: Little, Brown.

Duffy, F. H., McAnulty, G. B., & Schachter, S. C. (1984). Brain electrical activity mapping. In N. Geschwind & A. M. Galaburda (Eds.), *Cerebral dominance: The biological foundations* (pp. 53–74). London: Harvard University Press.

Evans, W. A. (1942). An encephalogrpahic ratio for estimating ventricular enlargement and cerebral atrophy. *Archives of Neurology (Chicago), 47,* 931–937.

Fender, D. H. (1987). Source localization of brain electrical activity. In A. S. Gevins & A. Remond (Eds.), *Methods of analysis of brain electrical and magnetic signals: EEG handbook* (rev. ser., Vol. 1). Amsterdam: Elsevier/North-Holland.

Flechsig, P. (1908). *Zentralblatt neurologie-psychiatrie, 27,* 50.

Fukuyama, Y., Miyao, M., Ishizu, T., & Maruyama, H. (1979). Developmental changes in normal cranial measurements by computed tomography. *Developmental Medicine and Child Neurology, 21,* 425–432.

Galaburda, A. M., Sherman, G. F., Rosen, G. D., Aboitiz, F., & Geschwind, N. (1985). Developmental dyslexia: Four consecutive patients with cortical anomalies. *Annals of Neurology, 18,* 222–233.

Galin, D. (1989). EEG studies in dyslexia. In D. J. Bakker & H. Van der Vlugt (Eds.), *Learning disabilities: Vol. 1. Neuropsychological correlates and treatment* (pp. 149–171). Amsterdam: Swets & Zeitlinger.

Gasser, T., Mocks, J., Lenard, H. G., Bacher, P., & Verleger, R. (1983). The EEG of mildly retarded children: Developmental classificatory and topographic aspects. *Electroencephalography and Clinical Neurophysiology, 55,* 131–144.

Geschwind, N. (1974). The development of the brain and the evolution of language. In N. Geschwind (Ed.), *Selected papers on language and the brain.* Dordrecht, The Netherlands: Reidel.

Geschwind, N. (1984). Cerebral dominance in biological perspective. *Neuropsychologia, 22,* 675–683.

Geschwind, N., & Behan, P. O. (1982). Left handedness: Association with immune disease, migraine, and developmental learning disorders. *Proceedings of the National Academy of Sciences of the U.S.A. 79,* 5097–5100.

Geschwind, N., & Galaburda, A. M. (1985a). Cerebral lateralization: Biological mechanisms, associations, and pathology: I. A hypothesis and a program for research. *Archives of Neurology (Chicago), 42* 428–459.

Geschwind, N., & Galaburda, A. M. (1985b). Cerebral lateralization: Biological mechanisms, associations, and pathology: II. A hypothesis and a program for research. *Archives of Neurology (Chicago)*, *42*, 521–552.

Geschwind, N., & Galaburda, A. M. (1985c) Cerebral lateralization: Biological mechanisms, associations, and pathology: III. A hypothesis and a program for research. *Archives of Neurology (Chicago)*, *42*, 634–654.

Geschwind, N., & Levitsky, W. (1968). Human brain: Left-right asymmetries in temporal speech region. *Science, 161,* 186–187.

Golden, G. S. (1982). Neurobiological correlates of learning disabilities. *Annals of Neurology, 12,* 409–418.

Harmony, T. (1984). *Functional neuroscience: Vol. III. Neurometric assessment of brain dysfunction in neurological patients.* Hillsdale, NJ: Erlbaum.

Harmony, T. (1989). Psychophysiological evaluation of children's neuropsychological disorders. In C. R. Reynolds & E. Fletcher-Janzen (Eds.), *Handbook of clinical neuropsychology* (pp. 265–290). New York: Plenum.

Haslam, R. H., Dalby, J. T., Johns, R. D., & Rademaker, A. W. (1981). Cerebral asymmetry in developmental dyslexia. *Archives of Neurology (Chicago) 38,* 679–682.

Hier, D. B., LeMay, M., Rosenberger, P. B., & Perlo, V. P. (1978). Developmental dyslexia: Evidence for a subgroup with a reversal of cerebral asymmetry. *Archives of Neurology (Chicago) 35,* 90–92.

Hinshelwood, J. (1900). Congenital word-blindness. *Lancet, 1,* 1506–1508.

Hinshelwood, J. (1902). Congenital word-blindness with reports of two cases. *Ophthalmic Review, 21,* 91–99.

Hounsfield, G. N. (1973). Computerized transverse axial scanning: I. Description of system. *British Journal of Radiology, 46,* 1016–1022.

Hynd, G. W., & Cohen, M. (1983). *Dyslexia: Neuropsychological theory, research, and clinical differentiation.* New York: Grune & Stratton.

Hynd, G. W., & Semrud-Clikeman, M. (1989a). Dyslexia and neurodevelopmental pathology: Relationships to cognition, intelligence and reading skill acquisition. *Journal of Learning Disabilities, 22,* 204–216.

Hynd, G. W., & Semrud-Clikeman, M. (1989b). Dyslexia and brain morphology. *Psychological Bulletin, 106,* 447–482.

Hynd, G. W., Semrud-Clikeman, M., Lorys, A. R., Novey, E. S., & Eliopulos, D. (1990). Brain morphology in developmental dyslexia, attention deficit disorder/hyperactivity. *Archives of Neurology, 47,* 919–926.

John, E. R. (1977). *Functional neuroscience: Vol. 2. Neurometrics: Clinical applications of quantitative electrophysiology.* Hillsdale, NJ: Erlbaum.

John, E. R. (1989). The role of quantitative EEG topographic mapping of "neurometrics" in the diagnosis of psychiatric and neurological disorders: The pros. *Electroencephalography and Clinical Neurophysiology, 73,* 2–4.

John, E. R., Prichep, L., Ahn, H., Easton, P., Fridman, J., & Kaye, H. (1983). Neurometric evaluation of cognitive dysfunctions and neurological disorders in children. *Progress in Neurobiology, 21,* 239–290.

John, E. R., Prichep, L. S., & Easton, P. (1987). Methods of analysis of brain electrical and magnetic signals. In A. S. Gevins & A. Remonds (Eds.), *Handbook of electroencephalography and clinical neurophysiology* (Vol. 1, pp. 449–496). Amsterdam: Elsevier.

John, E. R., Prichep, L. S., Fridman, J., & Easton, P. (1988). Neurometrics: Computer-assisted differential diagnosis of brain dysfunctions. *Science, 239,* 162–169.

Kaufman, A. S. (1979). *Intelligent testing with the WISC-R.* New York: Wiley (Interscience).

Kopp, N., Michel, F., Carrier, H., Biron, A., & Duvillard, P. (1977). Etude de certaines asymetries hemispheriques du cerveau humain. *Journal of the Neurological Sciences, 34,* 349–363.

Lehman, D. (1971). Multichannel topography of human alpha EEG fields. *Electroencephalography and Clinical Neurophysiology, 31,* 439–449.

Leisman, G., & Ashkenazi, M. (1980). Aetiological factors in dyslexia: IV. Cerebral hemispheres are functionally equivalent. *Neuroscience, 11,* 157–164.

LeMay, M. (1976). Morphological cerebral asymmetries of modern man, fossil man, and nonhuman primates. *Annals of the New York Academy of Sciences, 280,* 349–366.

LeMay, M. (1977). Asymmetries of the skull and handedness: Phrenology revisited. *Journal of Neurological Sciences, 32,* 243–253.

LeMay, M. (1981). Are there radiological changes in the brains of individuals with dyslexia? *Bulletin of the Orton Society, 31,* 135–141.

Livanov, M. N. (1969). The application of electronic-computer techniques to the analysis of bioelectric processes in the brain. In M. Cole & I. Maltzman (Eds.), *A handbook of contemporary Soviet psychology* (pp. 717–734).

Lyytinen, H., & Lorys-Vernon, A. (1988). Neurodevelopmental changes in ERP components associated with automatic attention (MMN). *Journal of Clinical and Experimental Neuropsychology, 11*(1), 28.

Matousek, M., & Petersen, I. (1973). Automatic evaluation of EEG background activity by means of age-dependent EEG quotients. *Electroencephalography and Clinical Neurophysiology, 35,* 603–612.

Moeschler, J. B., Bennett, F. C., & Cromwell, L. P. (1981). Use of the CT scan in the medical evaluation of the mentally retarded child. *Journal of Pediatrics, 98,* 63–65.

Morgan, W. P. (1896). A case of congenital word-blindness. *British Medical Journal, 2,* 1378.

Näätänen, R. (1990). The role attention in auditory information processing as revealed by event-related potentials and other brain measures of cognitive function. *Behavior and Brain Sciences, 13.*

Naeser, M. A. & Hayward, R. W. (1978). Lesion localization in aphasia with cranial computed tomography and The Boston Diagnostic Aphasia Examination. *Neurology, 28,* 545–551.

Oken, B. S., & Chiappa, K. H. (1986). Statistical issues concerning computerized analysis of brainwave topography. *Annals of Neurology, 19,* 493–494.

Parkins, R., Roberts, R. J., Reinarz, S. J., & Varney, N. R. (1987, January). *CT asymmetries in adult developmental dyslexics.* Paper presented at the annual convention of the International Neuropsychological Society, Washington, DC.

Pedersen, H., Glydensted, M., & Glydensted, C. (1979). Measurement of the normal ventricular system and supratentorial subarachnoid space in children with computed tomography. *Neuroradiology, 17,* 231–237.

Pelicci, L. J., Bedrick, A. D., Cruse, R. P., & Vannucci, R. C. (1979). Frontal ventricular dimensions of the brain in infants and children. *Archives of Neurology (Chicago), 36,* 852–853.

Petsche, H., & Shaw, J. (1972). EEG topography in evaluation of bioelectrical data from brain, nerve and muscle. In M. A. B. Brazier & D. O. Walter (Eds.), Handbook of electroencephalography and clinical neurophysiology (Vol. 5, Part B). Amsterdam: Elsevier.

Remond, A. (1955). Orientations et tendences des méthodes topographiques dans l'étude de l'activité électrique du cerveau. *Revue Neurologique, 93,* 399–410.

Rosenberger, P. B., & Hier, D. B. (1980). Cerebral asymmetry and verbal intellectual deficits. *Annals of Neurology, 8,* 300–304.

Rumsey, J. M., Coppola, R., Denckla, M. B., Hamburger, S. D., & Kruesi, M. J. P. (1989). EEG spectra in severely dyslexic men: Rest and word and design recognition. *Electroencephalography and Clinical Neurophysiology, 73,* 30–40.

Rumsey, J. M., Dorwart, R., Vermess, M., Denckla, M. B., Kruesi, M. J. P., & Rapoport, J. L. (1986). Magnetic resonance imaging of brain anatomy in severe developmental dyslexia. *Archives of Neurology (Chicago), 43,* 1045–1046.

Satterfield, J. H., Schell, A. M., Nicholas, T., & Backs, R. W. (1988). Topographic study of auditory event-related potentials in normal boys and boys with attention deficit disorder with hyperactivity. *Psychophysiology, 25,* 591–606.

Sattler, J. (1974). *Assessment of children's intelligence.* Philadelphia, PA: Saunders.

Satz, P., & Soper, H. V. (1986). Left-handedness, dyslexia, and autoimmune disorder: A critique. *Journal of Clinical and Experimental Neuropsychology, 8,* 453–458.

Semrud-Clikeman, M., & Hynd, G. W. (1990). Right hemispheric dysfunction in nonverbal learning disabilities: Social, academic, and adaptive functioning in adults and children. *Psychological Bulletin, 107,* 443–478.

Spitzer, R. L., Foreman, J. B. W., & Nee, J. (1979). DSM-III field trials: I. Initial interrater diagnostic reliability. *American Journal of Psychiatry, 136,* 815–820.

Stanovich, K. E. (1985). Cognitive processes and the reading problems of learning-disabled children: Evaluating the assumption of specificity. In J. K. Torgeson & B. Y. L. Wong (Eds.), *Psychological and educational perspectives on learning disabilities* (pp. 87–131). New York: Academic Press.

Stanovich, K. E., Cunningham, A. E., & Feeman, D. J. (1984). Intelligence, cognitive skills, and early reading progress. *Reading Research Quarterly, 19,* 278–303.

Synek, V., Reuben, J. R., & DuBoulay, G. H. (1976). Comparing Evan's index and computerized axial tomography in assessing relationships of ventricular size to brain size. *Neurology, 26,* 231–233.

Taylor, H. G. (1987). The meaning and value of soft signs in the behavioral sciences. In D. E. Tupper (Ed.), *Soft neurological signs* (pp. 297–335). New York: Grune & Stratton.

Taylor, H. G. & Fletcher, J. M. (1983). Biological foundations of "specific developmental disorders": methods, findings, and future directions. *Journal of Clinical Child Psychology, 12,* 46–65.

Von Economo, C., & Horn, L. (1930). *Zeitschrift für die gesamte neurologie and psychiatrie, 130,* 678.

Wada, J. A., Clarke, R., & Hamm, A. (1975). Cerebral hemispheric asymmetry in humans. *Archives of Neurology (Chicago), 32,* 239–246.

Weinberger, D. R., Luchins, D. J., Morihisa, J., & Wyatt, R. J. (1982). Asymmetrical volumes of the right and left frontal and occipital regions of the human brain. *Neurology, 11,* 97–100.

Witelson, S. F., & Pallie, W. (1973). Left hemisphere specialization for language in the newborn. *Brain, 96,* 641–646.

Wyngaarden, J. E. (Ed.). (1987). *Learning disabilities: A report to the U.S. Congress.* Washington, DC: National Institutes of Health, Interagency Committee on Learning Disabilities.

Yingling, C. D., Fein, G., Galin, D., Peltzman, D., & Davenport, L. (1986). Neurometrics does not detect neurologically normal dyslexics. *Electroencephalography and Clinical Neurophysiology, 63,* 426–430.

PART THREE

Neuropsychological Syndromes and Practice in Learning Disabilities

The most recent federal definition of learning disabilities represents an evolution in the definition first published in the *Federal Register* in 1976 as modified by the National Joint Committee on Learning Disabilities (NJCLD) (Wyngaarden, 1987). There are very few changes in the new definition. However, the changes that were incorporated are indeed significant. The most important changes include the notion that learning disabilities are due to central nervous system dysfunction, that deficits in social skills can constitute a learning disability, and the observation that learning disabilities may frequently co-occur with attention-deficit disorders (ADD) although ADD does not by itself constitute a learning disability.

The first section of this volume focused on the etiological formulations related to the presummed neurobiological basis of learning disability. Part Two presented views on clinical assessment and diagnosis, a clear prerequisite to identifying the phenotypes associated with learning disability. This section, Part Three, presents views on the clinical syndromes most commonly found in populations of the learning disabled. In addition to chapters regarding reading disorders, specific mathematics disorders, and speech and language disorders, a chapter on social-skills deficits and their associated disorders is included. Finally, the concluding chapters in this volume address practices associated with intervention among learning-disabled persons.

It has been approximately 130 years since Broca presented his views on the localization of the expressive speech center. In examining the ideas of Bouillaud, Broca found that lesions to the anterior cortex did indeed often lead to expressive speech deficits. He found it quite remarkable that in all of his cases the lesions were localized to the left frontal region (Hynd, 1988). Jackson, Wernicke, and others all contributed in the late 1800s in further articulating the organization of the central speech zones.

Concurrent to the observations made by clinicians regarding the lesions associated with speech comprehension and expression, other investigators were developing a body of case studies related to reading disabilities. As Aaron and Simurdak discuss in Chapter Nineteen, the emergence of the notion of developmental reading disability in which the deficits closely resembled those of brain-damaged subjects quickly found support in the literature. Both clinical and experimental evidence strongly argues that there is a neurological basis for reading disorders. In illustrating how these developmental deficits reflect neurological theory regarding brain organization, Aaron and Simurdak argue that at least three types of developmental reading disorders exist: (1) those with poor decoding but adequate comprehension, (2) those with poor comprehension but adequate decoding abilities, and (3) those with poor decoding and poor comprehension. A carefully thought-out diagnostic process illustrates the neurolinguistic relationships in these types of disabled readers. Through such a theoretically sound clinical differentiation scheme, one would expect that eventually reliably successful intervention procedures could be developed.

Although cases of specific mathematics disabilities due to brain damage are reported in the literature, relatively little is known about mathematics disorders compared to reading disorders. However, Keller and Sutton, in Chapter Twenty, integrate early attempts at understanding the theoretical basis of mathematics deficits with more recent evidence provided through cognitive psychology. This is especially important since there has been a renewal in the recognition that core curriculum in our schools needs to have a strengthened emphasis on mathematics education. As these authors point out, an integration of neuropsychological and cognitive approaches may not only lead to a better understanding of how mathematics abilities are conceptually organized and developmentally manifested in school-age children, but may lead to more productive strategies for instruction and intervention in the mathematically disabled child.

The federal definition of learning disabilities also notes that deficits in the production and comprehension of spoken language may constitute a learning disability. This is important since evidence increasingly indicates that nearly half of the children with language disorders also manifest learning problems in reading and mathematics. Other studies suggest that the connection between language disorders and other developmental learning disabilities may be even higher. In Chapter Twenty-one, Montgomery, Windsor, and Stark discuss the various cognitive and perceptual mechanisms that may underlie language impairment and attempt to relate these deficits to the frequent co-occurrence of reading disorders found in learning-disabled children. This discussion supports those ideas presented by Aaron and Simurdak in their earlier chapter and builds on the conceptual neurobiological model advanced in this volume. In this context, the literature related to symbolic representation, auditory perceptual processing, auditory memory, problem-solving abilities, cognitive style, and metalinguistic skills in language-impaired children is discussed and related to definitional issues.

While many specific learning disabilities may be related in some fashion to deficient language development and processing, the definition of learning disabilities now proposes that deficits in social skills may constitute a specific learning disability (Wyngaarden, 1987). Frequently, these children are thought to have a nonverbal learning disability and some evidence even suggests that social-skills deficits may be related in some fashion to learning problems in mathematics. Based on a social- developmental perspective, Semrud-Clikeman and Hynd critically review this literature in Chapter Twenty-two. Consistent with the literature regarding reading disabilities, there appear to be subtypes, or subpopulations, of children with nonverbal, social-skills learning disabilities. Semrud-Clikeman and Hynd review the literature on the nonverbal perceptual-organization-output (NPOOD) subtype, Denckla's left-hemisyndrome subtype, and the right-hemisphere learning-disability subtype proposed by Voeller. While there exists some evidence for each of these subtypes in terms of social-skills deficiencies, their incidence, degree of overlap with each other, and comorbidity with other neuropsychiatric syndromes such as ADD or depression is unclear. Since ADD does not by itself constitute a learning disability, a separate chapter on this topic was not included. Semrud-Clikeman and Hynd do address some of the important literature on ADD as it relates to nonverbal, social-skills learning disabilities, and Nieves in her earlier chapter expands on the possible connections between ADD and learning disabilities.

Clinical neuropsychology traditionally has focused greater attention on assessment and diagnosis and has shown less concern for treatment and educational intervention. However, this situation is changing primarily due to the work in cognitive rehabilitation. In this area, clinicians are implementing conceptually based cognitive rehabilitation techniques with adult head-injured patients and are providing remedial strategies based on a cognitive neuropsychological approach with patients who experience acquired language disorders.

Due to the effectiveness of theory-based intervention techniques with adult neurological patients, researchers have begun to investigate such strategies with reading- and/or learning-disabled children and adults. The fact is many of the remedial reading techniques have not been empirically validated for clinical intervention. For example, many remedial educators employ a traditional multisensory technique with children who experience developmental reading disorders specific to acquiring a sight vocabulary. However, well-controlled studies suggest that traditional multisensory techniques, particularly the kinesthetic component, may not be the appropriate strategy for treatment of either developmental or acquired dyslexia. Rather, language-based strategies, those facilitating word finding or phonemic analysis, may be more effective in improving word recognition and eventually fluent reading.

On a global level, much of the neuropsychological literature has dealt with subtyping of learning disabilities, but little of that data is concerned with treatment effects related to empirically derived subtypes. In a diagnostic framework the subtype studies have been conducted to account for the heterogeneity within the learning-disabled population. However, various types of intervention studies are desperately needed to ameliorate specific types of disabilities. The neuropsychological approach to specific reading disabilities assumes that the basis for the condition results from deficiencies in intrinsic psychological processes and cognitive skills related to the reading process. The concomitant issue at hand is whether or not these processes are amenable to remediation. Thus, in the third section of this volume interventions derived from field and experimental research are also reported and discussed.

Theoretically appropriate remediation studies could be accomplished on at least two levels of language functioning. First, following from the subtype literature, intervention studies could be conducted on individuals according to dysfunctions in word decoding, that is, specific coding operations or connections between specific codes such as letter–phoneme code connection, whole-word phonetic code connection, whole word–semantic code connection (Berninger, Chen, & Abbott, 1988), and word recognition. Second, when the task of reading advances beyond the level of word recognition, remediation studies need to be conducted on reading comprehension deficiencies. However, some evidence exists that disabled readers exhibit no "unique" deficit in comprehension and thus comprehension-strategy instruction for disabled and normal readers could be quite similar (PaLincsar & Brown, 1984). Perhaps this is the reason that has led Wise and Olson, in Chapter Twenty-three, to argue that theoretically appropriate remedial instruction must focus on disabled readers' primary deficits in phonological coding (which in highly heritable) and word recognition, while also supporting their need to make progress in the areas of vocabulary and comprehension, where there are no specific deficiencies. Specifically, their studies on remediation with talking computers have shown that disabled readers made consistent and substantial gains over control subjects in terms of word recognition, phonological coding based on segmented feedback, and attitude about reading.

In contrast, Bos and Van Reusen, in Chapter Twenty-four, present the data in support of the whole-language approach to reading intervention. The whole-language and metacognitive approach views reading as a language-based activity which also emphasizes the reading–writing connection and comprehension strategies in treatment research. Metacognitive instructional strategies are similar to the former notion of study skills but in addition more directly explain why, when, and how to use such strategies. Through the use of instructional methodologies based on cognitive/metacognitive processing strategies and cognitive behavior modification and intrinsic control mechanisms, these authors review effective intervention strategies used with learning-disabled students in the academic areas of reading comprehension, written composition, and verbal math problem solving.

Although these theoretical approaches exist, one reason for the general lack of treatment validity studies can be attributed to methodological problems inherent in remedial research. For example, field research lacks the precise control on intervening variables possible in laboratory studies. However, another reason for the lag in treatment studies is that learning-disabled children present with a unique protocol of strengths and weaknesses from which an individualized treatment plan is developed. In essence, there are few, if any, treatment plans that work effectively with all learning-disabled children. Thus, in the absence of group evaluative data, assessment of neurodevelopmental patterns can yield valuable information regarding normal and abnormal central nervous system functioning useful in the treatment of learning disabilities. The case-study approach presented by Lewandowski in Chapter Twenty-five illustrates how various models of neuropsychological assessment can be used to identify neuropsychological dysfunction in order for effective intervention to take place.

Even though recent advances in neuroscience and medicine have enabled us to better identify the etiological factors and neurological markers of learning disabilities, special educators have been reticent to accept the role of neuropsychology in the schools. As Kershner argues in Chapter Twenty-six, special education would be vastly improved if the neuropsychology of exceptionalities were established firmly as a core area within special education, as perceived by special educators. But in reality the neuropsychological approach will not become a widely accepted approach for understanding the childhood exceptionalities, including learning disabilities, until neuropsychological assessment consistently leads to effective and validated educational interventions.

Problematic of this endeavor, however, is the fact that not all learning-disabled children have a demonstrable neural basis to their disability. Thus, while the traditional neuropsychological model is useful in gaining an understanding of some learning-disability subtypes, it is ill suited as a theoretical framework for understanding others. In Chapter Twenty-seven, Hiscock and Hiscock describe some alternatives to the traditional medical model in understanding the etiology of learning disabilities and argue quite strongly that neuropsychological assessment and subsequent interpretations derived from these assessments typically have little or no impact on the learning-disabled child. These authors suggest rather than reject the neuropsychological model; clinical neuropsychologists should examine those functions that actually account for the learning disability. Specifically, the authors recommend a shift in emphasis be made from examining nervous system functioning, which pertains to the spinal cord and brain stem, to examination of higher cortical functions that are directly relevant to understanding the neural basis of reading, spelling, and math disabilities.

References

Berninger, V., Chen, A., & Abbott, R. (1988). A test of the multiple connections model of reading acquisition. *International Journal of Neuroscience, 42,* 283–295.

Hynd, G. W. (1988). *Neuropsychological assessment in clinical child psychology.* Newbury Park, CA: SAGE Publications.

Palincsar, A. S., & Brown, A. L. (1984). Reciprocal teaching of comprehension-fostering and comprehension-monitoring activities. *Cognition and Instruction, 1,* 117–175.

Wyngaarden, J. B. (Ed.). (1987). *Learning disabilities: A report to the U.S. Congress.* Washington, DC: Interagency Committee on Learning Disabilities.

CHAPTER NINETEEN

Reading Disorders: Their Nature and Diagnosis

P. G. Aaron
John Simurdak

I. Introduction

The association between neuropsychology and the study of reading disability goes back more than 100 years and had been an intimate one. The beginnings of such an association can be traced to the clinical descriptions of reading failure[1] in literate adults provided by neurologists such as Dejerine and Bastian which were published during the last decade of the nineteenth century (Bastian, 1898; Dejerine, 1891, 1892). The emergence of the notion of developmental reading disability[1] did not have to wait very long, for Pringle Morgan, a British physician, published the first case of developmental reading disability in 1896 and noted the similarity between "word blindness" in adults and "congenital word blindness" in schoolchildren.

---

1 The term "reading disability" is used in this chapter as a generic term to refer to all kinds of reading disorders, whether acquired or developmental. The term "reading failure" refers to the loss of reading skill in a literate adult. Other terms that are used to describe this condition are "word blindness," "acquired dyslexia," and "alexia." The term "developmental reading disability" refers to all kinds of reading disorders seen in children, whether these children have average, superior, or below-average IQ. "Specific reading disability" is one variety of developmental reading disability. An equivalent term is "dyslexia." Terms such as "congenital word blindness" and "strephosymbolia" were used in earlier literature to refer to specific reading disability.

Neuropsychological Foundations of Learning Disabilities, copyright © 1991 by Academic Press Inc. All rights of reproduction in any form reserved.

During the following years, several reports and monographs on developmental reading disability appeared and it has been suggested that Morgan's 1896 paper, *A Case of Congenital Word Blindness,* is the starting point for this interest in the study of reading disability in children (Pelosi, 1977). This might very well be true for many of the early publications that dealt with reading disabilities in children used terms such as "developmental alexia" and "congenital word blindness" to describe this condition (Dearborn, 1925; Fildes, 1921; Schmitt, 1918; Wallin, 1920). The free use of these terms indicates that many educators of this period were familiar with the neuropsychological perspective of reading disorders and were open to neuropsychological explanations of developmental reading disabilities. This state of congeniality, however, did not last very long and, as research in the psychology of reading progressed, two opposing views began to emerge regarding the etiology of reading disability. Physicians postulated a constitutional condition to explain developmental reading disability, whereas educators supported a pluralistic theory of causation which included psychological, educational, sociological, and linguistic factors. Even though the fields of education and neuropsychology continued to drift away from each other during the subsequent years, the recent development within the field of neuropsychology which assumes a linguistic posture and classifies reading failures as "deep dyslexia," "surface dyslexia," etc., on the basis of the patients' performance on reading tests, has created new opportunities for a rapprochement between pedagogy and neuropsychology.

One consistent finding that has emerged from the neuropsychological studies conducted during the past 100 years is that reading disability is not a single disorder but that there are several kinds of reading disabilities. One reason for the existence of different kinds of reading disability is that the reading process is mediated by several components and a breakdown of different components can result in different forms of reading difficulties. Even though acquired reading disabilities may not be directly comparable to developmental reading disabilities, it is reasonable to assume that the former are caused by the breakdown of specific components whereas the latter are caused by the failure of the same components to develop properly. For this reason, the model of reading process developed from neuropsychological findings can be useful in understanding the different kinds of developmental reading disabilities.

This chapter attempts to exploit the contributions made by neuropsychology and linguistics to the psychology of reading and presents a view of developmental reading disabilities and their diagnosis based on information available from neuropsychological, developmental, and experimental studies.

II. Components of Reading

In this section, it is proposed that the reading process is made up of two major components: decoding and comprehension. Evidence from neuropsychological, developmental, and experimental studies is presented to support this view.

A component is defined as an elementary information process that operates upon internal representations of objects and symbols (Sternberg, 1985). A process that is elementary enough to be labeled as a component depends upon the independence of the process from other processes as well as the desired level of theorizing chosen by the researcher. Leong (1988), for example, after studying children from fourth, fifth, and sixth grades, found that a three-component model of reading made up of an orthographic/phonological component, a morphological component (i.e., word knowledge), and sentence and paragraph comprehension provided a good fit for the data obtained. In contrast, Frederiksen (1982) breaks down Leong's first component into four components: encoding multigraphemic units, translating graphemic units into phonemic units, assigning appropriate speech patterns to word units, and retrieving the appropriate phonology from the lexicon. The choice of two components presented in this chapter is motivated by empirical as well as practical considerations. The empirical consideration is that the two-component view is in agreement with neuropsychological and experimental findings; the practical consideration is that the proposed model should lead to relatively easy diagnostic procedures that could be carried out readily and quickly without the need for sophisticated instruments and a plethora of tests.

A. Evidence from Neuropsychological Studies

During the closing decades of the last century, the issue of localization dominated the field of neurology and, consequently, investigators such as Dejerine, Redlich, and Brissaud (Geschwind, 1974) interpreted their clinical findings in neuroanatomical terms. As a result, patients who lost their ability to read were classified as having alexia with agraphia or as having pure alexia, these two forms of reading disorders being associated with lesions in different cortical areas. Almost all patients who had alexia with agraphia were reported to have had some degree of aphasia and deficits of comprehension (Geschwind, 1974, p. 408) even though the degree of reading and writing disturbance was more severe than the aphasic symptoms. The comprehension deficit in these patients was thought to be the result of lesions in the angular gyrus. Patients with pure alexia, on the other hand, were reported as having good comprehension for the spoken language; the reading deficit was considered to be due to the "language center" being disconnected from the visual centers. Dejerine's 1892 paper gives a clear description of such a case. The patient, Mr. C., was a well-educated businessman who, after having experienced weakness of right leg and right hand for some time, one day suddenly discovered that he could not read even a single word. The reading failure was so severe that he could not read the names of newspapers, signs, or even his own handwriting. His comprehension of the spoken language, however, was excellent and his speech was faultless. During the remaining 4 1/2 years of his life, he continued to run his business and play cards with friends. Autopsy revealed two major lesions: an older lesion which caused destruction of parts of the left occipital cortex and part of the splenium of the corpus callosum and a recent lesion in the angular gyrus caused by the stroke which led to his death. Dejerine concluded that the older infarct which disconnected the visual center from the language center was responsible for the reading failure. It is noteworthy that autopsy did not reveal any lesion in either Broca's or Wernicke's area. Geschwind (1974), who has reviewed the literature on alexia without agraphia, reports that since Dejerine's report 16 other cases have been recorded and the presence of aphasic symptoms is rarely reported. Cases of alexia with and without agraphia, therefore, suggest that comprehension can be affected independent of word-reading ability.

It is interesting to note that the dyslexic boy described by Morgan (1896) resembles the patients who have alexia without agraphia in having had normal comprehension skills. Morgan noted that the boy's oral language was good and the teacher who taught him thought that he could be the smartest lad in the school if the instruction were entirely oral.

The linguistic classification of patients with reading disorders into those having deep dyslexia and surface dyslexia (Marshall and Newcombe, 1966, 1973) also resembles the classification of reading failure as alexia with and without agraphia, with reference to comprehension. Deep dyslexic patients tend to read words aloud on the basis of their meaning and are not very good in using spelling-to-sound rules. Surface dyslexics, on the other hand, apply spelling-to-sound rules rather mechanically and often fail to comprehend the meaning of the words they have read. These neuropsychological studies of alexic patients indicate that the ability to read aloud is a component that is independent of comprehension.

B. Evidence from Developmental and Experimental Studies

The recognition that there are children who can pronounce the written word rather well but cannot comprehend what they have read has led to the concept of the syndrome of "hyperlexia." Compared to developmental dyslexia, the study of hyperlexia has a relatively short history even though the existence of children with this syndrome had been known for a long time. The term "hyperlexia" was used first by Silberberg and Silberberg in 1967 even though it was used only to point out a glaring discrepancy between word-decoding skill and comprehension ability and did not imply a pathological condition. Subsequent studies by Healy (1982), Healy and Aram (1986), and several others have, however, led to the characterization of the syndrome of hyperlexia as a form of reading deficit and define it as "a reading disorder caused by severe deficiencies in comprehension accompanied by extraordinary facility in decoding that had developed spontaneously and at a very young age" (Aaron, 1989, p. 158). Not only do hyperlexic children show a disso-ciation between pronunciation and comprehension but they also show a profile that is opposite to that of dyslexic children. For instance, Frith and Snowling (1983) compared the performance of 8 dyslexic children with that of 8 autistic children who showed hyperlexic tendencies and 10 reading-age-matched normal readers. These children were tested for their ability to select semantically appropriate words in a Cloze test. Their comprehension was also tested by requiring them to read sentences which contained homographs with different pronunciations (e.g., "He had a pink *bow*" versus "He made a deep *bow*"). It was found that in these tests, the dyslexic children showed the best performance and the autistic children the worst. The dyslexic children, however, did poorly on tests that assessed their phonological skills.

The dissociation between comprehension and pronunciation is further supported by genetic studies. DeFries, Fulker, and LaBuda (1987), using a multiple-regression technique for testing heritable and common environmen-tal contributions, found significant heritability for PIAT (Peabody Individual Achievement Test) word recognition and spelling and WISC-R digit span but not for PIAT reading comprehension. The data suggested that about 30% of the cognitive phenotype in reading disability is attributable to this heritable factor. Olson and his associates (cited in Pennington & Smith, 1988), who studied the same population of MZ, DZ, and control subjects, found signifi-cant heritability for nonword reading accuracy but not for sight reading for meaning. Commenting on these two studies, Pennington and Smith (1988) concluded that in specific reading disability, single-word reading, spelling, and digit span, but not reading comprehension, are genetically influenced.

The studies discussed so far examined subjects who had reading disabil-ity of one form or another. Do studies which have employed normal readers also indicate that decoding and comprehension are separate components? Jackson and McClelland (1979) tested two groups of university undergradu-ates differing in verbal ability on a number of information-processing tasks. In addition, they also measured these subjects' listening comprehension, reading comprehension, and the speed with which they accessed codes for visually presented letters. Analysis of data yielded two variables that accounted for nearly all the variance seen in reading ability. The two variables were speed of accessing codes for visually presented letters and ability to comprehend spoken material. Together, these two variables accounted for nearly 75% of the variance seen in reading skill. Palmer, McCleod, Hunt, and Davidson (1985) investigated the relationship between reading speed and reading and listening comprehension in college students of differing verbal abilities and found that reading speed varied with visual word processing while reading comprehension varied with nonvisual linguistic processing. They concluded that reading speed and comprehension should be treated as distinct abilities and that reading speed is more related to elementary information-processing tasks than is reading comprehension. These studies involving normal readers of differing verbal abilities suggest that decoding and pronunciation of the written word is a modular skill that is highly automatized, whereas comprehension is mediated by cognitive processes of a controlled nature.

Taken together, neuropsychological, developmental, and experimental studies are in agreement as to the componential nature of the reading process. In these studies, word processing and comprehension emerge as the two most important components. The diagnostic procedure described below is based on this two-component model of reading.

III. Differential Diagnosis of Reading Disabilities

A. Rationale of the Diagnostic Procedure

This componential view of reading process leads to the expectation that poor reading performance could be the result of weak decoding skill, poor comprehension ability, or a combination of these two. We can, therefore, expect to encounter three types of poor readers: (1) those with poor decoding but adequate comprehension skills, (2) those with poor comprehension but adequate decoding skills, and (3) those with poor decoding and poor comprehension skills. Children who have adequate comprehension ability but are poor in decoding ability are considered to have specific reading disability (SRD, or dyslexia) because their difficulty is limited to the written language; it does not encompass the spoken form of language. If these children show signs of poor reading comprehension, it is secondary to their decoding weakness. Children who have comprehension deficits but have adequate decoding skill are considered to have nonspecific reading disability (NRD). Children who are deficient in both comprehension and decoding are considered to have generalized reading disability (GRD). This form of classification can be readily accommodated within the two-route model of reading, which postulates that words could be read through a "phonological" route where the pronunciation of the word is realized without an intermediary semantic processing, or a "semantic" route, where meaning of the word could be realized without an intermediary phonological processing (Coltheart, 1980).

It is generally recognized that the decoding problem of the dyslexic (SRD) child is due to phonological weakness (Liberman & Shankweiler, 1985; Snowling, 1980). The phonological deficit manifests in the following symptoms: slow reading speed, errors in oral reading, poor spelling, errors of syntax in written language, and excessive dependence on context for reading. Collectively these symptoms constitute the syndrome of dyslexia. It appears that processing of syntactical elements of the language such as suffixes and function words as well as the ability to spell words correctly involve phonological skill. The dyslexic child, therefore, manifests weakness in these areas. In addition, being a poor decoder, the dyslexic child relies heavily on context and tends to use a "top-down" approach and guesses many words while reading aloud. Because their semantic skills are adequate, SRD children tend to perform normally in tests of listening comprehension. Given sufficient time, many of them reach the norm in reading comprehension as well. For documentation of these symptoms in poor readers with average or superior IQ, see Aaron (1989). These dyslexic children constitute about 2% of the general population of schoolchildren.

Children who can read aloud well but do not comprehend what they have read (NRD) constitute a proportion of children that is even smaller than that of dyslexics. These children have been known as "word callers" and their existence has been recognized by reading researchers (Jorm, 1983; Monroe, 1932). Hyperlexic children referred to earlier in this chapter represent an almost pure variety of this form of reading disorder. Neuropsychological studies of alexic patients provide a plausible explanation of the condition where words can be pronounced well but not understood (Funnell, 1983; Shallice, Warrington, & McCarthy, 1983). The patient described by Funnell was a 62-year-old man who, after brain damage, was found to be poor in reading and listening comprehension but was noted to have excellent word-reading ability. The patient, however, could not read nonwords, which led Funnell to postulate a lexical phonological route through which the pronunciation of the whole word is realized. The patient described by Shallice et al. (1983) was a woman who had a verbal IQ of 59 and was very poor in naming and comprehension skills. The observation that she could read regular and nonsense words correctly but not very irregular words led the investigators to conclude that the patient pronounced words by utilizing orthographic units that were smaller than the whole word. Children who can be classified as NRD tend to utilize a "bottom-up" process for reading. While they may not commit many oral errors when reading, their performance on tests of comprehension, whether listening or reading, is poor.

Finally, children who have both decoding and comprehension problems are classified as having general reading disability and these children constitute the bulk of children with reading problems. Children who belong to this category are also sometimes referred to as "the garden-variety poor readers." The reading performance of these children is generally in line with their general intellectual abilities. For this reason, they do not fit the general definition of learning disability which expects a significant discrepancy between reading potential and reading achievement. These children tend to do poorly on tests of comprehension and decoding as well as spelling. However, unlike dyslexic readers, these children do not rely excessively on context for word recognition and frequently their oral reading errors are meaningless and context inappropriate.

Traditionally, an IQ test such as the WISC-R is utilized to reach diagnostic decisions. There are, however, several problems in using the intelligence test for such diagnostic purposes. Because these problems are often discussed in journals, only the two most serious drawbacks will be mentioned here. The use of IQ as a measure of reading potential is based on the assumption that IQ exerts a unidirectional influence on reading performance but is not itself affected by the reading experience. Evidence, however, is accumulating to suggest that the verbal IQ itself may partly be the product of reading experience (Stanovich, 1986). This is because a major contributor to vocabulary growth is reading experience. The second most serious drawback of IQ-based diagnosis is that it does not lead to valid recommendations regarding remediation, intervention, and treatment procedures.

The diagnostic procedure described in this chapter utilizes, in the place of IQ, a measure of listening comprehension to predict the reading potential of the reader. There are several advantages in using listening comprehension in the diagnosis of reading disorders. First, listening comprehension and reading comprehension are closely interrelated because, beyond the input stage, they share the same cognitive mechanism (Aaronson & Ferres, 1984; Kintsch & Kozminsky, 1977). Second, the correlation between reading comprehension and listening comprehension is higher than the one obtained between reading comprehension and IQ (Kennedy, 1971; Stanovich, Cunningham, & Feeman, 1984). Finally, because the use of listening comprehension can differentiate between reading disorders that arise due to comprehension deficit and decoding weakness, diagnosis based on listening comprehension can lead directly to recommendations regarding reading remediation. Children with specific reading disability (dyslexia) need to improve their decoding skills, NRD readers need to improve their comprehension ability, whereas GRD children need attention in both these areas.

B. Tests and Tasks Used in the Diagnostic Procedure

The following tests and procedures are used to accomplish the differential diagnosis.

1. Test of reading comprehension. The passage-comprehension subtest from the Woodcock Reading Mastery Tests, Revised, Form G.
2. Test of listening comprehension. The passage-comprehension subtest from the Woodcock Reading Mastery Tests, Revised, Form H is converted and used as a test of listening comprehension. Each sentence in the test is read to the child by the examiner and the child is required to supply the missing word. The correlation between the reading comprehension test and the listening comprehension test, determined by administering these two tests to 180 children from grades three through eight, is .73. The listening comprehension test has a test retest reliability of .67.

Norms for the following tests (3–10) are presented in Appendices I and II.

3. A list of 38 words for assessing oral reading. These words are selected on the basis of certain spelling-to-pronunciation (grapheme–phoneme correspondence, or GPC) rules selected from literature (Calfee, Venezky, & Chapman, 1969; Wijk, 1966). The child is asked to read the words aloud and his responses are taped. The number of words correctly pronounced is compared against the norms for his grade.
4. Pronounceable nonwords. The 36 pseudowords used in this list are also based on the GPC rules mentioned in the preceding paragraph. The child is told that these are not real words but is asked to read them as best as he can. The responses are taped. A response is scored correct whether it is pronounced according to the GPC rules or by analogy. For example, the nonword *chind* is scored correct whether the "chi" part is pronounced as in *Chicago* or as in *China;* however, it is scored incorrect if it is given a /k/ value and pronounced as *kind*.
5. A list of 38 words to assess written spelling. This list contains the same words as the list of words used to assess oral reading. The examiner says each word, follows it up with a sentence in which the word is embedded, and says the target word again.

The previous three tests (3, 4, and 5) are useful in evaluating the decoding skill of the reader.

6. A list of function words. The 20 words in this list occur very frequently in written text (more than 500 times per 5,088,721 words of running text) (Carroll, Davies, & Richman, 1971). The function words in this list are matched for frequency and length with the content words in Test 7 (see below). The time taken to read aloud the list of function words is compared against the appropriate grade norms. Readers with decoding problems are also slow readers.
7. A list of content words. This list is made up of 20 content words that are nouns or verbs and are matched for length and frequency with the words in the function word list. The number of errors committed in reading

aloud this list is compared with the errors committed in reading the list of function words. Dyslexic readers tend to commit more errors in reading function words than content words; they are also slower in reading the function word list than the content word list. The other two groups of poor readers do not show such a discrepancy.

8. Cloze passages. The Cloze test is constructed by inserting 3-word multiple-choice items in the sentences from a selection of 24 graded passages. These 24 passages were taken from a corpus of 36 passages that have been calibrated for syntactic density and readability (Aquino, 1969; Miller & Coleman, 1967). The child is asked to read aloud two Cloze passages (forms A and B) that correspond to the grade equivalent of his performance on the reading comprehension subtest of the Woodcock Mastery Tests. By asking the child to read a passage that is in line with his reading comprehension ability, the decoding difficulty he might experience is reduced. The child is asked to read aloud and select one of the three multiple-choice words that fits the context. The number of incorrect choices made is the dependent variable. This is a test of reading comprehension and, because the decoding requirement is minimized, dyslexic children tend to do better in this test than the other two groups of poor readers.

9. Graded passages. The same passages used for the Cloze test are used in this test, but without the multiple word choices. In order to avoid practice effects, it is desirable to administer this test a day after the Cloze test had been given. As it was in the case of the Cloze test, the child is asked to read aloud the two passages (A and B) that correspond to the grade equivalent of his performance on the reading comprehension subtest of the Woodcock Mastery Tests. The number of errors as well as the nature of the errors committed are noted. In this test, SRD and GRD readers commit more errors than NRD readers. Poor readers with GRD tend to commit errors that do not fit the context; at times they produce neologisms. Because these types of errors are not characteristic of dyslexic children, performance on this test can be useful in separating SRD poor readers from GRD poor readers.

10. List of words obtained by decomposing the graded passage. There has to be an interval of a few hours between the administration of the graded passages and this list of words, the reason being that words that make up this list come from the graded passages. The child is asked to read the words aloud and the number of reading errors is noted. This figure is subtracted from the number of errors made in reading the corresponding graded passages. Normal readers commit fewer errors when they read the decomposed list than when they read the passage. The SRD reader, who relies heavily on context, uses a "top-down" processing strategy, and

makes more errors when reading the decomposed list than when reading the passage because the list does not have context clues. Such a discrepancy between errors committed while reading the passage and reading the list of words is not usually seen in GRD subjects.

C. The Differential Diagnostic Testing Procedure

The objective of the diagnostic procedure is to arrive at a decision as to which one of the three categories of reading disability (SRD, NRD, or GRD) the subject belongs. This is accomplished in two stages. During the first stage, an initial diagnosis is made by making use of the test of reading comprehension and listening comprehension. The initial diagnosis indicates whether there is a discrepancy between listening comprehension and reading comprehension or if both listening and reading comprehension are lower than the grade equivalent of the subject. The dyslexic child, by definition, has normal intelligence but poor decoding ability. As noted earlier, children with normal listening comprehension but lower reading comprehension are classified as dyslexic (SRD). Children who perform poorly on reading as well as listening comprehension tests have a basic comprehension deficit and are classified as having nonspecific reading disability (NRD). Children who do poorly on the listening comprehension test and even worse on the reading comprehension test have a double deficit (comprehension and decoding) and are classified as having generalized reading disability (GRD).

In the second stage, outlined below, the supplementary tests and tasks (items 3 through 10 in Section III,B) are administered to validate the diagnostic conclusions reached in the first stage.

Step 1. Administer the passage-comprehension subtest of the Woodcock Reading Mastery Tests, Form G. This provides a measure of the child's reading comprehension.

Step 2. Administer the passage-comprehension subtest of the Woodcock Reading Mastery Tests, Form H, as a test of listening comprehension. The examiner reads each statement to the child, who is then required to furnish the missing word. If the child asks that the sentence be repeated, the entire sentence is read once again, but no more. The word to be supplied by the child in each sentence is indicated by the examiner by saying "blank." Many of the first 24 sentences in this test include pictures as stimuli. While testing the child for listening comprehension, only the pictures and not the written sentences are shown.

Step 3. By referring to the Woodcock Reading Mastery Test examiner's manual, the raw scores obtained on the reading comprehension test and the listening comprehension test are transformed into standard scores and grade equivalents. While grade equivalents give a quick impression about the subject's performance relative to his age, standard scores are needed for further analysis.

Step 4. Apply the regression equation that is provided in Appendix II to the listening comprehension standard score. Note that each grade has its own regression formula. The regression formula for the grade the child is currently enrolled in has to be applied. By applying the regression formula to the listening comprehension score, we have now predicted the child's reading comprehension.

These regression formulas have been developed by administering these tests to 30 children from grades three through eight, a total of 180 children. The supplementary tests were also administered to these children and the mean and SD for Tests 3 through 7 are shown in Appendix II. Teachers and reading specialists can follow the model presented here and construct their own battery of supplementary tests based on the material taught in their school systems. Such a method of testing which is tied to students' curricula and is focused on measurement of pupil skills which, in turn, leads to instructional decisions and has, in recent years, gained popularity under the name of curriculum-based assessment (see Shinn, 1989).

Step 5. The next step is to compare the child's predicted reading comprehension score (obtained by applying the regression formula to the listening comprehension score) with the actual reading comprehension score he obtained on the Woodcock subtest, Form G. This comparison is made by converting into standard scores (1) the raw scores obtained on the reading comprehension test, and (2) the predicted reading comprehension scores obtained through the regression formula. In the Woodcock Reading Mastery tests this conversion is somewhat complicated, but by carefully following the instructions provided in the manual, this could be accomplished. After this, a score that is equivalent to one standard error of measurement (SEM) (provided in the examiner's manual) is added to the reading comprehension raw score and the corresponding standard score is obtained. Similarly, a score that is equivalent to one SEM is subtracted from the reading comprehension raw score and the corresponding standard score is obtained. Thus we have established the upper and lower limits for the standard score for reading comprehension. A similar procedure is followed in establishing the range of the predicted reading comprehension score. If the two bands (i.e., one for the standard score for reading comprehension actually obtained by the child and one for the standard score for the predicted reading comprehension) do not overlap, it can be concluded that there is a discrepancy between the obtained reading comprehension score and the predicted reading comprehension score and that the discrepancy cannot be attributed to errors of measurement.

If the child's predicted reading comprehension is at grade level, the standard score of his actual reading comprehension is below the predicted score, and if there is no overlap between the bands, the child is diagnosed as having SRD (dyslexia). If the child's predicted reading comprehension is below grade level and the standard score of his actual reading comprehension overlaps with the predicted standard score, the child is diagnosed as having NRD. If the child's predicted reading comprehension is below grade level and, furthermore, if the standard score of his actual reading comprehension is even worse so that there is no overlap between the obtained and predicted standard scores, the child is diagnosed as having GRD.

Step 6. The supplementary tests are administered to validate the initial diagnosis.

Poor performance on the following tests is indicative of decoding difficulty: word list reading, nonword reading, function word reading, and spelling. This, in combination with slow function word reading, committing more errors in reading a decomposed list than in reading the passages, and average or better performance in the Cloze test, is indicative of SRD, or dyslexia which is associated with weak decoding skill.

Normal performance in word list reading, nonword reading, function word reading, and spelling coupled with poor performance on the Cloze test indicates NRD, which is associated with a deficit in comprehension skill.

Poor performance in word list reading, nonword reading, function word reading, and spelling along with poor performance on the Cloze test indicates a GRD. These children are also slow in reading the function word list and have cognitive deficits that are pervasive. Individuals who have sustained pre- or postnatal brain injury are also likely to have general reading disability rather than specific reading disability.

Occasionally, it is possible to encounter a child who is referred to the psychology clinic for reading difficulty but is found to do well in standardized reading tests such as the Woodcock Reading Mastery Tests. Upon close testing, these children would be found to be extremely slow readers, with no other problem. These children are described as dysfluent readers (Aaron & Whitefield, 1990), and dysfluency appears to be a cognitive style. This condition can be detected by administering a timed reading test such as the Stanford Diagnostic Reading Test. In the tests described in this chapter, the function-word reading speed is useful in identifying extremely slow readers.

IV. Recommendations for Instructional Strategies

Logic would dictate that in order to improve reading skill the remediation strategy should focus on the weak component. Thus, in order to become a better reader, the child with poor decoding ability has to improve his decoding skill, the child with comprehension deficit needs improvement in comprehension skill, and the child with general reading disability needs attention in both decoding and comprehension. Unfortunately, this simple reasoning does not always work successfully. The reason for this state of affairs lies in the fact that reading performance is confounded by numerous variables such as the severity of the reading problem, reading experience, motivation, etc. A rule of thumb to remember is that reading is a skill and, like any other skill, improves with practice. Success in learning to read depends on the extent of the child's reading experience which, in turn, depends on the child's interest to read. Thus, the most important cue to successful remedial teaching of reading is to arouse and sustain the interest of the child in reading. Carried to excess any remedial method can become a boring exercise and eventually be detrimental to well-meaning remedial efforts. Thus, reading teachers and school psychologists should be willing to consider alternate approaches if a given method fails to produce satisfactory results within a certain period of time. This strategy is referred to as trial teaching.

V. Summary

The description of the nature of reading disabilities and the diagnosis of these disabilities described in this chapter are based on the belief that the reading process is multicomponential and a breakdown of different components can lead to different forms of reading disabilities. Neuropsychological, experimental, and developmental studies show that, at the most basic level, reading is made up of two components: decoding and comprehension. Consequently, a potential exists for the occurrence of three different kinds of disabled readers: those with poor decoding but adequate comprehension skills (specific reading disability or developmental dyslexia), those with adequate decoding skills but poor comprehension (nonspecific reading disability), and those with poor decoding and poor comprehension skills (generalized reading disability). This classification of developmental reading disability is partly derived from the findings of neuropsychological studies that investigated patients with acquired dyslexia.

Beyond the modality differences seen at the input stage, reading and listening comprehension appear to utilize the same cognitive mechanisms. Listening comprehension, therefore, can be used to predict reading comprehension. In fact, listening comprehension appears to be a better predictor of reading comprehension than IQ. The diagnostic procedure described in this chapter is based on this premise. The procedure arrives at initial diagnostic decisions by administering reading comprehension and listening comprehension tests. Subsequently, the validity of these decisions is evaluated by administering a series of reading-related tasks. This chapter concludes by illustrating the diagnostic procedure by describing three "typical" cases of reading disabilities.

VI. Illustrative Case Studies

The case studies that follow are actual cases referred to the School Psychology Clinic.

A. Case 1: SRD Child

Age: 11.3 years; Grade: 5; Sex: male.
WISC-R: VIQ 101; PIQ 129; FIQ 115.
Listening comprehension: 5.5 grade; standard score 110.
Predicted reading comprehension: 5.5 grade; standard score 97 (Range: 93–101).
Actual reading comprehension: 3.5 grade; standard score 86 (Range: 83–89).
Initial diagnosis: Decoding deficit; specific reading disability (dyslexia)

Results of supplementary tests:

Word list (no. correct)	Nonword reading (no. correct)	Spelling (no. correct)	Function words reading (time in sec)	Cloze (no. choice errors)		Graded passage reading (no. errors)		List of words from passage (no. errors)	
							Level		
				3A	3B	3A	3B	3A	3B
34	18	7	18.0	4	2	8	14	18	19

B. Case 2: NRD Child

Age: 12.4 years; Grade: 6; Sex: female.
WISC-R: VIQ 77; PIQ 105; FIQ 89.
Listening comprehension: 3.2 grade; standard score 76
Predicted reading comprehension: 5.2 grade; standard score 93 (Range: 89–97).
Actual reading comprehension: 4.7 grade; standard score 89 (Range: 85–93).
Initial diagnosis: Comprehension deficit, nonspecific reading disability

Results of supplementary tests:

Word list (no. correct)	Nonword reading (no. correct)	Spelling (no. correct)	Function words reading (time in sec)	Cloze (no. choice errors)		Graded passage reading (no. errors)		List of words from passage (no. errors)	
				Level					
				3A	3B	3A	3B	3A	3B
37	32	30	12.2	6	7	3	2	7	5

C. Case 3: GRD Child

Age: 10.7 years; Grade: 4; Sex: male.
WISC-R: VIQ 95; PIQ 96; FIQ 95.
Listening comprehension: 3.1 grade; standard score 84.
Predicted reading comprehension: 3.0 grade; standard score 81 (Range: 78–81).
Actual reading comprehension: 2.2 grade; standard score 69 (Range: 65–73).
Initial diagnosis: General reading disability

Results of supplementary tests:

Word list (no. correct)	Nonword reading (no. correct)	Spelling (no. correct)	Function words reading (time in sec)	Cloze (no. choice errors)		Graded passage reading (no. errors)		List of words from passage (no. errors)	
				Level					
				2A	2B	2A	2B	2A	2B
30	23	21	29.0	5	9	10	9	14	15

Acknowledgments

We wish to thank the Blumberg Center for Research Studies in Special Education for supporting the standardization project of the tests described in this chapter.

References

Aaron, P. G. (1989). *Dyslexia and hyperlexia: Diagnosis and management of developmental reading disabilities.* Boston, MA: Kluwer Academic Publishers.

Aaron, P. G., & Whitefield, J. (1990). Dysfluency-Fluency: Implications of a new cognitive style for reading consultation. *Journal of Reading, Writing and Learning Disabilities.* 6(4), 395–411.

Aaronson, D., & Ferres, S. (1984). The word-by-word reading paradigm: An experimental and theoretical approach. In D. E. Kieras & M. A. Just (Eds.), *New methods in reading comprehension.* Hillsdale, NJ: Erlbaum.

Aquino, M. R. (1969). The validity of the Miller-Coleman readability scale. *Reading Research Quarterly, 4,* 342–357.

Bastian, H. C. (1898). *A treatise on aphasia and other speech defects.* London: H. K. Lewis.

Calfee, R. C., Venezky, R. L., & Chapman, R. S. (1969). *Pronunciation of synthetic words with predictable and unpredictable letter-sound correspondences* (Tech. Rep. No. 11). Madison: University of Wisconsin Research and Developmental Center.

Carroll, J. B., Davies, P., & Richman, B. (1971). *Word frequency book.* New York: Houghton-Mifflin.

Coltheart, M. (1980). Reading, phonological recoding and deep dyslexia. In M. Coltheart, K. Patterson, & J. C. Marshall (Eds.), *Deep dyslexia.* London: Kegan Paul.

Dearborn, W. F. (1925). The etiology of word blindness. In E. Lord, L. Carmichael, & W. F. Dearborn (Eds.), *Special disabilities in learning to read and write* (Harvard Monograph Series, Vol. 2, No. 1). Cambridge, MA: Harvard University Press.

DeFries, J., Fulker, D., & LaBuda, C. (1987). Evidence for a genetic aetiology in reading disability of twins. *Nature (London), 329,* 537–539.

Dejerine, M. J. (1891). Sur un cas de cécité verbale avec agraphie, suivi d'autopsie. *Comptes Rendus des Seances de la Societe de Biologie et de Ses Filiales, 3,* 197–201.

Dejerine, M. J. (1892). Différentes variétés de cécité verbale. *Memoires de la Societe de Biologie, 9,* 61–90.

Fildes, L. G. (1921). A psychological inquiry into the nature of the condition known as congenital word blindness. *Brain, 44,* 286–304.

Frederiksen, J. R. (1982). A componential model of reading and their interrelation. In R. J. Sternberg (Ed.), *Advances in the psychology of human intelligence.* Hillsdale, NJ: Erlbaum.

Frith, U., & Snowling, M. (1983). Reading for meaning and reading for sound in autistic and dyslexic children. *British Journal of Developmental Psychology, 1,* 329–342.

Funnell, E. (1983). Phonological processes in reading: New evidence from acquired dyslexia. *British Journal of Psychology, 74,* 159–180.

Geschwind, N. (1974). *Selected papers on language and the brain.* Boston, MA: Reidel.

Healy, J. (1982). The enigma of hyperlexia. *Reading Research Quarterly, 17,* 319–338.

Healy, J., & Aram, D. M. (1986). Hyperlexia and dyslexia: A family study. *Annals of Dyslexia, 36,* 237–252.

Jackson, M. D., & McClelland, J. L. (1979). Processing determinants of reading speed. *Journal of Experimental Psychology: General, 108*(2), 151–181.

Jorm, A. F. (1983). *The psychology of reading and spelling disabilities*. London: Routledge & Kegan Paul.

Kennedy, D. K. (1971). *Training with the Cloze procedure visually and auditorially to improve the reading and listening comprehension of third grade readers*. Unpublished doctoral dissertation, Pennsylvania State University, University Park.

Kintsch, W., & Kozminsky, E. (1977). Summarizing stories after reading and listening. *Journal of Educational Psychology, 69,* 491–499.

Leong, C. K. (1988). A componential approach to understanding reading and its difficulties in preadolescent readers. *Annals of Dyslexia, 38,* 95–119.

Liberman, I. Y., & Shankweiler, D. (1985). Phonology and the problem of learning to read and write. *Remedial and Special Education, 6,* 41–55.

Marshall, J. C., & Newcombe, F. (1966). Syntactic and semantic errors in paralexia. *Neuropsychologia, 4,* 169–176.

Marshall, J. C., & Newcombe, F. (1973). Patterns of paralexia. *Journal of Psycholinguistic Research, 2,* 179–199.

Miller, G. R., & Coleman, E. B. (1967). A set of thirty six passages calibrated for complexity. *Journal of Verbal Learning and Verbal Behavior, 6,* 851–854.

Monroe, M. (1932). *Children who cannot read.* Chicago, IL: University of Chicago Press.

Morgan, W. P. (1896). A case of congenital word-blindness. *British Medical Journal, 2,* 1368.

Palmer, J., McCleod, C., Hunt, E., & Davidson, J. (1985). Information processing correlates of reading. *Journal of Memory and Language, 24,* 59–88.

Pelosi, P. L. (1977). The roots of reading diagnosis. In H. A. Robinson (Ed.), *Reading and writing instruction in the United States.* Newark, NJ: International Reading Association.

Pennington, B. F., & Smith, S. D. (1988). Genetic influences on learning disabilities: An update. *Journal of Consulting and Clinical Psychology, 56,* 817–823.

Schmitt, C. (1918). Developmental alexia: Congenital word blindness or inability to learn to read. *Elementary School Journal, 6,* 680–700.

Shallice, T., Warrington, E., & McCarthy, R. (1983). Reading without semantics. *Quarterly Journal of Experimental Psychology, 35,* 111–138.

Shinn, M. R. (1989). *Curriculum-based measurement.* New York: Guilford Press.

Silberberg, N., & Silberberg, M. (1967). Hyperlexia: Specific word recognition skill in young children. *Exceptional Children, 34,* 41–42.

Snowling, M. (1980). The development of grapheme-phoneme correspondence in normal and dyslexic readers. *Journal of Experimental Child Psychology, 29,* 291–305.

Stanovich, K. E., Cunningham, A. E., & Feeman, D. J. (1984). Intelligence, cognitive skills, and early reading progress. *Reading Research Quarterly, 19*(3), 278–303.

Stanovich, K. E. (1986). Matthew effects in reading: Some consequences of individual differences in the acquisition of literacy. *Reading Research Quarterly, 21*(4), 360–407.

Sternberg, R. G. (1985). *Beyond IQ: A triarchic theory of human intelligence.* New York: Cambridge University Press.

Wallin, J. E. (1920). Congenital word-blindness: Some analysis of cases. *Training School Bulletin, 71,* 37–47.

Wijk, A. (1966). *Rules of pronunciation for the English language: An account of the relationship between English spelling and pronunciation.* London: Oxford University Press.

Tests

Reading Test

Name _____ Grade _____

1. dog	20. except
2. cat	21. strong
3. pages	22. cold
4. chance	23. bring
5. larger	24. center
6. special	25. eggs
7. region	26. certain
8. decide	27. sing
9. girl	28. coming
10. uncle	29. songs
11. changes	30. became
12. discover	31. green
13. edge	32. children
14. fact	33. gone
15. large	34. cannot
16. cells	35. begin
17. city	36. game
18. page	37. moving
19. having	38. audible

Reading Test (Nonwords)

Name _____   Grade _____

1. gare	19. gend
2. duncle	20. cend
3. ract	21. grone
4. gar	22. chind
5. bace	23. gen
6. recide	24. pice
7. kaces	25. tite
8. gade	26. cad
9. skare	27. dit
10. chape	28. cilly
11. skar	29. cept
12. kute	30. colp
13. gite	31. kar
14. fedge	32. pare
15. git	33. sute
16. bage	34. kare
17. ling	35. par
18. gog	36. sut

Reading Test (Function Words)

Name _____   Grade _____

let
has
ago
off
why
any
yet
nor
will
much
also
must
even
such
once
soon
ever
upon
else
thus

Reading Test (Content Words)

Name _____   Grade _____

cat
run
men
boy
say
dog
she
man
bird
gold
book
feet
back
room
name
page
work
come
look
time

List 1

1.	dog	The *dog* makes a good pet.	dog
2.	cat	The *cat* is also a pet.	cat
3.	pages	There are many *pages* in the book.	pages
4.	chance	He has a *chance* of winning the game.	chance
5.	larger	Jane's house is *larger* than Bill's.	larger
6.	special	Christmas is a very *special* day.	special
7.	region	They live in the northern *region* of the country.	region
8.	decide	You must *decide* by tomorrow if you can come or not.	decide
9.	girl	She is a pretty *girl*.	girl
10.	uncle	You would like my *uncle*, but not my aunt.	aunt
11.	changes	When Bill goes swimming he changes his clothes.	changes
12.	discover	Did Columbus *discover* America?	discover
13.	edge	They live on the *edge* of the town.	edge
14.	fact	That is an interesting *fact*.	fact
15.	large	That is a *large* house, not a small one.	large
16.	cells	There are many *cells* in our bodies; you have to use a microscope to see them.	cells
17.	city	We live in the *city*, not in a village.	city
18.	page	Please turn to the first *page* of your book.	page
19.	having	Jim was *having* a good time.	having
20.	except	I like all kinds of food *except* spinach.	except
21.	strong	Bill is very *strong*. He is not weak.	strong
22.	cold	It is *cold* outside, but hot inside.	cold
23.	bring	Will you *bring* me my plate?	bring
24.	center	He hit it in the *center*, not outside.	center
25.	eggs	I had *eggs* for breakfast.	eggs
26.	certain	Are you *certain* of that, or are you not sure?	certain
27.	sing	I like to *sing* but not dance.	sing
28.	coming	John is *coming* home tomorrow.	coming
29.	songs	He knows many *songs* and he sings them.	songs
30.	became	Jill *became* a school teacher.	became
31.	green	The grass is *green*.	green
32.	children	Parents have *children*.	children
33.	gone	He must have *gone* home.	gone
34.	cannot	I *cannot* answer that question.	cannot

35.	begin	We will *begin* a new lesson tomorrow.	begin
36.	game	Basketball is a fun *game*.	game
37.	moving	They are *moving* to their new house.	moving
38.	audible	If the speech is *audible* you can hear it.	audible

Decomposed List of Words

away	dusting
table	task
skipped	thought
grandfather	was
corner	room
fast	lazy
window	started
her	alone
big	mother
someone	slowly
but	asked
Katy	and
legs	tall
neglected	the
ashamed	own
disliked	hurried
suddenly	made
finished	upstairs
little	more
living	tidy
again	she
said	dust
stood	heard
another	chair
talking	carefully

Cloze Test

Katy's mother asked her [to / and / for] dust the living room [in / the / and] to make her

own [days / room / thing] tidy. Katy disliked dusting. [He / Then / She] started to dust slowly.

[She / Many / They] neglected to dust one [in / of / for] the arms of the [home / hot / big] chair in

the corner. [Many / They / She] skipped the legs of [the / his / her] table by the window.

[When / And / In] another corner stood a [glass / main / tall] grandfather clock. She could

[not / then / but] reach the top, so [many / he / she] did not dust up [they / there / them] at all. Katy

thought [she / he / them] was alone in the [room / thing / top] but suddenly she heard

[rain / they / someone] talking. It was the [home / trained / grandfather] clock. It said slowly

[again / away / here] and again, "La-zy Ka-ty, [La-zy / cousin / sixteen] Ka-ty!" This made Katy

545

[in / up / so] ashamed that she started [this / her / more] task again, dusting more

[carefully / deeply / longer] . She finished dusting the [plants / fish / living] room and hurried

upstairs [for / the / to] her own room. The [long / little / water] clock there was also

[talking / tail / telling] to her. It said [as / in / so] fast as it could,“ [Good / Work / Busy] Katy, busy

Katy, busy [Katy / Mary / Jane] !”

Reading Passage

Katy's mother asked her to dust the living room and to make her own room tidy. Katy disliked dusting. She started to dust slowly. She neglected to dust one of the arms of the big chair in the corner. She skipped the legs of the table by the window. In another corner stood a tall grandfather clock. She could not reach the top, so she did not dust up there at all. Katy thought she was alone in the room, but suddenly she heard someone talking. It was the grandfather clock. It said slowly again and again, "La-zy Ka-ty, La-zy Katy!" This made Katy so ashamed that she started her task again, dusting more carefully. She finished dusting the living room and hurried upstairs to her own room. The little clock there was also talking to her. It said as fast as it could, "Busy Katy, busy Katy, busy Katy!"

Mean, SD, and Regression Formulas (Grades 3–8)

Norms (Grades 3–8)

Grade		3	4	5	6	7	8
Age	Mean	9.04	10.02	11.10	12.06	13.23	14.18
	SD	.75	.77	.63	.53	.54	.54
Grade	Mean	3.41	4.30	5.38	6.50	7.62	8.62
Reading Comprehension SS[a] (Form G)	Mean	99.43	101.43	102.31	102.30	108.00	101.97
	SD	10.25	17.45	11.95	12.24	10.44	11.60
Reading Comprehension GE[b] (Form G)	Mean	3.52	5.03	5.95	7.34	10.89	10.19
	SD	1.13	2.34	2.14	2.91	3.75	3.59
Listening Comprehension SS (Form H)	Mean	101.07	107.20	105.60	97.20	104.73	89.06
	SD	9.14	10.34	12.20	12.40	11.04	13.02
Listening Comprehension GE (Form H)	Mean	3.70	5.57	6.70	6.35	9.50	6.62
	SD	.99	2.27	2.96	2.57	3.33	2.96
Word Lists							
List 1 (no. correct)	Mean	31.63	33.47	36.71	37.07	37.23	37.69
	SD	5.93	8.31	1.41	1.23	.10	1.26
List 2, Nonwords (no. correct)	Mean	22.07	25.47	26.70	28.57	28.77	29.00
	SD	8.63	8.50	4.68	3.80	3.97	4.46
Function word list (no. correct)	Mean	18.33	18.30	19.00	19.67	19.93	19.78
	SD	2.41	3.96	2.23	.84	.25	.91
Content word list (no. correct)	Mean	19.60	19.33	19.80	19.73	20.00	19.62
	SD	.89	1.79	.48	.52	0.00	1.04
Spelling (no. correct)	Mean	23.37	27.27	32.60	33.80	36.90	38.66
	SD	7.44	10.24	5.28	4.57	3.00	3.28
Function words (time in sec)	Mean	20.53	21.87	13.80	15.23	9.83	12.47
	SD	14.92	15.56	4.30	3.34	2.05	3.84
Content words (time in sec)	Mean	12.97	16.40	12.23	17.00	9.23	11.28
	SD	4.57	9.65	3.37	18.71	2.10	2.94
Word List A from graded passages (no. errors)	Mean	3.60	3.53	1.47	2.03	1.20	1.78
	SD	3.76	3.87	2.03	2.80	1.03	1.31
Cloze A (no. errors)	Mean	4.83	5.83	4.63	5.10	5.43	3.44
	SD	2.95	3.87	2.85	3.41	2.61	2.42
Graded passages Passage A (no. errors)	Mean	4.20	4.03	3.23	2.93	2.67	2.44
	SD	3.41	4.58	3.55	2.92	1.94	1.81

[a] SS, standard scores.
[b] GE, grade equivalent.

Regression Formulas

Grade	Based on Standard Score
3	_____ = .725 (Listening SS) +26.1
4	_____ =1.15 (Listening SS) −22.2
5	_____ = .719 (Listening SS) +26.4
6	_____ = .608 (Listening SS) +43.2
7	_____ = .653 (Listening SS) +40.3
8	_____ = .519 (Listening SS) +55.7

CHAPTER TWENTY

Specific Mathematics Disorders

Clayton E. Keller
Joe P. Sutton

I. Introduction

Researchers have traditionally paid less attention to the mathematical abilities and performances of individuals with learning disabilities than to abilities in other academic areas (Hallahan, Kauffman, & Lloyd, 1985; Kosc, 1974; Rourke & Strang, 1983). In general, investigators have made (1) spoken language, (2) written language, and (3) perceptual and motor processes the main foci of their research (Wiederholt, 1974). There are several reasons, however, why disorders of mathematics should not be neglected.

First, mathematical knowledge and skills are integral components of our lives. As one indicator of their importance to human knowledge, preschoolers and even infants show the presence of quantitative abilities and competencies (Gelman, 1978). For example, Flavell (1985) summarizes the results of a study by Starkey, Spelke, and Gelman that suggests 6- to 9-month-old infants have some, albeit limited, concept of quantity because they are able to distinguish between groups of two and three objects on the basis of the quantities of the groups. As another indicator, the tasks of daily living and employment frequently place mathematical demands on us; balancing one's checkbook, managing money, cooking, and home repairs are a few common examples of tasks involving mathematics.

Second, the improvement of mathematical knowledge and skills, although always an emphasis in our schools, has become a fundamental part of current educational reform efforts. The majority of the major educational

Neuropsychological Foundations of Learning Disabilities, copyright © 1991 by Academic Press Inc. All rights of reproduction in any form reserved.

policy reports in the 1980s called for the strengthening of core curriculum subjects including mathematics (Ornstein & Levine, 1989). In 1989 the National Council of Teachers of Mathematics issued a new set of standards to address both content and teaching approaches of mathematics instruction in elementary and secondary schools.

And third, the prevalence of mathematics difficulties for persons with learning disabilities, while not as high as the prevalence of reading problems, is substantial. Kosc (1974) identified 6.4% of his sample of fifth-grade students in Czechoslovakia as dyscalculic, which he defines as a specific type of math disability. Norman and Zigmond (1980), in a descriptive study of the characteristics of students served as learning-disabled by the earlier Child Service Demonstration Centers, found that 8.1% of their sample had severe discrepancies solely in math while 13.1% were discrepant in both reading and mathematics. Learning-disabilities teachers in McLeod and Armstrong's (1982) survey served 26.2% of their students primarily for mathematics and an additional 40.3% when mathematics was an area of concern in addition to other difficulties. And, R. L. Carpenter's (1985) survey of elementary and secondary school learning-disabilities teachers indicated the average student spent a third of his or her time in the resource room for math instruction.

Research into disorders of mathematics among learning-disabled individuals should not only describe deficient performance, but should also be based on a theoretical explanation of the causal mechanisms for such performance (Keller, 1988). The study of specific mathematics disorders from a neuropsychological perspective can provide both rich descriptions of mathematical performance, especially through the use of detailed examples of particular individuals (e.g., Kosc, 1974, and Warrington, 1987), and a well-articulated causal theory with the search for brain–behavior connections. Overall, though, the neuropsychological work on mathematics disabilities has been characterized as poorly understood (Fletcher & Loveland, 1986) and controversial (Gurney, 1983).

We contend that, taken as a whole, neuropsychological research on math disorders is fairly consistent theoretically, especially if the heterogeneity of the math population is accepted. However, it does lack a sound grounding in the cognitive and mathematical components of the disabilities.

To support these assertions, we first review the current state of neuropsychological research on mathematics disabilities. We discuss the various disorders of mathematics described in the neuropsychological literature, considering also the neuropsychological processes implicated and the brain–behavior connections hypothesized. We next review the literature on mathematically related subtypes of learning-disabled individuals for the support it provides for the hypothesized causes of mathematical disorders and for the idea of a diverse population. Then we consider an information-processing viewpoint about mathematics performance as an example of a theory that accounts for the cognitive and mathematical demands of mathematical performance; we also discuss two examples of research that has combined neuropsychological and cognitive perspectives. Finally, we conclude with implications and suggestions about this melding of perspectives in the study of mathematics disorders.

II. Specific Mathematics Disorders from a Neuropsychological Perspective

Terms and Definitions of Mathematics Disorders

Sharma (1986) contends that many of the terms for learning disabilities in mathematics have been inconsistently and incorrectly used in an interchangeable fashion. Indeed, the variety of terms used at both general and specific levels among different researchers and clinicians echoes to earlier days in the field when, for example, Clements (1966) found 38 terms for minimal brain dysfunction.

Terms such as "learning disabilities in mathematics," "arithmetic disorders," "math disabilities," and "specific math disabilities" are generally considered to be broad, umbrella terms for a variety of disturbances and difficulties in mathematics. One subtle difference in the use of these terms appears in whether their definitions describe deficits in mathematical ability (e.g., Novick & Arnold, 1988) or in mathematical achievement or performance (e.g., Gurney, 1983). Such a distinction may be meaningful, as a deficit in one of these areas (ability or performance) may, but does not necessarily, appear with a deficit in the other.

The use of such terms extends beyond neuropsychology. Two terms which are somewhat general but are used more exclusively, though still with little consensus (Spiers, 1987), by those with a neuropsychological perspective are *acalculia* and *dyscalculia*.

1. ACALCULIA

Novick and Arnold (1988) define acalculia as an "acquired arithmetic disorder, the result of brain injury suffered after arithmetic skills have been mastered" (p. 132); Gaddes (1985) presents a similar definition. Kosc (1974) and Sharma and Loveless (1986) refer to this type of acquired math disorder, however, as "post-lesional dyscalculia;" Kosc uses acalculia then as a global term for a complete failure of mathematical abilities. Benton (1987) does not include the acquired aspect in his definition of acalculia and restricts this disorder to impairments with number operations.

Acquired math disorders—for which we shall follow Novick and

Arnold's (1988) and Gaddes' (1985) use of the term acalculia—are commonly divided into two groups, primary and secondary, based on whether the difficulties in mathematics are seen alone or in conjunction with disturbances in other cognitive or processing functions that may account for the math difficulties (Novick & Arnold, 1988). *Primary acalculia* appears to be synonymous with the terms "anarithmetia" or "true acalculia" (Benton, 1987; Gaddes, 1985; Spiers, 1987). Individuals exhibiting this particular math disorder demonstrate deficits in fundamental arithmetic operations and in the understanding of the concept of numbers yet maintain adequate language, memory, and visual–spatial skills (Novick & Arnold, 1988).

There are two main types of secondary acalculia. One, called *acalculia with alexia and/or agraphia for numbers* or *aphasic acalculia,* is an impairment in mathematics that manifests itself as difficulties with the oral and written production and comprehension of numbers yet preserved computational skills (Benton, 1987; Novick & Arnold, 1988). The problems an individual with this disorder has with the language (verbal and mathematical) components of mathematics interferes with his or her ability to perform the mathematical tasks successfully. In the other secondary acalculia, *acalculia secondary to visual –spatial disturbance* (Novick & Arnold, 1988), individuals with deficits in visual–spatial skills encounter serious problems with mathematics as their limitations interact with the many spatial demands of mathematical performance (e.g., the reading and writing of numbers, place value, and alignment).

A specific syndrome of acalculia that is firmly established in neurology is the Gerstmann syndrome (Gaddes, 1985). Individuals exhibiting this syndrome have difficulties performing arithmetical operations and with the orientation of number sequences (Kosc, 1974). They also show four characteristics: (1) left–right disorientation, (2) finger agnosia, (3) agraphia, and (4) acalculia (Gaddes, 1985; Rothstein, Benjamin, Crosby, & Eisenstadt, 1988). The Gerstmann syndrome is not limited to one type of acalculia (Benton, 1987).

2. DYSCALCULIA

Novick and Arnold (1988) define dyscalculia, also called developmental dyscalculia, as a "developmental arithmetic disorder, which refers to the failure to develop arithmetic competence" (p. 132). Kosc (1974) describes developmental dyscalculia as a structural "disorder of the maturation of mathematical abilities" (p. 166). In contrast to the acalculias and reflecting the developmental or maturational aspect of the definitions, dyscalculia is viewed primarily as a mathematics disorder for children (Gaddes, 1985; Kosc, 1974; Novick & Arnold, 1988). Though children with this disorder may make a variety of errors during math performance, their difficulties focus in the areas of understanding numbers, counting skills, computational skills, and solving word problems (Novick & Arnold, 1988).

Investigators have classified dyscalculia in various ways based on the symptomatology the disordered individual exhibits. One of the more developed classifications comes from Kosc (1974), who posited six types of developmental dyscalculia:

Verbal dyscalculia, an inability to name mathematical amounts, numbers, terms, symbols, and relationships;

Practognostic dyscalculia, an inability to enumerate, compare, and mathematically manipulate objects, either pictured or real;

Lexical dyscalculia, a disorder in reading mathematical symbols;

Graphical dyscalculia, a disability in writing mathematical symbols;

Ideognostical dyscalculia, a disorder in understanding mathematical concepts and in performing calculations mentally; and

Operational dyscalculia, a disability in performing computational operations.

Kosc suggested these dyscalculias could occur in different combinations and with other impairments.

There is also a dyscalculic version of the Gerstmann syndrome, called developmental Gerstmann syndrome. Children with this syndrome exhibit the same characteristics as adults with Gerstmann syndrome, though there is usually no documented neurological damage as there is in adults (Gurney, 1983). Spellacy and Peter (1978) found full sets of the characteristics of developmental Gerstmann syndrome in students with mathematics disabilities solely and in students with both mathematics and reading disabilities.

3. SUMMARY

Several dimensions are common throughout the various neuropsychological definitions of mathematics disorders; a focus on these dimensions may be more valuable to understanding the phenomena of math disabilities than attempts to master the diverse terminology of different researchers.

One dimension of the definitions considers whether the math disorder was acquired after the mastery of mathematical skills (e.g., Novick and Arnold's and Gaddes' acalculia; Kosc's and Sharma and Loveless' post-lesional dyscalculia) or either during or prior to the development of mathematical competence (e.g., developmental dyscalculia and most versions of dyscalculia). Closely connected to this dimension are dimensions of age (generally acalculia as a disorder for adults and dyscalculia for children) and etiology [acalculia results from brain injury; dyscalculia, according to Kosc (1974), from a congenital structural disorder of the parts of the brain concerned with mathematical abilities].

Another important dimension focuses on whether the mathematical difficulties are the result of disorders of other cognitive functions (secondary disorders) or appear despite all other abilities being intact (primary disorders)

(Novick & Arnold, 1988). Similarly, many definitions contain a dimension that addresses the component skills involved in mathematical performance. Some of the component skills are solely mathematical (e.g., Kosc's ideognostical and operational dyscalculias), though many are not (e.g., the two secondary acalculias and Kosc's verbal, lexical, and graphical dyscalculias). We now take a closer look at these component skills.

III. Neuropsychological Processes and Neuroanatomical Connections Implicated in Mathematics Disorders

Imagine a fifth-grade student calculating the answers to a worksheet of addition, subtraction, multiplication, and division problems; or a secondary school student producing a geometrical proof; or an adult trying to determine if it will be more economical to switch to a different home heating system. Each goes through numerous mental and physical processes to produce a result.

The various typologies of acalculias and dyscalculias reflect such analyses of the perceptual, linguistic, cognitive, and functional demands of performing mathematical tasks, as a disorder in satisfying any of these demands could potentially result in failure on the mathematical task (Strang & Rourke, 1985a). Thus, the neuropsychological processes implicated in mathematics disorders are many, as are the hypothesized brain–behavior connections that might cause the disorders (Spiers, 1987).

A. Localization of Abilities

The perceptual skills of visual–spatial organization, a skill needed in the comprehension and production of written mathematics, are mediated by the right hemisphere; whichever hemisphere is dominant for language controls the linguistic skills necessary for mathematical performance (Novick & Arnold, 1988). The higher-association areas of the dominant hemisphere play major roles both in reading and understanding word problems and in understanding mathematical concepts and procedures (Novick & Arnold, 1988).

The frontal lobes are the centers for quick mental calculations and abstract conceptualizing (Gaddes, 1985) and also for problem-solving skills and oral and written performance (Novick & Arnold, 1988). The parietal lobes mediate a variety of cognitive functions and play an integrative role in the cortical organization of the senses. Motoric functions and behaviors that involve tactile sensations, both of which can be involved in mathematical performance, are associated with the parietal lobes (Gaddes, 1985; Rothstein et al., 1988). Sequencing abilities are also controlled by the left parietal lobe (Novick & Arnold, 1988). The occipital lobes, the locus for visual experiences, control the visual discrimination of written mathematical symbols (Novick & Arnold, 1988) and are associated with geometry and routine calculations (Gaddes, 1985). Finally, mathematical skills involving auditory perception and long-term verbal memory are mediated by the temporal lobes (Gaddes, 1985). In addition, the dominant temporal lobe is responsible for the memory of series, basic math facts, and subvocalization during problem solving (Novick & Arnold, 1988). (See Table I for a summary of these mathematical ability–cortical connections.)

B. Localization of Disorders

Novick and Arnold (1988) suggest that primary acalculia, then, is associated with lesions in the parietal, occipital, and/or temporal lobes, primarily in the left hemisphere (Benton, 1987), though also, in rare instances, in the right hemisphere. Acalculia with alexia and/or agraphia for numbers is usually localized in the left hemisphere also or bilaterally. Acalculia secondary to visual–spatial disturbance generally results from injuries to the right parietal region and, occasionally, from bilateral damage. The Gerstmann syndrome is associated with damage in the area of the angular gyrus of the language-dominant (usually left) hemisphere (Benton, 1987). The subtyping work by Rourke, Strang, and their colleagues (Ozols & Rourke, 1985, 1988; Rourke & Finlayson, 1978; Rourke & Strang, 1978, 1983; Strang & Rourke, 1983, 1985a, 1985b) suggests that children with solely arithmetic disabilities exhibit right hemisphere dysfunction, whereas those with arithmetic, reading, and spelling deficits experience left hemisphere dysfunction. Share, Moffitt, and Silva's (1988) study found similar conclusions for boys and for girls with arithmetic and reading disabilities, but not for girls with solely arithmetic deficits.

TABLE I Abilities and Cortical Regions Associated with Mathematical Competence

Cortical region	Ability
Right hemisphere	Visual–spatial organization
Language-dominant hemisphere	Linguistic skills
Higher association areas of the dominant hemisphere	Reading and understanding word problems, understanding mathematical concepts and procedures
Frontal lobes	Quick mental calculations, abstract conceptualizng , problem-solving skills, oral and written performance
Parietal lobes	Motoric functions, use of tactile sensations
Left parietal lobe	Sequencing abilities
Occipital lobes	Visual discrimination of written mathematical symbols
Temporal lobes	Auditory perception, long-term verbal memory
Dominant temporal lobe	Memory of series, basic math facts, subvocalization during problem solving

C. Summary

It is necessary to evaluate the relationship between each of these component skills or processes and math performance singly to determine that deficits in the process do occur with poor mathematics performance; Hartje's (1987) review of spatial disorders, Siegel and Ryan's studies on memory skills (1988, 1989; Siegel & Linder, 1984), and Seron and Deloche's (1987) work on verbal skills represent such examinations of particular abilities. But, adding to the difficulties of parsing out such connections between specific neuropsychological deficits and underlying neuroanatomical dysfunctions is the likelihood, given the nature of mathematical tasks, that performance relies on a complex interaction or interplay of these various processes (Grunau & Low, 1987; Novick & Arnold, 1988).

For example, Grunau and Low (1987) collected cognitive measures (e.g., WISC-R subtests, Bender Visual Motor Gestalt Test, Porteus Maze, and Embedded Figures, among others) and task-related EEG activity data on a sample of adolescents. They used these measures in a stepwise discriminant analysis to classify those youth who performed below the median and those who performed at or above the median on arithmetic computation, concepts, and applications achievement tests. The spatial visualization and visual–motor coordination tasks distinguished the performances of the two groups on the calculation test; the EEG data indirectly suggested that calculation performance was not lateralized. Only the measure of figure–ground perception classified the groups on the arithmetic concepts test. Measures of spatial visualization, verbal ability, attention to visual detail, and motor balance predicted group membership on the applications test. Skills across different areas, some of which are and others which are not intuitively linked to the tasks, showed relationships to mathematical performance.

Research designs that can consider patterns or relationships among the component skills and processes will more closely match the interplay of these components during math performance. Designs that can find different types of patterns of these components will also better fit the heterogeneity of the learning-disabled population (McKinney, 1988; Nolan, Hammeke, & Barkley, 1983; Rourke, 1985; Satz & Morris, 1981). Subtyping designs meet both of these needs (Keller, 1988).

IV. Mathematically Related Subtypes of Learning-Disabled Students from a Neuropsychological Perspective

Emphases in subtyping research parallel the emphases found in learning disabilities research in general. A reading of major reviews on learning disabilities subtyping research indicates that studies involving reading or language disabilities are much more prevalent than subtyping studies investigating mathematics disabilities (McKinney, 1988; Rourke, 1985; Satz & Morris, 1981). Some research from a neuropsychological perspective has investigated patterns of performance on component skills and processes in samples of individuals with learning disabilities in mathematics. (For other math disabilities subtyping studies, see Cawley, Fitzmaurice, Shaw, Kahn, & Bates, 1979, and Keller, 1988.) The results of these subtyping studies provide insight on questions of the diversity of the math-disabled population and of the hypothesized brain–behavior connections in such disabilities.

A. Empirically Derived Subtypes

Spreen and Haaf (1986) cluster analyzed samples of individuals with learning disabilities in childhood (mean age of 10) and 15 years later using a set of achievement measures, subtests of intelligence tests, and neuropsychological measures, such as tests of right–left orientation, the Halstead Category Test, and the Purdue Pegboard. They were interested in determining how the subtypes would compare to those found by previous researchers, particularly whether the subtypes would represent reading disabilities solely or more general deficits. They also considered whether the same sample of learning-disabled individuals would produce similar subtypes in childhood and adulthood.

For one sample of learning-disabled children, Spreen and Haaf found six clusters: (1) one showed minimal impairment on all of the measures; (2) another had severely impaired performance on all of the measures; (3) two clusters had deficits in reading, spelling, and math, but with different patterns on the intelligence subtests and neuropsychological measures, one suggesting visual–perceptual deficits and the other linguistic problems; (4) one represented a reading disability; and (5) the last showed an arithmetic disability (the mean WRAT arithmetic score for the subtype was low relative to the other mean achievement scores).

A second sample of learning-disabled children produced a similar set of subtypes, though with the addition of a second reading disability cluster and a third cluster impaired in all achievement areas. Some subjects from the two childhood samples comprised the adult sample about 15 years later, along with some controls matched for age, gender, and socioeconomic status. A cluster analysis of the adult sample produced 9 clusters which tended to represent the clusters found at the younger ages, including the arithmetic disability subtype. Of the 11 individuals in the arithmetic disability cluster of the first sample, 6 were placed in the same type of cluster in adulthood.

Spreen and Haaf's study shows that within heterogeneous samples of learning-disabled individuals, some subtypes will evidence disabilities in mathematics relative to adequate performance in other achievement areas (similar to primary acalculia), some subtypes will show deficits in math along with deficits in other academic areas (analogous to the secondary acalculias), and some subtypes will show adequate math performance, either with or without disabilities in other achievement areas. Their study also shows that there is some consistency or stability in these subtypes over time; not only were there similar sets of subtypes at both ages but individuals were often placed in the same subtypes at both ages.

Other neuropsychological researchers have focused more specifically on mathematically related subtypes of learning-disabled individuals. Ackerman, Anhalt, and Dykman (1986) presented findings from two cluster analyses as part of a review of evidence suggesting a greater prevalence of math difficulties, especially in terms of automatization of skills, in individuals with either reading disabilities or attention deficits. In one cluster analysis, using adolescents with learning disabilities as subjects and WRAT subtest scores and WISC factor scores (verbal, spatial, and the ACID pattern consisting of the Arithmetic, Coding, Information, and Digit Span subtests) as clustering variables, Ackerman and her colleagues interpreted three subtypes as arithmetic-disabled and two as arithmetic adequate. Two of the arithmetic-disabled subtypes showed patterns on the WISC factors similar to each other, though different in degree; scores on the ACID and spatial factors were lower than scores on the verbal factor. In both of these subtypes, arithmetic scores were lower than reading scores. The other three subtypes, one arithmetic-disabled and two arithmetic adequate, had patterns on the WISC factors similar to each other, though again, different in degree: The ACID factor score was lowest, the verbal score was higher, and the spatial score was highest. For two of these subtypes, arithmetic achievement scores were equal to reading scores. Ackerman *et al.* did not interpret the differences, which seem minimal in terms of shape and degree, in the cluster patterns of WISC factors.

Ackerman *et al.*'s second cluster analysis (1986), this time using adults with learning disabilities as subjects and WRAT subtests and subtests from the Wechsler Adult Intelligence Scale (WAIS) as clustering variables, produced similar results. The pattern of performance on the WAIS subtests for the cluster of subjects whose arithmetic scores were lower than their reading scores was for the most part identical in shape, though not in degree, to the patterns for the other two subtypes (both of which had arithmetic scores similar to reading scores but the two sets of scores were different in degree of deficits).

B. Conceptually Derived Subtypes

A study by Nolan and his colleagues (1983) also examined patterns of performance on WISC-R subtests, the Luria–Nebraska Neuropsychological Battery, and some tests of tactile perceptions from the Halstead–Reitan Neuropsychological Test Battery for subtypes of learning-disabled children.

The methodology for this study was slightly different, as the three subtypes— a group with no achievement deficits, a subtype with low achievement in reading and spelling only, and a group with low math achievement only— were conceptually derived, that is, the researchers grouped subjects a priori in ways relevant to their research questions (McKinney, 1988); here the question centered on differences in the neuropsychological profiles for these particular groups. In contrast, the studies by Ackerman *et al.* (1986) and Spreen and Haaf (1986) used empirically derived subtypes, that is, subtypes that were formed on the basis of statistical procedures (McKinney, 1988).

Mean WISC-R subtest scaled scores were plotted for the three subtypes and differences among the groups on each subtest were tested separately with ANCOVAs (full-scale IQ, on which the groups differed, served as the covariate) and follow-up pairwise comparisons. There were group differences only on the Information and Arithmetic subtests. On the Luria–Nebraska scales, differences among the three subtypes were found only on the expressive speech, writing, and reading scales. There were no differences among the groups on the tactile perception tests used from the Halstead–Reitan Battery. The authors concluded that their results provided partial support for the theory that different types of learning-disabled children have different neuropsychological profiles, that support being from a different profile for the reading/spelling-disabled subtype relative to the other two groups.

A set of studies by Rourke, Strang, and their colleagues, though, has found different patterns of abilities for arithmetic-disability subtypes and has provided initial efforts at validating the subtypes in educationally useful ways. These researchers used three conceptually derived subtypes of learning-disabled students, ages 9 to 14: Members of one subtype had low achievement on all of the WRAT subtests (Group 1), individuals in another group had low WRAT reading and spelling scores relative to their arithmetic scores (Group 2), and individuals in the final subtype had low arithmetic scores relative to their reading and spelling scores (Group 3). The mean arithmetic scores for these last two subtypes, however, were virtually the same. The researchers then looked for different patterns of scores among the three subtypes on different sets of measures of neuropsychological abilities.

In Rourke and Finlayson (1978), the groups were compared on measures of (1) verbal and auditory–perceptual abilities, and (2) visual–perceptual and visual–spatial abilities from WISC-R subtest scores and a variety of other instruments. Groups 1 and 2 had similar patterns on both sets of measures: low on the verbal and auditory–perceptual measures and high on the visual–perceptual and visual–spatial measures. Group 3 showed the opposite pattern, namely, high scores on the verbal and auditory–perceptual measures and low scores on the visual–perceptual and visual–spatial measures. [Ozols and Rourke (1988) replicated these findings with a sample of 7- to 8-year-old learning-disabled children.]

Rourke and Strang (1978) compared the same subtypes of students on 13 measures of motor, psychomotor, and tactile–perceptual abilities, considering separately performance with the right hand, the left hand, and both hands together. They found no differences among the groups on the measures of motor abilities, while Groups 1 and 2 performed better than Group 3 on the psychomotor tasks. The groups differed in performance on the tactile–perceptual measure by the hand used for the tasks; students in Groups 1 and 3 tended to perform better with their right hands relative to their left hands, while Group 2 showed the opposite pattern.

Strang and Rourke (1983) compared the performances of just Groups 2 and 3 in terms of the numbers of errors made on the Halstead Category Test, an instrument designed to assess concept-formation and nonverbal reasoning abilities. Children in Group 2 made more errors than the students in Group 3 on two of the six subtests and on the total number of errors.

Strang and Rourke (1985b) summarized the adaptive behavior characteristics of learning-disabled individuals who exhibit the Group 3 pattern of performance on these neuropsychological measures, a pattern which they name as a " 'nonverbal perceptual–organizational-output disability' " (p. 307). Using data sources such as short- and long-term investigations of individuals with this pattern of abilities, cross-sectional studies, comparisons with the adaptive behavior characteristics of other subtypes, and analyses of case histories, they found that generally such individuals have difficulties dealing with novel situations and with changes, appear clumsy, have few close friends, are talkative, and misunderstand and do not use appropriately nonverbal communicative behaviors. In a similar vein, Ozols and Rourke (1985) found that subtypes of learning-disabled children varied on their performance of social sensitivity tasks requiring verbal and nonverbal responses in ways predicted by their patterns of performance on linguistic and visual–spatial measures.

Rourke and Strang (1983; Strang & Rourke, 1985a) also reported differences in the errors made by Groups 2 and 3 during math performance. Errors from the students' WRAT Arithmetic subtests were qualitatively analyzed. Children in Group 2 tended to make (1) fewer errors, (2) fewer different types of errors, and (3) fewer errors the researchers judged to be related to judgment and reasoning (Strang & Rourke, 1985a). Group 3 students, by contrast, made more errors and types of errors. Strang and Rourke (1985a) described seven overlapping categories of errors for Group 3 children: spatial organization, visual detail, procedural errors, failure to shift psychological set, graphomotor, memory, and judgment and reasoning. The authors felt that the results of the error analyses fit the patterns of performance on the neuropsychological measures. The error analyses also provided educational validation for these two subtypes: Despite having similar levels of achievement in mathematics, two conceptually identified subtypes showed differences both in patterns of neuropsychological abilities and in types of arithmetic errors.

The set of findings across these studies, especially for the contrasts between Groups 2 and 3, fits with the hypothesis that the localization of the specific mathematics disability of Group 3 is in the right cerebral hemisphere (Strang & Rourke, 1985a). Share *et al.* (1988) investigated the validity of this conclusion when gender was taken into account and when comparison to a nondisabled sample was provided. Though using different measures of the same neuropsychological abilities and different procedures for forming their subtypes, Share and his colleagues found support for the differential patterns in abilities between Groups 2 and 3 for boys, but not for girls. They also did not find nonverbal deficits (when compared to the nondisabled control group) in the girls' Group 3. Thus, gender differences may be worth examining in the findings from Rourke, Strang, and their colleagues.

C. Summary

Considered together, the neuropsychological subtyping studies involving the mathematics performance of individuals with learning disabilities at first seem to provide mixed support for the differentiation of mathematics-disability subtypes from the rest of the learning-disabled population on the basis of anything other than low math performance. The studies by Ackerman *et al.* (1986) and Nolan *et al.* (1983) (also Cawley *et al.*, 1979) do not show major differences in the shape or severity of the patterns of the variables investigated among subtypes with mathematics deficits and between such subtypes and subtypes without math difficulties. However, Spreen and Haaf's study (1986) shows that a mathematics-disability subtype (1) is separate from other subtypes, (2) has a pattern of performance on neuropsychological measures different from any other subtype, (3) shows stability over time, and (4) has somewhat consistent membership over time. The series of studies by Rourke and his colleagues shows that (1) learning-disabled students with arithmetic deficits can be classified into different subtypes based on the relationship of achievement scores; (2) such subtypes have different patterns of performance on neuropsychological variables; (3) these patterns support one neuropsychological theory about what would be expected; and (4) these subtypes are educationally relevant as each group makes different types and quantities of math performance errors. We believe a stronger case is made for the heterogeneous presence of math-disability subtypes than against them.

As a whole, these studies have many methodological weaknesses. The measures used are often of unknown quality psychometrically or of known poor quality. Information necessary to judge and understand the results of the cluster analyses (Blashfield, 1980) is not always reported. Group differences on numbers of measures within a study are tested with ANOVAs or AN-COVAs without, at least, correcting the alpha level for the multiple tests (e.g., Nolan *et al.*, 1983; Rourke & Finalyson, 1978; Rourke & Strang, 1978; Strang & Rourke, 1983).

The researchers do not externally validate the subtypes—that is, show the meaningfulness of subtype differences outside of differences on the subtyping measures—except in the set of studies by Rourke, Strang, and their colleagues. Important details about this validation procedure are missing though. Rourke and Strang (1983; Strang & Rourke, 1985a) do not describe the rules or hierarchical procedures used to classify the errors. They do not provide any figures on interrater agreement, which are important given the subjective nature of the task. They also do not indicate whether the error analysis was performed by someone "blind" to the information about an individual's subtype membership. Despite these limitations, though, the validation efforts by Strang and Rourke do represent an important effort to provide educationally and mathematically useful information about the subtypes they are proposing.

V. Summary of Mathematics Disorders

Although the use of terminology and definitions is varied and sometimes confusing, there is consistency in the neuropsychological literature about the phenomena of individuals who are unable to perform mathematical tasks successfully if one considers primarily the dimensions of the definitions and descriptions. There is also a fair amount of consistency about the deficits in component abilities and processes, along with their presumed cortical localizations, that may result in math disabilities as long as one is willing to accept heterogeneity in the population of individuals with math disorders, an assumption we think is warranted. Thus, on one hand, we see the neuropsychological literature on learning disabilities in mathematics as stronger than it has been characterized (e.g., Fletcher & Loveland, 1986; Gurney, 1983).

On the other hand, though, we find fault with the mathematical content of much of the neuropsychological work on mathematics disorders for four main reasons. First, the mathematical content is mathematically naive, simplistic, or inaccurate at times. Glennon and Cruickshank (1981), for example, note that one of Kosc's symptoms for operational dyscalculia (1974), that is, using fingers in the mental or written solution of problems, is developmentally and mathematically appropriate in some situations. Novick and Arnold (1988), in describing subskills involved in calculation, list "number comprehension and counting" (p. 136). What understandings of numbers and quantities and what particular counting skills are needed though? As Spiers (1987) discusses calculation, he states, "There are only four operations possible and the component steps of each operation are clearly specified. There can be no rule-exceptions to the 'grammar' of these operations without the production of an incorrect or unacceptable result" (p. 14). Although there is more, though not complete, validity to his statements when considering solely the standard algorithms for the four operations, the statements do not hold entirely, as there are variations in algorithms for the operations that will produce correct answers.

Second, the mathematics as described has limited educational utility. If deficits in component neuropsychological abilities and processes do relate to mathematical performance, research has shown that interventions which train these abilities do not consequently produce improvements in academic performance (Arter & Jenkins, 1979; Lloyd, 1984). Strang and Rourke's (1985a) error categories for their specific arithmetic-disability subtype— spatial organization, visual detail, procedural errors, failure to shift psychological set, graphomotor, memory, and judgment and reasoning—tell us little about the mathematical understanding these students have and the mathematical content on which their teachers should focus.

Third, the mathematical performances described at behavioral levels in much of the neuropsychological literature are often used as indicators of underlying ability or process deficits. Yet the behavioral descriptions are frequently unvalidated and sufficiently general to allow for the possibility of competing neurological explanations. For example, Strang and Rourke's (1985a) error analyses suggest the misalignment of numbers in columns is a type of spatial organization error, suggesting a spatial deficit. Another of their categories, graphomotor, which would indicate visual–motor difficulties, includes errors caused by large, poorly formed numbers. Such numbers, though, would also frequently lead to the misalignment of numbers. What type of processing problem would be indicated by such performance behavior? (Validation of the procedures used to classify math behaviors and error analyses would help to address such difficulties.) In addition, not only are there competing neurological explanations to these mathematical behaviors, there are also mathematical explanations that are often not considered. For one positive example, Hartje (1987) lists spatial disorders which may interfere with written calculation to produce certain types of errors, yet cautions against a one-to-one correspondence between the disorders and the errors because the errors could also be due to an incorrect or incomplete understanding of the number system.

And fourth, there is limited construct validity in relying solely on a neuropsychological explanation of mathematics disorders. How do deficits in neuropsychological processes and abilities cause disabilities in math? Why do deficits in some processes, say visual–motor skills, sometimes result in problems with mathematics and other times do not? Mechanisms must intervene between these abilities and performance in order for performance to be adversely affected by deficits in the abilities (Briars, 1983). And these mechanisms must account for the mathematical part of math performance. Instead of simply brain–behavior connections, neuropsychology should consider brain–cognition–behavior connections.

Cognitive psychology from an information-processing perspective and mathematics education provide a body of work that can (1) supply important components, such as error analyses, normative comparison data, and theoretical concepts about calculation, that are missing in the study of acalculia (Spiers, 1987), and (2) also address the mathematical shortcomings of neuropsychological research on mathematics disabilities. Some neuropsychological investigators have begun to utilize these combined perspectives in their studies.

VI. Contributions of a Cognitive Perspective

A. Cognitive Perspective

Cognitive psychologists from an information-processing perspective and mathematics educators have investigated (1) the cognitive demands of mathematical tasks, and (2) individuals' internal representations of knowledge and the strategies they use on those representations to meet such cognitive demands during performance (cf. T. R. Carpenter, Moser, & Romberg, 1982; Ginsburg, 1982; Hiebert, 1986; Lesh & Landau, 1983; Pellegrino & Goldman, 1987; Resnick & Ford, 1981; Romberg & Carpenter, 1986; Schoenfeld, 1987). Their work has produced, for example, (1) cognitively oriented theoretical frameworks for individual differences in mathematics (Briars, 1983; Resnick & Neches, 1984; Sternberg, 1984, 1985; see Keller & Lloyd, 1989, for a summary of these frameworks), (2) validated models of solving word problems (Briars & Larkin, 1984; Kintsch & Greeno, 1985), and (3) detailed accounts of the development of strategies to solve simple addition problems (cf. Keller & Lloyd, 1989, and Pellegrino & Goldman, 1987, for reviews of this research).

Siegler and Shrager's (1984) distribution of associations model provides one example of the type of work on mathematics coming from this perspective. Siegler and Shrager's model was designed to explain how and why a child uses different solution strategies to solve particular addition fact problems. According to their model, potential answers for each child have different probabilities of being the correct solution to the problems; these probabilities represent associative strengths between the problems and the answers. The child sets two parameters when solving addition problems: (1) a confidence criterion for judging associative strengths to determine when a generated solution should be accepted, and (2) the number of times the child will use a particular addition strategy (e.g., recall, counting, modeling) when solving the problem. The model posits that the child uses the most efficient strategies first and later uses less efficient strategies if the answers generated do not meet the confidence criterion. The model's predictions about relations among problems and possible answer associations, errors, latencies, and observable strategy use were supported in two experiments (Siegler & Robinson, 1982; Siegler & Shrager, 1984).

B. Cognitive and Neuropsychological Perspectives Combined

We are not the first to suggest that results from a cognitive perspective can play integral parts in the investigations of neuropsychologists. Deloche and Seron (1987) edited a book summarizing a variety of research programs that blend the two perspectives. Two of the lines of research that stand out as particularly strong examples are Seron and Deloche's work on the counting sequences of aphasics and children (1987) and Warrington's comprehensive case study of an individual with impaired calculation abilities (1987).

Seron and Deloche (1987) analyzed the production of counting sequences by aphasics according to cognitive models of number–sequence development. They examined the linguistic difficulties of these individuals in the task of producing counting sequences orally, with written digits, and with written words, a more typically neuropsychological analysis. But they also analyzed how the aphasics' difficulties affected the content of those sequences, which form an important foundation for other quantitative knowledge and skills. Their study highlights the lexical aspects involved in the development and understanding of counting sequence abilities. It also suggests the need for direct examination of how problems recalling and/or using number-word sequences might contribute to number-processing difficulties in some forms of acalculia.

Warrington's (1987) excellent description of her investigation of an individual with selected calculation impairments and dysphasia included a medical history, psychological test results, an assessment of the component parts of calculation skills, and comparisons to normative data on calculation skills. She tested the components of computation according to cognitive models of calculation skills to show what knowledge her patient still had about computation and what processes were impaired, thus affecting his performance. She argued convincingly, based on Groen and Parkman's (1972) chronometric retrieval-counting model for how basic addition facts are solved, that her subject's access to "the semantic entries of arithmetical facts" (p. 252) was impaired rather than that knowledge itself. He was "using the same processing strategies as a normal adult, the crucial difference being that the proportion of access failures . . . [was] much greater" (p. 253). Thus, instead of simply explaining her patient's calculation difficulties in general ways (e.g., his language difficulties impaired his ability to solve calculation problems), Warrington provided a more specific pinpointing of the math disability, one that interfaced the person's language deficits with the cognitive knowledge and process demands of the task.

C. Summary

The work of Seron and Deloche (1987) and Warrington (1987) are just two examples of the ways neuropsychology and cognitive psychology can be combined in the study of mathematics disabilities; Deloche and Seron's (1987) volume presents other research combining these two perspectives and undoubtedly more investigators will follow this direction. But what are the impediments to combining these perspectives successfully? We consider some in our concluding remarks.

VII. Conclusions and Implications

Neuropsychology has contributed much to the investigation and understanding of individuals with mathematics disabilities; but alone, in our opinion, it can only go so far in providing both a complete understanding of those individuals and information that is educationally useful. Research that includes a cognitive psychology perspective and its findings about mathematical knowledge and processes offers the possibility of providing more complete and educationally relevant findings. Indeed, each perspective adds an understanding of parts of the process of performing mathematical tasks that the other neglects.

But we think several concerns need examination for the combination of neuropsychological and cognitive perspectives to be successful. First, can these two perspectives really be merged? Are their underlying assumptions too disparate or even antithetical? If so, the combination of perspectives may result in research that is eclectic in the worst sense and not accepted by either discipline.

Second, how should the two approaches be combined? Are there ways of examining the understandings, processes, and errors during mathematics that are theoretically meaningful to both neuropsychology and cognitive psychology? Spiers (1987), for example, calls for error analyses in math-disabilities research that show a relationship to the central nervous system. Rather than the typical kinds of analyses that logically link errors to neuropsychological processes on the basis of descriptive similarities, we would suggest alternatively the need for a connection between error analyses and a sound cognitive psychology model. Then empirical compilations of types of errors, relating to changes or differences in conceptual and procedural knowledge, could be related to central nervous system theory. One problem with this suggestion, though, is that there is not a strong literature in cognitive psychology on the nature and development of mathematics abilities in learning-disabled individuals; such a literature would provide a stronger start at making behavior–cognition–brain linkages.

And third, how will individuals with mathematics disabilities ultimately benefit from this combined approach? Neuropsychologists, cognitive psychologists, and mathematics educators will increase their understanding of math disabilities. But these professionals will then need to develop and validate interventions based on this understanding that teachers can use to improve the knowledge and skills of learning-disabled individuals. Without increased attention to translating research into researched teaching practices, the gains in the understanding of mathematics disorders that neuropsychology has provided and will continue to provide will be diminished.

References

Ackerman, P. T., Anhalt, J. M., & Dykman, R. A. (1986). Arithmetic automatization failure in children with attention and reading disorders: Associations and sequela. *Journal of Learning Disabilities, 19*, 222–232.

Arter, J. A., & Jenkins, J. R. (1979). Differential diagnosis-prescriptive teaching: A critical appraisal. *Review of Educational Research, 49*, 517–555.

Benton, A. L. (1987). Mathematical disability and the Gerstmann syndrome. In G. Deloche & X. Seron (Eds.), *Mathematical disabilities: A cognitive neuropsychological perspective* (pp. 111–120). Hillsdale, NJ: Erlbaum.

Blashfield, R. K. (1980). Propositions regarding the use of cluster analysis in clinical research. *Journal of Consulting and Clinical Psychology, 48*, 456–459.

Briars, D. J. (1983). An information-processing analysis of mathematical ability. In R. F. Dillon & R. R. Schmeck (Eds.), *Individual differences in cognition* (Vol. 1, pp. 181–204). New York: Academic Press.

Briars, D. J., & Larkin, J. H. (1984). An integrated model of skill in solving elementary word problems. *Cognition and Instruction, 1*, 245–296.

Carpenter, R. L. (1985). Mathematics instruction in resource rooms: Instruction time and teacher competence. *Learning Disability Quarterly, 8*, 95–100.

Carpenter, T. R., Moser, J. M., & Romberg, T. A. (Eds.). (1982). *Addition and subtraction: A cognitive approach*. Hillsdale, NJ: Erlbaum.

Cawley, J. F., Fitzmaurice, A. M., Shaw, R., Kahn, H., & Bates, H., III. (1979). LD youth and mathematics: A review of characteristics. *Learning Disability Quarterly, 2*, 29–44.

Clements, S. D. (Project Director). (1966). *Minimal brain dysfunction in children* (National Institute of Neurological Diseases and Blindness Monograph No. 3). Washington, DC: U.S. Department of Health, Education, and Welfare.

Deloche, G., & Seron, X. (Eds.). (1987). *Mathematical disabilities: A cognitive neuropsychological perspective*. Hillsdale, NJ: Erlbaum.

Flavell, J. H. (1985). *Cognitive development* (2nd ed.). Englewood Cliffs, NJ: Prentice-Hall.

Fletcher, J. M., & Loveland, K. A. (1986). Neuropsychology of arithmetic disabilities in children. *Focus on Learning Problems in Mathematics, 8*, 23–40.

Gaddes, W. H. (1985). *Learning disabilities and brain function: A neuropsychological approach* (2nd ed.). New York: Springer-Verlag.

Gelman, R. (1978). Cognitive development. *Annual Review of Psychology, 29*, 297–332.

Ginsburg, H. P. (Ed.). (1982). *The development of mathematical thinking*. New York: Academic Press.

Glennon, V. J., & Cruickshank, W. M. (1981). Teaching mathematics to children and youth with perceptual and cognitive processing deficits. In V. J. Glennon (Ed.), *The mathematical education of exceptional children and youth* (pp. 50–94). Reston, VA: National Council of Teachers of Mathematics.

Groen, G., & Parkman, J. M. (1972). A chronometric analysis of simple addition. *Psychological Review, 79*, 329–343.

Grunau, R. V. E., & Low, M. D. (1987). Cognitive and task-related EEG correlates of arithmetic performance in adolescents. *Journal of Clinical and Experimental Neuropsychology, 9*, 563–574.

Gurney, R. (1983). The early detection of specific mathematical disabilities. *Cambridge Journal of Education, 13*, 28–32.

Hallahan, D. P., Kauffman, J. M., & Lloyd, J. W. (1985). *Introduction to learning disabilities* (2nd ed.). Englewood Cliffs, NJ: Prentice-Hall.

Hartje, W. (1987). The effect of spatial disorders on arithmetical skills. In G. Deloche & X. Seron (Eds.), *Mathematical disabilities: A cognitive neuropsychological perspective* (pp. 121–135). Hillsdale, NJ: Erlbaum.

Hiebert, J. (Ed.). (1986). *Conceptual and procedural knowledge: The case of mathematics*. Hillsdale, NJ: Erlbaum.

Keller, C. E. (1988). *Subtypes of learning-disabled students classified on the basis of cognitive processes comprising math performance*. Unpublished doctoral dissertation, University of Virginia, Charlottesville.

Keller, C. E., & Lloyd, J. W. (1989). Cognitive training: Implications for arithmetic instruction. In J. N. Hughes & R. J. Hall (Eds.), *Cognitive behavioral psychology in the schools: A comprehensive handbook* (pp. 280–304). New York: Guilford Press.

Kintsch, W., & Greeno, J. G. (1985). Understanding and solving word arithmetic problems. *Psychological Review, 92*, 109–129.

Kosc, L. (1974). Developmental dyscalculia. *Journal of Learning Disabilities, 7*, 164–177.

Lesh, R., & Landau, M. (Eds.). (1983). *Acquisition of mathematics concepts and processes*. New York: Academic Press.

Lloyd, J. W. (1984). How should we individualize instruction—or should we? *Remedial and Special Education, 5*(1), 7–16.

McKinney, J. D. (1988). Research on conceptually and empirically derived subtypes of specific learning disabilities. In M. C. Wang, H. J. Walberg, & M. C. Reynolds

(Eds.), *The handbook of special education: Research and practice* (pp. 268–282). Oxford: Pergamon.

McLeod, T. M., & Armstrong, S. W. (1982). Learning disabilities in mathematics— skill deficits and remedial approaches at the intermediate and secondary level. *Learning Disability Quarterly, 5,* 305–311.

Nolan, D. R., Hammeke, T. A., & Barkley, R. A. (1983). A comparison of the patterns of the neuropsychological performance in two groups of learning disabled children. *Journal of Clinical Child Psychology, 12*(1), 22–27.

Norman, C. A., & Zigmond, N. (1980). Characteristics of children labeled and served as learning disabled in school systems affiliated with Child Service Demonstration Centers. *Journal of Learning Disabilities, 13,* 542–547.

Novick, B. Z., & Arnold, M. M. (1988). *Fundamentals of clinical child neuropsychology.* Philadelphia, PA: Grune & Stratton.

Ornstein, A. C., & Levine, D. U. (1989). *Foundations of education* (4th ed.). Boston, MA: Houghton-Mifflin.

Ozols, E. J., & Rourke, B. P. (1985). Dimensions of social sensitivity in two types of learning-disabled children. In B. P. Rourke (Ed.), *Neuropsychology of learning disabilities: Essentials of subtype analysis* (pp. 281–301). New York: Guilford Press.

Ozols, E. J., & Rourke, B. P. (1988). Characteristics of young learning-disabled children classified according to patterns of academic achievement: Auditory-perceptual and visual-perceptual abilities. *Journal of Clinical Child Psychology, 17,* 44–52.

Pellegrino, J. W., & Goldman, S. R. (1987). Information processing and elementary mathematics. *Journal of Learning Disabilities, 20,* 23–32, 57.

Resnick, L. B., & Ford, W. W. (1981). *The psychology of mathematics for instruction.* Hillsdale, NJ: Erlbaum.

Resnick, L. B., & Neches, R. (1984). Factors affecting individual differences in learning ability. In R. J. Sternberg (Ed.), *Advances in the psychology of human intelligence* (Vol. 2, pp. 275–323). Hillsdale, NJ: Erlbaum.

Romberg, T. A., & Carpenter, T. P. (1986). Research on teaching and learning mathematics: Two disciplines of scientific inquiry. In M. C. Wittrock (Ed.), *Handbook of research on teaching* (3rd ed., pp. 850–873). New York: Macmillan.

Rothstein, A., Benjamin, L., Crosby, M., & Eisenstadt, K. (1988). *Learning disorders: An integration of neuropsychological and psychoanalytic considerations.* Madison, CT: International Universities Press.

Rourke, B. P. (Ed.). (1985). *Neuropsychology of learning disabilities: Essentials of subtype analysis.* New York: Guilford Press.

Rourke, B. P., & Finlayson, M. A. J. (1978). Neuropsychological significance of variations in patterns of academic performance: Verbal and visual-spatial abilities. *Journal of Pediatric Psychology, 3,* 62–66.

Rourke, B. P., & Strang, J. D. (1978). Neuropsychological significance of variations in patterns of academic performance: Motor, psychomotor, and tactile perception abilities. *Journal of Pediatric Psychology, 3,* 212–225.

Rourke, B. P., & Strang, J. D. (1983). Subtypes of reading and arithmetical disabilities: A neuropsychological analysis. In M. Rutter (Ed.), *Developmental neuropsychiatry* (pp. 473–488). New York: Guilford Press.

Satz, P., & Morris, R. (1981). Learning disability subtypes: A review. In F. J. Pirozzolo & M. C. Wittrock (Eds.), *Neuropsychological and cognitive processes in reading* (pp. 109–141). New York: Academic Press.

Schoenfeld, A. H. (Ed.). (1987). *Cognitive science and mathematics education*. Hillsdale, NJ: Erlbaum.

Seron, X., & Deloche, G. (1987). The production of counting sequences by aphasics and children: A matter of lexical processing? In G. Deloche & X. Seron (Eds.), *Mathematical disabilities: A cognitive neuropsychological perspective* (pp. 171–200). Hillsdale, NJ: Erlbaum.

Share, D. L., Moffitt, T. E., & Silva, P. A. (1988). Factors associated with arithmetic-and-reading disability and specific arithmetic disability. *Journal of Learning Disabilities, 21,* 313–320.

Sharma, M. C. (1986). Dyscalculia and other learning problems in arithmetic: A historical perspective. *Focus on Learning Problems in Mathematics, 8,* 7–45.

Sharma, M. C., & Loveless, E. J. (1986). The work of Dr. Ladislav Kosc on dyscalculia. *Focus on Learning Problems in Mathematics, 8,* 47–119.

Siegel, L. S., & Linder, B. A. (1984). Short-term memory processes in children with reading and arithmetic learning disabilities. *Developmental Psychology, 20,* 200–207.

Siegel, L. S., & Ryan, E. B. (1988). Development of grammatical-sensitivity, phonological, and short-term memory skills in normally achieving and learning disabled children. *Developmental Psychology, 24,* 28–37.

Siegel, L. S., & Ryan, E. B. (1989). The development of working memory in normally achieving and subtypes of learning disabled children. *Child Development, 60,* 973–980.

Siegler, R. S., & Robinson, M. (1982). The development of numerical understandings. In H. W. Reese & L. P. Lipsitt (Eds.), *Advances in child development and behavior* (Vol. 16, pp. 241–312). New York: Academic Press.

Siegler, R. S., & Shrager, J. (1984). Strategy choices in addition: How do children know what to do? In C. Sophian (Ed.), *Origins of cognitive skills* (pp. 229–293). Hillsdale, NJ: Erlbaum.

Spellacy, F., & Peter, B. (1978). Dyscalculia and elements of the Developmental Gerstmann Syndrome in school children. *Cortex, 14,* 197–206.

Spiers, P. A. (1987). Acalculia revisited: Current issues. In G. Deloche & X. Seron (Eds.), *Mathematical disabilities: A cognitive neuropsychological perspective* (pp. 1–25). Hillsdale, NJ: Erlbaum.

Spreen, O., & Haaf, R. G. (1986). Empirically derived learning disability subtypes: A replication attempt and longitudinal patterns over 15 years. *Journal of Learning Disabilities, 19,* 170–180.

Sternberg, R. J. (1984). Mechanisms of cognitive development: A componential approach. In R. J. Sternberg (Ed.), *Mechanisms of cognitive development* (pp. 163–186). New York: Freeman.

Sternberg, R. J. (1985). *Beyond IQ*. Cambridge: Cambridge University Press.

Strang, J. D., & Rourke, B. P. (1983). Concept-formation/nonverbal reasoning abilities of children who exhibit specific academic problems with arithmetic. *Journal of Clinical Child Psychology, 12,* 33–39.

Strang, J. D., & Rourke, B. P. (1985a). Arithmetic disability subtypes: The neuropsychological significance of specific arithmetical impairment in childhood. In B. P. Rourke (Ed.), *Neuropsychology of learning disabilities: Essentials of subtype analysis* (pp. 167–183). New York: Guilford Press.

Strang, J. D., & Rourke, B. P. (1985b). Adaptive behavior of children who exhibit specific arithmetic disabilities and associated neuropsychological abilities and deficits. In B. P. Rourke (Ed.), *Neuropsychology of learning disabilities: Essentials of subtype analysis* (pp. 302–328). New York: Guilford Press.

Warrington, E. K. (1987). The fractionation of arithmetical skills: A single case study. In G. Deloche & X. Seron (Eds.), *Mathematical disabilities: A cognitive neuropsychological perspective* (pp. 235–256). Hillsdale, NJ: Erlbaum.

Wiederholt, J. L. (1974). Historical perspectives on the education of the learning disabled. In L. Mann & D. A. Sabatino (Eds.), *The second review of special education* (pp. 103–152). Philadelphia, PA: JSE Press.

CHAPTER TWENTY-ONE

Specific Speech and Language Disorders

James W. Montgomery
Jennifer Windsor
Rachel E. Stark

I. Introduction

It is now generally accepted that learning-disabled (LD) individuals are a heterogeneous group [Hammill, Leigh, McNutt, & Larsen, 1981; National Joint Committee on Learning Disabilities (NJCLD), 1982]. Learning-disabled individuals may show varying degrees of difficulty in one or more of several areas of skill development: production and comprehension of spoken language, reading, mathematical ability, and social skills.

Although such specific skill areas can be identified, most current research indicates that an impairment of spoken language (and of the perceptual and motor skills that underlie language) is likely to be a common thread linking these areas (Snyder, 1984; R. E. Stark, Tallal, & McCauley, 1988; Wagner, 1986; but see Kamhi, Catts, Mauer, Apel, & Gentry, 1988, for a different view of the relation between spoken language and reading). Many authors have proposed the notion that a developmental language impairment may be manifested as a learning disability at a later point in development (Aram & Nation, 1980; Maxwell & Wallach, 1984; Wallach & Miller, 1988). Notably, Aram and Nation found that approximately 40% of a group of 63 pre-schoolers diagnosed as language impaired showed difficulties in mathematics

Neuropsychological Foundations of Learning Disabilities, copyright © 1991 by Academic Press Inc. All rights of reproduction in any form reserved.

and reading when they reached elementary school. Also, Roth and Spekman (1986) found that a group of LD children with apparently normal spoken language but impaired reading, written expression, and/or mathematics showed impaired narrative discourse skills relative to children who were developing language normally [hereinafter language-normal (LN) children]. As some authors have suggested (Strominger & Bashir, 1977; Tallal, 1980), it is plausible that the underlying mechanism(s) responsible for language impairment may also be responsible for other learning disabilities.

Estimates of the prevalence of spoken language impairments in the LD population vary. Certainly, such impairments appear to be pervasive. For example, Meier (1971) found that over half of the 284 LD second graders he screened were reported to be unable to correctly recall oral instructions. Approximately 20% of the children were unable to comprehend connected speech, had "immature speech," and showed "errors in oral expression." Semel and Wiig (1975) found that 76% of the 34 LD second to seventh graders they studied scored below the 10th percentile on a measure of receptive language skills; 56% did so on a measure of expressive skills.

One factor that may contribute to apparent differences in prevalence across studies is the terminology employed. A second contributing factor has been the initial lack of clear, agreed-upon definitions of LD and language impairment. The result is that somewhat different populations have been studied by different investigators. A variety of overlapping terms have been used to label children who exhibit a language impairment in the absence of other impairments: developmental dysphasics (e.g., Benton, 1964), developmentally language disordered (e.g., Tallal, 1988), language-learning disabled (e.g., J. Stark & Wallach, 1982), and specifically language impaired (Leonard, 1981; R. E. Stark & Tallal, 1981). The term "language impaired" (LI) will be used here to describe the characteristics of those LD individuals who demonstrate a language impairment.

Many of the linguistic characteristics of LI individuals are well documented and much-needed data detailing the expressive and receptive skills of these individuals are now available (see Tallal, 1988, for a review). In this chapter, we will discuss current proposals about the underlying perceptual and cognitive mechanisms that may be responsible for the characteristics of LI children. Particular attention will be given to the relation between language and reading and to the role of deficient rapid-rate auditory processing and phonological awareness in language and reading impairment.

In the Sections II and III the population of LI individuals will be defined and linguistic characteristics common to these individuals will be outlined. In the Section IV current proposals about causal factors underlying deficient linguistic and nonlinguistic abilities will be examined. In the Section V possible neurological correlates of language impairment will be outlined. In the

Section VI the relation between language and reading impairment will be discussed and implications for intervention summarized.

II. Definitions of Language Impairment

The population of LI individuals has been traditionally defined by exclusion (Tallal, 1988; Wallach & Butler, 1984). That is, those individuals evidencing a language impairment not associated with a primary diagnosis of global developmental delay, personality disorder, hearing impairment, acquired neurological lesion, or structural anomaly of the speech mechanism were considered to be LI individuals. Although this diagnostic approach has proved useful to a limited extent in identification of the population of LI individuals, it fails to describe the broader range of specific characteristics of this population. Information about specific characteristics is more likely to facilitate effective intervention.

It has become clear that the population of LI individuals is better defined in inclusionary terms, that is, through identification and description of the cognitive and linguistic characteristics that are common to LI individuals. Slightly different criteria have been used in defining the population of LI children by different investigators. However, it is generally accepted that LI individuals demonstrate significant deficits in expressive and/or receptive language relative to normal performance in other skill areas, notably in nonverbal cognition.

One of the difficulties encountered in developing an inclusionary definition, however, is the lack of generally agreed upon language measures for preschool children, elementary school children, or older children and adolescents. Language scales comparable to those that have been developed to measure intelligence do not exist. Few standardized tests measure receptive and expressive phonologic, morphologic, semantic, and syntactic abilities within a single instrument. None include pragmatic aspects in addition to purely structural aspects. Children may or may not be identified as language impaired, depending upon the test or tests employed. Attempts have been made to derive language ages by averaging the age-equivalent scores derived from a number of tests. This procedure is highly questionable, however, as the psychometric properties of the instruments employed may vary greatly and some may be more valid and/or reliable than others. In addition, it is not clear what difference in months or years should be required between such a derived language age and chronological age or mental age (e.g., performance or mental age) in order for a child to be identified as language impaired. A disparity of 1 year may have different implications when the child is 4 years of age and when he is 9 years of age.

A better procedure may be to consider the standard deviation derived from the child's score on each of a number of language tests, or to examine derived z scores. Pass–fail criteria may be set up for each test and the child may be required to fail more than one test before being classified as language impaired. Such a procedure has the advantage of enabling the diagnostician to examine the pattern of deficits exhibited by the child who is potentially language impaired, as well as determining the overall severity of the problem. Moreover, information about the pattern of deficits is important to the design of an effective intervention program.

In summary, LI individuals show a language impairment in the presence of normal vision and hearing and normal performance IQ, together with absence of frank neurological signs, obvious sensory or oral motor deficits, and behavioral–emotional problems. In general, definition of language impairment has centered on the use of batteries of standardized tests to determine linguistic and cognitive performance. Psychometric inadequacies of many tests commonly used with preschoolers have been identified (McCauley & Swisher, 1984) and it is clear that test results should be interpreted cautiously. Comparison of z scores to determine if performance on standardized tests is significantly below that expected at a given age level seems a more appropriate procedure (Swisher & Demetras, 1987).

III. Linguistic Characteristics

Although defined by specific criteria, the LI population is not homogeneous with respect to either type or severity of language impairment (Aram, Ekelman, & Nation, 1984; R. E. Stark & Tallal, 1981). Three general subgroups of LI individuals have been proposed. These include individuals with a primarily expressive impairment, those with a primarily receptive impairment, and those with both expressive and receptive impairments (Tallal, 1988). Language-impaired individuals may evidence difficulty in the morphologic, syntactic, semantic, pragmatic, and/or phonologic components of language.

Among other investigators, Snyder (1984) and Tallal (1988) have detailed difficulties that LI children, in general, may show. In brief, with regard to morphology and syntax, there is clear evidence that LI children's morphology is similar to that of LN children's in that the same set of grammatical morphemes (e.g., present progressive -ing, plural -s) is acquired in approximately the same order. However, LI children's acquisition of grammatical morphemes occurs at a later age and slower rate than that of LN peers (Johnston & Schery, 1976; Vogel, 1983). Some data indicate that LI children tend to produce grammatically less complex utterances than do LN children when the mean length of utterance is the same (Johnston & Kamhi, 1984). It has also been shown that LI children produce several syntactic structures less frequently than LN peers (Morehead & Ingram, 1973) and may produce ungrammatical sentences (Lee, 1966).

Leonard (1989), drawing on Pinker's (1984) model of language learnability, has hypothesized that LI children's deficit in grammatical morpheme acquisition may be linked to an impaired ability to perceive those morphemes regarded as being of low phonological substance. In Pinker's model, it is proposed that children acquire morphological distinctions by building paradigms that are formed through the process of perceiving and hypothesizing specific morphemes as particular members of the paradigm. Leonard has suggested that an impaired ability to perceive, and thus to create hypotheses with respect to, these morphemes leads to a deficit in grammatical morpheme knowledge. Moreover, Leonard has suggested that a difficulty with grammatical morphemes may lead to an impaired ability to parse unknown sentences, with consequent slower development in other areas of language development.

Language-impaired children acquire vocabulary items in a manner similar to younger LN children of the same language age (Camarata & Schwartz, 1985; Chapman, Leonard, Rowan, & Weiss, 1983; Schwartz & Leonard, 1985). They show the same range of semantic relations (e.g., agent + action) in their language as peers (Curtiss & Tallal, 1985; Freedman & Carpenter, 1976). Moreover, Dollaghan (1987) found LI and age-matched peers to perform similarly on several fast mapping tasks (i.e., constructing a representation for a novel word after one exposure). The LI children were less likely, however, to produce the complete phonological sequence of the novel word in a recall naming task. Vocabulary of recognition, as assessed by the Peabody Picture Vocabulary Test-Revised (Dunn & Dunn, 1981), is usually at a higher level in LI children than productive vocabulary as measured by the Vocabulary (Definition) Test of the Weschler Intelligence Scale for Children-Revised (WISC-R) (Wechsler, 1974) or the Stanford–Binet Intelligence Scale (Terman & Merrill, 1962), or by confrontation naming tests, for example, Kaplan, Goodglass, and Weintraub's (1983) Boston Naming Test (R. E. Stark, Bernstein, Condino, Bender, & Tallal, 1984). Related findings may be reflected in the works of Johnston and Kamhi (1984) and Curtiss and Tallal (1985), who have shown that some LI children express fewer propositions or ideas in sentences of equivalent length than do LN peers.

Several early investigations into the pragmatic skills of LI children indicated that these children show conversational deficits compared to LN peers. However, as Dudley-Marling (1985) has pointed out, many methodological concerns limit the value of this finding. More recent findings indicate that LI and LN children perform similarly in most respects in conversation. For example, Pearl, Donahue, and Bryan (1981) showed that LD children, in general, performed similarly to their peers in requesting clarification.

Language-impaired children may show less ability to adapt to listener feedback than LN peers (Brinton, Fujiki, & Sonnenberg, 1988) and less ability to change their communication style across listeners than language-age-matched peers (Fey & Leonard, 1984).

It has been suggested that certain cognitive, linguistic, and phonological skills develop in synergy (Camarata & Schwartz, 1985; Schwartz, Leonard, Folger, & Wilcox, 1980). That is, as performance demands increase in one skill area, performance in another may decline. For example, for some LI children, increased syntactic complexity may be associated with decreased accuracy and consistency of speech-sound production (Panagos & Prelock, 1982). In general, LI children's phonological skills are similar to those of younger LN children. That is, they show the same surface phonetic processes and the same underlying phonologic representations as younger children (Leonard, 1985; Shriberg, Kwiatkowski, Best, Hengst, & Terselic-Weber, 1986).

IV. Explaining Language Impairment: Some Proposed Causal Factors

Accumulating evidence suggests that a variety of nonlinguistic processing deficiencies may coexist with language impairment. In this section, some areas of perceptual and cognitive functions are discussed that are related to language and may be implicated in language impairment, namely, (1) nonlinguistic symbolic representational abilities, (2) auditory perceptual processing, and (3) auditory memory functions. Evidence with respect to other areas of cognitive functioning is also reviewed, namely, (1) problem-solving abilities, (2) cognitive style, and (3) metalinguistic skills in these children.

A. Symbolic Representational Abilities

Language-impaired children have traditionally been defined as having normal nonverbal intelligence, as evidenced by their ability to perform within normal limits on standardized nonverbal intelligence tests [e.g., performance subtests of the Weschler Preschool and Primary Scale of Intelligence (Weschler, 1963) and WISC-R (Wechsler, 1974)]. However, this notion has been challenged in light of recent evidence showing that LI children perform more poorly than LN children on a variety of nonstandardized cognitive tasks, many of which presumably require nonlinguistic symbolic abilities (Johnston & Ramstad, 1983; Johnston & Weismer, 1983; Kamhi, 1981; Kamhi, Catts, Koenig, & Lewis, 1984; Savich, 1984). These data have been taken as evidence that LI children suffer from a pervasive symbolic dysfunction.

One symbolic deficiency reported in studies of LI children is related to representational imagery. This imagery requires generation and manipulation of various mental representations of present or absent objects. Language-impaired children have been found to perform poorly on haptic recognition tasks in which blindfolded subjects feel geometric shapes and then choose the picture corresponding to that shape from a closed set (Johnston & Ramstad, 1983; Kamhi, 1981; Kamhi *et al.*, 1984). On imagery tasks requiring similarity judgments regarding the spatial orientation of two figures (i.e., mental rotation), LI children have been reported as slower than LN children although just as accurate in making their judgments (Johnston & Weismer, 1983). Finally, LI children are poorer at predicting future changes in position of an object in space (i.e., anticipatory imagery) (Savich, 1984). From such data, many investigators have concluded that a common symbolic deficit underlies LI children's linguistic and nonlinguistic difficulties.

These studies have not answered certain important questions, namely, (1) are such cognitive deficits related as the cause or the effect of language impairment?, and (2) what specific linguistic abilities (receptive and/or expressive) are influenced by such representational abilities? There is some evidence that a representational deficit may differentially affect receptive and expressive language abilities. Kamhi *et al.* (1984), for example, found that haptic recognition was highly correlated with receptive language abilities, in particular receptive vocabulary, but not with expressive abilities in LI children.

The conclusion that a common symbolic dysfunction underlies LI children's linguistic and nonlinguistic deficits is not shared by all investigators (see Tallal, 1988). First, not all LI children perform poorly on nonverbal tasks. In a haptic recognition experiment, R. E. Stark and Tallal (1980) found that LI and LN children matched for performance IQ did not differ with respect to oral or manual stereognosis. Second, linguistic and nonlinguistic abilities presumably require very different sorts of representations, rules, and computational processes (e.g., Curtiss, 1982). Thus there is no a priori reason to believe that a child impaired in one domain will be impaired in the other. Those who show dual impairments may, in fact, have mixed deficits.

As, by definition, LI children have normal nonverbal intelligence, it is confusing to find that they apparently suffer from subtle cognitive deficits. One possible explanation may be found in the different procedures used by different researchers in selecting LI children. An important component to the diagnosis of language impairment is establishment of a significant discrepancy between linguistic abilities on the one hand and nonverbal abilities as measured by standardized intelligence tests on the other, with linguistic abilities being at the lower level. Such a discrepancy has not always been established. Language-normal and language-impaired subjects have not always been matched on performance IQ prior to experimental testing. The reported group differences in representational abilities may in part be attributable to initial group differences in nonverbal intelligence. When matching of groups on the basis of performance IQ has been carried out, LI and LN children have shown the same degree of variability across performance subtests of the WISC-R (R. E. Stark, Tallal, Kallman, & Mellits, 1983). Even where this matching has been carried out, verbal IQ and full-scale IQ are likely to be lower in LI than in LN children. Verbal reasoning may be adversely affected and, in consequence, representational thinking may be affected also. Better understanding of the developmental relations among symbolic and linguistic processes will be gained when future research takes into account these various factors.

B. Auditory Perceptual Processing

1. SPEECH SOUND PROCESSING

A major finding from neuropsychological research (R. E. Stark & Tallal, 1980; Tallal & Piercy, 1974; Tallal & Stark, 1981; Tallal, Stark, & Mellits, 1985) is that LI children are poorer than LN children in identifying, sequencing, and remembering pairs of synthesized nonmeaningful consonant–vowel syllables. It has been suggested that these auditory perceptual difficulties reflect a rate-processing deficit (i.e., difficulty processing acoustic stimuli that incorporate a series of brief-duration segments or that are presented rapidly in series). Likewise, Elliot and her colleagues (Elliot & Hammer, 1988; Elliot, Hammer, & Scholl, 1989) have shown that LD children also have inferior speech discrimination in relation to nonmeaningful CV syllables. These syllables were distinguished by both temporal voice onset time (e.g., "ba" versus "pa") and temporal–spectral place-of-articulation (e.g., "ba" versus "da" versus "ga") cues. Significantly, both research groups have shown that performance on such auditory perceptual tasks is highly correlated with receptive language abilities in LI and LN children and discriminates the two subject groups with great accuracy.

It also has been argued that LI children may manifest an auditory perceptual learning disorder rather than a more basic, unchanging auditory perceptual deficit. Tomblin and Quinn (1983), in an auditory perceptual learning experiment with LN children, found that perceptual performance of LN children improved with training. However, it is not clear from their data whether the improved performance resulting from training is maintained over time. Certainly, the speech discrimination and sequencing abilities of LI children improve gradually with age even in the absence of special training. Bernstein and Stark (1985), in a follow-up study of 5- to 8-year-old LI children who exhibited auditory perceptual deficits, found that LI and LN subjects performed comparably on the same auditory rate-processing tests after 9 years of age. Despite apparently normal perceptual functioning at the time of follow-up, the LI children nonetheless remained language impaired. Unpublished data suggest that, if more difficult auditory rate–perceptual tasks had been used at time of follow-up, group differences might again have emerged. Elliot and her colleagues have shown that many LD children suffer from persistent "fine-grained" perceptual deficits well into the elementary school years (Elliot & Hammer, 1988; Elliot et al., 1989) and beyond (e.g., Elliot & Busse, 1987).

Despite the converging evidence that many LI and LD children suffer from an auditory rate-processing deficit, it cannot be concluded that language impairment is a direct result of such deficits. Some LN children also perform poorly on these perceptual measures. It may be that auditory perceptual and linguistic disabilities co-occur in LI children and are related to a third variable, that is, a more general information-processing deficit. It is clear, however, that LI children have difficulty with perceptual analysis of speechlike stimuli and that this deficit is highly correlated with receptive language (Tallal et al., 1985). What then might be the relation between this auditory perceptual deficit and higher-level linguistic abilities? This question has not been addressed by means of careful intervention studies.

As previously stated, many LI children show a significant deficiency in the use of grammatical morphemes compared to LN children (Johnston & Kamhi, 1984; Steckol & Leonard, 1979). Those grammatical morphemes that are especially difficult for LI children to acquire (e.g., plural -s, past tense -ed) are of low phonological substance, that is, they are not syllabic or they are unstressed syllables. Thus, these grammatical morphemes are characterized by shorter duration and lower amplitude relative to adjacent syllables in an utterance.

At the syntactic level, LI children do not appear to demonstrate a higher-level sequencing deficit in sentence production analogous to that found in the Tallal and Stark studies (Curtiss & Tallal, in press). That is, they do not produce sentences that violate the typical word-order constraints of English. In addition, LI and LN children do not differ with respect to the developmental progression from simple to complex sentence structures. By contrast, however, LI children do have difficulty in using word-order cues to interpret sentence meaning. These findings might suggest that phonological rather than morphological or syntactic deficits are primary in LI children. On the other hand, phonological and syntactic deficits may both reflect a general difficulty in analyzing the speech stream into component parts, including phonemes, morphemes, syllables, words, and phrases, and in resynthesizing component parts into new entities (syllables, words, and phrases).

Receptive and expressive language may relate differently to rapid-rate auditory processing deficits. Expressive language may be more highly correlated with speech articulation accuracy and rate of production of speech movements than with speech discrimination (R. E. Stark, Tallal, & Mellits, 1985). Two studies have suggested that speech discrimination and speech production capabilities may be related in LI children but in complex ways. R. E. Stark and Tallal (1979) showed that severely language-impaired children had greater-than-normal difficulty in controlling voice onset time in their productions of voiced and voiceless stops. Those who had shown some improvement in their speech discrimination abilities over a 1-year period showed least difficulty with this temporal aspect of speech production.

In a later study, R. E. Stark (1985) found that LI children were comparable to age-matched LN children in their production of stops in a naming task involving familiar words. On an imitation task in which nonmeaningful CVC syllables were presented from audiotape, both groups made stop and fricative errors. However, LI children made significantly more errors on both stops and fricatives than LN children on this imitation task.

2. SENTENCE PROCESSING

Language processing entails more than perceptual analysis of a transient acoustic signal. Comprehension develops through an interaction of lower-level perceptual and higher-level linguistic (e.g., lexical, phonologic, syntactic, semantic, pragmatic, and prosodic) processes. This interaction reflects the real-time nature of comprehension. The few existing developmental data suggest that normal children's comprehension is an interactive process (Montgomery, Scudder, & Moore, 1990; Tyler & Marslen-Wilson, 1981). To date, only one study has examined LI children's real-time language-processing abilities (Montgomery et al., 1990).

Using a word-recognition reaction-time paradigm, Montgomery et al. (in press) found that both normal and LI children used linguistic context to facilitate word recognition during sentence processing, suggesting that sentence processing is an interactive process for LI children also. Despite this overall group similarity, however, the LI children were slower to recognize words in sentences than normal children, suggesting that LI children are less efficient real-time language processors. It is possible that these LI children also had concomitant rate-processing disorders which may have further impeded word recognition. One ramification of LI children's real-time processing deficit may be that, when faced with interpreting unfamiliar language input containing new vocabulary and syntactic structures (e.g., as in language of the classroom), LI children will have difficulty identifying word boundaries and the constituent structures. In addition, LI children may need more time to process incoming speech, otherwise they may not fully process it all. Clearly, such inefficient linguistic processing may impede LI children's academic development.

C. Auditory Memory

Difficulty in encoding, storing, and/or retrieving information can impede learning. Research suggests that LI children have deficits in every major short-term memory (STM) function—stimulus encoding, storage, and retrieval. Most of what is known about LI children's memory abilities comes primarily from recall and naming studies.

Language-impaired children typically have been characterized as having "word-finding" difficulties. Compared to LN peers, LI children perform poorly on confrontation naming tasks (Leonard, Nippold, & Kail, 1983; Wiig, Semel, & Nyström, 1982), recall fewer words from lists, and produce more frequent hesitations, word substitutions, and fillers (e.g., "uh," "you know") during conversation. Such difficulties typically have been thought of as reflecting retrieval deficits.

Word-finding difficulties, however, may arise from deficient lexical storage, retrieval operations, or a combination of the two. Studies attempting to implicate specific retrieval deficits in LI children have yielded mixed results. In a series of experiments by Kail and his colleagues (Kail, Hale, Leonard, & Nippold, 1984; Kail & Leonard, 1986; Leonard et al., 1983) little evidence was found for specific retrieval deficits in LI children. Across a variety of naming and recall tasks, Kail and Leonard (1986) found LI and LN children to be comparable on parameters of word retrieval (e.g., use of semantic category cues, scanning speed). However, group differences emerged on parameters of lexical storage. That is, LI children were less likely than LN children to have stored the input. Kail and Leonard (1986) argued that most LI children's word-finding difficulties are mainly a manifestation of less elaborately represented lexical knowledge and not the result of specific retrieval deficits. Because LI children's lexical acquisition is delayed, words are less richly represented in long-term memory and thus less accessible for immediate retrieval. These data demonstrate how deficits in long-term memory (i.e., lexical memory) can influence STM functioning.

Little is known about LI children's lexical retrieval during comprehension. However, the study by Montgomery et al. (1990) cited previously suggests that LI children's slower word recognition may be related in large part to an on-line retrieval deficit (i.e., slow at retrieving linguistic properties of words during comprehension).

More recent studies directly examining the verbal STM processes in LI children have revealed specific retrieval deficits. Kirchner and Klatzky (1985), using a free-recall task, showed that LI children recalled fewer words, inserted more nonlist but semantically related words in recall, and were less likely to represent words phonologically in memory than LN children. The authors interpreted their findings to suggest that LI children use verbal rehearsal less efficiently and have less capacity to process verbal input than LN children.

These findings imply that LI children have less efficient "controlled" or deliberate processing abilities than LN children. However, the LI and LN children were shown to have comparable "automatic" semantic encoding abilities. These results could also be interpreted as additional support for the notions that LI children (1) represent lexical entries less richly, and (2) show a phonological processing deficit (i.e., poorer encoding and representation of phonological input). In a study examining LI children's memory-scanning speed, Sininger, Klatzky, and Kirchner (1989) showed that severely language-impaired children also demonstrate reduced memory-scanning speed compared to LN children.

Recall of story information has also been shown to be inferior in LI children. Graybeal (1981) showed that LI children recall less information about stories than normal children. Graybeal argued that LI children's story-recall deficit may reflect either deficient encoding or use of less efficient discourse-retrieval strategies.

Short-term recall also seems to depend on such factors as what one knows about the input (Chi, 1978) and what one chooses to attend to (Ceci, 1982), as well as one's ability to consciously invoke storage and retrieval strategies (Kail, 1979). These higher-level functions obscure the traditional memory constructs of "span" or "encoding" (Johnston, 1988). Thus, the poorer auditory memory performance of LI children probably also reflects their difficulty in using various metalinguistic and metacognitive functions. Indeed, LI children have been shown to possess less metalinguistic awareness for various aspects of language than normal children (Kamhi & Koenig, 1985; Kamhi, Lee, & Nelson, 1985; Liles, Schulman, & Bartlett, 1977) and less facility in the controlled and strategic processing of linguistic input (Ceci, 1983). Unfortunately, the available research has not specified a causal relation between LI children's STM and language deficits nor has it determined whether their STM deficits are specific to verbal memory. Future research needs to clarify these issues. Nonetheless, deficient memory and metacognitive abilities may contribute to academic difficulties.

D. Problem Solving

1. HYPOTHESIS TESTING

Language-impaired children are faced with numerous problems requiring the systematic generation and testing of specific solutions. Impairment in hypothesis testing has been regarded as a possible candidate for explaining language impairments to the extent that both abilities require the induction of some rule or solution to a problem. Weak hypothesis testing would certainly place LI children at great risk for learning failure.

Studies of LI children's hypothesis-testing abilities have reported mixed results. Initial studies comparing the nonlinguistic hypothesis-testing abilities of LI and LN children found essentially no group differences (Kamhi *et al.,* 1984; Kamhi, Nelson, Lee, & Gholson, 1985). A more recent study by Nelson, Kamhi, and Apel (1987) examined the role of both explicit and nonexplicit feedback on normal and LI children's hypothesis-testing performance within a discrimination-learning task. Results showed that the LI children performed less well (i.e., solved fewer problems and needed more trials to reach a solution) than the LN controls in both feedback conditions. Significantly, only the LI children benefited from explicit feedback regarding the correct hypothesis. The LN children performed comparably with and without explicit feedback. These findings suggest that LI children's hypothesis-testing difficulties may have stemmed from inefficient encoding of information. Language-impaired children may be less efficient at abstracting and storing the information necessary to solve a problem.

Compared to LN children, LI children have also demonstrated poorer performance on various analogical reasoning tasks requiring application of a sample solution to a new problem. For example, Nippold, Erskine, and Freed (1988) found that LI children were poorer at solving proportional, function, and verbal analogical reasoning problems. In particular, the LI children failed to transfer a modeled solution to a novel but similar problem, whether the problem was mediated linguistically or not, again suggesting difficulty in abstracting the relevant dimensions of a solution.

2. INFERENTIAL CONSTRUCTION PROCESSES

Another problem-solving disability exhibited by LI children is in making inferences. Compared to LN children, LI children demonstrate difficulty making various types of inferences (e.g., spatial and causal) in an attempt to organize and remember information. That is, LI children have difficulty going beyond what is explicitly stated in the input to derive more implicit meanings. Language-impaired children have difficulty making both verbal and nonverbal inferences (Crais & Chapman, 1987), thus demonstrating that deficient inference abilities are not confined to the verbal domain.

Although it might be reasonable to assume that LI children's nonlinguistic problem-solving difficulties are similar to their difficulty in discovering and hypothesizing different language patterns and rules from the ambient language, such an interpretation should be made cautiously. The conscious and controlled processes used in nonlinguistic tasks may be qualitatively very different from the presumably unconscious and automatic comparison processes evoked in language learning. Nevertheless, the question of what factor(s) are involved and whether the same factor(s) are responsible for LI children's difficulty in abstracting nonlinguistic and linguistic information must be asked.

E. Cognitive Style: Nonlinguistic and Linguistic Processing

Differences in cognitive style between LI and LN children have been suggested as a possible factor contributing to language impairment. Available research would suggest that, compared to LN children, LI children have a less reflective cognitive style (Catts, Condino, & Stark, 1982; Condino, 1983) and have less ability to engage in controlled cognitive processing (Ceci, 1982, 1983; Kirchner & Klatsky, 1985).

1. NONLINGUISTIC PROCESSING

Cognitive style (e.g., impulsive versus reflective) may affect the degree to which information is initially processed and subsequently used in solving a problem. Condino (1983) examined the relation between language ability, cognitive style (i.e., impulsivity versus reflectivity), and the processes presumably underlying problem solving (e.g. coding, memory, hypothesis generation, and evaluation and deduction). Condino examined only the first four processes. She found that a greater number of LI than LN children were classified as impulsive, whereas a greater number of LN than LI children were classified as reflective (on the basis of time and accuracy measures). Relative to LN peers, the LI children were also shown to be inferior on the coding, memory, and hypothesis-generation processes in problem solving, particularly coding. The coding process was found to be highly related to language ability and accounted for the group difference on the problem-solving tasks. These data suggest that LI children as a group are more impulsive problem solvers than LN children and possess poorer coding skills. Less efficient coding in turn appears to manifest itself in poorer hypothesis-generation and hypothesis-evaluation abilities. These findings along with others converge to suggest that LI children possess less efficient hypothesis-testing abilities and that this deficit may be related to a more basic coding (Condino, 1983) or encoding deficit (Nelson, Kamhi, & Apel, 1987). Alternatively, impulsivity and coding deficits could be a result of language impairment.

2. LINGUISTIC PROCESSING

Preliminary research findings suggest that LI and LN children are comparable in their automatic processing of relatively simple linguistic material (i.e., requiring limited processing capacity), but that LI children are less efficient than LN peers in controlled and strategic processing (Ceci, 1982, 1983; Kirchner & Klatzky, 1985). Ceci (1983) used an auditory lexical priming/picture-naming task to isolate children's automatic and controlled semantic processing abilities. From the pattern of reaction times across conditions, he inferred that the LI and LN children were similar in their automatic semantic processing abilities. However, the LI children, like younger LN controls, failed to benefit from semantically related primes or could not consciously "expect" a given cue type that would facilitate picture naming. These results suggested that the LI children had difficulty in the controlled aspects of semantic processing. Similarly, Kirchner and Klatzky's (1985) finding that LI children are poorer at using rehearsal to aid recall suggests that LI children have difficulty with the capacity-using, controlled aspects of linguistic processing.

The attentional abilities of LI children have not been widely investigated. However, it has been suggested that attentional deficits commonly co-occur with language impairment (e.g., Denckla, 1982). The specific relation between cognitive style and attentional/controlled processing functions and language impairment has yet to be determined. This relation is undoubtedly complex. For example, it has been found that hyperactive boys with attentional deficits but without language impairment or academic problems may perform poorly on certain tasks involving rapid auditory processing (Ludlow, Cudahy, Bassich, & Brown, 1983).

F. *Metalinguistic Awareness*

Metalinguistic awareness refers to the ability to treat language as an object of thought as opposed to using language directly in comprehension or production. It is the ability to think about the structural properties of language in a decontextualized way. Metalinguistic functioning is sometimes regarded as falling under the general rubric of metacognition—the ability to think about thinking (Flavell, 1979). Metalinguistic awareness coincides roughly with the development of other higher-level cognitive abilities (Franklin, 1981; Hakes, 1982; van Kleeck, 1982).

Compared to LN peers, LI children have been shown to have inferior metalinguistic abilities. For instance, LI children are poorer at detecting and revising syntactic and morphologic errors in sentences (Kamhi & Koenig, 1985; Liles *et al.*, 1977). They also have considerable difficulty with phonological awareness (Kamhi & Koenig, 1985; Kamhi, Lee, & Nelson, 1985). That is, they do not recognize that the speech stream can be analyzed into discrete linguistic units, for example, sentences into words, words into syllables, and syllables into phonemes. Detection of phonemes in the speech stream is especially problematic for LI children.

A more general metalinguistic ability, comprehension monitoring, has also been found to be deficient in LD children (Donahue, 1984; Donahue, Pearl, & Bryan, 1980). Comprehension monitoring refers to the ability to assess one's own state of comprehension. Compared to LN peers, LD children are less active in evaluating their understanding of a speaker's message and less likely to ask for clarification when they do not understand. Very little is known, however, about the comprehension-monitoring skills of LI children. Much debate exists about the role that metalinguistic awareness plays in the everyday language use of the child and to what extent such awareness is used during language acquisition (see Hakes, 1982, for a review). However, metalinguistic skills would appear to play a potentially important role in academic achievement, particularly in learning to read.

V. Neurological Correlates

It is frequently proposed that language impairment in children is related to abnormality or dysgenesis in the left cerebral hemisphere. Findings from the post-mortem studies of Galaburda and his colleagues (Galaburda & Kemper, 1979) have indicated that in adults with extreme and persisting language impairment and dyslexia, posterior lesions in the form of heterotopias are present in the left perisylvian area. It does not necessarily follow that milder forms of language impairment are accompanied by such anomalies.

Instead it has been proposed that language and language-related reading disorders might be related to less-than-optimal size relationships posteriorly in the left and right cerebral hemispheres. It has been demonstrated (Geschwind & Levitsky, 1968; Wada, Clark, & Hamm, 1975) that, in the majority of individuals (approximately 70%), areas of the cortex on the left side, especially the temporal plane, that is, the upper surface of the region of the temporal lobe behind the auditory cortex, are larger than the homologous areas on the right. Of the remainder, approximately 20% of subjects show reversed asymmetry (right temporal plane larger than left) and 10% show a lack of asymmetry. It was soon hypothesized that reversed asymmetry or lack of asymmetry in posterior perisylvian areas might be associated with language and learning disorders in children. The posterior location would accord well with the finding that LI children manifest rate-processing deficits when compared with normal children. However, evidence from CT scan studies in which right and left posterior perisylvian areas were measured in dyslexic and LI children have proved inconclusive (Haslam, Dalby, Johns, & Rademaker, 1981; Rosenberger & Hier, 1980). (See this volume, Chapter 18.)

It should be further noted that Wada *et al.* have reported sex differences with respect to anatomical asymmetries. These authors reported their results in the form of ratios of the length of the right temporal plane to the length of the left temporal plane. This ratio, over all subjects, was less than 1, reflecting the more usual longer plane on the left side. Of the individuals who showed a reversal of this pattern (right plane longer than left), the majority were female. Because there are many more males than females among language- and learning-disabled populations, the Wada *et al.* finding suggests that a predominance of reversed asymmetry in these populations is unlikely. This possibility, however, is being tested in a current study of LI children by Jernigan, Tallal, and colleagues. (P. Tallal, personal communication).

Another approach to the examination of the role of left-hemisphere functioning in LI children has derived from studies of children with known impairment to the left hemisphere. In these studies, the language of children with left and right hemiplegia and of children who have undergone left and right hemispherectomy have been investigated. Studies of carefully selected children who have sustained unilateral brain lesions or complete hemidecortication have shown that (1) right-hemiplegic children perform less well than left-hemiplegic children on measures of syntactic comprehension and formulation, semantic comprehension, and speech production (Rankin, Aram, & Horwitz, 1981); and (2) left-hemispherectomized children have more difficulty with syntactic comprehension and production than right-hemispherectomized children (Dennis, 1980). Although the Dennis study was carried out with a relatively small number of children, this work suggests that syntactic abilities are not as easily acquired by the right hemisphere as by the left. The right hemisphere may adopt different strategies in language learning than the left hemisphere, and these may lead to slower or less complete linguistic development than left-hemisphere strategies (Dennis, 1980; Dennis & Kohn, 1975; Dennis & Whitaker, 1976). In children in whom a malfunctioning left hemisphere is still present, the right hemisphere may be inhibited from making optimal use of compensatory strategies.

What might these findings suggest for LI children who do not show evidence of neurologic deficit or disease of either hemisphere? In many of these children, language impairment is more extensive and severe than in the carefully selected hemispherectomized subjects described above. Their language impairments may be more similar to those of children sustaining bilateral lesions or hemispherectomy in later childhood with greater possibility that the remaining hemisphere has suffered some damage as well.

The finding that LI children manifest attentional deficits (Denckla, 1982; Ludlow *et al.*, 1983) and impulsive behavior on cognitive tasks (Catts *et al.*, 1982; Condino, 1983), taken together with the observation that many LI children are also speech impaired, might suggest a frontal lesion or area of malfunction either bilaterally or in the left hemisphere only, in addition to, or instead of, a posterior deficit. A recent physiological study may provide support for this position. Lou, Henriksen, and Bruhn (1984) reported abnormally reduced regional blood flow (rCBF) bilaterally in 13 LI and/or attentional-deficit-disordered (ADD) children aged 6-1/2 to 15 years. The regions of hypoperfusion were both cortical and subcortical. They were, furthermore, different for different types of language disorder. Children with verbal dyspraxia (severe and persistent speech articulation disorder thought to be of a central nature) showed this anomaly in anterior perisylvian regions. Children with more global receptive and expressive language disorders had both anterior and posterior perisylvian hypoperfusion, while the one subject diagnosed as having verbal agnosia (word deafness) had bilateral posterior perisylvian hypoperfusion (involving cortical and subcortical areas) but normal perfusion in the left anterior perisylvian area. In addition, it is of interest that 11 children with ADD, only 6 of whom were language impaired, showed hypoperfusion of the mesial frontal lobe bilaterally, while the two children without ADD did not.

These findings, while still preliminary, suggest that different locations within the central nervous system may show malfunction in different groups of LI children. Thus, unless careful selection procedures are employed, heterogeneous groups may be included and deficits uncovered that reflect malfunction in central nervous system structures close to those associated with language functions but not necessarily essential to language functions. Associated deficits are certainly important to take into account in language intervention. However, conclusions with respect to causal relationships become all the more risky in studies that do not employ careful subject-selection procedures.

VI. Language Impairment and Reading

Reading is not an activity that is grafted onto spoken language in any simple manner. Reading requires much greater metaphonological awareness than does the comprehension or production of spoken language or of sign language in the deaf child or the hearing child of deaf parents. Humans are biologically well adapted to the learning of these interactive language systems, but not to the acquisition of reading. Reading of text is also a very different activity from speaking or listening. First, it is not an interactive process in the same sense. It must be carried out in the absence of paralinguistic cues and social context. Less ambiguity can be tolerated in written than in spoken text. Second, visual processing takes on a different role in reading and writing, where visual input is primary and static except as it is varied by eye movements, and in listening and speaking, where it is secondary and changes dynamically, at least in face-to-face interaction. Different association areas of the central nervous system are important for reading than for speaking and listening.

Nevertheless, almost all of the characteristics attributed to LI children are to be found in reading-impaired (RI) children also. There is considerable overlap between the two populations (Kamhi & Catts, 1989). This is not to say that all LI children become reading impaired or that all RI children have a history of language impairment. An understanding of the manner in which the characteristics shared by the two populations contribute to language impairment and to reading impairment might clarify the relationship between them. This relationship may be examined from the perspective of reading processes.

Reading is related to two main processes, namely, word recognition and reading comprehension. Available research suggests that much of the variance in reading disorder is attributable to deficits in word recognition (Stanovich, 1985). Reading comprehension also has a powerful influence on reading level. Both may require lower-level automatic skills and higher-level attention-demanding processes.

A. Word Recognition

Word recognition refers to the ability to decode and identify words from written text. For the beginning reader, it involves phonetic recoding and subvocal production of the printed word, except where visual word shapes are taught as a whole in relation to meaning. Certain word-reading and "spelling" tasks, for example, matching printed words from a 2- to 4- item closed set with a picture of an object, or selection of the initial or final letter to complete the printed form of a given familiar word, appear to be less difficult than word recognition, especially in the absence of picture or other word contexts (R. E. Stark, Ansel, & Heinz, in press). It may be that word retrieval is involved to some extent in word recognition, as the child attempts to find a word from his lexicon that matches the phonetic characteristics of the printed form. Word recognition may thus demand some of the same abilities as do naming and word fluency tasks, both of which present difficulty to LI and RI children.

A number of theories have been proposed to account for difficulty with word recognition, all of them relating to deficits in phonological processing (Liberman, Shankweiler, Fischer, & Carter, 1974; Wagner & Torgersen, 1987). Reading-impaired individuals have been reported as deficient in encoding, that is, representing phonological information in memory, retrieving phonological information from memory, using phonological memory codes to maintain verbal input in auditory short-term memory, and awareness of the phonological structure of the language. Word recognition depends upon the acquisition of phonological awareness, that is, the conscious awareness of the sounds of speech and the manner in which they succeed one another in words (Wagner & Torgersen, 1987). Such analytic skills are not present as a rule in children of less than 5 or 6 years (Shankweiler, Liberman, Mark, Fowler, & Fischer, 1979). The ability to abstract whole words from the speech stream is thought to emerge before the ability to abstract phonemes or syllables from an isolated word unit (Sawyer, 1988). Phonological awareness may, however, be related to preliterate word play and even to the acquisition of first referential words, in which alliteration and rhyming are used without conscious phonological awareness (Bradley, 1988; Vihman, 1981).

The question arises, then, is lack of phonological awareness related to the rapid-rate processing deficits that have been documented in LI children? The nature of rapid-rate processing deficits and the units of spoken language affected are still largely unknown. Experiments conducted by Tallal, Stark, Kallman, and Mellits (1980a, 1980b), however, suggest there may be such a relationship. Some of their older LI subjects (8 to 9 years in age) engaged in a concept-generalization task in which they had to categorize syllables as "d-initial" or "b-initial" and a segmentation task in which they had to indicate the order of occurrence of "d-initial" and/or "b-initial" syllables in words like *daddy* and *body*. However, their performance was significantly poorer on both of these phonological tasks than that of LN children matched with them for performance IQ. These same LI children had significant rapid-rate auditory processing and speech-discrimination problems.

Some LI children with delayed rapid-rate auditory processing may catch up with their peers in this respect sufficiently to begin to use intact metalinguistic abilities, for example, phonological awareness, in learning to read. Others may show no difficulty with rapid-rate auditory processing or speech discrimination in the preschool years or in kindergarten but may not be able to use these skills at a higher level of conscious awareness when they begin to read, for example, in learning phoneme–grapheme correspondence and the rules that relate the spoken and the written language forms of English.

It seems unlikely that rapid-rate processing is a simple or unitary phenomenon within the auditory nervous system. Different neural networks are probably involved when rapid-rate processing is used in auditory—motor learning for speech and in spoken-word recognition, for example. Affected children with severe articulation impairment may have difficulty with phonetic recoding, while those with normal speech but with difficulty in spoken-word recognition may have a related difficulty in printed-word recognition in reading, as recent data reported by Catts (1989) would suggest. Thus, the problems faced by different LI children as they begin to deal with phoneme–grapheme correspondence may be somewhat different and may require different strategies in intervention. On the other hand, many of the steps identified in early spoken language development, for example, word-initial sound learning, may be recapitulated in the young child's early attempts to read, in which case some commonalities across LI children might be expected. The work of Bradley and her colleagues (Bradley & Bryant, 1978, 1983) suggests that alliteration and rhyming, which are characteristic of preschool children's language, are also important for acquiring phonological awareness. By training poor readers in these skills in relation to spoken words and relating them to printed word forms, she and her colleagues were able to improve significantly the performance of these children in reading and spelling. This improvement was maintained over a 4-year period.

B. Reading Comprehension

Reading comprehension may be defined as the ability to abstract meaning from printed text, for example, of paragraph or story length. Reading comprehension therefore depends in part upon the prior acquisition of word recognition and of efficient and rapid decoding skills, sometimes referred to as bottom-up processing skills. It also depends upon the ability to predict upcoming words on the basis of semantic and syntactic content of preceding text, as well as upon a knowledge of semantic and syntactic rule systems (Smith, 1971). Top-down higher-level processing probably influences reading comprehension to an even greater extent than word recognition.

It has also been pointed out that there is a reciprocal relationship between language and reading, such that children with adequate reading comprehension are able to read to learn. In this way they acquire extended vocabularies and exposure to a variety of sentence structures not found in the same concentration in conversational speech or in formal instruction.

Clearly many higher-level cognitive abilities are important for reading comprehension, as well as motivational and attentional factors. The diversity of problems that RI children may present in these and other areas, such as poor visual acuity, poor visual discrimination, mixed laterality, or speech problems, has led educational researchers to protest that it is more useful in intervention to deal with factors that lie outside the reader, such as complexity of text, task demands, and type of discourse, than those that lie within. These investigators believe that the search for causal factors that might be addressed in intervention with children who have deficits in reading comprehension is doomed to failure (Lipson & Wixson, 1986). An interactionist perspective has been advocated instead, in which factors inherent in the reader, pedagogical factors, and factors inherent in the material to be read are all taken into account. Factors inherent in the reader include cultural and motivational factors as well as higher-level cognitive abilities and general knowledge. The emphasis in intervention is upon the conditions under which the child can and will learn.

VII. Summary

Similar problems are encountered in defining language impairment and reading impairment in learning-disabled children. Both may be defined on an inclusionary or an exclusionary basis. For both, inclusionary definitions depend upon the adequacy of the tests employed. Many in current use are psychometrically unsound. Nevertheless, it is clear that LI and RI children have characteristics in common and that many LI children go on to become reading impaired. It is not true to say that LI and RI children are all of normal or above-average intelligence with one isolated area of deficit. Instead, children in both groups are likely to display associated problems of various kinds and to be at the lower end of the normal scale in overall intelligence.

Because of the heterogeneity found in both groups, it is difficult to isolate causal factors. Post-mortem anatomical studies have been informative in the case of adults with severe and persisting reading impairment. They have not been carried out to any significant extent with RI or LI children. Neurophysiological studies have indicated very general relationships between language deficits and areas of hypofunction within the central nervous system. Further insights will likely come from such studies when the definition of impairment and types of impairments in language and reading become more precise.

Language-impaired children as a group show a delay or deficit in acquiring rapid auditory processing. Difficulty in processing signals that are low in redundancy as well as rapidly changing may be present and may affect speech discrimination. Language-impaired children may also have speech articulation problems and syntactic and semantic deficits. The relation between these aspects of language impairment and rapid auditory processing is unknown.

Reading-impaired children present difficulty with phonological awareness in the early stages of learning to read. This phenomenon could be related to rapid auditory processing. The difficulty impedes their early efforts at word recognition. Inefficient strategies of decoding and poor word recognition may, in turn, affect reading comprehension and overall reading rate. In the later stages of language learning and of learning to read, higher-level cognitive, cultural, and motivational factors may be more important than perceptual or motor factors. Representational thinking, problem solving, and inferencing need to be taken into account. If so, it may be that the emphasis in intervention should be different in beginning and more advanced language learners and readers whose performance is significantly below normal. Motivational and social factors, attentional abilities, and impulsivity probably need to be taken into account in both the earlier and the later stages of acquisition of language and reading.

References

Aram, D. M., Ekelman, B., & Nation, J. E. (1984). Preschoolers with language disorders: 10 years later. *Journal of Speech and Hearing Research, 27,* 232–244.

Aram, D. M., & Nation, J. E. (1980). Preschool language disorders and subsequent language and academic difficulties. *Journal of Child Development, 13,* 159–170.

Benton, A. L. (1964). Developmental aphasia and brain damage. *Cortex, 1,* 40–52.

Bernstein, L., & Stark, R. (1985). Speech perception development in language impaired children: A four year follow up study. *Journal of Speech and Hearing Disorders, 50,* 21–30.

Bradley, L. (1988). Rhyme recognition and reading and spelling in young children. In R. L. Masland & M. W. Masland (Eds.), *Preschool prevention of reading failure.* Parkton, MD: York Press.

Bradley, L., & Bryant, P. (1978). Difficulties in auditory organization as a possible cause of reading backwardness. *Nature (London), 271,* 746–747.

Bradley, L., & Bryant, P. (1983). Categorizing sounds and learning to read: A causal connection. *Nature (London), 301,* 419–421.

Brinton, B., Fujiki, M., & Sonnenberg, E. A. (1988). Responses to requests for clarification by linguistically normal and language-impaired children in conversation. *Journal of Speech and Hearing Disorders, 53,* 383–391.

Camarata, S., & Schwartz, R. G. (1985). Production of object words and action words: Evidence for a relationship between phonology and semantics. *Journal of Speech and Hearing Research, 28,* 323–330.

Catts, H. W. (1989). Speech production deficits in developmental dyslexia. *Journal of Speech and Hearing Disorders, 54,* 422–428.

Catts, H. W., Condino, R., & Stark, R. (1982). *Impulsivity in language-impaired children.* Paper presented at the annual convention of the American Speech-Language-Hearing Association, Toronto.

Ceci, S. J. (1982). Extracting meaning from stimuli: Automatic and purposive processing of the language-based learning disabled. *Topics in Learning Disabilities, 2,* 46–53.

Ceci, S. J. (1983). Automatic and purposive semantic processing characteristics of normal and language/learning disabled children. *Developmental Psychology, 19,* 427–439.

Chapman, K., Leonard, L. B., Rowan, L. E., & Weiss, A. L. (1983). Inappropriate word extensions in the speech of young language-disordered children. *Journal of Speech and Hearing Disorders, 48,* 55–62.

Chi, M. (1978). Knowledge structures and memory development. In R. Siegler (Ed.), *Children's thinking: What develops?* Hillsdale, NJ: Erlbaum.

Condino, R. (1983). *Characteristics of the problem solving process in children developing language normally and specifically language-impaired children for nonverbal visual tasks.* Unpublished doctoral dissertation, St. Louis University, St. Louis, MO.

Crais, E., & Chapman, R. (1987). Story recall and inferencing in language/learning disordered children. *Journal of Speech and Hearing Disorders, 52,* 50–55.

Curtiss, S. (1982). Developmental dissociations of language and cognition. In L. K. Obler & L. Menn (Eds.), *Exceptional language and linguistic theory.* New York: Academic Press.

Curtiss, S., & Tallal, P. (1985). *On the question of subgroups in language impaired children: A first report.* Paper presented at the Tenth annual Boston University Conference of Language Development, Boston, MA.

Curtiss, S., & Tallal, P. (1990). On the nature of the language impairment in language impaired children. In J. Miller (Ed.), *Pro-Ed.* Austin, TX.

Denckla, M. (1982). Language disorders. In J. A. Downey & N. L. Low (Eds.), *The child with disabling illness: Principles of rehabilitation*. New York: Raven Press.

Dennis, M. (1980). Capacity and strategy for syntactic comprehension after left or right hemidecontication. *Brain & Language, 10*, 287–317.

Dennis, M., & Kohn, B. (1975). Comprehension of syntax in infantile hemiplegia after cerebral hemidecortication. *Brain & Language, 2*, 472–482.

Dennis, M., & Whitaker, H. A. (1976). Language acquisition following hemidecortication: Linguistic superiority of the left over the right hemisphere, *Brain & Language, 3*, 404–433.

Dollaghan, C. (1987). Fast mapping in normal and language-impaired children. *Journal of Speech and Hearing Disorders, 52*, 218–222.

Donahue, M. (1984). Learning disabled children's conversational competence: An attempt to activate the inactive listener. *Applied Psycholinguistics, 5*, 21–35.

Donahue, M., Pearl, R., & Bryan, T. (1980). Learning disabled children's conversational competence: Responses to inadequate messages. *Applied Psycholinguistics, 1*, 387–403.

Dudley-Marling, C. (1985). The pragmatic skills of learning disabled children: A review. *Journal of Learning Disabilities, 18*, 193–196.

Dunn, L. M., & Dunn, L. M. (1981). *Peabody Picture Vocabulary Test-Revised*. Circle Pines, MN: American Guidance Service.

Elliot, L., & Busse, L. (1987). Auditory processing by learning disabled young adults. In D. Johnson & J. Blalock (Eds.), *Adults with learning disabilities: Clinical studies* (pp. 107–129). Grune & Stratton, New York.

Elliot, L., & Hammer, M. (1988). Longitudinal changes in auditory discrimination in normal children and children with language-learning problems. *Journal of Speech and Hearing Disorders, 53*, 467–474.

Elliot, L., Hammer, M., & Scholl, M. (1989). Fine-grained auditory discrimination in normal children and children with language-learning problems. *Journal of Speech and Hearing Research, 32*, 112–119.

Fey, M., & Leonard, L. B. (1984). Partner age as a variable in the conversational performance of specifically-language-impaired and normal language children. *Journal of Speech and Hearing Research, 27*, 413–423.

Flavell, J. (1979). Metacognition and cognitive monitoring: A new area of cognitive-developmental inquiry. *American Psychologist, 34*, 906–911.

Franklin, M. (1981). Metalinguistic functioning in development. In N. R. Smith & M. B. Franklin (Eds.), *Symbolic functioning in childhood*. Hillsdale, NJ: Erlbaum.

Freedman, P. P., & Carpenter, R. L. (1976). Semantic relations used by normal and language impaired children at Stage I. *Journal of Speech and Hearing Research, 19*, 784–795.

Galaburda, A. M., & Kemper, T. L. (1979). Cyto-architectonic abnormalities in developmental dyslexia: A case study. *Annals of Neurology, 6*, 94–100.

Geschwind, N., & Levitsky, W. (1968). Human brain: Left/right asymmetries in temporal speech region. *Science, 161*, 186–189.

Graybeal, C. (1981). Memory for stories in language-impaired children. *Applied Psycholinguistics, 2*, 269–283.

Hakes, D. (1982). The development of metalinguistic abilities: What develops? In

S. A. Kuczaj (Ed.), *Language development: Language, thought and culture* (Vol. 2). Hillsdale, NJ: Erlbaum.

Hammill, D. D., Leigh, J. E., McNutt, G., & Larsen, S. C. (1981). A new definition of learning disabilities. *Learning Disability Quarterly, 4,* 336–342.

Haslam, R. A., Dalby, J., Johns, R., & Rademaker, A. (1981). Cerebral asymmetry in developmental dyslexia. *Archives of Neurology (Chicago), 38,* 679–682.

Johnston, J. R. (1988). Specific language disorders in the child. In N. J. Lass, L. McReynolds, J. L. Northern, & D. E. Yoder (Eds.), *Handbook of speech-language pathology and audiology.* Philadelphia, PA: Decker.

Johnston, J. R., & Kamhi, A. G. (1984). Syntactic and semantic aspects of the utterances of language impaired children: The same can be less. *Merrill-Palmer Quarterly, 30,* 65–85.

Johnston, J. R., & Ramstad, V. (1983). Cognitive development in preadolescent language impaired children. *British Journal of Disordered Communication, 18,* 49–55.

Johnston, J. R., & Schery, T. K. (1976). The use of grammatical morphemes by children with communication disorders. In D. Morehead & A. Morehead (Eds.), *Normal and deficient child language* (pp. 239–258). Baltimore, MD: University Park Press.

Johnston, J. R., & Weismer, S. E. (1983). Mental rotation abilities in language disordered children. *Journal of Speech and Hearing Research, 26,* 397–403.

Kail, R. (1979). *The development of memory in children.* San Francisco, CA: Freeman.

Kail, R., Hale, C., Leonard, L. B., & Nippold, M. (1984). Lexical storage and retrieval in language impaired children. *Applied Psycholinguistics, 5,* 37–49.

Kail, R. & Leonard, L. B. (1986). Word finding abilities in language impaired children. *ASHA Monographs, 25.*

Kamhi, A. G. (1981). Nonlinguistic symbolic and conceptual abilities of language impaired and normally developing children. *Journal of Speech and Hearing Research, 24,* 446–453.

Kamhi, A. G., & Catts, H. W. (1989). *Reading Disabilities: A Developmental Language Perspective.* Boston, MA: College Hill.

Kamhi, A. G., Catts, H. W., Koenig, L., & Lewis, B. (1984). Hypothesis testing and non-linguistic symbolic abilities in language impaired children. *Journal of Speech and Hearing Disorders, 49,* 169–176.

Kamhi, A. G., Catts, H. W., Mauer, D., Apel, K., & Gentry, B. (1988). Phonological and spatial processing abilities in language- and reading-impaired children. *Journal of Speech and Hearing Disorders, 53,* 316–327.

Kamhi, A. G., & Koenig, L. (1985). Metalinguistic awareness in normal and language disordered children. *Language, Speech, and Hearing Services in Schools, 16,* 199–210.

Kamhi, A. G., Lee, R., & Nelson, L. (1985). Word, syllable and sound awareness in language disordered children. *Journal of Speech and Hearing Disorders, 50,* 207–212.

Kamhi, A. G., Nelson, L., Lee, R., & Gholson, B. (1985). The ability of language disordered children to use and modify hypotheses in discrimination learning. *Applied Psycholinguistics, 6,* 435–451.

Kaplan, E., Goodglass, H., & Weintraub, S. (1983). *Boston Naming Test*. Philadelphia, PA: Lea & Febiger.

Kirchner, D., & Klatzky, R. L. (1985). Verbal rehearsal and memory in language-disordered children. *Journal of Speech and Hearing Research, 28*, 556–565.

Lee, L. (1966). Developmental sentence types: A method for comparing normal and deviant syntactic development. *Journal of Speech and Hearing Disorders, 31*, 311–330.

Leonard, L. B. (1981). Facilitating linguistic skills in children with specific language impairments. *Applied Psycholinguistics, 2*, 89–118.

Leonard, L. B. (1985). Unusual and subtle behavior in the speech of phonologically disordered children. *Journal of Speech and Hearing Disorders, 50*, 4–13.

Leonard, L. B. (1989). Language learnability and specific language impairment in children. *Applied Psycholinguistics, 10*, 179–202.

Leonard, L. B., Nippold, M., & Kail, R. (1983). Picture naming in language impaired children. *Journal of Speech and Hearing Research, 26*, 609–615.

Liberman, I., Shankweiler, D., Fischer, F., & Carter, B. (1974). Reading and the awareness of linguistic segments. *Journal of Experimental Child Psychology, 18*, 367–375.

Liles, B., Shulman, M., & Bartlett, S. (1977). Judgments of grammaticality by normal and language disordered children. *Journal of Speech and Hearing Disorders, 42*, 199–209.

Lipson, M. Y., & Wixson, K. K. (1986). Reading disability research: An interactionist perspective. *Review of Educational Research, 56*, 111–136.

Lou, H. C., Henriksen, L., & Bruhn, P. (1984). Focal cerebral hypoperfusion in children with dysphasia and/or attention deficit disorder. *Archives of Neurology (Chicago), 41*, 825–829.

Ludlow, C. L., Cudahy, E. A., Bassich, C., & Brown, G. L. (1983). Auditory processing skills of hyperactive, language-impaired, and reading-disabled boys. In E. Z. Lasky & J. Katz (Eds.), *Central auditory processing disorders: Problems of speech, language, and learning*. Baltimore, MD: University Park Press.

Maxwell, S. E., & Wallach, G. P. (1984). The language-learning disabilities connection: Symptoms of early language disability change over time. In G. P. Wallach & K. G. Butler (Eds.), *Language learning disabilities in school-age children* (pp. 15–34). Baltimore, MD: Williams & Wilkins.

McCauley, R., & Swisher, L. (1984). Psychometric review of language and articulation tests for preschool children. *Journal of Speech and Hearing Disorders, 49*, 34–42.

Meier, J. H. (1971). Prevalence and characteristics of learning disabilities found in second grade children. *Journal of Learning Disabilities, 4*, 1–16.

Montgomery, J., Scudder, R., & Moore, C. (1990). Language-impaired children's real-time comprehension of spoken language. *Applied Psycholinguistics, 11*, 273–290.

Morehead, D., & Ingram, D. (1973). The development of base syntax in normal and linguistically deviant children. *Journal of Speech and Hearing Research, 16*, 330–352.

National Joint Committee on Learning Disabilities (NJCLD). (1982). Learning disabilities: Issues on definition. *ASHA, 24*(11), 945–947.

Nelson, L., Kamhi, A., & Apel, K. (1987). Cognitive strengths and weaknesses in language impaired children: One more look. *Journal of Speech and Hearing Disorders, 52,* 36–43.

Nippold, M., Erskine, B., & Freed, D. (1988). Proportional and functional analogical reasoning in normal and language-impaired children. *Journal of Speech and Hearing Disorders, 53,* 440–448.

Panagos, J., & Prelock, P. (1982). Phonological constraints on the sentence production of language-disordered children. *Journal of Speech and Hearing Research, 25,* 171–177.

Pearl, R., Donahue, M., & Bryan, T. (1981). Learning disabled and normal children's responses to non-explicit requests for clarification. *Perceptual and Motor Skills, 53,* 919–925.

Pinker, S. (1984). *Language learnability and language development.* Cambridge, MA: Harvard University Press.

Rankin, J. M., Aram, D. M., & Horwitz, S. J. (1981). Language ability in right and left hemiplegic children. *Brain & Language, 14,* 292–306.

Rosenberger, P. B., & Hier, D. B. (1980). Cerebral asymmetry and verbal intellectual deficits. *Annals of Neurology, 8,* 300–304.

Roth, F., & Spekman, N. (1986). Narrative discourse: Spontaneously generated stories of learning-disabled and normally achieving students. *Journal of Speech and Hearing Disorders, 51,* 8–23.

Savich, P. (1984). Anticipatory imagery in normal and language disabled children. *Journal of Speech and Hearing Research, 27,* 494–501.

Sawyer, D. J. (1988). Studies of the effects of teaching auditory segmenting skills within the reading program. In R. L. Masland & M. W. Masland (Eds.), *Preschool prevention of reading failure.* Parkton, MD: York Press.

Schwartz, R. G., & Leonard, L. B. (1985). Lexical imitation and acquisition in language-impaired children. *Journal of Speech and Hearing Disorders, 50,* 141–149.

Schwartz, R. G., Leonard, L. B., Folger, M. K., & Wilcox, M. J. (1980). Early phonological behavior in normal-speaking and language disordered children: Evidence for a synergistic view of linguistic disorders. *Journal of Speech and Hearing Disorders, 45,* 357–377.

Semel, E. M., & Wiig, E. H. (1975). Comprehension of syntactic structures and critical verbal elements by children with learning disabilities. *Journal of Learning Disabilities, 8,* 53–58.

Shankweiler, D., Liberman, I., Mark, L., Fowler, C., & Fischer, F. (1979). The speech code and learning to read. *Journal of Experimental Psychology: Human Learning & Memory, 5,* 531–545.

Shriberg, L. D., Kwiatkowski, J., Best, S., Hengst, J., & Terselic-Weber, B. (1986). Characteristics of children with phonologic disorders of unknown origin. *Journal of Speech and Hearing Disorders, 51,* 140–161.

Sininger, Y. S., Klatzky, R. L., & Kirchner, D. M. (1989). Memory scanning speed in language-disordered children. *Journal of Speech and Hearing Research, 32,* 289–297.

Smith, F. (1971). *Understanding reading: A psycholinguistic analysis of reading and learning to read.* New York: Holt, Rinehart & Winston.

Snyder, L. S. (1984). Developmental language disorders: Elementary school age. In A. L. Holland (Ed.), *Language disorders in children*. San Diego, CA: College-Hill.

Stanovich, K. (1985). Cognitive processes and the reading problems of learning-disabled children: Evaluating the assumption of specificity. In J. K. Torgesen & B. Y. L. Wong (Eds.), *Psychological and educational perspectives on learning disabilities*. Orlando, FL: Academic Press.

Stark, J., & Wallach, G. P. (1982). The path to a concept of language learning disabilities. In K. G. Butler & G. P. Wallach (Eds.), *Language disorders and learning disabilities* (pp. 1–14). Rockville, MD: Aspen.

Stark, R. E. (1985). *Developmental apraxia: A new perspective*. Invited paper, Boston University Conference on Language Development, Boston University, Boston, MA.

Stark, R. E., Ansel, B. M., & Heinz, J. M. (in press). *Spectral displays of speech as an aid to reading*, Proceedings of the conference on Treatment Efficacy. American Speech Language Hearing Foundation. San Antonio.

Stark, R. E., Bernstein, L. E., Condino, R., Bender, M., & Tallal, P. (1984). Four-year follow up study of language-impaired children. *Annals of Dyslexia, 34*, 49–68.

Stark, R. E., & Tallal, P. (1979). Analysis of stop consonant production errors in developmentally dysphasic children. *Journal of the Acoustical Society of America, 66*, 1703–1712.

Stark, R. E., & Tallal, P. (1980). Perceptual and motor deficits in language-impaired children. In R. W. Keith (Ed.), *Central auditory and language processing disorders* in children. Houston, TX: College Hill Press.

Stark, R. E., & Tallal, P. (1981). Selection of children with specific language deficits. *Journal of Speech and Hearing Disorders, 46*, 114–122.

Stark, R. E., Tallal, P., Kallman, C., & Mellits, D. (1983). Cognitive abilities of language-delayed children. *Journal of Psychology, 114*, 9–19.

Stark, R. E., Tallal, P., & McCauley, R. J. (1988). *Language, speech, and reading disorders in children: Neuropsychological studies*. Boston, MA: College-Hill.

Stark, R. E., Tallal, P., & Mellits, E. D. (1985). Expressive language and preceptual and motor abilities in language-impaired children. *Human Communication Canada, 9*, 23–28.

Steckol, K., & Leonard, L. B. (1979). The use of grammatical morphemes by normal and language-impaired children. *Journal of Communication Disorders, 12*, 291–301.

Strominger, A. Z., & Bashir, A. S. (1977). *A nine-year follow-up of 50 language delayed children*. Paper presented at the annual convention of the American Speech and Hearing Association, Chicago, IL.

Swisher, L., & Demetras, M. J. (1987). *Test-generated heterogeneity in children with specific language impairment*. Paper presented at a Conference on Language Acquisition and Language Impairment in Children, University of Parma, Parma, Italy.

Tallal, P. (1980). Language disabilities in children: A perceptual or linguistic deficit? *Journal of Pediatric Psychology, 5*, 127–140.

Tallal, P. (1988). Developmental language disorders. In J. F. Kavanagh & T. J. Truss (Eds.), *Learning disabilities: Proceedings of the National Conference*. Parkton, MD: York Press.

Tallal, P., & Piercy, M. (1974). Developmental aphasia: Rate of auditory processing and selective impairment of consonant perception. *Neuropsychologia, 13,* 1380–1381.

Tallal, P., & Stark, R. (1981). Speech acoustic-cue discrimination abilities of normally developing and language impaired children. *Journal of the Acoustical Society of America, 69,* 568–574.

Tallal, P., Stark, R. E., Kallman, C., & Mellits, E. D. (1980a). Developmental dysphasia: Relation between acoustic processing deficits and verbal processing. *Neuropsychologia, 18,* 273–285.

Tallal, P., Stark, R. E., Kallman, C., & Mellits, E. D. (1980b). Perceptual constancy for phonemic categories: A developmental study with normal and language-impaired children. *Applied Psycholinguistics, 1,* 49–54.

Tallal, P., Stark, R. E., & Mellits, E. D. (1985). The relationship between auditory temporal analysis and receptive language development: Evidence from studies of developmental language disorder. *Neuropsychologia, 23,* 527–534.

Terman, L. M., & Merrill, M. A. (1962). *Standford-Binet Intelligence Scale.* Boston, MA: Houghton-Mifflin.

Tomblin, B., & Quinn, M. (1983). The contribution of perceptual learning to performance on the repetition task. *Journal of Speech and Hearing Research, 26,* 369–372.

Tyler, L., & Marslen-Wilson, W. (1981). Children's processing of spoken language. *Journal of Verbal Learning and Verbal Behavior, 20,* 400–416.

van Kleeck, A. (1982). The emergencies of linguistic awareness: A cognitive framework. *Merrill-Palmer Quarterly, 28,* 237–265.

Vihman, M. (1981). Phonology and the development of the lexicon: Evidence from children's errors. *Journal of Child Language, 8,* 239–264.

Vogel, S. A. (1983). A quantitative analysis of morphological ability in learning disabled and achieving children. *Journal of Learning Disabilities, 16,* 416–420.

Wada, J. A., Clark, R., & Hamm, A. (1975). Cerebral hemisphere asymmetry in humans. *Archives of Neurology (Chicago), 32,* 239–246.

Wagner, R. K. (1986). Phonological processing abilities and reading: Implications for disabled readers. *Journal of Learning Disabilities, 19,* 623–630.

Wagner, R. K., & Torgesen, J. (1987). The nature of phonological processing and its causal role in the acquisition of reading skills. *Psychological Bulletin, 101,* 192–212.

Wallach, G. P., & Butler, K. G. (1984). *Language learning disabilities in school-age children.* Baltimore, MD: Williams & Wilkins.

Wallach, G. P., & Miller, L. (1988). *Language intervention and academic success.* Boston, MA: College-Hill.

Wechsler, D. (1963). *Wechsler Preschool and Primary Scale of Intelligence.* New York: Psychological Corporation.

Wechsler, D. (1974). *Weschler Intelligence Scale for Children-Revised.* New York: Psychological Corporation.

Wiig, E. M., Semel, E. H., & Nystrom, L. (1982). Comparison of rapid naming abilities in language-learning-disabled and academically achieving eight year olds. *Language, Speech, and Hearing Services in Schools, 13,* 11–23.

CHAPTER TWENTY-TWO

Specific Nonverbal and Social-Skills Deficits in Children with Learning Disabilities

Margaret Semrud-Clikeman
George W. Hynd

I. Introduction

Educators, researchers, and clinical practitioners have become increasingly cognizant of the interplay between deficits in social-skill development and learning disabilities. It has almost become a maxim that children with learning disabilities are at higher risk for social-skill delay (Pearl, 1987). However, as with most generalizations, it may well be that children with concomitant learning and social deficits comprise another manifestation of learning disability, that of the nonverbal learning disability (Semrud-Clikeman & Hynd, 1990). That is not to say that children with learning disabilities do not experience social difficulties, but that children with nonverbal learning disabilities may experience social interactions in a different manner than other learning-disabled children. This observation is particularly relevant since the National Institutes of Health interagency report to Congress recommending that particular difficulties in age-appropriate social-skill acquisition be recognized as a specific learning disability (Wyngaarden, 1987). It is not clear at this point whether social-skill deficits exist in isolation from learning failure or serious emotional disturbance.

The purpose of this chapter is to evaluate the evidence as to the existence of nonverbal learning disabilities as a separate disorder. A brief discussion of the development of social skills will first be presented followed by an examination as to possible explanations for delays in the attainment of age-appropriate social ability. Second, a review of the research findings as to the attainment of social perception and skills of learning-disabled children will be provided. Third, a discussion of the possible neuropsychological underpinnings of nonverbal learning disabilities and possible subtypes will be explored. Finally, the implications of these findings for future research and application will be discussed.

II. Components of Social-Perception Development

Social perception has been defined as "the child's ability to understand his social environment, *especially* in terms of his own behavior" (Myklebust, 1975 p. 96). Social skills are the specific behaviors used to interact with others (McFall, 1982). Social perception and resulting social skills are a function of development. The ability to project oneself into another's place becomes increasingly important in social-skill development. Popular children have been found to be most adept at effective communication, conversation initiation, and awareness and empathy of another's affective state. Perhaps most importantly, socially adept children show a well-developed ability to match their social skills with the demands of the current situation (Krudek & Krile, 1982). These skills were found to develop between the ages of 8 and 14.

Moreover, those skills that are associated with social success have been found to include the ability to conceptualize alternative scenarios, to anticipate consequences and act upon such anticipation, and finally, to utilize cause–effect reasoning (Bruno, 1981). Therefore, to experience social success, a child must accurately evaluate social situations and arrive at appropriate actions based on these perceptions.

Several components make up social perception. Among these are emotional recognition/labeling, prosody, and facial expressions and gestures.

It appears that the ability to accurately recognize and label emotion is an important component in social-skill development and increases in direct relation to age. Studies of normal and disadvantaged preschool children have found that emotional recognition and labeling are positively and significantly correlated with measures of intelligence and perceptual–motor skills (Izard, 1977). A strong relation between emotional recognition, social-skill development, and subsequent reading and arithmetic achievement has been demonstrated (Kirby & Asman, 1984).

The ability to recognize and label emotions may affect mother–child interactions and subsequently how the child interacts with his environment. These interactions later enable the child to organize his experience into a meaningful and predictable cognitive framework (Ainsworth, 1979). If a child has difficulty with interpreting facial expressions and gestures and thus does not respond appropriately to mother–child interactions, it is not unreasonable to propose that this most important relationship may be significantly altered.

Prosody is an integral part of emotional labeling and its comprehension is crucial to the development of social skills. Prosody involves the ability to express and understand the intonation and subsequent meaning of language (Ross, 1981). As such, prosody is thought to be one of the fundamental elements in the development of language.

Much of the prelinguistic child's learning is through visual and auditory perceptions of environmental sounds, visual–motor patterns and relations, and rhythms. These skills are felt to be disproportionately stored and processed in the right hemisphere during early ontogeny (Ley & Bryden, 1981). The right hemisphere develops faster than the left from 18–23 months of age, which may reflect a greater involvement of the right-hemispheric processes in infancy (Semrud-Clikeman & Hynd, 1990).

Consonant with the preceding discussion, facial expression has been found to play a crucial role in the development of social responsiveness. Vocalization, gestures, and exposure to the range of facial expressions have been found to contribute more substantially to the degree of social responsiveness than the meeting of the infant's physiological needs (Izard, 1982). Moreover, the infant's development of accurate perception of the mother's facial expression and gestures relates to the development of attachment behaviors and social adequacy (Ainsworth, 1979; Izard, 1977). Thus, the child who experiences significant difficulties in processing and retaining visual–spatial and auditory stimuli as well as in prediction of temporal events is likely to experience deficits in the understanding of human expressions and interactions as well as in the development of exploratory behaviors, cognitive reorganization, and individuation necessary for subsequent social-skill development (Kaslow & Cooper, 1978). In addition to the correct interpretation of facial expression, the child learns from these expressions how and when to appropriately display these affects (Mayo & LaFrance, 1979).

It is not unreasonable to speculate that children who are unable to acquire the ability to recognize, interpret, evaluate, and integrate the understanding of prosody, facial expressions, and experiences will be at risk for the development of significant difficulties in social competence. Moreover, such a disability may well be present early in development and go unrecognized until the age when peer interactions become crucial. Thus, these difficulties may be present at birth and subsequently unfold with development.

III. Cognitive Contributions to Social-Skill Development

Social-skill deficits may be the partial product of cognitive deficiencies. It may well be that learning-disabled children have the capability of performing appropriately but use these capacities poorly. Conversely, children with learning disabilities may have reduced capability, the source of which may be temporary or permanent (Goldstein & Dundon, 1987); Gresham & Elliott, 1987).

Rehearsal, elaboration, organization, and memory are all abilities that contribute to successful skill development in learning and social areas (Sternberg & Wagner, 1982). A number of studies have documented that children with learning disabilities have not developed these skills (Bauer, 1977; Kosteski, Goldstein, & Hasher, 1979, Torgesen, 1980). It is not established why these deficits occur in this population. One may speculate that learning-disabled children are able to perform these behaviors once they are specifically taught. Moreover, a second area of difficulty is that, although this population may acquire these skills, these children may be unaware that a particular strategy is needed. Knowing how and when to use these skills is an aspect of metacognition (Brown, 1975). Some studies indicate that children with learning disabilities experience significant deficits in when and how to use intact skills as well as what skills to utilize in specific situations (Torgeson, 1979; Trepanier & Casale, 1983).

In addition to metacognitive deficits, children with learning disabilities may have neuropsychological difficulties which, in turn, interact with these cognitive weaknesses. Evidence for involvement of right-hemisphere deficits (Rourke and Finlayson, 1978; Rourke & Fisk, 1981; Rourke, Young, Strang, & Russell, 1985), inherited deficiencies (Pennington, Bender, Puck, Salbenblatt, & Robinson, 1982), and/or prenatal, perinatal, or neonatal insult (Kinsbourne & Caplan, 1979) in children with nonverbal social learning disabilities has been demonstrated.

A combination of metacognitive weaknesses and neuropsychological deficits may contribute to nonverbal learning disabilities and social-skill deficits. It is important to examine the existing evidence as to the type and degree of social disability that exists in the learning-disabled population. Therefore, the following discussion focuses on the results of several studies of social deficits in children with nonverbal learning disabilities.

IV. Nonverbal Learning Disabilities

One of the first descriptions of social-skill deficits in learning-disabled children was made by Johnson and Myklebust (1971). They described this type of learning difficulty as a *nonverbal* learning disability. This disorder was defined as an inability to comprehend the significance of environmental cues, an inability to pretend or anticipate, and a failure in learning and appreciating the implications of gestures, facial expressions, caresses, and vocal intonation. The learning-disabled child was seen as unable to interpret the significance of integral nonverbal aspects of daily life even given the prerequisite intelligence to do so. In this way the nonverbal learning disability results in impairment of perception and imagery and thus presents a fundamental distortion of the total life experience. To lend further credence to their finding, Johnson and Myklebust (1971) found that children with these deficits also evidenced soft neurological signs.

In addition to the above difficulties, the following problems were found to be related to nonverbal learning disabilities: disturbed social relationships, poor self-help skills, difficulty learning right from left, difficulty learning to tell time, read maps, or follow directions, disturbances in math, and finally, problems in learning the meaning of the actions of others (Myklebust, 1975). As a direct result of these deficits, these children's poor social perception may well limit their resulting inner experience, consequently significantly imping-ing on reasoning and adaptive behavior. In this way nonverbal learning disabilities may have more profound effects than verbal learning disabilities in lieu of the fact that verbal deficits contribute little to nonverbal experience while nonverbal disabilities may contribute to misinterpretation of verbal information. Various investigators have documented a relationship between nonverbal learning disabilities and deficits in social perception (Gaddes, 1985), interpretation and emotion and visual–motor skills (Wiig & Harris, 1974), and inability to differentiate, interpret, and evaluate facial expressions (Badian, 1983).

A. Social-Perception Investigations

It has only been in the past 10–15 years that the learning-disabled child's social perceptual abilities have been consistently studied. In a review of five studies, Bryan (1974) concluded that children with learning disabilities tended to be more egocentric and lacked awareness of the affective state of others. Inability to appropriately gauge contextually experienced emotions was seen to result from the learning-disabled child's perceptual weakness that subsequently prevented the acquisition of appropriate cognitions related to emotional experience (Bachara, 1976). In contrast to normal children and adolescents, learning-disabled children have been found to experience signifi-cant difficulty in the interpretation of affective states. Visual perceptual, cogni-tive, or symbolic deficits have been postulated as possible explanations for these difficulties (Axelrod, 1982; Bruinicks, 1978; Bruno, 1981; Bryan, 1977; Gerber & Zinkgraft, 1982; Pearl & Cosden, 1982; Wiig & Harris, 1974). However, these findings have not been consistent, as several investiga-tors have not found significant differences between learning-disabled and normal subjects on social perception and interaction skills (Bryan, Donahue, & Pearl, 1981; Bryan & Wheeler, 1972; Bryan, Wheeler, Felcan, & Henek, 1976; Connolly, 1969; Maheady, Matiland, & Sainato, 1984; Richey & McKinney, 1978; Siperstein, Bopp, & Bak, 1978).

There are several possible reasons for the inconsistent findings of these studies. Variations in measures utilized, age of subjects, learning-disability diagnostic criteria, and number of subjects may partially account for the differing findings. Moreover, there was little attempt in most cases to control for attentional and/or verbal variables. It is perhaps surprising that none of these studies report how many children had codiagnoses of speech and language disability, attention-deficit disorder (ADD), or family histories of learning disability. Language disorders as well as ADD could easily affect performance on social-perception tasks. This omission is particularly disturbing since there is convincing evidence of the frequency of codiagnoses of language and attentional disorders with learning disabilities (Denckla, 1979; Hynd *et al.*, 1989). Therefore, these omissions would constitute a shared and important methodological problem in these studies.

Table I documents several difficulties with these studies. A number of conclusions can be drawn from Table I. First, not only are there differing criteria for establishing a diagnosis of learning disabilities between studies, but in 11 of 14 studies selection criteria are not provided, with sparse data on intelligence and achievement scores resulting in vague group definitions. One study that reported intelligence and achievement measures (Wiig & Harris, 1974) utilized different diagnostic criteria depending on the school the child attended. This factor alone places in serious doubt the interpretability of the results of this particular study. Second, of the three studies that evaluated speech and language abilities (Bachara, 1976; Bruno, 1981; Wiig & Harris, 1974), none reported appropriate scores. Language difficulties have been found to influence tests commonly used to diagnose learning disabilities (Hynd & Semrud-clikeman, 1989b). Third, sociometrics (a relevant variable in the study of social skills) is ignored in 11 of 14 studies with even teacher ratings rarely used. No study that evaluated children's social appropriateness in a natural setting (such as recess or unstructured play) assessed awareness of the child of his or her own behavior and the subsequent interpretation of the play situation. If indeed, as hypothesized by Torgesen (1979) and others, the ability to evaluate, organize, and elaborate on behaviors is deficient in learning-disabled children, it would be very significant to determine what attributions are made as well as the appropriateness of these attributions to the play situation.

While there are significant limitations to these studies, they do represent a first step in investigating nonverbal learning disabilities. In addition to social difficulties, these children are also frequently found to experience difficulties in the attainment of appropriate arithmetic skills.

B. *Arithmetic and Nonverbal Learning Disabilities*

Arithmetic deficits were included in Johnson and Myklebust's (1971) original definition of nonverbal learning disability. They described these chil-

TABLE I LD Studies of Social Interaction and Nonverbal Social Perception

Study	Group	Number M	F	Age	IQ	Achievement	Speech/language	ADD	Emotional assessment	Sociometric	Developmental history	Task	Findings	Comments
Axelrod (1982)	LD	16	16	Grade 8	NR[a]	In LD class, criteria NR	N/A[b]	N/A	No primary emotional problem; measures NR	LD teacher ratings	NR	PONS 3 subtests from 4-factor test of social IQ:	LD poorer at nonverbal social perception.	Subject selection not specified.
	Controls	24 21	26 22	Grade 8 Grade 9	NR	Chosen by school administrator	N/A	N/A	NR	NR	NR	expression grouping, missing cartoons, cartoon predictions	Visual channel was poorest for LD. PONS and expression grouping did not correlate with teacher rankings. Cartoon predictions correlated with teacher rankings.	One of the few studies that compared teacher rankings with test results.
Bachara (1976)	LD Control	25 25	— —	7–12 7–12	WISC-R IQ≧80 WISC-R IQ≧80	WRAT-Reading and Arithmetic; scores NR for either group	PPVT, ITPA scores NR for either group.	N/A N/A N/A N/A	N/A N/A N/A N/A	N/A N/A	N/A N/A	Both groups were administered the Bork Scales of Empathy—measures happy, sad, mad, and afraid	LD found more deficient in empathy. LD less able to perceive social situations and may experience interpersonal problems.	Definition of LD group and most measures are not reported. No exploration of the relation, if any, between the scores on the Bork and actual social functioning.

(continued)

TABLE I (Continued)

Study	Group	Number M	F	Age	IQ	Achievement	Speech/language	ADD	Emotional assessment	Sociometric	Developmental history	Task	Findings	Comments
Bruinicks (1978)	LD	15	8	NR Grades 1, 2, 4, 5	NR	Sight words Mean = 2.45 Math computation Mean = 2.81	N/A	N/A	Self-Esteem Inventory Mean = 65.65	Peer Acceptance Scale Mean = 2.54 (perceived) Mean = 2.26 (actual)	N/A	Both groups assessed as to need for inclusion, control, and affection in interpersonal relationships.	LD found to have lower social status and lower self-concept scores. Also were less accurate in assessing own status. No difference in interpersonal needs except LD greater need for expression of control.	No control for attentional variables. No IQ or S/L test reports. One of few studies with some measure of social status and/or skills.
	Controls	15	8	Matched to LD on grade and sex	NR	Sight words Mean = 4.22 Math computation Mean = 3.60	N/A	N/A	Mean = 73.39	Mean = 2.26 (actual and perceived)	N/A			
Bruno (1981)	LD	20	—	9-0 to 11-6, Mean = 10-5 for both groups	IQ range 90 115, Mean = 98.8, measure NR	Measures NR; differing basis for diagnosis. Selected from homerooms.	Eliminated children with severe naming problems	N/A	N/A	N/A	N/A	Test of Social Inference; Ss had to complete what picture was portraying. Also interviewed on 14 pictures for further information.	LD had more problems on TSI. LD responded to irrelevant details. LD errors were more illogical than control errors. LD had significantly more difficulty interpreting consequences.	LD selection questionable as used varying criteria. Article focuses significantly on attention as explanation for results but no attentional measures employed.
	Control	20	—			N/A	N/A	N/A	N/A	N/A	N/A			

Study	Group	N		Grade	IQ	Subject definition/achievement			Behavioral		Social	Measure	Results	Comments
Bryan (1977)	LD	21	2	NR Grades 3–5	IQ > 80	NR directly; reading achievement scores said to be "significantly below classmates."	N/A	N/A	Measure NR; no primary emotional problems.	N/A	N/A	PONS short form	Control group more accurate overall than LD: Both groups experienced difficulty interpreting the audio alone; LD had difficulty also with the visual alone.	No control for attentional variables. No measure of language skills or visual–spatial skills. Reading achievement measured, but not arithmetic or spelling—also not reported as discrepant to IQ. No measure of social-skill difficulty.
	Control	9	2	NR Grades 3–5	NR	No known problems.	N/A	N/A	No known behavioral problems.	N/A	N/A			
Bryan (1974)	LD	5	—	NR 3rd grade	NR	School defined measures—NR	N/A	N/A	N/A	N/A	N/A	Each LD child matched with control and observed in regular education classroom. Observations coded as to interactions with teacher and peers.	No differences between groups on time spent interacting with peers. LD ignored more often by peers. LD spent less time on task—poorest attention in arithmetic. Teacher 3 times more likely to respond to control than to LD.	No control for attentional variables. No assessment of social problems in LD. Achievement poorly reported. No IQ reported.
	Control	5	—	NR 3rd grade	NR	Teacher selected	N/A	N/A	N/A	No known social problems	N/A			

(continued)

TABLE I (Continued)

Study	Group	Number M	F	Age	IQ	Achievement	Speech/ language	ADD	Emotional assessment	Sociometric	Developmental history	Task	Findings	Comments
													Equal amount of positive interactions: LD> controls on negative interactions.	
Bryan and Wheeler (1972)	LD	10	—	NR Grades K, 1, 2, 4, 6	NR	School identified	NR	NR	NR	NR	NR	Classroom observation, coding of interactions, task-oriented, nontask oriented, interactions, and waiting	LD spent significantly less time engaged in task-oriented behaviors. Interactions frequency show no differences.	Although LDs were found to be off task more often no measure of attentional control was explored. Teacher selection of the subjects may have influenced the results. No measure of social skills for either group.
	Control	10	—	NR Grades K, 1, 2, 4, 6	NR	Measure NR; teacher rated as "normal"	NR	NR	NR	NR	NR			
Bryan, Wheeler, Felcan, and Henek (1976)	LD	13	4	NR Grades 3, 4, 5	NR	School identified, measure NR	NR	NR	NR	NR	NR	Subjects observed in communication with peers. Ratings based on rejection, information source, self-image, cooperation, competition, helping consideration,	LD gave more competitive statements to peers. Controls, more consideration statements from peers. No other differences.	Very poor reporting of criteria. No measure as to how LD or controls interpreted the interactions.
	Control	13	4	NR Grades 3, 4, 5	NR	NR	NR	NR	NR	NR	NR			

Study	Group	N		Age	IQ	Achievement						Test/Task	Results	Comments
Gerber and Zinkgraf (1982)	LD	8 15	— 7	7 & 8 10 & 11	88.25 84.63	School identified, measure NR NR	NR NR	NR NR	NR NR	NR NR	NR NR	Test of Social Inference	LD scored lower than control regardless of age. Younger < older social perception of 10 and 11 yrs. LD was same as 7 yr. old controls	Attempted to match subjects on basis of PPVT but not on any sociometric or emotional measure.
	Control	8 15	7 1	7 & 9 10 & 11	91.00 87.44	NR	NR	NR	NR	NR	NR			
Maheady, Maitland, and Sainato (1984)	Combined LD, SED, and EMR	72	—	7-0 to 11-11	Stanford–Binet LD X̄=93.17 SED X̄=92.58 EMR X̄=69.6	Woodcock & Key Math LD Reading X̄=2.0 Math X̄=2.9 SED Reading X̄=3.5 Math X̄=3.5 EMR Reading X̄=1.9 Math X̄=1.8	N/A	N/A	N/A	N/A	N/A	Social Interpretation Inference	LD and control answered more questions than EMR. Only significant group difference was for EMR. SED, LD, and EMR displayed more inappropriate behaviors than control.	Instrument may not have been sensitive to same type of cues found in classroom environment. Would have been useful to covary sociometric information with test results and teacher ratings.
				13-0 to 17-11	WISC-R LD X̄=89.08 SED X̄=96.25 EMR X̄=69.17							Social Interpretation task: S watched videotape and then answered interpretive questions. Teachers rated on 12 behaviors (e.g., misinterprets facial expressions)		
	Control	24	—	7-0 to 11-11	Otis–Lennon X̄=107.91 Range 93–129	LD Reading X̄=6.67 Math X̄=7.65	N/A	N/A	N/A	N/A	N/A		No relationship between classroom behavior and SIT.	
				13-0 to 17-11	X̄=111.75 Range 99–130	SED Reading X̄=5.07 Math X̄=6.30	N/A	N/A	N/A	N/A	N/A			
				7-0 to 11-11		EMR Reading X̄=4.17	N/A	N/A	N/A	N/A	N/A			

(continued)

TABLE I (*Continued*)

Study	Group	Number M	Number F	Age	IQ	Achievement	Speech/ language	ADD	Emotional assessment	Sociometric	Developmental history	Task	Findings	Comments
				13-0 to 17-11		Math $\overline{X}=4.18$ MAT Math $\overline{X}=5.76$ GE Reading $\overline{X}=5.76$ GE Natl. Ed. Dev. Test Reading $\overline{X}=67.8\%$ Math $\overline{X}=70.5\%$								
Pearl and Cosden (1982)	LD	24	19	Grades 6, 7, 8	WISC-R $\overline{X}=97.8$	Measure NR $\overline{X}=4.58$	N/A	N/A	N/A	N/A	N/A	Soap operas viewed with emotional subject. Five multiple-choice questions as to content of scene.	LD significantly less accurate covaried on IQ and significance remained; sex and grade not significant.	Controlled for IQ and investigated age and sex variables. No measure of emotional–social adjustment.
	Control	24	21	Grades 6, 7, 8	$\overline{X}=105.3$	Measure NR $\overline{X}=6.6$	N/A	N/A	N/A	N/A	N/A			
Richey and McKinney (1978)	LD	15	—	Grades 3 & 4	Group IQ measures	School identified, measure NR	N/A	N/A	N/A	N/A	N/A	Observations using the schedule for classroom activity norms: 12 categories provided for task-oriented, social, and affective behavior.	LD significantly more distractible than controls. No other differences.	No measure of ADD and yet the one variable found to separate the groups was attentional. Cannot be taken as evidence for no group difference in social perception or skills—often cited as such.
	Controls	15	—	Grades 3 & 4	Groups $\overline{X}$ IQ = 104.4 S.D. = 12.6	Reported to be "normal"	N/A	N/A	N/A	N/A	N/A			

Study	Group											Task	Results	Comments
Siperstein, Bopp, and Bak (1978)	LD	17	4	NR	School identified NR	N/A	N/A	N/A	N/A	Sec task	N/A	Students asked to rate same-sex peers on 4 questions: Who you like best, best athlete, smartest, best looking?	LD significantly less popular. No difference between groups as to isolate status. No LD was best liked, smartest. Same proportion found to be athletic and good looking.	One of few studies using sociometric measures. Teacher rankings as to status would have been interesting. Poor reporting of subject criteria.
	Controls	63	93	NR	N/A	N/A	N/A	N/A	N/A	Sec task	N/A			
Wiig and Harris (1974)	LD	15	2	14-10 to 18-8 $\bar{X}=16\text{-}1$	WISC or WAIS FSIQ $\bar{X}=113.8$ VIQ $\bar{X}=111.5$ PIQ $\bar{X}=114.82$ IQs ≥ 85 IQ $\bar{X}=116.53$	Gray Oral $\bar{X}=7.2$	Detroit Tests of Learning Aptitude scores NR	N/A	N/A	N/A	N/A	Video of female displaying 6 emotions: anger, embarrassment, fear, frustration, joy, and love. Ss circled emotion being portrayed.	LD misinterpreted emotions significantly more than controls. Qualitative differences were also observed—LD frequently substituted positive emotions for negative emotions.	Possible differences between groups on social skills not addressed. Sex effects not addressed. LD with scores in lower half of experimental task reported to have social problems—why was this not measured and what were their scores on other established tests in comparison to the group?
	Control	15	2	$\bar{X}=16\text{-}1$	Measure NR, reported to be "achieving"	N/A	N/A	N/A	N/A	N/A	N/A			

a NR, not reported.
b N/A, not assessed.
c subjects

615

dren as having difficulty in distinguishing differences in shapes, sizes, amounts, and lengths. These difficulties were found to be present early in life. Parents reported that these children infrequently played with puzzles, blocks, or construction-type toys. It appears likely that these children were born with an inability to discriminate and manipulate spatial and numerical relationships (Lansdown, 1978).

In support of the probable relationship between visual–spatial–imagery skills and arithmetic skills, evidence from studies of patients with right-hemisphere dysfunction seems relevant. Subjects with documented right-hemisphere damage showed difficulty with basic arithmetic skills (Weintraub & Mesulam, 1983). In the case of children, the acquisition of basic number concepts may be based on exploration of spatial and physical attributes of objects, an ability generally thought to be a right-hemispheric function. Moreover, arithmetic underachievers have been found to have unusual evoked potentials (EP's) in the right hemisphere from that of normal subjects (John, Karmel, & Corning, 1977). Electroencephalographic (EEG) studies have found right- as well as left-hemispheric contributions to math calculation (Dimond & Beaumont, 1972; Katz, 1980; Murphy, Darwin, & Murphy, 1977). Furthermore, Querishi and Dimond (1979), in a comparison of left-brain-damaged (LBD), right-brain-damaged (RBD), and normal individuals, found more deterioration of calculation in RBD subjects than in the other groups.

Luria (1980) emphasized the relationship between arithmetic operations, spatial imagery, and visual–spatial concepts. In a critical overview of arithmetic deficits, Gaddes (1985) concluded that medial posterior right-hemisphere dysfunction is involved in spatial perceptual and imagery difficulties as well as inferior achievement in arithmetic, geometry, map drawing, and mechanical–constructional skills. In addition, the interrelationships between arithmetic deficits, social intelligence, and right-hemispheric dysfunction were empirically strengthened by post-mortem studies of Turner's syndrome patients (Brun & Skold, 1968; Reske-Nielsen, Christensen, & Nielsen, 1982).

Therefore, it may be postulated that nonverbal social–emotional difficulties as well as arithmetic deficits are related to right-hemispheric dysfunction since both involve the manipulation of imagery, visuoperception, and spatial processes. In point of fact, a positive correlation between social-skill ability and arithmetic skills has been found (Badian, 1983). Children with excellent arithmetic skills were found to have good social adjustment, while children with low arithmetic ability evidenced significant emotional difficulties. Consonant with these findings, Kirby and Asman (1984) found that children with arithmetic deficits also experienced difficulty in learning appropriate social skills and applications. Further neuropsychological investigation into these interrelationships may prove to be highly productive.

V. Subtypes of Nonverbal Learning Disabilities

Several investigators have examined the interrelationships between visual–motor skills, social perception, and arithmetic (Badian, 1983; Denckla, 1978, 1983; Rourke & Strang, 1978; Voeller, 1986). Although there are some differences in classifications utilized by these researchers, there are more similarities in the behavioral manifestations than differences.

A. NPOOD Subtype

It has been suggested that central processing deficiencies can lead to social–emotional disturbances and learning disabilities (Rourke & Fisk, 1981). Rourke and Finlayson (1978) coined the subtype nonverbal perceptual-organization-output-disabled children (NPOOD). These children evidenced reading and spelling abilities at the average to above-average level, while arithmetic skills were significantly weaker accompanied by visuospatial deficits. Arithmetic errors by these children included weaknesses in spatial organization, procedural errors, a failure to recognize the need to shift operations, delayed visual–motor skills, and poor judgment and reasoning. Moreover, these children showed pronounced difficulty in adapting previously learned operations to novel situations (Strang & Rourke, 1983, 1985). This inability to shift operations and adapt to novel situations has a direct impact on these children's difficulty in adapting to novel social situations. The NPOOD child also shows bilateral tactile–perceptual weakness (more pronounced on the left side), bilateral psychomotor impairment (more in evidence on the left hand), and poorly developed visual–spatial–organizational skills.

Rourke (1982) hypothesizes that the conceptual development necessary for appropriate social behaviors is a right-hemispheric function and is established during the sensorimotor stage. In an attempt to provide empirical support for this hypothesis, Ozols and Rourke (1985) focused on the social functioning of the NPOOD child. Difficulty in attending to, labeling, and interpreting nonverbal social cues (gestures, facial expressions) were found to be representative of the NPOOD child. In addition, these children were found to have difficulty integrating new situations with previous learning, their social relations tended to be stereotypical and routinized, and their speech was characterized as monotonic and flat (Rourke, 1982). These children tended to overanalyze and attempted to use their language to verbally solve social problems for which nonverbal processing was most appropriate. As a result, the child with poorer math than reading skills tended to be more inattentive, disorganized, irresponsible, and possessed poorer social skills than children with reading problems (Badian & Ghubilikian, 1983).

To investigate possible differences in psychopathology between children with nonverbal versus verbal learning disabilities, Strang and Rourke (1985) assessed these two groups on the Personality Inventory for Children (PIC). The NPOOD children showed a significantly different profile that the linguistically deficient learning-disabled children and a profile more suggestive of psychopathology. The psychosis, social skills, anxiety, withdrawal, and depression scales were elevated on the PIC for the NPOOD but not the linguistically delayed learning-disabled children. This subsample was also found to have difficulty adapting to change, and they were clumsy, had few friends, and used language not to communicate but rather to make contact with the listener. In all the above studies the incidence of nonverbal learning disabilities was either equal between the sexes or in favor of the females.

Unfortunately, this group of disabled children is not typically identified until adolescence, and they are often initially diagnosed as depressed or socially maladjusted. Some NPOOD children were followed into adulthood and found to have continuing social-skill difficulties. Moreover, a significant number had been psychiatrically hospitalized for depression and/or suicide attempts. None of these subjects had been successful in their chosen careers or employment (Del Dotto, Rourke, McFadden, & Fisk, 1987; Rourke et al., 1985).

In a related study, Brumback and Staton (1982) hypothesized that depression, nonverbal learning disabilities, and ADD were all related to right-hemisphere dysfunction. When these children were treated with tricyclic antidepressants they showed significant improvement on visual–spatial difficulties and interpersonal abilities (Brumback, Staton, & Wilson, 1984; Ternes, Woody, & Livingston, 1987). Depression has been repeatedly found in adults with documented right-hemisphere damage (Kinsbourne & Bemporard, 1984; Ross, 1981; Weintraub & Mesulam, 1983; Wexler, 1980).

B. Denckla's Left Hemisyndrome

Denckla (1978) identified a subtype of learning-disabled child who possessed deficits in arithmetic, visual–spatial, and social perceptual skills. These children also possessed at least three left-sided motor-weakness markers including disorders in reflex, weakness, muscle tone, gait, dysarthria, and incoordination. In addition, difficulties were found in interpersonal skill development. Verbal reasoning, social linguistics, math skills, and gesture and expression abilities were all areas that showed significant dysfunction. Right-hemisphere dysfunction was postulated to be contributory to the above difficulties (Denckla, 1978, 1983).

C. Right-Hemisphere Syndrome

A further classification was developed by Voeller (1986). Her subtype bears a striking resemblance to the NPOOD and left-hemisyndrome descriptions. Empirical verification of right-hemisphere deficits was gathered from

CT scans, EEGs, and neuropsychological batteries prior to assessment of social skills. Fifteen children were found to present this profile. As a group, these children showed significant difficulty displaying appropriate affect, an inability to correctly interpret the emotional states of others, left-sided neurological deficits, and arithmetic difficulties. The children who presented with the above symptomatology were also found to evidence an increased incidence of ADD and motor impersistence (Voeller, 1986; Voeller & Heilman, 1988). Since motor impersistence has been found to be present in adults with documented right-hemisphere damage (Kertesz, Nicholson, Cancelliere, Kassa, & Black, 1985), it may well be that a link exists between attention-deficit disorders and right-hemisphere dysfunction in children. The evidence in support of this notion is conflicting however (Hynd *et al.*, 1990).

D. Summary

In summary, the preceding three classifications appear to be very similar. All contained children who experienced difficulties in math but not reading, had social-skill deficiencies, were unable to interpret gestures and facial expressions, and had left-sided neurological markers. Moreover, empirical evidence for the co-occurrence of attention-deficit difficulties was suggested. Rourke *et al.* (1985) also found a higher-than-average incidence of depression in the NPOOD children and adults. Denckla (1978) and Voeller (1986) do not address this issue. The co-occurrence of psychopathology, particularly depression, would appear to be an important area for further investigation, particularly given the results from treatment with antidepressants (Brumback & Staton, 1982; Ternes *et al.*, 1987).

VI. Evidence from Right-Hemisphere-Damaged Adults

Voeller (1986) attempted to provide evidence for the relationship of right-hemisphere dysfunction and social deficiencies. Certainly, the relationship between clearly documented right-hemisphere damage and nonverbal learning disabilities needs further investigation. Research with adults has provided most of the evidence regarding signs associated with right-hemisphere dysfunction. Although caution must be used in extrapolating adult results to children with neurodevelopmental disorders, it is nevertheless instructional to compare the observations from adults with those from children with suspected right-hemisphere dysfunction. Table II presents a summary of representative studies with RBD adults.

Several striking similarities appear when comparing the behaviors identified in children with possible right-hemisphere deficit and adults with documented RBD. For example, all of the studies reported in Table II that assessed for the presence of social-skills deficits reported their co-occurrence with

TABLE II Symptoms Associated with Right-Hemisphere Syndrome from Selected Studies

Authors	N/Sex	Deficit in social skills	Spatial orientation deficits	Interpretation of gestures and facial expression	Deficits in parody	Arithmetic deficits	Depression/ social withdrawal	Career difficulties	Attentional problems	Deficits in concept formation & problem solving	Area of damage	Treatment	Cause
Benowitz, et al. (1983)	5 M 1 F	Y	Y	Y	Y	N/A	NR[a]	NR	NR	N/A[b]	Temporal (2) Parietal (1) Global (3)	N/A	NR
Borod, Koff, Lorch, and Nicholas (1986)	12 M	Y	N/A	Y	N/A	N/A	N/A	N/A	N/A	N/A	Anterior & posterior (7) Posterior (5)	N/A	CVA
Dagge and Hanje (1985)	13 Sex NR	Y	Y	N/A	N/A	N/A	N/A	N/A	N/A	Y	Parietal (1) Perisylvian (4) Occipital (1) Basal ganglia (1) Internal capsule (2) Frontal (3)	N/A	CVA
Foldi (1987)	10 Sex NR	Y	N/A	Y	Y	N/A	N/A	N/A	N/A	Y	Temporoparietal (5) Frontotemporal (2) Middle cerebral artery (3)	N/A	Vascular
Heilman, Scholes, and	6 RBD[c] 4 M 2 F	N/A	N/A	Y	N/A	N/A	Neglect	N/A	N/A	N/A	Right temporoparietal	N/A	4 Infarcts 1 Encephalitis 1 Glioma
Watson (1975)	6LBD[d] 3 M 3 F	N/A	N/A	Y	N/A	N/A	N	N/A	N/A	N/A	Left temporoparietal	N/A	2 Glioma 3 Infarcts 1 Hematoma

Study	Sex								Lesion location		Etiology
Moya, Benowitz, Levine, and Finkelstein (1987)	10 M 8 F	Y	N/A	N/A	N/A	N/A	N/A	Y	Not directly reported. Most common area of damage: central gyrus, parietotemporal, frontotemporal, insular, basal ganglia	N/A	Stroke
Ross (1981)	1 M 1 F	Y Y	Y	N/A	Initially Y	Initially Y	N/A	N	Right posterior frontal and anterior parietal. M also had basal ganglia.	N/A	Stroke
Rourke, Young, Strang, and Russell (1985)	3 M 5 F	Y	NR	Y	Y	Y	N/A	Y	NR	NR	NR
Weinraub and Mesulam (1985)	7 M 7 F	Y	Y	Y	Y	Y	Y	Y	Right hemisphere	NR	Varied
Weinraub, Mesulam, and Kramer (1981)	RBD 6 M 3 F	N/A	N/A	N/A	N/A	N/A	N/A	N/A	Thalamus (1) Temporal (3) Frontal (1) Parietal (1) Temporoparietal (2) Frontotemporoparietal (1) None	N/A	6 CVA 2 surgical 1 head trauma

[a] NR, not reported.
[b] N/A, not assessed.
[c] RBD, right-brain damage.
[d] LBD, left-brain damage.

documented RBD (Benowitz et al., 1983; Borod, Koff, Lorch, & Nicholas, 1986; Dagge & Hartje, 1985; Foldi, 1987; Moya, Benowitz, Levine, & Finkelstein, 1986; Ross, 1978; Rourke et al., 1985; Weintraub, Mesulam, and Kramer, 1981). Spatial-orientation deficits were reported in five of the studies of RBD (Benowitz et al., 1983; Dagge & Hartje, 1985; Moya et al., 1986; Rourke et al., 1985; Weintraub & Mesulam, 1983). Less frequently, deficits in attention, arithmetic, and depression are reported in these patients. Consequently, evidence from adult patients with RBD does provide some supportive evidence for the hypothesis that children with deficits in social skills, with accompanying problems in spatial orientation, and in the interpretation of facial expression may have right-hemispheric dysfunction. This conclusion is supported by the observation that the brains of children seem functionally similar to the brains of adults (Hynd & Willis, 1988). Even in consideration of the rather poorly documented cases of functional reorganization following brain trauma in children (Piacentini & Hynd, 1988), there is little evidence that supports the notion that developmental disorders, such as learning disabilities, are accompanied by different patterns of cerebral organization. Thus, while there are developmental considerations as to when and how functional behaviors are attained (Hynd & Willis, 1988), there is little reason to suspect that our extrapolations from adult RBD cases to the child literature are unreasonable.

VII. Discussion

This review highlights several issues for discussion. First, the relationship between attention-deficit disorders and right-hemispheric dysfunction in children needs further study. Many of the children in these studies were described as flat, inattentive, lethargic, and apathetic.

A considerable body of evidence suggests that children with attentional problems comprise two subpopulations of attention-deficit disorder (Hynd et al., 1990). Children with attention-deficit disorder with hyperactivity (ADD/H) are described as motorically overactive (hyperactive), impulsive, inattentive, and have a higher incidence of co-occurring conduct disorder. Children with attention-deficit disorder without hyperactivity (ADD/WO) are described as inattentive, sluggish, poor at sports, impulsive, and have a higher number of co-occurring developmental learning disorders than ADD/H children. Children with ADD/WO also seem to be poorer in math achievement than ADD/H children and are slower and make more errors on rapid-naming tasks (Hynd et al., 1990). It remains to be determined if children with social-skills learning disabilities more typically suffer attentional and behavioral problems associated with ADD/H or ADD/WO subtypes of ADD. The data from the studies reviewed in this chapter, especially the reports by Rourke and colleagues and Voeller, obscure any definitive conclusions, as none of these reports carefully document co-occurring DSM-III or DSM-III-R psychiatric diagnoses (American Psychiatric Association, 1987). In fact, many of the reports on children with presumed nonverbal learning disabilities due to right-hemispheric dysfunction appear in book chapters with no confirming documentation (e.g., CT/MRI data of right-hemispheric involvement) (e.g., Rourke et al., 1985; Strang & Rourke, 1985). This is an important issue and deserves attention in future studies.

The role of selected thalamic nuclei that have been demonstrated to play a role in visual–spatial input and emotional expression (Kelly, 1985) needs to be further explored. Thalamic dysfunction may impede the allocation of attentional resources and as such may be implicated in learning and attention disorders (Hynd & Semrud-Clikeman, 1989a; Ojemann, 1974). The size (area and volume) and configuration of the corpus callosum may also be of interest as well in relation to the neurobehavioral deficits these children evidence.

Concurrently with attentional and learning problems, some evidence is present as to the possibility of increased likelihood of right-hemisphere mediation of sadness and depressed mood (Davidson, Schwartz, Saron, Bennett, & Galeman, 1979; Ladavas, Nicoletti, Umilta, & Rizzolatti, 1984; Tucker, Stenslie, Roth, & Shearer, 1981). The successful use of antidepressants in the treatment of attention deficit and possible right-hemisphere difficulties in children (Brumback & Staton, 1982; Ternes et al., 1987) would appear to be a promising avenue for future research with implications for eventual intervention.

A related concern is the late identification of children with right-hemisphere disabilities. Many of these children suffered social ostracism, emotional distress, and eventually poor vocational success. One can only wonder how many of these effects could be averted through early intervention. As school districts routinely screen incoming children for speech and language delays as well as readiness deficits, it may well be equally important to determine the child's social readiness through parent questionnaires, through observations of social skills in the classroom, and through inservice of teachers as to the early identification of social-skill deficits.

Sadly, interventions and outcome data are sparsely present for carefully defined subtypes of learning-disabled children, particulary in regard to children with nonverbal learning disabilities. Whether approaches that directly teach social skills or seek to strengthen metacognitive skills will be effective with this population is unknown at this time. Given the recent governmental mandate (Wyngaarden, 1987) for the provision of services for children with social learning disabilities, it is important to begin carefully documenting the outcomes of interventions with nonverbal learning-disabled children as well as their effectiveness with linguistically based learning-disabled children with social-skill problems.

Finally, careful diagnosis of social difficulties and their impact on subsequent learning needs to be more fully empirically validated with an eye to successful treatment. Hopefully, future studies will provide a stepping stone to effective treatment of children with nonverbal learning disabilities.

References

Ainsworth, M. S. (1979). Infant-mother attachment. *American Psychologist, 34,* 932–937.

American Psychiatric Association. (1987). *Diagnostic and statistical manual of mental disorders* (3rd ed.). Washington, DC: American Psychiatric Association.

Axelrod, L. (1982). Social perception in learning disabled adolescents. *Journal of Learning Disabilities, 15,* 610–613.

Bachara, G. (1976). Empathy in learning disabled children. *Perceptual and Motor Skills, 43,* 541–542.

Badian, N. A. (1983). Dyscalculia and nonverbal disorders of learning. In H. R. Myklebust (Ed.), *Progress in learning disabilities* (Vol. 3, pp. 235–264). New York: Grune & Stratton.

Badian, N. A., & Ghubilikian, M. (1983). The personal-social characteristics of children with poor mathematical computation skills. *Journal of Learning Disabilities, 16,* 154–157.

Bauer, R. H. (1977). Memory processes in children with learning disabilities: Evidence for deficient rehearsal. *Journal of Experimental Child Psychology, 24,* 415–430.

Benowitz, L. I., Bear, D. M., Rosenthal, R., Mesulam, M.-M., Zaidel, E., & Sperry, R. W. (1983). Hemispheric specialization in nonverbal communication. *Cortex, 19,* 5–11.

Borod, J. C., Koff, E., Lorch, M. P., & Nicholas, M. (1986). The expression and perception of facial emotion in brain-damaged patients. *Neuropsychologia, 24,* 169–180.

Brown, A. L. (1975). The development of memory: Knowing, knowing about knowing, and knowing how to know. In H. W. Reese (Ed.), *Advances in child development and behavior* (Vol. 10, pp. 103–152). New York: Raven Press.

Bruinicks, V. L. (1978). Peer status and personality characteristics of learning disabled and nondisabled students. *Journal of Learning Disabilities, 11,* 484–489.

Brumback, R. A., & Staton, R. D. (1982). A hypothesis regarding the commonality of right hemisphere involvement in learning disability, attentional disorder, and childhood major depressive disorder. *Perceptual and Motor Skills, 55,* 1091–1097.

Brumback, R. A., Staton, R. D., & Wilson, H. (1984). Right cerebral hemisphere dysfunction. *Archives of Neurology (Chicago),* 41, 248–249.

Brun, A., & Skold, G. (1968). CNS malformations in Turner's Syndrome. *Acta Neuropathologica, 10,* 159–161.

Bruno, R. M. (1981). Interpretation of pictorially presented social situations by learning disabled and normal children. *Journal of Learning Disabilities, 14,* 350–352.

Bryan, T. H. (1974). Peer popularity of learning disabled children. *Journal of Learning Disabilities, 7,* 621–625.

Bryan, T. H. (1977). Learning disabled children's comprehension of nonverbal communication. *Journal of Learning Disabilities, 10,* 501–506.

Bryan, T. H., Donahue, M., & Pearl, R. (1981). Learning disabled children's communicative competence on referential communication tasks. *Journal of Pediatric Psychology, 6,* 383–393.

Bryan, T. H., & Wheeler, R. (1972). Perception of learning disabled children: The eye of the observer. *Journal of Learning Disabilities, 5,* 484–488.

Bryan, T. H., Wheeler, R., Felcan, J., & Henek, R. (1976). "Come on dummy"; An observational study of children's communications. *Journal of Learning Disabilities, 9,* 53–61.

Connolly, C. (1969). The psychosocial adjustment of children with dyslexia. *Exceptional Children, 36,* 126–127.

Dagge, M., & Hartje, W. (1985). Influence of contextual complexity on the processing of cartoons by patients with unilateral lesions. *Cortex, 21,* 607–616.

Davidson, R. J., Schwartz, G. E., Saron, C., Bennett, G., & Galeman, D. G. (1979). Frontal versus parietal EEG asymmetry during positive and negative affect. *Psychophysiology, 16,* 202.

Del Dotto, J. E., Rourke, B. P., McFadden, G. T., & Fisk, J. L. (1987, February). *Developmental analysis of arithmetic disabled children: Impact on personality adjustment and patterns of adaptive functioning.* Paper presented at the International Neuropsychological Society meeting, Washington, DC.

Denckla, M. B. (1978). Minimal brain dysfunction. In J. S. Chall & A. F. Mirsky (Eds.), *Education and the brain* (pp. 223–268). Chicago, IL: University of Chicago Press.

Denckla, M. B. (1979). Childhood learning disabilities. In K. M. Heilman & E. Valenstein (Eds.), *Clinical neuropsychology* (pp. 535–573). New York: Oxford University Press.

Denckla, M. B. (1983). The neuropsychology of social-emotional learning disabilities. *Archives of Neurology (Chicago), 40,* 461–462.

Dimond, S. J., & Beaumont, J. G. (1972). A right hemisphere basis for calculation in the human brain. *Psychonomic Science, 26,* 137–138.

Foldi, N. (1987). Appreciation of pragmatic interpretations of indirect commands: Comparison of right and left hemisphere brain-damaged patients. *Brain & Language, 31,* 88–108.

Gaddes, W. H. (1985). *Learning disabilities and brain function.* New York: Springer-Verlag.

Gerber, P. J., & Zinkgraft, S. A. (1982). A comparative study of social-perceptual ability in learning disabled and nonhandicapped students. *Learning Disability Quarterly, 5,* 374–378.

Goldstein, D., & Dundon, W. D. (1987). Affect and cognition in learning disabilities. In S. J. Ceci (Ed.), *Handbook of cognitive, social, and neuropsychological aspects of learning disabilities* (Vol. 2, pp. 233–249). Hillsdale, NJ: Erlbaum.

Gresham, F. M., & Elliott, S. N. (1987). The relationship between adaptive behavior and social skills: Issues in definition and assessment. *Journal of Special Education,* *21*(1), 167–181.

Heilman, K. M., Scholes, R., & Watson, R. T. (1975). Auditory affective agnosia. *Journal of Neurology, Neurosurgery and Psychiatry, 38,* 69–72.

Hynd, G. W., Lorys, A., Semrud-Clikeman, M., Nieves, N., Huettner, M., & Lahey, B. B. (1990). Attention deficit disorder without hyperactivity (ADD/WO): A distinct behavioral and neurocognitive syndrome. *Journal of Child Neurology.* (in press).

Hynd, G. W., & Semrud-Clikeman, M. (1989a). Dyslexia and brain morphology. *Psychological Bulletin, 106,* 447–482.

Hynd, G. W., & Semrud-Clikeman, M. (1989b). Dyslexia and neurodevelopmental pathology: Relationships to cognition, intelligence and reading skill acquisition. *Journal of Learning Disabilities, 22,* 204–216.

Hynd, G. W., & Willis, W. G. (1988) *Pediatric neuropsychology.* Orlando, FL: Grune & Stratton [Allyn & Bacon].

Izard, C. E. (1977). *Human emotions.* New York: Plenum.

Izard, C. E. (1982). Comments on emotion and cognition: Can there be a working relationship? In M. S. Clark & S. T. Fiske (Eds.), *Affect and cognition* (pp. 229–240). Hillsdale, NJ: Erlbaum.

John, E. R., Karmel, B. Z. & Corning, W. C. (1977). Neurometrics. *Science, 196,* 1393–1410.

Johnson, D. J., & Myklebust, H. R. (1971). *Learning disabilities.* New York: Grune & Stratton.

Kaslow, F., & Cooper, B. (1978, January). Family therapy with the learning disabled child and his/her family. *Journal of Marriage and Family Counseling,* pp. 41–48.

Katz, A. (1980). Cognitive arithmetic: Evidence for right hemispheric mediation in an elementary component stage. *Quarterly Journal of Experimental Psychology, 32,* 69–84.

Kelly, J. P. (1985). Anatomical basis of sensory perception and motor coordination. In E. R. Kandel & J. H. Schwartz (Eds.), *Principles of neural science* (2nd ed., pp. 222–243). New York: Elsevier.

Kertesz, A., Nicholson, I., Cancelliere, A., Kassa, K., & Black, S. E. (1985). Motor impersistence: A right hemisphere syndrome. *Neurology, 35,* 662–666.

Kinsbourne, M., & Bemporad, B. (1984). Lateralization of emotion: A model and the evidence. In N. A. Fox & R. J. Davidson (Eds.), *The psychobiology of affective development* (pp. 259–291). Hillsdale, NJ: Erlbaum.

Kinsbourne, M., & Caplan, P. J. (1979). *Children's learning and attentional problems.* Boston, MA: Little, Brown.

Kirby, J. R., & Asman, A. F. (1984). Planning skills and mathematics achievement: Implications regarding learning disability. *Journal of Psychoeducational Assessment, 2,* 9–22.

Kosteski, D. M., Goldstein, D., & Hasher, L. (1979). *Organizational strategies in the memory of learning disabled and non-disabled children.* Paper presented at the meeting of the Eastern Psychological Association, Philadelphia, PA.

Krudek, L. A., & Krile, D. (1982). A developmental analysis of the relation between peer acceptance and both interpersonal understanding and perceived social self-competence. *Child Development, 53,* 1485–1491.

Ladavas, E., Nicoletti, R., Umilta, C., & Rizzolatti, G. (1984). Right hemisphere interference during negative affect: A reaction time study. *Neuropsychologia, 22,* 479–484.

Landsdown, R. (1978). Retardation in mathematics: A consideration of multifactorial determination. *Journal of Child Psychology and Psychiatry, 19,* 181–185.

Ley, R. G., & Bryden, M. P. (1981). Consciousness, emotion, and the right hemisphere. In G. Underwood & R. Stevens (Eds.), *Aspects of consciousness* (Vol. 2, pp. 216–239). London: Academic Press.

Luria, A. R. (1980). *Higher cortical functions in man.* New York: Basic Books.

Maheady, L., Maitland, G. E., & Sainato, D. M. (1984). Interpretation of social interactions by learning disabled, socially/emotionally disturbed, educable mentally retarded, and nondisabled children. *Journal of Special Education, 18,* 151–159.

Mayo, C., & LaFrance, M. (1979). On the acquisition of nonverbal communication: A review. In S. Chess & A. Thomas (Eds.), *Annual progress in child psychiatry and child development.* New York: Brunner/Mazel.

McFall, R. M. (1982). A review and reformulation of the concept of social skills. *Behavioral Assessment, 4,* 1–33.

Moya, K. L., Benowitz, L. I., Levine, D. N., & Finkelstein, S. (1987). Covariant defects in visuospatial abilities and recall of verbal narrative after right hemisphere stroke. *Cortex, 22,* 381–397.

Murphy, P., Darwin, J., & Murphy, D. (1977). EEG feedback training for cerebral dysfunction: A research program with learning disabled adolescents. *Biofeedback and Self Regulation, 2,* 288–295.

Myklebust, H. R. (1975). Nonverbal learning disabilities: Assessment and intervention. In H. R. Myklebust (Ed.), *Progress in learning disabilities* (Vol. 3). New York: Grune & Stratton.

Ojemann, G. A. (1974). Mental arithmetic during human thalamic stimulation. *Neuropsychologia, 12,* 1–10.

Ozols, E. J., & Rourke, B. P. (1985). Dimensions of social sensitivity in two types of learning disabled children. In B. P. Rourke (Ed.), *Neuropsychology of learning disabilities* (pp. 281–301). New York: Guilford Press.

Pearl, R. (1987). Social cognitive factors in learning disabled children's social problems. In S. J. Ceci (Ed.), *Handbook of cognitive, social, and neuropsychological aspects of learning disabilities* (Vol. 2, pp. 273–294). Hillsdale, NJ: Erlbaum.

Pearl, R., & Cosden, M. (1982). Sizing up a situation: Learning disabled children's understanding of social interactions. *Learning Disability Quarterly, 5,* 371–373.

Pennington, B. F., Bender, B., Puck, M., Salbenblatt, J., & Robinson, A. (1982). Learning disabilities in children with sex chromosome anomalies. *Child Development, 53,* 1182–1192.

Petrauskas, R. J., & Rourke, B. P. (1979). Identification of subtypes of retarded readers: A neuropsychological, multivariate approach. *Journal of Clinical Neuropsychology, 1,* 17–37.

Piacenti, J. C., & Hynd, G. W. (1988). Language after dominant hemispherectomy:

Are plasticity and equipotentiality theory viable concepts? *Clinical Psychology Review, 8,* 595–609.

Porter, J. E., & Rourke, B. P. (1985). Socioemotional functioning of learning disabled children: A subtypal analysis of personality patterns. In B. P. Rourke (Ed.), *Neuropsychology of learning disabilities* (pp. 257–280). New York: Guilford Press.

Querishi, R., & Dimond, S. J. (1979). Calculation and the right hemisphere. *Lancet, 1,* 322–323.

Reske-Nielsen, E., Christensen, A. L., & Nielsen, J. (1982). A neuropathological and neuropsychological study of Turner's Syndrome. *Cortex, 18,* 181–190.

Richey, D. D., & McKinney, J. D. (1978). Classroom behavioral subtypes of learning disabled boys. *Journal of Learning Disabilities, 11,* 297–302.

Ross, E. D. (1981). The aprosodias: Functional-anatomical organization of the affective components of language in the right hemisphere. *Archives of Neurology (Chicago), 38,* 561–569.

Rourke, B. P. (1982). Central processing deficiencies in children: Toward a developmental neuropsychological model. *Journal of Clinical Neuropsychology, 4,* 1–18.

Rourke, B. P., & Finlayson, M. A. J. (1978). Neuropsychological significance of variations in patterns of academic performance: Verbal and visual-spatial abilities. *Journal of Abnormal Child Psychology, 6,* 121–133.

Rourke, B. P., & Fisk, J. L. (1981). Socio-emotional disturbances of learning disabled children: The role of central processing deficits. *Bulletin of the Orton Society, 31,* 77–88.

Rourke, B. P., & Strang, J. D. (1978). Neuropsychological significance of variations in patterns of academic performance; Motor, psychomotor, and tactile perception abilities. *Journal of Pediatric Psychology, 3,* 62–66.

Rourke, B. P., Young, G. C., Strang, J. D., & Russell, D. L. (1985). Adult outcomes of central processing deficiencies in childhood. In I. Grant & K. M. Adams (Eds.), *Neuropsychological assessment in neuropsychiatric disorders: Clinical methods and empirical findings* (pp. 244–257). New York: Oxford University Press.

Semrud-Clikeman, M., & Hynd, G. W. (1990). Right hemispheric dysfunction in nonverbal learning disabilities: Social, academic, and adaptive functioning in adults and children. *Psychological Bulletin. 107,* 196–207.

Siperstein, G. N., Bopp, M. A., & Bak, J. J. (1978). Social status of learning disabled children. *Journal of Learning Disabilities, 11,* 98–102.

Sternberg, R. J., & Wagner, R. K. (1982). Automatization failure in learning disabilities. *Topics in Learning and Learning Disabilities, 1,* 1–11.

Strang, J. D., & Rourke, B. P. (1983). Concept-formation/nonverbal reasoning abilities of children who exhibit specific academic problems with arithmetic. *Journal of Clinical Child Psychology, 12,* 33–39.

Strang, J. D., & Rourke, B. P. (1985). Arithmetic disability subtypes: The neuropsychological significance of specific arithmetic impairment in childhood. In B. P. Rourke (Ed.), *Neuropsychology of learning disabilities* (pp. 302–330). New York: Guilford Press.

Ternes, J., Woody, R., & Livingston, R. (1987). A child with right hemisphere deficit syndrome responsive to carbamazepine treatment. *Journal of the American Academy of Child and Adolescent Psychiatry, 87,* 586–588.

Torgesen, J. K. (1979). Factors related to poor performance on memory tasks in reading disabled children. *Learning Disability Quarterly, 2,* 17–23.

Torgesen, J. K. (1980). Implications of the LD child's use of efficient task strategies. *Journal of Learning Disabilities, 13,* 364–371.

Trepanier, M. L., & Casale, C. M. (1983). Metamemory development in learning disabled children. In W. M. Cruickshank & E. Task (Eds.), *Academics and beyond* (pp. 182–193). Syracuse, NY: Syracuse University Press.

Tucker, D. M., Stenslie, C. E., Roth, R. S. & Shearer, S. L. (1981). Right frontal lobe activation and right hemisphere performance. *Archives of General Psychiatry, 38,* 169–174.

Voeller, K. S. (1986). Right hemisphere deficit syndrome in children. *American Journal of Psychiatry, 143,* 1004–1011.

Voeller, K. S., & Heilman, K. M. (1988, September). *Motor impersistence in children with attention deficit hyperactivity disorder. Evidence for right hemispheric dysfunction.* Paper presented at the 17th annual meeting of the Child Neurology Society, Halifax, Nova Scotia.

Weintraub, S., & Mesulam, M.-M. (1983). Developmental learning disabilities and the right hemisphere: Emotional, interpersonal and cognitive components. *Archives of Neurology (Chicago), 40,* 463–468.

Weintraub, S., Mesulam, M.-M., & Kramer, L. (1981). Disturbances in prosody: A right-hemisphere contribution to language. *Archives of Neurology, 38,* 742–744.

Wexler, B. E. (1980). Cerebral laterality and psychiatry: A review of the literature. *American Journal of Psychiatry, 137,* 279–291.

Wiig, E., & Harris, S. (1974). Perception and interpretation of nonverbally expressed emotions by adolescents with learning disabilities. *Perceptual and Motor Skills, 38,* 239–245.

Wyngaarden, J. B. (Ed.). (1987). *Learning disabilities: A report to the U.S. Congress.* Washington, DC: National Institutes of Health, Interagency Committee on Learning Disabilities.

CHAPTER TWENTY-THREE

Remediating Reading Disabilities

Barbara W. Wise
Richard K. Olson

I. Introduction

Although reading disabilities are but one type of learning disability, they are the most frequently studied type and thus the focus of this chapter. Are there remedial reading techniques which make more sense theoretically and which are more effective than others in improving the performance of reading-disabled children? Do optimal techniques vary with different children? Before attempting to answer these questions, this chapter discusses the definition of reading disabilities and reviews their genetic and neuropsychological bases, in order to provide a theoretical framework for assessing remedial approaches. The next section evaluates various remedial techniques according to their efficacy and consistency with neuropsychological evidence. The chapter concludes with our own current research on remediation using talking computers that provide auditory and visual feedback for difficult words in stories.

II. Definition of the Population

Population definition is an important first step in research on reading disabilities. Most studies of reading disabilities exclude children who read poorly because of obvious instructional deficiencies, assuming they would have achieved normal levels of literacy had they received normal instruction in good schools. This chapter likewise focuses on children who fail in reading despite normal education. Such children can be labeled reading disabled and receive special education services if they meet the legal criteria of a significant deficit in reading ability, despite normal sensory abilities, educational and emotional background, and intelligence (U.S. Department of Health, Education and Welfare, 1976).

Still controversial in research definitions of reading disabilities is the traditional and legal criterion of "normal intelligence." Most, but not all, of the studies reviewed in this chapter included this criterion in their selection of a reading-disabled sample, using some minimal score on an intelligence test as a criterion (e.g., IQ > 90 on the Wechsler Intelligence Scale for Children) (Wechsler, 1974). However, many experts now challenge the assumption that a discrepancy in reading performance relative to IQ defines a unique population (Siegel, 1989). In fact, the entire October, 1989, *Journal of Learning Disabilities* explores this controversy. Stanovich (1989) agrees that problems exist in using IQ tests for definitional purposes. Reading problems themselves can depress children's verbal IQs, and word-recognition problems relate similarly to phonological deficits across a range of IQ. However, since other reading problems relate to deficits in general intellectual ability, Stanovich recommends continuing to measure IQ and other reading-related abilities in research in order to understand different deficits.

III. Neuropsychological Basis of Reading Disabilities

Most educators agree that the goal of fluent reading is to understand printed text as adeptly as spoken language. Disabled readers cannot do this. Reading disabilities, by the definition above, cannot result from poor instruction, sensory deficits, or other extrinsic factors. Therefore, they must result from deficiencies in intrinsic psychological processes related to reading and learning to read. The neuropsychological question concerns *which* component processes of reading and related cognitive skills are deficient in reading disabilities, and whether these processes can be remediated.

This chapter focuses more on the causes and the remediation of problems in word recognition and related linguistic processes than it does on problems in comprehension. To justify this focus, we will review research that demonstrates (1) that word-recognition deficits constrain reading comprehension in disabled readers, (2) that word recognition, phonological coding, and related segmental language skills are uniquely deficient in most disabled readers, and (3) that the phonological deficit is highly heritable. We conclude the section with recent neuroanatomical evidence that suggests a possible pathway for genetic influences on phonological coding.

A. Reading Comprehension, Context, and Word Recognition

Some theorists would argue that our focus on problems in word recognition and phonological coding is misguided (Goodman, 1967; Smith,

1978). Goodman has characterized the reading process as a "psycholinguistic guessing game," wherein readers use context to guess the identity of unfamiliar words. According to Goodman and Smith, overuse of decoding strategies and inadequate attention to meaning and use of context primarily cause reading problems. However, Stanovich (1980) reported evidence directly contradicting this assertion. Stanovich found that good readers' word recognition shows very little influence of sentence context. On the other hand, disabled readers' word recognition benefits from appropriate context and suffers from inappropriate context. The central problem for disabled readers is *not* their inability to use context in identifying words, but rather their inefficiency in decoding words independent of context.

Word-recognition errors directly constrain reading comprehension, because misidentified words lead to faulty understanding. Yet even when disabled readers can correctly identify words, they may do so much less rapidly and automatically than normal readers do. This presumably costs them extra effort, leaving fewer attentional resources available for comprehending text (LaBerge & Samuels, 1974; Perfetti, 1985). Thus, their word-recognition problems hinder their reading comprehension both directly and indirectly.

Certainly, other problems can constrain reading comprehension in some readers. Conners and Olson (1990) analyzed independent contributions from skills in word recognition and listening comprehension to ability in reading comprehension, as measured by the Peabody Individual Achievement Test (PIAT) (Dunn & Markwardt, 1970). Reading comprehension depended very heavily on word recognition, as expected, since the PIAT tests comprehension of single sentences. However, listening comprehension also contributed substantial independent variance. Extended-path models were used to examine processes contributing to listening comprehension and word recognition. The models revealed that verbal intelligence [by Kaufman's (1975) verbal comprehension factor of the WISC] accounted for significant variance in listening comprehension. On the other hand, phoneme segmentation ability (described below) accounted for significant independent variance in word recognition and phonological decoding.

These results show that processes involved in word recognition and in verbal intelligence both affect reading comprehension. In the disabled reader with normal verbal intelligence, reading comprehension is secondarily constrained by poor word recognition. In the poor reader with relatively good word-recognition skills, comprehension is constrained by severely limited reading experience or relatively low verbal intelligence. Extreme cases fitting the latter profile have been labeled "hyperlexic" (Healy, Aram, Horowitz, & Kessler, 1982), while children with normal IQ and low word-recognition profiles are often called "dyslexic." The remedial needs of children whose primary deficits lie in word recognition will probably be quite different from those whose poor comprehension relates to primary deficits in verbal intelligence.

B. Unique Deficits in Component Reading and Language Skills

Researchers seek processes that relate causally to reading disabilities, as opposed to ones lagging due to reduced reading experience. Most research designs match disabled readers by age with normally reading controls. In such studies, the disabled readers typically lag in many skills, but the lags are difficult to interpret. Generalized frustration and expected failure in reading-related tasks may cause lower performance, and narrowed reading experience can cause secondary lags in comprehension or vocabulary. Finally, apparent relative deficits in skills may be difficult to interpret because of psychometric problems associated with test variance, reliability, and nonlinearity.

A useful approach for finding unique deficits in disabled readers is to match older disabled readers with younger normal readers on a reading skill (Bryant & Goswami, 1986). For example, fifth-grade disabled readers with second-grade-level word-recognition skills may be matched with average second-grade readers. The fact that these children perform in the same general range on other measures of reading-related skills eliminates psychometric problems of differential floor and ceiling effects. Also, the older disabled readers should have had at least as much reading experience as the younger normal group. Significant differences that emerge in reading-level-match comparisons can therefore be quite informative about unique deficits in disabled readers, and these deficits can suggest causal factors in reading disabilities.

Our own reading-level comparison matched older disabled and younger normal readers (mean ages 15.6 and 10.4 years) on their performance on the PIAT word-recognition test (Conners & Olson, 1990; Olson, Wise, Conners, Rack, & Fulker, 1989). The disabled readers had scored at least 1.5 standard deviations below the mean of a different *age*-matched normal comparison group on this test. The disabled group's reading comprehension, listening comprehension, and raw scores on the WISC verbal subtests were all significantly *higher* than their younger reading-level matches' scores. The comparison demonstrates a relatively greater problem in word recognition than in reading comprehension for the disabled group, a common result in studies of specific reading disability (Stanovich, 1985).

The comparison also examined tasks designed to measure two component processes of word recognition. *Phonological coding* ability is the ability to decode or sound out unfamiliar words. Our test of phonological coding measured subjects' combined accuracy and speed in oral reading of 85 pronounceable nonwords (e.g., *tegwop, calch*). Phonological coding is particularly important for beginning readers for decoding unfamiliar printed words, and recent research by Van Orden (1987) has shown that rapid phonological coding processes also function even in normal adult readers' recognition of familiar words.

A second task evaluated the ability to recognize specific *orthographic*, or spelling, patterns for words. Orthographic coding is essential in English, for reading homophones (e.g., *would, wood*) and "exception" words which violate common spelling-to-sound rules (e.g., *said, yacht*). Our orthographic task measured speed and accuracy for choosing the correctly spelled item versus its misspelled pseudohomophone foil (e.g., *rain, rane*) across 80 forced-choice trials. Phonological coding is ineffective in these choices, since sounding out yields the same pronunciation for both items. Instead, subjects had to recognize the correct pattern of letters for the target word.

The reading-level-match comparisons revealed very different results for the orthographic and phonological coding tasks. The older disabled group scored slightly but significantly higher than the younger normal group on the orthographic task. In contrast, the disabled group scored .78 standard deviations *below* the mean of the younger normal readers on the phonological coding task.

A phonological coding deficit in reading-level-match comparisons was first reported by Snowling (1980). Rack, Snowling, and Olson (submitted) conducted a metaanalysis of reading-level-match studies on phonological coding in nonword reading. Most studies that selected a sample with normal IQ and educational background reported the deficit. Sampling problems and methodological artifacts accounted for null results in most other studies.

Only one other task besides nonword reading yielded a significant deficit in the disabled group. This task required subjects to segment and blend phonemes within words, as in the "pig-latin" language game. Subjects had to strip the initial phoneme from a spoken word and pronounce the result of moving and blending the phoneme with an "ay" sound at the end of the word (e.g., *pig* becomes *igpay*). The disabled group performed .55 standard deviations below the younger reading-level-matched subjects. Path models revealed a strong influence from this task on disabled readers' phonological coding, as well as a similar deficit profile to phonological coding (Conners & Olson, 1990).

"Pig latin" involves segmental language skills similar to those evaluated in other studies of phonemic awareness and phonemic segmentation, several of which have also found deficits for disabled readers in reading-level-match comparisons (Bradley & Bryant, 1978; Snowling, 1981). Segmental language skills in prereaders are strong predictors of later reading ability (Bradley

& Bryant, 1983; Calfee, Lindamood, & Lindamood, 1973; Lundberg, Olofsson, & Wall, 1980), although reading experience also encourages the development of segmental language skills (Morais, Carey, Alegria, & Bertelson, 1979). Two studies to be reviewed later showed that preschool training in segmental language skills improved later reading performance. Taken as a whole, the evidence strongly suggests that deficits in segmental language skills constrain the development of phonological coding and word recognition in disabled readers.

C. Possibility of Visual Processing Deficits

A very different view has been taken by those who have proposed various visual processing deficits as causal factors in reading disabilities. However, Vellutino (1980) concluded from a number of studies that disabled readers have problems processing visual symbols only when verbal labels are involved. For example, disabled readers made no more reversals or other errors than normal readers did when copying letters from the unfamiliar (and thus not verbally encoded) Hebrew alphabet.

Other reports of visual deficits which do *not* involve verbal processing have appeared. Yet careful reviews and attempts to replicate most of these deficits have found serious flaws in reports of (1) abnormal eye movements (reported by Pavlidis, 1981; but see Olson, Kliegl, & Davidson, 1983; and Olson, Wise, Conners, & Rack, in press), (2) inadequate ocular dominance and convergence (Stein & Fowler, 1982; but see Bishop, 1986; Wilshire, 1989), (3) "scotopic sensitivity" (Irlen, 1983; but see Wright, 1989), and (4) foveal and peripheral processing differences (Geiger & Letvin, 1987; but see Klein, Berry, Briand, D'Entrement, & Farmer, in press).

Although the above visual deficits and attendant remediation are suspect, other differences in visual processes may exist between disabled and normal readers. Lovegrove, Martin, and Slaghuis (1986) reported that about 70% of specifically reading-disabled subjects suffered a deficit in "transient channel activity" that could be important in erasing the previous image when the eye moves (Breitmeyer, 1989). Disabled readers also make poorer judgements of double-flash temporal order, are less sensitive to flicker, and attenuate metacontrast less well than normal readers (M. Williams & LeCluyse, in press; Winters, Patterson, & Shontz, 1989).

These subtle deficits have not yet been shown to disrupt the processing of print. Some visual processing deficits could possibly result from the same general neurological factors that lead to problems in segmental language skills, which seem to be the primary cause of disabled readers' problems in phonological coding and word recognition. To address this issue, research must measure relevant visual and segmental language measures on the same subjects.

D. Genetic and Environmental Influences on Reading Disabilities

The relative influences of genetic and environmental factors are fundamental to questions about the neuropsychological basis of reading disabilities and their remediation. DeFries and Gillis (this volume, Chapter 2) review behavior–genetic methods and results from the Colorado Reading Project. In this section we will briefly consider some behavior–genetic results that bear directly on disabled readers' deficits in word recognition.

Olson *et al.* (1989) compared similarities in reading-related skills for identical, monozygotic (MZ), and same-sex fraternal, dizygotic (DZ) twin pairs. At least one twin in each pair scored at least 1 standard deviation below the word-recognition mean of a normal comparison group. Both MZ and DZ twin pairs share environmental factors equivalently. However, MZ twins share all the same genes, while DZ twins share only half their genes on average. Thus, greater similarity between MZ than DZ twins suggests a genetic etiology. Using DeFries and Fulker's (1985) regression model to determine heritability for group deficits (h^2g.) (see DeFries & Gillis, this volume, Chapter 2), we found that the disabled group's deficit in word recognition was about 40% due to genetic factors ($h^2g = .4$). However, most of the genetic variance in word-recognition deficits was linked to genetic variance in phonological coding. In contrast, most of the environmental variance in word-recognition deficits was linked to variance in orthographic coding.

More recent behavior–genetic analyses of a larger twin sample with a more reliable measure of word recognition have revealed somewhat higher heritability for deficits in word recognition than our previous analyses ($h^2g = .58$) (Olson, Wise, & Rack, 1989). However, the same pattern of results for phonological and orthographic coding emerged: The genetic covariance between deficits in word recognition and phonological coding ($h^2g = .62$) was substantially and significantly higher than the genetic covariance between word recognition and orthographic coding ($h^2g = .22$) Performance in orthographic coding may be largely due to environmental influences like exposure to print shared by both MZ and DZ twin pairs (and see consistent results from Stanovich & West, 1989).

The high genetic correlation between deficits in phonological coding and word recognition, coupled with the evidence for the unique severity of phonological coding problems, indicate a major genetically based constraint on the development of word recognition in most disabled readers. As discussed earlier, a minority of disabled readers in our sample did not have a unique phonological coding deficit. But consistent with our genetic hypothesis, the heritability of word-recognition deficits was significantly lower for those disabled readers who were relatively good phonological coders (Olson, Rack, Conners, DeFries, & Fulker, 1990).

Recent evidence has suggested a possible neuroanatomical pathway for genetic influences on phonological coding and segmental language skills. Studies have reported greater bilateral symmetry in the planum temporale among disabled readers (Galaburda, 1989; and see a review by Hynd & Semrud-Clikeman, 1989). Larsen, Hoien, Lundberg, and Odegaard (1989) have found specific links between bilateral symmetry and phonological coding problems. Seventy percent of their dyslexic sample had symmetrical plana temporale, compared to 30% of a normal sample. And all 5 of the 19 dyslexic subjects who had unique deficits in phonological coding relative to word recognition had symmetrical plana. No twin studies have yet measured plana symmetry, but its apparent link to phonological coding suggests the neuro-anatomical pattern could be heritable.

In summary, most disabled readers suffer unique deficits in phonological coding and related segmental language skills. Furthermore, these deficits are highly heritable and account for much of the heritable variance in word recognition, whereas environmental factors have more influence on ortho-graphic coding. High heritability does *not* predict that these deficits in word recognition or phonological processes must be permanent. Nonetheless, the genetic and neurological data do suggest that extraordinary effort may be required to improve disabled readers' phonological coding significantly. Thus, genetic influences may constrain the speed or ease of reading development, but environmental factors such as improved reading instruction and greater reading experience and exposure to print may compensate for genetic con-straints.

IV. Remedial Techniques

The phonological coding deficit is clearly established as the strongest predictor and correlate of reading disabilities. Theoretically based remedial strategies attempt either to remediate or to circumvent the deficit by teaching to strengths in other verbal skills. Before reviewing methods that acknowledge the phonological deficit, we will discuss some that ignore it.

A. Remedial Techniques Not Consistent with the Phonological-Deficit Theory

Severely disabled readers and their parents often become frustrated by the children's lack of success in reading despite their obvious intelligence and effort. Parents fear the consequences of long-term failure in reading and in other academic skills. Their desperation makes them ready targets for charis-matic speakers offering pseudomedical quick cures. But as *Wilshire* (1989) points out in reviewing such treatments, the notion of a cure is displaced, since reading disability is not a disease in the accepted sense of the word.

Wilshire (1989) discusses problems inherent in much remedial research. Field research lacks the precise control of intervening variables possible in laboratory studies. Also, control groups can be difficult to design into long-term studies, particularly when the experimenter expects positive results from a manipulation. Yet adequate control groups are vital in methodological research in order to distinguish treatment effects from those caused merely by the expectation of success on the part of the participants (placebo effects) or those resulting from the extra attention and structure of an experimental procedure (Hawthorn effects).

Wilshire (1989) finds inadequate control groups in nearly all the studies of "magic cures." He also points out even more glaring problems in studies of ocular-convergence training, tinted lenses, and use of megavitamins, antihistamines, and food additives. These studies demonstrate no pretreatment deficits in these processes in disabled readers relative to normals, nor do any related remedial programs show controlled evidence for improvement in reading (see also Bishop, 1986; and Wright, 1989). Educational "visual–perceptual" and "perceptual–motor" training programs also have long histories as remedial treatments, but reviews show them to be completely ineffective in improving reading (Bateman, 1979; Hammill, Goodman, & Wiederholt, 1974).

The notion of reading disability as a visual deficit is so entrenched historically that we expect continued research concerning this topic. Because of the recent evidence suggesting deficits in transient channel activity and flicker sensitivity, we also hope that continued research will investigate their possible relation to reading processes and remedial methods.

For the present, if any child *with or without a reading problem* has difficulties with visual acuity or convergence, prescriptive lenses or surgery can improve vision. But for children with word-recognition problems related to difficulties in segmental language skills, or for those with problems in listening and reading comprehension, programs that only address visual or perceptual problems will not improve reading.

B. *Programs that Address the Phonological Deficit*

Theoretically appropriate remedial techniques address the phonological deficit in three different ways. One way is to attempt to prevent later reading problems by strengthening phonemic awareness skills prior to beginning any reading instruction. If the deficit is not prevented, there are two other contrasting ways programs attempt to deal with it during reading instruction. On the one hand, programs can attempt to circumvent the problem by building on relative strengths in higher-level verbal skills like use of context and comprehension. On the other hand, many programs attempt to remediate the weakness, with concurrent training in phonemic awareness and in the association of phonemes with units of print during reading. We will discuss the three approaches of preschool prevention, circumvention by teaching strengths, and remediation during reading instruction.

1. PREVENTION OF THE DEFICIT: PRESCHOOL TRAINING IN PHONEMIC AWARENESS

Three findings argue for preschool phonemic awareness instruction for at-risk preschool children. First, preschool phonological skills predict later reading performance better than any other measure (see Wagner & Torgeson, 1987, for a review). Second, phonological deficits limit both word recognition and reading comprehension in disabled readers. And finally, training in these skills can lead to later improvement in reading ability for at-risk children.

Training in general auditory perception is no more likely than training in visual perception to improve reading (J. Williams, 1980). In contrast, phonemic awareness and segmentation training does generalize to improve the ability to learn word-decoding skills, (for reviews, see Berninger, Thalberg, DeBruyn, & Smith, 1987; Treiman, 1985). Bradley and Bryant (1983) performed the seminal work in this area. At-risk preschool children (with poor rhyming ability) were trained to categorize words by phonemic similarity; a control group learned to categorize words by concepts. Preschoolers with phonemic awareness training read better in first and second grades than the controls, but did no better in mathematics. However, since the phonemic training occurred concurrently with some instruction in letter–sound relationships, the question remained open whether phonemic training *by itself* would facilitate later reading.

Lundberg, Frost, and Petersen (1988) recently answered this question. Teachers trained in phonemic awareness theory and instructional methods participated in an 8-month field study. They taught preschoolers games about listening and rhyming, then segmenting and blending syllables within words, and finally manipulating phonemes within syllables. Training did not affect general language skills of vocabulary and listening comprehension. However, metalinguistic skills of rhyming, manipulating syllables, and especially phonemic segmentation skills increased dramatically for trained children. Reading and spelling benefited through second grade, showing that good early phonemic awareness training by itself can facilitate later reading.

Most studies, however, do merge phonemic awareness training with work on letter sounds and reading. A. Cunningham (1989) showed that phonemic awareness training benefited students significantly more when contextualized to use words and concepts from current reading lessons during school. Berninger *et al.* (1987) propose that some level of phonemic skill is needed to learn word decoding but that phonemic skills alone do not ensure the ability to learn decoding without continued instruction in reading.

Preschoolers' phonemic categorization skill does not completely predict later reading ability; factors like poor motivation or instruction also affect progress. Yet at-risk children trained in phonemic skills progress better in reading than at-risk controls (Bradley, 1989; Howard, 1986). Bradley suggests that preventing their failure is worth the cost of teaching an occasional child who might have acquired the skills independently. Scarborough (1990) reported an extremely high risk for later reading problems for 2-year-old children who had both a family history of dyslexia and evidence of a subtle language deficit in syntactic fluency. Preschool intervention could be especially valuable to help prevent reading problems in these children.

A few articles describe explicit training methods in phonemic awareness for kindergarten and elementary schoolchildren (Fox & Routh, 1984; Lewkowicz, 1980; Liberman & Shankweiler, 1979). The *Auditory Discrimination in Depth Program* (Lindamood & Lindamood, 1969) is a commercially available program that teaches phonemic awareness, segmentation, and blending. The program is unique in its explicit emphasis on concrete motor awareness of speech sounds as a mediating link for learning letter sounds, and it has led to improvements in phonemic skills and in reading among a wide range of early readers (Howard, 1986).

2. CIRCUMVENTION OF THE DEFICIT: PROGRAMS THAT TEACH TO STRENGTHS

Teaching to strengths in higher-level language skills can include the use of context for word recognition, the whole-language approach, and instruction in comprehension. We will evaluate all three types of approaches.

a. Use of Context. Some authorities recommend teaching prediction from context, avoiding any use of morphology or phonology in word-recognition instruction (Lipa, 1983). This follows Goodman's (1967) previously described suggestion that all children can learn to read "naturally" with enough exposure to meaningful literature, using prediction from context plus initial sound to guess words. Gentile, Lamb, and Riess (1985) even warn that instruction in decoding diminishes strengths of dyslexic children, causing hyperactivity and depression, although no data are presented to support their contention.

We have already mentioned that disabled readers actually use context more, though less proficiently, than good readers do to identify words

(Stanovich, 1980). Therefore, teaching them only to rely on context neglects the need to improve their understanding of how print associates with sound. Successful use of context requires sufficient word-recognition abilities to assess context confidently. Many disabled readers in our studies (to be discussed later) guess so much and so inadequately that they *do not know* whether or not they know a word; they require extensive training and support even to know when they should ask the computer for help or confirmation. Disabled readers' deficits in print-to-sound associations require that they learn to verify their attempt at a word using the print on the page, in terms both of meaning and of sounds.

b. Whole Language. The currently popular whole-language approach also teaches to strengths. It emphasizes reading as a language-based activity, the reading–writing connection, comprehension strategies, and reading interesting literature (Stahl & Miller, 1989). All of that is compatible with a language-based view of reading and of reading disabilities. The problem is that *some* whole-language advocates think that instruction below the word level is dry, rote, and unnecessary. Yet teaching the richness of English as an alphabetic system can be compatible with teaching strategies about language and thinking.

Calfee (1984) laments the current practice of ignoring English's "marvelous" alphabetic system or demeaning it as a low-level skill. He asserts the irrelevance of the "meaning versus word-decoding" question, suggesting that teachers learn about and teach all components of the reading process: decoding, vocabulary, and comprehension. Calfee and Drum (1987) advise teaching how and when to use decoding strategies and modeling and providing practice in their use in reading, quite compatible with whole-language and "metacognitive" ideas.

"Metacognition" means thinking about thinking—becoming aware and strategic about one's own thinking processes. Instruction in metacognitive strategies resembles what was formerly taught as study skills, except that metacognitive instruction directly explains why, when, and how to use strategies (Clark, 1988). This instruction is much more commonly applied to instruction in comprehension, which will be described later, than to word recognition.

However, metacognitive principles have also been successfully applied to word decoding. A. Cunningham (1989) found extra benefits for early training in phonemic segmentation and blending when it included contextualized instruction in how and why to use the strategies. The Benchmark School taught disabled readers to be aware of consistent patterns in words and to use them to decode new words by analogy (Gaskins *et al.*, 1988). Progress in word recognition and phonological coding correlated with instructional time and teacher adherence to the program, but the study included no control group. A different long-term experiment with low readers did show benefits relative to a treated-control group (Duffy et al., 1987). Trained teachers translated lessons about word-decoding skills into strategy lessons, explicitly showing how and when to apply the strategies in reading. Remedial readers in trained classrooms improved more in word recognition than students in classes where teachers had learned classroom management techniques and had taught word decoding as isolated skills. These studies demonstrate that instruction in decoding for children who need it can be compatible with whole-language and metacognitive strategy instruction.

c. *Comprehension Strategies.* Another type of instruction that bypasses the phonological deficit is remedial instruction in comprehension. As mentioned earlier, disabled readers suffer no *specific* deficit in comprehension. That is, disabled readers comprehend reading as well as or better than younger readers matched on word recognition, but worse than normal readers of their same age. This lag, rather than a unique deficit, suggests that general principles for good comprehension instruction for disabled and normal readers could be quite similar, and the metacognitive literature suggests this is generally the case.

Poor readers do not monitor their comprehension as well as age-matched good readers (Baker & Brown, 1984; Meyers & Paris, 1978), but they can learn to use good readers' strategies (Hansen & Pearson, 1983). Many studies have shown that aspects of successful comprehension strategy instruction are the same for remedial and normal readers: The instruction should be direct and explicit (Duffy et al., 1987), should model use and generalization, and should gradually reduce support (Palincsar & Brown, 1984). Palincsar and Brown have used "reciprocal teaching" with slow readers who have poor comprehension but adequate word-decoding skills. Students and teachers used prediction, question generation, and clarification strategies while they discussed the text being read. The teacher modeled the strategies and provided guided support as the students gradually began to lead the dialogue themselves. Trained students improved in comprehension more than controls, and gains were maintained 8 weeks after treatment and were transferred to noninstructed content subjects (Palincsar, Brown, & Martin, 1987).

The above studies selected remedial students with adequate decoding skills, but two studies have adapted similar techniques to account for disabled readers' deficits in word recognition and in short-term memory for verbal material (see Mann & Liberman, 1985; Mann, Shankweiler & Smith, 1984). J. Williams (1986) adjusted texts to the word-recognition levels of disabled readers and simplified, sequenced, and reviewed lessons in summarization and main-idea strategies to compensate for students' short-term memory deficit.

Trained subjects produced better summary paragraphs than other same-age nontrained learning-disabled controls, although results were nonoptimal due to insufficient training time. Hansen and Pearson (1983) improved inferencing and prediction strategies among fourth-grade remedial readers, using structured lessons and texts at appropriate word-recognition levels. The remedial readers improved on posttest comprehension measures. Interestingly, normal readers did not improve, expressing boredom with the lower-level texts.

Disabled readers generally receive much less training in reading comprehension than good readers do (Calfee & Drum, 1987; Maria, 1986). Certainly, comprehension instruction should not be postponed until word decoding approaches grade level; Bateman (1979) claims that remedial programs need at least 2 years to be effective. Delaying instruction in higher-level thinking strategies increases the disadvantages these children already suffer from their word-recognition and phonological deficits. Remedial programs should include comprehension instruction with appropriately graded materials, increasing the difficulty of the materials as remediated word recognition allows.

3. REMEDIATION OF THE DEFICIT: IN-SCHOOL TRAINING IN WORD-DECODING SKILLS

Whether phonemic awareness and decoding are specifically taught in school may be less crucial for normal than for disabled readers. Most children enter school able to count words and syllables and to categorize items by initial phonemes (Fox & Routh, 1980; Liberman & Shankweiler, 1979, 1985). Also, phonemic skills improve almost automatically for most children through the process of reading (Ehri, 1987; Ehri & Wilce, 1985). Normal children learn to read almost despite the methodology used and can decipher new and nonsense words through analogies with words that they have already learned (P.M. Cunningham, 1975–1976; Goswami, 1986). Yet this is not true for disabled readers, who begin school lagging in phonemic awareness and remain uniquely deficient at decoding new and nonsense words into adulthood, without specific remediation. This prognosis compels an attempt to remediate the deficiency.

Among specialists in reading disabilities, the longstanding controversy is not so much whether, but how, to remediate word-recognition skills— whether to teach subword or whole-word units. The common consensus is that field studies of early reading instruction show general advantages for decoding over whole-word approaches to teaching word recognition (Chall, 1983, 1989; Turner, 1989). Two recent extensive surveys concluded that benefits from early decoding instruction last into fifth and sixth grade (Anderson, Hiebert, Scott, & Wilkinson, 1985; Calfee & Drum, 1987). On the other hand, whole-word instruction may have special benefits for improving automaticity of word recognition (Warrren & Roseberry, 1988) or for use with exception words (Lovett, Rounsby & Barron, 1988).

Clark (1988) finds the same advantage for decoding over whole-word instruction in her extensive review of remedial methods for disabled readers. Many of the studies she reviews suffer from typical problems of field research: They fail to specify the instruction received by control groups or compare treatment gains only to the previous year's progress or to standardized yearly gains. Problems like these have led some to complain that "whether reading disorders are amenable to treatment and what constitutes effective treatment are questions that remain essentially unanswered" (Lovett *et al.*, 1988). This statement seems too strong to us. Some controlled studies do verify explicit benefits for disabled readers, including one by the just-quoted authors.

As far as what type of decoding instruction is best, Clark (1988) claims that most reading specialists favor "explicit, synthetic" phonics approaches which directly teach grapheme–phoneme correspondences and the blending of phonemes into syllables and words. Most blending programs in practice also include phonemic analysis and discrimination (e.g., Gaskins *et al.*, 1988; J. Williams, 1980). However, purely "analytic" methods abstain from segmentation and blending, expecting children to deduce sound–symbol relations while reading whole words in texts structured to use words with predictable sound–symbol relationships. Clark cites controlled research with disabled readers supporting explicit phonics but finds the research on analytic methods sparse and uncontrolled. She recommends explicit over analytic methods, because disabled readers' diminished knowledge of printed words hampers the development of analogic strategies. No study specifically compares the two methods, but the experimental studies that have shown benefits in phonological and word-recognition skills for disabled readers have all included explicit practice in blending.

J. Williams (1980) demonstrated benefits from explicit decoding instruction in a controlled field study. Disabled readers learned auditory syllabic and phonemic analysis of at first only nine phonemes and then learned to blend the phonemes using wooden squares as symbols. Later they learned letter names and the blending of letters and sounds to form word patterns. Trained children improved significantly more in phoneme analysis, blending, and reading transfer words than treated controls.

Roth and Beck (1987) reported a year's greater gain, relative to controls, for poor readers who used two microcomputer programs with digitized speech. Good and poor fourth-grade readers found pronounced words, or blended segments into words in gamelike formats, for three sessions per week for 20 weeks. The controls had the same classroom instruction as the experimental students, but unfortunately they had much less reading instruction, since computer sessions never occurred during classroom reading time. However, the fact that good readers showed no similar gains relative to their controls suggested unique benefits from decoding instruction for disabled readers.

Lovett *et al.* (1988) studied "accuracy-disabled" students with the severe decoding deficits typical of dyslexics and compared them with "rate-disabled" students with average word-recognition but slow reading rates. Students from both groups were taught decoding strategies for regular words and whole-word strategies for exception words (e.g., *said, have*). The children with decoding deficits learned more words taught both by decoding and by wholes than did controls who learned writing or study skills. However, the rate-disabled children showed relative gains only on words taught as wholes, supporting Roth and Beck's (1987) finding that only children with word-recognition difficulties may especially benefit from decoding training.

Vellutino and Scanlon (1987) found different benefits for the two kinds of instruction. Disabled readers initially learned more words by whole-word instruction, but phonemic segmentation training or a combination of the two led to greater gains in segmentation and word-recognition skills within only a 5-day training period. Error patterns reflected the type of training received, and students in combination training shifted gradually from holistic to analytic strategies. Interestingly, poor readers made no more reversal errors than good readers, but all readers in the whole-word condition made more reversals than those in the other conditions. Since combination training led to the best performance, the authors concluded that remedial reading instruction should include both types of training.

These previous studies suggest that disabled readers in general reap unique benefits from decoding instruction compared to good readers, and the last one suggests that the two types of instruction may offer them different kinds of benefits. A small subset of poor readers may not be able to benefit from decoding instruction. Lyon (1983) reported that 20 of 30 disabled readers profited from 26 weeks of synthetic phonics training. However, 10 children with especially poor sound-blending and auditory memory deficits did not benefit from phonics instruction. It may be that these severely disabled readers would require prior intensive training in phonemic analysis to have adequate skills to learn from this instruction. We have been studying the relative benefits of whole or segmented presentations of unknown words for different disabled readers, using microcomputers attached to high-quality speech synthesizers. The chapter will conclude with coverage of our ongoing work in this area.

V. Current Research with Computers and Speech Feedback

As a research tool, microcomputers with high-quality synthetic speech capabilities can mitigate some of the problems of long-term field research. Rozin and Gleitman (1977) complained about the difficulty of knowing how well teachers in the field comply with a prescribed experimental program. Good teachers understandably modify their teaching to help a child, but computers will continue to instruct as programmed. Also computers can give equal attention and structure to each tested methodology, thus avoiding the placebo and Hawthorn effects discussed earlier.

Such "talking computers" can also provide powerful remedial tools. In our programs, students read whole stories on the computer, requesting help by indicating, or "targeting," difficult words with a mouse. The computer highlights the targeted word and then highlights and simultaneously pronounces it, either in segments or as a whole word. Disabled readers can read harder stories than they could independently, with the computer support ensuring that they recognize every targeted word correctly. Without such feedback, disabled readers' already weak phonological associations deteriorate with every misread word because of the build-up of inconsistent print and sound associations. The immediacy of the paired orthographic and speech feedback offers a dynamic way of improving these associations. A computer program can be easily individualized, such that children choose stories of interest to them at their own instructional level and get feedback on the words they read. Other virtues of the computer include its motivational aspects and the fact that it can provide all help through earphones, anonymously and without embarrassment.

Preliminary studies had shown that disabled readers could understand the "Perfect Paul" voice on the DECtalk speech synthesizer almost as well as they could understand recorded human speech (Olson, Foltz, & Wise, 1986). Therefore, we designed short- and long-term studies using microcomputers attached to the DECtalk to investigate the benefits of different types of orthographic and speech feedback for disabled readers with varying cognitive profiles.

A. Short-Term Studies to Choose Subword Segments

Relative advantages of whole-word or segmented feedback could depend on the type of segment used. Whole words are simple to define and divide by spaces. The smallest orthographic unit is also fairly straightforward, if more difficult for beginning readers to grasp: Each grapheme corresponds to one speech sound, or phoneme. Most of the time, one letter stands for one phoneme (e.g., *b*, *a*; but *ch*, *th*). Intermediate between grapheme–phonemes and words are other units which might help disabled readers learn decoding skills, and much evidence supports that good readers do use them. Before studying long-term benefits of different-sized units, we needed short-term studies to determine the most helpful definitions and divisions of subword units.

The syllable is a unit that is easy to grasp in speech but difficult to see in print. Young children and nonreaders experience little problem segmenting spoken words into syllables compared to segmenting them into phonemes (Fox & Routh, 1980; Morais et al., 1979). In fact, prereaders count syllables per sentence more accurately than words per sentence (Ehri, 1987). Many studies verify adults' use of syllables in word recognition (e.g., Lima & Pollatsek, 1983; Taft, 1979). Scheerer-Neumann (1981) found that disabled readers learned more multisyllabic words presented with a space between syllables than words presented as wholes. And Rozin, Poritsky, and Sotsky (1971) found that second-grade disabled readers learned a rebus-style syllabic print as easily as good readers. Thus the syllabic unit is a good candidate for teaching decoding skills, but there is controversy in psychology about how syllables are divided.

We conducted a study to choose how to divide syllables to benefit printed word learning. Second-grade slow readers spent one half-hour learning a list of two-syllable words, half divided into vocalic center groups (VCGs) (e.g., ac/tor, gar/den) (Spoehr & Smith, 1973) and half into BOSS units which always preserve meaningful or "morphemic" units (e.g. act/or, gard/en) (Taft, 1979). After pretesting the items as whole words without speech feedback, the computer highlighted and pronounced the segments in sequence for three presentations apiece of each word. The children learned significantly more words trained with BOSS than with VCG divisions (Wise, 1987). Based on this study and on theoretical work by Kahn (1976), we decided to use rules based primarily on morphemes and secondarily on stress to determine syllabic boundaries in our long-term study.

Subsyllabic units influence spoken language errors and games (Treiman, 1983). Word games that divide syllables at an "onset-rime" (e.g., p/ig) boundary are much easier for children and adults to learn than are games that divide the syllable elsewhere (e.g., igpay easier than gaypi). Goswami (1986) found an onset-rime advantage for young readers' analogies from known words to new and nonsense words (e.g., advantage from beak to peak more than to bean).

We conducted three short-term studies to see whether below-average first-grade readers would show this same advantage learning 4-letter words (e.g., chip, salt) (Wise, Olson, & Treiman, 1990). A list-learning paradigm was used as in the syllable experiment, with half the words segmented and pronounced divided by onset-rime units during training (e.g., ch/ip, s/alt), and half divided after the vowel (e.g., chi/p, sa/lt). Letter-position effects were controlled, and in all three studies onset-rime presentations led to more gains in blending and retention of words than postvowel presentation did. Therefore, we decided to use onset rime as the subsyllabic unit in our studies.

A final list-learning study compared short-term benefits of different-sized units for poor and average first- and second-grade readers during two half-hour sessions 2 days apart. After pretesting, the computer highlighted and pronounced three each of 1-, 2-, and 3-syllable words by whole-word, BOSS-syllabic, onset-rime subsyllabic, and grapheme–phoneme units (Wise, 1987). All children learned by far the fewest words presented by grapheme–phoneme segmentation and were so frustrated that this condition was excluded from our subsequent long-term studies described below. All children learned many words from all other types of feedback. However, the poorer readers learned fewer multisyllabic words by onset-rime segmentation than by syllabic and whole-word presentations, consistent with Vellutino and Scanlon's (1987) short-term initial advantage for whole-word learning. We decided to attempt to evaluate whether onset-rime segmentation would show a long-term advantage for the development of phonological coding skill, despite its disadvantage for short-term learning in multisyllabic words.

B. Long-Term Studies

Teachers recommended third- to sixth-grade children from the lowest 10% of their readers to participate in our long-term studies. Many were in special reading programs, and all had verbal or performance IQs of at least 90. The children took pretests on timed and untimed word recognition, nonword reading, spelling, reading comprehension, and various language skills. Students were assigned to whole-word or segmented feedback or to an untreated control condition. Condition assignments were pseudorandom but balanced for grade and initial abilities in word recognition and phonological coding. After 10 weeks of training, students retook the same tests as posttests.

In the studies to be reported here, students read 4 or 5 days a week, for about 30 minutes a day, during time that would otherwise have been spent on reading or language-arts instruction. This was to assure that reading *instructional* time was similar for the untreated control and experimental conditions, though experimental subjects may have spent more time actually reading. Hawthorn effects could have affected comparisons between the control and the trained conditions, but not comparisons of feedback conditions, since structure and attention were equivalent for them.

Students chose stories from directories ranging from primer to sixth grade, each containing 20 to 30 stories and books. Directory assignment for stories depended mainly on number of syllables per word and secondarily on sentence length and story structure, since the children's primary deficit was in word recognition (Wise *et al.*, 1989). Students were assigned and reassigned to directories where they made about 2–5% oral reading errors.

Examiners trained the students first to attempt each word they were unsure of and then to ask the computer's help, checking to see whether the word they heard or blended made sense in the sentence. When the child targeted a word, the computer highlighted it or its segments in sequence in reverse video and then highlighted and simultaneously pronounced it for them. After 4–8 pages, at logical breaks in the stories, the computer asked, scored, and gave feedback about a main-idea comprehension question. It then reviewed five recently targeted words in a self-scored word-recognition test. Words on these tests were highlighted according to assigned segmentation condition, but without speech feedback. After training, examiners monitored the subjects' targeting and comprehension weekly, adjusting directory assignments accordingly.

The first semester included 45 students assigned to one of five feedback conditions: whole, syllable, subsyllable, combined syllable and subsyllable, or the comparison control group. Targeting rates were slightly and nonsignificantly higher on monitored than on independent days (33 versus 27 targets per session), (Wise *et al.*, 1989). Thus, subjects appeared to be effectively targeting most words when reading silently and independently. Segmented feedback resulted in significantly more gains in phonological coding as measured by gain in percentage correct on nonword reading (syllable, 13.6%; subsyllable, 17.5%, combined, 14.6%) compared to whole-word (6.0%) or control conditions (2.9%).

Pretest–posttest word-recognition gains were assessed in a test wherein most of the gained words had *not* been targeted during training. A planned contrast showed that experimental students read significantly and more than twice as many new words as the control subjects. (13.6 new words versus 5.2 by controls). All feedback conditions except combination feedback were significantly better by themselves than the control condition.

The results of the above study were generally consistent with our expectation that segmented feedback would specifically improve phonological coding, while both whole-word and segmented feedback would improve word recognition. Further satisfying outcomes included a very low attrition rate and enthusiastic responses on questionnaires from nearly all the trained subjects and their teachers (Wise *et al.*, 1989).

During the two semesters of the second year of the study, we dropped the combination condition but stretched our personnel resources to test and train another 119 experimental and 32 control subjects. Unfortunately this resulted in less effective training, and subjects' rate of detecting their decoding errors fell sharply to about half the 80% rate in the first semester. In the second year's study, trained children still gained significantly more than the control group in phonological coding (gain of 9.6% for trained versus 2.5% for untrained) and word recognition (13.0 versus 8 words), but the gains for all feedback conditions were nearly equivalent. Absolute magnitudes of gains were somewhat smaller than in the first study. However, in both studies, trained subjects improved more than three times as much as controls in phonological coding and almost twice as much in word recognition (more than twice in the first semester), far greater than the 15% greater effect generally attributed to Hawthorn effects (see Pflaum, Walberg, Karegianes, & Rasher, 1980).

We hypothesized that the significantly greater benefits from segmented feedback in the first than the second study resulted from subjects' appropriate targeting and attention to feedback, fostered by more training and attention from the examiners, leading to better awareness of decoding errors. Certain weaknesses in explicit instruction in the transfer of strategies to independent reading (see Duffy *et al.*, 1987), in active practice of the strategies (see Palincsar & Brown, 1984) and in substantial review of learned words (see Bateman, 1979), may have reduced differences between the feedback conditions.

We are attempting to ameliorate the problems of the second year by improving the computer programs rather than by increasing personnel. Our goal is to minimize required teacher time, realizing that ongoing human encouragement and direction will always be important. We have designed new programs and games to improve subjects' awareness of word errors, to give feedback about targeting behavior, and to provide active practice of the strategies and review of the words. The new program also includes explicit instruction about generalizing the contextual or segmentation-and-blending strategies to other reading.

VI. Summary

Remedial instruction must deal with most disabled readers' primary deficits in phonological coding and word recognition while also supporting their need to make adequate progress in other areas of reading where they are not "uniquely" deficient, such as vocabulary and comprehension. Principles of good comprehension instruction apply similarly to good and poor readers, so long as reading material is at an appropriate level and instruction simplified to compensate for possible short-term memory limitations. Benefits of preschool phonemic awareness training for at-risk children have been clearly established, and field and experimental research also show general benefits for training in word-decoding skills for disabled readers. Explicit training in segmenting and blending of phonemes appears most helpful for most disabled readers who have poor, but sufficient, phonological skills to profit from such instruction, and this instruction is even more beneficial when contextualized to show explicitly how to use it in actual reading. Whole-word instruction seems warranted for exception words and for training in automaticity.

Our own research on remediation with talking computers has clearly demonstrated their power both for research and as remedial tools. Experimental subjects made consistent and substantial gains over untreated controls in both studies in terms of word recognition, phonological coding, and attitude about reading, even though they all received equal instructional time in reading. The second study's lack of specific treatment differences indicates that much of this progress relates to factors common to all treatment conditions. Thus the immediacy of pairing print and sound, the motivational aspects of using a computer, and the fact of actually reading for 25 minutes a day with computer support for word-recognition difficulties all have probably contributed to the gains made by the trained children in both studies.

The improved program should clarify differential training benefits suggested by the first study and by earlier reported field and experimental research. We expect from our earlier studies that trained subjects in all feedback conditions will make substantially greater gains than the normal-instruction comparison group. It remains to be seen whether the long-term advantage for phonological coding from segmented feedback will be confirmed and whether relative benefits of whole-word or segmented feedback will depend on subjects' initial level of skill in phonological coding and phonemic awareness.

Acknowledgments

The research was supported in part by NICHD grants No. HD 11683 and HD 22223.

References

Anderson, R., Hiebert, E., Scott, J., & Wilkinson, I. (1985). *Becoming a nation of readers: The report of the Commission on Reading.* Washington, DC: National Institute of Education.

Baker, L. & Brown, A. (1984). Metacognitive skills and reading. In D. Pearson, M. Kamil, R. Barr, & P. Mosenthal (Eds.), *Handbook of reading research.* New York: Longman.

Bateman, B. (1979). Teaching reading to learning disabled and other hard-to-teach children. In L. B. Resnick & P. A. Weaver (Eds.), *Theory and practice of early reading.* Hillsdale, NJ: Erlbaum.

Berninger, V., Thalberg, S., DeBruyn, I., & Smith, R. (1987). Preventing reading disabilities by assessing and remediating phonemic skills. *School Psychology Review, 16*(4), 554–565.

Bishop, D. V. (1986). Unfixed reference, monocular occlusion and developmental dyslexia: A critique. *British Journal of Opthamology, 73*, 209–215.

Bradley, L. (1989). Rhyme recognition and reading and spelling in young children. In R. L. Masland & M. R. Masland (Eds.), *Pre-school prevention of reading failure.* Parkton, MD: York Press.

Bradley, L., & Bryant, P. (1978). Difficulties in auditory organization as a possible cause of reading backwardness. *Nature (London). 271*, 746–747.

Bradley, L., & Bryant, P. (1983). Categorizing sounds and learning to read: A causal connection. *Nature (London), 301*, 419–421.

Breitmeyer, B. (1989). A visually-based deficit in specific reading disability. Paper presented at the Rodin Satellite meeting of the Fifth European Conference on Eye Movements, Pavia, Italy. September 10, 1989.

Bryant, P. E., & Goswami, U. C. (1986). Strengths and weaknesses of the reading level design: A comment on Backman, Mamen, and Ferguson. *Psychological Bulletin, 100*, 101–103.

Calfee, R. (1984). Applying cognitive psychology to educational practice: The mind of the reading teacher. *Annals of Dyslexia, 34*, 219–239.

Calfee, R., & Drum, P. (1987). Research on teaching reading. *Handbook of research on teaching* (3rd ed.). New York: Macmillan.

Calfee, R., Lindamood, P., & Lindamood, C. (1973). Acoustic-phonetic skills and reading: Kindergarten through twelfth grade. *Journal of Educational Psychology, 64*, 293–298.

Chall, J. (1983). *Learning to read: The great debate* (updated ed.). New York: McGraw Hill.

Chall, J. (1989, March). Learning to read: The great debate 20 years later: A response to "Debunking the great phonics myth." *Phi Delta Kappan*, pp. 521–538.

Clark, D. B. (1988). *Dyslexia: Theory and practice of remedial instruction.* Parkton, MD: York Press.

Conners, F., & Olson, R. (1990). Reading comprehension in dyslexic and normal readers: A component skills analysis. In D. A. Balota, G. B. Flores d'Arcais, & K. Rayner (Eds.), *Comprehension processes in reading.* Hillsdale, NJ: Erlbaum. pp. 557–580

Cunningham, A. (1989). Phonemic awareness: The development of early reading competency. *Reading Research Quarterly, 24*, 471–472.

Cunningham, P. M. (1975–1976). Investigating a synthesized theory of mediated word identification. *Reading Research Quarterly, 2*, 127–143.

DeFries, J. C., & Fulker, D. W. (1985). Multiple regression analysis of twin data. *Behavior Genetics, 15*, 467–473.

Duffy, G., Roehler, L., Sivan, E., Rackliffe, G., Book, C., Meloth, M., Vavrus, L., Wesselman, R., Putnam, J., & Bassiri, D. (1987). Effects of explaining the reasoning associated with using reading strategies. *Reading Research Quarterly, 22*, 345–368.

Dunn, L. M., & Markwardt, F. C. (1970). *Examiner's manual: Peabody Individual Achievement Test.* Circle Pines, MN: American Guidance Service.

Ehri, L. C. (1987). Learning to read and spell words. *Journal of Reading Behavior, 17*, 5–31.

Ehri, L. C., & Wilce, L. (1985). Movement into reading: Is the first stage of learning visual or phonetic? *Reading Research Quarterly, 20,* 163–179.

Fox, B., & Routh, D. (1980). Phonemic analysis and severe reading disability in children. *Journal of Psycholinguistic Research, 9,* 115–119.

Fox, B., & Routh, D. (1984). Phonemic analysis and synthesis as word attack skills: Revisited. *Journal of Psycholinguistic Research, 76,* 1059–1064.

Galaburda, A. (1989). Ordinary and extraordinary brain development: Anatomical variation in developmental dyslexia. *Annals of Dyslexia, 33,* 67–80.

Gaskins, I., Downer, M., Anderson, R., Cunningham, P., Gaskins, R., Schommer, M., & the teachers of Benchmark School. (1988). A metacognitive approach to phonics: Using what you know to decode what you don't. *RASE: Remedial & Special Education, 9,* 36–66.

Geiger, G., & Letvin, J. (1987). Peripheral vision in persons with dyslexia. *New England Journal of Medicine, 316,* 1238–1243.

Gentile, L., Lamb, P., & Rivers, C. (1985). A neurologist's views of reading difficulty: Implications for instruction. *Reading Teacher,* pp. 174–182.

Goodman, K. (1967). Reading: A psycholinguistic guessing game. *Journal of the Reading Specialist, 6,* 126–135.

Goswami, U. (1986). Children's use of analogy in learning to read: A developmental study. *Journal of Experimental Child Psychology, 42,* 73–83.

Hammill, D., Goodman, L., & Wiederholt, J. (1974). Visual-perceptual processes: Can we train them? *Reading Teacher,* pp. 469–478.

Hansen, J., & Pearson, P. (1983). An instructional study: Improving the inferential comprehension of good and poor fourth-grade readers. *Journal of Educational Psychology, 75,* 821–829.

Healy, J. M., Aram, D. M., Horowitz, S. J., & Kessler, J. W. (1982). A study of hyperlexia. *Brain & Language, 17,* 1–23.

Howard, M. (1986). *Effects of prereading training in auditory conceptualization on subsequent reading achievement.* Doctoral dissertation, Brigham Young University, Provo, UT.

Hynd, G., & Semrud-Clikeman, M. (1989). Dyslexia and brain morphology. *Psychological Bulletin, 106,* 447–482.

Irlen, H. (1983). Address at the annual meeting of the American Psychological Association.

Kahn, D. (1976). *Syllable-based generalizations in English phonology.* Bloomington: Indiana University Linguistics Club.

Kaufman, A. S. (1975). Factor analysis of the WISC-R at 11 age levels between 6 1/2 and 16 1/2 years. *Journal of Consulting and Clinical Psychology, 43,* 2, 135–147.

Klein, R., Berry, G., Briand, K., D'Entrement, B., & Farmer, M. (in press). The accuracy of letter identification declines with increasing retinal eccentricity at the same rate for normal and dyslexic readers. *Psychophysics & Perception.*

LaBerge, D., & Samuels, S. (1974). Toward a theory of automatic information processing. *Cognitive Psychology, 6,* 293–323.

Larsen, J., Hoien, T., Lundberg, I., & Odegaard, H. (1989). *MRI evaluation of the size and symmetry of the planum temporale in adolescents with developmental dyslexia.* Stavanger, Norway: Center for Reading Research.

Lewkowicz, N. K. (1980). Phonemic awareness training: What to teach and how to teach it. *Journal of Educational Psychology, 72,* 686–700.

Liberman, I., & Shankweiler, D. (1979). Speech, the alphabet, and teaching to read. In L. B. Resnick & P. A. Weaver (Eds.), *Theory and practice of early reading* (Vol. 2). Hillsdale, NJ: Erlbaum.

Liberman, I., & Shankweiler, D. (1985). Phonology and the problems of learning to read and write. *RASE: Remedial & Special Education, 6*(6), 8–17.

Lima, S., and Pollatsek, A. (1983). Lexical access via an orthographic code? The BOSS reconsidered. *Journal of Verbal Learning and Verbal Behavior, 22,* 310–332.

Lindamood, C., & Lindamood, P. (1969). *Auditory discrimination in depth.* Boston, MA: Teaching Resources.

Lipa, S. (1983). Reading disability: A new look at an old issue. *Journal of Learning Disabilities, 16,* 543–557.

Lovegrove, W., Martin, F., & Slaghuis, W. (1986). A theoretical and experimental case for a visual deficit in specific reading disability. *Cognitive Neuropsychology, 3,* 225–267.

Lovett, M., Ransby, M., & Barron, R. (1988). Treatment, subtype, and word type effects in dyslexic children's response to remediation. *Brain & Language, 34,* 328–349.

Lundberg, I., Frost, J., & Petersen, O. (1988). Effects of an extensive program for stimulating phonological awareness in preschool children. *Reading Research Quarterly, 23*(3), 263–284.

Lundberg, I., Olofsson, A., & Wall, S. (1980). Reading and spelling skills in the first school years, predicted from phonemic awareness skills in kindergarten. *Scandinavian Journal of Psychology, 21,* 159–173.

Lyon, G. R. (1983). Subgroups of learning disabled readers: Clinical and empirical identification. In H. Myklebust (Ed.), *Progress in learning disabilities* (Vol. 5). New York: Grune & Stratton.

Mann, V., & Liberman, I. (1985). Phonological awareness and verbal short-term memory. In J. K. Torgeson & B. Y. L. Wong (Eds.), *Psychological and educational perspectives on learning disabilities* (pp. 133–159). Orlando, FL: Academic Press.

Mann, V., Shankweiler, D., & Smith, S. (1984). The association between comprehension of spoken sentences and early reading ability: The role of phonetic representation. *Journal of Child Language, 11,* 627–643.

Maria, K. (1986). Adapting the comprehension techniques for the learning disabled child. Paper presented to the Thirteenth annual conference of the New York Branch of the Orton Dyslexia Society, New York.

Meyers, M., & Paris, S. (1978). Children's metacognitive knowledge about reading. *Journal of Educational Psychology, 70,* 680–690.

Morais, J., Cary, L., Alegria, J. & Bertelson, P. (1979). Does awareness of speech as a sequence of phonemes arise spontaneously? *Cognition, 7,* 323–331.

Olson, R. K., Conners, F. A., & Rack, J. P. (In press). Eye movements in dyslexic and normal readers. In J. F. Stein (Ed.), *Vision and visual dyslexia.* London: Macmillan

Olsen, R., Foltz, G. & Wise, B. (1986). Reading instruction and remediation with the aid of computer speech. *Behavior Research Methods, Instruments, & Computers, 18,* 93–99.

Olson, R. K., Kliegl, R., & Davidson, B. J. (1983). Dyslexic and normal readers' eye movements. *Journal of Experimental Psychology: Human Perception and Performance, 9,* 816–825.

Olson, R. K., Kliegl, R., Davidson, B. J. & Foltz, G. (1985). Individual developmental differences in reading disability. In G. E. Mackinnon & T. G. Waller (Eds.), *Reading Research: Advances in theory and practice* (Vol. 4, pp. 1–64). Orlando, Florida: Academic Press.

Olson, R. K., Rack, J., Conners, F., DeFries, J., & Fulker, D. (1990). Genetic etiology of individual differences in reading disability. In L. Feagans, E. Short, & L. Meltzer (Eds.), *Subtypes of learning disabilities.* Hillsdale, NJ: Erlbaum. pp. 113–135.

Olson, R. K., Wise, B., Conners, F., & Rack, J. (1990). Organization, heritability, and remediation of component word recognition and language skills in disabled readers. In T. H. Carr & B. A. Levy (Eds.), *Reading and its development: Component skills approaches.* San Diego, CA: Academic Press.

Olson, R. K., Wise, B., Conners, F., Rack, J., & Fulker, D. (1989). Specific deficits in component reading and language skills: Genetic and environmental influences. *Journal of Learning Disabilities, 22,* 339–348.

Olsen, R. K., Wise, B. W., & Rack, J. P. (1989). Dyslexia: Deficits, genetic aetiology and computer-based remediation. *The Irish Journal of Psychology, 10,* 494–508.

Palincsar, A., & Brown, A. (1984). Reciprocal teaching of comprehension-fostering and comprehension-monitoring activity. *Cognition & Instruction, 2,* 117–175.

Palincsar, A., Brown, A., & Martin, S. (1987). Peer interaction in reading comprehension instruction. *Educational psychologist, 22,* 231–253.

Pavlidis, G. T. (1981). Do eye movements hold the key to dyslexia? *Neuropsychologia, 19,* 57–64.

Perfetti, C. (1985). *Reading ability.* New York: Oxford University Press.

Pflaum, S., Walberg, H., Karegianes, M., & Rasher, S. (1980, July). Reading instruction: A quantitative analysis. *Educational Researcher,* pp. 12–18.

Rack, J. P., & Olson, R. K. (1989, September 14). *Sources of variance in the phonological deficit in developmental dyslexia.* Paper presented to the Rodin Remediation Society, Bangor, Wales.

Rack, J. P., Snowling, M. J. & Olson, R. K., (submitted). The nonword reading deficit in developmental dyslexia: A Review.

Roth, S., & Beck, I. (1987). Theoretical and instructional implications of the assessment of two microcomputer word recognition programs. *Reading Research Quarterly, 22,* 197–218.

Rozin, P., & Gleitman, L. R. (1977). Reading: The alphabetic principle. In A. Reber & D. Scarborough (Eds.), *Toward a psychology of reading.* Hillsdale, NJ: Erlbaum.

Rozin, P., Poritsky, S., & Sotsky, R. (1971). American children with reading problems can easily learn to read English represented by Chinese character. *Science, 171,* 1264–1267.

Scarborough, H. (1990). Early Identification of Dyslexic Children: Familial Risk and

Preschool Behavior Characteristics. Paper presented at XVI meeting of the International Rodin Remediation Scientific Conference, September, Boulder, Co.

Scheerer-Neumann, G. (1981). The utilization of intraword structure in poor readers: Experimental evidence and a training program. In J. Kavanaugh & I. Mattingly (Eds.), *Language by ear and eye.* Cambridge, MA: MIT Press.

Siegel, L. (1989). IQ is irrelevant to the definition of learning disabilities. *Journal of Learning Disabilities, 22,* 469–479.

Smith, F. (1978). *Understanding reading: A psycholinguistic analysis of reading and learning to read.* New York: Holt, Rinehart, & Winston.

Snowling, M. J. (1980). The development of grapheme-phoneme correspondence in normal and dyslexic readers. *Journal of Experimental Child Psychology, 29,* 294–305.

Snowling, M. J. (1981). Phonemic deficits in developmental dyslexia. *Psychological Research, 43,* 219–234.

Spoehr, K. T., & Smith, E. E. (1973). The role of syllables in perceptual processes. *Cognitive Psychology, 5,* 71–89.

Stahl, S., & Miller, P. (1989). Whole language and language experience approaches. *Review of Educational Research, 59,* 87–116.

Stanovich, K. E. (1980). Toward an interactive-compensatory model of individual differences in the development of reading fluency. *Reading Research Quarterly, 16,* 32–71.

Stanovich, K. E. (1986). Cognitive processes and the reading problems of learning disabled children: Evaluating the notion of Specificity. In J. K. Torgeson & B. Y. L. Wong (Eds.), *Psychological and educational perspectives on learning disabilities.* New York: Academic Press.

Stanovich, K. E. (1989). Has the LD field lost its intelligence? *Journal of Learning Disabilities, 22,* 487–492.

Stanovich, K. E., & West, R. F. (1989). Print exposure and orthographic processing. *Reading Research Quarterly, 24,* 402–433.

Stein, J., & Fowler, S. (1982). Diagnosis of dyslexia by means of a new indicator of eye dominance. *British Journal of Ophthamology, 66,* 332–336.

Taft, M. (1979). Lexical access via an orthographic code: The BOSS. *Journal of Verbal Learning & Verbal Behavior, 18,* 21–39.

Treiman, R. (1983). The structure of spoken syllables: Evidence from novel word games. *Cognition, 15,* 49–74.

Treiman, R. (1985). Phonemic analysis, spelling, and reading. In T. Carr (Ed.), *The development of reading skills.* San Francisco, CA: Jossey-Bass.

Turner, R. L. (1989, December). The (great) debate: Can both Carbo and Chall be right? *Phi Delta Kappan,* pp. 276–283.

U.S. Department of Health, Education and Welfare (1976). Public Law 94-142. Washington, DC: USDHEW.

Van Orden, G. C. (1987). A ROWS is a ROSE: Spelling, sound and reading. *Memory & Cognition, 15,* 181–198.

Vellutino, F. (1980). *Dyslexia: Theory and research.* Cambridge, MA: MIT Press.

Vellutino, F., & Scanlon, D. (1987). Phonological coding, phonological awareness, and reading ability: Evidence from a longitudinal and experimental study. *Merrill-Palmer Quarterly, 33*(3), 321–363.

Wagner, R., & Torgeson, J. (1987). The nature of phonological processing and its causal role in the acquisition of reading skills. *Psychological Bulletin, 101,* 192–212.

Warren, B., & Rosebery, A. S. (1988). Theory and practice: Uses of the computer in reading. *RASE: Remedial & Special Education, 9*(2), 29–38.

Wechsler, D. I. (1974). *Examiner's manual: Wechsler Intelligence Scale for Children—Revised.* New York: Psychological Corporation.

Williams, J. (1980). Teaching decoding with an emphasis on phoneme analysis and blending. *Journal of Experimental Psychology, 72,* 1–15.

Williams, J. (1986). Teaching children to identify the main idea of texts. *Exceptional Children, 53,* 163–168.

Williams, M., & LeCluyse, K. (in press). The perceptual consequences of a temporal processing deficit in reading disabled children.

Wilshire, C. E. (September, 1989). Treatments for dyslexia: Proven of Unproven. Paper presented at the XV meeting of the Rodin Remediation Society, Bangor, Wales.

Winters, R., Patterson, R., & Shontz, W. (1989). Visual persistence and adult dyslexia. *Journal of Learning Disabilities, 10,* 641–645.

Wise, B. (1987). *Word Segmentation in Computerized Reading Instruction.* Doctoral dissertation, University of Colorado, Boulder.

Wise, B., Olson, R. K., Anstett, M., Andrews, L., Terjak, M., Schneider, V., Kostuch, J., & Kriho, L. (1989). Implementing a long-term remedial reading study in the public schools: Hardware, software, and real world issues. *Behavior Research Methods & Instrumentation, 21,* 173–180.

Wise, B., Olson, R. K., & Treiman, R. (1990). Subsyllabic units in computerized reading instruction: Onset-rime versus postvowel segmentation. *Journal of Experimental Child Psychology.*

Wright, J. D. (1989). Irlen lenses: Their claims have not been substantiated, Position paper of the Massachusetts Society of Eye Physicians and Surgeons. *Learning Disabilities Network Exchange, 7*(1), 1–4.

CHAPTER TWENTY-FOUR

Academic Interventions with Learning-Disabled Students: A Cognitive/Metacognitive Approach

Candace S. Bos
Anthony K. Van Reusen

I. Introduction

During the past two decades, increased attention has focused on the neuropsychological correlates of learning disabilities (LD). Studies examining children of normal intelligence who exhibit extreme difficulty in learning indicate that neuropsychological components have an important function in the learning process (e.g., Benton, 1975; Gaddes, 1985; G. W. Hynd & Obrzut, 1981; Rourke, 1985). However, when the demands of school move beyond the lower-level basic skills such as reading decoding and word recognition, math computation, and writing mechanics (spelling, capitalization/ punctuation, and handwriting), the relationship between learning disabilities and deficits in neurological functioning falls into uncharted territory. For example, the neuropsychological subtype literature in reading disabilities/ dyslexia would suggest that disabled readers could be subtyped according to the difficulties they encounter in decoding words (e.g., surface, direct, phonological, and deep dyslexia) (C. R. Hynd, 1986; G. W. Hynd & Cohen, 1983). However, these subtypes are based almost entirely on decoding aspects of reading with little consideration for the cognitive/metacognitive nature of the reading process, particularly reading comprehension. In addition, cognitive/ metacognitive models of reading are beginning to embrace the importance of

Neuropsychological Foundations of Learning Disabilities, copyright © 1991 by Academic Press Inc. All rights of reproduction in any form reserved.

motivation and attribution in the acquisition and application of the complex strategies involved in reading comprehension, an area rarely addressed in neuropsychological research with dyslexic students.

Consequently, this chapter focuses on the growing body of academic-intervention research emphasizing the use of instructional methodologies based on cognitive/metacognitive processing and cognitive behavior modification (CBM) and intrinsic control mechanisms (e.g., self-efficacy/advocacy training, attribution retraining, motivation strategies) (for reviews, see Bos, 1988a; Deshler, Schumaker, & Lenz, 1984; Licht & Kistner, 1986; Palincsar & Brown, 1987). Specifically, this chapter is organized around five areas which will (1) consider principles of learning and teaching related to intervention models associated with motivation, cognitive/metacognitive processing, and cognitive behavior modification, (2) review selected research related to effective strategies for teaching reading comprehension and text learning, (3) present research related to written composition instruction, (4) present intervention research related to verbal math problem solving, and (5) suggest a research agenda that might begin to establish the relationship between learning-disabled students' difficulties with complex cognitive/metacognitive strategies and neuropsychological functioning.

II. General Trends in Academic-Intervention Research

Five instructional trends have emerged from theories and academic research related to attribution and motivation, cognition/metacognition, and cognitive behavior modification. These include (1) the growing recognition of the critical role that self-concept and intrinsic motivation have in directing one's learning efforts and effectiveness, (2) the significance of schemata for activating current knowledge and learning new information, (3) the need to teach specific and general thinking processes and strategies necessary to meet academic demands, (4) the need to combine behavioral techniques with self-instructional methods, and (5) the need to provide intensive instruction which focuses on the acquisition, proficiency, maintenance, and generalization of skills and strategies.

A. Self-Concept and Intrinsic Motivation

One trend is the emerging importance of self-concept and intrinsic motivation in the effectiveness of academic interventions (Kurtz & Borkowski, 1987; Schunk & Rice, 1987). Research has demonstrated that LD students have lower self-concepts than their nonhandicapped peers with greater decrements for academic self-concept than for general self-worth (for a review, see Chapman, 1988). For many of these students, failure is perceived as due to attributes for which they have limited control, such as ability or external factors, rather than due to internal, controllable factors such as lack of effort or efficiency in learning (Tollefson *et al.*, 1982).

These student attributions differentially influence academic behavior and performance in various instructional conditions. For example, Pascarella, Pflaum, Bryan, and Pearl (1983) found that students identified as exhibiting internal locus of control demonstrated greater performance in low-structured conditions than in high-structured conditions. In contrast, students identified as having external locus of control demonstrated greater progress in high-structured conditions. Bendell, Tollefson, and Fine (1980) reported similar results with LD adolescents. The dilemma lies in the mismatch between LD students' attributions and the instructional conditions evident as these students move into secondary and postsecondary situations. For LD students to gain learning independence, less structured situations are suggested, yet these are the situations in which they have more difficulty. By providing highly structured situations, teachers may be perpetuating a learning dependency cycle on the part of LD students. That is, LD students may become dependent upon the instructional conditions, arrangements, and materials in order to demonstrate progress, which can undermine their development and use of self-directed and independent learning skills and strategies.

Related to the attributions of LD students is intrinsic motivation and its contributory nature to school success (e.g., Adelman & Taylor, 1983; Deshler *et al.*, 1984; Henker, Whalen, & Hinshaw, 1980). For example, LD adolescents have been reported to exhibit a lack of motivation regarding their personal, academic, social, and career success (White, Schumaker, Warner, Alley, & Deshler, 1980).

Interestingly, the goal of many intervention programs for LD students is to enhance and foster learning independence. Yet, in spite of this goal, many academic-intervention practices overlook the importance of intrinsic motivation in developing learner independence. These interventions oftentimes fail to include the student in the determination of learning needs or in establishing the value of learning specific skills, concepts, or strategies. However, when students have been included in major decisions, such as prioritizing needs and choosing instructional options, performance has been enhanced (Perlmuter & Monty, 1977; Van Reusen, Deshler, & Schumaker, 1989).

Based on these ideas and supporting research, several implications are clear. First, it is important that students are involved in the key aspects of learning and establish a commitment to learn or improve performance. This can be accomplished by assisting students in identifying their perceived strengths and weaknesses to improve and by prioritizing their needs and goals in view of in-school and out-of-school demands they face. Second, students should be involved in choosing and monitoring their goals. Ongoing conferences with students are helpful in fostering student motivation through monitoring, feedback, and adjustment of goals. Third, a variety of instructional options with regard to content, process, and materials should be provided to spark interest and motivation. Fourth, in an effort to enhance student self-concept and motivation, practitioners need to monitor the messages being communicated to students during instruction and feedback to ensure and promote independent achievement on the part of the student (Adelman & Taylor, 1983; Bryan, 1986; Van Reusen, Bos, Schumaker, & Deshler, 1987).

B. *Developing and Activating Schemata*

A second instructional trend focuses on the important role that knowledge structures and organizational frameworks play in the acquisition of information. Schema theory attempts to explain how this knowledge or information is structured in memory and how these structures affect incoming information. Schemata are data structures for representing generic concepts stored in memory (Anderson, 1984; Rumelhart, 1980). Conceptually, schemata are often hierarchical in nature and provide the organizational framework or scaffolding on which new information can be integrated and existing information can be retrieved. "Schemata are employed in the process of interpreting sensory data (both linguistic and nonlinguistic), in retrieving information from memory, in organizing actions, in determining goals and subgoals, in allocating resources, and generally, in guiding the flow of processing in the system" (Rumelhart, 1980, pp. 33–34).

Schema theory has been used particularly in the study of reading comprehension, memory, and content-area learning to explain the importance of prior knowledge for learning new information (Anderson, Reynolds, Schallert, & Goetz, 1977; Anderson, Spiro, & Anderson, 1978). Assumptions from schema theory have also been used to explain the powerful and consistent correlation between vocabulary knowledge and reading comprehension (e.g., Anderson & Freebody, 1981; Stahl & Fairbanks, 1986).

One of the characteristics of many LD students is difficulty in learning, organizing, elaborating, and retrieving meaningful information (e.g., Ceci, 1985; Scruggs, 1988; Torgesen, 1977). Therefore, techniques which foster the activation and development of schemata should be particularly fruitful for these students (Billingsley & Wildman, 1988; Bos & Anders, 1990a).

C. *Using Cognitive Modeling and Verbal Self-Instructional Procedures*

A third instructional trend relates to the use of cognitive modeling and verbal self-instructional procedures in teaching task-specific and general academic strategies. Research with such techniques was initially conducted with LD students in an effort to modify impulsivity and inattention toward academic tasks (Meichenbaum, 1977; Meichenbaum & Goodman, 1971). Meichenbaum (1977) referred to his methodology as cognitive behavior modification (CBM), which assumes that behavior can be modified through the regulation of cognitive processes. In CBM and other cognitive training methodologies, cognitive modeling plays an integral role in that verbalizations of observable behaviors and cognitive processes are used to model and mediate learning. Graham, Harris, and Sawyer (1987) suggest that at least six types of self-instructions can be used to assist students in activating and regulating appropriate strategies to mediate behavior: (1) problem definition, (2) attention focusing, (3) planning and response guidance, (4) self-reinforcement, (5) self-evaluation, and (6) coping and error-correcting options. The effectiveness of cognitive modeling and verbal self-instructional procedures for teaching cognitive strategies has been demonstrated in a variety of academic areas. For example, in the area of reading such procedures have been used to enhance reading comprehension and metacomprehension (e.g., Bereiter & Bird, 1985; A. W. Graves, 1986; Wong & Jones, 1982). These procedures have also been found to be successful in improving written composition (Englert & Raphael, 1988; Harris & Graham, 1985) and mathematics (Montague & Bos, 1986b; E. Smith & Alley, 1981).

The use of cognitive modeling has become recognized as an important aspect of strategy acquisition. For example, the learning-strategies intervention model developed at the University of Kansas (Deshler & Schumaker, 1986) utilizes cognitive modeling as part of its instructional methodology. However, for this type of cognitive training to be effective, selection and matching of the procedures to the student's age and metacognitive level are needed. For example, cognitive modeling and verbal self-instructional procedures were not as effective with young mildly retarded students (Brown, Campione, & Murphy, 1977). Wong and Wong (1988) argue that students with sophisticated learning-strategy repertoires may also be adversely affected due to the interference of the instructional techniques with processing routines that are at an automatic level. Thus, practitioners need to consider both age and metacognitive development factors in the use of such procedures.

D. Using Self-Regulatory Procedures

The fourth instructional trend focuses on the use of self-regulatory procedures. Inherent in the use of metacognitive and CBM intervention procedures is the importance of teaching students self-regulatory mechanisms. Efficient and effective learners are thought to regulate cognitive resources to strategically predict, plan, carry out, monitor, evaluate, and adjust their learning effectiveness toward the attainment of desired outcomes. Comparatively, LD students have been reported to approach tasks in a more passive manner (e.g., Torgesen, 1982) and exhibit a disorganized and impulsive response style (Keogh, 1977). Subsequently, many LD students are thought to be deficient in their use of self-regulatory strategies (Bos & Filip, 1984; Havertape & Kass, 1978; Torgesen, 1977).

In response to this passive learning style, some intervention researchers have altered traditional teacher-controlled behavioral management techniques (i.e., monitoring, recording, evaluating production) to emphasize student-controlled self-regulatory procedures focusing on process as well as production (Meichenbaum, 1977). For example, Hallahan and Sapona (1983) reported the results of an intervention in which self-monitoring was used successfully to increase the academic productivity and the on-task behavior of an LD student. Rooney, Hallahan, and Lloyd (1983) similarly reported the successful use of self-monitoring procedures to increase the attending behavior of LD students during language-arts activities in a regular classroom. Other research has replicated the effects of self-regulatory training (e.g., Englert, Raphael, Anderson, Stevens, & Anthony, 1989; Graham & MacArthur, 1988) and, consequently, a number of cognitive/metacognitive instructional models consider self-regulation an integral aspect (Deshler & Schumaker, 1986; Englert & Raphael, 1988; Harris & Graham, 1985; Palincsar & Brown, 1984).

E. Promoting Strategy Acquisition, Proficiency, Maintenance, and Generalization

The fifth trend deals with using instructional methods that are appropriate for different stages of strategy and skill learning (e.g., Bos & Vaughn, 1988; D. D. Smith, 1989). The stages include acquisition (initial learning), proficiency (consistent, accurate, and fluent usage), maintenance (consistent and independent usage over time), and generalization/adaptation (consistent and independent usage in similar and novel situations). An underlying assumption is that for instruction to be effective, it must incorporate the learner's prior experience with the strategy. Thus, instruction should be based on the learner's readiness at each stage of learning. The 8-stage instructional methodology developed as part of the Learning-Strategies Intervention model (Deshler & Schumaker, 1986) is one of the most recognized of the validated models for teaching strategies to LD and low-achieving students using this stage orientation toward strategy acquisition.

Other researchers who have focused their research on LD and other "at-risk" students have developed teaching methodologies based on notions of cognitive development suggested by Vygotsky (e.g., Bos and Anders, 1990b; Englert & Raphael, 1988; Palincsar & Brown, 1984). Vygotsky's sociocultural theory of cognitive development (1978) assumes that cognitive functioning grows out of social interactions during problem solving and practical activity. It is based on the premise that learning, including strategy acquisition and generalization, occurs during interactions or events between novices and experts which developmentally move from the level of social experience to individual experience (Diaz, Moll, & Mehan, 1986). This learning occurs in the "zone of proximal development" which Vygotsky (1978) described as ". . . the distance between the actual developmental level as determined by independent problem solving and the level of potential development as determined through problem solving under adult guidance or in collaboration with more capable peers" (p. 86). Methodologies developed on these premises tend to be less linear or stage oriented and more interactive, with dialogue between the novices and the expert a critical aspect of instruction. Reciprocal teaching (Palincsar & Brown, 1984) is probably the most frequently cited example of such methodology for "at-risk" learners. Regardless of the theoretical approach to strategy instruction, academic researchers have stressed the need for LD students to receive intensive instruction to promote strategy acquisition, maintenance, and generalization (Meyen & Leher, 1980).

How do the trends evident in academic-intervention research link to the neuropsychological functioning of learning-disabled students? At this point in the development of the learning disabilities field, the link is speculative at best (Hooper & Willis, 1989; Lyon, Moats, & Flynn, 1988). To date, most of the intervention studies upon which these trends are based have been conducted with heterogeneous groups of learning-disabled students, with little attention given to the specific nature of individual students' learning disabilities except for evidence of an aptitude–achievement discrepancy in the academic area under study (e.g., reading, math, written expression). One implication might speak to the robustness of the trends in that there is overall support for group effects regardless of the specific disabilities presumed to exist in the samples being studied. However at the same time, it brings to the forefront the need to increase efforts toward investigating aptitude–treatment interactions related to current intervention research.

III. Strategic Instruction in Reading Comprehension

In the field of reading, cognitive/metacognitive intervention studies have had their greatest impact on reading comprehension and learning from text. Given adequate word-recognition and decoding strategies, effective reading is strongly related to the strategies readers employ when interacting with the text to enhance understanding and learning (i.e., comprehension-fostering strategies) and to monitor comprehension and alleviate comprehension failures (i.e., comprehension-monitoring strategies) (Brown, 1980; Brown & Palincsar, 1982).

There is considerable evidence that LD students do not spontaneously employ task-appropriate strategies when reading (Bos & Filip, 1984; Wong,

1980; Wong & Jones, 1982). For example, Wong (1980) demonstrated that both second- and sixth-grade LD students were less effective than their normally achieving peers at comprehending implied information. However, by inserting questions/prompts, LD students' inadequate comprehension of implied information was alleviated. Bos and Filip (1984) demonstrated that seventh-grade students with learning disabilities were also less adequate than their average-achieving peers at spontaneously detecting text inconsistencies. But when cued to look for these inconsistencies, they were as able as their peers in finding them. This descriptive work in the area of reading comprehension built a strong case for teaching comprehension strategies to LD students. Intervention research with LD students has focused on a variety of specific comprehension-fostering and comprehension-monitoring strategies including paraphrasing, summarizing, and self-questioning (e.g., Clark, Deshler, Schumaker, Alley, & Warner, 1984; A. W. Graves, 1986; Jenkins, Heliotis, Stein, & Haynes, 1987; Wong, Wong, Perry, & Sawatsky, 1986) as well as several comprehensive comprehension strategies which are presented in the next sections (Bos & Anders, 1990b; Palincsar & Brown, 1984; Schumaker, Deshler, Alley, Warner, & Denton, 1982).

A. Multipass

Researchers at the Kansas University Institute for Research in Learning Disabilities adapted a well-known but unvalidated study strategy, SQ3R (Robinson, 1946), into a reading-comprehension and text-learning strategy (Multipass) (Schumaker et al., 1982). Multipass was taught as a three-substrategy learning strategy in which students made three passes through the textbook to learn information and answer questions posed in the chapter or by the teacher. The purpose of the first pass, Survey, was to familiarize the students with main ideas and organization of the chapter. The second pass, Size-Up, was designed to help students gain specific information and facts from the chapter without reading it verbatim. The Sort-Out pass allowed students to self-test over the materials presented in the chapter. A 10-step instructional methodology based on cognitive training and cognitive behavior modification was used which included determining students' current learning efficiency and obtaining a commitment to learn the strategy, describing and modeling the strategy, learning to an automatic level the steps in the strategy, and practicing the strategy in instructional-level and grade-appropriate materials while testing and providing feedback.

The strategy was investigated with eight LD secondary students using a multiple-baseline design across substrategies. Results indicated that students became substantially more proficient at each of the substrategies in terms of the procedures used and information gleaned from the chapter. On chapter content tests using objective formats, students' scores changed from failing before intervention to C's or better after intervention on both instructional and grade-level tests.

B. Reciprocal Teaching

Another comprehensive cognitive/metacognitive strategy, reciprocal teaching (Palincsar & Brown, 1984), is built on the assumptions that successful comprehension and text learning are based on six congitive/metacognitive activities:

1. Clarifying the purposes for reading and understanding the task demands,
2. Activating relevant background knowledge,
3. Allocating attention so that concentration can be focused on the major content,
4. Evaluating content for internal consistency and compatability within the text and with prior knowledge,
5. Monitoring ongoing activities to determine if comprehension is occurring, and
6. Making and testing predictions and interpretations (Brown, Palincsar, & Armbruster, 1984).

Usine these six activities as a guide, Palincsar and Brown (1984) selected four comprehension skills to teach, *summarizing* (self-review), *questioning, clarifying,* and *predicting.* The instructional methodology, reciprocal teaching, was based on Vygotsky's dialogic approach, in which the teacher and students took turns leading a dialogue about the text. Using this approach, the teacher and students read a section of text and then the leader (either a student or the teacher) asked questions, summarized the content, discussed and clarified any inconsistencies or difficulties, and made predictions about future content. Initially, the teacher employed cognitive modeling, prompting, and feedback to instruct the various comprehension strategies. Control of the discussions was gradually transferred to the students.

Palincsar and Brown's initial research (1984) studied the use of reciprocal teaching with seventh-grade students who were identified as poor readers with adequate decoding skills but deficient comprehension skills. Using one-on-one instruction, the 6 students in the reciprocal teaching group were compared with 6 students receiving instruction on locating information in text, 6 students who received the testing and daily assessments, and 6 students who served as pre- and posttest controls. A group of 13 average-achieving readers served as a normative group. In a second study, a multiple-baseline condition across groups was used in which groups of 4 to 7 students were taught by teachers. In both studies, qualitative improvements were evident in the students' dialogues, with the students gaining greater control of the four comprehension strategies. In addition the quantitative improvements on the comprehension tests were large and reliable. Almost all students who received reciprocal teaching improved in comprehension to the level set by the normative group. These effects were also durable in that maintenance probes showed no substantial drop in performance during an 8-week period.

C. Interactive Learning Strategies

Bos and Anders (1990b) have also investigated the use of comprehensive comprehension strategies for reading comprehension and vocabulary learning as it relates to content-area texts. Building upon an interactive teaching model (Bos & Anders, 1990a), they have incorporated Vygotsky (1978) assumptions about teaching processes and cognitive training procedures (Wong, 1985) to move an interactive model of teaching concepts to an interactive model for learning. The model itself is built on the following teaching–learning characteristics:

- activating prior knowledge,
- tying new knowledge to old knowledge,
- cooperative knowledge sharing and learning,
- predicting, justifying, and confirming concepts and text meaning,
- predicting, justifying, and confirming relationships among concepts, and
- purposeful learning (Bos & Anders, 1987).

Using interactive learning strategies, LD students worked in cooperative groups to first develop a brainstorm list based on the knowledge they had about the topic. Next, students surveyed the text to develop a clue list. Relevant information from the brainstorm was incorporated into the clue list. Then students organized concepts from the clue list into either a relationship map (Pearson & Johnson, 1978) or a relationship chart (Bos & Anders, 1987) and predicted the relationships among the concepts noted on the map or chart. These three activities served as prereading activities and set purposes for reading the text chapters which focused on clarifying and confirming concepts and their relationships. After reading the text cooperatively, the students worked together to make changes on the map or chart based on the information obtained from the text. The map or chart also served as a guide for studying.

In teaching this interactive learning strategy, teachers modeled the cognitive processes associated with developing a brainstorm, clue list, and map or chart and with clarifying and justifying learning, thus emphasizing the procedural knowledge associated with learning the strategy. Across the 6 weeks of instruction, the role of the teacher moved from that of "instructor" to that of "facilitator," with the students working in cooperative learning groups.

Several studies have been conducted using these interactive learning strategies. In one study (Bos & Reyes, 1989), bilingual, upper-elementary LD students were taught to use the strategy when reading and studying social-studies texts. In a second study (Anders *et al.*, 1990), middle-school LD students were taught to use the strategy with science texts. Results from both studies indicated that when students used the strategy, they were able to learn a substantial amount of information from content-area texts as measured on multiple-choice tests and written recalls. When using the strategy their learning was comparable to average-achieving students' learning and was maintained for a 6-week period. Analyses of videotapes of the teaching sessions and metacognitive interviews in which students reported their declarative, procedural, and conditional knowledge concerning the strategy indicate that, while procedural knowledge of the strategy was modeled and instantiated into the students' cognitive repertoire, conditional knowledge for the strategy was limited both in teaching and in learning.

D. Implications

Intervention research in reading comprehension and text learning has been most promising for "at-risk" learners and students identified as LD. Both the use of specific strategies such as summarizing or self-questioning and the use of more comprehensive strategies such as the ones described here have been shown to be fruitful with these learners. However, several cautions seem noteworthy. First, more emphasis needs to be placed on conditional knowledge and generalization in the instructional routines. Knowing when, where, and under which conditions to use different comprehension strategies is critical if LD students are to function successfully in regular classrooms. Providing opportunities for generalization may not be adequate if effort is not also geared to assisting them in developing the related conditional knowledge. Second, cognitive/metacognitive instruction is difficult. Bos and Anders (1990b), in their follow-up teacher interviews, found teachers regularly reporting that instructional methodology which requires the teacher to incorporate the teaching of declarative, procedural, and conditional knowledge is stimulating but taxing on the thought processes of the teachers. Third, learning cognitive strategies, particularly complex reading-comprehension strategies, requires systematic and intensive instruction over considerable time (Wong & Wong, 1988). It is important that in the learning process students have frequent opportunities to observe the benefits of learning and using cognitive strategies.

IV. Cognitive/Metacognitive Instruction in Written Composition

Like the area of reading comprehension, written composition also requires the orchestration of a variety of skills and cognitive processes. In the composing process, writers generate and organize their ideas and communicate those ideas using a written language system which requires them to attend to style, grammar, spelling, and punctuation/capitalization conventions. Effective writing encompasses the monitoring and regulation of such cognitive activities as planning, drafting, revising, and editing (Hayes & Flower, 1980; Scardamalia & Bereiter, 1986). Clearly, composing requires higher-order cognitive and metacognitive processes.

A number of studies have documented the difficulties LD students have with written composition. For example, Poplin, Gray, Larsen, Banikowski, and Mehring (1980) compared the written products of LD and normal students in grades three through eight using the Test of Written Language (Hammill & Larsen, 1978). While differences between younger LD and normal students were evident for writing conventions, LD students in later grades were significantly lower than normal students in composing skills as well as writing conventions.

Recently, there has been a growing interest in students' ability to use various text structures in their written compositions. Nodine, Barenbaum, and Newcomer (1985) compared the narrative text structures found in the stories of 11-year-old LD students, reading-disabled students, and nondisabled students. They found that while 71% of the nondisabled students and 47% of the reading-disabled students wrote stories (i.e., compositions containing a setting, conflict, and resolution all related to one another), only 30% of the LD students wrote stories. Thomas, Englert, and Gregg (1987) compared LD students' ability to generate different types of expository texts with the ability of low-achieving students matched for IQ and reading achievement and with normal achievers. Results indicate that LD students have substantial difficulties with expository prose. In comparison to normally achieving students, the LD students' writing reflected more mechanical errors and more irrelevant and redundant information. The LD students were also five times more likely than the normally achieving and matched subjects to terminate the piece prematurely. They tended to operate as though idea generation were an associative, serially driven process rather than a backward-looking process in which new ideas are selected and edited in relation to the topic (Englert & Raphael, 1988). MacArthur and Graham (1987) videotaped and interviewed fifth- and sixth-grade LD students during composing and found that the students reported that "finding the ideas" was the hardest part of writing. These students averaged less than 1 minute in prewriting activities.

Recent instructional interventions focusing on the composing process of LD students have drawn from researchers who focus their instruction on the cognitive processes associated with written composition and the recursive nature of those processes (D. H. Graves, 1983; Hayes & Flower, 1980; Scardamalia & Bereiter, 1986). Instructional models using this orientation generally include some amount and type of planning, drafting, revising and editing, and sharing or publication (Bos, 1988b; Florio-Ruane & Dunn, 1987). Several comprehensive strategy-instruction packages for teaching written composition to LD students have been investigated (Englert *et al.*, 1988; Graham *et al.*, 1987).

A. Cognitive Strategy Instruction in Writing

Englert, Raphael, and their colleagues (Englert & Raphael, 1988; Englert *et al.*, 1988) have utilized a process-oriented approach to teaching writing coupled with the explicit teaching of cognitive and metacognitive strategies designed to improve the expository writing of LD students. The intervention, Cognitive Strategy Instruction in Writing (CSIW) (Raphael, Kirschner, & Englert, 1986), teaches written composition of expository texts through the use of cognitive modeling and think alouds. The general components of the intervention reflect a process orientation: (1) daily writing, (2) sustained writing, and (3) the authenticity of audience through informed status and peer collaboration.

Think sheets assist students in organizing their written pieces. The use of think sheets and related questions represents the mature organization and thinking strategies in each writing stage. Each think sheet poses questions that prompt the writer to engage in certain cognitive/metacognitive activities. For example, the think sheet for prewriting poses the questions:

Audience: "Who will read my paper?"
Purpose: "Why am I writing this?"
Schema Activation: "What do I know about the topic?"
Organization: "How can I group/label my facts?"

During the planning stage, the students organize their ideas using different think sheets for each type of expository text. The different think sheets visually represented the different types of text.

Results from this instructional program suggest that positive benefits can result when LD students receive instruction in the thinking and dialogue that direct the writing processes of planning, organizing, writing, editing, and revising (Englert *et al.*, 1988). The writing of the LD students participating in the instruction became more sustained, the students became more aware and considerate of their audience, and they produced better-organized expository texts. The think sheets seemed to function as a scaffold for guiding and structuring the students' thinking and writing.

B. Self-Instructional Strategy Training

Graham and Harris (1987, 1989; Graham & MacArthur, 1988; Harris & Graham, 1985) have conducted a program of research with LD students using self-instructional strategy-training procedures for teaching written composition. The instructional components have been developed from assumptions drawn from (1) cognitive behavior modification (Meichenbaum, 1977), (2) the use of self-regulation training (Brown & Palincsar, 1982), and (3) the learning-strategies intervention model (Deshler & Schumaker, 1986). The package teaches task-specific strategies as well as metacognitive strategies. In the Graham and Harris studies, self-instructional training entailed criterion setting, self-instructions, self-assessment, and self-reinforcement. Harris and Graham (1985) used self-instructional training coupled with a specific strategy instruction to increase the use of action words, action helpers, and descriptive words in the written composition of two LD sixth graders. Results indicate increased use of these types of words when the students were asked to write stories about pictures. The improved performance generalized to the resource room and was maintained for 6 weeks.

In a subsequent study, Graham and Harris (1989) taught a specific story-grammar strategy using self-instructional training to 11 fifth- and sixth-grade LD students, and the specific story-grammar strategy plus self-regulation (i.e., criterion setting and self-monitoring) to a second group of 11 LD students. The strategy had five steps: (1) look at the picture, (2) let your mind be free, (3) write down the story-part reminder (W-W-W; What = 2; How = 2), (4) write down story-part ideas for each part, and (5) write your story—use good parts and make sense (Graham et al., 1987, p. 7). Using the mnemonic in the third step, students were instructed to think about seven story-grammar questions:

1. Who is the main character; who else is in the story?
2. When does the story take place?
3. Where does the story take place?
4. What does the main character do?
5. What happens when he/she tries to do it?
6. How does the story end?
7. How does the main character feel?

Results indicate that self-instructional strategy training improved LD students' written compositions. For example, prior to training only 36% of LD students' stories included at least six common story elements. After training, 86% of the stories met criterion, with the performance of the LD students after training being indistinguishable from a contrast group of normally achieving, competent writers. However, the self-regulation training provided to one group of students did not produce augmental effects on writing performance.

C. Implications

Like the reading-comprehension research, cognitive/metacognitive approaches to teaching written composition have also resulted in positive effects on LD students' learning. With these approaches a number of commonalities are evident. First, the emphasis has been placed on the processes associated with composing and the development of writing processes rather than individual skills. Second, attention has been given to the purposeful nature of writing through regard for audience, sharing of written pieces, and publication of some pieces. Third, the associated strategies have been taught explicitly to the LD students with control for learning gradually moving from the teacher to the student. Finally, an area of importance and intrigue is the component-analysis study conducted by Graham and Harris (1989) which demonstrated that self-regulation did not increase performance. Such component analysis of strategy instruction is critical if the teaching–learning process is to be as efficient as possible.

V. Cognitive Approaches to Mathematical Problem Solving

Only within the last decade has mathematical problem solving been recognized as an instructional priority (National Council of Teachers of Mathematics, 1980). In the latest mathematics report card, this area was targeted as one of great concern due to the significant number of students who experience difficulty in solving mathematical problems and due to its importance in today's technological society (Dossey, Mullis, Lindquist, & Chambers, 1988). Of the different instructional areas in math, mathematical problem solving is one in which cognitive and metacognitive instructional methodology seems particularly applicable (Schoenfeld, 1987).

Cognitive processing theory provides the theoretical framework for much of the recent research in mathematical problem solving because it addresses the complex interplay of numerous cognitive and metacognitive processes employed during problem solving (e.g., Kolligian & Sternberg, 1987; Montague & Bos, 1986a; Pellegrino & Goldman, 1987). Schoenfeld (1984) conceptualized problem solving as composed of two different types of problem-solving processes, tactical and managerial. Tactical processes are the algorithms and heuristics that problem solvers implement. Managerial processes are the metacognitive processes that effective and efficient problem solvers employ. In other words, problem solvers not only need to have a set of keys (tactical processes) to fit a lock (the problem), they need also to know how to select and use the "right key" (managerial/metacognitive processes).

Research with learning/math-disabled students indicates that delays in reasoning, cognitive/metacognitive processing, and reading have been associated with deficits in solving word problems. Lee and Hudson (1981) investigated the reasoning, reading proficiency, computation skills, and strategy efficiency of matched groups of seventh-grade LD and non-LD males. Although the groups were similar in the number of computation errors, the LD boys made significantly more errors in operation selection and reading. They also evidenced weaknesses in the areas of reasoning, selection of relevant information, determination of the correct and most efficient processes, assessment of correctness of response, estimation, and judgment. Englert, Culatta, and Horn (1987) found that irrelevant numerical information adversely affected the proficiency of LD students solving addition word problems. Irrelevant linguistic information however, did not affect problem-solving accuracy. Skirtic (1980) found delays in reasoning for junior-high LD students, with some students operating within the concrete-operations stage of Piaget's developmental sequence.

Learning-disabled students also have strategic deficits (e.g., Fleischner & Garnett, 1983; Pistono, 1980; Russell & Ginsburg, 1984). For example, Pistono (1980) found many of the LD primary students attempting strategic activity but failing to allocate and control their strategies adequately. Both Fleischner and Garnett (1983) and Montague and Bos (1986b) report observation data of LD students indicating that these students seem to lack knowledge of how to attack a problem.

Montague and Bos (1990) used video-stimulated interviewing to assess eighth-grade high-achieving (HA), average-achieving (AA), low-achieving (LA), and LD students' knowledge, use, and control of mathematical problem-solving strategies. The students' computational skills during problem solving were also assessed. Results indicate the LD students showed difficulty with control of math problem-solving strategies (i.e., knowing under which conditions to employ various strategies) and difficulty talking about those strategies (knowledge) when they were not watching the videotape and directly answering specific questions about how they solved the problems. As in the Lee and Hudson (1981) study, the LD students did not evidence computational difficulties in comparison to the other students.

A. Comprehensive Problem-Solving Strategies

Current math problem-solving intervention research with LD students has incorporated training regimens that focus on cognitive and metacognitive processing. The development of instructional models for teaching verbal mathematical problem solving to LD students has been dependent on the stages or strategies involved in solving problems. Polya (1945) described a 4-stage process: understanding the problem, planning, carrying out the plan, and looking back. Despite differences in terminology and number of components identified, recent models reflect similar conceptualizations (e.g., Gagne, 1983; Montague & Bos, 1986a; Uprichard, Phillips, & Soriano, 1984).

Based on models of mathematical problem solving and the documented strategic deficits of LD students, several researchers have implemented strategy-based instructional programs to teach mathematical problem solving (e.g., Fleischner, Nuzum, & Marzola, 1987; Montague & Bos, 1986b; E. Smith & Alley, 1981). E. Smith and Alley (1981) taught three sixth-grade LD students a verbal mathematical problem-solving strategy. The strategy consisted of the following seven steps: (1) read the problem, (2) reread the problem, (3) use objects to show the problem, (4) write the problem, (5) work the problem, (6) check your answer, and (7) show your answer. The acquisition steps from the learning-strategies intervention model (Deshler & Schumaker, 1986) were used to teach the strategy. Using a multiple-baseline design, an increase in accuracy was demonstrated for the students in both instructional and grade-level materials.

Montague and Bos (1986b) used an adaptation of the acquisition steps for the learning-strategies intervention model to teach six LD high school students how to solve 2-step word problems. The steps in the strategy were: (1) read the problem aloud, (2) paraphrase the problem aloud, (3) visualize, (4) state the problem, (5) hypothesize the number of steps and the operations to use, (6) estimate the answer, (7) calculate the solution, and (8) self-check. Using a multiple-baseline design, students made substantial improvement following intervention, evidenced generalization to 3-step problems, and maintained performance over a 3-month lapse in instruction and practice. Performance patterns over time indicate that the students adapted the 8-step strategy in various ways. For example, one student drew diagrams, hypothesized by showing the operation symbols, estimated by writing rounded numbers, and recorded the calculation check only for certain problems.

B. Implications

In relation to reading comprehension and written composition, the use of cognitive/metacognitive approaches with LD students in verbal mathematical problem solving is not as well investigated. Although there is growing interest in this area, it has been slow to transfer to the study of LD students. This seems primarily related to the traditional focus of the field on language-based deficits and interventions. However, cognitive/metacognitive-oriented intervention research for verbal mathematical problem solving with LD students appears promising. It will be important to continue with systematic investigation in this area, particularly attending to component analysis and generalization and to streamlining of the task-specific strategies and strategy instruction.

VI. Implications for Cognitive and Neuropsychological Research

The question to consider when viewing the neuropsychological functioning of LD students in relation to cognitive/metacognitive instructional research of complex academic skills is: Are we at a stage in both fields to pursue the systematic study of their link? It is our contention and that of C. R. Hynd (1986) and Lyon (1985) that such an agenda is possible to pursue. In the area of reading comprehension, Hynd suggests that based on aptitude–treatment interactions, students with deep or phonological dyslexia might particularly profit from comprehension strategies that provide visual representations of texts such as the interactive strategies suggested by Bos and Anders (1990a, 1990b). Students with surface, deep, or phonological dyslexia might profit from schema-activation procedures such as the ones that were evident in reciprocal teaching (Palinscar & Brown, 1984) and interactive learning strategies. Although aptitude–treatment interactions with LD students based on perceptual models of information processing have not been supported by research (e.g., Hammill & Larsen, 1974; Kavale & Mattson, 1983), some tentative evidence suggests that aptitude–treatment interactions based on cognitive/metacognitive models of instruction may be more advantageous (Lyon, 1985; Lyon et al., 1988).

How can such an agenda come to fruition? First, it is critical that instructional researchers provide more information concerning the cognitive and neuropsychological functioning of their subjects. Second, instructional effectiveness should be studied in terms of both individual students as well as groups of students. Questions such as the following need to be addressed: For which students did the instructional intervention result in gains or learning? Are there common neuropsychological, cognitive/metacognitive, and motivational characteristics among the students for which learning was evident? Third, it is imperative that the subtyping of LD students focus on a wide array of neuropsychological functioning and academic skills, not those primarily addressing lower-level skills. Fourth, collaboration between intervention researchers and those studying the neuropsychological functioning of LD students should allow for the most robust study of this area and allow for the greatest impact on instructional practice. This agenda is one that stirs anticipation in both fields because it directly addresses aptitude–treatment interactions and the link between a presumed neurological etiology and intervention.

References

Adelman, H. S., & Taylor, L. S. (1983). Enhancing motivation for overcoming learning and behavior problems. *Journal of Learning Disabilities, 16,* 384–392.

Anders, P. L., Bos, C. S., Scanlon, D., Gallego, M., Duran, G. Z., & Reyes, E. (1990). [Facilitating content learning through interactive strategy instruction with middle school learning disabled students.] Unpublished raw data.

Anderson, R. C. (1984). Role of the reader's schema in comprehension, learning and memory. In R. C. Anderson, J. Osborn, & R. J. Tierney (Eds.), *Learning to read in American schools: Basal readers and content texts* (pp. 243–258). Hillsdale, NJ: Erlbaum.

Anderson, R. C., & Freebody, P. (1981). Vocabulary knowledge. In J. T. Guthrie (Ed.), *Comprehension and teaching: Research reviews* (pp. 77–117). Newark, DE: International Reading Association.

Anderson, R. C., Reynolds, R. E., Schallert, D. L., & Goetz, E. T. (1977). Frameworks for comprehending discourse. *American Educational Research Journal, 14,* 367–382.

Anderson, R. C., Spiro, R. J., & Anderson, M. C. (1978). Schemata as scaffolding for the representation of information in connected discourse. *American Educational Research Journal, 15,* 433–440.

Bendell, D., Tollefson, N., & Fine, M. (1980). Interaction of locus-of-control orientation and the performance of learning disabled adolescents. *Journal of Learning Disabilities, 13,* 83–86.

Benton, A. L. (1975). Developmental dyslexia: Neurological aspects. *Advances in Neurology, 3,* 1–47.

Bereiter, C., & Bird, M. (1985). Use of thinking aloud in the identification and teaching of reading comprehension strategies. *Cognition and Instruction, 2,* 131–156.

Billingsley, B. S., & Wildman, T. M. (1988). The effects of prereading activities on the comprehension monitoring of learning disabled adolescents. *Learning Disabilities Research, 4,* 36–44.

Bos, C. S. (1988a). Academic interventions for learning disabilities. In K. Kavale (Ed.), *Learning disabilities: State of the art and practice* (pp. 98–122). Boston, MA: College-Hill, Little Brown.

Bos, C. S. (1988b). Process-oriented writing: Instructional implications for mildly handicapped students. *Exceptional Children, 54,* 521–527.

Bos, C. S., & Anders, P. L. (1987). Semantic feature analysis: An interactive teaching strategy for facilitating learning from text. *Learning Disabilities Focus, 3,* 55–59.

Bos, C. S., & Anders, P. L. (1990a). Toward an interactive model: Teaching text-based concepts to learning disabled students. In H. L. Swanson & B. Keogh (Eds.), *Learning disabilities: Theoretical and research issues* (pp. 247–261). Hillsdale, NJ: Erlbaum.

Bos, C. S., & Anders, P. L. (1990b). Interactive teaching and learning: Instructional practices for teaching content and strategic knowledge. In T. E. Scruggs & B. Y. L. Wong (Eds.), *Intervention research in learning disabilities* (pp. 161–185). New York: Springer-Verlag.

Bos, C. S., & Filip, D. (1984). Comprehension monitoring in learning disabled and average students. *Journal of Learning Disabilities, 17,* 229–233.

Bos, C. S., & Reyes, E. (1989, December). *Knowledge, use, and control of an interactive cognitive strategy for learning from content area texts.* Paper presented at the annual meeting of the National Reading Conference, Austin, TX.

Bos, C. S., & Vaughn, S. (1988). *Strategies for teaching students with learning and behavior problems.* Boston, MA: Allyn & Bacon.

Brown, A. L. (1980). Metacognitive development and reading. In R. J. Spiro, B. C. Bruce, & W. F. Brewer (Eds.), *Theoretical issues in reading comprehension* (pp. 453–482). Hillsdale, NJ: Erlbaum.

Brown, A. L., Campione, J. C., & Murphy, M. D. (1977). Maintenance and generalization of trained metamnemonic awareness by educable retarded children. *Journal of Experimental Child Psychology, 24,* 191–211.

Brown, A. L., & Palincsar, A. S. (1982). Inducing strategic learning from texts by means of informed, self-control training. *Topics in Learning and Learning Disabilities, 2*(1), 1–17.

Brown, A. L., Palincsar, A. S., & Armbruster, B. B. (1984). Instructing comprehension-fostering activities in interactive learning situations. In H. Mandl, N. L. Stein, & T. Trabasso (Eds.), *Learning and comprehension of text* (pp. 255–286). Hillsdale, NJ: Erlbaum.

Bryan, T. H. (1986). Self-concept and attributions of the learning disabled. *Learning Disabilities Focus, 1,* 82–89.

Ceci, S. J. (1985). A developmental study of learning disabilities and memory. *Journal of Experimental Child Psychology, 39,* 202–221.

Chapman, J. W. (1988). Learning disabled children's self-concepts. *Review of Educational Research, 58,* 347–371.

Clark, F. L., Deshler, D. D., Schumaker, J. B., Alley, G. R., & Warner, M. M. (1984). Visual imagery and self-questioning: Strategies to improve comprehension of written material. *Journal of Learning Disabilities, 17,* 145–149.

Deshler, D. D., & Schumaker, J. B. (1986). Learning strategies: An instructional alternative for low-achieving adolescents. *Exceptional Children, 52,* 583–590.

Deshler, D. D., Schumaker, J. B., & Lenz, K. (1984). Academic and cognitive interventions for LD adolescents: Part I. *Journal of Learning Disabilities, 17,* 108–117.

Diaz, S., Moll, L. C., & Mehan, H. (1986). Sociocultural resources in instruction: A context-specific approach. In *Beyond language: Social and cultural factors in schooling language minority students* (pp. 187–230). Sacramento: California State Department of Education, Bilingual Education Office.

Dossey, J., Mullis, I., Lindquist, M., & Chambers, D. (1988). *The mathematics report card: Are we measuring up?* Princeton, NJ: Educational Testing Service.

Englert, C. S., Culatta, B. E., & Horn, D. G. (1987). Influence of irrelevant information in addition word problems on problem solving. *Learning Disability Quarterly, 10,* 29–36.

Englert, C. S., & Raphael, T. E. (1988). Constructing well-formed prose: Process, structure, and metacognitive knowledge. *Exceptional Children, 54,* 513–520.

Englert, C. S., Raphael, T. E., Anderson, L. M., Anthony, H. M., Fear, K. L., & Gregg, S. L. (1988). A case for writing intervention: Strategies for writing informational text. *Learning Disabilities Focus, 3,* 98–113.

Englert, C. S., Raphael, T. E., Anderson, L. M., Stevens, D. D., & Anthony, H. M.

(1989, April). *Making writing strategies and self-talk visible: Cognitive strategy instruction in writing*. Paper presented at the annual meeting of the American Education Research Association, San Francisco, CA.

Fleischner, J. E., & Garnett, K. (Eds.). (1983). Arithmetic difficulties among learning disabled children: Background and current directions (Special issue). *Learning Disabilities, 2*(9).

Fleischner, J. E., Nuzum, M. B., & Marzola, E. S. (1987). Devising an instructional program to teach arithmetic problem-solving skills to students with learning disabilities. *Journal of Learning Disabilities, 20*, 214–217.

Florio-Ruane, S., & Dunn, S. (1987). Teaching writing: Some perennial questions and some possible answers. In V. Richardson-Koehler (Ed.), *Educators' handbook: A research perspective* (pp. 50–83). New York: Longman.

Gaddes, W. H. (1985). *Learning disabilities and brain function: A neuropsychological approach* (2nd ed.). New York: Springer-Verlag.

Gagne, R. (1983). Some issues in the psychology of mathematics instruction. *Journal for Research in Mathematics Education, 14*, 7–18.

Graham, S., & Harris, K. R. (1987). Improving composition skills of inefficient learners with self-instructional strategy training. *Topics in Language Disorders, 7*(4), 66–77.

Graham, S., & Harris, K. R. (1989). Components analysis of cognitive strategy instruction: Effects on learning disabled students' compositions and self-efficacy. *Journal of Educational Psychology, 81*, 353–361.

Graham, S., Harris, K. R., & Sawyer, R. (1987). Composition instruction with learning disabled students: Self-instructional strategy training. *Focus on Exceptional Children, 20*(4), 1–11.

Graham, S., & MacArthur, C. (1988). Improving learning disabled students' skills at revising essays produced on a word processor: Self-instructional strategy training. *Journal of Special Education, 22*, 133–152.

Graves, A. W. (1986). Effects of direct instruction and metacomprehension training on finding main ideas. *Learning Disabilities Research, 1*, 90–100.

Graves, D. H. (1983). *Writing: Teachers and children at work*. Portsmouth, NH: Heinemann.

Hallahan, D. P., & Sapona, R. (1983). Self-monitoring of attention with learning disabled children: Past research and current issues. *Journal of Learning Disabilities, 16*, 616–620.

Hammill, D. D., & Larsen, S. C. (1974). The effectiveness of psycholinguistic training. *Exceptional Children, 41*, 5–15.

Hammill, D. D., & Larsen, S. C. (1978). *Test of written language*. Austin, TX: Pro-Ed.

Harris, K. R., & Graham, S. (1985). Improving learning disabled students' composition skills: Self-control strategy training. *Learning Disability Quarterly, 8*, 27–36.

Havertape, J. F., & Kass, C. E. (1978). Examination of problem solving in learning disabled adolescents through verbalized self-instructions. *Learning Disability Quarterly, 1*, 94–100.

Hayes, J. R., & Flower, L. S. (1980). Writing as problem solving. *Visible Language, 14*, 388–399.

Henker, B., Whalen, C. K., & Hinshaw, S. P. (1980). The attributional contexts of cognitive intervention strategies. *Exceptional Education Quarterly, 1*(1), 17–30.

Hooper, S. R., & Willis, W. G. (1989). *Learning disability subtyping: Neuropsychological foundations, conceptual models, and issues in clinical differentiation.* New York: Springer-Verlag.

Hynd, C. R. (1986). Educational intervention in children with developmental learning disorders. In J. E. Obrzut & G. W. Hynd (Eds.), *Child neuropsychology* (Vol. 2, pp. 265–297). Orlando, FL: Academic Press.

Hynd, G. W., & Cohen, M. (1983). *Dyslexia: Neuropsychological theory, research, and clinical differentiation.* New York: Grune & Stratton.

Hynd, G. W., & Obrzut, J. E. (Eds.). (1981). *Neuropsychological assessment and the school-age child: Issues and procedures.* New York: Grune & Stratton.

Jenkins, J. R., Heliotis, J. D., Stein, M. L., & Haynes, M. C. (1987). Improving reading comprehension by using paragraph restatements. *Exceptional Children, 54,* 54–59.

Kavale, K. K., & Mattson, P. D. (1983). One jumped off the balance beam: Meta-analysis of perceptual-motor training. *Journal of Learning Disabilities, 16,* 164–173.

Keogh, B. (1977). Research on cognitive styles. In R. Kneedler & S. Tarver (Eds.), *Changing perspectives in special education* (pp. 318–342). Columbus, OH: Charles E. Merrill.

Kolligian, J., & Sternberg, R. J. (1987). Intelligence, information processing, and specific learning disabilities: A triarchic synthesis. *Journal of Learning Disabilities, 20,* 8–17.

Kurtz, B. E., & Borkowski, J. G. (1987). Development of strategic skills in impulsive and reflective children: A longitudinal study of metacognition. *Journal of Experimental Psychology, 43,* 129–148.

Lee, W., & Hudson, F. (1981). *A comparison of verbal problem-solving in arithmetic of LD and non-LD seventh grade males* (Research Rep. No. 43). Lawrence: University of Kansas, Institute for Research in Learning Disabilities.

Licht, B. G., & Kistner, J. A. (1985). Motivational problems of learning disabled children: Individual differences and their implications for treatment. In J. K. Torgesen & B. Y. L. Wong (Eds.), *Psychological and educational perspectives on learning disabilities* (pp. 225–255). Orlando, FL: Academic Press.

Lyon, G. R. (1985). Identification and remediation of learning disability subtypes: Preliminary findings. *Learning Disabilities Focus, 1,* 21–35.

Lyon, G. R., Moats, L. C., & Flynn, J. M. (1988). From assessment to treatment: Linkage to interventions with children. In M. G. Tramontana & S. R. Hooper (Eds.), *Assessment issues in child neuropsychology* (pp. 113–142). New York: Plenum.

MacArthur, C. A., & Graham, S. (1987). Learning disabled students' composing under three methods of text production: Handwriting, word processing, and dictation. *Journal of Special Education, 21,* 22–42.

Meichenbaum, D. H. (1977). *Cognitive behavior modification.* New York: Plenum.

Meichenbaum, D. H., & Goodman, J. (1971). Training impulsive children to talk to themselves: A means of developing self-control. *Journal of Abnormal Psychology, 77,* 115–126.

Meyen, E. L., & Leher, D. H. (1980). Evolving practices in assessment and intervention for mildly handicapped adolescents: The case for intensive instruction. *Exceptional Education Quarterly, 1*(2), 19–26.

Montague, M., & Bos, C. S. (1986a). Verbal mathematical problem solving and learning disabilities: A review. *Focus on Learning Problems in Mathematics, 8*(2), 7–21.

Montague, M., & Bos, C. S. (1986b). The effects of cognitive strategy training on verbal math problem solving performance of learning disabled adolescents. *Journal of Learning Disabilities, 19*, 26–33.

Montague, M., & Bos, C. S. (1990). Cognitive and metacognitive characteristics of eighth grade students' mathematical problem solving. *Learning and Individual Differences, 2*(3), 109–127.

National Council of Teachers of Mathematics. (1980). *An agenda for action: Recommendations for school mathematics of the 1980's*. Reston, VA: National Council of Teachers of Mathematics.

Nodine, B. F., Barenbaum, E., & Newcomer, P. (1985). Story composition by learning disabled, reading disabled, and normal children. *Learning Disability Quarterly, 8*, 167–179.

Palincsar, A. S., & Brown, A. L. (1984). Reciprocal teaching of comprehension-fostering and comprehension-monitoring activities. *Cognition and Instruction, 1*, 117–175.

Palincsar, A. S., & Brown, D. E. (1987). Enhancing instructional time through attention to metacognition. *Journal of Learning Disabilities, 20*, 66–75.

Pascarella, E., Pflaum, S., Bryan, T., & Pearl, R. (1983). Interaction of internal attributions for effort and teacher response mode in reading instruction: A replication note. *American Education Research Journal, 5*, 173–176.

Pearson, P. D., & Johnson, D. D. (1978). *Teaching reading comprehension*. New York: Holt, Rinehart, & Winston.

Pellegrino, J., & Goldman, S. (1987). Information processing and elementary mathematics. *Journal of Learning Disabilities, 20*, 23–32.

Perlmuter, L. C., & Monty, R. A. (1977). The importance of perceived control: Fact or fantasy? *American Scientist, 65*, 759–765.

Pistono, K. (1980). Certain aspects of problem solving of learning disabled and normal 6 and 7 1/2 year old boys as reflected in external cue incorporation on a memory task. *Dissertation Abstracts International, 41*, 3833A.

Polya, G. (1945). *How to solve it*. Princeton, NJ: Princeton University Press.

Poplin, M., Gray, R., Larsen, S., Banikowski, A., & Mehring, T. (1980). A comparison of components of written expression abilities in learning disabled and non-learning disabled children at three grade levels. *Learning Disability Quarterly, 3*, 46–53.

Raphael, T. E., Kirschner, B., & Englert, C. S. (1986). *Text structure instruction with process-writing classrooms: A manual for instruction* (Occasional Paper No. 104). East Lansing: Michigan State University, Institute for Research on Teaching.

Robinson, R. P. (1946). *Effective study*. New York: Harper & Brothers.

Rooney, K. J., Hallahan, D. P., & Lloyd, J. W. (1983). Self-recording of attention by learning disabled students in the regular classroom. *Journal of Learning Disabilities, 17*, 360–364.

Rourke, B. P. (Ed.). (1985). *Neuropsychology of learning disabilities: Essential of subtype analysis.* New York: Guilford Press.

Rumelhart, D. E. (1980). Schemata: The building blocks of cognition. In R. J. Spiro, B. C. Bruce, & W. F. Brewer (Eds.), *Theoretical issues in reading comprehension* (pp. 33–58). Hillsdale, NJ: Erlbaum.

Russell, R. L., & Ginsburg, H. P. (1984). Cognitive analysis of children's mathematics difficulties. *Cognition and Instruction, 2,* 217–244.

Scardamalia, M., & Bereiter, C. (1986). Research on written composition. In M. C. Wittrock (Ed.), *Handbook of research on teaching* (3rd ed., pp. 778–803). New York: Macmillan.

Schoenfeld, A. H. (1984). Heuristic behavior variables in instruction. In G. A. Goldin & C. E. McClintock (Eds.), *Task variables in mathematical problem solving* (pp. 431–454). Philadelphia, PA: Franklin Institute Press.

Schoenfeld, A. H. (Ed.). (1987). *Cognitive science and mathematics education.* Hillsdale, NJ: Erlbaum.

Schumaker, J. B., Deshler, D. D., Alley, G. R., Warner, M. M., & Denton, P. H. (1982). Multipass: A learning strategy for improving reading comprehension. *Learning Disability Quarterly, 5,* 295–304.

Schunk, D. H., & Rice, J. M. (1987). Enhancing comprehension skill and self-efficacy with strategy value information. *Journal of Reading Behavior, 19,* 285–302.

Scruggs, T. E. (1988). Nature of learning disabilities. In K. Kavale (Ed.), *Learning disabilities: State of the art and practice* (pp. 22–43). Boston, MA: College-Hill, Little Brown.

Skirtic, T. (1980). *Formal reasoning abilities of learning disabled adolescents: Implications for mathematics instruction* (Research Rep. No. 7). Lawrence: University of Kansas, Institute for Research in Learning Disabilities.

Smith, D. D. (1989). *Teaching students with learning and behavior problems* (2nd ed.). Columbus, OH: Merrill.

Smith, E., & Alley, G. (1981). *The effect of teaching sixth graders with learning difficulties a strategy for solving verbal math problems* (Research Rep. No. 39). Lawrence: University of Kansas, Institute for Research in Learning Disabilities.

Stahl, S. A., & Fairbanks, M. M. (1986). The effects of vocabulary instruction: A model-based meta-analysis. *Review of Educational Research, 56,* 72–110.

Thomas, C. C., Englert, C. S., & Gregg, S. (1987). An analysis of errors and strategies in the expository writing of learning disabled students. *Remedial and Special Education, 8,* 21–30, 46.

Tollefson, N., Tracy, D. B., Johnsen, E. P., Buenning, M., Farmer, A., & Barke, C. R. (1982). Attribution patterns of learning disabled adolescents. *Learning Disability Quarterly, 5,* 14–20.

Torgesen, J. K. (1977). Memorization processes in reading-disabled children. *Journal of Educational Psychology, 69,* 571–578.

Torgesen, J. K. (1982). The learning-disabled child as an inactive learner: Educational implications. *Topics in Learning and Learning Disabilities, 2*(1), 45–52.

Uprichard, A. E., Phillips, E. R., & Soriano, A. (1984). A conceptual schema for solving mathematical word problems with implications for instruction. *Focus on Learning Problems in Mathematics, 6*(1 & 2), 79–107.

Van Reusen, A. K., Bos, C. S., Schumaker, J. B., & Deshler, D. D. (1987). *The education planning strategy*. Lawrence, KS: Edge Enterprises, Inc.

Van Reusen, A. K., Deshler, D. D., & Schumaker, J. B. (1989). Effects of a student participation strategy in facilitating the involvement of learning disabled adolescents in the IEP planning process. *Learning Disabilities: A Multidisciplinary Journal, 1*(2), 23–34.

Vygotsky, L. S. (1978). *Mind in society*. Cambridge, MA: Harvard University Press.

White, W., Schumaker, J. B., Warner, M., Alley, G., & Deshler, D. (1980). *The current status of young adults identified as learning disabled during their school careers* (Research Rep. No. 71). Lawrence: University of Kansas, Institute for Research in Learning Disabilities.

Wong, B. Y. L. (1980). Activating the inactive learner: Use of questions/prompts to enhance comprehension and retention of implied information in learning disabled children. *Learning Disability Quarterly, 3*, 42–47.

Wong, B. Y. L. (1985). Issues in cognitive-behavior interventions in academic skill areas. *Journal of Abnormal Child Psychology, 13*, 425–442.

Wong, B. Y. L., & Jones, W. (1982). Increasing metacomprehension in learning disabled and normally achieving students through self-questioning training. *Learning Disability Quarterly, 5*, 228–238.

Wong, B. Y. L., & Wong, R. (1988). Cognitive interventions for learning disabilities. In K. Kavale (Ed.), *Learning disabilities: State of the art and practice* (pp. 141–169). Boston, MA: College-Hill, Little Brown.

Wong, B. Y. L., Wong, R., Perry, N., & Sawatsky, D. (1986). The efficacy of a self-questioning summarization strategy for use by underachievers and learning disabled adolescents in social studies. *Learning Disabilities Focus, 2*, 20–35.

CHAPTER TWENTY-FIVE

Neuropsychological Assessment: Case Studies

Lawrence Lewandowski

I. Introduction

A chapter containing case studies is often found toward the end of a book and attempts to integrate research with clinical issues. Assumptions are made that the reader is, by then, well acquainted with the topic and has mastered the jargon, definitions, key variables, and other prerequisite knowledge necessary to make sense out of the case studies. This chapter abides by these assumptions, expecting that the reader has acquired a sound knowledge base regarding the neuropsychology of learning disabilities. However, in order to best interpret the points raised in the case illustrations, several considerations will be addressed. First, a brief historical overview of neuropsychological assessment as related to learning disabilities will be presented. Second, different approaches to neuropsychological assessment will be highlighted. Third, a rationale for neuropsychological applications will be forwarded. And fourth, neurodevelopmental issues regarding learning disabilities will be discussed. This discussion will be followed by three case examples, illustrating three different neuropsychological batteries. The children selected as examples reflect individual differences in age, gender, and type and origin of learning problems. A chapter summary will highlight the similarities and differences across cases and reiterate some of the more important aspects of neuropsychological assessment of the learning-disabled child. The reader should derive a better sense of why, when, and how to use neuropsychological assessment as well as recognize its limitations, problems, and the need for evaluative research on this assessment model.

II. Historical Context

The fields of pediatric neuropsychology and learning disabilities emerged somewhat at the same time (over the past 25 years). Although the fields are reasonably distinct, they do share some overlap both in historic roots and in present practice. Both of these young fields can be traced, in some form, back to the late 1940s and early 1950s. At that time psychological testing of human abilities was advancing rapidly, and the study of adults with brain injuries (i.e., soldiers) was of interest to physicians and psychologists. These movements laid the groundwork for the field of "neuropsychology," a term promoted in a book by Hebb in 1949. The advances in clinical testing coupled with the findings about brain–behavior relationships in the brain-injured were soon applied to children. Werner, Strauss, Cruickshank, Kephart, and others noticed that children with cerebral palsy, certain forms of mental retardation, and other developmental problems showed many characteristics in common with the brain-injured adults. This included psychomotor incoordination or slowing, concrete thinking, difficulties in reading, writing, and speaking, and behavioral adjustment problems (Hallahan & Cruickshank, 1973).

While some psychologists became increasingly interested in the study of brain–behavior relationships, others joined educators in the search for interventions that would aid the children with known or suspected brain injury. Here the fields diverged into neuropsychology of adults (and children to a lesser extent) and a field within special education regarding the teaching of "brain-injured" children (Cruickshank, Bentzen, Ratzeburg, & Tannhauser, 1961). Gradually the field of neuropsychology would become specialized such that child neuropsychology would emerge as its own area of study and practice. Similarly, in the 1960s the field of learning disabilities was formed apart from existing disciplines in developmental disorders (i.e., mental retardation, cerebral palsy). Identification of learning disability was no longer contingent on medical diagnosis or proven neurological impairment. Nonetheless, definitions of learning disabilities from 1963 to the present time have included statements such as ". . . the term includes such conditions as perceptual handicaps, brain injury, minimal brain dysfunction, dyslexia, and developmental aphasia" (Federal Register, 1977).

Over the past 25 years the learning disabilities field has grown, changed, and been influenced by professional, social, and political agenda, yet it has still maintained its historic connection to brain-based disorders and thus its connection to neuropsychology. In fact, since the 1970s there has been a growing number of neuropsychologists working on the issue of specific learning disabilities, with advancement of research discoveries in neurology and neuroscience continuing to make an impact on the discipline.

While brain research continues to maintain a link to the learning disabilities field, there has been clinical application of neuropsychology. Many clinicians find neuropsychological assessment to be a viable approach to take with learning-disabled individuals. Neuropsychology provides a theoretical framework and empirical basis that has been often lacking in the study of learning disabilities. Furthermore, the work of Luria, Reitan, Gaddes, Rourke, and many others has documented the utility of neuropsychological assessment for the child with learning disabilities (see Hynd & Obrzut, 1981). Current history indicates a continuing research and clinical link between learning disabilities and child neuropsychology, a link not ordained by everyone in the learning disabilities field, but one that is sure to advance the scientific study of this developmental disability.

III. Neuropsychological Approaches

With regard to the learning disabilities field, assessment and identification practices have always varied widely. This is due in part to the lack of centralized direction within the field. For a long time state and local schools decided how to assess these youngsters. The federal government and its legislation PL94-142 (Education of All Handicapped Children's Act) avoided dictating assessment practice and gave schools loose guidelines on the assessment and identification of learning-disabled children. Consequently, theoretical and practical differences exist in assessment procedures across even adjacent school districts.

Within a school district there may exist a professional who chooses to apply a neuropsychological framework to the assessment and treatment of learning disabilities. If so, what is this psychologist likely to do when testing a child with suspected learning disabilities? In a recent survey, Leavell and Lewandowski (1988) found that most school psychologists with a neuropsychological orientation would adapt basic neuropsychology principles to their current psychoeducational assessment. That is, they would use the WISC-R, Bender, and other tests to provide neuropsychological information. A comparatively smaller percentage of school psychologists reported using more formal batteries such as the Halstead–Reitan Neuropsychological Battery for Children (HRNB-C) or the Luria–Nebraska Neuropsychological Battery-Children's Revision (LNNB-CR). These disparate neuropsychological assessment approaches highlight differences between qualitative and quantitative techniques (Luria & Majovsky, 1977).

The quantitative technique follows from a psychometric and experimental tradition. The typical assessment method is a standard battery that is fixed at the outset of testing, is administered in a prescribed manner, and makes use of norm-referenced comparisons (see Tramontana & Hooper, 1988). Decisions and interpretations are made in an actuarial fashion based on decision rules established by test authors. Such approaches have been accurate predictors of organic pathology as well as learning disabilities (see Reitan & Boll, 1973; Selz & Reitan, 1979), yet the Reitan batteries have been criticized for lacking flexibility (Luria & Majovsky, 1977), failing to delineate specific performance patterns among learning-disabled students (Hevern, 1980), and having an unstable factor structure with regard to the learning disabled (Gamble, Mishra, & Obrzut, 1988). The LNNB-CR has been criticized for some of the same inadequacies and, thus far, has been shown to discriminate learning disabilities but does not provide for reliable analyses of specific neuropsychological subtypes or profiles (e.g., Snow & Hund, 1985; Teeter, Boliek, Obrzut, & Malsch, 1986). Furthermore, neither approach (HRNB or LNNB-CR) has produced empirically validated neuropsychological treatment interventions proven successful with learning-disabled students. Rourke, Bakker, Fisk, and Strang (1983) point out some of the problems in applying neuropsychological assessment to the treatment of children. Subject heterogeneity and the uniqueness of selective brain dysfunction make group treatment interventions and evaluation studies virtually impossible. One way to tackle the heterogeneity issue is to determine neuropsychological subtypes of learning disabilities which then may be more conducive to neuropsychological treatment interventions. Subtype studies using the HRNB-C and LNNB-CR have attempted to determine neuropsychologically distinct groups of learning-disabled students which are theoretically best suited for certain intervention programs. Unfortunately, investigators have arrived at different subtypes based upon subject selection, tests employed, and subtyping method. To date, the evaluation of specialized treatment programs based on neuropsychological subtypes has been sparse (see Rourke, 1986).

The qualitative testing technique (see Luria & Majovsky, 1977) differs from the quantitative technique in philosophy and practice. It is a dynamic and flexible assessment method based upon the questions of the examiner and the individual differences of the child. The qualitative approach is not necessarily standardized or psychometric in design. Tests are selected on theoretical and practical grounds to assess abilities and functions of interest. Strengths and weaknesses are documented, and neuropsychological deficiencies as related to neurological systems are noted (Luria, 1966, 1973). This testing is only as long or as formal as the examiner feels is necessary. A good working knowledge of neuroanatomy, neuropsychology, and neuropsychological assessment is required. This method is not performed via technician as is sometimes the case with quantitative approaches. The advantages of such an approach seem obvious, however, there are dangers of inappropriate clinical inference, lack of consistency and specificity, absence of comparative group data, and examiner bias in diagnostic interpretations and treatment recommendations (see Meehl, 1954; Willis, 1986). With this method, much stock is put in the acumen and creativity of the examiner. Regardless of whether a psychologist uses a quantitative or qualitative assessment approach, questions remain as to the applicability of the neuropsychological information to the school setting (see Leavell & Lewandowski, 1988).

A third neuropsychological approach cited in the survey of Leavell and Lewandowski (1988) might be viewed as quasi-neuropsychological assessment. Little is known or written about psychologists with limited neuropsychological training who supplement a psychoeducational assessment with neuropsychological tests or invoke neuropsychological interpretations based upon psychoeducational instruments. This practice seems to be more prevalent in the schools than the two mentioned above, at least regarding assessment of learning disabilities. Such practice seems to be subject to a number of the criticisms mentioned thus far, particularly in relation to unsubstantiated clinical inferences, examiner bias, and lack of diagnostic and treatment validity mentioned above.

Despite the limitations of neuropsychological assessment approaches, there are positive aspects which will be highlighted by the case studies. Advantages to the neuropsychological approach include a theoretical basis, high identification accuracy, thorough assessment of lower and higher cerebral functions, and utilization of medical and neurodevelopmental information. This section hopefully served to caution the reader that no one assessment approach is inherently best and that neuropsychological assessment of children is not a long-established practice. In fact, all neuropsychological assessment and treatment approaches with the learning disabled are in need of ecological validation.

IV. Rationale for Neuropsychological Assessment

An obvious question given the concerns raised above is "why conduct neuropsychological assessment, particularly with learning-disabled children?" As previously noted and made clear in other chapters of this volume, neuropsychology has strong ties to the learning disabilities field. Research on the neurobiological underpinnings of learning disability has been fruitful (e.g., Geschwind & Galaburda, 1985; Pennington & Smith, 1988), and such findings have been correlated repeatedly with neuropsychological test data. The same neuropsychological test data can be used to differentiate children with and without learning disabilities with high accuracy (Selz & Reitan, 1979; Teeter et al., 1986). Some progress has been made on the determination of subtypes of learning disabilities that seem to differ in brain structure and function from one another and present with unique behavioral and learning characteristics (Rourke, 1989). Thus, the neuropsychological data base for learning disabilities is growing dramatically, and validation of brain-related "deficits" is being documented across techniques and samples.

What continues to lag behind are treatment-validity studies. One reason for the lack of treatment-validity evidence is that by nature neuropsychological assessment assumes individual uniqueness across patients. Thus, every assessment yields a unique protocol of strengths and weaknesses from which an individualized treatment plan emerges. There are no treatment packages that work effectively with brain-damaged or learning-disabled children. Therefore, treatment is administered on an individual basis, and evaluation studies of groups receiving similar treatments have not been forthcoming (see Rourke *et al.*, 1983). In the absence of group evaluation data, clinicians have relied on personal experiences (successes) in using neuropsychological assessment as a rationale for its applicability. Some clinicians like the fact that this assessment is predicted on the lawful principles of the central nervous system (CNS) (see Gaddes, 1980) and that neuropsychological tests can reliably differentiate between normal and abnormal CNS functioning (Reitan & Wolfson, 1985). Furthermore, it is possible to sometimes validate neuropsychological findings by documenting sites of brain damage which correspond to behavioral dysfunction (Reitan & Wolfson, 1985). This type of validation is seldom available to psychologists.

In the case examples to be presented the advantages of "knowing about the CNS" and "knowing where the damage is" should provide information to the reader that is helpful in reaching the best possible clinical representation of the child. From the neuropsychological perspective one must ask why any practitioner would want to overlook valuable biological (neuropsychological) information when assessing a child. The case studies will demonstrate that some children have neurophysiological characteristics which should be considered in the assessment and treatment of learning disabilities.

V. Developmental Considerations

As mentioned earlier, the specialization of pediatric neuropsychology is a relatively recent development. It came about due to the growing realization that adult and child neuropathology differed in many significant ways, necessitating different methods of diagnosis and treatment. The issue of rapid and malleable brain development in children versus a less plastic, more specialized adult brain also made professionals reexamine the field of child neuropsychology as more than a downward extension of adult neuropsychology. Gradually, the need for a stronger developmental focus with children took hold, and with it came the need to determine brain–behavior relationships in children across ages and types of CNS disorder. Consequently, different testing procedures and separate data bases were necessary for children (see Hynd & Willis, 1988; Tramontana & Hooper, 1988). Over the past 15 years these needs slowly have been met. Test batteries now exist for children, and numerous research studies on clinical subgroups of children have been performed (see Hynd & Willis, 1988; Lewandowski, 1985). Despite these clinical strides coupled with advances in brain science and cognitive science, there is still an incomplete understanding of how the brain works in the learning able or disabled child.

Over the past 10 years a better appreciation has been developed for ways in which the young brain differs from the adult brain. The CNS of a child proceeds through active phases of maturation. The development of brain structures and organization over time means that brain function can only evolve in concert with the developing brain organ. Thus, insults of various types and degrees and at various times during development may render a wide range of neuropsychological deficits. In children, the neuropathology most often encountered is congenital, diffuse, and static, as opposed to the acquired, often focal and progressive forms of pathology sustained by adults (Kolb & Wishaw, 1985; Spreen, Tupper, Risser, Tuokko & Edgell, 1984; Tramontana & Hooper, 1988). Because brain insults are present so early, the child is not in a position to recover function after an injury as adults do, but rather the child must overcome the injury in order to develop functions (i.e., motor, speech, etc.). Another feature of these early diffuse insults is that they may be genetic, biochemical, structural, or even electrical in nature and leave no structural evidence of brain damage, such as destroyed tissue found associated with many adult pathologies. Thus, with children who have soft neurological signs, EEG abnormalities, neuropsychological deficits, and learning problems, one might infer some type of brain "disturbance or dysfunction" rather than damage, disease, or injury (Spreen *et al.*, 1984).

Another characteristic of early brain impairment is that the small and vulnerable brain encounters pervasive insults (i.e., anoxia, hemorrhage, hydrocephalus, etc.) rather than the localized pathology found more frequently in adults (i.e., stroke, tumor, etc.). These diffuse types of pathology in a brain that may be relatively plastic (less specialized) in function can result in a child with a potpourri of physical, behavioral, and neuropsychological symptoms which change with age and fit no particular pattern or syndrome. One cannot assume that a child with early brain compromise will have typical brain development and organization. That is, the child may not be right-hand dominant nor left-hemisphere specialized for language processes like most individuals. Any preprogrammed brain specialization (if there is such a blueprint) may be altered in its functional representation.

Clearly the child brain differs from the adult brain physically, developmentally, and functionally. Clinical and research data bases on impaired and unimpaired groups of youngsters help the neuropsychologist make comparisons and tease out developmental, neurological, and psychological deviations from normality. Testing must be able to reliably measure these deviations and enable the clinician to build hypotheses as to the brain systems that are efficient and deficient. Knowledge of the features and outcomes of different types of disorders helps the clinician interpret test information and develop a management plan for the child. Because the brain of the child is dynamic, plastic, and immature, long-term plans and predictions are avoided. Changes in function are instead monitored closely via repeated neuropsychological testing (measure degree of change from baseline assessment) as well as neurologic and radiologic exams if necessary. Treatment interventions for children usually involve family and personal interventions as well as educational interventions. This is not only the case for learning-disabled children, but for all children with CNS compromise.

There are certain developmental considerations worth mentioning specifically for the child with learning disabilities. Usually these children have no known or proven form of brain pathology. Many people infer a brain etiology for learning disabilities (i.e., dyslexia) pointed out throughout this volume, and this is often suggested by neuropsychological testing results. Whether or not one believes with confidence in a brain explanation for learning disabilities, there are certain neurodevelopmental phenomena which have been observed repeatedly in this population (see Golden, 1981).

The child with subtle early CNS compromise has no apparent learning problems at birth or perhaps in preschool. However, if one examines large numbers of records of mildly neurologically impaired or learning-disabled children, one finds the following manifestations of CNS compromise across development. During the infancy period the reported problems consist of deviations in arousal, activity level, attention, temperament, sensory responsiveness, and muscle tone (Bayley, 1969; Gesell & Amatruda, 1941). Interestingly, these are the basic functions that the young nervous system is trying to regulate and master. The compromised CNS has difficulty mastering these somewhat elementary, yet developmentally important, functions. It is likely that less than complete mastery of these functions will hinder progress of the individual throughout the developmental period (Birch, 1964).

By the age of 6 to 24 months motor activities and skills take on greater importance. The compromised child tends to have delayed motor milestones, inadequate neuromuscular integrity, and incoordinated fine and gross motor function. Again, at a period when these functions (motor and physical mastery) are preeminent, the compromised child's nervous system seems overtaxed and unable to smoothly handle this phase of neurodevelopment (Gesell & Amatruda, 1941).

Between 2 and 4 years of age the typical child is rapidly advancing in language skills. At this same age psychologists and therapists get reports on the compromised child of speech delay, articulation problems, phonologic disorders, disfluency, and developmental language disorders. Once again the functions which seem developmentally most important are not performed well or easily automatized by the compromised child. There may be underlying auditory processing problems (i.e., poor phonetic ability) involved in the speech difficulty, a common accompaniment of learning disabilities.

During the 4- to 6-year-old period there are increased reports of perceptual–motor problems (Ilg & Ames, 1965). This is not to say that the compromised child has overcome the problems mentioned earlier. In some children these various manifestations of poor CNS integrity are cumulative, while others may show only one or two manifestations. Therefore, the 5-year-old may be inattentive, active, speech delayed, and now unable to draw, build, cut, print, or perform visual–motor tasks with ease. Since the child is often in a school setting by this time, there is usually someone who raises concern.

Between the ages of 7 and 12 years (the elementary school ages) these compromised children experience academic and learning problems. These problems usually involve some deficient linguistic process and most often affect reading and writing (de Hirsch, 1968; Orton, 1937). As the child advances in age the academic/learning manifestations of the CNS compromise become most salient, while activity, motor, and perceptual deficiencies become less pronounced. Frequently, the academic problems are joined by behavioral difficulties and social-skill deficits which can render the compromised individual "at risk" for vocational, social, and psychological adjustment difficulties (see Ceci, 1986).

The manifestations of early CNS compromise are far different from the effects of brain disease in an older adult. Neurodevelopmental patterns play a major role in helping professionals reach a clear understanding of learning disabilities. Thus, the pediatric neuropsychologist needs to operate with a different knowledge base, different testing purposes and procedures, and an awareness of how neuropsychological information can assist the student with a learning disability.

VI. Case 1

A. Background

Mike is a 10-year-old boy classified as learning disabled who attends a self-contained special education class. Both parents and school staff were interested in a comprehensive neuropsychological assessment to provide a more clear understanding of Mike's functioning and to determine whether present programming should be maintained or changed. Mike is the second in a family of three children with two professional parents. At 6 months of age he was diagnosed as having an infantile seizure disorder. Since that time Mike has been on anticonvulsive medication. Mike has a history of attentional difficulties, motor incoordination, and high activity level. Three years ago he was started on Ritalin, and parents report that he is more calm and attentive with the medication. Academic and social difficulties are presently of most concern. Mike performs inconsistently in school with the exception of math, which he fails routinely. Socially, Mike is immature, not highly regarded by peers, and prefers playing with much younger children.

B. Observations

It was easy to establish rapport with Mike and he seemed very motivated to do well on the tests. While walking to the testing room one could note his awkward gait, dysryhthmic movements, and mild speech-articulation errors. Mike was able to understand verbal directions and he followed instructions well. Mike stayed on task during the testing with two short breaks over a 2.5-hour period. Toward the very end of the session he became somewhat silly and impulsive. This was about the time his next dose of medication was due. Mike appeared to relish adult approval and he worked hard to attain it.

C. Results

The results of the Halstead–Reitan Neuropsychological Test Battery for Children and related tests are presented in summary form below.

WISC-R

Subtests	SS	Subtests	SS
Information	5	Picture Completion	10
Similarities	8	Picture Arrangement	8
Arithmetic	3	Block Design	10
Vocabulary	9	Object Assembly	8
Comprehension	8	Coding	8
Digit Span	6		
Verbal IQ	79	Performance IQ	91
		FSIQ = 84	

Trail Making Test
    Part A: 27 seconds; 1 error
    Part B: 55 seconds; 0 error   (within normal limits) (WNL)
Strength of Grip
    Preferred hand (right): 9 kg
    Nonpreferred hand: 9 kg   (weak in both; no dominance)

Tactile Form-Recognition Test
   0 errors for right and left hands   (WNL)

Tactile Finger Recognition
   Could not use a code (numbers or names)
      to identify fingers.
   He could wiggle the stimulated finger
      with 80% accuracy.

Category Test
   36 errors in first 66 trials; discontinued   (poor problem solving)
      due to difficulty.

Tactual Performance Test (6 block board)
   Dominant hand: 6' 30"
   Nondominant hand: 9' 15"
   Both hands: 7' 20"
   Total time: 23' 05"   (no strategy development)
   Memory: 6
   Location: 2

Seashore Rhythm Test
   Alternated same and different responses   (invalid)

Finger Tapping Test
   Dominant hand: 23
   Nondominant hand: 23   (low scores; no dominance)

Aphasia Screening Test
   Dyscalculia
   Constructional dyspraxia

Token Test (short form)
   Within normal limits

Benton Visual Retention Test (form C)
   Copy: 5 of 10   (dyspraxia)
   Retention: 5 of 10

Word Fluency Test
   25 words across three 60-second trials   (WNL)

Stanford Achievement Tests (school administered)
   Below 10th percentile in math for age
   At 25th percentile in reading for age

Motor Free Visual Perception Test
   Adequate
   Some Problems with visual closure and
memory

Visual Organization Test
   25 of 30 correct

Consistent with Block Design and Object
  Assembly (of the WISC-R)
Neurological Screening
  No sensory problems
  Intact cranial nerve function
  Reflexes WNL
  Rapid finger movements were slow and
    imprecise
  Poor balance on either foot
  Gross motor incoordination

    Mike is a pleasant, hard-working youngster with a history of early neurologic dysfunction and consequent neurodevelopmental problems. As is the case with a subset of learning-disabled students, Mike has a rather severe and generalized form of learning disability. Such children usually present with a low average IQ, and most, if not all, of the manifestations of early neurologic compromise. Mike has had this full expression of the disability, including attentional problems, overactivity, motor incoordination, speech difficulties, visual–motor problems, academic failure, and social-skills deficits. That these deficiencies are direct results of early neurologic insult is not the assessment issue here. More important is the *analysis* of function and dysfunction, patterns of performance, and brain–behavior relationships, leading to a thorough understanding of information-processing abilities and treatment implications.

    The neuropsychological test data are consistent with a serious and non-specific form of learning disability. There is evidence of neurocognitive limitations in both verbal and nonverbal domains. The WISC-R, Category Test, and Tactual Performance Test (TPT) all illustrate Mike's difficulty with abstract thinking, inferencing, and problem solving. His level of performance on these brain-sensitive tests is well below average expectations. A top-down perspective reveals difficulty at the higher levels of cognitive functioning, such that he does not easily generate solutions to new problems. On both the Category and the TPT tests Mike was unable to learn principles which would improve performance. Similarly, Mike has difficulty directing his own learning. Thus, he requires structure, cues, concrete examples, and associative learning.

    A bottom-up analysis reveals that Mike has intact sensory systems. With medication he appears to have the attentional and behavioral controls necessary to stay on task and receive information. This is borne out on most of the neuropsychological tests requiring sustained attention and/or information reception. He not only acquires information through all modalities, but it appears that he perceives adequately what he takes in. He can analyze information within a modality and, in some cases, transfer information across modalities. His memory skills, although not great, seem within low normal limits for both short- and long-term storage and retrieval. Yet, the ability to maintain, manipulate, and elaborate information in working memory is delimited. When information is symbolic, has little or no semantic meaning, or requires mental manipulation and the application of rules and abstractions (i.e., math), then Mike experiences difficulty. If the information is simple and requires little integration, elaboration, or abstraction, he may use it appropriately. This style seems to hold regardless of which modality receives the information or what type of information it is. Consequently, one sees no dramatic left–right hemisphere differences or extreme strengths and weaknesses. The variability in performance seems largely dictated by task demands and cognitive limitations.

In addition to the information-processing deficiencies cited above, Mike also has problems with what Luria (1966) termed the "execution or output" functions. Fine and gross motor incoordination, motor disinhibition and impulsivity, dysgraphia and dyspraxia, and speech misarticulation all contribute to production and execution difficulties. Consequently, most of Mike's achievements reflect less than his true potential and may not be accurate indicators of what he has learned. It is difficult to evaluate a child's abilities when all avenues of output are somewhat impaired.

Mike's neuropsychological profile illustrates subnormal performance on most of Reitan's brain-sensitive tests (i.e., Category, TPT, Finger Tapping, Seashore) as well as the neurological and aphasia screening tests. However, these data do not follow a particular pattern. Unlike adult profiles, Mike's performance shows no focal or lateralized signs, nor can one implicate only cortical functioning. The neuropsychological data likely reflects the early and diffuse nature of his impairment, which is somewhat corroborated by EEG abnormalities in central and posterior portions of both hemispheres. His chief symptoms of dyscalculia, constructional apraxia, dysgraphia, finger agnosia, and right–left confusion are congruent with a posterior brain disturbance (Luria, 1973). However, the motor, speech, thinking, and social difficulties are not easy to explain. These complex behaviors are controlled by elaborate brain networks which could be rendered dysfunctional by a wide range of cerebral insults (see Kolb & Wishaw, 1985).

One can see from the above analysis that isolating brain–behavior patterns in children with longstanding, diffuse, and subtle dysfunction is more complex than working with adults with acquired damage. Nevertheless, applying what is known about brain function/processing can assist in making a more thorough analysis of functions, providing one does not overinterpret or overgeneralize the data with neuropsychological inferences and neurological explanations. The attempt is made to understand Mike's present functioning in light of his neurodevelopmental history and documented neurophysiological abnormalities. Once all the data are put together one should better understand *why* Mike performs the way he does, *what* systems are efficient or deficient, and *what* makes sense in terms of educational interventions.

D. Conclusions and Recommendations

Mike is a youngster who has experienced CNS-related difficulties at every developmental age. What comes naturally for most children requires effort for Mike and results in imperfect productions. He is still hampered by early attention, motor, and speech problems, which are now overshadowed by neurocognitive and social deficits. As certain functions have become better integrated, other demands have revealed new dysfunctions. This is the outcome with a compromised CNS that never seems to have all the resources to handle life's challenges.

1. Despite Mike's shortcomings, he is remarkably hard working and motivated to perform. This positive attitude has been known to change as learning-disabled students get older and more aware of their problems. Thus, parents and teachers will need to work preventatively on any negative reactions to the academic deficiencies.
2. While high-level academic performance is not predicted, he should be able to master basic academic requirements, life skills, and job skills. In this effort, professionals will need to build on his strengths in the areas of language comprehension, associative learning, semantic memory, perseverance, and willingness to please. Conversely, staff must be careful not to overprogram in deficient areas such as math, drawing, writing, and inferencing.
3. Mike should benefit from a relatively structured, organized, distraction-free setting, where close teacher supervision can be provided. He will benefit from cues for completing certain tasks appropriately, help in making connections between ideas, and strategies for solving problems.
4. Efforts should be made to minimize any speech or manual difficulties. A computer is often useful in having a child create drawings through graphics or write stories that look presentable. Any way to obviate visual–motor and graphic difficulties should reduce frustration and provide creative ways for Mike to express his knowledge.
5. Also, Mike will need to be given social-skill training, perhaps utilizing verbal-mediation techniques. A small skill-building group with accepting peers might meet several needs.
6. Given that Mike is well behind his peers academically, he will need to continue working harder for less gain. This may include tutoring and even additional skill building (i.e., summer school) if he can tolerate it.
7. Although no major change in neurological status is predicted, medical

supervision for the seizure disorder and hyperactivity should be monitored closely. A repeat neuropsychological assessment is recommended within a year.

VII. Case 2

A. Background

Mary is an 8-year-old girl who should be in a regular third-grade class. The school referred Mary for a neuropsychological evaluation 3 months after she suffered a head injury in a car accident. Prior to the accident, Mary was reported to be an average student who was well behaved and liked by her peers. A head-on car collision caused Mary to be propelled into the dashboard of her father's truck. She suffered multiple fractures around the left eye and left side of the skull and a contusion over the anterior left hemisphere. Surgery was required to repair the fractures. She remained in a coma for 7 days after the accident. While she was in the hospital for several weeks it was noted that Mary had a right hemiplegia, aphasic speech, and dysarthria. These symptoms abated somewhat by the time she returned home. Mary returned to school on a half-day basis with placement in the third grade. The school realized that Mary could not function yet at that grade level so they returned her to the second grade. The school was not at all certain how to program for Mary, what services she required, what to expect from her, which hand she should write with, or whether or not she needed to wear protective headgear.

Mary lives on a farm with her parents and younger brother. Both parents were looking for any help possible in understanding and treating Mary's problems. At home Mary was not overprotected. She reportedly was back to climbing trees, wrestling with her brother, and riding the farm animals. In school, Mary was being handled cautiously by staff. She was not able to attend gym class or recess. Other children treated her as an invalid and wanted to do things for her. Mary was frustrated because she wanted to be one of the crowd, with no limitations or exceptions.

B. Observations

Mary came to the clinic for testing 3 months post-accident. Her right hemiplegia was noticeable but did not inconvenience her a great deal. A leg brace gave her walking support, and even running was possible for Mary. Her right arm had good mobility and reasonable strength, but a tremor occurred when she used her right hand. Her speech was usually intelligible, although dysarthria was noted, particularly with "s," "z," and "sh" sounds. Also, word-finding difficulties were noted. Behaviorally, Mary was active, impulsive, distractible, and disinhibited. At one point she got up on the test table and did a little dance. These behaviors were typical of how Mary now behaves in school, which apparently is quite different from her preaccident demeanor. It was necessary to structure the environment and provide contingent reinforcement in order to accomplish the evaluation conducted in three 2-hour sessions.

C. Results

Kaufman Assessment Battery for Children (K-ABC)

Subtests	SS	Subtests	SS
Hand Movements	5	Gestalt Closure	9
Number Recall	10	Triangles	5
Word Order	5	Matrix Analogies	7
		Spatial Memory	6
		Photo Series	5

Sequential Scale 80+/−8 Simultaneous Scale 76+/−7
Mental Processing Component 75+/−6

Peabody Individual Achievement Test
Mathematics: 20th percentile
Spelling: 30th percentile
Reading: 56th percentile

Spache
Oral Reading: 2.2 grade equivalent
Silent Comprehension: 1.8 grade equivalent

Token Test
Followed directions for up to four attributes

Word Fluency
8 words in three 60-second trials (expected mean is 21)

Motor Free Visual Perception Test
25 of 36 correct (27 is average for her age)

Visual–Motor Integration Test
4.8 year age equivalent (right hand intention tremor)

Ann Arbor Letter-Tracking Test
Adequate visual tracking for large and small print

Trail-Making Test
Part A: 33 seconds (WNL)
Part B: 93 seconds

Tactual Performance Test (TPT)
Discontinued due to failure and frustration

Purdue Pegboard Test
Right hand: 4 pegs in 30 seconds
Left hand: 11 pegs in 30 seconds

Finger-Tapping Test
  Right hand: 21
  Left hand: 33
Stereognosis Test
  Could identify five objects by feel in each hand.
  Could describe two of the objects but not name them (ribbon and paper clip).
Progressive Figures Test
  No problem
Color Form Test
  94 seconds and 4 errors (poor performance)
Socioemotional Assessment
  Low self-esteem
  Anxiety related to school

Mary has demonstrated improvement in all areas since her accident. Nonetheless, there remain significant neuropsychological difficulties, including general decline in cognitive and academic functioning (premorbid Otis–Lennon socre of 105) and more specific deficits in motor, language, and behavior-regulation functions. Her basic sensory and perceptual processes are intact, while higher-order cognitive skills such as reasoning, comprehension, and problem solving are presently curtailed (TPT, Category, K-ABC, Reading Comprehension).

Mary's profile is consistent with left-hemisphere brain dysfunction. Her word-finding difficulties (Word Fluency, Stereognosis), articulation problems, fragmented language usage, and motor problems on the right side (tremor, Purdue Pegboard, Finger Tapping) reflect common manifestations of left-hemisphere injury. Additionally, Mary's behavior is characteristic of anterior brain dysfunction as expressed by perseverative actions (Hand Movements, TPT), planning difficulties (TPT, Color Form Triangles), poor judgment, and difficulty modulating and regulating her own behavior. Concurrently, Mary's receptive language (Token Test), tactile (Stereognosis), visual (Motor Free, Ann Arbor Tracking, Gestalt Closure), and musical abilities (singing, humming) seem to be reasonably intact, suggesting relatively unaffected posterior and right-brain functioning.

D. Recommendations

There is little question that Mary had recovered many of her premorbid abilities within 3 months of the accident. Most recovery does occur within the first year after a head injury, therefore aggressive rehabilitation efforts are called for. The school should act proactively. In many ways Mary is not very different from other learning-disabled students with language-based academic problems. Therefore, a number of suggestions were made to the school with the understanding that the program would be closely monitored and updated as needed.

1. Mary should receive physical/occupational and speech therapy as part of her school program. The additional one-to-one attention as well as therapy geared toward her depressed physical and communication skills should improve her current level of functioning.

2. Mary should be allowed to use her left hand for refined school work while continuing to exercise and strengthen the right hand. There is no evidence to suggest that using her nonpreferred hand will interfere with motor or other development. Presently, tasks performed by her right hand frustrate and anger her. Trial teaching revealed that Mary could draw and write better with her left hand, however, right-hand performance could be improved by applying weight to the shoulder and arm (reduced tremoring).

3. The issue of whether Mary should wear protective headgear was referred to her physician. It seemed inconsistent to wear a helmet in school and go home to ride farm animals. Socially, it seemed preferable to have Mary look and behave as the other children. The headgear could be worn for adaptive physical education class or recess until the school was convinced Mary was out of danger.

4. It was suggested to lengthen Mary's school day gradually. She needed the time for increased therapy and academic remediation, as well as more interaction with peers. Besides, her after-school activities were far more tiring and risky than the school regimen.

5. Mary's placement in the second grade regular classroom seemed to be appropriate for the time being. She was with a teacher with whom she related well and someone well-suited to her needs. Special time with a learning-disabilities specialist was suggested to reinforce training in phonics, addition, and subtraction and to provide one-to-one structure and assistance.

6. Mary seems to perform best academically in a structured, rule-governed environment, with clear and consistent rules. She is impulsive, active, and manipulative, but can be helped to control behavior using structure and positive reinforcement. She gets frustrated easily, so close supervision, help, praise, and rewards serve to keep her going.

7. Mary performs better when tasks are divided into smaller parts and sequenced for her. She needs help in planning and strategy building. The use of games such as mazes, connect the dots, hide and seek, etc., also can be used to encourage Mary to plan ahead.

8. Mary needs improvement in the areas of attention, impulse control, and

social interaction. Behavioral changes since her accident have been difficult for school staff to understand. Cortical impairment, particularly in the frontal lobes, can serve to release control over one's own behavior. Without cortical executive control, her behavior may be subject to more primitive drives. Uninhibited and even aggressive behavior is not uncommon, and it is not necessarily intentional or volitional. One must be aware of the biological versus the environmental precipitants of such behavior, realizing that Mary's threshold for certain behavior has changed. Reteaching strategies of self control and automatizing acceptable behavior patterns will take concerted work on everyone's part. Cognitive behavior-modification approaches as outlined by Meichenbaum (1977) may be helpful.

9. Mary's self-esteem has suffered during this readjustment period. Despite her outgoing style, she is bothered by her perceived looks, particulary the helmet and leg brace, and by the difficulty with school work. Therefore, school and social activities should be geared toward creating success experiences for Mary. Parents, teachers, and peers will need to be sensitive to her needs. Positive peer interaction may need to be cultivated as Mary reenters the social milieu.

10. Mary's prognosis is viewed as optimistic. Her injury resulted in no penetrating lesion, and her contusion was not severe. Given her age and the resilience of youth, one would expect gradual recovery. That she has improved steadily over the past 3 months offers strong evidence that recovery will continue. How complete that recovery will be is difficult to predict. It is possible that Mary will experience some form of permanent learning disabilities, but she should have enough resources to compensate. Specialized treatment and educational services will also be crucial in offsetting any psychoeducational limitations.

11. Mary's functioning should be evaluated thoroughly at the middle and the end of the school year to determine progress and the need for program alterations. This first neuropsychological evaluation can be used as a baseline from which to compare future performance.

VIII. Case 3

A. Background

Joey is a 9-year-old boy who repeated second grade and is still struggling to keep up with his third-grade peers. He was referred for a neuropsychological assessment because of his early medical history and for a more complete understanding of his overall functioning. Joey was born preterm at 29 weeks gestation weighing approximately 1200 grams. His small head circumference was a concern to physicians, and a head sonogram indicated the occurrence of a mild subarachnoid hemorrhage which resolved with no major complications. Due to lung immaturity he remained on a respirator for 14 days after birth. Joey was taken off ventilation and sent home 1 month after birth. Although no major physical problems were reported, Joey's 6-month follow-up developmental exam revealed certain delays on the Bayley scales and neuromuscular testing. Joey was considered to show signs of dystonia (transient) with a possibility of mild cerebral palsy. By the time Joey was over a year old the transient dystonia had remitted and the suspicion of cerebral palsy was not confirmed. However, Joey still displayed delayed motor milestones and received a Bayley MDI score of 89. Joey's parents were asked to monitor his progress carefully and have him reevaluated once a year. It was mentioned that children with similar developmental courses have been known to later manifest learning problems. Joey's parents, now in their late 20s, educated and working, were the type to follow through on recommendations and seek additional resources on their own.

Joey attended preschool and kindergarten programs. In addition to motor incoordination, Joey demonstrated mild speech-articulation problems. However, he did not qualify for any special services at the time. In first grade Joey's performance was barely passable. His teacher noticed that he was different than most of the other children, particularly in following directions, remembering things from day to day, and grasping new information readily. Nonetheless, he had progressed sufficiently to move on to second grade. There, Joey encountered increasing learning failure and frustration. Reading and spelling were particularly difficult, and printing words was nearly impossible. Joey ended up repeating second grade at the request of his teacher. However, the strategy did not help Joey "catch up." He still had problems in reading, writing, and spelling that were not lessening. Finally, a referral to the school psychologist was made. After some initial psychoeducational testing the school psychologist decided that neuropsychological information might be helpful in delineating Joey's overall strengths and weaknesses.

B. Observations

Joey was tested in school in two 90-minute sessions. He was friendly and easy to work with despite being relatively soft spoken and introverted. He appeared to be a bit immature for his age in terms of interests, interactions, and language production. Joey was well dressed and groomed with no overt physical stigmata or behavioral peculiarities. Only mild articulation difficulties were noted. His gait and movements appeared to be somewhat uneven or disfluent, yet within the range of normalcy. Teacher reports and classroom observations indicated that Joey gets along with the students, although he tends to be quiet and on the fringe of the social milieu.

C. Results

WISC-R

Subtests	SS	Subtests	SS
Information	7	Picture Completion	10
Similarities	8	Picture Arrangement	9
Arithmetic	7	Block Design	10
Vocabulary	8	Object Assembly	9
Comprehension	10	Coding	8
Digit Span	(7)		

Verbal IQ 87   Performance IQ 93   FSIQ = 89

Diagnostic Assessment Battery (DAB) (Mean = 100, SD = 15)

Listening Composite	90
Speaking	79
Reading	69*
Written Language	68*
Mathematics	80

(* More than 1 standard deviation below full-scale IQ.)

Luria Nebraska Neuropsychological Battery-Children's Revision (LNNB-CR)

Motor Scale	63	(Mean = 50, SD = 10)
Rhythm	73*	
Tactile	62	
Visual	57	
Receptive Speech	71*	
Expressive Speech	70*	
Writing	74*	
Reading	74*	
Mathemetics	73*	
Memory	69	
Intelligence	59	
Pathognomonic	79	
Left Hemisphere	69	
Right Hemisphere	60	

(* Scores in the critical range based on Joey's age; high scores reflect poorer performance.)

D. Conclusions and Recommendations

In a variety of ways Joey represents a pretty common profile of a learning-disabled student. His history is marked by several medical and neuro-developmental abnormalities that suggest, but do not positively indicate, CNS dysfunction. Manifestations of this dysfunction have occurred across developmental stages and have been gradually overcome, with the exception of higher-level cognitive/academic deficiencies. As is often the case with learning-disabled children, Joey primarily demonstrates problems in the language areas. His verbal IQ is lower than his performance IQ and considerably lower than that of most of his peers. The LNNB-CR reveals significant difficulties on both receptive and expressive speech scales and on reading, writing, and mathematics scales. These are all heavily language-based test items. The DAB supports these findings, with significant deficiencies shown for reading and writing scales, and speaking to a lesser extent. Closer analysis of the profile reveals auditory memory and sequencing difficulties (Digit Span, Rhythm), as well as problems with phonemic analysis. Joey's problems with sound–symbol integration, sound blending, and phonetic segmentation resemble profiles referred to as dysphonetic readers by Boder (1973).

In addition to auditory and language problems, Joey demonstrated impaired tactile and sensorimotor performance, particularly on the right side of the body. These findings are in contrast to comparatively good scores on the visual (Teeter et al., 1986) and left-side sensorimotor scales. This pattern on the LNNB-CR is consistent with research findings implicating predominantly left-hemisphere deficits in reading-disabled youngsters (Galaburda, 1988; Leavell & Lewandowski, 1989). The data also suggest that, while reading and writing problems are the most glaring deficiencies, there are subprocesses (some call them neuropsychological functions) which underlie the learning disabilities. If these subprocesses are deficient due to cerebral impairment, then it is unlikely that training the deficit area will have positive effects. Therefore, for Joey, an educational program is designed to circumvent the weak functional system (phonetics) and capitalize on strengths.

1. Joey has most difficulty in areas highly valued in schools—language usage, working memory, reading, and writing. His strengths in visual and spatial functions could be largely overlooked. It would make sense to utilize visual aids such as pictures or demonstrations in teaching. Learning via lectures or reading will be incomplete unless supplemented by other modes and techniques.
2. Classes such as art, computer science, geography, and math can and should be constructed so as to capitalize on Joey's visual strengths and thereby provide some academic success.
3. Since both auditory and visual reception of information are intact, a

bimodal reading program is recommended. Rather than just rote phonics training, the bimodal approach presents Joey with words and sentences on a computer which concurrently says the word while it presents it. A picture representing the word is also available. Therefore, Joey cannot misread a word, and he has the benefit of associating and encoding the word orthography, pronunciation, and semantic picture. Reading vocabulary, rate, and word recall might all increase without intervention or intimidation from an adult.

4. Poor writing can be the result of a variety of deficiencies (i.e., general language, sequencing, motor, mechanics, spelling and punctuation, etc.). The assessment revealed that Joey can express himself better orally than in writing. Certain writing assignments can be first audiotaped and then written from the tape if necessary. This tends to initially increase the length and content of stories. The use of a computer for transcribing the stories then aids in editing for spelling, grammar, etc. The learning-disability specialist can use these techniques to draw better language expression from Joey and show him how to achieve polished products.

5. Spelling is not a high priority for a boy of his age and academic profile. Ensuring ongoing learning of important information and appropriate expression of ideas is foremost. Spelling should be taught in the context of reading and writing, but not used as an academic milestone that must be obtained.

6. As with most learning-disabled youngsters, Joey's individual needs must be understood by parents and professionals, who creatively can address his needs and be sensitive to the psychological effects of learning deficiencies.

7. In Joey's case the donut is larger than the hole. There is more working than not working. It is important not to allow the "hole" to become that which is dwelt upon. Multiple ways to minimize his deficiencies should be explored. Having tests read to him, getting extra time to complete tests, and using taped lectures and talking books are just some examples of the modifications available.

IX. Summary

Each of the three case studies has provided a slightly different approach or use for neuropsychological assessment. It is hoped that a better understanding of both the advantages and the limitations of such assessment has been attained. Unfortunately, brief case studies do not allow for the comprehensive analysis employed in neuropsychological assessment. Nor can one discuss the meaning of each test score, provide evidence in support of each interpretive comment, debate the pros and cons of specific recommendations, or state the rationale for using certain tests. An entire book on child neuropsychological assessment might be able to cover all the salient issues, examples, and research, at least more than this chapter (see Hynd & Obrzut, 1981; Tramontana & Hooper, 1988). All disclaimers aside, the purpose of this chapter was to expose the reader to different types of learning disabilities, neurodevelopmental problems associated with learning disabilities, various approaches used to assess learning disabilities, and ways in which one might apply neuropsychological assessment to children with such a handicapping condition.

This chapter, along with the rest of the volume's chapters, should have illustrated the contributions that neuroscience and neuropsychology have made and will make to the study of learning disabilities. Advances in neuroscience and medicine have enabled us to come closer to discovering etiological factors and neurobiological features of learning disabilities. Neuropsychological assessment has added to this knowledge base by reliably diagnosing learning disabilities in terms of discrete neuropsychological dysfunctions. The links between certain neurobiological anomalies and neuropsychological test performances are beginning to emerge. It will not be long before the CNS disturbances of Mike, Mary, and Joey are clearly documented and then related to neurodevelopmental problems that unfold in childhood and used to predict certain forms of learning and behavioral disabilities in school age. The matter of treating the disability will then be the area in greatest need of development and investigation.

References

Bayley, N. (1969). *Bayley Scales of infant development: Infant behavior record.* San Antonio, TX: Psychological Corporation.

Birch, H. G. (1964). *Brain damage in children.* Baltimore, MD: Williams & Wilkins.

Boder, E. (1973). Developmental dyslexia: A diagnostic approach based on three atypical reading parameters. *Developmental Medicine and Child Neurology, 15,* 663–687.

Ceci, S. J. (1986). *Handbook of cognitive, social, and neuropsychological aspects of learning disabilities* (Vol. 2). Hillsdale, NJ; Erlbaum.

Cruickshank, W. M., Bentzen, F. A., Ratzeburg, F. H., & Tannhauser, M. T. (1961). *A teaching method for brain injured and hyperactive children.* Syracuse, NY: Syracuse University Press.

de Hirsch, K. (1968). Clinical spectrum of reading disabilities: Diagnosis and treatment. *Bulletin of the New York Academy of Medicine, Series 2, 44,* 470–477.

Federal Register, 42, (1977, December 29). Assistance to states for education of handicapped children: Procedures for evaluating specific learning disabilities. Washington, DC: U.S. Government Printing Office.

Gaddes, W. H. (1980). *Learning disabilities and brain function: A neuropsychological approach.* New York: Springer-Verlag.

Galaburda, A. M. (1988). *The pathogenesis of childhood dyslexia.* Preprint from the Department of Neurology, Harvard Medical School, Cambridge, MA.

Gamble, C. M., Mishra, S. P., & Obrzut, J. E. (1988). Construct validity of neuropsychological instrumentation with a learning disabled population. *Archives of Clinical Neuropsychology, 3,* 359–368.

Geschwind, N., & Galaburda, A. M. (1985). Cerebral lateralization, biological mechanisms, association, and pathology: I. A. hypothesis and a program for research. *Archives of Neurology (Chicago), 42,* 428–459.

Gesell, A., & Amatruda, C. S. (1941). *Developmental diagnosis.* New York: Hoeber.

Golden, C. J. (1981). The Luria Nebraska Children's Battery: Theory and formulation. In G. W. Hynd & J. E. Obrzut (Eds.), *Neuropsychological assessment in the school-aged child* (pp. 277–302). New York: Grune & Stratton.

Hallahan, D. P., & Cruickshank, W. M. (1973). *Psychoeducational foundations of learning disabilities.* Englewood Cliffs, NJ: Prentice-Hall.

Hebb, D. O. (1949). *The organization of behavior.* New York: Oxford University Press.

Hevern, C. (1980). Recent validity studies of the Halstead Reitan approach to clinical neuropsychological assessment: A critical review. *Clinical Neuropsychology, 22,* 49–61.

Hynd, G. W., & Obrzut, J. E. (1981). *Neuropsychological assessment of the school-aged child.* New York: Grune & Stratton.

Hynd, G. W., & Willis, W. G. (1988). *Pediatric neuropsychology.* New York: Grune & Stratton.

Ilg, F. L., & Ames, L. B. (1965). *School readiness: Behavior tests used at the Gesell Institute.* New York: Harper & Row.

Kolb, B., & Wishaw, I. Q. (1985). *Fundamentals of human neuropsychology.* New York: Freeman.

Leavell, C., & Lewandowski, L. (1988). Neuropsychology in the schools: A survey report. *School Psychology Review, 17,* 147–155.

Leavell, C., & Lewandowski, L. (1989). *Neurolinguistic deficits and the left hemisphere in the reading disabled.* Presented at the International Neuropsychological Society meeting, Vancouver, B.C., Canada.

Lewandowski, L. (1985). Clinical subgroups among the learning disabled. *Journal of Learning Disabilities, 18,* 177–178.

Luria, A. R. (1966). *Higher cortical functions in man.* New York: Basic Books.

Luria, A. R. (1973). *The working brain.* New York: Basic Books.

Luria, A. R., & Majovsky, L. V. (1977). Basic approaches used in American and Soviet clinical neuropsychology. *American Psychologist, 11,* 959–968.

Meehl, P. E. (1954). *Clinical versus statistical prediction: A theoretical analysis and a review of the evidence.* Minneapolis: University of Minnesota Press.

Meichenbaum, D. (1977). *Cognitive-behavior modification: An integrative approach.* New York: Plenum.

Orton, S. T. (1937). *Reading, writing, and speech problems in children.* New York: Norton.

Pennington, B. F., & Smith, S. D. (1988). Genetic influences on learning disabilities: An update. *Journal of Consulting and Clinical Psychology, 56,* 817–823.

Reitan, R. M., & Boll, T. J. (1973). Neuropsychological correlates of minimal brain dysfunction. *Annals of the New York Academy of Sciences, 205,* 65–88.

Reitan, R. M., & Wolfson, D. (1985). *The Halstead Reitan neuropsychological test battery: Theory and applications.* Neuropsychology Press, Tucson, AZ.

Rourke, B. P. (1985). *Neuropsychology of learning disabilities: Essentials of subtype analysis.* New York: Guilford Press.

Rourke, B. P. (1986). *Neuropsychological assessment of children: A treatment-oriented approach.* New York: Guilford Press.

Rourke, B. P. (1989). *Nonverbal learning disabilities.* New York: Guilford Press.

Rourke, B. P., Bakker, D. J., Fisk, J. J., & Strang, J. D. (1983). *Child neuropsychology.* New York: Guilford Press.

Selz, M., & Reitan, R. M. (1979). Rules for neuropsychological diagnosis: Classification of brain function in older children. *Journal of Consulting and Clinical Psychology, 47,* 258–264.

Snow, J. H., & Hynd, G. W. (1985). A multivariate investigation of the Luria-Nebraska Neuropsychological Battery-Children's Revision. *Journal of Psychoeducational Assessment, 2,* 23–28.

Spreen, O., Tupper, D., Risser, A., Tuokko, H., & Edgell, D. (1984). *Human developmental neuropsychology.* New York: Oxford University Press.

Teeter, P. A., Boliek, C. A., Obrzut, J. E., & Malsch, K. (1986). Diagnostic utility of the critical level formula and clinical summary scales of the Luria-Nebraska Neuropsychological Battery-Children's Revision with learning disabled children. *Developmental Neuropsychology, 2,* 125–135.

Tramontana, M. G., & Hooper, S. R. (1988). *Assessment issues in child neuropsychology.* New York: Plenum.

Willis, W. G. (1986). Actuarial and clinival approaches to neuropsychological diagnosis: Applied considerations. In J. Obrzut & G. Hynd (Eds.), *Child neuropsychology: Vol. 2. Clinical practice.* Orlando, FL: Academic Press.

CHAPTER TWENTY-SIX

Neuropsychological Perspectives in Special Education

John R. Kershner

I. Introduction

Special education and nueropsychology have a natural affinity with many common bonds. Fundamentally, a link between the two was established as early as 1605 by Sir Francis Bacon's (1973) elegant, poetic arguments for the advancement of learning to King James I of England. Bacon included an outline for required research that was premised on the controversial claim, repugnant to theologians, that the brain was the seat of human "understanding." Their formal origins coincide historically with the founding of the first special class for mentally retarded children in Germany in 1860 (Hewett & Forness, 1974) and the concurrent publication of the French physician Pierre Paul Broca's phrenologically inspired but legendary paper the following year (Broca, 1861). When Broca reported that loss of speech and right-sided hemiplegia were associated with a left-sided cerebral lesion in the posterior part of the third frontal convolution, he set the stage for what was to become, simultaneously, a central theme in modern biology and a compelling dogma that assured a lasting alliance between special education and neuropsychology—the lateralization of the central nervous system.

Their coincidental beginnings in the same global, sociopolitical milieu more than 100 years ago favored strong early affiliations between the two in clinical and experimental research and in their respective earlier attempts to formulate rational and scientifically verifiable or refutable theoretical foundations. Political classical liberalism and the empirical tradition in philosophy, both epitomized by Locke (1892), combined with the influential work of the pedagogical neurologist, Sequin (1864), together induced the nascent special education movement from its inception to seek physiological explanatory models in diagnosis and in classroom teaching. Reciprocally but for different reasons, neurologists, physicians, and psychologists with an interest in brain–behavior relationships turned primarily to brain-damaged patients to test their ideas, to gain new empirical information, and to further their clinical expertise (see Wigan, 1844, 1985, for a prophetic account of psychological differences in function between the left and right cortical hemispheres of the brain). Thus, the die was cast through multiple common threads for a rich and mutually rewarding interplay between neuropsychology and special education as they evolved throughout the latter part of the nineteenth and into the twentieth centuries.

Special educators were oriented conceptually and dedicated philosophically to neuropsychology at a grass-roots level. Those now recognized as the earliest "neuropsychologists," although fewer in number compared to the professional size of the more rapidly expanding special education venture, similarly, were bound to working with individuals who were in need of special education services. The actual turn of events, however, shows unfortunately that only one-half of the promise has been fulfilled; special education in neuropsychology prospered, whereas the reverse application and synthesis of neuropsychological ideas in special education has been sporadic, elusive, and fraught with hard times. Indeed, the diagnosis, assessment, rehabilitation, and scholarly study of exceptional persons by professionals who are trained in experimental or clinical neuropsychology, without question, is one of the most dynamic frontiers in contemporary science. Significant advances in our knowledge of brain–behavior relationships across the entire spectrum of special education categories of exceptionalities are occurring at an unprecedented rate. For example, recent major neuropsychological texts report new, basic findings in the deaf (Poizner, Klima, & Bellugi, 1987); in Down syndrome patients (Nadel, 1988); in dyslexics (Geschwind & Galaburda, 1987); in the brain–injured, the emotionally disturbed, cases of chromosomal aberrations, dyspraxics, and the learning disabled (Molfese & Segalowitz, 1988); in subtypes of learning disability (Rourke, 1985); and in hyperlexics, autistic persons, mentally retarded individuals, and people with special talents (Obler & Fein, 1988). Notably, a predominant focus in the majority of this research is the localization and lateralization of cognitive functions in the brain.

This list is not intended to be all inclusive but simply a selective illustration of the point of departure that sets the organizing theme for this chapter. The point is that special education has had and continues to have a broad and vibrant impact on progress in neuropsychology. As a result, new and exciting inroads have been made in understanding both normal learning processes and learning processes in exceptional individuals who require special education. The scholarly tradition set in motion by visionary physicians like Wigan (1844, 1985), who were fascinated by what the exceptional brain might reveal about the origins of thought and the control of human behavior, has come of age. Neuropsychology has come of age. What, then, happened to frustrate the great expectations that were held for the reverse scenario—the successful integration of neuropsychological research and theory into theory and practice in special education? Despite outstanding pioneering efforts over the years, from Orton (1937) to Cruickshank (1966) and Gaddes (1980), to name a few, the rocky enterprise leading from neuropsychology to special education has produced largely dismal results and at times even spectacular failures. This is not to suggest an absence of scholarship or some success at integrating neuropsychological notions into special educational practice (e.g., Evans, 1982; Hartlage & Telzrow, 1983; Hynd & Cohen, 1983; Hynd & Obrzut, 1981; Kershner, 1988; Reynolds, 1981; Rourke, Bakker, Fisk, & Strang, 1983). Nevertheless, the collective impact of neuropsychology on special education, insofar as this can be inferred from major introductory texts (e.g., Kirk & Gallagher, 1983; Ysseldyke & Algozzine, 1984) and from omnibus, summary reviews of research and practice in special education (Wang, Reynolds, & Walberg, 1987, 1988, 1989), has been negligible in the extreme.

This chapter addresses the failure in special education to secure and sustain a pivotal role for neuropsychology. The chapter assumes that special education would be vastly improved if the neuropsychology of exceptionalities were established firmly as a core area within special education, as perceived by special educators. It assumes also that the unfulfilled role for neuropsychology in special education ought to have particular relevance, at least in terms of future potential, to issues in educational instruction.

Section II examines the mystery of what went wrong, made all the more mysterious in view of the great strides that were taking place at the same time in neuropsychology itself. The section begins with some little-known facts, by tracing the origins of the use of formative neuropsychological principles in educating exceptional persons, including consideration of brain laterality, to followers of Francis Gall, a physician of Vienna (later Paris), who founded and delivered lectures on the subject of phrenology beginning in 1796. This is followed by a brief historical account leading up to the present. It shows that neuropsychology as a formal discipline became restricted increasingly to a narrow conceptualization within special education as a medical-etiology model of exceptionality, while simultaneously, special education expanded to focus the greater part of its resources on high-incidence exceptionalities that were conceptualized more inclusively within behavioral, psychological, and environmental perspectives. At the same time, already threatened by a serious reduction in the scope of its territorial responsibilities, neuropsychology suffered from a terrible loss of credibility because of the broad-scale infusion of poorly documented, neuropsychologically based, remedial theories and claims into special education that were shown subsequently to be erroneous. One of these programs, the Tomatis Listening Training program (Tomatis, 1978), is used to illustrate the problems that such programs pose. Thus, aside from the acknowledged role of neuropsychology as a source of basic scientific knowledge regarding specific exceptionalities, the 1980s are presented as a time of fragility and even disillusionment for the status of neuropsychology in special education. Examples from the brain-laterality research literature are used to argue against the parochial view, represented by the medical-etiology model, that the future significance of neuropsychology to special education lies only or mainly in its unquestionable value as a repository of medical/ neuroanatomical facts and descriptive, neuroanatomical/behavioral correlations that have a direct bearing on etiology. The section stresses the need to view neuropsychology as an important theoretical dimension of cognitive processing in all exceptionalities, irrespective of etiology, rather than as one alternative model of exceptionalities, with severely restricted general usefulness across the field. The section argues for a reconceptualization of neuropsychology in special education and for special education to expand its research base, with an aim toward developing instructional approaches that are both tested adequately prior to implementation and consistent with valid neuropsychological theory.

Section III of the chapter examines a far-reaching dilemma that challenges the future of special education and the future of neuropsychology in special education. The dilemma came about in the 1960s by the creation of "learning disabilities" (LD) as a category in special education and by the "presumption of specificity," a key notion that defines what a learning disability is and rationalizes its very existence. Specificity refers to a presumed underlying neurological inefficiency that affects a domain-specific, cognitive process in LD, relatively dissociated from general intellectual skills and primary, affective development. Thus defined, LD is the largest by far of any of the exceptionalities served by special education. For special education, the political realities are profound; for if the unproven presumption of specificity were to be disproved, which could happen because it is after all an empirical question, special education services might be reduced in some states in the United States and in some provinces in Canada by as much as 50%! This chapter, however, addresses only the academic and theoretical side of the problem. The section explains that the specificity presumption has been a continuing source of friction in the unsettled relationship between neuropsychology and special education. In special education the consensual opinion is that the specificity claim implies the presence of brain damage and, consequently, the claim has been perceived as an unjustified attempt to extend the medical-etiology model of exceptionalities into high-incidence areas. The section argues that, by resting their case on an undocumented implication (pathological etiology) of a presumption (specificity), neuropsychologically oriented special educators further weakened the chances for neuropsychology to gain prominence in special education. Such an extension of neuropsychology into high incidence areas of special education without shifting away from the medical-etiology conceptual approach raises serious ethical and scientific questions. The section discusses research which supports the specificity presumption in a remedial context; however, consistent with the first section, emphasis is placed on the need for a reconceptualization of neuropsychology in special education. While the first section argues for a broader view of neuropsychology to go beyond the popular, medical-etiology model, the second section argues for a shift in models to a normal variance–individual differences conceptualization of etiology in high-incidence exceptionalities.

II. The Mystery

A. *Phrenologists Were Not All Wrong*

The earliest credit for a relationship between aphasia and lesions of the left cerebral hemisphere has been given to Marc Dax, who may have read a paper to that effect before the Medical Society of Montpellier, France, in 1836 (Hécaen, 1962). Not surprisingly, this claim of discovery, which was made by his son in a publication that appeared 4 years after Broca's landmark publication, has been disputed and remains an unresolved contention (Roberts, 1966). Of course, Broca is recognized correctly as the first to offer the discovery formally in a documented publication. In this connection, it is of considerable historical interest that a physician by the name of Mr. Hood, who was impressed by some of the reputable claims of the rightly debunked, pseudoscience of phrenology, reported in the *Transactions of the Phrenological Society* in 1822 that he treated a case of expressive aphasia with alexia, or acquired speech and reading disability (recognized now as Broca's aphasia), with the use of blood-letting leaches *applied over the patient's left temple* (Combe, 1845). This revelation suggests that knowledge of linguistic lateralization in diagnosis and *treatment* was known and documented well before either Dax's possible pronouncement in 1836 or Broca's excellent and influential publication in 1861.

Hood's patient was a literate, 65-year-old man who, on the evening of September 2, 1822, suddenly began to speak incoherently. Hood reported that "he had forgotten the name of every object in nature" even though the incident spared his memory, his ability to attend, his visual recognition of acquaintances, his perception and judgment, his verbal comprehension, and his bodily health. He could no longer read but could comprehend written passages if they were read to him. The only intelligible words remaining in his spoken language were "yes" and "no." But the story does not end there. According to Combe (1845), when the patient died on August 17, 1825, Hood reported, in the *Phrenological Journal*, Vol. 3, p. 28 (undated), that brain dissection confirmed the presence of two small anterior lesions in the left hemisphere and a right hemisphere that was entirely normal in appearance. Combe was so impressed by the implication of Hood's work for an asymmetry in cortical functions that he attended the brain dissection of a similar case of aphasia in 1836 which, indeed, confirmed the presence of a small anterior cavity in the left hemisphere while the "right hemisphere was entire."

Unfortunately and perplexingly, especially in the face of such dramatic behavioral observations that were confirmed by brain dissection and even carried over to influence efforts at rehabilitation, neither Hood nor Combe actually put forward the claim that language was lateralized! Their failure to draw the conclusion that seems in retrospect to be inescapable may be understood, perhaps, in the light of Combe's extensive and eloquent argument in the same text (Combe, 1845) in defense of the necessity for dual, mirror-image lesions in each hemisphere to disrupt any of the mental faculties. A theoretical mainstay of the phrenological position was that the plurality of localized brain functions (e.g., language, self-esteem, cunning, etc.), which they were among the first to argue, were represented topographically at mirror-image points in both hemispheres. With tissue damage localized to one side, they believed that the function in question could still be carried out by the homologous organ on the opposite side. Therefore, it appears that Hood and Combe failed to see the contradiction or to adjust their beliefs even though they were confronted with what seems to be a glaring anomaly. Without their apparent awareness, this anomaly separated their theoretical position from their observations and from their clinical practice. It may be that they were blinded by their tenaciousness in defending a mistaken, but rather prominent, theoretical point.

Moreover, Hood's well-documented clinical understanding of the relationship between aphasia and lesions of the left hemisphere in 1822 was guaranteed obscurity by the abundant controversial excesses of the phrenological movement, of which he was a part. For instance, the phrenologists claimed that individual differences could be ascertained in intellectual skills, in receptive and expressive language functions, and in personality characteristics by taking measurements of various physical dimensions of the head and face. In that they were really interested in the geography of the brain, they admitted to a degree of error in their methods which had to be indirect. However, they believed in a close correspondence between the brain's interior mapping and the external appearance of the skull. Consequently, they constructed and advocated the use of notoriously ill-conceived classification systems for criminals, for the mentally retarded, for personality archetypes, and for racial–cultural groups.

Just to give one illustration, no function was thought to be established better than the cerebellum, at the base of the brain, as the organ of sexual desire. Credit for this "discovery" was given to Dr. Gall, the founder of the movement. According to Combe (1845), in the course of treating a widow of irreproachable character for severe nymphomania, Dr. Gall, while suporting the patient's head during an intense fit of the disease, wa struck by the large size and heat of her neck. In the phrenologist's characteristic unscientific fashion, this initial observation led to many other "confirming" instances for the alleged brain–behavior connection between a hypertrophied and overheated cerebellum and uncontrollable sexual urges. It is not in the least surprising that the phrenologists were discredited resoundingly. The sad part of the story is that, mainly because of his association with the phrenologists, Hood's perspicacious observation of a functional correspondence between aphasia and the left hemisphere went unnoticed for another 40 years.

Nevertheless, in spite of the excesses and collapse of phrenology as a system, neuroscience was here to stay. In the 1840s and 1850s selective attributes of the phrenologist's theory strongly influenced the neuroscientists of the day, helping decisively to establish the principles that were to have a lasting effect on special education. Birth was delayed: The baby was not tossed out with the bath water. The modularity of the brain was argued forcefully by Combe (1845) and the brain's responsiveness to exercise and to sensory stimulation was supported staunchly by Sequin (1864), both having been inspired by Gall's system of phrenology. Mental deficiency and cretinism (a thyroid disorder) began to be understood as partial, mental disabilities that could coexist with average or even outstanding talent in art, music, and mechanical aptitude. The brain was perceived as a highly interconnected mosaic of discrete centers for potential abilities and disabilities. Indeed, although Combe was far from being an impassioned environmentalist, he went so far as to say that education could change a dull boy of 10 into a genius at 20. It was this sense of unfettered optimism that motivated Sequin's systematic training approach with the retarded in Paris and the spread of training facilities for the retarded throughout Europe and North America. Broca's historic publication in 1861 could not have been timed better to further encourage the establishment of special classes for the retarded and the establishment of neuropsychology as a key rationalizing force undergirding the special education movement.

B. Good Intentions but Definitional Chaos

Special education expanded quickly around the turn of the century to include classes for the deaf, blind, emotionally disturbed, physically handicapped, speech defective, and for those with chronic medical disorders as well as the intellectually gifted. Hence, with the exception of learning disabilities, by 1920 all of the traditional and contemporary categories in special education were in place. An embryonic understanding of neurology and psychology within special education began to emerge for each category and appeared certain, through their combination, to forge a knowledge base that would be useful to special educators across categories. Reality slowly curtailed the limitless enthusiasm that marked the earliest attempts at remediation, but humanitarian and scientific motives prevailed to assure a permanent place for neuropsychology in special education.

What happened next, however, had the unfortunate side effect of a restraining order for the rapid development and receptivity of neuropsychological ideas into special education. Learning disability as a category was about to be conceived, but the resultant definitional problems and methodological reservations that were brought to light fueled an imbroglio that remains unresolved to this day.

The momentous distinction between "endogenous" and "exogenous" causs of mental deficiency that was made by Binet and Simon (1914), by Larsen (1931), and by Strauss and Lehtinen (1974) lies at the root of a long cooling-off period for neuropsychology in special education. Strauss and Lehtinen (1947), who had the most to do with advancing the endogenous–exogenous distinction, made an appealing argument for brain injury as a special education category, to be differentiated from learning disorders due to constitutional factors. In an impressive monograph, they argued that such children demonstrated characteristic learning impairments irrespective of their intellectual level and that they required qualitatively unique remedial strategies. Then, as if this was not a sufficient challenge to any orderly synthesis between neuropsychology and special education, in a second related publication, Strauss and Kephart (1955) created the category of "normal brain injury"—children with learning difficulties who have normal IQs and no verifiable signs of brain damage. In effect, LD as a category was born. Neuropsychology, however, was in for hard times.

Special education groped in frustration for logical schemes and for objective methodologies to separate the mildly retarded, behavior disordered, and learning disabled. How and why does one infer brain injury if it cannot always be detected through observation and measurement? In the milder disorders the distinction between normal and exceptional became unclear and, partly as a result, a large number of special educators began to view neuropsychology more narrowly as a conceptual approach that was limited to those low-incidence exceptionalities in whom the existence of brain damage or neurological complications could be verified without doubt. Students with demonstrable brain injury, certain mental deficiency syndromes, chronic health impairments, and visual and hearing handicaps currently represent less than 10% of all exceptional students (Ysseldyke & Algozzine, 1984). These exceptionalities became rapidly the only noncontroversial areas for the application of neuropsychological knowledge. Furthermore, as the range of influence for neuropsychology withered, special educators welcomed alternative theoretical perspectives with relatively noncontroversial diagnostic procedures to identify the high-incidence exceptionalities. Behavioral, psychological, and environmental theoretical perspectives prospered and are now seen as alternative orientations with greatly increased scope for understanding etiology and for planning treatment in the high-incidence areas (Ysseldyke & Aglgozzine, 1984).

C. Remedial Therapies Come and Go

At the same time that neuropsychology was losing its appeal on philosophical and ideological grounds and because of the theoretical and methodological strength of paradigms that were seen as being in competition, neuropsychology became the staging ground for countless diagnostic and remedial approaches that have since largely been discarded. Such approaches included dietary interventions, perceptual–motor training, optometric training, and psycholinguistic process training (see Lloyd, 1988, for a review). In terms of their current impact on practice, these approaches may as well be aboard the space craft Magellan, on their way through interplanetary space to Venus. But lessons are to be learned by a detailed examination of at least one such remedial therapy. Therefore, this section discusses results from 1- and 2-year evaluations of the Tomatis Listening Training program (LTP), designed for use with LD children (Kershner, Cummings, Clarke, Hadfield, & Kershner, 1986, in press). The LTP is characteristic of many of the neuropsychologically inspired remedial programs whose collective failures have had a negative effect on the image of neuropsychology in special education.

It is not unusual for such programs to have things in common. For example, they typically share one deceptively attractive feature: They promise what readily available procedures cannot—optimism about reversing the academic deficiencies of exceptional children. Unfortunately, it is impossible to assemble a convincing argument to the contrary against the wildest remedial claim, however unsubstantiated or unbelievable, when research evidence indicates that available methods for LD children are ineffective in promoting long-term academic gains (Forell & Hood, 1985; Gittelman, 1985; Zarski,

1982). Longitudinal outcome studies find frequently that LD children fall behind increasingly in age-expected performance and this occurs regardless of whether or not they receive remedial instruction (Koppitz, 1971; Short, Feagans, McKinney & Appelbaum, 1986). The LTP is no exception in optimizing the advantage of this vulnerability. Unconfirmed reports of successful treatment for more than 15,000 children with langauge-related learning handicaps and several hundred others with dysfluent speech, autism, and a variety of emotional and psychosomatic ailments have provoked interest and controversy in Canada (Bergman & Warr-Leeper, 1981).

A second characteristic shared by many such programs is that they are introduced to special education and oftentimes adopted on a large scale prior to adequate field tests to demonstrate either their efficacy or their benefits relative to the financial expense of implementation. Again, the Tomatis LTP is no exception. Our literature search found only two unpublished studies and three doctoral dissertations. The unpublished studies (Palmaccio, Wilson, Metlay, & Risucci, 1984; Rourke & Russell, 1983) were exploratory in nature, not designed to generate definitive evidence and, consequently, their results are inconclusive (Cummings, 1985; Ontario Psychological Association, 1984). Two of the doctoral theses were nonexperimental studies without control groups (Donner, 1982; Neysmith-Roy, 1980). Even though they cannot be used legitimately as a basis for conclusive scientific evidence, both the unpublished studies and the theses have been a source of unqualified, positive commentary toward the LTP. The best controlled experiment turned out to be the third doctoral thesis (Schnitzer, 1974) which, unlike the other four studies, failed to find any indication of a favorable effect of the LTP. Also, unlike the other four studies, the latter thesis was not referred to very much by anyone.

A third property shared by many of these programs is their conceptual basis in esoteric theory that includes either speculative claims or assertions that are both speculative and clearly incompatible with accepted neuropsychological theory. In this instance, four central tenets of the LTP rationale are questionable statements about child neuropsychology. The LTP is based on the progressive lateralization, developmental view popularized by Lenneberg (1967) and on the ideas, popularized by Delacato (1966), that early neurodevelopmental stages can be recapitulated and that sensory stimulation can induce left-hemisphere specialization for language. According to the LTP rationale (1) from a perinatal, bihemispheric, or right-hemispheric locus, linguistic processing shifts gradually during childhood to the left hemisphere; (2) there is a cognitive and psychodynamic advantage associated with left-hemisphere specialization and with the strength or relative degree of that specialization; (3) learning disorders are caused by anomalous left-hemisphere specialization; and (4) left-hemisphere dominance for language can be increased by environmental manipulation or, in this case, by the Tomatis LTP. These tenets range in veridicality from (1) and (2), which are interesting theoretical hypotheses that have not been supported by experiment, to (3) and (4), which are current questions that, as yet, have not been resolved (Kershner, 1985). Of course, each of these hypotheses is subject to reevaluation as new evidence may indicate; but, the critical point to be emphasized is that programs ought to be grounded in credible theory that has substantial research backing.

Unfortunately, when such programs are unable to produce scientific evidence supporting their practical effectiveness neuropsychology suffers a double loss. Neuropsychology loses status by association, and some theoretical claims that may have merit in the long run may be rejected prematurely by association.

1. TOMATIS LTP

The LTP is a program of auditory training involving treatment primarily on the Electronic Ear, an "audio–vocal conditioning apparatus." The Ear has an input stage (cassette or child's spoken voice through a microphone), an output stage (child wears audio headsets with bone conductors), and two parallel frequency modification channels in between input and output. According to Tomatis, a French otolaryngologist, the Ear produces its beneficial therapeutic effect by increasing tympanic pressure and by exercising the two muscles of the tympanum, the malleus and stirrup bone muscles. Such "acoustic exercise" is directed at increasing the linguistic processing specialization of the left cerebral hemisphere. At the same time there is an attempt to reestablish three stages of auditory experience which, according to Tomatis' theory, characterize stages in the normal development of listening. During the first two stages, (1) "Filtered Sound" and (2) "Sonic Birth," the child listens passively to recordings of classical music and Gregorian chants. The first phase presents the frequencies which Tomatis theorizes would be heard through the liquid environment or amniotic fluid barrier of the unborn child. These recordings are filtered to exclude frequencies under 8000 Hz. Tomatis believes that this experience is a duplication and psychodynamic recapitulation of what children hear and feel emotionally before birth. In the second phase, the child is "reborn" into the full spectrum of the acoustic world by reintroducing the extrauterine frequencies between 125 and 8000 Hz. In the third and longest phase, the "Active Phase," the child responds orally to sounds coming from the Ear by repeating taped messages, by listening to classmates' filtered voices through the Ear as they read, and by listening to their own filtered voices in feedback as they read and speak into the Ear. During the third phase the intensity of feedback to the left ear (and by inference to the right hemisphere because of the greater strength of the contralateral auditory pathways) is reduced and the lower-band audio frequencies are filtered out as the higher (speech) frequencies are heightened correspondingly. Tomatis (1978) claims that such procedures applied clinically have been remarkably successful in remediating a broad range of auditory, linguistic, and academic deficits in thousands of LD children as well as boosting their motivation and self-esteem.

2. TOMATIS 1-YEAR EVALUATION

A packaged 100-hour LTP, that was prepared commercially for classroom use and distributed by the Tomatis Centre in Toronto, was evaluated. Trained Tomatis personnel collaborated with us in designing the study, in screening the children, and in implementing the LTP. The Tomatis personnel provided: (1) training for project and school staff to administer the LTP, (2) necessary equipment, (3) all equipment maintenance, (4) consultation and supervision of the program, (5) additional consultation as required by the research program, and (6) in-service programming for the school staff and introductory workshops for the parents.

In the first year (Kershner et al., 1986) 32 upper-middle-class LD children attending a private school participated in a traditional, pretest–posttest research design extending over the academic year, from September to May. The children ranged in age from 8 through 14. They were diagnosed as LD according to Ontario Ministry of Education guidelines, which exclude evident neurological disorder, emotional disturbance, sensory losses, and inadequate environmental or instructional opportunities. None were Attention-Deficit Hyperactive Disordered (ADHD) or taking stimulant medication. English was the main language spoken at home. The children were diagnosed individually on the basis of comprehensive psychoeducational assessments which included (1) WISC-R IQs > 80; and (2) at least a 2-year discrepancy between IQ and both reading comprehension and word recognition. Thus, the sample could be described as an auditory–linguistic subtype of LD children (Torgesen, 1977).

Because the LTP is adjunctive or complementary to formal instruction, it was necessary to combine the 100-hour, resource-withdrawal LTP with a full complement of regular remedial programming. The LD children were assigned randomly to an LTP or a placebo group. The placebo group throughout the first year received 22.5 hours of simulated experimental treatment comprised partly of mock LTP exercises on an Electronic Ear simulator (see the Year 1 report for greater details). The Ear simulator had no ear attenuation or frequency-modification capabilities. The children were withdrawn from art, music, and physical education for 6 hours per week of LTP treatment or for 1 hour per week of placebo treatment. Our purpose was not to match the groups for hours of treatment, but only to control for attention and expectancy effects. By design, therefore, both groups received special attention in Year 1 and both received the same amount of academic instruction, but only one group (LTP) participated in the Tomatis remedial program.

Comprehensive pretest–posttest assessments were carried out on tests of basic skills, academic achievement, personality, and neuropsychological functioning, which included a test of cerebral laterality. The children were assessed on measures of sight and auditory vocabularly, auditory discrimination, auditory word segmentation and phonetic synthesis, syllabication, visual word recognition, visual–motor sequencing, fine motor coordination, math computations and applications, spelling, four tests of reading ability, verbal fluency, self-esteem, and written language. The posttesting results revealed only a single treatment effect—the *placebo* group had improved more than the LTP group on a test of grapheme–phoneme correspondence and structural analysis of written words. Data on individual children were examined meticulously but unsuccessfully for any signs of an LTP treatment effect. There were significant gains over the year, but improvements occurred with the same frequency and magnitude in both experimental groups. As well one-on-one interviews were held with each child to search for any attitudinal changes that may have been undetected by our formal assessments. Additionally, parent and teacher questionnaires and special listening tests developed by Tomatis were examined. There were no indications whatsoever of a favorable LTP effect. This finding is similar to all other techniques in special education that do not directly teach to the deficit skill area.

Finally, the LTP's theoretical anchor in neuropsychology was put to test by examining dichotic listening results that were taken before and after treatment. The LTP claims to be able to induce changes in brain lateralization, changes that can be measured on tests of dichotic listening. Hemispheric specialization is measued commonly through this auditory competition task that sets up a rivalry between acoustic signals arriving at the left and right ears. The usual procedure in dichotic listening is to simultaneously project dissimilar verbal stimuli (for example, nonsense words or digit names) to the two ears and to observe which ear is better able to utilize its respective input for successful recognition or recall. A right-ear advantage on dichotic tests using verbal stimuli is interpreted as a direct indication, tempered by certain methodological qualifications, of the specialization of the left hemisphere for receptive speech. This inference is based on other evidence that (1) in most people it is the left hemisphere that is specialized for linguistic processing; (2) the contralateral auditory connections traveling between the right ear and the left hemisphere or between the left ear and the right hemisphere are prepotent over the ipsilateral (same-side) ear–hemisphere connections (Kimura, 1967;

Rosenzweig, 1951); and (3) the left hemisphere, when activated differentially by a language task, promotes attention selectively to the right side of space (Kinsbourne, 1970; Morais, 1978; Phillips & Gates, 1982). Therefore, if the left hemisphere is specialized for language, verbal information arriving at the right ear will be easier to perceive, remember, and recall than information arriving at the left ear (see Hughdahl, 1988, for a comprehensive survey of the dichotic literature).

The approach taken in analysis of the dichotic results was to perform an exhaustive search for treatment effects. We took this incautious approach (1) because of the large-scale failure of the other dependent measures to detect any LTP effects, and (2) because theoretically the dichotic test is a direct assessment of the underlying processing mechanisms that should be affected first by the LTP. Treatment effects should have been witnessed first and most robustly in changes in children's lateralization. Using eight different forms of statistical analysis on the same dichotic data failed to show any treatment effects or any changes over time in lateralization. A majority of children in both groups produced a right-ear advantage (REA), which is indicative of left-hemisphere lateralization.

3. TOMATIS 2-YEAR EVALUATION

Twenty-six of the LD children continued in the study for the second year. The purpose of our extended evaluation was to address the plausible argument that favorable treatment effects of such process-oriented, neuropsychological training programs may materialize over a longer span of time. A second purpose, discussed later in this chapter, was to test the LD specificity presumption. In the second year of the study the LTP and placebo activities were discontinued. The children received only regular instruction in mainstreamed small classes (student–teacher ratio = 8:1), rotating to different subjects through the day, where they were given a balanced curriculum of direct instruction in reading, writing, and arithmetic. The school program was based on the well-documented Orton–Gillingham multisensory approach (Cox, 1984). Remedial instruction focuses on language and arithmetic skills and is placed within the context of direct application to the actual task to be learned. It is noteworthy to point out that neuropsychological information had no bearing on the course of instruction.

As in Year 1, the treatment evaluation results in Year 2 are easy to summarize. The only significant treatment effect was produced by the better performance of the original *placebo* group compared to the LTP group on the Seashore Rhythm Test (Reitan & Davidson, 1974). The Seashore is a measure of sustained attention and auditory discrimination requiring a same–different decision between pairs of rhythmic (Morse code-like) patterns presented sequentially. This finding is critical because the Seashore was recommended specifically because of its sensitivity to the underlying auditory processing changes that are claimed to result from LTP treatment. Although there was no indication of a regression in auditory capabilities, the LTP children's relative lack of progress occurred in parallel with their poorer performance in phonics in our Year 1 report. These findings warrant a note of caution, especially for contemplated school applications of the LTP.

On the positive side, our Year 2 results demonstrated that LD children do not necessarily fall increasingly behind their nondisabled peers. Irrespective of their treatment group, on age-adjusted measures the LD children showed (1) stable performance in verbal and performance IQ and in reading and spelling on the WRAT (Jastak & Jastak, 1978), and (2) significant improvement in WRAT arithmetic, in written language on the TOWL (Hamill & Larsen, 1983), and in verbal fluency (Reitan, 1983).

Aside from our encouraging longitudinal results, treatment evaluation research cannot get more disappointing than our experience with the LTP. Regrettably, the LTP chronicle is representative of the inauspicious track record of systematic, instructional, and training programs in special education that have had a neuropsychological focus. Moreover, the increased pressure to restrict neuropsychology to high-incidence areas has been augmented by the frequency of failure for these kinds of programs and claims in the high-incidence exceptionalities (i.e., mild mental deficiency, behavioral and emotional disorders, learning disabilities). This is not in the least to imply an absence of potential, for the promise today may be even brighter than in the past. For instance, preliminary results have been encouraging for aptitude-by-treatment interactions (Hartlage & Telzrow, 1983; Lloyd, 1988). However, there are lessons to be learned from history and recommendations to be made.

D. Status Review and Recommendations

1. HOW THINGS ARE

Neuropsychology is barely mentioned in introductory texts in special education (e.g., Kirk & Gallagher, 1983; Ysseldyke & Algozzine, 1984) or in advanced comprehensive reviews of research and practice (Wang *et al.*, 1987, 1988, 1989). Generally speaking, its low profile is the result of its compartmentalization in special education as synonymous with the medical-etiology approach to exceptionalities. Of course, brief mention is usually made of neuropsychology in its established role in neuromotor assessment (Sheehan & Klein, 1989) and in basic research (Greenberg & Kusche, 1989). However, the consensual association between neuropsychology and the medical-etiology model has greatly restricted the breadth and extent of neuropsychology's influence in special education.

This medical-etiology compartmentalization has taken two forms. Neuropsychology plays an indispensable role in the medical-etiology approach to classification (McKinney, 1988; Reschly, 1987). This approach is traditional in special education and becomes useful whenever abnormal behavior patterns can be attributed to underlying biological pathology. Emphasis in this approach is placed on the kinds of descriptive information that are important in diagnosis and assessment and in the establishment of etiology. The abnormal behavior pattern is understood to be a direct result of a neurological deficit. Unfortunately, this idea of neuropsychology's relevance to special education, when it is the only view that one has, restricts neuropsychological considerations to the low-incidence exceptionalities and to the issue of etiology. The definitional problems in special education and competing philosophical approaches to exceptionality have worked to reinforce this view.

The second popular opinion of neuropsychology extends its conceptual role in low-incidence classification of the more severely impaired to educational treatment. Neuropsychology is seen as playing a principle role in teaching ideologies that owe their allegiance to the medical-etiology model (Colarusso, 1987; Lloyd, 1988; McKinney, 1988). These remedial approaches, of which the LTP is a good example, are referred to collectively as "process training" or "diagnostic-prescriptive" teaching. Their pedagogical objectives are aimed at correcting underlying neurological impairments and deficit training. Currently there is widespread dissatisfaction with such instructional approaches on both scientific and ideological grounds. On the one hand, they have not proven their worth empirically and, on the other hand, they are viewed as an irrational and unjustified intrusion of the medical-etiology model into low-incidence exceptionalities. Together, these two consensual, low-profile views of neuropsychology reflect a mixture of tradition, confusion, and disillusionment. Another conceptualization is needed.

2. DICHOTIC RESEARCH IN LD

Examples from research demonstrate that the consequences of compartmentalization extend well beyond political and academic realms. For instance, research in brain lateralization suggests that the medical-etiology model may have led to mistaken conclusions with LD children and with mentally retarded children. An important question regarding LD children, since Orton (1937) raised the issue, has been whether they are poorly lateralized for language. The poor-lateralization hypothesis implies the existence of an intrinsic, neurological deficit or maturational delay, a dysfunction that would be expected not to come and go, but to remain invariant across different learning situations. From the medical-etiology viewpoint, this hypothesis suggests that poorly established cerebral dominance, defined as a neuroanatomical condition, is the cause of learning impairments. As a result, several experiments using dichotic listening appeared to have confirmed the Ortonian hypothesis when they found a reduced REA or a left-ear advantage in their LD sample (see Bryden, 1988, for a review). What was unappreciated, however, is the extent to which brain function can be influenced by the surrounding social, psychological, and learning context. Dichotic listening measures *hemispheric patterns of activation*, not cortical structure (Levy, 1983). Empirical studies with the LD population have supported this notion (see Obrzut, 1988, for a review).

The fallacy of thinking that the Ortonian hypothesis could be confirmed by a simple test of dichotic listening was demonstrated clearly in a study in which the children's dichotic responses were recorded by having them respond in writing as well as orally (Kershner, Henninger, & Cooke, 1984). With digits as stimuli, a control group of nondisabled children showed the usual REA on one version of our dichotic task, which required them to write the numbers on a sheet of paper. The control group was tested only once, using the written response condition. The LD children, however, were tested twice: once in written recall and once in oral recall. The results showed that, when the LD children wrote their responses, they were lateralized more poorly than the normals; but in the oral recall condition they were lateralized more strongly compared to the normals. This study demonstrates (1) that when LD children are compared to nondisabled children they can be either more or less lateralized; and (2) that the same child can shift lateralization in dichotic performance, as a means of coping with task demands, from a left-hemisphere advantage to a right-hemisphere advantage. Thus the study identified a connection in LD between changes in brain processing and the altered demands of a learning task. The study did not identify a fixed anatomical cause of the LD problem. Etiology was not implied, nor does it need to be implied for neuropsychological research to have relevance to instruction. Irrespective of the direct cause of the abnormal behavior (e.g., LD), knowledge of how the brain processes information is an important dimension for understanding cognitive disabilities.

The point to be made from this research is that there is a potential role for neuropsychology in special education in helping to understand brain–behavior correlates in all exceptionalities, including LD, which is a high-incidence area. Such a reconceptualization will be necessary to begin to build the quality of collaboration needed to develop neuropsychologically valid theoretical models of instruction in special education. I have argued this case previously (Kershner, 1983) and I have worked out some of the details of how specific theories of brain processing can provide the conceptual foundations for theories of instruction in LD (Kershner, 1988).

3. DICHOTIC RESEARCH IN DOWN SYNDROME

High-incidence areas are not the only exceptionalities that have been induced to interpret research results too narrowly because of the limited perception of neuropsychology as a medical-etiology approach. Cerebral laterality research with individuals afflicted with Down syndrome, a chromosomal dysfunction that produces mental deficiency, has reported a reversed hemispheric pattern for language on the basis of studies showing an LEA in dichotic listening (for reviews, see Elliott, Weeks, & Elliott, 1987; Pipe, 1988). Many of these studies have been interpreted as evidence for a syndrome-specific reversal in the brain's structural substrate for processing language. Such a possibility has important ramifications for our understanding of the embryological pathogenesis in Down syndrome. Also, the availability of a large group of right-handed but right-hemisphere-dominant persons with mental deficiency would lead certainly to significant advances in knowledge of the relationship of anatomic cerebral asymmetries to mental development, cognitive aptitude, handedness, and other nonlinguistic cerebral specializations.

However, like the LD–laterality debate, it is simply the case that how the brain processes information can be shaped powerfully by such things as effort, mental set, and environmental surroundings. In fact, reversed asymmetries on measures of cerebral dominance can result from specific situational factors such as the relative activation of the hemispheres (Hiscock & Bergström, 1982; Kershner, Thomas, & Callaway, 1977; Levy, Heller, Banich, & Burton, 1983), the relative availability of limited hemispheric processing resources (Friedman, Polson, Dafoe & Gaskill, 1982; Kershner et al., 1984), and transient or habitual task strategies (Levy, Trevarthen & Sperry, 1973). Each of these factors can produce an LEA in dichotic listening without altering some fixed structural attribute of the brain. Thus the LEA for language stimuli that has been found in Down syndrome may have been produced by less exotic factors than reversed cerebral dominance: factors such as contextual arrangements, previous experience, processing strategy, attending and response biases, or an overload on left-hemisphere capacity.

In an attempt to test the reversal hypothesis, we conducted a dichotic experiment with mentally retarded, Down syndrome individuals in which we had some controls for context effects (Tannock, Kershner, & Oliver, 1984). To reduce the influence of such context effects we used a modified version of the selective listening, dichotic methodology that was developed by Hiscock and Kinsbourne (1980). In this methodology, memory demands are reduced and potential attention and reporting biases toward one ear are controlled by requiring focused recall from each ear on separate blocks of counterbalanced trials. Thus, instead of trying to recall all stimuli from both ears on each trial, the subjects attend and report on each trial exclusively from one ear, while they attempt to ignore the competing stimuli arriving at the unattended ear. Additionally, to maximize controlled performance from each channel, we placed a large drawing of a flesh-colored ear at the same side as the target ear, with frequent reminders to "listen only to this ear." Under these methodological constraints, the possibility for context effects is reduced by a considerable extent. Our results can be summarized very briefly: There was no support for the reversed-dominance hypothesis. Eight of our ten subjects showed at least a 1-digit advantage in favor of the right ear. But, perhaps most damaging to the reversal prediction, among the subjects who attended to their left ear on the first block of trials, four out of five produced a much larger number of intrusions from the right channel than correct responses from the attended left channel. A strong form of the reversal hypothesis cannot account for such performance in even one Down syndrome individual.

Of course, the question of hemispheric asymmetries in the mentally retarded and, more specifically, in Down syndrome is far from being resolved. Our findings do, however, suggest the need for greater caution in making inferences from such research because of methodological limitations. But, the point that is most germane to the present discussion is that this issue has as much to do with the medical-etiology model as it has to do with the tenuousness of the methodology. Even in low-incidence exceptionalities like Down syndrome, the medical-etiology conceptualization has had a limiting effect on research strategies and on scientific inference. From my point of view, understanding how context effects may influence lateralization is equally as important as knowing if language processing is located in the left or right hemisphere.

Neuropsychology in special education needs to be reconceptualized as an instrumental means for advancing our understanding of cognitive processes, not only etiology, and this new perspective warrants application in both low-incidence and high-incidence exceptionalities.

4. LARGER RESEARCH BASE NEEDED

Special education's definitional uncertainties and its vulnerability to unsubstantiated treatment claims are two additional factors that have diminished neuropsychology's appeal. Although these problems cannot be separated from the overriding conceptualization issue, they are largely empirical problems.

Political and ideological objections aside, the critical question in special education with regard to definitional status or category eligibility is whether educational instruction is effective. Which programs work with which children? The research pool needed to answer this question is virtually nonexistent; yet, the validity of any educational classification system for students rests entirely with its utility as an effective means of delivering appropriate instruction and training. Definitional questions need to be examined thoroughly in remedial research.

Expanding our theoretical and evaluation research base would also help to prevent the unwitting adoption of poorly researched programs and programs that are based on questionable theory. The first standard that any new program should meet is a reasonable degree of compatibility with current neuropsychological theory as determined by an assessment of the most recent research. The old adage "if it works use it" is an invitation to continued ignorance and any number of undesirable side effects. Blood-letting leaches were used on the same premise. Second, successful field trials need to precede any large-scale implementation and, then, implementation should have a rigorous evaluation component. Third, our vulnerability to excessive claims would be reduced proportionately as we are able to document what we do well and how we do it. For instance, both Kavale (1988) and Horn, O'Donnell, and Vitulano (1983) have pointed out that the gloomy, longitudinal outcome research in LD has not been entirely consistent and that problematic methodological issues warrant a more cautious, wait-and-see attitude. This view is supported by our longitudinal research with the LTP (Kershner *et al.,* 1990), which showed that, under fairly ideal instructional and environmental circumstances, some LD children can learn efficiently in most basic skill and academic areas.

The role for neuropsychology in this scenario, however, should be a very cautious one, which brings us back to the reconceptualization issue. At the moment, there are few if any firm implications for instruction from neuropsychological research; yet there is no question that special education would benefit from instructional strategies that dovetail compatibly with neuropsychological theory. History suggests two things: (1) a major, long-term effort will be needed to bridge the gap between theory and practice; and (2) the great potential that neuropsychology has in shaping instructional theory in special education is via its reconceptualization as a theoretical counterpart of cognitive science. Indeed without such a reconceptualization and without a strenuous effort to build a research base aimed both at the definitional problem and at the vulnerability problem, neuropsychology may remain as it is today, largely unconnected to theory and practice in mainstream special education.

III. Specificity Presumption

A. *What Determines Remedial Success in LD?*

The specificity presumption deserves discussion in a separate section because the future of neuropsychology may depend on the outcome of debates over its accuracy and on how one perceives its meaning. If it is false, those with a medical-etiology view will be convinced to continue to limit neuropsychology to low-incidence exceptionalities. The learning disabled will be perceived as no different from "garden variety" poor achievers and underachievers who do not require special education. Leaders in the field have argued that without the specificity presumption, the concept of LD would be meaningless (Stanovich, 1988; Swanson, 1988). If evidence is marshaled in its favor the controversy begun by Strauss and Kephart (1955) will be rekindled. Does specificity mean minimal brain damage? A few researchers have argued otherwise on scientific grounds (Ellis, 1985; Martin, 1986; Pribram & McGuinness, 1987), but most accepted definitions of LD imply that the answer is "yes." Such an extension of the medical-etiology approach into LD has always met with resistance on ethical and ideological grounds. The question of brain damage in LD is the topic of this section. However, first some evidence is presented that supports the specificity presumption.

According to the presumption, the LD child, who is selected very carefully according to the exclusionary criteria, suffers from a circumscribed neurological inefficiency that interferes with a delimited set of domain-specific cognitive processes. For the most part, this central nervous system dysfunction spares general intellectual ability. Such a restricted range of impairment, neurologically and cognitively, is referred to as a vertical domain to contrast it with disabling factors that operate across a broad sweep of tasks (e.g., below-normal IQ). By implication, IQ should not be instrumental in mediating new learning to the extent that educational task demands overlap with the underlying proximal cause of the disability. The other side of the coin suggests that achievement will covary with IQ in areas with little overlap with the neuronal basis of disability. The specificity presumption portrays LD as an insular, nonintellectual, cognitive impairment.

Thus, with some qualification, the specificity presumption leads directly to remedial predictions. Notably, phonological processing is acknowledged as a good possibility for the core locus of the LD child's modular learning impairment (Stanovich, 1988). But, this delimitation at the brain-cognitive level is focused less precisely in school achievement because impaired phonological processing can have an impact not only on visual word recognition in reading, but also on reading-related tasks like spelling and writing and even mechanical arithmetic. Arithmetic can be depressed because accurate performance requires verbal number concepts (Rourke & Fisk, 1988) and mental numerical operations that may both depend to some extent on phonology (Snowling, Stackhouse, & Rack, 1986).

This notion was examined in a very limited experiment which compared the relative value of IQ versus self-concept as predictors of achievement in LD children over a 2-year period (Kershner, in press). The sample consisted of a subset of 25 from the same LD children who were in the LTP study. The predictor variables were the WISC-R measure of IQ and the Coopersmith Self-Esteem Inventory (SEI) (Coopersmith, 1981). The SEI yields one overall estimate of self-concept by consideration of the child's expectations of success, acceptance, and personal strength in dealing with peers, family relationships, and school. The academic-achievement criterion variables were limited to those on which we had complete data sets on all subjects over the 2 years. These were the Wide-Range Achievement Tests of reading (word recognition), spelling, and arithmetic (WRAT) (Jastak & Jastak, 1978) and the Test of Written Language (TOWL) (Hammill & Larsen, 1983). Statistical comparisons are based on results that were obtained in September of Year 1 and in June of Year 2. Partial correlations were used to test for IQ–achievement relationships independently of self-concept and self-concept–achievement relationships independently of intellectual ability.

Analysis for pretest–posttest changes showed that IQ, reading, and spelling remained stable, while significant improvements occurred in SEI self-concept, arithmetic, and writing ability. Standard scores were used in all computations except self-concept, which produces only a raw score. The critical analyses were the partial correlations between the predictor variables, initial IQ and SEI, and the achievement-gain scores that took place over the two academic years. Controlling statistically for the effects of self-concept and chronological age, neither verbal IQ nor performance IQ was correlated with the achievement gains, whereas initial self-concept was correlated independently with the nonsignificant change in spelling (.69) and with the significant gains that occurred in both arithmetic (.58) and writing (.47), all $p < .01$. It is also important in arguing causality that the initial achievement scores did not correlate with the gains in self-concept. It appears that self-concept may be a causal factor in achievement, not simply a correlate.

The findings showed that the children's measured intelligence had no effect on their ability to profit from remedial teaching in areas that appear to be related closely to the proximal cause of their disability (phonological processing). The failure to find a relationship between IQ and reading may have been due to the attenuated range of the reading scores and absence of reading improvement; nevertheless, the failure to find a relationship between IQ and arithmetic and between IQ and writing, relative to the significant results obtained with self-concept, is consistent clearly with the specificity presumption.

The findings support the specificity idea and therefore the definition of LD in two important ways. First, the experiment suggests that the varied array of cognitive skills and knowledge that are measured on the WISC-R is not related causally to the neuropsychological substrate of the disability. Learning disability does, indeed, appear to be a modular information-processing disorder that is largely independent of IQ. Whether this is true at other IQ levels is an important question. These LD children produced WISC-R scores of mean = 99.0 and SD = 10.7 at the pretest and mean = 100.9 and SD = 13.5 at the posttest, so generalizability to LD children at higher or lower IQ levels is unwarranted. However, some evidence to suggest wider generality has been reported by Siegel (1988), who found no differences among LD children blocked into IQ groups of <80, 80–90, 91–109, and ≥110 on measures of reading (primarily word recognition), spelling, language, and memory. If we can generalize this dissociation of IQ from achievement (in areas that are related proximally to the disability) to lower and higher IQ levels, it could be argued, as Siegel (1988) has done, that IQ may be irrelevant to definitions of LD. I agree in theory that there appears to be no reason to limit LD to a particular IQ range. The very definition actually begs this conclusion. On the other hand, however, studies have shown that IQ tests and achievement tests do measure different abilities (Wright, 1987) and that an LD child's IQ level is an important factor in remedial success in academic areas further removed from, and unaffected by, the underlying specificity of the disorder. For instance, LD children with higher IQs are more likely to show treatment gains in reading when achievement is measured on a test of reading comprehension rather than on a test of word recognition (Kavale, 1988). Phonics is a primary factor in word recognition, whereas comprehension can be boosted by improved memory, test strategies, and relying more on content to extract the meaning of the passage. Hence, both IQ and achievement may be important considerations at the program level.

The second way in which the findings support the specificity principle is by suggesting that the widespread, generally impoverished, poorer performance of LD children may be due to their lower self-concept. Similar arguments have been made by Chapman (1988), Goldstein and Dunden (1987), and Rourke and Fisk (1988). The fact that LD children perform poorly across so many academic and experimental tasks would seem to falsify the specificity claim. However the substantial correlation between self-concept and achievement argues that much of the LD child's poorer achievement is caused by cognitive–motivational factors that may spread from a beginning, narrow cognitive area to negatively influence the child's general demeanor and overall performance. These findings demonstrate that LD children's feelings about themselves are a primary factor behind their poor achievement.

Thus, we have at least some support for the specificity principle. This being the case, the next question is whether acceptance necessarily implicates minimal brain damage in LD.

B. Deficit or Difference?

The most compelling scientific evidence in support of the existence of a neurological deficit comes from a small sample of four brains of dyslexics which all demonstrated structural abnormalities that were confined predominantly to cortical areas of the left hemisphere (cited in Geschwind & Galaburda, 1987). Such data are intriguing in their suggestion that an organic defect may be significant etiologically in large numbers of LD children; the cases are few but the sample represents all cases of dyslexia that have come to be examined in the laboratory. There are no nonconfirming cases.

Other evidence, however, suggests that these few examinations of the brains of dyslexics at autopsy may not be representative. The most comprehensive study on this question does not support the existence of minimal brain damage as a commonly occurring associative factor in LD. It stands to reason that a significant proportion of LD children should display some minor signs of organic involvement. Nichols and Chen (1981) reported the results of a study of 29,889 unselected children who were assessed shortly after birth for neurological symptoms and reassessed when they were 7 years old. The sample came from the Collaborative Perinatal Project begun in 1957 by the National Institute of Neurological and Communication Disorder and Stroke. Followup testing was carried out comprehensively on measures of child behavior, achievement, perceptual–cognitive ability, and neurological state. At the onset of the study, intercorrelations of 26 signs and symptoms of minimal neurological impairment failed to demonstrate the existence of anything resembling a single brain-damage syndrome; in fact there were few statistical associations among the measures. But, the most revealing finding came at the follow-up from a comparison of suspicious neurological signs between an LD group (defined by a discrepancy between IQ and achievement), composed of 8.36% of the sample, and a normal group, composed of 79% of the sample. Although 18% of the LD children showed neurological signs compared to 9% of the normals, the key result was that a huge majority of the LD children were free of any signs of organic impairment.

Comparing the scientific weight of these two sources of competing argument for teasing out the implications of the specificity presumption, at best, is a tenuous enterprise. The evidence confirming brain damage is extremely limited. The disconfirming evidence suggests a high degree of generalization, but it is always easier for spurious reasons to support the null hypothesis than to reject it. Nevertheless, however this question turns out, the existing equivocal data base presents a problem for neuropsychology in special education. The confirming evidence is used to justify the extension of the medical-etiology approach into theory, research, and practice in LD, but at the expense of neuropsychology's status because of the absence of conclusive evidence (Pribram & McGuinness, 1987). Inferring the existence of brain damage on any other than irreproachable evidence raises ethical issues as well. At the same time, the disconfirming evidence is used to argue against the validity of an intrinsic form of LD and, by implication, the value of understanding the neuropsychology of the disorder (McKinney, 1988). In either event, neuropsychology loses.

An alternative framework to the medical-etiology model may be needed for neuropsychology to gain an enduring and unquestionable position in the high-incidence exceptionalities. An attractive possibility that could be called a "normal variance–individual differences" model of exceptionality has been suggested in somewhat similar forms by several authors (Ellis, 1985; Martin, 1986; Pribram & McGuinness, 1987; Stanovich, 1988). First and foremost, this alternative conceptualization does not rest on the organicity question, but it can easily accommodate demonstrable neurological deficits under the wider umbrella of normal individual variability (Stanovich, 1988). Variation between individuals is the central dynamic of biological evolution. What is suggested is that the proper analogy to understand LD is obesity (Ellis, 1985) or physical height (Pribram & McGuinness, 1987), not measles. From this perspective, neither LD nor alleged LD subtypes are seen as discrete entities with invariant associated symptomatology. Instead, brain-cognitive processes are conceptualized as continuous distributions in multidimensional space. Divisions along any one dimension or between dimensions are completely arbitrary. Thus, the point at which someone becomes obese or tall or LD is a decision that we can make by social consensus.

A reconceptualization of neuropsychology in line with such a normal variance–individual difference model of exceptionalities would, I think, spark renewed interest in neuropsychology as an avenue to increase knowledge of individual differences at the level of brain processes. Trends in special education are moving in this direction. Such a shift would put neuropsychology in the high-incidence areas in special education in a better position to make recommendations for theories of instruction and on a firm scientific and ethical foundation.

IV. Addendum

This chapter attempted to sketch the historical origins and development of the most prominent neuropsychological perspectives in special education. It was assumed that current issues and controversies could be understood better in view of how and why they developed. No attempt was made to be all inclusive or to provide a comprehensive historical account. There was no intention to dispute the value of a medical-etiology orientation, only to challenge its limits when it is viewed as one exclusionary ideological motivation or as a singular research strategy. In particular, the use of the term medical etiology has no intended negative implications for either my medical friends or the continued high priority in science that must be given to seeking causal relations between events. Finally, it should be stressed that neuropsychology *in* special education, although their roots individually are fairly ancient, is of very recent origin. The interface between special education and neuropsychology is a rapidly unfolding dynamic. Innovative and promising technologies and new theoretical avenues promise to change the circumstances, the data base, and the arguments, and these changes are likely to occur in short order.

References

Bacon, F. (1973). *The advancement of learning*. London: Dent & Sons.

Bergman, I., & Warr-Leeper, G. (1981). *Critical appraisal of the Tomatis method: Theory and application*. Toronto: Ontario Speech and Hearing Association.

Binet, A., & Simon, T. (1914). *Mentally defective children*. London: Arnold.

Broca, P. (1861). Remarques sur le siège de la faculté du langage articule, suiviés d'une observation d'aphémie. *Bulletin of the Society of Anatomy, Paris*, Series 2, 6, 398–407.

Bryden, M. (1988). Does laterality make any difference? Thoughts on the relation between cerebral asymmetry and reading. In D. Molfese & S. Segalowitz (Eds.), *Brain lateralization in children* (pp. 509–525). Toronto: Guilford Press.

Chapman, J. (1988). Cognitive-motivational characteristics and academic achievement of learning disabled children: A longitudinal study. *Journal of Educational Psychology, 80*, 357–365.

Colarusso, R. (1987). Dragnostic-prescriptive teaching. In M. Wang, M. Reynolds, & H. Walberg (Eds.), *Handbook of special education: Research and practice* (Vol. 1, pp. 155–166). Toronto: Pergamon.

Combe, G. (1845). *A system of phrenology* (4th ed.). New York: Colyer; Boston, MA: Phillips & Sampson.

Coopersmith, S. (1981). *Coopersmith: Self-esteem inventory*. Palo Alto, CA: Consulting Psychologists Press.

Cox, A. (1984). *Structures and techniques-multisensory teaching of basic language skills*. Cambridge, MA: Educators Publishing Service.

Cruickshank, W. (Ed.). (1966). *The teacher of brain-injured children*. Syracuse, NY: Syracuse University Press.

Cummings, R. (1985). An evaluation of the Tomatis Listening Training Program. Unpublished doctoral thesis, University of Toronto.

Delacato, C. (1966). *Neurological organization and reading*. Springfield, IL: Thomas.

Donner, J. (1982). *Audio-psycho-phonological remedial training in relation to the psychosocial and personality adjustment of dyslexic boys*. Unpublished doctoral thesis, University of Ottawa.

Elliot, D., Weeks, D., & Elliot, C. (1987). Cerebral specialization in Down syndrome. *American Journal of Mental Retardation, 92*, 263–271.

Ellis, A. (1985). The cognitive neuropsychology of developmental (and acquired) dyslexia: A critical survey. *Cognitive Neuropsychology, 2*, 169–205.

Evans, J. (1982). Neuropsychologically based remedial reading procedures: Some possibilities. In R. Malatesha & P. Aaron (Eds.), *Reading disorders: Varieties and treatments* (pp. 371–388). Toronto: Academic Press.

Forell, E., & Hood, J. (1985). A longitudinal study of two groups of children with early reading problems. *Annals of Dyslexia, 35,* 97–116.

Friedman, A., Polson, M., Dafoe, C., & Gaskill, S. (1982). Dividing attention within and between hemispheres: Testing a multiple resource approach to limited capacity information processing. *Journal of Experimental Psychology: Human Perception and Performance, 8,* 625–651.

Gaddes, W. (1980). Learning disabilities and brain function: *Neuropsychological approach.* New York: Springer-Verlag.

Geschwind, N., & Galaburda, A. (1987). *Cerebral lateralization.* Cambridge, MA: MIT Press.

Gittelman, R. (1985). Controlled trials of remedial approaches to reading disability. *Journal of Child Psychology and Psychiatry, 26,* 843–846.

Goldstein, D., & Dunden, W. (1987). Affect and cognition in learning disabilities. In S. Ceci (Ed.), *Handbook of cognitive, social, and neuropsychological aspects of learning disabilities* (Vol. 2, pp. 233–249). Hillsdale, NJ: Erlbaum.

Greenberg, M., & Kusche, C. (1989). Cognitive, personal, and social development of deaf children and adolescents. In M. Wang, M. Reynolds, & H. Wallberg (Eds.), *Handbook of special education: Research and practice* (Vol. 3, pp. 95–129). Toronto: Pergamon.

Hammill, D., & Larsen, S. (1983). *Test of written language.* Austin, TX: Pro-ed Publishers.

Hartlage, L., & Telzrow, C. (1983). The neuropsychological basis of educational intervention. *Journal of Learning Disabilities, 16,* 521–528.

Hécaen, H. (1962). Clinical symptomatology in right and left hemispheric lesions. In V. Mountcastle (Ed.), *Interhemispheric relations and cerebral dominance* (pp. 215–243). Baltimore, MD: Johns Hopkins Press.

Hewett, F., & Forness, S. (1974). *Education of exceptional learners.* Boston, MA: Allyn & Bacon.

Hiscock, M., & Bergström, K. (1982). The lengthy persistence of priming effects in dichotic listening. *Neuropsychologia, 20,* 43–53.

Hiscock, M., & Kinsbourne, M. (1980). Asymmetries of selective listening and attention switching in children. *Developmental Psychology, 17,* 70–82.

Horn, W., O'Donnell, J., & Vitulano, L. (1983). Long-term follow-up studies of learning disabled persons. *Journal of Learning Disabilities, 16,* 542–555.

Hugdahl, K. (1988). *Handbook of dichotic listening: Theory, methods and research.* Toronto: Wiley.

Hynd, G., & Cohen, M. (1983). *Dyslexia.* Toronto: Grune & Stratton.

Hynd, G., & Obrzut, J. (1981). *Neuropsychological assessment with school-age children: Issues and procedures.* New York: Grune & Stratton.

Jastak, J., & Jastak, S. (1978). *Wide Range Achievement Test.* Los Angeles, CA: Western Psychological Services.

Kavale, K. (1988). The long-term consequences of learning disabilities. In M. Wang, M. Reynolds, & H. Walberg (Eds.), *Handbook of special education: Research and practice* (Vol. 2, pp. 303–344). Toronto: Pergamon.

Kershner, J. (1985). Ontogeny of hemispheric specialization and relationship of developmental patterns to complex reasoning skills and academic achievement. In C. T. Best (Ed.), *Hemispheric function and collaboration in the child* (pp. 327–360). Toronto: Academic Press.

Kershner, J. (1983). Laterality and learning disabilities: Cerebral dominance as a cognitive process. *Topics in Learning and Learning Disabilities, 3,* 66–74.

Kershner, J. (1988). Dual processing models of learning disability. In D. Molfese & S. Segalowitz (Eds.), *Brain lateralization in children* (pp. 527–546). New York: Guilford Press.

Kershner, J. (1990). Self-concept and IQ as predictors of remedial success in LD children. *Journal of Learning Disabilities, 23,* 368–374.

Kershner, J., Cummings, R., Clarke, K., Hadfield, A., & Kershner, B. (1986). Evaluation of the Tomatis Listening Training Program with learning disabled children. *Canadian Journal of Special Education, 2,* 1–32.

Kershner, J., Cummings, R., Clarke, K., Hadfield, A., & Kershner, B. (1990). Two-year evaluation of the Tomatis Listening Training Program with learning disabled children. *Learning Disability Quarterly, 13,* 43–53.

Kershner, J., Henninger, P., & Cooke, W. (1984). Written recall induces a right hemisphere linguistic advantage for digits in dyslexic children. *Brain & Language, 21,* 105–122.

Kershner, J., Thomas, R., & Callaway, R. (1977). Non-verbal fixation control in young children induces a left-field advantage in digit recall. *Neuropsychologia, 15,* 569–576.

Kimura, D. (1967). Functional asymmetry of the brain in dichotic listening. *Cortex, 3,* 163–178.

Kinsbourne, M. (1970). The cerebral basis of lateral asymmetries in attention. *Acta Psychologica, 33,* 193–201.

Kirk, S., & Gallagher, J. (1983). *Educating exceptional children.* Boston, MA: Houghton-Mifflin.

Koppitz, E. (1971). *Children with learning disabilities: A 5 year follow-up study* (pp. 115–126). New York: Grune & Stratton.

Larsen, E. (1931). A neurologic-etiologic study on 1,000 mental defectives. *Acta Psychiatrica et Neurologica, 6,* 37–54.

Lenneberg, E. (1967). *Biological foundations of language.* New York: Wiley.

Levy, J. (1983). Individual differences in cerebral hemisphere asymmetry: Theoretical issues and experimental considerations. In J. Hellige (Ed.), *Cerebral hemisphere asymmetry* (pp. 465–497). New York: Praeger.

Levy, J., Heller, W., Banich, M., & Burton, L. (1983). Are variations among right-handed individuals in perceptual asymmetries caused by characteristic arousal differences between hemispheres? *Journal of Experimental Psychology: Human Perception and Performance, 9,* 32–62.

Levy, J., Trevarthen, C., & Sperry, R. (1973). Perception of bilateral chimeric figures following hemispheric deconnexion. *Brain, 95,* 61–78.

Lloyd, J. (1988). Direct academic interventions in learning disabilities. In M. Wang, M. Reynolds, & H. Walberg (Eds.), *Handbook of special education: Research and practice* (Vol. 2, pp. 345–366). Toronto: Pergamon.

Locke, J. (1892). Concerning human understanding. In J. St. John (Ed.), *The philosophical works of John Locke*. London: Bell & Sons.

Martin, L. (1986). Assessing current theories of cerebral organization. In S. Ceci (Ed.), *Handbook of cognitive, social, and neuropsychological aspects of learning disabilities* (Vol. 1, pp. 425–439). Hillsdale, NJ: Erlbaum.

McKinney, J. (1988). Research on conceptually and empirically derived subtypes of specific learning disabilities. In M. Wang, M. Reynolds, & H. Walberg (Eds.), *Handbook of special education: Research and practice* (Vol. 2, pp. 253–281). Toronto: Pergamon.

Molfese, D., & Segalowitz, S. (Eds.). (1988). *Brain lateralization in children*. New York: Guilford Press.

Morais, J. (1978). Spatial constraints on attention to speech. In J. Requin (Ed.), *Attention and performance VII* (pp. 231–248). Toronto: Wiley.

Nadel, L. (1988). *The psychobiology of Down syndrome*. Cambridge, MA: MIT Press.

Neysmith-Roy, J. (1980). *Cognitive control functioning and spontaneous speech: Intensive case studies of audio-psycho-phonological remedial training with five dyslexic boys.* Unpublished doctoral thesis, University of Ottawa.

Nichols, P., & Chen, T. (1981). *Minimal brain dysfunction: A prospective study*. Hillsdale, NJ: Erlbaum.

Obler, L., & Fein, D. (Eds.). (1988). *The exceptional brain: The neuropsychology of talent and special abilities*. New York: Guilford Press.

Obrzut, J. (1988). Deficient lateralization in learning-disabled children: Developmental lag or abnormal cerebral organization? In D. Molfese & S. Segalowitz (Eds.), *Brain lateralization in children* (pp. 567–589). New York: Guilford Press.

Ontario Psychological Association. (1984). A review of the Tomatis method. Toronto: Author.

Orton, S. (1937). *Reading, writing, and speech problems in children*. New York: Norton.

Palmaccio, T., Wilson, B., Metlay, W., & Risucci, D. (1984). *Tomatis project follow-up study*. Unpublished.

Phillips, D., & Gates, G. (1982). Representation of the two ears in the auditory cortex: A re-examination. *International Journal of Neuroscience, 16,* 41–46.

Pipe, M. (1988). Atypical laterality and retardation. *Psychological Bulletin, 104,* 343–347.

Poizner, H., Klima, E., & Bellugi, U. (1987). *What the hands reveal about the brain*. Cambridge, MA: MIT Press.

Pribram, K., & McGuinness, D. (1987). Commentary: Brain function and learning disabilities. In S. Ceci (Ed.), *Handbook of cognitive, social, and neuropsychological aspects of learning disabilities* (Vol. 2, pp. 369–373). Hillsdale, NJ: Erlbaum.

Reitan, R. (1983). *Test of Verbal Fluency*. Indianapolis: Neuropsychological Laboratory, Indiana Medical Center.

Reitan, R., & Davidson, L. (1974). *Clinical neuropsychology: Current status and applications:* Washington, DC: Winston & Sons.

Reschly, D. (1987). Learning characteristics of mildly handicapped students: Implications for classification, placement, and programming. In M. Wang, M.

Reynolds, & H. Walberg (Eds.), *Handbook of special education: Research and practice* (Vol. 1, pp. 35–58). Toronto: Pergamon.

Reynolds, C. (1981). Neuropsychological assessment and the habilitation of learning: Considerations in the search for the aptitude x treatment interaction. *School Psychology Review, 10,* 343–349.

Roberts, L. (1966). Central brain mechanisms in speech. *UCLA Forum in Medical Sciences, 4,* 17–36.

Rosenzweig, M. (1951). Representation of the two ears at the auditory cortex. *American Journal of Physiology, 167,* 147–158.

Rourke, B. (Ed.). (1985). *Neuropsychology of learning disabilities: Essential of subtype analysis.* New York: Guilford Press.

Rourke, B., Bakker, D., Fisk, J., & Strang, J. (1983). *Child neuropsychology.* New York: Guilford Press.

Rourke, B., & Fisk, J. (1988). Subtypes of learning disabled children. Implications for a neurodevelopmental model of hemispheric processing. In D. Molfese & S. Segalowitz (Eds.), *Brain lateralization in children* (pp. 547–565) New York: Guilford Press.

Rourke, B., & Russell, D. (1983). *The Tomatis method applied to older learning disabled children: An evaluation* (Draft No. 1). Unpublished.

Schnitzer, L. (1974). *Listening, phonation, laterality, and reading effects of the aurelle therapy of Alfred Tomatis with reading difficulties.* Unpublished doctoral thesis, University of Toronto.

Seguin, E. (1864). *Idiocy and its treatment by the physiological method.* Albany, NY: Brandow.

Sheehan, R., & Klein, N. (1989). Infant assessment. In M. Wang, M. Reynolds, & H. Walberg (Eds.), *Handbook of special education: Research and practice* (Vol. 3, pp. 243–258). Toronto: Pergamon.

Short, E., Feagans, L., McKinney, J., & Appelbaum, M. (1986). Longitudinal stability of LD subtypes based on age and IQ achievement discrepancies. *Learning Disability Quarterly, 9,* 214–225.

Siegel, L. (1988). Evidence that IQ scores are irrelevant to the definition and analysis of reading disability. *Canadian Journal of Psychology, 42,* 201–215.

Snowling, M., Stackhouse, J., & Rack, J. (1986). Phonological dysplexia and dysgraphia–A developmental analysis. Cognitive Neuropsychology, *3,* 309–339.

Stanovich, K. (1988). Explaining the difference between the dyslexia and the garden-variety poor reader: The phonological-core variable difference model. *Journal of Learning Disabilities, 21,* 590–604.

Strauss, A., & Kephart, N. (1955). *Psychopathology and education of the brain-injured child* (Vol. 2). New York: Grune & Stratton.

Strauss, A., & Lehtinen, L. (1947). *Psychopathology and education of the brain-injured child* (Vol. 1). New York: Grune & Stratton.

Swanson, L. (1988). Toward a metatheory of learning disabilities. *Journal of Learning Disabilities, 21,* 196–209.

Tannock, R., Kershner, J., & Oliver, J. (1984). Do individuals with Down syndrome possess right hemisphere language dominance? *Cortex, 20,* 221–231.

Tomatis, A. (1978). *Education and dyslexia.* Quebec: Les Editions.

Torgesen, J. (1977). Memorization processes in reading disabled children. *Journal of Educational Psychology, 69,* 571–578.

Wang, M., Reynolds, M., & Walberg, H. (Eds.). (1987). *Handbook of Special Education: Vol. 1. Learner characteristics and adaptive education.* Toronto: Pergamon.

Wang, M., Reynolds, M., & Walberg, H. (Eds.). (1988). *Handbook of Special Education: Vol. 2. Mildly handicapped conditions.* Toronto: Pergamon.

Wang, M., Reynolds, M., & Walberg, H. (Eds.). (1989). *Handbook of Special Education: Vol. 3. Low incidence conditions.* Toronto: Pergamon.

Wigan, A. (1985). *Duality of the mind.* New York: Bogen & Simon. (Original work published 1844)

Wright, D. (1987). Intelligence and achievement: A factor analytic and canonical correlational study. *Journal of Psychoeducational Assessment, 3,* 236–247.

Ysseldyke, J., & Algozzine, B. (1984). *Introduction to special education.* Boston, MA: Houghton-Mifflin.

Zarske, J. (1982). Neuropsychological intervention approaches for handicapped children. *Journal of Research and Development in Education, 15,* 66–75.

CHAPTER TWENTY-SEVEN

On the Relevance of Neuropsychological Data to Learning Disabilities

Merrill Hiscock
Cheryl K. Hiscock

I. Introduction

Articles and monographs devoted to neuropsychological aspects of learning disabilities (LD) have proliferated in the past two decades. In light of the current popularity of neural explanations for LD, it may seem unfashionable and even anachronistic to question the usefulness of neuropsychological evidence. Nonetheless, in this chapter we do just that. We point out some of the factors that limit the value of neuropsychological assessments and ask if neuropsychology is not being "oversold" to educators responsible for teaching LD children.

Our argument begins with our observations of how LD children are handled in medical centers. Irrespective of whether a child is referred by parents, school officials, or a physician, the case typically is assigned to a multidisciplinary unit identified by a name such as learning disabilities clinic or developmental disabilities team. The unit includes specialists representing several clinical disciplines, for example, clinical psychology, neuropsychology, speech pathology, social work, occupational therapy, physical therapy, and special education. Typically the unit is directed by a physician, who may be a child psychiatrist, pediatrician, pediatric neurologist, or physiatrist. The child's history is taken, previous academic and medical records are examined, and the child is assessed by various team members. A meeting is then held to discuss the findings and to reach a consensus regarding the nature of the problem and recommendations for its amelioration.

A skeptical observer might characterize the evaluation process in the following way. The child has a problem that is by definition an educational problem, namely, difficulty in learning. Because the problem cannot plausibly be attributed to the child's home or school environment, those responsible for the child's education seek a biological explanation. Once general mental deficiency has been ruled out through psychological testing, a more circumscribed defect is suspected. At this juncture the child may be referred to the learning disabilities clinic, where the specialists assess those functions that they are trained to examine. Depending on the findings, the child is given a diagnostic label and the educational system is given a description of the child's "deficits" and perhaps some recommendations for teaching the child. Meanwhile, the child returns to school, where he or she continues to experience the learning problems that precipitated this chain of events.

Physicians, as a rule, do not ask schoolteachers for advice in treating children's medical problems. Why, then, do teachers seek medical help in treating children's educational problems? The answer seems to lie in the assumption that LD children suffer from a neurological disorder. But even if that assumption were universally correct, medical referral is not necessarily a logical or constructive step. To justify medical referral, the teacher must further assume that the child will benefit in some way by having a medical diagnosis.

Do LD children suffer from a neurological disorder and, if so, will medical diagnosis of that disorder help to ameliorate the learning problem? In the remainder of this chapter we examine the arguments and the evidence.

II. The Disease Model of Learning Disabilities

A. Rationale and Historical Development

Neural explanations for reading disability originated in the nineteenth-century and early twentieth-century observations of physicians such as Morgan, Hinshelwood, and Dejerine, who reported cases of congenital as well as acquired "word blindness" (see Benson, 1981; Benton, 1980; Geschwind, 1962; Spreen, 1989). Because acquired word blindness (alexia) in the adult was often associated with lesions involving the angular gyrus of the left cerebral hemisphere, congenital word blindness (congenital dyslexia) in the child was generally assumed to stem from an abnormality of the same region.

The existence of a distinct disorder called dyslexia, caused by a specific neurological abnormality, seems incompatible with the diversity of "symptoms" seen in LD children. However, once neurologically oriented LD theorists began to recognize the heterogeneity of LD, there was no shortage of neurological syndromes to serve as models for different subtypes of LD. Acquired alexia itself can be divided into three or four different syndromes (Benson, 1981; Friedman & Albert, 1985). In addition, LD can be modeled after adult neurological syndromes other than alexia. As pointed out by Spreen (1989), Orton proposed in 1937 that different varieties of dyslexia could be construed as developmental forms of alexia, agraphia, word deafness, apraxia, and mixed syndromes. Thus Orton's work foreshadowed contemporary subtyping efforts (e.g., Boder, 1973; Doehring & Hoshko, 1977; Kinsbourne & Warrington, 1963; Mattis, French, & Rapin, 1975; Myklebust, 1965; Petrauskas & Rourke, 1979; Rourke, 1989), many of which are influenced by neurological syndromes other than acquired alexia.

B. Empirical Support

Ordinarily a disease is diagnosed clinically on the basis of a characteristic symptom or cluster of symptoms. Depending on the degree to which the etiology and pathophysiology of the disease are understood, the clinical diagnosis may be confirmed by other evidence, such as the presence of a particular pathogen in a tissue culture. Learning disabilities researchers have attempted to specify the neuropathology underlying LD, but without much success.

A few autopsy studies suggest that certain individuals with severe language and learning disorders have structural defects in the cerebral hemispheres (Drake, 1968; Galaburda & Kemper, 1979; Galaburda, Sherman, Rosen, Aboitiz, & Geschwind, 1985; Landau, Goldstein, & Kleffner, 1960; Levine, Hier, & Calvanio, 1981). Most notably, Galaburda et al. (1985), who studied four consecutive brains of LD males, found that each brain had regions of deranged cortical organization (dysplasias) as well as clusters of displaced neurons (ectopias). These abnormalities, though distributed throughout the cortex, were most prominent in the perisylvian region of the left hemisphere. Whether these findings can be generalized to the entire population of LD children remains to be seen. Moreover, as acknowledged by Galaburda et al., the significance of the abnormalities cannot be determined in the absence of comparison data from brains of normal readers.

None of the four brains examined by Galaburda et al. (1985) showed the usual asymmetry of a cortical region known as the planum temporale, that is, none had a larger planum on the left side. Although symmetry in this region is fairly common, it is not so common that one would expect to find it in four consecutive cases. Galaburda et al. speculated that dyslexia is associated with a combination of planum temporale symmetry and cortical abnormalities rather than either characteristic by itself. In two studies based on CT scanning, it was reported that the usual left-sided superiority in the width of the posterior cerebral hemispheres was reversed in LD children (Hier, LeMay,

Rosenberger, & Perlo, 1978; Rosenberger & Hier, 1980), but these findings received little support in two other studies (Denckla, LeMay, & Chapman, 1985; Haslam, Dalby, Johns, & Rademaker, 1981).

It has been suggested that testosterone inhibits development of the left hemisphere prenatally (Geschwind & Behan, 1982; Geschwind & Galaburda, 1985). From this central hypothesis, Geschwind and his associates constructed a comprehensive model linking LD, sex differences, left-handedness, and immune-system disorders. Although Kinsbourne (1986, 1988) has confirmed some of the statistical correlations predicted by the model, he failed to find any concordance between cognitive and immune disorders. Since the statistical independence of LD and immune disorders would rule out a common causal factor (e.g., testosterone), Kinsbourne (1988) favors an explanation in terms of maternal immune disease, that is, cognitive deficit resulting from adverse effects of the mother's immune disease on the fetus, not from an endogenous influence such as fetal testosterone.

Anomalous hemispheric specialization can be distinguished in principle from pathological development of the left hemisphere. Learning disabilities conceivably could stem from an unusual pattern of hemispheric specialization, which is also reflected in weak, variable, mixed, or otherwise anomalous laterality (handedness, footedness, eyedness, visual half-field asymmetry, dichotic listening asymmetry, etc.). Beginning with Orton (1937), many writers have posited an association between anomalous laterality and LD. However, despite extensive study, consistent empirical support for this association is lacking (see reviews by Benton, 1975; Bryden, 1988; Corballis, 1983; Critchley, 1970; Geschwind, 1982; Gladstone & Best, 1985; Harris, 1985, 1988; Hiscock & Kinsbourne, 1980, 1982, 1987; Kershner, 1985; Kinsbourne & Hiscock, 1978, 1981, 1983; Leong, 1987; Naylor, 1980; Pirozzolo, 1985; Rudel, 1985; Satz, 1976; Vernon, 1957, 1971; Young & Ellis, 1981; Zangwill, 1962). Provided that the brain is healthy, anomalous lateralization of functions (as in many left-handers) appears to have little or no deleterious effect on the quality of the functions in question (Hiscock & Kinsbourne, 1987; Kinsbourne, 1988).

Another link between LD and brain dysfunction is the frequent occurrence of neurological abnormalities in LD children (Fabian & Jacobs, 1981; Gottesman, Hankin, Levinson, & Beck, 1984; Lowick & Spreen, 1990; Spreen, 1988, 1989; Tupper, 1987). These abnormalities include hard signs (unequivocal abnormalities of nervous system functioning) as well as soft signs. The latter may be understood either as less severe variants of hard signs or as characteristics (such as synergistic movements) that would have been normal at an earlier stage of development but should have disappeared with further maturation of the nervous system (Kinsbourne, 1975).

The association of neurological signs with LD helps to confirm the existence of brain dysfunction in a substantial proportion of individuals with LD, but the signs themselves are not helpful in understanding the neural factors responsible for the LD. Not only are the signs diverse within and across individuals, but they usually reflect dysfunctions that have little direct relevance to learning (Kinsbourne, 1973) and they are surprisingly variable over time (Lowick & Spreen, 1990). Yet, they do seem to index the severity of neurological impairment insofar as they are significantly correlated with long-term outcome (Spreen, 1989).

Various investigators have reported significant differences between LD children and controls in EEG or event-related brain potentials (ERP). Leisman and Ashkenazi (1980), for example, found spectral EEG differences between dyslexics and controls in the left parietal–occipital region during an eyes-closed resting condition. Dyslexic subjects showed greater shared activity (coherence) within a hemisphere, whereas controls showed greater coherence between corresponding sites of the left and right hemispheres. Using large samples of normal and LD children, as well as children at risk for neurological disorders, Ahn et al. (1980) demonstrated a strikingly high incidence of abnormal EEG findings in the clinical groups. Duffy and his colleagues (Duffy, Denckla, Bartels, Sandini, & Keissling, 1980; Duffy, Denckla, & Sandini, 1980), using a complex technique for the spatial mapping of EEG and ERP, found average differences between dyslexic boys and controls in the left posterior and medial frontal regions (see Duffy, McAnulty, & Schachter, 1984). Several other ERP studies have also yielded significant differences between LD children and controls (e.g., Bakker, Licht, Kok, & Bouma, 1980; Dainer et al., 1981; Johnstone et al., 1984; Shucard, Cummins, & McGee, 1984).

It is impossible to draw any simple conclusions from the EEG and ERP studies, for the studies differ widely not only with respect to details of the findings but also with respect to subject selection, choice of tasks, recording method, and data analysis. Pirozzolo (1985) has suggested that, in future studies, it may be necessary to study homogeneous subgroups of LD individuals so that specific ERP patterns can be related to specific kinds of reading problems. For the present, one can only conclude that the literature contains ample evidence of electrophysiological differences between LD children and their controls.

C. Interpretive Problems

Empirical support for the disease model of LD is constrained by the great diversity of symptoms. If there existed a disorder known as dyslexia, with pathognomonic signs or symptoms (e.g., letter and word reversals), then investigators could focus their attention on finding the corresponding neurological deficit. The diversity and variability of its symptoms suggest that dyslexia is not a unitary disorder but a broad category of disorders (Applebee, 1971). Each of the disorders (subtypes) has its own distinctive pattern of behavioral deficits and, presumably, its own pattern of underlying brain dysfunction.

The situation is further complicated by the existence of various classification schemes that are not readily related to each other. It is not even clear how one should go about delineating subtypes of LD children. Satz and Morris (1981) note that subtyping schemes traditionally have been based on a so-called "clinical–inferential" approach in which children are grouped according to (1) inferred etiology, (2) performance on cognitive tests, or (3) measures of academic achievement. Alternatively, LD subtypes may be defined using multivariate analysis of either cognitive skill or achievement data. Satz and Morris point out several pitfalls and shortcomings in each of these approaches to subtyping.

The subtyping problem complicates immeasurably the task of demonstrating a brain basis for LD. Instead of a single disorder, we face a bewildering variety of subtypes and classification schemes. In the midst of such confusion, it is difficult to specify the pattern of brain dysfunction that might be expected in any particular LD child.

III. Criticisms of the Disease Model

Many clinical psychologists find the medical model to be an unsatisfactory framework for understanding behavioral disorders. Korchin (1976) identified five problems associated with the medical model, which Phares (1988) has summarized as follows.

1. The model encourages biological rather than social or psychological views of mental problems. It becomes all too easy to tranquilize problems away rather than attack their psychological roots with psychological interventions.
2. Such a model stimulates us to view patients as passive recipients of medical treatment and wisdom. The patient becomes, not an active partner as in psychotherapy, but a passive consumer. The "doctor" becomes an authority figure and the "patient" an inferior figure; the relationship is not so much cooperative as it is authoritarian.
3. The model tends to inflate the value of a medical education for therapists and make the psychological skills of many mental health practitioners subordinate to those of the physician–psychiatrist.
4. The model can lead to an overemphasis on medical-like psychiatric

diagnoses and encourage a labelling and even stigmatizing process that is usually unproductive.

5. Finally, this model has a tendency to focus our attention on the pathologies and weaknesses of patients. It can easily obscure the presence of skills and latent coping abilities that exist in the patient. In short, an undue emphasis is placed on the negative. [p. 109]

Not all of these problems are as pertinent to LD as to psychopathology, but it is surprisingly easy to translate each one into words that do apply to LD. The first of the five problems, for example, reminds us of the tendency of "neurologize" LD and the consequent tendency to de-emphasize the environment in which the child must function and the possibilities for changing that environment.

The second problem may apply to any disorder of childhood simply because of the difference in status and power between the adult caregiver and the child "patient." It is unrealistic to expect the kind of cooperative relationship that might be established between a psychotherapist and his or her adult client. Nonetheless, the medical model of LD reinforces the child's passivity. This becomes clear if we contrast neurological concepts of LD with the Chinese and Japanese belief that children who fail to learn are either poorly motivated or not being taught effectively (Stevenson *et al.*, 1982). Educators are much less likely to hold the child responsible for academic failure if the child is seen as having a learning disability than if the child is thought to be unwilling to apply the necessary effort.

The relevance to LD of Korchin's third criticism varies from one setting to another. If the child is evaluated in a medical center, responsibility for directing and coordinating the work of the various specialists typically will reside with a physician who will integrate the findings of the different specialists and make the final decisions regarding diagnosis and recommendations. Apart from aggrandizing the importance of medical training, medical leadership of the clinical team tends to ensure that the psychoeducational perspective is subordinated to the medical perspective.

The fourth criticism stems from the third. If an educational problem (e.g., poor development of reading skills) is converted into a medical diagnosis (e.g., dyslexia), there may be increased risk of stigmatizing the child. Diagnosing and labeling may be even more harmful for LD children than for adults with mental disorders because (1) children may be more susceptible in general to the adverse effects of labeling, and (2) appropriate diagnosing of adults with mental disorders will, in some instances, lead to beneficial pharmacological intervention, but one would not expect this to happen in the case of LD (Werry, 1981). Although some individuals may feel that they have benefited from being labeled as learning disabled, we suspect that a diagnosis of LD is beneficial only when it supplants a less desirable label such as dull or mentally retarded, or when it attracts educational resources that otherwise would be withheld. Neither of these potential benefits logically depends on a medical or quasi-medical diagnosis.

Korchin's final criticism of the medical model is that the model emphasizes weaknesses rather than strengths. This probably applies to LD even more than to behavioral disorders in the adult. In fact, an emphasis on deficits is a defining characteristic of neuropsychological assessment (Lezak, 1983). Although the evaluation and treatment of LD children need not be focused entirely on weaknesses (Holmes-Bernstein & Waber, 1990), attention to the child's strengths ironically may be viewed as a manifestation of pessimism because it may lead to compensatory strategies designed to circumvent the child's deficits rather than strategies designed to overcome those deficits.

IV. Alternatives to the Disease Model

Many contemporary definitions of LD, such as the definition embodied in United States Public Law 94-142, incorporate the notion of an underlying processing deficit or a presumed central nervous system dysfunction. Thus, even if LD is not defined explicitly as a neurological disorder, the definition implies such a disorder. It is possible, however, to define LD in a way that does not beg the question of an underlying neurological defect.

Kinsbourne (1973) provides a useful general context for understanding LD:

> School problems result from factors of three types: environmental, emotional, and developmental. The great bulk of illiteracy in this country derives from socioeconomic adversity and cultural alienation that presents a primarily political rather than a medical challenge. But some children, even when offered adequate schooling under tolerable conditions, fail to achieve at a level to be expected from normally intelligent children at that age. Such children often also appear to be emotionally disturbed, and it may be difficult to decide what is the primary cause of the school failure. [p. 697]

Starting with this broad overview of school problems, Kinsbourne (1973) proceeded to pinpoint the central feature of LD as "unexpected school failure . . . the child doing less well than his parents or teachers expected" (p. 697). Learning disabilities, then, are seen not only as instances of academic underachieving but, more specifically, as underachieving that cannot be attributed to any of several common causes. This approach to LD, which has been described as diagnosis by *exclusion* and *discrepancy* (Leong, 1987), seems to have grown out of fashion. However, it enjoys the important advantage of being agnostic with respect to specific etiology. Learning disability is attributed to intrinsic factors, but the nature of those factors is an open question.

The "exclusion" part of this definition is difficult to avoid. Certain environmental factors—for example, incompetent teaching—as well as certain emotional factors—for example, grief reaction to the loss of a parent—must be excluded from the definition of LD if the definition is to have a meaning more specific than school failure or underachievement. Delineating LD in this way does not compel one to adopt a neurological model of LD. The critical question is whether the remaining factors are restricted by definition to the realm of known or presumed neurological abnormality.

The "discrepancy" component of the definition is more problematic. Diagnosing LD on the basis of discrepancy between ability and performance is often interpreted to mean that a child must have average or nearly average IQ in order to be categorized as LD, but there are logical as well as pragmatic arguments against restricting the LD label to children of average IQ (Cruickshank, 1980; Gaddes, 1985; Siegel, 1989; Spreen, 1989). On the other hand, dropping the requirement for normal intellectual ability tends to blur the distinction between LD children and children whose academic failure reflects below-average general intellectual ability (Leong, 1989).

The distinction between LD children and those who are intellectually dull can be reinstated by postulating processing deficits or central nervous system dysfunction in LD children (but not in dull children). However, as we stated previously, this begs the question of neurological abnormality. There are at least four alternative approaches to LD that do not require postulating the existence of a neurological deficit. These approaches emphasize, respectively, normal variation in academic skill, metalinguistic and cognitive development, speed of processing, and domain-specific knowledge.

A. LD as a Consequence of Normal Variation

A learning problem is a learning problem even if it reflects normal variation in some aspect of cognitive or linguistic development. As Galton pointed out more than a century ago (1869/1961), human abilities assort themselves according to a Gaussian distribution, with most scores falling near the population average. The greater the deviation from average, the less frequent the score. Approximately half the scores fall above the average and approximately half fall below. Applying Galton's principle to learning ability, we recognize that half of the children in any population will fall below the population average with respect to any given skill. Depending on the criteria for LD, a variable proportion of these below-average learners will be classified as LD.

In fact, somewhat more than half of the general population seems to fall below the average in intellectual ability. Spreen (1989) has recapitulated the evidence for a "heavy" tail at the lower end of the frequency distribution for IQ in the general population (Dingman & Tarjan, 1960; Roberts, 1952). It appears that a smaller distribution of IQs, with a mean of 32 and standard deviation of 16, is superimposed on the larger distribution with its mean of 100 and standard deviation of 16. The generally accepted explanation for this finding is that the smaller distribution reflects scores of brain-damaged individuals. Spreen points out an important corollary of this explanation: ". . . while brain damage may account for a large proportion of intellectually handicapped persons, another proportion can be viewed as part of the normal distribution of any multifactorial human trait" (p. 393).

Admittedly, many of the children falling toward the bottom of the normal IQ distribution would not be given an LD label. Those with the lowest scores would be regarded as mentally retarded. Others might be excluded from the LD category by a definition that demands average IQ or a substantial discrepancy between IQ and scholastic achievement. However, Spreen (1989) points out that skills more specific than IQ—such as reading ability—seem to be distributed in the same manner as IQs, that is, in a Gaussian distribution with an excess number of scores in the lower tail of the curve (Miles & Haslum, 1986; Yule & Rutter, 1976; Yule, Rutter, Berger, & Thompson, 1974). This implies that a disease model of LD can be only partly correct. Whereas the excess number of deficient scores may be attributable to neurological dysfunction, other equally low scores in the distribution may be attributable to normal variation. In Spreen's (1989) words, "This excursion into epidemiological studies leads . . . to the tentative conclusion that a certain proportion of dyslexics must be expected on the basis of a normal distribution of abilities alone. Not all dyslexics are necessarily neurologically impaired." [p. 393]

B. Metalinguistic and Cognitive–Developmental Explanations for LD

Processing-deficit models of LD are vulnerable to the criticism that they fail to account for the specificity and severity of children's learning problems (Morrison & Manis, 1982; Vellutino, 1979). Visuoperceptual impairment (Cruickshank, 1972) is a good example. To be plausible, the deficit must be sufficiently selective as to disrupt reading (or spelling or calculation) quite dramatically without having a marked effect on other functions. But what kind of visuoperceptual deficit would disrupt reading while sparing visual perception in other activities of the child's life? What kind of deficit would disrupt the reading of words while sparing the reading of letters and numbers? Empirical support for the perceptual-deficit hypothesis is weak, as is support for explanations based on deficits in serial ordering, attention, and short-term memory (Morrison & Manis, 1982).

The specificity of reading disability can be accounted for better by regarding it as a linguistic disorder. This perspective follows from the view that reading is parasitic on language (Rozin & Gleitman, 1977). Wagner and Torgesen (1987) delineated three lines of research in which reading acquisition is related to the processing of language sounds. One of these lines of research concerns "phonological recoding," or the translation of text into its phonological representation prior to lexical access (McCusker, Hillinger, & Bias, 1981). Another line of research concerns "phonetic recoding to maintain information in working memory." Especially for the beginning reader, an efficient speech-based storage system is required to facilitate the blending of sounds to form words (Baddeley, 1979, 1981).

Wagner and Torgesen (1987) describe a third line of research, which involves concepts with names such as phonological, linguistic, and metalinguistic awareness (e.g., Gleitman & Rozin, 1977; Lewkowicz, 1980; Liberman, 1970; Mattingly, 1972, 1984; Rozin & Gleitman, 1977). The basic premise is that awareness of phonological characteristics of the language conveys a number of advantages to the child who is learning to read. Difficulties in learning to read can be attributed to the child's lack of linguistic knowledge (normally acquired through experience in listening and speaking) or to the child's inability to apply this linguistic knowledge to the written word. The child who does not possess or cannot access adequate information about phonology "will find the correspondence between symbol and sound capricious at best" (Wagner & Torgesen, 1987, p. 192).

The importance of phonological competence is illustrated by Bradley and Bryant's (1985) finding that the ability of 4- and 5-year-olds to detect rhyming and alliteration is predictive of subsequent reading and spelling ability even after the effects of IQ, vocabulary, and memory are eliminated. Insofar as training in rhyming and alliteration was associated with improved reading and spelling, Bradley and Bryant (1985) established a causal link between phonological skill and the development of academic skills.

The psycholinguistic approach to reading may be applied to syntactic and semantic knowledge as well as phonological knowledge (e.g., Guthrie, 1973; Vogel, 1974; Wiig, Semel, & Crouse, 1973). Irrespective of level of analysis, the approach emphasizes "how children utilize the linguistic knowledge that they already have in order to learn to read" (Leong, 1987, p. 148). The child's experience in speaking and listening to speech provides a background of linguistic knowledge, for example, knowledge about the grammatical structure of sentences. To the extent that the child can access this implicit knowledge when learning to read, he or she will be able to extract information from written language.

Since the development of linguistic knowledge is a component of overall cognitive development, one could place children's acquisition of academic skills within a general cognitive–developmental framework. Chall (1983), for example, has described stages of reading development in the context of Piagetian theory. Reading is viewed as problem solving, and the child progresses from one reading stage to the next as a consequence of interacting with the environment. This approach has several advantages, including an ability to account for different manifestations of reading disability as stagnation at different developmental stages (Leong, 1987).

Ironically, the progression from phonological factors to broader metalinguistic factors and, ultimately, to cognitive development leads us back to a depiction of reading difficulties that sometimes transcends the realm of language. Indeed there seems to be increasing evidence that difficulty in learning to read may reflect a developmental problem more general than the poor reading itself (Crowder, 1984; Mann, 1984; Morrison, 1984; Wolford & Fowler, 1984). This does not necessitate a return to neurological-deficit models. On the contrary, the problems found to be associated with reading disabilities—for example, difficulty in learning irregular rule systems (Morrison, 1984) or failure to make efficient use of incomplete stimulus information (Wolford & Fowler, 1984)—differ considerably from the simple processing deficits of neurological models. Moreover, it is not generally known whether the problems associated with reading disability are causes, effects, or just correlates of impaired reading.

C. LD as Slowness

The speed with which verbal information is processed may have special relevance to reading difficulties (Denckla & Rudel, 1976; Leong, 1987; Wolf, 1984). Lovett (1984a, 1984b, 1987) has applied to LD the LaBerge and Samuels (1974) distinction between reading accuracy and reading automaticity. Dividing LD children into accuracy-disabled and rate-disabled subgroups, Lovett (1987) found that children in the former subgroup had pervasive impairments that included "all aspects of . . . reading systems and all indices of reading and spelling achievement" (p. 254). These children showed a profound inability to remember or produce sound–symbol correspondences in either reading or spelling. In contrast, the rate-disabled children resembled fluent readers in almost all respects except reading speed. The rate-disabled children were less accurate than fluent readers in reading connected text and in selecting the correct spelling of words from an array, but Lovett (1987) argued that the lower accuracy of rate-disabled children on these tasks was secondary to the slowness of their reading, which made them more susceptible to contextual interference.

Lovett's work indicates that at least one subgroup of LD children may lack many of the language-based abnormalities characteristic of LD. These rate-disabled readers exhibit instead a slowness that is specific to the processing of visual language. Rather than viewing accuracy- and rate-disabled subgroups as dichotomous categories, Lovett (1987) suggests that these two groups occupy different regions of a continuum ranging from normal fluent reading to disabled reading.

D. LD as a Lack of Domain-Specific Knowledge

The disease model of LD is explicitly rejected by Brown and Campione (1986), who argue that it leads to a misplaced emphasis on the hypothetical sources of a learning problem rather than the problem itself:

> The "leap to instruction" is a perennial problem in the area of learning disabilities. Imagine the following scenario. A child is first brought to a practitioner's attention because she is experiencing difficulty in reading. After she is subjected to a battery of diagnostic tests, it is determined that she has particular problems with auditory short-term memory and that this deficit is stable and reliable across situations and over time, in itself a controversial claim at best . . . . Traditionally, the most likely prescription for remediation would be practice on tasks of auditory short-term memory presented out of the context of any academic task of which auditory short-term memory could be assumed to be a component. The child may well show improvement on the auditory short-term memory task, but is it safe to assume that she will show a concomitant improvement in reading, the original source of her difficulty? [p. 1060]

This is not merely a criticism of models based on simple processing deficits such as auditory short-term memory, visual perception, serial ordering, and so forth. Brown and Campione's (1986) criticism is more fundamental: The authors reject the entire rationale for diagnosing and treating LD as if it were a medical disorder.

Brown and Campione (1986) point out two critical problems inherent in the traditional strategy for diagnosis and intervention. First, measurements of the underlying deficit (e.g., memory) tend to vary across time and settings. In addition, even if training should ameliorate the underlying deficit, that training may not transfer to the academic skill in question (e.g., reading). From the alternative perspective suggested by Brown and Campione, learning disorders are seen as failures to acquire specific information or skills. The deficit is dynamic, not static, and domain specific, not general. Accordingly, Brown and Campione advocate "dynamic assessment" methods, which focus on the academic skills in question and which attempt to determine not only the child's present knowledge in that domain, but also his or her potential for new learning, as well as the kind of assistance that will best facilitate learning. Remediation consists of expert guidance within a supportive context (cf. Vygotsky, 1978), which could be provided by a teacher, cooperative learning group, or computer-based tutoring system. Emphasis is placed on the achievement of conceptual understanding, rather than just accuracy and speed, and on the transition from externally assisted performance to independent competence.

V. Neuropsychological Assessment

In light of our examination of the disease model and some alternatives to this model, what can we conclude about the role of neuropsychological assessment in the diagnosis and treatment of LD children? To a large degree, one's valuation of neuropsychological assessment must hinge on one's belief in the disease model of LD. From the perspective of Brown and Campione (1986), for example, neuropsychological evaluation would be superfluous. Conclusions about deficits in visual perception or short-term verbal memory would be regarded with a skepticism based not only on doubts about the general validity of those conclusions across tasks and situations, but also about their relevance to the remediation of the child's learning problems.

What if one accepts the disease model of LD? Is neuropsychological assessment then useful? Or, to make the question more specific, what can one expect to learn, under the best of circumstances, from neuropsychological evaluation of an LD child?

A. Lesion Detection and Localization

The power of neuropsychological tests to find cerebral lesions is ascertained through clinicoanatomical correlation. Traditionally, post-mortem examination of the brain has provided the necessary information about size, locus, and nature of the lesion. The current availability of refined imaging techniques now makes it possible to identify structural lesions and localized physiological abnormalities in living patients. Either approach allows the neuropsychologist to determine whether a particular test is sensitive to, and selective for, lesions in a particular brain region.

The applicability of this confirmatory process to LD children is limited. Learning-disabled children in most instances will outlive the investigator, thus eliminating any opportunity for post-mortem examination, and there usually is no medical justification for exposing them to ionizing radiation or other risks inherent in the various imaging techniques (Haslam *et al.*, 1981). Therefore, the clinician must extrapolate localizing information from adult clinical populations. This extrapolation is a highly questionable process (Hiscock,

1990). Neuropsychological findings from one adult clinical population may not apply to another (cf. Sperry, 1982; Whitaker & Ojemann, 1977), and there is even less justification for generalizing from adults to children. The problem is compounded significantly if the adults' deficits are acquired but the children have a developmental disorder (See Towbin, 1978, for a description of the distinctive neuropathology associated with damage to the premature fetal- or neonatal brain.)

Without independent confirmation of lesion locus, the clinician does not know whether there is a lesion, much less where it is. Consequently, the term, dysfunction, is often substituted for the more concrete term, lesion. But the concept of dysfunction, when used in this way, is based on behavior and not the brain. A dysfunction is inferred from impaired performance in relation to appropriate norms. It cannot be localized except by establishing the existence of a corresponding structural or physiological abnormality. To claim that there is localized dysfunction (e.g., dysfunction of the left temporal lobe) on the sole basis of neuropsychological data is to imply the existence of a focal lesion for which there is no anatomical or physiological evidence. Given the small likelihood of ever confirming the existence of this putative lesion in an LD child, whether through autopsy or imaging, the neuropsychologist's diagnosis is well defended from disproof.

The concept of brain dysfunction in LD children resembles the concept of organicity in psychiatric patients. Traditionally, a patient suspected of organicity would be referred to a clinical psychologist, who often inferred organicity from the patient's performance on instruments such as the Wechsler Adult Intelligence Scale, the Minnesota Multiphasic Personality Inventory, and the Bender Motor Gestalt Test. If the patient appeared "organic" to the psychiatrist and if the psychologist's test battery suggested organicity, then the patient was declared to be organically impaired. In the absence of external criteria for organicity, the psychiatrist and psychologist operated within a closed system. Watson (1977) speculated that thousands of patients have been misdiagnosed as organic according to this circular logic. Whereas the validation of neuropsychological instruments with certain groups of adult patients puts the neuropsychologist on somewhat firmer ground, the parallel between diagnosis of brain dysfunction in LD and organicity in psychiatry is disturbing.

B. Lateralized Dysfunction and Anomalous Lateralization

Several hemisphere-related models of LD have been proposed and, with a modicum of ingenuity, many others could be added to the list of possibilities (Hiscock & Kinsbourne, 1982). Of these various models, two are particularly likely to be invoked as a result of neuropsychological assessment. One of these is the unilateral-deficit model, that is, the notion that LD children have dysfunctions that are largely restricted to either the left or the right hemisphere (e.g., Bakker 1979, 1981, 1983). The second is the claim that hemispheric specialization is absent, diminished, or delayed in the LD child (e.g., Witelson, 1977).

Can neuropsychological tests differentiate left- and right-hemisphere dysfunction in the LD child? This issue is similar to the issue of localization as discussed previously. Again there is no assurance that data regarding the effects of acquired lesions in adults can be extrapolated to developmental disorders in children. More relevant information comes from studies of children with unilateral lesions acquired early in life, including those who have had one hemisphere surgically removed. Early left-sided damage seems to have a disproportionate effect on the performance of certain sensitive tests of language and verbal memory, and early right-sided damage seems to have a greater effect on certain spatial functions (Dennis, 1980a, 1980b; Dennis & Kohn, 1975; Dennis & Whitaker, 1976, 1977; Vargha-Khadem & Isaacs, 1985; Vargha-Khadem, O'Gorman, & Watters, 1985). These effects, however, are often subtle, even in children who have had an entire hemisphere removed, and some of the conclusions are undermined by methodological and statistical flaws (Bishop, 1983). Consequently, there is little justification for inferring exclusively left-hemispheric dysfunction in LD children on the basis of poor performance on verbal tests. Bilateral dysfunction is more probable.

Laterality is particularly problematic because of the prevalent misconception that left- and right-hemisphere lesions can be readily distinguished on the basis of the discrepancy between verbal and performance IQ. Even in the adult, low verbal IQ is not a reliable indicator of acquired left-hemisphere damage, nor is low performance IQ a reliable indicator of right-hemisphere damage (Todd, Coolidge, & Satz, 1977). The ability of IQ tests to indicate side of unilateral brain damage acquired early in life is even less impressive (Dennis & Whitaker, 1977; Vargha-Khadem et al., 1985; Woods, 1980a, 1980b). Whereas the verbal–performance IQ discrepancy may differentiate a group of children with left-sided damage from a group with right-sided damage, such outcomes are not sufficiently frequent or robust as to justify making conclusions about lateralized dysfunction in the individual child.

As a rule, when one wishes to determine the presence of a lateralized cerebral lesion, relatively simple perceptual and motor tasks are more informative than tests of complex functioning (Smith & Campbell, 1979). Useful indices include limb weakness, impaired tactual perception, diminished motor control on one side, and reduced hand and foot size on one side of the body (Hiscock & Hiscock, 1990). These kinds of abnormality, if sufficiently pronounced, will be noted in a neurological examination. Neuropsychological assessment, because of the greater sensitivity of its measures, may identify subtle asymmetries that are missed in the neurological exam. Of course, as the degree of asymmetry decreases, so does the likelihood that the asymmetry is abnormal.

In addition to unfounded conclusions about left- or right-hemisphere dysfunction in LD children, neuropsychological assessment sometimes leads to the equally questionable conclusion that an LD child lacks the usual degree or pattern of hemispheric specialization. This conclusion usually is based on one or more of three measures: hand preference, foot preference, and eye preference. The child may show weak laterality, mixed laterality (e.g., right-handedness and left-eyedness), or laterality that is reversed relative to the norm. If so, the child is suspected of lacking the usual degree or pattern of hemispheric specialization. Unfortunately, however, laterality measures are not good predictors of hemispheric specialization (Hiscock & Kinsbourne, 1987).

Although there may be an elevated incidence of left-handedness among LD children, that finding is most plausibly attributed to pathological left-handedness (Harris & Carlson, 1988; Orsini & Satz, 1986; Satz, 1972, 1973). In other words, early damage to the left hemisphere may cause a number of potential right-handers to become left-handed. If so, there might be a statistical association between LD and left-handedness, but the association would not imply causation. It would only imply that, for a minority of left-handed children, early brain damage resulted in both LD and a switch from right- to left-handedness.

C. Diagnosis

Depending on what is meant by the word *diagnosis* (see Rourke, Bakker, Fisk, & Strang, 1983, for a discussion of diagnosis in neuropsychological practice), neuropsychological assessment can contribute to the diagnosis of LD even if the lesion (or dysfunction) cannot be reliably identified or localized. So long as diagnosis pertains to the description and classification of behavioral deficits, neuropsychological tests are appropriate (even though this kind of diagnosis is not necessarily helpful—Brown & Campione, 1986). If diagnosis is construed as the process of identifying the neurological basis of the LD, then neuropsychological evaluation is of limited use for reasons described previously. Neuropsychological assessment is an inquiry at the behavioral level of analysis. Questions about the existence or locus of lesions (or dysfunctions) are questions about brain anatomy or physiology. To answer such questions without having access to independent physiological or anatomical confirmation is to reduce neuropsychology to what Parsons (1977) has called "the new phrenology."

Neuropsychological tests provide data concerning perception, attention, memory, motor skill, language, and reasoning. The usefulness of this kind of information is a critical question. The disease model of LD justifies gathering this kind of information in an attempt to characterize the pattern of deficits underlying the learning problem. From other perspectives (e.g., Brown & Campione, 1986), this kind of information is useless. Although one could argue that no harm is done by collecting neuropsychological data, this middle-of-the-road position is difficult to defend simply because the considerable time and resources consumed by neuropsychological assessment could be used instead to perform a comprehensive analysis of the child's reading, writing, and arithmetic performance. In other words, neuropsychological assessment may be seen as a diversion of resources from the academic problem itself.

At worst, neuropsychological assessment reinforces the use of unfortunate concepts such as minimal brain damage (see Fry, 1968; Kinsbourne, 1975; Taylor, 1983) and contributes to the inappropriate use of neurological terms. One of us examined a boy with severe academic problems who previously had performed poorly on a clinical test of alternating hand movement. As a result of this finding (which was not noticeable on retesting), the boy had been assigned the diagnostic label of "dysdiadochokinesic." That the boy was referred for neuropsychological evaluation because of this unreliable sign indicates that concern for his learning problems had been subordinated to concern for a putative medical problem. In another instance, a school-aged girl with multiple handicaps was reported to have aphasia. This girl was blind and mentally retarded, and her hearing was impaired. When her longstanding difficulty in language development was labeled as aphasia, her parents became hopeful that her language problem could be successfully treated.

Neuropsychological assessment was not responsible for these rather extreme examples of mislabeling. In fact, the neuropsychologist repudiated the questionable labels. Nonetheless, these cases illustrate the contemporary tendency to "neurologize" educational problems. Inappropriate neurological labeling can divert the attention of professional caregivers from the learning problem to an extraneous or imagined medical problem; it can also distort the true nature of a disorder and contribute to unrealistic expectations regarding treatment and outcome.

D. Remediation

While describing how neuropsychological and other clinical findings might be translated into recommendations for treating the LD child, Mattis (1981) acknowledged that those recommendations tend not to be useful:

Quite often the elegant comprehensive multidisciplinary differential diagnostic evaluation of cognitive processes conducted in hospital based facilities results in recommendations that are naive as to their practicability or so obfuscated in technical jargon as to be of limited value to the school based reading specialist responsible for the treatment. . . . A crevasse of ignorance must be traversed as the hospital based clinician leaps from the familiarity of clinical findings and inferences to their implications for programmatic treatment by the school. [p. 105]

This criticism may be answered by asserting that the deficiency lies not in the disease model per se, but in the practitioner (Gaddes, 1985). This defense is not without merit. Mastering neuropsychological assessment skills is sufficiently challenging without the added burden of becoming expert in methods for teaching children with special needs. Even if the hospital-based diagnostic team includes a special education consultant, the gap between defining neuropsychological deficits and specifying remediation is not easy to bridge.

The main problem, however, is not the clinician's inability to bridge the gap between assessment and treatment but, rather, the existence of the gap itself. It is precisely this gap that necessitates what Brown and Campione (1986) called the "leap to instruction." If the assessment were more directly relevant to the problem, that is, to reading, spelling, or arithmetic, there would be much less of a gap to leap in translating the assessment into treatment.

Does addressing the disordered academic skill itself not constitute treating the symptom rather than the disease? Is it not more satisfactory to treat the underlying disease, much as the physician attempts to do in cases of somatic disorders? We would answer "yes" to both questions, but would add the obvious qualification that one cannot treat the underlying disease without having the means to do so. Assume that the disorder has been correctly diagnosed and the responsible cortical region correctly identified. What then? Surgery is unlikely to help. Medication is a possibility, but a rather remote one (Werry, 1981). Bakker and his colleagues (Bakker, Moerland, & Goekopp-Hoetkens, 1981; Bakker & Vinke, 1985) have claimed that hemisphere-specific stimulation is an effective treatment for certain subtypes of dyslexics, but other evidence is either largely negative (Grace & Spreen, 1990) or inconsistent with Bakker's model (Van den Honert, 1977).

Unfortunately, neuropsychological remediation of LD is often associated with a number of schemes, usually based on sensory stimulation or on perceptual or motor training (see Harris, 1985, 1988). Whereas some of these measures are merely unproven, others are generally regarded as either offbeat or exploitative, or both. None is known to be efficacious (Gittelman, 1983, 1985). The only remaining weapons in the neuropsychological arsenal are the more prosaic behavioral methods intended to "build up the brain," for example, rote repetition to improve verbal short-term memory. These are the kinds of methods criticized by Brown and Campione (1986), who pointed out that, even if the exercises yield some improvement in performance of a basic brain function (e.g., memory), the improvement is unlikely to transfer to reading, spelling, or arithmetic. It appears that Kinsbourne's (1975) advice of 15 years ago is still valid: "Pending the development of means for directly modifying central nervous system function, therapeutic effort should focus on the deviant behavior itself rather than on its hypothetical basis in neurologic abnormality." [p. 212]

E. Other Objectives

Stated in its most succinct form, our argument is that neuropsychological assessment seldom contributes to the amelioration of LD. We acknowledge, however, that there may be other reasons for performing neuropsychological evaluation of children with academic problems.

A potentially important function of the clinical neuropsychologist is to assist teachers and school psychologists in recognizing emergent medical problems in children and in making appropriate referrals. Neuropsychological assessment can be helpful in documenting acquired deficits and in understanding the reason for deterioration of a child's school performance. The assessment may help to determine the likelihood of a progressive disorder such as a neoplastic or demyelinating disease. Even in these cases, neuropsychological assessment may not be necessary, as an experienced neuropsychologist can often use historical and psychoeducational evidence to recommend an appropriate course of action, for example, referral to a pediatric neurologist. Thus, it is not the neuropsychological assessment per se, but the neuropsychologist's knowledge (as well as the neuropsychologist's ready access to medical specialists) that often proves most beneficial to the child.

Similarly, the neuropsychologist can contribute to the educational management of children with other medically treatable conditions such as attention-deficit disorder (ADD) and epilepsy. If the condition has not been previously diagnosed, neuropsychological assessment may contribute to its discovery. If the condition is being treated by a physician, serial neuropsychological assessment can help to determine treatment efficacy. Again, the assessment itself may be less important than the neuropsychologist's knowledge and experience. A competent and experienced neuropsychologist can inform school personnel concerning the behavioral and educational implications of the disorder and can often facilitate communication between educational and medical professionals.

Holmes-Bernstein and Waber (1990) describe an approach to evaluating children that overcomes many of the limitations of neuropsychological assessment. Although this "systemic approach" includes neuropsychological assessment procedures, the quantitative assessment constitutes only a small part of the evaluation. The approach emphasizes not the child's deficits but, rather, the child's problem-solving strategies and the significance of the child's characteristics within his or her own environment. Data from various sources are used to construct a "child–world system," which leads to interventions designed to minimize the mismatch between the child and his or her environment. Typically, changes in the environment as well as the child are suggested. Holmes-Bernstein and Waber's approach shares with Brown and Campione (1986) an adherence to certain of Vygotsky's views regarding reciprocal relationships between the child and his or her environment. This approach transcends the typical neuropsychological evaluation, with its narrow focus on brain dysfunction, and, consequently, it seems more compatible with the needs of the child.

Neuropsychological assessment can play a prominent role in efforts to identify preschool and kindergarten children at high risk for subsequent LD. Although determining risk for developmental disorders is a complex and difficult undertaking (Kopp, 1983), certain neuropsychological instruments, administered at a particular stage of development, may be helpful in screening for LD (Fletcher & Satz, 1984; Fletcher, Taylor, Morris, & Satz, 1982; Satz, Taylor, Friel, & Fletcher, 1978). Reliance on neuropsychological measures (as opposed to direct measures of reading, spelling, and arithmetic) can be justified by the children's lack of academic instruction at the time of screening. For example, one can assess motor or perceptual functions, but not reading skill, in kindergarten children who have not yet been taught to read.

Whether nonverbal neuropsychological predictors are superior to linguistic measures alone remains to be established (Jansky, 1978; Satz et al., 1978). The answer probably depends on several factors, including the subtypes of LD in question, the linguistic and nonlinguistic skills chosen as predictors, the criterion to be predicted, and the stage of development at which the criterion is measured (Fletcher, Satz, & Scholes, 1981). The contribution of nonverbal neuropsychological tests to early prediction of LD may reflect the sensitivity of those tests to a general developmental factor, as yet unspecified, that is correlated with the acquisition of academic skills (Fletcher et al., 1982).

Probably the best justification for neuropsychological assessment of LD children is the continuing need for knowledge about the nature and causes of LD. Learning disability is a scientific conundrum as well as a serious societal problem. Even if neuropsychological assessment seldom benefits the individual child, clinical assessments provide data that can contribute to a more adequate understanding of LD. Without further accumulation of data (and astute interpretation of the data), it is unlikely that our understanding of LD can be advanced substantially beyond the current level.

VI. Concluding Comments

Many readers will be familiar with the old joke about the drunken man who is observed in the middle of the night, searching for his lost keys under a streetlight even though the keys had been dropped halfway down the street. His rationale, of course, was that he could not expect to find the keys in the dark. Is it possible that clinical neuropsychologists, in assessing LD children, are behaving similarly? Are they searching the territory illuminated by their instruments rather than the murkier realms of reading, spelling, and arithmetic in which answers might be found?

Kinsbourne (1973) characterized the pediatrician's examination of nervous system functioning in the LD child as an exercise in "examining everything you know how to examine" (p. 699). He argued that the findings, which pertain to spinal cord and brain stem, are relevant to LD only indirectly and only because "any agent that damages one part of the nervous system is quite likely also to damage another part of it" (p. 699). Neuropsychological assessment represents a shift of emphasis to cortical functions that are more likely to be relevant to reading, spelling, and calculating. Yet, one could argue that neuropsychologists examine those functions that they know how to examine rather than those characteristics that actually account for the LD. The association between LD and abnormal cortical functioning should be somewhat stronger than the association between LD and abnormal brain stem or spinal cord functioning, but Kinsbourne's principal of "guilt by association" still applies. The presence of various impairments of cortical functioning in LD children informs us only that the brain is functioning abnormally and does not necessarily explicate the disability in reading or spelling or calculating.

Our argument should not be misconstrued to imply that the ultimate explanations for LD lie anywhere other than in the brain. Indeed we consider it tautological to claim that LD reflects certain characteristics of the child's brain. At issue, instead, is the degree to which neuropsychological constructs and tests are helpful in understanding and remediating LD. Neuropsychological research has helped to establish that at least some children with LD have demonstrable neural abnormalities. But neuropsychological research has also shown that LD children are a heterogeneous population. Even if the disease model of LD is useful in understanding some LD subtypes, the model may be ill suited as a framework for understanding others.

More than a decade ago Spreen (1976) cautioned neuropsychologists not to forget "that there are other positions, other interpretations for many of our data" (p. 446). In Spreen's words, "The neglect of alternatives shows a blind singlemindedness of purpose and leads to a further split of [neuropsychology and education]." [p. 446] In this chapter we describe some alternatives. We argue not that neuropsychological interpretations are invariably wrong, but that such interpretations apply only to certain cases of LD and, even then, tend not to be helpful to either the child or the teacher.

Neuropsychologists have debated the merits of alternative tests, test batteries, and subtyping schemes while overlooking the more fundamental question of whether lengthy and expensive neuropsychological evaluations benefit the child. Perhaps our doubts will impel others to examine more critically the degree to which neuropsychological assessment contributes to the welfare of the LD child.

Acknowledgment

The authors are grateful to Laura Johnson for her assistance in the preparation of this chapter, and to Dr. Che Kan Leong for his comments on a previous version of the manuscript.

References

Ahn, H., Prichep, L., John, E. R., Baird, H., Trepetin, M., & Kaye, H. (1980). Developmental equations reflect brain dysfunctions. *Science, 210,* 1259–1262.

Applebee, A. N. (1971). Research in reading retardation: Two critical problems. *Journal of Child Psychology and Psychiatry, 12,* 91–113.

Baddeley, A. (1979). Working memory and reading. In P. Kolers, M. Wrolstad, & H. Bouma (Eds.), *Processing of visible language* (pp. 355–370). New York: Plenum.

Baddeley, A. (1981). The concept of working memory: A view of its current state and probable future development. *Cognition, 10,* 17–23.

Bakker, D. J. (1979). Hemispheric differences and readings strategies: Two dyslexias? *Bulletin of The Orton Society, 29,* 84–100.

Bakker, D. J. (1981). A set of brains for learning to read. In K. C. Diller (Ed.), *Individual differences and universals in language learning aptitude* (pp. 65–71). Rowley, MA: Newbury House.

Bakker, D. J. (1983). Hemispheric specialization and specific reading retardation. In M. Rutter (Ed.), *Developmental neuropsychiatry* (pp. 498–506). New York: Guilford Press.

Bakker, D. J., Licht, R., Kok, A., & Bouma, A. (1980). Cortical responses to word reading by right- and left-earned normal and reading-disturbed children. *Journal of Clinical Neuropsychology, 2,* 1–12.

Bakker, D. J., Moerland, R., & Goekoop-Hoetkens, M. (1981). Effects of hemisphere-specific stimulation on the reading performance of dyslexic boys: A pilot study. *Journal of Clinical Neuropsychology, 3,* 155–159.

Bakker, D. J., & Vinke, J. (1985). Effects of hemisphere-specific stimulation on brain activity and reading in dyslexics. *Journal of Clinical and Experimental Neuropsychology, 7,* 505–525.

Benson, D. F. (1981). Alexia and the neuroanatomical basis of reading. In F. J. Pirozzolo & M. C. Wittrock (Eds.), *Neuropsychological and cognitive processes in reading* (pp. 69–92). New York: Academic Press.

Benton, A. L. (1975). Developmental dyslexia: Neurological aspects. *Advances in Neurology, 7,* 1–47.

Benton, A. L. (1980). Dyslexia: Evolution of a concept. *Bulletin of the Orton Society, 30,* 10–26.

Bishop, D. V. M. (1983). Linguistic impairment after left hemidecortication for infantile hemiplegia? A reappraisal. *Quarterly Journal of Experimental Psychology: Human Experimental Psychology, 35A,* 199–207.

Boder, E. (1973). Developmental dyslexia: A diagnostic approach based on three atypical reading-spelling patterns. *Developmental Medicine and Child Neurology, 15,* 663–687.

Bradley, L., & Bryant, P. (1985). *Rhyme and reason in reading and spelling.* Ann Arbor: University of Michigan Press.

Brown, A. L., & Campione, J. C. (1986). Psychological theory and the study of learning disabilities. *American Psychologist, 41,* 1059–1068.

Bryden, M. P. (1988). Does laterality makes any difference? Thoughts on the relation between cerebral asymmetry and reading. In D. L. Molfese & S. J. Segalowitz (Eds.), *Brain lateralization in children: Developmental implications* (pp. 509–525). New York: Guilford Press.

Chall, J. S. (1983). *Stages of reading development.* New York: McGraw-Hill.

Corballis, M. C. (1983). *Human laterality.* New York: Academic Press.

Critchley, M. (1970). *the dyslexic child* (2nd ed.). London: Heinemann.

Crowder, R. G. (1984). Is it just reading? Comments on the papers by Mann, Morrison, and Wolford and Fowler. *Developmental Review, 4,* 48–61.

Cruickshank, W. M. (1972). Some issues facing the field of learning disability. *Journal of Learning Disabilities, 5,* 380–383.

Cruickshank, W. M. (1980). "When winter comes, can spring . . . ?" In W. M. Cruickshank (Ed.), *Approaches to learning: Vol. 1. The best of ACLD* (pp. 1–24). Syracuse, NY: Syracuse University Press.

Dainer, K. B., Klorman, R., Salzman, L. F., Hess, D. W., Davidson, P. W., & Michael, R. L. (1981). Learning-disordered children's evoked potentials during sustained attention. *Journal of Abnormal Child Psychology, 9,* 79–94.

Denckla, M. B., LeMay, M., & Chapman, C. A. (1985). Few CT scan abnormalities found even in neurologically impaired learning disabled children. *Journal of Learning Disabilities, 18,* 132–135.

Denckla, M. B., & Rudel, R. G. (1976). Rapid "automatized" naming (R. A. N.): Dyslexia differentiated from other learning disabilities. *Neuropsychologia, 14,* 471–479.

Dennis, M. (1980a). Capacity and strategy for syntactic comprehension after left or right hemidecortication. *Brain & Language, 10,* 287–317.

Dennis, M. (1980b). Language acquisition in a single hemisphere: Semantic organization. In D. Caplan (Ed.), *Biological studies of mental processes* (pp. 159–185). Cambridge, MA: MIT Press.

Dennis, M., & Kohn, B. (1975). Comprehension of syntax in infantile hemiplegics after cerebral hemidecortication: Left-hemisphere superiority. *Brain & Language, 2,* 475–486.

Dennis, M., & Whitaker, H. A. (1976). Language acquisition following hemi-decortication: Linguistic superiority of the left over the right hemisphere. *Brain & Language, 3,* 404–433.

Dennis, M., & Whitaker, H. A. (1977). Hemispheric equipotentiality and language acquisition. In S. J. Segalowitz & F. A. Gruber (Eds.), *Language development and neurological theory* (pp. 93–106). New York: Academic Press.

Dingman, H. F., & Tarjan, G. (1960). Mental retardation and the normal distribution curve. *American Journal of Mental Deficiency, 64,* 991–994.

Doehring, D. G., & Hoshko, I. M. (1977). Classification of reading problems by the Q-technique of factor analysis. *Cortex, 13,* 281–294.

Drake, W. E. (1968). Clinical and pathological findings in a child with a developmental learning disability. *Journal of Learning Disabilities, 1,* 486–502.

Duffy, F. H., Denckla, M. B., Bartels, P. H., Sandini, G., & Keissling, L. (1980). Dyslexia: Automated diagnosis by computerized classification of brain electrical activity. *Annals of Neurology, 7,* 421–428.

Duffy, F. H., Denckla, M. B., & Sandini, G. (1980). Dyslexia: Regional differences in brain electrical activity by topographic mapping. *Annals of Neurology, 7,* 414–420.

Duffy, F. H., McAnulty, G. B., & Schachter, S. C. (1984). Brain electrical activity mapping. In N. Geschwind & A. M. Galaburda (Eds.), *Cerebral dominance: The biological foundations* (pp. 53–74). Cambridge, MA: Harvard University Press.

Fabian, J. J., & Jacobs, U. W. (1981). Discrimination of neurological impairment in the learning disabled adolescent. *Journal of Learning Disabilities, 14,* 594–596.

Fletcher, J. M., & Satz, P. (1984). Test-based versus teacher-based predictions of academic achievement: A three-year longitudinal follow-up. *Journal of Pediatric Psychology, 9,* 193–203.

Fletcher, J. M., Satz, P., & Scholes, R. J. (1981). Developmental changes in the linguistic performance correlates of reading achievement. *Brain & Language, 13,* 78–90.

Fletcher, J. M., Taylor, H. G., Morris, R., & Satz, P. (1982). Finger recognition skills and reading achievement: A developmental neuropsychological analysis. *Developmental Psychology, 18,* 124–132.

Friedman, R. B., & Albert, M. L. (1985). Alexia. In K. M. Heilman & E. Valenstein (Eds.), *Clinical neuropsychology* (2nd ed., pp. 49–73). New York: Oxford University Press.

Fry, E. (1968). A do-it-yourself terminology generator. *Journal of Reading, 11,* 428–430.

Gaddes, W. H. (1985). *Learning disabilities and brain function: A neuropsychological approach* (2nd ed.). New York: Springer-Verlag.

Galaburda, A. M., & Kemper, T. L. (1979). Cytoarchitectonic abnormalities in developmental dyslexia: A case study. *Annals of Neurology, 6,* 94–100.

Galaburda, A. M., Sherman, G. F., Rosen, G. D., Aboitiz, F., & Geschwind, N. (1985). Developmental dyslexia: Four consecutive patients with cortical anomalies. *Annals of Neurology, 18,* 222–233.

Galton, F. (1961). Classification of men according to their natural gifts. In J. J. Jenkins

& D. G. Paterson (Eds.), *Studies in individual differences* (pp. 1–16). New York: Appleton-Century-Crofts. (Original work published 1869)

Geschwind, N. (1962). The anatomy of acquired disorders of reading. In J. Money (Ed.), *Reading disability: Progress and research needs in dyslexia* (pp. 115–129). Baltimore, MD: Johns Hopkins Press.

Geschwind, N. (1982). Why Orton was right. *Annals of Dyslexia, 32,* 13–30.

Geschwind, N., & Behan, P. (1982). Left-handedness: Association with immune disease, migraine, and developmental learning disorder. *Proceedings of the National Academy of Sciences of the U.S.A., 79,* 5097–5100.

Geschwind, N., & Galaburda, A. M. (1985). Cerebral lateralization. Biological mechanisms, associations and pathology: II. A hypothesis and a program for research. *Archives of Neurology (Chicago), 42,* 521–552.

Gittelman, R. (1983). Treatment of reading disorders. In M. Rutter (Ed.), *Developmental neuropsychiatry* (pp. 520–541). New York: Guilford Press.

Gittelman, R. (1985). Controlled trials of remedial approaches to reading disability. *Journal of Child Psychology and Psychiatry, 26,* 843–846.

Gladstone, M., & Best, C. T. (1985). Developmental dyslexia: The potential role of interhemispheric collaboration in reading acquisition. In C. T. Best (Ed.), *Hemispheric function and collaboration in the child* (pp. 87–118). Orlando, FL: Academic Press.

Gleitman, L. R., & Rozin, P. (1977). The structure and acquisition of reading: I. Relations between orthographies and the structure of language. In A. Reber & D. Scarborough (Eds.), *Toward a psychology of reading: The proceedings of the CUNY conferences* (pp. 1–53). Hillsdale, NJ: Erlbaum.

Gottesman, R. L., Hankin, D., Levinson, W., & Beck, P. (1984). Neurodevelopmental functioning of good and poor readers in urban schools. *Developmental and Behavioral Pediatrics, 5,* 109–115.

Grace, G. M., & Spreen, O. (1990, February). *Effects of hemisphere-specific stimulation on academic performance and event-related potentials in dyslexic children.* Paper presented at the meeting of the International Neuropsychological Society, Orlando, FL.

Guthrie, J. T. (1973). Reading comprehension and syntactic responses in good and poor readers. *Journal of Educational Psychology, 65,* 294–299.

Harris, L. J. (1985). Teaching the right brain: Historical perspective on a contemporary educational fad. In C. T. Best (Ed.), *Hemispheric function and collaboration in the child* (pp. 231–274). Orlando, FL: Academic Press.

Harris, L. J. (1988). Right-brain training: Some reflections on the application of research on cerebral hemispheric specialization to education. In D. L. Molfese & S. J. Segalowitz (Eds.), *Brain lateralization in children: Developmental implications* (pp. 207–235). New York: Guilford Press.

Harris, L. J., & Carlson, D. F. (1988). Pathological left-handedness: An analysis of theories and evidence. In D. L. Molfese & S. J. Segalowitz (Eds.), *Brain lateralization in children: Developmental implications* (pp. 289–372). New York: Guilford Press.

Haslam, R. H. A., Dalby, J. T., Johns, R. D., & Rademaker, A. W. (1981). Cerebral asymmetry in developmental dyslexia. *Archives of Neurology (Chicago)*, 38, 679–682.

Hier, D. B., LeMay, M., Rosenberger, P. B., & Perlo, V. B. (1978). Developmental dyslexia: Evidence for a subgroup with reversal of cerebral asymmetry. *Archives of Neurology (Chicago)*, 35, 90–92.

Hiscock, M. (1990). Neural substrate of cognition and literacy: Biology as wish fulfillment? In. C. K. Leong & B. S. Randhawa (Eds.), *Understanding literacy and cognition: Theory, research, and application* (pp. 33–53). New York: Plenum.

Hiscock, M., & Hiscock, C. K. (1990). Laterality in hemiplegic children: Implications for the concept of pathological left-handedness. In S. Coren (Ed.), *Left-handedness: Behavioral implications and anomalies.* (pp. 131–152). New York: Plenum.

Hiscock, M., & Kinsbourne, M. (1980). Individual differences in cerebral lateralization: Are they relevant to learning disability? In W. M. Cruickshank (Ed.), *Approaches to learning: Vol. 1. The best of ACLD* (pp. 139–183). Syracuse, NY: Syracuse University Press.

Hiscock, M., & Kinsbourne, M. (1982). Laterality and dyslexia: A critical view. *Annals of Dyslexia, 32,* 177–228.

Hiscock, M., & Kinsbourne, M. (1987). Specialization of the cerebral hemispheres: Implications for learning. *Journal of Learning Disabilities, 20,* 130–143.

Holmes-Bernstein, J., & Waber, D. P. (1990). Developmental neuropsychological assessment: The systemic approach. In A. A. Boulton, G. B. Baker, & M. Hiscock (Eds.), *Neuromethods: Vol. 17. Neuropsychology.* (pp. 311–371). Clifton, NJ: Humana Press.

Jansky, J. J. (1978). A critical review of "Some developmental and predictive precursors of reading disabilities." In A. L. Benton & D. Pearl (Eds.), *Dyslexia: An appraisal of current knowledge* (pp. 376–394). New York: Oxford University Press.

Johnstone, J., Galin, D., Fein, G., Yingling, C., Herron, J., & Marcus, M. (1984). Regional brain activity in dyslexia and control children during reading tasks: Visual probe event-related potentials. *Brain & Language, 21,* 233–254.

Kershner, J. R. (1985). Ontogeny of hemispheric specialization and relationship of developmental patterns to complex reasoning skills and academic achievement. In C. T. Best (Ed.), *Hemispheric function and collaboration in the child* (pp. 327–360). Orlando, FL: Academic Press.

Kinsbourne, M. (1973). School problems. *Pediatrics, 52,* 697–710.

Kinsbourne, M. (1975). MDB—A fuzzy concept misdirects therapeutic effort. *Postgraduate Medicine, 58,* 211–212.

Kinsbourne, M. (1986). *Sinistrality and risk for immune diseases and learning disorders.* Paper presented at the meeting of the Child Neurology Society, Boston, MA.

Kinsbourne, M. (1988). Sinistrality, brain organization, and cognitive deficits. In D. L. Molfese & S. J. Segalowitz (Eds.), *Brain lateralization in children: Developmental implications* (pp. 259–279). New York: Guilford Press.

Kinsbourne, M., & Hiscock, M. (1978). Cerebral lateralization and cognitive development. In J. S. Chall & A. F. Mirsky (Eds.), *Education and the brain* (Yearbook of the National Society for the Study of Education, pp. 169–222). Chicago, IL: University of Chicago Press.

Kinsbourne, M., & Hiscock, M. (1981). Cerebral lateralization and cognitive development: Conceptual and methodological issues. In G. W. Hynd & J. E. Obrzut (Eds.), *Neuropsychological assessment and the school-age child: Issues and procedures* (pp. 125–166). New York: Grune & Stratton.

Kinsbourne, M., & Hiscock, M. (1983). The normal and deviant development of functional lateralization of the brain. In P. H. Mussen (Ed.), *Handbook of child psychology (4th ed.): Vol. 2. Infancy and developmental psychobiology* (pp. 157–280). New York: Wiley.

Kinsbourne, M., & Warrington, E. K. (1963). Developmental factors in reading and writing backwardness. *British Journal of Psychology, 54,* 145–156.

Kopp, C. B. (1983). Risk factors in development. In P. H. Mussen (Ed.), *Handbook of child psychology (4th ed.): Vol. 2. Infancy and developmental psychobiology* (pp. 1081–1188). New York: Wiley.

Korchin, S. J. (1976). *Modern clinical psychology.* New York: Basic Books.

LaBerge, D., & Samuels, S. J. (1974). Toward a theory of automatic information processing in reading. *Cognitive Psychology, 6,* 293–323.

Landau, W. M., Goldstein, R., & Kleffner, F. R. (1960). Congenital aphasia: A clinico-pathologic study. *Neurology, 10,* 915–921.

Leisman, G., & Ashkenazi, M. (1980). Aetiological factors in dyslexia: IV. Cerebral hemispheres are functionally equivalent. *Neuroscience, 11,* 157–164.

Leong, C. K. (1987). *Children with specific reading disabilities.* Amsterdam: Swets & & Zeitlinger.

Leong, C. K. (1989). The locus of so-called IQ test results in reading disabilities. *Journal of Learning Disabilities, 22,* 507–512.

Levine, D. N., Hier, D. B., & Calvanio, R. (1981). Acquired learning disability for reading after left temporal lobe damage in childhood. *Neurology, 31,* 257–264.

Lewkowicz, N. K. (1980). Phonemic awareness training: What to teach and how to teach it. *Journal of Educational Psychology, 72,* 686–700.

Lezak, M. D. (1983). *Neuropsychological assessment* (2nd ed.). New York: Oxford University Press.

Liberman, I. Y. (1970). Segmentation of the spoken word and reading acquisition. *Bulletin of the Orton Society, 23,* 65–77.

Lovett, M. W. (1984a). A developmental perspective on reading dysfunction: Accuracy and rate criteria in the subtyping of dyslexic children. *Brain & Language, 22,* 67–91.

Lovett, M. W. (1984b). The search for subtypes of specific reading disability: Reflections from a cognitive perspective. *Annals of Dyslexia, 34,* 155–178.

Lovett, M. W. (1987). A developmental approach to reading disability: Accuracy and speed criteria of normal and deficient reading skill. *Child Development, 58,* 234–260.

Lowick, B., & Spreen, O. (1990). *Persistence and changes of neurological signs in learning disabled subjects over a 15 year period.* Paper presented at the meeting of the International Neuropsychological Society, Orlando, FL.

Mann, V. A. (1984). Reading skill and language skill. *Developmental Review, 4,* 1–15.

Mattingly, I. G. (1972). Reading, the linguistic process, and linguistic awareness. In J. F. Kavanagh & I. G. Mattingly (Eds.), *Language by ear and by eye* (pp. 133–147). Cambridge, MA: MIT Press.

Mattingly, I. G. (1984). Reading, linguistic awareness, and language acquisition. In J. Downing & R. Valtin (Eds.), *Language awareness and learning to read* (pp. 9–25). New York: Springer-Verlag.

Mattis, S. (1981). Dyslexia syndromes in children: Toward the development of syndrome-specific treatment programs. In F. J. Pirozzolo & M. C. Wittrock (Eds.), *Neuropsychological and cognitive processes in reading* (pp. 93–107). New York: Academic Press.

Mattis, S., French, J. H., & Rapin, I. (1975). Dyslexia in children and adults: Three independent neuropsychological syndromes. *Developmental Medicine and Child Neurology, 17,* 150–163.

McCusker, L. X., Hillinger, M. L., & Bias, R. G. (1981). Phonological recoding and reading. *Psychological Bulletin, 89,* 217–245.

Miles, T. R., & Haslum, M. N. (1986). Dyslexia: Anomaly or normal variation? *Annals of Dyslexia, 36,* 103–117.

Morrison, F. J. (1984). Reading disability: A problem in rule learning and word decoding. *Developmental Review, 4,* 36–47.

Morrison, F. J., & Manis, F. R. (1982). Cognitive processes and reading disability: A critique and proposal. In C. J. Brainerd & M. I. Pressley (Eds.), *Advances in cognitive development: Vol. 2. Verbal processes in development.* New York/Berlin: Springer-Verlag.

Myklebust, H. (1965). *Development and disorders of written language: Vol. 1. Picture Story Language Test.* New York: Grune & Stratton.

Naylor, H. (1980). Reading disability and lateral asymmetry: An information processing analysis. *Psychological Bulletin, 87,* 531–545.

Orsini, D. L., & Satz, P. (1986). A syndrome of pathological left-handedness: Correlates of early left hemisphere injury. *Archives of Neurology (Chicago), 43,* 333–337.

Orton, S. T. (1937). *Reading, writing and speech problems in children.* New York: W. W. Norton.

Parsons, O. A. (1977). Human neuropsychology: The new phrenology. *Journal of Operational Psychiatry, 8,* 47–56.

Petrauskas, R. J., & Rourke, B. P. (1979). Identification of subtypes of retarded readers: A neuropsychological, multivariate approach. *Journal of Clinical Neuropsychology, 1,* 17–37.

Phares, E. J. (1988). *Clinical psychology: Concepts, methods, & profession.* Chicago, IL: Dorsey.

Pirozzolo, F. J. (1985). Neuropsychological and neuroelectric correlates of developmental reading disability. In C. T. Best (Ed.), *Hemispheric function and collaboration in the child* (pp. 309–326). Orlando, FL: Academic Press.

Roberts, J. A. F. (1952). The genetics of mental deficiency. *Eugenics Review, 44,* 71–83.

Rosenberger, P. B., & Hier, D. B. (1980). Cerebral asymmetry and verbal intellectual deficits. *Annals of Neurology, 8,* 300–304.

Rourke, B. P. (1989). *Nonverbal learning disabilities: The syndrome and the model.* New York: Guilford Press.

Rourke, B. P., Bakker, D. J., Fisk, J. L., & Strang, J. D. (1983). *Child neuropsychology: An introduction to theory, research, and clinical practice.* New York: Guilford Press.

Rozin, P., & Gleitman, L. R. (1977). The structure and acquisition of reading: II. The reading process and the acquisition of the alphabetic principle. In A. Reber & D. Scarborough (Eds.), *Toward a psychology of reading: The proceedings of the CUNY conferences* (pp. 55–141). Hillsdale, NJ: Erlbaum.

Rudel, R. G. (1985). Hemispheric asymmetry and learning disabilities: Left, right, or in-between? In C. T. Best (Ed.), *Hemispheric function and collaboration in the child* (pp. 275–308). Orlando, FL: Academic Press.

Satz, P. (1972). Pathological left-handedness: An explanatory model. *Cortex, 8,* 121–137.

Satz, P. (1973). Left-handedness and early brain insult: An explanation. *Neuropsychologia, 11,* 115–117.

Satz, P. (1976). Cerebral dominance and reading disability: An old problem revisited. In R. M. Knights & D. J. Bakker (Eds.), *The neuropsychology of learning disorders: Theoretical approaches* (pp. 273–294). Baltimore, MD: University Park Press.

Satz, P., & Morris, R. (1981). Learning disability subtypes: A review. In F. J. Pirozzolo & M. C. Wittrock (Eds.), *Neuropsychological and cognitive processes in reading* (pp. 109–141). New York: Academic Press.

Satz, P., Taylor, H. G., Friel, J., & Fletcher, J. M. (1978). Some developmental and predictive precursors of reading disabilities: A six year follow-up. In A. L. Benton & D. Pearl (Eds.), *Dyslexia: An appraisal of current knowledge* (pp. 313–347). New York: Oxford University Press.

Shucard, D. W., Cummins, K. R., & McGee, M. G. (1984). Event-related brain potentials differentiate normal and disabled readers. *Brain & Language, 21,* 318–334.

Siegel, L. S. (1989). Why we do not need intelligence test scores in the definition and analyses of learning disabilities. *Journal of Learning Disabilities, 22,* 469–478, 486.

Smith, A., & Campbell, A. (1979, February). *Neuropsychological diagnostic techniques: The Michigan Neuropsychological Test Battery.* Workshop presented at the meeting of the International Neuropsychological Society, New York.

Sperry, R. (1982). Some effects of disconnecting the cerebral hemispheres. *Science, 217,* 1223–1226.

Spreen, O. (1976). Neuropsychology of learning disorders: Post-conference review. In R. M. Knights & D. J. Bakker (Eds.), *The neuropsychology of learning disorders: Theoretical approaches* (pp. 445–467). Baltimore, MD: University Park Press.

Spreen, O. (1988). *Learning-disabled children growing up: A follow-up into adulthood.* New York: Oxford University Press.

Spreen, O. (1989). Learning disability, neurology, and long-term outcome: Some implications for the individual and for society. *Journal of Clinical and Experimental Neuropsychology, 11,* 389–408.

Stevenson, H. W., Stigler, J. W., Lucker, G. W., Lee, S., Hsu, C., & Kitamura, S. (1982). Reading disabilities: The case of Chinese, Japanese, and English. *Child Development, 53,* 1164–1181.

Taylor, H. G. (1983). MBD: Meanings and misconceptions. *Journal of Clinical Neuropsychology, 5,* 271–287.

Todd, J., Coolidge, F., & Satz, P. (1977). The Wechsler Adult Intelligence Scale discrepancy index: A neuropsychological evaluation. *Journal of Consulting and Clinical Psychology, 45,* 450–454.

Towbin, A. (1978). Cerebral dysfunctions related to perinatal organic damage. *Journal of Abnormal Psychology, 87,* 617–635.

Tupper, D. E. (1987). *Soft neurological signs.* Orlando, FL: Grune & Stratton.

Van den Honert, D. (1977). A neuropsychological technique for training dyslexics. *Journal of Learning Disabilities, 10,* 21–27.

Vargha-Khadem, F., & Isaacs, E. (1985, May). *The effects of early vs. late cerebral lesions on verbal learning and memory in children.* Paper presented at the meeting of the Society for Research in Child Development, Toronto.

Vargha-Khadem, F., O'Gorman, A. M., & Watters, G. V. (1985). Aphasia and handedness in relation to hemispheric side, age at injury and severity of cerebral lesion during childhood. *Brain, 108,* 677–696.

Vellutino, F. R. (1979). *Dyslexia: Theory and research.* Cambridge, MA: MIT Press.

Vernon, M. D. (1957). *Backwardness in reading.* Cambridge: Cambridge University Press.

Vernon, M. D. (1971). Reading and its difficulties. London: Cambridge University Press.

Vogel, S. A. (1974). Syntactic abilities in normal and dyslexic children. *Journal of Learning Disabilities, 7,* 103–109.

Vygotsky, L. S. (1978). *Mind in society: The development of higher psychological processes* (M. Cole, V. John-Steiner, S. Scribner, & E. Souberman, Eds. and Trans.). Cambridge, MA: Harvard University Press.

Wagner, R. K., & Torgesen, J. K. (1987). The nature of phonological processing and its causal role in the acquisition of reading skills. *Psychological Bulletin, 101,* 192–212.

Watson, C. G. (1977, March). Brain damage tests in psychiatric settings. *INS Bulletin,* pp. 10–12.

Werry, J. S. (1981). Drugs and learning. *Journal of Child Psychology and Psychiatry, 22,* 283–290.

Whitaker, H. A., & Ojemann, G. (1977). Lateralization of higher cortical functions: A critique. *Annals of the New York Academy of Sciences, 299,* 459–473.

Wiig, E. H., Semel, M. S., & Crouse, M. B. (1973). The use of English morphology by high-risk and learning disabled children. *Journal of Learning Disabilities, 6,* 457–465.

Witelson, S. F. (1977). Developmental dyslexia: Two right hemispheres and none left. *Science, 195,* 309–311.

Wolf, M. (1984). Naming, reading, and the dyslexias: A longitudinal overview. *Annals of Dyslexia, 34,* 87–115.

Wolford, G., & Fowler, C. A. (1984). Differential use of partial information by good and poor readers. *Developmental Review, 4,* 16–35.

Woods, B. T. (1980a). Observations on the neurological basis for initial language acquisition. In D. Caplan (Ed.), *Biological studies of mental processes* (pp. 149–158). Cambridge, MA: MIT Press.

Woods, B. T. (1980b). The restricted effects of right-hemisphere lesions after age one: Wechsler test data. *Neuropsychologia, 18,* 65–70.

Young, A. W., & Ellis, A. W. (1981). Asymmetry of cerebral hemisphere function in normal and poor readers. *Psychological Bulletin, 89,* 183–190.

Yule, W., & Rutter, M. (1976). Epidemiology and social implications of specific reading retardation. In R. M. Knights & D. J. Bakker (Eds.), *The neuropsychology of learning disorders* (pp. 25–39). Baltimore, MD: University Park Press.

Yule, W., Rutter, M., Berger, M., & Thompson, J. (1974). Over- and underachievement in reading: Distribution in the general population. *British Journal of Educational Psychology, 44,* 1–12.

Zangwill, O. L. (1962). Dyslexia in relation to cerebral dominance. In J. Money (Ed.), *Reading disability: Progress and research needs in dyslexia* (pp. 103–113). Baltimore, MD: Johns Hopkins Press.

Author Index

775

Asanuma, C., 212, *232*
Ashkenazi, M., 479, 490, 491, 492, *509,*
747, 770
Asman, A. F., 604, 616, *626*
August, G. J., 131, *141*
Auld, P. A., 414, *434*
Axelrod, L., 607, 609, *624*
Aylward, E., 189, *196*

Bachara, G., 607, 608, 609, *624*
Backman, J., 205, 208, 209, 219, 228, *231,*
238
Backman, J. E., 184, *196*
Backs, R. W., 497, 498, *510*
Bacon, F., 711, *736*
Badcock, D., 442, *471*
Baddeley, A., 204, *231, 753, 765*
Badian, N. A., 616, 617, *624*
Badien, N. A., 293, *304*
Baird, H., 495, 499, *506, 747, 765*
Bak, J. J., 607, 618, *628*
Baken, P., 414, *431*
Baker, J. G., 241, 243, *275*
Baker, L., 375, *379,* 643, *652*
Bakin, H., 32, 33, 34, *45*
Bakker, D., 108, *109,* 713, *740*
Bakker, D. J., 355, 359, 360, 366, *379, 380,*
382, 385, 391, *408, 467, 471,* 688, 690,
710, 747, 753, 758, 759, 761, 765, 771
Ball, D., 245, *280*
Bally, H., 134, *145,* 391, *410*
Banich, M., 728, *738*
Banich, M. T., 186, *197*
Banikowski, A., 670, *681*
Barbizet, J., 397, *408*
Barenbaum, E., 670, *681*
Barke, C. R., 661, *682*
Barker, B. M., 321, *328*
Barker, H. R., 321, *328*
Barker, W., 68, *75,* 505, *506*
Barker, W. W., 107, *110*
Barkley, R. A., 556, 558, 561, 562, *569*
Barnes, M., 86, *95*
Barnes, M. A., 205, 208, *238*
Barnett, D. W., 304, *305*
Baron, J., 201, 206, *231*
Barr, R., 359, *380*
Barrett, P., 20, *26*
Barron, R., 645, 646, *655*

Barron, R. W., 206, 207, 209, *231,* 361,
374, *382*
Bartels, P. H., 18, *25,* 495, 501, 505, *506,*
507, 747, 767
Bartels, S. G., 183, 187, *198,* 241, *278*
Bartlett, S., 584, 587, *598*
Bartlett, S., III., 557, 561, *567*
Bashore, T., 446, *469*
Basser, L. S., 101, *109*
Bassich, C., 587, 589, *598*
Bassiri, D., 643, 651, *653*
Bastian, H. C., 1, *6,* 475, *506,* 519, *545*
Batche, G. M., 321, 322, 323, *324*
Batchelor, E. S., 309, 310, 312, 313, 314,
315, 316, 317, 318, 319, 320, *324, 325*
Batchelor, R. S., 314, *324*
Bateman, B., 83, *92,* 639, 644, 651, *652*
Bates, E., 418, 419, *431*
Bates, H., III., 557, 561, *567*
Batheja, M., 414, 415, *431*
Bathurst, K., 414, *432, 433*
Bauer, D. W., 202, *239*
Bauer, J. N., 291, *305*
Bauer, R. H., 148, *175,* 244, 267, *275,* 606,
624
Bayley, N., 692, *708*
Beale, I. L., 411, *432*
Bear, D. M., 620, 622, *624*
Beaumont, J., 244, 248, *275*
Beaumont, J. G., 616, *625*
Beauvois, M. F., 202, *231*
Beck, B., *92, 96*
Beck, I., 645, *646*
Beck, P., 746, *768*
Bedrick, A. D., 487, 488, *509*
Behan, P., 18, *25,* 411, 412, *432,* 478, *506,*
746, *768*
Behan, P. O., 51, 71, *75,* 100, 108, 109,
110, 478, 479, *507*
Bellugi, U., 712, *739*
Belmont, L., 32, *45,* 413, *431*
Bendell, D., 661, *677*
Bender, B., 606, *627*
Bender, M., 577, *600*
Benjamin, L., 552, 554, *569*
Benjamins, D., 416, *433*
Bennett, D. E., 304, *304*
Bennett, F. C., 478, *509*
Bennett, G., 623, *625*
Bennett, L., 124, *142*
Benowitz, L. I., 620, 621, 622, *624, 627*

Subject Index